EMPIRE OF INDIA

Colonial and Indian Exhibition 1886

EMPIRE OF INDIA

SPECIAL CATALOGUE OF EXHIBITS

BY

THE GOVERNMENT OF INDIA

AND

PRIVATE EXHIBITORS

SIR THOMAS WARDLE

GYAN

Published by

GYAN

Gyan Publishing House
5, Ansari Road
Daryaganj, New Delhi-110002
Phone: 011-47034999, 9811692060
E-mail: books@gyanbooks.com

Distribution Network
gyanbooks.com
India, USA, Canada, UK, Australia

ISBN: 978-93-7169-555-8 (PB)

First Published, 1886

2nd Impression 2025

Printed at: Gyan Press, Delhi.

COLONIAL AND INDIAN EXHIBITION 1886: EMPIRE OF INDIA
Author: SIR THOMAS WARDLE

Colonial and Indian Exhibition, 1886.

EMPIRE OF INDIA.

SPECIAL CATALOGUE OF EXHIBITS

BY

THE GOVERNMENT OF INDIA

AND

PRIVATE EXHIBITORS.

LONDON:
WILLIAM CLOWES & SONS, LIMITED,
Printers and Publishers to the Royal Commission,
13 CHARING CROSS, S.W., AND AT THE EXHIBITION.
1886.

TABLE OF CONTENTS.

PART I.

CHAPTER VI.

Part I.—ECONOMIC COURT.

Part II.—ETHNOLOGY.

CHAPTER VII.

CHAPTER VIII.

PART II.

INDIAN SECTION.

EXECUTIVE STAFF IN LONDON.

EXECUTIVE COMMISSIONER,
Sir PHILIP CUNLIFFE-OWEN, K.C.B., K.C.M.G., C.I.E.,
Secretary to the Royal Commission.

COMMISSIONER FOR THE GOVERNMENT OF INDIA,
Sir E. C. BUCK, B.C.S.

OFFICIAL AGENT FOR THE GOVERNMENT OF INDIA,
J. R. ROYLE, Esq., C.I.E.,
Assistant Secretary to the Royal Commission.

SPECIAL OFFICER IN CHARGE OF ECONOMIC COURT,
Dr. GEORGE WATT, C.I.E., M.B., C.M.

HONORARY ARCHITECT,
C. PURDON CLARKE, Esq., C.I.E.

COMMISSIONER FOR H.H. THE NIZAM OF HYDERABAD,
Major NEVILL, C.I.E.

COMMISSIONER FOR H.H. THE MAHARAJAH OF MYSORE,
Colonel A. LE MESSURIER, C.I.E.

COMMISSIONER FOR H.H. THE THAKUR SAHIB OF BHOWNAGAR,
M. M. BHOWNUGGREE, Esq., C.I.E.

OFFICER IN CHARGE OF NATIVE ARTISANS,
Dr. J. W. TYLER, C.I.E., F.R.C.S.

CHIEF ASSISTANT TO THE OFFICIAL AGENT,
B. PLUCKNETT.

ROYAL COMMISSION AND GOVERNMENT OF INDIA SILK CULTURE,
T. WARDLE.

ASSISTANTS—

In Charge of the Commercial Enquiry Office .	Babu T. N. MUKHARJI.
In Silk Culture and Bombay Art Ware Court .	B. A. GUPTE.
In Art Ware Courts	W. D. FREETH. A. E. KEMPLEN. E. H. LLOYD. J. SEDMAN.
In the Administration Court	B. J. ROSE.
Literary Assistant	E. J. WADE, M.A.

PART I.

THE GOVERNMENT OF INDIA EXHIBITS.

PREFACE.

By Sir Edward C. Buck.

Secretary to the Government of India, in the Revenue and Agricultural Department, Commissioner for India.

The object of this Preface is to describe very briefly the scheme under which the collections of exhibits provided by or through the agency of the Government of India have been arranged. These collections, made with the assistance of the Governments of Presidencies and Provinces and of the Rulers of Native States, are distributed in three main divisions over the space allotted to the Government of India. The divisions are—

Scheme of arrangement of exhibits in Indian Courts.

I. The Art Ware Courts, containing specimens of Art Ware and ornamental fabrics from each Indian Province or State.

II. The Economic Court, in which are placed economical products and exhibits of agriculture and ethnology from the whole empire.

III. The Administrative Courts, containing exhibits contributed by administrative departments.

Art Courts. Primary arrangement geographical.

The primary arrangement of the division which comprises the Art Ware Courts is geographical, and not, as has hitherto been the case in all Exhibitions to which India has contributed, technical. In other words, Art exhibits are primarily divided with reference to locality, and not with reference to classification. It is true that, in the descriptive labels attached to each exhibit, an uniform classification has been followed in accordance with a classified list, which will be found on page 12 of this Catalogue, but the primary arrangement, both of exhibits and Catalogue, has reference to the place of manufacture, and not to the place which the exhibit occupies on the classified list. The cause of this departure from the usual system is to be found in the circumstance that in India the Art manufactures of any one place are, as a rule, so different in character from those of any other place that they ought not to be confounded by being brought under the same group. It is no exaggeration to say that a particular kind of Art Ware is often manufactured by one or two families only in a single locality. The absence, until a very recent date, of free communication throughout the country, the fact that the introduction of many Art trades in India is due to the importation by some ruling prince of one or two workmen from a country beyond the frontier, or from another State or Province, and the custom, consequent on a caste system of passing on every trade from father to son, are among the causes which have helped to maintain a practice so singularly conservative.

Advantage of geographical arrangement.

The geographical arrangement which has been followed in the Art Ware Courts has the further advantage of indicating, with considerable clearness, the changing complexion and character of Art manufacture as we pass from one part of India to another. It is easy to observe, for instance, the greater effect of Persian influence on many of the Art manufactures in the Punjab, when these are compared with those of Provinces further south; this circumstance being due to the fact that the Punjab has always been from its position the first province to be overrun by successive inroads of invaders from beyond the North-West Frontier. It is easy again to notice that many of the Art manufactures of large cities are of such a kind as could only have been supported by the patronage of a luxurious Court, such as that which existed under the Mogul Emperors at Delhi; or to form the conclusion from an examination of the Art specimens contributed by the capitals of decayed principalities, that the decline of much Indian decorative Art is due to the fact that manufacturers have now to work for a class of purchasers far poorer as well as less luxurious in habit than the wealthy nobles and princes of the courts of ancient times.

The observations contained in the preceding paragraphs are made with the object of giving one or two examples of the advantage of geographical arrangement, and not with the view of leading up to any review of the position and prospects of Indian Art, which would be beyond the scope of this Preface. It will not, however, be out of place to take advantage of the preceding remarks to explain that one important decorative Art has still survived with encouraging symptoms of vitality under the support of the wealthy members of the middle classes; this is the decoration of temples and house exteriors. The tendency in the present day is for wealth to accumulate in the hands of bankers and merchants, and the custom still prevails for men of this class to spend some part of their surplus wealth in decorating the houses of themselves and of the gods they worship with carving in wood and stone. It was thought desirable therefore that this living form of decorative Art should be given suitable prominence in the screens which form a double façade in front of the Provincial Courts. The idea of thus illustrating the decorative carving which ornaments so many of the streets and temples of India was originated on a small scale in one or two of the Courts of the Calcutta Exhibition of 1883, which were enclosed by carved balustrades on the level of the ground. But in order to avoid interference with the free passage of the public, it was decided by the Royal Commissioners that in London the carved work must be raised on arches, and it is satisfactory to know that this plan has rendered possible the imitation with greater closeness of the architectural style prevailing in India which confines the richest part of the carving to the arches of door-ways and to verandah balustrades. The carved screens have been constructed from a grant specially made for the purpose by the Royal Commissioners, and they form a convenient frame-work to the Courts containing the exhibits of each Province and Native State.

Art Court Screens.

The exhibits within the screens were in every instance collected under general instructions from the Government of India by special officers appointed by the Government or Prince ruling the Province or State. The names of the officers will be found on page 8 of this Catalogue. It is to their exertions that not only the complete illustration of Indian Art industries in the Art Ware Courts is due, but also the construction of the carved screens or façades which enclose those Courts; and in order to appreciate how great their exertions have been, it is necessary to understand the conditions under which a collection of Art manufactures has to be effected in India. Probably, however, no person who has not lived in Oriental countries can conceive how much labour is involved in getting together within a short period anything like a complete set of the Art-wares of a Province or State. No artisans in the world are more dilatory or less anxious to advertise their wares than the artisans of India. Except in the case of a few large dealers who have acquired the habit of dealing with English firms, liberal advances and constant supervision are required for the production of almost every one of the exhibits which the Art-ware Courts contain. The advantage of advertisement being little understood, the manufacturer has no incentive to send his wares for exhibition to a foreign country of which he has but a vague idea at the best, and as it is seldom the practice for any Indian artisan to keep any stock of his wares in hand, almost every single exhibit has had to be specially ordered by a Government official.

Exhibits in Art Courts collected by Provincial Officers.

Difficulties of collection.

In viewing the contents of each Art Ware Court, this circumstance must be remembered, because not only was the time, under the circumstances described, for preparing a complete illustration of Indian Art somewhat short, but also on account of the necessity of paying in advance for the greater part of the exhibits, financial exigencies made it impossible to provide specimens of a very costly character. On the other hand, the collection is in one respect believed to be more complete than that shown by India in former Exhibitions, in that an attempt has been made on this occasion to secure the illustration of every Art manufacture, however insignificant. Every industrial Art in every Province or Native State is illustrated by some one or more specimens. The Colonial and

Completion of an Industrial Art-survey of India.

Indian Exhibition, therefore, is the first at which a complete Art-survey of India has been effected.

The same may be said in respect of the useful products of India which are displayed in the Economic Court. This is the first Exhibition in connection with which anything like a complete economic survey of the Indian Empire has been attempted. Begun at the Paris Exhibition, continued at those of Melbourne and Calcutta, the economic survey of India has, at the Colonial and Indian Exhibition, reached its penultimate if not its final stage, and for the first time provides in a complete series of samples, which line the walls of the Economic Court, a scientifically arranged frame-work upon which to rest future investigation and enquiry. The main object, indeed, which the Government of India has attempted to obtain, conjointly with the equipment of the space allotted by the Royal Commissioners to the economic products of India, has been the collating in one book or economic ledger, as it can be called, of the information hitherto scattered through the reports and records which crowd the shelves of every official library, as well as that which is embodied in the valuable series of useful publications which have, since our occupation of India, from time to time been edited by private individuals. Experience has shown that the compilation of such a work must be based primarily on an actual collection of all the economic products which have to be surveyed and described and that without such a collection completeness and scientific accuracy are impossible. In this view the economic survey of India, while owing its initial existence to the former Exhibitions to which India has been called upon to contribute, will owe its final construction on a satisfactory basis to the Colonial and Indian Exhibition of 1886.

Economic survey of India.

The arrangement of the Economic Court is not, like that of the Art Ware Courts, geographical, but follows the scientific arrangement adopted in the classified list. The conditions of a collection of products differ much from those of a collection of Art-wares. Had any attempt been made to exhibit separately the products of each Province and each Native State of the Indian Empire, the undertaking, besides entailing great expense and trouble, would have involved the unnecessary reduplication of a very large quantity of material. Very few products are confined to a single Province, and a very large number are common to all. It would, therefore, have been plainly undesirable to entail upon each separate Government the labour and expense of providing a separate collection of products from each separate geographical area, merely in order to crowd the rooms of the Economic Court with repeated specimens of the same exhibits. Those who desire to learn the geographical distribution of any one product will find any information they may require in the scientifically arranged ledger to which reference has already been made, and copies of the first volume of which can be seen in the office of the Economic Court.*

Arrangement of Economic Court.

In arranging the disposition of the area allotted to economic products, it was found convenient that the Court should comprise also collections of Ethnological and Agricultural exhibits. The object of the former is two-fold; in the first place to give to the people of England some practical idea of the variety of races which are found in different parts of the great continent of India, as well as of the various manners in which ornamental fabrics are utilised as articles of dress; in the second place, to encourage an art which seems capable of attaining considerable excellence in India—that of clay modelling. The clay modellers in more than one Province of the Empire are in some respects equal to the best terra-cotta workers in Italy, and the system for the first time adopted in connection with this Exhibition of reproducing their work in plaster of Paris† seems likely to give prominence and encouragement to the plastic art of the country, since it will now be possible to meet any demand which may arise for such work with less risk of breakage and at a much smaller cost.

Ethnological exhibits.

The object with which the collection of agricultural implements has been made is also two-fold: first to give to the English public some insight into the agricultural methods and practices of the country, and second to invite the attention of manufacturers to the class of implements required by Indian agriculturists. The series is sufficiently complete to show that what the Indian agriculturist wants are simple and easily-handled

Agricultural exhibits.

* The "Dictionary of the Economic Products of India," compiled under the direction of the Government of India in the Revenue and Agricultural Department, by Dr. G. Watt, M.B., F.L.S.

† A system developed by Mr. J. Schaumburg, artist, attached to the Geological Survey Department of India.

implements, and that in this direction only is there any hope that the manufacturers of England can find any extensive outlet for agricultural machinery.

The third section of the space allotted to the Government of India is occupied by the Administrative Courts. The names of the various departments which have contributed to the equipment of these Courts will be found at page 13 of the Catalogue. With few exceptions, the exhibits in this class offer from their nature little attraction to the eye, yet the series of records and reports which have been provided will enable any persons who desire to make themselves acquainted with the details of the internal administration of India to ascertain the sources from which the best and most complete information is obtainable. The presence too of the Administrative Courts in the Exhibition building will help to give some practical notion of the vast machinery required for the administration of the Indian Empire, and in this view the contents of these Courts hold a significant position among the exhibits provided by the Government of India.

Administrative Courts.

Before concluding this brief review of the scheme under which the collections brought together by the Government of India have been effected and arranged, it is desirable to draw particular attention to four important exhibits, which lie perhaps outside the three sections which have been described. The first is the carved archway, or Nakarkhana, as it is called in the vernacular, which stretches across the central avenue in the foreground of the Art Ware Courts. This has been contributed to the Exhibition by the liberality of H.H. the Maharaja of Jaipur, and is characteristic, not only of the art of the country which he governs, but also of the enlightened munificence of this Prince. The second is the Animal Trophy, which has been furnished by the generous assistance of H.H. the Maharaja of Kuch Behar, a well-known and popular Prince and sportsman. But for this contribution the Indian Courts would have contained no striking illustration of the zoology of India. The third is the Burmese pavilion, which has been presented by the Chamber of Commerce of Rangoon, and contains an interesting exhibit of the two great products of that country, timber and rice. The fourth is the pair of double arches of inlaid stone from Agra. These have been presented to the British nation by the Government of the North-Western Provinces as an unique and faithful illustration of the architectural character of the celebrated "Taj Mahál of Agra"—the marble tomb of the wife of the Emperor Shahjehan. A historical description of these arches is given on page 194, and it is sufficient to state here that their connection with the Taj construction and architecture is so intimate that they may be accepted as a fragment of the mausoleum itself.

Four special exhibits.

Jaipur Nakarkhana.

Animal trophy.

It is necessary next to notice the connection with the Art Courts of the *Indian Art Journal*, of which special monthly numbers will appear during the period for which the Colonial and Indian Exhibition remains open. It has been truly observed that there are two powerful causes at work in the direction of degrading Indian art. The one is that of which mention has already been made, viz., the gradual decline of wealthy patronage; the other is the introduction of a cheaper and less artistic class of goods from Western countries. But the types of the old art remain in the country, and there appears to be some hope that through the education of the new generation of native artists in the right direction, and by spreading through the country a better knowledge of Oriental patterns, Eastern art may still struggle against the flood of Western ideas which threatens to obliterate the characteristic features which form its charm. The object of the *Indian Art Journal* is educational. It was launched under the patronage of the Government of India two years ago. Receiving liberal contribution from those officials and residents of India who are best able to supply suitable illustrations, and comprising, as it will, a continuous series of drawings from the Archæological Survey of the Empire, it is hoped that it will, by distribution among the schools and workshops of the country, help to feed the source from which new generations of artisans will imbibe their ideas of art and construction. The *Art Journal* has been advisedly brought within the scheme of the Indian sections of this Exhibition in order that advantage might be taken of the recent labours of the officers in every Province and Native State of the Empire to commence what is intended to be a complete series of historical descriptions illustrated by

"Indian Art Journal." *

* The *Indian Art Journal*, published by Mr. W. Griggs, Elm House, Hanover Street, Rye Lane, Peckham, London. The Archæological Survey Department is under the direction of Dr. J Burgess, C.I.E., LL.D., M.R.A.S., F.R.G.S.

typical examples of the art manufactures of India. It will be continued after the close of the Colonial and Indian Exhibition.

This Preface cannot be concluded without acknowledging the valuable contributions to the Indian section of the Colonial and Indian Exhibition, especially of the following princes, nobles, and Native gentlemen. Their voluntary and liberal aid has added greatly to the collections which find a place in the Indian Art Ware Courts.

Native Princes and Nobles whose contributions to the Colonial and Indian Exhibition are specially acknowledged.

His Highness the Nizam of Hyderabad; His Highness the Gaekwar of Baroda; His Highness the Maharaja of Mysore; His Highness the Maharaja of Jaipur; His Highness the Maharao Raja of Ulwar; His Highness the Maharaja of Kotah; His Highness the Maharaja of Jodhpur; His Highness the Maharaja of Bikanir.

INDIAN EMPIRE.

CHAPTER I.

AREA, 1,382,624 square miles; POPULATION, 253,891,821.

VICEROY AND GOVERNOR-GENERAL.—His Excellency the Right Honourable Sir Frederick Temple Hamilton-Temple, Earl of Dufferin, K.P., G.C.B., G.C.M.G., P.C., G.M.S.I., Viscount and Baron Clandeboye of Clandeboye in the County of Down, in the Peerage of the United Kingdom, Baron Dufferin and Clandeboye of Ballyleidy and Killyleagh, County Down, in the Peerage of Ireland, Vice-Admiral of Ulster.

LIST OF PROVINCES AND LEADING NATIVE STATES IN THE EMPIRE OF INDIA, REPRESENTED IN THE COLONIAL AND INDIAN EXHIBITION.

MADRAS.—GOVERNOR—His Excellency the Right Hon. Sir M. E. Grant Duff, C.I.E.—*Area in square miles*, 141,001; *Pop.*, 31,170,631; *No. in Skeleton Map*, XII.

BOMBAY.—GOVERNOR—His Excellency the Right Hon. Lord Reay, LL.D., C.I.E.—*Area in square miles*, 197,875; *Pop.*, 23,395,663; *No. in Skeleton Map*, III.

BENGAL.—LIEUTENANT-GOVERNOR—The Hon. Sir A. Rivers Thompson, K.C.S.I., C.I.E.—*Area in square miles*, 193,198; *Pop.* 69,563,861; *No. in Skeleton Map*, IV.

NORTH-WESTERN PROVINCES AND OUDH.—LIEUTENANT-GOVERNOR—The Hon. Sir A. C. Lyall, K.C.B., C.I.E.—*Area in square miles*, 11,236; *Pop.*, 44,849,619; *No. in Skeleton Map*. VI.

PUNJAB.—LIEUTENANT-GOVERNOR—The Hon. Sir C. U. Aitchison, K.C.S.I., C.I.E.—*Area in square miles*, 142,449; *Pop.*, 22,712,120; *No. in Skeleton Map*, VII.

CENTRAL PROVINCES.—CHIEF COMMISSIONER—C. H. T. Crosthwaite, Esq., C.S.—*Area in square miles*, 113,279; *Pop.*, 11,548,511; *No. in Skeleton Map*, IX.

BRITISH BURMA.—CHIEF-COMMISSIONER—C. E. Burnard, Esq., C.S.I.—*Area in square miles*, 87,220; *Pop.*, 3,736,771; *No. in Skeleton Map*, XI.

ASSAM.—CHIEF COMMISSIONER—C. A. Elliott, Esq., C.I.E.—*Area in square miles*, 46,341; *Pop.*, 4,811,426; *No. in Skeleton Map*, X.

COORG.—CHIEF COMMISSIONER—J. B. Lyall, Esq.—*Area in square miles*, 1,583; *Pop.*, 178,302; *No. in Skeleton Map*, XV.

AJMERE-MERWARA.—CHIEF COMMISSIONER—Colonel Sir E. R. C. Bradford, K.C.S.I., C.I.E.—*Area in square miles*, 2,711; *Pop.*, 460,722; *No. in Skeleton Map*, Ie.

CASHMERE.—NATIVE CHIEF—His Highness Maharaja Hartab Singh.—*Area in square miles*, 79,784; *Pop.*, 1,534,972. *Resident*—Colonel Sir Oliver St. John, K.C.S.I., R.E., B.S.C.

NIPAL.—NATIVE CHIEF—His Highness Maharaj-Adhiraj Prithivi Bir Bikram Sah.—*Area in square miles*, 54,000; *Pop.*, 2,000,000 (estimated by some at 5,000,000); *No. in Skeleton Map*, V. *Resident*—C. E. R. Girdlestone, Esq., C.S.

HYDERABAD.—NATIVE CHIEF—His Highness Nawab Mir Mahbub Ali Khan, G.C.S.I.—*Area in square miles*, 99,518; *Pop.*, 12,518,267 (including assigned districts); *No. in Skeleton Map*, XIII. *Resident*—J. G. Cordery, Esq., C.S.

MYSORE.—NATIVE CHIEF—His Highness Maharaja Cham Rajendra Wadiar, G.C.S.I—*Area in square miles*, 24,723; *Pop.*, 4,186,188; *No. in Skeleton Map*, XIV. *Resident*—J. B. Lyall, Esq., C.S.

BARODA.—NATIVE CHIEF—His Highness Maharaja Sayaji Rao Gaekwar.—*Area in square miles*, 8,570; *Pop.*, 2,185,005; *No. in Skeleton Map*, IIIa. *Agent to the Governor General in Baroda*—Major-General J. Watson, C.B., V.C., Bo.S.C.

RAJPUTANA STATES.

JEYPORE.—NATIVE CHIEF—His Highness Maharaja Madho Singh.—*Area in square miles*, 14,465; *Pop.*, 2,534,357; *No. in Skeleton Map*, Ia.

KARAULI.—NATIVE CHIEF—His Highness Maharaja Arjun Pal Deo.—*Area in square miles*, 1,208; *Pop.*, 148,670; *No. in Skeleton Map*, Ib.

BHARTPUR.—NATIVE CHIEF—His Highness Maharaja Jaswant Sing, G.C.S.I.—*Area in square miles*, 1,974; *Pop.*, 645,540; *No. in Skeleton Map*, I*b*.

DHOLPUR.—NATIVE CHIEF—His Highness Maharaja Rana Nihal Singh, Honorary Major in the British Army.—*Area in square miles*, 1,200; *Pop.*, 249,567; *No. in Skeleton Map*, I*b*.

KOTAH.—NATIVE CHIEF—His Highness Maharao Shatru Sal Sing.—*Area in square miles*, 3,797; *Pop.*, 517,275; *No. in Skeleton Map*, I*c*.

JODHPUR.—NATIVE CHIEF—His Highness Maharaja Jaswant Sing, G.C.S I.—*Area in square miles*, 37,000; *Pop.*, 1,750,403; *No. in Skeleton Map*, I*d*.

ULWAR.—NATIVE CHIEF—His Highness Maharao Raja Mangal Singh, Honorary Lieut.-Colonel in the British Army.—*Area in square miles*, 3,024; *Pop.*, 682,926; *No. in Skeleton Map*, I*f*.

BIKANIR.—NATIVE CHIEF—His Highness Maharaja Dungar Singh.—*Area in square miles*, 22,340; *Pop.*, 509,021; *No. in Skeleton Map*, I*g*. *Agent to the Governor General in Rajputana*—Colonel Sir E. R. C. Bradford, K.C.S.I., M.S.C.

CENTRAL INDIA STATES.

BHOPAL.—NATIVE CHIEF—Her Highness Nawab Shah Jahan Begum, G.C.S.I., C.I.E.—*Area in square miles*, 6,872, *Pop.*, 954,901; *No. in Skeleton Map*, II*a*.

GWALIOR.—NATIVE CHIEF—His Highness Maharaja Jayaji Rao Sindhia, G.C.B., G.C.S.I., C.I.E., Honorary General in the British Army.—*Area in square miles*, 29,046; *Pop.*, 2,993,652; *No. in Skeleton Map*, II*b*.

INDORE.—NATIVE CHIEF—His Highness Maharajah Tukaji Rao Holkar, G.C.S.I., C.I.E.—*Area in square miles*, 8,400; *Pop.*, 1,048,842; *No. in Skeleton Map*, II*c*.

REWAH.—NATIVE CHIEF—His Highness Maharaja Vyankatesh Raman Singh.—*Area in square miles*, 10,083; *Pop.*, 1,305,124; *No. in Skeleton Map*, II*d*. *Agent to the Governor General in Central India*—Sir L. H. Griffin, K.C.S.I., C.S.

TRAVANCORE.—NATIVE CHIEF—His Highness Maharaja Rama Varma.—*Area in square miles*, 6,730; *Pop.*, 2,401,158; *No. in Skeleton Map*, XII*a*. *Resident*—J. C. Hannyngton, Esq., C.S.

COCHIN.—NATIVE CHIEF—His Highness Raja Rama Varma, K.C.S.I.—*Area in square miles*, 1,361; *Pop.*, 600,278; *No. in Skeleton Map*, XII*b*. *Resident*—J. C. Hannyngton, Esq., C.S.

COOCH BEHAR.—NATIVE CHIEF—His Highness Maharaja Nripendra Narayan, Honorary Major in the British Army.—*Area in square miles*, 1,307; *Pop.*, 602,624; *No. in Skeleton Map*, XVI.

CHAPTER II.

OFFICERS AND COMMITTEES

CONNECTED WITH THE REPRESENTATION OF THE INDIAN EMPIRE AT THE COLONIAL AND INDIAN EXHIBITION, 1886.

At the Request of the Secretary of State for India in Council, and with the sanction of His Royal Highness THE PRINCE OF WALES, *Executive President of the Royal Commission, all the arrangements for the Indian Section of the Exhibition are entrusted to the Secretary to the Royal Commission,* SIR PHILIP CUNLIFFE-OWEN, K.C.B., K.C.M.G., C.I.E.

COMMISSIONER FOR INDIA.

SIR EDWARD C. BUCK, KT., B.C.S.

Secretary to the Government of India in the Revenue and Agricultural Department.

Official Collections in India were made under the general administration and direction of the Revenue and Agricultural Department of the Government of India.

I.—ADMINISTRATION.

By the following Officers—

Geology.

MEDLICOTT, H. B., Esq.

Meteorology.

BLANFORD, H. F., Esq.

Survey of India.

WATERHOUSE, Lieutenant-Colonel J.
STRAHAN, Major C., R.E.

Salt, Excise, Opium, Mints, Post Office, Government Printing, Education, Police, Sanitary and Medical, Public Works, Military, &c., &c.

Collections have been made under the orders of the Heads of the Departments concerned.

II.—ECONOMIC PRODUCTS.

By the following Officers—

Raw Products and Rough Manufactures.

WATT, Dr. G., C.I.E., on special duty with the Government of India Revenue and Agricultural Department.
MUKHARJI, BABU T. N., Revenue and Agricultural Department, Government of India.
Assisted by the Exhibition Committees in Bombay and Bengal, and the Chambers of Commerce at Calcutta and Bombay.

Timbers and Forest Produce.

RIBBENTROP, B., Esq., Inspector-General of Forests.
WHITTALL, R. H. C., Esq., Assistant-Inspector-General of Forests.
MANSON, F. B., Esq., Deputy Conservator of Forests, Bengal, on special duty.
Assisted by the Executive Officers working under the orders of the Inspector-General.

III.—ART WARE AND FABRICS.

By the following Committees and special officers appointed by the Governments of the various Provinces in India, or the Rulers of Native States—

MADRAS.

Committee.

HAWKES, Colonel H. P., Deputy Commissary General, President.

BIDIE, Dr. G., M.B., C.I.E.
HAVELL, E. B., Esq.
SHAW, J. C., Esq.
DEANE, C., Esq.
ORR, G. G., Esq.
LAWSON, C. A., Esq.
BENSON, C., Esq.
THURSTON, Dr. E.

BOMBAY.

Committee.

FORBES ADAM, The Honourable, Member of the Bombay Legislative Council, President.

OLLIVANT, E. C. K., Esq.
PORTMAN, Major A. B.
MACDONALD, Dr. D.
SULLEMAN, HAJI KARIM MAHOMED, Esq., (the late).
LEITH, E. T., Esq.
NANABHOY B. JEEJEEBHOY, Esq.
ATMARAM, VRIJBHUKAN DAS, Esq.
GRIFFITHS, J. Esq., Secretary.

BENGAL.

Committee.

COCKERELL, H. A., Esq., C.S.I., Member, Board of Revenue, President.

CRUICKSHANK, D., Esq., Vice-President
BERGER, H., Esq.
CUNNINGHAM, Surgeon-Major, D.D.
FINUCANE, M., Esq., B.C.S.
HENDERSON, J., Esq.
HILLS, C. R., Esq.
KESWICK, J. J. J., Esq.
KING, Dr. G.
LYALL, R., Esq.
MACDONNELL, Hon. A. P., B.C.S.
MAXWELL, J. D., Esq.
MILLER, R., Esq.
MURDOCH, J., Esq.
PEDLER, A., Esq.
RALLI, T., Esq.
RISLEY, H. H., Esq., B.C.S.
SIMSON, A., Esq.
TREVOR, Hon. Colonel S. T., R.E.
WATERHOUSE, Lieutenant-Colonel J., B.S.C.
JACKSON, M., Esq., Member and Secretary.

NORTH-WESTERN PROVINCES AND OUDH.

SMEATON, D. M., Esq., B.C.S., Director, Department of Agriculture and Commerce.
PITCHER, Lieutenant-Colonel D. G., Assistant Director, Department of Agriculture and Commerce.
GROWSE, F. S., Esq., C.I.E.
TYLER, Dr. J. W., C.I.E., Superintendent, Central Gaol, Agra.
CONSTABLE, A., Esq., Personal Assistant to the Chief Engineer, Oudh and Rohilkhand Railway.

PUNJAB.

KIPLING, J. L., Esq., Principal, Mayo School of Art, Lahore.

CENTRAL PROVINCES.

FULLER, J. B., Esq., B.C.S., Director, Department of Agriculture.

BURMA.

TILLY, H. E., Esq., Executive Engineer.

ASSAM.

DARRAH, H. Z., Esq., B.C.S., Director, Department of Agriculture.

COORG.

CLARKE, Colonel T. G., Commissioner of Coorg.
LEMESSURIER, Colonel A., Consulting Engineer, Bangalore.
McHUTCHIN, W., Esq., Executive Engineer, Mysore State Railway.

HYDERABAD STATE.

FITZGERALD, Colonel C. J. O., Commanding 3rd Cavalry, Hyderabad Contingent, Hyderabad.

MYSORE STATE.

LEMESSURIER, Colonel A., Consulting Engineer, Mysore, Bangalore.
McHUTCHIN, W., Esq., Executive Engineer, Mysore State Railway.

BARODA STATE.

Committee.

SADLER, Captain J. HAYES, Assistant Agent to the Governor General, President.
JACKSON, Major F. H.
RAO BAHADUR LAXMAN JAGGANATH.
RAO BAHADUR J. S. GADGIL.
TAIT, T. S., Esq.
REYNOLDS, P., Esq.
ABBAS S. TYABJI.
RAO BAHADUR RAOJI VITHAL.
RAO SAHEB HAR GOVINDAS DWARKADAS.
AMBALAL SAKARLAL DESAI.
DINSHA ARDESHIR TALEARKHAN, Honorary Secretary.

KASHMIR STATE.

ST. JOHN, Colonel Sir O., K.C.S.I., R.E., B.S.C., Resident in Kashmir.

NEPAL STATE.

GIMLETTE, Surgeon G. H. D., Residency Surgeon, Nepal, Katmandu.

CENTRAL INDIA STATES.

JOHNSTONE, J., Esq., Principal of the Residency College, Indore.

AJMERE AND RAJPUTANA.

BRADFORD, Colonel Sir E. R. C., K.C.S.I., M.S.C., Agent to the Governor General, Rajputana.
WHITEWAY, R. S., Esq., B.C.S., Settlement Officer, Ajmere-Merwara.
STRATTON, Surgeon-Major J. P., M.D., Resident, Eastern Rajputana States.
HENDLEY, Surgeon-Major T. H., in Medical charge, Eastern Rajputana States, and Honorary Secretary to the Museum Committee, Jeypore.
POWLETT, Colonel P. W., S.C., Resident, Western Rajputana States.
PEACOCK, Lieutenant-Colonel H. P., Political Agent, Alwar.
WYLLIE, Captain W. H. C., C.I.E., Political Agent, Kotah.
TALBOT, Captain A. C., S.C., Political Agent, Bikanir.
MUIR, Lieutenant-Colonel W. J. W., S.C., Political Agent, Harowtee and Tonk.
WALTER, Colonel C. K. M., S.C., Resident in Meywar.
EUAN-SMITH, Lieutenant-Colonel C. B., C.S.I., Political Agent, Bhartpur and Korowlee.

LIST OF NATIVE CHIEFS AND NOBLES

WHO HAVE RENDERED CONSPICUOUS ASSISTANCE IN THE EQUIPMENT OF THE INDIAN COURTS AT THE COLONIAL AND INDIAN EXHIBITION, 1886.

HYDERABAD.

HIS HIGHNESS THE NIZAM OF HYDERABAD, G.C.S.I.
Nawab Salar Jang.
Sardar Diler Jang, C.I.E.

MYSORE.

HIS HIGHNESS THE MAHARAJA OF MYSORE, G.C.S.I.
Diwan Sheshadri Iyer.

BARODA.

HIS HIGHNESS THE MAHARAJA (GAEKWAR) OF BARODA.

CENTRAL INDIA.

HIS HIGHNESS THE MAHARAJA SINDHIA OF GWALIAR, G.C.B., G.C.S.I., C.I.E.
HER HIGHNESS THE BEGAM OF BHOPAL, G.C.S.I., C.I.E.
HIS HIGHNESS THE MAHARAJA OF REWA.
HIS HIGHNESS THE MAHARAJA OF ORCHHA.
HIS HIGHNESS THE MAHARAJA OF DATIA.
HIS HIGHNESS THE MAHARAJA OF PANNA, K.C.S.I.
HIS HIGHNESS THE RAJA OF CHHATRAPUR.

RAJPUTANA.

HIS HIGHNESS THE MAHARAJA OF JAIPUR.
HIS HIGHNESS THE MAHARAJA OF JODHPUR, G.C.S.I.
HIS HIGHNESS THE MAHARAO RAJA OE ALWAR.
HIS HIGHNESS THE MAHARAO OF KOTA.
HIS HIGHNESS THE MAHARAJA OF BIKANIR.

MADRAS.

HIS HIGHNESS THE MAHARAJA OF TRAVANCORE.
HIS HIGHNESS THE RAJA OF COCHIN, K.C.S.I.

The Raja of Mandasa, Ganjam, C.I.E.
The Raja of Pithapur.
The Ranis of Tanjore.
The Zamindar of Sangamulsa, Vizagapatam.
The Zamindar of Mutto Kotham.

BOMBAY.

HIS HIGHNESS THE THAKUR SAHIB OF BHAVNAGAR, G.C.S.I.
HIS HIGHNESS THE RAO OF CUTCH.

BENGAL.

HIS HIGHNESS THE MAHARAJA OF COOCH BEHAR.
HIS HIGHNESS THE MAHARAJA OF HILL TIPPERAH.

Nawab Ahsanulla of Dacca.
Maharani Swarnamayi, C.I., of Kasim Bazar.
The Nawab Bahadur of Murshidabad.
Maharaja Girrijanath Rai of Dinajpore.
Maharaja Krishna Pratab Sahai Bahadur of Hatwa.
Raja Sir Sourendro Mohun Tagoro, Kt., C.I.E.
Babu Mohendro Lal Khan of Narajal, Midnapore.

NORTH-WESTERN PROVINCES AND OUDH.

HIS HIGHNESS THE NAWAB OF RAMPUR, G.C.S.I., C.I.E.

PUNJAB.

HIS HIGHNESS THE NAWAB OF BAHAWALPUR, G.C.S.I.
HIS HIGHNESS THE MAHARAJA OF PATIALA.

ASSAM.

THE MAHARAJA OF MANIPUR, K.C.S.I.

CHAPTER III.

Classified List, showing the Classes and Divisions under which Exhibits are ranged, and the general position they occupy in the Building.

CLASS A.—THE COUNTRY.

Div. I.—Physical Features	Economic Court Annexe.
II.—Natural History	Economic Court Annexe.
III.—Ethnology	Economic Court.

CLASS B.—THE ADMINISTRATION.

Div. I.—Department of Revenue and Agriculture.	Administration Court right of main entrance.
II.—Department of Finance and Commerce.	
III.—Home Department	
IV.—Department of Public Works	
V.—Legislative Department.	
VI.—Foreign Department.	
VII.—Military Department.	

CLASS C.—PRODUCTS AND PRIMARY MANUFACTURES.

Div. I.—Foods and Food Stuffs.	Economic Court opposite main entrance.
II.—Spirits, Wines, other Beverages and Vinegars.	
III.—Narcotics	
IV.—Oilseeds, Oils, Soap, and Perfumery.	
V.—Medicines, Drugs, Chemicals.	
VI.—Gums, Resins, &c.	
VII.—Dyes, Tans, Mordants, Pigments, and Paints.	
VIII.—Fibres and fibrous plants.	
IX.—Leather, Hides, Horns, &c.	
X.—Cane, grass, and Bamboo.	
XI.—Minerals and ores.	
XII.—Timbers	

CLASS D.—ARTS AND INDUSTRIES.

Div. I.—Fine Arts	Art-ware Court opposite main entrance.
II.—Decorative Art	
III.—Musical Instruments.	
IV.—Jewellery	
V.—Art manufactures in Metal.	
VI.—Art manufactures in Wood, Ivory, &c.	
VII.—Lapidaries' Work	
VIII.—Marble and Stone	
IX.—Pottery	
X.—Glass	
XI.—Textiles	
XII.—Embroideries	
XIII.—Leathers and Furs	
XIV.—Basket, Mat, and Straw work.	

CLASS A.—THE COUNTRY.

DIV. I.—*Physical Features.*

Sect. 1. Geography. 2. Meteorology. Geology.

DIV. II.—*Natural History.*

Sect. 1. Botany. 2. Zoology.

DIV. III.—*Ethnology.*

Sect. 1. Races of inhabitants. 2. Articles of personal adornment. 3. Articles of domestic use. 4. Articles of sport and war. 5. Articles of agricultural use. 6. Language and religion.

CLASS B.—ADMINISTRATION.

IMPERIAL DEPARTMENTS.

DIV. I.—*Department of Revenue and Agriculture.*

A star (*) denotes a minor Imperial Department under the administration of a Special Officer.

Sect. 1. Trigonometrical Survey, Topographical Survey, Cadastral Survey.* 2. Meteorology.* 3. Geological Survey.* 4. Agriculture. 5. Revenue. 6. Internal Trade. 7. Emigration.

DIV. II.—*Department of Finance and Commerce.*

Sect. 1. General Finance. 2. Salt.* 3. Customs. 4. Excise. 5. Opium. 6. The Mints.* 7. Stamps.* 8. Post Office.* 9. External Trade. 10. Government Printing.

DIV. III.—*Home Department.*

Sect. 1. Education. 2. Law and Justice. 3. Police. 4. Sanitary and Medical.* 5. Archæological Survey.* 6. Forests.* 7. Statistics and Gazetteers.* 8. Jails.

DIV. IV.—*Public Works Department.*

Sect. 1. Railways.* 2. Roads. 3. Irrigation.* 4. Public Buildings. 5. Telegraphs.*

DIV. V.—*Legislative Department.*

Sect. 1. Acts and Regulations.

DIV. VI.—*Foreign Department.*

Sect. 1. Native States. 2. Imperial Orders and Decorations.

DIV. VII.—*Military and Marine Department.*

Army Headquarters.

Sect. 1. Interior Economy of Army. 2. Military Education. 3. Soldiers' Exhibitions and Workshops. 4. Military Maps and Routes.

Military.

Sect. 1. Military Organisation. 2. Military Medical—Ambulance, &c.* 3. Army Clothing.* 4. War Matériel.* 5. Food and Transport.* 6. Horse Breeding and Army Remounts.* 7. Elephant Kheddahs.* 8. Indian Medals and Decorations. 9. Military Buildings.*

Marine.

Sect. 1. Dockyards and Ships.* 2. Marine Surveys.*

The Divisions show the Imperial Secretariat Departments of the Government of India.

The Sections show the Minor Departments and subjects with which they deal.

CLASS C.—PRODUCTS AND PRIMARY MANUFACTURES.

DIVISION I.—FOODS AND FOOD STUFFS.

OF A VEGETABLE NATURE.

Sub-Court XI., Sect. 1. Cereals and preparations from cereals—Flour, pearl-barley, &c.

Sub-Court XIII., Sect. 2. Pulses and preparations from pulses—Split-peas, peas, meal, &c. 3. Other grains and seeds—Buck-wheat, Amarantus, &c.

Sub-Court XI., Sect. 4. Bread, pastry, biscuits, and other manufactures from 1, 2, and 3.

Sub-Court VIII., Sect. 5. Vegetables, tubers, bulbs, roots, and stems—Potato, Aracaca, Yams, &c.

Sub-Court IX., Sect. 6. Fruits and nuts with models and drawings to illustrate these.

Sub-Court X., Sect. 7. Sugar, molasses, syrup, &c., &c. 8. Starches—Arrowroot, sago, tapioca, &c., &c.

Sub-Court VII., Sect. 9. Cattle food and fodder. 10. Foods used in times of famine.

Sub-Court XIV., Sect. 11. Spices and condiments—Pepper and mustard, olives, capers, cardamoms, cinnamons, ginger, &c., &c, 12. Essences and extracts.

Sub-Court IX., Sect. 13. Jams, jellies, preserved fruits, and other manufactures or preparations from fruits and vegetables. 14. Confectionery, sweetmeats, &c. 15. Pickles, chutnies, curry-powders, sauces, &c.

Sub-Court XI., Sect. 16. Other exhibits.

OF AN ANIMAL NATURE.

Sub-Court VI., Sect. 17. Preparations of meat, game, &c. 18. Preparations of fish, &c. 19. Other exhibits.

OF A MINERAL NATURE.

Sub-Court VI., Sect. 20. Salt, earths, &c.

DIVISION II.—SPIRITS, WINES, OTHER BEVERAGES, AND VINEGARS.

Sub-Court XII., Sect. 1. Spirits, spirits of wine, &c. 2. Wines. 3. Ale and porter. 4. Aërated waters, mineral water, and specially-prepared essences, &c., used in their manufacture. 5. Vinegar—malt and wine. 6. Other exhibits.

DIVISION III.—NARCOTICS.

Tea and Coffee Room, Sect. 1. Tea. 2. Coffee, coffee-beans, prepared coffee, and essence of coffee. 3. Chocolate, cocoa, and cocoa-beans.

Sub-Court XVI., Sect. 4. Tobacco and its preparations. (Shown in the Tobacco Room.) 5. Opium and its preparations. 6. Indian hemp, and its preparations. 7. Other exhibits.

DIVISION IV.—OIL-SEEDS, OILS, SOAP, AND PERFUMERY.

Sub-Court XXI., Sect. 1. Oil-seeds. 2. Prepared oils. 3. Soaps. 4. Perfumery-producing products. 5. Prepared perfumes, ottos, &c. 6. Wood ash. 7. Other exhibits.

DIVISION V.—MEDICINES, DRUGS, CHEMICALS.

Sub-Court XV., Sect. 1. Medicinal raw products 2. Prepared medicines and drugs—quinine, &c., &c. 3. Chemicals. 4. Poisons. 5. Other exhibits.

DIVISION VI.—GUMS, RESINS, &c.

Sub-Courts XXXIII. and XXXIV., Sect. 1. Gums and resins. 2. Catechu and its preparations. 3. Gambier and its preparations.

Sub-Court XXXVI., Sect. 4. Lac and its preparations.

Sub-Courts XXXIII. & XXXIV., Sect. 5. Varnishes, raw and prepared. 6. India-rubber, gutta-percha, &c., with their preparations and manufactures.

DIVISION VII.—DYES, TANS, MORDANTS, PIGMENTS, AND PAINTS.

Dyes of a Vegetable Nature.

Sub-Court XXXV., Sect. 1. Indigo.

Sub-Court XXXVII., Sect. 2. Safflower. 3. Madder. 4. Other exhibits.

Dyes of an Animal Nature.

Sub-Court XXXVII., Sect. 5. Lac-dye and cochineal. 6. Indian yellow dye or Peori. 7. Other exhibits.

Dyes of a Mineral Nature.

Sub-Court XXXVII., Sect. 8. Earths. 9. Mordants and dye auxiliaries. 10. Mixed dyes. 11. Other exhibits.

Tans.

Sub-Court XXXVIII., Sect. 12. Wattle bark. 13. Divi-divi pods. 14. Babul bark and pods. 15. Myrabolams. 16. Galls. 17. Other tans and tanning materials.

Pigments and Paints.

Sub-Court XXXVII., Sect. 20. Pigments. 21. Paints. 22. Inks, dry and liquid.

DIVISION VIII.—FIBRES AND FIBROUS PLANTS.

Of a Vegetable Nature.

(a) Textile Fibres.

Sub-Court XXIV., Sect. 1. Cotton, ginned and unginned. 2. Manufactures of cotton, not included in Class D.

Sub-Court XXV., Sect. 3. Jute. 4. Manufactures of jute.

Sub-Court XXIII., Sect. 5. Flax and its manufactures. 6. Hemp and its manufactures. 7. Sunn hemp (*Crotalaria juncea*) and its manufactures. 8. Bowstring hemp (*Sansevieria*) and its manufactures. 9. Manilla hemp and other plantain and banana fibres, with manufactures. 10. Aloe and Yucca fibres, with manufactures. 11. Rhea and other nettle fibres, with manufactures. 12. Coir and its manufactures.

Sub-Court XXII., Sect. 13. Fibres suitable as silk substitutes. 14. Other exhibits.

(b) Fibres suitable for Cordage.

Sub-Court XXII., Sect. 15. Cordage fibres. 16. Ropes, twine, &c., &c.

(c) Paper and Paper Materials.

Sub-Court XXVI., Sect. 17. Fibres suitable for paper manufacture. 18. Paper half stuffs. 19. Indian indigenous and hand-made paper. 20. European or machinery-made paper.

Of an Animal Nature.

(a) Silk.

Sub-Court XXVII., Sect. 21. Mulberry, silk-worms and insects, cocoons, waste, fibre, and thread. 22. Tussur silk-worms and insects, cocoons, waste, fibre, thread, and manufactures, not included in Class D. 23. Eri silk-worms and insects, cocoons, fibre, waste, thread, and manufactures. 24. Muga silk-worms and insects, cocoons, fibre, waste, thread, and manufactures. 25. Other exhibits.

(b) Wool.

Sub-Court XXVIII., Sect. 26. Indian and imported. 27. Manufactures of wool, not included in Class D. 28. Pashm and its manufactures. 29. Hair and its manufactures. 30. Other exhibits.

Of a Mineral Nature.

Sub-Court XXVIII., Sect. 31. Asbestos, &c.

DIVISION IX., LEATHER, HIDES, HORNS, Etc.

Sub-Court XXVIII., Sect. 1. Leather and the coarser manufactures therefrom. 2. Skins, hides, horns, &c. 3. Other exhibits.

DIVISION X.—CANE, GRASS, AND BAMBOO.

Imperial Court, Sect. 1. Canes, reeds, and bamboos. 2. Sedge mats and matting. 3. Palm (cane and leaf) mats and matting. 4. Screw pine and sital-pati mats. 5. Chicks and tatties. 6. Bamboo mats and matting. 7. Basket-work and cane furniture, not included in Class D. 8. Brushes and other small articles. 9. Thatching.

DIVISION XI.—MINERALS AND ORES.

Sub-Court XLI., Sect. 1. Minerals. 2. Coal. 3. Building materials, lime, sand, clay, &c. 4. Bricks, tiles, &c. 5. Stones, marble, &c. 6. Domestic pottery of every-day life, cooking utensils, water-jugs, &c., &c. 7. Ores. 8. Metals. 9. Metal wares used in every-day life, cooking utensils, &c.

DIVISION XII.—TIMBERS.

Sub-Courts I., II, and III., Sect. 1. Collections of timbers. 2. Wooden utensils and implements. 3. Other exhibits.

CLASS D.—ARTS AND INDUSTRIES.

DIVISION I.—FINE ARTS.

Sect. 1. Paintings and drawings. 2. Engravings, lithographs, &c. 3. Photographs, &c. 4. Sculpture.

DIVISION II.—DECORATIVE ART.

Sect. 1. Architectural designs and models. 2. Designs for manufactures. 3. Archæological drawings, models, &c. 4. Models in clay, wax, terra-cotta, plaster-of-Paris. 5. Decorative painting as applied to architecture. 6. Decorative painting as applied to articles of domestic use. 7. Decorative carving as applied to architecture. 8. Other works of decorative art not specified.

DIVISION III.—MUSICAL INSTRUMENTS.

Sect. 1. Wind instruments. 2. Stringed instruments. 3. Instruments of percussion.

DIVISION IV.—JEWELLERY.

Sect. 1. Gold and silver smiths' work, including filigrain, settings of precious stones, &c. 2. Enamelled jewellery.

DIVISION V.—ART MANUFACTURES IN METAL.

Sect. 1. Gold and silver plate. 2. Koft or damascened work. 3. Brass, copper, and mixed metal. 4. Brass and copper wares for sacrificial purposes—(*a.* modern), (*b.* ancient). 5. Arms and armour (*a.* ancient), (*b.* modern). 6. Cutlery. 7. Iron and steel wares. 8. Electroplated wares. 9. Enamels, other than jewellery.

DIVISION VI.—ART MANUFACTURES IN WOOD, IVORY, ETC.

Sect. 1. Carved furniture and carpentry. 2. Inlaid work. 3. Ivory carving. 4. Lacquered wares. 5. Wood carving.

DIVISION VII.—LAPIDARIES' WORK.

Sect. 1. Agate, jasper and cornelian wares. 2. Shells.

DIVISION VIII.—MARBLE AND STONE.

Sect. 1. Carved objects in marble. 2. Inlaid marble.

DIVISION IX.—POTTERY.

Sect. 1. Glazed pottery. 2. Unglazed pottery.

DIVISION X.—GLASS.

Sect. 1. Blown objects. 2. Moulded articles.

DIVISION XI.—TEXTILES.

Sect. 1. Cotton fabrics. 2. Wool fabrics. 3. Silk fabrics. 4. Other fabrics.

DIVISION XII.—EMBROIDERIES.

Sect. 1. Silk, cotton, or woollen thread. 2. Gold and silver.

DIVISION XIII.—LEATHERS AND FURS.

Sect. 1. Shoes. 2. Postins, belts, saddlery, &c. 3. Furs.

DIVISION XIV.—BASKETS, MATS, AND STRAW WORK.

CHAPTER IV.

CLASS A.—THE COUNTRY.

DIVISION I.—PHYSICAL FEATURES.

[*Exhibits under Section* (1) *Geography, and* (2) *Meteorology are placed in the Economic Court Annexe; those under Section* (3) *Geology in the Economic Court.*]

(1) Geography.

Maps.

1. **Raised Map of India.** Scale 1 in. = 32 miles.—This model has been made from the latest maps. On so small a scale as 1 in. = 32 miles it is necessary to greatly exaggerate the heights of the mountains, hence the vertical scale is twelve times the horizontal; though it is impossible to show minute features, great care has been taken to preserve the relative heights of the plains, plateaux, and hill tops. Geographical information is too scanty to allow of Burma or the countries north of India being accurately modelled; hence the representations of the hills end abruptly in those regions.

2. **Contour Map of India.** Scale 1 in. = 64 miles.—This map was prepared not to represent accurately the configuration of the hills, as its name perhaps implies, but to show the mean height of the mountain masses. On the map itself will be found a note describing how it was compiled, as also some tabular statements giving interesting information.

3. **Map of Principal River Basins.** Scale 1 in. = 96 miles.—A glance at this map shows that nearly all the large rivers of India flow into the Bay of Bengal. The most notable exceptions are the Indus, the Nerbudda, and Tapti. The Indus and Brahmapootra, rising from nearly the same place in Tibet, flow in exactly opposite directions, the one into the Arabian Sea, and the other into the Bay of Bengal. The tabular statements on the map itself give the lengths of the rivers and other interesting information.

4. **Irrigation Map.**—This map shows the canal system, and indicates clearly how the rivers of the Himalayas have been made to water the alluvial plains of the Punjab and of the North-Western Provinces. The width of the canals is necessarily much exaggerated, since, if drawn to scale, they would hardly be visible. This circumstance accounts for the apparent smallness of the area irrigated when compared with the net work of canals. The series of blocks in each province shows the actual areas under irrigation from canals, wells, and other sources, the latter head including tanks, lakes, and small rivers. The irrigation from canals is divided into snow-fed and river-fed irrigation, the difference between the two being that the former is independent of, and the latter dependent on, the annual rainfall. About half of the well area is said to be independent of annual rainfall, while almost all the irrigation from "other sources" is dependent on it.

5. **Railway Coal and Iron.**—This map shows the railways of India constructed to date as well as those which are in contemplation. The red dots denote places where iron, and the red splashes where coal is found.

6. **General Maps of India.**

7. **Civil Divisions.**—This map indicates (1) the Provinces under the British Government, and (2) the leading Native States of India, the former being coloured pink, and the latter yellow. A comparison of this map with the Meteorological and Geographical maps will show that a considerable portion of the yellow area, especially in North-Western Rajputana, where the country is desert, is dry and infertile.

8. **Map showing Density of Population.**—The interest of this map consists chiefly in the indication it gives of the way in which population crowds on the alluvial lands of the Ganges valley; a sure indication of the fertility of Bengal, the North-Western Provinces, and the south-east section of the Punjab. This map should be compared with the raised map on the table in the Economic Court.

9. **Distribution of Languages.** — It will be observed that the languages of Northern and Central India belong almost exclusively to the Aryan and those of Southern India to the Dravidian group. The total number of distinct Indian languages spoken in India was estimated at the last census in 1881 as 106.

10. **Distribution of Religions.**—Of the inhabitants of India about 74 per cent. are Hindus, 19 per cent. Muhammadans, 1 per cent Buddhists, and 7 per cent. Christians. Muhammadanism is most prevalent in the Punjab and in Bengal, in which provinces its followers number about one-half and one-third respectively of the population. Of the Christians, about two-thirds belong to the Madras Presidency.

11. **Missionary Stations.**—On this map the name of every missionary station is underlined in red, and close to it are placed the symbols which denote the societies of which there are representatives at that station. It will be seen that missionaries are considerably more numerous in the south of India than elsewhere, and the religion map shows that only in this part of India are Christians in any great numbers.

(2) Meteorology.

Ten charts are exhibited by the Indian Meteorological Department;* these may be arranged in three groups: the first group, charts 1 to 4 inclusive, dealing with the normal distribution of temperature in India; the second group, charts 5 to 8 inclusive, dealing with the normal distribution of rainfall; and thirdly, charts 9 and 10 dealing with the abnormal distribution of rain during famine years. The two years 1876 and 1877 were years of remarkable drought in different parts of India, and charts of the rainfall of those years are given to illustrate the vicissitudes of Indian rainfall.

The following is a brief descriptive notice of each of these charts:—

1. Chart of the mean annual isotherms.—This chart represents the mean distribution of temperature in India, on the average of the whole year, deduced from the observations of nearly 200 stations; and the temperatures dealt with in this chart have been corrected to their sea level equivalents.

It shows that when the temperature is reduced to its equivalent at sea-level, the hottest tract in India is a portion of the Deccan plateau, in the heart of the peninsula, extending between Bellary and Sholapur. Actually, owing to its elevation (about 1500 feet above the sea), the temperature of this plateau is 3° or 4° less than that shown on the chart; and the hottest region is really the eastern coast of the peninsula, from Vizagapatam southwards, and the plains of the Carnatic and Northern Ceylon, where the mean annual temperature is about 82°, or rather higher.

In the peninsula, or intra-tropical India, except as modified by the elevation of the country, the temperature increases steadily from the coast inland; and the west coast is cooler than the east coast.

In northern, or extra-tropical India, the western half, including Sind and Rajputana, has a higher annual mean temperature than the eastern half (including Bengal and Assam).

2. Isothermal Chart for January.—In the cold season, the temperature decreases, with the increase of latitude, more regularly and rapidly than at any other season of the year; and therefore the isotherms conform more nearly to the parallels of latitude. After allowing for elevation, there is a difference of nearly 25° between the Northern Punjab (the coolest region) and the southern extremity of the peninsula, which is exactly 1° of temperature for each degree of latitude, on an average.

3. Isothermal Chart for May.—This is the hottest month of the year in the greater part of India; the temperature of June and the subsequent months being reduced by the evaporation consequent on the monsoon rainfall.

The distribution of temperature in May is a very striking illustration of the thermal contrast afforded by land and water, when exposed to the same heating agency. The isotherms are a series of concentric curves, closely following the form of the land and the mountain boundaries, and increasing from a mean temperature of between 82° and 86° on the coast, to 96° (after correction for elevation) in Nagpur, the Nerbudda valley, Central India (Jhansi, Saugor, &c.), and Bikanir.

Of those stations, the temperature of which has been pretty accurately determined, the hottest, in the month of May, is Jhansi, with a mean temperature of 94·5° (as observed). Morar (Gwalior) and Wardha in Nagpur appear to be equally hot. The coolest region is Assam, where the rainfall of May is very copious.

4. Isothermal Chart for July.—The change in the distribution of temperature which distinguishes this chart from that of May is due to the cooling effect of the rains; and over the greater part of India the measure of this cooling varies as the copiousness of the rainfall.

The hottest region in India is now Upper Sind and the adjoining portion of Western Rajputana, a region which is practically rainless; any rainfall being rare and precarious.

Except that the Konkan and Malabar, which receive an exceptionally heavy rainfall, are cooler than any other part of Southern India, the peninsula has a nearly uniform temperature of about 83° (as reduced to sea level).

5. Chart of the average annual rainful:—This chart is based on the rainfall registers of about 1,300 stations.

The darkest tint on the chart indicates those tracts in which the average annual rainfall exceeds 100 inches. These are the west coast of the peninsula, the west coasts of Arakan, Pegu, and Tenasserim, the plains of Sylhet, and Cachar; the southern and western slopes of the Garo, Khasia, and Jaintia hills; and the southern face of the Central Himalaya, with a narrow strip of the plain at their foot. In some parts of these tracts the rainfall much exceeds 100 in.

The driest part of India is a portion of the Indus valley, extending from Bahawalpore to Hyderabad in Sind, and the Pat or Cuchee desert, which extends west of the Indus up to the Bolan Pass. In all this region the average annual rainfall does not exceed 5 in., and in some parts 3 in.

The mean annual rainfall of the whole of India proper, including Bengal and Assam, is about 42 in., varying, from an extreme of nearly 500 in. at Chera Poonji, in the Khasi Hills to about 3 in. at Jacobabad, in the extreme west, and to less than 20 in. around Bellary and at Tuticorin, in the extreme south of the peninsula.

The provinces most subject to dearth and famine are the North-Western Provinces, Behar, Rajputana, the Carnatic, the North Deccan, Hyderabad, Mysore, Orissa and the Northern Circars; all of which have an average rainfall

* A more detailed description of the Meteorological Department exhibits will be found in a "Memorandum to accompany charts of temperature of rainfall of India" by Mr. H. F. Blanford, F.R.S., Meteorological Reporter to the Government of India.

under 50 in., and a mean variability of 12 per cent. or more. Those provinces with an average rainfall of more than 50 in., and an average variability of less than 12 per cent. on either side of that average, enjoy practical immunity from famine.

6. Chart of the rainfall of the cold season.—This and the two charts next following show the distribution of rain during each of the three seasons into which the Indian year is naturally divided. The cold season of Northern India lasts from November to February; in the Punjab to the end of March. In the first month or six weeks of this season heavy rain is, as a rule, restricted to the Carnatic and Ceylon. In December it is more concentrated in Ceylon: the area of heavy rainfall travelling gradually to the south, up to the end of the year; when the north-east monsoon is established all down the Bay, and the weather clears up.

October and November are generally rainless, or nearly so, in Northern India; but, in December, the skies of the Punjab begin to be covered with cloud; and about Christmas, as a rule, rain sets in in the Upper Provinces, and snow falls on the mountains to the north and west. The rain is not continuous, nor much prolonged, but in general it is repeated two or three times in January and February, lasting on each occasion for two or three days. Most usually it begins in the Punjab, and subsequently extends to the east, sometimes reaching as far as Bengal. This is known as the cold weather rains of Northern India. Similar rain occurs in Assam, especially the upper part of the valley.

The greater part of the Bombay Presidency and the adjacent parts of Rajputana and Central India are, in general, rainless throughout the cold season and up to the end of May.

7. Chart of the rainfall of the hot season:—The rainfall of the spring months (March to May) is that which falls generally towards the evening, in local thunderstorms. It is fed by the sea winds, which set in from the cooler sea surface towards the heated interior of the country, when the distribution of temperature is becoming that represented in the isothermal chart of May. As the rainfall chart shows, it is practically restricted to the south and east of the peninsula, to Bengal, Assam, the Himalaya, and Arakan and Pegu; the greater part of the Bombay Presidency being almost or quite rainless; while the rainfall of the Southern Punjab, Rajputana, Central India, the North-Western Provinces and Oudh, and the western half of the Central Provinces, is extremely light, and in some years fails almost entirely.

8. Chart of the rainfall of the rainy season:—Except in the Carnatic and Ceylon, and also in the interior of the Himalaya, the rainfall of this season so far exceeds that of the remaining seasons of the year, that its distribution practically determines that of the whole year, as shown on the 5th chart of this series.

In Assam and Eastern Bengal, and there alone, the transition from the hot weather or spring rainfall to that of the rainy season proper is comparatively gradual. But in most parts of India, and more especially on the coasts, it is so abrupt as to be recognised in popular language as the *burst of the monsoon.*

On the west coast of India the monsoon blows rather from west than south-west In the northern part of the Arabian Sea the winds are frequently north-west, and generally from that direction in Beluchistan. Thus, the monsoon current that blows on Kathiawar and Cutch is by no means so damp a wind as that which prevails in the Konkan and Malabar; and to the north of Bombay the monsoon rainfall on the coast diminishes rapidly.

The aridity of North-Western India, including Sind, Khyrpur, Western Rajputana, Bahawalpur and the Southern Punjab, is thus explained. It is only occasionally and rarely that this portion of India is reached by a saturated current of air from the seas to the southward; and, except in the Northern Punjab, the prevalent winds during the monsoon are fed by air either from the Mekran coast or from the dry hilly country to the west.

On the Bay of Bengal the monsoon is from the south-west, changing to south and south-east in Lower Bengal, and blowing up the Gangetic plain as an easterly wind; while to the south of the Ganges and Jumna, the plateaux of Central India and the Deccan are swept by a strong west wind. Between this easterly wind on the north and the westerly branch of the monsoon on the south is a debatable region, where the winds are variable, the rainfall heavier and more regular and certain than either in the Gangetic plain on the one hand or in the Deccan on the other. This includes Chutia Nagpur, Orissa, the Central Provinces, and the eastern States of Central India. At frequent intervals during the monsoon, cyclonic storms, generated in the north of the Bay of Bengal, pass westwards across the Orissa coast, and travel along this debatable zone, sometimes passing right across India to Cutch and out to the Arabian Sea; at other times moving to the north-west, towards the Punjab, but always bringing a concentrated rainfall, and frequently causing more or less destructive floods.

9. Chart of the rainfall in 1876.—The year 1876 was that of the last great famine in Madras and the Deccan, owing to the failure of the rainfall of that year, following on a deficient rainfall in 1875. In the Carnatic, the rainfall of the year was 39 per cent. below the normal average; and the late autumnal rains, which give the chief supply to the tanks on which cultivation largely depends, failed almost completely. In Mysore and Bellary the deficiency was not less than 50 per cent., in Hyderabad 43 per cent., and in the Deccan 46 per cent. In Berar and Khandesh it was 23 per cent.; and elsewhere less; but it extended to the North-Western Provinces, where the rainfall was 16 per cent. below the average.

10. Chart of the rainfall in 1877.—In the year 1877, which was the year of drought in

the North-West Provinces and Rajputana in Northern and North-Western India, with the exception of the Punjab and in Central India, the deficiency of rainfall was very great. It amounted to 39 per cent. in the North-Western Provinces, to 45 per cent. in Rajputana, 31 per cent. in Central India, and to 22 per cent. in Behar. In Guzerat the deficiency was not less than 50 per cent. of the annual average.

Books.

11. Reports on the Meteorology of India from 1875 to 1883, 9 Quarto Volumes.
12. Original Observations at 6 Stations in India, 1879–1884, 6 Quarto Volumes.
13. Indian Meteorological Memoirs, 2 Quarto Volumes.
14. Indian Meteorologists' Vade-Mecum, Parts I. and II. and Tables, 3 Octavo Volumes.
15. Indian Meteorological Office, Telegraphic Code and Instructions. 1 Octavo Volume.
16. Report on the Calcutta Cyclone, 1864.
17. Report on the Midnapore and Burdwan Cyclone, 1874.
18. Report on the Vizagapatam and Backergunge Cyclone, 1876.
19. Report on the Madras Cyclone, 1877.

3. Geology.*

A Geological section, to natural scale (1 in. = 5,280 ft. = 1 mile), 40 ft. (480 miles) long, from Thibet to Amarkantuk in the Central Provinces, showing the profile and structure of the Himalaya, the plains, and peninsular India.

Maps.

The first 16 are general geological maps, the rest are of coal and mineral areas.

1. A geological map of India: scale 1 in. = 32 miles.
2 Geological sketch of the hills in the neighbourhood of the British Frontier from Quetta to Dera Ghazi Khan: scale 1 in. = 8 miles. All of tertiary and cretaceous formations.
3. A Geological map of Western Sind: scale 1 in. = 16 miles. All of tertiary and cretaceous rocks.
4. Geological map of the Province of Kathiawar: scale 1 in. = 16 miles. Principally of the Deccan trap, with a fringe of upper tertiary deposits.
5. Geological map of the Kashmir and Chamba territories: scale 1 in. = 16 miles. Shows the north-west termination of the Himalayas proper.
6. Geological map of a portion of the lower Narbada valley: scale 1 in. = 4 miles. It shows the cretaceous and Gondwana beds of Bág, between the Deccan-trap and the gneiss.
7. Geological map of the Punjab Salt-range: scale 1 in. = 4 miles. The only ground in which marine palæozoic rocks are known within (south of) the tertiary zone of the extra-peninsular region.
8. Geological map of the country between the Ganges and Ravi: scale 1 in. = 8 miles. This includes the Simla area of the Lower Himalayan region.
9. Geological map of the South Mahratta country: scale 1 in. = 16 miles. Shows the Bhima and Kaladgi basins of Vindhyan rocks at the southern margin of the Deccan-trap.
10. Geological map of the area north of the Sone and Narbada rivers occupied by the Vindhyan series: scale 1 in. = 32 miles. This is the main Vindhyan basin.
11. Geological map of the Darjiling hill territory: scale 1 in. = 4 miles. Shows the Gondwana coal-measures at the foot of the Sikkim Himalaya.
12. Geological map of the main Himalayan range in the Kumaun district: scale 1 in. = 4 miles.
13. Geological map of part of the Khasia hills: scale 1 in. = 4 miles. Shows the cretaceous and tertiary strata resting on the archæan rocks of the Shillong plateau at Chárápunji, and at the south border dipping under the plains of Sylhet.
14. Geological map of a portion of the Madras Presidency included in the Karnul and Cuddapah districts: scale 1 in. = 16 miles. This is the principal southern basin of Vindhyan rocks.
15. Geological map of Pegu Province of Burma: scale 1 in = 8 miles. The lower valley of the Irrawaddy between the Arakan and Pegu Yomahs of tertiary rocks, west of the Malayan gneissic axis.
16. Geological map of the neighbourhood of Madras: scale 1 in. = 4 miles.

Coal-field Maps.

17. The Wardha valley and Bandar coal-fields: scale 1 in. = 4 miles. Shows the Warora and Bandar fields of the Chanda district, the Pisgaon field in the Wun district of Berar and the Sasti and Antergaon fields in the Nizam's territories.
18. Geological map of the Pranhita Godavari valley: scale 1 in. = 8 miles. This is a great basin of Gondwana rocks with several outcrops of the coal measures, at Tandur, Chinur, Lingala, Madavaram-Damercherla, Bedanole, and the outlying field of Singareni.
19. The Warora and Wun coal-fields: scale 1 in. = 1 mile. The Warora colliery is the only one as yet established in this field.
20. Geological map of the northern part of the Jabalpur district and adjoining country: scale 1 in. = 4 miles. This is (prospectively) a very important mineral district, abounding in rich iron ores and adjoining good coal-fields (see special descriptive list).
21. The Umaria and Korar coal-fields: scale

* For a detailed description of Geological exhibits, see separate Catalogue by H. B. Medlicott, Esq., A.M., F.R.S., F.G.S., Director of the Geological Survey of India, copies of which may be had on application to the Assistant Secretary for India to the Royal Commission.

1 in. = 1 mile. These fields are at the western end of the great Gondwana basin of South Rewah. The actual outcrop of the measures, which is all that is shown on the map, seems small, but they extend indefinitely under flat covering strata.

22. The Karharbarí coal-field: scale 1 in. = 1 mile. One of the smallest of Indian coal-fields, but about the most prominent at present, as nearly half the output of Indian coal is derived from it.

23. The Daltonganj coal-field: scale 1 in. = 1 mile. This is the smallest of the Palamau fields, but the most promising.

24. The Aurunga coal-field: scale 1 in. = 1 mile. This is the largest of the Palamau fields.

25. The southern coal-fields of the Rewah Gondwana basin: scale 1 in. = 4 miles. This shows an immense stretch of coal country, as yet untouched; the measures crop out again on the north side of the basin.

26. The Jherria coal-field: scale 1 in. = 1 mile. This is a very large field next to the west of the great Raniganj field, but it is as yet untouched.

27. Geological map of the Rajmahal hills: scale 1 in. = 4 miles. Shows the numerous outcrops of the coal-measures along the western edge of the basaltic formation.

28. The Daranggiri coal-field in the Garo hills: scale 1 in. = 1 mile. This is the largest of the cretaceous coal basins of the Assam range.

29. The Naga hills coal-fields in Upper Assam: scale 1 in. = 8 miles. These are tertiary coal measures, but display a larger amount of coal than any others in India.

30. The Raniganj coal-field: scale 1 in. = 1 mile. Being the nearest to Calcutta this field was the first worked (in 1777); it is a very large and important field.

31. A general map showing the distribution of coal in India and the principal deposits of iron ore; scale 1 in. = 32 miles.

Books.

32. Palæontologia Indica, as published up to date.

33. Records of the Geological Survey of India, Volumes I. to XVII., 1868 to 1884.

34. Memoirs of the Geological Survey of India, Volumes I. to XXII.

35. Manual of the Geology of India, Volumes I. and II.

DIVISION II.—NATURAL HISTORY.

(*Exhibits under section* (1) *Botany are placed in the Economic Court; those under section* (2) *Zoology in the positions indicated in the list.*)

1. Botany.

It is not intended that the exhibits under this head should in any way illustrate the complete Botany of India, which is fully represented in the Museum and Library of the Royal Botanic Gardens at Kew. Exhibits are confined to a series of wooden glass fronted cases in the Economic Court containing specimens of the economic plants of India to which it is considered desirable to draw special attention.

2. Zoology.

As in the case of Botany, no attempt has been made to illustrate in any complete manner the whole Zoology of India, in view of the admirable collections already in existence at the British Museum and the Royal Zoological Gardens in Regent's Park. The following are the exhibits classed under this head:—

1. Hunting scene, illustrating, by means of stuffed specimens, the principal wild animals to be found in the jungles of Kuch Behar; contributed by His Highness the Maharajah of Kuch Behar. This exhibit is placed on the right hand side of the Grand Entrance Hall. It provides a very adequate representation of the large game of India, of which the most prominent examples find place in this trophy. Wild elephants, buffaloes, rhinoceros, tigers, leopards, and large deer, all represented, are far more common than any other kind of large animals of the forest throughout India.

2. A collection illustrating the more remarkable game birds of India, contributed by Sir Edward C. Buck, Commissioner for India.

A very complete account of the game birds of India has been published by Mr. A. O. Hume, C.B., and Major Marshall, R.E., a copy of which is placed for reference on table—in the Economic Court. It contains a full description of each bird exhibited.

DIVISION III.—ETHNOLOGY.

(*Exhibits under sections* (1) *Races of inhabitants are described in Chapter VI., Part II., and* (2) *Articles of personal adornment,* (3) *Articles of domestic use, and* (4) *Articles of sport and war, are described in Chapter VI., Part II.*)

(5) ARTICLES OF AGRICULTURAL USE.

The exhibits under this section comprise, *first*, a few scenes modelled in clay, illustrative of agricultural life and practice in Northern India and Bengal; and *secondly*, a collection of some of the principal implements and machines used in agriculture, carpentry, &c.

Agricultural Scenes.

1. An Indian Village (Northern India).

The model was executed by natives of Lucknow, other specimens of whose handiwork will be found in the North-Western Provinces and Oudh Art-ware Court, and of whom faithful portrait models, likewise their own handiwork, are shown close at hand.

Standing by the corner near the largest house and keeping the latter on the left hand, we see the Zamindar or landlord of the village in a house well representing the class of structure found in Oudh.

Seated in the verandah, unable himself probably to read or write in any but the roughest fashion, he is having the accounts of rent collections read out to him by the Putwari or Village Accountant, and dispensing rude justice, as evidenced by the groups below the threshold, where some unfortunate village wight is being beaten with shoes either for not paying his rent with proper punctuality or for some breach of village law or decorum. Near this house the village well tells its own tale, and close to it is the Brahman or village priest decorating with ceremonial the village idol. In the huts in front of the landlord's house are the various shops and occupations carried on under cover, such as are to be found in every large village in similar close proximity to the houses of the better class. Amongst this group of huts is to be seen a pair of bullocks laboriously working in a circle at the clumsy-looking but effectual mill, made out of trunks of trees, for pressing sugarcane. Behind the huts a group is engaged in shoeing a bullock—one of a yoke—the companion animal being tethered near the well and watching the operation anxiously from afar. To the right an old woman herds a drove of pigs, which do the scavengering of the village in company with the dogs, crows, and vultures, also to be noted busy near the pond on the carcases of dead cattle.

Looking to the right hand front corner, the ordinary mode of irrigation from wells by means of bullocks working on an inclined plane and raising water in a large leathern bucket or bag is shown, while in the corner to the left front is shown the method of raising water for irrigation by manual labour and swing baskets from ponds and rivers.

Close behind the huts to the left is shown a third method of irrigation by means of the balanced lever, and just behind the lever is the rude thatched shelter in which poor cultivators lie or sit out all night watching their crops from thieves, animal and human. In one field is to be seen ploughing, in another the operation of harrowing, as carried out with a log of wood. Close to the huts again is in one field an illustration of the method of irrigation, the whole duty of the water being regulated and exacted by means of small ridges raised on the surface of the field, the water being let into each compartment from the neighbouring one so soon as the water has served the turn of the latter. As crops, tobacco and yams are shown growing.

Near the well the bullocks are being fed, and between the fields is a scene of very common occurrence—a bullock having struck work has thrown himself down, and is being coaxed into rising by having his tail twisted.

2 & 3. Bengal Cultivators' Homestead. Of these models the first is a copy of the homestead of a well-to-do Hindu cultivator, who farms a holding of eight or ten acres, and the other of a Muhammadan cultivator of about the same standing.

The dwelling-house, which is raised on a plinth three or four feet high, is constructed of mud walls and a thatched roof, the peculiar bent eaves of which distinguish it from the village architecture in the tracts further west. It consists of a single room or compartment destitute of windows, and with doorways of the simplest construction, which are closed either with doors composed of rough planks, or, as shown in model No. 2, with a mat and bamboo screen. A portion of the verandah is screened off and serves as the family kitchen.

Facing the dwelling-house is the cultivator's cowshed enclosed in a bamboo fence. In one corner of the fence is an earthen pan or trough set up in mud, from which the cattle obtain their daily meal of chopped straw softened in water and flavoured with oil-cake and refuse or powdered rice.

A lean-to shed next to the cowhouse is devoted to the operation of husking rice. This is effected by means of a lever pestle or pounder, which consists of a heavy beam supported horizontally upon an upright block, and into one end of which the pestle, an iron-bound wooden peg, is inserted The operator keeps the machine in motion by stepping on and off the opposite end of the lever, and the rice to be bruised and husked is placed in a hollow below the pestle.

Between the cowshed and the cottage is a circular granary raised above the level of the ground to protect it from damp. It is made of bamboo matting, plastered within, and here the cultivator stores his harvest of rice for consumption or for sale when the market is favourable (provided that it has not already been pledged to the money-lender). Such portions as he needs from time to time are extracted from the window near the roof, which is reached by the ladder hanging beneath.

Near each cottage a palm-tree rears its elegant fan-crowned stem, and while the Hindu peasant may boast the beauty and profusion of the blossoms which adorn the *kadamb* tree shading his cowshed, his Muhammadan neighbour rejoices equally in the bright young leaves of a *pipal*.

Turning again to the Hindu cottage, the owner is seen returning from his work in the field, carrying his plough on his shoulder, and driving his plough oxen before him. The hour is noon, and the parched rice which formed his frugal repast in the morning has evidently not sated his appetite, for his face wears an appearance of pleased anticipation as he turns the corner and possibly gets a whiff from the earthen pot which contains the midday meal. The cattle too, appear to have caught sight of the food awaiting them in the trough, for, with outstretched necks, they are hastening to enter the enclosure of their shed.

The housewife, busy cooking, with all her platters around her, has not yet deigned to notice the return of her lord and master. Her son and little naked daughter, who were too hungry to wait, have already been served, and are busy eating.

Alongside of the cowhouse the sister-in-law

of the peasant is engaged in spreading on the wall, in the form of small round cakes, the manure obtained from the shed during the night. When dry these cakes serve as fuel; indeed, they constitute almost the only fuel available in those parts of India where forests have disappeared, and in order to cook his food the cultivator is obliged to stint his field.

A larger number of brass platters marks the Hindu as distinguished from the Muhammadan household, and the water pot of the latter differs in having a spout. In other respects the utensils are similar, and the earthen ones, such as the pot used for cooking the rice, the large jar for holding the day's supply of water, &c., are procured from the village potter at a trifling cost, paid in grain, and they are frequently renewed.

4. Ploughing and sowing (Bengal).

The cultivators here represented are both Muhammadans, a class which, though differing but slightly from the Hindus in physiognomy, can generally be distinguished by the presence of a beard. While one is ploughing with a pair of buffaloes, the other is sowing the field broadcast. Both wear protectors made of bamboo framework lined with palm leaves, which answer the double purpose of a hat and an umbrella.

Entering the field is the wife of one of the men. She carries his morning meal, which consists generally of cold rice, boiled the previous night and kept steeped in water. A swelling in the throat indicates that she is suffering from goitre, a disease prevalent in some parts of Bengal. The figure is a portrait model.

5. Rolling and Levelling (Bengal).

The clods raised by the plough or hoe are being imperfectly crushed and levelled by means of a bamboo ladder (in the North-Western Provinces it would be a log or plank) dragged over the field by a pair of oxen. To give the ladder weight the driver is standing upon it. Two men generally do this work, one relieving the other when tired. One man is off duty and is eating, in a corner of the field, the ordinary mess of coarse rice which his mother has brought from the distant village.

6. Hoeing and Weeding (Bengal).

The seated figure shows a cultivator weeding his rice-field. This operation is usually performed by hand, but a bullock rake is also used for thinning as well as weeding rice. Weeding by hand requires a practised eye, owing to the close resemblance which the young rice plants bear to the grasses which grow up in their midst.

In another field stand a *Buna* (*lit.* man of the woods) in the act of using a long-handled hoe. He comes of aboriginal stock, though now a semi-Hinduised labourer living in servitude and occupying the lowest caste status in the village community, to settle amongst whom he or his forefathers abandoned the freedom and independence of the forest. He is still so far faithful to his tradition as to prefer to the hoe in ordinary use an implement which allows of the free play of every muscle in his sinewy frame.

A third field gives an example of the mode of using the common hoe. The handle of this hoe runs almost parallel to the blade, and hence requires a stooping or sitting posture. One hand, it will be observed, grasps the handle above and the other below the blade. The figure is that of a Muhammadan, and he wears on his right arm a small silver tube containing some amulet or charm. He is going over the field a second time, and inverting and breaking the clods resulting from his first hoeing.

In the last field of the series is a straw hut supported on a bamboo platform and posts which is raised for the shelter of the man hired to watch the crops when they ripen.

7. Manure Cart (Bengal).

With the exception of the wheels and axle the cart is constructed entirely of bamboos, and in this respect differs from the carts in use in most other parts of India, where, owing to the greater scarcity of bamboos, wood is used for the body as well as the wheels. The vehicle is employed for every purpose of conveyance and carriage, and is the cultivator's waggon as well as his field cart. On the present occasion it is filled with about 12 cwt. of manure taken from the dust heap which is carefully preserved near each peasant's dwelling, and increased from day to day with the sweepings of the hearth and the surplus manure of the cowshed. The driver is carrying it to some adjacent field reserved for tobacco or other garden crop to which alone he can afford to apply manure. He keeps his team of sleek and lazy buffaloes from coming to a dead stop with an occasional prod with the stick which he holds in one hand, whilst with the other he pushes and shoves them into the right track; meanwhile he shows his opinion of the utility of reins by allowing them to lie idle before him.

8 & 9. Irrigating with the trough (Bengal).

In Bengal and the moister parts of India, where water is found at a moderate depth, or where marshes occur, the use of this and similar appliances enables the cultivator to dispense with the extra pair of oxen maintained for irrigation where deep wells are the rule.

The trough is generally the hollow stem of a palm open at one end and closed at the other; sometimes its place is taken by a leather or earthen bucket. It is attached to a bamboo or wooden lever or beam weighted at the opposite end with a clod of earth, a stone, or, as represented in one model, a basket full of wet earth.

A man standing on the opposite of the channel or reservoir from which the water is drawn depresses the lever with the weight of his body till the head of the trough is immersed; he then removes his weight, and the counter-weight at the other end raises the trough which discharges its contents.

The scene shows a tobacco field under irrigation. Seated near the man who is working the machine is another who has been relieved, and who is now regaling himself with a smoke from a *huqa* or water-pipe. He has probably had more than his fair share of this soothing enjoyment, for his fellow-labourer, who sits at the corner of the field regulating the flow of water into the different beds, is beckoning and calling to remind him that he would also like a turn at the pipe.

The pipe itself is of the simplest description. A cocoanut serves to form the bowl which holds the water. A hollow reed or stem passing into the shell connects the water with an earthen funnel-shaped vessel containing the tobacco with a few live coals. The smoke is drawn through a hole in the cocoanut shell above the level of the water. It is allowable for men of the same caste to use the same pipe, but when the person desiring a smoke is of a lower or a higher caste than the owner, he receives only the earthen funnel, and fixing it between the fingers of one hand he joins his palms, so as to form an air-tight hollow, and applies his mouth to an aperture left between the thumb and fore-finger.

The duplicate model shows the trough in the act of discharging water.

10 & 11. Irrigating with the Basket (Bengal).

This is another form of irrigation common to marshy tracts. Four strings are attached to the basket and held by two men standing opposite each other on either side of the channel or reservoir into which the water is to be lifted. Bending together they swing the basket into the lower pool, and with a re-actionary motion bring it full to the surface, and at the same moment discharge the water by raising the two strings on the off side.

Sometimes a larger basket is used, when four men work together, each holding one string.

By employing sets of baskets water is lifted several feet and carried long distances from reservoir to reservoir.

A sugarcane field is here shown as being irrigated by one lift. One man is engaged in a corner of the field tying up the canes. They are tied two or three together to afford mutual support against the action of the high wind, the dry leaves being used for this purpose.

In a corresponding model the basket is shown in the act of being filled.

12. Reaping (Bengal).

This is done throughout India with a small hand sickle worked in a stooping or sitting posture. Either a plain-edged or a saw-edged instrument is used, and as the plants are reaped, they are tied in small bundles by the reaper and laid on the ground. When the crop is cut before the straw is thoroughly dry, the sheafs are left for a day or two on the field if the weather is favourable. The model depicts the reaping of a crop of barley. In close proximity to the field is a temporary shed erected for the reapers, who are perhaps poor labourers coming from a distance to hire themselves out at this busy season. The hut is furnished with a rude straw mattress and the inevitable *huqa*. In a hole near the entrance are seen the ashes of last night's fire, at which (for it is winter) the reapers warmed themselves. It still conceals a smouldering cow-dung cake which will be raked up when the pipe is put into requisition.

13. Threshing with Bullocks (Bengal).

This mode of threshing is the one most commonly seen throughout India. In Bengal it is generally confined, in the case of rice, to crops grown on the lowlands, which are gathered close to the ear as the straw by long immersion in water is rendered tasteless and unfit for cattle.

The crop to be threshed is arranged three or four inches deep on a circular floor cleaned and prepared for the purpose. A wooden pole or bamboo is firmly fixed in the centre, to which three or four oxen are tethered. Driven round and round the pole in a line the oxen tread out the grain, which is then gathered up with the chaff and winnowed in the manner hereafter described. The team is usually driven by a boy, while a man keeps turning over the ears with a bamboo fork, but in the two models (which are duplicates) a man driving the bullocks is only shown. He is urging the laggard of his team by a twist of the tail.

14. Threshing by hand (Bengal).

Where rice is grown on the uplands it becomes an object to preserve the straw, which is three or four feet long, and, unlike the straw obtained from the lowland crops, is clean and wholesome fodder for cattle,—is, in fact, the chief cattle-food of Bengal. The crop is therefore reaped close to the root, and to keep the straw unbroken the ears are beaten out against an inclined board. Near the man engaged in this operation is a stack of unthreshed grain, from which he draws a supply from time to time.

15. Winnowing (Bengal).

It would hardly be possible to find a simpler or more tedious process than that of winnowing as practised in India. The trodden grain and chaff is gathered into a basket and poured out before the wind over and over again till the grain alone remains. Should, as frequently happens, there be no breeze stirring, it is artificially produced by the agitation of a piece of cloth or, as represented in the model, of a winnowing basket.

16. Castor Oil Press (Bengal).

This is a screw press of European invention. The seeds are filled into coarse jute bags and placed between the boards. Two men next tighten the screws from opposite sides by means of hand bars, and the pressure squeezes out the oil which gradually drips into a receiver placed below.

17. Pressing Sugarcane (Bombay).

This model, which shows method of crushing sugarcane in the Bombay Presidency, was prepared at Poona.

The mill consists of a pair of upright cylinders fixed in a wooden frame, and worked by cattle yoked to a cross bar or beam. The rollers act on one another by means of corresponding spirals rudely cut on the upper end of each. To the elongated axle of one roller is fitted the horizontal beam or cross bar, and the framework is sunk in the earth to a depth sufficient to bring the cross bar on a level with the shoulders of the cattle. They are thus enabled to throw their whole weight into the draught as shown in the model. When greater power is required a longer beam is used, and a pair of oxen are yoked to each end.

The rollers are fed, as they revolve with bunches of three or four canes, by two men who sit one on either side of the rollers. Owing to the faulty construction of the mill, the canes have to be passed twice and even oftener through the rollers before a fair proportion of juice is extracted. The juice is caught in a trough and runs through a spout into a large earthen vessel placed in the ground. It is removed twice a day into a large pan, and boiled till ready to crystallize, when it is poured into a cloth to drain and harden. It is then a crude brown sugar and ready for the market. The refuse canes or "trash" are sometimes given to cattle and sometimes used as fuel. In spite of the repeated crushing they retain a considerable quantity of juice, and in parts of Bombay the trash is purchased by the lower castes, who steep it in water, from which an inferior kind of sugar is extracted.

On a separate platform a woman is represented bringing in a bundle of canes, while a man is preparing them for the mill by lopping off the green tops and the hard roots.

The purple cane figured is the best variety grown in India, and has probably been introduced from the Mauritius.

Implements.

The chief characteristics to be observed in the collection of agricultural implements and machines referred to below are—

(1) The very small extent to which they are adapted to save hand labour.

(2) The preponderance of wood in their construction.

(3) The variations in form of the same implement.

In a country like India, where the daily wage of an adult labourer is from two to three pence, the incentive to that kind of mechanical invention which has for its object the saving of hand labour is almost entirely absent. Hand labour is the cheapest form of labour, and the invention, if exercised at all, is exercised in the direction of arming the hands and not superseding them.

The large proportion of wood used is due not only to the comparative scarcity of prepared iron and the greater costliness of manufacture in that metal, but to the fact that wood and bamboo, if less durable, are very much lighter. This is an important consideration where hand labour or weak cattle are the rule. Variations in form are the result, partly of altered prejudices or individual tastes, but broadly speaking, are attributable to the circumstance that the implements are not manufactured and kept in stock by some central establishment on whom the farmer may indent for what he requires, but are all made to order by rude artisans living in each village, whose function it is to construct and repair the tools and furniture of the village community.

Ploughs.

The implement used as a plough in India has no resemblance whatever to any English plough, but is not unlike the plough used in countries south of Europe. The only English implement with which it can be compared is the horse hoe, the work performed by which is similar. The Indian plough is quite deficient in splitting and gathering, and with the exception of some heavy varieties used for special purposes in Southern and Central India, makes a very shallow furrow which seldom exceeds three inches in depth. In no indigenous plough is the share formed to invert the soil, which is really scratched or torn as the plough passes through it. All Indian ploughs are without wheels, coulter or mould board, with a single stilt, and made of wood with an iron share. In the whole of the implement not a single screw, bolt or nut is used; the parts are fastened by mortise locks and by means of wedges. The yoke is tied on to the beam with a rope, and is in itself a peculiar contrivance suited only to humped oxen. The yoke is put on the necks of a pair of bullocks, and the plough attached to the middle by means of string and a peg which passes through the whole at the top of the beam. The angle of the ploughshare is regulated by the peg.

North-Western Provinces and Oudh. — 1. Cawnpore plough, ¼ full size. 2. Meerut plough, ¼ full size. 3. Bandelkhand plough, ¼ full size. 4. Kaisar improved plough, ¼ full size.

The weight of a full-sized native plough in the North-Western Provinces varies from 20 to 30 lbs., and the local price from 2 to 4 Rs. It does not invert the soil, and the furrow seldom exceeds three inches in depth. To obtain a fine tilth, such as is required for wheat, the plough is passed repeatedly over the field. The Bandelkhand plough is of the nature of a skim plough, and is used in the black or cotton soil tracts for cutting stubble and weeds before the ordinary plough is applied. An improved plough, called the *kaisar*, has been introduced by the Government Experimental Farm at Cawnpore, which, as it ploughs deeper than the native plough and completely inverts the soil, is useful for crops like sugar cane, which require a careful preparation of the ground. But some cultivators are averse to purchasing an earth-turning plough and maintaining it in addition to the native one necessary for sowing purposes. To meet this objection a duplex plough has been devised, which serves the double purpose of inverting the soil and of sowing like the native implement. In form it is just like the ordinary native plough of the North-Western Provinces, but is fitted with an extra sole for turning over the earth. This latter can be slipped in or off, and is fixed firmly on the step by means of wedges like the ordinary sole of the country plough. The duplex and the *kaisar* are purchased by cultivators to a limited extent.

Central Provinces.—1. Narbada valley drill plough, full size. 2. Nagpur plough, full size. 3. Bhandara plough, ¼ full size. 4. Chhattisgarh plough, ¼ full size. 5. Bullock hoe, Narbada valley and Nagpur plough, ¼ full size and full size.

The last on the above list is the same class of implement as the Bandelkhand plough, and is used for the same kind of land (black cotton soil). It is the plough in most general use in the Central Provinces. No. 1 is only employed when the seed is sown in October, and Nos. 2 and 3 for breaking up new land. No. 4 is peculiar to the Chhattisgarh country, where it takes the place of the bullock-hoe. It is used in thinning rice as well as in preparing land. Rice is universally sown broadcast in Chhattisgarh, and when the seedlings are six inches high the field is thinned out by ploughing.

Bombay.—1. Gujarat plough, ordinary. 2. Gujarat plough, heavy. 3. Khandesh plough. 4. Dharwar light plough. 5. Konkan heavy plough. 6. Konkan small plough.

The superior breed of cattle found in the Bombay Presidency admits of the use of heavier ploughs than are in vogue in other parts of the country. The wood used is generally some variety of *Acacia*, and the prices range from 2 Rs. for the light plough of Dharwar to 16 Rs. for the best description of heavy plough used in the same tract. No specimen of the latter is exhibited, as it is identical, except in weight, with the light plough. One is used for sandy soils, and the other for riddling the heavy and tenacious black soil of a deep-rooted grass by which it is frequently overrun.

The Gujarat plough is peculiar in having an adjustable share.

Four to eight pairs of oxen are employed to work the heavy ploughs, and the Khandesh plough makes a furrow seven inches deep, which is sometimes increased by weighting the body with stones. The length of the share in this plough is remarkable. The yoke is also unusually long, and the oxen stepping forward alternately utilize the length of the lever or beam.

The Konkan ploughs are employed only when the land has been softened by rain, and the lighter of the two is used even when the fields are covered to a depth of four inches with water. Hill cultivation is carried on with the light plough where the gradient is not too steep, and the beam of the plough is notched so that the pitch may be regulated to a small extent.

Madras.—1. Tinnevelli plough, ¼ full size. 2. South Kanara plough, ¼ full size. 3. Malabar plough, ¼ full size. 4. Bellary plough for unirrigated land, ¼ full size. 5. Bellary plough for irrigated land, ¼ full size. 6. Bellary plough for cotton soil, ¼ full size. 7. Bellary grubbers, heavy, ordinary wide and ordinary narrow, ¼ full size.

No. 1 illustrates the kind of plough in use in the Southern Districts of the Madras Presidency, Nos. 2 and 3 those in use in the Central District, and Nos. 4 to 7 those employed in the portions of the Presidency above the ghâts towards the Deccan. The share is generally of English iron, and for the rest any suitable kind of wood is adopted. The cotton soil plough (No. 6) is specially used on black cotton soil in the dry weather for the eradication of deep-rooted grasses, and the work is completed with the heavy grubber. The ordinary grubbers are used for preparing the land for sowing and also for covering the seed.

Burma.—1. Plough for level land. 2. Shan plough. 3. Plough for high lands.

The first is in general use in the plains for ploughing paddy fields. The second is used for early ploughing, chiefly on high lands. It is supposed to have been introduced from Upper Burma, where it is universally used by the Shan Tribes; the third is used in a very limited tract, and is a new importation. The share of this plough is of cast iron, and is believed to come from China *viâ* Bhamo.

Miscellaneous.—1. Plough and appurtenances from Bengal. 2. Plough from Ajmere, ⅛th full size. 3. Plough from Hyderabad, ⅛th full size.

These do not differ materially from the ploughs already described. The Bengal and Ajmere ploughs are allied to those employed in the North-Western Provinces and Oudh, while the Hyderabad plough resembles the implement in vogue in the Bombay Presidency.

Drills.—1. Four-coulter drill from Bombay. 2. Three-coulter drill from Bombay. 3. Two-coulter drill from Bombay. 4. Two-coulter drill from Bombay, for cotton seed. 5. Six-rowed drill from Madras, ¼ full size. 6. Three-rowed drill from Madras, ¼ full size. 7. Cotton drill (tube only) from Madras, full size. 8. Triple seed drill from the Central Provinces, model and full size. 9. Cotton drill, model and full size. 10. Drills (tubes) from Hyderabad, Ajmere, Bengal, &c., model and full size.

The use of seed drills is more characteristic of the agriculture of Southern than of Upper India, where the triple drill is indeed unknown, and the crops are generally sown broadcast, or when drilled, as in the case of wheat and barley, through a single tube attached to the plough. In Gujarat the 2, 3, 4 coulter drills are all used. In the Deccan the two-coulter drill is merely the three-coulter drill with the middle coulter and seed tube removed. In the Bombay Carnatic the four-coulter drill is used for all drilled crops except cotton. Here, if the seed is required to be sown deep, a heavier drill is used. There are, similarly, two varieties of the four-coulter drill in the Deccan—one light for sowing early rain crops, the other very heavy (200 lbs.), for wheat, gram, and other cold-weather crops. But sometimes in the Deccan the proper depth is secured by the removal of the middle coulter, which also makes the rows wider. Where the cultivator desires to insert a subordinate row crop between the rows of the principal crop, he either in the back journey uses the drill for this crop, or else a single tube, held by a woman, attached to the main drill, follows. Through this the seed of the row crop is dropped, sometimes on the seed deposited by the outer seed tube of the drill, and sometimes in the furrow made by the centre coulter of the drill, the seed tube of which is purposely stopped. All drills are drawn by one pair of oxen. The distance between the coulters is generally 11 or 12 inches, but it varies. The drills in the various tracts are remarkably similar.

The special cotton drills Nos. 4 and 9 are much alike, if not identical. Their peculiarity consists in the fact that the seed tubes are not fixed behind the coulter, but are separately held by sowers who follow the drill and keep the mouth of the seed tubes in the furrows made by the coulters. The implement can be used as a wide two-coulter drill for other crops, the seed tube and seed cup being fixed as in the ordinary seed drill.

The six-coulter drill of Madras is used in the central plateau above the ghâts, but only in free loose soils.

Bullock Hoes, Rakes, and Harrows.—1. Bullock hoe, Bombay. 2. Bullock rake, Bombay. 3. Bullock rake for special use in rice lands. 4. Harrows (three varieties from the Deccan, Gujarat, and Bombay Carnatic). 5. Wooden and iron toothed harrow from Madras, ⅛ full size. 6. Bullock hoes (sets of three), Madras, ⅛ full size. 7. Bullock hoe (on one frame), Madras, ⅛ full size. 8. Bullock hoe, Central Provinces, full size. 9. Bullock hoe, Central Provinces, full size. 10. Harrow from Ajmere, ⅛ full size.

The above implements are chiefly used for weeding standing crops. They are seldom employed in Upper India owing to the prevalence of the practice of sowing most crops broadcast. No. 1 is used everywhere in the Bombay Presidency except Gujarat. It is worked in pairs, one yoke being attached, so that both implements are drawn by one pair of oxen. Each hoe is very carefully guided by a separate man, the bullocks being driven between them. The bullock hoe can only be used when the crop has got a good start. It not only weeds close to the crop sown, but loosens the soil around the roots. The rows of crops themselves are weeded by hand. It is remarkable that this implement is not used in Gujarat, where the cultivators are certainly in advance of those of the rest of the Presidency. It is a neat implement, and requires very careful working.

The rake No. 2 works across the rows of young crops for the double purpose of taking out weeds to save hand-weeding and of thinning the rows. It appears to be a substitute for the bullock hoe, and is in vogue only in the Kaira District of Gujarat.

No. 3 works in fields covered with water. The long teeth pull up the weeds while the shorter ones lay them down in the soft mud. It is only used in rice lands, where weeds, must be eradicated and weakened before the seed is sown.

Harrows (No. 4) are put to a variety of uses, viz., to cover up seed sown by the drill, to scarify land not ploughed before sowing, as clod-crushers to follow the plough and prepare the seed-bed, and to weed between the rows of standing crops. The light implement with a long narrow blade (called *Rakhia* or *Pharát* in the Deccan, and *Balesál Kunti* in the Carnatic Districts) is used to cover up the seed. Frequently the blade and the prongs to which it is attached are removed, and the beam only is drawn over the sown land to cover in the seed. As a scarifier the largest-sized harrows are used. The driver usually stands on the beam, which is peculiarly adapted for this purpose. It is also customary first to use a heavy harrow drawn by four bullocks, and then to harrow the land with lighter implements drawn by one pair. Where the harrow works down the clods turned up by the plough, the heavier kinds are used. When employed for weeding, the length of the knife or blade is regulated by the distance between the tines of the drill by which the crop was sown.

The hoes and harrows from Madras and the Central Provinces are used for weeding standing crops and pulverizing the soil. They do not call for special remark.

Rollers, Clod-Crushers, &c.—1. Gujarat roller and clod-crusher, Bombay. 2. Kaira leveller, Bombay. 3. Deccan leveller, Bombay. 4. Konkan leveller, Bombay. 5. Plank harrow, Bombay and Madras. 6. Log harrow, Bombay, Madras, North-Western Provinces, Ajmere, &c.

The implement most commonly used in India for crushing clods and levelling the fields is a simple log of wood, flattened on one or both sides, which is fastened by ropes to the yoke and drawn across the field. To give it weight the driver and perhaps one or two other men stand upon it. In Upper India (where it is the only form of clod-crusher and leveller used, the smaller clods being broken up with a hand mallet when a fine tilth is needed) it is not generally sold, but either made by the cultivators themselves, when they happen to be the owners of trees, or borrowed from their friends. In Southern India a larger variety of implements are in use for preparing the field after ploughing. The Gujarat roller, besides crushing clods, levelling land for irrigation, and covering seed, is sometimes employed to roll young cereals. The Kaira leveller breaks up clods, fills up inequalities of rice land, which must be quite flat, and land intended to be irrigated. It works on the end, and when the resistance is great owing to the collection of clods, the driver can push the handle forward to lighten the draught. The Konkan leveller is a more elaborate implement. Besides levelling the rice fields, its great use is to draw the clods and earth to repair embankments so as to impound the water in the rains. The concave arrangement of the bamboo slats is designed to collect the excess earth. It must be noticed that the body of the implement is attached by rounded axles to the shafts, so that the implement can be thrown out of gear when the weight of earth collected is too severe. This leveller is necessary in making new rice land, and by it the embankments are formed. The driver can tilt the implement on either side to fill a hollow at will.

Miscellaneous.—1. Tobacco liner, Bombay. 2. Rice draw cart or sledge, Bombay. 3. Rice draw cart or sledge, Burma, ⅛ size.

As in England the seed drill with seed cup removed is used to mark out a field for planting cabbages, the drill being drawn across the field and then at right angles to the first journey, the cabbages being planted at the intersections, so is the tobacco liner used in Gujarat, and so effectively that the bullock hoes can pass safely close to young plants both along the rows and crosswise. No marks are set up, no steering poles to guide the driver, and yet the exactness of the work is remarkable. The implement, which is made of teak wood with iron tines, is used for other garden crops besides tobacco.

The rice sledge is a most ingenious contrivance. The platform is so made that all the parts give easily. On it the seedlings are laid in neat bundles, and it is drawn by bullocks over the embankments, and through the ruts and waterways of the rice fields where no carts could go, and yet without dropping one bundle of seedlings. The traces are attached to the end with curved rows. This sledge has probably been introduced into the rice-growing districts of the Deccan from Burma.

Hand Implements.—1. Picks and mattocks from Bombay, Madras, North-Western Provinces, &c. 2. Hoe or spade from Bombay, North-Western Provinces, Bengal.

The double-bladed picks and mattocks in ordinary use among labourers are of the English shape and not uncommonly of English manufacture. They are employed to a very limited extent, if at all, in agriculture; but for digging in hilly tracts, in mines, in the repair of roads, and the excavation of road metal, as in all other work of a similar nature where hard-pointed diggers are needed, the pick is used by day labourers or coolies, to whom they are usually served out by the employer or contractor.

Several special forms of picks are, however, used in agriculture for hoeing crops, working up the soil, digging out deep-rooted weeds which cannot be removed by the plough, &c. In general appearance they resemble the hoe, but the blade is pointed, the iron part much heavier than in the English hand hoe, and the handle, as a rule, much shorter. In Upper India, only the most paying crops, such as sugar-cane, potatoes, and other vegetables are cultivated with the pick, but among the ruder cultivators in hilly tracts it is the only instrument used for preparing the field. Amongst them it takes the place of the plough, of which it is probably the origin. All that is needed to convert the long-handled pick of the hill districts of Bombay for instance into a plough is to make it larger, add a stilt and put on a yoke.

For earth-work and digging purposes generally, whenever the nature of the soil does not require the use of the pick, the hoe (*ver.* Phaora) No. 2 is used. It appears to be an adaptation of the English hoe, but is much broader, and is really a spade with the handle bent at right angles to the blade. It is an invaluable instrument to the cultivator in digging earth for his hut, building the walls of his fields, cutting irrigation channels, and a hundred other purposes.

3. Weeding hook, Bombay, Bengal, &c. 4. Spud, Madras, North-Western Provinces, &c. 5. Scraper, Madras, North-Western Provinces, &c.

The weeding hook is used for weeding crops by hand, and for garden purposes generally. It is made in various sizes, and while some forms have an inner saw edge, others have two plain edges. As a rule the blade is made of steel welded on to the iron bar which is inserted into the wooden haft. In the North-Western Provinces, the spud or the scraper (No. 5) takes the place of the weeding hook. The spud is the favourite implement of gardeners, and the scraper, which differs from the spud in having a broader blade closing up to the handle which is bent, is indispensable to the agriculturist. For all sorts of digging and cutting which is done in England by the gardener's knife, shovel, billhook, hand hoe, &c., the scraper (*ver.* Khurpi) serves in India. The cultivator scrapes grass for his cattle with it, digs holes, grubs and weeds fields, and when required to cut string, peel fruit, &c., he makes it answer the purposes of a pocket-knife (a luxury of which he is rarely the possessor).

6. Sickle, Bombay, Madras, Central Provinces, North-Western Provinces, &c. 7. Choppers, North-Western Provinces, Ajmere, &c. 8. Billhooks, Madras, Bombay, Burma, &c. 9. Hatchets, Madras, North-Western Provinces, Bombay, &c.

The hand-sickle or reaping-hook is employed throughout India, and shows great similarity of form. In Bombay it is provided with a saw edge when used to cut rice, while the large millets are reaped with the plain edged sickle. The practice of carrying the sickle in a wooden scabbard is also peculiar to Southern India. Tall grasses as well as crops are gathered with the sickle, which also serves for the lopping and clearing of brushwood in Upper India, where the billhook is seldom used.

The chopper or chaffcutter (*ver.* Gandasa) is indispensable to every North-Western Provinces peasant who owns cattle. It is used principally for chopping up the stalks of the large millets, reaped between August and December. To this work the cultivator devotes himself after his day's labour in the field, and in two hours is able to chop enough fodder for one day's consumption of four oxen. The stalks are held in the left hand, and chopped with the chopper held in the right hand into pieces half an inch in length, as they are slowly moved over a flat log of wood.

Billhooks, as already noted, are not much in vogue in North-Western India, but in Burma, Assam, and Bengal, an instrument called *dáo* or *dá* is universally used for the purposes for which the billhook and hatchet are intended.

They bear, however, but a slight resemblance to the billhook, and vary a good deal in shape. Those used in Burma are said to be made of English or imported steel.

Hatchets of English manufacture are not much in favour, owing probably to the higher price and the difference in shape as compared with the native implement. The native hatchet is more pointed, and shaped to a thicker wedge than the English pattern; the blade is differently balanced, and the head formed to receive a round handle of an even thickness, which in case of breakage is not rendered useless, but can be shortened and re-inserted.

10. Knives from Madras, Burma, &c. 11. Nipper from Madras and Bombay. 12. Pruning scissors from Madras. 13. Poppy pricker and scraper from North-Western Provinces, Rajputana, &c.

The knife exhibited from Madras is used in the southern districts of the Presidency for cutting the ears of standing crops, and the specimen from Burma is a fruit-gatherer's knife.

The nipper is employed to pluck the leaves of the betel vine; the Bombay implement is fixed on the thumb of the operator.

The pruning scissors are apparently confined to the northernmost districts of the Madras Presidency.

Wherever opium is grown the poppy pricker and scraper is required. The former is made of three or four sharp-pointed bits of iron tied together with a thread. The latter is generally an iron spoon, but sometimes the shell of a bivalve or a metallic or wooden cup is used instead. The poppy heads when large enough are scratched every evening, and the sap which exudes and accumulates during the night is carefully scraped off and gathered next morning.

14. Winnowers from Madras, Bombay, Bengal, &c. 15. Sieves from Madras, Burma, &c. 16. Winnowing platform from Burma. 17. Basket from North-Western Provinces, &c. 18. Broom from Madras, &c. 19. Wooden fork from Ajmere.

The above are all connected with operations on the threshing floor.

The system universally adopted in India for winnowing is to pour out the broken chaff and grain from a height before a strong wind which drives off the chaff and light grains. The harvested crop is first trodden out with a team of oxen driven round in a circle over the threshing floor, which is generally an open space near the village and unprotected from the weather, and when the chaff has been sufficiently broken up it is poured out from a basket, trough or scoop (the form of which varies in different parts of the country) in the manner described. In Burma to obtain a greater height a platform is used. The process is a laborious one, and as the speed with which it is carried out depends entirely on a favourable wind, the garnered crops are usually at the mercy of the weather, and are not infrequently injured by rain. A simple winnower, which would render the cultivator independent of the wind, is much needed, but although many attempts have been made to introduce such a machine, they have hitherto been only partially successful.

20. Platform for driving away birds, &c. 21. Sling for driving away birds, &c. 22. Rainhood from Bombay. 23. Stool from Bombay. 24. Carrying pole from Bombay. 25. Rattle from Burma.

In India every field has to be watched night and day from the time the seed springs to the time the crop is reaped, to protect it from wild animals and birds. A platform is erected for this purpose in the corner of the field or on some commanding spot from whence the watcher (who is generally hired for the purpose) raises a shout from time to time, or uses his sling. Scarecrows consisting of tufts of grass and rags, or an earthen pot daubed with whitewash and raised on a pole, as well as many other contrivances equally rude are also used. In spite of these precautions, however, the injury done is often considerable, for even timid animals, like deer, soon learn to understand where no real danger is to be apprehended.

The rainhood or hat is a very characteristic feature of the Konkan, where all field work in the monsoon season is done in heavy rain. The leaves of the *palas* (*Butea frondosa*) are preferred, but teak leaves are often used. A similar hat is in fashion in Bengal, Assam, and elsewhere.

The stool is used by the cultivators in the Konkan as a seat in the muddy rice fields while pulling the seedlings ready for transplantation.

It is the practice in the same tract to raise the rice seedlings in a bed prepared with the ashes (called *rab*) obtained by burning the lopping of trees, brushwood, leaves, grass, &c., &c. This material is sometimes brought long distances from the jungle, and the carrying pole (*ver.* Baila) is used to assist the carrier. By the help of the Baila a man can bring 150 lbs. weight of grass, &c., at one time. The material is securely tied and the end of the pole inserted. The pad platform rests on the head of the carrier. The lower portion of the pole enables him to rest the bundle and easily raise it again, the pole being held erect.

34. *Irrigating appliances:* Bucket and pulley; Persian wheel; lever lift; swing basket; spoon bale, &c.

The lever lift and swing basket have already been described in the explanation of the models of agricultural scenes.

Wherever water has to be drawn from deep wells the bucket and pulley is employed. One or more buckets are used according to the diameter of the well, each being worked separately. The rope attached to the iron ring supporting the leather bucket is passed over a pulley and yoked to a pair of bullocks, which walk down an inclined plane formed of the soil obtained in digging the well. When water is at a great depth, or the need for irrigation is urgent, two pair of oxen work alternately. When the first pair reaches the bottom of the incline the rope is unyoked and the driver walks back with it and yokes it to the second team standing at the upper end. Meanwhile the first pair of oxen ascend, and while awaiting their turn feed at a trough placed near them. Besides the driver a second man is required to receive and empty the bucket. But in Southern India the plan followed is to have a spout or leather nozzle at the lower end of the bucket, to which a second rope is attached. Whilst the bucket is ascending full of water the rope is held taut so as to keep up the mouth of the nozzle, and on the bucket reaching the pulley the rope is slackened and the nozzle lowered to discharge the water. Another point of difference is that while in Upper India the oxen are turned round and walked up the slope, in Southern India they are taught to back up.

Irrigation by the Persian wheel is chiefly in vogue in hilly tracts, where water is obtainable at a moderate depth. It consists of an endless chain of small earthen jars, revolving round a drum placed over the well or reservoir, and rigidly fixed to a horizontal axis provided with spokes or teeth; an upright moving on a pivot armed at the lower end with a similar set of spokes, and a horizontal beam fixed to the upright to which the bullocks are yoked. The bullocks moving in a circle set the upright in motion, and its spokes, striking against those of the axle of the drum, causes the latter and with it the chain of earthen pots to revolve. A continuous stream of water is thus lifted, and being discharged into a trough flows into the distributing channel and thence to the field. The whole apparatus except the pots is of wood, and though of the rudest construction is very effective.

The spoon bale is used for distributing water over a field.

35. *Mills:* Sugar mills and evaporating pans; oil mills; rice mills, &c.

A description of the roller sugar mill of Bombay has already been given. This mill is also used in the Madras Presidency and in the Central Provinces, in one district of which a triple roller mill (wooden) is also employed. In lower Bengal the common mill is a horizontal double roller mill worked by the hand, but it is now fast being superseded by a vertical iron roller mill patented by Messrs. Thomson and Mylne of Bihea in Bengal.

The primitive pestle mill is, however, still the machine most generally used over the greater part of India for the extraction of cane-juice. The method of working it is shown in the model village. Into a cylindrical mortar of stone, three or four feet high, a wooden pestle is introduced and worked by means of a beam dragged round by oxen. The cane is cut into small pieces before being thrown into the mortar, and the juice runs through a vent into an earthen vessel placed below. The only parts of the machine which need renewal are the pestle and the beam; the stone mortars are imperishable and are often found marking the sites of flourishing villages which have long since passed away.

The indigenous oil mill is very similar in construction to the pestle sugar mill, but is worked by one bullock. A screw press is used in Bengal, which has already been described.

Hand mills are universally employed for husking and grinding grain, except in the Himalayan districts, where advantage is taken of the abundant water power. For bruising pulses and grinding flour, a millstone is used, and for husking paddy and other hard-shelled grains, a wooden pestle and mortar, which is worked either by the hand or the feet. In the latter case it consists of a heavy beam with an iron-bound peg fixed on the under-side at one end. The beam turns on an axle inserted in two upright posts, and a man (sometimes two men) by stepping on and off the shorter end causes the lever to rise and fall with his weight and pound the grain placed below the iron-bound peg. The hand pestle is a wooden pole iron-bound at both ends, with a handle cut in the centre. The grain to be pounded is placed in a wooden mortar fixed on the ground. It is used when a small quantity of grain is to be husked.

36. *Cotton machines:* Gins; scutching bow; spinning wheel; loom.

When the cotton has been cleaned by hand picking it is separated from the seed by a machine which consists of two wooden rollers about an inch thick turned by a handle attached to the lower one. The rollers are wedged tightly together in a frame, and, having screws or spirals cut on the projecting ends, turn in opposite directions.

The cotton thus separated from the seed is next scutched with a bow and mallet. The bow is shaped somewhat like a harp with a single string of catgut. The operator holding the bow horizontally by one hand twangs the cat-gut amongst the cotton with the dumb-bell-shaped mallet held in the other, causing the fibres to loosen and separate, and the dust and dirt to fly out.

To prepare the cotton for the spinning wheel it is rolled into small hollow rolls round a thin skewer.

The spinning wheel consists of a driving wheel and a spinning axle or spindle supported on an H-shaped stand. The driving wheel is made of a number of spokes fixed round each end of a central axle and connected across with a string so as to form a circular framework or cylindrical cage. Opposite the driving wheel is placed the spindle, an iron skewer revolving in two uprights. A driving band connects the spindle with the drum, which is turned with a removable crank handle. The spinner turns the handle with one hand, while in the other she holds a roll of cotton, and attaching it to the spindle as it revolves at a high rate of speed draws it out into thread which is wound round the spindle. When the spindle is full, the thread is wound off on a winder attached to the driving wheel in the place of the handle which is removed.

To prepare the warp a number of sticks are

planted in the ground in double row and in pairs. Round these sticks the thread is wound off a reel which revolves on a spindle. When the required amount of thread has been used the sticks are pulled up, and in their places a kind of bow inserted to preserve the cross of the thread, and on these the warp is adjusted. It is next soaked in rice water to give it stiffness, and after being stretched and brushed is fixed to the loom.

The loom differs but little from the English hand-loom. Its essential parts consist of the shuttle; a wooden frame or bar suspended from the roof for driving home the thread, and containing a comb of reeds or bamboo which keeps the threads or the warp apart, and the heddles which raise or depress every alternate thread of the warp and allow the shuttle to pass between. With such a loom the average speed at which a weaver can work is about a yard a day.

37. Models of vehicles from Madras, Central Provinces, &c.

Every well-to-do peasant keeps a cart, which in idle seasons he drives on hire. It is generally of the rudest construction, and made almost entirely of wood and bamboos. When used for the conveyance of passengers it is fitted with a rough hood made of mats or reeds. Tyres are only put on when the cart is of a superior class, or the country hilly and rough, and iron axles are seldom seen. In some parts of the country (Central Provinces, Madras, &c.) the wheel is composed of a solid disc of wood, and in one district of the Madras Presidency (Kurnool) discs of granite are also employed.

38. Collections of carpenters' and blacksmiths' tools from various parts of India.

These are mostly of European pattern, and very often, especially in the matter of chisels, of English make. There are one or two peculiar instruments used by the Indian carpenter, such as the *basula*, or adze, and the bow drill. The *basula* is the carpenter's chisel, plane, hammer, and anvil, all in one, and it is made of the best soft iron with a steel edge. With surprising dexterity he can with it square a block, smooth a board, or perform any other work for which a broad chisel or a rough plane is ordinarily used. The skilful use of this tool requires much practice, and the carpenter's son is taught to handle it from an early age.

The bow drill is everywhere preferred to a brace and bit, gimlet, Archimedæan, or any other form of drill.

The native carpenter also prefers a pulling saw with the teeth set backwards, and if he does buy an English saw, speedily alters the set of the teeth and substitutes a bent handle.

He is seldom provided with a bench or vice, as he prefers to work seated on the ground, and his prehensile toes serve every purpose for which a vice might be required.

Amongst the collection of blacksmiths' tools, the hand-bellows made of two kid skins show the ordinary description of bellows used in small smithies.

Additional Models in Administrative Court.

Exhibited by West of India Portuguese Guaranteed Railway Company.

Marmagao Harbour Works, West Coast of India—

I. General Model of the Harbour.
II. Model of Harbour Quay Wall.
III. Model of Harbour Breakwater.

Exhibited by Mysore State Railway Workshop, Bangalore.

831. Model of a Third Class Metre Gauge Railway Carriage, convertible into an ambulance.

832. Model of a Covered Metre Gauge Railway Goods Wagon.

Exhibited by V. H. Raroe, *Executive Engineer Mysore District.*

833. Model of a Mysore Tank and Bund, with sluices and gardens irrigated therefrom.

834. Model of a System of Canal Irrigation, with head-works.

Exhibited by H. H. Maharaja Dungar Singh, *of Bikanir.*

2730. Model of a Well (Kira), Bikanir, Rajputana.

CHAPTER V.

CLASS B.—ADMINISTRATION.

Arrangement of Exhibits and the Courts in which they are placed.

I.—Department of Revenue and Agriculture.

Sect. 1. Survey of India. — Administration Court.

Sect. 2. Meteorology. 3. Geological Survey. 4. Agriculture.—Economic Court Annexe.

Sect. 5. Land Revenue. 6. Internal trade. 7. Emigration.—Administration Court.

II. Department of Finance and Commerce.

Sect. 1. General Finance. — Administration Court.

Sect. 2. Salt.—Economic Court.

Sect. 3. Customs and Port Dues.—Administration Court.

Sect. 4. Excise. 5. Opium.—Economic Court.

Sect. 6. The Mints. 7. Stamps. 8. Post Office. 9. External Trade. 10. Government Printing.—Administration Court.

III. Home Department.

Sect. 1. Education. 2. Law and Justice. 3. Police. 4. Sanitary and Medical. 5. Archæological Survey.—Administration Court.

Sect. 6. Forests.—Economic Court.

7. Statistics and Gazetteers. 8. Jails.—Administration Court.

IV. Public Works Department.

Sect. 1. Railways. 2. Roads.—Administration Court.

Sect. 3. Irrigation. — Economic Court Annexe.

Sec. 4. Public Buildings. 5. Telegraphs.—Administration Court.

V. Legislative Department.

Sect. 1. Acts and Regulations.—Administration Court.

VI. Foreign Department.

Sec. 1. Native States. 2. Imperial Orders and Decorations.—Administration Court.

VII. Military and Marine Department.

Army Headquarters.

Sect. 1. Internal Economy of the Army. 2. Military Education. 3. Soldiers' Exhibitions and Workshops. 4. Military Maps and Routes. —Administration Court.

Military.

Sect. 1. Military Organisation. 2. Military Medical Ambulance, &c. 3. Army Clothing. 4. War Matériel. 5. Food and Transport. 6. Army Remounts and Horse-breeding. 7. Elephant Kheddahs. 8. Indian Medals and Decorations. 9. Military Buildings.—Administration Court.

Marine.

Sect. 1. Dockyards and ships. 2. Marine Surveys.—Administration Court.

The Divisions show the Imperial Secretariat Departments of the Government of India.

The Sections show the Minor Departments and subjects with which they deal.

The maps marked with an asterisk in the descriptive list which follows are reproduced and explained at length in a Statistical Handbook of the Indian Empire.

DIVISION I.—DEPARTMENT OF REVENUE AND AGRICULTURE.

(1.) Survey of India.

[The maps described in Chapter IV. under (1) Geography are also exhibits of the Survey of India Department.]

The exhibits of the Survey of India Department are so numerous that for economy of space a comparatively small number have been presented conspicuously by enclosing them in frames: these are representative specimens of the systems of survey pursued, and of the artistic methods of reproduction employed; but those who are interested in such special and technical subjects as map making, and geographical operations in general, will find a very extensive series of specimens of every order bound up in the numerous volumes laid on the table. To these volumes the attention of enquirers is directed.

The operations of the Survey of India embrace the whole practice of the delineation of ground and its cartographic reproduction. The peninsula of India has been covered by a great series of triangles, observed with instruments of precision, and calculated out with the greatest scientific accuracy. This great work, now completed, has occupied the great Trigonometrical Survey for a period of eighty years. The records of these operations will be found in the volumes (Nos. 24, 48, &c.) laid on the table, and to these the attention of enquirers is invited. These operations may be regarded as forming the primary order on which the subsequent detail surveys are based. The second order of surveying operations is termed the Topographical Survey, and it is produced by a branch bearing that title, by which an orographical delineation of ground, mostly of hilly nature, is compiled, so as to afford a general geographical map of the Empire suitable for the requirements of the military department and of the public in general. The third order of surveying is the cadastral, and it is executed by the Revenue Branch of the Survey of India; it is effected on a large scale, and the shape and area of each field are determined so as to serve the purposes of the fiscal authorities of the Government of India. In addition to the above there are other surveys, necessarily of a confidential nature, having reference to possible future military operations in foreign or transfrontier regions, such as may be indicated by the work of the Russo-Afghan Boundary Commission, now in progress; such surveys of an adventurous kind fall within the scope of the duties required to be performed by the officers of the Survey of India.

The history of the Survey of India from its inception in the last century will be found in the volume entitled "A Memoir on the Indian Surveys," which forms exhibit No. 49. The annual narrative of the operations of the Survey of India will similarly be found in the volumes of the General Report of the Survey of India, carried down to the year 1883-4, or the present time. These volumes comprise the Exhibit No. 45.

When the field surveys have been completed by the officers of the Survey of India—amongst whom are included the English officers who superintend, the European assistants who survey and check the field measurements and calculations, and the staff of native measurers who number many thousands—the original maps require to be compiled and copied in vast numbers, so as to become available for issue to the various officers of the State and to the public. This work is carried on at the headquarters or central offices established in Calcutta. These offices of the Surveyor-General are probably more extensive than any such appertaining to other Governments of the world, both in the large issue of maps required, which in 1884-85 numbered 235,636, as well as in the variety of arts practised therein: these offices, or sections, embrace drawing and compiling, engraving on copper, lithography in colours and monochrome, photo-zincography, heliogravure on copper, and collotype on gelatine; in addition a factory for the construction and repair of mathematical and surveying instruments is maintained; and lastly the work of Administration of the large field and fixed establishments, as well as the great Map, Record, and Issue Office, are conducted at the same centre in Calcutta.

Besides the above named offices there is a minor one conducted by the Superintendent of the Trigonometrical Branch, and it is located at Dehra Dun in the North-Western Provinces. It aids the central offices in compiling and drawing, and in photozincography, and at the same time carries on the special and technical processes of computing the great triangulation, of printing and publishing its own scientific volumes of records and data, of recording meteorological indications; and, being equipped with a photoheliograph of the largest size, solar photography is prosecuted under the auspices of the Royal Society of England. The records of these various operations will be found chronicled in the numerous exhibits (Nos. 24, 43 to 49) laid on the table of the Court of the Survey of India. G. C. DE PRÉE, COLONEL, *Surveyor-General of India.*

[1].—Railway Map of India. Lithographed. Scale, 1 inch equal 32 miles.

[2].—Map of India. Engraved on copper. Scale, 1 inch equal 96 miles.

[3].—Map of India. Engraved on copper. Scale 1 inch equal 64 miles.

[4].—Map of India. Engraved on copper. Scale 1 inch equal 128 miles.

[5].—Map of India. Engraved on copper. Scale 1 inch equal 256 miles.

The series of maps of India are exhibited so as to present the form in which the empire of India is available at all times to suit all purpose of administration of the Government of India. Being all engraved on copper, any number of impressions are available on the shortest notice.

No. 2 is a good specimen of the engraving done at the offices of the Survey of India established in Calcutta.

[6].—Plan of the city and environs of Mysore. Scale 12 inches equal 1 mile.

No. 6 is remarkable as the latest effort to depict ground by the system of true contours, which are obtained by levelling with the simple but efficient instrument the water level. It is also a good specimen of refined topographical surveying; and is also a good example of the photozincographic art as practised in Calcutta.

[7].—Map of Central Provinces. Engraved on copper. Scale 1 inch equal 16 miles.

[8].—Map of the Central India Agency. Engraved on copper. Scale 1 inch equal 16 miles.

These engravings are executed at the Survey of India Offices, Calcutta, by English engravers, who also supervise, and are assisted by, natives of India, men who have already attained considerable skill in this art.

[9].—Frame containing a full sheet of the Atlas of India. No. 28. Engraved on copper. Scale 1 inch equal 4 miles.

[10].—Frame containing one quarter sheet of the Atlas of India. No. 34, N.W. Scale 1 inch equal 4 miles.

[11].—Frame containing one quarter-sheet of the Atlas of India. No. 90, S.E. Scale 1 inch equal 4 miles.

[12].—Frame containing one quarter-sheet of the Atlas of India. No. 87, S.W. Scale 1 inch equal 4 miles.

[13].—Frame containing one quarter-sheet of the Atlas of India. No. 52, N.W. Scale 1 inch equal 4 miles.

[14].—Frame containing one quarter-sheet of the Atlas of India. No. 45, N.E. Scale 1 inch equal 4 miles.

[15].—Frame of specimens of heliogravure by the photo-electrotype process.

[16].—Frame of specimens of chalk-drawing and printing by lithography by Native of Bengal.

[17].—Frame of specimens of photo-collotype printing.

[18].—Frame containing specimens of heliogravure, obtained by the photo-etching process.

Various subjects executed by European experts, assisted by natives of India.

[19].—Double frame containing the proof and plate of the award certificate for the Calcutta Exhibition by the heliogravure-photo-electrotype process, after 5,000 impressions.

This exhibit is of considerable interest, inasmuch as the copper-plate, obtained by the heliogravuric process, is comparable with the resulting delicate printed impression.

[20].—Frame containing specimens of colour-printing by natives of Bengal, being a geological map of coalfields of the Rewah Gondowan Basin.

These lithographs were produced under the supervision of skilled English foremen.

[37].—Frame showing a standard sheet of the Guzerat Dang Forest survey, Sheet No. 49, section 7. Scale 4 inches equal 1 mile.

This sheet shows the latest style of topographical surveying in hilly forest-clad tracts, the contour lines being based upon trigonometrical levelling. It is reproduced by photozincography.

[38].—N. W. Provinces Survey, Sheet No. 18, N. W. Scale 2 inches equal 1 mile.

This sheet is one of the uniform series of maps depicting the plain or champain country of India. It is reproduced by photo-zincography.

[39].—Frame of a standard sheet of the Mysore Survey, Sheet No. 24. Scale 1 inch equal 1 mile.

[40].—Frame containing a standard sheet of the Deccan Survey, Sheet No. 18.

These two sheets represent the latest efforts of the Survey of India in producing an accurate topographical map of a greatly varying surface, showing also orographical feature.

[41].—Revised Sketch Map, illustrating the exploration of A—— K——, 1879-82, Great Tibet and Mongolia.

[42].—Index to the revised sheet of A—— K——'s exploration map of Great Tibet and Mongolia.

This remarkable exploration occupied the native explorer for nearly four years, during which he was cut off entirely from all knowledge of, or correspondence with, his friends in India; has obtained the following recognition :—(1) The Government of India have conferred on the explorer the honorary title of Rai Bahadur, and have presented him with the grant of a village in fee simple. (2) The Royal Geographical Society of England has presented a gold watch, a sum of money, and a letter of honour. (3) The Geographical Society of France has lately presented their gold medal to the explorer, accompanied by a graceful letter.

[21].—A raised map of India. Scale 1 inch equal 32 miles.

This model-map has been produced specially for this Exhibition. The elevated features are depicted with true accuracy, the vertical scale being arranged on the ratio of twelve to one of the horizontal scale.

[22].—Album of specimen sheets of various topographical maps.

[23].—Album containing specimens of the engraved sheets of the Atlas of India.

[24].—Album containing technical charts, illustrating the scientific operations of the Survey of India.

[25].—Album of specimens of engraved maps and miscellaneous subjects on copper.

[26].—Album of photozincographs of towns, cities, and sanataria on various large scales.

[27].—Album containing specimens of cadastral maps, reproduced from the original field surveys by photozincography.

[28].—Album of miscellaneous maps drawn on stone in monochrome.

[29].—Album of specimens of maps drawn on stone and lithographed in colours and chalk.

[30].—Album of 200 photographs of Art manufactures and buildings taken in the Calcutta International Exhibition of 1883–1884.

[31].—Album of 29 photographs of Indian jewellery, &c., taken in the Calcutta Exhibition.

[32].—Album Photographs of Indian silver-work, fabrics, and views, taken in the Calcutta Exhibition.

[33.]—Album of miscellaneous specimens of maps and plans reproduced by photozincography.

[34].—Album of specimens of vernacular writings passing through the Post-office of India, reproduced by photozincography.

[35].—Albums of Photozincographs of Ancient Muhamadan inscriptions from Gaur and Maldah.

[36].—Album of Indian Art Ware in the Calcutta Exhibition of 1883–84, reproduced in heliogravure.

[43].—Nine Volumes, containing the account of the operations of the great Trigonometrical Survey of India.

[44].—Seven Volumes, comprising the synopsis of the results of the operations of the great Trigonometrical Survey.

Fourteen Fasciculi of the synopsis of the results of the great Trigonometrical Survey of India.

[45].—Seven Volumes of the general report on the operations of the Survey of India, 1877–84.

[46].—Two Volumes. An account of the measurement of an arc of the meridian, by Capt. George Everest (subsequently Sir George Everest, C.S.I, late Surveyor-General of India), accompanied by a series of engravings of the instruments of precision used in the operation.

[47].—An Account of the measurement of two sections of the meridional arc of India, by Lieut.-Colonel Everest, F.R.S.

[48].—Abstract of the reports of the surveys and of other geographical operations in India for 1869–70, 1876–77, 1877–78. Printed and published by order of Her Majesty's Secretary of State for India.

[49].—Abstract of memoir on the Indian Surveys, by Clements R. Markham, C.B. F.R.S.

[50].—Twelve Maps of India, showing the moral and material progress of India, by order of the Secretary of State, by Trelawney Saunders, F.R.G.S

[51].—Statistical maps of India, prepared by order of the Government of India in the Revenue and Agricultural Department, consisting of

Native States of India.
Railways of India.
Irrigation of India.
Average General Contours of India.
Density of Population of India.
Rainfall of India.
Missionary Stations of India.
Crop Maps of various products of India.
Religions of India.
River Basins of India.
Languages of India.
Emigration of India.
External Trade of India.

(5.) Land Revenue.

Exhibits under Sections (2) *Meteorological Survey, and* (3) *Geological Survey, are described in Chapter IV.; those under* (4) *Agriculture in Chapter VI.*

1. Settlement map: showing which portions of India pay land revenue (*i.e.*, share of the profits from land) to Government, and of these, which pay sums fixed in perpetuity (permanent settlement), and which sums liable to periodical revision (temporary settlement).

2. Revenue rate map: showing the incidence per acre of the revenue paid to Government on all classes of land, and indicating the comparatively low rate on the permanently-settled area.

3. Land Revenue Settlement Reports of selected districts.

4. Land Revenue Administration Reports for 1883–84 from each province.

5. Stack's Memorandum on current Land Revenue Settlements in the temporarily-settled parts of British India.

6. Baden-Powell's Manual of the Land Revenue System and Land Tenures of British India.

7. Report of the Indian Famine Commission.
Part I.—Famine Relief.
„ II.—Measures of Protection and Prevention.
„ III.—History of Past Famines.
Appendices to the Report.

8. Famine Codes.

9. Cotton's Report on the Moral and Material progress of India, showing most recent statistics of Land Revenue income and charges.

Madras Revenue Survey.

Exhibitor, Colonel H. T. Rogers, R.E., *Superintendent, Revenue Survey.*

71. *Demarcation.* — Boundary demarcation sketch showing divisions.

72. *Demarcation.* — Eight division sketches showing fields.

73. *Demarcation.*—Land register.

74. *Survey.*—Boundary field book.

75. *Survey.*—Division field book.

76. *Survey.*—Field measurement book.

77. *Computation.*—Three boundary traverse sheets.

78. *Computation.* — Seven division traverse sheets.

79. *Computation.*—Area list.

80. *Mapping.*—Four village maps, scale 16 inches to 1 mile.

81. *Mapping.*—Village map, scale 8 inches to 1 mile.

82. *Mapping.*—Taluk map, scale 1 inch to 1 mile.

83. *Mapping.*—District map, scale ½ inch to 1 mile.

84. *Mapping.*—Atlas quarter sheet, scale ¼ inch to 1 mile.

85. *Mapping.*—Four reference sheets.

(6.) Internal Trade.

1. Internal Trade map: showing the division of India into blocks for the purpose of registering the Internal Trade.

Each province is divided, for purposes of registration, into "internal blocks," each of the other outlying provinces being, in regard to it, an "external block." In the registration of the sea-borne trade, each maritime province is the basis upon which the distribution of the trade is founded. Similarly, in the registration of internal trade some basis is required on which to reckon the distribution of the trade. The different provinces or blocks serve this purpose. The articles of which the traffic is registered are specified in a classified list prescribed by the Government of India. This list is supplied to the railway authorities who, from the weights given in the invoices received in their offices, prepare periodical returns showing the quantities of the articles carried between the different Provinces or "blocks." For this purpose the railway lines are divided into strips or lengths coterminous with the boundaries of blocks, and as invoices are ledgered in the railway offices, station by station, in the order of the stations on each line, it becomes a simple matter to set apart and deal separately with all the invoices belonging to each strip or length.

2. Internal Trade Reports of the several provinces for the year 1883–84.

(7.) Emigration.

1. Colonial Emigration map: showing the number of coolies emigrating annually from each district to the West Indies, Mauritius, Natal, and Fiji.

Indian or "Coolie" Emigration is practically confined to labourers recruited in India and conveyed under contract to work at particular industries in countries where labour is scarce. The movement is entirely wanting in the spirit of colonization which distinguishes the emigration of western nations, and it is governed by different conditions. Indian emigration supplies labour to three great industries—sugar, tea, and coffee. The terms offered by the different colonies are much alike. An adult labourer receives generally a shilling a day, free quarters, and medical attendance, and in some cases rations. He indentures for five years, and after a further residence of two years in the colony, during which he is free to seek his own employer on his own terms, he obtains a free passage to India. The number of Indians who have permanently settled in the colonies is very large. In Demerara (British Guiana), out of a population of 250,000, upwards of 80,000 are Indians; in Mauritius, which is exceptional in giving no return passage, 249,000 out of a total of 360,000 inhabitants are natives of India. There is still an immense field open for India in tropical and sub-tropical regions, where the white man cannot perform manual labour. Some idea of the magnitude of this labour field, as compared with India, may be gained from the fact that if a line be drawn from Calcutta to Bombay, the whole of India below that line will be just equal to Borneo. Nature in bestowing rich vegetable wealth on these regions has accompanied her gift with the drawback of a lazy population—lazy because the climate is enervating and because nature pours food into their lap. To these favoured lands the patient, sinewy, and hard-working Indian coolie is only waiting to be led by European enterprise and capital.

2. Inland Emigration map: showing the proportion of the population of each district emigrating annually to Assam, Burma, and Ceylon.

The population of Madras emigrates freely to Burma and the coffee plantations in Ceylon, and from the North-Western Provinces and Bengal there is a large migration to the Tea Gardens of Assam. The map deals chiefly with registered emigration, that is, emigrants who leave under contract to work, and who are brought for registration before a magistrate by whom the contract is examined and explained to the intending emigrant. There is a considerable amount of voluntary emigration within the limits of India and to neighbouring countries on the east coast for which complete information is not available.

3. Annual Reports on Emigration by the Protector of Emigrants, &c.

4. Reports by Messrs. Pitcher and Grierson on the system of recruiting coolies for the sugar-growing colonies.

5. Emigration Acts and Rules.

DIVISION II.—DEPARTMENT OF FINANCE AND COMMERCE.

(*Exhibits under section* (2) *Salt,* (4) *Excise, and* (5) *Opium, are described in Chapter VI.*)

(1) General Finance.

1. The Financial Statement for 1885–86.

2. The Finance and Revenue Accounts of the Government of India for 1883–84.

3. The Accounts of the Revenue and Expenditure and of the Debt of India for the years 1857–58 to 1882–83, Volumes I. and II.

4. The Finance and Revenue Accounts and Miscellaneous Statistics relating to the Finances of British India.

Part I., from 1st April 1876 to 31st March 1884.
Part II., do. do. do.
Part III., seventh issue.

5. License Tax Reports.

(3) Customs and Port Dues.

1. Report on the Administration of the Port Commissioners, Calcutta, for 1883–84.

2. Report on the Administration of the Port Commissioners, Rangoon, for 1883–84.

3. Bombay Port Trust Administration Report for 1883–84.

(6) THE MINTS.

1. Specimens in bronze of various Indian medals struck at the Calcutta Mint.
2. Photographs of Exterior and Interior of the Bombay Mint.
3. Specimens of Indian Silver and Copper Coins—from Bombay Mint.
4. Rupee in process of manufacture; blank cut from slip; milled and silver slip showing six bits cut out—from Bombay Mint.
5. Specimens of dies in various stages of manufacture, from blank die to finished die ready for coining—from Bombay Mint.
6. Reports on the working of the Calcutta and Bombay Mints for 1883–84.

(7) STAMPS.

1. Case contributed by Messrs. De La Rue and Company, showing all stamps used, whether for postal, judicial, or other purposes, in the Indian Empire.
2. Annual Reports for 1883–84 on the administration of the Stamp Department in the several Provinces.

(8) POST OFFICE.

Imperial.

1. Postal map: showing by means of colours the number of letters, &c., per head of population delivered annually by the Post Office of India in the different districts of the Indian Empire.
2. Post Office Administration Report for 1883–84.

Madras.

Exhibitor, Consulting Architect to Government.

101. Model of the new combined Post and Telegraph Office at Madras, scale 6 feet to the inch. This building is the last public work of interest completed in Madras. It is interesting, as all the details are of Eastern origin, and, with the exception of the pot-metal glass and rolled girders, the whole building was carried out by local workmen and local materials under the superintendence of Mr. R. F. Chisholm. (Around the model are specimens of the local materials and local workmanship.) The table was made by a Madras carver.

1. Model in pith of a postal mail runner.
2. Model in pith of a pony *Jhatka* (mail cart) used to convey mails in Madras.
3. Model of bullock *Jhatka* used for the same purpose.
4. Model of catamaran (native boat) used to convey mails between India and Ceylon.
5. Model of catamaran used in Madras harbour for landing and shipping mails.
6. Model of a *masula* boat used for the same purpose.
7. Model of a hide-covered basket boat used for passing mails in Madras.
8. Specimens of torches used by mail runners in certain districts of Madras.
9. Case containing silver and copper coins used in payment of postage in various parts of Madras.
10. Board used to count silver coins in Travancore State.

Bombay.

1. Model of a horse *dâk* rider of the Chhatila and Bhuj horse *dâk* division, Cutch.
2. Model of a camel *dâk* rider with mails.
3. Model showing mode of carrying mails across rivers in Sindh.
4. Model of a raft floated by means of a gourd used in the Bombay Presidency to convey mails across streams.

Bengal.

1. Model of a Combined Post and Telegraph Office in Lower Bengal, showing the interior of the building with establishment at work.

The building is on the standard plan for first class post offices at the headquarters of districts, and the model is on a scale of one-sixteenth the actual size. The upper story with the ceilings of the rooms on the ground floor can be raised so as to show the interior of the Post and Telegraph Office with the clerks of the different departments at work. The high wall round the Court-yard at the back of the building is constructed to secure privacy to the Hindu Postmaster's family who live with him in the upper story of the building.

2. Model of a postman.
3. Model of a mail runner carrying letter mails.
4. Model of a mail runner carrying parcel mails.
5. Model of apparatus used in Bengal to convey mails across streams in flood.
6. Model of a mail boat for delivery of letters to steamers at Diamond Harbour.
7. Models of boats for conveyance of mails on inland rivers.
8. Model of a *Tonga* (cart) used in parts of Bengal for the conveyance of mails and passengers.

North-Western Provinces and Oudh.

1. Model of a postman in the North-Western Provinces.
2. Model of a mail runner.
3. Model of a packer in the act of closing the mails.
4. Model of a *chaukidar* or watchman.
5. Models exhibiting mode of ferrying mails across rivers in flood in the North-Western Provinces.
6. Model of a description of mail cart made in the Postal Workshop, Aligarh, for use in different parts of India.

Punjab.

1. Models of mail coach and carriage used to convey mails and passengers between Umballa and Kalka on the road to Simla.
2. Model of *Tonga* or mountain car used

between Kalka and Simla to convey mails and passengers.

3. Model of Government bullock train cart for the conveyance of goods between Umballa and Simla.

Burma.

1. Model of mail boat maintained in Burma with rowers, mail bags, &c.
2. Model of Harbour postman with *Sampan* boat delivering letters in Akyab Harbour.
3. Model of native postmaster.
4. Model of postman.
5. Models of mail runners.
6. Model of convict postman in the Penal Settlement, Andaman Islands.
7. *Dáo* (bill-hook) used by mail runners to protect the mails.

Assam.

1. Specimen of buffalo horns sounded by mail runners in Assam to scare away wild animals.

Rajputana.

1. Bow and sheaf of arrows used to protect the mails in Rajputana.
2. Oil painting representing mode of conveying mails from Mount Abu, Rajputana.

9. External Trade.

1. Trade map illustrating the commerce of India with the rest of the world by sea.

This map indicates by coloured blocks the value of the exports from India to other countries, and the imports to India from other countries. Exports from India are coloured blue. Imports to India are coloured red. The imports to India from each country are shown twice—once in a red block on the country from which they are brought to India, and again as part of the large red block in the Arabian Sea. The exports from India are shown twice—once in a blue block on the country to which sent from India, and again as part of the large blue block in the Bay of Bengal. Exports and imports below £500,000 are not shown.

The total value of the external trade of India by sea is roughly one hundred and fifty-five million pounds sterling, of which ninety million pounds represent exports, and sixty-five millions imports. The total value of the commerce between India and the United Kingdom is eighty-six million pounds sterling, of which thirty-six millions represent exports, and fifty millions imports.

2. Trade Route map, showing the routes followed by trade in the commerce between India and countries across her frontier. Shows routes along which trade between India and other countries travels. The trade routes on the border are arranged in groups with reference to the external country. The relative importance of each route is indicated by the thickness of the line representing it.

The total value of the trade by land with countries across the frontier of the Indian Empire, from Sindh on the west to Siam on the east, is approximately eleven million pounds sterling, the imports and exports being nearly equally balanced. The trade with Afghanistan, Beluchistan, and Kashmir amounts to about three million pounds sterling; with Nepal to two and a half millions sterling, and with Upper Burma, including Karennee, to four and a quarter millions.

Reference should be made to the Statistical Atlas for particulars regarding the trade of India.

3. Review of the sea-borne trade of India, 1883–84.

4. The annual accounts of the sea-borne trade of India—

(*a*) Foreign trade . .	Volume I, 1883–84.	
(*b*) Coasting trade . .	" II.	"
(*c*) Trade of Aden and of the French and Portuguese possessions in India . .	" III.	"

5. The local accounts of the sea-borne trade of—

Bengal . . .	Volumes I & II.	1883–84.	
Bombay . .	"	"	"
Sindh . . .	"	"	"
Madras. . .	"	"	"
British Burma.	"	"	"

with the reviews of the above accounts.

6. Monthly accounts of the sea-borne trade, April, 1884 to March, 1885.

7. Review of the trade by land of India, 1883–84.

8. The accounts of the frontier trade (quarterly), 1884–85.

(10) Government Printing.

Imperial Department.

1. Type foundry specimens made by native workmen :—

Punches and Matrices; type cast from matrices made in India.

Electrotypes, Stereotype and Electrotype Plates; Metal Furniture Mould and Cast, with the cores for each size; Quotation Mould, Cast and Cores; Type Mould; Founders' Tools; Lead Mould; and a Composing Stick, &c.

2. Printing Inks made by Amritolall Ráy, Balliaghatta, Calcutta.
3. Bookbinders' Tools, made by Srirama Chundrá Chuckrabutty, Calcutta.
4. Specimens of Printing and Bookbinding by native workmen.
5. Portfolio containing specimens of miscellaneous printing.
6. Copy of the *Gazette of India*, published weekly.
7. Note on the working of the Press by E. J. Dean, Superintendent of Government of India Printing. (Contains also a detailed list of exhibits.)

Madras.

1. Specimen Book of English and Vernacular types, &c., in use in the Government Press, Fort Saint George.

2. Collection of Books in English and Vernacular languages, shown as specimens of printing and binding.

Bombay.

1. Specimens of work done by natives in the foundry of the Government Central Press, Bombay:—

Six Punches, of Marathi, Kanarese, and Guzarathi letters; Matrices, small Stereotype Plates, Copper Plate engraved and Electrotype Plate.

2. Specimens of printing appliances made of tamarind wood in the Press by native carpenters:—

Mallet, shooting stick, quoins, &c.

3. Printed Specimens of Oriental types used in the Press.

4. Specimens of printing and binding by native workmen.

5. Specimen of ruling and binding in country leather by native workmen in the Press.

6. Specimen of binding by reformatory boys working in the Press.

7. Pieces of pasteboard made by native workmen from Indian paper.

8. Map varnished, mounted on cloth and rollers in the Press. (The rollers were made in the Press.)

Bengal.

1. Collection of Government of Bengal Gazettes, showing printing in English and Vernacular.

2. Specimens (books) of printing and bookbinding.

DIVISION III.—HOME DEPARTMENT.

(1) Education.

Madras.

1. Photographs of colleges and schools in the Madras Presidency.

2. Collection of English and Vernacular school books.

3. Abacus, *i.e.*, reckoning machine.

4. Paper globes.

5. Maps used in village schools.

6. *Cadjan* books with packet of leaves of *Calatropis gigantea*, used for rubbing the *cadjan* to make the writing clear.

7. Wooden boards used as slates.

8. Wooden board with school drawings.

9. Ornamental boards with songs used on a festival called Mahanavami.

10. Book racks and wooden book stands.

11. Samples of paper used in village schools.

12. *Kadidamu*, made of rough cloth dyed with charcoal and the juice of certain leaves; used by native merchants instead of paper.

13. Specimens of ink, ink bottles, pens, styles, pencils, &c.

14. *Lapis Ollaris* pencils, with palmyra leaf stalk, used for cutting them.

15. Thread-lined board for ruling paper.

16. Muhammadan school-boys' silk bag.

17. Festival cards used in Muhammadan schools.

Bombay.

1. Photographs of colleges and schools in the Bombay Presidency.

2. Collection of English and Vernacular school books and maps.

3. Paintings, sketches, and designs by students of Sir Jamsetjee Jeejeebhoy's School of Art.

4. Model of an Indigenous school.

The 18 boys of different ages, sitting in three rows in front of the Brahman schoolmaster, sitting on a raised and cushioned seat, are of various castes and positions in life. The boys in the front row to the left of the master are the most advanced pupils of the school, being evidently able to read and write. They are represented as engaged in a writing lesson. Each boy writes his copy with a reed pen (No. 8) and has a school-boy's inkstand (No. 12) at his right hand. The careless boys have bespattered their dress with ink. The satchels or "*rumals*" (Towels, see No. 8) placed before each boy contain apparatus as detailed under No. 8. When the writing lesson is over, each boy will take out of his *rumal* his manuscripts for reading, or "*Bakhars*," and do his reading lesson. When this is done, he will do his arithmetic, and end his day's work with exercises in mental arithmetic. The second row is of less advanced boys, who have either finished or nearly finished the multiplication tables, which they write on their slates or sand-boards, and recite or intone together under the master's leadership. The third row on the right hand of the master is of beginners, who write the letters of the alphabet or easy multiplication tables on their slates or sand-boards (Nos. 5 and 6), as represented in the model.

The figures of the boys represent different castes. The first boys in the first and third rows, and the first two in the second, and the boy in the third row who is standing up, are boys of the Brahman or higher castes. The third boy in the first row is a Marwari boy (banker or trader); the rest, with darker skins and scantier apparel, are either *kunbis* (cultivators), *malees* (gardeners), or boys of other lower castes. The master makes those boys who pay him the largest fees sit near him, so that he may be able to pay them the greatest attention. The poorer boys who cannot afford to pay the master much sit farther off, and are comparatively neglected. In the model the boys sitting close to the master are evidently children of well-to-do parents, from their superior dress and ornaments.

5. Sandboard of a superior kind painted and varnished yellow, having a representation of Ganpati, the God of learning, with his two attendant goddesses "Ridhi" and "Sidhi" (Power and Success). A red powder (collected in the holder No. 10) is spread over this board, and the children learn to write upon it with a bamboo style or the hard quill (No. 11).

6. Sandboard of an inferior description. This sandboard is made of a kind of white clay, and is used with red sand (a specimen of which is collected in holder No. 10).

7. Boards with letters carved on them: are sometimes used by beginners. They trace the letters with the brass style, No. 11.

8. *Rumal* or satchel, literary towel, contains writing paper, copy slips, pen-holder with reed pens of sorts, a pair of scissors and pen-knife, manuscript letters for reading, "Bakhars" (mythological or historical stories), books of hymns or songs, and "Panchánga," or calendar of the year.

9. *Kalamdan*, or writing case with reed pens and inkstands.

10. Holders for red powder and red sand.

11. Styles of brass and bamboo.

12. Indigenous schoolboys' inkstand (the boys walk to school swinging their inkstands in the right hand, and with the "*rumal*" tucked under the left arm).

13. A schoolmaster's or man's inkstand, containing receptacles for red and black ink, sand, and gum.

14. The schoolmaster's cushion on which he reclines, used also by clerks.

15. Schoolboys' toys — *Vitti*, *Dandoo*, and *Chendoo—Anglicè* "cat, bat, and ball," tops of sorts, "*chakra*," or wheel.

16. Four figures representing the chief domestic occupation of native women of the poorer orders, viz.:—

A woman grinding corn;
A woman pounding rice;
A woman churning;
A woman fetching water.

The female children of these classes use toys in imitation of their occupations. The toys of native girls have thus a utilitarian aim, and in the course of playing, the little native girls learn a good deal of the simple domestic economy of native life. The figures illustrate the use of the toys, which are models on a smaller scale of the domestic utensils in common use.

17. Toys representing models of common domestic utensils, the use of most of which is shown by the four figures noticed under 16.

18. Infants' toys and appliances:—feeding spoons, rocking cradle, sleeping cot, rattles, cymbals, medicine boxes for holding domestic nursery remedies, &c.

Bengal.

1. Photographs of educational buildings and of scenes and ceremonies illustrating school life in Bengal.

2. English and Vernacular school books and maps.

3. Terrestrial globes in Bengali.

4. Specimens of map drawing.

5. Specimens of handwriting.

6. Specimens of drawing and painting.

7. Specimens of needle and fancy work done in girls' schools.

8. Collection of old manuscripts.

9. Bengali primers and copy books used in infant schools.

10. Writing materials; ink, ink-bottles, pens, boards, paper, &c.

11. Palm-leaves, used for writing on, with specimens of writing and iron stylus. (The edge on the head of the stylus is used for cutting the palm-leaf.)

12. Different kinds of accounts kept by native shopkeepers, traders, &c.

13. *Sampidi*, or wooden board fastened together in book form, used by shopkeepers in keeping petty accounts.

14. *Panjaka*, or Bengali almanac.

15. Horoscope in Sanskrit.

North-Western Provinces and Oudh.

1. Photographs of school buildings and groups of schoolboys.

2. Collection of school-books in English and Vernacular.

3. Curricula for village schools, normal schools, &c. &c.

4. Specimens of map drawing from boys' schools.

5. Specimens of penmanship from boys' schools.

6. Specimens of penmanship from girls' schools.

7. Embroidery work done in girls' schools.

8. Straw baskets, fans, &c., made by school-girls.

9. Ornamental writing, including specimens of *Tugra* penmanship, *i.e.*, words formed to represent animals, birds, and other objects. This a very complete and representative collection of specimens of a favourite art among the literate natives of Hindustan.

10. Wooden slates, used by beginners to practise handwriting.

11. Ink, inkstands, and reed and bamboo pens. Some of these last are highly ornamented.

12. *Kalamdáns*, or writing boxes, containing inkstands, pens, penknife, scissors, &c. The brass boxes are generally used by the banker class, those made of ebony by the writer class, called *kyastha*, and the coloured and ornamented boxes, fitted with ivory penknife, &c., by the aristocratic class, such as Rajahs and Nawabs.

13. Paper, common and ornamented. The paper ornamented with gold foil is commonly used for writing letters or petitions to persons of rank.

14. *Juzdán*, or satchel for holding books—done in embroidery.

15. *Baludán*, or sandpot, used instead of blotting paper.

16. *Rihal*, or stand for holding the Koran.

17. Specimens of the Koran copied in manuscript.

Central Provinces.

1. Photographs of schools and school life.

2. Linguistic map of the Central Provinces. In the Central Provinces most of the languages of India meet, and their multiplicity adds much to the difficulty of commencing schools. The census of 1881 records that there are twenty-six languages and mixed dialects in use in the Central Provinces, not including the dialects of the feudatory States.

3. Curriculum in English, Urdu, Marathi, Hindi, and Uriya.

4. Collection of school books and educational department rules.

5. Specimens of school work; model lessons, drawings, copy books, &c.

6. Map of the Central Provinces, used in village schools.

7. Wooden boards for exercises (also used by Marwaris (bankers) for rough notes of their day's transactions).

8. Brass *thali*, or plate, used in Guzarathi schools for the same purpose.

9. Specimens of paper, inkstands, pens, and pen-boxes or writing-cases.

10. Schoolboy's satchel.

11. Indian schoolmaster's *Koru*, or whip, after thirty years' service in an indigenous school in Jabalpur.

12. *Dandas* (sticks), used by schoolboys in reciting poetry. The sticks are clashed together at every pause in the verse recited.

13. Palm leaf prayer-book in Telugu, written with an iron stylus.

14. Carved book-rests, used by Muhammadans in reading the Koran, also by Hindus for the support of their *pothis* (prayer-books).

15. *Mistas*, or apparatus for ruling paper. The paper is pressed on the lines.

16. Specimens of work done by students of the Female Training School, Jabalpur.

17. Brahmanical map of the world. Mount Meru is the centre, surrounded by concentric circles of land and sea.

18. *Panchánga*. A Hindu calendar or almanac, so called because it gives information on five heads—1st, *tithi*, or date; 2nd, *war*, or day of the week; 3rd, *nakshatra*, or star in the lunar mansion; 4th, *yoga*, one of the twenty-seven divisions of the ecliptic; 5th, *karan*, one of the eleven astronomical periods. The general almanacs give other information, as dates of the months (Hindu, Christian, Muhammadan), days for marriages, thread ceremony, eclipses, &c., &c. These almanacs are from Nagpur.

19. Hindu books on Astronomy.

Muhurta Martand.—Contents: Lucky and unlucky days for every action or ceremony, *sanskaras* (purificatory rites or ceremonies), days for marriages, house building, pilgrimages, &c., miscellaneous events; coronation of kings.

Graha laghava. Contents: Description of the Sun and the Moon, description of Mars and other four principal planets, eclipses of the Sun and the Moon, rising and setting of the Sun and other planets, umbras of the planets, conjunctions, &c.

Muhurta Chintamani with Commentary. Contents: Auspicious and inauspicious days, constellations of the stars, conjunctions, purification rites and ceremonies, auspicious days for marriages, entry of a newly-married girl into her husband's house, sacrificial ceremonies, coronation of kings, pilgrimages, house building, &c.

20. Collection of Children's Toys.

The exhibits are more fully detailed in a brief note on education in the Central Provinces by Colin Browning, Esq., M.A., Inspector-General of Education in that Province.

Burma.

1. Set of photographs of school buildings.

2. Wooden model of a *Poongyi Kyaung*, or Buddhist Monastic School.

3. Wooden boards used as slates with soapstone (steatite), pencil attached. The surface is prepared by a coating of starch and charcoal powder, a fresh application of which is employed to efface the writing.

4. Blank exercise book, made of bamboo paper imported from China, and written on with soapstone pencils. The writing surface is prepared in the way described above, and made smooth by rubbing with bean leaves.

5. Bundles of palm leaves, trimmed and untrimmed, used for copying manuscripts.

6. Styles for writing on palm leaf and brush for oiling manuscripts. The style is studded by passing it through a small leather band round the fore-finger.

7. Writing-desks. The copyist when writing rests the palm leaf on the end of one of the cross pieces supporting the desk, and not on the lid.

8. Specimens of palm leaf manuscripts with gilt edges.

The palm manuscripts are preserved by oiling them with earth oil from time to time.

9. Palm leaf manuscript, containing a royal order making a grant of land for the construction of *Theni*, or building for the ordination of Buddhist priests.

10. Wooden and bamboo gongs with stand and mallet, used for assembling pupils.

(2) Law and Justice.

1. Reports on the Administration of Criminal and Civil Justice in the several Presidencies and Provinces.

2. Law Reports of the Calcutta, Madras, Bombay, and Allahabad High Courts.

3. Views of the High Court building, Calcutta.

4. Views of the Small Cause Court, Calcutta.

5. Views of the Police Court building, Calcutta.

6. Photographs of a double-storied Judge's Court-house on the standard plan, Bengal.

7. Photographs of a single and double Munsiff's (minor Civil Judge) Court-house on the standard plan, Bengal.

8. Photograph of the High Court, Bombay.

9. Photograph of the High Court, Allahabad.

(3) Police.

1. Annual Reports on the Administration of the Police Department in the several Provinces.

Drawings, plans and photographs of court houses and police stations, British Burma. Exhibited by Judicial Commissioner, British Burma.

(4) Sanitary and Medical.

1. Annual reports and other publications of the Medical Departments of the several Provinces.

2. Photographs of hospitals in Calcutta.

3. Photographs of medical buildings and hospitals in Bombay.

4. Five photographs showing arrangements for the removal of sewage adopted in —— Punjab.

5. Medicine Chest to accompany Surgeon-Major Hunter's work on Domestic Medicine.

Medical Works; — By Sur.-Major G. Y. Hunter; Sur.-Gen. Moore, Bombay; Brigade-Surgeon C. MacDowell: Sur.-Major G. Waters; Brigade-Surgeon H. V. Carter, M.D.; Sur.-Major W. Nolan, M.D.; Sur. I. Lucas, M.D.

Materia Medica of Western India. Dr. Dymock.

A collection of surgical instruments used by native surgeons. Exhibited by Inspector-General of Civil Hospitals, N.W. Provinces and Oudh.

Photographs of hospitals, Lahore District. Exhibited by Punjab Government.

(5) Archæological Survey.

1. Reports of the Archæological Survey in — volumes (illustrated).

2. Cole's Monograph of Ancient Monuments, with plates.

3. Dr. Rajendralala Mittra's Buddha Gya, illustrated.

4. Collection of photographs of Ancient Monuments and buildings in the North-Western Provinces and Oudh, under the care of the Archæological Division of the Public Works Department of the Province.

5. Collection of photographs of ancient buildings in Bijapur in the Bombay Presidency, now mostly used as public offices.

(6) Forests.*

Maps.

1. Map of India showing the distribution of Forest areas in Bengal, North-Western Provinces and Oudh, Punjab, Central Provinces, Ajmere Mhairwara, Coorg, Berar, Assam, and British Burma, on 1st April, 1885; scale 1 in. = 32 miles.

The areas of Forest lands under the Forest Department are as follows:—

Name of Province.	Area of Forests, in Square Miles.				
	Reserved.	Protected.	District.	Unreserved.	Total.
Bengal . .	4,882	2,298	4,313	...	11,493
North-Western Provinces and Oudh, School Circle.	764	...	...	...	764
Ditto, Central Circle	1,471	99	...	...	1,570
Ditto, Oudh Circle. .	1,194	17	...	...	1,211
Punjab . .	1,391	311	...	2,908	4,610
Central Provinces .	*19,440	...	...	404	19,844
Ajmere Mhairwara	145	...	...	...	145
Coorg . .	238	...	...	...	238
Berar . .	1,544	...	†1,889	‡931	4,364
Assam . .	2,342	§862	§6,390	...	9,594
British Burma, Pegu Circle.	2,811	...	...	...	2,811
Ditto Tenasserim Circle	716	...	...	...	716
Total .	36,938	3,687	12,592	4,243	57,360

2. Map of India, showing Forest distribution and rainfall, 1885, scale 1 in. = 32 miles.

3. Map of Bengal, Behar, and Chutia Nagpur, showing the distribution of Forest areas on 1st April, 1885, scale 1 in. = 16 miles.

4. Map showing the distribution of Forest areas in the North-Western Provinces and Oudh on 1st April, 1885, scale 1 in. = 4 miles.

4A. Map showing the distribution of Forest areas in the districts of Banda, Jhansi, and Lalitpur, North-Western Provinces, on 1st April, 1885, scale 1 in. = 4 miles.

5. Map showing the distribution of Forest areas in the Oudh Circle, North-Western Provinces, on 1st April, 1885, scale 1 in. = 4 miles.

6. Map showing the distribution of Forest areas in the Punjab, on 1st April, 1885, scale 1 in. = 16 miles.

7. Map showing the distribution of Forest areas in the Central Provinces, on 1st April, 1885, scale 1 in. = 16 miles.

8. Map showing the distribution of Forest areas in Ajmere Mhairwara, on 1st April, 1885, scale 1 in. = 4 miles.

9. Map showing the distribution of Forest areas in Coorg, on 1st April, 1885, scale 1 in. = 4 miles.

10. Map showing the distribution of Forest areas in Berar (the Hyderabad Assigned Districts), on 1st April, 1885, scale 1 in. = 4 miles.

* Specimens of Timber and Forest produce are described in Chapter VI.; the exhibits here referred to are confined to specimens of professional work, of which a more detailed description will be found in a list placed amongst the maps.

* Includes 1st and 2nd class forests.

† District unreserved forests.

‡ Unreserved forests managed by Forest officers.

§ Shown as unreserved forests.

11. Map showing the distribution of Forest areas in Assam, under the jurisdiction of the Chief Commissioner, with adjacent hills, on 1st April, 1885, scale 1 in. = 8 miles.

12. Map showing the distribution of Forest areas in British Burma, on 1st April, 1885, scale 1 in. = 4 miles.

13. Map of Forest reserves in Dehra Dun, Saharanpur, and Jaunsar Bawár, scale 1 in. = 1 mile, showing areas protected from fire in 1885.

14. Map of the Reserved Forests of Deota, Lambatach, &c., in Tehri-Garhwal, part of the School Circle, North-Western Provinces and Oudh, scale 4 in. = 1 mile.

15. Map of the Government Forests in the Jagirs of Dadhi and Raiengarh (Simla Hill States), part of the School Circle, North-Western Provinces and Oudh, scale 2 in. = 1 mile.

16. Map of the Ellichpur Taluk, Berar, scale 1 in. = 1 mile, showing Woods, Ramnas, and Grazing lands under the Forest Department.

17. Part of Sheet No. XIV. of the Melghat Taluk, District Ellichpur, Berar, scale 4 in. = 1 mile. [The levelled contour lines on this map were laid down with Tangent scale clinometer.]

Forest information on maps Nos. 1 to 13 was compiled by W. H. Reynolds, F.R.G.S., Officiating Superintendent of Forest Surveys, from existing surveys, sketches by Conservators of Forests, and other sources; maps Nos. 14 to 17 were drawn in the Office of the Superintendent of Forest Surveys.

18 to 67. Detailed maps in portfolios, North-Western Provinces and Oudh, School Circle.

68 to 131. Central Circle.

132 to 150. Oudh Circle.

151 to 159. Punjab.

160 to 200. Central Provinces.

201 to 215. Bengal.

216 to 237. Assam.

238 to 247. Berar.

248 to 254. Ajmere Mhairwara.

255 to 276. Coorg.

277 to 287. British Burma.

288 and 289. Trans-frontier.

Miscellaneous.

290. Traverse indicator. Designed by W. H. Reynolds, Officiating Superintendent of Forest Surveys, to facilitate the working of rectangular co-ordinates of traverse stations.

291 to 296. Skeleton maps and blue prints, &c. As it was represented that the hill shading on the maps was heavy and impeded their usefulness for forest purposes, the Superintendent of Forest Surveys had an experimental skeleton sheet drawn (No. 94), in which are shown not only the water-courses, roads, village-sites, and such other items as are generally shown in a skeleton sheet, but also the principal ridges and spurs. It did not, however, appear possible to limit the field work to the amount of detail shown in the skeleton map, because the amount actually required in each particular case was not known. Neither did it appear desirable to draw the fair sheets in skeleton only, partly for the same reason, and partly because such sheets would be useless for ordinary purposes, and for incorporation with the maps drawn by the Surveyor-General's department. It seemed, therefore, that work in the field must proceed as before, and that, if skeleton maps are required, they must be in addition to the shaded sheets. It was thought, however, that, if blue prints could be brought into use, Forest Officers would be in possession of maps which would be light enough to enable them readily to record information on them either by colour or in writing, while they would be in possession of all available detail without the additional expense of a second drawing and photozincographic process.

Nos. 291 to 296 have been prepared with this object, and blue prints have been in use for some time past in the office of the superintendent of Working Plans.

(7.) Statistics and Gazetteers.

1. Hunter's Imperial Gazetteer in nine volumes.

2. Gazetteers published in each Province.

3. Imperial Census Report, 1881.

4. Annual General Administration Report for each Province.

5. Selections from the Records of the Government of India.

6. Report on the Moral and Material Progress of India by Mr. James Sutherland Cotton.

6. Statistical Tables relating to British India.

(8) Jails.*

1. Jail Conference Report.

2. Reports on the working of Jails in each Province.

3. Model of a carpet loom.

4. Card samples of wool.

5. Implements used in manufacturing carpets.

6. Collection of elementary substances used in dyeing.

7. Model of a cotton carpet loom.

8. Collection of appliances used in the manufacture of paper.

9. Specimens of Prison uniforms used in Jails in Bengal.

DIVISION IV.

PUBLIC WORKS DEPARTMENT.

(1) Railways.

1. A Railway map of India on the scale of 32 miles to the inch. This map is published at the beginning of every year, and is perhaps the best map which is supplied by the Survey Department of the Government of India for general use. Its price is six rupees uncoloured,

* Jail manufactures, of which the principal are carpets, are shown in the Art-ware Courts; rougher manufactures in the Economic Court. Nos. 3 to 8 are exhibits of the Lahore Central Jail.

and eight rupees coloured. Copies can be obtained on reference to the Surveyor General's Office, Calcutta.

The total length of railway lines open in India on the 1st April 1885 was 12,004 miles, and the construction of 3500 miles more had been sanctioned.

2. Model of a Railway Carriage contributed by the Oudh and Rohilkhand Railway Company. The model has been constructed entirely by native workmen, and is a good illustration of the skill attained by the native mechanic in English joinery.

3. Administration Report on Indian Railways, Parts I. and II.

4. Statements showing Railways constructed and in progress—

Imperial State Railways.
Provincial State Railways.
Railways in Native States.
Guaranteed Railways.
Assisted Railways.

5. Annual Statement of the Financial Statistics of Indian State Railways.

6. Annual Synopsis of Transactions of Indian Guaranteed Railway Companies.

7. Return of Accidents on Indian Railways.

PHOTOGRAPHIC VIEWS OF THE OUDH AND ROHILKHAND RAILWAY.

(1.) Pontoon with Staging, fitted with three 20-ton cranes and three diggers, Ganges Bridge, Benares.

(2.) Pier No. 4. Ganges Bridge, Benares.

(3.) Ganges Bridge, Benares. No. 1. span from river, showing erection of girders for erecting platform of main girders.

(4.) Ganges Bridge, Benares, No. 1 span as seen from the north bank.

(5.) Ganges Bridge, Benares. View from down stream, North Bank, showing staging for girder, span No. 1.

(6.) Ganges Bridge, Benares. View from up stream, south bank, showing staging for girder, span No. 7.

(7.) Bridge over Burnah River, near Benares.

(8.) Bridge over Sai River, near Jaunpur.

(9). Bridge over Gumti River, near Jaunpur.

(10.) Bridge over Touse River.

(11.) Water Tower and Bridge over Gumti River, near Lucknow.

(12.) Bridge over Ganges River at Cawnpore.

(13.) Bridge over Ramganga River, near Bareilly.

(14.) Bridge over the Ganges at Rajghat.

(15.) Bridge over the Malin River.

(16.) Bridge Works, Banganga.

(17.) Bridge Works, Solani River.

(18.) Bridge over the Ganges Canal at Rurki.

(19.) Bridge over the Hindan River.

(2) ROADS AND BUILDINGS.

1. Map showing lines of communication in the Bombay Presidency and Sindh, Punjab, Assam, &c.

2. Photographs of suspension bridges in the Himalayas, Kumaon, North-Western Provinces.

3. Photographs of Bridges-of-boats over the rivers Indus and Attock, with working drawings, &c., of a Typical Boat Bridge used over Punjab rivers.

4. Series of Photos, illustrative of characteristic Native Bridges in the Himalayas, Punjab.

5. Sketch map of the Hindustan and Thibet Road (Punjab), with sketch showing one of the Galleries along the face of the Rogi Cliff and the Wangtu Bridge over the Sutlej, and eight photographs illustrative of the road.

6. Series of photographs illustrative of the architecture of the Punjab from the earliest times.

7. Photographs of modern buildings erected by the Public Works Department, Punjab.

8. Photographs of the principal public buildings in the Bombay Presidency, including views of Bombay City.

9. Photographs of the principal public buildings in the North-Western Provinces.

(3) IRRIGATION.

1. Annual Statements showing the Financial Results of Irrigation Operations throughout India.

2. Irrigation Reports of the several Provinces.

3. Irrigation map, Bombay Presidency (excluding Sindh), showing irrigation works.

4. Irrigation map, Sindh, showing the canals and embankments constructed, in progress, and proposed.

5. Map showing canals and irrigation works in the Bombay Presidency and Sindh.

6. Photographs of Irrigation Works, Bombay.

7. Series of photographs of the Ganges Canals in the North-Western Provinces.

MODELS OF IRRIGATION WORKS.

PUNJAB.

8. Model of the Sirhind Canal Head Works at Rupar.

This model shows the weir, with its under-sluices, across the Sutlej river and the Canal Regulator built on its left bank. When the raising now in hand is completed, the top of the weir will be 8 feet above the average river bed. The finished crest will be fitted with movable wooden shutters 2·5 feet in height. The weir is built of sandstone, the section being as shown on the model.

The under-sluices are constructed to pass off surplus water not required for the canal and to draw the deep channel of the river to the canal side. Each bay is provided with two iron gates aggregating 9·5 feet in height worked by a powerful traveller.

The canal regulating bridge consists of thirteen major and thirty-nine small-arched openings, which are provided with sluices worked by travellers moving along a line of rails on top of the Regulator.

9. Model of the Chupki Bridge 8 feet fall, and lock at 9 miles 2000 feet, Abohur Branch, Sirhind Canal.

This model shows the type of fall with lock employed on this canal. The water passes through notches which are so designed as to maintain the water above the fall at its normal depth in all stages of supply, thus preventing any acceleration or retardation of the velocity. No other means of regulation are used or found necessary. In passing over the semi-circular lips in front of the notches, the falling water assumes a veil shape and attains a wide even distribution before reaching the basin. The basin is made wide and deep, and is of a form which admits of the floor remaining intact under the severe action of the falling water.

The motion of the water is sufficiently steady and quiet before the earthen channel is reached to do no harm to the slopes. The lock is 120 feet long and 20 feet in width.

10. Bhowani Regulator at 2 miles 760 feet, Combined Branches, Sirhind Canal.

This model shows the masonry work built at the bifurcation of the Combined Branches into the Abohur and Bhattinda Branches. There is a fall of 3 feet into the Abohur, and of 2 feet into the Bhattinda Branch. Acceleration above is obviated by the use of notches, and the action of the water on the banks below is made practically *nil* by syphon walls under which the water has to pass. Navigation of the Combined and Abohur Branches is provided for by a lock. The exact distribution of the water desired between the Abohur and Bhattinda Branches is attained by the use of sleepers placed in vertical grooves.

11. Model of Mádhopur Head-Works.

The head of the Bári Doáb Canal is situated at Mádhopur in the Punjab on the River Ravi, about 5 miles below the point where it issues from the hills. The river at Mádhopur has a slope of 30 feet in a mile, and its bed is composed of large boulders and shingle.

The works comprise a weir 2445 feet long with a crest varying from 3 to 6 feet above the original bed of the river (M. S. L. 1133). and extending from the right (or Kashmir) bank to within 300 feet of the left (or British) bank.

This 300 feet is taken up by the under-sluices, which have 12 openings of 20 feet each, capable of being closed by iron gates; there being two to each bay, the lower being 3 feet in height and the upper 4 feet.

The floor of the outlet is fixed at a level of 1129·5.

Connected with and above the under-sluices is the inlet, which consists of a bridge with 23 arched openings of 10 feet span fitted with gates for regulating the supply to the canal, the level of the floor of inlet being 1133·3.

12. Model of Needle Dam across River Ravi and Regulator at Head of Sidhnai Canal.

The Sidhnai Canal is situated in the Punjab and takes off from the left bank of the River Ravi about 20 miles above its junction with the River Chenab.

The water in the river has been already drawn upon for irrigation in the upper part of its course, and the needle weir is necessary to maintain a steady supply in this Canal.

The dam consists of 32 openings of 20′ each giving a waterway of 640 cubic feet; it is closed by 2000 needles.

Bengal.

13. Model of Sone weir, and shutters.

14. Model of Four acres patent Dredger used in the Sone canals.

15. Model of Lock Gate used in the Sone canals.

Madras.

16. General models of Kistna Anicuts, Eastern and Western Delta.

Of these two models, one shows the head-works and a portion of the Anicut across the Kistna at Bezvada on the eastern bank, and the other the head-works and a portion of the Anicut on the western bank.

17. Cross section of Kistna Anicut.

The "cross section" of the Kistna Anicut is modelled to a larger scale and shows the wells on which the body walls are built, and the approximate position of the stone apron.

18. Model of Bezvada Head Sluice, Eastern Delta—2½ vents, showing shutters and gearing.

This model represents the Head Sluice attached to the Anicut across the Kistna river at Bezvada, the head of the Delta supplying the whole of the Eastern Delta of the Kistna. It was originally constructed in 1854, but heavy floods in the river have shown the necessity of raising and strengthening the original work. It is shown here as improved.

19. Model of Bezvada Under-sluice—2½ vents, showing the shutters and gearing.

This model shows the gearing used for raising the shutters of the under-sluices. Only one screw rod carried on the tramway is used for lifting the shutters; the shutters when raised are held up by means of a bar of iron placed through the hole in the T head attached to the shutter.

20. Model of Godavari Central Delta Head Sluice—one vent showing shutters and gearing.

This Head Sluice is attached to the Anicut across the Godavari at Dawlaishveram, the head of the Delta. The old work having failed, the sluice was rebuilt in 1878, and the design is one of the latest approved.

21. General Model of Grand Anicut and "Cauveri" and "Vennar" Regulators.

The Grand Anicut is an old native work between the Cauveri and Coleroon near the Head of the Tanjore Delta. It has been improved, under the British Government, and is now being further improved, while Regulators are being built across the Cauveri and Vennar Rivers which will enable the supply of water to over 800,000 acres of irrigated land in Tanjore to be controlled The model shows the works as they will be on completion.

22. Model of "Vennar" regulators, one vent showing shutters and gearing.

This model shows the gearing used for lifting the large shutters of these regulators. The two screws to raise one shutter are made to work exactly together by means of gipsy wheels and a chain working round in them.

23. General model of Lower Coleroon Anicuts and a portion of Intervening Islands.

This model gives a general view of the Anicut across the Coleroon river, some 50 miles lower down than the Grand Anicut, which irrigates a considerable extent of country in the Tanjore District, on the south side, and in the South Arcot District on the north side.

24. Lower Coleroon Anicut, one sluice of two vents showing shutters and gearing with the two adjacent arches.

This model shows one of the under-sluices of the Lower Coleroon Anicut, and a portion of the Anicut on each side.

25. Model of Staff boat from the Dowlaishweram Workshop.

This model shows the boat used by the officers of the Public Works Department and others, when travelling by canal.

(4) Telegraphs.

1. Administration Reports of the Indian Telegraph Department.
2. Telegraph map of India showing the lines open in 1885.
3. Photograph of the Central Telegraph Office, Calcutta.
4. Notices of the Indian State Telegraphs.

MILITARY DEPARTMENT.

(1) Military Organization.

The chief Exhibit of the Military Department is a series of life-size models showing the dress, arms, and accoutrements of the principal native regiments of the Indian Empire. The models are also intended to represent typical specimens of the class of men of whom each regiment is composed. The following is a detailed list by Lieutenant-Colonel A. C. Toker, Commanding 18th Bengal Infantry, under whose supervision the models were made:—

1. *11th Bengal Infantry.*—Model, Havildar Sewnundun Misser, Caste, Hindu (Brahmin) of Oudh. Enlisted May 1, 1864. Height 5 ft. 8½ in. Has served in Bhootan Campaign (1864–65) — Medal and Clasp; Afghan Campaign (1878–80)—Medal.

2. *11th Bengal Infantry.*—Model, Lance-Naick Hukdad Khan, Caste, Mahommedan (Pathan) of Rohilkund. Enlisted April 22, 1872. Height 5 ft. 11 in. Has served in Afghan Campaign (1878–80)—Medal. The Regiment is now commanded by Colonel P. H. F. Harris. It was raised at Cawnpore in 1825, and is composed of Hindus and Mahommedans (Hindustani) recruited in Oudh and the North-Western Provinces, It has served in the following campaigns:—Gwalior (1843) — Bronze Star (one Wing); Punjab (1848–49) — Medal with Clasps for Chillianwalla and Gujerat; China (1858–60)—Medal: Bhootan (1864–65)—Medal with Clasp; Afghan (1878–80)—Medal, and is at present on active service in Burma.

3. *Governor General's Body Guard.*—Model, Lance-Naick Shaikh Mahomed Jan, Caste, Mahomedan (Shaikh). Enlisted August 1, 1870. Height 6 ft. 2 in., weight 16 st. 4 lbs. The Body-Guard is now commanded by Captain C. W. Muir (Squadron Commander, 17th Bengal Cavalry). It was raised in 1762, and is armed with Lance and Sword. The Regiment is composed of Hindus and Mahommedans (Hindustani) and Sikhs. It is recruited in Oudh, North-Western Provinces, and the Punjab, and bears the following devices and distinctions:—"Java, Ava, Maharaipore, Moodkee, Ferozeshuhur, Aliwal, Sobraon."

4. *3rd Bengal Cavalry.* — Model, Lance-Duffadar Hoshyar Ali Khan, Caste, Hindustani Mahomedan (Ranghar). Enlisted May 1, 1876. Height 5 ft. 9in., weight 10 st. 12 lbs. Has served in Afghanistan (1878–80)—Medal with Clasps for "Ahmed Kheyl," "Kandahar," and Bronze Star for Kabul-Kandahar march. The Regiment, which was formerly the 4th Irregular Cavalry (2nd Regiment, Skinner's Horse), is now commanded by Colonel A. R. D. Mackenzie, A.D.C. It was raised on December 6, 1814, and is composed of Hindustani Mahommedans, Rajputs, Jats, and Sikhs, recruited in Delhi territories, North-Western Provinces, and Patiala. It has served in Afghanistan (1838–39)—Medal with Clasp for "Kelat" and Medal for "Ghuznee;" at Maharajpore (1843)—Bronze Star; in the Sutlej Campaign (1845–46)—Medal with Clasps for "Moodkee," "Ferozeshuhur," and "Aliwal;" and in Afghanistan (1879–80)—Medal with Clasp for "Kandahar" and Bronze Star for Kabul-Kandahar march.

5. *15th Ludhiana Sikhs.* — Model, Lance-Naick Bhola Singh, Caste, Jat Sikh. Enlisted June 20, 1872. Height 5 ft. 11 in., weight 9 st. 4½ lbs. Has served in Afghanistan (1878–80)—Medal, with Clasp and Bronze Star. The Regiment is now commanded by Colonel G. R. Hennessy, C.B., and was raised at Ludhiana in 1846. It is composed of Sikhs recruited from the Ludhiana Districts in the Punjab. It served in the Indian Mutiny (1857–59); in China (1860–62); in Afghanistan (1878–80), being present in the action of Ahmed Kheyl and the march to and action at Kandahar; and it was also in the expedition to Egypt in 1885, obtaining, in addition to the Medal, Clasps for Suakim and Tofrek.

6. *11th (P. W. O.) Bengal Lancers.*—Model, Duffadar Jowalla Singh, Caste, Jat Sikh. Enlisted, November 1, 1867. Height 6 ft., weight 14 st. 2 lbs. (armed and accoutred, exclusive of saddle, &c.). Has served in Afghanistan (1878–79)—Clasp and Medal for Ali Musjid. The Regiment is now commanded by Colonel A. H.

Prinsep. It was raised at Lahore, Punjab, by Captain Wale in August, 1857, and was formerly designated the 1st Sikh Irregular Cavalry. It is armed with Lance, Sword, and Carbine, and is composed of 4 Troops of Sikhs, 2 of Dogras. and 1 each of Punjabi Mahommedans and Pathans, It is recruited in the Punjab. Services of the Regiment since raised. Indian rebellion of 1857-58, including the final capture of Lucknow and many minor actions—Medal and Clasp for capture of Lucknow; China campaign of 1860 —Medal and Clasp for Taku Forts and Pekin; Umbeyla Campaign (1863)—Medal and Clasp; Afghan War (1878-79)—Medal and Clasp for Ali Musjid. A Squadron of the Regiment is serving as escort to the Commission for delimiting the Afghan Boundary.

7. *3rd Gurkha (The Kumaon) Regiment.*—Model, Sepoy Jokhoo, Caste, Goorun Hindu. Enlisted January 25, 1880. Height 5 ft. 2 in., weight 7 st. 8 lbs. The Regiment was raised at Hawulbagh (Kumaon) in 1815, and is composed of Gurkhas and a few hill-men recruited on the Nepal Frontier. It has served in the Mutiny at Delhi) 1857)—Medal and Clasp; in the Bhootan Campaign (1864-65-66)—Medal and Clasp; and in Afghanistan (1878-79-80)—Medal with Clasp.

8. *20th (Duke of Cambridge's Own) Punjab Infantry.*—Model, Sepoy Darwesh Khan, Caste, Mussulman (Sunni) of Bajour beyond N.W. Frontier. Enlisted October 26, 1883. Height 5 ft. 9¾ in., chest 35 in. Darwesh Khan is the son of an old sepoy who served with the Regiment in China. The Regiment is now commanded by Colonel H. W. Gordon, and was raised at Nowshera in August 1857 from 4th (Wilde's) and 5th (Vaughan's) Rifle Regiments, by Lieutenant (now Lieutenant-General Sir Charles, K.C.B.), Brownlow, and called the 8th Punjab Infantry. It is recruited chiefly in the Khyber, Peshawar, Kohat, Amritsar, and Sialkot Districts, and is composed of Mahommedans—2 Companies Afridis; 1 Company Pathans; 1 Company Khuttucks. Hindus—2 Companies Trans-Sutlej Sikhs; 2 Companies Dogras. The Regiment has served in the following campaigns and expeditions:—Punjtar (1858); the China War in 1860 (Taku Forts and Pekin); Umbeyla (1863); against the Ootman Khel Afridis in 1865; Hazara (1868); against Adam Khel Afridis and Kohat Pass in 1876; Jowaki Expedition (1877-78); Afghanistan, including Lughman and Ali Musjid (1878-79); Zaimukt Expedition (1880); Waziri Expedition (1881); Egypt (1882) (Tel-el-Kebir). At the present time 2½ companies are detached to form the Infantry Escort to the Afghan Boundary Commission.

9. *Merwara Battalion.*—Model, Havildar Azima, Caste, Merat. Enlisted August 1, 1865. Height 5 ft. 9 in., weight 10 st. 4 lbs. Has served in Afghan Campaign (1878-80)—Medal. The Regiment is now commanded by Major O. M. Creagh, V.C. It was raised at Beawar in 1822, and is composed of Mers and Merats, the former being the Hindu, and the latter the Mahommedan section of the same clan, and is recruited in Merwara, Rajputana. The corps has served in Central India (1854-57)—Medal, and Afghanistan (1878-80)—Medal.

10. *Deoli Irregular Force.*—Model, Havildar Girdhari, Caste, Meena. Enlisted September 7, 1867. Height 5 ft. 11 in., weight 11 st. 8 lbs. Has served in Afghan Campaign (1880-81)—Medal. The corps is now commanded by Colonel F. W. Boileau. It was raised at Deoli in 1857, and is composed of 2 Troops of Cavalry armed with Lances and Carbines and 8 Companies of Infantry. Cavalry consists of Sikhs from the Punjab; and Infantry is composed of Meenas from the Meenakherar in Rajputana. It has served in Kotah Campaign (1858)—Medal, and the Afghan Campaign (1880-81)—Medal.

11. *5th Bombay Light Infantry.*—Model, Havildar Hummuntoo, Caste, Hindu Camateo (Malee). Enlisted March 1, 1873. Height 5 ft. 9 in., chest 38 in., weight 12 st. 4 lbs. He was born and educated in the Regiment, and reads and writes English and Marathi. Has served in the Afghan Campaign (1880-81)—Medal. The Regiment is now commanded by Colonel R. A. C. Hunt. It was raised as the 1st Battalion of the 3rd Bombay Native Infantry in 1796 at Tellicherry, re-numbered 5th in 1823, and created "Light Infantry" in 1841. Its popular designation is "Kalee Panchween" (the black 5th), owing to its black facings. It is composed chiefly of Marathas, and recruited in Deccan and Concan. Has served in—Seedaseer, Seringapatam, Kahun, Beni Boo Ali: China (1860-62); Afghanistan (1879-80); and Left Flank Company, Persia.

12. *2nd Bombay Lancers.*—Model, Duffadar Abdoor Rahman, Caste, Mahomedan (Shaikh). Enlisted March 1, 1868. Height 5 ft. 9 in., weight 13 st. 10 lbs. (as photographed without arms). Has served in the Afghan Campaign (1879-80)—Medal. The Regiment is now commanded by Colonel C. J. Anderson. It was raised at Kaira in 1817, and is armed with Lance, Carbine, and Curved Sword. The Regiment is composed of Hindus and Mahommedans, recruited in the Bombay Presidency, Rajputana, and Central India, and has served in Central India (1857-58) and the Afghan Campaign (1879-80).

13. *29th (D. C. O.) 2nd Belooch Regiment of Bombay Infantry.*—Model, Naick Husain Ali, Caste, Gilzai Afghan. Enlisted April 2, 1867. Height 6 ft. ¾ in., weight 10 st. Has served in Afghanistan (1878)—Medal, Clasp, and Bronze Star; Egypt (1882)—Medal, Clasp, and Bronze Star. The Regiment is now commanded by Colonel T. Galloway, C.B. It was raised at Karachi in 1846, and is composed of Beloochis, Pathans, and Punjabis (Mussulmans), recruited in Sind, Beloochistan, and Afghanistan, and formerly in the Punjab also. It has served in Persian Campaign (1856-57)—Medal and Clasp; China Campaign (1862); against the Taepings under Gordon; Afghanistan Campaign (1878-81)—Medal and Clasp and Bronze

Star; Egypt Campaign (1882)—Medal and Clasp and Bronze Star.

14. *"Queen's Own" Sappers and Miners.*—Model, Subadar-Major Jeyram, Sirdar Bahadur. Subadar-Major Jeyram, Sirdar Bahadur, has seen long and varied service. He enlisted at Vellore in October, 1845, at the age of 18 years. His war services include Burmah, 1852, in which campaign he was at the capture of Pegu, November, 1852, affair at "Gongoo" in January, 1853 (Medal and Clasp). Also in the Afghan Campaign of 1879–80, and the expedition to the Lughman, Waziri, and Hissarick countries (Medal). He served in Egypt in 1882, was present at "Tel-el-Kebir" (Medal, Clasp, and Khedive's Bronze Star), and was selected to represent the Indian Contingent to visit England after the Egyptian War, 1882, receiving from the Empress of India at Windsor the title of "Bahadur" for service rendered in this campaign. The corps is now commanded by Lieutenant-Colonel A. F. Hamilton, R.E. Two Companies of Pioneers were first formed in September, 1780; in 1793 the establishment was increased to a Battalion of six Companies, and in 1803 a second Battalion was formed. In 1831 the 1st Battalion was placed under the command of Engineer Officers, and instructed as Sappers and Miners, and in 1834 the second Battalion was incorporated into the Sappers and Miners. In 1876 the corps was made a Royal Regiment and designated the "Queen's Own," and His Royal Highness the Prince of Wales was appointed Honorary Colonel. The chief operations in which Detachments of the Corps have been engaged are the following:—Relief of Wandiwash and battles of Porto Novo and Pollilore in 1781; Campaign under Sir Eyre Coote in 1782–83, and expeditions against the Dutch in Ceylon and against the French in Cuddalore; war against Tippoo Sultan in 1784 and 1792; siege and capture of Pondicherry in 1793; expedition against the Dutch Settlements in Ceylon and Malacca (1795–96), and attack and capture of Arrakerry in Mysore in 1800; expedition to Egypt (1800–02); Mahratta wars in 1803–04 and 1817–19; expedition to the Isles of Bourbon and France in 1810–12, and against Java in 1813; first and second Burmese wars in 1824–26 and 1852–53; Malacca expedition in 1832; Coorg war in 1834; Scinde and Afghanistan (1840–44); first and second China war in 1840–43 and 1860; Field Service in Persia (1857); Mutiny Campaign (1857–59); Abyssinia (1867); Perak (1875); Malta and Cyprus expedition (1878); Afghanistan (1878–79); Rampa expedition (1879); Egyptian war (1882), and Suakin in 1885.

15. *1st Madras Pioneers.*—Model, Private Mooneesamy, Caste, Malabar. Enlisted May 21, 1877. Height 5 ft. 11½ in., weight 12 st. 5 lbs. Has served in Afghan Campaign, 1879–80—Medal, and expedition to Mandalay, 1885. The Regiment is now commanded by Lieut.-Colonel E. H. Eyre. It was raised at Fort St. George in 1758, and is composed of Hindus and Mahommedans, recruited in Southern India. It has served in the following operations:—Campaign against Hyder Ali (1785), and against Tippoo Sultan, 1789–99, including the siege of "Seringapatam;"* against the "Pindaries" (1815), Mahratta Campaign, "Nagpore"* (1816), and "Seetabuldee"* (1817); 1st Burmese war, "Ava"* (1825); 2nd Burmese War, "Pegu"* (1852); Indian Mutiny, "Central India"* (1857–59); "Afghanistan"* (1879–80); Expedition to Mandalay, 1885.

16. *No 1 Kohat Mountain Battery.*—Model, Lance-Naick Bahawul Khan, Caste, Mussulman, Satti Rajput. Enlisted April 27, 1875. Height 5 ft. 11 in., weight 10 st. 11 lbs. Served in Jowaki Campaign (1877–78)—Medal and 1 Clasp, wounded in neck; Afghan Campaign (1878–79–80)—Medal and 2 Clasps, wounded in left leg; Akha Campaign (1883). The battery is now commanded by Captain J. C. Shirres, R.A. It was raised at Bunnu in 1851, under the title of No. 2 Punjab Light Field Battery, and armed with six 9-pr. smooth bore guns. It was then converted into No. 1 Kohat Mountain Battery in 1877, and armed with 7-pr. R.M.L. guns of 200 lbs., and is now about to be armed with four 7-pr. R.M.L. guns of 400 lbs. and two 7-pr. R.M.L. guns of 200 lbs. The Battery is composed of Sikhs, Hindus, and Punjabi Mahommedans, and is recruited in the Punjab. It has served in the following expeditions:—Frequent expeditions against frontier tribes between 1851–77; Jowaki (1877–78)—Medal and 1 Clasp; Afghan War (1878–79–80)—Medal and 2 Clasps; Waziri (1881); Akha (1883).

17. *3rd Sikh Infantry, Punjab Frontier Force.*—Model, Naick Bishen Sing, Caste, Malwai Jat Sikh. Enlisted May 1, 1873. Height 5 ft. 11 in., weight 11 st. 4 lbs. Has served in Jowaki Campaign, 1877—Medal and Clasp; Afghanistan (1879–80), present at Charasiah and Sherpur—Medal with 3 Clasps, and Bronze Star for march to Kandahar. The corps is now commanded by Colonel C. Griffiths, B.S.C. It was raised at Firozpur on the January 1, 1847, and is composed of two companies each of Malwa Sikhs, Manjha Sikhs, and Trans-Indus Pathans; one company of Dogras, and one company of Punjabi Mahommedans. It has served in the following campaigns:—Bozdar (1857), Indian Mutinies (1858–59), Sikkim (1860); Umbeyla (1863); Hazara (1868); Jowaki (1877); Afghanistan, including the march to Kandahar (1879–80); and against the Marri tribes in 1880.

18. *1st Punjab Cavalry.*—Model, Sowar Fazal Khan, Caste, Hazara Pathan. Enlisted November 23, 1878. Height 5 ft. 6½ in., weight 9 st. 5 lbs. Has served in Afghan Campaign (1878–80)—Medal and Clasp for Ahmed Kheyl 3rd Class Order of Merit for distinguished bravery at action of Patkau Shano Mahsud Waziri expedition (1881). The Regiment is now commanded by Colonel G. C. Bird. It was raised at Peshawar in 1849 by Lieutenant

* Borne on regimental colours and appointments.

H. Daly, 1st Bombay Fusiliers, and is recruited in the Punjab. It is composed of one squadron each of Sikhs, Pathans, and Hindustani Mahommedans, and one troop each of Dogras and Punjabi Hindus. It has served in North-Western-Frontier expeditions (1850-52)—Medal; Mutiny (1857-59)—Medal and three Clasps for Delhi, Lucknow, and relief of Lucknow; Afghanistan — Medal (1878-80)—Medal and Clasp for Ahmed Kheyl.

19. *1st Madras Light Cavalry.* — Model, Havildar Husain Khan. Enlisted December 3, 1864. Height 5 ft. 6¾ in. Served in Afghan Campaign (1879-80). The Regiment is now commanded by Colonel E. M. Cherry. It was raised in October, 1787, as the 5th Regiment, and became the 1st Regiment in February, 1788. It has been engaged in the following operations: — Reduction of the Fortress at Seringapatam (1799); Mysore country (1800); Mahratta country and Deccan, 1804-5 and 1807-8; with the Field Force at Kurnool (1813-14); in the Deccan and Elichpur (1814-15-16-17); Headquarters and two squadrons in Rangoon (1826); Coorg War ((1834); at the close of the Mutiny (1858); attached to the Kandahar Field Force during the second phase of the Afghan War from March 21, 1880, to April 29, 1881.

20. *Central India Horse.*—Model, Duffadar Sohan Singh, Caste, Sikh. Enlisted December 1, 1877. Height 5 ft. 8½ in., weight (in uniform) 12 st. Has served in Afghan Campaign (1878-80)—Medal with Clasp for "Kandahar," Bronze Star for "Kabul to Kandahar" march. The Regiment is now commanded by Colonel C. Martin, C.B. It was raised at Goona on April 5, 1860, for service ordinarily in Central India, but available for general service, and was originally called Mayne's Horse. The two Regiments of Beatson's Horse were incorporated with it in 1860, and the Regiment of Meade's Horse in 1861. It consists of two Regiments each of 625 Sabres, one Regiment being stationed at Agar, the Headquarters, and the other at Goona. The front ranks are armed with spears, and all have Swords and Breech-loading Carbines. It is recruited in the Punjab and the North-Western Provinces, and consists of Sikhs, Rangur Mahommedans, Jats, Pathans, and other Mahommedans. It has served in Afghanistan (1880)—Medal and Clasp and Bronze Star (including the march to, and action, at Kandahar).

21. *Malwa Bhil Corps.* — Model, Naick Jogria Deetia, Caste, Bheel. Enlisted June 6, 1869, in District of Sirdarpur. Height 5 ft. 2 in., weight 7 st. 18 lbs. Has served in pursuit of dacoits at Ali Rajpore in 1882. The Regiment is now commanded by Lieutenant-Colonel G. R. Peart. It was raised at Dilowra in 1840, and is composed chiefly of Bhils recruited in the hilly tracts south-west of Indore, viz., Dohud, Jhabwa, Ali Rajpore, and Dhar. It has served in the defence of Indore Residency in 1857; in the pursuit of dacoits of Kurod in 1881; and of Ali Rajpore in 1882.

22. *4th Regiment of Infantry, Hyderabad Contingent.*—Model, Jemadar Seopersad, Caste, Hindu (Lohar) of the Deccan. Enlisted March 11, 1865. Height 5 ft. 8¼ in., weight 11 st. 4 lbs. The Regiment is now commanded by Major J. G. Proudfoot. It was raised at Hyderabad in 1794, and is composed of Hindus and Mahommedans; recruited in the Deccan only since 1882; before this it was recruited from both the Deccan and Hindustan. It has served in the following campaigns:—Battle of Khundalah in 1799; Battle of Seringapatam in 1799; battle of Nagpore in 1817; battle of Nowah in 1858; capture of Copal in 1818; capture of Shorapur in 1858. Also action at Badaum in 1841, and many other actions against Rohillas and insurgents in the Deccan between 1849 and 1856.

23. *Her Majesty's 3rd Regiment, Cavalry, Hyderabad Contingent.*—Model, Trooper Abdool Kurreem Khan, Caste Mahommedan. Enlisted March 11, 1876. Height 5 ft. 10 in., weight 10 st. Has served in the 1st phase of the Afghan Campaign (1878-79)—Medal. The Regiment is now commanded by Lieutenant-Colonel C. J. O. FitzGerald. It was raised at Mominabad in 1816, and is composed of Mahommedans and Sikhs. Formerly it used to be recruited from Northern India, Punjab, and Deccan, but now it is restricted to the country south of the Nerbudda. It has served in the following campaigns:—Battles of Nowah (1812); Mahidpur (1813); Poona (1814); Kurnool (1838); Siege of Dharoor (1850); Central India Campaign (1857-58) — Medal with Clasp; Battle of Chichumba (1859)—Medal; Afghan Campaign (1878, 1879, and 1880)—Medal.

24. *No. 4 Field Battery, Hyderabad Contingent.*—Model, Havildar Shick Baffati, Caste, Mahomedan (Hindustani). Enlisted May 1, 1866. Height 5 ft. 7¼ in., weight 10 st. 4 lbs. Has not served in any Campaign. The Battery is now commanded by Lieutenant E. G. Nicolls, R.A. It was raised at Ellichpur in the Berars in 1811, and is composed of Hindus and Mahommedans; recruited before 1883 in Oudh, North-Western Provinces, and the Deccan, but since that date in the Deccan only. The armament of the Battery consists of two 6-pounder smooth-bore bronze guns and two 12-pounder smooth-bore bronze howitzers. It has served in the following Campaigns: — Operations against Insurgents in the Berar Valley (1841-42); Operations against the Rohillas in the Berars (1849); Central India (1857-58)—Medal with Clasp; Battle of Chichumba (1859)—Medal.

25. *32nd Punjab Pioneers.*—Model, Sepoy Nehal Singh, Caste Muzbi Sikh. Enlisted May 5, 1874. Age 29, height 5 ft. 8 in., weight 11 stone. The Regiment is composed almost entirely of Muzbi Sikhs, recruited principally from the Lahore and Amritsar Districts. It was originally raised from the gang of coolies working on the Madhopore Canal in June, 1857; marched down to Delhi, where it served till the capture. The following are the most important of the various field operations in which the regiment has been engaged :—Siege and capture

of Delhi in (1857); and of Lucknow in (1858)—Medal and Clasps; Expedition against the Kheyl. Wazieris on the North-Western Frontier in (1860): Eusufzai Field Force and Umbeyla (1863)—Medal and Clasps; Bhootan Campaign (1865-66)—Medal; Kabul Campaign; Southern Afghanistan; occupation of Kandahar and Girishk (1878-79); Northern Afghanistan; Action of Mazina (1880)—Medal; and Mahsood Wazieri Expedition (1881). For the last year the regiment has been employed in the construction of the Sind-Peshin Railway.

List of Articles of Indian Ordnance Manufacture sent as Exhibits from the Bengal Circle.

HARNESS AND SADDLERY.

Elephant Harness.

From the Harness and Saddlery Factory, Cawnpore:—Bands, back chain and throat; Breast Plates, Breechings, Cruppers with hip strap, Girths, Guddulahs, large and small; Lashings, Pads Saddle, Pieces Buckling, Saddles, wood with iron side plates; Stirrups, Traces, lead and wheel.

Camel Harness.

Saddle, Camel, riding complete.

Miscellaneous.

Specimens of Hides and Skins, as tanned and curried in the Factory. Models of all service pattern regimental tents.

(4) WAR MATERIEL.

Ordnance.

From the Foundry and Shell Factory, Cossipur:—Shells: 9-in. Studless Common, with gas check; 9-in. Studless Shrapnel, with gas check; 80-pr. Common Shell; 80-pr. Shrapnel Shell; 64-pr. Common Shell; 64-pr. Shrapnel Shell; 40-pr. Common Shell, with gas check; 40-pr. Shrapnel Shell with gas check; 25-pr. Common Shell; 25-pr. Shrapnel Shell; 9-pr. Common Shell; 9-pr. Shrapnel Shell; 7-pr. 200 lbs. Common Shell; 7-pr. 200 lbs. Shrapnel Shell; 2·5-in. Common Shell, with gas check; 2·5-in. Shrapnel Shell, with gas check; 6·3-in. Howitzer Common Shell, with gas check; one case Fuzes, direct action, in different stages of manufacture; Instruments for taking impression of vents, with staves, iron, in two pieces. No. 2; Instruments for taking impressions of boxes of rifled ordnance. Instruments for extracting projectiles, R.M.L; guns, 9 inch; Instruments for extracting projectiles, R.M.L. guns, 64-pr. Sights, Rifled Ordnance: Centre M.L. gun, 64-pr., 64 cwt. Hind; Fore M.L. gun, 2·5 in.; Tangent Scale M.L. guns, 9-in.; Tangent Scale M.L. guns, 46-pr., 64 cwt.; Tangent Scale M.L. guns, 40-pr., 35 cwt.; Tangent Scale M.L. guns, 9-pr. L.S., 8 cwt. 12°; Tangent Scale, M.L. guns, 2·5-in.; Tangent Crossbar M.L. guns, 40-pr., 35 cwt., and 25-pr., 18 cwt.; Trunnion Crossbar M.L. guns, 40-pr., 35 cwt., and 25-pr., 18 cwt.; Trunnion M.L. guns, 40-pr.

From the Gun Carriage Factory, Fatehgarh: Cart, complete, sick, Hawke's pattern (model, 1½ in. to the foot); Cart, complete, transport army (model, 2 in. to the foot); Planks, wood, 2 ft. by 6 in. by 1 in., Sāl; Planks, wood, 2 ft. by 6 in. by 1 in., Sissoo; Planks, wood, 2 ft. by 6 in. by 1 in., Teak.

From the Gunpowder Factory, Ichapur: Saltpetre, rough; Saltpetre, refined; Sulphur, refined; Charcoal, Indian Cylinder Urhur Wood; Timber Urhur, Dhall stalk, peeled, and unpeeled, grown on factory grounds; Barrels, powder, teak, with four copper hoops, whole; Grain from timber, urhur, dhall stalk, unpeeled, grown on factory grounds.

From the Small Arms Ammunition Factory, Dum Dum: M.H. Cartridges, in all stages of manufacture; Snider Cartridges, in all stages of manufacture; Enfield Pistol Cartridges, in all stages of manufacture; Copper Friction Tubes, in all stages of manufacture; 15 in. Seconds Timewood Fuzes, in all stages of manufacture; Service Signal Rocket, 1 lb.; Red Signal Rocket, 1 lb.; Long Light.

(5) FOOD AND TRANSPORT.

Collection of flour, pulses, salt, clarified butter, sugar, rice, coffee, tea, dried mangoes, &c., used by the British Indian troops. Exhibited by the Commissariat Store and Shipping Office, Calcutta.

Collection of models of carts, dulies, *mussucks* or water bags, cooking utensils, boilers, kegs, loading apparatus, tin cases, slings, water bottles, ambulances, &c., &c. Exhibited by the Commissariat Store and Shipping Office, Calcutta.

Collection of gunny bags, blouses or coats, blankets, belts, haversacks, shoes, turbans or *pagris*, drawers, fur coats for native officers, &c., &c. Exhibited by the Commissariat Store and Shipping Office, Calcutta.

MARINE.

1. Models of a slave dhow (Bustile) used on African coast.
2. A native sailing yacht (Kavia).
3. An Arab trader (Buglow), used on the African coast and Persian Gulf.
4. A native trader (Patimar), used on the Malabar coast.
5. A slave dhow (Dhow), used in the Persian Gulf.

Exhibited by the Director of India Marine.

CHAPTER VI.

A GUIDE TO

THE ECONOMIC AND COMMERCIAL COURT.

BY

GEORGE WATT, M.B.; C.M.; F.L.S.; C.I.E.

INTRODUCTION.

THIS Court occupies the first gallery to the left of the main entrance to the Exhibition building. In it will be found the collections of raw products and rough manufactures which have been made under the orders of the Government of India to illustrate the material resources of the Empire. These collections will be found to be arranged according to an industrial classification instead of being thrown together in provincial sections. An effort has been made to secure at least a small sample of every product, and where possible, a large quantity of all the more important and commercial ones. The smaller samples have been placed in tin boxes and arranged on the walls of the Court, thus constituting a ready index to the larger commercial exhibits displayed on the tables and trophies or in the glass cases dispersed throughout the body of the building. The former set of specimens has been called the "Index Collection." This will be found more complete and comprehensive in point of number and diversity of products, although not of so much practical value as the latter, or the set of larger samples known as the "Commercial Collection." Many economic products are used by the natives of India which have but a local interest. These appear in the index set only, but every product which is either known to commerce already, or which seems likely to be of value to Europe, has been represented in both sets.

The industrial classification followed in the arrangement of the collections will be found to be that adopted in the Exhibition "Classified List;" the exhibits which fall under Class C. being those which chiefly appear in the Economic Court. The following are the divisions laid down:—

I.—Foods.
II.—Beverages.
III.—Narcotics.
IV.—Oils.
V.—Medicines.
VI.—Gums.
VII.—Dyes and Tans.
VIII.—Fibres.
IX.—Skins and Leathers.
X.—Canes and Basket Work.
XI.—Minerals and Ores.
XII.—Timbers.

These Divisions are broken into Sections, which still further carry out the industrial classification. For convenience of arrangement, the Court has been divided into blocks separated by cross passages. In these blocks, beginning from the east end of the Court, the divisions have been distributed as follows:—

Block 1.—Timbers (Division XII.)

Block 2.—Food-Stuffs (Division I.); Beverages (Division II.); Narcotics (Division III.); Medicines (Division V.)

Block 3.—Oils (Division IV.); Fibres (Division VIII.); Skins and Leathers (Division IX.) Canes and Basket Work (Division X.)

Block 4.—Gums (Division VI.); Dyes and Tans (Division VII.); Minerals and Ores (Division XI.)

The divisions have been assorted into Sub-Courts within each of these blocks, and each Sub-Court contains the exhibits which fall under a section or group of sections. The index collection is so arranged on the walls as to appear exactly opposite the corresponding commercial collections. The Sub-Courts have been numbered with Roman figures, and these numbers are also given at the top of the pages of this catalogue.

The relation of the exhibits to the catalogue will be thus easily discovered, and it will be found that the specimens have been arranged and described in the alphabetical order of their scientific names within each Sub-Court. This system may be illustrated. Should the visitor be interested in the fibres of India, he will find these in the following Sub-Courts:—Sub-Courts XXI. and XXII., a general collection of the more important non-commercial fibres; Sub-Court XXIII., the minor commercial fibres, such as Rhea, Aloe, &c.; then the important commercial fibres thus—Sub-Court XXIV., Cotton; Sub-Court XXV., Jute; Sub-Court XXVI., Paper and Paper Materials.

The Exhibits of Tea, Silk, and Tobacco will be found in special rooms set apart for these products, and not in the Economic Court. Except therefore incidentally, they are not alluded to in this catalogue. A star has been placed against the names of all the economic products which are either introduced into India or at least are not known as indigenous wild plants. This will enable the reader, on turning over the pages, to discover the improvement which has been effected in India by the introduction of new products, and will reveal the relative extent to which this improvement has been carried in the various classes of products.

The catalogue, it will be observed, is arranged in two parts: Part 1, "The Economic Products of India, and Part 2, "Ethnology." In the Exhibition twelve Sub-Courts have been set apart for the exhibits corresponding to the latter, but it should be observed that these Sub-Courts have been designed in order to show the leading groups of inhabitants of India, and not to work out any ethnological classification; the title "Ethnological Sub-Courts" has therefore, been given purely for the sake of brevity. In these Sub-Courts will be found clay or plaster-of-Paris life-sized figures of the leading races of India, with a collection of objects of a more or less ethnological character, such as articles of personal adornment, of agricultural use, and implements of sport and war. This collection is intended to represent the leading features of Class A—"The Country." It is believed that the arrangement of these Sub-Courts within the Economic Court will tend in a measure to remove the monotony incident to a mere collection of grains, medicines, and fibres, the ethnological collections and life-size figures forming an interesting feature of the Court. By this arrangement also it is possible to place, in close proximity, models of the inhabitants of India, the crude appliances used by them, and the produce of their labour.

PART I.—THE ECONOMIC PRODUCTS OF INDIA.

Each Sub-Court is treated in this catalogue separately, the various chapters being introduced with brief notices of a general character. The figures of foreign trade have been obtained from Mr. J. E. O'Conor's "Annual Statement of the Trade and Navigation of British India." Very little of a trustworthy character can be learned regarding the internal trade of India, but the quotations given have been compiled from the most recent sources. The areas under cultivation of the various crops have been derived from the returns specially called for by the Revenue and Agricultural Department, and may be accepted as more accurate than anything hitherto published. It has been found impossible to mention in this catalogue, even by name, all the products of India, but a brief note has been given on the more important, care being taken to indicate, as correctly as possible, the regions where they are found. Under the direction of the Revenue and Agricultural Department, Government of India, a Dictionary of the Economic Products of India is now being published. This work is intended as a complete record of the productive resources of India. The first volume of the dictionary has already appeared, and it will be completed in other five volumes. It is contemplated that the numbers assigned in the dictionary to the various products may be adopted generally as museum and exhibition numbers, so as to insure accuracy and to facilitate international reference. The dictionary will thus become the detailed catalogue of the present collections, but it is believed that the present brief abstract catalogue and guide to the Economic Court will give all the information that the visitor to the Exhibition is likely to require.

For convenience of comparison the quotations of trade have, as far as possible, been expressed in pounds sterling, the rupee being accepted as equal to two shillings. The trade of India may here be compared with that of other countries. The total foreign trade (exclusive of re-exports of the six great commercial nations for the past five years was as follows, stated in millions of pounds sterling :—

	England.	France.	Germany.	United States.	India.	Italy.
1880 . .	634	340	285	310	122	91
1881 . .	631	336	297	318	126	96
1882 . .	654	335	316	303	130	95
1883 . .	666	330	326	318	137	98
1884 . .	622	315	—	290	133	—

Contrasting the trade of these countries during the past decade, Mr. O'Conor shows England to have remained almost stationary, or rather to have fallen off 0·6 per cent., while the trade of the other countries has increased—France 7·27 per cent., Germany 7·89 per cent., the United States 21·4 per cent., India 57·49 per cent, and Italy 3·14 per cent. In less than half a century India has grown into the fifth great commercial power in the world, and her foreign trade has increased 57 per cent. during the past decade, while the trade of the European nations as a whole has not increased more than 5 per cent.

The annual average revenue of India is about £70,000,000. Only a small proportion of this very large amount, however, is raised by taxation, the principal item being Land Revenue. The following may be given as the Indian revenue during 1884–5 :—

Land Revenue	£21,546,300
Opium	8,850,000
Salt	6,350,000
Stamps	3,578,000
Excise	4,013,500
Other Heads	6,294,000
Government Departments and Productive Public Works	19,359,400
Total	£69,991,200

The land revenue (or rather land rent) paid to Government is thus the largest single item of the Indian revenue, and salt is the only compulsory tax which falls upon the inhabitants. The total population of India is 252,000,000, and the area of cultivated land over 189,000,000 of acres. Dividing the average annual expenditure by the total of population, the administration of the Indian Empire costs a little over 5s. 6½d. per head, but not more than half that sum is actually paid by the people, the other half being raised by Government from State monopolies and Productive Public Works.

SUB-COURTS I., II., III.

(*These contain the special exhibits of the Forest Department or the articles enumerated in Division XII.*)

The Forest Department's Index Collection of Timbers occupies the first section of the Economic Court. It comprises upwards of 300 specimens of different Indian timbers, only a few of which are known commercially to Europe. As a special feature it may be noted that the collection has been made with the object of showing only such timbers as are utilised by the people of India. Mr. R. Whittall, Assistant Inspector General of Forests, undertook the supervision of the Forests Departments' collections.

On entering the Economic Court the first object which will naturally attract the attention of the visitor is—

The Arch of Timbers.

This trophy, constructed entirely of Indian timbers, is a frame-work with three ornamental arches. The middle portion is 22 feet broad, and rises to a height of 15 feet; the side parts are 12½ feet high. The total breadth of the trophy is 46 feet, and it is 5 feet in thickness.

The timber specimens used in its construction belong mostly to the Bengal Economic Museum, and have been lent by the Government of Bengal. The trophy thus includes the greater part of Mr. J. S. Gamble's collection described in his *Manual of Indian Timbers*. The specimens so described are marked with a letter followed by a number; the letter denotes the region from which each specimen was obtained. In addition to these collections a large number of new blocks of wood, furnished by the Inspector General of Forests, have also been built into the trophy.

The timbers thus brought together have been arranged on the trophy in geometrical patterns, and enclosed by fretwork panels of teak-wood in arabesque design. A border of alternating dark and light woods surrounds the entire framework. The pilasters are supported by large slabs of timber, bevelled to show the grain of the wood.

For the construction of the ornamental arches some of the principal Indian timbers procurable in Calcutta, viz., teak, *sál*, *sissu*, and pine have been used. The geometrical tracery of the panels forming the plinth on either side of the middle arch is of teak and *sissu*; whilst that of the pilasters on each side of the smaller arches is of teak.

The trophy has been designed and constructed by Mr. F. B. Manson, Deputy Conservator of Forests, Chutia Nagpur, Bengal.

A detailed list of the Indian timbers shown at the Exhibition has been drawn up by the Forest Department, but the following are the most important:—

1. ABIES DUMOSA, *Loudon*; Coniferæ.
2. A. SMITHIANA, *Forbes*.
3. A. WEBBIANA, *Lindl.* (*See* also 402.)
4. ACACIA ARABICA, *Willd.*; Leguminosæ. Babul (*Hind.*); Kikar (*Pb.*); Babla (*Beng.*). A moderate-sized tree, probably wild in Sind, Rajputana, Guzerat, and the Northern Deccan; common everywhere throughout the plains of India. The wood is very durable if well seasoned. Used extensively for wheels, well curbs, sugar and oil presses, rice-pounders, agricultural implements, and tool handles. In Sind it is largely used for boat-building, rafters, and for fuel, also occasionally for railway sleepers. Weight, about 45 lbs. a cubic foot. (*See* also 403, 484, 1051, 1128.)
5. A. CATECHU, *Willd.* (*See* also 648, 742, 1052, 1085, 1129.)
6. A. FERRUGINEA, *DC.*
7. A. LEUCOPHLŒA, *Willd.* (*See* also 485, 1130.)
8. ACER CÆSIUM, *Wall.*; Sapindaceæ.
9. A. CAMPBELLII, *Hook. f. & Th.*
10. A. LÆVIGATUM, *Wall.*
11. A. PICTUM, *Thunb.* (*See* also 404.)
12. ACROCARPUS FRAXINIFOLIUS, *Wight*; Leguminosæ.
13. ADENANTHERA PAVONINA, *Linn.*; Leguminosæ.
14. ADINA CORDIFOLIA, *Hook. f. & Bth.*; Rubiaceæ.
15. ÆGLE MARMELOS, *Corr.*; Rutaceæ. (*See* also 576, 747.)
16. ÆSCULUS INDICA, *Colebr.*; Sapindaceæ. (*See* also 405, 628.)
17. AILANTHUS EXCELSA, *Roxb.*; Simarubeæ.
18. ALANGIUM LAMARCKII, *Thw.*; Cornaceæ.
19. ALBIZZIA AMARA, *Boivin*; Leguminosæ.
20. A. LEBBEK, *Benth.* (*See* also 406.)
21. A. ODORATISSIMA, *Benth.*
22. A. PROCERA, *Benth.*
23. A. STIPULATA, *Boivin.*
24. ALNUS NEPALENSIS, *D. Don*; Cupuliferæ.
25. ALSTONIA SCHOLARIS, *R. Br.*; Apocynaceæ. Chatwan (*Beng.*); Satiún, chatiun (*Hind.*). A tall evergreen tree, found in the sub-Himálayan tract from the Jumna eastward, ascending to 3,000 feet. and in Bengal, Burma, and South India. The wood is used for boxes, furniture, scabbards, coffins, and other purposes, and is made into black boards in Burma. It is used occasionally in Darjíling, Assam, and Kachar for tea-boxes. Weight, about 28 lbs. a cubic foot. (*See* also 754.)
26. ALTINGIA EXCELSA, *Noronha*; Hamamelideæ.
27. AMOORA CHITTAGONGA, *Hiern.*; Meliaceæ.
28. A. CUCULLATA, *Roxb.*
29. A. ROHITUKA, *W. & A.*
30. A. SPECTABILIS, *Miq.*

*31. ANACARDIUM OCCIDENTALE, *Linn.*; Anacardiaceæ. (*See* also 630, 987.)

32. ANOGEISSUS ACUMINATA, *Wall.*; Combretaceæ.
33. A. LATIFOLIA, *Wall.* Dhaura (*Hind.*); Golra (*Raj.*); Khardhawa (*Banda.*) A large tree, met with in the sub-Himálayan tract from the Ravi eastward, ascending to 3,000 feet, in Central and South India. The wood is highly valued on account of its great strength and toughness, but it splits in seasoning, and unless kept dry is not very durable. Weight, about 65 lbs. a cubic foot. It is used for axe handles, poles for carrying loads, axles, in the construction of furniture, agricultural implements, and in ship-building. It has been recommended for sleepers. It gives a good fuel and an excellent charcoal. (*See* also 1055, 1132.)
34. ANOGEISSUS PENDULA, *Edgw.*
35. ANTHOCEPHALUS CADAMBA, *Bth. & Hk. f.*; Rubiaceæ. Kaddam, karam (*Hind.*, *Beng.*), Cadamba (*Tam.*). A large deciduous tree, wild in Northern and Eastern Bengal, Pegu, and the Western Coast; cultivated in Northern India. The wood is used for building, and in Assam, Kachar, and occasionally in Darjíling for tea-boxes. Weight, about 40 lbs. a cubic foot.
36. AQUILARIA AGALLOCHA, *Roxb.*; Thymelœaceæ. (*See* also 755, 992, 1087.)
37. ARTOCARPUS CHAPLASHA, *Roxb.*; Urticaceæ.
38. A. HIRSUTA, *Lamk.*
39. A. INTEGRIFOLIA, *Linn.* The Jack Fruit Tree; Kanthal, kathal (*Hind.*, *Beng.*). A large tree, cultivated throughout India, except in the northernmost part. Wild in the mountain forest of the Western Gháts, ascending to 4,000

feet. The wood is largely used for carpentry, boxes, and furniture, and is exported to Europe for cabinet work, turning, and brush-backs. Weight, about 40 lbs. a cubic foot. (*See* also 581, 633, 1090, 1133.)

40. BALANITES ROXBURGHII, *Planch.*; Simarubeæ. (*See* also 409.)

41. BALSAMODENDRON MUKUL, *Hook.*; Burseraceæ. (*See* also 762, 1056.)

42. BARINGTONIA ACUTANGULA, *Gærtn.*; Myrtaceæ

43. B. SPECIOSA, *Forst.*

44. BASSIA BUTYRACEA, *Roxb.*; Sapotaceæ. Phalwara (*Hind.*); Churi (*Nepal*); Chiura (*Kumaon*). A deciduous tree of the sub-Himálayan tract from Kumaon to Bhután, between 1,500 and 4,500 feet in altitude. Wood light-brown, hard. Annual rings marked by a dark line. Weight, 52 lbs. a cubic foot.

45. B. LATIFOLIA, *Roxb.* Mahúa (*Hind.*). A large, deciduous tree, indigenous in the forests of Central India; cultivated and self-sown throughout India. The wood is not much used, as the tree is so highly prized for its flowers that it is rarely felled; the timber has, however, been tried for railway sleepers in the Central Provinces Beddome says it is used for the naves of wheels, for door and window frames and panels, for furniture and country vessels. The *Mahúa* is described as the most generally useful tree of the regions where it occurs. (*See* also 410, 584, 709, 995, 1091.)

46. BAUHINIA PURPUREA, *Linn.*; Leguminosæ. (*See* also 411.)

47. B. RETUSA, *Ham.*

48. BEILSCHMIEDIA ROXBURGHIANA, *Nees.*; Lauraceæ.

49. BERRYA AMMONILLA, *Roxb.*; Tiliaceæ.

50. BETULA BHOJPATTRA, *Wall.*; Cupuliferæ. Bhujpattra (*Hind.*); Burj, burzal (*Pb.*). A moderate-sized deciduous tree found in the higher ranges of the Himálaya, forming the upper edge of arborescent vegetation, and ascending to 14,000 feet. The wood is extensively used in the inner arid Himálaya for building; it is elastic, seasons well, and does not warp. Weight, about 44 lbs. a cubic foot. (*See* also 412.)

51. B. CYLINDROSTACHYS, *Wall.*

52. BISCHOFFIA JAVANICA, *Bl.*; Euphorbiaceæ. Kein (*Hind.*); Uriam (*Ass.*); Boke (*Bomb.*). A deciduous tree, met with in Kumaon, Garhwal, Oudh, Gorakhpur, Bengal, South India, and Burma. In Assam the wood is esteemed as one of the best timbers, and is used for bridges and other works of construction. Beddome says it is employed by planters in the Nilgiris for building, and is sometimes called *Red Cedar*. Weight, 47 lbs. a cubic foot.

53. BOMBAX MALABARICUM, *DC.*; Malvaceæ. The Silk Cotton Tree; Semul (*Hind.*, *Beng.*); Letpan (*Burm.*). A very large deciduous tree, with branches in whorls, spreading horizontally; and stem with large buttresses at the base; met with throughout India and Burma. The wood is very light (from 20 to 30 lbs. a cubic foot) and is used for planking, packing-cases, and tea-boxes, toys, scabbards, fishing-floats, coffins, and the lining of wells. In Bengal and Burma the trunk is often hollowed out to make canoes. (*See* also 413, 908, 958, 1059.)

54. BORASSUS FLABELLIFORMIS, *Linn.*; Palmæ. (*See* also 585, 634, 711.)

55. BOSWELLIA SERRATA, *Roxb.*; Burseraceæ. Indian Olibanum Tree; Salhe, salga (*Hind.*). A moderate-sized, often gregarious tree, found in the intermediate northern and southern dry zones, the sub-Himálayan tract from the Sutlej to Nepal, and in the drier forests of Central and Southern India. The wood is used for fuel and for making the charcoal used in Nimar for iron smelting. It is light but not durable. Weight, about 34 lbs. a cubic foot. (*See* also 767, 1060, 1061.)

56. BRIEDEDIA RETUSA, *Spreng.*; Euphorbiaceæ. (*See* also 415.)

57. BUCHANANIA LATIFOLIA, *Roxb.*; Anacardiaceæ. Chirongi (*Beng.*); Charauli, Chironji (the fruit) (*Pb.*). A tree, leafless only for a very short time; found in the sub-Himálayan tract from the Sutlej eastward, ascending to 3,000 feet; throughout India and Burma. The wood is used for boxes, bedsteads, bullock-yokes, doors, window frames, tables, and the like. It seasons well, and is fairly durable if kept dry. Weight, 30 to 36 lbs. a cubic foot. (*See* also 635, 999).

58. BUCKLANDIA POPULNEA, *R. Br.*; Hammemalideæ.

59. BUTEA FRONDOSA, *Roxb.*; Leguminosæ. Dhak, kakria (*Hind.*); Palas (*Beng.*). A moderate-sized deciduous tree, found throughout India and Burma, extending in the North-West Himálaya as far as the Jhelum. The wood is practically useless; weight, about 40 lbs. a cubic foot. The late Dr. T. W. Sheppard introduced the charcoal for bleaching morphia. (*See* also 416, 1136.)

60. BUXUS SEMPERVIRENS, *Linn.*; Euphorbiaceæ. The Boxwood Tree; Shanda laghúne (*Afg.*); Chikri (*Kashmir*); Papri (*Pb.*). An evergreen shrub or small tree met with in the Sulaiman and Salt Ranges, North-West Himálaya, between 4,000 and 8,000 feet, in Bhutan about 6,000 to 7,000 feet; but scattered in different parts of the Himálaya, chiefly on a calcareous soil and often in remote localities. It is estimated that the cost per cubic foot of Indian boxwood delivered at Saharanpur from the Kelso forest would be Rs. 1-8; its further cost by rail from Saharanpur to Bombay would be at least Rs. 1-8 or total Rs. 3 per cubic foot. Considering 1 cubic foot as weighing 60 lbs., we have the cost per ton as Rs. 112, which could only be just covered by receipts if the very best description of wood were sent down. There is consequently little likelihood of much trade in boxwood from the Himálayan forests.

61. CÆSALPINIA SAPPAN, *Linn.*; Leguminosæ. The Sappan Wood; Bakum (*Hind.*, *Guz.*, *Beng.*); Patanga (*Tam.*, *Bomb.*). A small thorny tree of the eastern and western Peninsula and Pegu, cultivated in Central

India in plantations. Sapwood white, heartwood red. The wood takes a fine polish and does not warp or crack. Weight, about 60 lbs. a cubic foot. (*See* also 1138.)

62. CALLICARPA ARBOREA, *Roxb.*; Verbenaceæ.

63. CALOPHYLLUM INOPHYLLUM, *Linn.*; Guttiferæ. The Alexandrian Laurel; Sultana champa (*Hind.*, *Beng.*); Ponguyet (*Burm.*). An evergreen tree, cutivated in the western Peninsula, Orissa, South India, Ceylon, Burma, and the Andaman Islands. The wood is reddish brown, and moderately hard. It is used for masts, spars, railway sleepers, machinery; also for cabinet work. Weight, about 45 lbs. a cubic foot. (*See* also 1001.)

64. C. POLYANTHUM, *Wall.*

65. C. TOMENTOSUM, *Wight.*

66. CANARIUM BENGALENSE, *Roxb.*; Burseraceæ.

67. CARALLIA INTEGERRIMA, *DC.*; Rhizophoræ.

68. CARAPA MOLUCCENSIS, *Lamk.*; Meliaceæ.

69. CAREYA ARBOREA, *Roxb.*; Myrtaceæ.

70. CARPINUS VIMINEA, *Wall.*; Cupuliferæ.

71. CASEARIA GLOMERATA, *Roxb.*; Camydaceæ.

72. CASSIA FISTULA, *Linn.*; Leguminosæ. (*See* also 775.)

73. C. SIAMEA, *Lamk.*

74. CASTANOPSIS INDICA, *Alph. DC.*; Cupuliferæ. Banj katús (*Nepal*); Kashioron (*Lepcha*); Serang (*Ass.*). A moderate-sized evergreen tree met with in Nepal, Eastern Bengal, Assam, and Chittagong, ascending to 5,000 feet. The wood is very largely used for shingles in Darjíling. Weight 44 lbs. a cubic foot. The plant coppices freely, and is often pollarded and the branches burnt for manure.

75. CASTANOPSIS RUFESCENS, *Hook. f. & Th.*

76. CASUARINA EQUISETIFOLIA, *Forester*; Casuarinaceæ.

77. CEDRELA SERRATA, *Royle*; Meliaceæ.

78. C. TOONA, *Roxb.* The Toon or Indian Mahogany Tree; Moulmein Cedar; Tún (*Hind.*); Tuni (*Beng.*). A large tree, about 50 to 60 feet in height, growing in the sub-Himálayan forests, Bengal, Burma, and South India, ascending to 3,000 feet in the North-West Himálaya, and in Sikkim to 7,000 feet. The wood is durable and is not eaten by white-ants; it is highly valued and universally used for furniture of all kinds, and is also employed for door panels and carving. From Burma it is exported under the name of *Moulmein Cedar*, and as such is known in the English market. In Bengal and Assam, it is the chief wood for making tea-boxes, but is getting scarce on account of the heavy demand. Weight, 36 lbs. a cubic foot. (*See* also 1142.)

79. CEDRUS DEODORA, *Loudon*; Coniferæ. Deodar; Himálayan Cedar; Deodar (*Hazara, Kashmir, Garhwall, Kumaon*); Kelu (*Chenab to Jumna*). A very large and tall tree, found in the North-West Himálaya between 4,000 and 10,000 feet, extending east to the Dauli River, a tributary of the Alaknada below the Niti Pass, in the mountains of Afgháuistán and North Beluchistán. The wood is light yellowish brown, scented and moderately hard. Of the Himalayan conifers this affords by far the most durable wood. It is the chief timber of North-West India, and is used for all purposes of construction, for railway sleepers, bridges, and even for furniture and shingles. Weight, 36 lbs. a cubic foot. (*See* also 422, 1065.)

80. CELTIS AUSTRALIS, *Linn.*; Urticaceæ. (*See* also 424.)

81. CHICKRASSIA TABULARIS, *Adr. Juss.*; Meliaceæ. The Chittagong Wood; Chikrassi (*Beng.*); Boga poma (*Ass.*). A large tree, native to Eastern Bengal, South India, and Burma. The wood is used for furniture and for carving, having a beautiful satin lustre. Weight, about 52 lbs. a cubic foot.

82. CHLOROXYLON SWIETENIA, *DC.*; Meliaceæ. Satin Wood; Behra (*C.P.*); Halda (*Mahr.*). A moderate-sized deciduous tree, found in Central and South India, and Ceylon, The wood is used for agricultural implements, cart-building, furniture. and picture frames. In Madras it is prized for ploughs and oil-mills, and is found to stand well under water. It has been tried as a substitute for boxwood in engraving, but has not been found suitable; it is, however, good for turning. It is imported into England for cabinet-work and the backs of brushes. Weight, about 60 lbs. a cubic foot.

83. CINNAMOMUM GLANDULIFERUM, *Meissn.*; Laurineæ.

84. C. TAMALA, *Nees.* (*See* also 659.)

85. COCOS NUCIFERA, *Linn.*; Palmæ. (*See* also 660, 715, 895, 913, 1011.)

86. CORDIA FRAGRANTISSIMA, *Kurz.*; Boragineæ.

87. C. MACLEODII, *Hook. f. & Th.*

88. C. MYXA, *Linn.*

89. CORNUS CAPITATA, *Wall.*; Cornaceæ

90. CORYLUS COLURNA, *Linn.*; Cupuliferæ. (*See* also 636.)

91. CUPRESSUS TORULOSA, *Don.*; Coniferæ.

92. DALBERGIA CULTRATA, *Grah.*; Leguminosæ.

93. D. LANCEOLARIA, *Linn.*

94. D. LATIFOLIA, *Roxb.* The Blackwood or Rosewood of Southern India; Sitsal (*Beng.*); Sissui (Mar.). A deciduous tree, attaining a large size in South India; also found in Oudh, Eastern Bengal, and Central India. The wood is valuable for furniture, and is exported to Europe from the forests of Kanara and Malabar. It is good for carving and fancy work, and is used for the handles of knives, *kukris*, and other arms. Weight, about 55 lbs. a cubic foot.

95. D. SISSOO, *Roxb.* The Sissu (*Hind.*); Sissái (*Oudh*). A large deciduous tree of the sub-Himálayan tract from the Indus to Assam, ascending to 2,000 feet. The wood is very durable, seasons well, and does not warp or split. It is highly esteemed for all purposes where strength and elasticity are required. Clifford says that "in strength it is only inferior to *sál*, while in many other useful qualities it surpasses it, and has the advantage of being lighter. For felloes and naves of wheels and carved work

of every description, for framings of carriages and similar work, it is unsurpassed by any other wood, owing to its fine seasoning and standing qualities." It is extensively used for boat-building, carts, and carriages, agricultural implements, in construction, and especially for furniture. Weight, 47 lbs. a cubic foot.

96. DAPHNIDIUM ELONGATUM, *Nees;* Laurineæ.

97. D. PULCHERRIMUM, *Nees.*

98. DICHOPSIS POLYANTHA, *Bth. & Hk. f.;* Sapotaceæ.

99. DILLENIA INDICA, *Linn;* Dilleniaceæ. (*See* also 594.)

100. D. PENTAGYNA, *Roxb.*

101. DIOSPYROS EBENUM, *Kœnig;* Ebenaceæ.

102. D. EMBRYOPTERIS, *Pers.*

103. D. KURZII, *Hiern.* Andamanese Marble-Wood; Teakah (*Burm*); Pecha-da (*And.*). An evergreen tree of the Andaman Islands. Wood handsome, streaked black and grey. Weight, 60 to 80 lbs. a cubic foot. Much resembles Ceylon Calamander wood, is used for cabinet work, walking sticks, &c. Deserves to be better known.

104. D. MELANOXYLON, *Roxb.* Tendu (*Hind.*); Kend (*Beng.*); Tumri (*Mahr.*). A moderate-sized tree, common throughout India, but not in Burma. The wood is used in building, and for shoulder poles and carriage shafts, and the ebony or central black wood for all purposes of fancy work and carving. Weight, about 65 lbs. a cubic foot.

105. DIPTEROCARPUS LÆVIS, *Ham.;* Dipterocarpeæ. Kanyin, kanyin-neo (*Burm.*). A lofty tree of the tropical forests throughout Burma. Sapwood white, heartwood rough, reddish, soft. The wood is rarely used, but is occasionally employed for planking and rafters. Weight, about 44 lbs. a cubic foot. (*See* also 1068.)

106. D. TUBERCULATUS, *Roxb.* The Eng Tree; Eng (*Burm.*); Sooahn (*Talaing*). A large deciduous, gregarious tree, forming the "Eng forests" of Burma and Chittagong. The wood is very largely used in Burma for building, canoes, and house posts. Weight, about 53 lbs. a cubic foot. (*See* also 1069.)

107. D. TURBINATUS, *Gærtn. f.* (*See* also 1013, 1070.)

108. DOLICHANDRONE STIPULATA, *Seem.;* Bignoniaceæ.

109. DRIMYCARPUS RACEMOSUS, *Hk. f.;* Anacardiaceæ.

110. DUABANGA SONNERATIOIDES, *Buch.;* Lythraceæ. Bandorhulla (*Beng.*); Kochau (*Ass.*); Myoukgnau (*Burm.*). A tall deciduous tree, with light-brown bark; a native of Eastern Bengal (ascending to 3,000 feet), and of Assam and Burma. Wood grey, often streaked with yellow, soft; seasons well, neither warps nor splits. Canoes and cattle troughs cut out of it green, are at once used, even when liable alternately to wet and the heat of the sun. It is used in Northern Bengal and Assam very extensively for tea-boxes, for which purpose it is admirably fitted. Weight, 30 lbs. a cubic foot.

111. DYSOXYLUM BINECTARIFERUM, *Hk. f.;* Meliaceæ.

112. D. PROCERUM, *Hiern.*

113. ECHINOCARPUS DASYCARPUS, *Benth.;* Tiliaceæ.

114. EHRETIA WALLICHIANA, *Hk. f. & Th.;* Boragineæ.

115. ELÆOCARPUS LANCEÆFOLIUS, *Roxb.;* Tiliaceæ.

116. ELÆODENDRON GLAUCUM, *Pers.;* Celastrineæ.

117. ENGELHARDTIA SPICATA, *Bl.;* Juglandeæ.

118. ERIOLÆNA CANDOLLEI, *Wall.;* Sterculiaceæ.

119. E. HOOKERIANA, *W. & A.*

120. ERYTHRINA SUBEROSA, *Roxb.;* Leguminosæ.

121. ERYTHROXYLON MONOGYNUM, *Roxb.;* Lineæ.

122. EUGENIA ALTERNIFOLIA, *Wight.;* Myrtaceæ.

123. E. ARNOTTIANA, *Wight.*

124. E. JAMBOLANA, *Lam.* Jamoon (*Hind.*); Jam (*Beng.*); Jumbool (*Bomb.*). A moderate-sized evergreen tree, found wild or in cultivation all over India, from the Indus eastward, ascending to altitude 5,000 feet. Wood reddish-grey, rough, moderately hard, darker near the centre; no distinct heartwood. It is fairly durable and not subject to the attacks of white ants. Weight, about 48 lbs. a cubic foot. It is used for building, agricultural implements, and carts, also for well-work, as it resists the action of water. (*See* also 597, 717, 797.)

125. E. MANGIFOLIA, *Wall.*

126. E. OPERCULATA, *Roxb.*

127. EUONYMUS HAMILTONIANUS, *Wall.;* Celastrineæ.

128. EXCÆCARIA AGALLOCHA, *Willd.;* Euphorbiaceæ. (*See* also 1102.)

129. FAGRÆA FRAGRANS, *Roxb.;* Loganiaceæ.

130. FERONIA ELEPHANTUM, *Correa;* Rutaceæ. (*See* also 800, 1071.)

131. FICUS BENGALENSIS, *Linn.;* Urticaceæ. (*See* also 431, 919, 1105.)

132. F. GLOMERATA, *Roxb.*

133. F. RETUSA, *Linn.*

134. FLACOURTIA RAMONTCHI, *L'Herit.;* Bixineæ.

135. FRAXINUS FLORIBUNDA, *Wall;* Oleaceæ. Banarish (*Afg.*); Sum (*Pb.*); Kangu (*Nepal.*) A large deciduous tree, found in the Himálaya, from the Indus to Sikkim, between 5,000 and 8,500 feet. The wood is rough and hard and is used for oars, *jhampan* poles, ploughs, and other purposes. Weight, 46 lbs. a cubic foot.

136. GARCINIA SPECIOSA, *Wall.;* Guttiferæ.

137. GARDENIA LATIFOLIA, *Aiton, Roxb.;* Rubiaceæ.

138. GARUGA PINNATA, *Roxb.;* Burseraceæ. (*See* also 433.)

139. GIVOTIA ROTTLERIFORMIS, *Griff.;* Euphorbiaceæ.

140. GLUTA TAVOYANA, *Wall.;* Anacardiaceæ.

141. G. TRAVANCORICA, *Beddome.*

142. GMELINA ARBOREA, *Roxb.;* Verbenaceæ. Gumhár (*Hind.*); Gúmár, gúmbar (*Beng.*)

A moderate-sized, deciduous tree, met with in the sub-Himálayan tract from the Chenáb eastward and throughout India, Burma, and the Andaman Islands. The wood is easily worked and readily takes paint or varnish; it is very durable under water. Weight, 34 lbs. a cubic foot. Is highly esteemed for planking, furniture, domestic utensils, door panels, carriages, and palanquins, well-work, boats, toys, packing-cases, and all ornamental work; in Burma for carving images, clogs, and canoes. It would probably be a valuable wood for tea-boxes. It is the chief furniture wood of Chittagong, and is in some demand in Calcutta. (*See* also 434.)

143. GREWIA TILIÆFOLIA, *Vahl.*; Malvaceæ.

144. G. VESTITA, *Wall.* (*See* also 435.)

145. GYROCARPUS JACQUINI, *Roxb.*; Combretaceæ.

146. HARDWICKIA BINATA, *Roxb.*; Leguminosæ. Anjan (*Hind., Mar.*); Acha, alti (*Tam.*). A deciduous tree, found in the dry forests of South and Central India, generally gregarious in isolated belts or patches of greater or less extent. Most commonly found on sandstone, but also to be met with on trap and granite. Wanting in the western moist zone, and not found in Northern India, though it occurs as far north as the Banda district of the North-West Provinces. Perhaps the hardest and heaviest wood in India. Weight, 82 lbs. a cubic foot. At the Dehra workshops it has been used instead of brass for bearings for machinery, and has been found to wear well. It is used for bridge and house posts, and for ornamental work. It has been recommended for sleepers, but is probably too hard, heavy, and difficult to work to be much in favour. The Sone River piles of *anjan* were found after twenty years as sound as when first put in. (*See* also 436, 921.)

147. HEMIGYROSA CANESCENS, *Thw.*; Sapindaceæ.

148. HERITIERA LITTORALIS, *Dryand.*; Sterculiaceæ. Sundri (*Beng.*). A small gregarious tree, found in the coasts and tidal forests of Bengal, the Peninsula, Burma, and the Andaman Islands. Sundri wood is durable; it is heavy (weight, 67 lbs. a cubic foot), and does not float, and is extremely tough. It is used for a great variety of purposes, such as beams, buggy shafts, planking, posts, furniture, firewood; but chiefly in boat-building, for which purpose it is very extensively used in Calcutta, and particularly in the Government Dockyard at Kidderpore. It is the chief timber of the Sundarban forests. Its reproduction is most rapid. On all lands flooded by ordinary tides, a new growth of jungle springs up immediately; but on land above high-water mark it only establishes itself by slow degrees. It soon spreads on newly-formed islands on the sea edge of the forests.

149. HETEROPHRAGMA ROXBURGHII, *DC.*; Bignoniaceæ.

150. HOLARRHENA ANTIDYSENTERICA, *Wall.*; Apocynaceæ. (*See* also 807.)

151. HOMALIUM TOMENTOSUM, *Bth.*; Samydaceæ.

152. HOPEA ODORATA, *Roxb.*; Dipterocarpeæ. Thingan (*Burm.*); Rimda (*And.*). A large evergreen tree, found scattered in the evergreen forests of British Burma and the Andaman Islands. The wood is very durable. It is the chief timber tree of South Tenasserim. Boats made of it are said to last twenty years. It is used for house-building and canoes; also considered good for solid cart wheels. Weight, about 48 lbs. a cubic foot.

153. H. PARVIFLORA, *Beddome.*

154. HYMENODICTYON EXCELSUM, *Wall.*; Rubiaceæ. (*See* also 437, 809.)

155. ILEX DIPYRENA, *Wall.*; Ilicineæ. (*See* also 438.)

156. I. WIGHTIANA, *Wall.*

157. JUGLANS REGIA, *Linn.*; Juglandeæ. The Walnut; Akhrot (*Hind.*); Ákrut (*Beng.*); Charmaghz (*Pers.*). A large tree, wild in the North-West Provinces and the Sikkim Himálaya, and largely cultivated, especially in Afghánistán and Kashmír. The wood is extensively used for furniture throughout the Himálaya, its principal use being for gun-stocks. In Darjiling it is occasionally employed for shingles by the Bhutias, but is not so good as chestnut. Before it became scarce in the forests it was largely used for house-fittings, and many of the older houses in Darjíling have their doors and windows and other fittings almost entirely of walnut. It is not quite so heavy as European walnut, the Indian wood averaging from 28 to 46 lbs. a cubic foot. (*See* also 639, 1027.)

158. JUNIPERUS EXCELSA, *M. Bieb.*; Coniferæ. Himálayan Pencil Cedar; Apúrs, *Baluchistán*; Chalai, *Jhelam.* A moderate-sized tree of the arid tract of the North-West Himálaya and Western Tibet, extending eastward to Nepal; frequent in the mountains of Afghánistán and North Baluchistán. The wood is used in Quetta and Khelat for house-building, also mixed with stone for the walls of houses in Lahoul. Some of the temples in Kunawar are built of it, and it is there made into drinking-cups and walking-sticks. At Leh it is largely used as fuel, and is sometimes made into charcoal. Weight, 30 lbs. a cubic foot. (*See* also 1073.)

159. J. RECURVA, *Ham.*

160. LAGERSTRŒMIA FLOS-REGINÆ, *Retz.*; Lythraceæ. Jarul (*Beng.*); Taman (*Mar.*); Pymma (*Burm.*). A large deciduous tree, found in East Bengal, Assam, Burma, and on the West Coast, extending north to Ratnagiri. This is the most valuable timber of Sylhet, Kachar, and Chittagong, and in Burma is viewed as next after teak. It is used in ship-building and for boats and canoes, all kinds of construction, timber, and carts. The Ordnance Department use it for many parts of their gun-carriages. In South India it is employed for building, and in Ceylon for casks. Weight, about 45 lbs. a cubic foot.

161. L. LANCEOLATA, *Beddome.*

162. L. MICROCARPA, *Wight.*

163. L. PARVIFLORA, *Hook.* Bákli (*Hind.*);

Sida (*Beng.*); Tsambelay (*Burm.*). A large, deciduous tree of the sub-Himálayan tract from the Jumna eastward, Oudh, Bengal, Assam, Central and South India. The tree coppices readily. Wood tough, elastic, seasons well, works freely, and is fairly durable. It is used for ploughs and other agricultural implements, for construction, for buggy shafts and axe handles. It gives a very good charcoal. Weight, about 45 lbs. a cubic foot.

164. L. TOMENTOSA, *Presl.*

165. LARIX GRIFFITHII, *Hk. f. & Th.*; Coniferæ.

166. LEBEDIEROPSIS ORBICULARIS, *Mull.-Arg.*; Euphorbiaceæ. Garrar (*Hind.*); Parasu (*Kol.*); Garari (*Mar.*). A small, deciduous tree, met with in Bandelkhand, Satpura Range, and the forests southward to the Godavari mountains of South India. This tree coppices readily, and may, therefore, be specially recommended where fuel has to be produced in tropical parts of India, but it is also valuable as affording a useful wood for turning. Weight, 54 lbs. a cubic foot.

167. LOPHOPETALUM LITTORALE, *Kurz*; Celastrineæ.

168. L. WALLICHII, *Kurz.*

169. MACHILUS ODORATISSIMA, *Nees.*; Laurineæ. Dalchini (*Pb.*); Kawala (*Hind.*); Soom (*Ass.*); Dingpingwait (*Khásia*). A large tree of the outer Himálaya ascending to 8,000 ft., also of the Khásia Hills and Burma. In Assam it grows gregariously, in large forests, and is one of the trees on which the *muga* silk-worm feeds (*Antheræa assama*). The wood is used in Darjiling (where it is very common) for building, chiefly for native houses; also for tea-boxes. Weight, about 40 lbs. a cubic foot.

170. MAGNOLIA CAMPBELLII, *Hk. f. & Th.*; Magnoliaceæ. Red Magnolia; Lal champ (*Nepal*); Pendder (*Bhutia*). A large and tall deciduous tree of Sikkim and Bhután occurring between 7,000 and 10,000 feet in altitude. The wood is occasionally used for planking, but is now scarce. Weight, 25 lbs. a cubic foot.

171. MANGIFERA INDICA, *Linn.*; Anacardiaceæ. The Mango Tree; Am or Amb (*Hind.*); Thayet (*Burm.*). A densely-branched, large tree, wild on the Western Ghâts, the Chutia Nagpur Hills, and the Naga Hills; cultivated all over India for its fruit—the mango. The wood is used for planking, door and window frames; in Calcutta, for packing cases; and in Behar for indigo boxes; canoes and *masúla* boats are made of it. Weight, from 40 to 48 lbs, a cubic foot. (*See* also 446, 604, 816, 1155.)

172. M. SYLVATICA, *Roxb.*

173. MELANORRHŒA USITATA, *Wall.*; Anacardiaceæ. The Varnish Tree of Burma; Kheu (*Manipur*); Thitseeben (*Burm.*); Soothan (*Talaing*). A medium-sized deciduous tree, found in Manipur and Burma. The wood dark-red with yellowish streaks; it is used for tool handles, anchor stocks, and has lately been recommended for building, railway sleepers, gun-stocks, and other purposes. Weight, 56 to 60 lbs. a cubic foot.

174. MELIA AZEDARACH, *Linn.*; Meliaceæ. (*See* also 818.)

175. M. AZADIRACHTA, *Linn.* (*See* also 450, 721, 817.)

176. MELIOSMA ARNOTTIANA, *Wight*; Sabiaceæ.

177. M. WALLICHII, *Planch.*

178. MEMECYLON EDULE, *Roxb.*; Melastomaceæ.

179. MESUA FERREA, *Linn.*; Guttiferæ. (*See* also 819.)

180. MICHELIA CHAMPACA, *Linn.*; Magnoliaceæ. Champa (*Hind.*); Champa, champaka (*Beng.*). A tall evergreen tree, with yellow, sweetly-scented flowers; cultivated throughout India from the Ravi southward and up to 5,400 feet in the North-West Himálaya. Wild in Nepal, Bengal, Assam (ascending to 3,000 feet), Burma, and in the forests of the Western Ghâts as far as Kanara. The wood is soft and seasons well; it is used for furniture, house-building, carriage-work, and native drums. It is considered valuable in Northern Bengal for planking, door-panels, and furniture; and in Assam for building and canoes. Weight, 35 to 40 lbs. a cubic foot.

181. M. EXCELSA, *Blume.* White Magnolia; Bara champ (*Nepal*); Gók (*Bhutia*). A lofty, deciduous tree of the Eastern Himálaya, from 6,000 to 8,000 feet, and of the Khásia Hills. The wood is used for building, but chiefly for planking, door and window frames, and for furniture. This is the principal building and furniture wood of the Darjiling Hills. It is soft and light. Weight, about 33 lbs. a cubic foot.

182. MILIUSA VELUTINA, *Hk. f. & Th.*; Anonaceæ.

183. MILLETTIA PENDULA, *Bth.*; Leguminosæ.

184. MILLINGTONIA HORTENSIS, *Linn.*; Bignoniaceæ.

185. MIMUSOPS ELENGI, *Linn.*; Sapotaceæ. (*See* also 820.)

186. M. INDICA, *A. DC.*

187. M. LITTORALIS, *Kurz.*

188. MORINDA EXSERTA, *Roxb.*; Rubiaceæ. (*See* also 1159.)

189. MORUS CUSPIDATA, *Wall.*; Urticaceæ.

190. M. SERRATA, *Roxb.*

191. MURRAYA EXOTICA, *Linn.*; Rutaceæ.

192. MYRISTICA IRYA, *Gærtn.*; Myristicaceæ. This elegant wood seems more likely than any other to find a market in Europe. In point of texture it might be described as between walnut and oak.

193. MYRSINE SEMISERRATA, *Wall.*; Myrsineæ.

194. NAUCLEA ROTUNDIFOLIA, *Roxb.*; Rubiaceæ.

195. NEPHELIUM LONGANA, *Camb.*; Sapindaceæ.

196. NYCTANTHES ARBOR-TRISTIS, *Linn.*; Oleaceæ. (*See* also 1160.)

197. ODINA WODIER, *Roxb.*; Anacardiaceæ. Kiamil (*Hind.*); Jiyal (*Beng.*); Wodier *Tam.*). A moderate-sized or large deciduous tree with few branches, met with in the sub-Himálayan tract from the Indus eastward, ascending to 4,000 feet; common also in the forests of India and Burma. The wood is reddish-brown when ripe; it is used for spear-shafts, scabbards,

wheel-spokes, cattle-yokes, oil-presses, and rice-pounders; it might be good for cabinet-work. Weight, about 38 lbs. a cubic foot. (*See* also 454, 1076.)

198. OLEA CUSPIDATA, *Wall*; Oleaceæ. (*See* also 455.)

199. OUGEINIA DALBERGIOIDES, *Benth.*; Leguminosæ. Sándan (*Hind.*); Tunnia (*Banswara*); Telus (*Khandeish*). A moderate-sized deciduous tree, under certain circumstances gregarious, found chiefly in the sub-Himálayan tract from the Sutlej to the Tísta ascending to 5,000 feet, in central India and the western coast. The wood is used for agricultural implements, carriage poles, wheels, and furniture; also for building. It is tough and hard. Weight, 55 to 60 lbs. a cubic foot. A crystalline substance, probably magnesia, is sometimes found in the wood. (*See* also 456.)

200. PAJANELIA RHEEDII, *DC.*; Bignoniaceæ.

201. PARKIA INSIGNIS, *Kurz*; Leguminosæ.

202. PENTACE BURMANICA, *Kurz*; Tiliaceæ.

203. PHOTINIA LINDLEYANA, *Wight*; Rosaceæ.

204. PHYLLANTHUS EMBLICA, *Linn.*; Euphorbiaceæ. (*See* also 612, 834, 1166.)

205. PINUS EXCELSA, *Wall.*; Coniferæ. Piuni (*Afg.*); Chíl, chír (*Kashmir to Jaunsar*). A large gregarious tree, of the Himálaya, between 6,000 and 10,000 feet, from the Indus to Bhután, extending into the inner arid tract. The wood reddish and moderately hard; it is used for house-building, shingles, water channels, wooden spades, and other implements; also for torches, and from it turpentine is prepared. It gives an excellent charcoal for iron smelting. Weight, about 30 lbs. a cubic foot.

206. P. GERARDIANA, *Wall.* (*See* also 641.)

207. P. KASYA, *Royle.*

208. P. LONGIFOLIA, *Roxb.* The Long-leaved Pine; Nakhtar (*Afg.*); Chír (*Pb.*) A large gregarious tree, of the outer and drier Himálayan slopes, met with as low down as 2,000 feet and ascending to 7,500 feet. From Afghanistan eastward to Sikkim and Bhután. The wood is extensively used in some localities in the hills for building, shingles, tea boxes, and the bottoms of boats. It gives large quantities of resin, more than any of the other Himálayan pines, but the process is exhaustive. Weight, 36 to 45 lbs. a cubic foot.

209. P. MERKUSII, *Jungh.*

210. PISTACEA INTEGERRIMA, *Stewart*; Anacardiaceæ.

211*. PITHECOLOBIUM DULCE, *Bth.*; Leguminosæ.

212. PLANCHONIA LITTORALIS, *Van Houtte*; Myrtaceæ.

213*. PLATANUS ORIENTALIS, *Linn.*; Platanеæ.

214. PODOCARPUS BRACTEATA, *Bl.*; Coniferæ.

215. P. LATIFOLIA, *Wall.*

216. PONGAMIA GLABRA, *Vent.*; Leguminosæ. (*See* also 459, 839.)

217. POPULOUS CILIATA, *Wall.*; Salicineæ. (*See* also (461.)

218. P. EUPHRATICA, *Oliver.*

219. PREMNA LATIFOLIA, *Roxb.*; Verbenaceæ.

220. P. LONGIFOLIA, *Roxb.*

221. PROSOPIS SPICIGERA, *Linn.*; Leguminosæ.

222. PRUNUS ACUMINATA, *Wall.*; Rosaceæ.

223. P. PUDDUM, *Roxb.*

224. PTEROCARPUS INDICUS, *Willd.*; Leguminosæ. Andaman Redwood; Padauk (*Burm.*); Chalanga-da (*And.*). A large and lofty tree, found in Burma and the Andaman Islands. The wood is used for furniture, carts, gun-carriages, and other purposes. Heartwood, dark-red, close-grained, and hard. Weight, 45 to 60 lbs. a cubic foot. It is the most useful wood in the Andamans, where it grows to an enormous size. An interesting set of pieces of furniture made of this wood will be found in the Court. These have been prepared to demonstrate the adaptability of the wood for furniture and carriage building.

225. PTEROCARPUS MARSUPIUM, *Roxb.* Bija (*Hind.*); Hitun (*Kol.*); Vengai (*Tam.*). A large deciduous tree, of Central and South India, extending northward to the Banda District of the North-West Provinces. The wood is much used for door and window frames, posts and beams, furniture, agricultural implements, cart and boat building. Heartwood brown with dark streaks. Weight, 45 to 60 lbs. a cubic foot. (*See* also 465, 1080, 1167.)

226. P. SANTALINUS, *Linn. f.* The Sanders Red or Red Sanders Tree, sometimes also called Red Sandal wood; Rakta-chandan (*Beng.*); Lala chondana (*Bomb.*); Lal-Chandun (*Hind., Dec.*) A small tree of South India, chiefly in Cuddapah, North Arcot, Karnul, and other dry forests; cultivated in Bengal and other parts of India. The wood is used as a dye-stuff, and is largely exported from Madras to other parts in India. The colouring principle is called "Santalin." It is soluble in alcohol, and is sometimes used to dye cloth, imparting a pale pink colour. Beddome says it is used for building purposes and for turning. Weight, 72 lbs. a cubic foot. (*See* also 1168.)

227. PTEROSPERMUM ACERIFOLIUM, *Willd.*; Sterculiaceæ.

228. P. SUBERIFOLIUM, *Lam.*

229. QUERCUS ANNULATA, *Smith.*; Cupuliferæ. Barán, Brén (*Pb.*); Phaliant (*N.-W. P.*) A large evergreen tree, found in the valleys of the outer Himálaya, Garhwal, in Kumaon, Nepal, Sikkim (6,000 to 9,000 feet), Bhután, and Khásia Hills. The wood is not much esteemed in the North-West Himálaya; in Darjíling it is used for the same purposes as *Q. lamellosa*, but is not considered so good as that species. Weight, from 57 to 69 lbs. a cubic foot.

230. Q. DILATATA, *Lindl.* (*See* also 467.)

231. Q. GRIFFTHII, *Hk. f. & Th.*

232. Q. ILEX, *Linn.* The Holm Oak; Charrei (*Afg.*); Brekche (*Pb.*). A moderate-sized evergreen tree, met with in Afghánistán, Sulaiman Range, the arid tracts of the inner Himálaya, generally between 3,000 and 8,500 feet, westward to Southern Europe. The wood is largely used for tool handles, and pieces are brought from the Sulaiman Range for that purpose. It is also employed for agricultural implements, and yields good fuel and charcoal. Weight, 54 to 68 lbs. a cubic foot.

233. QUERCUS INCANA *Roxb.*

234. Q. LAMELLOSA, *Smith.* Shalshi, pharatsinghali (*Nepal*); Búk (*Lepcha*). A very large tree, of Nepal, Sikkim, Bhután, between 5,000 and 9,000 feet. It often attains 100 to 120 feet in height, with a girth of 20 to 30 feet, but old trees are very frequently hollow. Used for beams and posts in the construction of houses and bridges, and for door-posts, window-frames, rafters, and other house-building purposes. Weight, 57 to 63 lbs. a cubic foot. (*See* also 1170.)

235. Q. LANCEÆFOLIA, *Roxb.*

236. Q. LAPPACEA, *Roxb.*

237. Q. PACHYPHYLLA, *Kurz.*

238. Q. SEMECARPIFOLIA, *Smith.*

239. Q. SPICATA, *Smith.*

240. RHIZOPHORA MUCRONATA, *Lamk.*; Rhizophoreæ. (*See* also 1171.)

241. RHODODENDRON ARBOREUM, *Smith*; Ericaceæ.

242. RHUS COTINUS, *Linn.*; Anacardiaceæ.

243. SACCOPETALUM TOMENTOSUM, *Hk. f. & Th.*; Anonaceæ. (*See* also 469.)

244. SALIX TETRASPERMA, *Roxb.*; Salicineæ.

245. SALVADORA OLEOIDES, *Linn.*; Salvadoraceæ. (*See* also 471.)

246. S. PERSICA, *Linn.*

247. SANDORICUM INDICUM, *Cav.*; Meliaceæ.

248. SANTALUM ALBUM, *Linn.*; Santalaceæ. Sandalwood; Chandan, chandal (*Hind.*); Santa-ku (*Burm.*). A small evergreen tree, found in the dry region of South India. It grows naturally in the drier parts of Mysore, Coimbatore, and Salem districts, extending south to Madura and north to Kolhapur. It is met with generally at an elevation of from 2,000 to 3,000 feet, and seems to prefer poor soils, seeking the protection of hedgerows and scrub jungles. The heartwood is used for carving and for incense and perfume. It is an important article of trade in India, and is largely exported to China and Arabia. It has been found to be well suited for engraving. Weight 56 to 71 lbs. a cubic foot. (*See* also 844, 1045.)

249. SAPINDUS EMARGINATUS, *Vahl.*; Sapindaceæ.

250. SCHIMA WALLICHII, *Choisy.*; Tenstrœmiaceæ. Chilauni, goechassi (*Nepal*); Makusal (*Hind.*). A large evergreen tree, found in Northern and Eastern Bengal and Chittagong, ascending to 5,000 feet. The wood is used in Northern Bengal and Assam for many purposes, but chiefly for building. Many of the tea factories in Darjeeling have been built of it, and it has sometimes been used for bridges. As large quantities of the timber, well grown and straight, are available, it is to be hoped that it may be ere long in more extensive demand. Weight 42 to 50 lbs. a cubic foot.

251. SCHLEICHERA TRIJUGA, *Willd.*; Sapindaceæ.

252. SCHREBERA SWIETENIOIDES, *Roxb.*; Oleaceæ.

253. SEMECARPUS ANACARDIUM, *Linn. f.*; Anacardiaceæ. (*See* also 644, 845, 846.)

254. SHOREA OBTUSA, *Wall.*; Dipterocarpeæ.

255. S. ROBUSTA, *Gærtn.* The Sal Tree; Sál (*Hind.*). A large, gregarious tree (never quite leafless) of the north-east, moist and intermediate zones sub-Himálayan tract, from the Beas to Assam, eastern part of Central India, from the Ganges to the Godavari, extending westward to the longitude of Mandla, with an outlying patch on and around the sandstone hills of the Pachmarhi Range. Sál is the timber which in Northern India is the most extensively used. It is in constant request for piles, beams, planking, and railing of bridges; for beams, door and window-posts of houses; for gun-carriages; and above all for railway sleepers, the yearly consumption of which reaches some lakhs of cubic feet. Weight, 53 to 70 lbs. a cubic foot. It is used for making canoes in the hills of Northern Bengal, where it is found, perhaps, of the largest size now available. (*See* also 506, 1081.)

256. S. SIAMENSIS, *Miq.*

257. S. TALURA, *Roxb.*

258. S. TUMBUGGAIA, *Roxb.*

259. SIDEROXYLON TOMENTOSUM, *Roxb.*; Sapotaceæ.

260. SONNERATIA ACIDA, *Linn. f.*; Lythraceæ.

261. S. APETALA, *Buch.*

262. SOYMIDA FEBRIFUGA, *Adr. Juss.*; Meliaceæ. Indian Red Wood; Rohan (*Hind.*); Rohina (*Beng.*). A large deciduous tree of Central India and the Dekkan. The wood is used for construction, well-work, plough-shares, and oil-mills. Weight, about 73 lbs. a cubic foot. (*See* also 848.)

263. SPONGIAS MANGIFERA, *Pers.*; Anacardiaceæ. (*See* also 623.)

264. STEPHYGYNE PARVIFOLIA, *Hk. f. & Bth.*; Rubiaceæ.

265. STERCULIA URENS, *Roxb.*; Sterculiaceæ. (*See* also 943, 1082.)

266. S. VILLOSA, *Roxb.* (*See* also 944.)

267. STEREOSPERMUM CHELONOIDES, *DC.*; Bignoniaceæ.

268. S. SUAVEOLENS, *DC.*

269. STRYCHNOS NUX-VOMICA, *Linn.*; Loganiaceæ. (*See* also 890.)

270. S. POTATORUM, *Linn. f.* (*See* also 851.)

271. SYMPLOCOS RACEMOSA, *Roxb.*; Styraceæ. (*See* also 1177.)

272. TALAUMA HODGSONI, *Hk. f. & T.*; Magnoliaceæ.

273*. TAMARINDUS INDICA, *Linn.*; Leguminosæ. (*See* also 555, 624, 853, 1047.)

274. TAMARIX ARTICULATA, *Vahl.*; Tamariscineæ. (*See* also 1170.)

275. TAXUS BACCATA, *Linn.*; Coniferæ. The Yew, Saráp. (*Afg.*); Birmi (*Pb.*); Dingsableh (*Khásia*). A large evergreen tree of the Himálaya, from the Indus to Bhután, generally between 6,000 to 10,000 feet, and in the Khásia Hills; distributed to Europe, North Africa, Western Asia, Japan, and North America. The wood is used for bows, carrying poles, and

native furniture, and deserves to be better known and more extensively used, as it is very strong and elastic, and works and polishes beautifully. In some parts of the Himálaya and the Khásia Hills it is held in great veneration and called *Deodar* (God's tree); the wood is burnt as incense, the branches are carried in religious processions in Kumaon, and in Nepal the twigs are used to decorate houses at religious festivals. Weight, about 40 lbs. a cubic foot. (*See* also 854.)

276. TECOMA UNDULATA, *G. Don.;* Bignoniaceæ. (*See* also 476.)

277. TECTONA GRANDIS, *Linn. f.;* Verbenaceæ. The Teak Tree; Sáj (*Arab.*); Ságun (*Hind.*); Kyun (*Burm*). A large deciduous tree, found in Central and South India and Burma. Its northern limit may be defined by a line passing from the mouth of the Nerbudda up that river, and across to and down the Mahanadi; but in some places it extends farther north, and it is found as far as Jhansi and Banda. It is cultivated in Assam, Bengal, and the sub-Himálaya as far north as Saharanpur. This is the chief timber of India and Burma; it is exported largely for ship-building and the construction of railway carriages; in India it is used for all purposes of house and ship-building, for bridges, sleepers, furniture, and most other purposes. Weight, about 40 lbs. a cubic foot. (*See* also 1048, 1115.)

278. TERMINALIA ARJUNA, *Beddome;* Combretaceæ. Anjan, arjún (*Hind.*); Arjún (*Beng.*). A large deciduous tree, of the sub-Himálayan tract, Oudh, Bengal, Burma, Central and South India. The wood is used for carts, agricultural implements, boats, and for building. Weight, about 57 lbs. a cubic foot. (*See* also 1183.)

279. T. BELERICA, *Roxb.* (*See* also 477, 1185.)

280. T. BIALATA, *Wall.*

281. T. CHEBULA, *Retz.* (*See* also 855, 1184.)

282. T. MYRIOCARPA, *Henck. & Mull. Arg.*

283. T. TOMENTOSA, *W. & A.* Saj (*Hind.*); Piasal (*Beng.*); Toukkyan (*Burm.*). A large deciduous tree, of the sub-Himálayan tract from the Ravi eastward, ascending to 4,000 feet; Bengal, Central and South India, and Burma. The wood is largely used for house-building, carts, rice-pounders, ship and boat-building. It has been successfully tried for railway sleepers. It splits very much however, unless thoroughly seasoned. It is an excellent fuel, and makes good charcoal. Weight, about 71 lbs. a cubic foot. (*See* 1186.)

284. TERNSTRŒMIA JAPONICA, *Thunb.;* Ternstrœmiaceæ.

285. TETRAMELES NUDIFLORA, *R.Br.;* Datisceæ.

286. TETRANTHERA LAURIFOLIA, *Jacq.;* Laurineæ.

287. T. MONOPETALA, *Roxb.*

288. THESPESIA POPULNEA, *Corr.;* Malvaceæ.

289. TURPINIA NEPALENSIS, *Wall.;* Sapindaceæ. (*See* also 480.)

290. ULMUS INTEGRIFOLIA, *Roxb.;* Urticaceæ.

291. U. WALLICHIANA, *Planch.*

292. VACCINIUM LESCHENAULTII, *Wight;* Vacciniaceæ.

293. VATERIA INDICA, *Linn.;* Dipterocarpeæ.

294. VATICA LANCEÆFOLIA, *Bl.;* Dipterocarpeæ.

295. VIBURNUM ERUBESCENS, *Wall.;* Caprifoliaceæ.

296. VITEX ALTISSIMA, *Linn.;* Verbenaceæ.

297. V. LEUCOXYLON, *Linn. f.*

298. V. PUBESCENS, *Vahl.*

299. WENDLANDIA EXSERTA, *DC.;* Rubiaceæ.

300. WRIGHTIA TOMENTOSA, *Roum. & Sch.;* Apocynaceæ.

301. XANTHOPHYLLUM FLAVESCENS, *Roxb.;* Polygaleæ.

302. XYLIA DOLABRIFORMIS, *Benth.;* Leguminosæ. The Iron-wood Tree of Pegu and Arracan; Jambu (*Hind.*); Jamba, suria (*Mahr.*). A large deciduous tree, met with in the Chanda District, South India, Arakan, and Burma. The wood is used for boat-building, and for agricultural implements in Burma; also for carts and tool handles. In South India it is used for railway sleepers, posts, boat-building, and carts. It is hard, heavy, and difficult to cut, but a useful wood for piles and beams of bridges. Weight, about 63 lbs. a cubic foot.

303. ZIZYPHUS JUJUBA, *Lam.;* Rhamneæ. (*See* also 626.)

304. Z. XYLOPYRA, *Willd.*

EXHIBITORS.—The Chief Commissioner of the Andaman Islands exhibits an interesting set of furniture made of padank wood, and the Director of Kew a log of Deodar. The Assam Railway and Trading Company also show a large collection of their timbers and petroleum. Col. R. H. Beddome shows a complete set of his works, along with the other publications of the Forest Department. An interesting collection of timbers used in the construction of gun carriages is exhibited by the Madras Factory. On the Timber Trophy will also be seen a collection of horns, amongst which may be mentioned buffalo horns, exhibited by Messrs. Cuthbertson and Harper, of Calcutta.

SUB-COURTS IV. & V.

(*See* PART II.—ETHNOLOGY.)

SUB-COURT VI.

ANIMAL AND MINERAL FOOD-STUFFS.

SALT.—The most important product under this head is common salt. This is the only article of daily food which in India bears a direct tax. The collection of this tax formerly caused much annoyance to the people and did great injury to the internal trade of the country. The conditions of salt taxation which prevailed in the various provinces of India prior to the British conquests were for many years more or less perpetuated. The inequality of the tax necessitated, however, the maintenance of an elaborate and expensive protective system to prevent the cheaply-taxed salt of one province from being carried to another where it was less heavily burdened. The five principal sources of salt in India are the Salt Range in the Punjab, the salt lakes of Rajputana, a few other scattered salt lakes in various parts of the country, such as the Chilka lake in Orissa, sea water and the European imports. To regulate the transports over India, as late as in 1869 a fiscal line was maintained, which extended from the Indus to the Máhánadi in Madras, a distance of 2,274 miles. This was patrolled by 12,000 men, the annual cost of the system being £162,000. A similar line, 280 miles in length, was maintained in the north-eastern portion of the Bombay Presidency, extending from Dohud to the Runn of Cutch. Lord Mayo initiated the reform of this expensive fiscal system, and it has since been entirely removed. The duty has been so equalised as to do away with the necessity to interfere with inter-provincial trade.

The annual consumption of salt in India amounts to about 30½ million maunds (*e.g.*, £1,091,255 tons). and the total revenue derived therefrom in 1884–85 was £6,350,000. Even while paying this very large revenue, however, salt is still a cheap commodity. In Calcutta it sold in 1884–85 at 12·8 seers a rupee, that is, less than one penny a pound; it was even cheaper in Bombay, the purchase value of the rupee being 13·1 seers, and in Madras even still more so, namely, 16·4 seers per rupee, or a little over a halfpenny a pound. The inequality which exists at the present moment is governed mainly by the same causes which affect all other articles of merchandise—supply and demand. In Peshawar, near an important salt mine, as much as 40·6 seers may be had for the rupee, and in Kyouk Phyoo in Burma even as much as 80·01 may be got, while in Mirzapur, in the North-West Provinces, only 8·17 can be had. The average price throughout India as a whole in 1884–85 was 14·06 seers per rupee, or a little over three farthings a pound. Of this amount about two-thirds go to Government as duty.

The most important factor in regard to supply is railway freight, which, in an immense country like India, is a matter of supreme importance. Owing to the cost of freight the salt of Upper India is unable to compete with European salt at the Indian ports and for some considerable distance inland. For instance, Calcutta is supplied mainly with European salt, which finds its way as far inland as Benares, at which point it comes in contact with the salt of Rajputana.

The amount obtained as duty on imported foreign salt is a little over one-fourth of the total salt revenue. During 1884–85, 412,839 tons of foreign salt were imported.

There are four kinds of country salt met with in the bazars of India:—

305. Rock Salt.—By the natives this is regarded as the best, but mainly because it has not been boiled. It is obtained from the cis-Indus and trans-Indus salt mines.

306. Sea Salt.—This is extensively manufactured in the Madras Presidency under a system of Government supervision, the revenue obtained being over a million and a half pounds sterling.

307. Lake Salt.—This is procured from the Ajmere salt lakes on the water naturally evaporating during the hot season.

308. Earth Salt.—Common salt of a very impure quality is obtained by washing certain soils.

An interesting series of salt samples is exhibited by the Government of India. The Northern India Salt Department shows two blocks of Mayo Mines' Salt, together with a number of other samples of salt and salt ornaments. Katak salt is also represented. The Commissioner of Salt Revenue, Madras, contributes a valuable collection of Madras salts.

The following are the animal products of India which deserve to be separately mentioned:—

309. Bêche de Mer.—During the year 1884–85, 47,312 lbs., valued at Rs. 9,078, were exported from British Burma to the Straits. The imports amounted to Rs. 12,564.

310. Butter and Cheese. The exports of butter and cheese were very small. The imports during the year 1884–85 amounted to Rs. 524,459.

311. Fish-maws and Shark-fins.—The trade in fish-maws and shark-fins is increasing. The exports amounted to 791,780 lbs., valued at Rs. 5,76,629 in 1884–85, against 592,691 lbs., valued at Rs. 5,42,376 in the previous year. Bombay and British Burma supplied the bulk of the exports, of which Hong Kong took 383,396 lbs., the Straits 320,788 lbs., and the United Kingdom 83,113 lbs. The exports and imports amounted to Rs. 9,39,828.

312. Ghee.—The amount of exports of ghee during the year 1884–85 was Rs. 5,72,420 against Rs. 6,61,330 of the previous year. Bengal alone supplied half the quantity, and the remainder was chiefly exported from Madras and Bombay. Mauritius, Ceylon, and the Straits took the bulk of the exports chiefly going for coolie consumption. The import trade is increasing; it amounted last year to Rs. 4,85,396, or four times the value of the imports in the previous year. Bombay and Sind received the largest quantity. The whole foreign trade in ghee was, therefore, Rs. 10,57, 816. The inter-provincial trade in ghee for the last year amounted to Rs. 11,87,408.

313. Lard.—The exports of lard during the year 1884–85 were Rs. 2,83,054, of which Rs. 2,82,854 were from Bengal alone. There is no import trade in lard.

314. Salted Fish.—The exports of salted fish seem to be falling off; during the year 1884–85 they amounted to Rs. 2,64,805. Madras supplied the bulk of these exports, the supply going chiefly to Ceylon and the Straits. The imports amounted to Rs. 9,69,011, of which

Bombay, Madras, and Burma took the bulk. The internal trade in salted fish has been valued at Rs. 4,93,708.

EXHIBITORS.—Mr. T. H. Cripps of Madras contributes a collection of fish pickles.

SUB-COURT VII.

The exhibits arranged in this Sub-Court appear in the "Classified List," Division I., Sections 9 and 10.

FODDER AND CATTLE FOOD; HUMAN FOOD IN TIMES OF SCARCITY.

FEW agriculturists cultivate food of any kind for their unfortunate cattle. The Indian bullocks are allowed to graze over waste lands or fields, after the crops have been removed, and in this way pick up the bulk of their food as best they can. This is at most supplemented only by a feed of straw, cut up into small pieces and sometimes flavoured with oil-cake or other substances poured or sprinkled over the straw—the curry-stuff of the bullocks' diet. The question of provisioning Government cattle is, however, of pressing importance, and is engaging the attention of the authorities. Gram (*Cicer arietinum*) may be said to be the staple food given to these animals. Occasionally a small amount of oats is mixed with the crushed gram, and in Manipur and Burma unhusked rice is largely given to horses. The *dúb* grass (*Cynodon Dactylon*) is the principal grass for horses. This is the characteristic and delicate turf of roadsides and waste places, especially where sand prevails. The roots, as well as the stems, are highly nutritious. The grass-cutter digs up both root and stem, the result being that around large towns this beautiful and most useful grass is, practically speaking, being exterminated.

Fodder plants may be referred to two large sections—

(*a*) Grasses, *i.e.*, members of the *Graminaceæ* and *Cyperaceæ*.

(*b*) Herbs, bushes, or trees. (*See* Cattle Food and Green Fodder.)

The former are the principal fodder plants, but a few of the latter are beginning to be of importance in Europe and America, and in India of even still greater importance, since the question of grass-supply is becoming so serious. The following may be mentioned as important cattle food-stuffs. The *úrd* (*Dolichos biflorus*), *moth* (*Phaseolus radiatus*), and *guár* (*Cyamopsis psoralioides*) are also important fodder plants, and in the dry climate of Upper India *juar* (*Sorghum vulgare*) is even cultivated as a cattle-fodder. Popularly these are generally spoken of as green-food, and not as fodder, and the two most important families of plants affording such are *Leguminosæ*, or the family of the peas and pulses, and *Cruciferæ*, or the family of the cabbage and the turnip. There are in India, however, many most exceptional instances of green-foods belonging to families the least likely to prove nutritious or even wholesome. The whole subject therefore of fodder and green-food supply requires to be gone into in a much more extended manner than has hitherto been done, and it would seem probable that many useful facts may yet be brought to light. India possesses a large series of indigenous plants which cattle regularly feed on, and the fodder question may be more effectually solved by the cultivation of some wild plant than by attempts to acclimatize exotic *food plants* which at most can be grown during the cold season only, or on certain special and limited tracts of country. Attention might, for example, be directed to the subject of *Bœrhaavia diffusa*, the *gádha purna*; *Amarantus gangeticus*, the *lál-sag*; *A. polygamus*, the *chámpa-natiya*; *A. tristis*, and other allied species. *A. spinosus* enjoys the reputation of increasing the quantity and quality of the milk given by cows fed on it. There are in fact many indigenous plants which the natives can readily point out as those which cattle are fond of, and it would seem desirable that some half-a-dozen plants of this nature should be carefully cultivated with the double object of discovering the degree to which they are capable of improvement under cultivation, and whether cattle fed on such plants as a regular article of diet would be found to thrive. These are facts which can only be discovered by experiment; but of course it should be borne in mind that many of the green-foods lose their nutritious properties when dried like hay or preserved by ensilage. No class of plants can be so successfully preserved as the various grasses, and we may therefore enumerate here the leading Indian fodder-grasses, of most of which samples are shown at the Exhibition. The following are the principal fodder-grasses of India, the scientific names of which have been drawn out from Mr. Duthie's "Grasses," and the economic information derived very largely from Mr. Coldstream's MS. notes on the grasses of Upper India:—

INDIAN FODDER-GRASSES.

315. AGROSTIS ALBA, *Linn.*; Gramineæ. The Fiorin or White Bent Grass. Altitude 13,000 feet.

316. ALOPECURUS AGRESTIS, *Linn.*; Gramineæ. The Slender Fox-tail Grass. Is found on the plains of the Punjáb in damp places. It is described as a good fodder-grass, fresh or dry.

317. A. GENICULATUS, *Linn.* The Fox-tail Grass. Inhabits Northern India from Kumaon to Kashmir.

318. ALOPECURUS PRATENSIS, *Linn.* The Meadow Fox-tail Grass. North-West Himálaya; altitude 5,000 to 8,000 feet, also ascending to 13,000. Common in Kashmir and the Punjáb.

319. ANDROPOGON ISCHÆMUM, *Linn.*; Gramineæ. This is the *palwal* of Saharanpur and *Jarga* of Aligarh and Muttra. It is grown on barren, wet soils, and is considered one of the best

fodder-grasses, especially for making hay. It is eaten by cattle and horses, and the seed is regarded as nutritious. The name *palwal* is also given to *A. punctatus*, *Roxb.*

320. A. LANIGER, *Desf.* This is the *Juncus odoratus* of the older writers—the *búr*, *kháwi*, or *panní* of the Punjáb. When young, this grass may be grazed, will bear stacking, and last for 10 or 12 years. It flavours the milk, however, when much eaten.

321. A. MURICATUS, *Retz.* The Khas-khas or Panni of the Lower Provinces. This grass is eaten by cattle in times of scarcity, but only when it is young, *i.e.*, immediately after the old stems have been burned down; it will not stack. Captain Wingate says this is one of the fodder grasses of Gwalior. (*See* also 901, 989.)

322. A. PERTUSUS, *Willd.* Palwa (*N. W.-P.*; *Pb.*). This is regarded as one of the best grasses for stacking, remaining good for 12 or 13 years. It is described as excellent fodder for bullocks and horses, and is a favourite with buffaloes.

323. A. SCHŒNANTHUS, *Linn.* The Geranium or Rusa grass oil plant. This is not very good for grazing. It grows on swamps. Is wild in Central India, the North-West Provinces, and sparingly so in the Punjáb. It is a tall grass, too coarse to stack, but useful for thatching and for screens. (*See* also 991.)

324. ANTHISTIRIA CILIATA, *Linn.*; Gramineæ. The Kangaroo Grass of Australia or the Musel. This is regarded as one of the most useful of fodder grasses in India, and its cultivation should be extended. It luxuriates in a warm, temperate climate, and is reported to occur at Banda, Saharanpur, Garhwal, and Kumaon, ascending to 7,000 feet in altitude.

325. ANTHISTIRIA POLYSTACHIA, *Roxb.* Gandi (*Pb.*). It grows in swamps, is much eaten by buffaloes, and is fragrant when green. It lasts 10 or 12 years when stacked. Does not grow in situations where *Andropogon laniger* occurs.

326. APLUDA ARISTATA, *Linn.*; Gramineæ. Banjuri (*N.-W. P.*); Goroma (*Beng.*). A creeping grass found in hedges; used as fodder in Bundelkhand.

327. ARISTIDA DEPRESSA, *Retz.*; Gramineæ. Lámp or Lamba (*Pb.*). Mr. Coldstream says this cannot be cut with a scythe, as it is too fine; and is too light to stack. It is, however, particularly relished by cattle, and is nutritious.

328. A. SETACEA, *Retz.* The Shipur gadí, (*Madras*). This is the grass in Madras used for making *tatties*. According to Roxburgh cattle will not eat it, but Dr. Bidie says it is eaten by bullocks.

329. ARUNDINARIA RACEMOSA, *Munro*; Gramineæ. Extensively used in the Eastern Himálaya for fodder. Known in Nepal as *pathiu*. It occurs at an altitude of 7,000 feet.

330. AVENA FATUA, *Linn.*; Gramineæ. The Wild Oat. Collected for fodder. It occurs on the Himálaya, in Ladak, and also in Kumaon; altitude 9,000 to 11,000 feet.

331. A. PRATENSIS, *Linn.* The Meadow Oat Grass. This is found in Lahore, is viewed as a sweet fodder, and is recommended for cultivation on dry clay soils, at an altitude of 8,000 to 10,000 feet.

332. A. SATIVA, *Linn.* The Cultivated Oat. This is frequently cut as a green fodder, but it is only cultivated to a small extent in India. (*See* also 705.)

333. BAMBOO; Gramineæ. The leaves of various species of bamboo are regularly collected and given as fodder, especially to elephants. (*See* also 965.)

334. BROMUS ASPER, *Linn.*; Gramineæ. The Hairy-Stalked Brome Grass. Found on the North-West Himálaya in shady places.

335. B. SCHRADERI, *Kunth.* The Prairie Grass of Australia. This has been introduced by the Superintendent, Botanic Gardens, Saharanpur. Baron von Mueller regards it as one of the richest of all grasses, spreading readily from seed, particularily on fertile and humid soils.

336. CENCHRUS CATHARTICUS, *Del.*; Gramineæ. Bhurt (*N.-W. P.*). A grass of dry, sandy soils, much grazed. The grain, mixed with *bajra*, is eaten by the poorer classes.

337. C. ECHINATUS, *Linn.* Dhaman (*N.-W. P.*); Basla or Lapta (*Pb.*). Considerable difference of opinion exists as to the merits of this grass.

338. C. MONTANUS, *Nees.* Dhaman or Anjan (*Pb.*). An excellent fodder grass.

339. CHLORIS BARBATA, *Swartz.*; Gramineæ. Chhota takria (*Pb.*); Gandi or Gavung (*N.-W. P.*); Kondapulla (*South India*). A grass not much grazed; will keep in stack for four or five years.

340. CHRYSOPOGON ACICULARIS, *Retz.*; Gramineæ. The Chore-kanta (*Beng.*). Cattle do not eat this grass unless when very young; as soon as the spikes appear, they refuse to eat it, and indeed the spiny fruits are a great source of annoyance. Very common in Bengal along with the *Muthá* (No. 345) and the *Ulu* (No. 365).

341. C. GRYLLUS, *Trin.* Is grown in the plains and hills of the Punjáb and the North-West Provinces, and is a useful fodder-grass.

342. COIX LACHRYMA, *Linn.*; Gramineæ. Job's Tears; Sankrú (*Hind.*). Cultivated in Assam and Burma, where the grain is largely consumed as human food. In Bengal it springs up as a weed along with rice, and is cut for fodder. (*See* also 706.)

343. CYNODON DACTYLON, *Pers.*; Gramineæ. The Creeping Panic Grass; Dúb (*Lower India*); Tilla or Khabbal (*Pb.*). The properties of this grass are too well known to require any further notice than has already been given in the opening remarks regarding fodder.

344. CYNOSUROUS CRISTATUS, *Linn.*; Gramineæ. Found in the higher altitudes of the Himálaya, and is particularly valuable for its power to withstand droughts; this is due to the roots penetrating to considerable depths. It is cultivated for hay and fodder.

345. CYPERUS ROTUNDUS, *Linn.*; Cyperaceæ. The Muthá or Mustá. A grass-like Cyperaceæ

eaten by cattle. Very common in Bengal—Calcutta maidan. *Cyperus eleusinoides* is the *Deta* of the North-West Provinces.

346. Dactylis glomerata, *Linn.*; Gramineæ. Is a tall, perennial grass common in the Punjáb and the North-West Provinces Himálayas, and is valued in Europe as a fodder grass for cattle.

347. Eleonurus hirsutus, *Munro*; Gramineæ. Bhanjuri (*N.-W. P.*); Sin, Sewan, or Shewar (*Pb.*). Mr. Coldstream says this is nutritious and good for grazing and stacking. It will last for ten years. It is sweet when young, but becomes hard as it matures. The wilds of Bikanir owe their usefulness to this grass. It is eaten by elephants; grows rapidly, often attaining a height of eight feet. A fibre is prepared from the roots, and made into the brushes by weavers. It is supposed that this is the *Cusa* grass of ancient writers (*see Tod's Rajasthan, II.* 286). The grain is mixed with bajra and made into flour.

348. Eleusine ægyptica, *Pers.*; Gramineæ. Makra-jali (*Lower India*); Bhúra or Therna, madana (*Pb.*); Jharna, makra (*N.-W. P.*). This grass grows wild by roadsides and on pasture lands in the Punjáb and North-West Provinces. It is described as good fodder, cattle being fond of it. It may be stacked. A nearly allied small species (*E. scinda*), the *Bhobra*, is also common in the North-West Provinces. (*See* also 495.)

349. E. corocana, *Gærtn.*; *see* Millets. (*See* also 696.)

350. E. flagellifera, *Nees.* Gurdub (*N.-W. P.*); Ghatil (*Pb.*). This is an abundant creeping grass common on arid parts of the Punjáb. It is well known and useful; will stack for nine or ten years. Regarded as a specially good food for donkeys.

351. E. verticillata, *Roxb.* Therna or Jharna (*Pb.*). It is not very abundant, but is good for cattle, and will stack for twelve to fifteen years.

352. Eragrostis Brownei, *Nees*; Gramineæ. Bharu (*Aligarh*). A perennial grass, frequenting barren wet places; is eaten by cattle and horses.

353. E. ciliaris, *Linn.* A grass met with in the Punjáb, but not abundant; it is regularly grazed.

354. E. cynosuroides, *Retz.* The Dáb or dáboi (*N.-W. P.*); Kusha (*Beng.*); Dib (*Pb.*). A strong, coarse grass common in dry, barren ground and sandy places in the Punjáb, the North-West Provinces, and Sind. Cattle do not eat it as a rule, though it is liked by buffaloes.

355. E. diandra, *Roxb.* Bara bhurbhuri (*Muttra*). This is found in the plains of the Punjáb and North-West Provinces and on the Himálaya at low elevations; it is eaten by cattle, and the seeds are said to be nutritive.

356. Eragrostis pilosa, *Beauv.* Gádar Punch (the Jackal's tail) (*Pb.*). Buffaloes are said to relish this grass.

357. E. plumosa, *Linn.* The Phularwa (*N.-W. P.*). Is eaten by horses and cattle.

358. Festuca duriuscula, *Linn.*; Gramineæ. The Hard Fescue Grass. A good sheep fodder.

359. F. elatior, *Linn.* Met with at Binsár in Kumaon. Muller describes it as "well adapted for permanent pastures, has tender leaves, produces excellent hay, and is early out in the season. It is superior to rye-grass in produce."

360. F. gigantea, *Vill.* Is said in the North-West Himálaya to be a good forest grass.

361. Glyceria fluitans, *R. Br.*; Gramineæ. The Manna Grass. A perennial grass with tender foliage: delights in stagnant water, ditches, &c., covering their surface. Met with in Baspa valley and in Pangi; altitude 9,000 feet.

362. Hemarthria compressa, *R. Br.*; Gramineæ. Ransheru, buksha (*Beng.*). A perennial grass of the plains extending to the Punjáb. Cattle are said to be fond of it.

363. Heteropogon contortus, *R. & S.*; Gramineæ. The Spear Grass; Parba, banda, sarwar, lap (*N.-W. P.*); Sarwala, surwala (*Pb.*); Shervu (*Tel.*). When tender this grass is eaten, but when old it is refused, owing to the barbed fruits. It will keep good in stack for twelve years. This is the main fodder grass of Bandelkhand and of Dang Pahári near Gwalior. It makes good hay when the seeds fall off.

364. Hordeum vulgare, *Linn.*; Gramineæ. The Barley; Jab or jav. (*See* also 703.)

365. Imperata arundinacea, *Cyrill.*; Gramineæ. Ulú (*Beng.*); Usirh, sir, sil, bharwai (*Upper India*). A small grass, inhabiting the plains and hills of Bengal, the North-West Provinces and Sind. Very characteristic of Lower India, as, for example, on the Calcutta maidan. The fields are white with its silky flowers, which appear after the first rains. Only grazed when young; if allowed to mature cattle will not eat it. Much used for thatch.

366. Lolium perenne, *Linn.*; Gramineæ. The Hay or Perennial Rye Grass. Met with in Thibet; altitude 15,000 feet. Extensively grown in Europe along with clover, and is considered the most important of all the fodder grasses.

367. L. temulentum, *Linn.* The Darnel. Inhabits the plains and hills of North-West India. Often a common weed in corn-fields.

368. Melica ciliata, *Linn.*; Gramineæ. A perennial fodder grass met with in Kumaon, particularly desirable for sheep.

369. Oryza sativa, *Linn.*; Gramineæ. The Common Rice. Extensively given as green fodder in India. The straw cut up in small pieces is the cattle-food in the rice-producing provinces. The powder-like substance produced in the process of husking rice, called *kura*, and the water in which rice is boiled, are largely used in Bengal as cattle-food. (*See* also 504, 694, 723.)

370. Panicum antidotale, *Retz.*; Gramineæ. The Gamur or ghiri (*N.-W. P.*); Ghamur, garm, mangrur (*Pb.*); Chiman chárá (*Bomb.*). A tall grass common on the Gangetic plains, and in the Punjáb and Sind. Difference of opinion prevails regarding this grass; it is only eaten when young, but is even then considered bitter and saltish to taste.

371. P. COLONUM, *Linn.* The Shama (*Beng.*); Sanwak or samak (*N.-W. P.*); Samak (*Pb.*). An abundant grass throughout the plains, especially on cultivated soils: cattle are fond of it. This is one of the best grasses for forage, and will remain good in stack for five or six years. The grain is also collected and sold as *kher.*

372. PANICUM CRUS-GALLI, *Linn.* The Dhand or jal-sawank (*N.-W. P.*); Bharti (*Pb.*). Found on the plains, growing on moist soils; ascends to 6,000 feet. This is a coarse species, and cattle are not fond of it. The seeds are collected as an article of diet. The Hindus make *khir* from it on feast days.

373. P. FRUMENTACEUM, *Roxb.* The Shamúla or Sawan. The stems are given to cattle as fodder (*see* Milletts). (*See* also 697.)

374. P. HELOPUS, *Trin.* The Basaunta (*N.-W. P.*); Kuri (*Pb.*). This grass occurs on the plains and on the Himálaya up to 5,000 feet, chiefly on cultivated lands. It is considered a good fodder grass; will last seven years in stack. The grain is eaten by the natives in times of scarcity.

375. P. MILIACEUM, *Linn.* The Chena (*see* Millets). (*See* also 698.)

376. P. MILIARE, *Lamb.* The Lesser Millet; Shamay, kutki (*Hind.*); Chin (*Pb.*). This species grows in fields, and is scarcely met with in the jungles. It is very good for grazing. The seeds are an article of diet, and the straw is given as fodder.

377. P. PSILOPODIUM, *Trin.* Kutki (*N.-W. P.*); Chin. (*Pb.*). A common grass in fields, and to a certain extent cultivated in the North-West, and to a large extent in the Central Provinces under the name of *mijhri.*

378. P. REPENS, *Linn.* A perennial grass suited for river banks and swampy places; cattle are said to be fond of it.

379. P. SANGUINALE, *Linn.* Makur-gali, kewar (*N.-W. P.*); Bara takria (*Pb.*). This species is found on the plains of the North-West Provinces and the Punjáb, ascending the hills; frequent in Nepal. Is regarded as a good grazing grass. It lasts in stack seven to eight years.

380. PASPALUM SCROBICULATUM, *Linn.*; Gramineæ. The Koda (*Beng.*) (*see* Millets). (*See* also 699.)

381. PENNISETUM CENCHROIDES, *Rich.*; Gramineæ. This, like *Cenchrus montanus*, is known in the Punjáb as *Dhamán* and *Ajan.* A common grass on the plains and lower hills of the Punjáb and the North-West Provinces. One of the most nutritious of all the grasses, and very fattening. Good both for grazing and stacking. May be propagated where it occurs by simply loosening the ground after a good fall of rain. Will last fifteen to twenty years, if kept dry. Abundant in some parts of Bikanir, but is one of the first plants to give way to the plough, hence, as a wild plant, it is becoming rare. In Multan the seeds are collected as food.

382. P. TYPHOIDEUM, *Rich.* The spiked Millet or Bajra (*see* Millets). The green stalks chopped are used as fodder.

383. PHLEUM PRATENSE, *Linn.*; Gramineæ. The Timothy or Meadow Cats-tail grass. This plant is met with in the Himálaya; is considered one of the most valuable fodder grasses, especially for heavy moist soils.

384. PHRAGMITES COMMUNIS, *Trin.*; Gramineæ. The Common Reed; Dila (*Pb.*). In Ladak this is eaten by cattle, and in Lahoul is used for roofing. Sandals are made from the stems.

385. POA ANNUA, *Linn.*; Gramineæ. The Chirua (*N.-W. P.*). A good pasture grass, met with in the plains and hills of the Punjáb and North-West Provinces; is common in Europe.

386. P. PRATENSIS, *Linn.* The Smooth-stalked Meadow Grass. Found in Kashmir and Thibet. In Europe this is considered a good fodder grass, and valuable, as affording early hay.

387. POLLINIA ERIOPODA, *Hance.*, Gramineæ. The Bhábar Grass. Considerable interest has recently been raised in this grass as a paper material. It is regarded as a good fodder. (*See* also 937, 976.)

388. SACCHARUM SARA, *Roxb.*; Gramineæ. The Sara or shar. This, as indeed most other species of the genus, may be eaten as fodder when young or before flowering. (*See* also 938, 977.)

389. SACCHARUM SPONTANEUM, *Linn.* Káns, Káusi, káhi (*Pb.*); Rara (*Lucknow*). It is given when young as fodder to buffaloes.

390. SCIRPUS KYSOOR, *Roxb.*; Cyperaceæ. The Kasuri (*Hind.*); Kesur (*Beng.*); Kaseru (*Pb.*). A weed common on the borders of lakes and ponds. When fresh this is regarded as good forage. The tuberous roots are eaten by the poorer people.

391. SETARIA GLAUCA, *Beauv.*; Gramineæ. Bhandra or dissi (*N.-W. P.*). A common grass on the plains and lower hills of India.

392. S. ITALICA, *Beauv.* German Millet (*see* Millets). (*See* also 701.)

393. S. VERTICILLATA, *Beauv.* Kútta chirchitta, (*N.-W. P.*); Dora-byara (*Hind.*); Chirchira (*Pb.*). A grass found on the plains and hills of the Punjáb, and ascending the Himálaya to 6,000 feet in Naini Tal; also found in Nepal. It delights in a rich soil, especially on rubbish heaps. Cattle eat it when young or before the flowers appear, and the seeds are a favourite with birds. The rough awns representing the sterile flowers make it unpalatable to cattle.

394. SORGHUM HALPENSE, *Pers.*; Gramineæ. Bájra or Bara of *Bandelkhand*; Barú or Braham (*Pb.*). This is described by Muller as a rich, perennial grass. In Hazara, however, it is stated that fatal head affections often result from eating it, especially when young. It is common about cultivated lands, and is frequently grazed by cattle, and relished: will remain in stack for five years. The seed is collected and mixed with *bájra* flour, and in this form it enters largely into the food of the poorer classes of Bikanir. (*Tod's Rajasthan*, II., page 170.)

395. SORGHUM SACCHARATUM, *Pers.* The Chinese Sugar-cane. The grass is used as a valuable fodder for cattle. (*See* also 726.)

396. S. VULGARE, *Pers.* The Great Millet or Juar (*see* Millets). The dry stalks and leaves are chopped and given as cattle fodder. Indeed, it is sometimes grown solely for this purpose, the green stalks, before flowering, being cut up and given to cattle. In years of drought the stunted half-dried plants are said to become poisonous. (*See* also 702.)

397. SPOROBOLUS PALLIDUS, *Linn.*; Gramineæ. The Palanji (*Pb.*). This grass is not valued as a fodder, but the grain is eaten in times of scarcity.

398. S. TENACISSIMUS, *Beauv.* Usar-ki-ghas, kalusra (*N.-W. P.*); Kheo (*Pb.*); Tæmagerika (*Tel.*). This is the grass of the barren or *usar* lands. It is both good for grazing and for stacking, and will last for fourteen or fifteen years. Its long roots penetrate the soil in search of moisture. It is particularly good for horses.

399. TRAGUS RACEMOSUS, *Hall.*; Gramineæ. Bharchinti, charchinte choti (*Pb.*). This is common on cultivated lands, but is too small to be stacked. It is, however, a very nutritious grass, much grazed during the rains.

400. TRITICUM SATIVUM, *Linn.*; Gramineæ. The Wheat. The straw affords a valuable fodder for cattle. (*See* also 695, 727.)

401. ZEA MAYS, *Linn.*; Gramineæ. The Indian-corn. The green stalks are given as cattle fodder. (*See* also 704.)

CATTLE FOOD AND GREEN FODDER.

The herbs, bushes, or trees, the leaves and twigs of which are given to cattle, may be enumerated as follows:—

402. ABIES WEBBIANA, *Lindl.*; Coniferæ. The Himálayan Silver Fir. In the Panjáb Himálayas the twigs and leaves are cut and stored for use in winter. (*See* also 3.)

403. ACACIA ARABICA, *Willd.*; Leguminosæ. The well-known Babul tree. This is one of the most valuable of fodder-yielding trees. The green pods, the tender shoots, and the leaves are given as fodder for cattle, sheep, goats, and camels. The tree thrives in a dry climate, and is therefore specially valuable during a season of drought when other cattle-food fails. The road-side babúl trees of the North-West Provinces saved a large number of cattle from starvation in 1876-77, when a severe drought prevailed in many parts of the North-West Provinces.

The leaves of *Acacia Jacquemontii* (Benth.), and *A. modesta* (Wall.), and the pods of *A. leucophlæa* (Willd.), are also used as fodder. (*See* also 4, 484, 1051, 1128.)

404. ACER PICTUM, *Thunb.*; Sapindaceæ. A plant of the North-West Himálaya. The branches are lopped for fodder, as are also the branches of *A. villosum* (Wall.). (*See* also 11.)

405. ÆSCULUS INDICA, *Colebr.*; Sapindaceæ. The Indian Horse Chestnut. The thick foliage of this tree is greedily eaten by cattle, and is largely used as fodder in the Himálaya. (*See* also 16, 628.)

406. ALBIZZIA LEBBEK, *Benth.*; Leguminosæ. A large tree found in most parts of India. The leaves are used as camel fodder. The leaves of *A. odoratissima* (Benth.), and *A. stipulata* (Boivin) are also used as fodder. (*See* also 20.)

407. ALHAGI MAURORUM, *Desv.*; Leguminosæ. In Persian this shrub is called *shutar-khár*, or camel food, on account of its thriving in the deserts of Africa and Western Asia, and blossoming in the hot season while other plants die, thus affording food to camels at a time when other sources fail. It abounds in the arid tracts of Central India and the Punjáb. (*See* also 707.)

408. ANABASIS MULTIFLORA, *Moq.*; Chenopodiaceæ. Found in Punjáb; camels are fond of the plant.

409. BALANITES ROXBURGHII, *Planch.*; Simarubeæ. A small tree growing in the drier parts of India and Burma. The young twigs and leaves are browsed by cattle. (*See* also 40.)

410. BASSIA LATIFOLIA, *Roxb.*; Sapotaceæ. The well-known *mahuá* tree, the flowers of which are extensively used for the manufacture of country spirits; when given to cattle they are very fattening. (*See* also 45, 584, 709, 995, 1091.)

411. BAUHINIA PURPUREA, *Linn.*; Leguminosæ. A large tree found all over India. The leaves are given to cattle as fodder. The leaves of *B. racemosa* (*Lam.*) are eaten by buffaloes. (*See* also 46.)

412. BETULA BHOJPATTRA, *Wall.*; Cupuliferæ. A tree growing on the higher ranges of the Himálaya. The leaves are lopped for cattle-fodder. (*See* also 50.)

413. BOMBAX MALABARICUM, *DC.*; Malvaceæ. The Red Silk Cotton Tree. Grows all over India. The leaves and twigs are lopped for fodder. (*See* also 53, 908, 958, 1059.)

414. BRIEDELIA MONTANA, *Willd.*; Euphorbiaceæ. A tree of the sub-Himálaya. The leaves are used for fodder.

415. B. RETUSA, *Spreng.* A large tree of the sub-Himálaya. The leaves are used for cattle-fodder. (*See* also 56.)

416. BUTEA FRONDOSA, *Roxb.*; Leguminosæ. A tree found all over India and Burma. The leaves are used for cattle food, and are specially liked by buffaloes and elephants. In 1876-77 when drought prevailed in the North-West Provinces, the leaves of this tree were of great help to the cultivators in saving their cattle from starvation. (*See* also 59, 1136.)

417. CALLIGONUM POLYGONOIDES, *Linn.*; Polygonaceæ. A shrub found in Punjáb and Sind. The young shoots are relished by goats and camels.

418. CARDUUS NUTANS, *Linn.*; Compositæ. The Thistle plant. Eaten by camels greedily.

Also used as a cattle fodder in dry seasons, but the spines have to be removed.

419. CAROXYLON GRIFFITHII, *Moq.*; Chenopodiaceæ. A bush of the Punjáb, and a favourite food of camels, for which purpose, it is said, the plant is taken in large quantities to Multán.

420.* CARTHAMUS TINCTORIUS, *Linn.*; Compositæ. The plant is cultivated for its flowers—the safflower of commerce. Seed yields a lamp oil; they are given to fatten poultry. (*See* also 1005, 1139.)

421. CEDRELA TOONA, *Roxb.*; Meliaceæ. A large tree found in the plains. Seeds are used to feed cattle.

422. CEDRUS DEODARA, *Loudon*; Coniferæ. The Himálayan Cedar. Young shoots and plants eagerly browsed by goats. (*See* also 79, 1065.)

423. CELASTRUS SENAGALENSIS, *Lam.*; Celastrineæ. A spiny shrub of North-West India. The leaves used for fodder.

424. CELTIS AUSTRALIS, *Linn.*; Urticaceæ. A Himálayan tree, largely planted for fodder; said to improve the quality of milk. (*See* also 80.)

425.* CERATONIA SILIQUA, *L.*; Leguminosæ. The Carob tree. Lately introduced into India. Pods used as fodder.

426. CISSUS CARNOSA, *Lam.*; Ampelideæ. A climbing plant found at the foot of the Punjáb Himálaya; it is eaten by camels.

427. CORCHORUS OLITORIUS, *Linn.*; Tiliaceæ. The Jute plant. The leaves are eaten by cattle when the plant is cut for fibre, but generally they are allowed to rot in the field to serve as manure. (*See* also 547, 961, 967.)

428. CROTALARIA JUNCEA, *Linn.*; Leguminosæ. Sunn Hemp. This plant is largely cultivated for its fibre. When cut the leaves and tops are given to cattle. (*See* also 913a, 968.)

429. DAUCUS CAROTA, *Linn.*; Umbelliferæ. The Carrot. The leaves are given to cattle. The carrot is a valuable crop in seasons of drought, when the roots are used as human food and the leaves as fodder. Horses are very fond of carrots.

430. ERUCA SATIVA, *Lam.*; Cruciferæ. Cultivated to a small extent for its seed, from which a lamp oil is extracted. The crop is sometimes cut green and given to cattle, mixed with bad dried straw to give freshness to the food. (*See* also 665, 1015.)

431. FICUS BENGALENSIS, *Linn.*; Urticaceæ. The Banyan tree. The leaves and branches are largely used as elephant food. Other species of Ficus, *e.g. F. cordifolia* (Roxb.), *F. hispida* (Linn. f.), *F. nemoralis* (Wall.), *F. religiosa* (Linn.), *F. Roxburghii* (Wall.), *F. virgata* (Roxb.), &c., are also used as fodder. (*See* also 131.)

432. FLACOURTIA SEPIARIA, *Roxb.*; Bixineæ. A spiny shrub, the leaves of which are thrashed out for cattle fodder.

433. GARUGA PINNATA, *Roxb.*; Burseraceæ. A large weed of India and Burma. The leaves are used as fodder, especially for elephants. (*See* also 138.)

434. GMELINA ARBOREA, *Roxb.*; Verbenaceæ. A large tree, the leaves of which are used as fodder; deer are very fond of them. (*See* also 142.)

435. GREWIA ASIATICA, var. VESTITA, *Wall.*; Tiliaceæ. A small tree, found in the sub-Himálaya, Bengal, Central India, and Burma. The branches are lopped for fodder. (*See* also 144.)

436. HARDWICKIA BINATA, *Roxb.*; Leguminosæ. A large tree, found in the dry forests of South and Central India. The leaves are used as fodder. (*See* also 146, 921.)

437. HYMENODICTYON EXCELSUM, *Wall.*; Rubiaceæ. A large tree of the Western Himálaya, and South and Central India; the leaves are used as fodder. (*See* also 154, 809.)

438. ILEX DIPYRENA, *Wall.*; Ilicineæ. A small tree of the Himálaya. The leaves are used as fodder for sheep. (*See* also 155.)

439. IRIS KUMAONENSIS, *Wall.*; Irideæ. An herb common in the Punjáb Himálaya. In Ladák, the leaves are used for fodder.

440. JUGLANS REGIA, *Linn.*; Juglandeæ. The Walnut Tree. The twigs and leaves are used for fodder. (*See* also 157, 639, 1027.)

441. LAGENARIA VULGARIS, *Seringe*; Cucurbitaceæ. The Bottle-gourd. A climbing plant, cultivated all over India for its fruit, which is eaten as a vegetable. It is given to cows, cooked with rice, and is said to increase the yield of milk. (*See* also 526.)

442. LATHYRUS APHACA, *Linn.*; Leguminosæ. A plant, growing as a weed with the cold-weather crops. It is often pulled up and given to cattle as fodder.

443. L. SATIVUS, *Linn.* Chiefly cultivated as a green fodder, but it often appears as a weed if other crops are allowed to cover the fields after the removal of the crops. (*See* also 686.)

444. LONICERA HYPOLEUCA, *Dcne.*; Caprifoliaceæ. A small shrub of the arid tracts of the Punjáb Himálaya. Goats eat the leaves and are said to fatten on them. The leaves of *L. quinquelocularis* are also used as cattle fodder.

445. LYCIUM EUROPÆUM, *Linn.*; Solanaceæ. A thorny shrub of the drier plains of the Punjáb, Sind, &c. Camels and goats browse the plant.

446. MANGIFERA INDICA, *Linn.*; Anacardiaceæ. The Mango Tree. A tree cultivated all over India for its fruit. The green leaves were extensively used as fodder in the North-West Provinces during the drought of 1876–77. Cattle fed on them become diseased and their urine then affords the yellow peori dye. (*See* also 171, 446, 816.)

447. MEDICAGO DENTICULATA, *Willd.*; Leguminosæ. A field-weed in the plains of Northern India; largely gathered for fodder, and considered good for milch cows.

448. M. FALCATA, *Linn.* The Purple Medic or Lucerne. Cultivated for fodder in the Western Himálaya. *Medicago Sativa*, probably a cultivated variety of the above, is grown for fodder in many parts of India.

449. MEDICAGO LUPULINA, *Linn.* The Hop, or Black Medick, or Non-such. A common weed, frequently collected for fodder. It mixes well with grasses and clovers for artificial pastures.

450. MELIA AZADIRACHTA, *Linn.*; Meliaceæ. The Ním or Margosa tree. A tree found everywhere in India. In Hindustan, the leaves are largely used as camel fodder. The fruit of *M. Azedarach* (Linn.) is greedily eaten by goats and sheep. (*See* also 175, 450, 721, 817.)

451. MELILOTUS PARVIFLORA, *Desf.*; Legu-

minosæ. Found in most parts of India. The leaves are used for fodder and considered good for milch cows.

452. MUSA PARADISIACA, *Linn.*; Scitamineæ. The Plantain. The plantain tree, chopped into small pieces, is largely used as fodder in many parts of India. (*See* also 532, 606, 933, 973.)

453. MYRICARIA ELEGANS, *Royle*; Tamariscineæ. A small bush of the Western Himálaya. The twigs of this plant and of *M. germanica* (Desv.) are browsed by sheep and goats.

454. ODINA WODIER, *Roxb.*; Anacardiaceæ. A moderate-sized tree found in the forests of India and Burma. The branches are cut for fodder, especially for elephants. (*See* also 197.)

455. OLEA CUSPIDATA, *Royle*; Oleaceæ. A moderate-sized tree of the North-West Himálayas. The leaves are given to goats as fodder. (*See* also 198.)

456. OUGEINIA DALBERGIOIDES, *Benth.*; Leguminosæ. Found in the sub-Himálayan tracts, in Central India, and the West coast. The branches are lopped for fodder. (*See* also 199.)

457. OXYBAPHUS HIMALAICUS, *Edge.*; Nyctagineæ. A scrambling plant with a large carrot-like root, which is collected for winter fodder.

458.* PARKINSONIA ACULEATA, *Linn.*; Leguminosæ. The Jerusalem Thorn. A small tree naturalised in India. In Punjáb, the small branches are cut and given to goats as fodder.

459. PONGAMIA GLABRA, *Vent.*; Leguminosæ. A tree found all over India. Cattle are fond of the leaves. (*See* also 216, 839.)

460. POPULUS BALSAMIFERA, *Linn.*; Salicineæ. The Tacamahac. A large tree of the Himálayas. The branches lopped for fodder. The leaves of *P. ciliata* (Wall.), and *P. euphratica* (Olivier), are used as fodder for goats.

461. P. CILIATA, *Wall.* A large tree of the Himálayas. The leaves are used as fodder for goats. (*See* also 217.)

462. PREMNA INTEGRIFOLIA, *Linn.*; Verbenaceæ. A small tree of Northern India. The leaves of this plant and of *P. latifolia* (Roxb.) are a good fodder for cattle. (*See* also 840.)

463. * PROSOPIS DULCIS, Leguminosæ. Algaroba or Paray. An introduced plant. The succulent pods of this species and of *P. pubescens*, the screw mesquit bean, are largely used to feed cattle. *P. spicigera* (Linn.) is a native of the dry zones of India; its pods are used as fodder for camels, cattle, and goats.

464. PSORALEA PLICATA, *Delile*; Leguminosæ. A shrub of the arid plains of Punjáb; camels are fond of it.

465. PTEROCARPUS MARSUPIUM, *Roxb.*; Leguminosæ. A large tree of Central and South India. The leaves are a favourite food of cattle and goats, and are therefore in great demand. (*See* also 225.)

466. PUTRANJIVA ROXBURGHII, *Wall.*; Euphorbiaceæ. A moderate-sized, evergreen tree found in many parts of India. Leaves are used as fodder.

467. QUERCUS DILITATA, *Lindl.*; Cupuliferæ. A large tree of the Himálaya. The leaves are given to sheep and goats as fodder. The leaves of *Q. lanuginosa* (Don), and *Q. semecarpifolia* (Smith), are used for similar purposes. (*See* also 230.)

468. RHAZYA STRICTA, *Dcne.*; Apocynaceæ. A small shrub abundant in the Trans-Indus tracts. The leaves are very bitter but are used as fodder for goats after steeping for some days.

469. SACCOPETALUM TOMENTOSUM, *Hook f. & T. T.*; Anonaceæ. A large tree found in many parts of India. The leaves are used as fodder. (*See* also 243.)

470. SALIX ALBA, *Linn.*; Salicineæ. A large tree cultivated in the Western Himálaya. The branches are lopped for fodder. *S. Daphnoides* (Vill.), *S. elegans* (Wall.), and *S. tetrasperma*, Himálayan plants, used as fodder.

471. SALVADORA OLEOIDES, *Linn.*; Salvadoraceæ. A large, evergreen shrub of the Punjáb and Sind. The leaves are used as fodder for camels. The shoots and leaves of *S. persica* are used for the same purpose. (*See* also 245.)

472. SAPINDUS MUKOROSSI, *Gærtn.*; Sapindaceæ. A tree cultivated in Northern India. The leaves are given to cattle as fodder.

473. SAURAUJA NEPALENSIS, *DC.*, Ternstrœmiaceæ. A moderate-size tree of the Himálaya. The leaves are lopped for cattle fodder.

474. SESBANIA ÆGYPTIACA, *Pers.*; Leguminosæ. A shrub cultivated in many parts of India. The leaves and branches are lopped for cattle fodder.

475. SONCHUS OLERACEUS, *Linn.*; Compositæ. Milk Thistle. A common weed throughout India. Cattle are fond of it.

476. TECOMA UNDULATA, *G. Don.*; Bignoniaceæ. An evergreen shrub, common in the Sulaiman and Salt ranges and Western India. The leaves are used as cattle fodder. (*See* also 276.)

477. TERMINALIA BELERICA, *Roxb.*; Combretaceæ. Myrobalans. A large tree common in the plains. In Kangra, the leaves are considered the best fodder for milch cows. (*See* also 279, 510, 1185.)

478. TRIFOLIUM FRAGIFERUM, *Linn.*; Leguminosæ. Strawberry-headed clover. The plant is found in Kashmir and used as cattle food. *T. Partense* (Linn.), the red or broad leaved clover, is regarded as a good cropper where commoner clover had failed. *T. repens* (Linn.), is a valuable fodder plant, as it can be grown on dry and thin soils.

479. TRIGONELLA FŒNUM-GRÆCUM, *Linn.*; Leguminosæ. The Fenugreek. A small herbaceous plant, cultivated for its seeds, which are used as a condiment. They are also used to impart a pleasant smell to hay, or to render palatable damaged hay. (*See* also 678.)

480. TURPINIA POMIFERA, *DC.*; Sapindaceæ. A moderate-sized tree of Eastern Bengal. The leaves are used as fodder. (*See* also 289.)

481. ULMUS CAMPESTRIS, *Linn.*; Urticaceæ. The Elm. A large tree of the Punjáb Himálaya. The leaves afford good fodder, and the tree is often severely lopped on this account. *U. integrifolia* (Roxb.), and *U. Wallichiana* (Planch.), are also lopped for the same purpose.

482. VILLARSIA NYMPHOIDES, *Vent.*; Gentianaceæ. The plant is common in Kashmír about the lakes and is very largely used as fodder.

483. ZIZYPHUS NUMMULARIA, *W. & A.*; Rhamneæ. A spiny shrub, common in drier parts of west and south India. The leaves are beaten off the branches and given to cattle where fodder is scarce. (*See* also 515.).

HUMAN FOOD IN TIMES OF SCARCITY AND FAMINE.

484. ACACIA ARABICA, *Willd.*; Leguminosæ. The Indian Gum Arabic; Babul, kikar (*Hind.*, *Beng.*). The tree is wild in Sind, Rajputana, Guzerat, and the Northern Deccan, and common everywhere throughout the plains of India. The gum is highly nutritious, and in times of scarcity is much used as an article of food. (*See* also 4, 403, 1051, and 1128.)

485. A. LEUCOPHLÆA, *Willd.* Safed-kikar (*Hind.*). This tree is found on the plains of the Punjáb from Lahore to Delhi, and in the forests of Central and South India and Burma. The young pods and seeds and even the bark are eaten in times of scarcity. (*See* also 7, 1130.)

486. ALOE VERA, *Linn.*; var. OFFICINALIS; Liliaceæ. The Indian Aloe; Ghrita-kumári (*Beng.*). This variety is met with in a semi-wild condition in Bengal and the North-West Provinces. The pulp of the leaves is eaten by the poorer people in times of famine. (*See* also 750.)

487. ASPHODELUS FISTULOSUS, *Linn.*; Liliaceæ. A common plant abundant in the Punjáb plains; eaten as a vegetable in times of scarcity.

488. BAMBUSA ARUNDINACEA, *Ritz.*; Gramineæ. The Bamboo; Bans (*Beng.*, *Hind.*). The seed of this and other species of bamboo resembles unhusked rice. The grain is of great advantage to the poorer people when their crops fail. (*See* also 875, 903.)

489. BŒRHAAVIA DIFFUSA, *Linn.*; Nyctagineæ. The Spreading Hogweed; Gádha Púrna (*Beng.*). A troublesome weed found all over India. The leaves are eaten by the Santáls as a vegetable, and by the people of India generally during the times of famine. (*See* also 545.)

490. BETULA ACUMINATA, *Wall.*; Cupuliferæ. The Nagas of Manipur cut off the inner bark and sun-dry it into biscuits, which are eaten as an article of food.

491. CASSIA TORA, *Linn.*; Leguminosæ. The fœtid Cassia; Chákunda (*Beng.*). A gregarious undershrub, found everywhere in Bengal. The leaves are eaten during famine by the Santáls. (*See* also 779, 1141.)

492. COMMELINA BENGALENSIS, *L.*; Commelinaceæ. Kánchurá (*Beng.*). The leaves are eaten by the poor people as a pot-herb in times of scarcity.

493. DIOSPYROS TOMENTOSA, *Roxb.*; Ebenaceæ. This tree is found in the northern parts of Bengal and in the Punjáb. The kernels of the fruits and also the leaves are eaten by the people of Chutia Nagpur during famine.

494. EHRETIA LÆVIS, *Roxb.*; Boragineæ. A tree of the Sulaiman Range, Punjáb, sub-Himálayan Tract, Oudh, Bengal, Central and South India, and Burma. The inner bark is eaten in times of famine.

495. ELEUSINE ÆGYPTIACA, *Pers.*; Gramineæ. A common grass on the plains of the North-West Provinces and the Punjáb. Stewart says that the grain is eaten in times of famine. (*See* also 348.)

496. FICUS RELIGIOSA, *Linn.*; Urticaceæ. The Peepul Tree. The young leaf-buds are eaten in Central India, and, indeed, in most parts of India, during times of scarcity. (*See* also 1107.)

497. FLEMINGIA CONGESTA, *Roxb.*; Luguminosæ. Bara-salpan, (*Beng.*, *Hind.*). An erect, woody shrub of the pea family, common in the thickets and forests of the warmer parts of India. The seeds are eaten by the Santáls and other Chutia Nagpur tribes during famine. (*See* also 1152.)

498.* HIBISCUS SABDARIFFA, *Linn.*; Malvaceæ. A small, bushy plant cultivated in many parts of India. The capsules are eaten in times of famine. (*See* also 602.)

499. IPOMÆA ERIOCARPA, *Br.*; Convolvulaceæ. This plant is said to be eaten as a pot-herb in times of famine.

500. LOBELIA TRIGONA, *Roxb.*; Lobeliaceæ. An annual herb common in many parts of India. The leaves are eaten by the Santáls in times of scarcity.

501. MALVA PARVIFLORA, *Linn.*; Malvaceæ. A small, spreading herb in Upper Bengal, North-West Himálaya, the Punjáb, and Sind. The plant is frequently eaten as a pot-herb in times of scarcity.

502. MELOCHIA CORCHORIFOLIA, *Linn.*; Sterculiaceæ. An erect, branching herb or undershrub, generally distributed in the hotter parts of India from Kumaon (altitude 4,000 feet) to Sikkim, Malacca, and Ceylon. The leaves are eaten during scarcity.

503. NYMPHÆA STELLATA, *Willd.*; Nymphæaceæ. Common throughout the warmer parts of India. The roots and seeds are eaten, especially in times of scarcity.

504. ORYZA SATIVA, *Linn.*; Gramineæ. The wild forms of rice. Wild rice is very plentiful in the marshes and tanks of Bengal. It grows with marvellous rapidity, keeping above water and spreading all over the marsh. Grain is regularly collected and eaten, especially in times of famine. (*See* also 369, 694, 723.)

505. PANDANUS ODORATISSIMUS, *Willd.*; Pandaneæ. Keura (*Hind.*); Kéa (*Beng.*). A common, much-branched shrub, frequently planted on account of the powerful fragrance of its flowers. The lower pulpy parts of the drupes are eaten by the natives in times of scarcity.

506. SHOREA ROBUSTA, *Gærtn.*; Dipterocarpeæ. The Sál Tree. The fruit is eaten by the Santáls in times of scarcity; the seeds are regularly eaten in a certain preparation with *mahuá* flowers. (*See* also 255, 1081.)

507. Sida humilis, *Willd.*, var. morifolia, *Cav.*; Malvaceæ. An herb or under-shrub generally distributed throughout the hotter parts of India. The leaves are eaten by the Santáls in times of scarcity.

508. Spermacoce hispida, *Linn.*; Rubiaceæ. An herb or under-shrub found throughout India, from the Western Himálaya at Simla, ascending to 3,000 feet to Assam, and southward to Ceylon and Singapore. The leaves are used by the Santáls as an article of food in times of scarcity.

509. Suœda indica, *Moq.*; Chenopodiaceæ. A plant commonly met with on the salt ground near the sea. Roxburgh says that the leaves are very wholesome and form an essential article of diet with the poor during times of scarcity.

510. Terminalia belerica, *Roxb.*; Combretaceæ. Bahera (*Hind.*, *Beng.*). A large, deciduous tree, found throughout India, common in the plains and lower hills, extending to Ceylon and Malacca. The kernels of the fruit are eaten in times of famine. (*See* also 279, 477, 1185.)

511. Trianthema crystallina, *Vahl.*; Ficoideæ. A prostrate-branched herb, met with throughout India, from the Punjáb to Ceylon, excepting Bengal. The seeds are eaten in the Punjáb in times of famine.

512. Tribulus alatus. *Delile*; Zygophylleæ. A prostrate herb of Sind and the Punjáb. The seeds form a famine food.

513. T. terrestris, *Linn.* A low, trailing annual, common throughout India. The small, spiny fruits are said to have constituted the chief food of the people during the Madras famine.

514. Triumfetta rhomboidea, *Jacq.*; Tiliaceæ. The plant is eaten as a pot-herb in times of scarcity.

515. Zizyphus nummularia, *W. & A.*; Rhamneæ. A plant of the drier parts of the Punjáb, Guzerat, Deccan, and Konkan. (*See* also 483.)

THE NATIVE SHOPS.

On the left side of the Imperial Court will be found four small shops similar to those found in the average Indian village. These have been arranged so as to display the surplus stock of the exhibits which are shown in the Index Collection and arranged in Sub-Courts VIII., IX., X., XI., XII., and XVI. These shops have been constructed of bamboo and thatched with Indian straw, according to the system commonly seen in Bengal. The first shop is that of The Grain Merchant; the second The Fruit Seller; the third The Kabuli Dealer in Dried Fruits and Nuts, and the fourth The Spice Seller and Druggist.

On the opposite side of the path will be found The Indian Fish-wife, with around her a collection of models in clay of the more common fresh water fish of India.

SUB-COURT VIII.

This Sub-Court contains the specimens which in the Classified List are referred to Division I., Section 6. These may be grouped into (a) Vegetables and (b) Tubers.

VEGETABLES.

The vegetables met with in India may be referred to two well-marked sections: (*a*) indigenous, (*b*) introduced. The former are cultivated throughout the year, the majority ripening in the hot season, while the latter are sown and matured during the cold season. European fruits and vegetables, though often growing luxuriantly in India, rarely attain their peculiar and characteristic flavour. This doubtless is due, in a measure, to the fact of their being sown in autumn, thus maturing with the increasing heat of the approaching summer. The cabbage, cauliflower, turnip-stemmed cabbage, turnip, beet-root, radish, carrot, asparagus, artichoke, lettuce, onion, &c., are all regularly cultivated, but, with the exception of the cabbage, cauliflower, and radish, European vegetables are not eaten by the natives of India. The onion is forbidden because of some supposed relation to beef; this is the more surprising, since in some parts of India the onion succeeds admirably, Patna and Bombay onions being famous and even exported to Australia. The immense internal trade which has within recent years arisen in cabbage, cauliflower, and radish, especially in the vicinity of large towns, is remarkable; but these vegetables are rarely eaten by the natives of India until they are overgrown, and thus coarse from a European point of view.

Of the introduced tropical vegetables, the most important are the *brinjal* or egg-apple (*Solanum Melongena*), the *ochro* or ladies' finger (*Hibiscus esculentus*), and the Indian pumpkin or white melon (*Benincasa cerifera*). The last mentioned is supposed to be a native of Japan and of Java, and the two former of the West Indies.

Of the indigenous vegetables, India is the home of the cucumber and the melon, with a large series of allied plants, all of which yield valued fruits and vegetables. Just as Europe may be described as the home of the Cabbage family (*Cruciferæ*), so India may be viewed as the region of the Cucumber family (*Cucurbitaceæ*) of vegetables. These are the two most important kinds of Old World vegetables, and to the New World we are indebted for the Potato family (*Solanaceæ*), affording the potato, the egg-apple, and the tomato, as well as tobacco. In some parts of India the potato is grown most successfully, but as a rule the natives prefer the small wet ones to the better qualities. They are eaten hot in curries or cold in the form of a sweetmeat prepared by boiling the potato in ghee and flavouring ingredients.

Enough has been said, however, to indicate the leading features of the Indian vegetables and pot-herbs shown at the Exhibition. As nearly the whole of the pot-herbs are wild plants which require no cultivation, they illustrate one of the most striking features of India, for in few countries in the world are so many edible products to be procured for the trouble of collecting—edible products, too, which enter largely into the dietary of the mass of the people.

It is almost impossible to arrive at any definite idea as to the extent of the internal trade in vegetables. Nothing is more characteristic of the Indian village than its bazar or market-place, and it would be difficult to find a bazar where the egg-apple, the melon, the cucumber, the pumpkin, and the radish were not offered for sale alongside of rice, plantains, and chillies. Indeed, the potato, and, in the cold season, the cabbage and orange, are now offered in nearly every village bazar.

The published reports of the foreign trade in vegetables are mixed up with those of fruits, but, separating the two as far as possible, the following may be given as the exports of vegetables from India during the past five years:—1880-1, Rs. 204,604; 1881-2, Rs. 208,736; 1882-3, Rs. 243,942; 1883-4, Rs. 212,580; 1884-5, Rs. 219,630.

The bulk of the exports go from Bombay.

It is difficult to carry to Europe actual examples of Indian fruits and vegetables; a few, however, are shown, but the collection will be found to be supplemented by a series of accurate clay models both in SUB-COURTS VIII. AND IX.*

An enumeration of the *ságs* or green vegetables (*e.g.*, spinach) of India, as far as the aboriginal tribes are concerned, would mean a list of nearly one-half the plants found in the forests of any one region. There are, however, a large number, both cultivated and wild, which are regularly eaten and sold in bazars. Viewing these as of minor importance, the following are the principal vegetables shown in SUB-COURT VIII., arranged in the alphabetical order of their scientific names. No difficulty should be experienced in discovering the specimens, since they also are arranged alphabetically.

DIVISION I.—THE PRINCIPAL VEGETABLES.

516.* BENINCASA CERIFERA, *Savi.*; Cucurbitaceæ. The White Melon or Indian Pumpkin; Kumrá (*Hind.*). A climbing plant, cultivated all over India, frequently running over huts. Supposed to be originally a native of Japan and Java. This plant requires to be carefully distinguished from *Cucurbita Pepo* (DC.), but it may be known by the fruit being cylindrical, 1 to 1½ feet long, bright green, ultimately becoming smooth and covered with a bluish white, waxy bloom; flesh white. It is used in the following ways: (*a*) as a vegetable, (*b*) as a curry, and (*c*) as a sweetmeat called *hashmi*.

517. CUCUMIS MELO, *Linn.* The Sweet Melon; Kharbúja, Kharmuj (*Beng.*). Native of North-West India, Beluchistán, and perhaps West tropical Africa. It includes numerous varieties, which present differences both in shape and use of the fruit. Extensively cultivated in the North-West Provinces, on the sandy basins of rivers. From an agricultural point of view this is the most important species of the family. The flesh of the fruit is usually sweetish and pleasant, and is eaten by Europeans as well as by natives. (*See* also 637.)

518. C. MELO, *Linn.*, var. MOMORDICA (*sp. Roxb.*). This is one of the most marked varieties of *C. Melo.* It differs from the preceding chiefly in the form and nature of the fruit, which is cylindrical, quite smooth, 1 to 2 feet long, 3 to 6 inches in diameter. Dr. Roxburgh says of it: "The fruit is much eaten both by natives and Europeans. When young they are a good substitute for the common cucumber, and when ripe (after bursting spontaneously), with the addition of a little sugar, they are little inferior to the melon, and reckoned very wholesome."

519. C. MELO, *Linn.*, var. UTILISSIMUS (*sp. Roxb.*). The Kakri, Kánkur (*Hind.*, *Beng.*). Cultivated during the hot weather and the rains in Upper Bengal, the North-West Provinces and the Punjáb. This is an important article of food with the poorer classes during the hot weather months.

520. C. SATIVUS, *Linn.* The Cucumber; Khira (*Hind.*); Sasa (*Beng.*). A native of Northern India. The hot weather form has small egg-shaped fruits, and is sown in drills in February and March. The rainy season crop yields much larger fruits, some dark green, and others creamy white. These when full grown change in colour to a rusty brown. In addition to the above varieties, the fruits of *C. Hardwickii* (Royle), are sometimes met with; this is a wild species found on the Himálaya; it is known in Kumaon as *air alu.* The rainy season forms are the most common, and are universally eaten by natives of all classes as well as by Europeans. When gathered in a young state they are known as *gherkins*; in this condition they are pickled.

521. CUCURBITA MAXIMA, *Duchesne.* The Gourd or Squash Gourd; Kadu (*Hind.*). Cultivated all over India for its fruit. This plant produces the largest known cucurbitaceous fruits, some weighing as much as 240 lbs., and measuring nearly 8 feet in circumference. The fruit is wholesome, and when young is eaten as a vegetable. It is largely used in curry by natives of all classes. It should be observed that both this and the fruit of *Lagenaria vulgaris* are in English called "gourds."

522. C. MOSCHATA, *Duchesne.* The Musk Melon or Melon Pumpkin; Kharbúj (*N.-W. P.*). This is the commonest species of Cucurbita. It has erroneously been called *C. maxima* by many writers. The marbled leaves with white blotches, the angular peduncle of the female flower, together with the short calyx-tube, ending in leaf-like sepals, are characters which at once separate this species from all its allies.

* Models prepared at the Botanic Gardens, Saharanpur, under the supervision of Mr. J. F. Duthie.

523.* C. PEPO, *DC.* The European Pumpkin or True Vegetable Marrow. Cultivated for its fruit in European vegetable gardens.

524.* DOLICHOS BIFLORUS, *Linn.*, and *D. Lablab*, *Linn.*; Leguminosæ. The young pods are extensively eaten as vegetables. (*See* also 682.)

525.* HIBISCUS ESCULENTUS, *Linn.*; Malvaceæ. The Edible Hibiscus; Ochro of the West Indies; Gombo (*Fr.*); Bhindi (*Hind.*); Dhénras (*Beng.*). A herbaceous, annual bush, naturalised in all tropical countries; only met with in a cultivated state. The unripe fruit is a favourite vegetable. When young and tender, it is very mucilaginous, and is commonly eaten as a vegetable, or used to flavour soup. The natives eat it when mature, and chiefly in curries. (*See* also 924.)

526. LAGENARIA VULGARIS, *Seringe*; Cucurbitaceæ. The Gourd, Calabash, or Bottle Gourd; Kaddú (*Hind.*); Kudú, lau (*Beng.*). This climbing plant is found wild in India, the Moluccas, and Abyssinia. It is cultivated in the warm parts of America, Australia, and China, and extensively so in many parts of India, especially in the Upper Provinces and on the lower hills. It requires a rich sandy soil; the sowing takes place from February to July, and the gourd matures in three months' time. By Europeans this is boiled when young and used as vegetable marrow; by the natives it is sliced and cooked in curry. The young shoots and leaves are also eaten. The fruit assumes almost any form; it is sometimes as much as 6 feet long, and is frequently shaped liked a bottle; specially prepared ones are in fact used as such. The Nagás hollow them out into water and *zu*-beer bottles. The small variety called *tumri* is used for making the stringed instrument called the *sitar*. (*See* also 441.)

527. LUFFA ACUTANGULA, *Roxb.* The Torui (*Hind.*); Jhinga (*Beng.*). Met with in the North-West Himálaya and distributed to Sikkim, Assam, East Bengal, and Ceylon. Cultivated all over India, the sowing taking place from March to the beginning of June. This elegant obovate fruit with its angled or winged surface is one of the most abundant vegetables offered for sale in Indian bazars. The natives value it highly and eat it in curry. Roxburgh says that the half-grown fruits, when boiled and dressed with butter, pepper, and salt, are little inferior to green peas. Cut in round slices and made into *fricassée*, they constitute an excellent dish of vegetables.

528. L. ÆGYPTIACA, *Mill.*, *ex Hook. f.* The Dhundul (*Beng.*). A native of India, cultivated or naturalised in most of the hot countries of the world. In India it is common everywhere, and is often cultivated, especially in the plains. The seeds are sown from March to June, and the fruit ripens from June to October. The fruit is eaten by the natives in curry.

529.* MOMORDICA CHARANTIA, *Linn.* The Karela (*Hind.*); Karala (*Beng.*). Cultivated all over India on the plains. It is sown on rich soil in February and March, and the fruit ripens in April. It is of a bright orange-yellow colour, 1 to 6 inches long; is eaten cooked in curries, or sliced and fried; but a special treatment in hot water is necessary previous to cooking, to remove the bitterness. When sliced and dried, it remains good for many months.

530. MOMORDICA DIOICA, *Roxb.* The Gol kandra (*N.-W. P.*). Found throughout India at different altitudes up to 5,000 feet, generally in thickets, on banks of rivers, &c. The fruit, when green and tender, is eaten in curries by the natives. The tuberous root of the female plant is also eaten, and is larger than the male root.

531. MORINGA PTERYGOSPERMA, *Gærtn.*; Moringeæ. The Horse-radish or Ben-nut Tree; Sajna (*Beng.*). Wild in the sub-Himálayan tract from the Chenáb to Oudh; commonly cultivated in India and Burma. The fruit is a long whiplike pod. The leaves, flowers, and pods are very commonly eaten in curries by natives of all classes. After the pods are taken off the tree, the branches are universally lopped, and the leaves are then given to cattle as fodder. The root has a strong flavour of horse-radish, and besides being used in medicine as a vesicant, is said to be eaten by the natives. (*See* also 1030, 1075.)

532. MUSA PARADISIACA, *Linn.*; Scitamineæ. The plantain.

M. SAPIENTUM, *Linn.* The Banana; Kela (*Hind.*); Kala (*Beng.*). A perennial herb of 8 to 15 feet in height, extensively cultivated throughout India, nearer to the coast tracts than inland. The fruit is a common article of diet among both Europeans and natives, especially the latter. The various forms of the plaintain more properly should be classed as fruits than as vegetables. One form—the *kanch kolla* of Bengal—is, however, never allowed to ripen, its large fruits being cut up and eaten as a vegetable in curries. The young flowers are also regularly eaten. (*See* also 452. 606, 933, 973.)

533.* RAPHANUS SATIVUS, *Linn.*; Cruciferæ. The Radish; Muli (*Hind.*); Mulá (*Beng.*). An annual herb family, unknown in its wild state; cultivated here and there throughout the plains of India and up to 16,000 feet in altitude on the Himálaya. It is a cold-weather crop, but grows nearly all the year round on the hills. There are several varieties met with in India, the large, long, pale pink; the small, longish, pale pink; and the small, round, bright red. The last is raised generally in gardens from selected or European imported seed.

Var. *caudatus*—known in the vernacular as *mugra*. This extraordinary form is cultivated in the Punjáb and in Northern and Western India on account of its pods, which are used as a vegetable. It is generally believed that this plant is only *R. sativus* subjected to a peculiar treatment, viz., by being taken up and having all its roots cut off and then replanted. The habit of removing the tap-root as a vegetable and replanting the stock for the production of seed is quite common with the poorer classes.

534.* SOLANUM MELONGENA, *Linn.*; Solanaceæ. The Egg-apple, Brinjal; Baigún (*Hind.*); Begún (*Beng.*). This plant is extensively cultivated throughout India; there are many varieties as to size and shape of the fruit; the two most striking primary forms are readily recognised by their colour, the one being purplish green and the other white. The fruit is universally eaten in curry and sold in every bazar.

535. TRICHOSANTHES ANGUINA, *Linn.*; Cucurbitaceæ. The Snake Gourd; Chachinga (*Hind.*); Chichinga (*Beng.*). A native either of India or the Indian Archipelago. The pendulous, cylindrical, snake-like gourd, 3 feet long, is eaten cooked in curry, and is a common article of food.

536. T. CUCUMERINA, *Linn.* The Jangli-chachinda (*Hind.*); Ban-patol (*Beng.*). A pretty extensive climbing annual, found throughout India. The fruit is oblong, 1 to 4 inches long, striated with white and green when unripe, becoming red when ripe. It contains a red pulp which is eaten generally in curries, when unripe, but is very bitter.

537. T. DIOICA, *Roxb.* The Palbal (*Hind.*); Patol (*Beng.*). Cultivated during the rains throughout the plains of Northern India, from the Punjáb to Bengal proper and Assam. The fruit is oblong, smooth, about 2 to 4 inches long, green when unripe, and yellow or orange when ripe. It is eaten when unripe and always cooked, and is a much-esteemed vegetable. Natives generally make it into curry. (*See* also 859.)

538. T. PALMATA, *Roxb.* The Lal-indrayan (*Hind.*); Mákál (*Beng.*). Very common in most thickets, from the Himálaya to Ceylon and Signapore. The red fruit is very similar to the last-mentioned species. It is eaten when produced by cultivation, and is known in Upper India by the name *Lal-indráyan.*

DIVISION II.—GREEN VEGETABLES.

(*These are ságs or green vegetables similar to spinach.*)

539. AMARANTUS GANGETICUS, *Linn.*; Amarantaceæ. The Lál Ság. This is perhaps the most important *ság* in India.

540. A. OLERACEUS, *Linn.*; The Natya Ság. This seems in South India to take the place of the preceding in Bengal.

541. A. SPINOSUS, *Linn.* The Kánta-natiya. This makes a good spinach, but the spines must first be removed.

542. A. TRISTIS, *Linn.* The Mekanada (*Sans.*); Sirru-kirai (*Tam.*). This is cultivated more or less over India, and is highly spoken of as a pot-herb.

543. BASELLA ALBA, *Linn.*; Chenopodiaceæ. The Poi (*Hind.*). The succulent leaves and stems of this climber are extensively eaten as a pot-herb.

544.* BETA MARITIMA, *Linn.* The Beet-root: Palang (*Hind.*). The stems and leaves are largely eaten.

545. BŒRHAAVIA DIFFUSA, *Linn.*; Nyctagineæ. The Gádha púrna (*Beng.*); or Sindika (*Sans.*). Cultivated by the Santáls as a pot-herb. (*See* also 489.)

546.* BRASSICA CAMPESTRIS, *Linn.* Cruciferæ. The Rape. (*See* also 653, 997.)

546a.* B. JUNCEA, *H. f. & T.*, and B. NIGRA, *Koch.* The Mustard. The young leaves are eaten as pot-herbs. (*See* also 998.)

547. CORCHORUS OLITORIUS, *Linn.*; Tiliaceæ. The Jute. The young shoots and leaves are regularly eaten as a pot-herb. (*See* also 427, 961, 967.)

548. IPOMÆA AQUATICA, *Forsk.*; Convolvulaceæ. The Kalmi-sák (*Beng.*). This floating-Ipomæa is extensively eaten in Bengal as a pot-herb.

549. LYSIMACHIA CANDIDA, *Lindl.*; Primulaceæ. One of the most remarkable examples of pot-herbs on record. It is eaten by the Manipuris as a green vegetable, especially along with fish. This fact was discovered during the Manipur Boundary Commission.

550. MARSILEA QUADRIFOLIA, *Linn.*; Marsileaceæ. The Sushní-sák (*Beng.*). This sub-aquatic cryptogam (closely allied to the ferns) is regularly eaten as a pot-herb in Bengal.

551. OXALIS CORNICULATA, *Linn.*; Geraniaceæ. The Amrúl (*Beng.*). The whole plant is eaten.

552. PORTULACA OLERACEA, *Linn.*, and P. QUADRIFIDA, *Linn.*; Portulacaceæ. The Núniya (*Hind.*). This is regularly sold in the Calcutta market and in most bazars in Bengal; is an important vegetable with the poor.

553. RUMEX.; Polygonaceæ. Several species of sorrel are eaten as pot-herbs.

554. SESBANIA GRANDIFLORA, *Pers.*; Leguminosæ. The Basna (*Hind.*); Baka (*Beng.*); or Agati (*Tam.*). The large papilionaceous flowers and also the leaves of this elegant tree are eaten as a pot-herb.

555.* TAMARINDUS INDICA, *Linn.*; Leguminosæ. The Tamarind or Amli. The leaves are made into curry by the poorer classes. (*See* also 273, 624, 853, 1047.)

TUBERS, BULBS, ROOTS, AND STEMS.

556.* ALLIUM. The Onion, Garlic, Shallot. (*See* also 649.)

557. ALOCASIA INDICA, *Schott.*; Aroideæ. Mánkachú (*Beng.*). Generally cultivated around the huts of the poorer classes in Bengal. Its esculent stems and root-stocks are important articles of food in Bengal.

558. AMORPHOPHALLUS CAMPANULATUS, *Blume*; Aroideæ. The Ol (*Beng.*). A native of India and Ceylon, cultivated throughout the peninsula, in rich, moist soils. The corms are in common use as an article of food.

559.* ARRACACIA ESCULENTA, *DC.*; Umbelliferæ. The Peruvian Carrot. Experimentally introduced into India.

560.* BETA MARITIMA, *L.*; Chenopodiaceæ. The Beet-root. Cultivated over the greater part of India as a cold-season crop. The stem is extensively used as a vegetable; sugar is not made from it in India.

561. BRASSICA CAMPESTRIS, *Linn.*; Cruciferæ. Sub-species Rapa. The Turnip; Shalgham

(*Hind., Beng.*). Grown as a garden crop all over India. The stem and also the young leaves are eaten. The turnip is very watery, and, unlike the potato, contains no starch. The pungent essential oil gives it, however, a pleasant flavour, and although not very nourishing, it is a favourite vegetable, and is cultivated throughout India during the cold season.

562. COLOCASIA ANTIQUORUM, *Schott.*; Aroideæ. The Kachu (*Beng.*). Cultivated all over India on account of its corms, which constitute an important article of diet. In the wild state they are supposed to be unwholesome, an opinion confirmed by the fact that although every roadside in Bengal abounds with the wild plant the corms are not collected even by the poorest persons, but the succulent leaf-stalks are often collected and eaten.

563. COSTUS SPECIOSUS, *Sm.*; Scitamineæ. The Keú (*Beng.*). An elegant plant, with glossy leaves and white flowers; is common everywhere throughout India, especially so in Bengal, frequenting moist, shady places. The rhizomes are cooked in syrup and made into a preserve which is eaten by the natives.

564. CURCUMA ANGUSTIFOLIA, *Roxb.* Wild or East Indian Arrowroot. An abundant plant (wild and cultivated) in some parts of India, as, for example, at Travancore, where a good quality of arrowroot is prepared from the tubers. The flour, when boiled in milk, forms an excellent diet for patients and children.

565. DIOSCOREA, various species: Dioscoreæ. The Yam. There are several varieties (wild and cultivated) common all over India. The tubers are much appreciated.

566.* HELIANTHUS TUBEROSUS, *Linn.*; Compositæ. The Jerusalem Artichoke. Extensively cultivated as a vegetable.

567. IPOMÆA BATATAS, *Lamk.*; Convolvulaceæ. The Sweet Potato. Most probably a native of America, its cultivation in India becoming general in the eighteenth century. Cultivated to a limited extent in almost every part of India. It requires very little care, and grows in any soil. There are two kinds, the one with red, and the other with white, tubers. They are eaten by all classes of natives either roasted or cooked in curry.

568.* MANIHOT UTILISSIMA, *Pohl.*; Euphorbiaceæ. The Manioc or Tapioca plant. Introduced from America, now cultivated in Travancore and Burma. After being well boiled the root is eaten in fish curry by the natives. (*See* also 719.)

569.* MARANTA ARUNDINACEA, *Linn.*; Scitamineæ. The Arrowroot. An American plant, early introduced into India and now cultivated on a large scale, many native merchants dealing exclusively in native-made arrowroot. Several of these merchants have sent samples to the Exhibition. (*See* also 720.)

570. MUSLI. Several tubers are sold as articles of food and medicine under this name, but there are two important kinds:—(*a*) Black muslí, the tubers of *Curculigo orchioides*. (*b*) White muslí, the tuberous roots of *Asparagus adscendens*. These somewhat resemble the tubers known as Salep (which see), but according to many Indian authorities the white muslí is far superior to all the others. It forms with water an agreeable mucilage devoid of starch.

571. PUERARIA TUBEROSA, *DC.*; Leguminosæ. A climbing shrub of the sub-tropical tracts of the Western Himálaya, the Western Ghats, Chutia Nagpur, and Orissa. The roots, which are large and tuberous, are eaten by the hill tribes. Large specimens of this tuber are shown in the native shops along with vegetables.

572. SALEP MISRI. The tubers of two or three orchids are all sold under the name of Salep. Although several species of *Eulophia* are met with on the mountain tracts of India, they do not appear to afford the salep of our bazars. The commercial article comes from Persia, Afghánistan, and the Punjáb Himálaya. There are three forms, the Punjáb or palmate tuber, the Persian and Afghan, long ovoid and small round tubers. Part at least of these tubers is supposed to be derived from *Eulophia campestris* and *E. herbacea*. Round tubers are collected on the Nilgiris by the hill tribes and regularly eaten. These are vulgarly known as the "little man's potatoes." They seem to be the tubers of a *Ceropegia* (Asclepiadaceæ), and may prove the so-called Nilgiri *salep*. Similarly, many other substances are sold for *salep*, and the line which might be supposed to separate the *saleps* from the *muslis* is difficult to define in spite of the fact that the word *musli* (or *mushli*) means a tapering root. Both *salep* and *musli* yield a mucilage with water which is much prized by the natives, being supposed to be a mild food for infants and invalids.

573. SOLANUM TUBEROSUM, *Linn.*; Solanaceæ. Potato. Introduced into Europe in the 16th century, and into India in the 18th century. It is now cultivated throughout India in the plains, and on the hills up to 9,000 feet. The potato is eaten by almost all classes.

574. TACCA PINNATIFIDA, *Forsk*; Taccaceæ. The South Sea Arrowroot. Found in the Concan and southwards, also on the Parell hills near Bombay, cultivated at Travancore, forming an important article of trade. Its large round, tuberous roots yield a quantity of white nutritious fecula, resembling arrowroot.

SUB-COURT IX.

This Sub-Court contains the exhibits referred in the "Classified List" to Division I., Sections 5, 13, 14, and 15. These may be grouped into (a) Fruits, (b) Nuts, (c) Jams and Confectioneries, (d) Pickles.

FRUITS.

The fruits of the East are, it is believed, much overrated in Europe. Many of the best Indian fruits have been introduced from Europe, China, the West Indies and America. The most characteristic modern fruits of India are the mango, guava, litchi, pineapple, and plantain. The mangosteen is common in the Straits, and is regarded as the most delicately-flavoured fruit of the East. It is a remarkable fact that while the wild forms of many of the fruits of Europe are abundant as indigenous plants on the Himálaya, only a very few were cultivated before the arrival of Europeans, and the gooseberry, the currant, and the bramble, which have been carried to such perfection in Europe, are still uncultivated in India. The peach succeeds in the plains of India, but the effect of climate upon it is marked. In Bengal excellent peaches are to be had, attaining much of their European flavour and ripening into a soft pinkish pulp. The fruit reaches the market just before the mango, at the beginning of the hot season. In the Punjáb this soft condition is never attained. On the Western Himálaya peaches do not succeed well, the rains apparently preventing the ripening of the fruit, while on the Nilgiris. at the same altitude, peaches are wonderfully good. The apricot shows a somewhat similar behaviour. In Afghánistán, Kashmír, and Chamba, excellent apricots are obtained, and indeed the tree, if not indigenous to Afghánistán, is quite naturalised, at an altitude between 6,000 and 9,000 feet. It is grown in the Punjáb, although not in the plains of India generally; but in the Punjáb, and along the Himálayan chain, the fruit is very inferior to the Kashmír and Afghán apricot. Even at Simla, only a few miles east of Chamba, the apricots are very inferior, and this degeneration increases on passing still further east and south-east, until, in the moister mountain regions of Darjiling, Assam, and the Nilgiris, it cannot even be cultivated.

The grapes of Kashmír and Afghánistán are famous, but, owing to the period of plucking and the method of packing, they have lost their natural flavour before they reach the plains of India. A very considerable trade is, however, done by the Kabuli merchants in small circular boxes of grapes. His Highness the Maharajah of Kashmír has successfully introduced the wine-grape, and in another part of the Exhibition will be found samples of wine and spirits produced in his dominions.

The foreign trade in fruits is comparatively small, the cocoa-nut being the chief article. The exports during the past five years were as follows: — 1880-81, 8,37,438 rupees; 1881-82, 4,25,029 rupees; 1882-83, 3,16,280 rupees; 1883-84, 3,93,348 rupees; 1884-85, 8,97,912 rupees. It was found impossible to convey to London a collection of actual fruits, but the models shown will help to compensate for this.† The Kabuli fruit-seller is so conspicuous a feature of the Indian bazar, that the idea was entertained of arranging the fruits in the form of a shop.

The following are the principal Indian fruits. The * indicates those which are not indigenous, although now extensively cultivated or even naturalised.

575.* Achras Sapota, *Linn.*; Sapotaceæ. The Sapodilla Plum or Sapota. A native of America; fruit not much appreciated, but surreptitiously sold in the streets as mangosteen.

576. Ægle Marmelos, *Correa*; Rutaceæ. The Bael Fruit. This sacred fruit is extensively used in the green state as an astringent medicine, but when ripe it is much eaten by the natives, and by Europeans is made into sherbet. (*See* also 15, 747.)

577.* Ananas sativa, *Linn.*; Bromeliaceæ. The Pineapple; Anárus (*Beng.*). A native of America; fruit highly esteemed. Quite naturalised in the Eastern Peninsula. (*See* also 900.)

578.* Anona reticulata, *Linn.*; Anonaceæ. The Bullock's Heart: Nóna (*Beng.*). The fruit ripens during the latter part of the rainy season, and is eaten by the natives only. (*See also* 902.)

579.* Anona squamosa, *Linn.* The Custard Apple; Ata (*Hind.*, *Beng.*). A West Indian fruit which under cultivation in India seems to have greatly improved. In the central tableland it is naturalised even more so than the preceding. (*See* also 903.)

580.* Artocarpus incisa, *Linn.* The Bread Fruit. A native of Java, Amboyna, and the neighbouring islands. Not met with to any great extent in India, although it is plentiful in Ceylon.

581. A. integrifolia, *Linn.*; Urticaceæ. The Jack Fruit; Kánthál (*Hind.*, *Beng.*). This large fruitescence is 12 to 18 inches in length, and 6 to 8 inches in diameter. It ripens during the rains, and is extensively eaten by the natives. The unripe fruit is made into curry. (*See* also 39, 633, 1090, 1133.)

582. A. Lakoocha, *Roxb.* The Lakúcha; Mádár (*Beng.*). The fruit is eaten by the natives.

583.* Averrhoa Carambola, *Linn.*; Geraniaceæ. The Karmal (*Hind.*). The fruit is eaten raw by the natives, and made into an agreeable jelly by Europeans.

584. Bassia latifolia, *Roxb.*; Sapotaceæ. The Butter or Mahuá Tree. This is indigenous to the forests of the central table-land of India, growing in gregarious clumps in the *sál* forests. The preserved flowers constitute an important article of food to the aboriginal tribes, and are now exported to Europe for the purpose of feeding cattle. A good spirit is also distilled from them. (*See* also 45, 410, 709, 995, 1091.)

585. Borassus flabelliformis, *Linn.*; Palmæ. The Palmyra Palm; Tál (*Hind.*, *Beng.*). A tall palm, with cylindrical stem, cultivated throughout the warmer parts of India, being capable of existence at a much greater distance from the sea than the cocoa-nut. The seed is sold in Bengal under the name of ***talsans***. It is viewed as a delicacy. The yellow pulp of the ripe fruit surrounding the seed is, with the addition of a little lime, made into a much-relished jelly. It is also fried into cakes, or by being mixed with flour and other ingredients. (*See* also 54, 634, 711.)

† These models were made at the Botanic Gardens of Saharanpur under the supervision of Mr. J. F. Duthie, and by the Krishnagarh modellers employed by the Government of India.

586. CAPPARIS SPINOSA, *Linn.*; Capparideæ. The Caper Berry. The ripe fruit is either eaten raw or made into pickles.

587.* CARICA PAPAYA, *L.*, Passifloreæ. The Papaw or Papaya Tree. An American plant extensively grown in Bengal. The green fruit is cooked and eaten as a vegetable in curries. The ripe fruit is by many persons regarded as one of the best and most wholesome of fruits.

588. CARISSA CARANDAS, *Linn.*; Apocynaceæ. The Karenja Fruit. The unripe fruit is pickled, and ripe one made into tarts and jelly.

589.* CITRULLUS VULGARIS, *Schrad.*; Cucurbitaceæ. The Water-melon; Turbuza (*Hind.*). The fruit is large, ovoid, green and smooth; the flesh whitish-yellow or pinkish. There are several distinct varieties, all of which are much appreciated in India as refreshing fruits, but they are inferior to the water-melons of Europe.

590. CITRUS AURANTIUM, *Linn.*; Rutaceæ. The Orange; Narangi (*Hind.*). (*b*) Var. *Bigaradia.* The Seville Orange. (*c*) Var. *Bergamia.* The Bergamot. The forms of this justly popular fruit are probably natives of China. The orange is brought from the Khasia hills to Calcutta, appearing in the markets about the beginning of the cold season.

591.* CITRUS DECUMANA, *Willd.* The Shaddock, or Pomelo; Batavi nebu (*Beng.*). Probably a native of Java. There are two forms of the fruit, one with whitish and the other with pinkish pulp; they are favourite fruits both with Europeans and natives.

592. CITRUS MEDICA, *Linn.* The Citron, Lemon, Lime. These fruits appear to be all natives of India. (*See* also 785.)

593.* CYDONIA VULGARIS, *Tourn.*; Rosaceæ. The Quince. Cultivated in North-Western India to Afghánistán, ascending to 6,000 feet in altitude. The ripe fruit is eaten; it is also made into preserve, and often used to flavour marmalade and other preserves.

594. DILLENIA INDICA, *Linn.*; Dilleniaceæ. The Chálté (*Hind., Beng.*). An abundant tree in Bengal and other parts of India. The persistent and succulently-developed calyx around the fruit is eaten either raw or cooked. (*See* also 99.)

595. DURIO ZIBETHINUS, *DC.*; Malvaceæ. The Durian or Civet-cat Fruit Tree. A large tree of the Malay islands, wild in South Tenasserim, and cultivated as far north as Moulmein. The fruit called the Durian has a strong offensive smell, but is eaten greedily by the Burmese, and it is stated that as many as 40,000 are annually sent to Upper Burma.

596.* ERIOBOTRYA JAPONICA, *Lindl.*; Rosaceæ. The Loquat or Japan Medlar. A tree of the Apple family, cultivated in Japan, China, Australia, and Southern Europe. Introduced from China into Bengal. The fruit has somewhat the flavour of the apple.

597. EUGENIA JAMBOLANA, *Lam.*; Myrtaceæ. The Jam (*Hind. Beng.*). The tree is found wild or in cultivation all over India. The fruit is of the size of a pigeon's egg, and is eaten by all classes of people. It is a sub-acid fruit of very little value. (*See* also 124, 777.)

598. EUGENIA JAMBOS, *Linn.* The Rose-apple; Golab jám (*Beng.*). The tree is indigenous to the Sikkim Terai. It is commonly cultivated in gardens. The fruit is small, yellowish, and is eaten raw or is made into a preserve.

599.* FICUS CARICA, *Linn.*; Urticaceæ. The Common Fig; Anjir (*Hind.*). Probably a native of Afghánistán and Persia, extending to Europe; introduced into India. The figs of a better quality than those grown in India are annually brought into the Punjáb from Afghánistán and Persia.

600.* FRAGARIA VESCA, *Linn.*; Rosaceæ. The Strawberry. This is a native of temperate regions, and is abundant on the Himalaya. The cultivated form is purely an introduction from Europe, the plant never having been cultivated by the natives from an indigenous stock. It thrives remarkably in the plains of the Punjáb and at Dinapore in Behar, but does not seem to be able to withstand the rains of Bengal.

601.* GARCINIA MANGOSTANA, *Linn.*; Guttiferæ. The Mangosteen. A native of the Straits, cultivated in Burma. This is said to be the most delicious of all known fruits.

602. HIBISCUS SABDARIFFA, *Linn.*; Malvaceæ. The Rozelle; Patwa (*Hind.*). This bush is cultivated in many parts of India. The red calyx when dried is eaten by the natives as an acid article of diet, like tamarind, and by Europeans it is made into tarts, and also into a jelly, which can scarcely be distinguished from red currant jelly. (*See* also 498.),

603.* LYCOPERSICUM ESCULENTUM, *Miller*; Solanaceæ. The Love-apple or Tomato. A native of tropical America, cultivated in many parts of India for its red and sometimes yellow fruits, which are eaten chiefly by the European population.

604. MANGIFERA INDICA, *Linn.*; Anacardiaceæ. The Mango; Am (*Hind., Beng.*). Indigenous to the eastern side of India, only naturalised in the west. The tree blossoms from February to April, and the fruit ripens from May to July. The green fruit is sliced and cooked in curry; it is made into pickle with salt, mustard oil, and chillies, and also into preserves and jams by being boiled and cooked in syrup. The natives dry the slices of the green fruit to make their *Am chúr.* The mango is by far the most popular fruit in India. There are good mangoes and bad mangoes. In the former the pulp is deliciously flavoured, and of a consistence somewhat like butter; in the latter it is stringy, and tastes strongly of the carrot with a little turpentine. There are small, yellow, and rose-cheeked mangoes, large mangoes both yellow and green. The thick juice is by the natives squeezed out, spread on plates and allowed to dry, in order to form the thin cakes known as *Amsatta.* (*See* also 171, 440, 816, 1155.)

605. MORUS INDICA, *Linn.*; Urticaceæ. The Mulberry; Tút (*Beng.*). Cultivated throughout North India as a fruit tree.

606. MUSA PARADISIACA, *Linn.*; Scitamineæ. The Plantain. (*See* also 532, 933, 973.)

606*a*. MUSA SAPIENTUM. The Banana. Natives

of India and the Malaya. (*See* "Vegetables," in Sub-Court VIII.).

607.* NEPHELIUM LITCHI, *Camb.;* Sapindaceæ. The Litchi. Native of South China and Siam, introduced into Bengal at the end of the eighteenth century. The fruit is round, red, or chocolate-brown. The jelly-like pulp is eaten.

608.* OLEA EUROPÆA, *Linn.;* Oleaceæ. The Olive. The tree has been introduced on the Himálaya and the Nilgiris. There are some six or seven species of *Olea* met with in India, none of which appear to have been cultivated with the object of ascertaining how far they might come to afford the much prized olive-oil. *O. cuspidata* comes very near to the true olive, and it is therefore surprising that it has never been carefully cultivated.

609.* OPUNTIA DILLENII, *Haw.;* Cacteæ. The Prickly Pear. A native of America, naturalized in South India. (*See* also 934, 975.)

610.* PHŒNIX DACTYLIFERA, *Linn.;* Palmæ. The Date Palm; Pindi khejúr (*Beng.*). The date palm has existed from prehistoric times in the warm dry zone extending from the Indus to Senegal. It is cultivated and self-sown in South Punjáb and Sind. The date is eaten both by the natives and Europeans; the entire fruit is superior to the form met with in which the fruits are crushed.

611. PHŒNIX SYLVESTRIS, *Roxb.* The Wild Date; Khejúr (*Beng.*). Wild and cultivated throughout India. The fruit is eaten by the natives of the lower classes, but the tree is chiefly of value on account of its saccharine juice, from which date-sugar is prepared. (*See* also 724, 936.)

612. PHYLLANTHUS EMBLICA, *Linn.;* Euphorbiaceæ. The Emblic Myrabolam; Amla (*Beng.*). A tree of the dry forests of India and Burma. The fruit is of the size of a small gooseberry; it is eaten by the natives either raw or preserved. It is also made into a sweetmeat with sugar, and by the Europeans into tarts and jellies. A half-ripe fruit if chewed has the effect of making water taste sweet. (*See* also 834, 1166.)

613.* PHYSALIS PERUVIANA, *Linn.;* Solanaceæ. The Cape Gooseberry; Trepári (*Beng.*). Indigenous to tropical America, but in some parts of India it is quite naturalized. The small yellow berries are largely eaten, and make the best jam to be had in India.

614.* PRUNUS ARMENIACA, *Linn.;* Rosaceæ. The Apricot. Probably a native of China, generally cultivated in the north of India, and naturalized in Afghánistán, Kashmír, and Chumba. The fruit is largely eaten by all classes, fresh or dried. The dried fruits brought by the Cabulis in strings, if well washed and soaked in water over night, make an excellent stew with a pleasant and peculiar flavour not quite that of the apricot.

615.* P. AVIUM, *Linn.* The Bird Cherry. Cultivated in the North-West Himálaya; it flowers in April and May, and the fruit ripens in June.

616.* P. CERASUS, *Linn.* The Sour Cherry. This exists in the north of India as a cultivated plant only. The fruit is eaten by all classes, but is very inferior to the European cherry.

617.* P. COMMUNIS, *Huds.* The Plum. Cultivated from Garhwál to Kashmír, on the Western Himálaya. The ripe fruit is large, yellow, sweet, and juicy. The Bokhara Plum. This plum is met with in a dry state in the Indian bazars. The plant from which it is obtained is not known, but there seems little doubt but that it is a variety of this species. A chutney is generally prepared from it, which is much relished by the natives.

618.* PRUNUS PERSICA, *Benth. and Hook.* The Peach. Commonly cultivated in the cooler parts of India up to an altitude of 10,000 feet, especially in the North-West Himálaya. But it succeeds admirably in Bengal and in many other parts of the plains of India, fruiting towards the close of the cold season. The fruit is eaten as a delicacy.

619.* PSIDIUM GUYAVA, *Linn.;* Myrtaceæ. The Guava; Péyara (*Beng.*). An introduced tree from America and the West Indies. The fruit is universally eaten by the natives. Europeans use it chiefly in the form of stew or of "Guava jelly" and "Guava cheese."

620.* PUNICA GRANATUM, *Linn.;* Lythraceæ. The Pomegranate; Dalim (*Beng.*). A native of Persia, Afghánistán, and Beluchistán; introduced into India proper. (*See* also 841, 1169.)

621. RIBES. It is a somewhat remarkable fact that, while both the gooseberry and the black currant are wild on the North-West Himálaya, these popular European fruits are never seen in cultivation in European gardens at hill stations, nor have the indigenous forms been cultivated by the hill tribes. (Compare with similar remark under 600.)

622.* SPONDIAS DULCIS, *Willd.;* Anacardiaceæ. The Otaheite Apple. A native of the Society Islands and of Fiji.

623. S. MANGIFERA, *Pers.* The Hog Plum; Amra (*Beng.*). Wild and cultivated throughout India from the Indus eastwards, and southwards to Malacca and Ceylon. The fruit is eaten raw when ripe, and in the green state it is pickled or cooked in curry. (*See* also 263.)

624.* TAMARINDUS INDICA, *Linn.;* Leguminosæ. The Tamarind; Tentúl (*Beng.*). Probably indigenous in Africa; diffused through India and the tropics generally. The acid pulp of the pods is used in curry by the natives. It forms a pleasant cooling drink when sweetened with sugar. (*See* also 273, 555, 853, 1047.)

625.* VITIS VINIFERA, *Linn.;* Ampelideæ. The Grape; Angúr (*Hind., Beng.*). The grape has its most easterly point of distribution in Afghánistán, where it seems to be indigenous. (*See* also 728.)

626. ZIZYPHUS JUJUBA, *Lamk.;* Rhamneæ. The Jujube or Chinese Date; Kúl (*Hind., Beng.*). Common throughout India and Burma, both in a wild and cultivated state. The fruit is eaten by all classes of people, and also preserved in chutney. (*See* also 303.)

627. Z. VULGARIS, *Lamk.* The Common Jujube or Indian Plum. The tree occurs both wild and cultivated. The fruit is eaten by the natives, and when dried constitutes the jujubes of the shops.

NUTS.

In India this term is more comprehensive than in Europe. It covers not merely the commoner nuts, but such seeds as the ground-nut and the seeds of the edible pine. Most nuts are eaten as luxuries either raw or roasted, but the almond is a regular ingredient in the Indian rice dish known as *pillao*. The almond is also a sacred offering common to the Hindu and the Jain, and it is a remarkable fact that India is indebted for its entire supply of this nut to the Mahommedan traders of Afghánistán and Persia. The so-called "country almond" of India has no resemblance to the true almond. The betel-nut is an ingredient of *pán*—the mildly stimulating preparation chewed by the natives everywhere in India. The hazel-nut and the walnut are largely imported into India from Afghánistán and Central Asia, being, in many cases, not only carried across the Himálaya by Afgháns, but conveyed by the same enterprising dealers to every town and village in India. The cocoa-nut has been classed as a fruit in the Trade Returns, and to prevent confusion in the quotations of imports and exports it has been left in that position, although it should more correctly appear as a nut.

The following are the leading Indian nuts:—

628. ÆSCULUS INDICA, *Colebr.*; Sapindaceæ. The Himálayan Horse-chestnut. (*See* also 16, 405.)

629.* ALEURITES MOLUCCANA, *Willd.*; Euphorbiaceæ. The Belgaum Walnut. A handsome tree introduced from the Malay Archipelago, but now common in many parts of the peninsula, especially in South India. (*See* also 986.)

630.* ANACARDIUM OCCIDENTALE, *Linn.*; Anacardiaceæ. The Cashew Nut. A small evergreen tree introduced from South America; naturalized in the coast forests of Chittagong, Tennasserim, and the Andaman Islands. (*See* also 31, 987.)

631.* ARACHIS HYPOGÆA, *Linn.*; Leguminosæ. The Ground-nut or Earth-nut. A South American annual extensively cultivated in India, and especially so in South India. The nuts or seeds are largely exported on account of the oil they contain. They are universally offered for sale by fruit-sellers, and in India are roasted and eaten as nuts. (*See* also 993.)

632.* ARECA CATECHU, *Linn.*; Palmæ. The Betel-nut. A tall elegant palm, with thin, straight stem, cultivated throughout India. The ruminated albuminous seed or nut forms a very important article of trade in India. The following are the imports and exports during the past five years:—

FOREIGN IMPORTS AND EXPORTS.

	Value.	Value.
	Rs.	Rs.
1880-81 . . .	23,29,395	96,930
1881-82 . . .	20,19,918	53,545
1882-83 . . .	21,68,061	77,199
1883-84 . . .	34,06,458	52,417
1884-85 . . .	33,44,551	32,099

The foreign imports are chiefly from Ceylon, the Straits and Sumatra, and the exports to Zanzibar, Mauritius, and Mozambique. The transports or inter-provincial coasting trade amounted in 1883-84 to Rs. 55,21,614, and the exports by land to Rs. 7,52,441. (*See* also 652.)

633. ARTOCARPUS INTEGRIFOLIA, *Linn.*; Urticaceæ. The Jack Fruit. The dry seeds of this aggregated fruit are roasted and eaten as nuts. (*See* also 39 581, 1091, 1133.)

634. BORASSUS FLABELLIFORMIS, *Linn.*; Palmæ. The Palmyra Palm. The *talsans* or seeds of this palm are universally eaten as nuts. (*See* also 54, 585, 711.)

635. BUCHANANIA LATIFOLIA, *Roxb.*; Anacardiaceæ. The Chirauli-nut. A common tree of the sub-Himálaya. The nut is commonly eaten as a substitute for almonds. (*See* also 57, 999.)

636. CORYLUS COLURNA, *Linn.*; Cupuliferæ. The Indian Hazel-nut. A moderate-sized tree of the North-West Himálaya. The nut is smaller than the European hazel-nut, but nearly as good in point of flavour; it forms an important article of food in some parts of the North-West Himálaya. It is probable, however, that the true hazel is also brought to India by the Cabulís, as both forms are met with in the bazars. The chief import trade of Hazel-nuts is from Afghánistán and Kashmír. (*See* also 90.)

637. CUCUMIS, SP. The seeds of the various forms of melon are roasted and eaten as nuts. (*See* also 517.)

638. EURYALE FEROX, *Salisb.*; Nymphaceæ. The Gorgon-nut; Makhana (*Beng.*). A spiny water-lily not uncommon on the lakes of India. The black seeds are roasted in hot sand and eaten as nuts.

639. JUGLANS REGIA, *Linn.*; Juglandeæ. The Walnut; Akrot (*Hind.*). A large tree not uncommon on the Himálaya. Extensively cultivated in the North-West and Punjáb Himálaya and in Afghánistán, a large annual supply coming to the plains of India by the Cabulí and other traders from the hills. The nut ripens from July to September. It has been said that a single tree will often yield over 20,000. There are several well-known forms of this nut, the soft-shelled kind from Kashmír and Chumba being regarded as the most superior of all. This is, however, scarcely known in trade; it bears the name of *Kaghazi akhrot*. (*See* also 157, 1027.)

640. NELUMBIUM SPECIOSUM, *Willd.*; Nymphæaceæ. The Sacred Lotus. (*See* also 722.)

641. PINUS GERARDIANA, *Willd.*; Coniferæ. The Neosa or Edible Pine. A moderate-sized tree found in the dry arid parts of the North-West and Punjáb Himálaya, extending into Afghánistán, at altitudes of from 6,000 to 9,000 feet. The seed is collected and stored for winter use. It forms an important article of food in the regions where the tree is found, and is brought to India by the Afghán traders. (*See* also 206.)

642. PISTACIA VERA, *Linn.*; Anacardiaceæ. The Pistachio Nut. A small tree of Western

Asia and Afghánistán. This nut is perhaps the most striking feature of the collection of fruits, nuts, and resins offered for sale by the Afghán fruit-seller. It is brought to India in large quantities, and is eaten by all classes of people. (*See* also 1037.)

643.* PRUNUS AMYGDALUS, *Baillon*; Rosaceæ. The Almond. This is cultivated in Afghánistán, Persia, Kashmír, and even in the Punjáb. A large quantity of these nuts is annually carried across the Himálaya to India by Afghán traders, along with the pistachio, the pomegranate, the raisin, and the grape. (*See* also 1040, 1079.)

644. SEMECARPUS ANACARDIUM, *Linn.*; Anacardiaceæ. The Marking-nut. An extremely abundant tree throughout the central table-land of India and along the sub-Himálaya. The fruit-stalk of this plant becomes succulently enlarged. As it matures, it changes to a bright orange colour and is then edible, being either eaten fresh or after being roasted in ashes. The nut produced on the apex of this stalk is also eaten, and is known as the Malacca-bean or Marsh-nut. The juice from the unripe shell is powerfully astringent; a black varnish is prepared from it and mixed with lime-water; this constitutes a good marking-ink for cotton. (*See* also 253.)

645. TERMINALIA CATAPPA, *Linn.*; Combretaceæ. The Country Almond.

646. THEOBROMA CACAO, *Linn.*; Sterculiaceæ. The Cacao or Chocolate Bean. A large, exceedingly handsome tree, common throughout India. The coiled-up embryo of this seed is extensively eaten by the natives of India. By Europeans it is generally served up as a dessert, the nuts floating in a cold dilute syrup. (*See* also 737.)

647. TRAPA BISPINOSA, *Roxb.*; Onagraceæ. The Singara-nut. The common aquatic weed found floating on tanks and lakes. The persistent calyx develops around the fruit into a barbed structure which serves as an anchor. This starchy nut is universally eaten, and indeed in some parts of the country forms an important article of food. It is stated that in Kashmír 30,000 persons are dependent upon this wild plant for food during certain months. The value of the plant to the poorer people cannot be over-estimated.

JAMS, CONFECTIONERIES, AND PICKLES.

EXHIBITORS.—A large collection of preserved fruits, jams. and pickles are exhibited. Of these mention may be made of the special show made by Mr. P. Vencatachellum; by Messrs. C. Kistnasawmy Chetty & Sons; by Mr. T. H. Cripps, of Madras; the Great Eastern Hotel Company, Limited, Calcutta; Mr. Nusserwanji Cursetji Ahmednagar; Messrs. Manockji Poonjiajee & Sons, Bombay.

SUB-COURT X.

This Sub-Court contains the exhibits which fall into Division I., Sections 11 *and* 12.

CONDIMENTS AND SPICES.

To the native of India, spices and condiments are indispensable. He will eat contentedly, by the stream side, a meal of uncooked flour and water, provided it is flavoured with a few green chillies. No luxury is more extensively indulged in than *pán*—the stimulating preparation of betel-leaf, lime, and betel-nut—chewed by nearly every native in India. Turmeric (or *haldí*) is an essential ingredient in curry—the Indian national dish. It is unnecessary, however, to discuss the spices and condiments collectively, since a brief notice will be found in the succeeding pages of each of the more important ones. Suffice it to say, that the total value of the foreign trade (*e.g.*, imports and exports) for the year 1884–85 amounted to Rs.1,10,46,842—a trade which, expressed at par, may be valued at a little over one million of pounds sterling. The principal articles of this trade are betel-nuts, pepper, ginger, cloves, and cardamoms. Cutch, which is largely eaten as a condiment in *pán*, has been treated as a dye-stuff, since its chief use is in dyeing and tanning. This remark also applies to turmeric. The trade in cutch and in turmeric has not, therefore, been included in the above quotation; but, on the other hand, the minor condiments (such as coriander, cummin, &c.) which, in the Government published trade returns, are given as seeds, have been relegated to their true place and included in the above.

The following are the principal Indian spices and condiments, arranged in the alphabetical order of their scientific names; the specimens are shown in a like order.

648. ACACIA CATECHU, *Willd.*; Leguminosæ. The Catechu, Cutch, or Káth. A common tree, in most parts of India and Burma. The extract obtained by boiling down chips of the heartwood forms the cutch of commerce. This substance is chiefly employed in dyeing and tanning, but it is also largely used as a drug, especially in America. The value of the catechu exported from India during 1884–85 and the preceding four years was as follows:—1880–81, Rs.42,66,415; 1881–82, Rs.25,30,840; 1882–83, Rs.30,52,434; 1883–84, Rs.35,32,000; 1884–85, Rs.28,20,785. The bulk of these exports consisted in Burma or Pegu cutch, but Bombay and the North-West Provinces also export a considerable amount, the cutch or *káth* of the latter being more particularly interesting, since it is of a different nature. It is paler coloured than Burma cutch, and is baked into large cubes somewhat resembling gambier. Instead of being boiled down to a thick extract and then cast into large masses, twigs are placed in the concentrated decoction and the *káth* allowed to crystallize. The substance thus obtained is afterwards thrown into cubes about 1½ inches in

size. The result of this treatment is the production of a much purer article, and this or gambier is the form of catechuic acid eaten in *pán* by the natives of India. (*See* also 5, 742, 1052, 1085, 1129.)

649.* ALLIUM; Liliaceæ. The onion and the garlic are extensively cultivated all over India. The onion is supposed to be a native of Western Asia, but exists in India only under cultivation. The onions of Patna and Bombay are, however, of a very high quality and are now being exported. It is surprising how powerfully the climate of India seems to affect the onion. In one province excellent onions are to be had while in another they are very inferior. The garlic is eaten to a much greater extent than the onion by the natives of India, the aggregated white bulb being offered for sale in every bazaar. (*See* also 556.)

650. AMOMUM SUBULATUM, *Roxb.;* Scitamineæ. The Greater Cardamom; Bara-eláchi (*Beng.*). A native of Nepal. The Greater Cardamom is much used in the preparation of sweetmeats on account of cheapness. This, as well as the Lesser Cardamom, also form ingredients of the *pán* betel-leaf preparation. (For trade quotations *see* Elettaria.)

651. APIUM GRAVEOLENS, *Linn.;* Umbelliferæ. Wild and Cultivated Celery; Ajmud (*Hind.*). A native of Europe, Egypt, Abyssinia, and of Asia from the Caucasus to the Himálaya and Beluchistan. Cultivated in different parts of the plains of India. The small fruits are eaten as a spice by the natives, who never cultivate the plant for any other purpose; in consequence it has quite a different appearance from the garden celery cultivated by Europeans.

652.* ARECA CATECHU, *Linn.;* Palmæ. The Areca or Betel-nut. This has already been mentioned under Nuts, which see. (*See* also 632.)

653. BRASSICA; Cruciferæ. The seeds of the various forms of Mustard, Rape, and Cole are used as condiments. They are, however, chiefly of interest as oil-seeds. (*See* also 546, 997.)

654.* CAPSICUM; Solanaceæ. Two or three species yield the various forms of Chillies, and Red pepper or Cayenne pepper. They are all natives of America, although now extensively cultivated in India.

655. CARUM CARUI, *Linn.;* Umbelliferæ. Caraway Seed; Jira (*Beng.*); Zira (*Hind.*). Wild in Kashmír and the North West Himálaya, cultivated as a cold season crop throughout the plains. The seed is used entire or powdered, in curries, cakes, and confectionery.

656.* C. COPTICUM, *Benth.* The True Bishop's Weed; Ajowan (*Hind.*). Cultivated from the Punjáb and Bengal to the South Deccan. The aromatic seed forms an ingredient of the preparation, *pán*.

657. C. ROXBURGHIANUM, *Benth.;* Ajmud (*Hind.*). Is extensively cultivated and eaten like parsley; the seed is also used in flavouring curry.

658.* CARYOPHYLLUS AROMATICUS, *Linn.;* Myrtaceæ. The Cloves; Lang (*Hind.*); Lavang (*Sans.*). Indigenous in the Moluccas; cultivated in South India. The unexpanded and dried flowers form the cloves of commerce. They contain a pungent, aromatic oil, to which their peculiar property is attributable. They appear to have been known to the Sanscrit writers but not to the Romans. One of the earliest Sanscrit medical writers (*Charaki*) gives them the name of *Lavanga*, a word which exists to this day in many parts of India. In Bombay cloves are known as *Lavang*, in Bengal as *Lavanga*, and to the Hindustanis as *Laung* or *Lang*. The early Arabian writers called them *Karaufal*, a name which may have been derived from the Greek. Arabian and Persian writers, however, speak of cloves as coming from Batavia. Cloves were known in Europe after the discovery of the Moluccas by the Portuguese. The cloves imported into India during the year 1884–5 were valued at Rs.11,09,841, the bulk of which came from Zanzibar.

659. CINNAMOMUM; Laurineæ. Two or three species afford the various forms of Cinnamon. *C. Zeylanicum* (Breyn.), or Ceylon Cinnamon, is the true Cinnamon of modern commerce; *C. Tamala* and *C. obtusifolium* yield part of the so-called Cassia Lignea—the Indian Cinnamon. The exports of cinnamon from India during the year 1884–5 were valued at Rs.7,931, and the imports at Rs.2,640. The Ceylon Cinnamon of European commerce does not appear to have been the Cinnamon of the ancients. Everything points to the probability that the Cassia Lignea of China and India was the much-prized Cinnamon of antiquity. Ceylon Cinnamon appears to have been first discovered about the thirteenth century, and it was not cultivated until the eighteenth. Cassia is mentioned by one of the earliest Chinese herbal writers in 2700 B.C. (*See* also 84.)

660.* COCOS NUCIFERA, *Linn.;* Palmæ. The Cocoa-nut; Narikel (*Beng.*). A native of the Indian Archipelago, most probably having been brought to India, Ceylon, and China about 4,000 years ago, and conveyed to America and Africa at even an earlier date. It is chiefly abundant on the coast, disappearing altogether about 150 miles inland. There are two or three varieties. They flower in the hot season, and the nuts ripen in September to November. The albuminous layer from the interior of the shell is largely eaten as a condiment. It is preserved in sugar and made into various sweetmeats. In the published trade returns the Cocoa-nut is treated as a "Fruit." (*See* also 85, 715, 894, 912, 1011.)

661.* CORIANDRUM SATIVUM, *Linn.;* Umbelliferæ. The Coriander. Widely cultivated throughout India; indigenous to the Mediterranean and Caucasian regions. As a condiment this seed forms one of the indispensable ingredients of native curry. During the year 1884–5 the exports of coriander were valued at Rs.1,56,505.

662.* CUMINUM CYMINUM, *Linn.;* Umbelliferæ. The Cumin; Jira (*Beng.*). Widely cultivated in the Punjáb plains, Rajputana, and in the Deccan. Indigenous to the upper regions of the Nile, but carried at an early age to Arabia, India, and China. It was an important for invalids under the name of evalenta or revalenta. In India it is largely grown as a winter crop, and it is universally eaten, both by natives and Europeans. In the Punjáb, excluding perhaps the more arid tracts, it is grown everywhere in the plains and hills, up to an altitude of 11,000 feet in the Himálaya. It is also common in the North-West Provinces, the Central Provinces, and in Bengal.

685.* GLYCINE SOJA, *S.&Z.*; Leguminosæ. The Soya Bean; Gari-kulay (*Beng.*); Bhat, bhatwan (*Hind.*). This plant is densely clothed with fine ferruginous hairs, is sub-erect. It is met with in the tropical regions and the outer Himálaya, from Kumaon to Sikkim, the Khásia and the Naga Hills to Upper Burma. Dr. Stewart mentions a field of *bhat* having been observed in Bissahir in the Punjáb, altitude 6,000 feet. The plant is met with in a state of cultivation. Dr. Roxburgh first saw it from seed received from the Moluccas in 1798. De Candolle views Soya, and apparently correctly, as a native of Cochin China, Japan, and Java. But he remarks that "it is of modern introduction into India." "There are no common Indian names" for it. This seems to be a mistake; the plant is well known in India under the names given above. In Manipur and the Naga Hills it is one of the most abundant of pulses. In the Naga Hills it is known as *Tsu dza*, a name not unlike *Soja*, but at the same time it may be viewed as related to the old Chinese name *Shu*. The Soya most likely reached India from China, passing by way of the mountain tracts of Assam. The importance of these hills in settling questions of the nativity of cultivated Indian and Chinese plants has not been fully appreciated, and we might fairly anticipate that many statements at present accepted as facts will be considerably modified with an extended knowledge of the wild and cultivated plants of the Assam and Chinese frontier. The thorough exploration of the region indicated is very desirable. Soya is an important article of food in Tibet. It is made in India into a sauce called "Soy." The advisability of extending its cultivation on the Himálayan tracts was pressed on the Government of India in 1882 by Professor Kinch, and the attention of local Governments also was called to it, but it does not appear to have made much progress.

686. LATHYRUS SATIVUS, *Linn.*; Leguminosæ. The Jarosse of Gesse; Khesari (*Beng.*). This pulse is common in the Northern Provinces of India, from the plains of Bengal to Kumaon, where it reaches 4,000 feet in altitude, generally cultivated, but in some places wild. When cultivated, it is sown about the close of the rains (October) in heavy clay soils and on land hardened through submersion, and occasionally in rice-fields before the rice is cut. Its cultivation in the North-West Provinces and Oudh is more common in the eastern districts and in parts of Allahabad and Azimgarh. It is also extensively grown in Bengal and other parts of India. It is chiefly used as a green fodder for cattle, and seems to spring up as a weed of other and has only an abortive mace. (*See* also 1032.)

670.* NIGELLA SATIVA, *Linn.*; Ranunculaceæ. The Black Cumin or Kálá jírá (*Hind.*). A native of South Europe and of the Levant; extensively cultivated, the seeds constituting a favourite spice with the natives of India.

671. OCIMUM BASILICUM, *Linn.*; Labiatæ. The Common or Sweet Basil; Babui túlsi (*Hind.*, *Beng.*). The seeds and also the leaves are eaten as a cooling condiment. (*See* also 827.)

672.* PEUCEDANUM GRAVEOLENS, *Benth.*; Umbilliferæ. The Dill or Sowá. A native of tropical and sub-tropical India. Often cultivated in the plains of India. The seed is eaten in curry.

673. PIPER BETEL, *Linn.*; Piperaceæ. The Pán-leaf Pepper. The leaves of this plant, along with a little catechu, areca-nut, and lime, flavoured with spices, constitute the preparation known as *pán*. This is chewed by the natives of India as a mild stimulant, especially after meals. It colours the mouth and saliva a deep red colour. The trade in this leaf is entirely for Indian consumption.

674.* P. CUBEBA, *Linn.*; Cubebs. A native of Java and Sumatra; cultivated in India.

675. P. LONGUM, *Linn.* (Chavica Roxburghii, *Miq.*). One of the forms of Long Pepper; Pipul (*Beng.*); Pippali (*Sans.*). A perennial shrub of Eastern India, Nepal, and East Bengal; of Java, Ceylon, and the Philippines. The dried unripe fruit constitutes the long pepper of India.

676. P. NIGRUM, *Linn.* The Black Pepper; Kálá marich (*Hind.*). A climber extensively cultivated in South India, where it is indigenous. Introduced from India into the Straits. The berries are largely eaten as a condiment in curry, and when reduced to a powder constitute the black pepper of Europe. The value of pepper exported during the last five years was as follows:—1880-1, Rs.10,32,771; 1881-2, Rs.8,01,463; 1882-3, Rs.23,06,721; 1883-4, Rs. 16,13,362; 1884-5, Rs.19,25,973. The imports of pepper (presumably chiefly black pepper, for 1884-5 amounted to Rs.10,05,891, the bulk of which came from the Straits, a remarkable fact, since the plant is a native of India introduced into the Straits.

677.* PIMPINELLA ANISUM, *Linn.*; Umbelliferæ. The Anise. Introduced into India by the Mahomedans from Persia. It is now grown in North India. The seed is used in confectionery. The export of anise during the year 1884-5 was valued at Rs. 14,854. (*See* also 1036.)

678. TRIGONELLA FŒNUM-GRÆCUM, *Linn.*; Leguminosæ. The Fenugreek; Methi (*Hind.*). Cultivated in some parts of India, wild in Kashmír and the Punjáb. The seed is commonly used by the natives as a condiment in curry. (*See* also 479.)

679. ZINGIBER OFFICINALE, *Roscoe*; Scitamineæ. The Ginger; Adrak (*Hind.*); Ada (*Beng.*); Ardraca (*Sans.*); Zanjabil (*Arab.*). A native of the warmer parts of Asia, but not known in its wild state. Cultivated in many parts of India

for its rhizome. The value of the ginger exported from India during the last five years was as follows: —1880-1, Rs.628,822; 1881-2, Rs.5,31,172; 1882-3, Rs.6,55,542; 1883-4, Rs.10,60,978; 1884-5, Rs.15,68,570. It appears from the above figures that the export trade in ginger has increased considerably and promises a still greater increase in the future.

PREPARED SPICES, CONDIMENTS, AND CURRY POWDERS.

The same Exhibitors who have already been referred to as showing Jams and Chutneys show also Spices and Curry Powders.

SUB-COURT XI.

The exhibits which fall into Division I., Section 2, are shown in this Sub-Court.

THE PULSES.

These may be briefly defined as leguminous seeds which are boiled and eaten as a regular article of diet. One of the most curious and interesting features of an Indian bazaar is the baskets of whole and split pulses, peas, beans, and lentils of all colours,—white, black, brown, green, grey, red, &c.—shown by the dealers. This has been taken advantage of in the arrangement of the collections shown, in the form of a grain merchant's shop.

There are probably not more than two or three kinds of pulse exported from India, but as the quotations of sea-borne trade are given collectively, the relative amounts of each kind cannot be accurately expressed. In the trade returns gram is also treated separately instead of being included with the other pulses. It may be stated of the pulses as a whole, that they form an exceedingly important article of internal trade, and including gram the exports are by no means inconsiderable. During the year 1884-85 they amounted to 923,198 cwt., valued at Rs.26,28,955. The imports are small, and the total foreign trade in these pulses may approximately therefore be put down at £260,000, but this large sum must bear but a small relation to the internal trade. The total area under pulses is 48,000,000 of acres, but as these are chiefly grown as cold season crops, the same land yields in addition a crop of some other product, such as wheat or rice.

680.* Cajanus indicus, *Spreng.*; Leguminosæ. The Pigeon-pea; Arhar dál (*Hind., Beng.*). This is apparently a native of equatorial Africa. Cultivated in most parts of India, constituting an important article of food. There are two chief varieties: *C. flavus* (DC.), with the pea plain yellow, known in the vernacular as *thor*; and *C. bicolor* (DC.), with the pea veined with purple, known as (*arhar*). The latter is the one most commonly cultivated in the North-West Provinces and Oudh, while in the Central Provinces and the Deccan *thor* takes the place of *arhar*. It is grown mostly as a subordinate crop along with *juar*, *bajra*, and cotton, *sunn*, jute, &c., and by itself to a comparatively much smaller extent. The leaves are considered an excellent fodder; the stalks are used for roofing, basket-making, and tubular wicker-work fascines (*bira* or *ajar*) used to line wells to prevent the earth from falling in.

681.* Cicer arietinum, *Linn.*; Leguminosæ. The Common Gram, or Chicken-pea; Chena or Chola (*Hind., Beng.*). Originally a native of the countries to the south of the Caucasus and to the north of Persia. It was probably carried into India by the Western Aryans at an early date, and prior to the time of its cultivation in Europe. There seems some probability that the plant may have also been indigenous in Greece. Cultivated throughout India in any soil, giving, however, the largest return in heavy soils. There are two sorts—one, a large reddish grain; the other, a small light-brown one. The exports for the last three years were as follows:—

	Cwts.	Rs.
1882-83 . .	312,953	8,28,647
1883-84 . .	392,694	11,99,796
1884-85 . .	314,965	9,28,848

Madras and Bengal supplied the bulk of the exports, the major portion of which was consigned to Mauritius and Ceylon. (*See* also 1020.)

682. Dolichos biflorus, *Linn.*; Leguminosæ. The Horse-gram; Kurti-kalai (*Beng.*); Kulthi gahat (*Hind.*). There are two very distinct varieties of this pulse—the one an erect annual (var. *uniflora*), the other a twining herb (var. *biflora*), met with chiefly in a state of cultivation as a pulse crop on the tropical and subtropical Himálaya, to Burma and Ceylon. It is sown either singly or along with other grains; it seems to succeed best near the coast. The sowing is made in October and November, generally in dry, light, rich soils; and the crop is reaped in February. The grain is eaten by the poorer classes of natives, and is also given to horses and cattle. The pods are flat and curved like a sickle; they are given to cattle. The straw is a useful fodder. (*See* also 527.)

683. D. Lablab, *Linn.*; The Indian Bean; Sim, Makhum-sim (*Beng.*); Sim (*Hind.*). Wild and cultivated throughout India; ascends to 6,000 to 7,000 feet on the Himaláya. There are several varieties of this bean. Roxburgh describes thirteen cultivated. Most of the forms are eaten cooked in curry by the natives as a vegetable or bean, not as a pulse. When young and tender, the pods constitute a good substitute for the common French beans.

684.* Ervum Lens, *Linn.*; Leguminosæ. The Lentil; Masúri (*Hind.*). This appears to be originally a native of Western Asia, Greece, and Italy. At a very early date it was introduced into Egypt as a cultivated plant, and from this centre it spread east and west, reaching India probably about 2,000 years ago. The meal from this pulse is sold in Europe as a food for invalids under the name of evalenta or revalenta. In India it is largely grown as a winter crop, and it is universally eaten, both by natives and Europeans. In the Punjáb, excluding perhaps the more arid tracts, it is grown everywhere in the plains and hills, up to an altitude of 11,000 feet in the Himálaya. It is also common in the North-West Provinces, the Central Provinces, and in Bengal.

685.* GLYCINE SOJA, *S.&Z.;* Leguminosæ. The Soya Bean; Gari-kulay (*Beng.*): Bhat, bhatwan (*Hind.*). This plant is densely clothed with fine ferruginous hairs, is sub-erect. It is met with in the tropical regions and the outer Himálaya, from Kumaon to Sikkim, the Khásia and the Naga Hills to Upper Burma. Dr. Stewart mentions a field of *bhat* having been observed in Bissahir in the Punjáb, altitude 6,000 feet. The plant is met with in a state of cultivation. Dr. Roxburgh first saw it from seed received from the Moluccas in 1798. De Candolle views Soya, and apparently correctly, as a native of Cochin China, Japan, and Java. But he remarks that "it is of modern introduction into India." "There are no common Indian names" for it. This seems to be a mistake; the plant is well known in India under the names given above. In Manipur and the Naga Hills it is one of the most abundant of pulses. In the Naga Hills it is known as *Tsu dza*, a name not unlike *Soja*, but at the same time it may be viewed as related to the old Chinese name *Shu*. The Soya most likely reached India from China, passing by way of the mountain tracts of Assam. The importance of these hills in settling questions of the nativity of cultivated Indian and Chinese plants has not been fully appreciated, and we might fairly anticipate that many statements at present accepted as facts will be considerably modified with an extended knowledge of the wild and cultivated plants of the Assam and Chinese frontier. The thorough exploration of the region indicated is very desirable. Soya is an important article of food in Tibet. It is made in India into a sauce called "Soy." The advisability of extending its cultivation on the Himálayan tracts was pressed on the Government of India in 1882 by Professor Kinch, and the attention of local Governments also was called to it, but it does not appear to have made much progress.

686. LATHYRUS SATIVUS, *Linn.;* Leguminosæ. The Jarosse of Gesse; Khesari (*Beng.*). This pulse is common in the Northern Provinces of India, from the plains of Bengal to Kumaon, where it reaches 4,000 feet in altitude, generally cultivated, but in some places wild. When cultivated, it is sown about the close of the rains (October) in heavy clay soils and on land hardened through submersion, and occasionally in rice-fields before the rice is cut. Its cultivation in the North-West Provinces and Oudh is more common in the eastern districts and in parts of Allahabad and Azimgarh. It is also extensively grown in Bengal and other parts of India. It is chiefly used as a green fodder for cattle, and seems to spring up as a weed of other crops. The seeds are very irregular in form, generally wedge-shaped, grey coloured, and minutely spotted with a dark line. They have in Europe the reputation of causing paralysis of the lower extremities. In the Proceedings of the Government of the North-West Provinces for 1866, pp. 265 to 295, Dr. Irving gives an interesting account of the prevalence of a form of palsy in the Barrah and also in the Khyragarh divisions of the Allahabad district. He attributes the disease to the habit of eating, as an article of daily food, the *khesari* vetch. He bases his opinion on the fact that the peculiar disease is met with only in districts where this pulse is eaten as a regular article of food. The disease appears suddenly, having none of the premonitory symptoms of paralysis. The sufferer having shown no previous disease which could be supposed to give origin to palsy, suddenly becomes paralysed. There is no pain, and the affected part, instead of becoming deformed, continues to grow. The disease is confined to the lower limbs, and is much more prevalent amongst men than women, but boys are often found quite lame. The symptoms and history are entirely in favour of the disease being of a paralytic nature and not rheumatic, such as might result from exposure to wet and cold. It would thus seem desirable to discourage the cultivation of this plant as a food crop. The split pea is largely used to adulterate *dál*, from which it can scarcely be distinguished when sold in the split form. It is used, in fact, by the poorer classes as an occasional substitute for other pulses, but is hard and indigestible. It is, however, only injurious when eaten continuously as a regular article of food. The troops under General Elphinstone in the first expedition to Cabul suffered very much from the fact of their having to mix this pulse with their food. Pigs fed on the *khesari* are said to lose the use of their limbs, but fatten well. (*See* also 443.)

687. PHASEOLUS ACONITIFOLIUS, *Jacq.;* Leguminosæ. The Moth or Mothi (*Hind.*). Found from the North-West Himálaya to Ceylon, ascending to 4,000 feet in altitude. Cultivated as a hot-weather or *kharif* crop in the plains, in dry, light, sandy soil. In many parts of India it is quite as much cultivated as *úrd*. In the North-West Provinces and Oudh it is grown as a sole crop and also among millets. It is not possible to give the total area in India which is annually under this pulse, but it is by no means an unimportant crop. The grain is used as food by the natives, but is not considered wholesome. It is also used as cattle-food, and is regarded as fattening. The leaves and stalks are also given to cattle.

688. P. MUNGO, *Linn.* (*a*) Var. *Max* (Roxb.). The Mung or Mug (*Hind.*). This is sometimes spoken of as "green gram." It is a native of India, but has been cultivated for at least 3,000 years. It is met with throughout the plains, and ascends to 6,000 feet in the outer ranges of the North-West Himálaya. It requires a strong, rich dry soil; is seldom grown alone, being a subordinate crop in fields of millet or cotton. The ripe grain is wholesome and nutritious, much esteemed, and commands a comparatively high price. The crushed stalks and leaves are prized as fodder for cattle. (*b*) Var. *Radiatus* (Linn.). The Mash-kolai (*Beng.*); Urd mash (*Hind.*). This variety differs from *P. Mungo* proper in having longer and more trailing stems, in the plant being much more hairy, in the seeds being fewer, larger and longer, and usually of a dark colour. It has two distinct sub-varieties—one with large black seeds, ripening in August and September, and the other with smaller green seeds, ripening in October and November. Both are, however, sown at the commencement of the rains. The soil which suits the crop is of the heavier kind. It is cultivated in most parts of the plains as a subordinate crop with millet or cotton.

689. P. TRILOBUS, *Ait.* The Mungani (*Beng.*). Common throughout India, wild and also frequently cultivated; it ascends in the North-West to 7,000 feet in altitude. Seeds are gathered and eaten by the poor. It affords good fodder.

690.* PHASEOLUS VULGARIS, *Linn.* The Kidney or French Bean or Haricot. Cultivated, for the sake of its young pods, in all parts of India, chiefly in gardens. The green pods are cut up into slices, boiled, and eaten by Europeans; they are scarcely, if ever, used by the natives.

691.* PISUM ARVENSE, *Linn.*; Leguminosæ. The Grey or Field Pea; Desi Mattar (*Hind.*, *Beng.*). This is supposed to be originally a native of Greece and of the Levant, and is probably the parent of *P. savitum.* It is cultivated in many parts of India during the cold weather. It produces small, round, compressed, greenish, and marbled peas. It bears some resemblance, in appearance of grain and in mode of cultivation, to *Lathyrus sativus*, the latter being frequently mixed with it.

692.* P. SATIVUM, *Linn.* The Common Pea; Mattar, Gol mattar (*N.-W. P.*). An annual, climbing by means of tendrils; a native of the south of Europe. Cultivated in many parts of India during the cold weather, and extensively so by Europeans. It includes the white pea, known as *Cabuli* and *Patnai*, according as they are large or small. *P. sativum* is more valuable and prolific than *P. arvense.* It is one of the oldest and most valuable of cultivated legumes.

693. VIGNA CATIANG, *Endl.*; Leguminosæ. The Chowlí of India; Barbati (*Beng.*); Urohi Mahorpat (*Ass.*). Universally cultivated in the tropical zone of India on account of the grain, which forms one of the summer crops raised along with the millets; it ripens in October and November. The pod is sometimes as much as two feet in length, and contains a number of seeds. These constitute a considerable article of food, but the crop is not much valued, on account of the seed being difficult of digestion. In Bengal the young green entire pods are cooked in curry. The leaves and stems are used as cattle-fodder. This plant is said to afford a green dye. (*See* Dyes.)

SUB-COURT XII.

GRAINS.

This sub-Court includes the exhibits which fall under Division I., Section 1, Cereals; and Section 3, Other Edible Grains and Seeds.

THE GRAIN TROPHY.

The idea of this structure is taken from the famous tomb of Itmád-ud-dowlah at Agra, the beautiful marbled geometric mosaics having been imitated by glass panels of coloured grains. On the outside elevations there are eight large panels, two of which are devoted to rice, two to wheat, two to Indian-corn, one to barley and oats, and one to millets and Job's tears. Sixteen smaller panels are filled with the pulses, and the remainder with other edible grains and oil-seeds. The interior is thatched with grains in ear and Indian-corn cobs. In the four corners of the room are shown commercial samples of the grains, and in the centre a group of three women (in clay) "grinding at the mill."

Near by will also be found the cases containing the special display of wheats prepared by the Bombay Commercial Committee, and the collections of rice from Bengal and Burma.

CEREALS.

These may popularly be described as Rice, Wheat, Barley, Oats, Indian-corn, and the various forms of Millet.

In Bengal, Burma, Orissa, and the eastern portion of Central India, the southern part of Madras and the western districts of Bombay, rice is the principal food. In the Punjáb, the North-West Provinces and Oudh, Behar and the northern part of the Central Provinces and Guzerat the poorer classes live on millets (*juar* and *bajra*) grown in the rains, and also on barley and gram; the richer only use wheat and rice. In the southern part of the Central Provinces, Berar, the Bombay Deccan, and the northern part of Madras, the larger millets, *juar* and *bajra*, are the staple foods. In Mysore the small millet, *ragí*, is the principal article of food. In Assam rice is the staple, supplemented with Indian-corn and Job's tears. Wheat is chiefly grown for export, and to the inhabitants of India rice is the most valuable of all the Cereals.

The grains constitute an important item in India's Foreign Trade. In 1884–85 the imports were 54,532 cwt., valued at Rs. 1,70,972 and the exports 38,294,889 cwt., valued at Rs. 13,62,45,269. At par this large foreign trade might be expressed at 15½ million pounds sterling. The recent rapid growth of the wheat trade is almost unprecedented in the history of any other product, and it seems to promise a still greater development.

I.—RICE.

694. ORYZA SATIVA, *Linn.*; Gramineæ. Rice Dhánya, Tandulam, Vrihi, Arunya (*Sans.*). (*See also* 369, 584, 723.)

Wild Rice.—In the marshes and tanks of Bengal, wild rice—*uri* or *jará-dhan*—is very plentiful. This is exceedingly like some of the forms of the cultivated *áman* rices. As the water rises in the tanks it grows with great rapidity, spreading from the tanks over the neighbouring fields until it becomes the cultivator's greatest enemy. It, however, yields a grain which is regularly eaten, the ears being tied together to prevent the grain shaking into the water. When ripe, the fishermen pass over the fields and lakes in their boats and collect the harvest of wild grain. The *uri* may possibly be the source of the aquatic or *áman* rices. It seems probable, however, that the habit of cultivating the plant originated in China. On the lower hills of India another wild rice occurs, viz., *Oryza coarctata* (Roxb.). This grows on dry rocky soils and yields an edible grain. Structurally this differs very much from the cultivated hill rices, otherwise it might be inferred that it was the source of the *áus* rices or those which do not require to be half submerged.

The Peculiarities of the Cultivated Rices.—Some forms are temperate and grow on the hills, often ascending to 8,000 ft. in altitude. Others occur on the inundated plains or over deep marshes, luxuriating in a tropical climate; the latter frequently grow up with the rising water until they attain a height of as much as 20 ft.

Soil, climate, and mode of cultivation, during the lapse of centuries, have doubtless all combined to produce from a common stock the multitude of forms with which we are familiar. As far as the plains are concerned, rice crops may be referred to two or three primary groups, according to the method of cultivation, season of the year when cultivated, and length of the period required for ripening. These groups receive various names in different districts and provinces, but correspond to each other pretty constantly, being earlier or later, as the result of special peculiarities in climate and soil or season of rainfall. The average condition in Bengal may be expressed as follows:—

1st. *The Aus or Asu Crop.*—The forms thrown into this group are the early or autumn rices. They are sown from April to May, on comparatively high lands not inundated during the rains. The seed is generally sown broadcast, and the field is carefully kept free from weeds during May and the first half of June. The crop is harvested from July to August, or even not till September. The forms of *áus* are the least valuable of all the rices; about one-sixth of Bengal rice belongs to this group.

2nd. *Aman Crop.*—This crop comprises the late or cold-season rices. Owing to their ripening on inundated fields, they are sometimes called the floating rices. They are referred to two important sub-groups:—

(*a*) *Chotan áman.*—The early and better sorts of *áman;* these are generally transplanted into the field from a seed-bed.

(*b*) *Boran áman.*—The coarser forms of *áman*, which grow habitually in deep water. They are sown for the most part broadcast in *bíls* or low-lying lands: they are only occasionally transplanted.

The weeding required for the *áus* crop is often sufficient for a combined *áus* and *áman* crop. As the height of the water rises over the inundated fields the *áman* crop may be observed to grow with marvellous rapidity, as much as 9 in. having been recorded in 24 hours at the beginning of the rains. When submerged through a sudden flooding for more than three days the crop is completely destroyed. This is the chief danger to the *áman* rices.

The *áman* is the principal crop of rice in the plains, after the harvest of which the land generally remains undisturbed until the end of February, when preparations for the new *áus* crop commence. Sometimes, however, winter crops of pulses and oil-seeds are taken off the higher *áman* lands.

3rd. *The Boro Crop.*—The hot-season rices come under this heading. They are transplanted from the seed-bed or sown broadcast from December to February and harvested in April to May. The forms of this group yield an abundant crop of very coarse and hard rice, chiefly consumed by the poorer classes. They are quick-growing rices, one kind of which is known as the *shatia* or 60-days' rice, because in that period, from sowing to harvest, it yields its crop. Only a very limited amount of these rices is cultivated; they are suitable for *churs* or low-lying lands. They are, however, of much value to the poor, since the coming of this crop in the hot season tends to lower the then high rates of other classes of rice. A peculiar kind of *boro* rice is known as *raida* or *bhasha-naranga.* This is sown along with the ordinary boro rice in December. The young stems are shorn when the *boro* crop is removed, but this does not seem to injure the *raida.* It continues to grow, and yields its crop in September or October, having been thus ten to eleven months on the field.

Five crops of rice a year.—A proprietor of an estate with a fairly mixed soil, according to this system, might have three, if not four, or even five, harvests of rice every twelve months, thus:—

(1) *Aus* harvest, from July to August.
(2) *Chotan áman*, from October to November.
(3) *Boran áman*, from December to January.
(4) *Boro*, from April to May.
(5) *Raida*, from September to October.

Two harvests are all but universal in Bengal, with an occasional third but smaller one; two crops are frequently taken off the same field. Of these groups of rices the *áus*, *boro*, and *raida* cannot be used at religious ceremonies as offerings to the Hindu gods; but these, together with the *boran áman*, are the rices eaten by the million, the finer classes of *áman* being, from their high price, restricted to the rich. A remarkable fact which may be here noted is that the *áus*, *áman*, or *boro* rices of one district are often so different from those of another, that if interchanged the one will not grow on the fields on which the other has flourished for centuries. Here the European farmer is confronted with a problem scarcely known to his scientific agriculture; but although it is difficult to follow his reasonings, the rice cultivator of India will detect the one from the other with a perfectly marvellous degree of certainty.

Some forms of rice are scented, while the majority have no smell whatever. Scented rices are common, for example, in Orissa and Behar, and are much prized by certain classes of people. The richer natives eat the long, thin, white *chotan áman* rices; while the short, thick, more or less reddish rices—the so-called Patna rices—are those eaten by the mass of the people of India. The Mahommedans prefer an absorbent rice, such as that from Pilibhit. In Burma, amongst many other high class rices, a grain is produced which, while largely used for industrial purposes, is regarded as unwholesome as an article of food. One of the most curious peculiarities and one recently brought to light regarding rice is that while the great mass of rices contain only one grain within the husk, two or even three grains are regularly present in certain rices.

TRADE RETURNS IN RICE.—It has been calculated that in India, out of a total area of 167,000,000 acres of land under crops, nearly 60,000,000 acres are annually under rice cultivation, and of this Bengal has 37,500,000 acres. The Indian rice trade (excluding Burma) is chiefly for home consumption. This statement may be proved by comparing the area under rice and the exports to foreign countries with those for wheat or any other important product. Allowing for imperfections, it will be found in round figures that, raised from one-third of the area under rice, the exports of wheat are relatively greater and much more valuable than the rice exports. In certain parts of Bengal a surplus of rice is raised for export, but the foreign market is chiefly met by Burma. Within the past few years, however, the foreign trade in rice may be said to have been almost ruined. This in a large measure is due to the fact that sugar can now be got in Europe nearly as cheap as rice, and at the same time the abundant harvests of wheat both in Europe and America have reduced the price of wheat to a point lower than has been known for the past hundred years. Of late an important item in the rice export trade has been the demand for the grain as a source of spirit. Sugar and wheat being at the present moment at such a low figure, rice has, however, failed to hold its own. At the same time the Burmese cultivators, from a mistaken idea of raising the rate, have withheld supplies until the prices obtained in Europe do not correspond with those paid in Burma. The heavy export duty (nearly 15 per cent.) levied on rice has also greatly helped to produce the present depression in the rice trade. The following were the exports and imports of rice during the last three years:—

RICE IN THE HUSK.

		Cwt.	Rs.
1882-83	Imports	38	110
	Exports	228,567	362,363
		228,605	362,473
1883-84	Imports	2,001	3,808
	Exports	208,144	332,012
		210,145	335,820
1884-85	Imports	2,081	6,761
	Exports	349,396	694,106
		351,477	700,867

RICE NOT IN THE HUSK.

		Cwt.	Rs.
1882-83	Imports	501	2,232
	Exports	31,029,721	84,400,909
		31,030,222	84,403,141
1883-84	Imports	423	2,038
	Exports	26,831,715	83,288,786
		26,832,138	83,290,824
1884-85	Imports	3,997	18,622
	Exports	21,702,136	71,227,870
		21,706,133	71,246,492

EXHIBITORS.—Messrs. Rowett exhibit 30 samples of Rangoon Rice.

II.—WHEAT.

695.* TRITICUM SATIVUM, *Lam.*; Gramineæ. Common Wheat; Genhu (*Hind.*); Godhuma (*Sans.*).

Wheat is one of the most ancient of all foodstuffs, and it is extremely difficult to ascertain the source from which it was originally obtained. It nowhere exists in India, China, or Mongolia except in a state of cultivation, but evidence seems to favour the idea that it spread to these countries from the Euphrates Valley.

Wheats are grouped primarily into what are known as *soft* and *hard* wheats. Soft wheats are in most demand for the United Kingdom, while the hard forms go chiefly to the Mediterranean, being used in the manufacture of maccaroni and preferred by the natives of India; a coarse flour made from hard wheat is in India known as *suji*. Each of these two classes of wheats are referred to groups according to colour, white or red, and again according as the grain is bearded or beardless. The best Indian wheats are the fine, soft, white forms.

Various professional opinions have been given regarding these, which may be briefly summarised. They all possess in a marked degree the character of great dryness, with a distinct beany and almost aromatic flavour. The flours prepared from them are ricey, yielding a bread of a close texture, but having a hard and brittle crust. These characteristics do not, however, detract from their usefulness in any important degree, and if liberally mixed with other wheats they yield very superior bread. The bread supplied to our British troops in India is made entirely of Indian flour, and seems good and light. In fact the "chief characteristics of the Indian wheats are just those in which the wheats grown in Europe are most deficient. Their great dryness and soundness render them invaluable for admixture with English wheats that are in any degree out of condition through moisture. . . . Added to their dryness, the thinness of the skins of these wheats, and consequent greatness of the yield of flour, must always place them in the front rank as a 'miller's' wheat whenever they are handled with reasonable intelligence and skill."

The superior nutritive quality of bread as compared with rice, Indian-corn, potatoes, and other well-known foods containing starch, depends upon the proportion of gluten or nitrogenous compounds present in the flour. The elasticity of bread is also due to the gluten, and consequently it is generally believed that upon this constituent depends the yield of bread from flour. But this is not the case, unless at the same time a high percentage of gluten be associated with a high degree of dryness, for it is upon dryness that the yield of bread mainly depends.

Indian wheats do not appear to have found their way to any appreciable extent at least into the Scotch market. This seems to be mainly due to the difference of the Scotch system of baking as compared to the English, the flours from Indian wheats not being strong enough for the Scotch system of public baking.

Indian wheats were not much known or appreciated in the European markets previous to the year 1871–72. From that year some attention was given to the subject, and the Government of India, following up the movement, abolished in January 1873 the export duty of 3 annas per maund. The result was that the exports rose suddenly, and the wheat trade has since then steadily increased. The low rate of exchange has also greatly assisted the development of this new and now most valuable export trade.

The total area under wheat cultivation in 1884–85 has been calculated at 20,306,464 acres; the Punjáb having had nearly 8 million acres, the North-West Provinces 5 million, the Central Provinces 3½ million, Bombay 2¼ million, and Bengal nearly a million acres. The outturn of grain from irrigated land is often as high as 15 maunds an acre, but it varies to 6 maunds on the unirrigated land. The cost of cultivation in the Central Provinces has been estimated at Rs. 15† to Rs. 16 an acre for unirrigated lands, and Rs. 22 to Rs. 24† for irrigated, and this may be viewed as a fair average for all the wheat-producing districts. The total exports and imports for the years 1883 to 1885 were as follows:—

		Cwts.	Rs.
1883–84	Imports	188,310	7,75,772
	Exports	20,956,495	8,87,75,610
	Total	21,144,805	8,95,11,382
1884–85	Imports	17,783	57,789
	Exports	15,831,754	6,30,91,402
	Total	15,849,537	6,31,49,191

† This might be viewed as equivalent to from £1 to £2 an acre.

Wheat sold in 1884–85 in the Central Provinces at 25·5; Bombay at 14·6; North-West Provinces at 19·9; Punjab at 24·7; Bengal at 17·2; and Madras at 12·2 seers per rupee.

EXHIBITORS.—Collections of wheat are shown from the Punjáb, the North-West Provinces, the Central Provinces, Bombay, Sind, and Bengal. Deputy Surgeon General J. Shortt, M.D., F.L.S., exhibits samples of Spelt wheat (*Triticum spelta*) from the Shevaroys, Madras Presidency.

The Director of Agriculture, Central Provinces, contributes a large collection of wheat samples.

The Bombay Committee, having undertaken the exhibition of wheat samples from all India, have, in conjunction with the Bombay Chamber of Commerce, shown collections from the Punjab, North-West Provinces, Central Provinces, Bombay Presidency, including Sind, and also from Bengal. The Bombay Flour Mill Company, Limited, have sent samples of various descriptions of flour.

III.—MILLETS.

Where rice is not cultivated as the staple food, the millets are exceedingly important. This is the case in a marked degree in wheat-producing districts, thus showing conclusively that the bulk of the wheat is grown essentially for foreign trade. With the exception of Burma, rice is grown almost entirely for home consumption; and where rice cannot be cultivated, the millets invariably take its place as the staple food-crop of the mass of the people. The total area of land under millets has been estimated as 33,228,867 acres, of which Bombay has 13 million, Madras 7½ million, the North-West Provinces 5½ million, the Punjáb nearly 5 million, and Berar a little over 2 million acres. In Bengal millets are scarcely cultivated excepting to a small extent by the hill tribes. The exports of millets to foreign countries during the past two years were as follows:—

JUAR AND BAJRA EXPORTS.

	Cwts.	Rs.
1883–84	248,110	6,51,613
1884–85	245,633	6,99,137

The following are the more important millets arranged alphabetically:—

696. ELEUSINE COROCANA, *Gærtn.*; Gramineæ. Ragí or Marúa Millet. A procumbent grass, most probably a native of India, and widely cultivated during the rainy season, but chiefly in South and West India. It has been grown in Egypt during modern times; is mentioned by Sanscrit authors under the name of *Rajika* but apparently was not known to the Arabs, Greeks, or Romans. This is looked upon as the staple grain of Mysore, being stored in huts. A fer-

mented liquor is made from it, as also a kind of beer. Ragí in 1884–85 sold in Madras at 28·4 seers per rupee. (*See* also 349.)

697. PANICUM FRUMENTACEUM, *Roxb.* Gramineæ. Shamula or Sawan. This is the most rapid growing of all the millets, affording, through its early ripening, a cheap grain which comes into market before the main autumn food-crop is harvested. It is subject to the danger of destruction through excessive rain and blight. The grain is wholesome and nourishing, and is a favourite with the poorer class. (*See* also 373.)

698.* P. MILIACEUM, *Linn.* Chena or the Common Millet. This is viewed as a native of Egypt and of Arabia, and was evidently introduced at a very early date into India. Its cultivation is pre-historic in Europe, Egypt, and Asia. In point of value as a food-stuff, it is supposed to be inferior to *Setaria italica* (Beauv.), and fetches accordingly a much lower price. It also grows very much more slowly than that species, but has one advantage of great importance to the poorer hill tribes, viz., it may be successfully cultivated on indifferent soils up to an altitude of 10,000 ft. The straw is of no use as a fodder, and is accordingly thrown away. (*See* also 75.)

699. PASPALUM SCROBICULATUM, *Linn.* Gramineæ. Koda or Khodon Millet. A native of India, luxuriating in light, dry, loose soils, being cultivated in the rainy season. It is far more extensively grown than any of the other minor millets, owing to the readiness with which it may be cultivated. It is a common and cheap grain, and is an important article of food with the poorer classes, particularly those who inhabit the mountains and the more barren parts of the country; but it is considered unwholesome, as it tends to produce diarrhœa. It is said to have an intoxicating effect. The straw is given as fodder to cattle. (*See* also 380.)

700. PENNISETUM TYPHOIDEUM, *Rich.* The Spiked Millet or Bajra. A native of tropical Asia, Nubia and Egypt. Cultivated to a large extent in Northern and Southern India, especially on the Coromandel Coast and in the North-West Provinces during the rainy season. The grain is used chiefly by the lower classes of natives, and is eaten in the cold season. It is considered heating, but more nutritious than rice. Bajra in 1884–5 sold in the North-West Provinces at 24·6 seers per rupee. The fodder is much used. (*See* also 382.)

701. SETARIA ITALICA, *Beauv.* Gramineæ. German or Italian Millet, the Kangni of the North-West Provinces. This is supposed to be a native of China, Japan, and the Indian Archipelago. It is, however, extensively cultivated in India, both on the plains and on the hills ascending to 6,000 ft. above the level of the sea. Two crops may be taken off the same field a year, but this millet is chiefly grown as a subsidiary crop; there are two varieties. The grain is much approved as an article of food. The flour is made into pastry and is valued as a food for invalids. The Brahmins especially esteem it. The grain is in demand as a food for cage-birds. The straw is not much valued. (*See* also 392.)

702. SORGHUM VULGARE, *Pers.* Gramineæ. The Great Millet or Guinea corn; Juar, cholum (*Hind.*). This is perhaps the most important of the millets, and with *bajra* is regularly exported. According to some authors, this plant is viewed as indigenous to India and China. It is cultivated in Lower Egypt at the present day under the name *dhurra*, and an analogous form is wild in equatorial Africa. De Candolle inclines to the view that it is more probably a native of Africa than of Asia. Juar in 1884–5 sold in the Punjab at 36·3 seers per rupee. (*See* also 396.)

IV.—BARLEY.

703. HORDEUM VULGARE, *Linn.* Gramineæ. Barley. A native of Western temperate Asia; cultivated from remote ages.

Barley is cultivated to a considerable extent in North India, about 4,551,372 acres being annually under the crop. There are two principal varieties, one of which has two rows of grain in the ear. (*See* also 364.)

V.—INDIAN CORN OR MAIZE.

704.* ZEA MAYS, *Linn.* Indian-Corn or Maize. As this, after the millets, is perhaps the next most important Indian food-stuff, it may not be out of place to say something regarding it here. In his 'Origin of Cultivated Plants,' De Candolle has shown conclusively that maize was unknown before the discovery of America. *Zea* is a remarkable illustration of a genus containing only one species, a genus that has little in common with its nearest allies. Roxburgh, who wrote shortly after the beginning of the present century, says it was in his time cultivated in gardens as an ornament, "but nowhere on the continent of India as an object of cultivation on a large scale." There are now over $2\frac{1}{4}$ million acres annually under this crop. The rapidity with which it has spread all over the empire, until it must now rank as an important food-crop, is a powerful proof of its being a modern introduction, since so useful a plant was certain to have taken its present position thousands of years ago had it existed in the country at all.

While cultivated extensively in every district in India it is not exported, but is either eaten green as a vegetable, or matured as a grain-crop; it is not made into flour to any great extent. To the hill tribes this is now an important article of food. In South India it may be grown all the year through. There are many varieties, some with white grains, others yellow, dark red, orange or mottled. A collection of many thousand cobs is shown on the grain trophy. (*See* also 401.)

VI.—OATS.

705.* AVENA SATIVA, *Linn.* Oats. Introduced into India within the past fifty years, this crop has only gained favour in the neighbourhood of cantonments as a food-supply for horses. It is accordingly chiefly met with in Northern India. With copious watering, a valuable crop of green fodder may be obtained in the cold season. Oats do not appear to be cultivated in India as an article of human food; there were in 1884–85 exported 87,725 cwt. valued at Rs. 1,89,751. The annual imports are trifling, but the export trade is capable of considerable development should necessity arise. (*See* also 332.)

VII.—JOB'S TEARS.

706. Coix lachryma, *Linn.* Job's Tears. This curious grain might almost be described as unknown to the natives of India generally except as a weed of cultivation: in Chutia Nagpur it is common, but never eaten by the Kolarian tribes. To the hill tribes on the eastern frontier, however, it is an important article of food. In Manipur it is regularly cultivated by the hill tribes, a white and a black form of the globular grain being equally abundant. The Karens, a tribe in Burma, use a long variety for ornamental purposes, sewing the pretty shining grains all over their costumes, and so also the Angami Nagas ornament their ear-rings with this form. Specimens of Job's Tears are shown from Assam and the Naga Hills, as also decorative articles ornamented with the grain. (*See* also 342.)

OTHER GRAINS AND SEEDS.

This includes the forms of the grain-yielding species of amarantus and buckwheat. The former in some parts of India, as, for example, on the Punjáb Himálaya, is a most important article of food. During the autumn the terraced hill-sides are speckled with the golden plots of this crop. There are two primary varieties, one green, becoming yellow when ripe, the other dark red. The garden plant known as Love-lies-bleeding is also to a limited extent cultivated for its grain, but it is admittedly an introduced plant; while *Amarantus paniculatus* (Miq.), var. *frumentaceus* (Buch.), the *báthu* of the hills, seems in all probability to be indigenous. Buckwheat, *Fagopyrum esculentum* (Mœnch), the *chin*, although cultivated in many parts of India, is by no means an article of much importance. The seeds are ground to flour and made into thin cakes. The grain is chiefly sold for the purpose of feeding fowls, pheasants, &c. A curiosity in the way of food-grains may be mentioned in *Perilla ocimoides* (Linn.), a member of the Labiatæ or mint family. This is regularly cultivated for its small aromatic seeds—*kenia* of the Naga Hills. Of amarantus and buckwheat fairly good collections are shown.

SUB-COURT XIII.

This includes the articles enumerated in the "Classified List," Division I., Sections 7 and 8.

SUGARS, STARCHES, AND TODDY.

Sugar.—Of the products enumerated in this list (excluding rice and wheat, which are dealt with in another chapter), sugar and palm-toddy are the most important. From the latter sugar is largely prepared, so that the two are intimately related. Sugar is in fact obtained from two forms of the so-called sugar-cane, and from four species of palms, viz., *Phœnix sylvestris*, the Indian Date-palm, or toddy palm of Bengal; *Borassus flabelliformis*, the Palmyra or toddy palm of South India, Bombay, and Burma; *Cocos nucifera*, the Cocoa-nut palm, and *Caryota urens*, the Sago palm. The bulk of the Indian sugar is derived, however, from *Saccharum officinarum*, the Indian sugar-cane, and experimentally from *Sorghum saccharatum*. The interest in beet-sugar, so far as India is concerned, consists mainly in the influence it has exercised over our exports of raw sugars. France, Austria, and Germany, in order to foster and develop the beet-sugar trade, have instituted a protective system of giving bounties to home refiners, and have at the same time levied upon all foreign sugars heavy import duties. This system has naturally led to a vast extension of beet cultivation and of refining operations. Over-production has, however, caused ruinous reduction in prices of sugar; cane-sugar falling in exact ratio with beet. This has naturally caused the bankruptcy of numbers of beet-growers and of some of the largest refiners, a financial crisis having occurred in Vienna in consequence of these failures. India is, however, but indirectly affected by the beet-sugars of Europe; it is Mauritius which exercises the greatest influence on our markets. Very little indeed of the immense stock of sugar accumulated in Europe has found its way to India; still the imports during 1884–85 were very nearly twice those of the previous year. The explanation of this may be looked for in the threatened failure of the Indian crops, the general improvement of the country, and the increased facilities of transport. One of the chief obstacles to Indian-grown sugars participating more largely in the demand for refined sugars is our defective system of expressing the juice—a system which causes ruinous fermentation.

In his review of Sea-borne Foreign Trade of British India for 1883–4, Mr. J. E. O'Conor gives an interesting *résumé* of the present position of the Indian sugar trade. In March, 1882, the import duty of 5 per cent. on sugar was "taken off, with other import duties, and the remission was vehemently opposed by the representative, in the Legislative Council, o the mercantile community of Calcutta, on th ground that it would assuredly bring about the extinction of the sugar industry in Bengal. The prediction so far has been singularly falsified, and if the trade should collapse now, after having had for two full years since the abolition of the duty a far more flourishing existence than it had ever previously known, its decay must be attributed to other and wholly different causes than the removal of a protective duty. The larger portion of the exported sugar consists of molasses and jaggery or *gúr* while almost the whole of the imports are given under the heading 'Refined Sugar.'" Since the above was written, however, the exports of raw sugars or *gúr* * have greatly decreased, and the imports of refined sugars immensely increased. It is difficult to define absolutely the causes which have induced this change in the sugar trade. The tide of imports has continued to flow towards India, and Calcutta, which has been hitherto a large exporting port, is now receiving not only sugar freely, but is expecting molasses also, from Mauritius.

To the Indian refiner, the development of the Indian internal trade is far more important than any idea of increased exportation, and there cannot be a doubt but that the trade will become immense as the prejudice against refined sugars amongst the natives of India is removed. It has been calculated that 2,000,000 tons of raw cane-sugar are annually produced in India.

The following may be given as the Imports and Exports of sugar during the last three years:—

IMPORTS OF SUGAR (REFINED SUGARS).

		Cwts.	Rs.
1882–83	Refined	669,348	1,08,56,003
	Unrefined	3,324	13,607
	TOTAL	672,672	1,08,69,610
1883–84	Refined	729,321	1,14,61,689
	Unrefined	7,588	22,012
	TOTAL	736,909	1,14,83,701
1884–85	Refined	1,613,067	2,13,89,937
	Unrefined	3,807	18,440
	TOTAL	1,616,874	2,14,08,377

EXPORTS (CHIEFLY RAW SUGARS OR *gúr*).

		Cwts.	Rs.
1882–83	Refined	111,274	13,01,331
	Unrefined	1,207,424	67,86,428
	TOTAL	1,318,698	80,87,759
1883–84	Refined	203,693	22,86,004
	Unrefined	1,426,827	71,46,181
	TOTAL	1,630,520	94,32,185
1884–85	Refined	55,323	7,14,940
	Unrefined	1,015,596	47,45,755
	TOTAL	1,070,919	54,60,695

The bulk of the exports go from Madras. In 1885, Great Britain received refined sugar, 10,855 cwt., and unrefined, 785,547 cwt. Of the imports Bombay receives the major portion, the supply coming chiefly from Mauritius (1,265,362 cwt.).

The following are the principal sources of sugar and starch in India; a number of the plants which should appear in this list have, however, been referred to already under "Tubers," and need not be again described:—

707. ALHAGI MAURORUM, *Desv.*; Leguminosæ. The Camel Thorn or Persian Manna. A widely-spread shrub of the Gangetic valley and of the arid northern zones; distributed to South Africa, Egypt, Asia Minor, and Greece. The manna, or sugary excretion obtained naturally from this plant is chiefly collected in Khorasan, Kurdistan, and Hamadan, and imported into Bombay. Dr. Dymock, of Bombay, contributes a good sample of this substance. (*See* also 407.)

708. ARENGA SACCHARIFERA, *Labill*; Palmæ. The Java Sago Palm. A Malayan tree, often cultivated in India, but said to be wild in Orissa and Burma. The sago from the interior of the stem, although inferior in flavour to that of the true sago palm, is nevertheless an important article of food. Sugar, wine, and vinegar are also prepared from the sap.

709. BASSIA LATIFOLIA, *Roxb.*; Sapotaceæ. The Butter or Mahúá Tree. A large tree indigenous to the forests of the central table-land of India. The flowers constitute an important article of food; they yield sugar and spirit. (*See* also 45, 410, 584, 995, 1091.)

710. BETA MARITIMA, *L.*; Chenopodiaceæ. The Beet-root. The manufacture of sugar from the beet-root has, within recent years, become one of the most important industries of Europe, but the plant in India is only grown as a vegetable.

711. BORASSUS FLABELLIFORMIS, *Linn.*; Palmæ. The Palmyra Palm. Yields wine and sugar. (*See* also 54, 585, 634.)

712. CALOTROPIS GIGANTEA, *R. Br.*; Asclepiadeæ. The Madar. A small shrub found all over India, chiefly in waste lands. The tribes of the Western Ghâts are said to make an intoxicating drink called *bar* from its milky sap. (*See* also 769, 910, 960, 1095.)

713. CANNA INDICA, *Linn.*; Scitamineæ. The Indian Shot. A herbaceous plant common all over India, chiefly in gardens, where it is grown as an ornamental plant. The root-stock contains starch, and may be cooked for food.

714. CARYOTA URENS, *Willd.*; Palmæ. The Bastard Sago. A beautiful palm of the western and eastern moist zones of India, affording good sago.

715. COCOS NUCIFERA, *Linn.* The Cocoa-nut Palm. Yields palm wine and sugar. (*See* also 85, 660, 895, 913, 1011.)

716. CURCUMA ANGUSTIFOLIA, *Roxb.*; Scitamineæ. The Wild or East Indian Arrowroot. Grows in abundance in the forests of the Deccan and in Malabar. An arrowroot is prepared from its tubers.

717. EUGENIA JAMBOLANA, *Lam.*; Myrtaceæ. In Goa a wine, very faintly resembling port, is prepared from the fruit of this tree. (*See* also 124, 597, 797.)

718. HONEY. Indian honey is of a very inferior quality to that of Europe.

719.* MANIHOT UTILISSIMA, *Pohl.*; Euphorbiaceæ. The Tapioca. Commonly cultivated in the equatorial or tropical regions, especially in America from Brazil to the West Indies; introduced in South India.

720.* MARANTA ARUNDINACEA, *Linn.*; Scitamineæ. The Arrowroot. Introduced from America and now extensively cultivated in India. Yields the true arrowroot of commerce. (*See* also 569.)

* Molasses are scarcely if at all exported from India.

721. Melia Azadirachta, *Linn.*; Meliaceæ. The Ním, or Margosa. A large tree planted and self-sown throughout the greater part of India and Burma; yields a kind of toddy. (*See* also 175, 450, 817.)

722. Nelumbium speciosum, *Willd.*; Nymphæaceæ. The Sacred Lotus of Padma. An aquatic herb common throughout India, extending as far to the north-west as Kashmir. The starchy tubers are eaten; so also are the tubers of the water-lilies. (*See* also 640.)

723. Oryza sativa, *Linn.*; Gramineæ. The Rice. The common rice is largely used as a starch, and also in the distillation of spirits. (See under "Cereals.") (*See* also 369, 504, 694.)

724. Phœnix sylvestris, *Roxb.*; Palmæ. The Indian Date-Palm. This palm is one of the chief sources of palm sugar, and of toddy. It has been calculated that there are about 168,000 acres under date-palm, cultivated as a source of sugar, and chiefly in a belt of country running north from Calcutta towards the foot of the Darjeeling Himálaya. (*See* also 611, 936.)

725. Saccharum officinarum, *Linn.*; Gramineæ. The Sugar-cane. A native of Asia, most probably from the Gangetic region to Cochin China. Grown extensively in the North-West Provinces, Bengal, the Punjáb, and to a much less extent in other parts of India for the manufacture of sugar. It is calculated that there are about 1,922,000 acres annually under the cane, which may be assumed to yield 2,000,000 tons of coarse sugar. Of the exports of raw sugar, it is not possible to ascertain how much was actually obtained from the sugar-cane, but a comparison of the total exports from all sources with the probable production will give an approximately reliable idea of the immense consumption of sugar in India. The exports were only a little over one million cwt. against two million tons of sugar-cane produced.

726.* Sorghum saccharatum, *Pers.*; Gramineæ. The Chinese Sugar-cane. Probably a native of tropical Africa, cultivated in North India. (*See* also 305.)

727.* Triticum sativum, *Lam.*; Gramineæ. The Common Wheat. Used in distillation. (*See* under "Cereals.") (*See* also 400, 695.)

728.* Vitis vinifera, *Linn.*; Ampelideæ. The Vine. Attempts have been made to manufacture wine in Kashmír on European principles and with considerable success. His Highness the Maharajah exhibits samples of his wines and spirits. (*See* under "Fruits.") (*See* also 625.)

ADJUNCTS TO BEVERAGES AND TO DISTILLATION.

A large number of substances are used in India to take the place of the hops of Europe. These are sometimes employed like hops as simple bitters, or are added to the liquor, because it has been ascertained that a larger quantity of alcohol is produced from a given weight of grain when an astringent seed or bark is present during fermentation and distillation. At other times adjuncts are added to drug the liquor, and for this purpose some of the most poisonous narcotics are used. It seems probable that the sacred *Soma* was of this nature, rendering a beverage more pleasant and intoxicating. The following are a few of the important bitters and narcotics used in India in the preparation of beverages:—*Anamirta Cocculus* (fruits); *Acacia arabica*, *A. ferruginea*, and *A. leucophlœa* (the bark); *Cannabis sativa*—Indian hemp used as *ganja*, *charas*, *bhang*, or *majun*; a species of *Cnestis* employed by the inhabitants of Manipur (the stem); a fungus found on the inflorescence of a sedge (*Rhyncospora aurea*) used by the Khasias; *Datura fastuosa* (the seeds burned on charcoal, an empty vessel being inverted to catch the smoke; when full the beverage is suddenly thrown into the smoke and is thereby made intoxicating); *Ligustrum robustum* (the bark) accelerates fermentation.

This list is of course very incomplete, but it may be remarked that no subject seems deserving of more attention than this, both on account of its economic interest and because of the fact that adjuncts to beverages are extensively used for criminal purposes. We know very little about the plants of this class used by the aboriginal tribes of India. The Santals, for example, are said to use *Ruellia suffruticosa* (Roxb.) (the *chaulia*), when they wish to prepare a pleasant beverage from rice, but add *Clerodendron serratum* (Spreng.), the *Saram lutur*, to make this intoxicating.

Exhibitors.—Messrs. Turner, Morrison & Co., Calcutta—Raw and Refined Sugars; Messrs. Carew & Co., Rosa Sugar Refined Sugars; Mr. H. H. Abdoollah, of Colootolla, Calcutta—Arrowroot.

SUB-COURTS XIV. & XV.

NARCOTICS AND STIMULANTS.

The following are the substances which naturally fall into this section:—Tea, Coffee, Cocoa, Tobacco, Rum and other Spirits, Wines, Beers, and Ales, Vinegar, Opium, Indian hemp. Objection may be taken to cocoa being placed here, but, while not a narcotic, it is more nearly related to tea and coffee than to any other substance. The total imports and exports of narcotics for the year 1884–5 were valued at Rs.18,05,63,986 (=£18,056,398).

729. Beers and Ales. The imports of beer, ale, and porter during the year 1884–5 amounted to Rs.24,99,272. The Indian hill breweries are now of the greatest importance and turn out annually a large amount of very superior beer, which has begun to visibly tell upon the imports of foreign beers. The quantity imported in 1884–5 was 194,531 gallons less than in 1883–4. A selection of hill beers are shown, the more important being those from Madras and the Punjáb.

730. Camellia theifera, *Griff.*; Tenstrœmiaceæ. Tea. The area in India under the tea

plant has been put down as 266,286 acres, 188,428 being in Assam and Cachar, 55,698 in Bengal, 8,427 in the North-West Provinces, 8,172 in the Punjáb, 5,551 in Madras, and 10½ acres in Burma. The imports of tea into India amounted to about 4 million pounds, valued at Rs.32½ lakhs. A large proportion of this was green tea intended for the Persian and Afghánistán markets. The exports were 64,162,055lbs., valued at Rs.4,04,47,592. The total exports and imports during 1884-5 were thus Rs.4,37,03,069 (=£4,370,306). It would appear that the imports of Indian teas into Great Britain have risen from 25½ million pounds in 1875 to 66 million pounds in 1884, while in the same period the imports of China teas have fallen from 170½ million pounds to 144½ million pounds, the proportion of Indian teas imported into Great Britain, compared to the total imports, having, during the past 10 years, risen from 13 to 31·4 per cent. This gives a consumption of about 2 pounds per head of population. Samples of tea will be found in the Tea Room.

731. CANNABIS SATIVA, *Linn.*; Urticaceæ. Indian Hemp. Hemp is in India almost exclusively cultivated on account of its narcotic property:—

(*a*) In Eastern Bengal the plant is cultivated for the agglutinated female flower-tops known as *ganjá*. This is sold in two forms—round and flat—and the drug is always smoked, a small quantity being mixed with tobacco. In 1883-4 2,493 acres were under *ganjá*. This gave employment to 1,972 persons with a yield of 8,982 maunds. The cultivation, manufacture, and sale is regulated by law. Permission is granted on license, and the produce is compulsorily placed in Government stores. There are two charges made by Government—a license to trade and sale, and a direct duty per maund on actual amounts removed from store. During the year 1883-4 the Bengal Government realized a net revenue of Rs.19,73,713, being a charge of Rs.335 a maund on amount consumed. The consumer paid from Rs.16 to Rs.23 a seer, or Rs.640 to Rs.800 a maund (*e.g.*, £64 to £80 for 84 lbs.).

(*b*) In the North-West Provinces the cultivation of *ganjá* is prohibited, but *bhang* or the young leaves and twigs are largely collected from the semi-wild plant. These are made into a greenish intoxicant liquor known as *hashish*. The supply of *ganjá* consumed in these provinces is imported from the Central Provinces, Bombay and Bengal. Including *bhang*, the consumption in 1883-4 amounted to 6,690 maunds, which gave a total revenue of only Rs.5 53,356. There is no direct duty levied on amount consumed, and the revenue is raised entirely by farming the retail shops. The Government obtained in this way only Rs.82·11 per maund, while in some parts at least of these provinces the drug was retailed at the same price as in Bengal.

(*c*) In the Punjáb *ganjá* is very little used, but the consumption of hill-grown *bhang* is very extensive. From Kashmír, Ladak, and Afghánistán *charas* is largely imported into the Panjáb. This is a resinous-like substance found on the flower tops and twigs, collected by rubbing the flower tops between the hands or by causing men to run violently through the fields. The resin or *charas* adheres to their naked bodies and is scraped off. It is commonly reported that from Nepal a fine quality of this substance, known as *momea*, is obtained. Dr. Gimlette, Residency Surgeon, Nepál, reports, however, that as far as Katmandu and its neighbourhood are concerned the name *momea* is unknown except as applied to an extraordinary medicinal preparation in which human fat forms an important ingredient. Dr. Gimlette further states that, as far as he is aware, *charas* is, in Nepál, prepared by rubbing the flower-tops between the hands. A small amount of *charas* is produced in Sind by causing men clad in skins to run through the fields. The chief supply of *charas* comes to India, however, from across the Punjáb frontier, and is conveyed under a permit system (but free of duty) nearly all over India. On reaching the frontier of Bengal it has, however, to pay the heavy duty of Rs.8 a seer. About 600 maunds of *charas* are annually consumed in the Punjáb, but the imports are over 5,000 maunds. As this large amount enters and passes over India almost quite free of duty, it naturally affects most materially the Indian-grown *ganjá* and *bhang*. It is stronger than *ganjá* and fetches a slightly higher price in Bengal; but in the Punjáb it is sold at Rs.4 to Rs.13 a seer (2 lbs.); and in Bombay for about Rs.2 a seer. The total revenue derived in the Panjáb from hemp narcotics was in 1883-4 only Rs.1,44,640, or a revenue of Rs.31 a maund on consumption.

(*d*) In Bombay *ganjá* is very extensively cultivated, the consumption being over 9,000 maunds, and the revenue only Rs.1,61,599, or about Rs.17 a maund. There is no fixed duty, but the revenue is realized, as in the North-West Provinces and the Punjáb, by farming the retail shops. *Ganja* is sold in Bombay at Rs. 2 a seer.

(*e*) In the Central Provinces cultivation of *ganjá* on a large scale takes place according to a system very much similar to what prevails in Bengal. The shops are farmed, but over and above a fixed duty per maund is levied on amounts removed from the stores. The production in 1883-4 amounted to 6,356 maunds, and the local consumption to only 768 maunds. The total revenue realized from all sources amounted to Rs.1,29,207, or Rs.168·7 per maund on amounts consumed locally. Removals from the stores to other provinces appear to pay no duty, so that exports from the Central Provinces may be put down in Allahabad free of duty, while from Bengal the same article pays Rs. 5 a seer to Government.

(*f*) Assam consumes annually a very considerable amount of Bengal *ganjá*, and the provincial treasury is credited with a large revenue therefrom: this in 1883-4 amounted to Rs. 363 a maund, the total revenue being Rs. 2,31,691.

(*g*) Madras cultivates *ganjá* and *bhang* to a certain extent, and doubtless it imports these substances from neighbouring provinces also; but a separate account of the revenue derived therefrom is not published, so that the condition of the Southern Presidency cannot be compared with other parts of India. Hemp narcotics are apparently not consumed in Burma.

A very great inequality thus exists in the revenue derived from hemp narcotics in the various provinces of India. The substance, in one or other of its forms, is more or less used all over India,—either smoked as *ganjá* and *charas*, or consumed as *hashish* liquor, or eaten in the form of special sweetmeats, known as *majun*, the last two forms being preparations from *bhang*. The total consumption in 1884 for all India amounted to only 16,378 maunds, leaving, as shown by the published figures of production, 11,264 to be either in stock or consumed without paying duty.

Intimately associated with the religious systems of Hinduism hemp intoxication has become an established luxury, and has been inherited by the corresponding classes of Mahomedans. It should be recollected that habitual indulgence in hemp is nowhere so prevalent as habitual alcoholic intemperance. Hemp-narcotism does not establish the same irresistible craving as alcohol. The indulgence is rather accidental or occasional, than habitual, so that it is more widely diffused than might at first sight be inferred. The agricultural classes who, of course, constitute the bulk of the population of India, rarely, if ever, indulge in hemp narcotics. It is the artizans, mendicants, and domestic servants who are the chief consumers; the middle and upper classes partake of hemp only at certain religious observances, and even then, but to a small extent. These facts necessarily narrow the community who partake in this indulgence, and it is probable that a percentage of two persons in every 1000 of population would express very nearly the number of consumers. The utmost that a man could smoke of *ganjá* per annum has been estimated at one and a-half seers. (*See* also 911, 770.)

732.* COFFEA ARABICA, *Linn.;* Rubiaceæ. Coffee. The condition of the Indian coffee trade is unsatisfactory, the quantity exported for the year 1884-5 having been smaller than for the year 1883-4. While values have declined, the exports can scarcely be said to have advanced for the past five years. Much of the Indian coffee goes to Arabia, Persia, Egypt, Turkey in Asia, and even to Mauritius. Ceylon and the Straits send to India large quantities of coffee; 10½ lakhs of rupees worth having been received in 1884-5, and chiefly by Bombay. The total imports and exports in 1884-5 were valued at Rs.1,35,10,658. The collections of Indian coffee will be seen in the Tea Room.

*NICOTIANA TABACUM, *Linn.;* Solanaceæ. Tobacco. Perhaps no other plant is so much used by the inhabitants of the world as tobacco. It has been calculated that one-fourth of the entire human family use it. The exports of leaf and manufactured tobacco from India during the year 1884-5 were valued at Rs.14,99,902, and the imports at Rs. 8,42,081. The total value of the Indian trade for 1884-5 was thus Rs. 23,41,983 (=£234,198). The imports of foreign cigars have begun to be materially affected by the growing demand for Indian cigars. These cigars have within recent years greatly improved in quality, and the majority of Anglo-Indian smokers decidedly prefer Indian to imported cigars.

There are two distinct species of tobacco plant met with in cultivation in India:—

733. (*a*) *Nicotiana rustica* (Linn.). This species is easily recognized by its greenish flowers and stalked ovate leaves. The leaves are coarser and much crumpled, but dry readily. This is generally known as Turkish tobacco. It is by no means so plentiful as the next species, but is often met with in certain isolated localities; it is a remarkable fact that it nowhere in India appears self-sown.

734. (*b*) *Nicotiana tabacum* (Linn.). This is the form generally cultivated in India, and in some parts of Bengal it is quite naturalised. It is often self-sown and frequents lanes and roadsides in the vicinity of villages; the uncultivated islands and sandbanks on the Hugli river above Calcutta are almost covered with wild tobacco appearing in the cold season and flowering in the beginning of the hot weather. Botanists agree in regarding tobacco as of American origin: it is certainly not a native of India, although cultivated throughout the country.

An assortment of the leading kinds of Indian tobaccos and tobacco-leaf is shown in SUB-COURT XV., but the visitor is referred to the special tobacco-room, where he will not only have the opportunity of examining a much more comprehensive collection, but (if a smoker) may even try the different kinds of Indian tobaccos.

EXHIBITORS. From Trichinopoly: Messrs. R. Ethirajulu Bros.; T. B. Mulusawmy, Mudalior & Co.; N. Sawminathe & Co.; Naelamagum Pillais; T. M. Mariya Pillay & Bros.; M. Cupanna, Pillay Bros.: T. M. Subramania, Pillay & Co.; P. N. Ammia, Pillay & Co.; P. Narrainsawny Pillay; Messrs. J. Henke & Co., Calicut.; Parthasarathy Naidu, Madras; Roberts & Co., Coconada.

735.* PAPAVER SOMNIFERUM, *Linn.;* Papaveraceæ. The Opium. Poppy has been known from a remote period. It seems to be a cultivated form of *Papaver setigerum* (DC.), a native of the shores of the Mediterranean, Spain, Sicily, Greece, and the Island of Cyprus. As this wild form has not been met with in Eastern Asia, the probability is that the cultivated plant was introduced into India. But if this idea be accepted, the existence of Sanscrit names and a large series of vernacular names suggest a very early introduction, probably little short of 3000 years ago. At the present day opium cultivation is circumscribed. Except in Native States it is retained as a Government monopoly. Certain districts are permitted to cultivate the plant, but cultivators wishing to grow it must obtain a license. An advance of Rs. 12 to Rs. 13 an acre is made in two instalments, one before the seed is sown, and the other two months after. The seed is sown broadcast in October; the plants progress slowly through December and January, but in February they are in full flower, and the crop commences to yield at once. The petals are carefully collected, care being taken not to break or injure the plants in any way. For this purpose women and children are busily employed, moving about up to their waist in the field; the petals are purchased for packing purposes. At the same time, the half-ripe capsules are systematically scratched with an instrument called the *cheni* or *maharni*. This is made of four small knives tied together, the blades appearing like the teeth of a comb. The scratching is done in the afternoon, and in the morning it is found that the milky sap has exuded and hardened over the wounds. This is carefully scraped off and preserved in an earthen vessel. The operators move over the field, returning in regular order to the same capsules after a definite interval, and thus scratch each capsule four to eight times. After all the opium has been removed, the capsules are cut off and dried. The seeds are taken out and sold for oil, and the empty capsules are purchased by the druggists. There is restriction, but no compulsion, put on the opium cultivation, but it is remarkable that, while it is a highly remunerative crop, the cultivators are often averse to taking it up. Debiting the wages of the cultivator, the rent of land, and all other charges, it costs about Rs. 48·4 to cultivate an acre of land with poppy. The advance is given free of interest, and comes in opportunely at a time when the cultivator requires money. Government purchases the opium at from Rs. 4·8 to Rs. 6 a seer, and each acre yields from ten to fifteen seers of opium. At the same time some twenty seers of petals, valued at Rs. 4, and five to six maunds of seeds with the capsules over and above, are obtained from the acre, and these are marketable articles, and, what is no doubt an important consideration, the opportunity is afforded of illegally retaining a small amount of the opium. There is a certain market, and the returns highly remunerative; but in the face of many advantages opium production is not popular, and efforts to extend poppy cultivation have been resisted keenly. The exports of opium during the past six years were—

	Cwts.	Rs.
1879–80 . .	144,630	14,32,33,143
1880–1 . .	127,484	13,60,01,477
1881–2 . .	123,913	12,43,21,418
1882–3 . .	126,789	11,48,13,764
1883–4 . .	126,585	11,29,44,601
1884–5 . .	118,599	10,88,26,060

During 1866–7 the value of the exports amounted to Rs. 11,32,60,388. It would appear that the total value of opium exported has not fluctuated much during the past two decades, but has averaged from fourteen to eleven million of pounds sterling. The bulk of the exported opium finds its way to China, but the increased cultivation in Southern and South-Western China has caused a considerable decrease in the consignments to Hong-Kong, and a corresponding increase in the exports to the Treaty Ports. Persian opium has also improved greatly in recent years, and, being cheaper than the Indian article, has begun to have a distinct effect on the market. The foreign exports by no means represent the total trade in the drug. There is an immense internal consumption of what is known as Excise opium. This is retailed to the Indian consumer as a decoction or in the form of two smoking mixtures known as Chandu and Madak. The total annual revenue derived by Government from provision opium, i.e. opium sent to China, is close upon nine million pounds sterling, and about £800,000 is realized by Government from excise opium, i.e. opium consumed in India.

Dr. P. Wier, Principal Assistant and Opium Examiner, Benares Agency, has furnished an interesting descriptive catalogue of the collection of specimens intended to represent the products of the opium poppy (*Papaver somniferum*, var. *album*) as cultivated in the Benares Opium Agency. The following abstract may be accepted as applicable to the entire collection of opium samples shown at the Exhibition :—

A[1]. *Crude Opium.*—The juice derived from the incised unripe capsules of the opium poppy and delivered by the cultivators to the officers of the Agency for transmission to the Central Opium Factory at Ghazipur, where it is made up into "Provision Opium" for the China market, or into "Excise Opium" for Indian consumption.

A[2]. *Opium powder.*—Opium of the Benares Agency dried and reduced to powder over the steam-table at 200° Fahr. Payment by Government for opium is made according to its value as ascertained by assay, *i.e.*, by finding the amount of dry powder resulting from drying 100 grains of the sample on the steam-table at 200° Fahr. Opium, of which 100 grains yield, when so dried, 70 grains of powder, being taken as the standard and paid for at the rate of Rs. 5 per seer (8*s.* 0¼*d.* per 2 lb. 0·914 oz.).

A[3]. *Provision opium cake.*—As prepared for the China market.

A[4]. *Section of a provision opium cake.*—Through a diameter.

A[5]. *Half of shell of a provision opium cake* from which the opium has been removed to allow the inner surface of shell to be seen. The provision opium cake consists of a central mass of opium (A[1]) weighing 3 lbs. 0·342 oz. at the standard consistence of the Agency, viz., 70° in the Benares, 75° in Behar Agency: the central mass of opium being enclosed in a shell about 6″ in diameter and ½″ thick, composed of a number of layers of "leaf" (B[1]) held together by a paste called "lewa" (A[6]), consisting of 7·714 ozs. of opium at standard consistence broken up with water till it is of a consistence of 52°·50.

A[6]. *Lewa.*—The paste by which the layers

of the shell of the provision opium cake (A[3]) are held together. In the preparation of lewa all the opium of inferior quality unfit for the central mass of a cake by reason of its consistence or the presence in undue quantity of passewa (A[7]) is used, supplemented if necessary by good opium: the passewa delivered is also employed to the extent of 5 per cent. in making lewa, to give greater adhesiveness to the paste.

A[7]. *Passewa.*—A dark coffee-coloured fluid which collects in the bottom of the vessels in which the freshly-collected juice of the capsules is placed by the cultivators when brought home. The shallow vessels are tilted to such a degree that the passewa can drain off and be collected and sent in separately for weighment. The reason for its separation is that passewa, if allowed to remain in opium, injures the physical characters of the drug, causing it to look black and liquid, whilst at the same time it gives the drug an unduly high assay when tested by evaporation on the steam-table. Passewa consists of the most soluble of the principles of opium dissolved in dew or in moisture absorbed from the atmosphere; it has a peculiar smell, is strongly acid in reaction, and contains meconic acid, resin, morphia, and narcotine.

A[8]. *Abkári or Excise cake of Benares drug.*—This consists of opium, the produce of the Benares Agency, which, by exposure to the sun in shallow wooden trays, has gradually become inspissated to such a consistence that 100 grains when dried on the steam-table at 200° Fahr. yield 90 grains at least of solid matter. The opium having reached this consistence is well mixed up and trampled into a homogeneous mass, which is then cut up into portions of 2 lb. 0·914 oz. weight, which are moulded into cakes in a hand-press, stamped by a brass stamp bearing the device of an Imperial crown and the legend "Benares Abkari," and are then wrapped in two folds of Nepal paper (prepared from the bamboo), the inner paper being smeared with a few drops of poppy oil (A[10]), to prevent it adhering to the surface of the cake. The cake is then bound up with a piece of string. Sixty cakes so prepared (A[9]) are packed in two tiers into a chest of *sál* or mango wood, and the seams being dammered the chest is sewn up in a gunny cover. The chest is now ready for issue to the treasury officers of the various districts of the North-Western Provinces, Oudh, and Central Provinces, by whom the excise opium is issued on sale to the licensed vendors who retail it. The excise opium as retailed is consumed either as a decoction or as prepared into madak or chandu for smoking in an opium pipe. B[12] is a specimen of a chandu pipe. Chandu (B[10]) is an inspissated filtered decoction of opium. Madak (B[11]) is similarly prepared, the drug being boiled and strained through muslin: but after it is strained and somewhat thickened it is mixed with roasted shreds of *pán* leaf and then tossed in a brass vessel over a charcoal fire until ready for use.

A[9]. *An Abkári cake packed up* in two layers of Nepal paper secured by a piece of string.

A[10]. *Poppy oil* obtained by compression from poppy seed (A[11].)

A[11]. *Poppy seed.*—The seeds obtained from the ripe capsules of *Papaver somniferum.* The best seed is yielded by capsules which have not been lanced. The seeds by pressing yield a bland oil, which at the opium factories is used in the manufacture of excise opium, a few drops being smeared on the inner paper wrapper to prevent this adhering to the Abkari cake (A[8] and A[9].)

B[1]. *Leaf.*—The technical term applied to the material of which the layers of the cake shell (A[3], A[4], A[5]), are composed. "Leaf" consists of the petals of the poppy flower formed into circular cakes from 8″ to 12″ in diameter and about $\frac{1}{16}$″ thick.

B[2]. *Trash uncleaned.* B[3]. *Trash cleaned for packing* B[4]. *Trash cleaned for caking.*—Trash is the departmental name for a coarse powder employed in the manufacture and packing of the opium cakes. It consists of the leaves of the poppy plants which have been left standing after the collection of the capsules until they have become quite dry under the influence of the hot April winds, when they are removed and broken up into a coarse powder. Trash for caking consists of packing trash which has been refined by being sifted first in sieves of 8 meshes to the inch, finally in sieves of 40 meshes to the inch. The newly-made provision cake (A[3]) is rolled in this trash to prevent its sticking to the cup in which it is placed for storage.

B[5]. *Opium, Malwa crude.* B[6]. *Opium, Malwa, in lump ready for caking.* B[7]. *Abkari cake of Malwa drug.*—For the consumption of the North-West Provinces and Oudh, and of the Central Provinces, the opium used in the manufacture of excise cakes is received from Malwa and Rajputana, being purchased there by an officer of the department and sent to Ghazipur packed in cotton bags. The Malwa opium differs from the opium sent in by the different districts of the Benares Agency in being of an oily nature due to the fact of the cultivators throwing the newly-collected drug into a vessel of linseed oil (B[8]) obtained from the white linseed (B[9].) After arrival at Ghazipur the crude Malwa opium is made up into excise opium cakes after inspissation in the sun in the same way as excise manufactured from the Benares, the oil which exudes during the process of inspissation being carefully mopped up (it is used up afterwards in preparing dammer), and the cakes after being moulded are wrapped up in a single sheet of Nepal paper and kept for six or eight weeks unpacked on racks that any oil that may separate may be recovered. At the end of this time the cakes are readjusted to the correct weight, and finally packed up for despatch in the same way that the Benares excise cakes (A[8] and A[9]) are.

B[8]. *Linseed oil.*—Obtained by pressing firm B[9]. *White linseed.*—And used by the cultivators in Rajputana for receiving and storing their crude opium, the idea apparently being to prevent the opium from drying and thereby losing weight.

B[10]. *Chandu.* B[11]. *Madak.*—Prepared from excise opium for smoking as detailed under (A[8].)

B[12]. *Chandu pipe.*—Used for smoking chandu, together with the apparatus, a lamp with glass shade set on a brass tray on which also stands a small brass box to contain the chandu. The pipe is furnished with a long cleaning rod and with a shorter iron needle on which a measure of chandu is prepared for smoking over the flame of the lamp and then held to the bowl of the pipe.

B[13]. *Earthen bowl set in cleft bamboo handle.* — Used to measure a *khorak* or dose of the cold infusion of opium which is used as a beverage.

C[1]. *Morphia, crude cake, first stage.* C[2]. *Morphia, crude cake, last stage.* C[3]. *Morphia, pure.*—Certain of the alkaloids of opium are recovered and their salts manufactured at the Ghazipur Opium Factory. The raw material is contributed by both Opium Factories (Patna and Ghazipur), and is composed of—

1. *Dhoi* or washings of vessels, in which the cultivators have stored their opium sent in by the district officers.

2. Confiscated opium, *i.e.*, all opium sent in from the districts which, on examination at the Sadr Factory, is found by the opium examiner to be so much adulterated as to be unfit for use in lewa-making.

3. Burnt opium unfit for use in lewa-making.

4. Contraband opium unfit for use in lewa-making.

The alkaloids are extracted in the following way:—

A quantity of the raw material is broken up in a sufficient quantity of warm water to form a semi-fluid mass. This is thrown on a blanket filter, and the filtrate is set aside, the residue being washed again and again till no more extract can be obtained. The filtrate is transferred to a vat heated by steam and slowly concentrated. When sufficiently inspissated, a solution of chloride of calcium is added to it. The mixture having been allowed to settle is filtered, and the filtrate is reduced over the steam-table for a few days and then set out in copper pans to crystallize. After two days the contents of the pans are submitted to pressure, and a quantity of dark fluid is expressed; the crude morphia (C[1]) which remains is dissolved in hot water, filtered, and allowed to crystallize. This is repeated some ten or twelve times with pressing until the colouring matter has, as far as possible, been removed. The white cake (C[2]) of crude morphia is then dissolved in hot water and again filtered, and the morphia in the filtrate is precipitated from the acid solution by the addition of a sufficiency of liquor ammonia (manufactured at the factory, sp. gr. ·898.) The precipitated morphia is then strained off on a fine muslin filter, and washed frequently with distilled water until the nitrate of silver test shows that all chlorides have been removed. If the morphia is wanted for store purposes in the pure state, it is now collected, dried, tested, weighed, and stowed away in earthen jars. If hydrochlorate or morphia is desired, the drying stage is omitted; the damp morphia freed from chlorides is dissolved in distilled water, acidulated with hydrochloric acid by means of heat; the solution is filtered, powdered charcoal (C[12]) is added, together with distilled water, and the mixture is heated in a porcelain basin on a sand-bath, filtered and allowed to settle. The water is drained off, and the crystals of hydrochlorate of morphia (C[4] and C[5]) are collected, pressed, and dried. After having their purity tested and ensured, the crystals are packed in earthenware jars and closely corked down and stored until required for issue.

C[4]. *Morphia hydrochlorate.*—An illustration of its mode of crystallizing in long silky needles.

C[5]. *Morphia hydrochlorate.*—In crystals as issued from the Ghazipur Factory to the various medical depots.

C[6]. *Morphia hydrochlorate.*—In powder, the crystals C[5] having been rubbed down in a mortar.

C[7]. *Morphia acetate.*—In powder.

C[8]. *Morphia sulphate.*—In powder. The acetate and sulphate are prepared at the factory as required by dissolving pure morphia (C[3]) in warm water, to which a sufficiency of either acid, acetic or sulphuric, has been added to ensure perfect solution, after which the mixture is filtered, slightly reduced in bulk by heat, and allowed to cool. The crystals which separate are collected, powdered, tested, weighed, and stored for issue as required.

C[9]. *Codeia.*—In crystals.

C[10]. *Codeia crystals powdered.* — After the crude morphia cake (C[2]) has been dissolved and the morphia has been precipitated from the solution by liquor ammonia and removed, the mother liquor remaining is warmed over the steam-table to expel the ammonia: the fluid portion is then decanted from any precipitate that may have collected and is concentrated and treated with liquor potassæ. The precipitate which falls is collected, washed, dried, and dissolved in spirit and water and allowed to stand. The codeia crystallizes out, and is dried, tested, weighed, powdered, and stored away until required for issue.

C[11]. *Narcotine.*—The marc left on the blanket filter after the meconate of morphia has been extracted from the raw material is placed in wooden tubs, and distilled water, acidulated with hydrochloric acid, is added. The mixture having been well stirred is allowed to stand over night; it is then thrown on a blanket filter, the filtrate collected and treated with liquor ammoniæ, and the narcotine precipitated and allowed to settle. The water is poured off and the precipitate collected on a cloth and dried in the sun. It is then dissolved in boiling spirits of wine and filtered, and the solution is set aside to crystallize. This process is twice repeated.

The narcotine crystals now thoroughly purified are collected, dried, tested, weighed, and stored in glazed earthenware jars until required for issue.

C^{12}. *Charcoal, vegetable.*—For obvious reasons the use of animal charcoal as a decolorizing agent is inadmissible in India, owing to the prejudices of the natives. After numerous experiments with the wood of various trees, it was found that the charcoal most suited to the uses of the Laboratory Department of the Ghazipur Opium Factory was that derived from the *dhak* or *palas* tree (*Butea frondosa*), of which C^{12} is a specimen.

D^1. *Chest used for packing provision opium.*—(A^3) Cakes for export to China. It is made of the wood of the mango tree (*Mangifera indica*), obtained chiefly from Behar, where the chests are made up by native contractors.

D^2. *Compartments used in packing provision opium.*—Cakes made of the wood of the *seemul* tree (*Bombax malabaricum*). This is obtained from the Patna Opium Factory, Saw Mill Department.

D^3. *Mat of bamboo.*—*B. Arundinacea*, used in packing provision opium.

D^4. *Gunny cover.*—Sewn outside the provision opium chest after it has been packed and dammered.

In packing provision opium for China, which is done at the Ghazipur Factory at the rate of 500 chests per diem, 40 provision cakes (A^3) are put into each chest (D^1), 20 in the lower tier and 20 in the upper, each 20 cakes in each tier of every chest packed during the day being of identical weight. The cakes in a tier are kept separate by partitions of *seemul* wood (D^2), and each cake is firmly but not too tightly packed in its compartment by a dunnage composed of trash (B^2, B^4). Between the upper and lower tier of packed cakes is interposed a bamboo mat (D^3). The chest having been packed, has the lid nailed down; the seams are then dammered, and the chest is sewn up in a gunny cover (D^4), stamped with the distinctive device of the Agency and with the serial number of the chest, which is now ready for despatch to the store godowns in Calcutta.

In the case of excise opium 60 cakes (A^9) are packed in two tiers in a smaller sized chest made of *súl* wood (*Shorea robusta*), no dunnage being used, the packed cakes fitting tightly into the compartments. A gunny cover is sewn over the chest after it has been nailed down and dammered. (*See* also 831, 1035.)

736. Spirits.—While a very large internal trade is carried on in the distillation of *Arack* and spirits of various qualities, very little of this is, however, exported. The exports of rum, for the years 1882–83 and 1883–84, amounted to 2 and 4½ lakhs of rupees respectively, but in 1884–85 they suddenly declined to Rs. 244. The total value of the foreign trade in spirits, *e.g.*, the imports and exports of spirits, for the year 1884–85 amounted to Rs. 62,98,329. This trade appears almost stationary; brandy has given way to whisky.

737. Theobroma Cacao, *Linn.*; Sterculiaceæ. Theobroma; Cacao, or Coco or Chocolate Tree. The Chocolate tree is a native of parts of Brazil and other northern portions of South America, extending also into Central America as far north as Mexico. Coco has within recent years been introduced into India and is now being cultivated commercially in some parts of the Madras Presidency. (*See* also 646.)

738. Vinegar.—In India vinegar is made from toddy, the fresh juice of the palmyra and cocoanut palms, and also from the inspissated juice, jaggery, by dissolving it in water and exposing the solution to air in very large earthen jars, half submerged. The dried flowers of the *Bassia latifolia* (Mahua), also yield an excellent vinegar. The vinegar from the sugar-cane juice is of a poorer quality, containing not more than 2 per cent. of acetic acid. At Peshawar a superior quality is made from grapes which is quite fit for table use. The manufacture of vinegar is carried on chiefly in Mahomedan centres, the Hindus rarely using it except as medicine. The Indian vinegar is very inferior in quality to European, and is entirely consumed within the country in the manufacture of pickles, &c.

739. Wines.—The total of the imports of wines into India during the year 1884–85 came to Rs. 33,60,698. His Highness the Maharaja of Kashmir exhibits a selection of wines and spirits prepared in his kingdom. The white wine obtained at the Calcutta International Exhibition a gold medal for its purity and superior quality.

Excise Exhibits.

740. The Excise department has contributed a most interesting collection of spirits and drugs along with many appliances and instruments used in smuggling. The model shown of the ordinary still used all over India is one quarter actual size.

The total annual revenue derived by Government from Excise is on an average £4,000,000.

Exhibitors.—E Dyer & Co., Solon. The Castle Brewery Co., Nilgiris. Khidderpore Distillery, N. W. P. Cursetjee & Sons, Ahmednagar. Karwar Distillery, Karwar. H.H. The Maharaja of Kashmir. Albion Distillery, Calcutta. Rosa Distillery, Shahjehanpore. R. W. Morgan, Madras.

SUB-COURT XVI.

DRUGS, MEDICINES, CHEMICALS, AND POISONS.

The exports of drugs and medicines for the past five years were:—

	Rs.
1880–81	11,59,659
1881–82	8,66,165
1882–83	12,51,361
1883–84	8,23,973
1884–85	16,31,730

The Imports were:—

		Rs.	Total Imports.
1880–81	General Imports	32,75,327†	
	Government Imports	3,96,534	36,71,861
1881–82	General	38,18,880†	
	Government	2,90,369	41,09,249
1882–83	General	39,16,727†	
	Government	68,676	39,85,403
1883–84	General	36,28,443†	
	Government	1,09,930	37,38,373
1884–85	General	35,82,778†	
	Government	1,52,282	37,35,060

The Imports of Chemicals for the last five years were:—

	Rs.
1880–81	13,75,296
1881–82	13,27,278
1882–83	12,63,456
1883–84	14,53,541
1884–85	18,98,571

The most important chemicals imported into India are Alum, Arsenic, Copperas, Sal Ammoniac, Sulphur, and Sulphuric Acid.

Dr. George King, Superintendent of the Calcutta Botanic Gardens, has furnished the following brief note regarding the present position of Indian Cinchona:—

"The Government Cinchona plantation in Sikkim was begun in 1862, since which time it has been gradually extended, until it now (1886) contains 4,912,111 trees. The Cinchonas cultivated are chiefly of the two sorts which yield the red and yellow bark of commerce. Red bark is the produce of the single species *Cinchona succirubra.* Yellow bark is, however, yielded by the two species known as *Calisaya* and *Ledgeriana.* Besides these species there are in the plantation about 385,100 trees of a hybrid Cinchona, which yields excellent bark.

"The outturn of bark from the plantation amounted last year to 339,201 lbs., bringing the whole outturn, since the plantation began to yield, up to 3,256,927 lbs. Almost the whole of this large quantity of bark has been manufactured on the plantation into Cinchona febrifuge, a medicine which has proved an excellent cure for the malarious fever so common in all tropical countries, and the low price of which puts it within reach of the poorest. During the past eleven years about 68,473 lbs. of this medicine have been consumed in India.

"The total cost of the plantation has been under eleven lakhs of rupees. The actual profit on the sale of Cinchona products from the beginning of the plantation to the present time amounts to Rs. 4,95,513 (£49,513), while the saving to Government by the substitution in its Dispensaries and Hospitals of Cinchona febrifuge for Quinine amounts to over twenty-five lakhs of rupees (£250,000).

"The Government plantation on the Nilgiris contained on 31st March, 1885, 1,618,744 Cinchona trees of various sorts. During the official year 1884–85 these plantations yielded a crop of 118,017 lbs. The financial results of the Nilgiri plantations since their commencement show a net surplus of profit of Rs. 5,51,743 (£55,174). Cinchona trees have also been planted largely by private individuals in the Nilgiris, Wynaad, Travancore, and Coorg, but the Cinchona enterprise has never commended itself to any extent to the planting communities in the Eastern Himálaya and Assam."

Exhibitors of Cinchona.—The Governments of Bengal and Madras, and Messrs. E. Parry & Co.

It has been found by private cultivators in the Madras Presidency that *C. Ledgeriana* is one of the most useful plants. It is best cultivated at low altitudes, and will scarcely grow above 4000 feet. Its cultivation is thus more economical than the forms of Cinchona which require a colder climate.

The Imports of Quinine were—

		Rs.	Total Imports.
1875–76	General Imports	1,91,619	
	Government Imports	16,650	2,08,269
1876–77	General	3,34,437	
	Government	2,69,734	6,04,171
1877–78	General	6,58,509	
	Government	98,782	7,57,291
1878–79	General	6,50,005	
	Government	58,947	7,08,952
1879–80	General	8,60,072	
	Government	1,16,307	9,76,379
1880–81	General	4,29,515	
	Government	1,66,173	5,95,688
1881–82	General	9,98,631	
	Government	1,70,666	11,69,297
1882–83	General	6,48,912	
	Government	1,511	6,50,423
1883–84	General	7,25,227	
	Government	4,069	7,29,296
1884–85	General	5,86,650	
	Government	683	5,87,333

There are over 1,300 plants reputed by the natives of India to possess remedial properties. Many of these are of no value whatever, although some are endowed with high mythical virtues. There are, however, about 100 indigenous drugs which have attained almost a European reputation, and which most thoroughly deserve to be more extensively used. Nepal aconite is, of course, well known to Europe, but recent investigations have revealed the fact that true Monk's-hood is not only an abundant plant on the Himalaya, but that much of the aconite obtained from Nepal and sold in the Indian bazars as *A. ferox*, is in reality the root of *A. Napellus.* Dr. Gimlette, the Residency Surgeon in Nepal, has given this subject much attention, and his collection of roots, purchased from the special Nepal drug collectors, has been accompanied with flowering botanical specimens of the plants from which each kind of root is obtained. *Chaulmugra* and *Pongamia* oils have recently attracted much attention. *Mishmi Tita* (the

† These figures include Camphor, a substance which will be found described under "Extracts."

root of *Coptis Teeta*) and *Atis* (the roots of (*Aconitum heterophyllum*) are extremely useful tonics. *Datin*, or the alkaloid from the bark of *Alstonia scholaris*, seems likely to take a distinct place as an antiperiodic, and could be produced in India to an absolutely unlimited extent. No Indian drug stands in higher fame with the natives of India than the specially prepared pulp of the unripe *bael* fruit. This is a valuable astringent, and will often succeed in the cure of diarrhœa and dysentery when all other drugs have failed. The better qualities of the Kumaon *Káth*, or Catechu, extract from *Acacia catechu*, seem every bit as good medicinally as the Gambier imported from the Straits. The natives of India prefer the Indian-grown aloes to the imported article, and there would seem every reason for supposing that for ordinary dispensary purposes at least they are quite as good. *Atropa belladonna* is an extremely plentiful plant in some parts of the Himálaya, but not only are its properties quite unknown to the natives of India, but large quantities of the drug are annually imported into India. The seeds of *Cæsalpinia Bonducella* are highly esteemed as a domestic medicine for fever. The root of *Calotropis gigantea* is used in leprosy and syphilis, and in dysentery it is believed by the natives to be quite as effectual as ipecacuanha. The various species of *Cassia* are all employed as external applications for skin diseases, and a powder of the seeds of *C. auriculata* has the reputation of being almost a specific for purulent ophthalmia. The Tinnevelly Senna leaves are little inferior to the imported article, and a large trade is done in them all over India.

The inner bark of *Hymenodictyon excelsum* is a valued astringent. The powder of *Mallotus philippinensis* and the seeds of *Vernonia anthelmintica* are useful anthelmintics. The roots of *Picrorhiza Kurroa* and the stems of *Swertia Chirata* are most useful tonics. The *Ispaghul* (*Plantago ovata*) has the reputation of being useful in renal affections, and *Abroma augusta* as valuable in cure of dysmenorrhœa. No Indian drug seems more deserving of careful examination, however, than the bark of *Holarrhena antidysenterica*, the *Kurchi* bark. This attained at one time a high reputation in France, but fell into disuse from the inert adulterants which were mixed with the bark. The seeds of this tree—*Indrajau* of the Sanscrit writers—are considered as possessed of carminative and astringent properties, and are viewed as very valuable in chronic chest affections. It is needless, however, to specialise one more than another for each of the following drugs, if not likely to displace in dispensary practice many of the imported drugs, possess distinct remedial properties and deserve to be made more generally known.

The following are the principal contributors to this Court: Dr. W. Dymock, Bombay; Dr. George King, Calcutta; Mr. J. F. Duthie, Saharanpur; Mr. J. A. Murray, Karachi; Dr. Gimlette, Nepal; and Dr. Moodeen Sheriff, Madras.

DRUGS.

741. Abrus precatorius, *Linn.;* Leguminosæ. Indian or Wild Liquorice Root (*Eng.*); Liane á reglisse (*Fr.*); Gunchi, rati (*Hind.*). A beautiful climber, met with all along the Himálaya, ascending to altitude 3,000 feet, and spreading through the plains of India to Ceylon and Siam. There are three principal varieties:—1st. With rose-coloured flowers, and red seed with black eye. 2nd. With dark-coloured flowers, and black seed. 3rd. With white flowers, and white seed. The root and the seed are used in native medicine: the former is said to possess some of the properties of liquorice and the latter is boiled and eaten as a pulse; the powdered seed, if injected into the blood, is fatal in about twenty-four hours.

742. Acacia Catechu, *Willd.;* Leguminosæ. Catechu (*Eng.*); Cachou (*Fr.*); Catechu (*Ger.*); Khair (*Hind.*). A moderate-sized, gregarious, thorny, deciduous tree, common in most parts of India and Burma, extending in the sub-Himálayan tract westward to the Indus. The extract known as the Catechu or Cutch is used medicinally as an astringent in fevers and other maladies. (*See* Extracts.) (*See* also 5, 648, 1052, 1085, 1129.)

743. Aconitum ferox, *Wall.;* Ranunculaceæ. Indian or Nepal Aconite; Kat Bish (*Beng.*); Bachnab (*Bomb.*). Temperate sub-alpine Himálaya, from Sikkim to Garhwál, altitude 10,000 to 14,000 feet. The mass of the roots sold as Aconite are derived from this species, but several others are no doubt used as adulterants. Dr. Bidie says the roots of *Methonica superba* are in Madras used as an adulterant. The root is highly poisonous, and is largely used by the natives criminally as an arrow poison. As a medicine, it is regarded as heating and stimulant and useful in fever, cephalalgia, affections of the throat, dyspepsia, and rheumatism. *Bish* appears to have been known to the Hindu doctors from the earliest ages. It is much used as an external application, the root being formed into a paste (*lep*) and spread upon the skin in neuralgia, boils, &c. Internally it is chiefly used in the treatment of chronic intermittent fevers (*Dymock*). Europeans use it as a substitute for true aconite. Dr. Gimlette, Residency Surgeon, Nepal, has sent a large series of Nepal aconites, accompanied with botanical specimens of the plants from which the roots were obtained. This collection has thus facilitated, in a remarkable degree, the identification of the Indian aconites. It seems proved beyond all doubt that much of the so-called Nepal aconite is obtained from *A. Napellus*.

744. Aconitum heterophyllum, *Wall.* Ati-visha (*Hind.*). West temperate Himálaya, from Kumaon to Hasora, altitude 8,000 to 13,000 feet. The root is pleasantly bitter, and is regarded as a valuable, mild antiperiodic, aphrodisiac, and tonic, checking diarrhœa. It may be administered internally with safety owing to the absence of Aconitia or other poisonous properties. It is

especially useful in convalescence after fever. As a tonic the dose is five to ten grains, three times daily, and as an antiperiodic from twenty to thirty grains of the powdered root every three or four hours. This root is often adulterated with that of *Asparagus sarmentosus* (*satamuli*). Two kinds are met with in the market —(*a*) gr y shrivelled tubers, larger and longer than (*b*) white, the daughter off-shoots broken from the former. The latter fetch the best price. They are slighly scarred from the abrasion of rootlets, and are generally two inches long, with a thin tap-like extremity, often bifurcated. They should break with a short starchy fracture, presenting a white surface (*Dymock*). The *atis* is eaten fresh by the hillmen of Kanáwár as a mild tonic.

745. A. NEPELLUS, *Linn.* This is the true Monks'-hood, or Wolves'-bane Aconite. This plant is met with in the temperate alpine Himálaya from 10,000 to 15,000 feet, ascending in stunted alpine forms to the highest limits of vegetation. The root is generally said to be the most poisonous of all the species of the genus yielding the true aconite of chemists' shops, from which Aconitia, the most virulent of poisons is obtained. Ewets, however, regards *A. ferox* as the more poisonous.

746.* ACORUS CALAMUS, *Linn.*; Aroideæ. The Sweet-flag; Bach (*Hind.*). A semi-aquatic perennial, with indefinitely branched rhizomes, a native of Europe (?) and North America; cultivated in damp, marshy places in India and Burma, altitude 3,000 to 6,000 feet; exceedingly common in Manipur and the Naga hills, often apparently quite wild on the cultivated fields, spreading from the division walls. The aromatic rhizome or root-stock is considered emetic in large doses, and stomachic and carminative in smaller doses. It is a simple useful remedy for flatulence, colic, or dyspepsia, and a pleasant adjunct to tonic or purgative medicines. It is also used in remittent fevers and ague by the native doctors, and is held in high esteem as an insectifuge, especially for fleas. (*See* also 985.)

747. ÆGLE MARMELOS, *Correa*; Rutaceæ. The Bael Fruit. A small tree of the sub-Himálayan forests from the Jhelam eastward, Central and South India, Burma. The medicinal properties of this plant are as follows:—

(*a*) The UNRIPE FRUIT is cut up and sun-dried, and in this form is sold in the bazars in dried whole or broken slices. It is regarded as astringent, digestive, and stomachic, and is prescribed in diarrhœa and dysentery, often proving effectual in chronic cases after all other medicines have failed. It seems especially useful in chronic diarrhœa; a simple change of the hours of meals and an alteration in the ordinary diet, combined with bael fruit, will almost universally succeed. (*b*) The RIPE FRUIT is sweet, aromatic, and cooling, and made into a morning sherbet, cooled with ice, is pleasantly laxative and a good simple cure for dyspepsia. The dried ripe pulp is astringent and used in dysentery. (*c*) The ROOT BARK is sometimes made into a decoction and used in the cure of intermittent fever. It constitutes an ingredient in the *dasmal* or preparation from ten roots. (*d*) The LEAVES are made into poultice, used in the treatment of ophthalmia, and the fresh juice diluted is praised in catarrhs and feverishness. (*e*) The ASTRINGENT RIND of the ripe fruit is used in dyeing and tanning. (*See* also 15, 576.)

748.* ALOE SUCCOTRINA, *Lam.*; *A. Perryi*, *Baker*, Liliaceæ. Socotrine Aloes of Commerce; Mussabar (*Hind.*). *A. Perryi* is indigenous to the island of Socotra and *A. socotrina* to South Africa. In small doses the drug is used as a stomachic tonic; in larger doses, purgative, and indirectly emmenagogue. It is a remedy of great value in constipation caused by hysteria and atony of the intestinal muscular coat. It is also very useful in atonic dyspepsia, jaundice, amenorrhœa, and chlorosis. Locally applied, dissolved in glycerine, it is valued as a stimulant application in skin diseases, and for this purpose it is generally combined with Myrrh, constituting the *Musáubár* of Bombay.

749.* ALOE VERA, *Linn.* Indian and Barbados Aloe; Ghikuwári (*Hind.*); Ghritakumári (*Beng.*). The resinous extract is generally known as Sibr (*Pers.*). There are many varieties of this plant met with in cultivation throughout India, some of which have gone wild, as, for example, on the coast of South India. As a medicine the *inspissated juice* from the forms of this species is regarded as but little to that from the preceding. It is an aperient, and deemed highly beneficial to persons predisposed to apoplexy. The *fresh juice* from the leaves is said to be cathartic, cooling, and useful in fevers, spleen, and liver disease, enlarged lymphatic glands, and as an external applicant in certain eye diseases. The *pulp* of the leaves is, in native practice, applied to boils, and is regarded as acting powerfully on the uterus, and is useful as an emmenagogue. It is also largely employed in veterinary medicine. The *root* is supposed to be efficacious in colic. Indian Aloes, valued at Rs.740, were exported during the year 1884-5 from Madras to the Straits. The quantity imported was valued at Rs.27,657.

750. VAR. OFFICINALIS, sp., *Forsk.* Ghritkumári (*Beng.*). This is the form met with in a semi-wild condition in Bengal and the North-West Provinces. (*See* also 486.)

751. VAR. LITTORALIS, sp. *Koening.* Chotákanvar (*Hind.*, *Dec.*); Shiru-katrazh-ai (*Tam.*); Chinna-kalabanda (*Tel.*). It has become quite naturalised on the coast of the south of the Madras Presidency.

752.* ALPINIA GALANGA, *Swz*; Scitamineæ. The Greater Galangal (*Eng.*); Galanga (*Port.*); Kulanján (*Beng.*). A perennial plant, native of Sumatra and Java, now cultivated in East Bengal and South India. The rhizomes are aromatic, pungent, and bitter, and are used in the form of an infusion in fever, rheumatism, and catarrhal affections. They are sometimes used as carminative or fragrant adjuncts in complex prescriptions, but they have nothing peculiar in their properties or action. The seeds are also prescribed medicinally. The exports of Galangal during the year 1884-5 were valued at Rs. 6,465 and the imports at Rs. 33,078.

753.* ALPINIA OFFICINARUM, *Hance.* The Lesser Galangal. This is the article which is most frequently sold in the bazars under the names of *kulinjan, kolijana, panki-jer*, or *chanda-pushpi*. The root-stock is a native of China, and is largely exported to Europe and India. This is the Galangal of the European shops. It is a stomachic tonic, used by native practitioners to reduce the quantity of urine in diabetes. It is, when chewed, used to correct foul breath, and the juice swallowed stops irritation in the throat. Dr. Moodeen Sheriff of Madras described in 1869 an *Alpinia* under the name of *A. Khulanjan*, which would appear to be the plant afterwards named *A. officinarum* (Hance).

754. ALSTONIA SCHOLARIS, *R. Br.;* Apocynaceæ. The Chatiun (*Beng.*). A tall evergreen tree of the sub-Himálayan tract, from the Jumna eastward, ascending to 3,000 feet, Bengal, Burma, and South India. The bark is used as an astringent tonic, anthelmintic, alterative, and antiperiodic. It is a valuable remedy in chronic diarrhœa and the advanced stages of dysentery. It is also useful in catarrhal fever. The milky juice is applied to ulcers, and, mixed with oil, in ear-ache. (*See* also 25.)

755. AQUILARIA AGALLOCHA, *Roxb.;* Thymelæaceæ. Eagle-wood, Aloes-wood, Lignum-aloes, Calambac-wood, Agila, Akyaw; Agar (*Hind.*). A large evergreen tree of East Bengal, Burma, Malayan Peninsula and Archipelago. The fragrant resinous substance is considered cordial by some Asiatic nations. It has been prescribed in gout and rheumatism. (*See* also 36, 992, 1087.)

756. ARTEMISIA MARITIMA, *Linn.;* Compositæ. The Worm-seed or Santonine. This plant is met with in Western Himálaya, from Kashmír to Kumaon, altitude 7,000 to 19,000 feet, Western Tibet; in Salt Plains, altitude 9,000 to 14,000 feet, abundant. Commercially, it is obtained from Russia. The flower-heads are largely used for their anthelmintic, deobstruent, and stomachic tonic properties. In the form of a poultice they are used to relieve pain caused through stings of insects and poisonous bites. Santonine is chiefly employed in the treatment of round and thread worms. It has the peculiar property of causing objects to appear yellow to patients under its action.

757. ARTEMISIA VULGARIS, *Linn.* The Indian Worm-wood; Nagadona (*Hind.*). A tall, aromatic, shrub-like herb found throughout the mountain tracts of India, altitude 5,000 to 12,000 feet on the West Himálaya, Khásia hills, Manipur, and the mountains of North Burma. It has stomachic and tonic properties, and is used as a febrifuge. Dr. Wight states that the leaves and tops are used in nervous and spasmodic affections connected with debility; an infusion is given as a fomentation in ulcers. The drug may be used as an inferior substitute for cinchona in intermittent fevers; it is also employed in dyspepsia, and as an anthelmintic, and in liver diseases.

758. ASPARAGUS ADSCENDENS, *Roxb.;* Liliaceæ. Found in Rohilkhand. The tubers of this species of *Asparagus* are used as a demulcent and tonic and as a substitute for salep.

759. A. SARMENTOSUS, *Willd.* A climber, found in Upper India and the Deccan. The root is mucilaginous and considered nourishing and aphrodisiac. Boiled with oil, it is applied to cutaneous diseases.

760. ATROPA BELLADONNA, *Linn.;* Solanaceæ. The Deadly Nightshade. A plant found wild in Kanáwár at 8,500 feet. The officinal parts are the leaves and the dried root. They are powerfully sedative, anodyne, and antispasmodic. The drug is generally prescribed in the form of an extract or tincture. In cataract and other eye affections, in which it is desirable to dilate the pupil or to keep the edge of the iris free, it is invaluable in surgical practice. In rheumatic and scrofulous iritis it is a relieving agent.

761.* BALSAMODENDRON KATAF, *Kth.;* Burseraceæ. The African Bdellium. This gum-resin reaches Bombay from Berbera, the purer kinds very much resembling Myrrh, with which it has been confused by many authors.

762. BALSAMODENDRON MUKUL, *Hook.* The Gum Gugul or Indian Bdellium. A small tree, found to grow in the arid zone, Sind, Kathiawar, Rajputana, and Khandesh. Indian Bdellium is used in native medicine as a demulcent, aperient, carminative, and alterative; especially useful in leprosy, rheumatism and, syphilitic disorders. It is also prescribed in nervous diseases, scrofulous affections, urinary disorders and skin diseases, and is employed in the preparation of an ointment for bad ulcers. (*See* also 41, 1056.)

763.* B. MYRRHA, *Nees.* The Myrrh; Ból (*Hind*). A small tree of Arabia and the African coast of the Red Sea. Often cultivated in Western India. Myrrh is beneficial in dyspepsia, amenorrhœa, and chlorosis, and is a useful stimulant and astringent to all ulcerations or congestions of the mucous membrane. It is a useful application to old, foul, and indolent ulcers, and a valued wash for the mouth and gums, and a gargle in ulcerated sore throat. It is a stimulant expectorant, much admired as a remedy for pulmonary affections, especially the asthma of the aged. Meer Mahommed Hussain says it is hot and antispasmodic. Hakims use it for intestinal worms. It is detergent, siccative, astringent, and aperient, a disperser of cold tumours, and one of the most important of medicines, as it preserves the humours from corruption. Dissolved in milk it is dropped into the eye in purulent ophthalmia. It is said to cause abortion, and is useful in fever and epilepsy. Dose in pill, powder, or emulsion, 10 to 30 grains; of tincture ½ to 1 fl. drachm. (*See* also 1057.)

764.* B. OPOBALSAMUM, *Kunth.* The Balsam or Balm of Gilead. A small-branched tree found on both sides of the Red Sea south of 22° north latitude. It is also recorded from several places on the Nubian Coast and in Abyssinia. It is met with on the Asiatic side at Ghizandad in

Arabia, at Aden, and Yemen. It is in all probability introduced into Palestine. The wood and the fruit are imported and chiefly used as medicines by the Yunani Hakims of India. The fruit is considered to be a powerful carminative and digestive; it is also praised as a stimulant expectorant, and is usually administered in combination with tragacanth.

765. B. Roxburghii, *Arn.* The Gugala (*Beng.*). A small tree of East Bengal and Assam. (*See* also 1058.)

766. Berberis Lycium, *Royle;* Berberideæ. The Kashmal (*Hind.*). An erect rigid shrub of the North-West Himálaya, from 3,000 to 9,000 feet. The medicinal extract from the root, known under the name of *Rasout*, is highly esteemed as a febrifuge and as a local application in eye diseases. In chronic ophthalmia it has been used with success when combined with opium and alum. (*See* also 1093, 1134.)

767. Boswellia serrata, *Roxb.;* Burseraceæ. The Indian Olibanum; Guggulu (*Sans.*). A moderate-sized gregarious tree of the intermediate, northern, and southern dry zones, sub-Himálayan tract from Sutlej to Nepal, the drier forests of Central India from Berar to Rajputana, and southward to the Deccan and to the Circars and the Konkan. Frequent on the eastern slopes of the Pegu Yomah and Martaban in Burma. The Guggulu of the Sanskrit was regarded as a demulcent, aperient, alterative, and a purifier of the blood. The gum at the present day is used in rheumatism, nervous diseases, scrofulous affections, and skin diseases. It is regarded as a diaphoretic and astringent, and is used in the preparation of ointment for sores. It is also prescribed with clarified butter in syphilitic diseases: with cocoa-nut oil for sores, and as a stimulant in pulmonary diseases. The Olibanum is also given in bronchorrhœa and chronic laryngitis, employed both internally and in the form of fumigation. An ointment has been prepared from it which is said to be a good stimulant application to carbuncles, ulcerations, boils, &c. The Mahomedans consider it hot and dry, and to have dessicative, astringent, and detergent properties. Mixed with gum acacia it is used as a corrective for foul breath. If given for any length of time in ʒi doses it is said to reduce obesity. (*See* also 55, 1060, 1061).

768. Cæsalpinia Bonducella, *Roxb.;* Leguminosæ. The Fever-nut: Nátá (*Beng.*). A sub-scandent prickly bush found all over India, especially in Bengal, Burma, and South India. The seed is tonic and antiperiodic, and is largely used by the natives instead of quinine, being pounded with black pepper. This preparation is used as a tonic in fevers, and the powder is also made into an ointment with castor oil, and applied externally in hydrocele. An oil is extracted from the leaves which is used in palsy and rheumatism. The oil expressed from the seeds is used as a cosmetic. In Persia and India the seeds are considered to be hot and dry, useful for dispersing swellings, restraining hæmorrhage, and keeping off infectious diseases. They are also given internally in leprosy, and are thought to be anthelmintic. Necklaces of the seeds strung upon red silk are worn by pregnant women as a charm to prevent abortion.

769. Calotropis gigantea, *R. Br.;* Asclepiadeæ. The Madar (*Hind.*). A small shrub found all over India, chiefly in waste land. The root-bark and juice of this plant are used in medicine for their emetic, diaphoretic, alterative, and purgative properties. In the treatment of dysentery the dried bark of the root is stated to be an excellent substitute for ipecacuanha. The bark, root, and dried milky sap may be used in small doses in certain cutaneous affections, such as leprosy and secondary syphilis; the root-bark, in large doses, acts as an emetic. A preparation from it is administered to promote secretions, and is stated to be useful in enlargements of the abdominal viscera, intestinal worms, cough, ascites, anasarca, &c. The flowers are considered digestive, stomachic, tonic, useful in asthma, catarrh, and loss of appetite. (*See* also 712, 910, 960, 1095.)

770. Cannabis sativa, *Linn.;* Urticaceæ. The Hemp; Ganja, bhang (*Beng.*, *Hind.*). An annual bush wild (or perhaps only naturalised), extensively cultivated on account of its narcotic properties. The narcotic of hemp is highly valued as a medicine, having anodyne and antispasmodic properties. It is stimulant, then anodyne, sedative, and antispasmodic. It is also said to be diuretic and parturifacient. It is useful in tetanus, hydrophobia, delirium tremens, infantile convulsions, various forms of neuralgia, and other nervous affections. It has also been employed in cholera, menorrhagia, and uterine hæmorrhage, rheumatism, hay fever, asthma, cardiac functional derangement, and skin diseases attended with much pain and pruritus. (For further information *see* under Narcotics.) (*See* also 731, 911.)

771. Cassia Absus, *Linn.;* Leguminosæ. A shrub, common all over India. One of the sources of the medicinal senna leaves. The seeds reduced to a powder are applied beneath the eyelids in the form of an ointment in ophthalmia. They are very bitter, somewhat aromatic and mucilaginous, and as such, have been found very useful in mucous disorders.

772. *C. alata, *Linn.* The Dádmardan (*Beng.*, *Hind.*). A small shrub, very probably introduced from the West Indies into India. The leaves are regarded as an excellent medicine for ringworm. Taken internally they act as an aperient, and a tincture has been found to operate in the same manner as senna. They are also used in other skin diseases, and are considered useful in snake-bite.

773.* Cassia angustifolia, *Vahl.* The Indian or Tinnevelly Senna. Cultivated in many parts of India. Senna is extensively employed as a simple and mild purgative. The objections urged against the drug are its taste and the tendency to gripe which it manifests, combined with a somewhat irritant action. The Tinnevelly Senna is much milder than the Alexandrian obtained from *C. acutifolia* (Delile).

774. C. AURICULATA, *Linn.* A shrub of Central and South India. The seed is a valuable application in that form of the purulent ophthalmia known in India by the name of 'country eye-sore.' The bark is highly astringent. A decoction or infusion of the leaves is much esteemed as a cooling medicine by the Singhalese, and also as a substitute for tea. (*See* also 1140.)

775. C. FISTULA, *Linn.* The Indian Laburnum or Purging Cassia; Amaltás (*Hind.*). A moderate-sized deciduous tree of the sub-Himálayan tract, ascending to 4,000 feet, and common throughout India and Burma. The pulp of the fruit or the root-bark is generally used as simple purgatives. This drug is described as lenitive and useful in relieving thoracic obstructions. It is often combined with tamarinds. Externally it is useful in gout and rheumatism. The flowers are made into a confection known as *gul-kand;* this is viewed as a febrifuge. The bark and the leaves, like those of most other species of this genus, are valued external applications in skin diseases. (*See* also 72.)

776. C. OBOVATA, *Colladon.* The Country or Jamaica Senna. A shrub common all over India. The whole plant is sold in the bazars as a substitute for the true Senna, under the name of country Senna. Its action is similar, though much inferior, to Tinnevelly or Mecca Senna.

777. * C. OCCIDENTALIS, *Linn.* The Negro Coffee. An annual, common in Bengal, South India, and Burma. The leaves, roots, and seeds are alexipharmic, useful in the expulsion of corrupt humours and to relieve cough, especially whooping cough. An infusion of the root is considered by the American Indians to be an antidote against various poisons. The whole plant is purgative. In the French-African colonies the seeds are called 'Negro coffee.'

778. CASSIA SOPHERA, *Linn.* The Kál-kashúnda (*Beng.*). A common shrub in the Himálayan Tarai, Bengal, Burma, and South India. The bark, leaves, and seeds are used as a cathartic, and the fresh juice of the leaves is viewed as a specific in ringworm; it is made into a plaster combined with sandal-wood. The plant is supposed by the Hindus to have expectorant properties and by the Mahomedans as useful as a remedy for snake-bites, the root being given with black pepper.

779. C. TORA, *Linn.* The fœtid Cassia; Chakunda (*Hind., Beng.*). A common weed, growing all over India and Burma, exceedingly common on waste places around villages. The leaves are used as an aperient; both leaves and seeds constitute a valuable remedy in skin diseases, chiefly ringworm and itch. The root rubbed to a pulp with lime-juice has almost specific powers in the case of ringworm. (*See* also 491, 1141.)

780.* CINCHONA CALISAYA, *Weddell;* Rubiaceæ. The Calisaya Bark. Cultivated in Sikkim at moderate elevations. Yields one of the most valuable of the Cinchona barks, rich in alkaloids, among which quinine forms ½ to ⅓. The bark and powder form the officinal parts, being powerfully antiperiodic, tonic, and astringent; the two former properties are due to the presence of quinine. The leaves also possess tonic and antiperiodic properties. (*See* also introductory remarks to Drugs, &c.)

781.* C. CONDAMINEA, *Humb.* The Loxa or Crown Bark. Cultivated at high elevations on the Nilgiris, in Ceylon, and in Sikkim. The bark is rich in alkaloids, of which more than one half is quinine.

782.* CINCHONA SUCCIRUBRA, *Pavon.* The Red Bark. Cultivated in the Nilgiris and other hills of South India, at the plantations of Rangbi and Poomong in Sikkim, on the hills east of Toungoo in Burma, and in parts of the Satpura range in Central India. At first it was experimentally cultivated by Government, but Cinchona has so far proved itself a profitable investment as to have induced several tea companies to form new gardens or to set apart portions of their old plantations for the purpose of cultivating this and other Peruvian bark-yielding species. (*See* the account of Cinchona in the introductory remarks to this Chapter.)

The following were the exports of the cinchona bark for the past five years:—1880-81, Rs. 7,24,705; 1881-82, Rs. 4,58,340; 1882-3, Rs. 7,90,861; 1883-84, Rs. 4,06,453; 1884-85, Rs. 9,86,110.

The exports chiefly went to the United Kingdom and Italy.

783. CINNAMOMUM ZEYLANICUM, *Breyn.* The Ceylon or true Cinnamon; Dalchini (*Hind.*). A tree indigenous to the forests of Ceylon up to 8,000 feet in altitude. Kurz says it is also met with in the forests of Tenasserim. Cinnamon is a tonic and heating medicine. The leaves are, like the bark, aromatic, and they yield oil of cloves. The liber or bark also affords oil, but cinnamon bark is chiefly used as a condiment. The bark is removed by making longitudinal incisions on the twigs; it coils up naturally, and when dry is then broken off.

784. CISSAMPELOS PAREIRA, *Linn.;* Menispermaceæ. The False Pareira Bark. A climber common both to the Old and New Worlds. The dried root is used as a mild tonic and diuretic in advanced stages of acute and chronic cystitis and catarrhal affections of the bladder; the bark possesses similar properties.

785. CITRUS MEDICA, *Linn.;* Rutaceæ, Var. 1, *medica* proper. The Citron (Eng.); Cedratier (*Fr.*); Cedro (*It.*); Bijaura (*Hind.*); Begpura (*Beng.*). Cultivated in many parts of India—Assam, Calcutta, Chutia Nagpur, North-West India, Bombay; also in Persia. Citron rind is hot, dry, and tonic; the pulp cold and dry; the seeds, leaves, and flowers hot and dry; the juice refrigerant and astringent. (*See* also 592.)

786. Var. 2, *Limonum.* The Lemon (*Eng.*); Limonier, more generally Citronnier (*Fr.*); Limone (*It.*); Citrone (*Germ.*); Bara nimbu (*Hind.*). Cultivated abundantly in the south of Europe; also in India. Citric acid is made of the fruit of this variety. There are three officinal parts: (1) the outer part of the rind; (2) the essential oil of the rind; (3) the juice of

the ripe fruit. The rind is said to be stomachic and carminative. Lemon oil is carminative in doses of from two to four drops. It has been applied in some cases of ophthalmia, but with doubtful results. Lemon juice is highly valued as an antiscorbutic and refrigerant; primarily antalkaline, secondarily, antacid. It forms the best remedy for scurvy, and an excellent drink in fever and inflammatory affections. It has met with success in acute rheumatism, dysentery, and diarrhœa; recently it has been recommended as a simple antiperiodic. It also forms an antidote to acro-narcotic poisions.

787. Var 3, *Acida.* The Sour Lime of India; Libu, nebu (*Hind.*); Jambíra (*Sans.*). Grown in Burmah and Bengal. This variety yields the juice used medicinally. A pickle of the fruit is an effectual medicine for indigestion.

788. Var. 4, *Limetta.* The Sweet Lime of India; Mitha nebu (*Beng., Hind.*). Commonly cultivated in most parts of India and Burma. Indigenous in the Nilgiris.

789. Coptis Teeta, *Wall.*; Ranunculaceæ. The Coptis or Mishmi Títa. Met with in east Assam, in the temperate region of the Mishmi hills. The dried root is recommended as a pure bitter tonic, useful in general debility, convalescence after fevers, nervous diseases, atonic dyspepsia, and in mild forms of intermittent fever. It has been found to produce excellent results. This drug was first made known by Griffith during his Mishmi explorations. There seems every reason to think that this would prove a most valuable addition to our list of tonic medicines could the supply be increased, so as to admit of its becoming better known. It is imported into the plains of India done up in small baskets.

790. Croton Tiglium, *Linn.*; Euphorbiaceæ. The Purging Croton; Jaypál (*Beng.*). A small tree, cultivated in many parts of India and Burma. The seed is used as a powerful drastic purgative. In over-doses it acts as an acro-narcotic poison. The croton oil expressed from the seed possesses powerful hydragogue cathartic properties. Its acts externally as a rubefacient and counter-irritant. It is useful in dropsy, obstinate constipation, and apoplexy.

791. Curcuma aromatica, *Salisb.*; Scitamineæ. Wild Turmeric; Yellow Zedoary; Cochin Turmeric; Jungli-haldi (*Hind.*); Ban-Halud (*Beng.*). The round, short rhizomes of this plant are of a pale yellow colour, and possess at all times an agreeable fragrant smell and a warm aromatic taste. They are used medicinally, being regarded as tonic and carminative, and hold an important place in native perfumery.

792. C. Zedoaria. *Roscoe* (*non-Roxb.*). The long and the round Zedoary.; Kachura (*Hind.*). A not uncommon plant, wild in the moist forests of India. The rhizomes possess aromatic, stimulant, and carminative properties. They are employed in native practice as a stomachic, and also applied to bruises and sprains.

793. C. Zerumbet, *Roscoe* (*non-Roxb.*). The maha-buri-bach (*Beng.*). The rhizomes of this plant are warm and aromatic, and are largely used in native medicine.

794. Datura fastuosa, *Linn.*; Solanaceæ. The Black Datura; Kala dhatúrá (*Beng., Hind.*). A small shrub, found all over India, in waste places; flowers purple. The leaves act as antispasmodic when smoked by persons labouring under asthmatic complaints. The seeds are used as a poison for criminal purposes. Var. *alba.* The white Datura; Safed-dhatúrá (*Hind.*). A large, spreading annual, 2 to 4 feet high; flowers white or nearly so. The leaves of this form, and of the preceding, are applied as local anæsthetics Heated they are applied locally in painful affections of the eye. The whole plant is poisonous; taken in excess it produces maniacal delirium.

795. Datura Stramonium, *Linn.* The Stramonium or Thorn Apple. A coarse annual, met with in the temperate Himálaya, from Kashmír to Sikkim. The seed is used criminally, but is also prescribed medicinally, especially in asthmatic complaints. The leaves are applied to boils and ulcers, and are smoked with tobacco for asthma. The uses are in fact very similar to those of *D. fastuosa.* All Daturas produce dilatation of the pupil, and have been recommended as substitutes for Belladonna. Var. *Tatula.* The young fruits, strung on threads and imported into India from Persia, seem to be those of this species. It is common everywhere around the villages of Afghánistán. The name by which these young fruits are sold is *sharbhuli* in Bombay and *maratia múghú* in Madras. They are said to be sedative and slightly intoxicating.

796. Echium, sp.? Boragineæ. The drug known in India as *Gao-zabán* is supposed to be an undescribed species of this genus. The flowers sold as *Gul-i-Gao-zabán* are of two kinds —purple coloured, with a tube nearly one inch long, narrow, and slightly bent; yellow, straight, almost campanulate, and about three-quarters of an inch long. The leaves are thick and fleshy with curious glandular scars, each ending in a hair. These flowers must belong to two widely different plants. (*See* also *Onosma.*)

797. Eugenia Jambolana, *Lam.*; Myrtaceæ. The Jaman (*Hind.*); Kálájám (*Beng.*). A moderate-sized tree, found wild or in cultivation all over India, from the Indus eastward, ascending to altitude 5,000 feet. The bark is astringent and used in cases of dysentery, and the decoction as a tooth gargle. The fresh juice of the bark is given with goat's milk in the diarrhœa of children. A vinegar, prepared from the juice of the unripe fruit, is an agreeable stomachic and carminative; it is also used as a diuretic. The expressed juice of the leaves is employed alone or in combination with other astringents in dysentery. A considerable interest has recently (in Europe and America) been raised in the seeds of this tree as a drug useful in the treatment of diabetes. This property appears to be quite unknown to the natives of India. (*See* also 124, 597, 717.)

798. Euphorbia antiquorum, *Linn.*; Euphorbiaceæ. A shrub with three-angled branches, common on the dry hills of the Peninsula. The

juice which flows from the branches is used as a purgative to relieve pain in the loins. It is an acrid irritant in rheumatism and tooth-ache. When taken internally it acts as a drastic purgative. It is also employed in nervine diseases, dropsy, palsy, deafness, and amaurosis. A plaster prepared from the roots and mixed with assafœtida is applied externally to the stomachs of children suffering from worms. The bark of the root is purgative, and the stem is given in the form of a decoction in gout. The plant is supposed to ward off lightning, and is generally kept in tubs or pots on the roofs or other exposed parts of native houses.

799. E. NERIIFOLIA, *Linn.* The Mansa sij (*Beng.*); Sunhi, Vujri (*Sans.*); Gangichú (*Pb.*); Thor (*Bomb.*). A small tree or bush with cylindric stem. Cultivated near villages in most parts of India. It is considered a sacred plant by the Mechis of the Sikkim Terai and Bhután Duars, and is consequently often found on deserted village sites. The plant is sacred to *Mansá*, the goddess of serpents. The root, mixed with black pepper, is employed in cases of snake-bite, both internally and externally. Every part abounds with an acrid milky juice, employed to remove warts and cutaneous eruptions. The milky juice of an undetermined species of *Euphorbia*, probably this one, is applied to incipient abscesses, and is said to be effectual in preventing suppuration. It is also considered purgative and rubefacient.

800. FERONIA ELEPHANTUM, *Correa;* Rutaceæ. The Wood Apple; Kathbél (*Hind.*, *Beng.*). A large tree of the sub-Himálayan forests, from the Ravi eastward, Bengal, South India, Chanda district in the Central Provinces. The fruit is aromatic and used as a stomachic stimulant in diseases of children. The gum, resembling gum-arabic, acts as a demulcent in bowel affections. the unripe fruit is described as astringent, and is used in combination with *bél* and other medicines in diarrhœa and dysentery. The ripe fruit is said to be useful in hiccup and affections of the throat. The leaves are aromatic and carminative. In Mahomedan medical works the leaves are described as astringent, the fruit as cold and dry, refreshing, astringent, cardiacal, and tonic, a useful remedy in salivation and sore throat, strengthening the gums and acting as an astringent. Sherbet made from the fruit increases the appetite, and has alexipharmic properties. The pulp, applied externally, is a remedy for the bites of venomous insects; if not obtainable, the powdered rind may be used. The fruit is sometimes employed to adulterate *bél* fruit. (*See* also 130, 1071.)

801.* FERULA ALLIACEA, *Boiss.;* Umbelliferæ. The Indian Assafœtida; Hing (*Hind.*). By Eastern doctors this form of Assafœtida has, from the remotest times, been held in great esteem, and was once regarded as worth its weight in silver. In Europe its use as a medicine has of late years greatly diminished. In Hindu medical works it is directed to be fried before it is used. It is highly esteemed as a carminative and condiment, also as an antispasmodic. If taken daily it is said to prevent the attacks of malarious fever. The fruit is considered stimulant. (*See* the next species). (*See* also 1103.)

802.* F. NARTHEX, *Boiss.* The Assafœtida of Europe; Hing (*Hind.*, *Beng.*). A native of Kashmír, Persia, and Afghánistán. The gum-resin is a powerful antispasmodic, expectorant, and anthelmintic, a nervine stimulant, and a feeble laxative. It is useful in hysterical affections, also in spasmodic affections such as asthma, whooping-cough, angina pectoris, flatulent colic, &c. It produces remarkable effects in pneumonia and bronchitis in children. The leaves possess sudorific and carminative properties. In ring-worm assafœtida is applied as a paste. The exports of assafœtida during the year 1884-85 amounted to Rs. 31,857, and the imports to Rs. 3,50,076. Nearly the whole of the imports were from Persia. (*See* also 1104.)

803. GARCINIA MORELLA, *Desrous;* Guttiferæ. The Gamboge. An evergreen tree, found in the Khásia Hills, East Bengal, and West Coast of India. Gamboge is used as a warm purgative, and considered a valuable hydragogue cathartic. It possesses anthelmintic properties, and is a valuable medicine for dropsical affections, amenorrhœa, and obstinate constipation. (*See* also 1019, 1109.)

804. GENTIANA KURROO, *Royle;* Gentianaceæ. The Himálayan Gentian; Kútki (*Hind.*, *Beng.*). Common in Kashmír and North-West Himálaya, altitude 5,000 to 11,000 feet. The root is used as a bitter tonic, and as a substitute for true Gentian. On the hills it is viewed as a febrifuge, and is largely exported to the plains along with *Picrorhiza Kurrooa* (Royle), as the officinal *karrí or kútkú*. Atkinson says that five tons of this drug are annually exported from the hills to the plains.

805. GYNOCARDIA ODORATA, *R. Br.;* Bixineæ. The Chaulmugra. A glabrous tree, met with in the forests of the Malayan Peninsula and Eastern India, as far north as Assam, extending thence to the west along the base of the Himálaya to Sikkim. The seeds are alterative, tonic, and in large doses emetic. They yield an oil which is in India generally used in the cure of skin diseases, scrofula, &c. This oil is also largely prescribed for consumption and rheumatism, and as a specific against syphilis. The active principle of the oil, Gynocardic acid, has been separated and much recommended as an excellent form of administering the drug. In the treatment of phthisis the *Chaulmugra* oil has gained a European reputation, and a reputation which seems daily to be increasing. When the patient comes under the influence of the medicine, it at first causes watery diarrhœa, but this rapidly subsides, followed by a great desire for food, which, if not satisfied, results in nausea. If rubbed freely upon the chest, both back and front, the relief to the cough is very marked. Mr. Christy, in his 'New Commercial Plants,' publishes certain letters from private persons who speak in the highest terms of the use of the oil in the cure of rheumatism. He recommends that the oil should be liquified by heat and then well rubbed into the parts affected.

806.* HELLEBORUS NIGER, *Linn.*; Ranunculaceæ. The Black Hellebore or Christmas Rose; Kála-kútkí (*Beng.*). A small, perennial herb, with black, jointed, definite rhizomes, having numerous interlacing rootlets. A native of Central and South Europe, with the Altai Mountains as its southern limit. Ainslie says, with a degree of hesitation and doubt, that the plant which yields this drug is met with in Nepal. Sir W. O'Shaughnessy, in his 'Bengal Dispensatory,' speaking of this drug, simply gives an abstract from Ainslie, and most modern authors have done the same. Even Ainslie derived his information, however, from Dr. Kirkpatrick, who writes that it is known in Nepal as *kutka*, and that it also reaches India by way of the Red Sea. Dr. Dymock, in his valuable work on the 'Materia Medica of Western India,' does not allude to hellebore or to any Indian substitute for it. As a matter of fact the black hellebore plant has never been found in Asia in a wild state. Mahomedan physicians do, however, prescribe a drug which is known as hellebore, as also many other drugs which neither grow nor are imported into India. Dr. Royle explains this by stating that the Mahomedans obtained their medical science from the Arabian physicians who, in their turn, learned it from the Greek authors. European plants have thus come to be known by name in India, and Royle includes in his list of such the roots of the black hellebore, remarking that the druggist, trusting to the indifference of the physician and the ignorance of the patient, substitutes for such drugs others with supposed similar properties. *Actæa spicata* seems to be the plant substituted for hellebore by most Indian druggists: it is an indigenous herb and abundant on the higher Himálaya.

807. HOLARRHENA ANTIDYSENTERICA, *Wall.*; Apocynaceæ. The Kurchi or Conessi Bark. A tree, common in the sub-Himálayan tracts, Bengal, Burma, Central and South India. *Kurchi* bark is medicinally used as a tonic and febrifuge; but it is chiefly esteemed for its antidysenteric properties. That it is always a sure remedy for dysenteric affections has been borne out by the statements of many medical practitioners, both native and European. The seeds (known as *Indrajau*) are considered by the Arabic and Persian writers as possessed of carminative and astringent properties, and are used in chronic chest affections, such as asthma, and also in colic and diuresis. For many years great confusion existed about the identity of this plant. Through an early mistake it received the name of *Wrightia antidysenterica*. Partly on this account the bark was in India adulterated with that obtained from *Wrightia tinctoria*, and hence Conessi Bark fell into disrepute owing to the inert action of the adulterant. (*See* also 150.)

808. HYDROCOTYLE ASIATICA, *Linn.*; Umbelliferæ. The Asiatic Penny-wort; Bráhmamanduki (*Hind.*); Thálkuri (*Beng.*). A small herbaceous plant, found in damp places in Bengal and South India. The leaves have been made official in the 'Indian Pharmacopœia.' They are described as alterative, tonic, and when locally applied, stimulant; they are used in leprosy with good results. In secondary or constitutional syphilis they are of great value. In ulcers and skin diseases they are prescribed both internally and externally. On the Coromandel Coast the leaves are applied to bruises.

809. HYMENODICTYON EXCELSUM, *Wall.*; Rubiaceæ. A large deciduous tree with smooth bark, met with on the dry hills at the base of the Western Himálaya, throughout the Deccan, Chutia Nagpur, and Central India to the Anamallays, also in Tenasserim and Chittagong. The inner bark is bitter and astringent, and is used as a febrifuge. This drug seems likely to attain a European interest, and it is at present being experimented with by Mr. Christy. (*See* also 154, 437.)

810. HYOSCYAMUS NIGER, *Linn.*; Solanaceæ. The Henbane. A coarse erect herb of the temperate western Himálaya, altitude 8000 to 11,000 feet from Kashmír to Garhwal, cultivated in the Sahranpur Botanic Gardens, and in the neighbourhood of Agra and Ajmere. The dried leaves are described as anodyne, sedative, and antispasmodic. A preparation from the leaves is useful in nervous irritability, mental excitement, sleeplessness, and various other mental disorders. As an external application this drug has been employed in neuralgic and rheumatic affections, painful glandular enlargements, irritable ulcers and hæmorrhoids. In diseases of the eye it is a valuable remedy.

811. ILLICIUM ANISATUM, *Linn.*; Magnoliaceæ. The Star Anise; Anasphal (*Hind.*). Indigenous to China and Japan. There are two imperfectly known species of this genus met with in the mountains on the eastern frontier of India—*I. Griffithii*, on the Khásia hills, in Bhután and *I. Majus*, in Tenasserim. While the, *Star Anise* has long been in use in China and Japan, it has only been employed in modern times in India. It is viewed as of great service in flatulent and spasmodic affections of the intestinal canal. It is chiefly employed in Europe to flavour spirits, the greatest consumption being in Germany, France, and Italy.

812.* IPOMŒA BONA-NOX, *Linn.*; Convolvulaceæ. The Moon-flower, a name derived from the fact that the large, white, and sweetly-scented flowers open only at night; Kulmi-latá (*Beng.*). A native of America, early introduced into India, and in some parts of the country now quite naturalised. The dried capsules and seeds, as well as the flowers, leaves, and roots, are included amongst the medicines supposed to have some merit as remedies against snake-bite.

813. I. HEDERACEA, *Jacq.* The Káládáná (*Hind.*). A common plant, widely cultivated in India, where it is also apparently wild. The seed is used medicinally. The author of the 'Makhzan-ul-Adwiya' says that this drug is a drastic purgative, useful in the treatment of bilious and phlegmatic humours, and that it acts also as an anthelmintic. Roxburgh was the first to make the seed known to European physicians, and it now holds an important position as a useful and cheap substitute for Jalap. The drug is administered in the form of a tincture, an extract, a compound powder, or a resin, supplying the place of the corresponding preparations of Jalap. The resin appears to be the most satisfactory form of administering the medicine, the dose of which is 4 to 8 grains.

814.* JATROPHA CURCAS, *Linn.;* Euphorbiaceæ. The Physic Nut; Bag-berenda (*Hind.*, *Beng.*). A soft-wooded, evergreen shrub, indigenous to America, cultivated in most parts of India. The seed yields an oil which is used as a purgative and emetic, and also as an application in cutaneous diseases. In overdoses it acts as an acro-narcotic poison. The diluted oil forms a useful embrocation in chronic rheumatism. The leaves are extensively used in the Cape de Verd Islands as a lactagogue, in the form of a decoction or cataplasm to the mammæ. (*See* also 1026.)

815. MALLOTUS PHILIPPINENSIS, *Mull.;* Euphorbiaceæ. The Kamala or Kaméla (*Hind.*). A small tree of the sub-Himálayan tract from the Indus eastward to Bengal (ascending to 4,000 feet in altitude), Central and South India, Burma, and the Andaman Islands. The powder prepared from the tricocous fruit is used as an anthelmintic, vermifuge, and purgative medicine. It is also said to possess cathartic properties. Recently it has been discovered by Professor W. T. Thiselton Dyer that the African Waras powder is not, as was formerly supposed, identical with the Indian *Kaméla*, but is in fact the glandular hairs from the pods of *Flemingia congesta*, a common wild plant in India and Africa. (*See* also 1154.)

816. MANGIFERA INDICA, *Linn.;* Anacardiaceæ. The Mango; Amb (*Hind.*); Am (*Beng.*). A densely-branched tree supposed to be wild in certain isolated tracts, such as in the Western Ghâts, Chutia Nagpur, and in Manipur and the Naga hills; cultivated all over India for its valuable fruit. The ripe fruit is laxative. The bark is used as an astringent, valuable in hæmorrhages, diarrhœa, and other discharges. The decoction of the kernel, either alone or in combination with *bel* and ginger, is generally prescribed in diarrhœa. The juice of the kernel, as a snuff, is employed to stop nasal bleeding. The kernel is also described in the 'Indian Pharmacopœia' as an anthelmintic, and containing a large quantity of gallic acid, is said to be highly useful in bleeding piles and menorrhagia. The unripe fruit has the reputation of being useful in ophthalmia, and the seeds in asthma. (*See* also 171, 446, 604, 1155.)

817. MELIA AZADIRACHTA, *Linn.;* Meliaceæ. The Ním or Margosa Tree. A large tree planted and self-sown throughout the greater part of India and Burma. The fruit is used medicinally as an antiseptic, purgative, emollient, and anthelmintic. The bark is known as astringent, tonic, and anti-periodic, and is used in intermittent and other fevers, in constitutional weakness, and during the convalescent state after fever and other diseases. The leaves are stimulant and applied to ulcers and skin diseases of long standing. They are also used in the form of poultices to disperse glandular tumours, and in the form of a pulp in cases of pustular eruptions and small-pox. The oil obtained from the seeds effects suppuration of scrofular glands, and is given in leprosy. The gum is said to have stimulant properties. (*See* also 175, 450, 721.)

818. M. AZEDARACH, *Linn.;* The Persian Lilac, Bastard Cedar or Bead Tree; Mahá-nímb (*Hind.*); Mahá-ním (*Beng.*). A tree, with smooth, grey bark, commonly cultivated throughout India, and believed to be indigenous in the outer Himálaya, Siwalik tract, and the hills of Baluchistán. The bark is extremely bitter, and is employed as an anthelmintic in the form of decoction. In large doses it exercises narcotic influence on the constitution. The fresh berries and leaves are supposed to be poisonous. The flowers and leaves are applied as a poultice to relieve nervous headaches. The juice of the leaves is administered internally, and is said to be anthelmintic, anti-lithic, diuretic, and emmenagogue. The bark and leaves are used internally and externally in leprosy and scrofula. A poultice of the flowers has the reputation of being useful to kill lice and to cure eruptions of the scalp. (*See* also 174.)

819. MESUA FERREA, *Linn;* Guttiferæ. The Nagesar (*Hind.*, *Beng.*). A middle-sized tree, met with in the mountains of Eastern Bengal, the Eastern and Western Peninsulas, and the Andaman Islands. The dried fragrant flowers constitute the *Nagesar* or *Nage-kesar* of the bazars. They are mild, stimulant, astringent, and stomachic, useful in thirst, stomach irritation, and excessive perspiration. A paste made of the flowers with butter and sugar is used to stop bleeding from piles. The bark is a mild astringent and aromatic. The kernels yield by expression a fixed oil known as *Nahur* oil, useful in the treatment of itch. (*See* also 179.)

820. MIMUSOPS ELENGI, *Linn.;* Sapotaceæ. The Bakul (*Beng.*); Mólsarí (*Hind.*). A large, evergreen tree, much cultivated; said to be wild in the Western Ghâts, Burma, Ceylon, and the Andaman Islands. The bark is an astringent tonic, and in decoction forms a good gargle to promote salivation. Water distilled from the flowers is used as a stimulant medicine, and also as a perfume. The unripe fruit is astringent, and when chewed affords firmness to the teeth. The dried and powdered flowers are snuffed by persons labouring under the disease known in Bengal as *Ahwa*, which is generally accompanied by headache, strong fever, and pain in the neck. It relieves the pain in the head by inducing copious discharges from the nose. The bruised seeds are applied locally within the anus in cases of constipation of children. (*See* also 185.)

821. MUCUNA PRURIENS, *DC.;* Leguminosæ. The Cowhage Plant; Alkusa (*Beng.*). An annual climber common in the forests, and a

very attractive plant on account of its golden brown, velvety pod, covered with irritating hairs. In Hindu medical works, the seeds of this plant are described as a powerful aphrodisiac. The root is tonic and useful in nervine diseases. Ainslie says, that a strong infusion of the root, mixed with honey, is prescribed by the Tamil doctors in cholera. The hairs of the pod are known as a vermifuge in the West Indies. The 'Pharmacopœia of India' recommends that cowhage should be administered as an electuary with treacle or honey. The pods dipped in the vehicle should be then scraped until the mass obtains the consistency of an electuary. A table-spoonful for an adult or a tea-spoonful for a child followed by a purgative expels the worms.

822. MYRICA SAPIDA, *Wall.*; Myricaceæ. The Káiphal (*Hind.*, *Beng.*). A moderate-sized tree on the outer Himálaya, ascending to 6,000 feet in altitude, and extending to the Khasia hills and Burma. The bark is the most valuable product of this tree. It is considered heating, stimulant, and useful in diseases caused by the derangement of phlegm, such as catarrhal fever, cough, and affections of the throat. It is also employed as a rubefacient and sternutatory. In cholera cases, the body of the patient is rubbed with the powder made of the bark and ginger to bring about reaction. It is also used as an astringent gargle.

823. NARDOSTACHYS JATAMANSI, *DC.*; Valerianeæ. The Spikenard: Jatamansi (*Hind.*, *Beng.*). A plant of the alpine Himálaya, altitude 11,000 to 15,000 feet; from Kumaon to Sikkim, ascending to 17,000 feet. The root is aromatic and bitter in taste. It is supposed to possess tonic, stimulant, and antispasmodic properties, and is often employed in the treament of epilepsy, hysteria, and convulsive affections; it is also considered to be deobstruent, diuretic, and emmenagogue, and recommended in various diseases of the digestive and respiratory organs. *Jatamansi* is regarded as useful in jaundice, affections of the throat, and as an antidote for poisons. It is popularly believed to have the power of promoting the growth and blackness of the hair. It has been noticed by Ainslie that in Lower India, the people prepare a fragrant and cooling liniment from this drug, to be applied to the head and used internally as a blood-purifier. (*See* also 1033.)

824. NEPHRODIUM FILIX-MAS, *Richard*; Filices. A common fern on the Himálaya and lower hills of India from 4,000 to 10,000 feet in altitude. The dried rhizome is officinal in the 'Indian Pharmacopœia,' being anthelmintic, especially serviceable in the treatment of tape-worm.

825. NERIUM ODORUM, *Soland.*; Apocynaceæ. The Sweet-scented Oleander; Karabi (*Beng.*). A large shrub of Central India, Sind, Afghánistán, and the outer Himálaya, to 5,500 feet. Often cultivated. There are two varieties, one with white flowers and the other with red. All parts of the plant, especially the root, are recognised by the natives as poisonous, and as such are used for criminal and suicidal purposes. When used medicinally over-doses of the root are productive of serious and even fatal effects. A preparation of the root is sometimes used to procure abortion. In skin diseases, such as leprosy and inflammatory affections, the root and bark are highly beneficial. In the form of a paste it is recommended to beapplied to ulcers on the penis. The juice of the tender leaves forms a remedy for ophthalmia. The decoction of the leaves is said to reduce swellings, and the paste made from the bark is a medicine for itch and ringworm. According to Mahomedan physicians the root is a powerful resolvent and attenuant.

826. NYCTANTHES ARBOR-TRISTIS, *Linn.*; Oleaceæ. The Harsinghar (*Hind.*); Sephalika (*Beng.*). A small tree of Central India, extending to Bengal and Burma; cultivated throughout India. The leaves are useful in fever and rheumatism. The fresh juice of the leaves is given with honey in chronic fever. A decoction of the leaves, prepared over a gentle fire, is recommended by several writers as a specific for obstinate sciatica. Six or seven of the young leaves are rubbed up with water and a little fresh ginger, and administered in obstinate fevers of the intermittent type. The powdered seeds are used to cure scurfy affections of the scalp. (*See* also 196, 1160.)

827. OCIMUM BASILICUM, *Linn.*; Labiatæ. The Common Sweet Basil: Bábáitulshi (*Beng.*). An erect, herbaceous annual, indigenous in Persia and Sind; growing throughout India. The seed is mucilaginous and cooling, given in infusion in gonorrhœa, diarrhœa, and chronic dysentery. The juice of the leaves forms an excellent nostrum for the cure of ringworm, and the bruised leaves for scorpion stings. The seeds and flowers also possess stimulant diuretic and demulcent properties. Diaphoretic and expectorant actions are also ascribed to the plant; a cold infusion of the seed relieves after-pains of parturition. (*See* also 671.)

828. OLDENLANDIA CORYMBOSA, *Linn.*; Rubiaceæ. The Daman-papar (*Hind.*); Khet-papra (*Beng.*). A herbaceous plant found throughout India ascending the hills to altitude 5,000 feet. There seems no doubt but that all the allied species to this plant are used indiscriminately with this particular one. The plant is considered an important medicine in the treatment of fevers which have their origin in the derangement of the bile. The whole of the plant is used medicinally in the form of a decoction combined with aromatics. It acts as an alterative when given in low forms of fever.

829. ONOSMA BRACTEATUM, *Wall.*; Boragineæ. It seems probable that part at least of the so-called *gao-zabán* of Indian druggists' shops is obtained from this plant. (*See* "Echium.")

830. O. ECHIOIDES, *Linn.* The root of this plant is one of the principal sources of the medicinal and dye root sold as *rattanjot*.

831.* PAPAVER SOMNIFERUM, *Linn.*; Papaveraceæ. The White Poppy; Opium. An annual, cultivated throughout India. Opium is primarily a stimulant, and secondarily a narcotic anodyne and antispasmodic. In over-doses it acts as a powerful poison, causing sleep which passes into coma, attended by slowness of respiration, feeble pulsation, cold perspiration, and contraction of pupils, followed by death. In inflammation it has been extensively used either alone or in combination with other medicines. In spasmodic affections, patients have been found to obtain immediate relief by a few doses of opium. In simple or cancerous ulceration of the stomach, diarrhœa, and dysentery, and in the diseases of the genito-urinary organs, it is of the highest value. It is also highly esteemed as the most effectual remedy in tetanus, acute rheumatism, and delirium tremens. It is also useful as an external application in various rheumatic, neuralgic, and other painful affections, also in ophthalmia and other diseases of the eye. According to the Sanscrit writers, the poppy-seeds are demulcent and nutritive, and useful in cough and asthma. (*See* also 735, 1035.)

832. PADALIUM MUREX, *Linn.;* Pedalineæ. The Bara-gokhru (*Hind., Beng.*). A weedy herb of the Dekkan Peninsula and Ceylon. The mucilage of the fresh leaves and stems is highly valued by the people of South India as a medicine for gonorrhœa and dysuria. The fruits are demulcent, diuretic, antispasmodic, and aphrodisiac. The juice is a good gargle and used in aphthæ as a local application. The plant makes a good poultice.

833. PEGANUM HARMALA, *Linn.;* Rutaceæ. The Hurmal (*Hind.*). The seeds are known as *Isband Lahori.* A bush 1 to 3 feet in height, much branched and densely clothed with leaves, met with in Kashmír, the North-West Himálaya, and the plains from Sind and the Punjáb, to Delhi and Agra. *Hurmal* is an alterative medicine in atrabilis, and also in diseases supposed to arise from cold humours, such as palsy, lumbago, &c. For administration a concentrated decoction is mixed with sweet oil and honey, or the crushed seeds are boiled in wine down to one-fourth of the original bulk of the latter, and the mixture strained. The infusion or tincture acts as a stimulant emmenagogue and produces slight intoxication like *Cannabis sativa.* The decoction of the leaves is given for rheumatism, and the root acts as a vermifuge.

834. PHYLLANTHUS EMBLICA, *Linn.;* Euphorbiaceæ. The Emblic Myrobalan; Amla, aonla (*Hind.*); Amlaki (*Beng.*). A moderate-sized tree in the dry forests of India and Burma. The fruit constitutes the *Emblic myrobalan.* It is purgative when fresh, but when dry is used as an astringent in bowel complaints and hæmorrhages. It is useful in diarrhœa and dysentery, and is regarded as an antiscorbutic. It contains a large proportion of gallic acid. The flowers are employed as a refrigerant and aperient. The bark is astringent. An extract from the root is used medicinally. The fresh juice is cooling, refrigerant, diuretic, and laxative. The exudation from the incisions on the fruit is used as an external application in inflammation of the eye. (*See* also 612, 1166.)

835. PICRORHIZA KURROOA, *Royle;* Scrophularineæ. The Katki (*Hind., Beng.*). A low, more or less hairy, herb of the alpine Himálaya from Kashmír to Sikkim, altitude 9,000 to 15,000 feet. The root is bitter, acrid, and stomachic, and in large doses acts as a moderate cathartic. It is used in fever and dyspepsia and in many purgative preparations. Antiperiodic virtues have been attributed to it by Dr. Tripe.

836. PLANTAGO OVATA, *Forsk.;* Plantagineæ. The Ispaghul. A stemless herb found in Sind and the Punjáb plains and North-West India to Baluchistán, Afghánistán, Arabia, Egypt, and Spain. The seed is demulcent and mildly astringent; it is useful in febrile, catarrhal, and renal affections. It is chiefly used in diarrhœa and dysentery. The bruised seed forms a good emollient poultice. The mucilage is a cooling demulcent drink. It is said that this medicine often cures the chronic diarrhœa of children after all other drugs have failed.

837. PLUMBAGO ROSEA, *Linn.* and P. ZEYLANICA; Plumbagineæ. The Rakta-chitra (*Hind., Beng.*). Shrubby perennials, most probably natives of India, and extensively cultivated in gardens, especially the former. Medicinally the two plants are not distinguished. The root is a well-known vesicant capable of raising blisters within twelve or eighteen hours; it may be used as a cheap substitute for cantharides, with the additional advantage of not causing irritation of the genito-urinary organs. Internally it acts as a stimulant, and in large doses as an acro-narcotic poison. It is also used as a powerful sialagogue, and in South India is highly valued as a remedy for secondary syphilis and leprosy.

838. PODOPHYLLUM EMODI, *Wall.;* Berberideæ. Found in the interior ranges of the Himálaya, altitude 8,000 to 14,000 feet, extending from Sikkim to Hazára; it appears at 6,000 feet in Kashmír. Dr. Stewart says that the fruit of this plant is used medicinally at Lahoul. Apparently *Podophyllum* root is not known as a medicine to the natives of India, and no mention is made of the root of this extremely common Himálayan species having been experimented with as a substitute for the American-imported drug.

839. PONGAMIA GLABRA, *Vent.;* Leguminosæ. The Karanj (*Hind.*); Karanja (*Beng.*); A small tree found in the Central and East Himálaya, extending to Ceylon and Malacca. It is commonly met with in the Concans. The seed and the expressed oil are used externally in skin diseases, and for this purpose the oil has been found extremely useful, and deserves to be introduced into European medical practice. A poultice of the leaves is applied to ulcers infested with worms. Ainslie states that the juice of the root may be used as a wash for foul sores. (*See* also 216, 459, 1039.)

840. PREMNA INTEGRIFOLIA, *Linn.;* Verbenaceæ. The Arni (*Hind.*); Ganiari (*Beng.*). A small, deciduous tree of Oudh, North Bengal, South India, Ceylon, Tenasserim, and the Andaman Islands. The root is bitter and stomachic,

and is given in decoction as a cordial and tonic. It forms an ingredient of *dasamula*, a native preparation. The leaves are bitter and carminative, and rubbed along with pepper are administered in colds and fevers. The whole plant is used in the form of decoction in rheumatism and neuralgia. (*See* also 462.)

841.* PUNICA GRANATUM, *Linn.*; Lythraceæ. The Pomegranate; Anar (*Hind.*); Dalim (*Beng.*). A small tree or bush cultivated throughout India, probably wild in the North-West. The fresh juice of the fruit is an ingredient of cooling and refrigerant mixtures for dyspepsia. The rind of the fruit is used as an astringent in diarrhœa. The seed is stomachic, the pulp cardiac and stomachic. Pomegranate peel, with opium and an aromatic, such as cloves, is an efficacious remedy in chronic dysentery and diarrhœa. A decoction of the bark followed by a purgative acts as an anthelmintic. The efficiency of the decoction of the root-bark as a remedy for tapeworm is now well established in India. (*See* also 620, 1169.)

842. RHEUM EMODI, *Wall.*; Polygonaceæ. The Indian Rhubarb; Hindi-revand-chini (*Hind.*); Bangalu-revan-chini (*Beng.*). A large herb, frequent in parts of the Punjáb Himálaya from 7,000 to 14,000 feet. The Indian rhubarb is an astringent tonic and purgative. It is less active than the imported rhubarb, and has been often pronounced worthless. This is probably owing to the fact that an inferior variety reaches the plains, while the action of the fresh root has been found to be equal to that of the true rhubarb.

843. *RICINUS COMMUNIS, *Linn.*; Euphorbiaceæ. The Castor-Oil Plant; Arand (*Hind.*); Reri (*Beng.*). Castor oil is a mild and efficacious purgative, useful in costiveness, tympanitis, fever, inflammation, &c. It is much valued in chronic rheumatic diseases. The root is useful in various forms of rheumatism, such as lumbago, pleurodynia, and sciatica, &c. The root-bark is used as a purgative and alterative in chronic enlargements and skin diseases. The fresh juice of the leaves is used as an emetic in poisoning by opium and other narcotics, and a decoction or poultice may be used as a lactagogue. (*See* OILS and OIL-SEEDS.) (*See* also 1043, 1172.)

844. SANTALUM ALBUM, *Linn.*; Santalaceæ. The White Sandal-wood tree; Chandan, Sufed-chandan (*Hind.*); Chandan (*Beng.*). A small, evergreen tree of the dry regions of South India. Sandal-wood is a bitter, cooling, and astringent medicine, useful in biliousness, vomiting, fever, thirst, and heat of the body. An emulsion of the wood is applied to the skin in erysipelas, prurigo, and sudamina. It also acts as a diaphoretic. A yellow volatile oil is distilled from the wood, which has been reported as a remedy for gonorrhœa. This has of late been tried as a substitute for copaiba in European practice. (*See* also 248, 1045.)

845. SAUSSUREA LAPPA, *C. B. Clarke*; Compositæ. The Costus; Kut, kust (*Hind.*). A tall, stout herb, met with in Kashmír, altitude 8,000 to 12,000 feet. *Kust* is collected in large quantities and exported to the Punjáb, where it finds its way all over India, and is shipped from Bombay and Calcutta to China and the Red Sea; a small quantity finds its way to Europe. It has been used in Hindu medicine from the earliest ages. It is said to be aphrodisiac, tonic, and aromatic, stimulant and useful in diseases arising from deranged air and phlegm, also in asthma and for resolving tumours. *Kust* is an ingredient in a stimulating mixture given by the natives for cholera. It was formerly smoked as a substitute for opium. The dried powder is used in the preparation of a stimulating ointment for ulcers; it is a useful hair-wash; the root is a valuable perfume and is a preservative to woollen cloths.

846. SEMECARPUS ANACARDIUM, *Linn. f.*; Anacardiaceæ. The Marking-nut Tree; Bhela (*Hind.*, *Beng.*). A deciduous tree of the sub-Himálayan tract from the Sutlej eastward, ascending to 3,500 feet; abundant also in the forests of India, extending to Chittagong but not to Burma. The acrid juice of the marking-nut is a powerful vesicant, and is applied externally to cold swellings. The ripe fruit is regarded as acrid, heating, stimulant, digestive, nervine, and escharotic, and is used in dyspepsia, piles, skin diseases, nervous debility, &c. In Goa, the nut is used internally in asthma after having been steeped in butter-milk, and is also given as a vermifuge. (*See* also 253, 644.)

847.* SESAMUM INDICUM, *Linn.*; Pedalineæ. The Gingelly or Sesame oil (*Eng.*); Benne-oil, Huile de Sesame (*Fr.*); Sesamol (*Germ.*); Mitha tél, krishna-tél (*Hind.*). Commonly cultivated in India, and in nearly every tropical country; probably introduced into India two or three thousand years ago; apparently a native of the Sunda Islands. There are three varieties of *til* seed—black, white, and red. The black kind is the best suited for medicinal use. Sesamum seed is considered emollient, nourishing, tonic, diuretic, and lactagogue. It is said to be especially serviceable in piles, by regulating the bowels and removing constipation. Ground to a paste with water it is given with butter in bleeding piles; sweetmeats made of the seed are also beneficial. A poultice of the seed is applied to ulcers; a powder made from the roasted and decorticated seed is used as an emollient both externally and internally. Both the seed and the oil are used as demulcent in dysentery and urinary diseases. Sesamum oil has been employed as a substitute for olive oil in the preparation of *Linimentum calcis*. The seed if taken largely is capable of producing abortion. In amenorrhœa a warm sitz bath containing a handful of seeds has been found very efficacious. In decoction the seed is said to be emmenagogue; the same preparation, sweetened with sugar, is prescribed in cough; a compound decoction with linseed is used as an aphrodisiac; a plaster is applied to burns, scalds, &c.; a lotion from the leaves is used as a hair-wash and is supposed to promote the growth of the hair and make it black; a decoction of the root is said to have the same properties. (*See* also 1046.)

848. SOYMIDA FEBRIFUGA, *Adr. Juss.*; Meliaceæ. The Rohun Tree. Found in the hilly districts of North-West, Central, and South India, extending southward to Travancore. The bark is astringent, tonic, aphrodisiac, and a powerful febrifuge, being an excellent substitute for the Peruvian Bark. It was entered in the Edinburgh and Dublin Pharmacopœiæ as early as the beginning of the present century. The decoction of the bark is used in intermittent fevers and general debility, in the advanced stages of dysentery, in diarrhœa, and in other cases requiring astringents. If taken in too large doses it is apt to derange the nervous system, occasioning vertigo and stupor. (*See* also 262.)

849. STRYCHNOS COLUBRINA, *Linn.*; Loganiaceæ. The Kuchila lata (*Hind.*, *Beng.*). A plant of West Deccan Peninsula, from the Concan to Cochin. The wood is supposed to constitute the *Lignum colubrinum* of old writers, the Pao de Cobra of the Portuguese, from its efficacy, imaginary or real, in the treatment of the most venomous snake-bites, even of the *Cobra de Capello*. According to Horsefield it has been employed in intermittent fevers. It is also used as an anthelmintic to cure cutaneous affections, and to alleviate the pain and swelling from confluent small-pox. In an overdose it occasions tremour and vomiting, but in smaller doses it may be used as a vermifuge, and also in quartan agues.

850. S. NUX-VOMICA, *Linn.* The Nux-vomica Tree; Kuchlá (*Hind.*); Kuchilá (*Beng.*). A small tree found throughout tropical India, altitude from the plains to 4,000 feet; rare in Bengal, common in Tenasserim and Madras. Nux-vomica seed produces a sort of intoxication, for which it is habitually taken by some natives as an aphrodisiac. In over-doses it acts as a virulent poison. Medicinally the seed is used in dyspepsia and diseases of the nervous system. It is very useful in palsy, relaxation of the muscles and tendons, debility and chronic rheumatism. It has been recommended in neuralgic affections, atonic diarrhœa, and chronic dysentery, also in habitual constipation, prolapsus of the rectum, spermatorrhœa, &c. It has also been employed in intermittent fevers, epilepsy, diabetes, anæmia, chlorosis, and other affections. (*See* also 269.)

851. S. POTATORUM, *Linn. f.* The Clearing Nut; Nirmali (*Hind.*, *Beng.*). A tree attaining to forty feet, found in the Deccan Peninsula, extending north-west to the Sone river, Prome, and Ceylon. The seed is chiefly used as a local application in eye diseases. Rubbed with honey and a little camphor, it is applied to the eyes in lachrymation or copious watering from them. Rubbed with water and rock salt it is applied to chemosis in the conjunctiva, it is devoid of poisonous properties, and is used in native practice as an emetic, as a remedy in diabetes, gonorrhœa, &c. Its chief use, however, is as a means of clearing muddy water, hence its Anglo-Indian name, *clearing nut*. Dr. Pareira suggests that this property depends upon the albumen and casein which it contains. Mahomedan writers describe it as cold and dry; when applied externally to the abdomen it relieves colic; it strengthens the sight, and is used as a remedy in snake-bite. (*See* also 270.)

852. SWERTIA CHIRATA, *Ham.*; Gentianaceæ. The Charayatah (*Hind.*); Chirétá (*Beng.*). A small, erect, herbaceous plant two to five feet in height, twigs four-angled or quite round, leaves opposite and stem clasping, the lower two to three inches in length. Met with in the temperate Himálaya, altitude 4,000 to 10,000 feet, from Kashmír to Bhután and Khásia mountains, altitude 4,000 to 5,000 feet. The medicinal herb, as met with in the bazars, consists of bundles of dried twigs of brownish colour, and very bitter but pleasant taste. The whole plant is used medicinally, but the root is said to be the most powerful. The natives consider it as tonic, stomachic, and febrifuge, and prescribe a decoction or infusion of it, in the quantity of a small tea-cupful, twice daily. It is more bitter than English Gentian, and although little used in Europe, it is reported to be especially serviceable in the dyspepsia of gouty subjects. Chiretta possesses the property of a bitter tonic, but unlike most other medicines of this class, it does not constipate the bowels but rather tends to produce a regular action.

853. *TAMARINDUS INDICA, *Linn.*; Leguminosæ. The Tamarind Tree; Amli (*Hind.*); Tentul (*Beng.*). Cultivated throughout Burma and India as far north as the Jhelam; probably indigenous in Africa. The ripe fruit is refrigerant, digestive, carminative, and laxative, useful in bilious disorders such as burning of the body, costiveness, and in intoxication from spirituous liquors or datura, &c. The shells of the ripe fruit are burnt and their ashes used in medicine as an alkaline substance, along with other medicines of the sort. The pulp of the ripe fruit, as well as a poultice of the leaves, is recommended to be applied to inflammatory swellings. A gargle of tamarind water is recommended in sore throat. The seed is said to be astringent and used as a poultice to boils. The leaves crushed with water and expressed yield an acid fluid, useful in bilious fever and scalding of the urine; made into a poultice they are applied to reduce inflammatory swellings and to relieve pain. A poultice of the flowers is used in inflammatory affections of the conjunctiva; the juice expressed from them is given internally for bleeding piles. The bark is considered to have astringent and tonic properties. (*See* also 273, 555, 624, 1047.)

854. TAXUS BACCATA, *Linn.*; Coniferæ. The Yew; Sarap, badar (*Afg.*); Birmi (*Kashmir*); Tcheiray gulab (*Nepal*). An evergreen tree of the Himálaya, from the Indus to Bhután and the Khásia hills. The leaves contain a volatile oil, tannic and gallic acids, and a resinous substance called taxin. Yew leaves and fruits have been given for their emmenagogue, sedative, and antispasmodic effects. At the present time, yew is never used in regular medical practice in

Europe, the principal interest attached to it having reference to its poisonous properties. The leaves and young branches act as a narcotic poison, both to the human subject and to certain animals, but more especially to the horse and cow. (*See* also 275.)

855. TERMINALIA CHEBULA, *Retz.*; Combretaceæ. The Harra (*Hind.*); Haritaki (*Beng.*). A large, deciduous tree of the sub-Himálayan tract, from the Sutlej eastward, ascending to 5,000 feet; Bengal, Assam, Chittagong, Central and South India. The chebulic myrobalan was highly extolled by the ancient Hindus as a powerful alterative and tonic. It is also described as laxative and stomachic. Seven varieties of haritaki are mentioned by the older writers, of which two are at present recognised,—the large ripe fruit called *haritaki*, and the unripe fruit called *jangi haritaki*. Chebulic myrobalans are used in fever, cough, asthma, urinary diseases, piles, intestinal worms, chronic diarrhœa, costiveness, flatulence, vomiting, hiccup, heart diseases, enlarged spleen and liver, ascites, skin diseases, &c. In combination with emblic and beleric myrobalans, and under the name of *triphala*, or the three myrobalans, a preparation is extensively used by the Hindus as an adjunct to other medicines in the treatment of many diseases. (*See* also 281, 1184.)

856.* THEVETIA NERIIFOLIA, *Juss.*; Apocynaceæ. The Exile or Yellow Oleander; Kolkaphul (*Beng.*). This plant is commonly cultivated in tropical America, and has been introduced into India, and is now almost naturalised in Bengal. The milky juice is highly poisonous. The bark is bitter, cathartic, and a powerful febrifuge. In large doses it acts as an acrid purgative and emetic, and in still larger doses as a powerful poison. The oil extracted from the kernels is said to be emetic and purgative. Dr. Warden of Calcutta has been recently experimenting with this plant.

857. TINOSPORA CORDIFOLIA, *Miers.*; Menispermaceæ. The Gulancha. A climbing shrub found throughout tropical India. The stem, leaves, roots, and watery extract are all used in Hindu medicine. The entire plant is regarded as a valuable alterative and tonic, and useful in general debility, fever, jaundice, skin diseases, rheumatism, urinary diseases, irritability of stomach, and syphilitic affections. *Gulancha* is also regarded by the natives in certain parts of India as a specific for the bites of poisonous insects and venomous snakes.

858. TODDALIA ACULEATA, *Pers.*; Rutaceæ. The Toddalia. A large, scandent shrub, covered with prickles, met with on the Himálaya from Kumaon eastward to the Khásia hills, ascending to altitude 5,000 to 6,000 feet; also common throughout the Western Peninsula and Ceylon. The root-bark is an aromatic tonic, stimulant, carminative, and antiperiodic; useful in constitutional debility, and in convalescence after febrile and other exhausting diseases. Toddalia, under the name of Lopez root, was formerly esteemed in European practice as a remedy for diarrhœa, but has long fallen into disuse.

859. TRICHOSANTHES DIOICA, *Roxb.*; Cucurbitaceæ. The Parvar (*Hind.*); Patól (*Beng.*). Throughout the plains of North India from the Punjáb to Assam and East Bengal. The leaves constitute a bitter tonic. The fresh juice of the unripe fruit is often used as a cooling and laxative adjunct to alterative medicines. In bilious fever a decoction of *patola* leaves and coriander in equal parts is given as a febrifuge and laxative. An alcoholic extract of the unripe fruit is said to be a powerful and safe cathartic. The bulbous part of the root is a hydragogue cathartic. The root acts like *Elaterium*, for which it can be substituted. The old Hindu physicians placed much confidence in this drug in the treatment of leprosy. (*See* also 537.)

860. TYLOPHORA ASTHMATICA, *White & Arn.*; Asclepiadeæ. A slender, twining plant, met with in North and East Bengal, Assam, Cachar, Chittagong, and Burma to Malacca, Deccan Peninsula. Common in the hotter districts of Ceylon. The dried leaves are emetic, diaphoretic, and expectorant, useful in over-loaded states of the stomach and other cases requiring the use of emetics. It has also been found useful in dysentery, catarrh, and other affections in which ipecacuanha has been employed.

861.* UNCARIA GAMBIER, *Hunter*; Rubiaceæ. The Gambier, Pale Catechu, or Terra Japonica. An extensive scandent bush, native of Ceylon and the Malay Archipelago, distributed to Java and Sumatra. Gambier, under the name of *Catechu*, is in India used as an astringent, for various purposes. Catechu lozenges are useful in hoarseness, relaxation of the throat, uvula, and tonsils, in sponginess and ulceration of the gums, salivation, &c. They may be employed in diarrhœa, pyrosis, and other cases in which astringents are indicated. (*See* Extracts.)

862. VALERIANA OFFICINALIS, *Linn.*; Valerianeæ. The Common Valerian. A very abundant herb found in North Kashmir, Sonamurg, altitude 8,000 to 9,000 feet. The Valerian of the Indian druggists' shops is no doubt chiefly the root of *V. Wallichii* or *Hardwickii*, extremely abundant plants throughout the alpine Himálaya. The root and underground stem are stimulant and antispasmodic. The root constitutes a useful drug in hysteria, epilepsy, chorea, and allied affections, advanced stages of fevers, and low asthenic inflammations. As an antispasmodic it is much inferior to asafœtida. In excessive doses it causes headache, mental excitement indicating a deranged state of the nervous system.

863. VERNONIA ANTHELMINTICA, *Willd.*; Compositæ. The Buckche (*Hind.*); Somraj (*Beng.*). A common plant in India, especially on the Himálaya. The seed is of great repute as a medicine for white leprosy and other skin diseases. It is mentioned also as an anthelmintic. It is used internally for removing phlegm and intestinal worms, and in the form of poultice or plaster it is said to disperse cold tumours. In Travancore, the bruised seeds are largely employed with lime-juice for destroying pediculi. The seed is also a valuable tonic, stomachic, and

diuretic; it is given in anasarca and used in plasters for abscesses.

864. VIOLA SERPENS, *Wall.*; Violaceæ. A common herb (the commonest of all the Indian violets), met with in the moist woods throughout the temperate Himálaya, Khásia hills, Pulney and Nilgiri mountains, and Ceylon, altitude 5,000 to 7,000 feet. The flowers are diaphoretic and laxative, the seed diuretic, and the root emetic.

865. VITEX NEGUNDO, *Linn.*; Verbenaceæ. The Nirgandi (*Hind.*); Nishinda (*Beng.*). A small tree or bush widely distributed throughout India. The root is tonic, febrifuge, and expectorant. The leaves are aromatic, tonic, and vermifuge, and given in decoction with the addition of long pepper, in catarrhal fever with heaviness of head and dulness of hearing. A pillow stuffed with the leaves is placed under the head to relieve headache. The juice of the leaves is applied to ulcers. An oil prepared with the juice of the leaves is applied to sinuses and scrofulous sores. Dr. Fleming remarks that the leaves are discutient and useful in dispersing swellings of the joints from acute rheumatism, and of the testes from suppressed gonorrhœa. The dried fruits act as a vermifuge.

866. WITHANIA COAGULANS, *Dunal.*; Solanaceæ. The Púnír-ke-Bij (*Hind.*). A rigid undershrub, frequent in the Punjáb and Sind. The dried fruits are used in dyspepsia and flatulent colic and other intestinal affections. They are said to be alterative and diuretic and useful in chronic liver disease. In the form of an infusion they are employed along with the leaves and twigs of *Rhazya stricta*. They are also used to coagulate milk in the process of cheese manufacture.

867. W. SOMNIFERA, *Dunal.* The Asgand (*Hind.*). An erect bush found throughout the drier, sub-tropical part of India; frequent in West Hindustan, rare in Bengal. The root is regarded as tonic, alterative, and aphrodisiac, and is used in consumption, emaciation of children, debility from old age, rheumatism, &c. It has also narcotic, diuretic, and deobstruent properties. The ground root and bruised leaves are employed as a local application to carbuncles, ulcers, and painful swellings. The leaves are very bitter, and are given in infusion in fevers. The fruit is diuretic. The Telinga physicians suppose the root to be alexipharmic.

868. XANTHIUM STRUMARIUM, *Linn.*; Compositæ. The Chhota-gokhru (*Hind.*): Bun-okra (*Beng.*). A weed, met with everywhere throughout the plains of India, and a source of great annoyance to the cultivator. Common in waste places, river-banks, and especially so in the vicinity of villages. The whole plant is supposed to possess powerful diaphoretic and sedative properties. It is generally administered in the form of decoction, and is said to be very efficacious in long standing cases of malarious fever. The root is a bitter tonic, useful in cancer and strumous diseases.

EXHIBITORS.—Baroda Durbar, a large collection of indigenous drugs; also Sirish Chundere Dutta, of Calcutta, a collection of special preparations.

POISONS.

869. A most interesting collection of the indigenous poisons of India has been specially prepared by Babu Taraprasanna Roy, F.C.S., F.I.C., and by Babu Ramchandra Mittra, under the supervision of Dr. Warden, Professor of Chemistry, Medical College, Calcutta. Among the more curious objects shown in this collection may be mentioned the *sui*, or poisoned spines from the powdered seeds of *Abrus precatorius*.

SUB-COURTS XVII. & XVIII.

(*See* PART II.—ETHNOLOGY.)

THE BAMBOO TROPHY.

This structure is intended to exhibit the bamboos of India and to show the multifarious uses to which they are put. The idea of such a trophy was first suggested by Mr. Ribbentrop, Inspector-General of Forests, and through the active co-operation of the Forest Officers it has been found possible to bring together one of the most perfect collections of the bamboos ever exhibited. Mr. F. B. Manson designed and constructed the trophy, and took the greatest pains to see that the names of the various bamboos used were carefully preserved, so that the merits of the species might be compared side by side. The trophy consists of an arch over the central transverse path leading from the Art-ware Courts. It is formed of a platform 12 by 10 feet in size, supported on four columns and raised 12 feet above the floor. This platform is reached on the East and the West sides by flights of steps. The steps are covered with pieces of split bamboo arranged in geometrical patterns; the floor of the platform is similarly ornamented. There are forty steps, twenty on each staircase, the designs being all different. Ten species of bamboo have been used in this ornamental work, four steps to each species. Two species only have been used in the decoration of the platform. The railing is made of *Bambusa Brandisii*, and some 30 species of bamboo in all are used in constructing the trophy, an index set of which is exhibited on the adjacent walls of the Court. A number of very interesting objects made of bamboo have been hung all over the trophy, but these might be multiplied indefinitely and volumes written on the uses of the various species of bamboo. They are cut up and split into bands in the manufacture of mats of every degree of fineness. Thin strips tied with strings are made into excellent *tatties* or door mats. Hollow bamboos when beaten and then split open into flat pieces are used for the seats of chairs, tops of tables, and of beds. The greater part of the people in Eastern India and in the Malay Peninsula live entirely in houses constructed of bamboo. Models of such houses are exhibited in the Ethnology Sub-Courts. Bamboo bridges supported on a multitude of bamboo uprights are frequent all over India. The larger hollow species are well suited for aqueducts, water-pails, pots, cups, and other vessels. A single joint of a green bamboo is frequently used as a cooking-pot. Spoons, knives, and other domestic utensils are made of bamboo, and a joint of a small bamboo makes a useful tobacco pipe. All sorts of agricultural implements and the appliances for spinning cotton and wool, as also for reeling silk, are often constructed of the same material. Poles for carrying loads are universally made of bamboo.

The fisherman makes his oars, masts, fishing appliances, baskets and fish traps, and even his hooks, of bamboo. Excellent fishing-rods made of the solid bamboo are in universal use all over India. Bamboo rafts are not uncommon, being chiefly used by fishermen. Bamboo is extensively used for making spear-shafts, bows and arrows, crude scabbards and handles for swords, knives, and axes. The Nagas of Manipur defend the approaches to their villages by burying, in an erect position, sharp-pointed knives of bamboo (*pangis*) among the leaves and soft soil.

All sorts of curious musical instruments are made of bamboo, from the fife to the crude violin which has often two or three strings, also of bamboo. The Nagas make a sort of Jew's harp from the bamboo, and in the Malay Peninsula Æolian harps are made of the village bamboo clumps. A selection of the better stems of the clump is made, and these are perforated in a peculiar way so as to keep up whistling in all tones at once as the wind blows through the culms. Soft and liquid notes like that of the flute are produced, but with the undulations of the atmosphere these swell into the deep and full tones of the organ.

The following are the principal species of bamboo contributed by the Forest Department:—

870. ARUNDINARIA FALCATA, *Nees.*; Gramineæ. A native of the Himálaya, from the Ravi to Bhután; in the west never descending below 4,500 feet; in the east coming down to near the plains. Specimens have been sent from Kurseong (8989†) under the name of *Choyak*.

871. ARUNDINARIA FALCONERI, *Benth. & Hook. f.* Met with on the Himálaya from Kumaon to Nepal. Specimens were sent under this name from Kurseong (8986), bearing the vernacular name *dhungria*; these appear to be Dendrocalamus Hamiltonii.

872. A. HOOKERIANA, *Munro.* Found in Sikkim between the altitudes of 4,000 and 7,000 feet. Specimens are exhibited from Darjeeling (8987), received under the vernacular name *Singhani*.

873. A. KHASIANA, *Munro.* A native of the Khásia hills, altitude 5,000 feet. Specimens have been received from Assam (8959) under the name *U-Kadac namlang*. This species is extensively cultivated and used for wattle and dab-walls.

874. A. WIGHTIANA, *Nees.* A native of the Nilgiri hills. The specimens exhibited (9001) came from the Nilgiri hills.

875. BAMBUSA ARUNDINACEA, *Retz.* Kantabans (*Orissa*); Bad (*Buxa*); Bariala (*Darjeeling*); Kyaka-wa (*Burm.*). Common all over Burma, in the large alluvial plains, especially in the neighbourhood of streams and paddy cultivation. Also frequent in Bengal, Central and South India, extending north as far as Dehra Dun. Specimens have been received from Burma (8940); Bengal (8974, 8982, and 8996); from Madras (8997, 8999, 9002). Used for house and fence purposes; it will last for four or five years. (*See* also 488, 904).

876. B. BALCONA, *Roxb.* Balcoa bans (*Beng.*). A native of Bengal and Assam. This is regarded as the best bamboo in Bengal, being very useful for building and scaffolding purposes. The leaves are larger than those of *B. Tulda* and not pubescent. Specimens have been received from Bengal (8976, 8977, and 8990); Assam (8962).

877. BAMBUSA BRANDISII, *Kurz* (8931). Syn.—*Dendrocalamus Brandisii* (Kurz). Wabo (*Burm.*). A gigantic species with stems often 120 ft. high and 30 in. in circumference. Common in the tropical forests of the eastern slopes of the Pegu Yoma and of Martaban up to about 3,500 ft. elevation. Often cultivated in gardens, the young shoots being eaten and the mature stems used as water vessels. Specimens have been received from Burma (8931, 8943).

878. BAMBUSA MASTERSII, *Munro.* Ka-sejbrai (*Khásia*). A native of the Khásia hills, altitude 4,000 to 5,000 ft. The specimens exhibited were received from Assam (8953); this is a smaller species than *B. nutans*, which it much resembles.

879. B. NUTANS, *Wall.* Ka-sejong (*Khásia*); Mahlu (*Lepcha*). A native of Nepal, Sikkim, and the Khásia hills, altitude 4,000 to 5,000 ft. A wild and cultivated species, very common near villages, the stems being largely used as *chongas* or water-pots, basket-work, and for building huts. The specimens exhibited came from Assam (8952, 8965) and Bengal (8975).

880. B. POLYMORPHA, *Munro.* Kya-thoungwa (*Burm.*). A native of Burma. The specimens exhibited came from Burma (8934).

881. B. SPINOSA, *Roxb.* Behor (*Beng.*); Kotoha (*Ass*). A native of Bengal, Assam, Burma, and South India; cultivated in North-West India. This species is closely allied to *B. arundinacea*. The specimens exhibited were received from Assam (8961).

882. B. TULDA (*Roxb.*) (891). Tulda (*Beng.*); Thaik-wa (*Burm.*). The common Bamboo of Bengal. It is also frequent in the open forests

† Numbers given by the Forest Department.

of Pegu and more rarely along the alluvial clayey banks of streams in the hills. The wood is strong and the culms are used for roofing, scaffolding, mats, basket-work, and other purposes. The specimens exhibited came from Burma (8937), Assam (8964), Bengal (8978, 8993).

883. BAMBUSA VILLOSULA, *Kurz.* Tabendine (*Burm.*). An almost simple-stemmed, rarely tufted, bamboo, met with on limestone hills of Martaban and Upper Tenasserim. The specimens exhibited were received from Burma (8941).

884. B. VULGARIS, *Wendl.* Ka-serengjai (*Burm.*). Cultivated throughout India; said to be a native of the southern and central parts of Ceylon. It is cultivated on the Khásia hills, altitude 500 ft. It is used for building and making boats. The specimens exhibited came from Assam (8955).

885. CEPHALOSTACHYUM PALLIDUM, *Munro.* Beti (*Burm.*). A thin, climbing bamboo, native of Ava and the Mishmi hills. It is used by the Assamese for making hand-punkahs and for other purposes. The specimens exhibited came from Assam (8972).

886. C. PERGRACILE, *Munro.* Tinwa (*Burm.*). Common in upper mixed forests of Burma, and often gregarious. The specimens exhibited were received from Burma (8933).

887. DENDROCALAMUS HAMILTONII. *Nees* and *Arn.* Tama (*Nep.*); Pao (*Lepcha*); Ka-sejlai (*Ass.*). A native of Sikkim, Bhután, and Assam. It grows gregariously, on hill-sides, up to 5,000 ft. The stems are 40 to 60 ft. high, and are largely used as *chongas* or water-pots, basket-work, and for building huts. The specimens exhibited were received from Assam (8954) and Bengal (8992).

888. D. LONGISPATHUS, *Kurz.* Waya (*Burm.*). An evergreen, tufted bamboo, frequently found along the banks of streams in the upper mixed forests, and also in the tropical forests all over Burma. The specimens exhibited came from Burma (8938).

889. DENDROCALAMUS STRICTUS, *Nees.* (8932). Male Bamboo; Myinwa (*Burm.*); Baus Kaban (*Hind.*). Met with throughout India and Burma. It occurs wild on the Khásia hills; altitude 6,000 ft. The stems are used for roofing, wattle, and basket-work. They are also made into fishing-rods and spear handles. The specimens exhibited were received from Assam (8958), Burma (8932), Bengal (8979, 8980, 8981), and Madras (8998, 9000).

890. DINOCHLOA MACLELLANDII, *Kurz.* Watha-Bok (*Burm.*). A native of Chittagong and Burma. The specimens exhibited were received from Burma (8936).

891. GIGANTOCHLOA AURICULATA, *Kurz* (8939). Talagu (*Burm.*). Found in the low forests of Southern Pegu, where it is rather rare. It is also met with in Chittagong and Arracan. The specimens exhibited came from Burma (8939).

892. G. MACRASTACHYA, *Kurz.* Wa-net (*Burm.*). A native of Chittagong and Burma. The specimens exhibited were received from Burma (8942).

893. MELOCANNA BAMBUSOIDES, *Trin.* Múlo (*Beng.*); Kayoung-wa (*Magh*). The common gregarious bamboo, native of Eastern Bengal, Chittagong, Arracan, and Tenasserim. It is of good quality, durable, straight, and with straight knots, and is very largely cut and exported for house-building, mats, and other purposes. The specimens exhibited were received from Bengal (8995).

894. OXYTENANTHERA ALBOCILIATA, *Munro.* Wa-pyu-gale (*Burm.*). A native of Burma. The specimens exhibited were received from Burma (8935).

The following specimens of Bamboo were received under vernacular names and cannot be identified:—From Bengal: (8944) *Bhuddume*, Beng., *Moyah*, Magh; (8945) *Katt a Buriala*, Beng., *Orain*, Magh; (8946) *Molu*, Beng., *Khaiya*, Magh; (8947) *Dolu*, Beng., *Mra*, Magh; (8948) *Kalachari*, Beng., *Tangya*, Magh; (8949) *Ura*, Beng., *Targoo*, Magh; (8950) *Nayanshuk*, Beng., *Benk*, Magh; (8951) *Lotta*, Beng., *Nasai*, Magh; (8983) Salia; (8984) Kusanga; (8985) Belengi; (8988) Filing; (8994) Doloo. From Assam: (8956) *Ka-sejech*; (8957) *Ka-seskien*; (8960) *Bhenda*; (8963) *Jati*; (8966) *Deo*; (8967) *Tarai*; (8968) *Dalua* or *Dalow*; (8969) *Nal*; (8970) *Kakoah*; (8971) *Sakthoi*.

THE COCOANUT PALM.

895. Mr. M. C. Pereira, Head-Assistant, Government Medical Storekeeper, Bombay, exhibits a most interesting collection of objects made from the common cocoanut palm. This collection will be found near the Bamboo trophy. Mr. Pereira gives a brief description of his collection as follows:—

(1) Coir (*Kábál, Káthá*).—The fibre made of cocoanut husk; in this state it is used for stuffing cushions, pillows, beds, making rope mats, &c., &c.

(2) Spoon (*Ulki*).—Used in the cook-rooms of Europeans, and by the natives for drinking gruel (rice *conjee*); has the advantage over the metallic one of not being corroded.

(3) Drainer (*Zárá*).—Used for draining food fried in *ghee* (clarified butter) or oil.

(4) Ladle (*Doho*).—Used for water.

(5) Ladle, small (*Buddi*).—Used by natives for taking out oil for daily use from an earthen vessel containing the yearly or quarterly stock. It is not corroded by the oil.

(6) Hubble bubble (*Gudgudi*).—This is the *hookah* of the poorer classes.

(7) Beads (*Mani*).

(8) Vinegar (*Shirká Amti*).—Made of the juice (*toddy*) of the cocoanut palm.

(9) Pickle (*Lonche, Achár*).—Made of the pith of the top of the fresh tree with vinegar of the juice (*toddy*) of the same palm.

(10) (*Pogi*).—The spathe of the blossom.

(11) Rib (*Kadi Hirkúte*).—The rib of the leaf.

(12) Broom, Goa (*Kersunî, Butará, Zadû*).—Made of leaf ribs; it is much used for sweeping purposes.

(13) Strainer (*Mandorá*).—The bracts of the tree by which the leaves are held firm to the tree. Used for straining (*toddy*), cocoanut juice and cocoanut milk, and for general straining in the cook-room.

(14) Woolly floss (*Burá*).—Much used as a styptic for cuts by the *toddy* drawers and cultivators.

(15) Blossom (*Kontî*).—The blossom in the state when it is tapped for drawing juice (*toddy*).

(16) Chain (*Sanklî, Kargotá*).—Used round the waist to retain the loin cloth. The size is for a child. Set in metal may be used as a watch guard.

(17) Drum (*Dholkî*).—Made of a piece of the trunk of the cocoanut tree.

(18) Wood piece of rafter (*Barod Wánsa*).—Made of the lower part of the tree, 10, 20, and 25 feet in length.

(19) Oil (*Khobrel*).—Oil expressed in the native mills for commerce.

(20) Oil (*Muthel*).—Oil extracted from fresh cocoanuts by rasping fine, drying, and pressing between coir and twisting with hands or by extracting the milk and separating the oil by heat. Used internally in lieu of cod-liver oil, and externally for ulcers with good results.

(21) Hair oil.—Cocoanut hair oil.

(22) Liquor (*Daru, Rashi, Urákh*).—Spirituous liquor 60° under proof, distilled from cocoanut juice (*toddy*) and drunk hot.

(23) Punch (*Queimado, Portuguese name*).—The punch is made of the liquor of the cocoanut palm with spices and sugar from the recipe of the Portuguese. There is no native name for it, and is only known to the native Christians of Bombay. Drunk hot for a cold, one or two cupfuls.

(24) Liquor (*Fhenidárû Port Do brado, double.*)—Liquor made of cocoanut (*toddy*) juice by re-distillation, 20° under proof; formerly much used for making medicinal tinctures and country brandy.

(25) Cocoanut (*Nárel*).—This fruit takes a year to ripen.

(26) Sweet-meat (*Nárlipák*).—Prepared from the kernel of the nut.

(27) Sweet-meat.—Prepared from the kernel with saffron.

(28) Splints (*Kambî*).—Made of (*poguy*) the spathe of the blossom used for this purpose by the *toddy* drawers and natives of Goa, &c.

(29) Door mats.—Made of the fibre, of many shapes and sizes, by natives and in the jails.

(30) Buggy Mats.—Made of the fibre, of many shapes and sizes, by natives and in the jails.

(31) Carriage Mats.—Made of the fibre, of many shapes and sizes, by natives and in the jails.

(32) Floor Mats.—Made in Malabar and in the Bombay jails, of different sorts and colours.

(33) Cage (*Pinjará, Khuri*).—Made of the rib of the leaf.

(34) Horn (*Pipánî Tontora*).—Made of the leaf of the palm; gives a loud sound when fresh.

(35) Horn, small size (*Dhaktî Pipánî*).—Made of the leaf of the palm; gives a loud sound when fresh.

(36) Toy Parrot (*Popat*).—Made by children of the leaf of the palm; when new, it looks better.

(37) Toy Parrot in Cage (*Pinjaryât Popat*).—Made by children of the leaf of the palm; when new, it looks better.

(38) Leaf-woven Cudjan (*Zavlî*).—The leaf of the tree used for thatching houses; has the advantage over tiles of keeping the house cool.

(39) Root (*Mûl*).—Used medicinally, astringent, and as a gargle for sore mouth.

(40) Rope (*Káthá, Sumbha*).—This is extensively used.

(41) Oil Bottle (*Dowlá*).—Hung beneath the labour cart with castor-oil and brush in it for lubricating axles.

(42) Nut, immature (*Khakota*).—Used medicinally as an astringent; children are fond of it.

(43) Trough (*Panshira*).—Trough made of cocoanut tree, used for catching water drawn from a well with a Persian wheel for irrigation purposes (model).

(44) Conduit (*Panhál*).—A conduit put under the hole of the trough for conveying water for irrigation purposes.

(45) Adapter (*Nalá*).—Piece of the adapter used for connecting the native still to the condenser.

(46) (*Tuntuna*).—Native musical instrument, used by the poorer classes.

(47) Beam (*Báhál*).—Piece of beam of the shape used for houses. It is also used for fishing stakes in the sea; generally two cocoanut trees make a stake 60 to 70 ft. long.

(48) Rosary Box.—Made of immature cocoanuts.

(49) Charcoal Powder (*Kolsá*).—Burnt shell used for preparing black and lead-coloured washes for houses.

(50) Broom (*Zádû*).—Made of the ribs of the leaf, used by the Bombay and other municipalities for sweeping roads, streets, yards, &c.

(51) Broom (*Záddû*).—Made of the stems of the blossom and nuts; used by the cultivators for collecting dry leaves for (*rab*) burning on the fields.

(52) Crab Trap (*Kathimbrá Dhoderá*).—Made of the stem of the leaf.

(53) Fish Trap (*Malai*).—Made of the ribs of the leaf.

(54) String of Pots (*Mál*).—This is made of fibre of 60 or 70 ft. in length, and about fifty or sixty earthen pots fixed to it and put on the Persian wheel (*rahat*), which in rotating brings up the pots filled with water and takes down the empty ones.

(55) Violin (*Sárangî*).—Used by the lower classes of natives, particularly the gosavies (a class of professional beggars).

(56) Sling (*Shinká*). — Used for keeping sundry articles of food out of the reach of cats, rats, and ants, by hanging it on a hook to the

ceiling. Tied to the ends of a bamboo serves for carrying water-pots, baskets, &c. The small one is used by milkmen for carrying milk for sale.

(57) Flesh Glove (*Hátáli*).—Used for washing and rubbing cattle and horses.

(58) Tar with Acetic Acid (*Kartel*).—Made by burning the shells in a pot with a small hole in the bottom, placed on another heated by fire on all sides. Used by the natives for ringworm and skin diseases.

(59) Rope (*Dore*).—Made of various sorts and sizes.

(60) Brush (*Chavár*).—Made of the husk of the nut, for cleaning sieves, washing baskets and rice-drainers (*Shibum*).

(61) Sugar, molasses (*Gúl*).—Made of the juice (*toddy*) in Goa.

(62) (*Band*).—Peeled from the outer part of the stem of the leaf. Is used as a cord by the *toddy* drawers.

(63) Cocoanut, gilded (*Karyácha Nárel*).—Offered by the higher classes of Hindus to appease the sea on the cocoanut fair day. At weddings the bridegroom and bride carry it in their hands.

(64) Husk (*Sál, Charád, Sodán*).—Used as fuel, especially for baking purposes and for making fibre.

(65) Scoops.—Made of the shell. The round and deep ones are used as drinking cups.

(66) Neck Belts (*Pattá*).—Used for yoking bullocks and buffaloes to carts, ploughs, oil-mills, &c.

(67) Sack (*Thaili, Jali*).—Used for sending out articles; a somewhat similar one is attached to the cart for carrying straw or grass.

(68) Tooth-brushes (*Dáton*).—The pedicels of the blossom are used as tooth-brushes.

(69) Brushes (*Kunchá, Kuchrá*).—The peduncles of the blossom are used for whitewashing houses, &c.

(70) Blind (*Dol-Dhápan*).—Used for blinding bullocks and buffaloes while yoked to the Persian wheel, oil-mills, &c.

(71) Nest (*Gharta, Gharbá*).—Made by birds out of the fibre of the leaf.

(72) Soap (*Sabu*).—Made of cocoanut oil, has larger percentage of water than any other soap.

(73) Puzzles and Toys.—Rings, whips, neck-ties, rattles, crosses, &c.

(74) Bats for Cricket.—Made of the wood (cocoanut).

(75) Oil-Cakes (*Pend*).—Oil-cake from the native mill.

(76) Patimar (Ship) (*Fatemári*).—Toy made by the boys of the fishermen class.

(77) Boat, fishing (*Hodke*).—Toy made by the boys of the fishermen class.

(78) Kernel (*Khobre*).—Dry kernel.

(79) Stem (*Jhintár*).—Used as a broom.

(80) Charpai, Cot (*Khát Báj*).—Used by the natives (model).

(81) Potash (crude) (*Khár*).—The ash of the stem of the leaves; they produce 20 per cent. of ash.

(82) Cocoanut, abortive (*Vánzá Nárel, Váhil*).—Used as floats for beginners in swimming.

(83) Spadix.—The spadix prepared for drawing juice (*toddy*). A thin slice is cut from the palm stem three times a day. The juice flows from this and drips down into an earthen pot suspended on purpose. A small piece of the leaf is fixed above to prevent the bottom of the pot from touching the point, the sheath of the leaf covering the mouth of the pot to keep out flies. (*See* also 85, 660, 715, 913, 1011.)

This well-known and useful palm requires considerable care and cost to bring it to the state of bearing fruit. The ripe good-sized nuts from an old tree are kept in a well of water for three months, until they germinate; they are then put into the ground in beds of fifty or a hundred and watered every day. In three months more they begin to grow up, and after three years or more they may be transplanted in regular spaces of 15 to 20 ft., watered regularly every other day, and manured occasionally. In about twelve or fifteen years they come to bearing, but the yield is in proportion to the care taken to water and manure; at this stage the value of the tree is from Rs. 25 to 30 each.

SUB-COURTS XIX. & XX.

(*See* Part II.—ETHNOLOGY.)

FIBRES OF INDIA.

The "Classified List" shows the vegetable fibres of India grouped under Division VIII., Sections 1 to 20. In the Exhibition, however, the more important of these fibres have had separate Sub-Courts assigned to them, such, for example, as Cotton, Jute, Rhea, and other commercial fibres and paper materials. There still remains an extensive and interesting series of fibres which are regularly used by the natives of India, although the large majority are quite unknown to the textile manufacturers of Europe. There are, for example, over 300 fibre-yielding plants in India; at least 100 of these afford strong and useful fibres. The more important of these are shown in the Sub-Courts XXI. and XXII. Before proceeding, however, to take up each of these Sub-Courts with the object of enumerating the more prominent exhibits shown, it may not here be out of place to say something of the Indian foreign trade in fibres collectively. Cotton is by far the most important fibre in India, the manufactured cottons being the most valuable articles of import trade. The Indian foreign trade in cotton during the year 1884–85 was valued at over £41,000,000 (the rupee, for convenience, being calculated at par), and the total foreign trade in fibres (i.e., imports and exports) amounted to over £53,500,000, being a decline from the previous year of £1,000,000, in the exports of raw cotton. The exports of manufactured cottons improved during the year by nearly £1,000,000; jute remained, practically speaking, stationary, and the exports of raw silk, of wool, and the imports of paper, fell off considerably. The Government imports of paper appear to be increasing; last year they amounted to £137,109, or 100 per cent. more than in 1881-2. Although steam machinery has driven handlooms largely out of the market, still there survives in every village the weaver who, with the crudest of appliances, produces from home-spun yarn a coarse though very strong and durable fabric ornamented with a simple but elegant border; but of the extent of the internal trade in fibres little or nothing can be learned.

The following tabular statement of the more important fibres will give some idea of this foreign trade during the past two years:—

The Textile Industries for 1883-84 *and* 1884-85.

		1883-84. Rupees.	1884-85. Rupees.
Sub-Court XXIV.			
Cotton, raw	Exports	14,38,31,278	13,28,63,673
	Imports	9,25,820	16,25,980
	Total	14,48,33,098	13,44,89,653
Cotton, manufactured.	Exports	2,85,31,710	3,33,80,297
	Imports	25,10,83,306	24,55,78,331
	Total	27,96,15,016	27,89,58,636
Sub-Court XXV.			
Jute, raw	Exports	4,59,26,353	4,66,13,684
	Imports	1,267	1,364
	Total	4,59,27,620	4.66,15,048
Jute, manufactured.	Exports	1,33,41,447	1,54,38,696
	Imports	4,14,491	3,61,943
	Total	1,37,55,938	1,58,00,639
Sub-Court XXIII.			
Flax and its manufactures.	Exports	5,457	—
	Imports	11,15,486	10,55,745
	Total	11,20,943	10,55,745
Hemp and its manufactures.	Exports	6,91,826	5,85,808
	Imports	2,09,335	2,55,474
	Total	9,01,161	8,41,282
Coir and its manufactures.	Exports	15,30,629	21,43,241
	Imports	1,06,630	1,13,554
	Total	16,37,259	22,56,795
Cordage and rope.	Exports	4,92,068	3,53,389
	Imports	3,90,584	3,52,413
	Total	8,82,652	7,05,802
Sub-Court XXVI.— Paper—			
Raw materials	Exports	3,63,659	3,70,533
Manufactured	Exports	1,733	—
	Total	3,65,392	5,70,533
General	Imports	37,49,127	33,21,026
Government	Imports	16,68,148	13,71,095
	Total	54,17,275	48,92,121
The Silk Room.			
Silk, raw	Exports	62,76,117	46,35,613
	Imports (mostly from China)	96,95,749	74,75,633
	Total	1,59,71,866	1,21,11,246
Silk, manufactured.	Exports	28,57,336	32,85,627
	Imports	1,20,13,481	1,27,33,536
	Total	1,48,70,817	1,60,19,163
Sub-Court XXVIII.			
Wool, raw	Exports	75,58,409	71,35,760
	Imports	6,51,368	6,18,212
	Total	82,09,777	77,53,972
Wool, manufactured.	Exports	12,07,003	11,83,427
	Imports	1,21,70,531	1,23,43,397
	Total	1,33,77,534	1,35,26,824
	Grand Total	54,68,86,348	53,53,97,459

SUB-COURTS XXI. & XXII.

THE MORE IMPORTANT FIBRES OF INDIA.

On the walls of these Courts basket-work and matting are displayed, and below these the index collection of the principal vegetable fibres of India. The following is a brief enumeration of a few of the leading fibres shown in these Sub-Courts:—

896. Abroma augusta, *Linn.*; Sterculiaceæ. Ulatkambal (*Beng.*). A small bush, widely spread, native or cultivated, throughout the hotter parts of India. The bark of the twigs yields a much-valued fibre, which deserves to be more generally known. The plant is a perennial, stands coppicing, and yields three crops of fibre-twigs a year. This fibre might be used with advantage as a substitute for silk. It resembles jute, but is much more durable.

897. Abutilon asiaticum, and A. indicum, *G. Don;* Malvaceæ, Country Mallow; Petári (*Beng.*). These two plants are so nearly allied botanically, that, from an economic point of view, they may be regarded as one and the same. *A. asiaticum* (G. Don), is chiefly met with in Western India and Ceylon, while *A. indicum* (G. Don), is widely distributed throughout tropical India, to Prome, Pegu, and Ava (but not found in Malacca). The stems contain good fibres suitable for cordage. These exceedingly abundant wild plants deserve attention.

898. *Agave americana, *Linn.;* Amaryllideæ. American Aloe; Vegetable Silk. A native of America, but naturalised in many parts of India. The leaves and the root yield an excellent fibre. (*See* also 963.)

899. A. vivipara, *L.* The Bastard Aloe. This is altogether a much less robust plant than *A. americana*, and produces viviparous buds upon an erect stem. The leaves are less fleshy and erect instead of reflexed. The flowering stem

is less than half the height of that of *A. americana*, and much thinner and red-coloured.

900.* ANANASSA SATIVA, *Linn.*; Bromeliaceæ. The Pine Apple; Ananas (*Hind.*). This and all other members of the Bromeliaceæ now met with in India were introduced from America. The leaves, which require to be steeped in water for 18 days, yield a beautiful fibre, which, but for the difficulty of extraction, would be largely used. (*See* also 577.)

901. ANDROPOGON MURICATUS, *Retz.*; Gramineæ. Khas (*Hind.*); Khas-khas (*Beng.*). A grass abundant on sandy banks in Bengal, Upper India, the Coromandel Coast, and Mysore, where it is commonly planted to divide fields. The roots are in India made into the aromatic-scented mats which are hung over doors and kept wet to cool the atmosphere in the hot season, and are also in great demand for making fans, &c. (*See* also 321.)

902.* ANONA RETICULATA, *Linn.*; Anonaceæ. Bullock's Heart; Nona (*Beng.*). A small tree, common everywhere; by some authors regarded as wild in some districts, but it is chiefly met with in cultivation. A good fibre is prepared from the bark of the young twigs. (*See* also 578.)

903.* A. SQUAMOSA, *Linn.* Custard Apple; Sa-ripha (*Hind.*). A small tree, the sweet-sop of the West Indies, naturalised in Bengal and the North-West Provinces. An inferior quality of fibre may be prepared from the twigs of this tree. (*See* also 579.)

904. BAMBUSA ARUNDINACEA, *Retz.*; Gramineæ. Bamboo; Bans (*Beng.*). A common bamboo of Central and South India and Burma. This and several other species of bamboo have been proposed as a source of paper fibre. The fibre extracted from the young shoots makes excellent paper, but there are practical difficulties which almost preclude the possibility of bamboo ever becoming a paper supply to any appreciable extent. (*See* also 488, 875.)

905. BAUHINIA RACEMOSA, *Lam.*; Leguminosæ. Banraji (*Beng.*); Vanaraja (*Sans.*). A small tree found all over India. A strong fibre is made from the inner bark. This is used for cordage, but is not durable in water. It yields a good bast and slow match. (*See* also 1092.)

906. B. VAHLII, *W. & A.* Maljan, Malu, Jallaur (*Hind.*); Chehur (*Beng.*). This is one of the most extensive, as it is one of the most abundant and most useful, of Indian climbers. It is found all along the lower Himálaya, from the Chenab eastward, in North and Central India, and Tenasserim. Its uses are, perhaps, more numerous than those of any other forest plant, and of these the strong cordage from the bark is certainly not the least important.

907. BŒHMERIA NIVEA, *H. & A.*; Urticaceæ. Rhea Grass; China Grass; Riah (*Beng.*). This yields one of the finest, and at the same time strongest fibres in Asia. In India there are many species of Bœhmeria, however, and it seems probable that in concentrating our attention on conquering the difficulties against introducing this particular species, we may have overlooked others of equal merit. Nearly every province in India has one or two indigenous species of rhea, and most of these are regularly resorted to by the natives as sources of strong fibre; the fibres obtained are quite unknown to Europeans. A large collection of rhea and allied rhea fibres will be found on the tables, which will richly repay inspection. *B. malabarica* is a bush or small tree of the moist, tropical or extra-tropical regions, and might be cultivated over an extensive area of the plains of India. Mr. W. A. Talbot, Deputy Conservator of Forests, Kanara (along with an extensive series of other fibres), sends a good sample of the Malabar rhea.

908. BOMBAX MALABARICUM, *DC.*; Malvaceæ. Silk Cotton Tree; Simal (*Hind.*); Simul (*Beng.*). A large tree, with thorny, buttressed stems and showy flowers, appearing in Bengal in January and February. The seeds are surrounded by a floss of cottony hairs, too short to be spun, but largely used for stuffing pillows, &c. The inner barks of the stem and of the branches also yield good fibres, suitable for cordage. (*See* also 53, 413, 958, 1059.)

909. BROUSSONETIA PAPYRIFERA, *Vent.*; Urticaceæ. The Paper-Mulberry Tree. A small tree, said to be wild in the Martaban hills, but is more peculiarly a native of Japan, China, Polynesia, and Siam. The Japanese make paper from the bark, and the Burmese construct their curious papier-mâché school slates (*Par abaik*) from it. The Tapa cloth of the South Sea Islands is also made from Broussonetia, and so also is the Karen paper mulberry cloth. (*See* also 966.)

910. CALOTROPIS GIGANTEA, *R. Br.*; Asclepiadaceæ. Madar (*Hind.*); Akanda (*Beng.*). A small shrub, common throughout India. The silky floss from the apex of the seed is used for stuffing pillows, and has been proposed as a paper fibre. Attempts have been made to spin this silky floss, but it has been found too short in staple and too light for ordinary purposes. The bast fibre from the bark has, however, attracted considerable attention, and is constantly spoken of as one of the best of Indian fibres. The chief difficulty in utilising it seems to reside in the inability to rapidly and cheaply separate and clean the fibre, and in the shortness of the fibre when extracted. A large set of samples are on view also of strong and very durable string made from this fibre. (*See* also 712, 769, 960, 1095.)

911. CANNABIS SATIVA, *Linn.*; Urticaceæ. Hemp. Most probably a wild plant in the mountain tracts of Northern India. It is chiefly, if not exclusively, cultivated on account of its narcotic principle. Several attempts have been made to use the stems rejected after the separation of the narcotic, but these have uniformly failed. It has been found that the narcotic-yielding plant affords only a miserable fibre, and, in the plains of India at least, it seems impossible to produce a profitable crop of hemp fibre. On the hills, especially at Kumaon, the plant is often cultivated for its fibre, and coarse cloth is made of it by the hill-people. From the Government reports of the foreign trade of India in 1884-85,

there would appear to have been 9092 cwt. of hemp, valued at Rs. 2,14,178 imported, and 73,029 cwt., valued at Rs. 5,82,679, exported. How far these figures allude to the true hemp it is impossible to ascertain, for it must be recollected that a series of widely different fibres are often spoken of as "Hemp," such as Manilla-hemp, Sunn-hemp, &c. (*See* also 731, 770.)

912. Cochlospermum gossypium, *DC.*; Bixineæ. The Yellow Silk-Cotton Tree; Kumbi, Galgal (*Hind.*). A small, deciduous tree in the forests at the base of the North-West Himálaya, from the Sutlej eastward to Central India, the Central Provinces, Chutia Nagpur, the Deccan, and to Prome in Burma. The floss from the seeds is extremely soft and silky, and if found useful could be procured in India to an almost indefinite extent. The Rev. A. Campbell, of the Free Church Santal Mission, has furnished, along with many other extremely interesting products from the forests around his station, a large sample of this fibre, which will be found to resemble in many respects the *Kapok* or seed-hairs of *Eriodendron anfructuosum.* (*See* also 959, 1066.)

913.* Cocos nucifera, *Linn.*; Palmæ. The Coir or Cocoanut Fibre; Narikel (*Beng.*). The thick, fibrous pericarp yields the valuable coir fibre of commerce. A fibre from the leaf-stalks is also prepared, but compared to the coir it is unimportant. The foreign trade in unmanufactured coir for the year 1884–85 was valued at Rs. 1,20,799 and of manufactured at Rs. 21,35,996. Excellent samples of stair-carpets and door-mats made of coir will be found in the Court and around the "Rope Trophy." (*See* also 85, 715, 895.)

913a. Crotalaria juncea, *Linn.*; Leguminosæ. The Sunn Fibre. (*See* also 968.)

914. Cyperus tegetum, *Roxb.*; Cyperaceæ. The Grass-matting of Bengal. The subject of mat-grasses is exceedingly obscure, but it seems probable that any large *Scirpus* may be used for this purpose. The better qualities of Calcutta mats are made from *C. tegetum*, but as this plant is not found near Calcutta (although common in Orissa and Chutia Nagpur), the prepared mat fibre must be imported. The commoner mats are made of *C. articulatus*, *C. procerus*, and *C. exaltatus.* The grass-mats of the Sandwich Islands are made of *C. lævigatus*, a species common in Madras, but apparently never made into mats in India. Ceylon mats are made of a species allied if not identical with *C. malaccensis.* Grass-mats are made in Bombay from *Scirpus subulatus.*

915. Daphne papyracea, *Wall.*; Thymelæaceæ. Set barúwa, satpura (*Hind.*); Gande, kaghuti (*Nepal*). A large shrub or small tree found on the Himálaya from the Indus to Bhutan, between altitudes of 3,000 and 9,000 feet; also on the Khasia and Naga Hills. From the bark of this plant is prepared the famous Nepal paper and also strong ropes. Interesting samples of this fibre and of paper made from it are on view both in this Sub-Court and also in the Sub-Court devoted to paper materials. (*See* also 969.)

916. Debregeasia bicolor, *Wedd.*; Urticaceæ. A large shrub of the Salt Range and of the North-West Himálaya ascending to altitude 5,000 feet. The fibre is made into twine and ropes. It is very strong and may be viewed as allied to rhea.

917. Edgeworthia Gardneri, *Meisn.*; Thymelæaceæ. A large, elegant bush, almost leafless when covered with its clusters of yellow, sweet-scented flowers. Found along the Himálaya from Nepal to Sikkim and Bhutan and Manipur. The strong, tough fibre obtained from the long, straight, sparsely-branched twigs of this bush must be viewed as one of the best fibres in India. The finest Nepal Paper is made of it. (*See* also 970.)

918. Eriodendron anfractuosum, *DC.*; Malvaceæ. The White Cotton Tree; Safed simal (*Hind.*). A tall, deciduous tree of India and Burma, found throughout the hotter parts. This yields the Kapok fibre of Java recently introduced to European commerce by the Dutch. It is obtained from the seeds being a soft, silky floss resembling that afforded by the red cotton tree, *Bombax malabaricum*, and from the yellow silk cotton, *Cochlospermum Gossypium.* In South Canara a fibre is also extracted from the stem which is said to be suitable for the manufacture of paper. (*See* also 957.)

919. Ficus bengalensis, *Linn.*; Urticaceæ. The Banyan Tree; Bar (*Hind.*); Bat (*Beng.*). One of the most characteristic of Indian trees. A coarse rope is made from the bark and from the aërial roots, and paper is also reported to have been formerly largely prepared in Assam from the bark. A large series of rope fibres will be found on the tables, obtained from various species of Ficus, one of the finest being that from *F. Tsiela.* (*See* also 131, 431, 1105.)

920. Girardinia heterophylla, *Decaisne*; Urticaceæ. The Nilgiri Nettle; Awa, alla, bichua (*Hind.*). An exceedingly common, large, herbaceous plant of the forests of the warm temperate regions. It is common throughout most of the hill districts of India and Burma, but especially upon the Himálaya. There are two if not three distinct species, each of which yields admirable fibres. *G. zeylanica* is the true Nilgiri Nettle, although commercially the fibres of all three have come to bear that name. It is chiefly met with on the mountains of South India. *G. heterophylla* is the characteristic form on the Himálaya. It affords a fine, silky fibre, used in Sikkim for ropes and coarse cloth resembling *gunny.* Roxburgh says of it:—"The bark abounds in fine, white, glossy, silk-like, strong fibres." A very serious practical difficulty exists against an extended use of these strong fibres in the stinging hairs. These cause great annoyance to the persons employed to extract the fibre, and even after being manufactured into cloth the poisonous property has not been completely destroyed, but on the contrary often causes great irritation to the person wearing garments made of this cloth.

Mr. E. G. Chester, Deputy Conservator of Forests, Darjeeling, contributes a good sample of this fibre.

921. HARDWICKIA BINATA, *Roxb.*; Leguminosæ. Aojan (*Hind.*); Acha (*Tam.*). A large, deciduous tree of the dry forests of South and Central India. The bark yields a strong and valuable fibre, much used for ropes by the inhabitants of the forests where it abounds. (*See* also 146, 436.)

922. HELICTERES ISORA, *Linn.*; Sterculiaceæ. Maror-phal, kapasi, bhandu (*Hind.*); Antmora (*Beng.*). A large, dense shrub of the tropical or sub-Himálayan regions; from the Punjáb to Bengal, South and Central India, and Burma. The fibre extracted from the bark is strong, white, and very useful for cordage, rough sacking, and canvas. (*See* also 971.)

923. HIBISCUS CANNABINUS, *Linn.*; Malvaceæ. Deccani Hemp; Hemp-leaved Hibiscus; Ambarei (*Hind.*); Mesta-pat (*Beng.*); Garnikura (*Sans.*). A small, herbaceous shrub, with prickly stems, apparently wild, east of the Northern Gháts. Largely cultivated, especially in the North-West Provinces and the Punjáb, for its fibre, which is stronger, though not so good as *Sunn* (*Crotalaria juncea*). In Sind this is considered the best fibre for nets and ropes. It is the chief fibre used in the manufacture of paper in the Dacca district, Bengal. It is also employed for this purpose in the Madras Presidency. A very interesting fibre, and deserves more attention. It is sometimes met with as an adulterant of jute. Mr. F. B. Manson, Deputy Conservator of Forests, Chutia Nagpur, Bengal, exhibits a large series of samples of this fibre and also of ropes made of it. (*See* also 972.)

924.* H. ESCULENTUS, *Linn.* The Edible Hibiscus; Ochro of West Indies; Gombo (*Fr.*); Bhindi (*Hind.*). A herbaceous annual bush, naturalised in all tropical countries; only met with in a cultivated state in India. The bark yields a strong, useful fibre, deserving of more attention, especially by paper-makers. The plant is extensively cultivated, as a vegetable, and the fibre might therefore be procured at a reasonable rate. (*See* also 525.)

925. H. FICULNEUS, *Linn.* Kapasiya (*N.-W. P.*). A native most probably of the southern provinces, naturalised in the Punjáb, Bengal, the Circars, and the Concan. A small herbaceous and annual bush, which should be sown at the beginning of the rains. Like most other members of the Malvaceæ this yields a valuable fibre. Roxburgh says:—"In none have I found so large a quantity, equally beautiful, long, glossy, white, fine, and strong as in this. To these properties may be added the luxuriant growth and habit of the plant, rendering it an object of every care and attention, at least until the real worth of the material is fairly ascertained." Like many other of Roxburgh's valuable economic discoveries, this has remained for nearly a century without having been taken any advantage of. The immense success of jute has obscured not a few fibres which, although not so easily and cheaply separated, would be far more valuable were they to be substituted for many of the purposes to which jute is now put. Of these may be mentioned the fibres of the various species of *Hibiscus*, *Abroma*, *Abutilon*, and *Sida*.

926.* HIBISCUS SABDARIFFA, *Linn.* The Rozelle Fibre. A small bush, cultivated in many parts of India, which is largely made into jelly. The stems yield a good, strong, silky fibre. This is obtained by retting the twigs when in flower. (*See* also 498, 602.)

927. H. TILIACEUS, *Linn.* The Bola or Chelwa of the Coast of Bengal. This large bush is exceedingly plentiful on the coast; its abundance and the ease with which it might be still further extended over tracts of country where little else will grow, being powerful reasons for the utilisation of the plant being carefully considered. It yields a useful and strong jute-like fibre, extensively used for cordage. It is said to gain in strength when tarred. The fibre is readily separated from the green or unsteeped branches, the work of preparation being less tedious than with the other fibre-yielding plants of the genus. It appears to be well adapted for making ropes, mats, and possibly paper. A large series of samples of this fibre is shown from the Sunderbuns and Burma, contributed, amongst many other extremely interesting economic products, by the Forest Officers of these regions.

928. H. VITIFOLIUS, Linn. Bun-kapas (*Beng.*). A common bush throughout India. The bark yields a strong, silvery fibre, a beautiful sample of which is exhibited by Mr. G. A. Richardson, of Buxar, Bengal.

929. LAPORTEA CRENULATA, *Gandich.*; Urticaceæ. A tree of Sikkim, Assam, Eastern Bengal, the West Coast, Ceylon, and Burma. This yields a good fibre, which can be made into ropes and coarse cloth.

930. MAOUTIA PUYA, *Wedd.*; Urticaceæ. Poi (*Hind.*). A shrub, with white leaves, found in the Himálaya from Garhwal eastward, Assam, and the Khásia Hills and Burma, chiefly in old cultivations and up to 4,000 feet in altitude. It yields a strong fibre of excellent quality, very much resembling rhea; this is made into fishing nets, net-bags, twine, and cloth. It seems highly probable that this plant could be more easily cultivated than the true rhea, and that the fibre would be found quite as serviceable. A large sample of this fibre is exhibited by the Government of Assam. Compare with the remarks under Bœhmeria.

931. MARANTA DICHOTOMA, *Wall.*; Scitamineæ. Pati (*Beng.*). A reed-like plant found in Eastern Bengal, Assam, the Coromandel Coast, and Burma. The stems are slit into strips, and plaited into the so-called *Shital-pati* mats. These are smooth mats which, owing to their coolness, are largely used in the hot weather for sleeping on. Some of the finest cost about £5 each, but the ordinary kinds average from Rs. 2 to Rs. 3.

932. MARSDENIA TENACISSIMA, *W. & A.*; Asclepiadaceæ. A climbing shrub found in Kumaon, Oudh, Behar, Bengal, and Ava. It yields the silky fibre sometimes known as

"Rajmahal hemp," one of the strongest and finest of all fibres, and yet at the present day one completely neglected.

933. MUSA PARADISIACA, *Linn.;* Scitamineæ. The Plantain; Kela (*Hind.*, *Bomb.*); Kela (*Beng.*). Various species of plantain are extensively cultivated throughout India, and several wild forms occur in the sub-tropical forest. A beautiful fibre is obtained from the stem of the Indian plantain, though inferior to that of the Manilla-hemp. Considerable attention has of late years been attracted to the subject of plantain as a source of paper. It seems probable that a good future is before the paper industry of India, and that amongst many other fibres the thousands of plantain stems which by the natives are annually thrown away as useless may yet come to be greedily purchased for paper manufacture. The chief difficulty consists in the fact that the cultivated plantain stems would have to be collected over a wide area, since it would scarcely pay to cultivate the plant exclusively as a paper material. The wild plantains, on the other hand, frequent the inaccessible recesses of the forests where the question of freight to the paper mill would prove fatal. *Musa textilis* affords the Manilla-hemp of commerce. Large quantities of this fibre are annually imported by Messrs. Harton and Co., and other Indian rope manufacturers; samples of their ropes, made of this fibre, are to be seen on the "Rope Trophy." Attempts to introduce this plant into the plains of India have been made but with little success. An effort is now, however, being put forth to acclimatise the plant in the Andaman Islands, and the experiment so far seems successful.

934.* OPUNTIA DILLENII, *Haw.;* Cacteæ. The Prickly Pear; Naghana (*Hind.*). An erect, fleshy, and thorny shrub common all over the arid and dry regions and often planted as a hedge; introduced but now naturalised in India. A coarse fibre is obtained from this plant which might be found suitable for paper. Dr. Bidie writes from Madras:—"This abounds in every part of the country, and has become such a nuisance that large sums are expended annually in cutting it down, and burying it, on sanitary grounds. This plant has taken such a hold of certain tracts of country that the supply would certainly never be in the least affected by the utilisation of the fibre as paper material." (*See* also 609, 975.)

935. PAVONIA ZEYLANICA, *Cav.;* Malvaceæ. Bala (*Sans.*). A much-branched shrub common in the North-West Provinces, Sind, the Western Peninsula, and Ceylon. It yields a fibre of excellent quality. *P. odorata* affords a similar fibre, and both these plants deserve to be more carefully cultivated and their fibres tested. Mr. J. W. Cherry, Deputy Conservator of Forests, Salem, Madras, sends a large sample of this fibre along with many other extremely interesting fibres.

936. PHŒNIX SYLVESTRIS, *Roxb.;* Palmæ. The Wild Date Palm; Khajur (*Hind.*). A palm, with ashy grey foliage; cultivated throughout India. The fibrous leaflets and the fibre from the petioles are made into mats, ropes, and baskets. The fibre produced by cutting the leaves into strips may come to be used as a paper material. (*See* also 611, 724.)

937. POLLINIA ERIOPODA, *Trim.* (ERIOPHORUM COMOSUM), *Wall.;* Gramineæ. Babar or Baboi Grass. An abundant grass in many parts of India. This has now become one of the principal paper materials in India. It is largely used by the Bally Paper Mills near Calcutta. Interesting collections both of the grass, of paper half stuff, and of paper made from it will be found in Sub-Court XXVI. The fibre is also extensively made into strings, cords, and ropes. (*See* also 387, 976.)

938. SACCHARUM MUNJA, *Roxb.;* Gramineæ. Munj Grass. This grass is very common in North India, especially in the Punjáb. It is useful in the manufacture of strong ropes, strings, mats, and paper. For ropes it is much valued on account of its elasticity and strength, and a power of resisting moisture, common to few other fibres. The flower-heads and sheaths of this plant constitute one of the best paper grass materials in India. For this purpose it is largely used by the Upper India Paper Mills near Lucknow. The *bán-múnj* is the flower sheath from which the natives prepare a fine thread. (*See* also 388, 977.)

939. SANSEVIERIA ZEYLANICA, *Willd.;* Liliaceæ. The Bow-string Hemp. A stemless bush with a rosette of leaves; common on the coast of South India. Mr. H. J. Porter, Deputy Conservator of Forests, Madras, exhibits an admirable example of this interesting fibre. (*See* also 978.)

940. SESBANIA ACULEATA (*Pers.*); Leguminosæ. Dhanicha (*Beng.*). This bush is found in Bengal and South India. A strong fibre is extracted from its stalks, and made into ropes and fishing nets. The fibre is much valued because of its high power of endurance under water. It is superior to jute in strength and durability, and is best suited for the manufacture of cordage, for which purpose it is preferred to either sunn-hemp or jute.

941. SIDA RHOMBIFOLIA, *Linn.;* Malvaceæ. Swet-berela (*Beng.*). This small, gregarious bush is abundant in many parts of India, especially so in Bengal. The bark yields a large quantity of very flaxy fibre. Mr. G. A. Richardson, Deputy Conservator of Forests, Buxar, Bengal, sends, among many others, an excellent sample of this fibre. Two or three allied species are equally common and yield similar fibres, especially *S. humilis*, and they are all characterised by great strength, average length, and fineness. Mr. Cherry, Deputy Conservator of Forests, of Salem, Madras, contributes a beautiful sample of *S. carpinifolia*.

942. STERCULIA GUTTATA, *W. & A.;* Sterculiaceæ. A common tree of South India. The bark yields a valuable cordage fibre. The younger parts abound with very strong, white, flaxen fibres, of which the inhabitants of South India manufacture a kind of coarse cloth.

943. S. URENS, *Roxb.* Gulu, kulu, tabasi, karrai (*Hind.*); Odla (*Ass.*). A large tree met with in the sub-tropical forests of Bengal, Assam, Burma, and South India. The inner bark yields a good strong light-coloured fibre. (*See* also 265, 1082.)

944. S. VILLOSA, *Roxb.* Udal, udar (*Hind.*). A moderate-sized tree of the sub-Himálayan tract from the Indus eastward; common in forests throughout India and Burma. The tree is highly valued on account of the fibre obtained from the inner bark, which is coarse but strong, and is made into ropes and bags. The tree is so highly valued for its fibre that in the more accessible forests it may be said to occur chiefly as a bush, from the habit of constantly lopping its branches for the fibre they contain. Mr. H. G. Young, Assistant Conservator of Forests, Cachar, Assam, contributes an admirable sample of this, along with many other very valuable fibres. (*See* also 266.)

945. URENA LOBATA, *Linn.*; Malvaceæ. Bun-ochra (*Beng.*). A common shrub in India, found in waste places. It abounds in strong fibre, which is considered suitable for the manufacture of sacking and twine.

946. VILLEBRUNEA APPENDICULATA, *Wedd.*; Urticaceæ. Bun Rhea (*Ass.*); Lipic, lipiah (*Nepal*). A small tree of the north-eastern Himálaya, Khásia Hills, and Chittagong. It yields an extremely valuable fibre of a rich brown colour, strong, and flexible: this is made into ropes, nets, and coarse cloth in Sikkim and Assam. It seems highly probable this may prove one of our most useful rhea-like fibres. The tree grows freely and quickly and coppices readily. Mr. F. S. Barker, Assistant Conservator of Forests, Assam, sends a good sample of this fibre, along with a large supply of string made from it.

947.* YUCCA GLORIOSA, *Linn.*; Liliaceæ. Adam's Needle; the silky grass fibre. A native of America from Carolina to Mexico and Texas. Introduced into India, met with in gardens in Bengal, occasionally naturalised in the Madras Presidency. The fibre which it yields resembles in many respects that of the *Agave*, and is applicable to similar purposes. There are several species, all of which yield excellent fibres; but *Y. gloriosa* is the principal one, and may be taken as the type of the others. The root is said to be employed as a substitute for soap. (*See* also 979.)

EXHIBITORS.—Forest officers in the several Provinces have assisted largely in the collection of Fibres shown in Sub-Courts XXI. and XXII.

SUB-COURT XXIII.

COMMERCIAL FIBRES.

In addition to cotton and jute, there are about half-a-dozen other fibres which may be regarded as at present of value to Europe. The first and most important of these is undoubtedly Rhea. Strenuous efforts have, within recent years, been made to bring this fibre into greater importance; but the high price of the fibre, together also with its exceptional strength and durability, unfit it for many purposes. Perhaps no fibre is more beautiful in texture than rhea, but fabrics made of it are stiff and crease readily, and it is next to impossible to ever hope to wear out a dress of rhea cloth. These are undoubtedly obstacles to a greatly extended application of rhea, but where durability is desired, no fibre known can compare with rhea in this respect. Now that the question of the separation of the fibre has been overcome, there seems every hope of a greater future for rhea, but it will never be a favourite with the cultivator, since it is a very exhausting crop. It has been urged that a mistake has been made in confining investigations too closely to one species, since almost every province of India has one or more indigenous forms of rhea. It is assumed that one of these may yet be discovered more serviceable to the textile industries and calculated to meet demands which rhea proper is not likely to do. A rhea, a little less durable, not quite so strong, more easily separated and less exhaustive to the soil, would at once be accepted. The Glenrock Company, Limited, of the Wynaad, Madras, exhibit an interesting collection of their fibres in this Sub-Court, showing not only rhea grown on their plantations, but also two or three of the allied rhea fibres. Special attention is desired to the *Debregeasia* fibre which Mr. Minchin describes as the so-called wild rhea of South India. This fibre is well known to the natives of India, and seems one of those which will rapidly attain a high position in the European markets. An allied plant, *Villebrunea appendiculata*, yields the wild rhea of Assam, a fibre certainly inferior to none in India. The various species of Nilgiri nettles are better known, although they do not offer so much hope of a future development. The Glenrock Company also show, in addition to the above, pine-apple fibre and manilla-hemp. A large assortment of aloe fibre is also on view, as well as a selection of the better class fibres allied to jute.

It is not deemed necessary to enumerate in detail all the fibres shown in this Sub-Court, since the leading fibres of India have already been described under Sub-Courts XXI. and XXII., and the descriptions there given may be consulted. The selection shown in Sub-Court XXIII. has been made with the object of placing more prominently before the public the fibres of India which seem most likely to become of importance.

EXHIBITORS.—Messrs. Reinhold Bros., Calcutta; The Glen Rock Company, Limited, Madras.

SUB-COURT XXIV.

COTTON.

Cotton is the most valuable article of Indian export trade. In India there are 14,000,000 acres annually under cotton, not including

Bengal and Assam; of these provinces the cotton returns are not published. The following are the quantities and values of the cotton exports for the past five years.

	Cwts.	Rs.
1880-81 .	4,541,539	13,24,17,341
1881-82 .	5,627,453	14,93,59,595
1882-83 .	6,168,278	16,04,90,174
1883-84 .	5,979,494	14,38,37,278
1884-85 .	5,066,057	13,28,63,673

The exports for 1884-85 were about 15 per cent. smaller in quantity and 7½ per cent. less in value than those for 1883-84. This depression, Mr. O'Conor explains, was due to a short and inferior crop of Bombay cottons.

The following analysis of the exports for the year 1884-85 shows the chief markets to which Indian cottons are consigned:—

Presidency from which exported.	Weight in Cwts.	Value in Rupees.
Bengal . .	288,976	68,82,064
Bombay . .	4,064,609	10,88,52,143
Sindh . .	71,660	17,45,986
Madras . .	557,877	1,34,72,806
British Burma	82,935	19,10,674
Total . .	5,066,057	13,28,63,673

Country to which exported.	Weight in Cwts.	Value in Rupees.
United Kingdom . .	2,134,762	5,58,86,298
Italy . .	740,647	1,90,78,004
France . .	577,169	1,52,80,431
Austria . .	575,645	1,55,54,204
Belgium . .	533,933	1,41,88,184
China . .	236,600	58,51,838
Germany .	85,353	23,19,504
Other Countries	181,888	47,05,210
Total . .	5,066,057	13,28,63,673

It is remarkable how unimportant India is as a supply of cotton for the English market. Out of the whole exports for 1884-85, the Continent imported direct 2,513,807 cwt. and England 2,134,762, but nearly half the amount consigned to England was re-exported again to the Continent of Europe. To the English manufacturer, therefore, Indian cotton is, comparatively speaking, of secondary importance; Italy offers the largest market.

Much confusion still exists with regard to the forms of cotton met with in cultivation in India, and it may therefore be of service to repeat here the characters of the leading species. There are in India three species of *Gossypium* which yield cotton, but of these there are many varieties and hybrids, giving origin to the numerous forms known to the cultivator and manufacturer by local and technical names. The three species may be briefly defined:—

949.* GOSSYPIUM ARBOREUM, *Linn.*; Malvaceæ. This is known as *Narma*, *manua* or *radya* cotton in India generally, and in Mysore as deo kapás. It does not appear to be cultivated to a great extent on account of its cotton. It sometimes attains the height of a small tree; more frequently it is a densely-branched bush, with purple flowers, often with a yellow centre. The leaves are thicker and more glossy than those of the next species; they are three-fourths segmented or even cut to the base, into 5 or 7 lobes (mostly 5, never 3); the segments are contracted below, narrow ovate, linear, acuminate or ovate lanceolate, not one-fourth as broad as long; the central lobe often has, on either side, a small supplementary segment or tooth in the deep rounded lateral sinus. Bracteoles of the flowers ovate, cordate acute, toothed or entire. Seeds free from each other, covered with a white cotton over-lying a dense green down; cotton not readily separable from the seed.

This is now viewed as a native of tropical Africa.

950.* G. BARBADENSE, *Linn.* There are many very distinct cultivated forms referred to this species. Whether the accepted type is the original condition of the plant, however, or is itself only one of the numerous cultivated forms, can only be determined when the whole subject of the wild cottons of America (the wild cottons which exist as such at the present day) has been carefully worked out. At the time of the discovery of America, the forms of cotton now referred to this species were being cultivated from the West Indies to Peru, and from Mexico to Brazil. Accepting this as evidence that they were the cultivated forms of an indigenous species—the more so since, as far as can be learned, they were not known to the Old World before the discovery of America—we may adopt the general view and regard them collectively as "the American cottons." According to some botanists these are referred to a number of distinct species, or by others are reduced to varieties under a somewhat hypothetical species. Parlatore relegated the numerous conditions to three species, which answer to *Gossypium hirsutum*, *G. barbadense*, and *G. religiosum*, Linn. The authors of the 'Flora of British India' group a number of forms, including the above, into one species, namely, *G. barbadense*.

G. barbadense may be distinguished from the other species as follows:—Leaves, sub-glabrous, broader and more cordate than those of the preceding species, having rounded ears at the base: blade about half cut into three to five lobes, each broad ovate, acuminate, more than half as broad as long (often very acuminate and then almost sub-lanceolate). Floral bracteoles, larger and broader than in the preceding species, obtuse, deeply laciniate. Flowers yellow with a crimson spot. Seeds black and naked, *i.e.* destitute of adnate pubescence (except var. *religiosum*), free from each other or cohering in a kidney-shaped mass. *Cotton* readily separable from the seeds, white, tawny, or almost brown.

This may be reduced to three varieties :—

951. *Var.* 1*st.* — *Barbadense* (proper). The Bourbon cottons and the Barbadoes, New Orleans, Sea Island, Uplands, Egyptian, Georgian, Florida and Alabama cottons. The much-prized cotton cultivated in Western India and known as Dharwar appears to be a form of New Orleans.

952. *Var.* 2*nd.* — *Religiosum* (sp. Roxb.). Nankeen Cotton. The distinguishing feature of this cotton seems to be that the seeds are clothed with tawny pubescence and enclosed in cotton of the same colour. Apparently this was introduced into India at a much earlier date than the forms referred to the first variety, and as it exists at the present day it might be more correctly viewed as a hybrid, hence the fact of the seeds being pubescent.

953. *Var.* 3*rd.* — *Acuminatum* (sp. Roxb.). Peruvia or Kidney Cotton. The cottons which fall into this variety are distinguished chiefly by the peculiarity of the black naked seeds cohering together in a kidney-shaped mass. It is probable that these are even still earlier introductions than the forms of *religiosum*, and Roxburgh seemed to incline to the opinion that they were indigenous. They are sometimes spoken of under the name of *Gossypium peruvianum.* The following are the principal commercial forms:—Brazilian, Pernambuco, Maranham, and Peruvian and the Ukan paruthi and Judi paruthi of Madras, and the long kidney cottons of the Garo and Khásia hills.

It seems probable that instead of *Gossypium hirsutum* (Willd.) being constituted into a fourth variety, it should be viewed as a distinct hybrid between *G. herbaceum* and *G. barbadense.* It is chiefly characterized by having greenish tomentose seeds surrounded by fine, long, silky cotton, and by having purple flowers with the leaves of the American forms. A good deal of the Berar and Surat cottons, and also the nudum yerra prathi, and semparuthi of South India, are of this nature.

954. Gossypium herbaceum, *Linn.* There seems no doubt about this species having been originally a native of Asia, and of India in particular. A wild species, closely allied, is said to occur in Sind at the present day, which may prove the parent of the cultivated forms. Its cultivation has, however, spread all over the world—it is common in Europe, Asia, and the United States. To admit of comparison with the species described above, the diagnostic characters of this species may be here given:—Leaves very hairy; often quite hirsute; about half cut into three to five lobes, mostly three; lobes ovate; oblong, acute, or acuminate; about half as broad as long. Floral bracteoles ovate, cordate, acute, toothed or entire. Flowers yellow with a purple centre, or rarely wholly yellow or white or purple. Seeds ovoid, free from each other, covered with greyish or greenish down, cotton white or yellow. The most characteristic features of the plant are its very hairy leaves, half segmented, the majority having only three lobes or five, very rarely seven. The bracteoles are those of *Gossypium arboreum*, and are quite unlike the laciniated bracteoles of *G. barbadense.* The purple flowers and green tomentum of some of the forms have most probably been derived by hybridism with *G. arboreum;* some such hybrid being again crossed with *G. barbadense* to produce a few of the cultivated forms, such as *G. hirsutum*, which possesses the characters of all three species.

There seems to be little doubt that *G. herbaceum* has been hybridised freely with both of the preceding species, and that many of the cultivated forms of cotton met with in India are of this nature. Efforts appear to have been made to improve the indigenous plant by crossing it with the superior though less hardy and introduced species.

The hybrids and cultivated forms of this species may conveniently be referred to two sections:—

955. *Var.* 1*st.* — *herbaceum* (proper). This includes the Bengal or Dacca cottons, and many of the Berar and Surat—such as the Kumari hatti of South Kanara and Punasa pratti of Ganjam, as also some of the China cottons.

956. *Var.* 2*nd.*—*obtusifolium.* This is the small blunt-leaved form met with in Ceylon, and on many of the hill tracts of India.

Cotton is the principal article of export trade from Bombay. There are eight leading kinds: *Hinganghát* and *Amráoti* from the Central Provinces, Berár, Khándesh, the Nizam's country, and the North Deccan; *Broach* and *Dholera* from Gujarat, Kathiawar, and Cutch; *Saw-ginned Dharwar* and *Coompta* from the Southern Maratha Districts and Sholapur; *Westerns* from Madras; and *Iráni* from Persia.

Exhibitors.—The Bombay Committee having agreed to take charge of the exhibition of samples of raw cotton, cotton yarns, and cloth for all India, have, with the co-operation of the Bombay Chamber of Commerce and Bombay Millowners' Associations, sent collections of varieties of cotton grown in Bombay, Madras, North-West Provinces, Sind, Bengal, and Assam; also cotton yarn and cloth prepared by the City of Bombay Spinning and Weaving Company, Limited; Empress Spinning Company, Limited; Leopold Spinning, Bleaching and Manufacturing Company, Limited; Connaught Mills Company, Limited; Manockji Petit Manufacturing Company, Limited; and Morarji Gokuldas Spinning and Weaving Company, Limited.

From Bengal:—Messrs. Ernsthausen and Oesterly, at the instance of the Bengal Commercial Exhibition Committee, have prepared a special collection of cottons. Mr. Duthie, of Saharanpur Botanic Gardens, contributes a collection of North-West Provinces' cotton; and Mr. Darrah, Director of Agriculture, Assam, sends Assam cottons. Mr. R. L. Heinick, Bengal; Mr. T. W. Cherry, Madras; Mr. F. Copeland, Punjáb, also exhibit.

SILK COTTON.

Interest has recently been taken in the subject of "silk cotton" or kapok. The following are the plants which yield this floss, enumerated in the order of their importance:—

957. *Eriodendron anfractuosum* (DC.). Malvaceæ. The Kapok or White Silk Cotton; the Elavamparuthi of Madras. This tree is particularly plentiful in the Konkan, but it grows in most parts of India, and its cultivation could be extended. As a road-side tree, while affording shade, it might thus be made to yield a distinct revenue to the country. Examples of this silk cotton have been contributed by the officers of the Forest Department. (*See* also 918.)

958. *Bombax malabaricum* (DC.). The Simul or Red Silk Cotton. This is the commonest of the silk cotton trees, occurring throughout the peninsula, but more particularly on the eastern side, ascending the hills to 4,000 feet in altitude. (*See* also 53, 413, 908, 1059.)

959. COCHLOSPERMUM GOSSYPIUM (DC.). The Kambi of Galgal. A common tree of the lower hills of India from Garhwal, Bandelkhand, Behar, Orissa, and westward to the Deccan. It has large yellow flowers, and is not uncommon in cultivation throughout the country, especially in South India. It would seem that samples of this form of silk cotton have been consigned to Europe and declared as such, so that its peculiar merits have not apparently been definitely determined. The fibre is soft and silky, but very short. The Reverend A. Campbell, of the Santal Mission, Chutia Nagpur, exhibits a large sample. (*See* also 912.)

960. *Colotropis gigantea* (R. Br.). The Madar.

This and other members of the Asclepiadaceæ and Apocynaceæ yield silky hairs—the coma of the seeds. These are generally classed as silk cottons, but, with the exception of *madar*, none of these have as yet been experimented with. The natives of India regard the *madar* silk cotton as much cooler than simul, and affirm that it has a soothing effect when used in pillows. (*See* also 712, 769, 910, 1095.)

SUB-COURT XXV.

JUTE.

961. This fibre is prepared by retting the stems of *Corchorus capsularis* and *C. olitorius*, Linn., two species of closely-allied plants. The former has a spherical fruit, flattened at the top; it is the species which yields the fibre in Central and East Bengal. The latter has an elongated fruit, and is the species cultivated in the vicinity of Calcutta. The genus Corchorus has representatives in all the warm, moist regions of the world —Asia, Africa, and America. Geographical evidence cannot therefore be resorted to in efforts to determine the ancestral home of the jute-yielding species. *C. olitorius* is the Jew's Mallow. It is cultivated in Egypt and in Syria as a vegetable, and in many other parts of the world. By some authors it is viewed as a native of Western India and of Kordofan. In Bengal, where both *C. olitorius* and *C. capsularis* are cultivated for the fibre, they do not appear to exist in a wild condition.

The first commercial mention of the word "Jute" is in the customs returns of the exports for 1828. In that year 364 cwt., valued at Rs. 620, of raw jute were exported to Europe. The manufacture of gunny-bags and cloth was then entirely in the hands of Indian peasants, but the trade must have been limited, since there do not appear to have been any foreign exports in these jute manufactures. Jute mills were, however, early established in Dundee, and a large export trade in raw jute sprang into existence. Down to the year 1854 little or no effort was made to improve the Indian jute manufactures, but in that year the "Ishera Yarn Mills Company" was established near Serampore. Three years later the Company, now known as the "Baranagore Jute Mills," was established, and in 1863-64 the "Gouripore Jute Factory" was founded. Factories sprang up rapidly in every direction around Calcutta. There are now twenty-three large jute mills at work in India, and in 1884-85 the exports of raw jute amounted to Rs. 4,66,13,684, and the exports of manufactured jute to Rs. 1,54,38,696. Expressing these figures at par, we have the startling fact that the value of the foreign trade in jute in 1828 was only £62 sterling, but during 1885 it was £6,205,238. As a present fluctuation the jute trade is not in a very flourishing condition, over-production having caused a fall in prices. During the past few years, however, the exports of Indian manufactured jutes have been steadily improving, and the exports of raw jute apparently falling off. Little more than forty years ago the peasant handlooms of India met the home and also the foreign demand for Indian-made gunny-bags, but the opening out of steam factories in India has not only absorbed this trade, but has greatly extended the foreign market. This is illustrated by the fact that in 1850-51 the exports of handloom manufactures were valued at £215,978; in 1884-85 they were only £51,882. There were no European factories at work in India in 1850, so that the exports of manufactured jute which appear in the trade returns for that year must have been entirely hand-loom made. But even with twenty-three large factories at work the foreign trade in raw jute is four times as valuable to India as her exports of manufactured jute. In estimating the total value of jute to India care must be taken not to regard the quotations of imports and exports of jute and jute manufactures, declared as such, as indicating the actual extent of the trade. Leaving out of account the large quantity of jute used up annually by the people of India themselves for agricultural and internal trade purposes (home trade), an immense number of gunny-bags leave India in the foreign produce trade filled with wheat, rice, and other grains and seeds, and are therefore not included in the returns of exports of gunny-bags. Through the kindness of a Calcutta jute merchant the following figures have been procured for the total Bengal trade in jute manufactures during the year 1882. The commercial year does not correspond with the Government financial year, so that a slight difference exists between the figures compiled by merchants and those published by the Government of India. There were exported 41,523,607 power-loom made gunny-bags (this is given by Government as 41,156,766); but according to the Calcutta brokers there were sold in Calcutta over and above 77,519,164 gunny-bags. About one-half of these are shown in the Government reports of coasting and railway-borne trade to have been sent from Bengal to other provinces to be used in the home and foreign grain trade. Of the balance no record is preserved by Government in any form. These bags were of course used in the Bengal home and foreign grain trade. It should thus be carefully observed that the published figures of exports of manufactured jutes as such represent probably little more than one-third the actual trade in these bags. Mr. J. E. O'Conor, in his 'Review of the Trade of India' for 1884–85, while speaking of the exports of manufactured jute, says, "the whole trade in jute manufactures" was valued at Rs. 1,54,38,696 (=£1,543,869), but in his 'Annual Statement of Trade and Navigation,' he shows that power-loom gunny-bags to the value of Rs. 74,44,577 (over and above the foreign exports) were sent from Bengal to other provinces. If to this we add the value of the bags used up in Bengal itself, the whole value of the Bengal trade in jute manufactures cannot have been far short of 3 crores of rupees (£3,000,000). Since 1882 the exports to foreign countries of jute manufactures have greatly improved; last year, for example, 77,841,776 gunny-bags left India, or, including hand-loom bags, 82,779,207 were exported, while nearly 40 millions were in addition sent to other provinces, and probably about the same number used up in Bengal itself.

The total value of the foreign jute trade during 1884–85 has been published as Rs. 6,24,15,687. and it is amusing to observe that raw jute is actually being imported into India, Arabia having sent raw jute to the value of Rs. 583. The imports of manufactured jutes were valued at Rs. 6,61,943, chiefly from Ceylon, Great Britain, and the Straits.

The very interesting collection of jute samples and manufactures now on view was prepared by the Bengal Commercial Committee. (*See* also 547, 967.)

Exhibitors.—The Indian Jute Manufacturers Association undertook the preparation of the special show of raw and manufactured jute. Messrs. Jardine Skinner and Co., Calcutta, exhibit jute manufactures, as also the Barnagore Jute Factory, Kamarhatty Co., Sibpur Jute Manufacturing Co., and Messrs. Byrack and Brothers, Dacca.

SUB-COURT XXVI.

PAPER AND PAPER FIBRES.

The art of paper-making in India dates from the great emperor Akbar, and was first practised in Kashmír. Rapidly it spread all over India, displacing the birch-bark used by the hill tribes and the palm-leaves by the people of the plains. It is probable, however, that the art of Nepal paper-making came from China to the inhabitants of the eastern Himálaya long anterior to the introduction of the paper industry by Akbar. Even at the present day the paper-making of the natives of India is very much like their glass-blowing, since it very largely consists in remaking from paper-waste.

In a country teeming with fibres, it is a surprising fact that the question of a paper-fibre should still be under consideration. European writers seem always to forget the immense size of the continent of India, and that a few hundred miles are of little consideration in most Indian questions; but when this assumes the form of railway freight upon a bulky article, it becomes prohibitive even to industries that can afford to pay more than paper-making. To cultivate fibre specially for paper has many drawbacks, and but one need be mentioned—the cost of land near commercial centres is so high as to almost preclude the idea of the cultivation of paper-fibres. But the paper-fibre must be, like esparto, fit almost for immediate immersion in the vats, for paper-making can never pay for cultivation and separation of fibre, even where land can be got at a merely nominal rent. No fibre known to commerce can compete with jute in point of cheapness, yet the paper-maker can afford to purchase jute waste and jute cuttings only, so that but for the demand for an altogether different purpose, the paper-maker could never procure jute. The two most important indigenous paper grass-fibres in India are *munj* grass and *bhabar* grass. These are now being largely used by our Indian paper mills, the supply at a remunerative price being the chief obstacle. The roots and lower stems of rice have been suggested as a paper material, and if it is proved that these are worth the trouble of collecting, the supply might be practically unlimited, but it is doubtful whether the paper-maker could pay sufficient to cover freight and expense of collection. It has been demonstrated that bamboo affords excellent paper, but practical difficulties exist which have, for the present at least, dispelled the hopes once entertained of the immense tracts of bamboo forest becoming of commercial value.

The most valuable paper materials in India are old rags, waste gunny-bags, and *sunn* ropes.

The exports of rags and other paper materials for the last five years were:—

	Rs.
1880–81	2,97,774
1881–82	2,37,120
1882–83	3,54,014
1883–84	3,63,659
1884–85	3,70,533

The following is the analysis of exports for the year 1884–85:—

Presidency from which exported.	Value.	Country to which exported.	Value.
	Rs.		Rs.
Bengal . . .	3,22,288	United States . .	3,21,451
Bombay . .	47,341	United Kingdom .	47,300
Madras . .	904	Ceylon	1,063
		Other countries .	719
Total . .	3,70,533	Total . .	3,70,533

The imports of paper and pasteboard for the last five years were:—

		Rs.	Rs.
1880–81	General Imports . . .	48,60,076	
	Government Imports .	7,87,990	
			56,48,066
1881–82	General	47,31,342	
	Government	6,58,546	
			53,89,888
1882–83	General	33,42,989	
	Government	11,07,865	
			44,50,854
1883–84	General	37,49,127	
	Government	16,68,148	
			54,17,275
1884–85	General	35,21,026	
	Government	13,71,095	
			48,92,121

EXHIBITORS.—The Bengal Exhibition Committee undertook to supervise the collections of paper, and as the result the special show-case exhibited was designed by Mr. Grieve, Manager, Bally Paper Mills, under directions of Messrs. George Henderson & Co., Calcutta. The paper materials, the half stuffs and manufactured papers are shown side by side. A large and interesting collection of jail and native-made papers have been collected from all parts of India. The papers manufactured by the Bally Paper Mills, and by the Upper India Paper Mills, Lucknow, are shown in the paper trophy.

It is needless to attempt to specialise the leading fibres of India which might be used in paper-making. It has already been indicated that the only obstacle is one of price. Any fibre may be used for paper, but the following are a few of those most deserving of mention:—

962. ADANSONIA DIGITATA, *Linn.*; Malvaceæ. The Baobab Tree or the Monkey Bread Tree of Africa. Cultivated in some parts of India to a small extent. The bark yields a strong useful fibre, which seems likely to come into use in paper manufacture.

963.* AGAVE AMERICANA, *Linn.*; Amaryllideæ. The American Aloe. A native of America, now naturalised in many parts of India. The leaves and the root yield an excellent fibre, which may become an important paper material. In experiments performed at the Bally Paper Mills, it was discovered that one of the greatest difficulties in the way of agave fibre for paper manufacture was the fact that the young leaves yielded too fine a pulp; the best leaves were those three years old. A mixture was found injurious, and therefore a difficulty exists in the necessity of getting uniformity. (*See* also 898.)

964. ANTIARIS TOXICARIA, *Leesch.*; Urticaceæ. The Travancore Sacking Tree. A gigantic tree of the evergreen forests of Burma, Western Ghâts, and Ceylon. It seems probable that the bark of this tree may come into use as a paper fibre.

965. BAMBOO. Mr. Routledge, in his pamphlet on 'Bamboo as a Paper-Making Material,' makes the following remarks: "Of all the fibre-yielding plants known to botanical science, there is not one so well calculated to meet the pressing requirements of the paper trade as 'bamboo,' both as regards facility and economy of production, as well as the quality of the 'paper-stock' which can be manufactured therefrom." While this is doubtless correct, there are practical difficulties which render it extremely improbable that bamboo will ever come into use as a paper material. The difficulty of getting a continuous supply of young shoots without injuring, if not killing, the clumps, after two or three years, the heavy charges likely to be incurred in conveying the material from malarious jungles to the mill, and the fact of the scales and young stems being covered with hairs which cannot be removed, render the bamboo practically unsuitable for paper-making. Experiments recently conducted have proved that a clump of bamboo is killed after a very few years if a large percentage of the shoots be systematically removed. The natives of India and of China, however, do make paper from bamboo, and do not appear to regard it as absolutely necessary to use the young shoots only. (*See* also 333.)

966. BROUSSONETIA PAPYRIFERA, *Vent.*; Urticaceæ. A small tree, said to be wild in the Martaban hills. The Japanese make paper from the bark. There is, perhaps, no plant that offers a better future than this as a source of paper fibre, and if extensively cultivated by the villagers as a hedge, would undoubtedly become a distinct source of revenue. Samples of native-made Broussonetia paper are exhibited. (*See* also 909.)

967. CORCHORUS OLITORIUS, *Linn.*; and C. CAPSULARIS, *Linn.*; Tiliaceæ. The Jute Plant. These plants are extensively cultivated for their fibre. The rejections and cuttings are largely employed in paper-making both in India and Europe. (*See* also 427, 547, 961.)

968. CROTOLARIA JUNCEA, *Linn.*; Leguminosæ. The Sunn. The plant is extensively cultivated all over India for its fibre. The waste is utilised in paper manufacture, but it would never pay to cultivate the plant solely for paper, and the uses of *sunn* are limited, so that the amount of waste available is comparatively small. (*See* also 428, 913*a*.)

969. DAPHNE LONGIFOLIA, *Meisn.*; D. PAPYRACEA, *Wall*; and D. WALLICHII, *Meisn.*; Thymelæaceæ. The barks of the above plants are used in the manufacture of paper. The so-called Nepal paper is prepared from the bark of the first two. As these plants, however, require a warm-temperate climate, the cultivation would have to be conducted on the hills and therefore at a distance from commercial centres and paper mills, so that, although this affords a remarkably strong paper, the fibre does not seem likely to ever become of much importance.

Extensive collections of Nepal papers are exhibited. (*See* also 915.)

970. EDGEWORTHIA GARDENERI, *Meisn.*; Thymelæaceæ. A large, elegant bush, found along the Himálaya from Nepal to Sikkim and Bhután, and recently found plentiful on the mountains of Manipur, extending to the northern frontier of Burma.

The finest Nepal paper is said to be made from the fibre of this plant, which is purer and cleaner than the paper from *Daphne papyracea*. The same remarks as have already been made with regard to a possible development of the trade in *Daphne* fibre is applicable to this plant also. (*See* also 917.)

971. HELICTERES ISORA, *Linn.*; Sterculiaceæ. A large shrub in the tropical and sub-tropical regions of India. The fibre from the bark might become serviceable as a paper material were it not for the fact that it will scarcely pay to cultivate for paper alone any fibre that requires to be extracted. The plant could be cultivated to any extent throughout India as a hedge. (*See* also 922.)

972. HIBISCUS CANNABINUS, *Linn.*; Malvaceæ. The hemp-leaved Hibiscus. A small, herbaceous shrub, apparently wild on the Northern Ghâts, largely cultivated for its fibre, especially in the North-West Provinces and the Punjáb. This is the chief fibre used in the manufacture of paper in the Dacca district, Bengal, and largely so also in the Madras Presidency. The fibre is too valuable, however, to be cultivated on a commercial scale for the purpose of paper alone. (*See* also 923.)

973. MUSA PARADISIACA, *Linn.*; Scitamineæ. The plantain. (*See* also 452, 532, 933.)

974. M. SAPIENTUM, *Linn.* The Banana. Considerable attention has of late years been attracted to the subject of the *Musa* fibre, as affording a paper material. It has been stated that a great future is before the paper industry of India, and that the enormous quantities of plantain stems which are annually thrown away by the natives of India as useless may yet come to be greedily purchased for paper manufacture. The principal objection to this idea is that unless cultivated within a definite area, it would never pay to collect the stems all over the country, unless some simple process could be suggested by which the people could reduce the stems to fibre so as to lessen the charges of freight.

975.* OPUNTIA DILLENII, *Haw.*; Cacteæ. The Prickly Pear. An erect, fleshy, and thorny shrub common all over the arid and dry zones of India. Originally brought from America, but now quite naturalised. Dr. Bidie, speaking of the Madras Presidency, says: "This abounds in every part of the country, and has become such a nuisance that large sums are expended annually in cutting it down and burying it, on sanitary grounds." If found suitable as a paper material, this nuisance might be converted into a source of wealth. (*See* also 609, 934.)

976. POLLINIA ERIOPODA, *Trim.*; Gramineæ. The Bharbar or Bhabui Grass. A grass met with throughout the central table-land of India from Bengal to Madras and the North-West Provinces and Central India; in some parts of the country extremely abundant.

As a paper material this grass has been reported as little inferior to esparto, and the paper made from it as of good quality. The great drawback to the fibre is that it would not pay to cultivate the grass purely for the purpose of a paper supply, and the wild plant has to be collected over wide and distant areas. The question of freight is in India one of most serious consequence, for if a bulky substance has to be carried for great distances by railway, the price of the article is enhanced to a prohibitive extent. The Indian paper mills are largely using *bhabar* grass, and samples of paper and paper-stuff made of it are exhibited by the Bally Paper Mills. (*See* also 387, 937.)

977. SACCHARUM SARA, *Roxb.*; Gramineæ. The Munj Grass. The grass is common from Bengal to North India. Munja and several other species of *saccharum* are largely used in the Upper India Paper Mill near Lucknow. Indeed, this is one of the most valuable of Indian paper materials, in some respects being even superior to *bhabar* (*Pollinia*) grass. The great obstacle to it is the difficulty of procuring a large and constant supply, and the fact that, from greed, the collectors reap the grass too near the ground, injuring materially the quality of paper through the amount of hard stems mixed with the leaves. (*See* also 388, 938.)

978. SANSEVIERIA ZEYLANICA, *Willd.*; Hæmodoraceæ. The Bowstring Hemp; Murba (*Beng.*). A stemless bush found on the coast of Bengal extending to the Madras Presidency, and common on the Coromandel Coast. The fibre from the leaves make a very superior paper, but the price of the fibre precludes an extended use. (*See* also 939.)

979.* YUCCA GLORIOSA, *Linn.*; Liliaceæ. The Adam's Needle. A native of America introduced into India. It yields, like Agave, an excellent fibre suitable for paper manufacture, but it is too valuable to be put to paper manufacture alone, and the fibre not being used in the textile industries to any appreciable extent, it is impossible to obtain a large supply of waste. (*See* also 947.)

SUB-COURT XXVII.

HIDES AND LEATHER, HAIR, WOOL, FEATHERS, AND HORNS.

Of the exhibits shown in this Sub-Court by far the most important are hides, skins, and leather. The exports of raw hides and skins in 1884–85 were valued at Rs.2,85,85,798 (£2,858,579), and of tanned hides and skins at Rs. 2,07,57,603 (£2,075,760). The former is almost entirely a Bengal trade, and the latter a Madras trade. Of cattle hides 8,374,409 were exported, and of skins 4,551,567. These figures represent 13 million animals, which either die or are killed annually to meet the export trade, but when the immense amount of leather used up in India itself is taken into consideration, it is probable that the annual death-rate of cattle in India is little short of 20 millions. The most important item of the Indian woollen trade is the imports of manufactured goods. During the year 1884-85 these were valued at Rs.11,83 427.

The following are the principal exhibits shown in this Sub-Court:—

HIDES.

980. The exports and imports of Raw Hides for the last five years were:—

	Exports. Rs.	Imports. Rs.
1880-81 . .	1,87,49,466	1,62,484
1881-82 . .	1,81,03,501	93,434
1882-83 . .	1,94,61,080	1,24,400
1883-84 . .	2,18,54,983	92,668
1884-85 . .	2,52,30,702	58,248

The following is the analysis of the exports of raw hides for the year 1884-85:—

Presidency from which exported.	Value.	Country to which exported.	Value.
	Rs.		Rs.
Bengal. . .	2,13,06,270	United Kingdom .	1,54,17,148
British Burma	17,79,393	Italy	36,18,314
Bombay . .	12,35,882	United States . .	29,09,332
Sindh . . .	8,23,560	Austria . . .	15,91,897
Madras . .	85,597	France	5,31,641
		Straits	5,08,028
		Egypt	5,07,056
		Other countries .	1,47,286
Total . .	2,52,30,702	Total . .	2,52,30,702

The exports and imports of dressed or tanned hides for the last five years were:

	Exports. Rs.	Imports. Rs.
1880-81 . .	35,21,015	1,08,417
1881-82 . .	45,29,429	1,29,498
1882-83 . .	54,36,591	1,32,185
1883-84 . .	51,43,279	1,47,768
1884-85 . .	57,10,517	97,627

The following is the analysis of the exports of hides (dressed or tanned) for the year 1884-85:—

Presidency from which exported.	Value.	Country to which exported.	Value.
	Rs.		Rs.
Madras . .	43,73,641	United Kingdom .	55,79,604
Bombay . .	8,79,961	Italy	1,06,965
Bengal. . .	4,52,969	France	6,417
British Burma	3,948	Austria . . .	5,300
		Straits	5,448
		Persia	3,019
		Aden	2,049
		Other countries .	1,715
Total . .	57,10,517	Total . .	57,10,517

SKINS.

981. The exports and imports of raw skins for the last five years were:—

	Exports. Rs.	Imports. Rs.
1880-81 . .	24,46,557	1,21,914
1881-82 . .	21,94,692	1,00,224
1882-83 . .	27,72,419	1,23,929
1883-84 . .	29,08,663	1,48,475
1884-85 . .	33,55,096	1,21,289

The following is an analysis of the exports of raw skins for the year 1884-85:—

Presidency from which exported.	Value.	Country to which exported.	Value.
	Rs.		Rs.
Bengal. . .	32,72,721	United States . .	15,74,775
Madras . .	45,142	United Kingdom .	15,37,643
Sindh . . .	30,335	France	1,63,507
Bombay , .	6,863	Italy	50,808
British Burma	35	Hong-Kong . .	8,125
		Austria . . .	13,042
		Other countries .	7,196
Total . .	33,55,096	Total . .	33,55,096

The exports and imports of skins (dressed or tanned) for the last five years were:—

	Exports. Rs.	Imports. Rs.
1880-81 . .	1,26,18,615	3,34,499
1881-82 . .	1,46,60,302	3,71,710
1882-83 . .	1,67,67,613	3,42,828
1883-84 . .	1,67,30,438	2,50,274
1884-85 . .	1,50,47,086	2,13,077

The following is the analysis of exports of skins (dressed or tanned) for the year 1884-85:—

Presidency from which exported.	Value.	Country to which exported.	Value.
	Rs.		Rs.
Madras . .	1,14,39,018	United Kingdom .	1,23,60,874
Bombay . .	32,96,984	United States . .	16,27,913
Bengal. . .	2,83,421	Austria . . .	6,85,247
Sindh . . .	27,663	Straits	1,91,514
		France	1,67,754
		Other countries .	13,784
Total . .	1,50,47,086	Total . .	1,50,47,086

LEATHER, HORNS AND BRISTLES.

982. The exports and imports of leather (unwrought and manufactured) for the past five years were—

	Exports. Rs.	Imports. Rs.
1880-81 . .	32,247	7,83,428
1881-82 . .	27,682	8,92,399
1882-83 . .	32,428	10,30,383
1883-84 . .	45,757	12,37,431
1884-85 . .	36,945	13,56,646

The imports of leather, boots and shoes for the last five years were:—

	Rs.
1880-81	5,92,401
1881-82	8,03,501
1882-83	9,28,490
1883-84	10,41,244
1884-85	9,87,953

The export trade in leather, boots and shoes during the year 1884-85 amounted to only Rs. 46,917.

Exhibitors.—Bombay Committee, Mr. A. E. Laurie, Assistant Conservator of Forests, Chamber of Commerce, Bombay; Munshi Babu Ram, Cawnpore; Mr. Amba Datt Joshi, Almora; Mr. F. Duthie, Saharanpore Government Harness and Saddle Factory, Cawnpore; Deputy Conservator of Forests, Bengal; Mr. Pootan, Cawnpore; Mr. T. B. Fry, Bombay; Messrs. Begg, Sutherland & Co., Cawnpore; Messrs. Hinde & Co., London, exhibit Indian pig-bristles.

WOOL AND PASHM.

983. The exports and imports of raw wool for the last five years were:—

	Exports. Rs.	Imports. Rs.
1880-81 . .	1,01,41,371	7,23,434
1881-82 . .	81,45,513	7,54,350
1882-83 . .	79,04,058	6,89,313
1883-84 . .	75,58,409	6,51,368
1884-85 . .	71,35,760	6,18,212

The following is the analysis of the exports of raw wool for the year 1884-85:—

Presidency from which exported.	Value.	Country to which exported.	Value.
	Rs.		Rs.
Bombay . .	57,58,951	United Kingdom .	71,14,295
Sind . . .	13,65,768	United States . .	10,464
Bengal. . .	9,220	France	10,290
Madras . .	1,821	Other countries .	711
Total . .	71,35,760	Total . .	71,35,760

The exports and imports of woollen manufactures for the last five years were:—

	Exports. Rs.	Imports. Rs.
1880-81 . .	21,02,752	1,29,91,299
1881-82 . .	19,66,830	1,12,12,320
1882-83 . .	15,83,494	98,48,725
1883-84 . .	12,07,003	1,21,70,531
1884-85 . .	11,83,427	1,23,43,397

The following is the analysis of the imports of woollen manufactures for the year 1884-85:—

Presidency to which imported.	Value.	Country from which imported.	Value.
	Rs.		Rs.
Bengal. . .	53,58,117	United Kingdom .	1,17,75,763
Bombay . .	50,13,207	Germany . . .	2,25,260
British Burma	14,66,457	Persia	1,08,837
Madras . .	3,85,692	Austria . . .	59,729
Sindh . . .	1,19,924	Belgium . . .	54,696
		France	48,759
		Straits	41,083
		Other countries .	10,29,270
Total . .	1,23,43,397	Total . .	1,23,43,397

FEATHERS.

984. The exports of feathers for the last five years were—

	Rs.
1880-81	2,69,447
1881-82	2,89,659
1882-83	3,04,253
1883-84	4,76,389
1884-85	6,33,017

The following is an analysis of the exports of feathers for the year 1884-85:—

Presidency from which exported.	Value.	Country to which exported.	Value.
	Rs.		Rs.
Bengal . .	5,52,609	United Kingdom .	5,51,788
Bombay . .	36,178	Hong.Kong . .	47,564
British Burma	22,962	Straits	31,690
Madras . .	21,268	Australia . . .	1,572
		Other countries .	700
Total . .	6,33,017	Total . .	6,33,017

Exhibitors of Wool:—Messrs. Davee Sahai Chumba Mull, Amritsar, Punjáb; Messrs. Divi Sahai Prub Dial, Amritsar and Bikanir Durbar.

In this section of the Court will also be found an interesting set of the snakes of India contributed by Col. R. H. Beddome, and two special collections of birds. Mr. E. C. Buck's game birds of India, and Mr. E. J. Moore's special show of Assam birds. It was not intended that the Exhibition should deal with collections of the Natural History of India, but the Kuch Behar trophy may be accepted as representative of the leading animals of India. Fine collections of Indian Butterflies has been contributed by Private T. Allen and Drummer Juett, of the Royal Fusiliers.

SUB-COURT XXVIII.

The Exhibits shown in this Sub-Court appear in the "Classified List" under Division IV.

THE OILS, OIL-SEEDS, SOAP, PERFUMERY.

Oil-Seeds.—In Mr. J. E. O'Conor's 'Trade and Navigation Returns' the oil-seeds are given under the heading "Seeds." A few of these may possibly be used as spices and condiments; or may be distilled for their essential oils. This is an unavoidable difficulty, but the amounts of doubtful or undefined seeds are comparatively small, so that the returns under "Seeds" may be accepted as meaning "Oil-seeds." In his review of the sea-borne foreign trade for 1884-85, Mr. O'Conor says of these seeds: "This trade has developed in recent years into one of the first importance, exceeding greatly the trade in wheat, rice, jute, both raw and manufactured combined, indigo, or tea, and being exceeded only by cotton and opium. The way in which this trade has augmented during the last six years will be apparent from the figures placed below:—

	Cwts.	Rs.
1879–80	7,091,469	4,68,58,929
1880–81	10,229,109	6,34,52,089
1881–82	10,466,098	6,05,40,987
1882–83	13,139,206	7,20,03,365
1883–84	17,355,588	10,08,37,583
1884–85	18,250,688	10,74,52,035

"The trade increased during the year in quantity by a little more than 5 per cent., in value by 6½ per cent. The increase in five years was about 78½ per cent. in quantity, and 69½ per cent. in value.

"Linseed, rape-seed, til or gingelly seed (sesame), poppy seed, earthnuts, and castor seed are the principal kinds of seed. They have here been mentioned in the order of their respective aggregate values last year, thus—

	Rs.
Linseed	4,91,29,344
Rape-seed	2,68,35,906
Sesame	1,92,30,128
Poppy	40,91,595
Earthnuts	36,14,063
Castor	21,03,379

"Their values amounted to 1,050 lakhs, all other kinds together representing only 24½ lakhs in value."

Prepared Oils.—The enormous amount of oil-seeds exported from India is out of all proportion to the quantity of prepared oils. It has been repeatedly pointed out that mills for the preparation of oil in India would seem likely to prove highly remunerative. The following are the exports of prepared oils for the six years ending March, 1885:—

	1879–80.	1880–81.	1881–82.
Gallons	4,205,815	4,999,184	4,305,176
Rupees	56,94,532	58,11,394	46,82,274

	1882–83.	1883–84.	1884–85.
Gallons	3,644,632	4,337,151	5,120,504
Rupees	41,62,768	49,59,768	53,40,411

Of these exports nearly three-fourths are castor oil: of cocoanut oil, the only other oil of any importance, 1,553,887 gallons, valued at Rs. 16,20,128, were shipped to the United Kingdom and France in 1884–85.

The above quotations include small quantities of animal, essential, and mineral oils in addition to the vegetable oils. The exports of animal oils do not seem to be of much importance, though the value has gradually increased from Rs. 3,478 in 1880–81 to Rs. 61,618 in 1884–85. The import trade is also improving, the figures in 1880-81 and 1884-85 being Rs. 24,246 and Rs. 33,253 respectively. The trade in essential oils is of more importance; but the exports have decreased in value from Rs. 3,40,452 in 1882–83 to Rs. 1,85,917 in 1884-85. The imports have improved from Rs. 29,611 in 1880–81 to Rs. 41,542 in 1884-85. The export trade in mineral oils is not extensive; during the last year it was valued at Rs. 27,165. The imports, on the other hand, are of great value. They consist almost exclusively of kerosine oil from the United States. This oil has increased from 9,692,269 gallons five years ago, to 26,299,091 gallons last year, the corresponding values being Rs. 46,58,820, and Rs. 1,11,00,507.

There are over 300 plants known in India to yield oils or perfumes, but the following may be enumerated as the most interesting and useful:—

985.* Acorus Calamus, *Linn.*; Aroideæ. An essential oil, used by perfumers. (*See* also 746.)

986.* Aleurites moluccana, *Willd.*; Euphorbiaceæ. The Candle-nut or Belgaum Walnut. This contains 50 per cent. of oil—*kekuna oil*. (*See* also 629.)

987.* Anacardium occidentale, *Linn.*; Anacardiaceæ. The Cashew Nut or Cardole. This plant yields two distinct oils—a bland oil obtained from the kernels and cardole from the outer shell of the nut. Of the former 40 per cent. is obtained, and of the latter 29 per cent. (*See* also 31, 630.)

988. Andropogon citratus, *DC.*; Gramineæ. The Lemon Grass.

989. A. muricatus, *Retz.* The Khas-khas (*See* also 321.)

990. A. Nardus, *Linn.* The Citronella.

991. A. Schœnanthus, *Linn.* The Geranium or Rusa Oil Grass. (*See* also 323.)

992. Aquilaria Agallocha, *Roxb.*; Thymelæaceæ. The Agar or Eaglewood. (See also 36, 755, 1087.)

993.* Arachis hypogœa, *Linn.*; Leguminosæ. The Ground-nut or Earth-nut. The cultivation of this nut may be described as a modern industry, the trade in oil, as a substitute for olive oil, having, within the past thirty or forty years, developed in an almost unprecedented manner. The exports from India of the seed were in 1878–79 valued at Rs. 1,68.420, but in 1884-85 they amounted to Rs. 36,14,063, and the exports from French ports in India a little less than that amount, so that the total exports from India are just under half a million of pounds sterling. France is said to import from all countries 33½ million francs worth of the nuts, of which India supplies only 2½ million. so that even with its present flourishing condition, the trade has by no means reached its greatest possible development. The seeds contain 52 per cent. of oil. (*See* also 631.)

994. BASSIA BUTYRACEA, *Roxb.*; Sapotaceæ. The Indian Butter Tree. A vegetable butter is extracted from the seed, which makes good soap.

995. B. LATIFOLIA, *Roxb.* The Mahúa. (*See* also 45, 410, 709, 1091.)

996. B. LONGIFOLIA, *Willd.* The Mahúa of South India. The seed of this and of the preceding yield good oils.

997.* BRASSIAC CAMPESTRIS, *Linn.*; var. 1, *campestris* proper (*Sinapis dichotoma*, Roxb.). The Cole seed; var. 2, *glauca*—The Sarson or Rape; and var. 3, *Toria* (*Brassica glauca*, Royle); Cruciferæ. The trade in rape seed has rapidly increased from 1,255,580 cwt., valued at Rs. 67,10,228 in 1880–81 to 4,521,933 cwt., valued at Rs. 2,68,35,906 in 1884–85, or 260 per cent. in quantity, and nearly 300 per cent. in value during the last five years. Of the total quantity exported last year England took 1,881,207 cwt., and France 1,194,328 cwt. (*See* also 653.)

998. BRASSICA JUNCEA, *H. f. & T.* The Indian Mustard. The names Rape and Mustard are very obscurely applied to the forms of this and the preceding. The subject requires to be more carefully worked up. The internal trade returns are sometimes published as "Rape," at other times as "Mustard," or again under the joint heading "Rape and Mustard." The true mustard is scarcely met with in India. Collectively the foreign exports of rape and mustard for the year 1884–85 were 4,559,281 cwt., valued at Rs. 2,70,99,632—nearly £3,000,000. (*See* also 546.)

999. BUCHANANIA LATIFOLIA, *Roxb.*; Anacardiaceæ. The Chirauli. The oil is obtained from the kernels of this fruit, but owing to these being so much eaten, the oil is rarely prepared. (*See* also 57, 635.)

1000. BUTTER. Indian butter is very inferior to that of Europe, and is chiefly used in the form of ghi or clarified butter.

1001. CALOPHYLLUM INOPHYLLUM, *Linn.*; Guttiferæ. The Alexandrian Laurel or Sultana Champa. The fresh seeds yield a quantity of fragrant, green oil. A curious fact regarding this oil is that, though it cannot compete with castor oil for industrial purposes, in the Calcutta market it fetches about four times the Calcutta price of castor oil in Burma. The oil is said to be chiefly used for burning. (*See* also 63.)

1002. CAMELLIA THEIFERA, *Griff.*; Ternstrœmiaceæ. Tea Seed Oil. An excellent sample of this oil is contributed by the Forest Department of Assam. It is a limpid, clear, tasteless oil of an amber colour resembling olive oil.

1003.* CAMPHOR. This term is technically given to a number of gum-resins derived from (1) *Cinnamomum camphora*, Nees,—the Chinese camphor; (2) *Dryobalanops camphora*, Colebr.,—the Barus or Sumatra camphor; and (3) *Blumea balsamifera*, DC., Ngai camphor.

1004. CANANGA ODORATA, *H. f. & T.*; Anonaceæ. This yields the perfume Ilang-Ilang.

1005. CARTHAMUS TINCTORIUS, *Linn.*; Compositæ. The Safflower or Kusum. The seed of this plant yields an oil useful for burning, as it gives out very little heat: it is also eaten, and is said to be an ingredient in "Macassar hair-oil." (See also 420, 1139.)

1006. CARUM CARUI, *Linn.*; Umbelliferæ. The Caraway. A valuable essential oil, called Caraway oil, is obtained from the seed; this is used in medicine, also as a perfume for soap.

1007.* CARYOPHYLLUS AROMATICUS, *Linn.*; Myrtaceæ. The Cloves. The colourless or yellowish essential oil obtained from the flower-buds and flower stalks is extensively used in the manufacture of perfumery.

1008. CINNAMOMUM ZEYLANICUM, *Breyn.*; Laurineæ. The important Cinnamon oils are obtained from this plant, and are of three kinds, viz., oil extracted from the bark, from the leaves, and from the root. These oils are largely used in perfumery, especially the first.

1009. CITRUS MEDICA, *Linn.*, var. LIMETTA; Rutaceæ. The Sweet Lime of India. The essential oil known as the "Essence of Lemon" is extracted from the rind of the fruit. It is extensively used in perfumery.

1010. CLEOME VISCOSA, *Linn.*; Capparideæ. Sometimes known as Wild Mustard. A thin, light oil is expressed from the seed, which is likely to prove useful where a very liquid oil is required. The plant being a common weed in Bengal, the oil could be prepared to any extent.

1011.* COCOS NUCIFERA, *Linn.*; Palmæ. The Cocoanut. The well-known cocoanut oil is extracted from the kernel of the fruit, about 36 per cent. being obtained. It is largely exported to Europe, where it is used in the manufacture of candles and soap. During the year 1884–85 cocoanut oil to the value of Rs. 16,20,128 was exported. (*See* also 85, 660, 715, 913.)

1012. CROTON TIGLIUM, *Linn.*; Euphorbiaceæ. The Purging Croton. The seed yields a valuable medicinal oil, which is used as a drastic purgative.

1013. DIPTEROCARPUS TURBINATUS, *Gærtn. f.*; Dipterocarpeæ. Gurgun or Wood Oil. The wood oil obtained from this tree (as also from one or two allied species) is used in painting houses and ships, as well as in medicine—a remedy for skin diseases. (*See* also 107, 1070.)

1014. ELLETARIA CARDAMOMUM, *Maton.*; Scitamineæ. The Lesser Cardamom. An oil is extracted from the fruits by distillation. (*See* also 664.)

1015. ERUCA SATIVA, *Lam*; Cruciferæ. The oil expressed from the seed is largely used in Upper India for burning purposes. (*See* also 430, 665.)

1016. EUPHORBIA DRACUNCULOIDES, *Lam.*; Euphorbiaceæ. Chaqul-Púputː. The oil obtained from this tree is used as a drying oil and for burning. In 1843 the London brokers pronounced it more valuable than linseed oil.

1017. EXCÆCARIA SEBIFERA, *Müll. Arg.* Euphorbiaceæ. The Chinese Tallow Tree. The seed yields an oil resembling white and solid tallow; it is pure and inodorous, and is employed in the manufacture of candles.

1018. GARCINIA INDICA, *Choisy.*; Guttiferæ. The Kokum Butter, as the oil from the seed of this plant is called, is recommended for many medicinal purposes.

1019. G. MORELLA, *Desv.* The Gamboge Tree. A semi-solid fat or kokum obtained from the seed is burnt as a lamp oil by the rich, and eaten as a substitute for *ghí* by the poor. (*See* also 803, 1109.)

1020. GOSSYPIUM HERBACEUM, *Linn.*; Malvaceæ. The Cotton Seed Oil. The various forms of cotton seed all yield good oils capable of being refined. About 28 per cent. of oil to the weight of seed is obtained. Cotton oil is useful for lamps.

1021. GUIZOTIA ABYSSYNICA, *Cass.*; Compositæ. The Niger-seed and Oil. The seed yields a limpid, clear, pale, sweet-tasted oil, used for culinary purposes.

1022. GYNOCARDIA ODORATA, *B. Br.*; Bixineæ. The Chaulmagra Oil. The oil obtained by expression from the seeds is a valuable remedy for cutaneous diseases.

1023. HELIANTHUS ANNUUS, *Linn.*; Compositæ. The Sunflower. A clear, fluid oil, resembling ground-nut oil, is obtained from the seed of this plant; about 22 per cent. may be expressed.

1024. JASMINUM GRANDIFLORUM, *Linn.*; Oleaceæ. The Spanish Jasmine.

1025. J. SAMBAC, *Aiton.* The Arabian Jasmine. The flowers of this and the preceding are largely used in the preparation of perfumed oils and ottos.

1026. JATROPHA CURCAS, *Linn.*; Euphorbiaceæ. The Physic Nut. The seed yields about 30 per cent. of a pale-coloured oil: it is used for burning in lamps, and in medicine as a purgative. (*See* also 814.)

1027. JUGLANS REGIA, *Linn.*; Juglandeæ. The Walnut. The kernels yield about 32 per cent. of oil; this is largely expressed in Kashmir. (See also 157, 639.)

1028. LINUM USITATISSIMUM, *Linn.*; Lineæ. The Linseed Oil. The well-known Linseed oil is obtained from the seeds of this plant, which yield about 38 per cent. of oil. Upwards of five million cwt. of this seed, valued at three crores of rupees, are annually exported from India. The figures of the export trade of Linseed during the last five years show an increase from 5,997,172 cwt. in 1880–81 to 8,746,596 cwt. in 1884–85, *i.e.*, nearly 46 per cent. The diversion of this trade from Calcutta to Bombay is very striking; in 1880–81 Calcutta exported 4,065,341 cwt., and Bombay only 1,925,524 cwt., whereas in 1884–85 they exported 3,757,018 cwt., and 4,989,578 cwt., respectively. The bulk of the exports go to the United Kingdom, viz., 4,731,138 cwt., France receiving only 1,656,659 cwt., and the United States 1,231,437 cwt.

1029. MELALEUCA LEUCADENDRON, *Linn.*; Myrtaceæ. The Cajput Oil Tree. The leaves of this tree yield Cajput oil, largely exported from the Malay Archipelago. It is used in medicine as a stimulant and diaphoretic.

1030. MORINGA PTERYGOSPERMA, *Gærtn.*; Moringeæ. The Horse-radish Tree. The Ben or Moringa oil of watch-makers is obtained from the seeds of this plant; it is used for medicinal purposes. Very little, however, is extracted in India, but, as the tree is very common, the subject appears to deserve attention. (*See* also 531, 1075.)

1031. MURRAYA KŒNIGII, *Spr.*; Rutaceæ. The clear, transparent oil known as *Simboli*, or *Limboli*, is obtained from the seeds of this tree.

1032. MYRISTICA MOSCHATA, *Willd.*; Myristaceæ. The mace and the nutmeg both yield an essential and a fixed oil. The former enters largely into the composition of European perfumery, especially Frangipani. A soap, known as Banda soap, was once upon a time prepared from the fatty oil or butter of nutmegs. (*See* also 669.)

1033. NARDOSTACHYS JATAMANSI, *DC.*; Valerianaceæ. The Spikenard. The root is largely used in native perfumery. (*See* also 823.)

1034. OLEA FERRUGINEA, *Royle*; Oleaceæ. In Afghánistán an oil is obtained from this tree, which would doubtless take an important place in the oil trade were it procurable in large quantities; it is as good in quality as the ordinary olive oil. The olive tree, *Olea europea*, Linn., has been introduced in the hills, and there seems no reason why India might not take a place amongst the countries which supply the olive oil of commerce. Olive kernels yield 44 per cent. of oil, and olive pulp 39 per cent.

1035.* PAPAVER SOMNIFERUM, *Linn.*; Papaveraceæ. The Poppy. An oil is expressed from the seeds and is used for culinary purposes and as a demulcent medicine; the seeds yield 45 per cent. of oil. The trade in poppy seeds is a fluctuating one. Last year 660,000 cwt., valued at £400,000, were exported; this was an increase of 28 per cent. in quantity and 35 per cent. in value over the figures of 1883–84. France receives about half the exports. (*See* also 735, 831.)

1036.* PIMPINELLA ANISUM, *Linn.* The Anise Seed. An essential oil obtained from the fruit is largely used in the preparation of cordials. It is also employed for scenting soaps and pomatums. (*See* also 677.)

1037. PISTACIA VERA, *Linn.*; Anacardiaceæ. The Pistachio Nut. The oil extracted from the kernels is used medicinally as a demulcent and restorative. (*See* also 642.)

1038. POGOSTEMON PATCHOULY, *Pellet*; Labiatæ. The Patchouli. An essential oil is obtained from this plant and used as a perfume.

1039. PONGAMIA GLABRA, *Vent.*; Leguminosæ. The seed yields a red-brown, thick oil, used for burning, and medicinally as a very valuable application for diseases and irritation of the skin. (*See* also 216, 459, 839.)

1040. PRUNUS AMYGDALUS, *Baillon.*; Rosaceæ. The Almond Oil. Is largely used in perfumery, and as a medicine; the kernels contain 53 per cent. of oil. (*See* also 643, 1079.)

1041. RHUS SUCCEDANEA, *Linn.*; Anacardiaceæ. The seed yields a fine, yellowish-white wax, known in commerce as "Japan Wax." (*See* also 1114.)

1042. RHUS WALLICHII, *Hook.* The seed yields a fine, yellowish-white wax, similar to that obtained from the preceding.

1043.* RICINUS COMMUNIS, *Linn.*; Euphorbiaceæ. The Castor-oil Plant. The seed yields by expression the well-known Castor-oil. The annual export of the oil from India is above three million gallons, valued at about thirty lakhs of rupees. In Castor seed the trade is still comparatively small, but it has grown very quickly, the figures for 1880-81 and 1884-85 being 76,461 cwt., value Rs. 4,33,858, and 476,396 cwt., value Rs. 21,03,379 respectively. Last year France took the largest quantity (194,190 cwt.). (*See* also 843, 1172.)

1044. ROSA ALBA, *Linn.*; Rosaceæ. The Rose Oil or Otto of Roses. Is largely made in the North-West Provinces and the Punjab.

1045. SANTALUM ALBUM, *Linn.*; Santalaceæ. The True Sandal-wood. The roots yield a scented oil, largely used as a basis in the manufacture of different kinds of ottos. The seed by expression gives a thick viscid oil, which is burnt in lamps. (*See* also 844.)

1046. SESAMUM INDICUM, *Linn.*; Pedalineæ. The Gingelly or Sesame-oil. Large quantities of oil are extracted from the seed of this plant by simple expression; 51 per cent. being obtained. This oil is in India used for culinary purposes, and to anoint the body; also in soap manufacture and as a lamp oil. The annual export of the seed is nearly two million cwt., valued at about £1,200,000. The export of til or gingelly rose from 1,907,008 cwt., value Rs. 1,31,26,933 in 1880-81, to 2,853,382 cwt., value Rs. 1,97,97,536 in 1883-84; but in 1884-85 it decreased to 2,646,484 cwt., value Rs. 1,92,30,128. The bulk of this seed is shipped to the Continent, principally to France and Italy. (*See* also 847.)

1047.* TAMARINDUS INDICA, *Linn.*; Leguminosæ. The Tamarind. The seed yields a clear, bright oil free from smell and suitable for culinary purposes. In times of famine they are roasted and eaten, but ordinarily they are thrown away as useless. The oil which may be prepared from them appears to have escaped the attention of the natives, but it might be expressed in large quantities. (*See* also 273, 555, 624, 853.)

1048. TECTONA GRANDIS, *Linn.*; Verbenaceæ. The Teak Tree. The oil obtained from teak-wood is used as a varnish for wood-work. (*See* also 277.)

1049. TERMINALIA CATAPPA, *Linn.*; Combretaceæ. The Indian Almond. The seeds yield a limpid oil resembling almond oil. It does not get rancid so readily as the true almond oil.

1050. VATERIA INDICA, *Linn.*; Dipterocarpeæ. The Piney Varnish or Indian Copal Tree. The seed yields a solid, concrete fat, suitable for the manufacture of candles and soap. (*See* also 293, 1084.)

EXHIBITORS.—Dr. Kanni Lal De, C.I.E., Calcutta; Dr. Moodeen Sheriff, Madras; Mr. Abbhai Naidu, Herbarium keeper, Madras Museum; North-West Provinces Soap Manufacturing Company, Mirut.

PERFUMERY.

In the foregoing enumeration of the oils and oil-seeds of India, a few of the more important perfumes have been alluded to, but it is necessary in this place to specify the collections of prepared perfumes and essences.

I.—*A Collection of Essential Oils or Atars from Indian Herbs, Flowers, Fruits, &c. Exhibited by* DR. KANNY LOLL DEO, RAI BAHADUR, C.I.E., F.C.S., &c.

1. Aghor Chandau (*Aquillaria Agallocha*). 2. Ajvan Atar (*Ptychotis Ajowan*). 3. Aimb Atar (*Mangifera Indica*). 4. Bedmûsk Atar (*Salix Caprea*). 5. Bela Atar (*Jasminum sambac*). 6. Bakul Atar (*Mimusops elengi*). 7. Chameli Atar (*Jasminum grandiflorum*). 8. Champa Atar (*Michelia Champaca*). 9. Dalchim Atar (*Cinnamomum Zeylanicum*). 10. Dona Atar (*Artemisia Indica*). 11. Gunda Atar (*Tagetes erecta*). 12. Golab Atar (*Rosa Damascena*). 13. Hena Atar (*Lawsonia inermis*). 14. Jafran Atar (*Crocus sativus*). 15. Jui Atar (*Jasminum auriculatum*). 16. Kamla Nebu Atar (*Citrus aurantii*). 17. Kaora Atar (*Pandanus odoratissimus*). 18. Kurankusha Atar (*Andropogon iwarancusa*). 19. Kurna Atar (*Citrus Limoni*). 20. Khuskhus Atar (*Andropogon muricatum*). 21. Labanga Atar (*Caryophyllus aromaticus*). 22. Mati Atar (Rock Oil). 23. Mouri Atar (*Fœniculum Panmourium*). 24. Nagkesor Atar (*Mesua ferrea*). 25. Nebur Atar (*Citronella*, Ceylon). 26. Pan Atar (*Chavica*, Betel). 27. Pachapal Atar (*Pogostemon patchouli*). 28. Payara Atar (*Psidium guava*). 29. Susa Atar (*Cucumis sativus*). 30. Sassiferus Atar (*Camphora grandiflora*). 31. Sewly Atar (*Nyctanthes arbortristis*). 32. Soûnti Atar (*Chrysanthemum Roxburghii*). 33. Sohag Atar (from mixed herbs). 34. Sulpha Atar (*Anethum Sowa*). 35. Chandan Atar (*Santalum album*).

II.—*List of Perfumes and Essences Exhibited by* R. H. BANA AND CO., *Navsari.*

Guards Bouquet, 1 bot.; Lisbon Water, 1 bot.; Fragrant Lavender Water, 1 bot.; Eau de Millefleurs, 1 bot.; Esprit de Boquet, 1 bot.; Jockey Club Bouquet, 1 bot.; Esprit de Rose, 1 bot.; Frangipanni Boquet, 1 bot.; Eau de Jasmin, 1 bot.; Royal Hunt Bouquet, 1 bot.; Essence of Randeletia, 1 bot.; H. H. Guicowar's Perfume, 1 bot. Essence of Nutmeg; Extract of Black Pepper; Flavouring Essence; Extract of Ginger; Extract of Capsicum; Essence of Lemon; Essence of Coriander; Essence of Cloves; Essence of Orange; Essence of Rose; Essence of Cinnamon; Essence of Carraway.

SUB-COURTS XXIX.—XXXII.

(*See* Part II.—ETHNOLOGY.)

SUB-COURT XXXIII.

GUMS AND RESINS.

The gums of India have been entirely overlooked, and the result is that not a single Indian gum is to-day of any commercial value. The so-called East Indian Gum-arabic is gum brought from the Red Sea ports to Bombay and thence re-exported to Europe. The following are the principal gum and resin-yielding trees of India:—

1051. Acacia arabica, *Willd.*; Leguminosæ. The Indian Gum-Arabic; Babul, Kikar (*Hind.*). Wild probably in Sind, Rajputana, Guzerat, and the Northern Deccan; cultivated throughout the greater part of India except in the most humid regions on the coast. The gum is a tolerable substitute for the true gum-arabic, but the mucilage is weak, and the red colour often objectionable. It exudes chiefly in March and April, each tree yielding about 2 lbs. In the bazaars it occurs in the form of irregular and broken tears, agglutinated in masses, each tear about half an inch in size, and brown or red to light straw colour. This gum is very wholesome, and in times of scarcity is often eaten. The principal English supply is from Egypt; France obtaining its gum from Senegal. (*See* also 4, 403, 484. 1128.)

1052. A. Catechu, *Willd.* Common in most parts of India and Burma, extending in the sub-Himálayan tract westward to the Indus and eastward to Sikkim. Admirable samples of this gum have been contributed by the Forest Department. It exists in the form of large transparent round tears of clean gum. The solution affords a useful and strong adhesive gum. (*See* also 5, 648, 742, 1085, 1129.)

1053. A. Modesta, *Wall.* Phulahi (*Pb.*). Found in the Sulaiman and Salt Ranges, the sub-Himálayan tract, between the Indus and the Sutlej, and the northern part of the Punjáb plains. The gum is used in native medicine and calico-printing. It occurs in small, round, smooth, sub-translucent tears. It is used by the Lucknow printers under the name of *bábúl*.

1054. Acacia senegal, *Willd.* Khor (*Sind.*). The tree is chiefly found in Sind and Ajmere; abundant in West Africa north of the Senegal river. It yields a gum which is collected and sold in Sind with that of *A. arabica.* The gum exudes naturally from the tree in large quantities. Trade in this gum from Sind and Rajputana is capable of the utmost development. This is supposed to be one of the commercial forms of gum-arabic—the gum known as White Senar or Picked Turkey. This tree is also said to yield the white gum of the upper Nile.

1055. Anogeissus latifolia, *Wall.*; Combretaceæ. Dhawa (*Hind.*). Found in the sub-Himálayan tract from the Ravi eastward, and Central and South India; very plentiful in Melghát. It yields a gum which is extensively sold for use in calico-printing. It occurs in clear, straw-coloured, elongated tears adhering into masses, sometimes honey-coloured or even brown from impurities. As an adhesive gum it is inferior in strength to gum-arabic, in consequence of which it commands a much lower price in Europe, the more so since it is nearly always mixed with the bark of the tree, sand, and other impurities, and adulterated with the brown tears which are probably derived from some other plant than *Anogeissus*. In India the reputation of this gum stands high with the calico-printers, especially of Lucknow, and it is probable it possesses some specific peculiarity justifying this preference, since it is used with certain dye-stuffs, such as with *haldi* (*Curcuma longa*), while gum-arabic or *bábúl* is used with madder (*Rubia cordifolia*). *Dhawa* or *bakli* gum is generally collected in April. (*See* also 33, 1132.)

1056. Balsamodendron Mukul, *Hk.*; Burseraceæ. The Gum Gugul; Guggul (*Hind.*). Met with in the arid zones of Sind, Kattiwar, Rajputana, and Khandesh. It yields the gum-resin known as *Gugul* and also as *Indian Bdellium.* This occurs in vermicular or stalactitic pieces, is of a brown or dull green colour, and has a bitter, acrid taste. It is not brittle, and swells when heated, diffusing a disagreeable odour. It is also used in medicines like Myrrh. (*See* also 41, 762.)

1057.* B. Myrrha, *Nees.* The Myrrh; Bol (*Hind.*). This is at least one of the trees from which the Myrrh of commerce is obtained, but it does not seem to be determined whether *B. Myrrha* is the plant which yields the true Myrrh or not. The article occurs in the form of tears of irregular shape and variable size: it is somewhat translucent, of a reddish-yellow or reddish-brown colour, has an agreeable, aromatic odour, and a bitter acrid taste. It is partly soluble in water, alcohol, and ether, and is chiefly used in medicine. In Bombay—the great emporium of Myrrh—there are four kinds met with in the bazaars, viz.:—(1) The African Myrrh, known in Bombay as *karam* or *bandar-karum*; this is regarded as the true Myrrh, or that of best quality. On the bags containing Myrrh arriving from Africa they are opened and sorted into four kinds, of which the best qualities are re-exported to Europe; (2) Arabian, or *meetiya*, mostly sold in Bombay as true Myrrh, for which it might easily be mistaken; (3) The Siam Myrrh, also called *meetiya*, from which it can hardly be distinguished; this is largely imported into Calcutta and Bombay where it is known as *chinai-bol;* (4) The Persian Myrrh, the source of which is unknown: in 1882, 1,000 cwts. were imported into Bombay. Myrrh is chiefly adulterated with inferior qualities, or with the gums and resins derived from other species of *Balsamodendron.* (*See* also 763.)

1058. Balsamodendron Roxburghii, *Arn.* Gugala (*Beng.*). A small tree of Eastern Bengal, Assam, and Berar. It yields a gum-resin of a greenish colour, moist, and easily broken, having a peculiar cedar-like odour; it is largely supplied to the Bombay market from Oomraoti, and is much used by masons to mix with fine plaster. (*See* also 765.)

1059. Bombax malabaricum, *DC.*; Malvaceæ. The Silk Cotton Tree; Simul (*Hind.*). A common tree throughout the hotter forests of India and Burma, ascending the Himálaya to 4,000 ft. in altitude. It yields a brown gum (*mocha-ras, i.e.,* juice of *mocha*) used in native medicine. This belongs to the dark or Mor nga series, and, like the other false Tragacanth gums, is of little commercial value. It is collected by the Bhils and wandering tribes of Western India and sold by the druggists at Rs. 4 per maund of 37½ lbs. An interesting series of samples of this gum has been contributed by the officers of the Forest Department from almost every province in India. These have put at rest all doubt as to the large, red, inflated, gall-like masses sold as *Mocha-ras* being actually the produce of this tree. Great doubt for long existed regarding this point in consequence chiefly of the fact that these round masses are sometimes known as *Supári-ka-phul,* the flowers of the betel-nut palm. (*See* also 53, 413, 908, 938.)

1060.* Boswellia (species not determined); Burseraceæ. The true Frankincense or Olibanum of European Commerce; Kundur (*Hind.*). It is probable that several species yield Olibanum, of which *B. Carterii* is perhaps the most important. The frankincense trees inhabit the Somali Coast of Africa to Cape Guardafui and also the South Coast of Arabia. (The reader is referred to Sir George Birdwood's extremely valuable paper on the species of Boswellia published in the Linnæan Society's Transactions.) The Arabs, as early as the tenth century, carried Olibanum to India, and the Indian names for it have, through the lapse of time, become almost hopelessly mixed up with those given to the Indian species of this genus, and also with those given to the *Balsamodendrons.* It is impossible therefore to definitely fix the names of the balsamiferous plants, but Mahomedan writers distinguish several kinds of the imported or African and Arabian Olibanum:—1st. *Kundur Zakur,* or male Frankincense. This is esteemed the best quality, and consists of deep yellow tears. It should burn readily and not emit much smoke. 2nd. *Kundur Unsa,* or female Frankincense. 3rd. *Kundur Madharaj.* This consists of artificially-prepared tears, made by shaking the moist exudation in a basket. 4th. *Kishur Kundur* or *Kashfa.* This consists of the bark of the tree coated with the exudation. This is the *Dhúp* of the Bombay market, and under that name forms a distinct article of commerce. 5th. *Dukák Kundur,* or dust of Olibanum. This meets the demand of the Indian and Chinese markets, the finer qualities of Olibanum being exported from Bombay, after assortment, to Europe. Olibanum, as met with in European commerce, may be described as a dry gum-resin, consisting of tears often an inch in length, and of an ovate or oblong, clavate or stalactitic form, and mixed with impurities. The pieces are light yellow to brown, or pale green or colourless. The odour is balsamic and resinous, especially while being burned. In taste it is bitter and terebinthinous, softening in the mouth. By heat it softens without actually fusing, decomposing at high temperatures. (*See* also 55, 767.)

1061. B. serrata, *Roxb.* Sometimes called the Indian Olibanum Tree; Salhe, Salei, Sale, Lúban (*Hind.*). It is probable that the name *Gugul* should have been restricted to this plant, but modern use has extended it to include *Balsamodendron Mukul.* There are two varieties of this plant, both of which yield the so-called Indian Olibanum:—1*st.*—*Serrata* proper. A moderate-sized tree of the forests at the base of the Western Himálaya, from the Sutlej to Nepal southward to the Deccan, the Circars, and the Konkans. This is *B. thurifera,* Roxb., and is characterised by the *leaflets* being sessile, pubescent, coarsely crenate serrate; *racemes* axillary, shorter than the leaves. The gum-resin, *Salai gugul,* occurs as a transparent golden yellow, semi-fluid substance which slowly hardens with lime. Dr. Moodeen Shariff says that when it is found in this massive form it is known as *Gandah ferozah.* It is pungent, having a slightly aromatic taste and balsamic resinous odour. It becomes opaque when immersed in alcohol or in water, the proportion of resin to gum being much smaller than in Frankincense. The opaque, soft, whitish mass produced by water when rubbed in a mortar forms an emulsion. Indian Olibanum is consumed almost entirely in Central and Northern India, and is never exported. 2*nd.*—*Glabra,* sp., Roxb. A moderate-sized tree of North-West India. *Leaflets* nearly or quite glabrous, and generally entire or nearly so; *racemes* terminal, sub-panicled. It seems probable that this form yields the solid rounded pieces or tears described by some authors as of Indian origin, owing to the substance drying more rapidly than the gum-resin from *B. serrata.* Royle mentions having picked tears off the trees, and states that these burned rapidly with a bright light, diffusing a pleasant odour. (*See* also 55.)

1062. Butea frondosa, *Roxb.*: Leguminosæ. The Bengal Kino: Dhak, Palás (*Hind.*); Palas (*Beng.*). A small, distorted tree, found throughout India and Burma, extending to the North-Western Himálaya as far the Jhelam. It yields a gum which is sold as "Bengal Kino." This occurs in the form of fragmentary pieces of a deep claret colour mixed with similarly-shaped particles of grey bark. The purer qualities are met with in round tears, often bright claret coloured and free from dirt. It may be purified by solution in water. The brilliant ruby-red coloured tears are translucent and very brittle, heat rendering them more so instead of melting the gum. This gum is generally known as *kamarkas* in the bazaars of the North-West Provinces. With age it darkens and becomes opaque. In native medicine it is largely used as an astringent—a substitute for true Kino. It is also largely used in tanning. An aqueous solution of this gum is, by the action of persulphate of iron, changed into a dirty green colour; a larger quantity occasions a green precipitate. Acids precipitate an orange or dirty yellow pigment from the solution. A few drops of caustic potash change the colour to crimson, becoming grey with excess, until the whole of the colour is destroyed. Similar changes are effected by the action of caustic soda and ammonia. The addition of a carbonate of potash or of soda deepens the colour of the solution, but not so much as caustic potash does. Metallic solutions like acetate of lead precipitate the whole of the colouring matter. Attempts were made to fix these colours in the fibre of cotton, silk, wool, &c., with different mordants, but the colours, though permanent, were all imperfect. This gum has been found to contain a large portion of tannin. This fact, together with its cheapness, shows that it would be highly valued in the arts, especially in that of tanning leather. It is said to be used in purifying indigo.

1063.* CANARIUM COMMUNE, *Linn.;* Burseraceæ. The Jangli Badam (*Hind.*). A tree, native of the Malay Peninsula, but occasionally cultivated in India. The concrete resinous exudation *Elemi* is chiefly imported from Manilla, and is said to have the same properties as Balsam of Copaiva. It was formerly believed that the gum of *C. commune* was identical with *Elemi.* This has recently been shown to be a mistake.

1064. C. STRICTUM, *Roxb.* The Black Damar Tree; Kala Dammar (*Hind.*, *Beng.*). A tall tree of South India. It yields a brilliant resin, used medicinally or as a substitute for Burgundy Pitch. This is obtained by making vertical cuts in the bark and setting fire to the tree. Two years afterwards the resin is obtained from the incisions.

1065. CEDRUS DEODORA, *Loudon;* Coniferæ. The Deodar or Himálayan Cedar; Deodár (*Hind.*); Devadáru (*Sans.*). A tall handsome tree, abundant in the North-Western Himálaya. It yields a true resin, and by destructive distillation, an oil, dark-coloured and resembling tar. This is used medicinally. (*See* also 79, 422.)

1066. COCHLOSPERMUM GOSSYPIUM, *DC.;* Bixineæ. The Kúmbi or Gabdi (*Hind.*). A small tree met with in the dry hills of Garhwál, Bandelkhand, Behar, Orissa, and the Dekkan; commonly planted near temples. It yields a clear, white gum (*Katira* or *Katila*, see also under *Sterculia urens*), which, according to Baden Powell, is used in shoemaking. It may be employed as a substitute for gum tragacanth. This seems to be the gum-hog said to be exported from Calcutta to America, in which a future trade may possibly come into existence. It has been found valuable in the art of marbling of paper and in book-binding. (*See* also 912, 959.)

1067. DIPTEROCARPUS ALATUS, *Roxb.;* Dipterocarpeæ. The Garjan (*Beng.*). A tree found in Chittagong, Burma, Tenasserim, and Andaman Islands. It yields a wood-oil and a dirty-brown resin.

1068. D. LÆVIS, *Ham.* Placed under *D. turbinatus*, Gærtn., in Fl. Br. Ind. A common tree in the tropical forests of Burma. It yields a resin and a large quantity of wood-oil. (*See* also 105.)

1069. D. TUBERCULATUS, *Roxb.* The Eng. A large tree met with in Chittagong and Burma. From the stem exudes a clear yellow resin. (*See* also 106.)

1070. D. TURBINATUS, *Gærtn. f.* The Gurjun Oil Tree; Kanyin (*Burm.*). This tree occurs in the Eastern Bengal and in the Eastern Peninsula from Chittagong and Pegu to Singapore. The wood-oil which it affords is used in painting houses and ships. (*See* also 107, 1013.)

1071. FERONIA ELEPHANTUM, *Correa;* Rutaceæ. The Wood-Apple; Bilin, Kat-bel (*Hind.*); Kath-bel (*Beng.*). A middle-sized tree occurring wild or in a cultivated state throughout India in dry situations from the Punjáb eastward and southward to Ceylon. It yields a brownish or reddish gum with a small proportion of clear yellow tears; this is soluble in water and occurs in irregular and semi-transparent tears. It is said to be used by dyers and painters, particularly miniature painters and chintz printers. It is also employed in making ink and varnish, and is used by bricklayers in preparing certain cements and plasters. The *Pharmacopœia of India* pronounces it as superior to gum-arabic for medicinal purposes. It is precipitated by acetate of lead. (*See* also 130, 800.)

1072. HOPEA ODORATA, *Roxb.;* Dipterocarpeæ. The Rock Dammar of Commerce. A tree found occasionally in the evergreen forests of British Burma and the Andaman Islands. It yields a yellow resin, from which the Andamanese prepare a sort of wax.

1073. JUNIPERIS EXCELSA, *M. Bieb.;* Coniferæ. The Himálayan Pencil Cedar. This tree occurs in the arid tract of the North-West Himálaya and Western Tibet, extending eastward to Nepal, and westward to the mountains of Afghánistán and Baluchistán. It yields a resin, from which the preparation known as *Dhúp* is made in some parts of India. The *Dhúp* of Bombay commerce is the *Boswellia* bark imported from Aden. *See Boswellia.* (*See* also 158.)

1074.* LIQUIDAMBAR ORIENTALIS, *Miller;* Hamamelideæ. The Liquid Storax; Siláras (*Hind.*). A handsome tree, resembling a plane, often growing to the height of 40 feet and forming forests in the south-western part of Asia Minor. *Liquid Storax* or *Rose Malloes* is imported into Bombay from Asia Minor, and is much used in Hindu medicine. It is largely exported from

Bombay to China, where it has for many centuries been used as a medicine, having been formerly carried into China by the Arabs as far back as during the Ming dynasty, A.D. 1368–1628. The method of extraction of Liquid Storax is curious. It is carried on by Turcomans. They strip off the outer bark and reject it. The inner bark is then scraped off and thrown into pits until a sufficient quantity has been collected. By boiling in a copper vessel the Liquid Storax is collected by skimming the boiling liquid. The boiling is said to be done with brackish water. The residual bark is then placed in hair bags and subjected to pressure, when a further proportion of the oleo-resin is obtained. The dried and compressed bark is then made into cakes, and this constitutes the fragrant cakes formerly common and well known in Europe under the name of *Cortex Thymiamatis*. The resin is opaque and greyish-brown, of the consistence of honey. Dr. Dymock says that in Arabic and Persian works there are three kinds generally described—1st, that which exudes naturally; 2nd, that which is obtained by pressing the bark; and 3rd, that which is obtained by boiling it. These three kinds are, however, not distinguished in commerce.

1075. MORINGA PTERYGOSPERMA, *Gærtn.*; Moringeæ. The Horse-Radish Tree; Sajiná (*Hind.*, *Beng.*). A small distorted tree wild in the forests of the Western Himálaya and Oudh, commonly cultivated in India and Burma. It yields a gum which is white as it exudes, but which gradually turns to a mahogany or claret colour as it dries. It is used in native medicine. This is one of the gums often called *mocharas*, and false tragacanth or gum-hog of European writers. (*See* also 531, 1030.)

1076. ODINA WODIER, *Roxb.*; Anacardiaceæ. The Ging of Kuni Gum; Kiamil (*Hind.*); Jiyal (*Beng.*). A middle-sized tree occurring throughout the hotter parts of India, from the extreme north-west and along the foot of the Himálaya to Assam, Burma, Tenasserim, the Andaman Islands, and Ceylon. The gum as it exudes from the tree is white (*kanne-ki-gond*), but becomes black (*jingan-ki-gond*), and is reduced to a powder when it falls to the ground. The former is much more valuable than the latter. This gum is often used with the gum of *Anogeissus latifolia* in calico-printing, and the Brahmins of Bengal use it to stiffen their Brahminical strings. It is found exuding from the trees about October in great stalactitic masses, the thin tips of which are perfectly translucent. The larger masses resemble dirty jelly, quite soft and very adhesive, and dry rapidly, leaving a varnished-like appearance on the fingers. (*See* also 197, 454.)

1077. PINUS EXCELSA, *Wall.*; Coniferæ. The Raisalla (*Hind.*). A handsome pine found on the Himálaya. The plant is very resinous; the wood is used for torches, and from it turpentine may be prepared.

1078. P. LONGIFOLIA, *Roxb.* The Long-leaved Pine; Chil, Chir (*Pb.*); Salla, Sapin, Kolan (*Gurhwal* and *Kumaun*); Gandha Bizoza (*Bomb.*). The commonest of the Indian pines occurring on the outer North-Western Himálaya, to Sikkim, Bhután, and Burma. It appears about 2,000 feet in altitude, and ascends to nearly 8,000 feet. It yields a true resin, which, when distilled, forms turpentine; tar also is prepared from the tree. There are two kinds of resin: (1) the *berja* sort, which comprises the tears exuding naturally from the bark; and (2) the *bokhar berja*, or the resin produced by making deep and long incisions into the sap-wood. In Bengal the resin is known under the name of *Gandh biroza*.

1079.* PRUNUS AMYGDALUS, *Baill.*; Rosaceæ. The Almond; Badam (*Hind.*). This tree yields the Badam or Hog Tragacanth exported from Persia into Bombay, and re-exported to Europe. It is used as a substitute for the true Tragacanth. The Hog-gum of European commerce is obtained from a tree (*Symphonia globulifera*, Linn.; Guttiferæ), a native of tropical South America and the West Indies, and recently discovered in Africa. (*See* also 643, 1040.)

1080. PTEROCARPUS MARSUPIUM, *Roxb.*; Leguminosæ. The Indian Kino. A tree met with in the plains of the Western Peninsula and Ceylon. It yields the red gum-resin called "Kino"—a valuable astringent, much used in medicine. The juice is extracted when the tree is in blossom by making longitudinal incisions in the bark. The juice is collected in a receiver and dried. The hardened juice consists of blackish-red, angular, pea-like grains, partially soluble in water, but almost entirely in spirits of wine. It may be used as a source of tannin if sufficiently cheap. (*See* also 225, 465, 1167.)

1081. SHOREA ROBUSTA, *Gaertn.*; Dipterocarpeæ. The Sál Tree. A very large tree, met with in the tropical Himálaya, and along its base from Assam to the Sutlej; also in the eastern districts of Central India, and on the western Western Bengal. The tree, when tapped, exudes large quantities of a whitish aromatic resin, used in native medicine; also employed as an incense, and to caulk boats. It occurs in large stalactitic masses from a pale creamy colour to a dark brown, nearly opaque, and very brittle. It has no taste or smell; to a small extent it is soluble in alcohol, almost entirely so in ether, and perfectly so in turpentine and the fixed oils. It is chiefly used as a substitute for dammar by boat-builders. The conservation of the *sál* forests has put a stop to the practice of notching the trees, and thereby made the supply of *sál* resin in large quantities quite improbable. Bombay is supplied with *rál* (or *sál*) from Singapore, and the resin is imported in large quantities. American resin is, to a large extent, displacing *sál* or *rál* resin, although the latter is quite as good for medicinal purposes. (*See* also 225, 506.)

1082. STERCULIA URENS, *Roxb.*; Sterculiaceæ. The Gúhú (*Hind.*). A soft-wooded tree of North-West India, Assam, Behar, the Eastern and Western Peninsulas, and Ceylon. It yields a gum called *Katila* or *Katíra*. This belongs to the pale or tragacanth series. It is inferior to tragacanth, but is issued to the Government Hospitals in Bombay instead of that gum. It has been repeatedly valued in Europe, and has been pronounced worth only some twenty shillings a cwt. It is largely used in Bombay in the manufacture of native sweetmeats. The watery solution, after separation of the gelatinous mass, has been found useful in imparting a gloss to silk. It should be mixed with an equal quantity of ordinary gum-arabic. (*See* also 265, 943.)

1083.* TRAGACANTH. A gum obtained from several species of *Astragalus*, inhabiting South Europe, Asia Minor, and Persia. It is used in the arts as a substitute for glue. It is of a dull white colour, translucent, inodorous, and tasteless. In India the following gums are used as substitutes for tragacanth: — *Cochlospermum Gossypium*, *Sterculia urens*, and *Prunus Amygdalus*, imported into Bombay and Persia.

1084. VATERIA INDICA, *Linn.;* Dipterocarpeæ. The White Dammar of South India, or Piney Varnish, or Indian Copal; Kahruba or Sandras (*Hind.*). A large tree of the western moist zone; on the Western Ghát from Kanara to Travancore, ascending to 4,000 feet in altitude. On wounding the tree the resin known as the *Peini* or *Piney Dammar* is obtained. Under the influence of gentle heat it combines with wax and oil, and forms an excellent resinous ointment. The resin of this tree is, with that from *Shorea robusta*, known as *rál;* it is imported into Bombay from Singapore in casks and bales, value Rs. 6 per cwt. It forms an excellent varnish resembling Copal. It is also burnt as a candle, giving off smoke with a pleasant smell. Specimens vary in colour, denseness, and fragrance. It occurs in much larger masses than *sál* resin, is more porous and much lighter coloured. Some consignments of *rál* are of a light greenish colour, homogeneous, vitreous on fracture, while others are of a yellow amber colour and vesicular. *Rál* is sold all over India by native druggists; a large consignment came from Cawnpore for the Colonial and Indian Exhibition declared as *Acacia Catechu* gum. (*See* also 293, 1050.)

EXHIBITORS. — The Officers of the Forest Department.

SUB-COURT XXXIV.

EXTRACTS AND INSPISSATED SAPS.

The following are the principal Extracts, Oleo-resins, and Inspissated Saps, met with in India (excluding those such as Opium, &c., which appear as Narcotics or as Drugs):—

1085. ACACIA CATECHU, *Willd.;* Leguminosæ. The Catechu or Cutch; Katha (*Hind.*); Khayer (*Beng.*). Found throughout the Himálayas from the Punjáb to Sikkim, ascending to 5,000 feet in altitude; also common in Burma. The resinous extract is used in medicine and in tanning leather; it is known as *Cutch* or *Catechu*. It is prepared by boiling down a decoction from chips of the wood. There are several kinds of catechu met with in commerce. In Kumaon, while the decoction is being boiled down, twigs are placed in the liquid. Upon these a crystalline substance known as *Kath* is deposited. This is collected and afterwards made into cubes of a grey colour; it is sold all over India, and is the form of cutch eaten in *pán*. In Burma and Bombay the decoction is boiled down to a solid consistence and thrown into leaf moulds, or is baked into cakes and balls. This is the ordinary Cutch of commerce, and instead of being of a pale greyish colour is deep reddish-brown, with a glassy fracture. *Kath* is never exported, but Cutch is largely so. Compare with the extract from *Uncaria Gambier*, the Gambier of commerce, and the extract from *Areca Catechu*, Palm Cutch. (*See* also 5, 648, 742, 1052, 1129.)

1086. A. SUNDRA, *DC.* Met with in Western Peninsula, Ceylon, and Burma. Yields catechu of good quality.

1087. AQUILARIA AGALLOCHA, *Roxb.;* Thymelæaceæ. The Agallocha, Aloe-wood, or Eagle-wood; Agar (*Hind.*); Agura (*Beng.*). A large tree of Sylhet and Tenasserim; distributed to the Malay Peninsula and Archipelago. The wood, impregnated with an odorous resin, is the much prized *Agallocha*. Chips of this wood are boiled, and the water thereafter distilled, in order to prepare *Agar-atar*, a perfume much admired by the people of India. (*See* also 36, 755, 992.)

1088.* ARECA CATECHU, *Linn.;* Palmæ. The Areca Nut or Betel Palm; Supári (*Hind., Beng.*). A palm cultivated throughout tropical India. A decoction of the nut yields an inferior resinous extract, known sometimes as "Areca or Palm Catechu." The ripe nut is boiled in an earthen or tinned copper vessel, and the nuts, together with the boiling water, are poured over a basket. The water is caught in a vessel and allowed to thicken of itself, or is thickened, by further boiling, into a black, very astringent catechu. This substance is apparently rarely, if ever, exported from India, but may be procured from Madras and Mysore, where a considerable local trade is done in this form of Cutch. It exists in large slabs about an inch in thickness, prepared on the leaves of the teak-wood tree. Compare with *Acacia Catechu* and *Uncaria Gambier*.

1089. ARGEMONE MEXICANA, *Linn.;* Papaveraceæ. The Mexican Poppy; Buro-shiálkánta (*Beng.*). A spiny, herbaceous plant, introduced into India within historic times. The milky sap, on drying, forms a substance somewhat resembling opium.

1090. ARTOCARPUS INTEGRIFOLIA, *Linn.;* Urticaceæ. The Jack Fruit Tree; Panas (*Hind.*); Kánthál (*Beng.*). Cultivated throughout India, and wild in the mountain forests of the Western Gháts. The bark yields a very dark-looking gum, with a resinous fracture, soluble in water. The juice is used as a valuable birdlime, and as a cement. A sort of Caoutchouc is said to be obtained from it which is elastic, leathery, water-resisting, and capable of removing pencil marks. (*See* also 39, 581, 633, 1133.)

1091. Bassia latifolia, *Roxb.*; Sapotaceæ. The Mahúa Tree. Indigenous in the forests of Central India, cultivated and self-sown throughout the warmer regions, very gregarious, often associated with the *sál*. It yields a white, milky juice or gummy substance, from incisions and from cracks in the bark. The discharge of this gum is facilitated by a process of ringing the trees practised in Chutia Nagpur during the fruiting season. It does not seem to be of any economic value. (*See* also 45, 410, 584, 709, 995.)

1092. Bauhinia racemosa, *Lam.*; Leguminosæ. A small, crooked, deciduous tree met with in the sub-Himálayan tract, from the Ravi eastward, and in Oudh, Bengal, Burma, and Central and South India. An oleo-resinous extract which might be used as a varnish, is said to be extracted from this plant. It is a pale brownish oleo-resin when fresh, but dries into a deep brown resembling Japan-varnish. (*See* also 905.)

1093. Berberis Lycium, *Royle*; Berberideæ. The Kashmal (*Hind.*). *B. aristata*, DC., *B. asiatica*, Roxb., and *B. vulgaris*, Linn., can scarcely be distinguished from *B. Lycium*, L., even by botanists, and may therefore be expected to be used indiscriminately by the natives. They are thorny bushes, common along the Himálaya; *B. asiatica*, Roxb., coming down to the lower hills of the plains. Royle says that from *B. Lycium*, L., is prepared the extract known as *Rasat*, *rasaut*, *rusot* in Hindi, or *Rasanjana* in Sanskrit. Mr. J. F. Duthie, Superintendent of the Botanic Gardens, Saharanpur, contributes good samples of this substance. (*See* also 766, 1134.)

1094. Blumea balsamifera, *DC.*; Compositæ. A sub-bushy plant met with on the tropical Himálaya from Nepal to Sikkim, altitude 1,000 to 4,000 feet, extending to Assam, the Khásia Hills, Chittagong, Burma, and the Straits. The whole plant smells strongly of camphor, and in Tenasserim camphor to a small extent is actually prepared from it. This is known as Ngai or Blumea camphor.

1095. Calotropis gigantea, *R. Br.*; Asclepiadeæ. The Madár (*Hind.*); Akand (*Beng.*). A bush very common in waste lands all over India. This species, and also *C. procera*, yields Gutta-percha. Dr. Riddell first drew attention to this gutta, and was followed by Royle, and still later by Mr. Baden-Powell. Samples of the milky juice are exhibited by Mr. Manson, Deputy Conservator of Forests, Chutia Nagpur. (*See* also 712, 769, 910, 960.)

1096. Camphor. The name "camphor" is technically given to a number of gum-resins, more or less resembling each other, derived from (1) *Cinnamomum camphora*, Nees, the well-known Camphor Laurel, which yields China or Japan Camphor; (2) *Dryobalanops Camphora*, a large tree of the Malay Archipelago which yields Barus or Sumatra Camphor; (3) *Blumea balsamifera*, DC., and *B. densiflora*, which yield Ngai or Blumea Camphor.

1097. Caoutchouc, or India-rubber. The following are the principal Indian plants which are known to yield this most valuable substance:—(1) *Alstonia scholaris*, R. Br.; Apocynaceæ. A common tree widely cultivated throughout the plains of India, and exceedingly useful, as it is highly ornamental. (2) *Artocarpus Chaplasha*, Roxb.; Urticaceæ. A common Burmese tree. (3) *Chonemorpha macrophylla*, G. Don.; Apocynaceæ. Met with in the moist forests throughout India, extending from Kumaon in the Himálaya to Travancore, Ceylon, Malacca, and the Andaman Islands. (4) *Cryptostegia grandiflora*, R. Br.; Asclepiadeæ. A common plant of West India; cultivated in India. (5) *Ficus elastica*, Bl.; Urticaceæ. A tree very abundant in Assam, its western limit being Darjiling. It yields the Indian Caoutchouc or true India-rubber. (6) *F. laccifera*, Bth. Yields India-rubber sparingly and of inferior quality. (7) *F. obtusifolia*, Roxb. Yields an inferior rubber. (8) *Parameria glandulifera*, Benth.; Apocynaceæ. An extensive climber on the borders of the tidal forests of Burma, extending to Malacca, Singapore, Andaman Islands, Java, and Borneo. Recently this plant has attracted considerable attention as a source of India-rubber. (9) *Urceola elastica*, Roxb.; Apocynaceæ. Yields what is after No. 5 the best Indian India-rubber, and is to some extent being experimentally cultivated in India. This yields the Borneo Rubber. (10) *U. esculenta*, Bth. The same as No. 9, and often used indiscriminately with it; a wild plant in Tenasserim. (11) *Willoughbeia edulis*, Roxb.; Apocynaceæ. A native of Chittagong; yields fairly good Caoutchouc. (12) *W. martabanica*, Willd. A native of Tenasserim. Of the preceding, No. 5 is the only true commercial product; Nos. 9 and 10 have been experimented with. The following are the Caoutchouc-yielding plants from other parts of the world, well known commercially, most of which are being cultivated in India:—(13)* *Castilloa elastica*; Urticaceæ. Central American Rubber. (14) **Hevea*, various species; Euphorbiaceæ. The Para Rubber. (15) **Landolphia*, various species; Asclepiadaceæ. The African Rubber. (16)* *Manihot Glaziovii*; Euphorbiaceæ. The Ceara Rubber. A glance at these lists will show that Caoutchouc is obtained chiefly from four natural orders—*Euphorbiaceæ*, *Urticaceæ*, *Asclepiadeæ*, and *Apocynaceæ*—and the arrangement of these orders as given is that of their importance in the supply of rubber.

1098.* Cinnamomum Camphora, *Nees*; Laurineæ. One of the sources of the Camphor of Commerce; Kafúr (*Hind.*); Karpúr (*Beng.*). A tall tree, with smooth, shining leaves, native of China and Japan. Camphor is a crystalline volatile substance prepared by boiling chips of the wood in a retort. The chemical substance passes off with the steam and condenses upon straw placed in the summit of the retort for that purpose. It is afterwards purified by sublimation and made into cakes. It is largely imported into India, and a considerable export trade is done in Indian refined China Camphor.

1099. EUPHORBIA ANTIQUORUM, *Linn.*; Euphorbiaceæ. A bush with three-angled branches and stems, found on the arid hills above Coimbatore, and on the lower dry slopes of the Himálaya from Kashmír eastward. One of the forms of the resinous substance known in Europe as *Euphorbium* is prepared by boiling down the fresh milky juice of this plant. The true or original *Euphorbium* is the extract of *E. resinifera*, supplied to Europe from Morocco and Barbary. This substance is chiefly used in the preparation of the anti-corrosive paint employed for the bottom of ships. It closely resembles gutta-percha; it is partially soluble in oil, and may be applied to steam joints instead of red-lead. The gutta-percha-like substance has been called *Cattimando*; it is the *Doof* of the Hindus —a much-prized medicine.

1100. E. CATTIMANDOO, *Elliot.* Katti mandu (*Tel.*). A small tree with five-angled stems. The milk yields the true *Cattimandu* used as a cement; common in Vizagapatam district. This contains sufficient caoutchouc to make it a profitable source of supply.

1101. EUPHORBIA TIRUCALLI, *Linn.* A small tree. Dr. Riddell says the milk hardens after having been boiled and becomes brittle; whilst warm it is as ductile as *madár* gutta-percha.

1102. EXCÆCARIA AGALLOCHA, *Willd.*; Euphorbiaceæ. A small, evergreen tree of the tidal shores of Bengal, Burma, and the Andaman Islands. The wood contains a poisonous sap, which causes the eyes of men engaged in hewing down the trees to become swollen. This hardens into a black, caoutchouc-like substance. (*See* also 128.)

1103.* FERULA ALLIACEA, *Boiss.*; Umbelliferæ. The Medicinal Asafœtida of the Natives of India; Hing (*Hind.*); Hingu (*Sans.*). This plant supplies the Asafœtida which is most used by the natives of India; a large trade is done in Bombay. It is a solid-brown gum-like substance contained in skins mixed with impurities and certain portions of the plant. The thick, fleshy roots of the Asafœtida-yielding plants are cut or scratched, when a milky juice exudes. This hardening forms the fœtidly-scented gum-resin. Surgeon-Major W. Dymock, Medical Store-Keeper, Bombay, contributes a good specimen of this along with many other interesting extracts and resins. (*See* also 801.)

1104.* F. NARTHEX, *Boiss.*, *Fl. Orient.* Generally supposed to be the source of the Asafœtida of European Commerce. A perennial herb of Afghánistán. *Hingra* is chiefly imported from Afghánistán. The gum-resin occurs in irregular masses, opaque, white when broken, and ultimately becoming brownish-pink. Sometimes met with in India in the form of a ferruginous powder. It occurs also in tears, or flat pieces, or "stone" formed by mixing with sand. It is recognised by its bitter, acrid taste, and by its fœtid but not purely alliaceous odour. (*See* also 802.)

1105. FICUS BENGALENSIS, *Linn.*; Urticaceæ. The Banyan Tree; Bor (*Hind.*); Bur, But (*Beng.*). A large tree, wild in the East Himálayan tracts, planted throughout India. It yields an inferior caoutchouc, which by the natives is made into bird-lime. (*See* also 131, 431, 919.)

1106. F. ELASTICA, *Bl.* The India-rubber Tree; Bar, Attah Bar (*Beng.*). A large, evergreen tree of the North-Eastern Himálaya, eastward to Assam and Arracan. Government has a large plantation of it in Assam. This tree yields the India-rubber of Indian commerce. An experimental plantation has now for some years existed in Assam, but as yet it has not commenced to bear. The India-rubber of Assam at the present day is purely an article of trade with the hill tribes, who prepare the substance and carry it into the valley of Assam for sale. Samples of this rubber are exhibited by the Assam Government. *See* "Caoutchouc."

1107. FICUS RELIGIOSA, *Linn.* The Peepul; Asawat (*Beng.*). A large tree with suddenly pointed leaves; wild in the sub-Himálayan tract, Bengal, and Central India. The bark yields a tenacious milky juice, which hardens into a substance resembling caoutchouc. (*See* also 496.)

1108. GARCINIA COWA, *Roxb.*; Guttiferæ. The Cowa (*Hind.*). A tall, evergreen tree of East Bengal, Assam, Chittagong, Burma, and the Andaman Islands. It yields a kind of Gamboge of a somewhat paler colour than that produced by *G. Morella*.

1109. G. MORELLA, *Desv.* The Gamboge Tree. An evergreen tree of the forests of the Khásia Hills, East Bengal, the Western Peninsula, and Ceylon. This tree produces the true Gamboge, which is used in medicine and in the arts as a paint. The chief trade-supply is obtained from Siam, in the form of cylindrical pieces or sticks into which it has been melted. In Ceylon, it is collected by cutting off thin slices of the bark, about the size of the hand. Upon the exposed surface the gum collects, and is scraped off when sufficiently dried. (*See* also 803, 1019.)

1110. GUTTA-PERCHA. A commercial term for the inspissated milky sap of several plants of which nearly all (or at least all the important ones) belong to the natural order *Sapotaceæ*. The word gutta-percha is of Malayan origin; it signifies the gum or *gutta* of the tree known as *percha*. The gutta-percha of commerce is, however, chiefly the *gutta-taban* or *Dichopsis Gutta*, a tree of Perak. As it reaches the market, however, this is largely adulterated, often consisting of the inspissated saps of some five or six different plants mixed together, of which a fig and bread-fruit tree, yielding inferior India-rubber, are most probably the largest adulterants. Gutta-percha seems to have come into the notice of Europe in the year 1845 (from the Straits), its important uses soon causing an immense demand. It is principally used in coating telegraphic cables, it being a perfect insulator, while of such a nature as to withstand, in a remarkable degree, the action of water. It is, in fact, much more durable when entirely submerged than when exposed to a moist atmosphere. About 10 years have been stated to be the period it will withstand the variations of climate in the air; 20 years if enclosed in iron tubes; but 20 years, when it has been submerged, have no appreciable effect upon the article. This is due to the fact that under the influence of light and air it slowly becomes oxidised, being converted into a brittle resin soluble in hot alcohol. This is the great defect of gutta-percha, for when oxidised it loses its plastic nature. Under water, and at great depths in the sea, it is, however, very durable, hence its value as an insulator for submarine cables. Chemically, gutta-percha is almost identical with India-rubber, but it differs physically, being tough and inelastic. Since the date gutta-percha was made known to Europe, perhaps no substance has developed more rapidly, and, with India-rubber, its uses may be said to be so many and so important as to make it perfectly indispensable to commerce. The demand is, however, rapidly exterminating the plants, and it would seem desirable that, to meet future necessities, plantations should be made wherever *gutta*-yielding plants can grow. It would seem that the Sunderbands might prove suitable for this purpose, and if so, extensive tracts of practically useless country might be made to yield a distinct revenue. The following are the principal gutta-yielding plants:—(1) *Alstonia scholaris*, R. Br.; Apocynaceæ. Satian, satwin (*Hind.*); Chatwan (*Beng.*). One of the many forms of this tree has recently been discovered to be the source of the *Gutta-pulei* of Singapore. The Satián has long been regarded in India as yielding an inferior India-rubber. (2)* *Achras Sapota*, Linn.; Sapotaceæ. The Sapota Tree. Largely cultivated in Bengal on account of its fruit; it yields the Mexican chicle-gum, a substance closely resembling gutta-percha. (3) *Bassia mottleyana*, De Vriesse; Sapotaceæ. (4) *Calotropis gigantea*, R. Br.; Asclepiadeæ. (5) *C. procera*, R. Br. (6) *Dichopsis elliptica*, Benth.; Sapotaceæ. The *panchoti*, a large tree of the Western Ghâts; it yields the Indian Gutta-percha. (7) **D. Gutta*, Benth. & Hook. The finest Gutta-percha. A large tree indigenous to the Straits and the Malayan Archipelago. The enormous demand for Gutta-perchas exterminated this exceedingly valuable plant from all accessible places. It flourishes most on the sides of the hills near Perak. There are two forms, one with red flowers known as *tuban-merut* and the other with white flowers, *tuban-pateh*. Singapore and Penang are the chief collecting depôts. (8) **Dichopsis obovata*, Clarke. An evergreen tree of Tenasserim, extending to Malacca and Penang. Kurz says it yields gutta-percha. (9) *D. polyantha*, Benth. The Tali (*Beng.*); Sill-kurta (*Cachar.*). A tree, 30 to 40 feet in height, occurring in Sylhet, Chittagong, and Pegu. Kurz says it produces a good quality of gutta-percha in large quantities, probably not inferior to that of Singapore. (10)* *Dyera costulata* Hook. f.; Apocynaceæ; and (11)* *D. laxiflora*, Hook. f. Trees which inhabit the forests of Malacca, Singapore, and Sumatra. They yield the *gutta-jelutong* of commerce. (12) *Euphorbia Cattimandoo*, Elliot; Euphorbiaceæ. The Kati Mandu (*Tam.*). This yields the *Cattimandu* cement of the Madras Presidency. It contains sufficient caoutchouc to make it a profitable source of supply, if not of India-rubber, at least of gutta-percha. (13) *E. neriifolia*, Linn. The Mansa-sij. Yields a milky sap which, on drying, much resembles gutta-percha. (14) *E. pulcherrima*, Willd. Dr. Riddell recommends this, as also the next species, as suitable for the preparation of gutta-percha. (15) *E. resinifera*, Willd. This plant yields the gum known as *Euphorbium*, now largely used as an anticorrosive paint for the bottoms of ships; it comes chiefly from Morocco and Barbary. Its resisting the action of water depends upon its resemblance to gutta-percha. (16) **E. Tirucalli*, Linn. The Lankasij (*Beng.*); Sehud (*Hind.*); Tiru kalli (*Mal.*); Sha-soung-leknyo (*Burm.*). A small tree cultivated throughout India and used as a hedge. Dr. Riddell says this yields a fairly good gutta-percha. (17)* *Payena Maingayi*, C.B.C.; Sapotaceæ. A tree of Malacca and Penang, said by Maingai to abound in gutta-percha.

1111. KINO. *See Butea frondosa*, Roxb., Bengal Kino, and *Pterocarpus Marsupium*, Roxb., the true Kino.

1112. MELANORRHŒA USITATA, *Wall.*; Anacardiaceæ. The Black Varnish Tree of Burma. A large, deciduous tree found in Manipur, Burma, and Tenasserim. The black varnish made from this plant is much used by the Burmese in their lacquer-work as a size in gilding, for writing in palm-leaf books, and for many other purposes.

1113. PWENYET or POONYET. Pwenyet, sometimes called Black Dammar. A honeycomb black resin, met with in Burma, formed by a hymenopterous insect (*Trigona læviceps*). This insect seems to obtain the resinous matter from the following plants:—*Hopea odorata*, Roxb., the *Thingan* of Burma; *Dipterocarpus lævis*, and *D. turbinatus*, Gærtn. (= *lævis*, Ham.), the Wood-oil Tree, the *Kanyengnee*; and *Canarium bengalense*, Roxb.; probably also from *Shorea obtusa*, Thitya, which exudes a white resin. The insect must, however, obtain its resinous supply chiefly from the first two of these, as the others are not common. It constructs its hive in the hollows or bifurcations of trees, the crevices of rocks, or on the ground. A trumpet-shaped entrance is constructed of the resinous matter, protruding often for about a foot in length, and gracefully widening to about the same extent. To obtain the hive the trees have in the majority of cases to be hewn down, each yielding about 4 lbs. The principal use of *Poon-yet* is for caulking boats, for which purpose it is mixed with earth-oil or petroleum. It is first boiled in water; thereafter it is kneaded with petroleum until it attains the consistency of putty.

1114. RHUS SUCCEDANEA, *Linn.*; Anacardiaceæ. A tree about 30 feet high, met with in the temperate Himálaya, from the Jhelam to Assam, and on the Khásia Hills. The seed yields a pure white wax, made into candles in Japan. The stems of this and also *R. vernicifera* are in Japan and China scratched at the age of 4 or 5 years. From these incisions an exudation is obtained which constitutes the varnish used in Japanese and Chinese lacquer-work. (*See* also 1041.)

1115. TECTONA GRANDIS, *Linn.*; Verbenaceæ. The Teak Tree; Ságun (*Hind.*). Found in Central and South India and Burma. The wood-tar from this tree may be used like coal-tar, but with much less permanent effects.

1116. TURPENTINE. An oleo-resin, obtained chiefly from various species of Coniferæ. Several turpentine oleo-resins are also obtained from Anacardiaceæ, of which may be mentioned the Chian or Cyprian Turpentine. There are several samples of crude turpentine on view chiefly obtained from *P. longifolia*; contributed by the officers of the Forest Department.

1117. VARNISH. Various substances used in solution with spirit, or in the natural condition, or after being liquified by heat. Of the commercial varnishes the following may be mentioned as the most important:—(1) Lac or Spirit Varnish. (2) Burmese Varnish, *Melanorrhœa usitata.* (3) Cingalese and Indian Varnish, *Semecarpus Anacardium.* (4) Japanese Varnish, *Rhus succedanea.* (5) Doon Varnish, *Doona zeylanica.*

1118. WAX. Indian wax is of a very inferior quality. It comes chiefly from the hills, and is the produce almost entirely of wild or semi-wild bees.

EXHIBITORS.—The Officers of the Forest Department.

SUB-COURT XXXV.

INDIGO.

1119. INDIGOFERA TINCTORIA, *Linn.*; Leguminosæ. The Indigo Plant; Nil (*Beng., Hind.*); Nila (*Sans.*). Roxburgh says that the native place of the plant is unknown, for, though it is found in a wild state over most parts of India, it is generally not remote from places where it is or has been cultivated. The existence of Sanskrit and other vernacular names render the Asiatic origin highly probable; the more so when it is recollected that many other species of *Indigofera* are unquestionably indigenous to India. The lands most suited for indigo cultivation are low-lying and sandy churs in the neighbourhood of rivers, periodically enriched by alluvial deposits. The crop grown on high loamy soils is also, however, of a superior quality, although it requires much more careful cultivation. There are two sowings of indigo in the year,—one in the spring and the other in the rains. The soil requires careful ploughing and harrowing, and is, sometimes, manured before the sowing, at other times when the plant is growing. The seed is sown broadcast at the rate of 15 to 17 seers to the acre. The plant is ripe for cutting just as the flowers begin to appear. The crop is reaped with the sickle, and brought to the factory, where the process of extracting the dye immediately commences. This, roughly speaking, consists in steeping, beating, boiling, and straining. The cuttings of the plant are steeped from 11 to 15 hours in a water vat. Thereafter, the greenish liquid is drained off into a lower beating vat; in this vat 7 or 8 men standing up to their waists agitate the liquid by means of sticks, lashing methodically to a song, so as to keep the liquid in constant motion. The oxidation of the green colouring matter is thereby effected into the dark blue particles of indigotine. The liquid is then allowed to stand until these particles settle down, when the surface water is carefully drained off and the blue sediment conducted into the boiling vat. The boiling goes on for about 5 hours, and the semi-liquid substance is then repeatedly passed through a cloth strainer for the separation of the dye particles from the water. The dye matter is allowed to dry, and afterwards subjected to an increasing pressure for about 12 hours. It takes the form of firm slabs 3½ inches thick, which are cut into cubes by means of a wire, and are then ready for being stamped and finally dried. The substance known in the market as Madras Indigo is prepared from the dried leaves instead of the fresh green twigs used in Bengal and the North-West Provinces. The ripe plant is dried in sunshine and thrashed to separate the stems from the leaves, which are then stored. In the course of four weeks the leaves undergo a change in colour from green to pale blue-grey. They are then macerated into water and the dye extracted in the usual way.

The total area under cultivation of indigo is as follows:—

	Acres.
Oudh	16,857
N.-W. Provinces	412,064
Bengal	†710,000
Punjáb	153,889
Madras	321,339
Central Provinces	126
Bombay	5,185
British Burma	10
Total	1,619,470

There are 197 factories working in Bengal, 1,963 in the N.-W. Provinces and Oudh, and 1,254 in the Madras Presidency, of which a large number are under European management. In his Review of the Trade of British India with other countries for 1878-79, Mr. J. E. O'Conor writes:—"The manufacture of indigo is of all forms of enterprise now known in India, that which was first taken up by Europeans, who still retain the monopoly of the manufacture of this article, at any rate so far as concerns

† The actual area under indigo in Bengal is open to some doubt. The figure here given has been taken from Dr. McCann's Report on the 'Dyes and Tans of Bengal,' a work compiled from information contributed by District officers to the Bengal Economic Museum.

the better kinds exported to foreign markets. European marks of indigo are guarantees of quality, and the exports from India have hitherto consisted almost exclusively of such marks, though lately there has been some extension of cultivation in the North-Western Provinces under native supervision, the produce of the plantation being supplied to Europe. Practically, however, as yet the whole quantity produced from year to year in European factories is shipped from India, the inferior qualities of native manufacture being retained for consumption in the country."

The Exports of Indigo for the past five years are:—

	Cwts.	Rs.
1880–81 .	61,870	3,57,15,814
1881–82 .	150,363	4,50,90,802
1882–83 .	141,041	3,91,29,970
1883–84 .	168,590	4,64,09,906
1884–85 .	154,629	4,06,88,996

The following is an analysis of the exports for the year 1884–85:—

Presidency from which exported.	Value.	Country to which exported.	Value.
	Rs.		Rs.
Bengal . . .	3,02,33,957	United Kingdom .	1,86,78,506
Madras . . .	94,35,208	Unit·d States . .	68,68,080
Bombay . .	6,34,295	France	47,45,076
Sindh . . .	3,85,536	Egypt	33,55,468
		Austria . . .	33,21,077
		Germany . . .	11,98,000
		Persia	9,08,124
		Turkey in Asia .	8,10,953
		Italy	3,60,435
		Other countries .	14,43,277
Total .	4,06,88,996	Total . .	4,06,88,996

The imports are not of much importance in comparison with the exports; the figures for the last five years are:

	Cwts.	Rs.
1880–81 . .	2,119	46,218
1881–82 . .	2,238	25,265
1882–83 . .	1,909	64,530
1883–84 . .	1,631	31,563
1884–85 . .	2,173	35,491

"In explanation of the decline of exports to Persia, one of the British Consuls in that country offers an explanation which is interesting. He says that the extension of opium cultivation in Persia has brought so much money to the Persian peasantry, that they are discarding their coarse home-woven indigo-dyed shirts, and are substituting for them fancy prints from Manchester, not so durable but pleasanter to the eye. If this is correct, the competition of Persian with Indian opium in China acts upon this country in more ways than one. The decline in the exports to Persia is not so serious as yet, but this statement suggests that the indigo trade might suffer seriously if such a change in dress were to be introduced generally in Egypt, Persia, and Asiatic Turkey. These three countries took about 24,000 cwt. of indigo last year." (J. E. O'Conor's 'Review of the Trade of India, 1884–85.') There are other blue or indigo-yielding plants known in India and in other parts of the world, one or two of which have assumed almost commercial importance. In China, indigo is prepared from three distinct plants, according to the climate of the region where cultivated:—*Isatis tinctoria* at Shanghai and Chusan; *Polygonum tinctorium* at Ichang, and *Strobilanthes flaccidifolius* largely in the province of Chekiang. (*See* Fortune's 'Residence among the Chinese,' page 189.) In Egypt *Tephrosia Apollinea*, and on the Niger *Tephrosia toxicaria* (plants allied to *Indigofera tinctoria* of India), yield indigo. In the West Indies *Randia aculeata* is grown for this purpose, affording a good quality of indigo,

The following are a few of the more important Indian plants known to yield the chemical substance Indigo:—

1120.* Cicer arietinum, *Linn.*; Leguminosæ. The Gram. The leaves of this plant are said to yield indigo. (*See* also 681.)

1121. Isatis tinctoria, *Linn.*; Cruciferæ. The Woad or Dyer's Weed. A member of the cabbage family. This plant is common in Western Thibet. It yields indigo, and for this purpose is said to be cultivated in Afghánistán.

1122. Marsdenia tinctoria, *R. Br.*; Asclepiadeæ. The plant yields a blue dye resembling indigo. This is prepared by the hill tribes in many parts of India, as, for example, in Sikkim. An allied plant, *Gymnema tigens*, also yields a blue dye. (*See* also 1156.)

1123. Strobelanthes flaccidifolius, *Nees.*; Acanthaceæ. This is the indigo plant of Assam and the eastern mountain tracts extending into China (*see* Dyes). (*See* also 1176.)

1124. Vigna Catiang, *Endl.*; Leguminosæ. The Chowlee of India; Barbati (*Beng.*); Urohi Mahorpat (*Ass.*). Universally cultivated in the tropical zone of India on account of the grain, which forms one of the summer crops raised along with the millets, and ripening in October and November. Regarding this plant a curious fact has recently been brought to light. A piece of cloth dyed a beautiful green colour came from Assam as a sample of dyeing as practised by the Khamptis. A reference was at once made for a sample of the plant from which this dye was extracted, when a half-rotten and fragmentary bundle of what appeared to be *Vigna Catiang* was received. The process of extracting the dye is as follows:—Crush the creeper and leaves of the *Urohi mahorpat* in a "*denki*" or pestle and mortar to extract the juice, thereafter mix with this the juice of Thekara tenga (*Garcinia pedunculata*) ¼th to ¾th of Urohi juice. Leave standing in the sun for four hours, when the mixed juices or dye solution will be ready for use. The article to be dyed should be dipped into this, squeezed and dried, the process being repeated three or four times.

1125. Wrightia tinctoria, *R. Br.*; Apocynaceæ. The leaves yield an indigo-blue used along with the seeds of *Cassia Tora*. This is said to be prepared in South India.

Exhibitors.—An interesting collection of green leaf indigo is exhibited by the Bengal Exhibition Commercial Committee, by Messrs. William Moran & Co., Messrs. Jardine Skinner & Co., Messrs. Shoene Kilburn & Co., Messrs. Begg Dunlop & Co., and Messrs. J. Thomas & Co., of Calcutta, Messrs. H. W. Jewsbury & Co., London, and The Indigo Co., London, Agents, Gillanders, Arbuthnot, & Co., Calcutta. The model of an indigo factory will make intelligible the brief account given of the process of indigo manufacture. Messrs. Parry & Co., and also Messrs. Croysdale & Co., of Madras, exhibit dry leaf indigo, and the Assam Government has contributed a sample of Strobilanthes indigo.

SUB-COURT XXXVI.

LAC.

1126. Coccus lacca, *Linn.*; Hemipteræ. The Lac Insect (*Eng.*); Laque (*Fr.*.); Lack (*Ger.*); Lacca (*It.*); Lakh (*Hind.*); Gálá (*Beng.*); Lâkshâ (*Sans.*). This insect is indigenous to the forests of India, and occurs in aggregated masses around the twigs of certain trees, especially *Butea frondosa* and *Ficus religiosa.*

Lac is the resinous incrustation formed on the bark of the twigs through the action of the lac insect. When the larvæ or grubs of the *Coccus lacca* escape from their eggs, they crawl about in search of fresh sappy twigs. When satisfied, they become fixed, and form a cocoon by excreting a resinous substance. The male cocoon is ovoid in shape, the female circular. For about two-and-a-half months the insects remain within their cocoons in the lethargic state, but structural changes have been accomplished by which they have reached the mature or imago condition. The male escapes from his cocoon by backing out at the ventral opening. The female has also become mature; but since destined to remain in its present position, it renews activity and commences to throw up around itself a more perfect coating of resin, until its body becomes completely encrusted. It is supposed that there are about 5,000 females for one male. Upon the circular body of the female there are three openings, which become developed, as the incrustation proceeds, into three filamentous tubes. One serves the purpose of an anal opening, and through it impregnation is also accomplished; the others are breathing stomata. When the male escapes from his cocoon, he at once commences to crawl over the females. The impregnated female, after depositing her eggs below her body, commences to construct cells round each with as much precision as the bee forms its comb.

The irritation caused by parasitic insects to vegetable tissues results in the formation of many curious and extraordinary structures, some of which are economically of great use to man, such as gall-nuts, lac, &c. In the case of the lac insect, the plants chosen are those naturally possessed of resinous principles, but still the insect exercises a curious influence over this resinous sap, changing its properties entirely. The *Coccus lacca* penetrates the bark of the twig by its proboscis or penetrator until it reaches the sap-wood; from there it sucks its nourishment and transforms the sap into the resinous excretion—lac—which it encrusts around itself. As time advances, further changes are visible; the female body enlarges considerably and becomes brilliantly coloured. The red colour is due to the formation of a substance intended as food for its offspring. The eggs germinate below, and the larvæ, eating their way through the body of the mother (thereby causing her death), make their escape to repeat this strange story.

After the larvæ escape the old encrusted twigs are removed and cut up into pieces 4 to 6 in. in length. These form the stick-lac of commerce. They are spread upon a flat floor and a roller passed over them by which the resinous crust is broken from off the twigs. The wood is carefully removed, and the resin thrown into tubs of water, where it is either beaten with a wooden pestle or trodden by men. The liquid becomes red coloured, and one washing after another is performed. The washings are carefully preserved and afterwards evaporated, when a red substance is obtained which is made into cakes and dried like indigo. This is the lake-lac or lac-dye of commerce (*see* Dyes). By the washings the resin has been freed from its impurities, and now exists in a fine pulverized or granular state. This is the seed-lac of commerce. After drying, the seed-lac is placed in bags 10 ft. long and 3 or 4 in. in diameter. These are stretched across charcoal fires until the lac begins to melt. The operators then commence to twist the sacks in opposite directions, holding them every now and again over specially-prepared glazed porcelain troughs, or simply the stems of the plantain slit down the middle, and thus formed into smooth, glazed, natural troughs. Through the pores of the cloth the melting lac is forced, and dropping upon the troughs it spreads out in thin sheets. These are removed and allowed to dry, any impurities being broken out of the thin flakes. When packed in bags these become the thin pieces known in commerce as shell-lac or shellac. Sometimes, and especially with the coarser qualities used for home consumption, the melted lac is let drop into rounded pieces about 1 to 1½ in. in diameter. These constitute button-lac, and if formed into larger masses, sheet or piece-lac.

The quality of lac varies chiefly according to the tree upon which the insect feeds. The best lac is *kusum* lac or lac from the *kusum* tree (*Schleichera trijuga*), next *dhak* or *palas* (the *Butea frondosa*), then *pipal* (*Ficus religiosa*). The *kusum* is said to last for ten years, while all others are only good for two or three years. The *kusum* lac twigs are of a light golden colour, from which orange shellac is manufactured. This sells in London for about £10-12 per cwt. of best quality, *i.e.* "fine lac orange D.C." The other qualities are known as "liver" or "native orange," maximum price £8-9 per cwt.; "garnet" £7-8 maximum; "native leaf" and "button" being generally about £3-6 or £3-8 per cwt. The best lac comes from Siam.

Lac is frequently adulterated with orpiment, or still more frequently with common resin, which may be detected by its smell on crushing the lac.

In India lac is dissolved in native spirits and coloured; in this form it is used as a varnish for carpentry and furniture: mixed with sulphur and some colouring agent, it is formed into the sticks, *batti*, like sealing wax, which are used by the toy-makers to coat their wooden wares. In Europe it is largely made into sealing wax, and dissolved into spirits it forms spirit varnish. It is made into cement, into lithographer's ink, and is used to stiffen hats and other articles constructed of felt.

The exports and imports of stick lac during 1884-85 amounted to Rs. 90,449, and the exports of manufactured lac to Rs. 59,91,453. The export trade in lac dye has declined considerably during the past five years, namely, from Rs. 1,30,201 in 1880-81 to Rs. 1,274 in 1884-85, the aniline dyes having entirely driven it out of the foreign market.

The following are a few of the plants on which the lac insect is found.

(1.) *Acacia arabica*, Willd.; Leguminosæ. The Babul or Kikar. In Sind and Guzerat yields large quantities of lac. (*See* also 4, 403, 484, 1051, 1128). (2.) *Butea frondosa*, Roxb.; Leguminosæ. The Dhak or Palas. (3.) *Ficus religiosa*, Linn.; Urticaceæ. The Aswat or Pipal. (*See* also 496, 1107.) (4.) *Schleichera trijuga*, Willd.; Sapindaceæ. The Kusum or Kusumb. This is the most important of all the lac trees. It is a native of the sub-Himálaya, Central and South India, and Burma. (5.) *Shorea robusta*, Gærtn.; Dipterocarpeæ. The Sal Tree. The ease with which this plant coppices, and its power of endurance and rapid growth, make it one of the best trees for lac cultivation. (6.) *Zizyphus jujuba*, Lam.; Rhamneæ. The Ber or Kul. Although the lac yielded by this tree is inferior in quality, the ease with which it may be propagated makes it a good lac-yielding tree, suited especially to the Punjáb.

Exhibitors.—The Bengal Commercial Committee undertook the responsibility of procuring a collection of lac exhibits to represent the industry. They have procured contributions of lac samples from the following firms: Messrs. Jardine Skinner & Co., Messrs. Schoene Kilburn & Co., and Messrs. Angelo Brothers, of Calcutta. A very large collection of lac samples is exhibited. The Forest Department shows an interesting series of samples from all parts of India.

SUB-COURTS XXXVII. & XXXVIII.

THE DYES AND TANS OF INDIA.

The influence of aniline has been more destructive to the tinctorial and textile industries of India than is commonly supposed. These cheap colours have not only depraved the tastes of the people, but have demoralised their indigenous industries. The soft delicacy and harmony of colour which formerly characterised Indian fabrics has given place to the brilliant tints, and coincident with this degeneration, the reputation for durability formerly enjoyed by Indian die-stuffs has been destroyed. Not only have the textile industries been thus irreparably injured, but most of the indigenous tinctorial industries have been completely ruined. Ten years ago the exports of Safflower from India were valued at £70,000; last year they had fallen to one-tenth that sum. Lac-dye to the amount of £10,000 was exported five years ago; last year the exports were only £1000. The imports of Cochineal were in 1880 valued at nearly £70,000: last year, as the result of a steady decrease, they fell to £30,000. The exports of Indigo were valued in 1884-85 at £4,000,000, showing a falling off from the previous year of nearly £60,000.

These remarkable changes have their counterpart in the imports of aniline dyes, which last year were valued at over £100,000, while only a few years ago they were unknown in the Indian markets. It seems almost unfortunate that India cannot follow the example given by the Persian Government in prohibiting the importation of aniline dyes.

India, famed as the country of the beautiful red *manjit* dye, imported last year from Persia nearly £34,000's worth of *manjit*, while it exported only about £200's worth. Not less striking is the fact that Saffron — a dye-stuff obtained from an abundant and indigenous plant in Kashmír — was imported last year from France to the value of £34,000. Even Myrobalans come to India now-a-days from Ceylon, while the mountain tracts of the central tableland of India contain an inexhaustible supply.

The inference to be drawn from these extraordinary facts seems irresistible—the dye-stuffs of India have been neglected. Although famed for its dyes, with the single exception of Indigo, India does not possess at the present moment a single dye-stuff of importance to European commerce. The very extensive knowledge of indigenous dyes possessed by the people is daily threatened through the rapid diffusion of aniline colours. There are over 300 dyes and tans known to the inhabitants of India, and the majority of these are regularly used. The dyes are frequently extremely difficult to extract, and the auxiliary stuffs used are often so numerous that it is sometimes difficult to determine which gives the colour. It may happen that no single ingredient will give a colour of any kind, and yet the combination, when put through the tedious and intricate process known only to the native dyer, produces the most lovely and permanent shades. The *chay*-root of Madras may be mentioned as an illustration of this kind, and it is to be feared that the knowledge of the process by which the red colour characteristic of the Madras handkerchiefs will soon be lost. Few countries in the world can show either a greater or a more varied series of dyes than India. Every village has its dyer if not its calico-printer, and the people are fond of coloured garments. But aniline colours are rapidly taking the place of the more expensive but permanent vegetable dyes, just as European steam calico-printing is steadily carrying ruin to the homes of the Indian calico-printers.

The only dye-stuff which seems to have prospered, in spite of introduction of aniline colours, is turmeric, but is doubtful how far this may be due to the root being put to other than tinctorial purposes. In 1881–82, the exports of turmeric were valued at £36,000, but last year they had reached the sum of £73,000.

The total value of the exports in dyes† and tans from India during the past six years was as follows:—

Rs.		Rs.
1879–80, 3,23,78,321	.	1880–81, 3,80,64,188
1881–82, 4,78,96,893	.	1882–83, 4,16,60,377
1883–84, 4,90,75,636	.	1884–85, 4,40,81,039

The Indian imports of dyes and tans are insignificant when compared with the exports. During the past six years they were:—

Rs.		Rs.
1879–80, 14,52,344	.	1880–81, 22,03,537
1881–82, 17,14,906	.	1882–83, 20,66,395
1883–84, 25,14,222	.	1884–85, 21,50,569

The following are a few of the more important dyes and tans:—

1127. Abir. A white, perfumed powder which is mixed with a colouring substance (*Gulal*). This, as a religious observance, is thrown by the Hindus at each other, during the Holi carnival. In some parts of the country it is used dry, in others made into a solution and ejected from a syringe. There are many different kinds of this powder, almost each province having a series of *abirs* peculiar to itself. They are generally red coloured, though some are yellow, brown, green, or even black. In most cases, alum is a necessary ingredient in the *abir*, the colour being produced only when alum is added to the other ingredients. The chief colouring materials used are *Sappan* wood, *tesu* flowers (*Butea frondosa*), saffron or sandal-wood. The odours are produced by zedoary, deodar, cloves, agar-wood, costus-root or by musk. The modern *abir* of Bengal is flour-coloured with aniline dyes.

1128. Acacia arabica, *Willd.*; Leguminosæ. The Indian Gum Arabic Tree; Babul, kikar (*Hind.*). A small, thorny tree, common everywhere in India. The bark is a powerful astringent, and is one of the tanning substances most extensively used in India. The seeds, pods, and leaves are also used in tanning, but more rarely than the bark. Leather tanned with *babul* is of a buff colour. The pods and the bark yield a yellow or brown dye, with alum as a mordant. Salts of iron deepen this colour into black. (*See* also 4, 403, 484, 1051, 1126.)

1129. A. Catechu, *Willd.* Catechu, Cutch; Khair, katha (*Hind.*). A tree, 30 to 40 feet high, abundant in the forests of India and Burma. It yields a valuable extract similar to Gambier. This is used as an astringent in medicine, and in dyeing and tanning. It is known as Cutch or Catechu, and possesses 45·55 per cent. of dark-coloured mimotannic acid. A solution of Catechu is, by the action of lime or of alum, changed into a dull red colour, which constitutes a fairly good dye, and is used for that purpose in some parts of India; the extract may be used or the heartwood broken up and boiled with lime. Cutch is largely employed by the calico-printers to produce metallic shades. The bark is also used as a tan and very largely so in tanning fishing lines and nets. (For further information *see* under Extracts and also Condiments.) (*See* also 5, 648, 742, 1052, 1085.)

1130. A. leucophlœa, *Willd.* Reru, safed kikar (*Hind.*). A tree met with in North, South, and West India and Burma. In Burma the leaves are used in dyeing and give a black colour; the bark affords a red colour. The latter is also valued as a tan, imparting a pinkish shade to the leather similar to that produced by A. Jacquemontii. (*See* also 7, 485.)

1131. Adhatoda Vasica, *Nees.*; Acanthaceæ. Arusa (*Hind.*); Bakas (*Beng.*); Adhatodai, (*Tam.*). A small, sub-herbaceous bush, often gregarious, found everywhere in Bengal, and in the sub-Himálayan tract, ascending to 4000 ft. in altitude. One of the most abundant plants in India, especially so at the foot of the Himálaya. A yellow dye, obtained from the leaves by boiling, is used for dyeing coarse cloth. It gives a greenish-blue when combined with indigo.

1132. Anogeissus latifolia, *Wall.*; Combretaceæ. Dhawa, dhaura (*Hind.*); Daura (*Mahr.*). A denizen of the Himálayan forests and of the mountain tracts of the central table-land of India extending to the hills of South India. It yields a gum used by calico-printers, especially so when printing with turmeric. Dr. Dymock says that the leaves are used in Bombay as a tan. They were analysed by Dr. Lyon and were found to contain as much tannin as those of the Sumach tree. Mr. Duthie reports that they are also used as a tan in the N.W. Provinces. (*See* also 33, 1055.)

1133. Artocarpus integrifolia, *Linn.*; Urticaceæ. The Indian Jack Tree; Panas (*Hind.*); thal (*Beng.*). A low but densely-branched tree, met with all over India and Burma. The wood, or the sawdust from it, yields on decoction a yellow dye, employed to colour the Burmese priest's cloth. To some extent it is also used in Madras and other parts of India and in Java.

† Excluding Cutch and Gambier which are given as Extracts.

It is fixed with alum, and often intensified by a little turmeric. (*See* also 39, 581, 633, 1090.)

1134. BERBERIS ARISTATA, *DC.*, and B. LYCIUM, *Royle;* Berberideæ. The Barberry; Chitra, rasaut (*Hind.*). Thorny shrubs, with small, simple, spiny leaves, met with throughout the Himálaya. The former is found from the Sutlej to Bhután (altitude 6,000 to 10,000 feet) to the western ghâts; the latter seems to be confined to the North-West Himaláya. A yellow dye, obtained from the root, is used in tanning and colouring leather. From the wood is obtained a decoction, which is boiled down to form the resin-like substance known as *rusot.* The roots of several other species are used as dyes, *B. Nepalensis* affording a paler colour than the dye-stuff usually met with in Europe. A perfectly unlimited amount of barberry might be obtained from India.

1135.* BIXA ORELLANA, *Linn.;* Bixineæ. The Arnotto Dye; Latkan (*Hind.*). A graceful shrub, with handsome white or pinkish flowers and echinate red capsules; originally a native of America, now largely cultivated in India for the red or orange dye obtained from the pulp which surrounds the seed. This pulp gives a beautiful flesh colour, largely used in dyeing silks. It is altered by certain combinations into orange, deep orange, or red, the brighter orange and red colours being obtained in combination with the red powder of *Mallotus philippinensis.* The dye is exported to Europe chiefly from the West Indies, and is used to colour cheese and other edible articles, such as chocolate, &c. It may be extracted from the seeds direct, or the pulpy matter may by boiling be separated from the seeds and made into cakes like those of lac or indigo. In this form it is generally sold in Europe.

1136. BUTEA FRONDOSA, *Roxb.;* Leguminosæ. Bengal Kino Tree; Dhak (*Hind.*); Palas, palash (*Beng.*); Kinsuka (*Sans.*). A small, distorted tree with bright orange flowers, found all over India. The dried flowers, called tesu, are used as a yellow dye, the dye being extracted by simply steeping or boiling in water. The colour is, however, fleeting, but may be made less so by using alum or lime as a mordant, which also deepen the colour. Sometimes myrobalans are employed for this purpose, or the dye is combined with arnotto (*Bixa Orellana*). The gum also yields a bright vermilion colour which may be isolated; as yet this has not been put to any industrial purpose on account of its being difficult to fix. The flowers of the climbing species, *B. superba,* are also sold under the name of tesu. (*See* also 59, 416.)

1137.* CÆSALPINIA CORIARIA, *Willd.;* Leguminosæ. This is the American Divi-divi or Sumach. It has been successfully introduced into India, especially in the Madras Presidency. The sinuous pods of this plant are used for tanning leather.

1138. C SAPPAN, *Linn.* The Sappan Wood; Bakam (*Hind.*). A small, thorny tree of the Eastern and Western Peninsula and Pegu. Cultivated in Central India. The wood yields a valuable dye, which is largely exported. The dye is also said to be prepared from the pods (*taira*), from the pith, from the bark, or from all together. The pods are used in Monghyr along with proto sulphate of iron to give a black colour. Sappan wood is largely used in calico-printing, its price being about 12 Rs. a cwt. Chips of the wood steeped in water yield the red colour. This is intensified by alkalis. Combined with turmeric and sulphate of iron, it gives the colour known as Kalejai. With indigo it gives (*sausni*) purple. Sappan colour, however, is not permanent, being formed through the presence of the soluble substance Brazilin. (*See* also 61.)

1139.* CARTHAMUS TINCTORIUS, *Linn.;* Compositæ. The Safflower; Kusum (*Hind.*). An annual, herbaceous plant, with large, yellow flower-heads, cultivated as a dye-crop all over India. The flowers yield both a red and a yellow dye; and the seeds give a useful oil. To prepare the red dye, the yellow is first carefully removed. This is done by reducing the flowers to a powder and sprinkling over this a little water or oil. The powder after a time is carefully rubbed in the hand or squeezed in bags under the feet while pure water is being poured over it. After a time, the yellow dye is completely removed. This is either rejected as useless or is used as a base colour before the red. After the removal of the yellow dye, an alkali is mixed with the powdered flowers and rubbed in with the hand. On placing this mixture on a strainer, the bright red solution is obtained. This is one of the most beautiful of all Indian dies, but it is fleeting. The cultivation of safflower was once upon a time one of the most important industries in Bengal. The trade is now almost entirely ruined, aniline having driven it completely out of the market. Messrs. Modan Mohan Bysack and Brothers of Dacca exhibit samples of their safflower. (*See* also 420, 1005.)

1140. CASSIA AURICULATA, *Linn.;* Leguminosæ. Tarwar (*Hind.*). A common shrub in South and Central India. The bark is one of the most valuable of Indian tans, and is also, like myrobalans, used to modify dyes. It gives a buff colour to leather. The flowers yield a yellow colouring matter. (*See* also 774.)

1141. C. TORA, *Linn.* The Fœtid Cassia; Chakunda (*Hind.*); Tarota (*Dec.*); Prabanatha (*Sans.*). A gregarious under-shrub, from 1 to 2 ft. in height, found everywhere in Bengal, widely spread and abundant throughout India. In Mysore the seeds of this bush are regularly sold to the indigo dyers, who use them to produce certain effects with indigo which they cannot otherwise produce. In experimenting with these seeds Mr. Thomas Wardle of Leek discovered, however, that they yield a beautiful yellow colour, which may be usefully employed in silk-dyeing. This property appears to be quite unknown to the natives of India, although other species of *Cassia* afford freely the same colouring material on macerating a powder of the dry ripe seeds. (*See* also 491, 779.)

1142. CEDRELA TOONA, *Roxb.;* Meliaceæ. The

Toon or Indian Mahogany Tree; Tun (*Hind.*). A tree about 50 to 60 ft. in height, abundant in the plains of India and lower hills, ascending to 6,000 ft. in altitude. The flowers yield a red and a yellow dye (in Bengal generally known as *Gulnari*); said to be used in Mysore for dyeing cotton. The flowers are boiled to extract the colour, which is known as basanti in the North-West Provinces. It is fleeting, and apparently only used by the poorer classes. In Burma it is used in conjunction with safflower. (*See* also 78.)

1143. CERIOPS CANDOLLEANA, *Arnott.*; Rhizophoreæ. Often called a Mangrove (*see* RHIZOPHORA); Goran (*Beng.*); Mada (*And.*). A small evergreen tree, met with on the muddy shores and tidal creeks of India and the Andaman Islands. The bark is used for tanning. This and *C. Roxburghii* are economically not distinguished, both being used under the name of *garan* or *goran.* They impart a good red colour to leather. They are exceedingly valuable tans, and deserve to be brought more prominently to the notice of European tanners.

1144. COCCUS CACTI, *Linn.*; Hemiptera. Cochineal Dye. The dried bodies of the female insects; obtained commercially from America and Central Asia, but recently procured in small quantities from Rajputana and South India. Experiments to extend, in South India, the rearing of this insect, appear, practically speaking, to have failed. The plant on which it feeds is abundant and quite naturalised. The dye is held in high esteem.

1145. C. LACCA. Lac Dye. A dye obtained by the evaporation of the liquid in which stick-lac has been washed. As a European article of trade, lac-dye seems to have been driven out of the market completely by aniline, and to a limited extent also by cochineal. It is used by the natives as a dye, but chiefly in colouring leather. The European lac manufacturers, who formerly used to prepare the dye as a by-product have discontinued doing so, since it does not now pay them to boil down the washings of lac for the dye. (*See* also 1126.)

1146. COSCINIUM FENESTRATUM, *Colebrooke*; Menispermaceæ, Jar-ki-huldi (*Dec.*); Haldi-Gach (*Beng.*); Maru munjil (*Tam*); Manipussupu (*Tel.*). An extensive climber of the forests of the Western Peninsula, extending to Ceylon and the Straits. The chips of wood yield a yellow dye. Dr. Bidie remarks:—"This wood contains much colouring matter, akin in properties to that of turmeric," hence the name *jar-ki-haldi* or *gach-haldi.*

1147.* CURCUMA LONGA, *Roxb.*; Scitamineæ. The Turmeric; Haldi (*Hind.*). Turmeric is cultivated all over India. The rhizomes yield a valuable yellow dye, which, with alkalis, changes into a deep red. (*See* also 663.)

1148. CYNOMETRA RAMIFLORA, *Linn.*; Leguminosæ. Shingr (*Beng.*); Irapu (*Tam.*); Myenka-pen, myinka (*Burm.*). A large evergreen tree of the Sunderbans, South India, and Burma, in tidal forests. Frequent from Chittagong to Tenasserim; also in the Andaman Islands. Skinner says that chips of the wood give, in water, a purple dye.

1149. DATISCA CANNABINA, *Linn.*; Datisceæ. Akalber (*Hind.*); Bhang-jala (*Pb.*); Bayr-bunja (*Sind.*). A tall, erect herb, resembling hemp, hence the specific name; met with in the Punjáb Himálaya. Said to give a red and yellow dye.

1150. DELPHINIUM SANICULÆFOLIUM (*Boiss.*); Ranunculaceæ. Asbarg, ghafiz (*Pb.*); Zarir (*Arab.*); Asfrak, trayaman (*Pers.*). A small, herbaceous plant, met with in the Himálaya on dry hills from the Jhelam to the Indus, and distributed to Afghánistán. The dried flowers are brought from Afghánistán to Multan, where they are used along with *akalbér* (*Datisca cannabina*) and alum, to impart a sulphur yellow die to silk.

1151. ERIOBOTRYA BENGALENSIS, *Hook. f.*; Rosaceæ. Berkung (*Lepcha*). A small tree of the Eastern Himálaya, altitude 4,000 ft.; also in the Khasia Hills, Chittagong, and Ava. The bark is said to be used in Nepal for dyeing scarlet.

1152. FLEMINGIA CONGESTA, *Roxb.*; Leguminosæ. The Waras of Africa; Bara-salpan, bhalia (*Beng.*). An erect, woody shrub, common in the thickets and forests of the warmer parts of India. The glandular hairs from the pods yield with alcohol a red colour. The Kamela dye of India has for long been exported to Europe under the idea that it was the same thing as the Waras of Africa. This mistake was only recently detected by Prof. W. T. T. Dyer, Director, Royal Botanic Gardens, Kew, and it is remarkable that while both plants are equally common in India, the dye property of only the one—Kamela—was discovered by the natives of India. Mr. Wardle regards the Kamela as a better dye-stuff than the Waras. Professor Lawson, Director of the Botanic Gardens, Madras, exhibits a sample of the Indian Waras dye.

1153. LAWSONIA ALBA, *Lam.*; Lythraceæ. Henna, Mmendi (*Hind.*). Wild in Baluchistan and on the Coromandel Coast, and perhaps also in Central India; cultivated throughout India. The henna dye is used to give the nails, hair, &c., an orange colour. For this purpose the freshly-gathered leaves are pounded with catechu or lime; with indigo it is sometimes used to dye the hair black. As a dye for fabrics it is very fleeting, and, therefore, rarely used.

1154. MALLOTUS PHILIPPINENSIS, *Mull.*; Euphorbiaceæ. Punag, kamalaguri (the dye powder), *Beng.*; Kamela, kamal (*Pb.*); Kapila (*Bomb.*); Kapli, kapila (*Tam.*). A small tree of the sub-Himálayan tract, from the Indus eastward (ascending to 4500 ft.) to Bengal, Central and South India, Burma and the Andaman Islands. The dye is obtained from epidermal glands of the fruit. It gives a rich red colour used in dyeing silk and wool, and does not require a mordant. About 80 per cent. of resin is extracted from the colouring agent through the means of alcohol. Dr. Schlich says the root also yields a red dye. The bark is largely used in tanning leather in the North-West Provinces. (*See* also 815.)

1155. MANGIFERA INDICA, *Linn.*; Anacardiaceæ. The Mango Tree; Am (*Hind.*); Amra (*Sans.*). A densely-branched tree, wild on the Western Gháts, the Chutia Nagpur Hills, and the Naga Hills; cultivated all over India for its fruit. The bark and the leaves yield a yellow dye not much used, but the dry unripe fruit is largely used as a mordant, especially in dyeing with safflower. The leaves are also used in tanning by the poorer classes in Oudh. The bark is said to be used in the Dacca district, Bengal, as tan. (*See* also 171, 446, 604, 816.)

1156. MARSDENIA TINCTORIA, *R. Br.*; Asclepiadeæ. Kali lara (*Nepal*); Ryom (*Lepcha*). A climbing shrub of the North-East Himálaya and Burma. The leaves of this plant yield an indigo blue dye which, by combinations, may be deepened into black. This is the indigo plant of Sikkim. (*See* also 1122.)

1157. MORINDA ANGUSTIFOLIA, *Roxb.*; Rubiaceæ. Asugach (*Ass.*); Kchai-tun (*Phekial*); Chenung, chengrung (*Caro*); Yeyo (*Burm.*). An erect bush, or small tree, of the tropical Himalaya, wild and cultivated from Nepal eastward, ascending to 4000 ft., also met with in Assam, the Khasia and Naga Hills, Chittagong and Tenasserim. This may be recognised from the other species by the caudate-acuminate leaves, taper-into the petiole, and the fruit 1 in. in diameter or less, consisting of five free and turbinate black drupes. Bark and wood yield a good yellow dye. Brandis remarks this species is "cultivated in toungyas in Burma as a dye."

1158. M. CITRIFOLIA, *Linn.* A small tree cultivated or wild (?) throughout the hotter parts of India, Burma, and Ceylon. It may be recognised from the preceding species by the leaves being elliptic, acute, or obtuse, shining; fruit, of many drupes coalescent into a fleshy, globose head, 1 in. in diameter. The "Flora of British India" has reduced the form of this plant to the following varieties:—Var. 1st. *citrifolia* proper, *Roxb.*; *Fl. Ind.* i. 541. The Al (*Hind.*): Ach, aich or achhu (*Beng.*); Ala, bartondi (*Bomb.*); Munja pavattary (*Tam.*); Ye-o, Nyaw kyee or nyau-ki (*Burm.*); Suranji, a common trade name. Supposed to be truly wild in Malacca. Largely cultivated throughout India. This is the chief dye-yielding form. Var. 2nd. *bracteata*, sp. (*Roxb.*); *Fl. Ind.* i. 544. The Hurdi, huldi, kung (*Hind., Beng.*): Nagakunda (*Bomb.*). Roxburgh regards this form as a native of Ganjam in Orissa, and Thwaites views it as wild in Ceylon. It is not unfrequent in the forests of the Andaman Islands (*Kurz*), and here and there in the forests of the Terai near the Tista (*Schlich*). Var. 3rd. *elliptica.* A form met with in the Concan, Malacca, &c.; in point of foliage intermediate between *M. angustifolia* and *M. citrifolia.*

The young roots, root-bark, and even chips of wood of the above varieties yield a valuable red dye. With regard to the cultivation of the *al*, Mr. Buck, in his account of the dyes and tans of the North-Western Provinces, states that an acre will produce about 10 maunds of root, one-third of each class. He gives the following classes of the dye-stuff:—1st class.—Thin rootlets (*Hargharka, bhara bar*). 2nd class.—Middle sized (*Lari, jharan, pachmer*). 3rd class.—Thick roots (*Pachat, ghatiya*). The *bhara*, or thin, thread-like rootlets yield the true dye. The thicker roots are very inferior, and often almost worthless. The *bhara* fetch about Rs. 8 a maund, the second quality Rs. 4, and the third Rs. 2. The plant takes three and a-half years to reach maturity; the cultivator therefore requires a high price, which he cannot now obtain. On placing a few twigs of *al* in pure water, at first a yellow colour is extracted, but if allowed to ferment, or if a little alkali be added in the course of two or three days the solution becomes purple red. The process of dyeing, as actually practised by the Indian dyers, is tedious, and, in consequence, the use of this dye-stuff is rapidly disappearing through the introduction of the cheap and more showy aniline dyes. The colours produced vary from reddish yellow to dark brown. The thread or fabric is previously prepared by being steeped for three or four days in powdered castor oil seeds and cow-dung with water. After washing it is soaked in a decoction of myrobalans, then in alum. It is next removed, washed, dried, and thereafter boiled in the dye solution. It is finally sized and beaten smooth with wooden clubs. *Al* is largely used in dyeing the cotton yarn afterwards spun into fancy borders for the garments of the poorer classes. It is sometimes employed for silk, *e.g.*, with the *eri* silk; but the chief use of al is to dye the coarse *Kharua* cloth. Fabrics dyed with *al* are said not to be attacked by white ants; and it is commonly stated that on this account the dye is used for certain purposes such as to dye the cloth used to cover account-books.

1159. M. TINCTORIA, *Roxb.* This is considered by many Indian botanists to be but a wild form of *M. citrifolia*, Linn. It is probable, however, that var. *bracteata* is the wild form of that species, and that this is a distinct and almost entirely wild species. It may be distinguished from the preceding by the leaves being acute at both ends, glabrous or pubescent, but not shining; fruit, of many drupes coalescent into a head, generally less than 1 in. in diameter. The following are the forms of this species recognised by the "Flora of British India":—Var. 1st.—*Tinctoria* proper, Roxb.; "Fl. Ind." i. 543. The Al, ak acha, auch (Hind., Beng.). *Var. 2nd.*—*Tomentosa*, sp., Heyne, as in "Kurz," ii. 60. Not unfrequent in the dry forests of Prome. Dye obtained from the interior of the wood of old trees. Var. 3rd.—*Multiflora*, sp., Roxb.; "Fl. Ind." i. 546. In Nagpore and Berar where it is called aál. Var. 4th.—*Aspera*, sp., W. & A.; Prod., 420. The plant which Roxburgh called *M. exserta*, and which was republished by Beddome, Kurz, and Gamble, is pronounced by the "Flora of British India" to be a mere sexual condition of either *M. citrifolia* or *M. tinctoria*, being a condition in which the stamens are exserted from the mouth of the corolla; it cannot therefore be regarded even as a variety. It will be observed that *M. citrifolia* (Linn.), in the above notes is kept up as distinct from *M. tinctoria*, (Roxb.), but it may be added that while they both receive the same names in the jungles, *M. citrifolia* is the form which is most frequently met with under the name of *Al* or *Ach*, and is the chief source of the dye of commerce. In some parts of India the dyers make a distinction between *al* and *ach*, but it is believed that they allude to different qualities of the dye-stuff and not to the products of different species. (*See* also 188.)

1160. NYCTANTHES ARBOR-TRISTIS, *Linn.*; Oleaceæ, Harsinghar, shinghar (*Hind.*). A small shrub of Central India, ascending to altitude 3000 ft., and extending to Bengal and Burma. Cultivated throughout India. The lower or tubular portion of the corolla constitutes the dye material. It is orange-coloured and yields a beautiful but fleeting orange or golden dye, sometimes used for silk. *Harsinghar* is sometimes used in combination with turmeric. Half a seer of the dye-stuff is said to be sufficient to colour 60 yards of silk cloth. (*See* also 196, 826.)

1161. OCHRE. The essential ingredient is peroxide of iron, whether as an anhydrous red hæmatite or the hydrated brown and yellow limonites, but there is a wide range in the proportion of this colouring matter that may be contained in a marketable "Ochre," from the pure pigment manufactured on a large scale at Katni by crushing the rich hæmatite ore occurring there, down to the ochreous clay (layering) largely used as a black *khaki* dye in Manipur, although it contains only nine per cent. of limonite. These instance the great range in the mode of occurrence of this substance,—from the metallic lode in very ancient rocks down to the most recent alluvial clays. The old rocks of India are peculiarly rich in ores of iron, and these have naturally affected all the later derivative formations. The basaltic formation covering so large an area of Western India is another primary source of ferruginous matter; beds of bole (a variety of ochre) are not unfrequent in it. From these stores were derived the characteristically ochrey rock known as laterite, which occurs so widely throughout India. Originally deposits of iron peroxides, such as those already mentioned, whether in veins or in beds, pure or mixed with clay, would in most cases yield an unlimited supply; but in a collection of ochres made promiscuously from native sources a large number would probably be of secondary origin, *i.e.*, local and superficial decomposition products of rocks or minerals containing iron in some other state of combination. The occurrence of these small local sources would be innumerable, but the supply would of course be limited; hence the need for competent observation in each case. The ochres are of course chiefly used as pigments, but a few are also employed as dyes, such as the *khaki* ochres and red hæmatite.

1162. OCHROCARPUS LONGIFOLIUS, *Bth. & Hook. f.*; Guttiferæ. Suringi (*Mahr.*); Sura-ponna (*Tel.*). The flower-buds are known as Lambada Nagkesara. A large, deciduous tree of the Western Ghâts. The dried flower-buds are used for dyeing silk; they are about the size of cloves and are of a red colour. Dr. Dymock says that the *Nagkesar* referred to in "Spon's Encycl." under the name of *Mesua ferrea* are the flower-buds of this plant.

1163. OLDENLANDIA UMBELLATA, *Linn.*; Rubiaceæ. Chay Root (sometimes called Indian madder); Surbuli (*Beng.*); Cheri-vello (*Tel.*); Saya-wer, Imburel (*Tam.*). A small bush or herb found on sandy soils. Abundant in certain tracts of the Madras Presidency from Orissa southward. It occurs also in Ceylon and North Burma. The bark of the root gives a beautiful red. It is curious that this dye does not appear to be used in Bengal; the root from the Puri district, Orissa, is entirely exported to Madras. Drury, in his 'Useful Plants of India,' Appendix D., states that a much cheaper, though less durable, dye may be prepared from the bark of the root of the Deccan plant known as *Cherinji*, when used with a leaf called *jagi*. It seems probable from the similarity in the word *Cherinji* with the Telugu name *cheri-vello* for the above species, that the *Cherinji* may prove another species of *Oldenlandia*, and it is possible that by *jagi* is meant *Jasminum grandiflorum*, L.

1164. PEORI DYE. This curious dye-stuff is obtained from the urine of cattle fed entirely on mango leaves. It is usually met with in the bazaars of the Punjáb in roundish balls known as *Hardwari peori*. A considerable trade is carried on in this dye at Monghyr in Bengal. The smell is exceedingly offensive, and even after repeated washings, the dye imparts the smell of cow's urine to cloth dyed with it. It, however, gives a bright yellow, and seems to be composed of magnesia and purreic acid; the latter substance may be separated by treating the dye solution with dilute muriatic acid. *Peori* is also the name applied to chrome yellow, which this substance very much resembles. Cow urine (*peori* or *peri*) is chiefly used as a pigment. A very similar yellow colour is produced from the pollen grains of *Cedrus Deodara*. Mr. Duthie, Superintendent of the Botanic Gardens, Saharanpur, has contributed a specimen of deodar yellow.

1165. PERISTROPHE TINCTORIA, *Nees.*; Acanthaceæ. Bet or Batia-rung (*Beng.*); Ghátípitta-pápada (*Bomb.*). A common, bushy plant in Bengal, occurring everywhere in the woods around Calcutta, the flowers appearing in October. It is said to be largely cultivated in Midnapur, Bengal. It yields the red dye used to colour the *Masland* mats of Midnapur. The twigs yield dye, being cut into small chips for this purpose.

1166. PHYLANTHUS EMBLICA, *Linn.*; Euphorbiaceæ. Amla, Aonla (*Hind.*, *Beng.*). A moderate-sized tree in the dry forests of India and Burma. The fruit is the Emblic Myrobalan, used as a medicine and in dyeing and tanning. The leaves are also used in tanning in most parts of India along with *Terminalia*, *Shorea*, &c.; in fact the leaves of this plant are regarded as one of the best tans by the Bengal tanners. A black dye is obtained from the fruit, along with the ordinary myrobalans and sulphate of iron. Recently Mr. Wardle has shown that the leaves afford a valuable yellow dye for silk; this does not appear to be known to the natives of India. (*See* also 612, 834.)

1167. PTEROCARPUS MARSUPIUM, *Roxb.;* Leguminosæ. Gum Kino; Bija, Bijasar, Salbia (*Hind.*). A large tree of Central and South India, extending northward to Banda in the North-West Provinces; often cultivated in gardens. This yields gum Kino, a resinous substance known in Europe for upwards of a century. It is the dried juice which exudes copiously on the stem being artificially wounded. This substance is sometimes used as an auxiliary in dyeing and tanning, and the heartwood of the tree, cut up into chips, may also be used to give a yellow dye. (*See* also 225, 465, 1080.)

1168. PTEROCARPUS SANTALINUS, *Linn. f.* The Sanders Red or Red Sanders Tree, sometimes also called Red Sandalwood; Lal-chandan, Raktachandan (*Hind., Beng.*). A small tree of South India, chiefly in Cuddapah, North Arcot, Karnul, cultivated in Bengal and other parts of India. The wood is used as a dye-stuff, and is sent largely from Madras to other parts in India. It is chiefly employed to "mark idols and the forehead in ceremonies." The colouring principle is called "Santalin." It is soluble in alcohol, and is sometimes used to dye cloth, imparting a pale pink colour. (*See* also 226.)

1169.* PUNICA GRANATUM, *Linn.;* Lythraceæ. The Pomegranate; Granades; Anar, Darim, Damu (*Hind.*). A small tree, or large shrub, wild in some parts of the North-Western Himálaya; cultivated throughout India. The flowers are said to be used in Bellary to give a light red dye. The fruit-rind (*Náspal*) is astringent, and is a valuable tan. It is said to be used in the tanning of morocco leather, imparting to it the characteristic colour. It is often used as a dye-auxiliary, especially with turmeric or indigo. Dr. McCann says the "bark gives a yellow, or with alum and *Cassia Fistula*, a red dye," and Mr. Buck, that it gives a greenish decoction. Mr. Wardle has succeeded in extracting a good yellow for silk-dyeing from the rind. (*See* also 620, 841.)

1170. QUERCUS LAMELLOSA, *Sm.;* Cupuliferæ. Shalshi, Budgrat (*Nepal*); Buk (*Lepcha*). A large, handsome tree, with broad, serrate leaves, silvery below, with many regular parallel veins; met with in Nepal and eastward to Sikkim, Bhután, the Naga Hills, and the mountains on the Burma-Manipur frontier. In Darjeeling the bark is used for tanning. (*See* also 234.)

1171. RHIZOPHORA MUCRONATA, *Lamk.;* Rhizophoreæ. The Mangrove Tree; Bhara (*Beng.*). A small tree, frequent in tidal forests from Arracan and Pegu to Tenasserim, and on the tidal shores of West India and the Andaman Islands. The bark is good for tanning. Mr. Christy recommends this to be used as a preliminary preparation for cheap leathers. The skins should be about half prepared in India and exported to Europe in that condition, to be redone and have the colour improved by myrobalans or other tanning materials. Mangrove Bark has been exported to Europe, but leather prepared with it is always inferior in colour and quality. Except therefore as a preliminary tan, or in the preparation of cheap leathers, it is not likely to become an article of much European trade. (See also 240.)

1172.* RICINUS COMMUNIS, *Linn.;* Euphorbiaceæ. The Castor Oil Plant or Palma Christi; Arendi (*Hind.*). A large shrub, indigenous in Arabia and North Africa; cultivated throughout India. The seeds are used by Indian dyers to assist in the isolation of certain colours such as with *al* (*Morinda citrofolia*); they seem also to have the power of rendering dyes more permanent. (See also 843, 1043.)

1173. RUBIA CORDIFOLIA, *Linn.;* Rubiaceæ. The Indian Madder; Manjit (*Hind.*). A small, herbaceous climber, often growing in festoons over the neighbouring vegetation forming masses of 6 to 8 ft. in length. There are two easily recognised primary forms met with in India. It is worth distinguishing these, as this may assist to explain the fact that one consignment of madder is often found to be much inferior to another.

Var. 1*st*. *Cordifolia* proper. Leaves, four in a whorl, more or less cordate on petioles not more than 1 in. long; generally five costate, rarely three, veins impressed; surface rough or hispid. This is the form chiefly met with on the Himálaya, appearing in Afghánistán and distributed eastward to Sikkim and Bhután, altitude 8,000 ft., to the Khásia and Naga Hills, Burma, South India, and Ceylon. It seems nowhere to be cultivated, but is largely collected as a wild dye-stuff and carried to the plains to be sold. The root and lower or ground twigs are the dye-yielding portions.

Var. 2*nd*. *Khásia*. Leaves on petioles, generally 1, 1½ or 2 inches long; three costate, rarely five, often almost with a solitary midrib, smooth, not hispid, and veins not impressed. This form appears to be richer in the dye-principle than the preceding, but in both cases the plants must be of the same age, otherwise comparison will be impossible, since the dye only appears when mature. This form is met with in Sikkim, but it attains its greatest development eastward in the Khásia and Naga Hills. It seems nowhere to occur to the west of Sikkim. This may probably prove the plant to which Roxburgh wished to assign the name *R. manjista*. The dye twigs are rarely as thick as a pencil, the bark is smooth and thin, and the wood purple red. When mounted on paper a dried flowering specimen will be found to impart its colour freely to articles placed in contact with it, a fact which never occurs with *R. cordifolia* proper.

1174. RUBIA SIKKIMENSIS, *Kurz.* An extensive sub-woody climber; branches with long internodes and retrorsely scabrid; leaves 3 to 6 by 1 to 2 inches, sessile, or nearly so, four in the whorl, elliptic or ovate lanceolate, three, rarely five, costate. This is the largest and the most handsome species in the genus, growing along the ground or over bushes and small trees, with branches often 3 to 4 yards long, and the whorls of leaves as much as a foot apart. It makes its appearance in Sikkim and is distributed eastward to the Khásia and Naga Hills, where it is perhaps the most common species. Apparently the Lepchas of Sikkim do not know that this plant yields the madder dye, but the thick coarse roots with soft corky bark (many times thicker than the roots and twigs of *R. cordifolia*) which are sold in the bazars at Darjeeling and throughout India belong to this species, though they are probably collected as an adulterant to the *manjit*. The idea of this oversight is strengthened by the fact that until 1874 the plant was not named or even known to exist. Specimens had of course been collected, but they escaped attention, having remained for many years unpublished in the larger Herbaria, and the roots and stems which are regularly used as dyes, and even exported from Sikkim for this purpose, appear to have been mistaken for those of *R. cordifolia*. In the Naga Hills and in Manipur this species alone supplies the brilliant red dye used by the hill tribes to colour their cloths, hair decorations for spears, shields and earrings, &c., as well as to stain their cane and bamboo plaited work. The process of extracting the dye is curious. It was personally observed in Manipur, and the following brief account gives the ingredients and method of extracting the dye as practised by the Nagas and Manipuris. A woman brought with her the following:—1st. Two or three bundles of the root and stem of *R. sikkimensis*, Kurz. 2nd. A slab of the bark of *Quercus fenestrata*, Roxb., and of *Alnus Nepalensis* (either being used). 3rd. A bundle of twigs and leaves of *Symplocos racemosa*, Roxb. 4th. A packet of the seed of *Perilla ocimoides*—a grain eaten in the Naga Hills (see Grains). 5th. Two skeins of cotton thread, one of which was of a faint yellow colour and the other white. The former had been treated by a mordant prepared from No. 3. 6th. Two earthen vessels. 7th. A small basket. To prepare the second skein of cotton with the mordant, the woman sat down and set fire to the bundle of twigs and leaves of *Symplocos racemosa*. When completely burned to ashes, these were carefully collected and placed in the corner of the basket and a little water was sprinkled over and allowed to soak for a few minutes; then more water was sprinkled, until ultimately a yellowish liquid began to strain through and trickle into one of the earthen vessels placed below the basket. When enough saline liquid had been thus collected the second or unprepared skein of cotton was placed in the vessel and boiled for some time; after which it was removed, wrung out, and the now yellow and mordanted skein was hung up to dry. The next stage was then proceeded with. The woman and her assistant commenced to pound the chips of *Rubia sikkimensis*, using about equal proportions of root and stem. When this had been done the powder was mixed (about a quarter as much as powdered madder) with a handful of the seeds of *Perilla*, and intimately combined and rubbed together by the hand on a stone. This mixture was then placed in the second earthen vessel and boiled with about three proportions of water to one of the mixed powder. When boiling, the prepared skein of cotton was plunged into the solution, which was now of a deep red colour. It was turned round and round in the boiling liquid upon the extremity of a small twig, and when dyed to the required depth, it was removed and allowed to strain off the surplus liquid. Thereafter it was washed several times and hung out to dry. The second skein was treated in a like manner only that the bark No. 2 was added to the solution. This had the effect of deepening the colour to dark red or brown.

1175.* Rubia tinctorium, *Linn.* The European Madder. Leaves subsessile, four to six in a whorl, elliptic or lanceolate, penninerved, 2–4 by ½–1¼ in. acuminate margins, and nerves beneath prickly. Cultivated in Kashmír, Sind, and distributed to Afghánistán and westward to Spain; wild or cultivated. The venation is so distinct from the 3-5 sub-parallel nerved condition of the preceding species, that a glance at the feather-veined form of this plant would be enough to enable any ordinary observer to say for certain whether the madder he was examining was the true European plant or the Indian forms, *R. cordifolia* or *R. sikkimensis*. It is believed that this plant is much more extensively cultivated in India than we have any actual evidence of at present. Dr. Aitchison says that the roots of *R. Kotschyi*, Boiss, are used to colour the hard-boiled eggs required by the Afgháns at a certain festivity. The interest in this consists in that while *R. cordifolia* is described by that author as "a very common weed in the hedges all over the country, always in damp localities, from Kumaon to Alikhel," it is not the madder dye-yielding plant of these regions. This fact seems to support the opinion already given regarding the form of *R. cordifolia* met with on the western extremity of the Himálaya. Stewart's remarks in his "Punjáb Plants" would almost lead one to the same conclusion, for he affirms that *R. tinctorium*, Linn., is the dye-yielding species of the Punjáb Himálaya, being cultivated in the upper Sutlej valley at Kanáwar, beyond the Indus in Gandava, and abundantly at Kabul. The Indian-grown madder from this species may be recognised by the fact of its always occurring in short broken pieces instead of in long twigs as with *R. cordifolia* or *R. sikkimensis*.

1176. Strobilanthes flaccidifolius, *Nees;* Acanthaceæ. Assam Indigo Rúm, Rámpát (*Ass.*); Khúma, Khúm (*Manipur*). A shrub, wild and cultivated in Assam and Eastern Bengal, altitude 1000 to 4000 ft. It yields indigo. This plant grows freely on the plains of Manipur, in a climate not very different from that of many parts of Bengal, Behar, or the North-West Provinces, and might be extensively cultivated in Assam. It does not require the flooding which is necessary for the early growth of the Bengal indigo plant, and is therefore not exposed to the danger of having its colour extracted during an exceptionally rainy season. In fact in many respects it possesses properties eminently suited for a profitable indigo crop, and in China at least, the dye is produced on a large scale and of a quality pronounced finer than the dye obtained from any other plant. It is propagated freely by cuttings, yields prunings twice or three times a year, and is perennial. Its cultivation might be combined with that of the Bengal indigo plant. The *rúm* would flourish on the higher dry lands in the plantation, yielding its crop probably in the cold and the hot season, while the ordinary indigo might be grown in the low-flooded lands and occupy the attention of the planter during the rest of the year. At present an indigo factory is silent for more than half the year, but with *Strobilanthes flaccidifolius* this need not be so. In Manipur the *khúma* is largely cultivated, and the dye is extracted for home use; nearly every owner of a farm cultivates a small plot of it and prepares his own dye. The twigs, about a foot long, are twice or three times a year plucked and deposited in large earthen pots filled with water. In these primitive vats they are left for the required time, and when ready the decoction of a greenish colour is poured into another pot and violently shaken or stirred by a few twigs. A little lime is generally added, and when the transformation of green into blue indigo has been effected, the liquid is poured into a small earthen vessel and boiled down, more and more being added until from the evaporation of the liquid the vessel becomes filled with the dye-stuff. A little lime is then placed in the mouth of the vessel, which is thereafter placed in the sun to complete the drying of the dye. In this form it is stored for family use or sold in the market. The dye, in combination with turmeric, is employed to produce shades of green; with lime and turmeric, browns and almost reds; with lime alone, deep blue black; with safflower, purple; and so on as in the ordinary combinations with indigo. A large series of Assam blue cloths are shown both in the Economic and in the Assam Art-ware Courts—these are nearly all dyed with the indigo from this plant. (*See* also 1123.)

1177. SYMPLOCOS RACEMOSA, *Roxb.*; Styraceæ. Lodh (*Hind.*, *Ben.*, *Bomb.*); Chamlani (*Nepall*). A common, small tree found in the low hills of Bengal, Orissa, Chutia Nagpur, and the Terai, altitude 2,500 ft., and distributed to Assam, Burma, and China. The dye property is said to reside in the thick, corky, grey bark; it yields a good yellow. It is chiefly used as an auxiliary with other dye-stuffs, and in addition to imparting its own colour and thus modifying the shade, it is supposed to produce other effects in sharpening and fixing the colours. No other dye substance is so extensively used by the Indian dyers, and its peculiar properties therefore deserve to be more carefully investigated than has been done hitherto. It is used for apparently the same purpose by the most remote and diverse tribes,—from the Kolarian races of the central table-land of India to the wild tribes on the Assam-Chinese frontier. In the Central Provinces the *lodh bark* is considered one of the best tans. (*See* also 271.)

1178. TAMARIX.—There are six species of Tamarisk met with in India, which all bear the generic vernacular name of *Jhau*. They afford galls which are highly prized on account of the very great amount of tannin they contain. They are regarded as one of the most valuable of Indian tans, and a considerable export trade is now done in them. The following are the most important species:—

1179. TAMARIX ARTICULATA, *Vehl.*; Tamariscineæ. A bush or coniferous-looking tree, abundant in Sind and the Punjáb, often cultivated. This is the *Farás* of the Punjáb and the *Asrelei* of Sind. (*See* also 274.)

1180. T. DIOICA, *Roxb.* A small tree frequent in river banks from Sind and the Punjáb to Assam and throughout the Western Peninsula to Burma; frequent also on the sea coast. This is the *Lei* of the Punjáb, the *Gaz* or *lao* of Sind, and the *Lal Jhau* of India generally.

1181. TAMARIX GALLICA, *Linn.* A small tree or gregarious bush, common throughout India near rivers and on the sea coast. This is the true *Jhau* of Indian writers, and the *Jhavuka* or *Shavaka* of Sanskrit literature.

1182. TERMINALIA.—Several species of trees belonging to this genus afford valuable tans. The barks of all are rich in tanning materials, and the fruits of at least two constitute the so-called myrobalans of commerce, viz., *T. Chebula*, the Chebulic or Black Myrobalan, and *T. belerica*, the Beleric Myrobalan. The young twigs of *T. Chebula* are nearly always covered with galls, which, by the natives of India, are used both in dyeing and tanning, and in the manufacture of ink. These galls do not appear to have been exported from India hitherto, although they could be supplied to an unlimited extent. The following are the more valuable tannin-yielding Terminalias:—

1183. TERMINALIA ARJUNA, *Beddome*; Combretaceæ. Anjan, Arjun (*Hind.*, *Beng.*). A large tree of the sub-Himálayan tracts of the North-West Provinces and Oudh, extending to Bengal, Burma, Central and South India. The fruits are described in the "Flora of British India" as one to two inches long, nearly glabrous, ovoid, or obovoid-oblong, the wings not very broad, their striations curving much upwards. The bark is a tonic and astringent, used sometimes in dyeing and tanning, serving as a concentrator of colour rather than as a dye material. It is, however, said to give a black dye with *bábúl* (*Acacia arabica*). (*See* also 278.)

1184. T. CHEBULA, *Retz.* The Chebulic or Black Myrobalan; Harra (*Hind.*): Haritáki (*Beng.*). A large tree, attaining the height of 80 to 100 feet, abundant in North India from Kumaon to Bengal, and southward to the Deccan tableland; also in Ceylon, Burma, and the Malayan Peninsula. The fruit is described as ¾ to 1¼ inch long, ellipsoidal or obovoid from a broad base, glabrous, more or less, 5-ribbed when dry. The bark is used for tanning and dyeing, and the fruit is the "Black Myrobalan;" this is reported to be of better quality than the Myrobalans from *T. belerica*. These Myrobalans are exceedingly valuable. In dyeing they are mixed with water, and after being allowed to soak for a time, the solution is ready. The cloth is steeped once or twice and dried, and then placed in the dye solution. With iron salts they give a black dye; they are used along with turmeric and indigo in the production of a green, and with catechu, they give a brown. With alum, the fruits are said to afford a yellow dye. In all these instances, however, the *harra* is a concentrator or vegetable mordant to the actual colours. The young twigs of the tree are often covered with galls; these are used in dyeing and tanning, and in the preparation of ink along with iron. The Rev. A. Campbell, Santal Missionary, Chutia Nagpur, exhibits an interesting series of Myrobalans, Terminalia galls, and Terminalia bark. The various Forest Officers throughout India have also contributed largely, and with the special show case furnished by the Chamber of Commerce of Bombay, the collection of Indian Myrobalans now on view is believed to be one of the largest and most complete ever exhibited. (*See* also 281, 855.)

1185. TERMINALIA BELERICA, *Roxb.* The Beleric Myrobalan; Bahera (*Hind.*). A deciduous tree, attaining a height of 60 to 80 feet, common in the plains and lower hills throughout India (except in the desert regions of West India). The fruit is described as ½ to ¾ inch in diameter, globular, suddenly narrowed into a short stalk, smooth, covered by a close, fulvous tomentum; when dried they are obscurely five-angled. This is one of the Myrobalans regularly exported from India, and is largely used in dyeing and in tanning and for making ink. The leaves and the fruits together are often used in tanning. (*See* also 279, 477, 501.)

1186. T. TOMENTOSA, *W. & A.* Saj, Asan (*Hind.*); Piasal, Usan (*Beng.*). A large tree of the sub-Himálaya from the Ravi eastward, ascending to altitude 4,000 feet, also in Bengal, Central and South, India, and Burma. The fruit is described as 1 to 2 inches long, glabrous or hoary obovoid, oblong, wings broad, striations carried horizontally to the edge. The bark is used for tanning and dyeing black, and the ashes yield a lime, often eaten by the natives in *pán*. It imparts the characteristic red colour to native leather, and cut up in small pieces and boiled for 6 or 8 hours, it gives a brown dye; along with the bark of *Mimusops Elengi* it is employed to give a red dye to jute. (*See* also 283.)

1187. WOODFORDIA FLORIBUNDA, *Salisb.*; Lythraceæ. This is sometimes called "Dyers' Flowers;" Dawi, Dha, Dhaula (*Hind.*). A small, much-branched bush, when in flower becoming simply purple, from its having numerous flowers all along the branches. Common throughout India, ascending on the Himálaya to altitude 5,000 feet. The flowers give a red colour used sometimes in silk dyeing. Alum or lime is employed as a mordant with it. These flowers are, however, more often used in combination with other dye-stuffs, particularly with *Al* (*Morinda*). The leaves are said to be sometimes resorted to as a tan along with the flowers, the latter imparting their colour to the skin. The leaves, along with the bark of *Zizyphus xylopyra*, constitute the tanning mixture of Bandelkhand, taking the place of *bábúl* (or Indian Wattle), so frequently used in most parts of India.

1188. WRIGHTIA TINCTORIA, *R. Br.*; Apocynaceæ. Bhur-kurri (*Bomb.*); Dudhi (*Banda*); Haya Marak (*Sans.*). A small tree, common in the Peninsula, ascending to 4,000 feet in altitude. The seeds are said to be used as an adjunct in dyeing, and the leaves yield an indigo prepared in Mysore.

EXHIBITORS: — A large collection of the wooden blocks used in calico-printing are exhibited, but chiefly from Madras and Jeypore.

OTHER EXHIBITS USED MAINLY FOR DECORATIVE PURPOSES.

Throughout the Imperial Court a large collection of photographs furnished by Messrs. Bourne and Shepherd, and Messrs. Johnston and Hoffmann of Calcutta, and by the Bombay and Madras Exhibition Committees, and the various native states of India.

A large selection of these will also be found in the Art Ware Courts and in the picture gallery. Those especially selected for the Imperial Court illustrate the every day life of the people of India, their trades and industries, together with an assortment to show Indian cities and mountain scenery. On the walls of the court will also be found Colonel Tanner's admirable water-colour sketches of Himalayan scenery, and sketches in water colours of a certain number of the races of people met with in India. Of the latter, a Hindu artist employed by the Government of India has furnished some life-like illustrations which have been greatly admired. These, together with Mrs. E. M. Hunter's water-colour drawings of the typical hill tribes of the North-Western Himalaya, have proved most attractive. A collection of photographs taken during the Gilgit Mission, together with portraits in oil of Major General Lockhart, General Barrow, C.B., and Captain Giles are also to be seen on the walls of the Court.

A very large assortment of domestic pottery will be found displayed throughout the Court, those from each province being grouped near the corresponding Ethnological sections: near by are also to be seen glass cases containing peasant jewellery, amongst which may be mentioned a most interesting collection of old brass work used for sacrificial purposes, contributed by Mr. J. H. Rivett Carnac, of the Opium Department. Mr. B. A. Gupte of Bombay has furnished a most instructive collection of objects used as charms in the Bombay Presidency.

SUPPLEMENTAL LIST OF PRODUCE *exhibited by* HIS HIGHNESS THE HONOURABLE THE MAHARAJAH OF VIZIANAGRAM, in the MADRAS PRESIDENCY.

1. *Oriza sativa*, commonly called Paddy; grown in wet lands, and used as a staple food by the people of the country, and shipped to the home market also. Several qualities.

2. *Cynosurus coracanus*, commonly called Raggy. This is a dry crop, and is used largely by the working and poorer classes as their staple food.

3. *Holcus spicatus*, commonly called Combú. This is also a dry crop, and is used by the working and poorer classes as food.

4. *Triticum vulgare*, or Wheat. This is grown near the hills.

5. *Holcus saccharatus*, commonly called Cholam. This is a dry crop, and is used in the shape of puddings and cakes. Also given to poultry.

6. *Panicum miliaccum*, or Millet. This is used as food by the poor.

7. *Panicum italicum.* This is the canary-seed of the Northern Circars, and is used as food by poor people, and makes splendid puddings.

8. *Zea Mays*, or Indian corn. In the unripe state this is boiled or toasted before being eaten. Not much praised by those who can afford to buy other grains.

9. *Glycine tomentosa*, commonly called Madras Horse-gram. Is the common food for horses in the Southern Presidency, and is much used by the lower classes as an article of diet.

10. *Phaseolus radiatus*, or Green-gram. This pulse is wholesome, and used by the natives almost daily as an article of diet.

11. *Citysus Cajan*, commonly called Red-gram. Used as an article of diet by the natives of the country.

12. *Trigonelia fœnum-græcum.* This is chiefly used as condiment by the natives, and by native practitioners in the affections of the bowels.

13. *Cicer arietinum*, Gram. This pulse is chiefly grown in the Northern Provinces, but also Madras. Used by natives in curries, but in Bengal it is common food for horses.

14. *Phaseolus Max*, commonly called Black Ulandu, used as an article of diet by the natives.

15. *Coriandrum sativum*, or Coriander fruit. Grows abundantly all over India. Used by natives as stomachic and gentle stimulant, and also as condiment with curries.

16. *Sesamum orientale*, commonly called 'Gingelly seed.' An oil is obtained from this by expression which is universally eaten by the natives, and also used in the process of dyeing silk of a pale orange colour. Large quantities are shipped annually for the home market.

17. *Pespalum frumentaceum.* This small grain is used by the poorest as an article of diet.

18. *Terminalia Chebula*, commonly called Myrobalans used by Native doctors as an astringent medicine. Is much employed in dyeing, and largely shipped for the home market.

19. *Curcuma longa*, commonly called Turmeric. Used as condiment in curries, and by dyers is employed in yellow and green.

20. *Strychnos potatorum*, commonly known as the clearing nut. Used by native practitioners as an astringent and for clearing muddy water by rubbing hard one of the seeds round the inside of the water pail. The impurities subside, and the water is found clear and tasteless.

21. *Strychnos Nux-Vomica.* A poison; in small doses it is a tonic, and is used by the natives largely in medicine.

22. *Ricinus communis.* Castor Oil. Chiefly used for producing lamp oil, and largely shipped for home market.

23. *Anacardium occidentale*, commonly called 'Cashew nut.' The pulp is eaten after being toasted.

24. *Semecarpus Anacardium*, or the Marking nut. The juice of the shell is used by native practitioners in venereal, scrofulous, and leprous affections. An oil is prepared from it by boiling, which is considered as a valuable application in rheumatism in the form of a blister.

25 Aloe fibre; used for making ropes, &c. Jute fibre; used for making gunnies, ropes, &c. Udda Nara; chiefly used for tying purposes.

26. A model of an up-country village.

A COLLECTION OF INDIGENOUS DRUGS. Exbited by the BARODA DURBAR. This contains 200 examples, together with a pharmacopœia, which is too technical to be included in this Catalogue.

PART II.

A GUIDE TO THE ETHNOLOGICAL MODELS AND EXHIBITS SHOWN IN THE IMPERIAL COURT.

BY

GEORGE WATT, M.B., C.M., F.L.S., C.I.E.

In point of interest to the student of Ethnology, India is second to no other country. Wave after wave of invaders have conquered and colonised her rich fertile plains, driving the older inhabitants to the more inaccessible mountain recesses. Since the seventh century of the Christian Era her history has been carefully recorded, and the effects of modern invasions can with almost absolute certainty be traced out. Two thousand years before Christ India was, however, invaded from the north-west by a powerful and highly intellectual people generally designated the Aryans. Crossing the Upper Indus, these people conquered the Panjáb, and following the great alluvial basins of the Ganges and Indus which isolate the Himálayan chain from the central table-land of India, they ultimately took Oudh, and extended their possessions into Bengal. They found these fertile plains inhabited by various races—the people collectively designated in modern works (and used here from want of a more accurate term) as the Indo-Turanians. It is accepted that these pre-Aryan inhabitants at a still more remote period were in their turn but invaders, who entered India most probably by crossing the passes on the eastern extension of the Himálayan chain. The struggle which took place between the Aryan invaders and the various Indo-Turanian tribes resulted in the expulsion of the latter to the more inaccessible mountain recesses, or their ultimate absorption into the lower grades of the social and religious system of the Aryans, or, as they may now be called, of the Hindus. The Indo-Turanians are by popular usage designated the *Aboriginal Races of India.* The intrusion of the Aryans may be assumed to have isolated the Kolarian and Dravidian sections of this Turanian family, compelling so many to occupy the central table-land of India, and the others to recede into the valleys and mountain tracts of the Himálaya. According to some writers, the Dravidians were more recent invaders than the Kolarians, and crossed the Himálaya by the more western passes. They have many peculiarities, especially in their more advanced arts, which recall the Assyrians, and, according to the indications of similarity of language, they would seem to have left in Beluchistan the Brahuí tribe, and pushing across the gap of country between the Indus and the Nerbudda, left again the Gonds in the Central Provinces, the Uraons in Chutia Nagpur, and the Malers in Rajmahal, and to have finally matured into a great and powerful people in the Madras Presidency, ramifying into numerous tribes, of whom the Tamil and the Telugu are the more important. There are at the same time peculiarities in the Dravidians which bring to mind some of the Mongolian races of the eastern extremity of the Himálayan chain. The Khasias of Assam speak a language which, like some of the more primitive dialects of the Dravidian tongue, may be described as monosyllabic in the agglutinative stage of progression. Their compound words are mere juxtapositions of roots which have their independent powers as well. There are several other languages in the mountains of Assam that show a similar relation to the agglutinated tongue of the Dravidians, and it is singular that amongst these people the strange social habit should prevail of the youths of both sexes before marriage living together in a common house instead of with their parents. This habit has been incorrectly attributed to some of the Kolarians. It is practised by all the Nagas of Assam, and by the Uraons and Malers of the central tableland of India, but by none of the Kolarians. It would be unwise, however, to dwell too far upon suggestions based upon social habits, suffice it to say that, according to some writers, the Dravidians are accepted as the aboriginal inhabitants of the Madras Presidency who spread from somewhere near Tanjore over distant tracts of country, reaching even to Ceylon, and in Burma giving origin to the Talaings.

The Aryan conquests of the Indo-Turanians did not result in the construction of a great and united empire. The humble position assigned to the conquered, engendered bitter animosities against the conquerors; and when the faith of Buddhism was preached, it was the Indo-Turanians that first embraced its tenets and rallied around the standard that gave them social and religious equality with their conquerors. Important revolutions had also taken place on the northern frontier of India, which resulted in the complete isolation of the Aryan conquerors from their parent stock. Forced to intermarry with the aboriginal people of India, they degenerated, and were ultimately no more the pure and intellectual people who had conquered India, but were contaminated both in blood and in religion. Under Asoka, the Buddhist Emperor, India, however, became a united nation, and from 250 B.C. and for a thousand years Buddhism was universal. A period of great darkness followed the great Buddhistic epoch. Hinduism began to reassert itself, and the faiths of Vaishnava, Saiva, and Jaina claimed an almost equal division of the people. Buddhism was exterminated. The old dynasties disappeared, and just as the Rajput races were triumphant (about the 7th century), they were confronted by the bitterest enemies to their faith—the Mahommedan invaders. For a second thousand years a great religious struggle ensued, and new blood obscured once more the ethnological history of the races of India; and as one result the faith of Islam claimed nearly one half her inhabitants.

Thus during two great and important periods the Indus was crossed by invaders, who passed south and south-east along the vast alluvial basin, and conquered and colonised the more fertile tracts of country. The great Buddhistic monuments and the Hindu art and architecture mark the former civilisation, and the Indo-Saracenic edifices the latter. India has thus passed through 4,000 years of almost incessant change, and it is therefore not to be wondered at that her 253 millions of people should be broken into a number of distinct and a multitude of transitional races. The advent of western civilisation was however the commencement of another era of change and evolution, and one destined, at no distant future, to efface completely race independence. Aryan persecution drove to the mountain recesses the aboriginal tribes which exist at the present day. These were preserved during the reign of Mahomedan tyranny, but the social and religious liberty and equality of the present day, when combined with the vast advantages of unmolested trade and commerce, seem destined to efface completely race distinctions. It will soon be difficult to study the peculiarities of the races of India, and the task of working out their origin, which even now is involved in the greatest obscurity, will, in the future, be perfectly impossible.

It has not been deemed desirable to enter upon the debatable questions of more advanced anthropology; the present catalogue is confined to a brief description of the people as they are found at the present day. To aid the visitor to understand the ethnological objects shown in the Court, clay, or in some instances plaster-of-Paris, castes have been prepared of the more important races of the people. These have been arranged in twelve sub-courts, corresponding as near as possible to the leading provinces and native states of India. The ethnological objects have been draped upon the models according to the fashion in which they are worn, or have been arranged on stands and in glass cases near to their respective sub-courts.

The following are the sub-courts in the order in which they will be found, commencing from the main entrance into the Court:—

Sub-court IV. . The Andaman and Nicobar Islands.
Sub-court V. . Burma.
Sub-court XVII. . Assam (the upper portion of the Valley).
Sub-court XVIII. . Bengal (Chutia Nagpur).
Sub-court XIX. . Assam (the Lower Assam).
Sub-court XX. . Bengal (Darjiling, Chittagong and Urissa).
Sub-court XXIX. . Bombay.
Sub-court XXX. . Madras.
Sub-court XXXI. . Central India, Rajputana and Central Provinces.
Sub-court XXXII. Mysore, Coorg, and Hyderabad.
Sub-court XXXIX. North-West Provinces and Nepal.
Sub-court XL. . Panjab.

SUB-COURT IV.

THE ANDAMAN AND NICOBAR ISLANDS.

A chain of small volcanic islands on the eastern side of the Bay of Bengal stretches from a point south of the promontory of Lower Burma to Sumatra, running parallel to Tenasserim and the Malay Peninsula. More correctly, these islands occur between the 6th and 14th degrees of north latitude, and near the meridian, 93 E. of Greenwich. These are collectively known as the Andaman and Nicobar Islands. The most northern—the "Great Andaman" is broken into three islands by narrow stream-like channels. These are designated North, Middle, and South Andaman. Still to the south is "Little Andaman," and still farther, the two groups of islands known as the Nicobars. South Andaman has for nearly a century been held as the Indian Penal Settlement, and Port Blair is its capital.

"The tribes which inhabit the Andaman group are Negritos, and seem to have all descended from a common source. They are entirely distinct from the inhabitants of the Nicobar Islands, who are allied to the Malays. There are, at least, nine Andamanese tribes speaking mutually unintelligible languages, all of which are, however, formed after a common type of construction, and although in two of them an occasional resemblance in roots can be traced, the relational words and particles, post positions, prefixes and suffixes which form the principal peculiarity of the language, are totally different for the different tribes." (*A. J. Ellis Ann. Address. Phil. Society.*)

Mr. E. H. Man, in his most interesting account of the *Aboriginal Inhabitants of the Andaman Islands*, gives a detailed account of these primitive savages. It is unfortunately impossible to do more in this catalogue than to touch upon a few of the striking peculiarities of this extremely interesting people. According to the Census of 1881, there are in all about 15,000 people in the Andaman Islands, but of these, according to the most careful estimates, it would appear that in the Great Andaman there are scarcely more than 2000 aboriginals, and in the Little Andaman not more than 1000 to 1500. Nearly four-fifths of the entire population are therefore convicts, and these are distributed over thirty scattered stations.

The Andamanese are short of stature, the average height of the males being 4 feet 10¾ inches, and that of the females 4 feet 7¼ inches. They are well built, active and cheerful. The colour of the skin, while varying slightly, is intensely black, and often shining like the hue of a black-leaded stove. The average age has been estimated at twenty-two years, and fifty years is viewed as extreme old age. At this period the hair generally begins to turn grey. It is frizzly and seems to grow in spiral tufts, although the roots are in reality uniformly distributed. The majority of the women shave the hair entirely, or have only two small parallel ridges from the crown to the nape of the neck. Although the men are sometimes seen to shave like the women, the style of dressing the hair is generally distinct. Formerly the almost universal habit prevailed of having only a circular patch of hair about six inches in diameter on the crown of the head. Modern fashion has given origin however to new and more fanciful styles, and it is customary to see the skull-cap-like tuft with the lateral sides much higher than the central patch. Occasionally also they are seen with a piece about two or three inches broad shaved clean between the forehead and the nape of the neck.

Marriage never takes place until both parties have attained maturity: the usual age of the bridegroom varies from eighteen to twenty-two, and of the bride from sixteen to twenty. Although the men go absolutely naked, or are dressed at most with ornaments, the women wear an apron of leaves, and are scrupulously virtuous and modest. When very angry, a man does not stamp his foot, he places his left hand palm uppermost between his teeth and glares fiercely at some object on the ground near the offender. When in good spirits, the eyes sparkle and the surrounding skin is wrinkled. Women show their surprise by striking the thigh. In beckoning, the head is nodded vertically and a hand outstretched, the fingers with the knuckles uppermost being waved towards himself. They cannot count more than one, two, but when a higher number than two is desired, they describe the objects as "several," "many," "very many," "innumerable." To count nine the nose is tapped with the tips of the fingers in successive order, commencing with the little finger, while saying "one," with the next, "two," the third, with the remark "and this," so on, "and this" being repeated with each remaining finger until the nine have been counted, the thumb of the second hand is then clenched and both hands held up. To count "one" the forefinger of either hand is held up and the word "*ubatul*" uttered.

The Andaman language has already been alluded to: it is agglutinative. Capt. Temple conceives that "the roots are all properly monosyllabic, which generally end with a consonant, but these monosyllables are frequently extended by the addition of a vowel or diphthong, or the same preceded by a consonant, in which the real meaning lies in the first syllable, though it has now been lost, while the expansions serve as modifications." It has been estimated that the language changes materially every hundred years; a remarkable peculiarity is the fact that each substantive, adjective and verb generally ends in *da*, which is usually dropped before post positions and in construction: for human objects the words end in *re*.

In an interesting account of the Great Nicobar Islanders, Mr. Man publishes a number of most instructive facts. He has now made known the existence beyond all possible doubt of an aboriginal race in the interior of the Nicobar, perfectly distinct from the Malay-like race of the Coast. These people are known as the *Shom Pen*. Mr. Man estimates that there are perhaps 6000 souls on the Nicobar Islands, of whom perhaps about 1000 belong to Shom Pen. While the Nicobarese are described as of mixed Malay, Burmese, and Siamese blood, Mr. Man accepts the Shom Pen as of pure origin. They are aboriginal inhabitants of the islands who have been forced by the Nicobarese to seek the protection from their conquerors afforded by the mountain fastnesses. They have many interesting peculiarities, but space cannot be found to allude to them; suffice it to add that they cook their food in a vessel made from the bark of a tree, and have not got even the primitive knowledge of the potter's art possessed by the people of the Coast, and apparently the metals are quite unknown to them.

ETHNOLOGICAL EXHIBITS.

SUB-COURT V.

THE ETHNOLOGY OF BURMA.

Further India may be referred to two great sections, Lower Burma and Upper Burma. The former used to be known as British Burma, and the latter Native or Independent Burma; but the conquests of the past few months have destroyed for ever this distinction, and have extended the British dominions from the mouth of the Pakchau river (10° north latitude), in the extreme south of Tenasserim, to the frontier of China (24° north latitude), the area of Further India thus brought under British rule being about four times what it was a few months ago. Burma may now be defined as the vast basins of the Irrawaddy, the Sittang and the Salween, extending from the water-sheds which separate Chittagong, Kachar, Manipur, Assam, and China, to the Bay of Bengal, with the long strip of Tenasserim skirting the kingdom of Siam. Upper Burma is, however, too imperfectly known to justify an attempt being made in this brief ethnological catalogue to include the tribes which have so recently become British subjects. The Census report of 1881 reveals many facts of Lower Burma not generally known, and it will suffice for the present purpose to deal almost exclusively with the lower province.

Lower Burma comprises an area of 87,220 square miles, and has a population of 3,736,771. The smallest district is about the size of an average English county, and the largest as great as four or five counties put together. But although the area is large, the population is sparse and confined, the inhabitants being chiefly distributed over the lower hills and along the banks of the rivers and streams. In 1835 it was estimated that there were only 280,024 persons in British Burma, and since the Census of 1871 the population has increased very nearly one million, or nearly one-seventh of the present population. This most unprecedented increase may be viewed as due to three causes: (*a*) More perfect Census returns; (*b*) Immigration of labourers from India; (*c*) Immigration from Upper Burma, the inhabitants of Ava seeking the protection of British rule from the misrule which so long characterised independent Burma. Still, however, in spite of rapid growth and great prosperity, the density of population in Lower Burma is remarkably low, being only 42·8, or a little more than that of Russia. The late Census revealed the fact that in Burma there are only 87·7 females to every 100 males, whereas in Madras there are 102·3, and in Bengal 101·1.

Viewing the people of Burma according to religion, there are 3,251,584 Buddhists, 143,581 Natworshipers, 88,177 Hindus, 166,881 Mohammedans, and 84,219 Christians. The Buddhists are the most numerous and most important, forming as they do 87 per cent. of the population; but on turning to the question of increased population, it is found that the Buddhists have increased 32·8 per cent., Natworshipers 32·2, Hindus 40·6, Mohammedans 69·1, and Christians 61·0 per cent. The conversion of the Karens may be accepted as approximately explaining the increase of Christians, for of the total Christian community, 77,355 are native converts, of whom 55,874 are Baptists.

The question of race or nationality is much more troublesome. Dr. Mason, in his '*Burma; its People and Natural Products*,' says Burma may be defined as "bounded by the Tais or Shans on the east; the Malays on the south; the Caffres and Hindus on the west, and the Tartars and Chinese on the north. Within these limits are embraced a great variety of tribes, with a still greater variety of appellatives. More than fifty names may be found in books, but a large portion are synonymes, and nearly all may be referred to four great families—the Talaing, the Burman, the Karen, and the Shan."

In some of the notices of other Ethnological Groups within the Imperial Court, it will be found an effort has been made to separate the races into Hindu (or Aryan), semi-Hinduised, and Aboriginal races. This course cannot be followed in Burma, since, with the exception of the Mons (the people now known as the Talaings), all the other inhabitants are the descendants of successive invaders who have settled in the province. At the same time, intermarriage and the amalgamation of religious ideas have in the lapse of centuries produced intermediate tribes between all the great races of Burma, until it is now sometimes difficult to determine to which section a tribe belongs. The same process which has in Hindustan produced the semi-Hinduised races has been operating in

Burma, and corresponding communities perplex the anthropologists. In no case is this more marked than with the

I.—The Mons, or Talaings.

The Mons are generally admitted to be the only race in Burma that have any claim to be regarded as aboriginal. Seven centuries before the Christian era, the fertile lower basins of the Irrawaddy, the Sittang and the Salween were inhabited by a savage race supposed to have been the Mons. These people were conquered by invading traders of the Dravidian family from India. The latter received the name of Talaings from the name of the ancient country of Telinga, from which they came. After conquering the Mons, they settled amongst them as colonists, ultimately becoming so intermixed, that when found by the Burmese the two races were collectively designated Talaings. But by this time the Talaings had also embraced the then new religion, Buddhism, and they were thus able to give to their Tartar (the Burmese) conquerors the religion and literature which they now possess. The Dravidians have left little or no trace of their colonisation among the Mons, save their name and a few Hindu sculptures at Thatone (the early seat of the Talaings before their removal to Prome) and at Pagat. The name Mon has many affinities in the Turanian and Kolarian races, as for example the Munda of Chutia Nagpur, and it is remarkable that in addition to this similarity of name, the first six numerals in the languages of both these peoples are the same. The Munda language has, however, proceeded into the agglutinative stage, while the Talaing is for the most part monosyllabic, and is closely related to the languages of Cambodia and some of those of Assam.

II.—The Burmans.

The oldest inhabitants in Burma after the Talaings are the branches of the great Mramma family. Some tribes living in the hills of Northern Arakan, though belonging by origin to the same race, are at present so different in habits and speech that they cannot be classed with the dwellers of the plains. Under the Mramma family are included the Arakanese, Burman, Tavoy, Choringtha, Yaw, and Yabein languages and races. The Burmese tradition claims for them a western origin and a connection with the Solar Aryans; but it is much more likely that they came from the tableland of Tibet, and followed the Mons until they gradually expelled the latter from the fertile regions which they were found to be inhabiting, and soon the invaders overthrew the kingdoms of Prome and Pegu. The race which now inhabits Lower Burma is formed of the descendants of Burmans, who intermarried with the vanquished Talaings in Upper Burma, the race is purely Burman.

The Talaing and Mon languages are now almost extinct, although Talaing is still spoken in a few fishing villages in the Tenasserim coast. Burman is the language generally spoken; it is not an Aryan language, but approximates more to Chinese than to the Indian languages; it is monosyllabic and tonal. The alphabet is not, however, symbolic, but is derived from the Sanskrit through the Vali.

The religion of the country is Buddhism. Brahminism, however, appears to have penetrated into Burmah, as is proved by statues of Indian gods found in Burma. The Buddhism of Burma in its present form is more Theism than Atheism.

Hill Tribes of the Tibet-Burman Family.

There are a large number of very different hill tribes who appear to belong to the Mramma group, such as the Sak, Chaw, Kwaymi, Kún, Mro, and Shandú. These tribes mostly live near the Kaladan river and its tributaries. Space cannot be afforded to go into the subject of these tribes in detail. The Sak people live in the Akyab district, and do not appear to tattoo themselves to any appreciable extent. The Chaws are a small tribe in Northern Arakan, and appear to be related to the Kukis. The Kwaymís (or dog-tails), or Kamís, differ but little in appearance from the Mros. They are found in Northern Arakan and Akyab. The Kúns dress like the Kwaymís, but speak a distinct language, containing many words common to the Manipuris. The Mros are quiet and inoffensive, and are probably related to the Nagas. The Shandús are the most warlike tribe, and exist in large numbers outside the Burmese boundary. They are probably a branch of the great Kukí race, and they are said to be pressing upon the Kwaymís and Mros.

III.—The Karens.

The Karens are a hill race said to be aborigines of the mountain tracts of Burma. They are divided into two great tribes, the Sgans and the Pghos; the language spoken by these tribes is monosyllabic tonal, like Burmese, but it is quite distinct, differing in its construction, as well as in the words. There are innumerable subdivisions of the great Karen tribe. The Sgans are represented at the Exhibition by closely allied tribes of Gechos, Bghais and Pakus; these tribes live in the hills in the Toungnoo district, they cultivate *taungyas* (patches of forest land cleared by fire on which rice and other products are sown broadcast) on the side of the hills, and oranges, betel-nuts, and betel-pepper in the valleys. They live in bamboo huts, and the villages are often shifted once every two or three years as the culturable land in the neighbourhood becomes exhausted.

A large number of the Karens had abandoned the hills before the English occupation of Lower Burma, and settled down in the plains. The numbers of these settlers have largely increased during the English occupation, and the Karens now constitute an important section of the cultivating population of the Delta District of Lower Burma. According to the last census returns the Karens numbered about 500 000, or nearly one-seventh of the population of Lower Burma. They are more steady and harder workers than the Burmans; they are in fact the first agriculturists in Burmah. They are a shy race, and generally avoid contact with strangers. This shyness is probably the result of the centuries of oppression which they have endured at the hands of the Burmans; the remembrance of the injuries they had suffered, and from which English rule saved them, has made the Karens very loyal to the English Government. During the present troubles in Burma, they have on more than one occasion done good service in dispersing and capturing rebels.

The Karens worship nats or the spirits of trees, rivers, mountains, &c. They also carry offerings to the Buddhist monasteries, but in case of epidemics or other calamities, it is to the spirits and to the Burmese monks that they appeal for help. They have a tradition that white men coming from the West would bring them a white book which would reveal to them the true religion. When the Baptist missionaries appeared with the Bible the hill tribes thought the prophecy fulfilled, and large numbers of them adopted Christianity. The American Baptist missionaries and the French Roman Catholic priests have converted large numbers of these people, and the number of Karen Christians is probably not under 100,000.

The principal tribes of the Karens are known by different names in different parts of Burma; in the south (Tenasserim) they call themselves Sgans and Pghos; in the north (Pegu and Irrawaddy) the Sgans call themselves Pates (descendants of the father), or Fragha Kanyan (men *par excellence*), and the Burman Karens or white Karens; the Pghos in the north call themselves Mutis (descendants of the mother), and the Burmas call them Talaing Karens. The name of Karen is not used by the Karens themselves, and is the name under which the Burmans designate all the Karen tribes, the legend of the Karens regarding their name is that they were once a powerful nation with an independent king, the Burmans attacked them and all but exterminated their race, sparing only one man and one woman. The man was married to a Burman woman and the woman to a Talaing; hence the names under which they are now known, "descendants of the father," or Burman Karens, and "descendants of the mother," or Talaing Karens.

The Chins.

It is difficult to assign an exact place to the Chins. By language they are related to the Pwo-Kareens, but in other respects they are more allied to the hill tribes of the Mramma family. They are a very widely distributed people, being found on both sides of Arakan Yoma, also in Thayetmyo and Prome districts to the east of the Irrawaddy River. In Upper Burma there are also large numbers of Chins. The most remarkable peculiarity of this people is that they tattoo the faces of their young girls, so as not to leave even the eyelids free.

The Torengthús.

The Torengthús are an isolated tribe which have not yet been definitely classed with any of the other races of Burma. They resemble in dress the Shans, but their language is tonic and closely related to that of the Pwo-Karens. They are a clannish, taciturn race. Their name signifies "hillman," but they have settled like the Shans on the plains and cultivate on the permanent system. They call themselves Pao.

IV.—The Shans.

The Shans are not an indigenous race to Burma, but are immigrants from the Shan States, where they extend from Ava to Bankok. These people are of the same family as the Ahoms and Kamtis of Assam. It has been from the Shan states and not from Siam proper that the various branches of the Shan family have emigrated into India and Burma. The Shans are careful cultivators and hard-working men. They are also great traders and pedlars.

The only other race found in Burma which deserves a separate though brief notice is

The Salúns.

The Salúns (or Selungs) may be described as a tribe of sea-gipsies, who live in the dry weather in their boats, and during the monsoons seek a temporary shelter in huts built on the lee-side of the islands. These wild people pay no taxes. In personal appearance they are between the Malayas and the Burmans. Their language has affinities to the tongue of the former and belongs to the Malay-Polynesian group of agglutinating languages. They live on fish, turtle, and wild pigs, hunting the latter with a special breed of dogs. The sea-slug and the edible swallows' nests are their principal articles of trade, in return for which they procure coarse rice. Like the Parsís, they expose their dead to the elements, erecting for this purpose a wooden platform, upon which the body is exposed; for some time they desert the island or portion of the island in which a dead body is placed. They make extremely neat boats, the lower portion being a large tree and the upper made of plaited bamboos; they are expert boatmen.

SUB-COURT XVII.

THE PROVINCE OF ASSAM.

Assam occupies the north-east corner of the Indian Empire. It is bounded on the north by the eastern extremity of the Himálaya, on the north-east and east by the Native State of Manipur and the wild regions of Upper Burmah, and on the south and west by Bengal. It is generally spoken of as consisting of three distinct and well marked sub-divisions, viz.: the Brahmapútra valley, the Súrma valley, and the intervening hill tracts. The first comprises the six "Assam Valley Districts," the next the plains of Kachar and Sylhet, and the last the "Hill Districts." The total area of the province has been determined as 46,341 square miles, and the population 4,881,426. The geographical features and climate of the regions embraced under the province are extremely varied, and this fact has undoubtedly much to do with the marvellous multiplicity of races of inhabitants. At the same time Assam seems to have been a natural gate to India, through which, from the north and east, successive waves of immigrants appear to have passed, and may perhaps have left in the province some of the isolated colonies which now exist. The Santals of Chutia Nagpur, for example, have a tradition that they entered India through the north-east Himalaya, passing most probably down the Brahamaputra valley and along the north bank of Ganges, and at the present day they are tending to move back towards Assam. Within historic times the Shan tribes successively invaded, conquered, and settled in the province, and from India immigration of Aryan races has for many years steadily taken place. The inhabitants of Assam are thus very distinct, and may be referred to five great sections: 1st. The group of Non-Aryan races, collectively spoken of as BODO. This includes among many others the Kacharís, Lalungs, Gáros, the Chutyas, Mech, and the Koch. 2nd. The SHAN tribes, or the Ahoms, Khamtís, Singphos, and Shans. 3rd. The BHUTAN tribes, or those which inhabit the mountain tracts of the Upper or the north, north-western side of Assam, namely, the Akas, Daflas, Mirís, Mishmis, and Abors. 4th. The NAGAS, or the hill tribes of the north-eastern frontier from the Singpho country, south along the Patkoi mountains to the North Kachar hills. These include, among others, the Angamís, Kucha-Nagas, Rengmas, Semas, Lhotas, Banferas, Jaktungias, Hathigorias and the various races of Manipur Nagas. 5th. The ARYAN races, or the immigrants from India. Of these a very considerable number are non-Aryan races, attracted to Assam from the mountain tracts of the central portions of India to the lucrative employment of tea plantations. It is impossible in the present brief catalogue to allude even by name to all the tribes met with in Assam. In the Native State of Manipur alone, for example, there are perhaps not less than ten quite different tribes, each distinct in language and social customs, although inhabiting but narrow valleys isolated by mountain ranges little more than a few thousand feet in altitude. The census report for 1881 gives the following aboriginal population as under British rule:—Abor, 821; Ahom, 179,314; Bhutia, 1,340; Chutiya, 60,232; Dafla, 549; Dyko, 707; Gáro, 112,104; Hajung, 4,354; Kachári, 281,611; Khamti, 2,883; Khasia, 104,830; Koch, 230,382; Kuki, 10,812; Lalung, 47,650; Langam, 1,895; Madhi, 13,159; Mál, 1,239; Maw, 282; Manipuri, 40,443; Matak, 220; Mech, 57,890; Mikir, 77,765; Miri, 25,636; Mishmi, 681; Naga, 104,650; Nepalese, 3,991; Rabha, 56,499; Rajbansi, 106,376; Santals, 7,397; Santengs, 47,815; Sarania, 4,718; Shans, 275; Singhu, 1,774; Tippera, 3,984; and Totla, 2,539, or in all 1,317,022. The following are the principal Assam aboriginal tribes:—

1. THE BODO GROUP, OR THE KACHARIS, LALUNGS, GÁROS, CHUTYAS, MECH, AND KOCH.

These races constitute more than one-third of the population of the Assam valley. The Mech and Koch will be found described under Bengal, but the Mikirs and Khasias have been added to this group and described in this place, because they are at least more nearly related to the Bodo tribes than to any others.

THE KACHARIS.

Little or nothing seems to be known of the origin and history of this people. They call themselves *Bara*. It is possible that they may at one time have been the dominant race of the Brahmaputra valley, an idea which receives support from many of the rivers having names commencing with "Di":—Diputa, Dibong, Dikhu, &c., Di being the Kachari word for water. The Kacharis have no definite idea of a supreme being, and their religion is one of fear. In appearance the Kachari is somewhat like the Nepali, approximating to the Mongolian type, with projecting cheek-bones. Those of them that have not become tainted with Hinduism are at liberty to eat anything, and in their deportment they compare favourably with the other dwellers in the plains, for they have a bold, independent, manly bearing. They are excessively clanish, and will stand by each other for good or for evil to the last extremity.

THE GÁROS.

The Gáro tribes are found inhabiting the Gáro hills, which divide Assam from Bengal. They are a branch of the great Bodo or Kacharí race which extends from Tipperah to the Nepal *tarai*. At the last census it was ascertained that there were 112,091 Gáros. Many of the Gáro tribes have been to a certain extent Hinduised, but those whose homes are on the higher hills have altogether escaped Brahmanical influences. The Gáros inhabiting the hills of the interior are born depredators, and before the subjugation of their country in 1866, they were always raiding upon their lowland neighbours. It is said that about two fifths of the Gáro hill population are slaves. The slaves, however, are well fed and cared for, and are generally the best looking people in the village. Their costume is very simple. They suspend in front of the person a small piece of dark striped home-made cloth, and deck the hair with feathers. The women wear some twenty or thirty large brass ear-rings two to four inches in diameter in each ear, and throw over their shoulders a small red silk shawl. The Gáro implements of husbandry are a hoe, a heavy short sword, called a *dao*, and a battle axe called *lumbiri*. They are not particular as to what they eat, and they rear for food kine, goats, swine, dogs, cats, fowls, and ducks. From their hills they obtain deer, wild hogs, frogs, snakes, &c., all of which they eat. They cultivate cotton (a remarkable form, namely a kidney cotton with pods often six inches long), Indian-corn, rice, millet, &c. They depend upon the cotton which they sell to obtain those necessaries which their hills do not afford. They seldom sell the produce they bring to market, but barter it for what at the time they require. They are lively, good-natured, hospitable, frank, and honest in their dealings, until contaminated by contact with the people of the plains of India. They burn their dead, and bury the ashes. They formerly immolated human victims in honour of the dead, but the inhuman practice has been discontinued.

Mikirs.

The Mikirs live partly in the Assam valley, and partly in the Northern Kachar and Jaintia hills, but they are concentrated in the low mountainous tract in the Nowgong District. According to tradition current among them they were the original inhabitants of the Jaintia hills, from which they were driven by more powerful races. The Mikirs call themselves "Arleng," which simply means "a man." In an able paper upon the Mikirs, Mr. C. J. Lyall shows that they are more nearly related to the Bodo than to the Khasia races. The Census of 1882 gives the total number of Mikirs at 77,765, divided into three tribes, viz., Chintong, Ronghang and Amri. Although the Mikirs emigrated from the Jaintia hills and settled within the territories of the Assam kings, they long remained subject to demands from Kachar and Jaintia. They however acknowledged their principal allegiance to the Assam sovereign, whom they paid a tribute in kind consisting of cotton, mats, &c. The Assamese people however looked upon the Mikirs with contempt, and they therefore kept themselves aloof in their forests, distant from all civilising influences. In 1838, a settlement of land revenue was made with the Mikirs which raised them into a position of equality with the other Assamese cultivators, and so much improved their material condition that they began to send their children to school. The Mikirs have always been a peaceful people, except on one occasion when they were instigated by the Jaintia insurgents to rise against Government. But they speedily settled down as soon as their grievances were redressed. A Mikir house is generally built on a platform ten or twelve feet high, under which the pigs and fowls are kept. All the members of a family live together, however numerous they may be. The Mikirs follow the *jûm* system of cultivation, which consists in clearing forest lands, setting the trees on fire, when dry, and sowing the seeds broadcast on the ashes thus formed after the first fall of rain. The Mikir villages are therefore temporary habitations, as the people must move to new forest lands when those adjacent to the village have been exhausted. The only implement necessary for such a wasteful system of cultivation is a hoe called the *dao*, which among all the wild tribes on the eastern frontier is not only the only agricultural implement, but the only instrument for household work of all kinds, and it is the principal weapon both in war and chase. In these forest clearings, which are mostly made on slopes of hills, the only crops raised are cotton and summer rice. In the plains some of the Mikirs have now learnt the use of plough, and they have commenced to raise winter rice with its assistance. The Mikirs give offerings to various spirits presiding over their hills, streams and marshes. But the principal deity is called Arnam Kethe, or the Great God, to whom pigs are offered. The Mikirs have as yet been very little influenced by Hinduism. They do not marry early. Any young man wishing to marry a girl has to serve in the house of his father-in-law for a term, generally two years before he can carry his wife to his own home. Polygamy is not prohibited if a man can afford to maintain more than one wife. Intercourse among the different sexes before marriage is entirely unrestrained. The Mikirs burn their dead, and the funeral ceremony is held with drinking, singing and dancing.

The Khasias.

The Khásias are found occupying the Khásia hills. They are much more civilised than most of their neighbours. Their language may be best described as monosyllabic in the agglutinative stage of progression. Their compound words are mere juxtapositions of roots which have their independent powers as well. The Khásias are divided into several states, under hereditary chiefs. They are a short thickly-set muscular race, with strongly marked Mongolian features; they are of an active disposition, and are fond of martial exercises. Their chief points may be briefly stated :—Colour tawny or yellow; nose depressed, forehead flat and broad, face broad, flat and squarish, with high and rounded cheek-bones; skull globular rather than square; eyes middle-sized and black, with a yellow tinge in the eye-ball; eyelids obliquely set but less acutely than in the Chinese; mouth large and prominent, hair black, thick and long, tied up in a knot at the back. In the males the beard is remarkably sparse, moustache full, legs muscular, calves over-developed, carriage ungraceful. The dress of the men is a waist cloth and long shirt without sleeves. The women wear a cloth of striped red and white cotton or eri-silk, in the form of a loose garment tied round the breast. They do not drink milk, but are fond of the flesh of animals, especially of that of swine. Fish also forms a part of their food. They believe in the transmigration of souls; after death human beings are transformed into monkeys, crabs, tortoises, frogs, &c. A future state is not denied, but it is treated with indifference. They have, it appears, a name for the Supreme Being, but they pay more devotion to inferior spirits who reside on the hills, or in rocky dales and in groves. They have neither temples nor idols connected with their ancient faith. They are much addicted to consulting auspices, especially the appearances of eggs on being broken. Marriage is contracted by the parents. When arranged, the young man and his friends go to the bride's house, and are fed and housed for that day. On the morrow the bride is taken with her friends to the bridegroom's house and feasted, and next day the bridegroom returns with the bride to her house, where they take up their abode. The children in all questions of lineage and personal rights follow the mother, not the father. Whatever the husband may have earned in wedlock goes to the wife and children, but all property coming from his family reverts to them, as also his corpse after death. They bury their dead and erect grave-stones of rough slate. All over the Khásia hills are found long, upright, rough pillars or monoliths of irregular shape, often arranged in groups around one or two horizontal ones. It is the custom of the Khásias, in fact, to erect on the waysides and approaches to villages fantastically-formed oblong stones in commemoration of their deceased. The last census gave the number of Khásias as 107,431.

The Jaintias or Santengs.

The Jaintias (or Santengs as they call themselves) are found inhabiting the Jaintia hills. There is practically no difference between them and the Khásias. They are an active, energetic race of men and fond of martial exercises. They are never found without their arms, which are generally a sword and shield and a bow and arrow. It is a common practice with them to use poisoned arrows against wild beasts, but they have never been known to use them against their fellow-men. Their common food comprises rice, millet, maize, *kachu* (an aroid tuber), and arrowroot, all of which they cultivate. They eat the flesh of animals, including that of the leopard. They are dependent to a large extent, however, upon other tribes for their clothing, and their indigenous costume is being destroyed by the adoption of imported articles. Their dress is much the same as that of the Khásias. Their religious ideas and customs are also very similar. The Raja of Jaintia, at the time of his deposition by the British, was Hinduised to some extent.

2. Shan Group, or the Ahoms, Khamtis, and Singphos.

The Ahoms.

More is known about the Ahoms than of about the other races of Assam. They are the descendants of a tribe of Shans who migrated from the upper basin of the Irrawaddy. They crossed the Patkoi hills and entered Assam about the year 1228 A.D. From ruling over a small portion of Upper Assam they extended their dominions, conquering the Bodo tribes until the advent of the Burmese in 1810, and the annexation of Assam in 1826 by the British, overthrew the Ahom empire.

The Ahom system of Government was personal service in lieu of taxation. About 1640 they became Hindus, and except in the records preserved by their priests (*deodhas*), they have forgotten their ancient faith and original tongue. The latter is said to closely resemble the Khamti. The census returns 179,283 persons as Ahoms. The better class of Ahom farmers dress in Muga-silk costumes with a hat which very much resembles that worn by the Lepchás of Darjiling.

The Khamtis or Shans.

The Khamtis are found located in Assam, where they have settled within the last hundred years. They originally came into the Brahamaputra valley from the Bor-Khamtí, a mountainous region between Assam and the valley of the Irrawaddy. Like the Ahoms, they immigrated from the Shan kingdom of Pong, the ancient capital of which was Mogoung.

Although on many occasions the Khamtís have rendered assistance to Government, they themselves rebelled in 1839 and massacred a large number of British subjects. In consequence of this they were divided into four sections and located in different districts. According to the last census, they are now chiefly found around Lakhimpur, and number only about 2883 persons. They are far in advance of all the other north-eastern frontier tribes in knowledge, arts, and civilisation. They are Buddhists, and have regular establishments of priests well versed in the recondite mysteries of the religion, and a large portion of the laity can read and write in their own language. They are dark in complexion and coarse in features, with the Mongolian (or rather Tartar) peculiarities strongly developed. Their arms are the *dao*, a kind of short sword, and a round shield of buffalo hide. The men commonly wear tight-fitting jackets of cotton cloth, dyed blue, a white muslin turban so arranged as to leave exposed the top knot, into which their long hair is twisted; this is left projecting somewhat over the forehead. Their nether garment is of coloured cotton of a chequered pattern, or silk, more or less ample according to the rank of the wearer. The costume of the women is plain but neat. They wear their hair drawn up from the back and sides into a massive roll, so much in front as to appear to form a continuation of the frontal bone. The roll is encircled by an embroidered band, the fringed and tasselled ends of which hang down behind; the lower garment, generally of dark-coloured cotton cloth, is folded over the breasts under the arms, and reaches to the feet; in addition to this they wear a coloured scarf round the waist, and a long-sleeved jacket; their ornaments are amber earrings, and coral and other necklaces. Their priests are expert carvers in ivory; and the chiefs work in gold, silver, and iron, forge their own weapons, and make their wives' jewels. The women are skilled in embroidery; they make elaborately-worked bags for their husbands and for sale also, embroidered bands for the hair, and other pretty things; they are, nevertheless, capable of bearing a very severe share of the out-door farm work.

The Singphos.

The Singphos are found in Assam, where they have settled since the commencement of the present century. They are divided into three clans:—Tenghai, Mayho and Nimbrong. They are a fine athletic race, above the ordinary standard in height, and capable of enduring great fatigue, but their energies are greatly impaired by the use of opium and spirits, in which they freely indulge. Their features are of the Mongolian type, and their complexion varies from a tawny yellow, or olive, to a dark brown. The national weapons of the tribe are the heavy short sword or *dao*, admirably adapted for close quarters in war, and for clearing the jungle and preparing the ground in peace; a spear with a short shaft used for thrusting, and a strong cross-bow with bamboo arrows. They use shields of buffalo hide, four feet long, and helmets sometimes of that material, sometimes of thick plaited rattan work, varnished black and decorated with boars' tusks, &c. The men tie the hair in a large knot on the crown of the head, and wear a jacket of coloured cotton and chequered under-garment of the same material, or of silk. The dress of the women consists of one piece of coloured cotton cloth, often in large, broad, horizontal bands of red and blue, fastened round the waist, a jacket, and a scarf. Married women wear the hair in a large broad knot on the crown of the head, fastened with silver bodkins with chains and tassels. Maidens wear their hair gathered in a roll resting on the back of the neck and similarly secured. They all wear as ornaments bright pieces of amber inserted in perforations in the lobe of the ear. The men tattoo their limbs slightly, and all married women are tattooed on both legs from the ankle to the knee in broad parallel bands. The Singphos understand the smelting of iron, and *daos* of their make are celebrated for their temper and durability. They manufacture their own wearing apparel. They have a confused notion of a Supreme Being, but they propitiate only malignant spirits called *Bhuts*, of which there are three—the *Mer-Bhut* or spirit above, the *Ga-Bhut* or spirit below, and the household *Bhut* or *penate*. They sacrifice fowls, pigs, and dogs, and on special occasions buffaloes. They bury their dead, but in the case of a man of note the body is kept for two or more years in order that the scattered relatives of the deceased may have time to attend his funeral.

3. The Bhutan Group, or the Bhutias, Akas, Daflas, Miris and Abors.

The people of Assam accept these tribes as of Tibetan origin; there are in all 27,000 of these people in Assam. (The Bhutias will be found under the account given of the tribes of Bengal.)

Daflas or Domphilas.

The people known as the Daflas comprise numerous cognate tribes independent of each other. They inhabit the hill passes on the north of the British districts of Darrang and Lakhimpur. The number settled within the British territory is only 549, as ascertained by the census of 1882. The name Dafla (or Daphla), which should be written "Domfila," as the word is pronounced in Lakhimpur, is given to them by the people of the plains. They call themselves Niso or Nising, or Bangni, meaning simply "men." Physically, the Daflas are not so well made as the Miris, and are also less laborious. The Dafla colonies in the plains often suffer terribly from sickness, causing entire depopulation of newly-formed hamlets. They generally bring their hair on to the forehead, where it is wound up into a ball, through which a skewer of wood or metal is pierced, or a silver arrow in the case of a chieftain; and there are thirty to forty chieftains in each inter-tribal clan. The Daflas have a habit of slightly contracting their eye-brows, which gives them a haughty appearance. They repudiate polyandry as a sin that should be visited by death. The eastern Daflas are superior in physique to those inhabiting the western part of the hills. The Daflas claim relationship with the Abors, but they repudiate any connection with the Miris, although the language and religion of both are practically the same. They worship spirits, designated Yápum and Oram, who delight in the offering of a white goat or a fowl. The sun has a place among the Dafla deities, but their great god is "Wi," of whom the Dafla speaks in hushed tones for fear of giving displeasure. The Daflas gave frequent trouble to the British authorities, the chief cause being the right to a tax called Posa, consisting of one double cloth, one single cloth, one handkerchief, one bill-hook, ten head of horned cattle and eight pounds of salt to every ten houses, which the Daflas claimed to collect directly from villages within British territories. After much trouble this tax was commuted into money payments which the Dafla chiefs receive direct from the Government authorities.

The Hill Miris.

The Hill Miris occupy a portion of the hill country between Assam and Thibet, but a large number have settled in the plains where they have proved themselves good agriculturists and expert boatmen. They live in small communities under hereditary chiefs, and in some instances the head of one family has obtained sufficient influence to be acknowledged as chief over clusters of communities. Their villages are small, and placed in some position difficult of access, and the safety of the community is committed to the care of the chief. They are entirely ignorant of arts and manufactures, and are dependent upon others for their clothing, implements of husbandry, &c. They belong to the Mongolian family, and used formerly to acknowledge allegiance to the Ahom kings of Assam. They cultivate rice, millets, Indian-corn, sweet-potatoes, tobacco, &c., but they rarely rear sufficient for their own consumption. They eke out their subsistence by fishing and hunting, and by bartering the wild products of their hills for the necessaries of life. They eat the flesh of all animals from the elephant to the mouse. That of a tiger is prized as food for men; it gives them strength and courage. It is not suited for women; it would make them too strong-minded. The costume of the ladies of this clan is elaborate and peculiar. A short petticoat is secured to a broad belt of leather; over this is worn a small petticoat made of filaments of cane woven together. It is about a foot in length and is fastened tight round the loins. Their upper garment consists of a band of plaited cane-work, girding the body close under the arms, and from this a fragment of cloth depends and covers the breasts. The men have fine muscular figures, many of them over 5 feet 8 inches in height. Their dress does not err on the side of superfluity. Polygamy is practised to a great extent by the chiefs, and when a man dies, his son or heir becomes the husband of all the women except his mother. A woman is valued more on account of her family than her good looks. Wives are bought; three buffaloes, thirty pigs, and a number of fowls being sometimes demanded as the price of a girl. Their religious observances are confined to the slaughter of animals in the name of the sylvan spirits, and vaticination by the examination of the entrails of birds, the deities have been invoked after such sacrifices. They profess a belief in a future state, and have an indefinite idea of a god who presides in the region of departed souls. They bury their dead fully clothed and equipped with arms, travelling pouch and caps; a store of food, cooking utensils, and ornaments, according to this position in life, are deposited along with the body in the grave. The Hill Miris are the most powerful and numerous of the tribes residing on the mountains east of Bhutan: according to the last census they numbered 25,636.

The Abors.

The Abors are found located in the hill country between Assam and Tibet and between the Mishmís and Hill Miris. This name is given to them by the Assamese, and signifies barbarous and independent. The name they give themselves is Pádam. The Abors and Miris are supposed to have come from the same stock, the Miris having entered the Assam hills at an earlier date than the Abors. In the last census it was ascertained that there are 821 Abors settled in British territory. They are a wild, savage people, without knowledge of the arts. Their implements of husbandry are their long straight swords, with crooked bamboos to scrape the earth, and pointed sticks with which to make holes to receive the seed. They have strongly-marked Mongolian features, and are of a rather uniform olive complexion. They are taller than some of the tribes on their frontiers, but are clumsy-looking and sluggish. Their arms are cross-bows and common bows with arrows, the latter used with and without poison, very long spears, daggers, and long straight cutting swords. The dress of the men consists primarily of a loin cloth of the bark of a certain tree. It answers the double purpose of a carpet to sit upon and a covering. It serves also as a pillow by night. Those living near the Assam frontier are better clad. Some wear coloured coats without sleeves, some long Thibetan cloaks; they weave a thick cotton cloth which is made into jackets. The dress of the females, as ordinarily seen, consists of two cloths, blue and red in broad stripes, one round the loins forms a petticoat just reaching to the knee; it is retained in its position by a girdle of cane-work; the other is folded round the bosom. Their necks are decorated by strings of beads reaching to the waist, and the lobes of the ears are enormously extended for decorative purposes. Round the ankles are worn broad bands of finely-plaited cane-work, sometimes of a light blue tinge. All females with any pretensions to youth wear suspended in front from a string round the loins a row of from three to a dozen shell-shaped embossed plates of bell metal, from about six to three inches in diameter, the largest in the middle and the others gradually diminishing in size as they approach the hips. In features and complexion the Abor women are a coarse type of the Chinese. Their religion consists in a belief in certain sylvan deities, to each of whom some particular department in the destiny of man is assigned.

The Digáru Mishmis.

The Mishmis are a people found occupying the hills in the north-eastern frontier of Assam. They are divided into many clans, of which the Digáru Mishmis are one; the name Digáru being derived from the river passing through their country. They were formerly known as Tain Mishmis. Though extremely wild-looking, the Digárus are comparatively inoffensive, but they are exceedingly dirty, and almost equally dishonest. Agriculture is carried on by them in the most rude and simple manner, and their supply of food-grains is necessarily scanty. They do not, however, confine themselves to a vegetable diet, but eat the flesh of almost any animal. They do not congregate in villages, but build their houses apart from each other in the densest and most inaccessible parts of the forest. The dress of all classes is very scanty, and that of the lower orders scarcely decent; but the chiefs wrap themselves in comfortable long cloaks of Tibet wool.

The females dress better than the males. They wear a coloured cloth in the form of a petticoat, and a bodice sometimes covered with a thicker cloth. Both men and women wear the hair long, and gather it into a knot on the top of the head. They are extensive polygamists. Each man may have as many wives as he can afford to purchase, the price ranging from a pig to a bonus of 20 oxen. The Mishmis are a short, sturdy race, of fair complexion for Asiatics, with well-knit figures. They are as active as monkeys and vary much in feature, generally exhibiting a softened phase of the Mongolian type. Their religion is confined to the propitiation of demons, whenever illness or misfortunes visit them. They appear to have no notion of a Supreme Being.

The Chulikáta Mishmis.

The Chulikáta Mishmis inhabit the hill country bordering on Assam, between the Digáru and the Dibong, and on both banks of the hill-course of the latter river. The Assamese call them Chulikáta in consequence of their habit of cropping the front hair on the forehead. Their villages extend across the sub-Himálayan range to the borders of Tibet. They are greatly detested and mistrusted by their neighbours on account of their kidnapping women and children, whom they carry away with them to their hills. They come down in innocent-looking parties, apparently bent only in bartering the merchandise they carry with them. But on finding an unprotected village, they pounce on the women and children and carry them away captive to their hills. They are a trading people, and large parties are always on the move trading with Tibet. The colour of the Chulikáta Mishmi varies from dark brown to the fairness equalling that of a European brunette. Among the girls many are good-looking, but they mar themselves by their peculiar method of cropping the hair. Their features are of a coarse Mongolian type, faces flat and broad, the nostrils wide and round, and the eyes small and oblique. They have learned to utilize for clothing many of the fibrous plants that grow wild in their hills, as well as cotton and wool. Both men and women are great smokers. Their favourite weapons are straight Tibetan swords, daggers, bows and cross bows, poisoned arrows and oblong shields of buffalo hide. They seem altogether devoid of religious feeling, their creed being "men die and worms eat them." There are only some 680 Chulikáta Mishmis in British territory.

4. The Naga Group or the Angamis, Kucha-Nagas, Rengmas, Lhotas, Semas, Banferas, Hathigorias, etc.

The mountainous region which may be defined as south of the Sibsagar District and a continuation of the Northern Kachar Hills connecting the Manipur with the Patkoi hills, and thus trending in a north-easterly direction, is the home of the numerous tribes which are generically designated Nagas. They may be referred to two groups, the southern and the northern.

(a) *Southern Group of Nagas.*

Angámi Nágás.

The Nágás are the most numerous and the most powerful of all the wild races inhabiting the north-eastern frontier of India. They are divided into numerous tribes, of whom the Angámis occupy the most prominent position, both on account of their numbers and their turbulent and warlike habits. A remarkable feature common to all the Nágás is the absence of the bow and arrow, and the use in sport and war of a long, often richly ornamented, spear with a correspondingly large shield, in this respect recalling to mind the Zúlús of South Africa.

Since the occupation of Assam by the British, the Angámi Nágás have been a source of constant anxiety to the frontier authorities. They have committed numerous outrages by raiding on the villages in their neighbourhood, on which occasions they have either massacred the inhabitants or carried them away as slaves to their inaccessible hills. Many expeditions have been undertaken against them, often with doubtful results. The last, in 1878, was, however, conducted on a larger scale, and the result has been that under a wise and clever civil officer, they have been consolidated into a peaceful and faithful community. The region occupied by the Angámis has now come to bear the designation of the Nágá Hills. The sportsman may explore this region with as much personal comfort and security as if these wild hills had been for half a century under British rule.

The Nágá Hills may be defined as an open mountainous region, with a moderate rainfall, a beautiful climate, and a fertile soil. The land is well cultivated, and the hill sides are covered with terraces, on which an abundant harvest of rice, cotton and other valuable crops are reaped. The term "Angámi" is unknown among the people themselves, but they address each other "Tengima." They are a stalwart hardy race, with a brown complexion, flat nose, and high cheek bones. They are brave, but at the same time treacherous and vindictive. Their warrior dress is highly picturesque. A dark blue or black kilt, with rows of conch shells, covers the lower part of the body; a plain, homely cotton cloth, generally brilliantly dyed red and blue, hangs loosely from the shoulders; strings of various-coloured beads ornament the neck in front, a conch shell being suspended behind; and the wild boar supplies ear ornaments, the tusks combined with tufts of goat's hair (dyed red) being worn as ear-rings; but they also wear ear-rings of brass wire. The long flowing locks of human hair, taken from victims or foes, intermixed with red-coloured goat's hair, and ornamented with shells, not only form the most valued neck and breast ornament, but proclaim the prowess of the wearer in the field, for none but he who has secured a number of human heads is allowed to don such an insignia of honour. The Angámi armlets are massive pieces of ivory, and the calves of the legs are protected by rings of dyed rattan cane, or neatly plaited yellow and red leggings; these are generally worked on the legs, and allowed to remain until they wear out.

The women are short in stature and extremely plain looking. All the drudgery of the family has to be performed by them, not only the indoor, but also field work, such as bringing of fuel and drawing of water. The young women are gaily dressed in white cloth with broad blue stripes, but the old women wear scarcely any coloured garments. Among certain Angámis a sip of nicotine is a rare luxury. This is prepared by the old women, who smoke all day and spit into a vessel placed near them for this purpose. This liquid is boiled down, and in a condensed form is given to the men, who carry it in small vessels. These they present to each other on meeting as a friendly saluation. The tip of the finger is dipped in the nicotine and then placed on the tongue.

The most remarkable feature of the Angámi Nágá is the fact that each village is broken into independent sections or *khels*, a stone wall separating completely each section. The villages are located on the summits of hills, and powerfully fortified with walls and ditches, the trenches and approaches being often filled with sharply-pointed bamboos (*pánjis*). The young men and women of each *khel* live together in a common house and not with their parents, and are chiefly employed in keeping watch on the other *khels*. After marriage the women are absolutely chaste, unfaithfulness constituting a blood feud between the men.

Lhotas.

The Lhotas occupy the hills north of the Angámi county, and bordering on the valley of Dimapur. Wokha may be regarded as their capital. In many respects they resemble the Angámis, but instead of the happy, open, and independent expression, they are sulky, intensely lazy, and habitual drunkards. They are careless in the matter of dress as compared with the Angámis. They wear a black bearskin fur over the brow and around the head, and instead of the Angámi flowing badge of honour, they bear across the breast a wooden ornament about a foot in breadth and 3 inches in depth, which is richly ornamented with shells.

The Lhotas are under the jurisdiction of the Deputy-Commissioner of the Nágá Hills.

Kucha-Nágás and the Manipur Nágás.

The Kucha-Nágás occupy the mountainous region south of the Angámi country, and connecting it with Manipur and the Northern Kachar hills, or what may be more expressly defined as the southern portion of the Barel range lying between the Dhaneswari and the Barak rivers. They speak a different dialect and are less warlike than the Angámis, but in other respects these two tribes are closely allied.

Still to the south and south-west, until the frontier of Kachar is reached, are the Kolya and Kwaphis, or the Nagas of the Western side of the valley of Manipur. These are a timid race of people with no form of organised government. In features they resemble the Kacharis, and since they are not migratory, but are attached to their homes and villages, they are generally viewed as earlier inhabitants than the Manipuris, Kukis, and other tribes who have now come to hold the more fertile tracts of country. Their houses are peculiar, the gables are turned to the streets, and the front or gable beams are crossed above the roof, and often ornamented by carvings of a crude kind with horns of animals and tufts of orchids attached to them. The further gable is lower than the front one, so that the ridge pole slopes backwards. Immediately in front of each house is the burial-place of the dead, who are buried in coffins made of hollow trunks of trees, with a large stone placed over them to mark the spot. This curious habit may be accepted as indicating a former state of cannibalism, the family being thus able to protect their dead. Indeed, among many of the Nágá tribes, the tradition exists that they themselves were cannibals at one time, and eat all things that once had life except the horse. They point with disdain to their distant neighbours as being cannibals at the present day. Throughout the whole of the Nágá tribes the dog is the favourite article of food and fetches a higher price than a sheep or goat; indeed the latter can with difficulty be procured. The dog is fed on rice, and thus reared as an article of food. A great luxury is to feed the dog as hard as it can be with rice, and then kill it and rapidly cook it rice and all. The Nágás, like most hill tribes, abstain from the use of milk or cheese, and eggs are never eaten until they are quite rotten. The Kwaphis (or Kowpois) are fond of sitting on the stones which cover their deceased relatives. They then appear to enjoy themselves greatly, and are exceedingly loquacious. They smoke violently, pipes containing green tobacco, but they admit that the pleasure of doing so is nothing compared to that derived from holding in the mouth a sip of the water from the bowl of the pipe after being well impregnated with the fumes of the smoke passing through it. Kwaphis do not indulge in very elaborate garments, but, unlike all other Nágás, what they do wear are artistically embroidered, the fringe being brightened by alternate tufts of cotton and the bark of an orchid, which remains of a brilliant yellow colour. The Nágás on the eastern side of Manipur are perhaps the most degraded of the race, and this is probably due to the persecution they have been subjected to by the migratory Kukis or Lushais, who have for many years in successive waves passed through their country, and lived almost entirely by raiding upon these simple people.

The Tonkhul and Lahúpa tribes are the most powerful of the eastern Manipur Nágás. The section Lahúpa has received that name from the Manipurís, in allusion to the fact of their wearing a basket helmet which the other Tonkhuls do not do. The Tonkhuls are a tall race of men with large heads and heavy stolid features, somewhat resembling the Angámis. The dress is very scanty, a piece of cloth folded around the waist, a portion hanging down in front; but even this is dispensed with when the only article of dress is a ring of deer's horn or ivory worn on the person. In holiday attire they wear, thrown boldly across the shoulders, a large flowing white sheet, with red stripes. But perhaps the most striking feature of the Tonkhul is the remarkable way in which the hair is cut, all the hair on either side of the head being carefully shaved off so as to leave a narrow ridge passing like a cock's comb over the head.

The villages are situated on the sides of the hills near the summit, but the houses are very primitive. On the birth of a child fowls are sacrificed, and the women of the village treated to liquor. The child has chewed rice placed in its mouth, and is thereafter immersed in water heated to near the boiling point. This is supposed to prevent, in after life, rheumatic pains. At puberty the male child assumes the ring above described, and the ears are perforated so as to admit of small bales of cotton wool,—the Tonkhul ear ornament. The only weapon of war used by the Tonkhul is a long, heavy spear, which is thrust, as it is too heavy to be thrown, two hands being used.

The southern portion of the tribe use the bow and arrow, frequently poisoned, but this may have been borrowed from the Lushais and other tribes to the south. The religion of the Tonkhul, like most other hill tribes, is a form of demon worship. He has some idea of a Supreme Being who is benevolent, and who inhabits space, but the evil spirits who reside between heaven and earth are those most to be concerned about. Their ideas of a future state are that after death they go to the West, where there is another world; in this future state they live and die, men six times, women five times; after this they are turned into clouds.

The Murring tribes occupy a portion of the country south of the Tonkhuls, on the hills lying between Manipur and the Kabo valley, but intermixed with them are to be found villages of the Khongjai Kukís, and further to the north the raiding Chasad Kukis, and on the east of Manipur, bordering on the Kwaphís are the Kom Kukís. The Kukís are modern immigrants into Manipur from the Chittagong hill tracts.

(*b*) *Northern Group of Nágás.*

Banfera Nágás.

Among the Northern Nágás, one of the most curious tribes is the Banferas. They inhabit but a small tract of country, and have only a very few villages. They are, however, bold and fearless, and tattoo the face in a remarkable manner, which, when taken along with their striking features, gives them a most pronounced expression, forcibly recalling some of the American Indians. This idea is enhanced by the fact that they wear on the head a crown of long flowing feathers taken from the tail of the wild cock. They are also fond of hair ornaments, but unlike the Angámis the hair is generally dyed yellow instead of red. Tufts of this yellow hair are attached to their *dao* or sword (which has a truncated point) to their shield, and to their elbows and knees, projecting backwards. The monkey's skull is also a favourite ornament, two rows being generally arranged along the small basket which they carry on the back.

SUB-COURTS XVIII. & XX.

THE PRESIDENCY OF BENGAL.

The Presidency of Bengal (or the Lower Provinces) comprises four strongly defined regions, viz., Bengal proper, Behar, Orissa, and Chutia Nagpur. These cover an area of 193,198 square miles, and constitute a territory nearly as large as Spain, or more than half as large again as Great Britain and Ireland. Under the Lieutenant-Governor of Bengal there are nine Commissioners and forty-five district officers, with, in each district, two or more sub-divisional officers. A sub-division is about the same size as an average English county, *e.g.*, 717,677 acres. The census of 1881 revealed the fact that in this vast territory, and under the administration briefly indicated, there are 69,536,861 persons—a population about equal to France and the United Kingdom taken together. This gives for each square mile of the whole presidency 360, but in Bengal proper there are 506 persons; the North-West Provinces have 403; Madras, 221; Bombay Presidency, 133; the Panjab, 159; the Central Provinces, 102. Comparing with these figures one or two European countries, England and Wales have 445; Scotland, 121; Russia in Europe, 35; and Norway only 13. In Bengal a single sub-divisional officer is governing therefore about the same number of persons as are to be found in an English county. This fact is the more remarkable when it is recollected that instead of being collected into large self-governing towns, the inhabitants of Bengal are thickly dispersed in hamlets and homesteads. Only about one village in every 1,000 contains 5,000 inhabitants. Bengal, with nearly three times the population of England, has only about half the number of towns and villages, and, moreover, 309.336 persons live habitually in boats on the great rivers which traverse the rich alluvial plains. But, what is still more wonderful, the 70,000,000 of people met with in Bengal are broken into a number of distinct and antagonistic races; people widely dissimilar in race, religion, and social customs. There are 43,452,806 Hindus, 21,704,724 Mohammedans, 128,153 Christians, 155,809 Buddhists, and 2,092,369 aboriginal and other tribes not referred to these great religious communities. It is impossible to define what is meant by a Hindu, and doubtless a large number of the aboriginal people at the census may have returned themselves as Hindus. Viewing, however, the better known castes, the following analysis of the Hindus of Bengal may be given: higher castes, 4,897,426; intermediate, 2,777,124; trading, 963,159; pastoral, 4,115,377; persons engaged in preparing cooked articles of food sold in that state, 924,984; agriculturists, 6,875,197; servants, 2,804,003; artizans, 4,482,471; weavers 1,619,344; labourers, 546,839; fish and fruit sellers, 142,417; boatmen and fishermen, 2,131,433; dancers and musicians, 43,255; and others, 731,341. Under Hindus have been included 1,365,215 persons who by nationality are aboriginals, but who have individually left their own faith and been converted to Hinduism, and also 10,618,451 supposed aboriginal races who have wholly merged into the lower grades of the Hindu system. These are the so-called semi-Hinduised tribes, such as the Bagdís, Baurís, Bhuinyas, Chámárs, Chandals, Doms, Dosadhs, Háris, Kochs, Máls, &c., &c.

The aboriginal tribes who at the present day remain pure and uncontaminated by either Hinduism or Mohammedanism number about 2,091,226. These may be viewed by provinces, or according to an ethnological classification. The census report refers them to Western aborigines, viz., the Dravidian and the Kolarian races of Western Bengal, of Orissa, and of Chutia Nagpur, with the groups of Feudatory States attached to these; and, second, Eastern aborigines, or the more or less Mongolian races of the Himálayan ranges, extending through Sikkim to the Tibetan frontier. This classification is, however, open to considerable ambiguity, from the overlappings of these races; and for the purposes of this brief catalogue of the models and ethnological exhibits shown in the Imperial Court, it is perhaps preferable to follow a provincial system. The writer has to acknowledge the valuable assistance rendered by the Rev. A. Campbell, of the Santal Mission, in preparing the following brief descriptions of the people of Chutia Nagpur:—

Section—Chutia Nagpur.

(a) *Kolarian Races.*

The Santáls.

The Santáls belong to what is known as the Kolarian group of aboriginal races, and their language points to a Turanian origin. They number 1,087,202, and are found inhabiting "a strip of Bengal extending for about 350 miles from the Ganges to the Baitarni, bisected by the meridian of Bhágalpur, or 87° east longitude." They are somewhat nomadic, and their traditions keep alive the memory of their many migrations. But although given to change on very slight provocation, they are not nomads in the proper sense of the term. They are splendid backwoodsmen, and have great skill in clearing forest land, and bringing it under cultivation, and in this capacity their services are much in request in the tea districts of Assam and Kachar. They are short of stature, but are strongly built, with exceptionally long bodies. They are very dark-complexioned, often having black short curly hair. The eyes are full and round, but the hair of the eye-brows does not always follow the form of the bone. They are a happy, good-natured people, and have little care beyond the supply of their present wants. They are fond of hunting and field sports, and annually they meet in their thousands for two days' organised hunting. They are fond of strong drink, and a home-brewed ale flows freely at all their feasts and merry-makings. They are not a warlike race, but in their insurrection of 1854 they showed courage of a high order. Their arms are the bow and arrow and a serviceable battle-axe. Their religion partakes of a fetish character, but they neither make nor worship idols. Their religious ceremonies are all intended to propitiate malignant spirits, who, they believe, have power to send all manner of sickness and calamity upon them. They burn their dead, and consign a piece of the charred collar bone to the waters of the Damuda river.

The Múndáris or Múnda Kols.

The Múndáris, or Múnda Kols, belong to what is known as the Kolarian group of aboriginal races. They are found in Chutia Nagpur, inhabiting the district of Lohardugga, and number 591,858. Their language is closely allied to that of the Santáls, and is therefore Turanian in origin. The Múndáris are an agricultural people, and have long been settled in their present habitat. They are light-hearted and good natured, but extremely indolent. At their numerous festivals and marriage feasts they indulge, to intoxication, in strong drink. They are passionately fond of dancing and hunting. Although at present peacefully inclined, they were formerly warlike and turbulent. Their arms are the bow and arrow, and a heavy battle-axe. Their religion is more shamanistic than fetish. They make no images of their gods, nor do they worship symbols. They offer sacrifices in "high places" and in groves dedicated to the worship of their deities. They burn their dead, but bury a portion of the charred loins in an urn, over which a heavy slab is placed. A large number of the Kóls have become Christians.

The Hos or Larka Kóls.

The Hos, or as they are also called the Larka Kóls, belong to the Kolarian group of aboriginal races. They are found located in Singbhúm, a district of the Chutia Nagpur Province, and number about 190,000 souls. They are intimately allied to the Múndáris, both in language and customs. They have been less influenced by the Aryan races than many of their cognates, and even at the present day the exclusiveness of the Hos is remarkable. Physically they are a much finer people than any other of the Kolarians. The males average 5 feet 5, or 5 feet 6 inches in height; and the females 5 feet 2 inches. In features they are variable; some approaching the Aryan type, and others the Mongolian. They were formerly a warlike people, as the name, Larka Kól, or fighting Kól, implies. Their arms are the bow and arrow and battle-axe. They are now peaceful cultivators. Like the other Kolarian tribes, they are fond of dancing and music. They are also addicted to intoxication. Their dress at the present day is a narrow strip of cloth for the males, a broader piece worn like a petticoat by the older females, and the common Indian dress, or *sárí*, worn by the younger women, but tradition says they formerly dressed in aprons made of leaves. They cremate their dead, and bury a piece of the charred bone under a huge slab. Their religion is the same as that of the Múndáris.

The Bhumij.

The Bhumij belong to the Kolarian group of aboriginal races. They are found located chiefly in the Manbhúm district of the Province of Chutia Nagpur, and number about 300,000 souls, although in the census report they appear to have been confused with the Hindus and Kóls. They are closely allied, both in language and customs, to the Múndáris and Larka Kóls. They are less exclusive than many of their cognates, and those who live amongst Bengalis have retained very few of their ancient customs. They were formerly very turbulent, and were always ready for a fray or foray; and they had many conflicts with the British Government before their country was finally settled. Their arms are the bow and arrow and a battle-axe. They are short of stature but strongly built, and in complexion they are variable, ranging from a dark chocolate to a light-brown colour. They are all agriculturists, and live in commodious, well-built houses, and are generally well-to-do. Like the other members of the Kolarian family, they are fond of dancing and music. In former years they were in the habit of kidnapping children and sacrificing them at the shrine of a local goddess named *Rankíní*, in this respect resembling the Khonds who inhabit the mountains far to the south, in the province of Orissa.

(*b*) *Dravidian Races.*

The Uráons.

The Uráons belong to what is known as the Dravidian group of aboriginal races. They are found located in the Province of Chutia Nagpur, and number in all probability about half a million, but they appear to have been returned as Hindus or Kóls in the census report. Their language is closely allied to Tamil and to the other Dravidian tongues. They are a small race, averaging 5 feet 2 inches in height, but there is a perfect proportion in all the parts of their form. They are dark complexioned and by no means well favoured. They are industrious cultivators, and the youth of the tribe are known all over Bengal as hardy day-labourers. Music and dancing are their national pastimes. They begin to dance as soon as they can walk, and to sing as soon as they can talk. The dress of the men is the scantiest possible with decency. That of the women consists of a waist cloth of brown cotton reaching to the knee, the upper part of the body being left uncovered. In the more civilised tracts of country the persons of young females are decently clad in the coarse cotton cloth of the country. Like the Nagas of Assam the young people live in a common house and not with their parents. They believe in the existence of a Supreme Being, but the sole object of their religious ceremonies is to propitiate the malignant spirits, who, as they believe, are continually thwarting his benevolent intentions. They burn their dead on the funeral pyre.

The Mals and Malers, or the Paharias.

The Mals and Malers, or Paharias, the Hillmen of Rajmahal; according to most authors, they belong to the Dravidian group of aboriginal races. They inhabit the Rajmahal Hills, and number about 150,000 souls. They were the first of the aboriginal races of Bengal to attract the attention of the British. They are described as early as 1796 as "being destitute of manufactures, and but little acquainted with agriculture, and subsisting principally by plunder," and their incursions into the low country for the purpose of plunder were accompanied by every species of cruelty. Since then, however, they have settled down to agriculture, and have become law-abiding and industrious. Their houses are built with cane, and their numerous out-houses, e.g., styes and well-stored granaries, bespeak plenty and comfort. They cultivate in their hills a variety of Indian-corn and also millets; these grains constitute their principal food. They also cultivate pine-apples and plantains, and sell these fruits to the inhabitants of the lowland country. They are of average stature and dark complexion, with remarkable short square noses and prominent eye-brows with acutely pointed eyes. They indulge in dancing, but are said only to do so when under the influence of liquor, to which they are very much addicted. The unmarried adults of both sexes are excluded from the family residence; the bachelors and maidens reside in separate quarters of their own, after the same fashion as the youths of the Angami Nagas in Assam. The Malers are short of stature and of light make, and fairer than most other aboriginal tribes. They dress well, and are fond of gaudy colours and ornaments. Considerable confusion still exists regarding the Mals and Malers. By some authors they are treated as sub-divisions of a common tribe, by others as quite distinct. The former inhabit the southern ranges near Rámgarh, while the latter are more abundant on the heights of Damun. The Máls, like the Kóls, are fond of dancing, and are almost Hinduised, refusing to eat beef or food not cooked by themselves; while the Malers are far less cheerful, and never dance, but eat anything they can procure. The census report includes them as semi-Hinduised tribes, giving their numbers as follows: Mals, 125,238; Malers, 2,388; and Mal Paharias, 13,260. According to other authorities, the Malers only are Dravidians.

(c) *Semi-Hinduised Tribe, most probably of Dravidian origin.*

The Bhuiyas.

The Bhuiyas, or Bhuinyas, are a semi-Hinduised aboriginal tribe, very numerous in the Province of Chutia Nagpur, although not confined to it; they number about 60,000. It is thought probable that they belong to the Dravidian rather than to the Kolarian family, but having lost their own language, and having adopted many of the customs of the Hindus, nothing positive can be discovered as to their origin. They possess traditions of having once constituted a powerful nation, and from the qualities which they still display this may be regarded as very probable. They are a dark-brown, well-proportioned race, with black straight hair, plentiful on the head but scant on the face. They are of middle height with figure well-knit. They are capable of enduring great fatigue, but they do not usually present the muscular development of hill-men. In many districts they are the hereditary guardians of the passes, and hold their lands on a service tenure. Their arms would appear to have been a sword and shield, and they still indulge in their war-dance, but since they have been disarmed a stout stick has taken the place of the sword Their dress depends upon their station in life, the male portion of the poorer classes are often scantily enough clothed, but the women are generally decently clad in cotton cloth. They burn their dead in the funeral pyre as the Hindus do.

Section—The Hill Tracts of Orissa.

The Khonds.

The Khonds or Kandhs inhabit the mountainous tract lying between Orissa on the north and the Presidency of Madras on the south, or more correctly in the tract of country between the Godavari and the Mahanadi. This is known as the Kandhmáls, and it is partly under the jurisdiction of Madras and partly of the small native state of Bod—one of the eighteen tributary states to Orissa.

The Khonds attracted the attention of the British Government in 1855, owing to their practice of offering human sacrifice to their earth god *Pennu*. The victims were called *Toki* or *Keddi*, or more vulgarly *Meriahs*, and were procured from a low caste of Hindus—the Páns—who lived in the Khond country and traded with the Hindus of the plains, from whom they either purchased or kidnapped children. The Khonds regarded with great veneration the *Meriah* children, and fed them with the utmost care until the time they were required for sacrificial purposes. The greatest cruelty was then however perpetrated. The bodies were literally torn to pieces and life taken by the most inhuman devices. Each worshipper carried away from the sacrifice a small piece of the *Meriah* flesh, and this on arrival at the distant village was the object of further devotion before being consigned to *Pennu*. This was ultimately accomplished as follows:—A small hole having been dug in a selected field, the head man of the village approached this spot by walking backwards, and with his hands behind his back, deposited the sacred offering in the hole and covered it with earth without looking at it. Fortunately human sacrifice is now almost completely abolished, and it is of course viewed as criminal and punished by law. The priests are a distinct class who may not eat with the laymen, but this restriction does not extend to liquor. Personal feuds are generally settled by the head man, who exercises a patriarchial power. A blood feud may be averted by the criminal escaping to another village and claiming the protection of the head man, whose slave he becomes. Few hill tribes have stronger convictions regarding hospitality, and hence the protection afforded by this system of a village of refuge.

The Khond language belongs to the group generally designated Dravidian. The Khonds, although they live in villages, do not practice any trade other than agriculture. They are fond of sport. They live chiefly upon rice and pulses, but eat the animals killed in sport. Their huts are of wattle and daub, thatched with grass. The male dress consists of a piece of cloth wrapped round the waist, without any head-dress. They go armed with an axe and sometimes carry bows and arrows. The women have a short piece of cloth passed once or twice round the body which does not reach below the middle of the thigh, and the bosom is uncovered.

The Khonds are very fond of tobacco, which they smoke in a kind of cigarette made of a rolled leaf filled with cut tobacco. The men are also very partial to liquor which they make from rice and *mahua* flowers (*Bassia latifolia*). The villages are often enclosed by wooden stockades similar to those built by the Nagas of Assam.

Section—The Hill Tribes of North Bengal—Sikkim.

The Lepchas.

The Lepchas are in all probability the aboriginal inhabitants of the valley of Sikkim, a confined region of perhaps not more than sixty miles in breadth, hemmed in by Nepal on the west and Bhutan on the east. Sir J. D. Hooker's admirable account of these timid and peaceful mountaineers is the most complete and accurate yet published, but from want of space only a brief abstract can be here given, but the reader is referred to the *Himalayan Journals* (vol. 1, pp. 127 to 136). The Lepchas are a fine, frank, open-hearted and free-handed race, fond of change and given to out-door life. They have no word for plough in their language, and follow the nomadic form of agriculture known as *júm* cultivation. The Lepcha is a singularly marked Mongolian in features, and a good deal too in habit; but still he differs from his Tibetan prototype, though not so much as from his nearest neighbours, the people of Nepal and of Bhutan. An attentive study of the Lepcha in one respect entirely contradicts our preconceived notions of a mountaineer; he is timid, peaceful and no brawler, qualities which are all the more remarkable from contrasting so strongly with the brave warriors on the west and the quarrelsome cowards on the east. A group of Lepchas is exceedingly picturesque. They are of short stature—four feet eight inches to five feet—rather broad in the chest, and with muscular arms, but small hands and slender wrists. The face is broad, flat, and of eminently Tartar character, flat-nosed and oblique-eyed, with no beard and only a little moustache; the complexion is sallow, or often a clear olive; the hair is collected into an immense tail, plaited flat or round.

Their intercourse with one and another is scrupulously honest; a present is divided equally. They are constantly armed with a long, heavy, straight knife called *ban*, but never draw it on one another; family and political feuds are alike unheard of amongst them. Polyandry is unknown amongst them and polygamy rare. Their dress consists of a cotton vesture, which is loosely thrown round the body, leaving one or both arms free; it reaches to the knee and is gathered round the waist. Its fabric is close; the ground colour white, ornamented with longitudinal blue stripes prettily worked with red and white. In cold weather an upper garment with loose sleeves is added. A hat when worn is generally extravagantly broad and flat-brimmed, with a small hemispherical crown very much like the Assam Ahom hat.

In diet, the Lepchas are gross feeders, but rice constitutes the chief sustenance. Pork is a staple dish, but all kinds of animal food are also eaten. Marriages are contracted in childhood, and the wife is purchased by money or by service. The females are generally chaste and the marriage tie is strictly kept. Its violation is heavily punished by divorce, beating or slavery. The Lepchas profess no religion, though acknowledging the existence of good and bad spirits. To the good spirits they pay no heed. "Why should we?" they say. "The good spirits do us no harm; the evil spirits who dwell in every rock, grove and mountain, are constantly at mischief, and to them we must pray, for they hurt us."

Several modern writers have pointed out that the Lepchas of Sikkim very closely resemble isolated mountain tribes found in some of the loftier Himalayan valleys far to the west. According to the Census, there are about 4000 Lepchas.

The Limbus.

The Limbus inhabit portions of Sikkim and also cross into Nepal. They are described as hardy and industrious. They cultivate grain and rear cows, pigs and poultry. Sir J. D. Hooker says that they once ruled in eastern Nepal. "Although not divided into castes, they belong to several tribes. All consider themselves as the earliest inhabitants of the Támbar valley, though they have a tradition of having originally emigrated from Tibet, which their Tartar countenance confirms. They are more slender and sinewy, than the Lepchas, and neither plait their hair nor wear ornaments. Instead of the *ban* they use the Nepal *kukri*, a curved knife or bill-hook; while for the striped kirtle of the Lepchas are substituted loose cotton trousers and a tight jacket; a sash is worn round the middle, and on the head a small cotton cap."

"Their habits are so similar to those of the Lepchas, that they constantly intermarry. They mourn for, burn, and also bury their dead, raising a mound over the corpse, erecting a head-stone, and surrounding the grave with a little paling of sticks; they then scatter eggs and pebbles over the ground." "The Limbu language is totally different from the Lepcha." According to the last Census returns, there are about 5000 Limbus, exclusive of those in Nepal.

Bhutanis, or Bhutias.

Bhutan may be said to stretch from the eastern boundary of Sikkim eastward along the Himálaya to the country inhabited by the Akas, Daflas and Miris. It is limited on the south by Koch Behar and Assam. It may be referred to two well-defined regions (*a*) the Dwars or lower and southern ranges and tarai, and (*b*) the upper and loftier regions extending to the frontier of Tibet. The greater portion of the Dwars is now under British rule, and about 6000 Bhutias are therefore British subjects. They are described under Bengal because of the Bhutias of Darjiling being better known than those further to the east on the Assam frontier.

The Bhutias may be described as a Tibetan race, with a language which is best defined as a dialect of Tibetan blended with words and idioms taken from the countries on which they severally touch. Their religion is a form of Buddhism, the observances being accompanied with the most remarkable noises. Clarionets of brass, or even silver, but with the poor of wood, with reeds, are violently played, while horns, shells, cymbals, drums and gongs complete the deafening clamour. They are polyandrists, but the marriage tie is so loose that chastity is quite unknown. Intercourse of the sexes is in fact so promiscuous that inheritance has to be set aside, property passing to the Raja, and not to the children, from the difficulty to determine parentage.

The Bhutias are a short, square-built people, with broad, flat faces, small oblique eyes, and a low, short and flat nose, with a large mouth. They seem always happy and healthy, and the women in Darjíling have the reputation of being stronger than any man from the plains. They are excessively dirty, and almost never wash. Their garments consist of a long, flowing robe, wrapped round the body and secured in its position by a leather belt round the waist. The boots are made of red and white felt, with buffalo-hide soles; the uppers are prolonged like leggings, up almost to the knees. A cap, made of fur or coarse woollen cloth, completes the habiliment. Their food is of the very coarsest, and their cookery most primitive. All classes are addicted to intoxication. Mr. Robertson, in his *Account of Assam*, says: "Every element of deterioration is comprised in their government, both secular and spiritual. Their energies are paralysed by the insecurity of property; their morals are degraded, and their numbers reduced by the unnatural system of polyandry and the excessive prevalence of monastic institutions. Yet, under all these disadvantages, some redeeming traits of character occasionally prove them to be still connected with the more elevated of their species by the links of a common sympathy."

The Bhutiás from Tibet, according to Sir J. D. Hooker, have all the virtues with but few of the vices of the Bhutias proper, and are more accessible and less sulky. They are dressed in loose blanket robes, girt about the waist by a leather belt, in which they place their iron or brass pipes, and from which they suspend their long knives, chop-sticks, tobacco-pouch, tweezers, tinder-box, &c. The women are dressed in long flannel petticoats and spencers, over which is thrown a short sleeveless striped cloak, drawn round the waist by a girdle of broad brass or silver links, to which hang their knives and scissors. Both sexes wear silver rings and ear-rings set with turquoises, and square amulets upon their necks and arms. The hair is plaited in two tails, and the neck is loaded with strings of coral and glass beads, and great lumps of amber, glass and agate.

The Mechs.

The Mechs are the western branch of the great Bodo or Kachari race; they inhabit the *tarái* lying immediately below the Darjíling Himálaya. Closely allied to the Mechs, and inhabiting the same region, are the Dhimáls, and according to the census there are about a thousand of each of these clans. They are a squalid, unhealthy-looking people, typical of the region they inhabit. In reality, however, they are not unhealthy, as their sallow complexion does not indicate a sickly constitution. They are nomadic cultivators, so little connected with any one spot that their language possesses no word for village. They never cultivate the same field beyond the second year, or remain in the same village for more than five or six years. They have no artisan communities, and admit no strangers into their villages. What articles they require, and which they cannot make, they purchase from neighbouring villages. They have no buffaloes, few cows, no sheep, but a good many goats, and a great abundance of pigs, poultry, and ducks. Each family tends its own stock and no animals are sold. They despise trade and do not therefore barter further than suits their own necessities. They are averse to working for strangers, whether as soldiers, menials, or carriers. Among themselves they have neither servants nor slaves, all Bodos or Dhimals are equal. Their clothes are made by their women, the females wear *eri*-silk garments and the men cotton. Rice is the principal article of food, wheat and barley are unknown to them. Fish of all sorts are eaten, and all animals save oxen, dogs, cats, monkeys, elephants, bears, and tigers.

The religion of the Mech and the Dhimál is distinguished, like their manners and customs, by the absence of anything barbarous, ridiculous or incommodious. It consists of the worship of the sun and moon and of the terrene elements, but the rivers are the principal elements of their adoration. Their rites consist of offerings, sacrifices, and prayers, but these even are few and simple; they consist of invocations for protection for the people, their crops and domestic animals. Hogs are the most common sacrifices, and eggs are very common offerings.

The Kochs.

These are a branch of the great Bodo race, closely allied to the Mechs and Dhimáls, and they inhabit the *tarái* further to the east bordering on the Dwars of Assam. The Maharaja of Kuch Behar is the head of this race, and following his noble example, the better classes of his people are rapidly becoming civilized.

Section—The Hill Tribes of East Bengal —Tipperah and Chittagong.

"Rising from the rice swamps and level land of the Chittagong district, of which it forms the eastern boundary, there stretches out a vast extent of hilly and mountainous country inhabited by various hill races." So writes Col. T. H. Lewin in his admirable little book "The Wild Races of South-eastern India." This wild region is bounded on the south and east, as far as the Blue Mountains, by the province of Arracan; on the north by the Fenny river, which divides the Chittagong hill tracts from hill Tipperah; while to the north and north-east it borders with Upper Burma and Manipur.

Col. Lewin divides the people of this region into two great generic sections:—

A. *The Khyoungtha, or Children of the River.*

These are of pure Arracanese origin, and speak the ancient dialect of Arracan and conform in every way to the Buddhistic customs. Under this section, however, is included the Chuckma tribe, although they do not all speak Arracanese.

The tribes of this section live near the streams, from which they take their respective clan names. They are collected into village communities under a Roaja, or head man. Those to the south of the Karnafúlí river are subject to a chief called Bohmong, while those to the north owe allegiance to the Mong Raja. The position of the Roaja, or village head, is more an honourable than a profitable one: he is chosen by the villagers, and appointed by the Chief, to whom he must present a *nuzzer* on his nomination being ratified.

B. *The Toungtha, or Children of the Hills.*

The tribes included under this section speak numerous and distinct dialects. They included the Tipperah, Kumi, Mrús, and Khyengs tribes, who are tributary to the British; the Bungís Pankhos, more or less tributary; and the Lushas and Kukís and the Shendús, entirely independent tribes.

Reference has been made in another page to the raiding Kukís, who for many years have continued, wave after wave, to migrate into Manipur, and even still further to the north. Space cannot, however, be afforded for a detailed account of the people of the Chittagong hill tracts. Suffice it therefore to conclude with another passage from Col. Lewin: "The Toungtha are distinguished from the Khyoungtha in many ways. Their villages are, generally speaking, situated on lofty hills and in places difficult of access. The men wear hardly any clothes at all, and the petticoat of the women is scanty, reaching barely below the knees, while their bosoms are left uncovered after the birth of the first child. Previous to that the unmarried girls wear a narrow breast-cloth. Both men and women are much given to dancing together. The women do not hold so high a position among them as among the Khyoungtha, and upon them falls the greater part of the labour of life. Their religion is simple—it is the religion of nature. They worship the terrene elements, and have vague and undefined ideas of some divine power which overshadows all. They were born and they die, for ends to them as incomputable as the path of a cannon-shot fired into the darkness. They are cruel, and attach but little value to life. Reverence or respect are emotions unknown to them; they salute neither their chiefs nor their elders; no form of greeting exists in their many tongues, neither have they any expression conveying thanks." "Great licence is allowed before marriage to the youth of both sexes, between whom intercourse is entirely unchecked." Marriage with them is more a civil contract than a religious ceremony. It is entered into by the mutual agreement of the contracting parties, and can be dissolved at their joint request."

"Each village is a small state, owing fealty and allegiance to no one save their own special leader. A man may leave one chief, and transfer himself and his family to the village of another; hence it happens that the power of different chiefs, which depends upon the size of their respective villages, varies considerably from time to time, according to their success or popularity."

SUB-COURT XXIX.

THE BOMBAY PRESIDENCY.

The Bombay Presidency forms a strip of more or less mountainous country skirting the Western Coast of India. There are 16,508,440 inhabitants in the Presidency, chiefly Marathas, Gujaratis, Musalmans, Christians, and Parsis, with, in addition, a few distinct though little known aboriginal tribes, of whom the more interesting are the *Thakúrs*, *Katkaris*, *Warlis*, *Son Kolis* and *Bhíls*. It has been thought sufficient to confine attention chiefly to the exhibits shown in connection with these aboriginal tribes. The collections will be found, however, to be extensive and interesting. They have been mainly prepared by Mr. John Griffiths, Principal of the Bombay School of Art, assisted by district officers, and more particularly by Mr. W. F. Sinclair, C.S. The following account of the above Bombay aboriginal tribes will be found to allude to their peculiar articles of dress and adornment, to the weapons used by them both in sport and war, and to their agricultural implements and domestic appliances. On the walls of the Court will also be found the characteristic forms of domestic pottery, metal utensils, peasant jewellery, and basket work, met with in the Presidency.

The ratio of population to area is 132·8 persons per square mile. But if Sind and the Island of Bombay are excluded, the ratio is raised to 174·1. The greatest density prevails in Gujarat, while the lowest occurs in the Thar and Parkar district. Gujarat has 281, Konkan 237, Deccan 144, Ka[illegible]tic 149, while Sind has only 50 inhabitants to the square mile. The Presidency covers an area equal to that of Hungary with the population of Spain. Sind is equal in extent to Roumania, while the population is less than that of Switzerland. The Deccan has the population of Ireland, with a little more than the area of Portugal; take away the collectorate of Ahmednagar, and it is about the size of Scotland. The Karnatic extends over an area a little below that of Greece, and has a population a little above that of Switzerland. Gujarat is about the same size as the State of Vermont, but its population is larger and stands about half-way between that of Saxony and Wallachia. The following are the principal aboriginal tribes of Bombay:—

The Katkaris or Kathodis.

The Katkaris are a non-Aryan forest tribe inhabiting the same region as the Thakurs. They are found in the Thana and Kolaba districts, as well as on the borders of Poona, Nasik, and Bhor. As their name indicates, they are makers of Cutch. They very much resemble the Thakurs, but are regarded as less peaceful, poorer, and wilder; they never use the plough, and subsist chiefly upon forest produce. They kill and eat almost any animal, and have a bad reputation as thieves. Their principal weapon is the bow, and their only implement the *Koita*, or bill-hook. They are undoubtedly brave and skilful huntsmen, and it may be doubted whether their present degradation is not as much due to the extermination of animals as to their own reckless and drunken habits. Their characteristic industry, the boiling of the *Khair* wood in the preparation of Cutch, has been stopped by Government in the interests of forest conservancy, the tree having been almost entirely exterminated by them. Their bow is peculiar in having two bamboo-strings, one loose, but available should the other get broken. The arrows used for large game have flat iron heads, two-edged, those for birds are often tipped with basalt pebbles. Being poor, their jewellery is primitive and inartistic, consisting chiefly of wire or of plaited grass. A very similar race of men is found both in the Central Provinces and in the North-West Provinces, and known by the same name, from their principal employment being the preparation of Cutch.

The Warlis (or Várlís).

The Wárlis (or Várlís) or highlanders are a non-Aryan hill and forest tribe met with in the Thana district. Unlike the Thakurs and Katkaris, instead of being scattered over a wide area in isolated colonies, they are confined to a small tract of country. Although many of them are extremely uncivilised, they show that under favourable circumstances they are capable of much improvement. They generally use the plough. In dress the poor resemble the Thakurs, and the rich imitate the Hindús.

The word Wárli possibly comes from Váráli or up-landers. In olden times the Wárlis were of sufficient importance to give the name Várálát to one of the seven Konkans. They were in 1882 returned in Thana as 70,015 souls. They are very innocent and harmless, but immoderately fond of liquor. Among themselves they are extremely sociable. With strangers they are timid at first, but with Europeans whom they know they are frank and truthful. They follow no regular craft or calling. None of them are in the army, in the police, or in any branch of government service, except the Forest Department. Their love for the forests is so great, that though there may be plenty of waste land ten or twelve miles from them, and though they may be very anxious to get land, they cannot be induced to go so far from their woods. During the monsoon they are generally employed as day labourers in the fields, and during the dry weather they gather and sell grass and firewood. They are also employed as domestic servants by farmers to whom they generally pledge themselves for service for a given number of years in consideration of loans raised for marriage expenses. They are passionately fond of sport, and will take their guns into the forest and stay there for days together shooting deer, short-horned antelope, peacock, and jungle and spur fowl. They live in small communities, often under their own headmen, and seem to avoid neighbours, except Kolis, Katkaris, or Thakurs. They eat rice and other grains, and all kinds of meat except beef, bison, *nilgai*, or white-footed antelope. They are fond of fowls, and always cook them for their wedding and other feasts. They also eat land crabs. The bamboo is eaten largely for some months before the rain sets in. The men go with their heads uncovered, and on their bodies wear rarely anything but a loin cloth. The women wear a robe, one end of which is drawn over the shoulders and breasts. They worship the spirit of the tiger, or Vaghia, which speaks to them through the medium of one of themselves when possessed for the time being of the spirit. They have, however, embraced a certain amount of Hinduism, and in the house of the well-to-do idols are often seen, and the poor come to worship them. The bodies of those who die of skin diseases, such as ulcers or leprosy, are buried, but those who die of other diseases are cremated.

The Son Kolis.

Son Kolis are the maritime division of a non-Aryan race, very widely distributed in the Bombay Presidency, and found in every possible condition of life.

The *Son* or Golden *Kolis* have their headquarters in the Konkan, and their chief, or *Sar Patel*, lives at Alibag in the Kolaba district. His authority, depending on caste convention, is exercised equally in the neighbouring Native States, and was acknowledged by his tribesmen in British India, while Alibag was still native territory. The Son Kolis live by fishing, by the coasting trade, and to some extent by agriculture. They were great pirates up to the beginning of this century, and are still brave and skilful seamen in small craft, though they never go on long ocean voyages. The Indian Government has long employed them in pilot vessels and lifeboats, and in their own small open smacks they fish out of sight of land all through the stormy season. The dress of a Koli at work consists of a plain string girdle, with a red cotton handkerchief made fast behind and brought up and tucked through the girdle in front as a fig-leaf, the end flying loose; a red cap, varying in shape according to the peculiar fashion in the village or town; and an iron knife subject to similar variation, but never having a handle. This is secured by a lanyard round the neck. His holiday dress is that of the general Hindu population, and his ornaments resemble theirs. The Koli women used not to wear the "*choli*" or bodice, but now many do, and the chief difference between their ornaments and those of other Hindu women is that a Koli wife offers the bangles of her right arm to the sea at her wedding, to earn its favour for her husband, and never wears them again.

Their chief household gods are Khandoba, Bahiri, and Bhanani, and their principal places of pilgrimage are in the Deccan, at Karli, Jejuri, and Nasik. Social disputes are settled by the opinion of the majority of the men at a meeting under the control of the Kori *pátel*, or headman. Against an unapproved-of decision, an appeal is made to the chief, the *Sar pátel* of Kolaba. It is said that the family of the *Sar pátel* exercise unlimited power over the Kolis, and in former days could even put them to death. At every marriage a fee of two shillings (R. 1) is paid to the *Sar pátel*, and he gets a handful from every boatload of fish that comes ashore.

The Bhíls.

The Bhíls of Bombay differ in no essential respect from those found in Central India and Rajputana. (*See* the account given under Sub-Court XXXI.)

The Thakurs.

The Thakurs are a non-Aryan hill tribe, who inhabit the Northern Sahyàdris and North Konkan. They are a simple and well-disposed people who subsist mainly on a coarse, dwarf species of millet. They seldom use the plough, and their system of cultivation is therefore extremely primitive. They are truthful, honest, and harmless. They are hardworking, the women doing quite as much work as the men. They live in huts of wattle and mud, with roofs of palm leaves. If there is an open space available near their dwellings they grow vegetables. They are very particular about their drinking water, always choosing a spring or a good well, and take great pains to keep the water pure. Though generally temperate, they drink freely on special occasions, such as marriages and caste meetings. They have a firm belief in the power of evil spirits. They are fond of sport, and, when game was more abundant than at the present day, hunting constituted an important occupation. They use the matchlock, and in some parts of the country even percussion firearms, but a short broad-bladed pike is their tribal weapon. They are not fond of the bow and arrow, and only rarely wear a sword; although every Thakur carries a *koita*, or short bill-hook, an instrument used for almost every peaceful purpose. This is worn on the right hip, with the back turned forwards, and is contained within an *akhadi* or crutch made of wood or of buck-horn. It is attached to a girdle of twine, which is curiously plaited and tasselled. On the girdle is also suspended a leathern pouch, of which the front is neatly perforated and ornamented with mica. The Thakur is full-dressed with his rope-belt pouch, *koita*, a brown blanket, and a small breech-cloth.

The writer is indebted to Mr. A. B. Gupte, of Bombay, for the preparation of the above account of the Western Presidency.

SUB-COURT XXX.

THE ETHNOLOGY OF THE MADRAS PRESIDENCY.

The Madras Presidency, or the south-eastern Peninsula of India, may be briefly defined as a long stretch of country skirting the east coast from Orissa to Cape Comorin, being limited on the north and north-west by the Central Provinces, Hyderabad, Mysore and Coorg. It comprises an area of 141,001 square miles, and has a population of 31,170,631. It has thus a density of 221 souls per square mile. and in this respect stands third in the list of Indian provinces, namely Bengal 442, the North-West Provinces 403, and Madras 221. A period of great depression fell upon South India during the famine of 1876–78, and the evil effects of that calamity will not be effaced for another decade. Instead of an increase of population since the census of 1871, Madras showed in 1881 a decrease of 462,897; but assuming that the average increase of 7·95 per square mile actually took place, but for the famine, Madras should now have had 34 instead of 31 millions of inhabitants.

Analysing the most recent returns, the people of Madras, according to religion (or sect), caste and language, are as follows: — 28,497,666 Hindus; 1,933,571 Mohamedans; 711,072 Christians; 24,962 Janias; and 3360 others. This gives for every 1000 persons, 914 Hindus, 62 Mohamedans, 23 Christians, and 1 others. The Hindus are approximately 15,399,686 followers of Siva, 10,494,408 of Vishnu, 64,580 Lingaits, and 2,538,992 Hindus not defined. Roughly speaking, the Telugus, or people of the north, are chiefly Vishnuvites, and the Tamils, or those of the south, Sivites. The remarkable hold Christianity has taken upon Madras is striking when compared with other provinces, and of the Christian community 473,353 are Roman Catholics. Mahomedanism has made within recent years rapid progress in Malabar.

With the exception of the Brahmins settled in Madras, the Hindus of South India are not Aryans. They are Dravidians or Turanians, who have adopted the most advanced form of the Aryan caste system. The castes were originally few, but they have increased and multiplied to a degree that baffles systematic enquiry. The census report of 1881 enumerates 19,044 caste names, but reduces these to 257 sub-heads of castes, and 15 occupation main heads.

With reference to the languages of Madras, 28,853,267, or 92·56 per cent., speak a Dravidian language (Tamil, Telugu, Malayalam, Kanarese or Tulu); 2,054,604 speak Aryan or rather Indian, or better still Hindustan languages (Uriya 1,128,495, Hindustani 696,103, and Marhatti 230,006). Expressing these figures according to every 1000 of population, 925·6 speak a Dravidian language, 68·3 Indian, 4·7 Kolarian, 1·1 English, and 0·3 other languages.

But under the generic heading Hindu have been included all the semi-Hinduised races, as well as the aboriginal tribes. It would seem desirable to try as far as possible to clear up this ambiguity, for while it may have been impossible to avoid generalisation in the compilation of a census, it is highly desirable in the interests of science that a more explicit investigation be made. It has been determined that these two classes number about 6,700,000 persons, or 23 per cent. of the so-called Hindus of Madras. The census report alludes to this community as Pariahs (Tamil and Telugu), and the toddy-drawing, fishing and leather-working castes, the *Oddars* or earth-diggers, and *Kallars* and *Marwars*. These seven classes alone number 5,726,199, the balance being to a large extent purely aboriginal tribes; but it is remarkable that the Palis are treated as aboriginal, and the Vellálas not; that the Puliyars and Mulcers of the Annamalis are omitted, while the Kaders are included as aboriginals. The following may be enumerated as the more important aboriginal tribes of Madras:—Badagas, 24,398; Irulas, 37,055; Todas (or Tudus), 689; Kurumbas, 7,875; Erakalas, 48,883; Enádís, 69,099; Koravas, 55,645; Védans, 51,854; and Malayálís, 67,396.

It would be beside the purpose of a catalogue to describe more of these races than are represented by the collections at the Exhibition, but although the Tamil and Telugu are fully shown, they are too well known to require description. It may be added, however, that the Dravidians are almost confined to Madras. Offshoots of the family exist in Ceylon, in the Central Provinces and in Bengal, and according to some authorities, the Brahuí tribe of Beluchistan speak also a Dravidian language. Accepting this as correct, it is further assumed that the Dravidians entered India from the north, crossing the Lower Indus. On the trail of their journey to South India, according to this hypothesis, they would appear to have left the Brahuí in Beluchistan, and pushing across the gap of country between the Indus and the Nerbudda, left again the Ghonds in the Central Provinces, the Uraons in Chutia Nagpur, and the Malers in the Rajmahal hills. This assumption is favoured by the numerous resemblances in Dravidian to Assyrian art; but on the other hand, there is nothing to disprove that the Dravidians were not in South India in prehistoric times, the offshoots alluded to being but migrations from a common aboriginal centre not far from Madura or Tanjore. It is desirable however to describe here only the tribes that are primitive, and the above remarks must be viewed as giving a sufficiently complete notice of the more civilized Dravidian races.

The Todas.

The Todas (or the Tudas), though an insignificant race in point of numbers, have attracted much attention, owing to their peculiar features, their patriarchal mode of life, their simple religious ideas, and their primitive manners and customs. The Todas occupy one of the four divisions of the Nilgiris, called Todánad, the other three being the Mekanad, the Peranganad, and the Kundanad. The legends current among the Todas and the neighbouring tribes point to a jungle tract of low hills near Hasanur as the original home of the race, and it is supposed that they migrated to and settled in their present country within the last few hundred years. Various conjectures have been made about the origin of the Todas, but most authorities view them as the remnant of a Dravidian tribe who occupied the country before the later invaders of the same race took possession of it and drove them to mountain fastnesses and inaccessible jungles. The idea of their Dravidian origin is corroborated by their language, which is a dialect of the Kanarese. In physical appearance, however, the Toda resembles more the Aryan of North India than his brother Dravidians of the South; tall in stature, with well-proportioned limbs, well-formed expressive and intelligent eyes, a long and generally aquiline nose, a profusion of hair on the head and the face, with a complexion of dull-copper hue. The women are tall and stalwart, fairer in complexion than the men, with comely features. They part their hair in the middle, and allow it to hang on the shoulders, loose, or in carefully prepared curls. The dress of the Toda is very simple; it consists of a sheet of thick coarse cotton cloth, with which the body is wrapped from the neck down to the knees. The women wear the same dress, though in a slightly different fashion. They wear in addition ornaments made of solid brass; these are often very heavy, a pair of armlets generally weighing as much as six pounds. A Toda village, called Mand or Matt, generally contains five huts, three for the people to dwell in, one used as a dairy, and the fifth as a fold for the cattle. The inhabitants are all related to each other, and, indeed, consider themselves as one family.

The Todas are a purely pastoral tribe, their chief wealth being herds of buffaloes; they subsist mainly on milk, supplemented by a little agricultural produce which they receive as tribute or tithe from their neighbours, the Badagas, in return for the right of cultivating land situated within the Toda country. Although the Todas slay buffaloes in funeral ceremonies in order to provide the soul of the deceased with means of subsistence in his journey to the unknown, they consider the animal as sacred, and pay as much reverence to it as the Hindus do to the cow. They consider the milk as the "divine fluid." Each village has a common pasture ground on which the herds possessed by the different households graze together and under the care of the village priest, who milks them and divides the milk among the different families. None but the priest can enter the dairy. So much is the buffalo venerated by the Todas that bells worn by certain buffaloes in former times become objects of worship under the name of *Konten Der*, or *Mani Der*, or the bell-gods. The bell-gods of a village are carefully preserved in the priest's house, but they are considered the property of the present bell-cow of the herd. The bell-cow is viewed as the direct descendant of the original and now sacred bell-cow.

The priest who milks the cows is known as the *Pálal*, and the herdsman priest as the *Kavilál;* these men lead ascetic lives, and are venerated by the people as holy personages. A priest if he chooses can give up his celibate life and marry. Besides the bell-gods, the Todas also worship the sun and the moon, and a hunting god called Betikhán.

The Todas practice polyandry, but the custom is now gradually falling into disuse. In former times infanticide was common among them, but this has now been entirely stopped. The Todas perform two funeral ceremonies, one immediately after the death, called the green funeral, and the other called the dry funeral, performed after some months. On the occasion of the green funeral the body is burnt on a funeral pile, and two buffaloes slaughtered. On the occasion of the dry funeral, which takes place within twelve months after the death, a large number of buffaloes, sometimes the whole property of the deceased, are slaughtered amidst feasting, dancing, and religious ceremonies. Formerly on such occasions they made a reckless slaughter of the buffaloes in honour of and as a provision for the departed, but they have now been compelled by the Government authorities to fix a limit on the number of animals to be killed.

According to the census report of 1881, the Todas numbered only 689 souls. It is supposed that they were more numerous in former times than now. The cause of the decline is attributed to polyandry, infanticide and opium.

Badagas.

The Badagas are a Hinduised tribe who live on the lower slopes of the Nilgiris. In appearance they differ little from the Hindu races of the plains, but they have a separate language of their own, which is described as a dialect of the Kanarese. In Todánad they pay a revenue or tribute to the Todas for the land they cultivate. This tribute consists of a portion of field produce paid annually under the name of *Gudu.* According to the census of 1881 the Badagas in the Madras Presidency number 24,398.

Irulas.

The Irulas are a hill tribe inhabiting a portion of the Nilgiri Hills. Their features are of a Mongolian type, with prominent cheek-bones and a short and flat nose; but their language is a dialect of the Tamil. They are Hindus by religion, and followers of Vishnu, under the name of Rangaswámi. They are believed by the neighbouring tribes to possess the power of charming the tiger. They live by cultivating small patches of land near the villages, in a careless haphazard way, from which they obtain millets and amarantus seeds. They are fond of bananas, which they plant extensively round their villages. The Irulas also supplement their field and garden produce by yams, which they dig for in the forests. They also collect wood, honey and bees-wax in the jungles, which they sell to the people of the plains. They are known to be able to coat their bodies with a substance which prevents the bees from stinging them, and they accordingly fearlessly approach and destroy the wild hives, carrying off the honey. The Irulas are supposed to be an offshoot of the Vidar or hunting tribe. They bury their dead, placing the body in a sitting posture in the grave. They were returned by the last census as numbering 37,055.

Kurumbas.

The Kurumbas inhabit the lower slopes of the Nilgiris, and are also found in Coimbatore, Malabar and largely in Mysore. Their number, according to the last census (1881), in the Madras Presidency, was 7,875. The Kurumbas are described as small in stature, with a squalid and somewhat uncouth appearance, arising from their peculiar physiognomy, their matted hair and almost nude bodies. They live in villages called *Mottas*, around which they cultivate patches of land with millets and amarantus. Like the Irulas, they supplement their agricultural food supply by digging up roots, by selling jungle produce, such as honey, resin, gall-nuts, &c., and by catching wild game in nets. Some of the Kurumbas worship Siva, while others pay homage only to their own deities, one of which is named Kuribattráya, or lord of many sheep. The language of the Kurumbas is a dialect of the Tamil. The Kurumbas supply priests to the Badagas, who perform religious ceremonies at harvest time and offer sacrifices to deities on occasions of blight, murrain or other evils. For these services, the Kurumba priest, called Kani-Kurumba, is paid in money as well as in grain. The Kurumbas have no religious marriage ceremony. The bridegroom chooses a girl, whom he brings home, and the wedding is celebrated with a feast. They burn their dead. After death they prepare a car, hung with cloth, under which they place the body, and round which they dance for some time. The body is then burnt, along with the car and the cloths.

The Kurumbas, though now an insignificant race, played at an early age an important part in the history of South India. They occupied the southern part of the present Presidency of Madras and the Native State of Mysore, where they are still numerous. This country was called by the name of Kurumba-bhumi, or the country of the Kurumbas. Tradition speaks of them as a brave race, but cruel and constantly engaged in strife, not only with their neighbours but also among themselves. They are said at first to have had no religion, but to have been subsequently converted to the Jaina faith by an ascetic. This act raised a host of enemies against them, and Adondai king of Tanjore, taking advantage of this fact, made war upon them. Though twice defeated, he eventually subdued the Kurumbas, drove them from the country, settled another tribe in it called Villazher, and changed the name of the country from Kurum-ba-bhumi to Tonda-Mandalam. Thus, according to tradition, the Kurumbas have undergone the fate of all the earlier settlers, they have been ousted from position and power by successive waves of invaders from the West and the East.

SUB-COURT XXXI.

RAJPUTANA, CENTRAL INDIA AND THE CENTRAL PROVINCES.

The tract of country in the heart of India which comprises the native States of Rájputáná and of Central India and the Central Provinces of British India is generally viewed as the home of three important aboriginal tribes—the Minás, the Bhíls and the Gonds. This country is extremely wild and diversified in its physical aspects. On the west lies the vast expanse of the Bikánir desert, traversed by camel caravans and the scene of endless mirages; the middle portion is broken by low hills and innumerable mountain rivulets, amid which the Bhíl hunts with his primitive bows and arrows, having remained totally unaffected by the vast changes which have gone on immediately outside his forest abode; on the east stretches a large area of forest lands which in the maps of the last century were marked as the "Unexplored Regions."

The Aryan advent into this part of the country took place in comparatively recent times, and in the history of many of the native principalities is related in painful detail how by force, treachery or intrigue, the simple-minded children of the soil were gradually ousted by the more civilised immigrants. Kings and princes in Northern India, driven from their own possessions by the political upheavals which were constantly occurring, found refuge among the wild hilly or desert regions, and there built strongholds, and carved out for themselves new kingdoms. Some of these rose to great power and grandeur, the most noted being that of Ujain in ancient, and that of Gwalior in modern times. The foundation of new kingdoms and principalities in this style went on till the end of the last century, when the consolidation of British power in India practically put a stop to it. Tonk, Bhopal, Bhartpur, Sindia and Holkar's Dominions are notable examples of such modern principalities. But notwithstanding these changes, the inaccessibility of the country has rendered this region a stronghold of aboriginal power no less against the Aryan, but the Hindu power, as also against the inroads of the Mussulmans. Aided by the natural strength of the country, and by the bravery of its people, the petty states of Rajputana and Central India maintained their independence when other parts of India succumbed. Thus in these tracts, while on the one hand the aboriginal population occupy a respectable position, on the other the Hindu refugees have been able to preserve many of their ancient customs and traditions totally unaffected by modern changes. It is not possible to embody in a short catalogue an account of the various races and tribes inhabiting such a vast area: a short description of the three principal aboriginal tribes is therefore all that can be attempted.

The Mínás.

The Mínás and the Bhíls are supposed to be the aboriginal inhabitants of Rajputáná and of Central India. Driven from their possessions in Upper India, the Rajput clans migrated to the wild country to the south, and gradually ousted the original inhabitants, carving out for themselves new kingdoms. The annals of Rajputáná are full of traditions how the Mínás were massacred and dispossessed of their lands by the Rajput clans, until the whole tribe was driven to mountain fastnesses or absorbed by the Hindu community as one of its intermediate castes. Unlike the Hinduised aboriginal people in other parts of India, where they generally occupy the lowest position in the Hindu society, the Mínás, by their bravery and importance, have been able to secure for themselves a status immediately below that of the Rajputs. They even claim to be half-blood Rajputs, an assertion which may now be accepted as extremely probable, for extensive intermixture of blood between the pure Rajputs and the primitive inhabitants of the country must have taken place. The physical appearance of the Mínás, which is decidedly Aryan, confirms this supposition. The Mínás now inhabit different tracts of country in Rajputáná, and are found in large numbers in Jaipúr and Alwár. In Bhartpúr and Dholpúr they number about 20,000. In Jaipúr and Alwár they occupy a respectable place in the Hindu Society. In the former State they are the hereditary guards of the State property, and possess the right of coronating the prince on his accession to the throne. The Mínás are noted for their thieving propensities, especially those residing in the wild tracts, who are famous as "savage and daring marauders," who "cultivate least and plunder most, maintaining incessant guerilla warfare with the State authorities, and who are at the lowest range of the social scale, caring little for caste rules." The Mínás of the plains are however becoming more civilized, and have adopted agriculture as their profession or accepted service as village policemen. The Mínás eat flesh and drink spirits. They do not seclude their women like the Rajputs. They swear by the Rajput dagger (*katar*).

Two other races are found in Rajputáná who are closely allied to the Mínás, viz., the Meos and the Mers. They also claim to be half-blood Rajputs. The Meos are largely found in Alwár and Bhartpúr. They have been converted to the Mohamedan religion. "Mers" signifies a "hillman," a name given to them on account of their inhabiting a narrow tract of hilly country called Merwaner. This tribe is closely related to the Mínás in their appearance and customs.

The Bhíls.

The Bhíls probably belong to the Kolarian race, or the earliest inhabitants of India. The Bhíls were the original inhabitants of Rajputáná and Central India. They still form the bulk of the population in the Aruali range of hills, in Meywar and Sirohi. These wild regions, for administrative necessities, have been called "Bhíl Tracts." The Bhíls, like the Mínás, have got a bad name for their lawless and predatory habits. They claimed the right of levying black mail throughout their country, and they have often given much trouble to the chiefs, to whom they owe nominal allegiance. Many expeditions have been undertaken against them, but not with any permanent results, as it has been found difficult to pursue them to their native fastnesses. They have however been pacified by lenient measures adopted by the British Government, and by inducing them to take service in the irregular force called the Malwa Bhíl Corps. Bhils have thus been engaged to subdue Bhíls, and the result has proved highly satisfactory. A model of a Bhíl soldier will be found in the vestibule. The Bhíls are subdivided into a number of clans. Their religion consists in the worship of local deities, with a slight admixture of Hindu mythology. They are very much afraid of witchcraft, which often leads them to commit great cruelties to persons suspected of practising the black art. They burn their dead. There are three models in the court, two males and one female. The men fight with the bow and arrow, and the women are experts in the use of the sling and stone.

The Gonds.

The Gonds are one of the most important aboriginal tribes of India. They are supposed to be a branch of the Turanian race (Dravidians), who occupied the plains of India after the Kolarians and before the advent of the Aryans. They rose to great power in the sixteenth century in the country formerly called Gondwana, which now forms the greater part of the Central Province. As late as 1853 this tract of country was a *terra incognita* to foreigners. The hilly and inaccessible nature of the country enabled the Gonds to hold out for a long time against the encroachments of the Aryan invaders. In the sixteenth century three powerful kingdoms were ruled by Gond kings, viz., Garhá-Mandla, Deogarh, and Chanda. The Gond power was subverted by the Marhattas, and, as in other parts of India, the Gond cultivators were driven step by step to "stony summits and upland valleys inaccessible to the plough, and only culturable by the rude expedient of burning the forest and sowing in the wood ash." Those who remained in the plains were absorbed into the Hindu community, and formed the "lowest stratum of the Hindu social system, being allowed to take rank above none but the most despised outcasts." The Gond of the hill, however, still maintains his primitive form of worship, though Hindu deities and Hindu rites and ceremonies have obtained a prominent place. For instance, the seven principal deities of the Gonds have all Hindu names, viz., Narain Deo, Suraj Deo, Mátá Devi, Bará Deo, Khair Mátá, Thákur Deo, and Ghanaswim Deo. Besides these seven principal gods, the Gonds believe in the existence of spirits who preside over the forests, and these they propitiate by sacrifices, in order to induce them to be lenient. The Gonds perform many remarkable ceremonies on the birth of a child and during the celebration of marriage rites. They have seven different forms of marriage, one being known as Langina, in which the bridegroom serves his would-be father-in-law for a number of years before he can get his bride. The Gonds consider cremation as the most respectable mode of disposing the dead, but it is seldom practised on account of the expense. The physical appearance of the Gonds is thus described:—A little below the average height of Europeans, and in complexion darker than the generality of the Hindus; bodies well-proportioned, but features rather ugly—a round head, distended nostrils, wide mouth, thickish lips, straight black hair, and scanty beard and moustaches. Both hair and features are decidedly Mongolian. In character the Gond is generally faithful, trustworthy, and truthful, but ignorant and uncivilised. (The writer has been favoured by the above account of Rajputáná, Central India and the Central Provinces, as well as that of the Panjab, from Mr. T. N. Mukharji.)

SUB-COURT XXXII.

MYSORE, COORG, AND HYDERABAD.

The aboriginal inhabitants of these States are so similar to those met with in Madras and Bombay that it has been deemed unnecessary to describe them in this brief catalogue."

SUB-COURT XXXIX.

THE NORTH-WEST PROVINCES AND OUDH.

The North-West Provinces and Oudh may be said to be bounded on the south by the Ganges and the Jumna, commencing from Arrah in Bengal, and extending to the water shed of the Satluj in the Punjáb; on the north by the line of perpetual snow and the kingdom of Nepal. They comprise the tract of fertile country lying between the Ganges and the Jumna; Bundelekand, or the hilly region south of the Jumna—the home of the Bundellas; Rohilkand, or the fertile plain north of the upper portion of the Ganges; with the Himaláyan mountainous tract, inhabited by the Kumaonis and Gurhwalis, still to the north and extending to the line of perpetual snow. The province of Oudh, once an independent kingdom, but now administered by the Government of the North-West Provinces is the rich agricultural country stretching from the Ganges to the frontier of Nepal. It is drained by the Gúmtí, the Gagra, and the Raptí.

There are in all 44,107,869 persons in these provinces, of whom 38,053,394 are Hindus, 5,922,886 Mohamedans, 79,957 Jainas, and 51,632 mixed races, the greater portion Christians. Under the heading of Hindus, however, 427,629 persons have been included, who while now-a-days participating in some of the practises of the Hindus and even of the Mohamedans, are outside the restrictions of caste, and are the true descendants of the early aboriginal inhabitants of these provinces. It should not be forgotten that a large proportion of the successive waves of invaders who entered India through Afghanistan settled in these provinces in the first instance before spreading over the rest of India. These are the Aryans, and they gave to the North-West Provinces and Oudh the names of Aryavartta and Aoydiah. Here the Western (or Aryan) civilizing influence was first exercised, and it is but natural that the extermination, or rather the absorption of the aboriginal or non-Aryan races should accordingly be more complete in these provinces than in any other part of India. There are, in fact, but few aboriginal tribes, and those that do exist are by no means as pure as the aboriginal tribes of Bengal, or still more so of Assam. A few of the more readily recognisable may, however, be here referred to. The Thárus and Bogshás inhabit the sub-Himalayan forests which constitute the northern boundary, just as the Bhíls, Gonds, Saharias and Kóls dwell in the forests south of the Ganges and the Jumna, which form the southern boundary of these provinces. The Thárus in the north, and the Kóls in the south have retained many of the simple virtues of the untutored savage, and to such people the forest is the natural home. The remaining tribes (Kanjars Doms, Banmánushís, Nats, Kanchans and Cherús) live in the intervening deforested plain, and lead a precarious life as thieves, gang-robbers, jackal-hunters, trappers, fowlers, jugglers and acrobats—savages whom the surrounding civilisation has demoralised rather than improved, because it has failed to assimilate, and whom Manu described as "sinful and abominable wretches," never to be permitted to reside within the haunts of men. (See *Nesfield's Caste System and Essay on Thárus and Bogshás* in 'Calcutta Review,' January, 1885.) Much has been written regarding the scattered and half assimilated aboriginal tribes of these provinces, but the reader is particularly referred to the 'Gazetteer,' written by Mr. E. F. T. Atkinson, and to the Census Report of 1881.

THE MAHRÁS AND BOGSHÁS (OR BHUKSAS).

About two hundred years ago Dehrá Dun, including Sirmor and Bischar, were conquered by the Rajá of Gurhwal, Pradip Shah, and for some time they formed part of his kingdom. The parts of these districts lying east of the Jumna river were personally governed by the Rajá of Gurhwal, and the rest were given back to the local Rajás on condition of their paying a certain amount of annual tribute. Affairs continued in this state till 1803 A.D., when the whole of the Gurhwal country was conquered by the Gurkhás.

The Mahrás of Dehrá Dun appear to belong to the same race as the Mahrá clan of Kumáon and Gurhwal. They both claim to be descendants of the famous Ahir Nand Mahrá of Mathra, who is spoken of in the Prem Ságar and other Hindu religious works. According to tradition the Mahrás of Dehrá Dun are Khassia Rajputs, and are said to be the illegitimate children of a Mahrá in Gurhwal. The Bogshás inhabit the country from the west bank of the Kitcha to the Ganges.

The Bogshás consider the Mahras of Dehrá Dun as their equals in rank among the Rajputs, and it would appear that Mahra is perhaps only a local name for some of the Bogshas who live in the Dun, where they settled about the eleventh century. They began to be called Mahrás from the time they adopted the profession of Cutch manufacturers. But both these people look on their neighbours, Thárus, as below them, inasmuch as the latter rears and eats fowls. The Mahrás and Bogshás are Hindus by religion. They are great hunters. Those residing in the Nepal Tarái shoot game with bows and arrows. They keep cattle and also cultivate. As a rule, however, they are indolent, and object to all labour that is not necessary for subsistence. They are fond of tobacco and spirits, but their women are not allowed either.

The Thárus.

The settlement of this tribe in the extensive tracts of the Tarái dates in all probability from some period subsequent to the arrival of the Bogshás. The Kitcha river may be said to divide the Bogshás from the Thárus; the latter extending from the east bank. The Thárus, like the Mahrás and Bogshás, also claim to be Rájputs, the descendants of an ancient Chitoor Ráná; and, according to some authorities, their tribal name Tháru is derived from *Thartharawa*, the tremblers, in allusion to their timidity as compared with the warrior Rajputs. Sir H. Elliot seems disposed to think they are of Tibetan origin, although they now speak Hindi.

The Thárus of the present day are divided into six sub-branches, viz., Sonsá, Khunká, Rajiá, Dhungrá, Gusai, and Kásá. They intermarry with their own castes, excepting near-blood relations. They are also said to intermarry with Bogshás, but in very rare cases. Their occupation consists in agriculture, hunting and gold-washing They are migratory and greatly addicted to drink. They rear fowls and eat them, but water is taken by other Hindus from their hand without any scruple.

The crops reared by them are chiefly rice of the finest quality, known in trade as the Pilibhit, perhaps the most expensive rice in India. Their houses are constructed of a frame-work of wood with walls of wattle and date. The use of burnt clay seems unknown to them. Their huts however are much neater and on a much larger scale than those of the people of the plains, and are kept scrupulously clean. For smith's work they employ men from the plains. They practice no handicrafts beyond perhaps basket-weaving, the work being ornamented in a peculiar manner with shells.

Thárus, it may be noted, hunt in the forests with dogs, of which they keep a large and savage breed. Fortunately, the Tháru considers field rats a delicacy, and persistently searches for them, a taste inspired no doubt by a sense of self-preservation, for the rats would otherwise largely multiply and destroy the crops.

Bhutís.

The Bhutís are by most writers described as a cross between the Khasia Rajputs and the Hunias—the people who occupy the higher Western Himálaya. They are nomadic, and live chiefly in tents, and almost entirely monopolise the trade across the mountains. During the winter months they move to lower altitudes to graze their cattle, sometimes even going so low down as to the *tarai*, where they often resort to agricultural pursuits. In some respects they resemble the Bhutias of the Eastern Himálaya; like them they are extremely dirty in their person and dress, but instead of in two tails the women plait their hair into a number of small tails, which hang down all over the neck and shoulders, commencing from the forehead. They are professional beggars, the children following the traveller for some distance from their camp, entreating for *bakshish*.

The Kanjars.

This is one of the tribes, probably aboriginal, that still leads the life of the wandering outcasts ot human society. They have lagged behind the rest of the inhabitants in the march of progress, and lead a vagrant life. Nothing apparently comes amiss to them, for the jackal even is eaten. The Kanjars are the gipsies of the North-West Provinces.

The Bandelas.

The tribe of spurious or Chattri family of Rajputs who give the name to Bandelkhand. These differ greatly from the Rajputs of the Duáb and of Oudh both in habits and costume as well as in language, and, unlike them, do not disdain to engage in agricultural pursuits. They are supposed to have been driven to the country they now inhabit about the thirteenth century, in consequence of the Mohamedan conquests of Oudh. They resemble in many respects Dhandelas and Ponwars, with whom they intermarry. Their character for honesty does not stand high, and they are reputed a turbulent race, as was evinced at the time of the mutiny.

SUB-COURT XI.

THE INDEPENDENT STATE OF NEPAL.

The little kingdom of Nepal may be defined as that portion of the Himalayan chain north of Oudh and Bengal, between the head basin of the Gogra on the west, and the Sikkim Valley on the east. It includes the loftiest mountain in the world—Mount Everest (or as it is called by the hill men, Deodunga—Mount of God). Khatmandú is the capital of the State, and in many respects is one of the most beautifully situated and most interesting cities in the world. Numerous photographs of Nepal, kindly contributed by Messrs. Bourne and Shephard, and by Messrs. Johnston and Hoffmann, of Calcutta, may be seen throughout the Imperial Court. The most striking feature of the street scenery is the marked Chinese or modern Buddhistic architecture of certain buildings in close proximity to the most hideous Tantric forms of the Hindu style. The models to represent the province of Nepal will be found near those of the North-West Provinces and Oudh, and the writer has only to add that the following notes regarding the people of Nepal have been obligingly furnished by Dr. Gimlette, the Resident Surgeon, who has also furnished all the Nepal objects which are now on view throughout the Exhibition.

The Newars.

The Newars, a race of mixed Indian and Mongolian origin, form the bulk of the inhabitants of the valley of Nepal proper — the dynasty of the Newar Rajas was overthrown by the Gorkhalis in 1767 after a long and desultory war. Their language appears to be of Tibetan origin, and bears little or no resemblance to any dialect of Hindustan.

The trade, agriculture, and handicrafts of Nepal are still in their hands. They are industrious on working days, but indulge in very numerous holidays. Two-thirds profess Buddhism and are called *Buddhimargis*, the other third are Hindus, and are called *Sheomargis*. The *Buddhimargi* are divided into three classes: I. *Banhras*, with 9 sub-divisions; II. *Udas*, with 7 sub-divisions; and III., a class with 30 sub-divisions, including agriculturists or the *Jaffas* (who comprise one-half of all the Newars), painters, carpenters, workers in iron, &c. There are, besides, 8 classes of outcasts, such as *dhobies*, *mehters*, &c. Pure Buddhism is unknown, and caste distinctions are universal among all Newars. Even Class I., the *Banhras*, from whom the Buddhist priesthood is recruited, worship certain Hindu deities. Buddhism is indeed rapidly dying out, and no doubt will soon be entirely replaced by Hinduism.

Sheomargi Newars are divided into 14 classes, grouped into the ordinary Hindu divisions; *Brahmans*, *Chatriyas*, *Kshatriyas*, *Vaisyas*, and *Sudras*. One class of Chatriyas, the Mallah, are supposed to represent the first Newar dynasty, the sovereigns of which were Hindus.

The Newars are of a cheerful, careless disposition, more fitted for peaceful occupations than for arms, although they made a gallant stand against the Gorkhalis for many years. As a rule, a Newar has but one wife at a time, but the marriage tie is readily dissolved by mutual agreement. A Newar girl is married when a child with ceremony to a *bael* fruit which represents the god. When she feels inclined to quit her human husband, she has only to put two *bael* fruits in his bed, and may then leave his house without further notice. She is never supposed to become a widow, and is at liberty to choose another partner after the death of her first. This easy custom has of late years been discouraged by the Government, particularly by the late Jung Bahadoor. A husband is now able to proceed in the Law Courts against a wife who has left him, and against the man with whom she has run off. This, however, he seldom does, preferring, as a rule, to look out for a new wife. It is still not uncommon for a Newar husband to turn off a wife of whom he is tired, the discarded lady returning to her father's house. Notwithstanding these ideas on the subject of the connubial state, the Newars are decidedly a happy people; they specially excel as agriculturists, and work most diligently in their fields, raising two crops a year, the principal one being rice. The plough is little used, all trenching being done by a *kodali* of peculiar shape.

The Khas.

This race forms the bulk of the military class in Nepal, as well as of that portion of the population designated Gorkhalis. The latter is a rather indefinite term, and strictly means inhabitants of the province of Gorkha, from whence came the conquerors of Nepal in 1767. A still more indefinite designation, but in common use, and applied mainly to the Khas, Brahman and Rajput, is Parbattia, meaning merely a dweller in the hills. The Khas tribe apparently sprang from connections formed between Brahman refugees from the plains of India at the time of the Mohamedan conquest, and the women of hill tribes, and probably also from converts to Hinduism among the aboriginal hill tribes. They wear the sacred thread and have been ranked since their origin with the second order of Hinduism, the Kshatriya. Owing to this mixed descent there is a good deal of indefiniteness about the Khas type of feature, but it is far less Turanian than that of the other inhabitants of Nepal. They, as a rule, are slightly-built men, often with Rajput features.

They are passionately devoted to arms, and the object of their ambition is to serve in the Nepalese army; failing this, they occupy themselves in agriculture, but without the industry of the Newars. Hindus by religion and descent, they are far less scrupulous in their observances of the minor points of the ceremonial law than the Hindus of the plains, but remain, however, quite as bigotted on the main principles. Caste in Nepal is upheld by the law of the country, and offences against it are severely punished in the courts. One general rule is, that every Hindu is liable and must on no account refuse to take water from the hand of any other Hindu.

The Khas language is a dialect of Hindi, and is the common language throughout the different tribes of Nepal. Marriage customs are similar to those of the Hindus of the plains; the race has been split into clans, the members of which intermarry; a Khas will not marry in his own clan.

The Magars.

A hill tribe, originally inhabiting the central and lower parts of the mountains between the rivers of Rapti (of Gorakhpur) and the Manchangdi. They have now become more or less scattered throughout Nepal, and the Nepal army is largely recruited from them.

They are of a decidedly Tartar type of feature, and speak a language which may almost be considered a dialect of the Tibetan tongue; the large majority speak also Parbatia, the language of the Khas tribe, and particularly those who have served in the Nepal army have adopted to a great extent Khas habits and feelings.

Originally Buddhists, they early threw in their lot with the rising race of Gorkha, and adopted Hinduism. They do not wear the sacred thread, and hold an undefined sort of rank between the second and third Hindu orders. They do not eat buffalo meat or pork, and are inclined to be lax in their observances of ceremonial. They are divided into numerous clans. In the matter of marriage no Magar will give his daughter to a social interior, or will take money in exchange for her. They are most particular to avoid marrying with a member of the clan (or tribal section) to which they themselves belong, but never intermarry outside the limits of the tribe; the marriage of widows is not permitted. Both Magars and Gurungs are superstitious to the last degree.

The Gurungs.

This tribe, from which the Nepalese army is also largely recruited, came originally from a tract of country between that inhabited by the Magars and the snows.

They are powerful, sturdy men with a strongly-marked Turanian cast of feature, and approach the Tibetan type in appearance and habits more nearly than their southern neighbours. Gurungs resemble Magars closely in social customs; their Hinduism is even less orthodox than that of the latter; they eat buffaloes and pigs, and drink spirits freely. The Gurung language is still spoken, and closely resembles that of the Magar, with some differences of dialect. The tribe is also divided into numerous clans which, with certain exceptions, intermarry. A Gurung will not marry a girl belonging to the same clan as himself, nor with one belonging to another tribe. Gurungs and Magars eat together freely while bachelors; after marriage certain restrictions are observed. They do not wear the sacred thread of the Hindus.

SUB-COURT XI.

ETHNOLOGY OF THE PUNJAB.

The fertile plains of Northern India, watered by the five tributaries of the Indus, viz., the Jhilam, the Chenab, the Ravi, the Bias and the Sutlaj, have received the name of Punjab, or the land of the five rivers. The Aryan immigrants from the West early settled in this province, and called it Brahmavartta, or the land of the gods. Here the Hindu religion had its birth, and the most ancient sacred literature in the world was written. Here also the Sikh faith saw the light of day, and since the Gupta dynasty, of whom came the illustrious Asoka, originated in the Punjab; Buddhism also may, in a measure, be said to have had its beginning in the land of five rivers. The present British province of the Punjab has the valley of Kashmir on the north; the river Jamná on the east, separating it from the adjoining province of the North-West Provinces and Oudh: the desert of Rajputana on the south; and Afghanistan on the west. It has an area of 142,250 square miles, with a population of 22,704,000 inhabitants (exclusive of the fluctuating military population), or 159 persons to the square mile. The country may be divided into four well marked physical regions:—

(1) The Himalayan tract, comprising the Kangra Valley and various feudatory native states on the Himalaya. This has an area of 19,840 square miles, with a population of 1,539,000 souls, mostly Hindu of the Rajput family, speaking a dialect of the Hindi language.

(2) The submontane tract along the foot of the Himalaya, which comprises 6680 square miles, with a population of 2,998,000, residing in large agricultural and pastural villages. The religion followed by the people of this tract is like that of the plains further to the south; the language spoken is Hindi on the east and Punjabi on the west.

(3) The Eastern Plains, which comprise the most fertile part of the province (except on the south, where it touches the Bikánir desert) have an area of 35,020 square miles, with a population of 10,358,000. In most parts of this region the rainfall is abundant, the soil fertile, and large towns and villages occur. The population consists of Jats and Rajputs, Hindu on the east, Sikh in the centre, and Mohamedan on the west. The language varies in the same way, being Hindi on the east, the dialects of Rajputana on the south, and Punjábi in the centre and west.

(4) The Western Plains; these comprise the arid tract of country bordering on Afghanistan, where the rainfall is scanty and cultivation confined to near the rivers. This country is sparsely inhabited, the population being Afghan and Biluch on the west, and Jat and Rajput in the other parts. This tract has an area of 59,890 square miles, and a population of 4,885,000 souls.

(5) The Salt Range Tract occupies the north-west corner of the province, between the Safedkoh and the Sulaiman range of mountains. It comprises an area of 21,020 square miles, with a population of 2,924,000, mostly Musalmans, speaking Pashtu in some parts and Punjábi dialects in others.

Taking the province as a whole, the Punjab, owing to its closer proximity to the Mohamedan countries to the west, has a larger proportion of Musalmans than any other part of India, and the Sikh religion having had its origin in it, the province naturally contains almost all the followers of this tenet, for the religion of Nának has made but very little progress outside the Punjab. Out of a total population of 22,712,120, the followers of Mohamed number 11,662,434; Hindus, 9,252.295; Sikhs, 1,716,114; Jainas, 42,678; Christians, 33,699; Buddhist, 3251; other religions, 1649.

The following figures give the languages spoken in the province:—Hindustáni and its dialect Bagri, 4,328,254; Punjábi and its different dialects, 14,216,259; Sindhi and its dialect Jatki, 1.609,888; the hill languages (Kashmiri, Dagri, Garhwali, &c.), 1,554,786; Bengali, 2891; Pashtu, Persian and Bilochi, 935,711. Besides the above, members of other nationalities, such as Europe, Asia, Africa, reside in the province, and speak their own languages. English is spoken by 27,584 persons.

Ethnologically, the tribes of the Punjab are pre-eminently Aryan. The close promixity of the province to the supposed original home of that great branch of the human race and its early occupation by them have led either to the expulsion of the aboriginal tribes, or to their total absorption into the lowest castes. Even among the Himalayas, Mongolian features are less prevalent than in the eastern extremity of the mountain chain. As in other parts of India, the Hindus of the Punjab are divided into various castes, following distinctive professions; the Brahmans occupy the first place, the Rajputs the second, the trading and landowning classes the third, the cultivating and artisan classes the fourth, and last of all the workers in leather; the menial servants, and the persons who lead a vagrant life, fill the lowest place in the Hindu community. In the Punjab, however, another caste claims equal rank with the Rajput. This is the Jat. The Musalmans chiefly belong to the Biluch or the Pathan tribe, but many of the Hindus in the West have become converted to Mohamedanism, such as the Aons, the Ghakkars, the Mers, and also numerous Jats, Rajputs, and Gujars. The following is a brief account of the three principal tribes of the Punjab, the tribes which may be regarded as peculiar to the province, viz., the Jats, the Biluchs, and the Pathans.

The Jats.

The Jats number 4,432,750. They are the yeoman peasants of the Punjab. They are honest, industrious, and manly, and are respected by the Hindus. The Sikh religion, the fundamental doctrine of which may be said to be the fatherhood of God and the brotherhood of man, found early favour among the Jats. Under the impulse of this new religion, and actuated by the persecution which the Musalmans of Delhi directed against them, the Jats soon became a military people. They greatly aided the British in the subversion of the Mohamedan empire, and carved out independent principalities for their chiefs, of which the last development was the powerful kingdom of Ranjit Singh, the Lion of the Punjab. The bravery of the Sikh soldiers during the Sikh war is a matter of history. On the conquest of the Punjab, the Jats took kindly to the British rule, and they now afford one of the most important elements in the Indian army.

The Biluchs.

The Biluchs number 355,238 in the Punjab. They are natives of Biluchistan, who have migrated into the province within the last few hundred years. The Biluchs claim descent from Mai Hamza, an uncle of Mohamed. The political organisation among the Biluchs is tribal, the chief enjoying the privileges of a limited monarch. In physical appearance the Biluch is shorter and more slender than the Pathan. He has a manly bearing, is frank and open in his manners, and fairly truthful, as well as "faithful to his word, temperate, and enduring, looking upon courage as the highest virtue." He is nomadic in his habits. He does not seclude his women, but he is extremely jealous of female honour, and punishes adultery with death. The Biluchs follow the Mohamedan religion, but are extremely ignorant of the tenets of that faith. In the Punjab they are divided into fifty-one different tribes.

The Pathans.

The Pathans in the Punjab number 859,582. They occupy Afghanistan and the hills to the north-west of the Punjab. They are a strong, stalwart race, but bloodthirsty, cruel, vindictive, and extremely superstitious. Their language is Pashtú, and by religion they are Mohamedans. Many of the Rajput converts to the Musalman religion call themselves Pathans, and are proud of the designation of Khan, which a Pathan always affixes to his name. The Pathans in the Punjab are divided into eighty-nine sub-tribes.

ART WARE COURTS.

CHAPTER VII.

Screens—Rajputana—Central India—Bombay and Baroda—Bengal—Nepal—North-West Provinces—Punjab—Kashmir—Central Province—Assam—Burma—Madras—Mysore and Coorg—Hyderabad.

CLASS D.

ARTS AND INDUSTRIES.

The Entrance Gateway and Ornamental Screens or Walls forming the divisions of Art Ware Courts.

ENTRANCE GATEWAY.

The Art Ware Courts are entered through a Gateway, contributed by His Highness the Maharaja of Jeypore, and carved by his subjects. The gateway is surmounted by a Nakarkhana,* or Drum-house, such as is usually found over the entrance to royal residences or temples in which musicians play at stated intervals, and in regular order, certain tunes in honour of the sovereign or god, after which other strains are added at the will of the performers.

In the kiosk on the top are arranged all the musical instruments which are usually played in a drum-house. On the front of the platform has been carved the Shamsha or picture of the sun, which is symbolical of the descent of the lords of Jeypore, and of the Rajput chiefs of the solar race, and is, moreover, according to the Ain-i-Akbari, or Institutes of the Emperor Akbar—"a Divine Light" which God directly transfers to Kings without the assistance of men. It is affixed to the gates or walls of palaces.

On the opposite side will be found a representation of the moon, from which the Indrabani, the other great branch of the Rajput race, represented by the Rajas of Jaisalmir and Karauli, is said to have sprung. On the same beam below the cornice on the front of the gate is engraved the motto of the Jeypore house, "*Yato dharm stato jaya,*" † in Sanskrit with Latin and English versions. The Latin "Ubi virtus ibi victor" better expresses the meaning of the original than the English "Where virtue is—is victory," but, however worded, the idea is as appropriate for the entrance of a great Exhibition as it is for the motto of a State which has in many ways acted up to it. On the corresponding beam at the back the motto, "Ex Oriente lux,"—from the east comes light,—has been carved.

The central kiosk can be closed with *purdahs* or curtains of *mushu*, that is, cotton and silk cloth (silk alone was forbidden to be worn by Mussulmans at prayer time, hence the fashion) of Indian make such as is used in Hindu palaces. To support the curtains *chobs* or metal poles have been provided.

The banners on the rails are respectively the *panch-rang* or five-coloured flag of Jeypore; a small copy of the standard given to the late Maharajah at the Imperial Assemblage at Delhi by Her Majesty the Queen-Empress; the *Mahi maratib* or symbol of the highest nobility given by the Moghul Emperors, which was much prized. It consists of the golden head of a fish and of two gilt balls, all borne on separate poles. These symbols were brought from Delhi in the reign of the Emperor Feroksha, and so great was the honour deemed that the musicians in the Jeypore Nakar-khana played for three days and nights consecutively, and the whole city was given up to rejoicing.

RAJPUTANA COURT SCREENS.

The Jeypore Sub-Court.

The gateway at the entrance of the Rajputana Court and the screens which form the walls of the Jeypore bays, have been primarily constructed to afford more space for the display of exhibits, but they have been carved wherever possible to illustrate the position of wood-carving in the country. Jeypore, as a whole, is essentially a land of stone and stone-carvers, but, owing to the patronage of many wealthy bankers, who live in Shaikhawati, the northern district of the State, a large number of carpenters have settled in the great towns situated in that sandy tract, which is almost devoid of timber. Some of the better workmen, in past days, may, however, have been attracted from Delhi by the Mussulman Nawabs of Fatehpur and Jhinjhuni, formerly rulers in the district. In the unsettled times which preceded the British supremacy, the great capitalists of India, who were for the most part Marwaris of the branch of the Jain faith known as Oswals, sought safety, for which, of course, they well paid, among the chiefs and nobles who lived in Bikanir, Marwar, and Shaikhawati, in other words, on the verge of the country marked on our maps as the Great Indian Desert. In this way large towns have sprung up, such as Fatehpur, Nawalgarh, Jhinjhuni, Ramgarh and Chirawa, and here the bankers or Seths and their retainers have lived securely, while their

* Also termed *Naubat-khana* from the larger drum used in it.

† Literally: "Where virtue or righteousness is there is the victory."

agents or *gumasthas* have earned in distant places, even as far as Hongkong on the one hand, and Zanzibar on the other, heavy interest on their capital. As the agents left their families at their homes, and retained little money, the heads of the firms ran but small risk.

The Seths have built magnificent temples and houses, and as good durable wood was scarce, they imported it from distant places and had it carved into door-frames, windows or balconies. Wonderful old traditional designs have thus been preserved.

Following this rule, Surgeon-Major T. H. Hendley suggested that the timber necessary for constructing the Jeypore Screen should be cut and joined in Bombay, and be then brought to Jeypore, where the Shaikhawati carpenters should be allowed to enrich it by carving without unnecessary European interference. The scheme was adopted. The measurements of the screens were fixed in accordance with those laid down by the Royal Commission, and Colonel Jacob of Jeypore supplied a design for the screens and an elevation for the entrance gate.

The general design is the modified Saracenic in vogue in Upper India and Rajputana. The only instructions issued to the wood-carvers were that as great a variety of patterns should be employed as possible, the ornament to be purely Indian, and no attempt to be made to work on other than the traditional lines. The men draw rough outlines with a pencil or even the graver, and each carver has done what was right in his own eyes, subject to the approval of the *mistris* or master-workmen, who had to judge whether the whole work would be in harmony or not.

The screens were cut and joined by the Bombay Saw Mills Company, and the *Nakar-khana* by Mr. Wimbridge, Head of the East-India Art Furnishing Company, of Gawalia Tank Road, Bombay.

Bhartpur, Karauli, and Dholpur Sub-Court.

The front screen consists of a carved red sandstone architrave and false arch, supported on carved pillars, and surmounted by a perforated sandstone screen, also of the same stone, and 10 ft. long by 2½ ft. high. Above the screen, and to break the monotony of a horizontal line, are placed in the centre a perforated imitation of a nearly semi-circular fan-light, and at the two ends a couple of small turrets surmounted by cupolas.

The style of architecture cannot be exactly defined, as the screen in reality is a mixture of copies of parts of several local buildings, fitted to the dimensions required; thus the pillars, false arch, and architrave are taken from the interior of the Khanwas Mahal (now used as the Residency); the perforated work in screen is a copy of similar works in the *masjid* at the Wazipur gate of the city; the central bit is borrowed more or less from a semi-circular fan-light in the city, and the cupolas on the turrets placed at the ends are similar to those used to cover portions of the palace.

Generally speaking, the screen is a representation of local architecture in details, but not as a whole. It is made throughout of red sandstone procured from the celebrated quarries in the immediate vicinity of the city of Karauli, and has been constructed entirely by local stone-masons and stone-carvers, under the general supervision of the State Public Works Department. It has cost altogether Rs. 308-6-2; and has taken five months to complete, during which time an average of ten masons were daily employed on it.

The side screen consists almost entirely of perforated work (*Jalli*) in panels. The panels are formed by vertical pillars and horizontal architraves, 6 in. wide, which enclose the perforated work. In the central panel a small false arch is substituted for this.

The screen is throughout a representation of the perforated sandstone screens largely used in the city of Bhartpur and neighbourhood, and known as *Jalli*. The pillars and false arch are in general imitation of local work in similar positions.

The stone used throughout is a light brown or salmon coloured sandstone from the Rupbat quarries. It is much used in the city, easily worked, and admits of very fine work. The screen has been manufactured throughout by the local masons from designs supplied them.

Western Rajputana Sub-Court.

The Jodhpur screen is of carved teak wood; it was designed and made at Jodhpur by Jodhpur artists and workmen. The architecture is the modified Delhi adopted in Rajputana.

Ulwar Sub-Court.

The front portion of the screen consists of panels of white marble, perforated and carved in relief, fitted in a frame-work of black marble and teak wood, and supported upon three beautifully carved white marble pillars, 8 ft. high each. A decorative design of glass-work, on which the crest and arms of His Highness the Maharao Raja are emblazoned, surmounts this portion of the screen.

The side portions of the screen consist of panels of red sandstone carved on both sides. The designs of the pillars and panels are taken from carvings existing in the Ulwar Palace, and are of pure Hindu style. The glass-work decoration is also taken from the Ulwar Palace, three rooms in which are entirely ornamented with work of this description. The screen is altogether of Ulwar workmanship, and the marble is from the celebrated quarries of Makrana, Rajputana.

There are quarries of white, pink, and black marble in the Ulwar State, the quality of the first-mentioned being perhaps the finest obtainable in India for statuary purposes.

Kotah Sub-Court.

The screen for the Kotah section of the Rajputana Court consists of a front and side piece made of Shisham wood (*Dalbergia Sisu*) and inlaid with ivory. This style of work is much practised in the town of Etawah in the Kotah State. The architectural design is Hindu, and has been copied from old buildings in the City of Kotah.

Ajmere Sub-Court.

This screen is designed to represent a sample of the ordinary street architecture in the Ajmere City. The archways or arcades are similar to the description usual in verandahs of houses, serais, shop fronts, &c. These arcades are often surmounted by a system of ornamental bracketing and open carved work, supporting upper balconies. In this screen the balconies are of course omitted, to conform to the limits imposed by the dimensions of the Exhibition Courts. The architecture is spoken of in Ferguson's 'History of Architecture' as the "Mixed Hindu Style." The materials generally used in street architecture of this kind are a mixture of cut stone and stone masonry and plaster work, the whole being either whitewashed or decorated by painting in bright water colours. In some cases the entire work is of cut stone or of marble.

This model is carved in wood and painted white to represent the original type as nearly as possible.

Bikanir Sub-Court.

The Bikanir ornamental screen is a simple wooden structure, 10 ft. 6 in. high, of a total length of 20 ft., divided into two bays, each 12 ft. 6 in. broad, by two central (one in front and one in rear) and two side supports, each 1 ft. 3 in. broad. The entrances into each bay are 8 ft. high in the centre, sloping off to 6 ft. 6 in. at the sides, and the upper portion is 2 ft. 6 in. broad, having in addition a crenelated edge along the façade facing the central avenue. The screen has no pretensions to architectural design, and was constructed to show to the best advantage a style of decoration applicable to wood, stone, earthenware, ivory, and glass, and believed to be peculiar to Bikanir, of which the following is a brief description:—On the surface of the wood, which had been previously well scrubbed with liquid clay and allowed to dry, the outlines of a flower pattern were stencilled with a bag of powdered charcoal through perforated paper. Successive layers of liquid clay were then applied with small squirrel's-hair brushes within the outlines of the pattern, each layer being allowed to dry before the next application, until a raised surface bringing out the stalks, leaves, and petals with sufficient distinctness had been produced. The whole surface was then fixed by a coat of paint, and when this was dry gold leaf was applied over all. The ground-work, black, with a red border, on the portion intended to face the central avenue and the adjacent Courts of Central India and Ajmere, and red with a black border in the interior of the Bikanir bays, was then painted in, the flower pattern standing out in gilt relief.

The Central India Court Screen.

On the right hand side facing the Bombay Court, the Central India screen consists of three bays, each about 10 ft. in length. The central bay is higher than those flanking it, and is intended to illustrate Buddhist and Hindu sculptures as found in Central India. The pillars are modelled on, though not exactly copied from, sculptures existing at Khajurahu in Bundelkhand. At the base of each is a large female figure, with smaller figures on either side, and above these, groups of small figures arranged in tiers, each of a different design, the whole being in high relief. The cross-beam uniting the pillars illustrates Hindu style both in figures and in ornamentation. The centre is occupied by an image of Ganeshji. This mixture of styles was adopted in order to take an opportunity of showing Buddhist and Hindu figures together. The bays flanking this central gateway are somewhat lower, and consist of one pillar at each extremity, supporting, with the help of the central pillars, horizontal screens of Gwalior stone-carving in relief. These pillars are of simpler style than the central pair, but are also modelled on the carvings of Khajurahu. The stone screens consist of panels and plaques, in various designs, some copied from the Sanchi Tope, near Bhopal, others from the fort at Gwalior, and others again planned by the workmen themselves.

On the left hand side facing the Bombay Court, the style of screen is altogether lighter. Here, again, there are three bays, but the central one consists of an arch in the middle about 5 ft. broad, flanked by two narrow passages about 2 ft. broad. There is no horizontal screen in the central portion of this bay, which is simply an archway, but the side portions are fitted with glazed tiles. One flanking bay is fitted with perforated stone-work from Gwalior, and the other with perforated wood-carving from Ujjain. The three pairs of pillars supporting these three bays are all of similar style, differing only in elaborateness of carving, and are copied from the kind of pillars often seen in temples and dwelling-houses in Indore and its neighbourhood. The perforated stone panels and wood-carvings are, as before, partly copied from actual buildings, partly designed by the workmen.

The outer pillars of the portion of the screen first described, and all six pillars of the second portion, are surmounted by brass pinnacles made at Rutlam, and copied from temples.

The Bombay and Baroda Court Screen.

The screen, the general design for which was made by Mr. Griffiths, the Superintendent of the Bombay School of Art and Secretary to the

Bombay Committee for the London Exhibition, consists of two lengths, each of 80 ft. long, made up of eight open bays, 10 ft. wide. In addition to these are the four ends, each 12 ft. wide, the total length of the screen being 208 ft., with a uniform height of 10 ft. The design of the screen has been made with a view to illustrate as fully as possible the characteristic wood-carving of the Presidency.

The cost of the screen is met by a grant from the Royal Commission and contributions from Native States. The amount assigned by the Royal Commission to Bombay, including Baroda, was Rs. 4,500, which was supplemented by contributions of Rs. 4,000 from his Highness the Gaikwar of Baroda, Rs. 4,000 from His Highness the Thakursaheb of Bhavnagar, and Rs. 2,000 from His Highness the Rao of Cutch. His Highness the Nawab of Junagad undertook to fill in two bays at a cost of Rs. 1,700.

The sections belonging to the Royal Commission, to His Highness the Gaikwar of Baroda and to His Highness the Rao of Cutch were executed by native artizans under the superintendence of Mr. Wimbridge, of the East India Art Manufacturing Company, Bombay. The carved details for the Royal Commission and Cutch sections have been selected by Mr. Wimbridge from Mahafiz Khan, Shapur, Dastar Khan, and Rani Sipri mosques at Ahmedabad, and the detail for the Baroda section from various houses in Surat.

The Bhavnagar section, which comprises four of the richest bays, was constructed in Bhavnagar itself, under the immediate supervision of Mr. Proctor Sims, the State Engineer, assisted by a very intelligent native *mistry*. The details of the work are taken from the old palace, and from some of the old houses in the town.

The Junagad section was likewise carried out locally by Dalpat Nathu.

The work is executed in teak.

The Bengal Court Screens.

The screens of the Bengal Art Ware Court are an attempt to illustrate, chiefly by means of *papier mâché* castings, the styles of architectural ornament characteristic of the best Hindu and Muhammadan buildings in Bengal proper.

The Northern, or Hindu screen is adapted from the temple of Krishna at Kantanagar near Dinajpur, built between 1704 and 1722 A.D. This temple forms an excellent example of the brick architecture of Lower Bengal, and one of its chief constructive peculiarities, the bent cornice, supposed by the late Mr. Ferguson to have been copied from the common bamboo hut of the country, has been reproduced in the screen. The entire surface of the building is covered with terra-cotta reliefs, representing for the most part figure-subjects taken from the daily life of the people. From some of the best of these casts have been made in a mixture of *papier mâché* and plaster of Paris, coloured to match the originals, and attached to the screen so as to represent the general effect of the temple. It should be added that the form of the five central arches was determined by the requirements of the Exhibition, and bears no resemblance to anything at Kantanagar. The side arches, on the other hand, though not quite correct in their proportions, give a fair idea of the style of the pointed arch which the Bengal school borrowed from Muhammadan architecture. Maharani Swarnamayi, M.C.I., of Kasimbazar, in Murshidabad, contributed Rs. 3,000 to the construction of this screen, which has been presented by her to the Bengal Art Gallery.

Muhammadan Screen.

The Southern or Muhammadan screen was designed by Mr. Jules Schaumburg, Artist to the Geological Survey of India, on the lines of the architecture of the ancient city of Gaur and its suburb Pandua. Gaur became the capital of Bengal under Muhammed Bakhtyar Khilji in A.D. 1198, increased greatly in size and wealth up to its sack by Sher Shah, the Afghan Governor of Behar in 1537, and was finally abandoned in 1575, under Akbar, in consequence of a pestilence which devastated the city. The general idea of the screen was derived from the Qadam Rasul Mosque built by Nusrah Shah in 1530, the flat pilasters bulging outwards at the bottom are adapted from the tomb of Sultan Ghyasuddin (1211–1227), known as the Eklahi Mosque at Pandua, while the detailed ornamentation consists of casts taken from the remains of these and other buildings preserved in the Indian Museum, Calcutta. The painted design at the west end of the screen is a composition from carved stones and tiles in the Museum, and is intended to represent the enamelled tiles with which the Gaur and Pandua buildings were overlaid. For the colouring of this design Mr. Melik Beglar, of the archæological Survey of India, is the authority. Instances are not wanting in the museum to show that the same patterns were used indifferently for low relief and for encaustic tiles. The Muhammadan screen was constructed at the cost of Nawab Ahsanulla, of Dacca, and presented by him to the Bengal Art Gallery.

The construction of both screens has been carried out by Babu Sarat Chander Ghose, Honorary Assistant Engineer, Bengal Public Works Department. The painting has been executed by Mr. W. G. Carpenter, of the firm of Messrs. Walsh, Lovett & Co., Calcutta. Babu Hera Lal Dass contracted for and supplied all the castings of which the decorations on both screens consist.

The Nepal Court Screen.

The front face of the screen, which is double, consists of a large central plaque and two smaller side plaques of carved birch wood, divided and bordered by panels of carved *satisal* wood.

The central plaque is a copy, half the actual scale of a window above the entrance of an ancient Newar Vihar or monastery in the town of Patan. The original window must be from two to three hundred years old. All the details have been faithfully copied in the replica.

The side plaques are copies on a reduced scale of windows frequently seen in old Newar buildings—either monasteries, temples, darbars, or private dwellings.

The inner face of the screen is of carved birch wood, the patterns shown being reproductions of types of ancient Newar decorative carving.

The double row of pillars and arches supporting the screen are copied from the enclosure of the temple at Tripureswar on the banks of the river Baghmati near Khatmandu.

The carving of the front face of the central arch is supposed to represent cloudy sky, the winged figures being angels, or the substitute for them in Newar mythology, and the dragons symbols of lightning.

The architecture is that of all ancient Newar buildings; unfortunately the work represented is fast falling into disuse from a variety of causes, and workmen capable of producing it are not easy to collect. Since the Newars have been a conquered race, they have lacked the means of gratifying their undoubtedly artistic instincts, and the Gurkhalis or dominant class in modern Nepal have no appreciation of beauty in architecture.

North-West Provinces and Oudh Court Screens.

The screens fall into three divisions:—

(1) A row of marble pillars inlaid with precious stones.

(2) That portion of the screens enclosing the smaller of the two sections into which the Court is divided.

(3) The portion including the larger section.

Division (1) has been taken from a large number of pillars of similar design now lying in the Fort at Agra, and constitutes a gift from the Government of the United Provinces to the National collection at South Kensington. The inlaid work on the pillars is similar to much of that on the world-famed Taj, and it is supposed that they were constructed in view of extending the buildings known as the Diwan-i-khas. Before, however, the pillars could be erected, Agra was taken and held for a time by Sooraj Mull, the neighbouring Raja of Bhartpur, by whom the pillars were apparently buried previous to the town being recovered from him.

Quite recently, during the progress of excavating foundations for a guard-house, the pillars were accidentally discovered and unearthed. It may be possible some day to restore and erect those left in some suitable locality, but the cost of doing so is, at the present time of financial pressure, prohibitive. So far as these pillars have been restored, the work is that of Nathuram Mistri. These pillars have been erected in the form of a recess outside the Indian Palace.

Division (2) consists entirely of stone-carving executed at Muttra and Agra for the Royal Commission. The light graceful work in white stone filling in the two ends of the Court was executed by workmen at Muttra, from designs approved by Mr. F. S. Growse, C.S., C.I.E., to whose exertions and taste the native arts of the Provinces are so deeply indebted.

The whole of the front was executed by Agra workmen under the direction of Nathuram Mistri from the designs of Dr. J. W. Tyler, C.I.E., of Agra. The trellised screens are faithful copies of similar screens in the Taj and at Fatehpur-Sikri, respectively, while the open arches are in like manner copies of work to be seen in the Agra Fort and Fatehpur Sikri.

Division (3) consists entirely of wood-work. The ends of the Court are here again furnished by workmen from the districts of Bulandshahr and Mainpuri, in the employ of Mr. Growse, and working from his designs. The doors in the centre at one end are in the style of work known as *Tar kashi*, or brass wire inlaid on wood, an art which had sunk very low until Mr. Growse revived it.

The frontage to the extent of 50 feet is occupied by carved wood-work, the greater portion of which has been dug out of ancient houses in Lucknow City under demolition as ruinous from age. Necessarily, to adapt the screen to the dimensions insisted on, some fresh wood has to be added, but in the main this portion represents the style of doors, arches, &c., to be seen in the Lucknow bazars. Owing to the decay of the older part of the city, house demolition is an every-day occurrence, and not a few doors, as delicately carved as in this example, are to be found a prey to white ants and weather in the timber yards.

The remaining portion of the frontage was executed at Farrukhabad from the designs and under the superintendence of Seth Janki Das, a wealthy merchant of that city, and is a copy of the frontage of a verandah erected a few years ago in the Seth's house.

The Punjab Court Screen.

The screen of wood wrought for the Punjab Court owes its simplicity to several considerations, the most important of which was the desirability of occupying as little as possible of the floor-space. Another was the fact, that in order to get the work ready in time it was distributed to various hands in different places, and the adoption of a uniform design simplified the execution, while care had to be taken not to exceed the sum allowed by the Royal Commissioners. There are two arcades, each of 100 feet in length, closed by four end arcades of three arches, each 12 ft. 6 in. in length. One of the longer arcades is wrought in shisham (*Dalbergia sisu*), the cabinet wood of the Punjab, and was made at Udoki, a village in the Amritsar district, by a large family of Sikh carpenters, headed by Gopal Singh and Ganga Singh. Carpentry has long been a favourite occupation of the Sikhs, and this portion is a fair sample of their skill. The pillars are slightly varied in detail, and the proportion of the parts is according to the received canons of to-day as derived from Moghul architecture. The spandrils or *mihrabs*, owing to the conditions involved in the sizes specified on the sketch plan furnished as a guide, are somewhat insignificant in their proportions, but there are numerous examples of precisely this form, both in old and modern work. The horizontal panels are in framed geometric lattices (not perforated), locally known as *Pinjra*, literally "cage-work," strongly resembling the lattice work of Arabic architecture. This is, perhaps, the most characteristic feature of Punjab wood-work, and it is valuable as producing a peculiar effect of repose. One set of the horizontal panels is in shisham wood inlaid with ivory, and was made at Bassi Ghulam Hussain, near Hoshiárpur. The cresting and the finials are forms in actual use. The whole of the work, indeed, is such as is wrought for the best class of constructions every day in the Punjab.

The similar length opposite is in deodar or Himalayan cedar (*Cedrus deodara*), and is the work of various hands in Lahore, notably Chanda Singh and Lena Singh, also Sikhs. Deodar wood is full of resin, and consequently is not attacked by insects, and it is extremely durable. It is practically the building timber of the Province.

The end arcades—two in shisham and two in deodar—are designed in a different style, known among Punjab workmen as Akbari. It is doubtful whether this older type of woodwork is correctly referred to the time of Akbar; but the name serves well enough to indicate a finer and more delicate fashion than is now usually followed. The square Hindu shaft and other minor details are characteristic of this style, and in older work a peculiar crispness and brightness of execution, combined sometimes with excessive minuteness, are noticeable. These ends were wrought at Amritsar by Ram Singh, Kirpa Singh, Lena Singh, and others.

The Kashmir Court Screen.

"The screen for the Kashmir Court," writes Sir Oliver St. John, Resident in Kashmir, "is copied from the verandah of an old wooden mosque near Chakoti, on the Kashmir Murree Road, to which the attention of travellers is invited in Ince's handbook. The date of its erection was not, as far as I could find, anywhere marked on the building, but tradition and the character of the carving seem to point to the earlier part of the last century. Until fifteen or twenty years ago the mosque appears to have been in tolerable preservation, but latterly it had been suffering much from the depredations of tourists and art-collectors, who stripped off every bracket or other piece of carving that could be got at, until the building became a mere wreck of what it had been. Two years ago it was still further spoilt by repairs made to fit it for the purpose of a house for the road police, and the destruction was finally completed by the earthquake of 1885, which left it little more than a ruin. Before that catastrophe, I had obtained the permission of the Maharaja to take away the pillars and arches of the verandah which shaded the mosque on two sides, to put them up in Srinagar as a model to wood carvers; but finding the building practically a ruin, I had all carving worth removal taken to Srinagar. Besides the verandah there are a number of beams and cornices and a doorway, of which unfortunately the pediment had been stolen by a French art-collector. The pillars, brackets, and architrave beam of the screen are almost an exact copy of the original both in design and proportion. The side bays, 6 ft. 3 in. each, are identical, and the front bays differ only in that the original arches, each 5 ft. 2½ in. span, have become pillars 10 feet apart surmounted by brackets. The railing at the top is *pinjra* work, such as is commonly made and used throughout Kashmir at the present day. The carving was done under my supervision by eight carpenters, paid at the rate of 5 to 7 annas (say, 5½*d.* to 8*d.*) a day, and took them about four months. Their only tools were the small native chisel and heavy adze, and as regards the ornament, they had no assistance from me except in the drawing of some of the more difficult patterns on the wood. I had, however, to repress their inclination to add detail. Left to themselves, every bare space would have been covered with chisel work.

"In the original the pattern on every pillar and every spandril was different. The greater length of the adaptation has necessitated repeating each twice. The material is deodar wood."

The Central Provinces Court Screens.

The screens which form three sides of each of the Central Provinces Courts are the handiwork of native carpenters at Nagpur, and are very fair specimens of the wood-carving which is very characteristic of the Central Provinces. The art of carving in wood, and to a less degree in stone, is perhaps the only one in which these Provinces can hold their own against other Provinces in India. It is no uncommon thing to find even in small villages houses with carved teak fronts of considerable beauty, and in several towns there are streets with carved wooden frontages displaying very considerable taste and skill. Carved wood plays an important part in Nagpur architecture, and the Maratha palaces in the vicinity of the city are distinguished by their high verandahs of black teak often very elaborately carved.

The screens were designed by a native artist after illustrations in Ferguson's 'Architecture,' and were carved under the superintendence of the Curator of the Nagpur Museum, Mr. Dasabhay Mahalakshmivala.

The Assam Court Screen.

The Assam ornamental screen is composed almost entirely of bamboo and cane, but a kind of mat locally known as *sital patti* and some native silk cloths have been also used in its manufacture. There are really two screens, one for each side of the court. These differ from each other only in pattern, the main idea being exactly the same in each. This consists of a sentry box at one end occupying two feet of the length. The remaining sweep of 18 feet is divided into two by a bamboo pillar resting in a socket of lacquered wood. The whole length of the screen (20 feet) is covered by a board 20 feet long, 2½ feet wide, and 10½ feet from the ground. The under-surface of this board is covered with the best *sital patti* matting. The workmanship is so fine that twenty-three strips of the *patti* go to one inch. Below the board and at right angles to it along the central line, in a series of six panels, separated from each other by bamboo bars and enclosed in bamboo frames. Each half of the space of eighteen feet contains two small and one large panel. The panels all differ in design and consist of intricate figures worked out by native artists and formed in very fine cane. Along the two edges of the long boards runs a fringe of hanging cane-work, six inches deep, worked out like the panels, but in different designs. The board is partially supported by brackets also of cane-work.

The Burma Court Screen.

The screen of the Burma Court is made of carved teak with *kalaga* (or cloth hanging) panels. The upper part resembles the carving placed round the eaves and gables of Burmese monasteries, palaces, and shrines. The small flame-like pinnacles perhaps point back to a former fire-worship era. The frame-work just below is an example of the ordinary wood-carving of the country, and the *kalagas* or *appliqué* work, which are placed as panels, are part of the hangings used as screens, roofings, or backgrounds at open-air festivals or in-door feasts. The pillars are ornamented in red and gold in a manner common in shrines and monasteries. The workmanship is purposely that met with on objects commonly made in Burma.

The Madras Court Screens.

The carved screens for the Madras Court are in a style of the Dravidian architecture of Southern India of the Vijaynagar period, i.e. about the 15th or 16th century. Avoiding as far as possible the grotesque eccentricities of the style, it is attempted to show that South Indian carvers are capable of much good work. The columns are fluted and ribbed and crossed at intervals with bands of elaborate ornament. The upper portion is cut in representation of a *chatty*, or earthen vessel, from which the capital springs in the shape of a lotus. Above this two richly-carved brackets assist in supporting the long beam on which the upper portion or entablature of the screens rest. The Hindu architects use an elaborate system of brackets in place of the arch construction of Saracenic and European builders. The long beam is divided into panels filled with various designs of foliage, birds, gryphons, and other monsters of Hindu mythology. What might be called the frieze of the entablature is divided into panels by carved upright struts. The panels themselves are each divided into three niches, the design being adapted from the metal shrines in which the Hindus place the images of their gods. The centre of each of these is filled with pierced foliage, generally in representation of the tree of life, and in the spandrel between the niches, a cobra with distended hood is coiled up. The variety of the patterns on the screen and the treatment of animal forms will give a good idea of the facility for ornamental design possessed by most oriental handicraftsmen. The screen is constructed of Burma teak by a Madras carpenter, Ramalingam Asari. The general design was prepared by the Superintendent of the Madras School of Arts and executed under his direction by about twenty Madras carvers, the smaller details being designed by Minakshi Asari, a carver from Ramnad, in the Madura District. The difficulty of getting a sufficient number of expert carvers in Madras city and the short time allowed for the work prevented the design being carried out in its entirety.

The Mysore and Coorg Court Screen.

The screen for the Mysore and Coorg Court encloses a space of about 70 feet in length by 12 feet in width. The front elevation is divided into seven bays of 10 feet each, the Mysore Court of five bays being separated from the Coorg Court of two bays by a partition. The designs for the pillars and arches are copied from the Daria Daulat Bagh (the Garden Palace, built by Tippoo Sultan at Seringapatam, and long occupied by the Duke of Wellington, then Colonel Wellesley), reduced to half the original dimensions. The pillars, panels, &c., are made of different kinds of Mysore timber, the carving being executed by local carpenters. The plain panels above the arches of the front elevation and at the sides and top of the three partition screens are filled in with photographs of Mysore scenery, &c., and native mythological paintings.

The Hyderabad Court Screen.

Except in the centre piece or gateway, the height of the screen is 10½, and that of the arches, 8 feet from the ground. The arches may be numbered 1 to 7. Nos. 1 and 7 are intended to show the brass work of the province. The pieces (front and back) forming the arches, and those in front of the sentry-boxes, are of brass *repoussé* work. The designs were left entirely to the native workmen, supervision being only exercised to prevent any European ideas from creeping in. The pieces forming the recesses in the sides of the frame which pertain to these arches are of brass fretwork mounted on wood, coloured black, so as to show the design. The fronts and backs of the supports facing the sentry-boxes are draped with Aurangabad *San-*

geen, an inferior kind of satin used for trowsers. The centre panels over the brass arches are fitted up with cotton carpets from Warangal, and the smaller panels on either side of the carpets with the brass plates commonly used by the labouring classes.

The second and sixth arches are of *Bidri* ware, *i.e.*, blackened pewter inlaid with gold, silver, or copper. Silver is the metal most commonly used, but the arch pieces in the case of the Screen have been inlaid with brass. The central panels, over the arches, are fitted with the beautiful silk carpets for which Warangal is famous, and the panels on either side of the carpets, as well as those at the back, are trays, the designs inlaid on which represent "Brahma," "Vishnu," "Surya," and "Ravana" in silver. The pieces forming the recesses in the sides of the supports in this particular portion of the Screen are mere imitations of *Bidri* ware, being designs in silver leaf on wood painted black. The costliness of the real article is perhaps sufficient excuse for its not having been used throughout.

The third and fifth arches—those on either side of the central piece—are entirely of lacquer work. The different portions of the screen have been so designed as to be separately utilized in a variety of ways.

The central portion of the screen, or, as it may well be termed, the central gateway, is a Tazzia, such as is commonly constructed during the Mohorram festival, to represent the Mausoleum of Hassain and Hussain. It is constructed of paper, talc, and tinsel, and is chiefly interesting as showing the ingenuity and labour bestowed upon it, all the designs being punched out by hand. In the small arches stand two "Buraks," effigies of the celestial steed on which the Prophet visited Paradise.

It will be seen from the above brief description that while the ornamental arts of the province have been fairly represented in the screen, its architecture has not been shown except in the cornice work over the several arches, the designs of which have been copied from the façades of one or two old Mosques about the place.

RAJPUTANA STATES.

JEYPORE.

Div. I.—Fine Arts.

1. *Paintings and Drawings.*

[538-544].—Reproductions of the Illustrations of the Emperor Akbar's copy of the Razm Namah, or Persian version of the Mahabharata or Great Indian Epic.

The originals were the work of the greatest artists of the day (A.D. 1588). The paintings were photographed and enlarged, and the colours applied to them by Jeypore artists, with the originals before them as a guide.

[545-556].—A Collection of valuable Old Persian Historical Paintings, from the library of the Maharaja.

[557-623].—A Series of Native Paintings, representing mythological scenes and characteristic figures.

The collection of portraits of the Maharajas is exhibited by the Jeypore Museum.

[1366-1393].—A Series of Designs for Jeypore enamel work.

2. *Engravings, Lithographs, &c.*

[1016].—A Copy of Memorials of the Jeypore Exhibition, in 4 vols. Imp. 4°.

This work was written by Surgeon-Major T. H. Hendley, and published at the sole cost of H.H. the Maharaja, by W. Griggs, Peckham. Volume iv. is devoted to the Razm Namah.

3. *Photographs.*

[836-884]. Photographs of Views in Jeypore, photographed by Lala Din Dyal, of Indore, and coloured by Jeypore artists on the spot.

[885-944].—Photographs of places in the Jeypore State, by the Photographer of the Maharaja.

[1001-1015].—Khetri Photographs, by Ismail Yusuf.

Exhibited by the Raja of Khetri.

Div. II.—Decorative Art.

1. *Architectural Designs and Models.*

[417].—Model in Brass of the Cenotaph of Maharaja Sawai Jey Singh II., Founder of Jeypore.

The original is near Jeypore.

[418].—Model of the Hawa Mahal, or Palace of the Wind, Jeypore.

[419.—Model of the Kiosk for Garuda (the vehicle of Vishnu), in front of the temple of Jagat Siromani, at Amber, about 300 years old.

[420].—Model of a Gateway in brass and coloured gilt of Jeypore house or temple.

[427].—Model of a marble shrine, full size.

This is a copy of a shrine in a Jeypore street.

[743].—Brass Model of a Temple.

3. *Archæological Drawings, Models, &c.*

[439-458]. — Models in painted wood of astronomical instruments of Maharaja Sawai Jey Singh II., in the observatory at Jeypore.

4. *Models in Clay, Wax, &c.*

[428-438 and 459-518].—A Collection of Models in Papier Maché, representative of various native figures, castes and trades.

5. *Decorative Painting as applied to Architecture.*

[624-642].—Decorative Tiles and Plaques, painted on screens.

8. *Other Works of Decorative Art.*

[421-426].—Models of Bullock Cart, *palki*, portable throne, palanquin and chair.

Made in the State workshops.

[519-521].—The *Mahi Maratib* or Fish Insignia, given by the Emperor Farukshir to the Maharaja of Jeypore.

[522].—The *Panch Ranga*, or five-striped and five-coloured banner of Jeypore.

[532].—Copy on a small scale of the banner given to the Maharaja of Jeypore by the Queen Empress at the Imperial Assemblage at Delhi.

[524-527].—Sunshade, Peacock-plumes and Fly-whisks used by princes.

No. 526 represents a pair of imitation *morchals* used by religious beggars as a parody on royalty.

[953-954.]—Designs for the Feathers of State, flywhisks or *morchals*.

[1920].—Lal-dyed Wood.

[2063].—Collection of Kites.

[2083].—Specimens of Caligraphy in glass and on paper, &c.

Div. III.—Musical Instruments.

1. *Wind Instruments.*

[535-537.] Long horn and flute.

2. *Instruments of Percussion.*

[533-4 & 536.] Large and small drums and cymbals.

Div. IV.—Jewellery.

1. *Gold and Silversmiths' Work, including Filigrain, Settings of Precious Stones, &c.*

[1473-1475.] Hookah mouthpiece, parcel gilt and jewelled, and silver necklace and bracelet.

[1551-1557 & 1582-3.] Gold and silver necklaces and bracelets and brooch and pin, ornamented with garnet beads and pendants.

[1591-1632.] Specimens of silver jewellery, including necklaces, armlets, bracelets, anklets, rings and charms.

[1633-1645 & 1647.] Gold ornaments, consisting of necklaces, armlets and bracelets.

[2084-89, 2099 & 2171-2191.] Samples of peasant jewellery, consisting of anklets, toe-rings, &c.

[2197-2233.] Collection of jewellery, including gold and silver brooches, solitaires, sleeve links, shirt buttons, hair pins, lockets, scarf pins, earrings, also silver rosary, necklace, cross and bracelets.

The forms of Indian jewellery are as endless as is the demand for it. In prosperous times all classes invest their savings in this manner, and no girl can become a bride without, for her position in life, a really considerable outlay on ornaments for her person, which serve as her dowry, and as a provision for her family in times of need. Sooner or later, however, her gold and silver are sure to be sold or find their way to the melting pot, and thus it is that the most ancient forms are found in the base metal ornaments which are worn by the poor, especially by the Brinjaras or wandering grain merchants, for the material of which they are made has no great intrinsic value.

2. *Enamelled Jewellery.*

[1501-1525.] Enamelled jewellery, consisting of lockets, bracelets and brooch.

[1646.] Silver enamel betel case.

[1648-1711, 1731-1740 & 2298-2300.] Gold enamelled ornaments, including necklaces, rings, bracelets, charms, sleeve links, pins, earrings, &c., many of the articles being studded with precious stones. One of the necklaces is formed of plaques set with turquoises.

The Jeypore enamel is of the kind termed Champlévé, the outline being formed by the plate itself, while the colours are placed in depressions hollowed out of the metal. These colours are metallic oxides, and are made to adhere by fire; they are applied in succession for each single tint or group of tints. It is this necessity of repeated exposure to varying temperatures, depending upon the different lengths of time required by the colours before they fuse, that makes the art of the enameller so difficult, and the risk run at every stage of course greatly increases the value of the ornament. The red colour is the most difficult to apply, and for this hue Jeypore is famous.

Div. V.—Art Manufactures in Metal.

1. *Gold and Silver Plate.*

[1451-1460.] Silver trays and boxes.

[1461-1472.] Coffee pot, rosewater sprinkler, vases, goblets, spoons and paper knife.

[1476-1480.] *Surahis*, hookah and *chillum*, boxes, &c.

[1487.] Silver umbrella or canopy.

[1491-1494.] Silver plated poles.

2. *Koft or Damascened Work.*

[1481-1488.] Damascened articles, including antimony holder, trays and vases.

[1490.] Vase of true gold damascened on steel.

3. *Brass, Copper and Mixed Metal.*

[655-672 & 674-681.] A collection of lamps and trays, &c., in engraved brass work, the designs being taken from the ceilings and doors of tombs near Delhi.

[682-737, 739, 741-2, 746-750, 772 & 828-835.] Engraved articles in brass, including trays, lamps, figures, *surahis, abkhoras*, vases, *lotahs*, betel cases, soap boxes, urns, paper knives, sugar basins, censers and hookahs.

The bulk of the collection is sent by the Jeypore School of Art.

[777–780.] Copper trays with silver incrustations (Tanjore pattern). From Jeypore School of Art.

[781–820 & 823–4.] Domestic utensils, including *lotahs*, cups, betel boxes, cooking pots, candle stands, spittoons, spice box, plates, strainers, hookahs and pen case, &c.

[955.] Image in brass of the 23rd Jain lord.

[2070–2072.] Pen case, sand box, and gum box.

[2196.] Water cup, half-plated.

[2270–2275.] Brass *Hastawas*, engraved and grooved, also tray and fruit box.

4. *Brass and Copper Wares for sacrificial purposes.*

[738, 740, 751–771, 821–2 & 825–6.] Bells, brass swing, brass and copper lamps, incense burner, Ganges water vessel, salver and throne.

[733–776.] Portable set of sacrificial implements.

[744–5.] Images in brass of Garuda and Parasnath.

[2195.] A brass *sakhi*.

5. *Arms and Armour.*

[1394–1443].—Battle Axes, Swords, Daggers, Knives, Spears and Shields.

This collection was purchased for the Royal Commission by Mr. C. Purdon-Clarke.

[1444–1450, 1584–1590 and 2065].—Small Shields, Sword-scabbards, Lance-tops and Daggers (the *Katar* and *Jamaya*).

7. *Iron and Steel Wares.*

[827].—Iron Padlock.

9. *Enamels other than Jewellery.*

[1496–1500].—Gold Enamelled Boxes, Trays and Scent Phial.

[2297].—Enamel Ark and Cover.

DIV. VI.—ART MANUFACTURES IN WOOD, IVORY, ETC.

1. *Carved Furniture and Carpentry.*

[2064] —Khetri Folding Bed.

3. *Ivory Carving.*

[1526–1533].—Specimens of Carved Ivory, consisting of paper-knife, figures of elephant and tigers, knife handles and powder horn.

4. *Lacquered Wares.*

[960–966].—Lacquered Figures of Horse, Peacocks and Parrots.

[1017–1163].—A Series of Teakwood Panels painted with scenes from the Razm Namah or Persian version of the Mahabharata and then lacquered, intended to serve as bookcovers or panels for cabinets. They are copies of originals done by the best artists in the time of Akbar (A.D. 1588).

[1164–1213].—A Series of Lacquered Panels depicting mythological scenes and figures.

[1214–1279].—A Collection of objects illustrative of the incised lacquer work of Jeypore, consisting of bottles, betel boxes, vases, cups, plates, *lotahs, surahis, abkhoras*, &c.

Exhibited by the Jeypore School of Art.

[1280–1317].—Articles in Coloured Lacquer Work including toys, cups, *chukries*, &c.

[1318–1365]. — Lacquered Ornaments and Figures, including bracelets, chessmen, camels, elephants and toys.

[2081–2].—Lacquered Slates.

Small wooden articles, such as tobacco or opium boxes and bedstead legs, are made in almost every town in Rajputana. They are turned on a lathe, and lac is applied to them as they are rapidly revolved. The lac adheres, and is then polished. In many cases sticks of different colours are employed, so as to produce the variegated variety of the work characteristic of the province. In the School of Art at Jeypore a good deal of incised lacquer is produced. Several coats of lac of different colours are applied one over the other to the articles as they are turned in the lathe, and figures of different colours are produced by scratching down to the different layers with sharp tools.

5. *Wood Carving.*

[528].—A full sized Carved Door from Chirawa in the Khetri Estate.

[529].—Copy of a portable Shrine of wood, painted and lacquered. It is dedicated to Jagannath.

[943–654].—Cross Screens carved in wood.

[1534–1550.—Examples of Betel Nut Carving in walking sticks, animals, birds, flowers, &c.

[1942–2025].—Collection of Sanganir Printing Blocks, for stamping cloths.

These were made by four families whose ancestors came from Mooltan.

[2026–2061]. — Stamps used for printing raised patterns on plain cloth.

These are employed for stamping the borders of the white clothing used by Mahommedans each time the garment is washed.

[2080].—Book Stand.

[2253–2265].—Specimens of Carving in Mace Wood, lacquered and painted, consisting of staffs, powder-horn, knives and hookah. Lent by the Maharaja.

[2295–2296].—Carved Picture Frames.

DIV. VII.—LAPIDARIES' WORK.

1. *Agate, Jasper, and Cornelian Wares.*

[1558–1581].—A Collection of Garnets, including necklaces of garnets and rock crystals, as well as separate stones.

[2265-6]. — Specimens of Garnet with the original matrix and with dodecahedral crystal.

The Jeypore garnets are in very great demand throughout India and in Europe, and are so cheap and superior that they have practically driven the produce of other mines out of the market. The stones are found in the Jeypore, Oodeypore, and Kishengarh States, but the best are quarried in the first-named territory, at a place not far from Rajmahal on the Banas river. The matrix in which the stones are imbedded is mica schist or serpentine, and the crystals are usually of dodecahedral form. The colours vary from yellow with a brown tinge to purple; the latter are the most valuable, and are the real almandine or noble garnets.

Div. VIII.—Marble and Stone.

1. *Carved Objects in Marble.*

[1-86, 112, 113, 114, 118, 120—135, & 530].—Images of Brahma, Vishnu, Siva, Sarasvati, the ten great incarnations of Vishnu, the regents of the nine planets, and other figures of Indian mythology.

[87-109, 117, & 531-532].—Images of the Jain lords.

[110 & 116].—Krishna as a flute player.

[111].—A Jain image (full size).

[115]. Image of Janaki or Sita, wife of Rama and daughter of King Janaka. Carved in red marble from Baldeogarh of Jeypore. Sent by Jeypore School of Art.

[119].—Mahadeva or Siva, with Paravati his wife, the Ganges flowing from his hair. Cut in chlorite from Dungarpur, and oiled.

[136.]—Marble window and frame, made of Makrana stone.

This was made by the Public Works Department, for Mr. C. P. Clarke, on behalf of the Royal Commission. The stone is procured from Marwar, near the Sambhar Lake.

[137 & 138].—Panels in white Makrana marble, from Maharaja Jai Singh's cenotaph at Gehtore, near Jeypore.

[139 & 140].—Window panels of carved marble.

[141-151].—Carved black, white, red, and pink marble; and chlorite, showing figures of elephants, camels, bulls, &c.

[152].—White marble image of Balarama.

[153].—White marble tracery panel.

[2192-4].—Images of Radha Kishen, in stone and white and black marble.

Div. IX.—Pottery.

1. *Glazed Pottery.*

[154-190].—Large vases in semi-translucent pottery, the most of it made in the School of Art and town of Jeypore.

[191-291, 400-415, 945-952, 967-1000, 2267-2269, & 2276-2294]. — Vases, jars, *surahis*, water-vessels, pilgrim bottles, and *abkhoras*.

[292-315.]—Plates.

[316].—Picture of Chandra Mahal.

[317].—Amber palace gate.

[318-320].—Decorative tiles.

[321-384].—Collection of jugs, *lotahs*, pilgrim-bottles, vases, *surahis*, jars, *abkhoras*. Sent by Jeypore School of Art.

[385-399].—Plates and large vases, sent by ditto.

[416].—Model of a Jain shrine.

The shrine is supposed to be dedicated to Parswanath, the twenty-third Jain lord who is placed under the canopy. It is covered with lucky Jain symbols, and represents the seat or throne made by Indra, upon which the Jain lords preached the doctrines.

[2101-2142].—Porcelain jars, *surahis*, *lotahs*, vases, tiles.

It was not until the opening of the School of Art in 1866 that pottery of any value was made in Jeypore, but since that date a large quantity has been produced. Practically it is the same as that for which Delhi has been long noted. The yellow clay and felspar, which are the principal ingredients in its manufacture, are obtained in the state, and the cobalt and copper, with which it is coloured, are also found near Bhagore on the property of the Rajah of Khetri, a feudatory of Jeypore. The vessels are formed in moulds, and, after union of the separate parts, are coated with powdered white felspar mixed with starch, and are then painted. The blue colour, which is most characteristic of the work, is obtained from an oxide of cobalt (which is known under the name of Syepoorite or Jeypoorite), and the green from an oxide of copper, which is associated with it in the mines. The ware is then dipped in a transparent glaze of glass, and when dry goes to the kiln. Only one baking is required.

Div. X.—Glass.

2. *Moulded Articles.*

[2062].—Collection of glass bead necklaces worn by women at Jeypore.

[2143-2170].—Coloured glass *surahis*, vases, cups.

Div. XI.—Textiles.

1. *Cotton Fabrics.*

[1729-30 & 1744].—Examples of Sanganir cloth, stamped with gold and silver.

[1773-84]. — Scarves, sheets, and veils of Sanganir cloth.

[1785-1841 & 1867-1880].—Series of Sanganir patterns on *rezi* or country cloth.

[1842-60].—Country checked cloths.

[1861-1866].—Sanganir patterns on English cloth.

[1881-1917].—Handkerchiefs, petticoats, corsets, towels, *durris*, &c.

[1939].—Cotton carpet.

[2241-2252].—Collection of very old specimens of Sanganir chintzes of fine pattern. Lent by H. H. the Maharaja.

2. *Wool Fabrics.*

[1932-38].—Cloak, rug, and Hindu and Mussulman prayer carpets.

[1940-41].—Woollen carpets.

3. *Silk Fabrics.*

[1495].—Four silk curtains or *purdahs.*

[1763-1772].—Series of Bandhana cloths, in which the patterns of different colours are produced by knotting.

Div. XII.—Embroideries.

1. *Silk, Cotton, or Woollen Thread.*

[1712-14, 1716-18, 1721, & 1726].—Embroidered corset or breast cloth, cap, handkerchief, veils, bag, baby's robe, and antimacassar.

[2234-2240.]—Collection of embroideries from Jeypore Girls' School, consisting of table mats, napkins, &c.

2. *Gold and Silver.*

[1715, 1719-20, 1722-25, 1727-28].—Embroidered cap, slippers, antimacassars, &c.

[1741].—Collection of silver lace.

[1742-43].—Collection of gold lace.

Div. XII.—Leathers and Furs.

1. *Shoes.*

[956-959].—Samples of shoes worn in Jeypore.

2. *Poshtins, Belts, Saddlery, &c.*

[1923-27 & 1929-31].—Complete set of saddlery from Khetri, also camel trappings, belt with powder-horn and accoutrements.

Div. XIV.—Baskets, Mats, and Straw Work.

[1918, 1919, & 1921].—Aloe fibre ropes and door-mat.

[2066-2069].—Cup, water bottle, and betel boxes, made of *kuskus* grass.

KOTAH.

Div. IV.—Jewellery.

3. *Gold and Silversmiths' Work, including Filigrain, Setting of Precious Stones, &c.*

[2902-2904]. — Kotah City silver ware. Hookah snakes.

Nothing remarkable in the manufacture.

[2905-6].—Jhalawar City silver ware. Rose-water sprinkler. Sword hilt.

Div. V.—Art Manufactures in Metal.

Loan Exhibits.

5. *Arms and Armour, ancient.*

[2907-2910].—Kotah matchlocks. Shield and dagger.

Div. VI.—Art Manufactures in Wood, Ivory, Etc.

2. *Inlaid Work.*

[2911-2916].—Etawah ware, small boxes, powder horn, combs.

This method of decoration is peculiar to the small town of Etawah, in the Kotah State. The articles are made of Shisham wood (*Dalbergia Sisu*), or of buffalo horn, inlaid with ivory and mother-o'-pearl, and are principally used for ornamental purposes. The industry is confined to two or three families belonging to the Khati caste, who turn out their work very slowly, though it is as a rule carefully and strongly executed. Specimens may be bought at Kotah, or ordered direct from the maker, Sheo Lal Sitaram, in Etawah.

4. *Lacquered Wares.*

[2918-2919].—Indragarh lacquered ware, cups and water jars.

These articles are manufactured at the small town of Indragarh, in the Kotah State. The cups are made of Khirni wood (*Mimusops indica*) or *Kauki*, which is obtained at Indragarh. The clay of which *surahis* are made is also found at Indragarh. The cups are made by the Khati caste, and the *surahis* by *Kumhurs.* The lac is first reduced into small thin pieces of about an inch wide and 6 inches long. The cups are revolved in a lathe (*Kharad*), and the pieces of lac applied, which, when thus heated by friction, adhere to the wood. The ornamental work on the cups is then done by means of a small fine chisel. Lac when melted is put upon *surahis* with a small piece of iron. About 1000 cups of various patterns and 100 *surahis* are turned out every year.

Div. XI.—Textiles.

1. *Cotton Fabrics.*

[2920-2938].—Kotah muslins, dyed cloths.

Kotah Muslin.—This manufacture is carried on in the City of Kotah by certain Mahommedan and Hindu weavers. The muslin is woven in hand-looms of cotton thread imported from Europe, and purchased in Bombay and Calcutta. About Rs. 25,000 worth of muslin is annually made at Kotah, turban pieces being in greatest demand. The weavers sell muslin retail to a small extent, but for the most part dispose of it wholesale to cloth merchants for export to Nimach and other places in British India. The price runs from Rs. 4 to Rs. 15 a "*than,*" a "*than*" being equal to 12 yds.

Dyed Cloth.—This is a pleasing style of work in a variety of colours practised in the town of Baran in the Kotah State, and affords occupation to 108 families of the "Khatri" caste. It consists of two processes, viz.:—1st., dyeing the cloth; and 2nd., producing a pattern by tying up with cotton thread small portions of the cloth in pieces about the size of a threepenny piece, and often much smaller. The tying is so tightly and thoroughly done that when dipped in a second dye these spots retain their original colour. Very intricate patterns of pagodas, trees, animals and birds are produced in two or three different colours. Each portion of the pattern that is required of one colour has to be knotted at one time; it is then dyed, and the second set of knots tied, and so on. The effect is almost that of crape when the pattern is a close one. Washing takes away from this appearance, and renders the cloth quite flat. Prices vary from Rs. 4 upwards.

Div. XII.—Embroideries.

1. *Silk, Cotton, or Woollen Thread.*

[2939–2943].—Shergarh embroidered cloths, Kotah jail carpet.

Shergarh Cloths.—These comprise rugs, saddle-cloths and elephant trappings made of English broadcloth, embroidered with floss silk of various colours. The work is done at Kotah by two families of the Machi caste. Saddle-cloths are the only articles for which there is any great demand, and they are generally made for local sale.

Prices from Rs. 20 upwards, according to the size of the cloth to be embroidered.

AJMERE.

Div. I.—Fine Arts.

3. *Photographs.*

[3824].—Photographs of the Mayo College Buildings.

[3825].—Photograph of Jaipur House.

[3826].—Photograph of Jodhpur House.

[3827].—Photograph of Oodeypur House.

[3828].—Photograph of Jhalawar House.

[3829].—Photograph of Ulwar House.

[3830.]—Photograph of Tonk House.

[3831].—Photograph of Kotah House.

[3832].—Photograph of Bhurtpore House.

[3833].—Photograph of Principal's House.

[3834.]—Photograph of Ajmere Residence.

[3835, 3836, 3837].—Panorama of ground and S. E. boarding houses from top of Mayo N. E. College, and from the Jaipur Residence.

Div. IV.—Jewellery.

1. *Gold and Silversmiths' Work, including Filigrain, Setting of Precious Stones, &c.*

[3838].—Silver Ornaments: Bracelets or *poonchi* in Hindi, worn on wrist.

[3839].—Necklace, called *hamail.*

[3840].—Hanging for Armlet. Worn by richer class of women.

[3841].—Silver Flower, worn about wrist. Called *hathphul* in Hindi.

[3842].—Necklace, *Jhalra*, worn by rustic women.

[3843].—Bracelet, *Kankni*, generally worn by all classes of women.

[3844].—Bracelets.

[3845].—Necklet, *Timniya*, is of different shapes, and is worn by almost every Hindu woman in Marwar.

[3846–8].—Flower, worn round neck by rustics.

[3849].—Bangle.

[3850].—Anklets. Called *neoni* in Hindi, worn by rustic women on ankle.

[3851].—Necklace.

[3852].—Bracelets, *Gujri*, worn by all classes of richer women.

[3853].—Flower, worn round neck.

[3854].—Plum (silver), worn in hair on top of head; woman's ornament.

[3855].—Ear-rings, *Nagla*, worn on top of lobe by rustic women.

[3856].—Ear Ornaments, worn on bottom of lobe.

[3857].—Necklet, worn round neck.

[3858].—Forehead Ornament, hook in parting of hair to hang round top of forehead.

[3859].—Gold ornaments. Necklet, worn tight round neck.

[3860].—Nose ring.

Div. XI.—Textiles.

Sect. 1. *Cotton Fabrics.*

[3803].—Cotton curtains, 6 ft. by 5 ft. 6 in.

[3804].—Cotton carpet, 7 ft. by 4 ft.

[3861].—Large stamped cloth, *Jajam*, used as carpets.

[3862].—Large stamped handkerchiefs.

[3863].—Pieces of stamped cloth, worn round shoulders.

[3864].—Turban of variegated colours.

Pagris are generally softer and lighter in texture than other native cloths, the ordinary dimensions being 13 yds. long by 10 in. wide.

[3865].—Turban of 84 colours.

[3866].—Turban of 84 colours.

[3867].—Covering (with figures of peacocks and birds), *Choondri*, worn by women.

[3868].—Covering, green.

[3869].—Covering, yellow.

[3870–1].—Coverings, rosy.

[3872].—Covering, with squares of variegated colours.

[3873].—Red cloth.

[3874].—Coarse cloth with squares thereon, *Charkhana*. This is a kind of check *susi*, the varieties being black and white check or red and blue. It is superior in make to the ordinary *susi*.

[3875–6].—Chintzes, blue.

[3877].—Coarse-lined cloth, *Susi*.

This is a narrow cotton fabric used only by Mahomedan women for making trousers. It is distinguished by having stripes lengthwise down the piece of a different colour from the ground work. The patterns most common are dark blue with white stripes, or blue and red stripes. The fabric is plain woven.

[3878].—Cloth of variegated colours.

[3879].—Red blanket.

[3880].—Small carpet for praying on.

[3881].—Waterproof.

2. *Wool Fabrics.*

[3801].—Woollen carpet, 12 ft. by 9 ft.

[3802].—Woollen carpet, 4 ft. 6 in. by 3 ft.

GENERAL STATEMENT.

1. *Ornaments and Jewellery.*

1. The *nath*, a small nose ring, one side of which is ornamented with pearls.

2. *Tussi*, a necklace with pendants fixed with silk.

3. *Tunnia*, a necklace fitting rather close to the neck, with several rows of small beads suspended.

4. *Gajra*, a flexible bracelet made of squares or irregular circular studs mounted on silk.

5. *Jhella*, a fringe hanging over the forehead on either side. Some of these are richly jewelled.

6. "Amulets," a small square case to contain written prayers or charms, prettily ornamented.

False jewellery is made of brass, zinc, and other metals, which is largely worn by the lower classes.

Jewellery is as much worn by men as women. It is of the same general style as that of Delhi and Lahore, but the ornaments noted are peculiar to Rajputana alone.

Ornaments are worn by women on the head, forehead, ears, nose, neck, arms, wrist, and fingers. There are several varieties, too numerous to detail minutely. The Ajmere jewellery is inferior to the very fine jewellery of Jeypore and Delhi.

2. *Cotton Manufactures, Plain Cloth.*

The varieties of cloth manufactured are very limited, being only seven in number.

The cultivation of the cotton plant is extensively carried on in Ajmere-Merwara, and raw cotton is exported largely to Bombay from the Beawar market.

1. *Pagris* (turbans). These are generally softer and lighter in texture than other native cloths, the ordinary dimensions being 13 yds. long by 10 in. wide. Those made from native thread are used by the rural population. Those made from English thread are fine specimens of native muslins, with beautiful borders, in which gold thread is often tastefully introduced. The trade in *pagris* is rapidly increasing.

The cotton manufactures of Ajmere-Merwara consist of cloth worked with native thread, both coloured and plain, and cloths worked with English thread.

2. *Takri* or *reza.* These are stiff white cloths made from native thread, resembling the Garha of the Punjab; they are largely used for garments by the rural population for their cheapness and durability. They are also extensively used for calico printing, bed-covers, and floor-cloths.

The native thread is decidedly inferior in quality to that of the Punjab. The cloth made from this thread is coarse.

3. *Saptah.* This is a kind of coarse muslin of narrow width, usually made from English thread or a combination of English and native thread woven together. It is used for scarfs.

Cloths worked with English thread are gradually giving way before Manchester cloths, the demand for which is rapidly increasing.

The process of manufacture is the same as it is elsewhere; the hand-looms are of the simplest and rudest construction.

NOTE.—The machine-made muslins of Manchester and Bombay have entirely superseded the manufacture of *saptah* cloth, which in these days is seldom made or sold in this district.

4. "*Khes.*" The fabric is remarkable chiefly as exhibiting a different kind of weaving. In Ajmere the pattern is generally plain, the thread of the weft is entwined alternately with those of the warp, so that the make of the fabric appears diagonal or corner-wise across the fabric instead of the thread crossing at right angles. It is made by certain Kuli weavers from Bhartpore and other places, and chiefly used for upper wrappers (*chadars*), but being made of coarse native thread are far inferior to the Punjab *khes.*

All native cotton fabrics are made in one or other of three styles:—

1st.—Plain cloths wove with a single thread.

2nd.—Cloths with a longitudinal stripe.

3rd.—Cloths with diagonal patterns.

5. "*Dhotis.*" This fabric is only a variety of the *tukri* cloth. The *dhoti* is a sheet worn round the waist by Hindus; they are seldom made in Ajmere, as the demand for them is almost nil, the people preferring the produce of the Bombay cotton mills.

The weaving of towels, table linen, *dasoti*, cloth of sorts is only practised in the Ajmere jail; these cannot be counted as a class of indigenous manufactures.

6. "*Susi.*" This is a narrower cotton fabric, used only by Mahomedan women for making trousers; it is distinguished by having stripes lengthwise down the piece of a different colour from the groundwork. The commoner patterns are dark blue, with white stripes, or blue with red stripes. The fabric is plain woven.

The native fabrics are not so conspicuous for regularity of workmanship or softness and fineness of texture as they are for durability.

7. "*Charkana.*" This is also a kind of check *susi*, the varieties being black and white check, or red or blue. It is superior in make to the ordinary *susi.*

3. *Cotton Prints.*

The *tukri* cloth is largely used for the purpose of printing. The cotton prints of Ajmere are far inferor to those of Jeypore both in purity and brilliancy of dyes. The favourite colour is dark red, the main ingredients used being *al* (the root of the *Morinda citrifolia*), and manjít (*Rubia*). It is effected by dipping the cloth in boiling solution of the dyes.

Varieties of colours are also obtained by the combined used of indigo and turmeric; the colours are generally permanent.

Calico printing is done without dipping the cloth in any colouring solution. The cloth is damped and stretched in wooden blocks, on which the floral patterns project in strong relief are charged with colour and then pressed down on the cloth. The bed covers and printed floor cloths of Nayanagar are the best in the district.

4. *Transient Colours.*

The principal ingredients used by the dyers of Ajmere are safflower, turmeric, and indigo.

These colours are particularly remarkable for their excellence, and are much prized throughout Rajputana.

Native cloth is seldom used, as it is too coarse for colouring purposes; the cloth in common use is English muslin. The varieties of these colours are—

Keladar orhni, pamcha, kesarani pila, dhanak. The design slightly varies in each case, but is almost the same, the ground being coloured black, red, yellow, or azure blue with striped or spotted border, and the field covered by imitations of plantain fruit surrounded by small squares of various colours.

The trade in coloured cloth and red *pagris* is largely carried on in Ajmere. The people of Marwar and surrounding Native States depend on the dyers of Ajmere for their requirements. The annual exports are put down at four lakhs.

The *chunnis*, worn by females, are spotted sheets, or cloths, with a pattern made by tying up tight little knots, so that when the whole is dyed the parts remain uncoloured.

Printing in gold and silver leaf is also common in this district.

5. *Woollen Cloth.*

There is not much to report on this head. No great care is taken of the wool, which in this district is coarser than the Punjab wool, and all that is woven from it is blanketing, generally coarse and hard. The Todgurh blankets are the best of the whole.

In certain parts of the district, *saris* (under-garments of females) are made of wool, which are used mostly by Jat women. They are woven by the Balae weavers, who are met with in almost every village in the district.

6. *Embroidery.*

There is only one establishment, giving employment to about 15 persons. Embroidery is principally employed in articles of dress and edging of garments. The solid and rich kind is called *karcholi*, and is unknown in Ajmere. The art cannot be said to be in a flourishing state, as there is little or no demand for such things.

The few men who know the art in Ajmere can work well, and are in no way inferior to the Delhi workmen.

7. *Wood Manufactures.*

The turners of Ajmere are chiefly employed in making rosaries, combs, &c., of sandalwood, which are purchased in large quantities by the pilgrims, who resort to the Durgah Khwaja Sahib. The carpenters generally work in *babul* wood, which is the only wood procurable in the district.

There are some clever carpenters in Ajmere, who can imitate the most intricate design, and can build carriages, Bareilly carts, &c.

8. *Leather Manufactures.*

Ajmere-Merwara cannot boast of any varieties of leather manufactures beyond the few things required to satisfy the immediate wants of the rural population, viz., *chams* (buckets for raising water from wells), shoes, and leather trunks (*jamdanis*). Workers in leather are met with in almost every village, but belong to a class of people who will not make the slightest alteration or improvement in the designs bequeathed to them by their ancestors. This is not, however, the case in Ajmere, Nasirabad and Nayanagar, where, especially in the first two, a marked improvement has been displayed during the last ten years. European imported leathers are now freely used, and shoes of various sorts suited to the taste of all classes of people, particularly imitation of English shoes. Ornamental shoes are made, false *tila* and *muskesh* made of brass gilt being the material worked on leather or cloth over leather.

9. *Ivory Manufactures, Lacquered Ware.*

Ivory bangles, &c., are made by the turners of Ajmere. Lacquered wares consist chiefly of bangles (commonly called *churis*); they are made of a style similar to the Delhi make, though inferior to it in workmanship.

The illumination of lacquered ware is effected by the use of colours, chiefly red and yellow metal foils and small pieces of mica.

10. *Work in Precious Metal, Gold and Silver Ware, and Fabric woven with Gold and Silver Wire and Thread.*

Silver and gold tinsel, spangles and thread are made in Ajmere, besides various sorts of lace. The popular opinion is that Ajmere lace is better in quality than the Delhi and Jeypore lace, as the *kundla* (silver ingot) here is particularly pure, being never allowed to be alloyed with more than a fixed quantity of copper.

Next to Delhi and Jeypore, Ajmere is the principal place from which Rajputana chiefly receives its supplies of fabric of this class, the demand for which is immense.

11. *Metal Manufactures.*

There is not much to report, the metal manufactures of Delhi, Moradabad, and Jeypore are imported here in such large quantities that the indigenous manufactures are dying out.

12. *Marble.*

White, Purbutpura.—Quarried near Purbutpura, about 5½ miles to the south of Ajmere, by the Mayo College Division. Can be had in all sizes suited to building purposes.

White with Green Streaks, Jamon-ki-chowki.—Quarried near Jamon-ki-chowki, about 9 miles to the south-west of Ajmere, by Mayo College Division. Can be obtained in all sizes suited to building purposes.

Green, Bussi.—Quarried near Bussi, 12 miles to the north of Ajmere, by Mayo College Division.

White; Pink, Kanipura.—Quarried near Kanipura, 14 miles to the north-east of Ajmere, by Mayo College Division.

Black, Khojar-ki-chowki. — Quarried near Khojar-ki-chowki, at the end of the 7th milestone of the Ajmere-Nasirabad road, by Mayo College Division.

BIKANIR AND TONK.

Div. I.—Fine Arts.

3. *Photographs.*

[2601].—Photographs.
Taken by Shiri Shunkar Narain, Bombay, Photographer to School of Art.

Div. II.—Decorative Art.

1. *Architectural Designs and Models.*

[4252].—One bullock tonga, with pair of bullocks. Made at Tonk.

6. *Decorative Painting, as applied to Articles of Domestic Use.*

[2602 & 2603].
The wood is overlaid with successive coatings of liquid clay applied with a brush and worked into a raised pattern, then gilt and painted. Price varies according to size and workmanship of article, about Rs. 25 being that of a small cabinet.

8. *Other Works of Decorative Art not specified.*

[2604–2616].—Lacquer on pottery.
Articles of common china ware are lacquered as above. This work is also done on stone, glass, ivory, &c. The price of jars and vases is from Rs. 2 to Rs. 5. The ornamental screen is a specimen of this work on wood. It is very effective.

Div. IV.-V.—Art Manufactures in Metal.

1. *Gold and Silversmith's Work, including Filigrain, Setting of Precious Stones, &c.*

[2617—2639].—Bikanir.
Fairly good work can be procured at Bikanir, especially in chased silver; jewellery and arms are also set with precious stones. Prices of course vary, workmanship being about annas 4 per rupee's weight. These are excellent examples of the Bikanir chased silver work.

3. *Brass, Copper, and Mixed Metal.*

[4253].—One brass tray, chased.
Made at Tonk.

5. *Arms and Armour.*

[2640–2686].—Bikanir ancient armour.
These are all ancient arms sent on loan. Matchlocks and percussion-cap guns are also made. Prices vary from Rs. 3 to Rs. 10 per gun.

[4254–4257].—Two muskets and two daggers.
Made at Bundi. Matchlocks, plain, price Rs. 25 each. Daggers, plain, Rs. 15 each. The Bundi smiths used to be noted for their good metal.

6. *Cutlery.*

[2687 & 2688].—Bikanir cutlery.
Common scissors, &c., are made up to a maximum price of annas 4.

Div. VI.—Art Manufactures in Wood, Ivory, Etc.

1. *Carved Furniture and Carpentry.*

[2689 & 2690].—Bikanir wood carving.
The wood-carving of Bikanir is excellent. Prices vary with workmanship, from Rs. 10 to Rs. 100 for a door frame, and Rs. 5 to Rs. 40 for a pair of doors.

3. *Ivory Carving.*

[2691–2705].—Bikanir ivory carving.
Bangles, boxes for holding antimony and opium, and salt-cellars, are made. Prices from R. 1 to Rs. 30.

4. *Lacquered Ware.*

[2706–2715].—Bikanir wood and lacquer.
Articles in wood are lacquered and painted. Price varies from R. 1 to Rs. 20, according to size of articles.

[4258 & 4259].—Two shields.
Made at Shahpura. Price of each shield, Rs. 25. Cost of each boss and grip, Rs. 13 as. 8. Total, Rs. 38 as. 8.

5. *Wood Carving.*

[2716–2739].—Bikanir wooden models of idols, elephants, camels, horses, oil-press, country cart, camel plough, churn, spinning wheel, bullock cart, a well, street doors, carved cabinet, glove boxes. Lacquered walking sticks, carved bracelets and pillars, rotating frame, and chair in glass and lacquer work.

DIV. VIII.—MARBLE AND STONE.

1. *Carved Objects in Marble.*

[2740–2746].—Bikanir stone carving. Stone models of Maharaja Guj Sing's cenotaph, and of a banker's house; also carved trellis, plaques, and window.

These and objects of Hindu worship, and figures of animals are carved in red sandstone. Value, according to size and workmanship, from Rs. 10 to Rs. 115.

2. *Unglazed Pottery.*

[2747–2759]. — Bikanir pottery. Nohar-Bikanir earthen jars, boxes, tobacco pipes, and pumice stones.

These are made at Bikanir and other large towns in the State; up to a maximum price of 4 annas.

DIV. X.—GLASS.

2. *Moulded Articles.*

[2760–2763].—Bikanir glass ware.

Bikanir glass ware is lacquered; prices vary.

DIV. XI.—TEXTILES.

1. *Cotton Fabrics.*

[2764–2783].—Bikanir cotton.

Prices vary from R. 1 to Rs. 25, according to quality of material used.

2. *Wool Fabrics.*

[2784 & 2785].—Bikanir serges.

These are made both at Bikanir city and in the districts. They are considered the best in Rajputana. Price, Rs. 3 to Rs. 25, according to quality for a piece 8 by 1½ yards.

[4251].—Felt cloak.

3. *Silk Fabrics.*

[2786 & 2787].—Bikanir hair embroidery.

Embroidery is worked on articles of dress for men and women. Prices vary from R. 1 to Rs. 65, according to quality of materials used.

DIV. XII.—EMBROIDERIES.

1. *Silk, Cotton, or Woollen Thread.*

[4260].—One saddle or table cover.

Made at Chupra of Tonk.

2. *Gold and Silver.*

[2788–2804].—Bikanir embroidery. Bodices, jackets, and shawls of dancing girls.

DIV. XIII.—LEATHERS AND FURS.

1. *Shoes.*

[2805–2810].—Embroidered leather. Prices vary from R. 1 to Rs. 10.

2. *Poshtins, Belts, Saddlery, &c.*

[2811–2821].—Bikanir leather ware. Water-bottles, lacquered and plain, camel-saddle, pipes, silver-mounted and lacquered, embroidered bridles and belts, cuirass leather, powder-flask and pouch.

These are made at Bikanir and other large towns. The water-bottles and camel-saddles of Bikanir are used throughout Rajputana; prices vary from Rs. 2 to Rs. 7 for bottles, and Rs. 15 to Rs. 60 for camel-saddles.

DIV. XIV.—BASKETS, MATS, AND STRAW WORK.

[2822 & 2823].—Reni Bikanir straw ware. Embroidered *Khos* fans with ivory handles.

These are made at Reni; when used they are sprinkled with water, which brings out the perfume of the grass roots of which they are made. Price, from Rs. 1 to Rs. 20.

KARAULI.

DIV. I.—FINE ARTS.

3. *Photographs, &c.*

[4301].—Album of views of Karauli.

Strictly speaking, not an exhibit; sent, however, as an interesting contribution calculated to illustrate local architecture, dress, &c.

DIV. II.—DECORATIVE ART.

1. *Architectural Designs and Models.*

[4304–4305].—Specimens of designs by local artists.

These are made out by the masons engaged in the local manufacture of carved stone work. The drawings are rough. They convey, however, a fair idea of the design.

7. *Decorative Carving as applied to Architecture.*

[4306–4327].—Carved sandstone screen for front of Karauli Bay, Provincial Court.

This carved work in sandstone is a speciality, the sandstone, red and white, of the Karauli quarries being especially adapted for the work.

[4330–4333].—Carved sandstone pedestal for revolving screen.

The carved trellis-work screens are especially handsome. The front screen and pedestal are good examples of this industry.

Div. IV.—Jewellery.

1. *Gold and Silversmiths' Work.*

[4334–4335].—Local manufacture of jewellery, as gold and silver necklaces, ear-rings, &c.

The ordinary articles of native jewellery are manufactured by the resident gold and silversmiths, nothing especially needing notice. The exhibits, a necklace and nose-ring, are fair specimens of local work.

Div. V.—Art Manufactures in Metal.

2. *Koft or Damascened Work.*

[4341].—In handles, to swords, daggers, &c.

The exhibit, a sword with damascened handle, is a fair example of the work in silver. Handles damascened in gold are more expensive.

3. *Brass, Copper and Mixed Metal.*

[4342].—*Lotas, thallies*, hooka stand, &c.

In addition to the usual *thallies, lotas* and other domestic vessels usually made in brass, a special kind of hooka bowl is made. This consists of brass, covered with a mixture of quicksilver and lead, and worked in an effective manner. The exhibit is a specimen of this class of work.

5. *Arms and Armour.*

[4343–4345].—Swords, spears, daggers, matchlocks, &c.

The exhibits, a shield and two daggers, are specimens of the ordinary weapons of the country, manufactured by the local smiths. Some very fair imitations of breech-loading guns have also been of late turned out by the Raj workshops.

Div. VI.—Art Manufactures in Wood, Ivory, Etc.

4. *Lacquered Wares.*

[4352].—Boxes, hooka stems and bowls, cups, bed-posts, &c.

Some very pretty wooden articles turned on a lathe and covered with delicate and neat shades of lacquer, are turned out by the local manufactures; *singardans* (of which the exhibit is a specimen), glass *lotahs*, hooka stems, bed-posts and several sorts of ingenious toys are the articles principally manufactured.

Div. VIII.—Marble and Stone.

1. *Carved objects in Marble and Stone.*

[4356–4358].—*Pathrotas*, cups, &c.
[4359–4362].—Animals, carved.
[4363–4364].—Plaques.

The *pathrota* is a large bowl used for storing coin. The small kinds, of which exhibit No. 4356 is a specimen, have covers. These, as well as the carved plaques (No. 4363–4364) are manufactured from the local sandstone above referred to, and the smaller animals from a softer kind of stone, somewhat resembling soapstone.

Div. XI.—Cotton Fabrics.

1. *Cotton Fabrics.*

[4371–4373].—Cotton cloths, locally manufactured and dyed in *ál* and indigo.

The exhibits are specimens of the local industry, both as regard manufacture and dyeing.

Div. XIII.—Leather and Furs.

1. *Shoes.*

[4376].—Manufacture of shoes in leather.

The exhibit is a specimen of a peculiar pointed shoe used by the Maharaja and higher officials.

BHARTPUR.

Div. I.—Fine Arts.

3. *Photographs, &c.*

[4381–4382].—Photographic views of Bhartpur and Díg. Painting of H. H. the Maharaja.

Strictly speaking, not exhibits; sent, however, as interesting contributions calculated to illustrate local architecture, &c.

Div. II.—Decorative Art.

7. *Decorative Carving as applied to Architecture.*

[4386–4403].—Carved sandstone work in side screen, for Bhartpur and Karauli Bay.

The carved screen illustrates generally the local industry of stone-carving, which is carried on to a considerable extent; the stone from the local quarries especially lending itself to fine and delicate carving.

Div. V.—Art Manufactures in Metal.

3. *Brass, Copper and Mixed Metal.*

[4411].—Local work in brass, &c.

The exhibit, a hooka bowl, is a special kind of work, consisting of a covering of quicksilver and lead on brass.

Div. VI.—Art Manufactures in Wood, Ivory, Etc.

3. *Carved Furniture and Carpentry.*

[4416–4418].—Local work in the manufacture of *ruths*, carts, &c.

The exhibit, a model of *baili* (or country carriage), and bullocks, illustrates generally the character of work turned out by the local carpenters.

3. *Ivory Carving.*

[4421].—Local work in ivory.
This local industry is mainly confined to the manufacture of ivory *chauris*, of which the exhibit is a fine specimen.

5. *Wood Carving.*

[4422].—Local work in wood.
This industry is mainly confined to the manufacture of sandalwood *chauries*, as illustrated in the exhibit.

DIV. VIII.—MARBLE AND STONE.

1. *Stone Carving.*

[4426-4427].—Carved work, consisting of *pathrotas*, cups, &c.
The two exhibits (stone cups), illustrate the general nature of the industry, which is mainly confined to the manufacture of such articles, as well as plates, grindstones, &c. These are all made of sandstone from the local quarries.

DIV. IX.—POTTERY.

2. *Unglazed Pottery.*

[4431-4432].—Local work in clay.
This industry comprises the manufacture of all clay domestic utensils in use amongst the poorer classes.
The exhibits are samples of a hooka bowl and stem, and a *chilum*. The former contains the water through which the smoke from the tobacco burned in the latter is drawn.

DIV. XI.—TEXTILES.

Cotton Fabrics.

[4434].—Local manufacture of cloth.
The exhibit is an example of the common country cloth locally manufactured and worn.

DIV. XIV.—BASKETS, MATS AND STRAW WORK.

[4436-4439].—Local manufacture of hand-fans.
These hand-fans are made from the leaf of the palm-tree, skilfully plaited, the plaits being coloured to produce a pattern.

DHOLPUR.

DIV. II.—DECORATIVE ART.

7. *Decorative Carving as applied to Architecture.*

[4458-4461]. — Dholpur ornamental sandstone screen work.
The stonework, numbered 4458, is in two layers of colour, red and white, the white being carved in pattern showing a relief on the red ground.
The others are perforated screen work.

DIV. V.—ART MANUFACTURES IN METAL.

3. *Brass, Copper and Mixed Metals.*

[4462].—Dholpur Kalli, or Hubble Bubble.
Formed in brass, studded with copper and moulded, over which ornamental chisel work is done and then plated. Price at 1/8 a seer, with a wooden carved Naicha.
[4463].—Baseri ornaments.
Made in brass moulding, mostly used by native women of lower class.

6. *Cutlery.*

[4464].—Dholpur nut cracker.
The handles are made of brass and the blade of steel; it can be converted to a dagger by taking out the pin and turning the handles.

DIV. VI.—ART MANUFACTURES IN WOOD.

4. *Lacquered Wares.*

[4465-4466].—Bari wood stands for bedsteads, Indian clubs.
Carved wood-work, painted and varnished.

JODHPUR.

DIV. I.—FINE ARTS.

1. *Paintings and Drawings.*

[3001-6].

3. *Photographs.*

[3007-10].

DIV. II.—DECORATIVE ART.

4. *Models.*

[3011-13].

DIV. III.—MUSICAL INSTRUMENTS.

[3014-16].
[3017].— *Setar* (guitar).
Is generally worked with ivory; its price varies according to workmanship, from Rs. 4 to Rs. 200. It is a favourite instrument with singers and others fond of music.
[3017-18].

DIV. IV.—JEWELLERY.

[3019-30].
[3023].—*Timniya*, neck ornament, made of gold and silver.
Varies in price from Rs. 20 to Rs. 500 accord-

ing to weight, is of different shapes, and is worn by almost every Hindu woman in Marwar.

[3024].—*Tora*, anklet, foot ornament made of silver.

Chiefly used by Brahmins as a marriage present to the bride. Price from Rs. 60 to Rs. 150.

Div. V.—Art Manufactures in Metal.

[3033].—Wine holder used by Rajputs when drinking.

1. *Silver Plate.*

[3031-35].

[3043-48].—Jalore wine flasks and vessels.

3. *Brass, Copper, and Mixed Metal.*

Jodhpur pot, boxes, lamp, plates, &c.

[3049-50].—*Pachbedra* inkstands and penholders.

These are used by shopkeepers and official class.

4*a*. *Brass, &c.*

[3051-52, 3053].—Nagore rolling lamp and scales.

[3051-52].—*Lotandiya*, rolling oil-lamp made of brass or iron.

This lamp is so constructed that it will roll on the ground without upsetting the oil-box or the light being put out. Price from R.1 to Rs.2

[3053].—*Kanti*, jewel scales.

Made at Nagaur; is used for weighing jewels and is exported to other countries.

5. *Arms, &c.*

[3067-74].—Jodhpur arms—swords, shields, daggers.

[3090-93].—*Talwar*, swords.

[3075-100].—Sirohi arms—swords, shields, daggers,

Sirohi swords are famous in Rajputana; their prices (from Rs.2 to Rs.200) vary according to the quality of the steel, as also of the workmanship of sword hilts, which are generally worked with silver and gold.

6. *Cutlery.*

[3101-13].

[3114].—*Sigari*, firepan.

Made at Nagaur, and used by the well-to-do people during the cold season. Price from 1 R. to Rs.50, according to finish and work.

7. *Iron, Steel, &c.*

[3114-21].

8. *Wood Carving.*

[3115-16].—*Tionchi*, tripod.

This is a very beautiful folding water-stand, and was much admired at the late Calcutta Exhibition. Price from R.1 to Rs.3

Div. VI. Art Manufacture in Wood, Ivory, Etc.

3. *Ivory Carving.*

[3128-29].—*Surmadani*, antimony box.

Made at Pali and chiefly purchased by gentlemen visiting that place as samples of Marwar ivory-carving.

5. *Wood Carving.*

[3122-42].

[3143]. — *Hindora*, cradle made of wood carved, coloured, and gold gilt.

[3143-71].

These cradles vary in value according to the material used, size, and finish, from Rs.20 to Rs.2,000. Made at Jodhpur and exported to Bombay, Guzerat, &c. Used for swinging Hindu gods.

[3144].—*Singhasan*, throne made as above.

Used for seating Hindu gods.

Div. VIII.—Marble and Stone.

1. *Marble, Stones, &c.*

[3172-78].—Jodhpur cup, box, vase, smoking-pipes, &c. *Piyala* bowls made of marble.

Made of Makrana marble. Marble is largely exported from Makrana (in Marwar) to other countries.

[3179-94].]—Jaisalmir saucers, cups and paper weights. Cups, saucers, and paper weights.

These are made of yellow limestone, blended with red ochre-like substance, and other stones, and are well polished. Price Rs.2 to Rs.4 a piece.

Div. XI.

1. *Cotton Fabrics.*

[3195-230]. — Jodhpur cloths, shawls, and turbans.

These are chiefly made at Jodhpur and Nagore, and are used by the well-to-do people.

[3237-42].—Pali cloths.

[3231-36].—Pipar cloths.

[3243-45].—Sambhar cloths.

2. *Wool Fabrics.*

[3247-62].

[3247-60.]—These shawls and petticoats are prepared by Jat and Vishnoi women in their leisure hours, chiefly at Alai, Khajwana, Indana, &c., in the Nagaur District (Marwar). They have been largely purchased by European gentlemen of late.

4. *Other Fabrics.*

[3263-70].—These are made at Merta.

[3271-73.]—These plumes are made of pure silver leaves finely cut, and generally washed with gold, and are tied over turban on marriage occasions.

Div. XII.

2. *Embroidery.*

[3271–80].

[3274–78].—These are made of coloured silk and lace, and are tied over turban, and are much in demand.

Div. XIII.

1. *Shoes.*

[3281–87].

2. *Belts, Saddlery.*

[3288–302].

ULWUR.

Div. I.—Fine Arts.

1. *Paintings and Drawings.*

[4011–4013].—Ancient painting. A processional Sowari of Akber II. in three parts (framed).

This is a painting of historical interest, depicting in minute detail as it does a procession in the time of the Mogul Emperors. Sir Charles Theophilus Metcalfe, resident at Delhi, is seated on one of the elephants.

[4014].—A painted photograph of His Highness the Maharaja of Ulwur.

The photograph was taken by Messrs. Bourne and Shepherd of Calcutta, in January 1884, and was coloured by "Chotoo," an artist in the service of His Highness the Maharaja of Ulwur.

[4015].—Book illustrations. A page of the Gulistan (framed).

There exists in the library of His Highness the Maharaja of Ulwur a manuscript of the Gulistan which is said to have cost over one lakh of rupees. The border of each page is beautifully illuminated in gold, and the designs on no two pages are alike. This is a specimen of one of the pages in the manuscript.

[4016].—Book illustrations. A painted border copied from one of the pictures in the library of His Highness.

This is a specimen of one of the border designs which native artists paint round religious pictures or pictures of great personages.

3. *Photographs.*

[4017].—A set of Ulwur views (seventeen in number).

These views were taken in 1885, by Lala Din Dyal, a photographer in Central India.

Div. II.—Decorative Art.

2. *Designs for Manufactures.*

[4018].—A coarse kind of chintz (samples of which are exhibited) is printed in Ulwur, and is largely used by the common people in the State. This is exported also to Afghanistan by Cabul merchants, who come and purchase large quantities of it every year.

3. *Archæological Drawings, Models, &c.*

[4019].—A soapstone model of the tomb of Maharaja Bakhtawar Singh (made to scale).

This is a model of the cenotaph of Maharaja Bakhtawar Singh, the second chief of Ulwur, and is considered an edifice of pure Hindu style of architecture.

5. *Decorative Painting as applied to Architecture.*

[4020].—A panel of decorative painting, with looking-glass in centre.

This species of decorative painting, interspersed with small pieces of variegated glass, is found in the Shish Mahals of native chiefs, and there are three rooms in the Maharaja's palace decorated in this style.

8. *Other Works of Decorative Art not specified.*

[4021].—Book-binding.

This species of book-binding is peculiar to Ulwur. The designs are believed to be Tartar in origin. The covers exhibited are the property of the Royal Commission.

Div. III.—Musical Instruments.

2. *Stringed Instruments.*

[4022–4024].

No. 4022 is an ordinary "Sitar" with ivory work inlaid in wood made in Ulwur. (Loan.) No. 4023 is a Kutchwa, another kind of *Sitar* made in Ulwur. (Loan.) No. 4024 is a *Bin* with two gourds, lacquered and painted with gold in Ulwur. (Loan.)

Div. IV.—Jewellery.

1. *Gold and Silversmith's Work, including Filigrain, Setting of Precious Stones, &c.*

[4025–4029].—1. A silver *Chuskidan*, wine-bottle and glass stand (Rajput). 2. A *Khasdan* or betel-holder. 3. A *Surahi* (water-bottle). 4. A milk-jug. 5. Two pairs of bracelets.

These articles have been made by silversmiths in the service of His Highness the Maharaja of Ulwur, and are specimens of the filigree and chased work done in the Ulwur State. Bracelets of this description are also made in gold.

Div. V.—Art Manufactures in Metal.

2. *Koft or Damascened Work.*

[4030].—A betel-nut cutter.

There is only one man in the service of His Highness that does this damascened work.

3. *Brass, Copper, and Mixed Metal.*

[4033–4033].—Brass tumblers with chased work.

Made in Ulwur.

5. *Arms and Armour.*

[4034].—Steel sword (Modern).
A sword made in Ulwur. (Loan.)

[4035].—*Zafar Lakiya.*
Native chiefs generally use this as a support when sitting. (Loan.)

[4036].—*Shamsher Dam-i-Lamancha.*
This is a sword with pearls let into the blade. (Loan.)

[4037].—*Katar Fouladi.*
A steel poniard, with bas-relief gold work representing in alto relief the pictures of Hindu gods and goddesses. (Loan.)

[4038].—*Katar Fouladi.*
A steel poniard, having an iron handle with golden koft work. (Loan.)

[4039].—*Katar Fouladi.*
A steel poniard, showing on its handle a species of koft work. (Loan.)

[4040].—*Katar Fouladi.*
A steel poniard having an iron handle with silver koft work. (Loan.)

[4041].—*Katar Dohra Fouladi.*
A double dagger, made in Ulwur. (Loan.)

[4042].—*Khanjar Fouladi.*
A steel dagger, with an agate handle worked in gold and studded with jewels. (Loan.)

[4043].—*Churi Fouladi.*
A steel knife, with a silver handle having black ornamental work on its surface. (Loan.)

[4044].—*Churi Derh Khami.*
A steel knife with pearls let into the blade, made in Ulwur. (Loan.)

[4045 & 4046].—*Dao Kheri.*
Steel hatchets (ancient). (Loan.)

[4047].—*Gurz Fouladi.*
Steel mace (ancient). (Loan.)

[4048].—*Pesh Kabz Fouladi.*
Steel dagger, with a handle of rhinoceros horn and a scabbard with enamelled work on silver, made in Ulwur. (Loan.)

[4049].—*Aarsi Fouladi.*
A steel mirror (ancient). (Loan.)

[4050].—*Sipar-i-Fouladi.*
A steel shield, with Koft work on the margin, and having four steel bosses. (Loan.)

[4051].—*Sipar-i-Fouladi.*
A steel shield. (Loan.)

[4052].—*Sipar-i-Chirmi.*
A shield made of rhinoceros' skin, with golden bosses. (Loan.)

[4053].—*Saz-i-Banduq.*
A belt, with powder-horn, and four other articles.

[4054].—*Butli-Saz.*
A powder-horn, made of wood and inlaid with ivory. (Loan.)

[4055].—*Zira-Tikra.*
A coat of mail made in Ulwur.

[4056].—*Dastana Fouladi.*
A pair of gauntlets (ancient). (Loan.)

[4057].—*Khod.*
A silver antlered headpiece, bearing various weapons in miniature. (Loan.)

[4058].—*Banduh-i-Sindhi.*
A flint lock musket, made in Sindh. (Loan.)

[4059].—*Kaman Fouladi.*
A steel bow. (Loan.)

[4060].—*Kaman Seeng.*
A bow made of horn. (Loan).

[4061–4064]. — Four quivers with arrows (ancient), made in Ulwur. (Loan.)

[4065].—Stock of a gun made of mango wood with steel locks and springs. Made in Ulwur.

[4066 & 4667].—Two spear-heads. Made in Ulwur.

6. *Cutlery.*

[4068].—A box of skinning knives.
Containing four big and two small knives and a pair of scissors, made in Ulwur.

Div. VI.—Art Manufactures in Wood, Ivory, Etc.

1. *Carved Furniture and Carpentry.*

[4069].—A toonwood frame for toilet glass.
Design of carving and turrets taken from one of the old tombs extant in Ulwur.

[4070].—A small bookshelf.
Made in Ulwur.

3. *Ivory Carving.*

[4071].—An elephant.
The *jhool* is enamelled, the rider is supposed to be the god Sitaram, and the driver Hanuman the monkey.

[4072].—An ivory antimony case, with pearls round the top of the cover.

[4073].—Ivory perforated screen work.
Made in Ulwur.

[4074.]—An ivory scent-box.
Made in Ulwur.

[4075.]—An ivory ball.

4. *Lacquered Wares.*

[4076 & 4077].—Two lacquered trays.

[4078–4081].—Four sets of bed supports.
Made in Ulwur.

Div. VIII.—Marble and Stone.

1. *Carved Objects in Marble.*

[4082.]—1. Marble screen of Court.

Div. IX.—Pottery.

1. *Glazed Pottery.*

[4083 & 4084].—*Hukkas.*
The one represents a Rajput leathern Hukka, and the other an ordinary Hukka used by the generality of people.

[4085–4098].—*Surahis.*
Earthen goblets of different colours and designs.

[4099 & 4100].—*Jhajris*, water-holders.

[4101 & 4102].—*Dibbas*, boxes.

[4103–4113].—*Chillums*, tobacco holders.
Showing the various descriptions.

[4114-4119].—Tumblers with covers.
[4120-4127].—Drinking vessels and jugs.
[4128].—Earthen imitation cocoa-nut *Hukka.*
[4129]—Earthen cup with cover.
[4130 & 4131].—Small boxes.
[4132-4135].—Saucers.

Div. XI.—Textiles.

1. *Cotton Fabrics.*

[4001-4005].—Cotton *Durris.* Ulwur Jail manufacture.

[4136-4191].—Pieces of coarse chintz. Ulwur manufacture.

2. *Wool Fabrics.*

[4006-4010].—Woollen carpets. Ulwur Jail manufacture.

Div. XII.—Embroideries.

1. *Silk, Cotton, or Woollen Thread.*

[4192 & 4193].—*Meo Chadars.*
[4194-4196].—Jatni dress, consisting of a head-dress, a petticoat, and a bodice.

2. *Gold and Silver.*

[4197].—An *Angarkha* (coat).
Ulwur embroidery of this description in gold and silk thread is much admired for the designs and for the fineness of the workmanship. Embroidery of all descriptions is done in Ulwur.

Div. XIII.—Leather and Furs.

1. *Shoes.*

[4198 & 4199].—Two pairs of shoes.
Made in Ulwur; peculiar for their lightness.

Articles not specified in Class D.

[4200].—Indra Biwan.
An elephant-carriage drawn by four elephants, in which the Maharaja with his Court drives in procession on the Dashara festival from his palace.

[4201].—*Barahdari.*
A *Shamiana* or tent made in Ulwur.

[4202-4205].—Four embroidered broadcloth *Purdahs*, with gold fringe and tassels.

MEYWAR.

Div. II.—Decorative Art.

[3674].—Glass Mosaic.
Coloured glass inlaid in Plaster, used in interior wall decorations; one example represents a ceiling border, and the other an arch spandril.

Div. V.—Manufactures in Metal.

Iron and Steel Wares.

[3677].—Iron goad for driving elephant.
Iron inlaid with gold and silver.

Div. VI.—Art Manufactures in Wood, Ivory, Etc.

3. *Ivory Carving.*

[3678].—Flower cut out of ivory.
This represents no established industry. Is exhibited as an example of delicate hand work.

Div. X.—Glass.

[3687-89].—Tassel ornaments made of glass.
These ornaments are worn chiefly in turbans, and are made of glass, two sticks of which are exhibited with the ornaments.

Div. XII.—Embroideries.

[3691].—Silk cords worn over shoulder and used for attaching daggers.

CENTRAL INDIA STATES.

Div. I.—Fine Arts.

1. *Paintings and Drawings.*

[411].—Datia. Water-colours in native style.
Portraits of H.H. Maharaja of Datia on horseback.

[437].—Alipura. Water-colours in native style.
A tiger seizing an antelope. The picture forms a Persian inscription.

[769].—Indore. Painting on ivory.
Portrait of H.H. Maharaja Holkar.

[770-772].—Oil painting.
By a native artist, Ram Lal, of Maharaja Holkar's Court.

3. *Photographs.*

[342].—Chhatrapur. Views.
Album of views of Chhatrapur State.

[773-776].—Indore. Views.
By Lala Din Dayal of Indore. These views of the Sanchi Tope, near Bhopal, are exceedingly good. Other specimens of his work will be found in the rotating frames, No. 890.

4. *Sculpture.*

[249-253].—Dhar. Small stone figures.
Not high-class work, but newly started.

[458-464]. — Mandsaur, Gwalior State. Figures of gods, or in stone.
Nos. 460-464 are old and curious.

DIV. II.—DECORATIVE ART.

4. *Models in Clay.*

[465-493].—Gwalior. Figures of clay.

Figures of various classes of natives, as well as gods.

7. *Decorative Carving as applied to Architecture.*

[174 & 175, 200-202]. — Indore. Carved pillars, &c.

No. 174 is an elaborate piece of work, modelled partly on Buddhist carvings.

DIV. III.—MUSICAL INSTRUMENTS.

1. *Wind Instruments.*

[343-345].—Chhatrapur. Wooden pipes.

[346].—Brass trumpets.

[438].—Alipura. Brass trumpets.

2. *Stringed Instruments.*

[254 & 255].—Dhar. Guitars.

Inlaid with ivory and strung with wire.

3. *Instruments of Percussion.*

[439].—Alipura. Brass cymbals.

DIV. IV.—JEWELLERY.

1. *Gold and Silver Jewellery.*

[267 & 268].—Rutlam. Silver ware.

[347 & 348].—Chhatrapur. Silver ware.

[440].—Alipura. Gold ware.

[494, 495].—Jhansi. Gwalior State. Gold and silver rings. These are of exceedingly light and fine workmanship.

[777-790].—Indore. Gold and silver ware.

No. 780 is a good specimen of native ornament, and several of the bracelets are of good workmanship.

2. *Enamelled Jewellery.*

[269-271].—Rutlam. Enamelled ware.

[791-828].—Indore. Enamelled ware.

Both kinds of work are similar. It is not real enamel, but consists of thin gold or silver leaf cut into fine and elaborate designs, and laid on glass of various colours. Good specimens are Nos. 808 and 811.

[869].—Indore. Small enamelled box.

DIV. V.—ART MANUFACTURES IN METAL.

1. *Gold and Silver Plate.*

[256].—Dhar. Rose-water sprinkler of silver.

A pretty design in the shape of a bird.

[349-351].—Chhatrapur. Silver boxes.

[441].—Alipura. Gold scent-box.

[496].—Gwalior. Silver scent-box.

[829-834].—Rampura. Indore State. Scent-stands, salvers, rose-water sprinklers, &c.

Nos. 831 and 832 are good specimens in silver *repoussé* work ornamented with gold.

2. *Damascened Work.*

[420-422].—Datia. Sword-hilt, paper weight, &c.

Gold on steel.

3. *Brass, Copper, and Mixed Metal Wares.*

[1-36].—Rewah. Base metal ornaments, bracelets, armlets, anklets, &c., chiefly of zinc.

Some very handsome designs.

[239].—Charkhari. Brass.

Old and curious set of chessmen.

[176 & 177, 203-208, 272].—Rutlam. Brass pinnacles for domes and pillars, hookahs, &c.

Good, though plain workmanship.

[353-354, 363-364]. — Chhatrapur. Brass vessels, locks, lamps, &c. Nos. 363 and 364 are curious. The former is a spherical lamp of perforated brass work, which can be rolled along the ground when lighted. The latter is a lock containing a double-barrelled pistol.

[355-362].—Base metal ornaments.

[386-396].—Orchha. Brass vessels, and figures of animals. Nos. 388 and 395 may be noted.

[412].—Datia. Brass lock.

[497-534, 537]. — Ujjain. Gwalior State. White metal vessels, hookahs, &c.

Very effective in appearance.

[535 & 536].—Old brass vessels.

[835-848].—Indore. Brass vessels, walking-sticks, &c.

4. *Brass and Copper Ware for Sacrificial purposes.*

[538-545].—Ujjain. Gwalior. Brass images. Nos. 538 and 539 may be noted.

[849-867].—Indore. Set of brass vessels used in Hindu worship.

5. *Arms and Armour.*

(a) *Ancient.*

[240-247]. — Charkhari. Old matchlock, sword, coat of mail, &c.

The sword is of great weight. It is said that Raja Bijara Bahadur Singh of Charkhari used to tie the head and four legs of a camel together, and cut them through with one blow of this weapon.

[365].—Chhatrapur. Old arrow.

(b) *Modern.*

[127-132].—Sarungpur, Dewas State, S.B. Lance-heads and butts. Plain, but well made.

[257].—Dhar. Sword with ornamental hilt.

[273].—Rutlam. Shield, made of hide.

[366-372].—Chhatrapur. Knives, daggers, shield, spear-head. No. 371 may be noted.

[397 & 398]. — Orchha. Matchlock and powder-horn.

[413-419]. — Datia. Shield lance-head, battle-axe, dagger. No. 413 shows good work. It is a small inlaid shield with three daggers fastened to it, to serve as offensive weapons.

[429 & 430].—Bijawar. Whip with pistol, lance-head with pistol.

[442 & 443].—Alipura. Battle-axes.

[452-457].—Panna. Battle-axe, lance-head, and butt, matchlock and sword.

The sword and axe contain inlaid work, gold on steel.

[546-566].—Gwalior. Matchlocks, powder flask, mace, daggers, knives, swords, bow and arrows, shields.

The matchlocks are well made though plain. Of other arms, note Nos. 551, 560, 561, 563, 566. The last is a hide shield with real enamel bosses.

[868].—Rampura. Indore State sword.

Plain sword with well-tempered blade.

6. *Cutlery.*

[274 & 275].—Rutlam. Penknife, pair of pincers.

7. *Iron and Steel Wares.*

[133-138].—Sarungpur. Dewas State, S.B. Bits for horses. Very severe bits, used only by natives of India.

[373-375].—Chhatrapur. Betel-nut cutter, trident for spearing fish, steel mirror.

No. 375 may be noted.

Div. VI.—Art Manufactures in Wood, Ivory, Etc.

1. *Carved Furniture and Carpentry.*

[77-111].—Rewah. Wooden toys.

Turned in a lathe and painted in various colours.

[112-115].—Sandalwood combs.

[276-297].—Rutlam. Wooden pipes, vases, wine-glasses, &c.

Of very neat designs, with tasteful patterns painted outside.

[298.]—Set of 10 Cocoanut-shell bangles.

[376-378].—Chhatrapur. Neatly carved box, ebony hookah, folding table.

[567-573].—Gwalior. Legs for bedstead, walking-stick, toys, &c.

3. *Ivory Carving.*

[116-122].—Rewah. Combs and figures of animals.

[258, 259].—Dhar. Paper-cutter and sword-hilt. Good carving in handle of knife.

[299-306].—Rutlam. Scissors, paper-cutter, &c. Neatly made.

[445-447].—Alipura. Combs.

[870-877].—Indore. Bracelets.

4 *Lacquered Wares.*

[37-76].—Rewah. Ornaments, e.g., necklaces, bangles, earrings, also snuff boxes.

These designs are very fine and of considerable variety.

[307-320].—Rutlam. Imitation fruits and vegetables.

[878-889].—Indore. Bangles.

Various and tasteful patterns.

5. *Wood Carving.*

[448].—Alipura. Carved window.

[178-179, 209-212, 890].—Indore. Carved frames, &c.

These are to hold stone and wood panels and tiles in the screen. No. 890 is a carved pillar supporting carved rotating frames for holding pictures. The design is by a native *mistri* of Indore, Nand Ram. Four female figures appear to hold up the frames, and the pillar is surmounted by another figure. There are thirty-two frames, each bordered with a different pattern.

[891-893].—Sandalwood carving from Rampura, in Indore State, *Chauri*, penholder, and fan. No. 893 is entirely made of sandalwood.

[213-216].—Ujjain, Gwalior State. Carved panels, perforated work—not very minute.

Div. VIII.—Marble and Stone.

1. *Carved objects in Marble and Stone.*

[379-383].—Chhatrapur. Cups and bottles of soapstone.

[399-406].—Orchha. Boxes, cups, plates of soapstone.

[431-436].—Bijawar. Boxes, hookah-stand, bottle, of soapstone.

[449].—Alipura. Betel leaf of soapstone. Well carved.

[180-199, 217-226, 237-238]. — Gwalior. Panels and plaques, both perforated and in relief. This is exceedingly fine work. Nos. 217 and 218 are especially worthy of notice.

[574-585].—Jugs, cups, &c. Good carving on Nos. 574, 581, 584 and 585.

Div. IX.-Pottery.

1. *Glazed Pottery.*

[227-236].—Indore. Tiles.

New industry in these parts, capable of improvement with encouragement. Exhibited in screen.

[384].—Chhatrapur. Blue jar.

[586-628]. — Mandesar, Gwalior State, Water-bottles and vessels, cups and saucers, hookah-stands, &c.

Never before exhibited. Not high class pottery, but would improve with encouragement.

Div. X.—Glass.

2. *Moulded objects of Glass.*

[629].—Gwalior. Square piece of dimmed glass, with pattern, chiselled on the glass.

[894-896].—Indore. Bangles.

Tasteful designs.

Div. XI.—Textiles.

1. *Cotton Fabrics.*

[123-124].—Rewah. Country carpets.

Strongly made and in suitable colours.

[139–173].—Sarangpur, Dewas State, S.B. Fine cloths, turbans, loin-cloths, female dresses, &c., chiefly bordered with silk.

These cloths are chiefly yellow, some made of natural yellow cotton. They are well known in Central India for their excellence. Nos. 144 & 159 are good specimens.

[260].—Dhar. Country carpet.

[321–331]. — Rutlam. Striped and dyed cloths, and chintz.

[407–410].—Orchha. Turbans, head-dresses, &c., of muslin.

No. 409 is a good specimen.

[630–638, 662–667]. — Gwalior. Chanderi muslins, turbans, loin cloths, &c.

Nos. 630, 635, and 662 may be noted. This is the finest cloth manufactured in Central India. The muslin is exquisitely fine, and is usually left white; the silk and gold lace borders are exceedingly handsome; and in some cases the silk is coloured differently on either side.

[639–661].—Gwalior city. Check muslins, dyed cloths, and country carpets.

The dyed cloths are of great variety, and some of the pale shades are very pretty.

[668–683]. — Ujjain, stamped floor cloths, table cloths, head dresses, handkerchiefs, &c.

Stamped cloths of good quality, and including a considerable variety of patterns.

[684–683]. — Mandesar stamped cloths, &c.

Like the Ujjain cloths only with more variety.

[897–903].—Indore state. Maheswar muslins, loin-cloths, native ladies' dresses, &c.

These muslins are second only to those of Chanderi, are made in tasteful colours, with silk or gold lace borders. Nos. 898, 900, 903 may be noted.

[904–925].—Indore city, women's dresses, and other cloths, and caps.

These are stamped cloths of common quality, but of good material. The imitation gold and silver cloths are very effective. See especially Nos. 922–925.

2. *Wool Fabrics.*

[125–126].—Rewah. Carpets.

Blue on white ground. Colouring and workmanship excellent.

[424].—Datia. Rug.

[744–751].—Gwalior state. Gwalior city. Carpets and rugs.

Tasteful blending of colours.

[752—755]. — Jhansi. Carpets and rugs. Similar to those of Gwalior.

3. *Silk Fabrics.*

[261].—Dhar. Silk rug.

[756–759].—Chanderi, Gwalior state. Native ladies' dresses, &c.

Very handsome fabrics, especially No. 759, which is deep crimson on one side and green on the other, with a broad gold lace border.

[926].—Maheswar. Indore state.

White silk with crimson border.

4. *Other Fabrics.*

[760–764].—Gwalior city. Hempen rugs.

Coloured only one side, after manufacture.

Div. XII.—Embroideries.

1. *Silk, Cotton, and Woollen Threads.*

[332–333].—Rutlam. Horse-trappings, mouthpieces for hookah. Trappings No. 332 embroidered with wool and silk.

[425].—Datia. Chessboard.

Embroidered with cotton.

2. *Gold and Silver Embroidery.*

[248].—Charkhari. Chessboard.

Handsome old gold embroidery.

[262–266].—Dhar. Scent-stand, cap, sword-belt, mat, bag.

No. 264 is a good piece of work.

[334–337].—Rutlam. Imitation gold and silver embroidery, handkerchiefs, mouthpieces for hookahs, &c.

[426–427].—Datia. Handkerchief and cap. Handsome gold embroidery.

[450–451].—Alipura. Pouch, and gun-cap holder. Silver embroidery.

Div. XIII.—Leathers and Furs.

1. *Shoes.*

[338–339].—Rutlam. Shoes for upper and lower classes. Embroidered and spangled.

[385].—Chhatrapur. Bundelkhandi shoes. With large flaps at sides.

[428].—Baoni. Bundelkhandi shoes.

[765–768].—Barnagar, Gwalior State. Shoes, plain and embroidered.

These shoes are well known in Malwa.

[927–929]. — Indore city. Ordinary native shoes worn by Mahrattis and others.

Embroidered and plain.

BOMBAY.

Div. I.—Fine Arts.

1. *Paintings and Drawings.*

*[51-65].—Figures and Landscapes in oil and water colour.

Collection of paintings illustrating native life in Bombay, by Mr. Horace Van Ruith.

[76].—Drawings from Cutch.

Illustrating the holiday procession of His Highness the Rao, native dinner parties, artizans at work, and scenes from every-day life at Cutch—by a native of Cutch.

[77 & 78].—Figure subjects.

*Painting of a *nách* girl and a Vanjari woman, by Jagannath Anant.

*[82].—Sketches in water colour, of typical figures of the Bombay army.

Painted by Mr. A. C. Lovett, Gloucestershire Regiment.

†[83].—Water-colour drawings.

A collection illustrating Bombay flora and fungi, drawn from nature, by Isaac Benjamin. Exhibited by Dr. K. R. Kirtikar, Thana (Economic Court).

3. *Photographs.*

[101].—Street architecture.

A collection of photographs of some of the carved wooden houses at Nasik and Yeola.

†[102].—Artizans at work at Bombay, Yeola and Nasik.

4. *Sculpture.*

[200].—Marble bust of Shamaldas Parmanandas, late Diwan of Bhavnagar.

Executed by Vala Hira, an ex-student of the Bombay School of Art, and now engaged on work in the Bhavnagar state.

Div. II.—Decorative Art.

Architectural Designs and Models.

*[65-75].—Designs for bas-relief.

Designs for bas-reliefs for the Darbar Hall at Limri (Kathiawar), by Mr. Horace Van Ruith, subjects being from Indian life and history.

[202].—Model of a tomb in ivory and ebony.

Model of the tomb now being erected in white and black marble at Junagad, to the memory of the late Nawab—made by Dalpat Nathu, and Atmaram Nathu.

[203].—Working drawings of the Bhavnagar section of the carved screen No. 1728.

These drawings were made by the native foreman carpenter, Harilal Parshotam, who had charge of the work.

[204].—Perspective view of a marble cenotaph at Bhavnagar.

This cenotaph or *chhatri* is in course of erection in the middle of a large tank in the centre of the town, from designs by Mr. J. Griffiths, of the Bombay School of Art. It is being built entirely of Italian marble, at a probable cost of £25,000.

[205].—Full size detail drawings of pierced marble screen.

For the cenotaph described above.

[206].—Perspective view of the Takhtsingji Hospital, Bhavnagar.

[207].—Detailed drawings of the same.

This building is under construction from design by Mr. W. Emerson. The style is Hindu, and is being built of a reddish trachyte obtained from quarries near Bhavnagar. The probable cost will be £50,000.

4. *Models in Clay, Wax, Terra-cotta, Plaster of Paris.*

[311 to 313].—Plaster busts of the Honourable J. B. Peile, Mr. E. H. Percival, and Gowrishankar Udeyshankar, C.S.I., formerly Prime Minister of Bhavnagar.

Executed by Vala Hira a Kathiawar mason.

[301 to 310, 315 & 316, & 49].—Models of fruit, animals, and workmen from Gokak; model of an elephant from Surat, models of palanquins from Junagad, and figures from Poona and Sawantwari.

Made at Gokak in the Belgaum District, carved in wood and painted. Surat produces a number of toys similar to the elephant exhibited, consisting of camels, horses, cows, and other familiar animals and birds.

5. *Decorative Painting as applied to Architecture.*

[351].—A decorative panel in *Chunam* (mortar) from Bhavnagar, illustrating house decoration in Kathiawar.

7. *Decorative Carving as applied to Architecture.*

[201].—Perforated window in soapstone.

From Rewa Kantha.

8. *Other Works of Decorative Art not specified.*

[381].—A marble screen.

This screen forms part of the cenotaph being erected at Bhavnagar. Exhibited near the inlaid marble pillars from Agra.

[377].—Necklaces and bracelets.

Made of fragrant powders moulded into shape.

[378 to 380].—Fans made of feathers from Cutch.

[382 & 383].—Wooden spoons used for sacrificial purposes from Junagad.

[21 to 23].—Horn work from Sawantwari, Ink-stand and Cornucopias.

[388 to 390].—Bison's horn-work from Ratnagiri.

* In the Albert Hall.

† In the Imperial Economic Court.

Made at Vigiadurg in the Ratnagiri district. The horn is imported from Malabar and Cochin.

[391].—Papier mache basket from Ahmedabad.

[392 & 393].—Bangles made of wood and lac, and lined with tinsel, decorated with spangles or dyed red, from Ahmedabad and Surat, where they are largely used by Gujarathi women.

[396].—Bookstand from Surat. Used by Musalmans in their schools and mosques.

[397].—A native account-book made of native-made paper and leather from Nasik.

*[398].—A collection of spangles.

These are applied by Hindu women to their foreheads.

[399].—A state carriage from Bhavnagar.

This was made at Cambay. It is only used by ladies of the palace on state occasions or at marriage festivals. Exhibited in the grounds near the fountains.

[400].—Silver ornaments for bullocks and driver of the above.

[401].—Collection of rhinoceros-horn work, consisting of bangles, cups, boxes, &c.

From Cambay.

*[4912 to 4922].—Sticks, clubs, ropes, &c., from Aden.

Div. III.—Musical Instruments.

1. *Wind Instruments.*

[406-411].—*Páwa, Sharnái* (flutes) and shell from Bhavnagar.

2. *Stringed Instruments.*

[451 & 452].—*Satárs* from Cutch and Poona.

[453-456].—*Tamburi, Satár, Bin,* and *Sárangi* from Bhavnagar.

3. *Instruments of Percussion.*

[487].—Drum from Cambay.

[488-494].—Drums from Bhavnagar.

Div. IV.—Jewellery.

1. *Gold and Silversmiths' Work, &c.*

[501].—Ornaments worn by Jewish women at Aden.

[502].—Ornaments worn by Somali women at Aden.

The work is massive and the execution bold in treatment.

[503].—Ornaments worn by Arab women, Aden.

[504].—One pair of bracelets from Cutch.

[505-507].—Bracelets from Ahmednagar.

[508-511].—Gold head ornaments from Belgaum and bangles from Junagar.

The head ornaments are worn by Maratha women.

[$\frac{701}{1}$ to $\frac{701}{28}$].—Collection of jewellery made principally at Bhavnagar.

Court jewellery exhibited by His Highness the Thakur Sáheb of Bhavnagar. The articles are from 25 to 75 years old. $\frac{701}{2}$ a pair of gold anklets (*phulsankla*); $\frac{701}{10}$ a large earring inlaid with precious stones (*toti*), worn by Rajput ladies; $\frac{701}{13}$ gold ornaments for the hair (*chamari*), worn by children; $\frac{701}{23}$ four gold finger ornaments, worn by females at the ends of the fingers and thumb at marriage ceremonies; and $\frac{701}{25}$ a gold necklace (*champákali*), may be noted as good specimens.

[$\frac{702}{1}$ to $\frac{702}{9}$].—Collection of gold and silver articles from Bhavnagar.

Exhibited by His Highness the Thakur Sáheb of Bhavnagar. $\frac{702}{1}$ a cocoanut covered with gold plate, and mounted with precious stones (*shrifal*), is held in the hand of a leading male member of a house on all religious ceremonies. $\frac{702}{2}$ a gold seat of the god Shiva, and gold serpent who overshadows Shiva (*Jatádhári* and *Nág*) were used by the late Thakursaheb.

[540].—Collection of imitation jewellery from Poona.

Brass gilt to illustrate the gold and silver ornaments worn by Maratha women.

Div. V.—Art Manufactures in Metal.

1. *Gold and Silver Plate.*

Lent by H.N. the Rao of Cutch.

[541-697].—Collection of Cutch silver ware.

A very large collection is sent for exhibition, which fairly illustrates the industry as now carried on in Cutch.

[771-818].—Collection of silver plates from Ahmadnagar.

The work is similar to that of Cutch. Exhibited by Messrs. Cursetji & Sons.

[819-821].—Silver pots from Poona, Junagar and Ahmedabad.

3. *Brass, Copper and Mixed Metal.*

[901-951]. — Brass and Copper pots from Nasik.

Pots turned on the lathe at Nasik are in large demand among Hindus who visit the sacred city on pilgrimage.

*[952-980].—Brass and copper cooking and household utensils, &c., from Bombay.

These are made in most of the principal towns of the Presidency.

[1001-1003]. — Copper and brass *repoussé* work, made at the Bombay School of Art.

[1004 & 1005].—Brass perforated windows from Ahmedabad.

The designs are copied from the windows in the Rani Sipri and Shah Allam mosques, Ahmedabad.

[1006-1011].—Perforated brass panels from Ahmedabad.

* In the Imperial Economic Court.

[1012-1014].—Dies used in gold and silver work and brass padlocks from Junagad.

[1015-1020].—Brass pots from Poona.

[4904-4906]. — Silver-gilt brass pots from Cutch.

[4907].—Three brass puzzle boxes from Cutch.

4. *Brass and Copper Wares for Sacrificial Purposes (modern).*

[1021-1068]. — Idols, cups, stands, lamps, bells, &c.

Nasik and Poona supply these articles, which are required in every Hindu family.

4. *Brass and Copper Wares for Sacrificial Purposes (ancient).*

[1069-1100]. — Idols, cups, stands, lamps, bells, &c.

Sent for sale by Sitaram Govind of Nasik.

5. *Arms and Armour.*

[1101].—Bows and arrows, daggers, swords and spear-heads (modern) from Palanpur.

[1102 & 1103].—Sword and dagger (modern) from Vadasinor.

[1104].—Dagger from Junagad.

[1105 to 1107].—Matchlocks, daggers, battle-axe (ancient). From Bhavnagar.

*[1108 to 1120].—Bows, arrows, daggers, and spears, &c. (modern). From Aden.

[1121 to 1295, 1401 to 1500, 1603 to 1700, 1801 to 1844].—Collection of decorative arms (modern), consisting of shields, swords, daggers, battle-axes, &c.

Decorative arms in imitation of old work are now extensively made in Cutch for supplying the demand created by collectors of curios, who buy them for decorative purposes.

6. *Cutlery.*

[1297 to 1300].—Betel-nut knives, from Limri and Junagar.

[4901 to 4903].—Penknives from Cutch.

7. *Iron and Steel Wares.*

[1296].—Padlock.

From Junagar.

9. *Enamels, other than Jewellery.*

[891 & 892]. — Enamelled perfume holders from Cutch.

Div. VI.—Art Manufactures in Wood, Ivory, Etc.

1. *Carved Furniture and Carpentry.*

[1301 & 1302].—Carved cabinets exhibited by Messrs. Mulchand-bhai Hattising and Brothers, Ahmedabad (Private Exhibitors' Court).

These are adaptations from the architecture of Ahmedabad.

[1303 & 1304].—Carved black wood table and chair. Made in the State engineer's workshops at Bhavnagar by Kalian Karsan.

[1308].—Cabinet from the Ratnagiri School of Industry.

[1309 & 1310].—Carved teak sideboard black wood buffet. Designed in the Hindu-Saracenic style, and exhibited by Mr. E. Wimbridge (Private Exhibitors' Court).

2. *Inlaid Work.*

[1351 to 1353].—Portfolio and glove-boxes.

Inlaid work from Cutch.

[24 to 31].—Jugs, urns, bowls, vases, &c.

Exhibited by the Sawantwari State.

[1729].—Sandalwood cabinet.

A specimen of Bombay inlaid work.

3. *Ivory Carving.*

[1375 to 1377].—Paper knives from Cutch.

[1501/1 to 1501/7].—Humming-top, rose-water bottle, egg-shaped box for opium, &c.

From Bhavnagar.

4. *Lacquered Wares.*

[1 to 20].—Cabinets, chairs, tables, brackets, &c.

Exhibited by the Sawantwari State, and collected by Col. G. R. C. Westropp, Political Superintendent, Sawantwari.

[1601].—Toys from Nasik.

[1602].—A collection of toys made at Mahuwa Bhavnagar State.

[4912, 4923-4942].—Tea poy, boxes, flower-stands, &c., from Hyderabad (Sind).

5. *Wood Carving.*

[1701-1706].—Carved picture frames, brackets and flower stand.

From the establishment started by Mr. De Forrest, of New York, which is under the supervision of Mr. Maganbhai Hattising of Ahmedabad.

[1707-1712].—Carved brackets, vase, clock-case and inkstand.

Exhibited by Messrs. Mulchand-bhai Hattising and Brothers, of Ahmedabad.

[1713].—Carved doorway.

Exhibited by Mr. Maganbhai Hattising on behalf of Mr. F. De Forrest (Private Exhibitors' Court).

[1714 & 1715].—The Cutch portion of the carved screen exhibited by H.H. the Rao of Cutch.

[1716-19].—The Royal Commissioners' portion of the carved screen exhibited by the Bombay Committee.

[1720 & 1721].—The Junagar portion of the carved screen exhibited by H.H. the Nawab of Junagad.

[1722].—The Baroda portion of the carved

* In the Imperial Economic Court.

screen exhibited by H.H. the Gaikwar of Baroda.

[1723.]—The Bhavnagar portion of the carved screen exhibited by H.H. the Thakursaheb of Bhavnagar.

[1724-1726.]—Carved box from Lunvada and frames from Ahmedabad.

[1727.]—Carved sandal wood and inlaid cabinet from Surat.

[1728.]—Carved window from Muddebihal, Bijapur.

[1732.]—Carved doorway from Surat.

This is a good specimen of wood carving (used in ordinary houses) as carried on at Surat, where there are several workshops, at which doors, shutters, and cupboards may be bought ready made. Exhibited to the left of the Gwalior gateway.

*[1733.]—Carved screen.

Extra piece similar to the screen in front of court. Exhibited by Mr. E.Wimbridge, Bombay.

[1734-1736.] — Specimens of sandal wood carving from Kanara.

Div. VIII.—Marble and Stone.

Carved Objects in Stone.

[402-403.]—A pair of carved plates from Dhrangadra.

Div. IX.—Pottery.

1. *Glazed Pottery.*

[2001-2117, 2195-2200, 2207-2218.—Collection of glazed pottery from the Art Pottery Works, Bombay.

Executed under the supervision of Mr. G. W. Terry, by a Sind potter and a number of ex-students of the Bombay School of Art. Some of the designs are in imitation of the Sind ware, and some are selected from the ancient wall-paintings at the Ajanta caves.

[2118-2134.]—A collection of glazed tiles.

These tiles, which are made at Hala in Sind, are reproductions of various features on the exterior and interior of the tombs at Hyderabad. Exhibited in the Indian Palace Courtyard.

[2201-2206.]—Glazed pottery from Ahmedabad.

2. *Unglazed Pottery.*

[2301.]—Unglazed pot from Bombay.

[2302-2348].—A collection of pots, *chilams* (pipe-bowls), &c., from Ahmedabad.

Selected from native shops, in which a large variety of unglazed pottery is exposed for sale.

Div. X.—Glass.

Blown Objects.

[2401.]—Collection of glass ware from Kapadwanj, Kaira District.

The shapes of the little vessels are very quaint and beautiful, and they are remarkable for their irridescent properties and good colour, resembling antique and old Venetian glass.

* In the Imperial Economic Court.

Div. XI.—Textiles.

1. *Cotton Fabrics.*

[2501 & 2502]. Cotton curtains printed with gold and silver leaf, from Ahmedabad.

This industry is now nearly extinct in the Presidency. There is only one man at Ahmedabad who carries on the work.

[2503].—Cotton prints used for making quilts, from Ahmedabad.

[2504].—Cotton print used as a bed cover.

[2505-2513].—Cotton prints exported to Siam, where they are used as loin cloths.

A large trade in these fabrics is carried on between Ahmedabad and Pethapur on one side, and Siam on the other.

[2514-2518].—Cotton prints worn by Gujarathi women.

[2519-2527].—Collection of cotton prints used as turbans and scarves, from Ahmedabad.

[2528-2529].—Cotton prints used as floor cloths, from Broach.

[2530-2549].—Cotton prints worn by Gujarathi women.

[2550].—A coverlet from Junagad.

[2551].—Cotton print used for quilts from Jalgaon in Khandesh.

[2552].—Cotton quilt from Broach.

[2553-2556].—Cotton fabrics from Cambay.

[2557-2560].—Cotton waistbands from Jat, in the Satara district.

[2561-2600 & 2601-2651].—Cotton fabrics from Sind.

[2601].—Ten specimens of cotton fabrics from Bhavnagar.

[2652-2679].—Cotton prints from Cutch.

Among this collection are specimens in good colour and design, which may be used for ceilings or floor-cloths.

[2683-2687].—Specimens of cotton printing in thickened oil paint, from Adhoi, Morvi State.

[2701-2753].—Carpets (*satranjis*), curtains, rugs, and counterpanes.

These are specimens manufactured at the Ahmedabad, Ahmednagar, Karachi, Surat, Thana, Ratnagiri, and Bijapur Jails.

[2688 & 2689].—Carpets from Nawalgund, Dharwar.

2. *Wool Fabrics.*

[2901 & 2902].—Felt rugs from Jath, in the Satara district.

3. *Silk Fabrics.*

[3001-3008].—Silk double brocades or *kinkhabs* from Surat.

Instead of using gold and silver thread for the weft, as formerly, differently coloured silk itself is used at Surat for producing a large variety of these fabrics which are in demand among the Musalmans of this presidency for jackets, caps, &c.

[3009 & 3010].—Silk single brocades from Surat.

[3011 & 3012].—Silk fabrics used by Musalman women from Surat.

[3013].—Silk cloth used for petticoats by Gujrathi women from Ahmedabad.

[3014 & 3015].—Silk fabrics dyed by the process of knot-dyeing (*bandhána*) from Ahmedabad.

Knot-dyeing is extensively practised at Jamnagar, Porbandar, Ahmedabad, and Bombay.

[3016-3018].—Silk fabrics worn by Maratha women from Yeola.

[3019-3022].—Silk fabrics used for bodices, from Belgaum.

[3023-3026].—Silk fabrics from Surat used for trousers by Bhoras.

[3027-3030].—Silk fabrics (satin) from Jamnagar.

[3031 & 3032].—Silk fabrics from Cambay, worn by Gujrathi women.

[3033].—Silk fabric from Yeola, used by Maratha women for bodices.

[3034].—Six samples of silk fabrics from Porbandar used for bodices.

Samples of knot-dyeing.

[3035-3042].—Silks from Thana.

These are specially made for the use of European ladies for dresses.

[3043 & 3044].—Silk handkerchiefs, from Thana.

[3045].—Silk quilt.

This manufacture is a speciality of Broach. Each little square of the material is woven, and filled with cotton while on the loom.

[3046].—Silk quilt from Viramgam.

[3047-3054].—Silk fabrics from Bijapur used for bodices.

The silk is of excellent quality, and the design and colour good.

[3101-3106].—Handkerchiefs from Cutch.

Specimens of knot-dyeing.

4. *Other Fabrics.*

[3201-3205].— Gold and silk brocades from Ahmedabad, used for jackets, trousers, petticoats, and bodices.

[3206-3208].—Gold and silver brocades worn by women as *sádis*.

These are made to given sizes for being utilized as hangings.

[3209-3222].—Gold, silver and silk brocades or *kinkhabs* from Ahmedabad.

Ahmedabad is famous for its *kinkhabs*, which were formerly extensively used by native princes and noblemen. The square pieces now exhibited are used as coverings to presents given by wealthy natives.

[3223-3236].—Gold, silver, and silk brocades from Ahmedabad.

This variety is thinner and cheaper than the above. It is called *Banársi* on account of its resembling the work manufactured at Benares. No. 23 (3223) is a square piece used for covering presents, and is an excellent typical example of the work.

[3237]. — Gold and cotton brocades from Ahmedabad, worn by Hindu ladies.

[3238-3243] —Gold and silk brocades from Surat.

Exported to Siam, and worn by the Siamese as loin-cloths. Nos. (3240) to (3243) are specially made to order of convenient sizes for being utilized for screens.

[3244].—Gold and silk brocades from Surat.

It is called a *jaridáno* because the design is partly worked in gold and partly in silk. The inscription in the design means "blessings to the wearer."

[3245]. — Gold and cotton brocade from Yeola.

[3246-3250].—Silk and gold fabrics from Yeola.

Yeola supplies a large quantity of these fabrics for native use, which are required particularly during marriage ceremonies. No. 46 (3246) is a specimen of work woven red on one side and yellow on the other. It is worn by men as a loin-cloth during meal-times and while performing religious ceremonies. Exhibited in the Silk Court.

[3251-3285].—Silk and cotton fabrics from Ahmedabad.

This variety is called *Mashru*, which in Persian means "cleverly woven," from the fact that the cotton warp is so covered by the silk weft as not to be visible. This material is used only by Musalmans.

[3286].—Gold and cotton scarf exhibited by H.H. the Nabab of Junagar.

[3287-3290].—Gold, silk and cotton fabrics from Nawanagar.

Nos. (3288 & 3289) are typical examples of knot-dyeing.

[3291].—Gold and silk end of *sádi* from Nawanagar.

[3292].—Gold and silk fabric from Surat. Used for bodices.

[3293-3300].—Gold, silk and cotton fabrics from Ahmedabad.

[3301-3307].—Silk and cotton fabrics worn by Maratha women from Yeola.

[3308-3310].—Silk and cotton fabrics from Bijapur.

[3311-3313].—Silk and cotton fabrics from Tatta used as loin-cloth.

[3314-3318].—Silk and cotton fabrics from Nasik printed with thick colour.

These fabrics are printed with thickened oil-colour, on which, while wet, gold leaf or powdered talc is applied.

[3319].—Silk, cotton and gold fabrics from Yeola.

[3320-3322].—Silk and cotton fabrics used for bodices from Belgaum.

[3323 & 3324].—Silk and cotton fabrics from Surat used for trousers.

[3325].—Silk and cotton brocade from Surat. Called *Nabábi Himro* from the fact of this particular pattern being exclusively used for the last four generations for the dresses of the Nababs of Surat. Exhibited by Haji Allibhai Tajbhai.

[3326-3360].—Collection of silk, gold and silver borders from Ahmedabad.

Largely used by native women for bodices and petticoats.

[3361-3368].—Silk, gold and silver borders from Surat.

[32].—Carpet.

Exhibited by the Sawantwari State.

[3369-3374, 3427-3428, 3429-3433].—Pile carpets from the Karachi, Thana, Shikarpur and Hyderabad (Sind) Jails, &c.

[3375-3396]. — Collection of turbans from Bombay and Cambay.

[3327-4000].—Collection of caps from Surat. Worn by native lascars.

[3401-3404].—Silver and gold fabrics from Bombay. Specimens of knot-dyeing.

[3405-3419].—Silver and cotton fabrics from Bijapur, Yeola, Nasik and Hyderabad.

[3421-3426].—Silk and gold fabrics from Cutch. Specimens of knot-dyeing.

Div. XII.—Embroideries.

1. *Silk, Cotton, or Woollen Thread.*

[3701 & 3702].—Embroidered borders from Surat.

This variety of embroidery is called *Reshmi bharat kám*, and is a speciality of Surat. In former days these borders were much used by the Pársis and Gujaráthis for their women's dresses, but of late the introduction of foreign silks has replaced this practice to a great extent.

[3703].—Interior lining to the *Rath* or carriage —page 28, and the covering cloths to the pair of bullocks drawing the *Rath*.

Specimen of patchwork of pieces of silk, most deftly stitched on without pattern by native tailors at Bhavnagar. (With the carriage in the Gardens.)

[3704-3716].—Table-covers, scarves, dresses, &c., embroidered at Hyderabad.

[3721-3735].—Cushions, slippers, doyleys, table-cloths, &c., from Cutch.

[3736-3742].—Embroidered scarves and petticoats from Cutch.

These are particularly good specimens of Cutch work. They illustrate one of the chief domestic industries of the women of Cutch.

[3743].—Embroidered coverlet from Gondal.

2. *Gold and Silver.*

[4001]. Embroidered saddle-cloth from Dhrangadra.

[4002].—Embroidered saddle (complete) from Palitana.

[4003 & 4004].—Embroidered coat and jacket from Surat.

[4005-4019, 4021-4059].—Caps, slippers, borders, curtains, cushions, &c.

Specimens illustrating the different kinds of embroidery from Surat, Cutch and Hyderabad (Sind). No. (4017) is a good specimen of embroidery called *bádláni*, where the design is worked in flattened gold or silver wire—carried on extensively at Surat, and is done by women.

[4401].—Scarlet and gold covering to the *rath* or carriage. Recently executed at Bhavnagar for exhibition. (With the carriage in the Gardens.)

[4699].—Saddle and bridle. Made at Kundla-Bhavnagar.

Div. XIII.—Leather and Furs.

1. *Shoes.*

[4501-4529, 50, 4530-4534].—Shoes, slippers, and sandals from Ahmedabad, Surat, Junagad, Ratnagiri, Cambay, Satara, Sawantwari and Aden.

The collection illustrates the varied and fantastic shapes of shoes, as worn by the different sections of the native community.

2. *Poshtins, Belts, Saddlery, &c.*

[394 & 395].—Embossed leather covers used for account books.

Principally made at Ahmedabad.

[4695].—Eleven books.

Exhibited by the manager of the *Times of India*, as specimens of bookbinding by native workmen of Bombay.

[4696-4698, 4701-4714]. — Leather water-bottles (chargle) from Dhrangadra, and a collection of bottles made of skins from Cutch and Ahmedabad.

Div. XIV.—Baskets, Mats, and Straw Work.

[33-48].—Baskets, fans, boxes, mats, &c., from Sawantwari.

Khaskhas embroidered in gold thread and ornamented with quills and beetle-wings.

[4801].—Mats from Bhavnagar.

Used as seats for water vessels carried on woman's head.

[4802-4822].—Baskets and mats from Aden.

[384-387].—Cane baskets, &c., from the Ratnagiri and Thana Jails.

BARODA.

Div. I.-III.—Photographs, Etc.

[230-236, 241, 242].

Photographic views of some of the principal streets of Baroda, and of places where cloth is printed and brick and pottery work done. One of the photographs represents a state procession at Baroda, headed by the Maharaja seated on an elephant, with a golden howdah and canopy.

Div. IV.—Fine Art.

Gold and Silver Work, Jewellery, &c.

[301-375, 401-403]. — Amreli *lotas*, cups, rose-water vase, Baroda necklaces, anklets, plates, head ornaments, hookahs, model of an elephant with howdah, &c.

The numerous gold and silver articles are mostly ornaments in common use amongst Gujratis and Marathis. A silver hookah with raised burier is particularly worthy of notice. The model of an elephant and howdah is made of solid silver, and is a copy of the elephant and howdah used by H. H. the Gaekwar on state occasions.

Div. V.—Art Manufactures in Metal.

3. *Brass, Copper and Mixed Metals.*

[410–430].—Salvers, bullocks, worshipping set, peacocks, lamp-stands, &c.

Among the numerous brass exhibits may be noticed a complete set of articles used by the Hindoos when worshipping their household gods. The locks made in Baroda are very interesting samples of finished blacksmith's work.

5. *Arms and Armour.*

[459–502].—Axe, hatchet, dagger, shields, bow and arrows, sword-handles, lance, club, &c.

Among the articles of armoury may be noticed some fine samples of inlaid gold, silver and ivory work of a decorative character, also some old arms lent by the Baroda Durbar.

6. *Cutlery.*

[512–517].—Nut-crackers, screw-knife, &c.

Div. VI.—Art Manufactures in Wood, Ivory, Etc.

Wood Work.

[251–262, 518–614].—Cloth printing blocks, artificial fruits, lacquered works, Billimora inlaid sandal wood, ivory and tin work, pigeon-house, Dumni wood images, *rath*, backwall, &c.

The pigeon house is elaborately carved, and is in imitation of the Indo-Saracenic style of architecture. The lacquered articles of the Sunkheda wood turners show an application of an old industry, capable of much larger development. The bullock-carriage is a rich pattern of silver inlaid and enamelled work, and is used by the Hindu aristocracy. The *rath* is a model of a curious old-fashioned carriage, now rapidly becoming obsolete. The inlaid sandal and ivory boxes are made at Billimora, in the Southern Division of the Baroda State, where large business is done in these articles. The backwall is a fine kind of carved work representing some of the designs found on the front of native houses. The door is particularly well carved.

Horn.

[214].—Carved and polished horn in shape of a peacock.

Div. VIII.—Marble and Stone.

3. *Stone.*

[615–623.]—An old temple in miniature size, box, rings, &c.

Div. IX.—Pottery.

[631–680].—Water-jugs, toys, flower-vases, hookahs, &c.

The pottery work is an old industry of Patan, where one family is said to possess the secret—capable of further development.

Div. X.—Glass.

[750–793].—Glass, &c., bangles of different sorts.

Large collection of glass bangles made at Baroda, much worn in Gujarat.

Div. XI.—Textiles.

[801–942].—Women's garment, ***Musroos***, caps, stockings, gloves, purse, *saris*, &c.

The textile fabrics contain many noticeable patterns of designs for cotton and silk garments.

Div. XII.—Embroideries.

[969–1000].—Teapoy covers, waistcoat, caps, bodices, horse saddlery.

The embroidered articles contain a complete set of native silver saddlery used by noblemen of Baroda. The gold, silver and silk embroidery work is also worthy of note.

Div. XIII.—Fragrant Plants.

[215–218].—Fans.

Used in the hot weather. When the grass part is wetted it gives a fragrant smell.

Div. XIV.—Perfumery.

[1–12].—Attar.

The attars are highly concentrated essences of Indian flowers, herbs, &c. Some contain essence drawn from earth, giving the fresh smell of the ground after a first shower of rain The essences are so rich that but few drops are required to make an ordinary bottle of scent.

BENGAL.

Div. I.—Fine Arts.

The art of painting as practised by the natives of Bengal has not as yet reached any very great excellence. The paintings from Puri and Shahabad are most worth notice as illustrating the indigenous art of the country. Those from the Calcutta Art Studio show more finish and training. The engravings and lithographs shown by the studio should also be noticed. The Calcutta School of Art are exhibiting in the Educational Court specimens of the work of this nature done by pupils. Mr. Scott has sent his paintings, at the request of the Committee, to complete their set of illustrations of the scenery of Bengal.

Photography is practised by several European and native firms in Calcutta. The latter are not as a rule successful, and no specimens of their work are shown. Messrs. Bourne and Shepherd have lent the collection of photographs mentioned below.

1. *Paintings.*

[1007-1014].—From Darjiling.

These paintings were executed by Tibetans, and are in the style of those used for decorating the interiors of Tibetan monasteries. No. 1014, illustrative of the Buddist belief in purgatory is worth notice. Accompanying it is a translation to which reference should be made.

A set of paintings of Darjiling and Bengal scenery by Mr. A Scott.

From Kalighat.—A set of mythological and other paintings.

[7, 10, 662].—From Puri.

Executed by Uriyas, illustrating the figure of the temple of Jagannáth and the ceremonies performed therein, and other mythological subjects.

[101].—From Shahabad.

A set of mythological paintings.

3. *Photographs, &c.*

A set of photographs taken by Mr. T. F. Peppe, illustrating the handicrafts of Behar.

A set of photographs and scenery and architectural remains in Bengal.

A set of photographs of Darjiling and Bengal scenery taken by Messrs. Bourne and Shepherd, Calcutta.

[2203].—From Dinapur.

A set of designs cut out in paper by Moulvi Karim Baksh.

4. *Sculpture.*

Small figures of deities and animals are carved out of stone in Gaya, Dainhát, and other places. They have been classed under Division VIII. Section 1. Sculpture has, however, almost died out in Bengal. The temples of Orissa and the ruins in Chutia Nagpur and elsewhere prove that in ancient times sculpture was a flourishing industry. Images of gods and goddesses, desecrated by Kálapahár, lie scattered at Jájpur and other places in Orissa, and the temples are adorned with images sculptured out of red sandstone. Formerly the sculptors of Dainhát, a town in Bardwán, annually turned out a large number of images of Krishna and the Sivaite symbols, but the trade has declined. The Hindu caste engaged in sculpturing is called *Bhaskar*. Stucco mouldings are found on many houses in Bengal. Those in Dacca are most remarkable for their beauty. The specimens shown were obtained with difficulty, as the work is but little in demand and the industry is dying out.

[268-272].—Stucco mouldings from Dacca.

No. 268 has been lent by Babu Mohim Chandra Basák of Dacca.

Div. II.—Decorative Art.

4. *Models in Clay.*

The Krishnagarh clay models are the best in Bengal. This industry had its origin in the manufacture of idols, and gradually extended its scope to the representation of native social life and of mythological scenes. The establishment of the Krishnagarh trade is said to be due to Dr. Archer, but it has received a great impetus from the encouragement given to it at the Calcutta International Exhibition of 1883-84. The models from Nadiyá mentioned below are good specimens of this work. The life-sized figures placed in the other Indian courts, and constructed under the orders of the Revenue and Agricultural Department of the Government of India have been made entirely by Krishnagarh modellers. In Calcutta clay models are made of an inferior description. They are, however, in some cases covered with tinsel work, and the effect is remarkably good. The figures of Kali and Durga shown in the court are good examples.

Clay models of fruit, &c., are made in Saran, Muzaffarpur, Dacca, Bardwán, and other places, but they are not good.

[3877, 3881].—From Calcutta.

No. 3877 represents the figure of the goddess Durgá, wife of the god Siva, the destroyer. The annual festival held in her name in Bengal is known as Durgá Pújá, and forms the greatest holiday amongst the Hindus.

[1577-1580].—From Nadiyá.

Small models of fisherman, bhisti, &c. are made by Rakhaldas Pal of Ghurni in Krishnagarh, a sub-division of Nadiyá district. No. 1578 is a model of an indigenous *páthsálá* of Bengal. No. 1579 is a model of a Krishnagarh market called Goáribázár.

[580, 582, 602, 648, 663, 665, 667, 672 and

689].—From Púri, models of gateways of the temple of Jagannáth and some surrounding temples at Púri.

Nos. 582, 689, 665, and 663 are respectively the north, south, east, and west gates of the famous temple at Puri. The main gate in the east is called *Sinhadvár* or the "Lion gate." No. 666 is a collection of models of Jagannáth or the "Lord of the world" and his companions, such as Suvadrá, Balarám, and Sudarsan, with Lakshmi and Sarasvati. Nos. 580, 581 and 667 are temples of Bimalá (one of the innumerable manifestations of Durga), Lakshmi, the goddess of wealth, and Sarasvati, the Indian muse. No. 648 is tho *Múktí-mandap* or the "Platform of salvation."

[**106, 107, 139** and $\frac{311}{183}$].—From Sarun; models of pumpkins, *karela*, orange and *ákrot*.

Presented to the Government of Bengal by Mahárájá Krishna Pratab Sahai of Hatwa. The imitation fruits and vegetables exhibited under this head are made of clay, and simply coloured; but those exhibited under Division VI., Section 4, are lacquered.

5 *Decorative Painting as applied to Architecture.*

No. 3873 from Calcutta. is a doorway covered with imported prints. This style of decoration is common to the Marwari and Hindustani shop-keepers of Bengal, who decorate the doors, ceilings, and walls of their shops, &c.. with papers printed with the figures of gods and goddesses of the Hindu mythology.

6. *Decorative Painting as applied to articles of Domestic use.*

No. 2183, from Gayá, painted earthen pots. Three painted earthen pots which have been lent by Babu Bihárilál Bárik of Gayá. Some artistic taste is shown in the painting.

No. 1539. from 24-Parganás. is a collection of painted earthen pots purchased from Kálighát, one of the chief shrines of Bengal, situated some two miles south of Calcutta. The painting and the pottery are both very rough.

8. *Works of Decorative Art.*

[3675, 3676].—From Dinajpur, artificial fruits made of pith.

In this class may be included the moulded bricks and encaustic tiles found in old temples in Bengal. The decorations on the Hindu and Muhammadan screens are good examples of this style of work.

[669].—From Puri, a pith model of Balarám's car.

Pith models and ornaments are made in Puri and Dinajpur. No finish or artistic excellence is shown in the work, which is remarkably rude and gaudy.

Div. III.—Musical Instruments.

Exhibited by Rajah Sir Sourindro Mohan Tagore, Kt., Mus. Doc., C.I.E.

The following list is taken from a catalogue drawn up by him, and his classification has been adhered to. The Rajah wishes the collection to be presented, after the close of the Exhibition, to some public institution in Great Britain.

1. *Stringed Instruments* (*Tata Yantra*).

A. *Drawing-room Instruments.*

(*a*) Played upon with a *mizrab* (steel plectrum).

[4001].—*Mahatí Vina.*

A very ancient instrument said to have been invented by the Sage Národa. It is the best and most difficult of all Hindu musical instruments.

[4002].—*Kachchhapí Vina.*

A classical instrument known at present as *Kachuá Setár.* The instrument owes its name to the shape of the gourd which is flat like the back of the *Kachchhapi* (tortoise).

[4003].—*Tritantri Vina.*

Also an ancient instrument: now going by the general name of *Setár* (or "three wires") given to it by Amir Khusru in the 13th century. The hollow of this instrument is sometimes made of wood. In other respects the instrument is just like the *Kachchhapí.* Originally it had three wires.

[4004].—*Bipanchi Vina.*

The hollow of this instrument is made of a peculiar kind of gourd known in Bengal as the *Tith Láu.*

[4005].—*Sur-bahara.*

A large-sized *Kachchhapí Víná*, invented about 60 years ago by Gulam Muhammed Khan of Lucknow. It is especially adapted for the playing of *Klápas*, *Rágas*, and *Ráginis.*

[4006].—*Shauktika Vina.*

The hollow of this instrument is made of mother-o'-pearl. In every other respect it is just like the *Kachchhapí.*

[4007].—*Bharata Vina.*

A modern instrument, formed out of the *Rudra and Kachchhapí Víná.*

[4008].—*Nadesvara Vina.*

A very modern instrument, formed out of the violin and *Kachchhapi Víná.*

[4009].—*Kairata Vina.*

The instrument has one gourd and six frets. It is something like the *Mahatí Víná.*

(*b*) Played upon with an iron *jawa* (plectrum).

[4010].—*Prasaraní Vina.*

The instrument is a *Tritantí Víná*, with two finger-boards. A modern invention.

[4011].—*Sur-Sringara.*

The instrument is a combination of the *Mahatí*, *Kachchapí*, and *Rudra Víná*, devised by the celebrated *Víná*-player, Piyár Khan.

(*c*) Played upon with a wooden *jawa* (plectrum).

[4012].—*Rudra Vina.*

The instrument is known at present as *Rabáb*, and in Arabia as *Rubeb.* It is extensively used in Persia, Afghanistan, and the North-Western Provinces of India.

[4013].—*Saradiya Vina.*
The *Sarod*, by which name the instrument is known at present, is mostly used in the Upper Provinces. It was formerly used as an outdoor instrument in royal processions.

(*d*) Played upon with a bow.

[4014].—*Sarangi.*
A very sweet-toned ancient instrument intended to accompany the female voice. The instrument is generally used in performances of Hindustani Nautch-girls.

[4015].—*Alabu Sarangi.*
Called by some European writers on Hindu music "The Indian Violin." The surface of this instrument is like that of the violin, having a hollow gourd under it. The instrument is known to be a very old one.

[4016].—*Taus* or *Mayuri.*
A form of the *Esrár.* The instrument derives its name from the figure of the peacock (*Mayur*) which is attached to the end of the hollow.

[4017].—*Mina Sarangi.*
Another form of the *Esrár.* With the exception of the finger-board, the whole instrument is made of one entire piece of gourd. The instrument derives its name from the figure of the fish (*Mína*) which is attached to the end of the hollow.

[4018].—*Sursanga.*
The instrument is formed out of the *Esrár* and *Setár.* In fact, it is the *Esrár* without the side wires. The first instrument of this kind is said to have been made by Sebaram Dass of Vishnupur (an ancient city of Bengal).

(*e*) Played upon with the tips of the fingers.

[4019].—*Tumburu Vina.*
Better known as *Tumburu.* The invention of this instrument is attributed to the celestial musician Tumburu. The instrument is intended to accompany vocal or instrumental performances, and is the indicator of the key-note adopted.

[4020].—*Mochanga.*
A very ancient instrument. It has to be held with the teeth, by means of the left hand, and the wire to be gently tapped with the fore-finger of the right hand. The instrument gives only one note.

B. *Pastoral Instruments.*

(*a*) Played upon with a wooden *jawa* (plectrum).

[4021].—*Ananda Lahari.*
An instrument mostly used by singing beggars. It consists of one cat-gut, the variety of sounds produced by which is due to the different degrees of tension to which it is subjected.

(*b*) Played upon with a bow.

[4022].—*Sarindi.*
A rude form of the *Sárangí*, and known to be an ancient instrument; now generally used by *Durwáns* (door-keepers), &c.

[4023].—*Chikara.*
The instrument is generally used by *Durwáns*, *Syces* (grooms), &c., &c. The strings of the instrument are made of horse-hair.

(*c*) Played upon with the tip of the finger.

[4024].—*Ektara.*
Used exclusively by *Vairágís* and *Báuls* (religious mendicants), for accompanying pastoral songs. The instrument is mounted with one string.

[4025].—*Gopiyantra.*
Used exclusively by *Vairágís* and *Báuls* (religious mendicants), for accompanying pastoral songs. The instrument is mounted with one string, the different sounds being produced by the compression or otherwise of the fingers with which the lower part of the instrument is held.

Wind Instruments (*Sushira Yantra*).

A. *Drawing-room Instruments.*

"Flute" species.

[4026].—*Bansi.*
The Indian flute, made of bamboo wood. The invention of the instrument is ascribed to the Hindu Deity Krishṇa, who is said to have been very fond of it.

[4027].—*Sarala Bansi.*
The Indian flageolet. The instrument has to be held straight before the mouth when played upon.

[4028].—*Laya Bansi.*
Like the *Sarala Bansi.* The instrument has to be held straight before the mouth; but it has to be blown into from one extremity of the lips.

[4029.]—*Benu.*
The *Benu* is a popular instrument with the people of Orissa. A classical instrument, about four feet six inches in length, and made of bamboo wood.

B. *Outdoor Instruments.*

(*a*) "Reed" species.

[4030].—*Kalama.*
So called, because of its likeness to the *Kalam* (pen).

[4031].—*Shanayi.*
As played in the *Nahabat.* The *Nahabat* is an Indian brass band played on festive occasions and marriage processions. The musicians are invariably made to sit on an elevated position, generally over gates or triumphal arches, &c. This band had its origin in the Muhammadan period, and is still in use. The *Shánáyí*, called *Sharná* in Persian, is said to have been a favourite instrument with the Moghul Emperor Akbar Shah.

[4032].—*Shanayi.*
As used by the people of Orissa.

(*b*) "Horn" species.

[4033].—*Sringa.*
The Indian horn. The instrument is said to have been a favourite of the Hindu Deity Siva.

[4034].—*Rana Sringa.*
An instrument formerly used in military bands. It is now used in religious processions.

[4035].—*Turi.*
The Indian trumpet; used on occasions of war, and also with the *Nahabat.*

C. *Used in Religious Service.*

"Shell" species.

[4036].—*Sankha.*

A very ancient instrument, formerly used on warlike, religious, and festive occasions; now only on the latter. This instrument might, not inappropriately, be called the father of wind instruments. In days of yore, *Sankhas* of various descriptions were in use, such as the *Pánchajanya* (used by Krishna), *Devadatta* (used by Arjjúna), &c. The *Sankha* is also used in Buddhist temples. The instrument is sometimes called by Europeans the "conch trumpet."

[4037].—*Gomukha.*

Another kind of conch, somewhat resembling the mouth of the cow, whence it derives its name.

[4038].—*Barataka.*

A large-sized conch made of the *Káwri* shell.

D. *Pastoral Instruments.*

With double tubes.

[4039].—*Tubri.*

Called *Tiktiri* in Sanskrit. A rude instrument used by snake-charmers.

3. Percussion Instruments made of Metals (*Ghana Yantra*).

A. *Drawing-room Instruments.*

[4040].—*Mandira.*

The sound of this instrument is produced by two cups made of bell-metal striking against each other. The *Mandirá* is used to measure out the time in a musical performance.

[4041].—*Khattali.*

The castanets of the Hindus. The instrument consists of two steel bars.

B. *Used in Religious Service.*

[4042].—*Ghanta.*

A ringing bell used at the time of worship.

4. *Pulsatile Instruments covered with Skin* (*Anaddha Yantra*).

A. *Drawing-room Instruments.*

Played upon with the hands.

[4043].—*Mridanga.*

An ancient instrument, said to have been invented by the Hindu Deity Brahmá. The *Mridanga* is intended to accompany classical forms of songs and hymns. It is sometimes played with the *Mahatí Víná*, *Rudra Víná*, &c.

[4044].—*Dholaka.*

The *Dholaka* is generally used to accompany songs sung in *Játtrá*, *Pánchálí*, *Half-Akrái*, and other semi-operatic performances.

[4045].—*Banya* and *Tabla.*

The *Bányá* is played upon with the left hand and the *Tablá* (sometimes called the *Dáhiná*) with the right. This pair is a modern invention; the idea being taken from the *Mridanga*, the left end of which is represented by the *Bányá*, and the right end by the *Tablá.*

B. *Used in Religious Service.*

[4046].—*Dhak.*

Formerly known as *Dhakká*, and used in the war-field, but now the instrument is used on occasions of religious festivities, such as the *Durgá Pujá*, *Charak Pujá*, &c. The right-hand side of the instrument is played upon with two sticks. The left-hand side is not touched at all.

[4047].—*Khol.*

Chiefly used to accompany the *Kírtana* and other religious songs.

C. *Pastoral Instruments.*

[4048].—*Dindimi.*

A smaller variety of the *Khanjaní.*

[4049].—*Jhanjh Khanjani.*

The instrument is supplied with two small cymbals which make a jingling sound when it is struck upon.

[4050].—*Nyastaranga.*

The *Nyástaranga*, a trumpet-shaped instrument, has to be placed upon the vocal chords, sounds from which produce by vibration a clear reedy note upon the instrument. It is believed that an instrument of this description is scarcely to be met with in any other part of the world than India. It is known in Sanskrit as the "*Upánga*," and is extensively used by Hindus in the North-Western Provinces, and particularly at Mathurá and Brindában.

(*a*) Works composed or edited by Rajah Sir S. M. Tagore, Kt., C.I.E.

English.

[4185].—Six Principal Rágas of the Hindus.

With lithographic illustrations. Original. Royal 4to., pages 110.

[4186]. — Eight Principal Rágas of the Hindus.

With lithographic illustrations. Original. Royal 4to., pages 162.

[4187]. — Ten Principal Avatáras of the Hindus.

With lithographic illustrations. Original. Royal 4to., pages 157.

Sanskrit.

[4188].—The Five Principal Musicians of the Hindus.

A brief exposition of the essential elements of Hindu music, as set forth by the five Celestial musicians of India. An offering to the Fifth International Congress of Orientalists, held in Berlin, in September, 1881. Royal 4to., pages 28.

English, with Sanskrit and Bengali Translations.

[4189].—The National Anthem.

Translated into Sanskrit and Bengali verses and set to twelve varieties of Indian melody. Demy 4to., pages 32.

1. *Wind Instruments.*

[923 & 990].—From Darjiling.

These are received from Tibet. No. 923 is a flute made of human bone. No. 990, a pair of trumpets. Used to call the Tibetans to worship.

[3483].—From Midnapur.

No. 3483 is a copper horn, locally called *shinga* (from *shringa*, a horn). It is generally used by the Vishnavites, or the followers of Vishnu, when singing their holy songs, *sankirtans*. It was purchased in the Calcutta bazaar.

3. *Instruments of Percussion.*

[3484].—From Cuttack.

Gongs are extensively manufactured in the district of Cuttack. No. 3484 is an ordinary one purchased in the Calcutta bazar.

DIV. IV.—JEWELLERY.

Gold and Silversmiths' Work, including Filigrain, &c.

Dacca, Cuttack, and Calcutta are the chief centres in Bengal of the manufacture of jewellery, though jewellers are found in nearly every bazar. The higher classes wear gold jewellery, which is made chiefly in Calcutta. The different shapes of gold jewellery most worn are shown in the collection of cheap jewellery mentioned in sub-section *a*. It is said that the demand for Dacca silver ware has increased of late, while that for Cuttack ware has diminished. The Hill Tipperah work is very like that made in Cuttack, and is also worth notice.

[461–557, 3062–3285]. — Cuttack — filigrain and silver wire ware, personal ornaments, baskets, boxes, *áttardán*, and *guláLpásh*, &c.

Jewellery to suit European taste, such as necklets and necklaces, bracelets, lockets, pendants, and brooches, hair-pins, shoe-buckles, and other articles, are extensively manufactured for export. *Attardáns*, *gulábpáshes*, and *pánbáttás* are in considerable demand among the natives of Bengal.

[231–233, 368–370]. — Dacca — silver wire ware, personal ornaments, boxes, *huká*, and models of elephant, house, &c.

Nawáb Ahsanullá has lent a very good collection. No. 233, a silver box, is one of the most remarkable features.

[1018, 1020, 1028, 1032, and 1038].—Darjiling—personal ornaments, necklaces and pin for tying ladies' cloth, &c.

No. 1018 is made at Sikkim, 1032 at Bhutan, the rest in Tibet.

[2031, 3678–3880]. — Dínájpur — gold and silver ornaments.

Exhibited by the Máháráján of Dínájpur.

[1125, 1126]. – Monghyr—silversmith's work, not being personal ornaments.

Silver fishes.

[1864 (three different sorts)].—Rájsháhí—silver ornaments.

[1456–1468].—Hill Tipperah—silver wire work, personal ornaments, flower-vase, envelope case, &c.

A good collection has been lent by the State of Hill Tipperah. No. 1456, an envelope case, is worthy of special notice.

Sub-section a.

1502–1516, 3452, 3455–3473].—Calcutta—cheap jewellery, consisting of personal ornaments made in metal and gilted.

The ornaments exhibited under this head are chiefly used by women who are too poor to afford real gold or silver ornaments, and by native dancers and singers. The articles are brought from Bonpásh Kámárpara in the district of Bardwán, a seat of some expert *kámárs* (blacksmiths), some of whom carry on their manufacture hereditarily, to Calcutta, where they are washed and gilded by Muhammadans, who are the professional electroplaters of Bengal.

Metal Ornaments.

[925, 926, and 969].—From Darjiling, coat and shawl fasteners, bracelets, &c.

Made in Tibet.

[1952–1960].—From Dinájpur.

[36, 43, 44, 47–50, 54, 55, 2186–2188, 2190].—From Gayá.

Collected by Dr. R. Macleod.

[2689 and 2691].—From Patna.

[1288, 1289, 1291–1298].—From Santál Parganás.

Nos. 1289, 1291 to 1293, 1295, 1297, and 1298 have been presented to the Government of Bengal by the sub-divisional officer of Pákaur.

[$\frac{87}{10}$–$\frac{87}{31}$, $\frac{87}{40}$–$\frac{87}{49}$].—From Sarun.

The whole of the collection under this head has been presented to the Government of Bengal by Mahárájá Krishna Pratab Sahai Bahadur of Hatwa.

[102–108].—From Shahabad.

Sub-section b.

Glass, Lac, and Horn Ornaments, Plain and Tinsel Work.

[2193, 2804, and 3012–3019].—From Bhagalpur.

[3422, 3424–3430, 3432, 3434, 3435, 3438–3451, 3453, 3454 (?)].—From Calcutta.

The manufacture of bangles is a thriving industry. The set shown comprises nearly all the different patterns in general use.

[3423, 3431, 3433, 3436, 3437]. — From Cuttack.

Purchased in Calcutta bazaar; said to be made in Cuttack.

[208].—From Darbhangah.

[1951].—From Dinájpur.

Sub-section c.

[2172].—Gayá crystal beads (worn as necklaces).

Div. V.—Art Manufactures in Metal.

1. *Gold and Silver Plate Wares.*

But little gold or silver plate work is executed by the natives of Bengal. Their forte lies rather in filigrain. A large collection is shown and catalogued under Division IV, Section 1.

[1021, 1036, and 1037.—From Dárjíling.

Nos. 1021 and 1037 are cups with covers, respectively called *phorpa* and *rukta*. No. 1036 is a case for an image. These were made in Tibet.

[2947].—From Murshidábád.—An *árákdan*.

3. *Brass, Copper, and Mixed Metal Wares.*

[3612-3621].—From Bírbhúm, plates, cups, dishes, water-pots, washing basins, ewer, spoons, &c.

The estimated value of No. 3612, two pairs of *tasturi* (dishes), No. 3614, three cups, and No. 3621, three pairs of spoons, is Rs. 10.

[4217-4231]. — From Calcutta Government School of Art, plates, *lotahs*, and cups, &c.

A collection of copper *repoussé* work made by the students of the Government School of Art, Calcutta. No. 4218, a water-vessel, popularly called *dawthunay ghati*, is much used in Orissa. No. 4219, *karanga ghati*, a speciality of the Nadiya district, is used by mendicants. No. 4226 is a plate for offering *pushpa* or flowers to the deities, and hence called *pushpa-pátra*. The central figure in it represents the figure of Vishnu, the preserving principle of the Hindu trinity. Nos. 4227-4230 are small cups for holding *chandan* or the sandal-wood paste for devotional purposes. No. 4231 is a *támra kúnda* or copper bowl used for giving baths to the favourite Hindu god *Sálgram*. All the articles exhibited under this head have been made by Babu Saratchandra Dás except No. 4221, a *lota*, made by Babu Upendranath Dás. No. 4217 is a shield made of brass. In design it is the same as No. 4216 exhibited under Section 8 of Division V.

2. *Damascened Work, Bidri Ware.*

The name of this ware is said to be derived from Bidar, a town in Hyderabad, from which place the industry is reported to have been introduced into Bengal. The best bidri ware in the Lower Provinces is made in Purniah. Babu Maheslal of that town says that it has been in existence in that district for about 200 years. There is a very marked difference between the ware as manufactured in Bidar and in Purniah. In Bidar the ground colour is as a rule white, while the ornamental patterns are in black; in Purniah the ground is black, the tracings and figures being of silver and white. No. 2997 lent by the Nawab of Murshidabad is, however, a *hukka* with black ground, the inlaid metal being gold. The annual outturn of this ware is declining in Bengal, the reason is probably a change in the tastes of the people. The cost of bidri-ware is high, and those who can afford the luxury seem to prefer plain silver utensils to those made of *bidri*.

[2949 ,2950, 2956, 2957, 2960, 2976, 2977, and 2984].—From Murshidabad, *húká* inlaid with gold and silver, and *sarposh*, or cover for *chillam*, plate, &c.

The last three specimens are lent by the Nawab Názim of Murshidábád.

[2595-2599].—From Patna, *húká, khásdán, ábkhorá*, &c.

Nos. 2595-2507 are lent by Moulvi Syed Fazal Imán, No. 2598 by Hawab Syed Welayet Ali Khan, C.I.E., and No. 2599 by Babu Rai Jaikrishna.

[1176-1182, 2001-2019, 3403, & 3404].—From Purniah, *húká, pándán, tasturi, gelás*, &c.

Nos. 3403 and 3404 are lent by Babu Maheshlal of Purniah. Nos. 2018 and 2019 are also lent respectively by Babu Dharam Chand and Syed Reza Ali, of Purniah.

3. *Brass, Copper, and Mixed Metal Wares.*

Vessels of bell-metal, brass, or copper are used in every native household. Hindus use brass and bell-metal ware for domestic purposes, and copper for religious purposes. Muhammadans prefer tinned-copper vessels. Brass or bell-metal ware is made in most of the towns of Bengal. Khankra near Murshidabad and Jhanjharpur near Darbhangah have the best reputation for plain polished work. The shapes are generally good, but little or no carved work is done. Hugli, Gayá, Moharbhanj, and Calcutta are the only places where there is any carving worth notice, and it cannot bear comparison with that executed in other provinces. The cut figures of gods and goddesses from Gayá and Moharbhanj are quaint in design, but without finish.

[1625-1627]. — From Bírbhúm, waterpots, *húkas*, cups, dishes, spoons.

[1544, 1545, 1594, 3477, 3480, 3481, 3486-3488 3820-3826, 3828-3832, 3836-3838, 3842, 3843, 3846-3848, 3850, 3851, 3853-3860, 3867, 3872, 3882, 3887-3889, 3891-3894].—From Calcutta, spittoons, water-cups, drinking-vessels, *chillumchis*, plates, large bowls, &c.

This collection has been purchased in the Calcutta bazar. It consists of articles manufactured in Calcutta city or brought from the districts of Bánkurá, Bardwán, Howrah, Midnapur, and Murshidabad. Nos. 3847 and 3848, two large brass spittoons (*pikdán*) and smaller ones of the same form, are specialities of the village of Belur in the Howrah district; Nos. 3837, 3838, 3882, *chillamchis* or washing bowls, and the *pushpa pátras* or copper plates for offering flowers to the gods, are only manufactured in Calcutta; *pánbáttá* No. 3850, and *karanga ghoti* No. 3858, are specimens of best bell-metal articles manufactured in the district of Murshidabad; No. 3867 a copper *chakra* was made in Simla, Calcutta. It was intended for the crowning piece of a temple dedicated to Siva; No. 3887 a collection of bell-metal wares of Murshidabad is exhibited by the Superintendent, Zoological Gardens, Calcutta.

[201-204].—From Darbhangah, ewers and betel-boxes.

These are manufactured in Jhanjharpur. No. 201 is an ewer having a long neck and a spout, locally called *jhari*; No. 202 with a short neck and a spout like the first is called *madhosinghi.*

[919-922, 927, 928, and 1025].—From Darjiling.

These are used for *pújá* services by the Llámás of Tibet. No. 919 is a copper pot used for holding holy water; No. 920 is a brass lamp used for Tibetan monasteries; No. 921, *mani*, is a prayer wheel made of brass and copper; No. 922 is a bell-striker used in worship. Nos. 927 and 928 are needle cases used by the Tibetans; No. 1025 is a case for keeping images.

[45/34, 46, 2184/48, 53/49, **98**, and **99**.]—From Gayá.

Nos. 45/34, **98** and **99** are plates stamped with foot prints of Vishnu; they are called *Vishnupáds.*

[1564-1566, 1568, 1569, 1571, 1573-1575, 1590, 1591, and 1595].—From Hugli, ewer, jugs, glass, dishes, and *lotahs*, &c.

These are manufactured in Jehanabad subdivision of the district of Hugli.

[716-719, 727, 722, 746-748, 764-767, 769, 2953-2955].—From Murshidabad, plates, dishes, cups, water-pots, and betel-boxes, &c.

[2312/3 and 2812].—From Patna.

[1183, 3362/2020, 3405, 3406].—From Purniah.

These are *sarposhes*, or covers of *chillams*, for smoking. Both brass (1183 and 3362/2020) and copper (3405 and 3406) are used for this manufacture.

[1894, 1895].—From Rangpur.

Nos. 1894 and 1895 are known as *chilmári* cups owing to the fact of their having been manufactured in Chilmari, a *thάná* in Rangpur district. No. 1894 is a nest of nine bell-metal cups, locally called *gánjá bati*, and No. 1895 is a tumbler with a cup below and another at the top with a small plate covered over with a conical cover. The latter is called *ganja gelás*, and is generally used for carrying tiffin, &c. These have been presented to the Government of Bengal by Babu Shyamá Charan Rai, naib of Báhárbanda, in the district of Rangpur.

[86/3 & 86/9, 86/11, 86/13, 86/15, and 86/17].—From Sarun.

Sub-section a.

Metal Images of Hindu Deities.

[3474, 3476, 3478, and 3479].—From Calcutta.

These were collected from the Calcutta bazaar and are said to be made in Moharbhanj near Cuttack.

2163/21, 2165/25, 3/26, 37/27, 38/28, 39/29, 51/30, 40/31, 52/32, **85**, **95**, and **97**.]—From Gayá.

[1898].—Tinsel work, from Rangpur.

This is a *mukut* or headdress of the goddess Durga. The framework is made of *sola* (pith), the decorative work being done with peacock's feathers, talc and tinsel embroideries. It has been presented by Babu Govindalál Rai, a zemindar of Rangpur district.

8. *Electroplated Wares.*

Electroplating of old articles is done by several native firms in Calcutta.

[4216].—From Calcutta Government School of Art, a shield.

Made of copper and electroplated with silver. The design of the shield is taken from the Temple of Jaggannáth at Púri. Made by Babu Bhútnáth Kharmakár, teacher, metal repoussing class, Government School of Art, Calcutta

5. *Arms and Armour.*

The manufacture of arms and armour in Bengal is nearly extinct. In Monghyr a large number of match locks and swords used to be turned out. Specimens of the work are shown in the Imperial Court. With the exception of the swords from Sikkim, no ornamentation is used. Some of the Darjiling *kukaris* have their scabbards covered with silver filigree work.

[1022-1024].—From Darjiling, swords with cases, called *tiring.* They have been received from Sikkim.

[1143].—From Monghyr, spearhead.

[2985].—From Murshidábád, a *peshkabaz* (knife).

Lent by the Nawab Nazim of Murshidábád.

[4163].—From Mr. G. A. Richardson, Baxár, a sword with a cloth covering.

[110, 111, 113].—From Shahabad, mace, sword, and dagger.

6. *Cutlery.*

But little cutlery is made in Bengal except the rudest description. Prem Chand Mistri, of Hanchanagur, in the Bardwán district, makes scissors, knives, &c., for the Stationery Department of Government. A case of his manufactures is shown in the Imperial Court. The Simhat cutlery is slightly ornamented, and the shapes of the sacrificial knives are remarkable.

[1576, 1596, & 1597].—From Nadiyá, *kátári, dáo, bânti*, &c.

From Simhat, Nos. 1576 and 1597 are chiefly used for cutting cocoa-nuts, splitting bamboos, &c. They are extensively used all over Bengal by *gharámis*, or men employed for erecting huts and bungalows. No. 1596 is used by native women for peeling vegetables and cutting fishes.

[1892].—From Rangpúr, a *kharga*, sacrificial knife.

The colloquial term of *kharga* is *khândá.* It is used for sacrificing animals at the shrines of Hindu deities. It has been presented by Babu Madhusudan Banerji, zemindar of Gopalpur, in Rangpúr district.

[2889].—From Santál Parganás, a *kharga*, sacrificial knife.

Presented to the Government of Bengal by Mr. E. McL. Smith, subdivisional officer, Pákaur, Santál Parganás.

[**1475**].—From Tipperah Hill Tracts, *kharga* (sacrificial knife).

Presented to the Government of Bengal by His Highness the Maháráján of Hill Tipperah.

Div. VI.—Art Manufactures in Wood, Ivory, Etc.

2. *Inlaid Work.*

Monghyr is the only district where inlaid wood work is executed. It consists of highly-polished ebony inlaid with ivory. The demand for this work is but small and is apparently diminishing. It is reported that there are but six or eight carpenters (Hindus) now engaged in the industry, and that a large number of men who used to do this work are now employed on the East Indian Railway—an occupation that is more lucrative than the indigenous industry of the town.

[1113, 1114, 1117-1124].—From Monghyr, desk, bracket, ruler, watch-case, and plaques, &c.

No. 1119, a desk, is perhaps the best-executed specimen.

3. *Ivory Carving.*

The ivory carving of Murshidabad is said to be the best in Bengal, but the work is carried on also in Patna, Dacca, Orissa, Rangpur, Hill Tipperah, and Sarun. The style of the Murshidabad carvings is somewhat conventional and lacks life. Some native chiefs in Behar and Orissa employ artists on this work. The Murshidabad work is fostered by the Maharani Swarnamáyi, M.C.I., and the Nawab of Murshidabad. It is, however, said to be on the decline. The ivory fans and mat-work shown were made in Bengal, though it is probable that this class of the industry was imported from Assam.

[2075 & 2077].—From Chittagong, chess-men and buttons.

[597, 598, 600, & 604].—From Cuttack, stick, watch-case, chain, and snuff-box.

No. 597, a stick, is a fair specimen of Cuttack ivory-carving.

[235].—From Dacca.

A fan lent by Nawab Ahsanullah of Dacca. An ivory mat also lent by the Nawáb is catalogued in Division XIV.

[1933-1935].—From Dinajpur, models of goddess Durga, a bullock cart, and a native woman going to bathe.

Lent by the Maharaja of Dinajpur and were made in Murshidabad.

[720, 742-745, 751-759, 763, 771, 774, 797, 798, 2912-2924, 2966, 2971-2975, 2980, 2982, 2987, 2988, 2990, 2991, & a *pálki* without number].—From Murshidabad, country bullock carts, *pálkis*, boats, ploughmen and ploughs, gods and goddesses of Hindu mythology, and personal ornaments, &c.

Mahárání Swarnamáyi, of Kasimbazar, M.C.I., has offered No. 798, an elephant with state howdah and figures, and No. 797, a carved stick, as presents to Her Majesty the Queen-Empress of India and His Royal Highness the Prince of Wales, respectively, at the close of the Exhibition. Nos. 2971-2975 and the remaining last six numbers have been lent by the Nawáb Báhádur of Murshidabad.

Among the other carvings are figures of:—

(1) The goddess of *Dassabhujá* (from *dasa*, ten, and *bhuja*, a hand), or ten-handed *Dúrgá* with her attendants; (2) *Hara Párvati*, *i.e.*, *Hara* or *Siva*, the destroying principle of the Hindu Trinity, and his wife *Parvati* (another name of *Durgá*), the *Sakti*, or the principle of energy, with their attendants, *Nandi* and *Bhringi*; (3) *Káli*, one of the innumerable manifestations of *Dúrgá*; (4) Car of *Jagannátha*, or "the Lord of the World," the eighth *avatár* or incarnation of *Vishnu*, the protecting principle of the Hindu Trinity; (5) *Sarasvati*, the Indian muse and the consort of *Brahmá*, the creating principle of the Hindu Trinity; (6) *Ganesa*, the elephant-headed son of *Siva* and *Párvati* and "the god of good luck and remover of difficulties and obstacles," whose help is invoked by the Hindus at the beginning of any new enterprise or literary composition.

[$\frac{2265}{1}$, $\frac{83}{27}$, $\frac{2434}{28}$, $\frac{2436}{30}$, $\frac{2437}{31}$, $\frac{2438}{32}$, & $\frac{2439}{33}$].—From Patna, Bullocks with plough, *palki* with bearer, cow, figure of a *Ganesa*, and card-case, combs, &c.

[1887 & 1888].—From Rangpur.

Fans like No. 235, from Dacca, described previously. These have been lent by Babu Govindalál Rai, Zemindar of Tájhát, Rangpur.

[89].—From Sarun, a pair of armlets.

Presented to the Government of Bengal by Mahárájá Krishna Pratab Sahai, Bahadur, of Hatwa.

[1480 & 1481].—From Tipperah Hill Tracts.

No. 1480, an ivory hat, and No. 1481, an ivory fan are presentations from His Highness the Mahárájá of Hill Tipperah, Agartala, to His Royal Highness the Prince of Wales.

4. *Lacquered Wares.*

3603, 3605-2607].—From Bírbhúm, betel boxes, dishes, lamp-stand, &c.

The lacquered wares of Ilambazar in Birbhum and of Murshidabad are the best in Bengal. The models of fruits and vegetables are not good, nor is much artistic taste shown in the colouring of the other articles, but the surfaces are well polished and evidence care in the manipulation of the lacquer. The only exhibits in this class that have any pretensions to design are the cups and boxes from Patna, but the workmanship on them is so rude and unfinished as to render them hardly worth notice.

[1632].—From Bardwán, models of fruits.

[1601, 1602, 1606, 1621, 1622].—From Bírbhúm, stick, chain, paper-weight, and models of fruits and vegetables, &c.

[2837 & 2839].—From Muzaffarpur, Toy boxes.

[749, 750, 760-762, 2939-2946, 2951, 2952, 3008, 3995, 3997, & 3998].—From Murshidabad, cups, tumblers, sticks, paper-weights, *húká* pipes, and bedstead legs, &c.

Some of the gold-spangled articles, which form the major portion of the collection under this head, are worthy of notice. Of the other lacquered articles, Nos. 2939 and 2942, *Pánch-rangá* (literally meaning five coloured), bedstead legs, and a walking-stick respectively are fair samples.

[2310, 4098, 4099].—From Patna, cups and boxes.

[1190, 1191, 1207, 1208, 1210 & 1216].—From Purniah, cups and vessels of sizes.

Manufactured in Kisoriganj.

[121].—From Shahabad, playing cards.

These cards are made of pieces of talc lacquered and painted.

5. *Wood Carving.*

No specimens of Bengal wood carving have been shown at late exhibitions. From the collection now shown it is evident that the art still exists, though it is not much practised. The Bengalis' skill in carpentry has been recognised, and the models now shown are good samples of it. In Calcutta a large amount of European furniture is made by natives, but it has not been considered necessary to show specimens though the work is good. The Gayá carving or that sent by the Calcutta School of Art is perhaps the best. The Dárjíling doorway and pillars are interesting, as they show the style affected by Tibetans. It is believed that had the Committee received information earlier, it would have been possible to obtain carvings from Orissa and the Hugli district, where it is understood there are many good pieces of old work.

[4184].—From Barakhar, model of one of the Barakhar temples.

The dimensions and details of this model are accurate. It was constructed by Ritter R. Von Schwarz under his personal supervision and on the spot.

[4232-4236].—From Calcutta Government School of Art.

No. 4232 is a *gámbhár* wood (*Gmelina arborea*, Rox.) jewel-box carved after Hindu ornamental designs, by Babu Harish Chandra, the teacher of wood carving in the School of Art, Calcutta. The five copper *repoussé* electro-plated panels fixed on the top and sides are made by Babu Saratchandra Das, a student of the same school. The designs in these are taken from Bhubaneswar temple in Orissa. Nos. 4233 and 4234, two teakwood carved panels, respectively represent carved figures of *Káttáyani*, the martial goddess of the Hindu Pantheon, and *Vabáni*, another incarnation of the same order.

[3624-3626].—From Bírbhúm.

Nos. 3624 and 3625 are figures of women. No. 3626 is a tripod carved out of a single piece of wood.

[3900].—From Cuttack, model of the great temple at Puri.

The model is not supposed to be accurate. It was constructed by Mr. Davis at the Cuttack Government workshops.

[981-983, 985-989, 992-1001, & 1003].—From Dárjíling.

No. 981 is a gateway, and Nos. 982 and 983 are pillars of a Tibetan monastery. The rest are masks used in religious dances by Llamas of Tibet.

From Dinajpur.—Model of the temple of Kantanagar.

The dimensions and details of this model are accurate. It was constructed by Babus Madhub Chunder Ray, Executive Engineer, Public Works Department, and Kali Sankar Chatterjee, Assistant Engineer, Public Works Department, under their personal supervision.

[1931].—From Dinajpur, portion of a carved stone pillar.

Lent by the Mahárájá of Dinajpur.

[$\frac{2180}{52}$, 69 to 74, $\frac{2189}{7379}$, & 4190].—From Gayá.

No. $\frac{2180}{52}$ is an old piece of carving taken from the balcony of a house, and Nos. 69 to 74 are specimens of old wood carving taken from the caves of shop fronts. The first was lent by Most Narayan Sijwarin of Gayá and the other pieces by Babu Bihari Lal Barik.

Nos. $\frac{2189}{7379}$ are pieces of a new doorway made to the order of Dr. R. Macleod, by Bull *mistri* of Gayá at a cost of Rs. 100.

No. 75 on the uppermost piece of the doorway (beginning on the left hand side of the spectator) has carved on it the figure of a peacock, a figure of a decorated horse with rider, the decorated figure of an elephant, and a flower.

No. 76 on the middle piece of the doorway has carved on it in the order named from left to right the figures of two peacocks; a two-headed stag; the figure of Ram Chandra and of Sita; the figure of two peacocks; the figure of Hanuman (monkey god) prostrating before the idol of Bhagwan; a two-headed stag; two peacocks.

No. 77, on the lower piece of the doorway has carved on it in the same order the figure of two hermits worshipping Siva; the figure of Mahadev riding on a bull, with two followers on each side; the figure of Vishnu riding on *garur* (a bird), with the figure of Mahabir standing with a *yadá* (a club) in his hand; the figure of Ganes; the figure of Bhagwan riding on a *garur*, and the figure of Mahabir with a *gada* (club) in his hand; the figure of Mahadeb riding on a bull with two followers; the figure of a three-headed Brahma (the goddess of fire) riding on a swan with two followers.

No. 4190 is a fancy box exhibited by Bíhári *mistri* of Gayá.

[1252, 1253].—From Maldah.

No. 1252 is a copy of a carved door frame of the entrance to a house in Maldah district. No. 1253 is a carved wooden frame.

[2872, 2874].—From Muzaffarpur.

No. 2872 is a portion of a carved cornice of a balcony, and No. 2874 is a carved wooden pillar. Cornices and pillars carved in this style are found on the fronts of houses and shops in Behar.

[4175.]—From Mr. G. A. Richardson, Baxár, a snuff-box.

[115].—From Shahabad, a pair of sandals.

Sub-section a.

Turned Wood Work, Wood, and Horn Ornaments, &c.

[1593/22, 1593/32].—From Hugli, *Húká* pipes, rulers, buttons, &c.

Manufactured in the Jehanabad sub-division of the district.

[2867/13].—From Muzaffarpur, one *húká* pipe.

This is partly embroidered with *khaskhas*.

[1139–1142].—From Monghyr, personal ornaments.

No. 1139 is a set of buffalo horn ornaments; Nos. 1140 and 1141 are ornaments made of ebony; and No. 1142 is a set of betel-nut ornaments—each set consists of a necklace, a pair of bracelets, a pair of earrings, and a brooch.

[91].—From Sarun, a stick.

This is made of betel-nuts joined together. The handle is made of ivory. It is presented by Mahárájá Krishna Pratab Sahai of Hatwa to the Government of Bengal.

Div. VII.—Lapidaries' Work.

1. *Agate, Jasper, and Cornelian Wares, &c.*

[1015–1017].—From Dárjíling, amber necklets.

Called *peshil*, made in Tibet.

2. *Shell Manufactures.*

[1699, 1700, 1743–1751, 1758–1760, 3490, 3491, and **19–21**].—From Bankura, bracelets and rings.

Shell ornaments have been in use in the country from prehistoric times, und even goddesses are said not to have considered it beneath their dignity to decorate themselves with them. A legend exists of a family quarrel in the house of Siva, the great god of eternity, destruction, and regeneration, whose consort, Sakti, the goddess of energy, and the original Mother of the Universe, threatened to leave him because he was too poor to give her a set of shell bracelets. The story is still sung by religious mendicants who obtain as alms a handful of rice from every house visited. The old shell ornaments were very rude and uncouth in construction, being simply thick rings sawn off an entire conch shell, with a little lacquering on the outer surface. The work has, however, improved, and among the specimens sent from Bankura and Dacca may be found many which are really artistic in design and well-finished. Dacca is believed to be the oldest seat of this industry, and the calling in that town is hereditary.

[3623].—From Bírbhúm, bracelets.

[250–259, 357–367].—From Dacca, bracelets, napkin rings, and buttons.

These bracelets are only used by Hindu ladies.

[2021–2030].—From Dinajpur, bracelets, bangles, rings, &c.

These have been exhibited by the Mahárájah of Dinajpur. No. 2022 is a *chur* (bracelet) set with stones.

[1251].—From Maldah, armlet.

[770 (3 pairs)].—From Murshidábád, bracelets.

Div. VIII.—Marble and Stone.

1. *Carved Stone Wares.*

The carved stone ware of Bengal has not much artistic merit. The images made in Bardwán and Gayá are evidently copies of forms that have been handed down from father to son, and have as would be expected, lost any artistic feeling they may once have possessed. The images of animals are but little better than those of deities. The Gayá and Mánbhúm vessels are better, but the former are being spoilt by a tendency to cover them with gilding.

[1634].—From Bardwán.—An image of Sri Krishna.

[2169/11, 2168/12, 2167/13, 2166/14, 2164/15, 28/16, 27/17, 34/19, 29/20, 31/21, 32/22, 33/23, 1527/33–1527/37, 1527/39–1527/68, **80–82**, 3876/83, **84**].—From Gayá, black marble jars, plates, &c., and figures, idols, mendicants, animals, &c.

Gayá Public library has lent a very good collection. The stone wares manufactured by the stone carvers of Gayá, locally called *Song Trash*, are the best of the kind in Bengal. They are purchased to a large extent by pilgrims who visit Gayá.

[1851, 1853, 1854, 1855, 1856, 1857, 1858, 1859, 2112, 2113, 2156, 2157].—From Mánbhúm, plates, dishes, cups, *pán dibás*, lamps, &c.

The district of Mánbhúm stands first in Bengal in producing soap or pot stone utensils. The price of the articles is cheap, and the demand for the plates is large in the district and in the surrounding places.

[8000].—From Monghyr, two large plates.

These have been presented to the Government of Bengal by Messrs. Ambler & Co., of Monghyr. A large collection of their manufactures is shown in the Imperial Court under class C, Division XI.

Div. IX.—Pottery.

The pottery made in Bengal is generally more remarkable for its shape than for its external finish or decoration. The best shapes are found in the collection from Dinajpur. The collection of the manufactures of Messrs. Burn & Co.'s Raniganj Pottery works is worth attention. The pottery in it is decidedly the best in Bengal, though it is not as a rule oriental in character. The Calcutta School of Art while under Mr. Schaumburg's control, commenced a course of instruction in the manufacture of pottery. The specimens shown are made from designs drawn in the school, the pots having been baked in the bazar.

1. *Glazed Pottery.*

[1651–1655, 1657, 1658, 1660, 1663, 1664, 4051–4089, 4301, 4303–4310].—From Bard wán, vases, wall brackets, goblets, tea-cups, milk jugs, ash pots, fern-boxes, tripod garden seats, washing basins, carved ridge and flat, tiles, &c., of sizes for roofing and flooring.

A collection of pottery made at Messrs. Burn & Co.'s Pottery works at Raniganj. Nos. 4057 and 4058, two large arabesque vases, and Nos. 4059 and 4060, a pair of Grecian pattern small vases, deserve special notice. The tiling also is good.

[1556].—From Khulna, a collection of 13 different samples of cups, tea-pots, *huka* bottoms, oil-pots, and *pándibas*.

Made and exhibited by Madhu Sudan Pal, Kánjia village.

[92,93].—From Sarun, a collection of black and red pottery wares, consisting of cups, saucers, flower-pots, goblets, tea-pots, &c.

This trade is carried on in the Sewan sub-division. It is said to have been introduced from Azamgarh, a district in North-Western Provinces, celebrated for this manufacture. The articles exhibited under this head are presented to the Government of Bengal by Mahárájá Krishna Pratab Sahai of Hatwa.

2. *Unglazed Pottery.*

From Bardwán, Statuettes, vases, &c.

Made by Messrs. Burn & Co., Raniganj Pottery works.

[4203–4215].—From Calcutta Government School of Art, vase, flask, bracket, &c.

No. 4203, "Lizard pattern;" No. 4208, "monkey pattern;" No. 4209, "Trinity pattern," *i.e.*, bearing figures of *Brahma*, *Vishnu*, and *Mahesvar*, the creating, preserving, and destroying principles of the Hindu Trinity; No. 4210, "medallion pattern;" No. 4211, *Hangsha* or "swan pattern;" No. 4212, "Lotus pattern;" No. 4213, *Tábiz* or "armlet pattern;" No. 4214, "crown pattern;" and No. 4215, "festoon pattern."

[1936-1941, 1943, 1945, 1946, 1950, 3042, 3043, 3046-3051, 3631, 3632, 3634, 3635, 3638, -3640, 3643-3645, 3650-3655].—From Dinajpur, Water-pots, betel-boxes, oil-pots, *húka*, *chillam* with *sarposh* or cover, lampstand, ink-pots, bowls, incense burner, &c.

Nos. 1936 to 1950 have been received from the Mahárájá of Dinajpur.

[702, 703, 706, 708, 714, 728, 731, 732, 739].—From Murshidabad, goblets, milk-pots, tumblers, cups, &c., grey and black varieties.

[$\frac{2322}{1}$].—From Patna, pots and vessels of sizes, 18 samples.

[**2 & 7**].—From 24-Parganas.

These pots were made in Sundarbans, and presented to the Government of Bengal by Mr. A. Simson, Member, Bengal Exhibition Committee.

DIV. X.—GLASS.

Glass ware is made in most of the villages of Bengal from pieces of broken bottles. The only place where an attempt is made to turn out articles with any pretence to beauty is Patna. Some of the colours and shapes are remarkably good, but the manufacture is still in its infancy, the shapes are not even, and the workmen show a strong inclination to copy designs in catalogues of glass ware sold by European firms. There are but two artizans in Patna who can make this glass, their names are Mya Jahu and Hussain Baksh. Considering that the size of the combined workshop and dwelling-house belonging to either of these men is not more than 15 ft. × 21 ft., and that their appliances are of the rudest description, the results of their work are remarkably good.

[2397, 2537].—From Patna, flower vases, goblets, tea-cups, saucers, jugs, water-pots, glasses, milk jugs, spittoons, *húka* bottoms, &c.

DIV. XI.—TEXTILES.

1. *Cotton Fabric, Plain Muslins.*

With the exception of the celebrated Dacca muslins, *tasar* silks, and the silks of Murshidabad and Bankura, the fabrics of Bengal are not of a high order of excellence. Notwithstanding the supersession of native-made cotton fabrics by the cheaper piece goods of Manchester which has taken place generally throughout the country, the former are still woven in small quantities in every district. The collection of cotton fabrics bought in Howrah Bazar, and those made in Dinajpur and in the Chittagong and Tipperah Hill Tracts show generally the style of native-made cloths worn in Bengal. The colours in the cloths from the Hill Tracts are firm and durable while the designs are generally good. In the collection bought in the Howrah Bazar, it is believed that no Indian dyes with the exception of indigo are used. The twist and the dye is imported and the *dhuti* or *sarí* woven in the villages. The country-woven cloths are more durable than the imported piece-goods, but owing to their comparatively high prices, they are not generally worn. A manufacture of considerable interest is that of *kotki* cloth in Darbhangah and Muzaffarpur. It is of the same colour as the *khaki* worn in the best weather by troops, and it is superior to *khaki* in that it does not change colour or fade. In Dinapur the firm of Messrs. Thakur, Prosad, Shaw and Co., make ordinary cotton fabrics of European fashion, such as table-cloths, towels, sheets, dusters, and light fabrics for wear in the hot weather. A large collection is sent by that firm. The fabrics are good and it is understood that there is a considerable demand for them. In Patna good plain *dhuties* and *saris* are made, and in the Midnapur and Rajshahi Jails good coloured *pardahs* and *durries*. Of all Bengal manufactures none have attained greater celebrity than the muslins of Dacca. Many very fine specimens are exhibited by the Nawab Ahsanulla and Messrs. Nitai Charan and Jago Bandhu Baisrak of that town. The muslins are now generally made of English twist, but the fine sorts are made of Indian twist. The weaving of the latter is carried on generally during the rains and in the early morning and evening, as there is not enough moisture in the air at other times, and the warp would break. In dry hot weather while weaving the finest fabrics it is necessary to keep shallow vessels of water beneath the net, the evaporation from which keeps the warp moist. The price of the muslins made at the present time varies from Rs. 5 to Rs. 150 for a piece of one yard by ten yards. In former days, however, far finer muslins used to be made and higher prices were asked.

[237, 240, 242, 260, and 275-281].—From Dacca.

The first three are lent by Nawab Ahsanulla of Dacca, and the rest are sent for sale by Messrs. Nitai Charan, Baisak & Co.

[1185].—From Purniah, *Kotki* cloth.

The colour of this cloth as well as of No. 2857/36 from Muzaffarpur, resembles *khaki* and fabrics made of the celebrated Nankin cotton. It does not fade. In the district of Darbhangah, where the industry is said to be of great antiquity, the cotton is called *banga*.

[2857/36].—From Muzaffarpur, *Kotki* cloths.

Sub-section a.

Striped, figured, bordered, &c.

[1629, 3627-3630].—From Birbhum, sheets, coloured *purdahs* and *sairanchis*.

[1].—From Champaran, one black *satranchi* or *darri*.

[1328-1330, 2051-2074, 3685, 3686, 3690, 3691, 3695, 3696, 3698].—From Chittagong, coloured, checked and striped *lúngis*, towels, wrappers, &c.

[3897/1417, 3886/1418, **1419**, 3885/1420, 3899/1421, **1422**, 3898/1423, 3884/1426, **1429-1431**, 3687-3689, 3692-3694, 3697, 3699, 3700, 3806, 3810-3815].—From Chittagong Hill Tracts, wrappers, breast and loin cloths, turbans, coats, bed-sheets of Tipperah, Mugh, Lushai, Chakma, Khumi, and Bunjogi men and women.

Nos. 3687 to 3815 have been lent by Mr. A. Simson, Member Bengal Exhibition Committee.

[608, 609].—From Cuttack, *dhutis* and *sáris*.

These are presentations to the Government of Bengal from the Khondmehal estate.

[263, 315, 4164].—From Dacca, gold bordered *sári* and *chádar* and plain striped *than*.

[1058]. — From Dárjíling, one *Pangdhen* cloth.

Made in Tibet and used by women only.

[2032-2036, 3657-3673]. — From Dinajpur, *dhutis*, *sáris* and wrappers for children, men, and women.

A collection of the cloths commonly used in the district.

[2174/3] —From Gayá, a *darri*.

Used for bedding purposes, lent by Gayá Public Library.

[3492-3500, 3681-3683, 3701-3743, 3752, 3753, 3756-3759, 3761-3764, 3768-3770, 3800]. —From Howrah, *saris*, *dhutis* and *chádars*.

A collection of cloths purchased at a weekly fair held in Howrah. It contains specimens of cloths manufactured in the districts of Bardwán, 24-Parganás, Bankura, Hugli, Cuttack, Nadiya and Dacca.

[17 and eight others].—From Midnapur, *pardahs* of various coloured patterns.

Manufactured in the Midnapur Jail.

[1334, 1335].—From Noákhálí, sheets and mosquito curtain cloth.

[1961-1963]. — From Pabná, *dhutis* and *chádars*.

These are perhaps the finest plain *dhutis* and *sáris* produced in Bengal. Those like No. 1961, a pair of black bordered *dhuti*, and No. 1963, a pair of sheets, are only made to order, and are used by rich and well-to-do persons of Lower Bengal.

[2531/11, 2533, 2534, (2723-2725)/(25-27), (2727-2735)/(28-36), (2299, 2529, & 2736)/37, (2737-2765)/(38-66), (2215, 2217, 2243)/67, (2261, 2262, 2263)/67, (2523, 2582, 2587)/67, (2588 & 2766)/67, (2528, 2536, & 2767)/68, (2525 & 2768)/69, 2769/70, 2770/71, 2321/72, 2772/73, (2774-2776)/(74-76), (2778-2720)/(77-89), 2793/92, 2313/93, (2795-2800)/(94-99), (2209-2211)/(100-102), and 3684.]

From Patná, a collection of bedsheets, table covers, tea table cloths, doylies, towels, and handkerchiefs of various sizes and patterns, *darris*, &c.

Nos. 2531/11 and 3684, sample pieces of coloured checks used for coats and pantaloons, &c., are respectively lent by Rai Jai Krishna of Patna, and Messrs. Thakur Prosad, Shaw and Co., Dinapur. Nos. 2533 and 2534, two middle-sized *darris*, have been lent by Syed Luft Ali Khan, C.I.E.

[1885, 1896].—From Rangpur, floor cloths (*satranchis*).

Presented to the Government of Bengal by Babu Govindlál Rái, zemindar, Tázhát, and Babu Mahimáranjan Rai, zemindar, Kákiná, respectively.

From Rájsháhi, one *pardah*.

Made in the Rájsháhi Jail.

[4174].—From Mr. G. A. Richardson Baxár.

A cap used by Bhutanese.

[1522-1526, 1538, 1582-1588, 1592, 4095, 4096].—From Sháhábad, *Darris* and *Pardahs*.

Made in the Buxar Central Jail.

[1357-1370, **1371-1385**].—From Tipperah, *Charkháná* cloths.

Charkháná or coloured checks are made in Mynamati, and known as Mynamati cloths. They are said to have been prepared from cotton grown in the State of Hill Tipperah. The patterns exhibited are chiefly checks and stripes, some of which display considerable taste.

From Tipperah Hill Tracts—

[3862/1482, 3861/1483, **1484**, 3866/1485, 3896/1486, 3863/1487, 3685/1488, **1489**, 3684/490, & **1491-1496**].—Wearing apparel of

Tipperah, Manipuri, and Kuki men and women —a Kuki bag and a Kuki rug.

Presented by the State of Hill Tipperah to the Government of Bengal.

Sub-section b.

1. *Cotton Fabrics Printed with Country Block prints.*

Bengal is very backward in the production of printed goods. Formerly *sáris, dhutis, chadars* or wrappers, and quilt covers, &c., printed with *deshi chhap* or country block prints were much in use among natives of Bengal, but since the introduction of cheap European piece goods the trade has almost become extinct. Calcutta and the districts of Darbhangah, Sarun and Patna are the only places in Bengal where this art is still carried on to a small extent. Specimens from Patná show that the fabrics are only stamped in colours, but the Calcutta specimens have been made in a different manner. In these the patterns are first struck off with carved tamarind wood (*Tamarindus Indica,* Linn.) blocks besmeared with a peculiar sort of dye-stuff, and then boiled in a dye solution which leaves a reddish colour in the cloths. This colour does not fade.

From Calcutta.

Ten pieces of sample cloth.

[2311].—From Patná.

No woollen fabrics are made in Bengal, with the exception of carpets. The fabrics and rugs sent from Darjiling are interesting both in colour and design, but they were made in Tibet and Sikkim. The carpets made in the Hazáribágh and Bhagalpur jails are perhaps the best in Bengal. The Patna carpets are bad, the dyes being for the most part aniline and the texture thin. The floor covers made in Shahabad are gaudy, but are in great demand among the natives.

2. *Woollen Fabrics.*

Manufactured in the Bhagalpur Central Jail. The description and patterns exhibited are as follows :—

[$\frac{4091}{68}$, $\frac{4093}{201}$, $\frac{4092}{485}$, $\frac{4097}{313}$, $\frac{4090}{322}$, **540**, $\frac{1548}{721}$, $\frac{1547}{783}$].—From Bhagalpur, carpets of various sizes and patterns.

No. $\frac{4097}{68}$ *subji* (green) pattern, 8 stitches, 8 ft. by 3 ft. 6 in. No. $\frac{4093}{204}$ Persian B pattern, 10 stitches, 8 ft. by 4 ft. 6 in. No. $\frac{4092}{485}$ new shawl pattern, 14 stitches, 7 ft. by 4 ft. No. $\frac{4097}{313}$ new shawl pattern, 10 ft. by 8 ft. 4 in. No. $\frac{4090}{322}$ *pardah* pattern, 14 stitches, 7 ft. by 2 ft. 11 in. No. **540** *subji* pattern, 14 stitches, 7 ft. 3 in. by 3 ft. 8 in. No. $\frac{1548}{721}$ old shawl pattern, cream border, black ground, coarse wool, 8 stitches, 11 ft. 5 in. by 6 ft. 5 in. No. $\frac{1547}{787}$ crescent pattern, white border, claret ground, coarse wool, 8 stitches, 5 ft. 3 in. by 5 ft.

[891–899, 913, 976, 978, 979, 1055, 1060–1063 & 3895].—From Dárjíling, carpets, hats, shawl, blankets, coats, &c.

All these specimens, except No. 976, are manufactured in Tibet and used by Tibetans. No. 976 is made in Sikkim.

[$\frac{4094}{6}$].—From Hazáribágh, one carpet, Persian pattern.

The size of this is 7 ft. by 3 ft. 6 in. Price Rs. 38$\frac{1}{2}$; made in Hazáribágh Central Jail.

[$\frac{2600}{7}$].—From Patná, one carpet, called in the vernacular of the district *kalin-wooni.*

Lent by Syed Lufft Ali Khan, C.I.E., of Patná.

[4170, 4171].—From Sháhábád.

Two pieces of woollen fabrics received from L. Maude, Esq., Arrah.

3. *Silk Fabrics.*

[1733–1742, 1752–1757, **1–3, 5–11, 13** and **15–18**].—From Bánkurá, plain, twilled and figured silk and *tasar* gown pieces, coloured and figured *dhutis, sáris,* scarves, necties, coloured bed-sheets, quilt cloths.

The chief silk producing districts in Bengal are Murshidabad and Bánkurá. Large collections are sent from these places and also from Midnapur. Some very handsome pieces of silk are also sent from Darjiling. They are probably of Chinese design and were imported to the district through Tibet and Sikkim. A large collection of *tasar* pieces is also shown.

[1161–1167, 2805–2818, 3025–3033].—From Bhagalpur, *Tasar,* plain, twilled, striped and square patterns.

Nos. 1161, and 3025, "nine threaded" twilled and square pattern *tasars,* natural colours, are the best and strongest. The others are worth notice for the different dyes used.

[1630 and 3622].—From Bírbhúm, plain and dyed *tasar.*

No. 3622, the dyed *tasar* piece, has been presented to the Government of Bengal by Babu Ramchandra Das.

[1906–1910].—From Bográ, gown piece, *shari,* handkerchiefs, curtain cloth, &c.

No. 1908 is a thin checked silk cloth, locally called *kapardhúl,* used for making mosquito curtains for Rajas, Maharajas and wealthy people.

[902–912, 974, 975, 977, 1044, 1045, and 1054]. —From Darjiling, coats, hats, dancing dresses, &c.

Manufactured in Tibet from figured silks. Nos. 902–906 are dancing dresses worn by Tibetans. These dresses are worn loose without girdle.

[2178].—From Gayá, *tasa saris.*

Ordinary specimens of cloth much used by native women for sacred purposes. They have been lent by Babu Rangabahadur Singh, Gayá.

[1517, 1518, 1521, 1589, 1598, and 1599].—From Hugli, white and dyed silks, waistband, *tasar* fabrics, &c.

Manufactured in the Jehanabad sub-division. No. 1599, *dhúpchháyá* or shot silk, and No. 1518, *charkhána* silk, are perhaps the best.

[1228–1233].—From Maldah, white gown pieces, dyed and bordered *saris,* &c.

Maldah is noted for dyed silks. The colours

represented in the present collection are *saris* Nos. 1228 *mayur-kanthi* or peacock-neck colour, 1229, *asmani* or sky colour, and 1230 *dhúpchháyu* (literally sunshine and shade), a shot silk.

[1826 and 1828-1830].—From Mánbhúm, *tasar thán, dhuti*, and mosquito curtain cloth.

Nos. 1828 and 1829 are fair samples of plain and twilled *tasar* produced in the Chutia Nagpur Tributary States. The industry is carried on hereditarily by men and women of the *Tânti* or Hindu weaver caste, of whom there are about 250 persons engaged in this trade. Of the three places, Raghunathpur, Shibnagar, and Singbazar, where these fabrics are chiefly manufactured, Raghunathpur cloths are perhaps the best in texture and fineness.

[1494-1497].—From Midnapur, plain and figured silks, figured neckties, coloured checks, &c.

Nos. 1494 and 1495 are good specimens of white silks, plain and figured. They are manufactured chiefly from *Marchband* silk, which is the best of the kind for whiteness, and glossy and soft texture. The silk is prepared in parganá Chetua. There are several filatures in the district of Midnapur, especially in the Ghatal sub-division.

[741, 773, 780-785, 795, 800, 2958, 2959, 2961, 2962, 2970, 2995].—From Murshidábád, gown pieces, *saris*, table cloths, handkerchiefs, &c.

No. 2970, Baluchar *sari* is lent by the Nawab Nazim of Murshidábád. Mahárání Swarnamayi, of Kásimbázár, has also lent two Baluchar *saris* (Nos. 2961 and 2962 with figures of gods and goddesses woven at the ends) and one silk cloth, No. 2958, Nos. 773, 783, 784, and 795 are unbleached silk pieces called *corah*. They are also called *garád*, which has a similar meaning to *shaugáli*, the term applied to the finest Dacca muslins, *i.e.* those that are worthy of being offered as presents.

[585-589 and 592].—From Orissa Division, *tasar* cloths, white and coloured.

The Barambá and Moharbhanj States have respectively presented to the Government of Bengal Nos. 592 and 585-589.

[$\frac{2702}{4}$, $\frac{2703}{5}$, $\frac{2704}{6}$, $\frac{2705}{7}$, $\frac{2707}{8}$, $\frac{2708}{9}$, $\frac{2709}{10}$, $\frac{2710}{11}$, $\frac{2711}{12}$, $\frac{2712}{13}$, $\frac{2791}{90}$, $\frac{2792}{91}$, $\frac{2576}{134}$, $\frac{2577}{135}$, $\frac{2576}{136}$, and $\frac{2579}{137}$].—From Patna, silk and *tasar* fabrics, plain and dyed, and silk *dhutis* and *saris*, &c.

Messrs. Thakur Prosad Shaw & Co., Dinapur, have exhibited a large and valuable collection under this head.

[1881-1883].—From Rangpur, silk *sari* and *endi* cloths.

These have been presented to the Government of Bengal by Babu Padmanáb Ghosal, Superintendent of Kutabpur, Rangpur district.

[1863].—From Rájsháhí, a pair of *matka* cloths.

Manufactured from threads prepared from pierced mulberry cocoons. These are chiefly purchased by *Baniyahs*, inhabitants of Jaipur and Jodhpur

[4176].—From Mr. G. A. Richardson, Baxár.

Manufactured in Bhutan.

Printed Silk Fabrics.

Sub-section a.

[786].—From Murshidábád.

Berhampur, in the district of Murshidábád, is celebrated for these printed silk goods.

Textiles, Mixed Fabrics, Silk and Cotton.

Section 4.

[4,12 and 14].—From Bánkurá, plain *thán* wrapper and *garva súti* cloth.

[1171-1175, 2192, 2819-2824, 3020-3024, 3034 3040].—From Bhagalpur, *bafta* cloth (plain, twilled and checked), and *bafta* turban pieces.

[247, 267 and 317].—From Dacca, plain *mugá* striped muslins.

The local vernacular name for these is *Azizullá* or *Ajiji*, a term generally applied to cotton fabrics having stripes of *mugá* silk, just as the hand embroidery in *mugá* upon cotton fabrics is called by its generic name of *kasidá*.

[1598].—From Hugli, *garva súti* cloth.

The District Officer of Hugli describes this as a purely tasar fabric, but it is believed to be made of both *tasar* and cotton.

[1227, 1234-1244].—From Maldah.

These dyed silks are chiefly used for dresses of females and children, and for *doláis* or wrappers.

[1827].—From Mánbhúm, *garva súti* cloth.

Made of *tasar* and cotton.

[$\frac{2713}{14}$, $\frac{2714}{15}$, $\frac{2715}{16}$, $\frac{2706}{17}$, $\frac{2716}{18}$, $\frac{2717}{19}$, $\frac{2718}{20}$, $\frac{2719}{21}$, $\frac{2720}{22}$, $\frac{2721}{23}$, $\frac{2722}{4}$, and $\frac{2212}{103}$].—From Patna, *bafta* cloth sheets, &c.

Most of these are exhibited by Messrs. Thakur Prosad Shaw & Co., Dinapur.

Silk and Wool.

Sub-section a.

[1059].—From Dárjíling, a coat.

Used by Llamas of Tibet.

Jute and Cotton.

Sub-section b.

[1886].—From Rangpur, *Mekii* cloth, a *darri*.

Presented by Babu Govindalál Rai, zemindar, Tajhat.

[1836, 2896, 4184].—From Santál Parganás, pack saddles.

Div. XII.—Embroideries.

The embroideries of Dacca, Calcutta, Patna, Murshidabad, and Sarun have attained a considerable celebrity. The Dacca *kasida* work and the Calcutta *chikan* work are perhaps best known to Europeans, though the Patna, Murshidabad, and Sarun work is more prized by natives of India. The latter is probably of foreign origin, the work having been introduced from the North-Western Provinces and elsewhere by artists who have settled in these provinces. The collections of Dacca and Calcutta embroideries are believed to be the most comprehensive that have yet been made. For the former the Committee are indebted to the Nawab Ahsanulla. Messrs. Nitai Charan and Jagobandhu Baisak, of Dacca, have also sent a very extensive collection, the whole of which is for sale. The collection of Calcutta *chikan* work was made by the late Mr. H. H. Locke, member of the Bengal Exhibition Committee. The specimens of Sarun work, sent by the Maharajah of Hatwa, the Maharani Swarnamayi, and the Nawab Nazim of Murshidabad, are most valuable and excellent samples of the work.

Loom-embroidered Fabrics, Silk, Cotton or Woollen Thread.

Sub-section a.

[239, 264, 265, 284–289, 291–293, 295, 301–305, 307–309].—From Dacca, Loom worked *jámdáni* pieces, both white and coloured.

No, 239, *shaburgá chowaldáná* piece, lent by Nawab Ahsanullah of Dacca.

Cotton and Gold Mixed.

Sub-section b

[262, 310, 311].—From Dacca.

Hand-embroidered Fabrics, Silk, Cotton, or Woollen Thread.

Sub-section c.

[241, 245, 266, 283, 321–337, 356, 3817].—From Dacca, silk and *mugá* embroidered muslins, satins, shawls, gowns, &c.

Nos. 241 and 283, *shamudra lahar* (literal meaning "sea wave"), are used by Moguls for turbans.

No. 332, a silk embroidered shawl, and No. 3817, a *mugá* thread embroidered fabric, better known as *jhábbá kasidá*, are good specimens. The demand for *kasidá*, *i.e. mugá* or *tasar* silk embroidered pieces, is considerably on the increase. They are largely exported by Arab merchants to Aden, Persia, and Turkey for turban pieces. The black net used for No. 337 is imported. The *kasidá* cloths are principally made of English twist. The silk embroidery in colours upon scarves, shawls, gowns, &c., is carried out by a set of workmen called *sardárs.*

One hand-embroidered *sari* is exhibited by Srimuthy Ganderbeshwari Ishrami, a native lady, of Kuch Behar.

Silk, Cotton, and Wool.

Sub-section c.

[4101-4105].—From Calcutta, one *chikan* embroidered *tasar* dress, consisting of four skirt pieces, eight flouncings, four pieces of insertion, one piece plain fabric, and three handkerchiefs.

Maker, Shaik Golab, *chikanwálá*, Calcutta. Cost of the dress is Rs. 57-8, and three handkerchiefs Rs. 31.

[4106-4108].—Two *chikan* embroidered *tasar* dresses, consisting of two skirt pieces, two pieces each containing seven strips of insertion, and six yards of plain fabric.

Maker, Muhammed Hossein, *chikanwálá*, Calcutta.

[4109-4114].—One *tasar* silk dress, consisting of six flouncings, five flounces (different), four pieces insertion, one sash, one piece containing two pockets, and ten and a-half yards of plain fabric.

Maker, Kasim Ali, *chikanwálá*, Calcutta. Cost Rs. 54-12.

[4115-4118].—One baby's robe, *chikan* embroidered on Rádhánagur muslin, consisting of one body piece, one skirt piece, four yards trimming, and one foot plain fabric.

Maker, Kasim Ali.

[4119-4124].—From Calcutta, one *chikan* embroidered *korah* silk dress, consisting of one piece flouncing, one piece flouncing (different), one piece insertion, one sash, one piece containing two pockets, and fifteen yards of plain fabric.

Maker, Satobur, *chikanwálá*, Calcutta.

[4125].—Three handkerchiefs.

Maker, Satobur, *chikanwálá*, Calcutta.

[4126].—Three handkerchiefs.

Makers, Satobur, *chikanwálá*, Calcutta; Morabuk, *chikanwálá*, Calcutta.

[4127].—Two handkerchiefs.

Maker, Satobur, *chikanwálá*, Calcutta.

[4128-4133].—One *chikan* embroidered *tasar* dress, consisting of six flouncings, five flouncings (different), four insertions, one sash, one piece containing two pockets, and one piece plain fabric eighteen feet four inches long.

Maker, Kásim Ali, *chikanwálá*, Calcutta.

[4134-4137].—One Rádhánagur muslin embroidered baby's robe, consisting of one body piece, one skirt, four yards of trimming, and one foot of plain fabric.

Maker, Kasim Ali, *chikanwálá*, Calcutta.

[4138].—Two embroidered handkerchiefs.

Maker, Kasim Ali, *chikanwálá*. Calcutta.

[4139].—Six embroidered handkerchiefs.

Maker, Mahomed Hossein, Calcutta.

[4140].—Two pieces *korah* silk for dress.

Supplied by (?) Babu Radha Shyam Gooyee, Calcutta.

[4141] —Two pieces *korah* silk for dress.

Supplied by Satobur, *chikanwálá*, Calcutta.

[4142].—One embroidered China silk dress.

[4143].—One *tasar* dressing gown.

[4144].—Eight yards of *chikan* embroidered muslin flouncings.

[4145 & 4146].—Two babies' frocks.

[4147 & 4148].—Two babies' robes.

[4149].—One child's frock.

[4150].—Four yards of trimming.

[4151] —Four yards of trimming.

[4152].—Four yards of insertion.

From Nos. 4142 to 4152 are exhibited for sale by Satobur, *chikanwálá*, Calcutta.

[4153-4163].—A collection of ninety-four *chikan* embroidered muslin handkerchiefs of various sizes and patterns.

These are exhibited for sale by Kásim Ali, *chikanwálá*, Calcutta.

[4165]. — Two *chikan* embroidered *tasar* dresses.

Exhibited for sale by Shaik Gloáb, *chikanwálá*, Calcutta.

[4167 & 4168].—From Dárjíling.

Two fine specimens of silk embroidery purchased from a Bhutia dealer in Calcutta. These are worn by the higher classes in Thibet.

[1250].—From Maldah, *Sujni*.

This is used by native gentlemen both as a carpet and bedsheet. The stuffed ornamental needlework is done by females.

[772, 2965].—From Murshidabád, *Námbáli sujni*.

No. 772, a silk *námábali*, *i.e.*, a sheet interwoven with the names of different gods and goddesses of the Hindu mythology, is generally used by Hindus at the time of their morning prayer (*anhik*). It is sometimes used as a sacred wrapper by Hindu men and women of advanced age. It is lent by Babu Lukshmi Kánta Bág, Murshidabad. No. 2965, embroidered *sujni* (*see* remark against No. 1250 above), is lent by the Nawab Nazim of Murshidábád.

[A, B, C].—From Nadiyá, three samples of *sujni*.

[668, 675].—From Puri, *sujnis*, red and white.

[$\frac{95}{35}$, $\frac{9}{7}$].—From Sarun, embroidered pillow-cases.

Such pillow-cases are used by rich men only. These are presented to the Government of Bengal by Mahárájá Krishna Pratab Sahaí of Hatwa, Sarun.

Gold and Silver.

[1638].—From Bírbhúm.

[3052-3061, 3802-3805, 3818, 3819].—From Calcutta, gold and silver fabrics, fringes, crown, turban, cap, wreath, embroidered *húká* pipes, &c.

Gold and silver sheets like Nos. 3804, 3805 are said to have been manufactured in Calcutta from imported thread. They are specially used for dresses of native dancing girls. Turban, cap, and crown are also used by native professional singing parties, *játrá-walás*, and theatrical companies.

[2-4].—From Champaran.

[340, 341, 351-353].—From Dacca, dresses, fabrics, and caps.

Messrs. Nitái Charan Basák & Co., of Nawábpur, Dacca, have sent a good collection of Dacca fabrics for sale. No. 340 is a black net gown, richly embroidered with gold, and priced Rs. 1,200. *Jari patkas*, or silver embroidered cloths, like No. 341, are used by respectable Muhammadans, and caps, Nos. 351-353, are used by other wealthy natives.

[4166].—From Dárjíling.

This is a breast-piece with fine embroidery in gold. It is used for dresses of Llamas and other respectable people of Tibet.

[2925, 2926, 2963, 2964, 2967, 2968, 2979, 2992, 2994, 2996-3007, 3009-3011]. — From Murshidabad, canopy, *palki* cover, gowns, jackets, dresses, bodice, prayer carpets, caps, &c.

No. 2963, *chope chandni*, an embroidered canopy with fringes, price Rs. 1,518-2, and No. 2964, a *chhattri* or cover of a palanquin, value Rs. 2,000, have been lent by Mahárání Swarnamayi of Kasim Bazar, Murshidábád.

[58-65, 67-82, 84, 85, 2202, 2204-2206, 2580, 2581, & 2594].—From Patná, caps, slippers, money-bags, belts, *zerandez pan*, *kanthá*, &c.

[96 & 97].—From Sarun, native slippers and *zinposh* (saddle cloths).

The saddle cloth No. 97 is a beautiful piece of gold embroidery. Its price is Rs. 600. Both this and No. 96 have been presented to the Government of Bengal by Mahárájá Krishna Pratab Sahai of Hatwa, Sarun.

Silk and Gold Mixed Embroideries.

[339, 342-346].—From Dacca.

No. 339, gold and silk embroidered gown, is used by European ladies; Nos. 342-345, embroidered *saris*, by Nepalis and wealthy native ladies. These have been exhibited by Messrs. Nitai Charan Basák & Co., of Nawábpur, Dacca.

Gold Embroidered Ornaments.

Sub-section d.

[347-350, 354, 355].—From Dacca, necklets and dancing bracelets.

Div. XIII.—Leathers and Furs.

1. *Boots and Shoes.*

[980, 1046, 1056 and 1064].—From Dárjíling.

No. 980, a pair of shoes called *shotshi;* No. 1046, 1056 and 1064, three pairs of boots called *lum*. Made by Tibetans.

2. *Belts and Saddlery.*

[900, 901, 924, 929, 1026, 1027, 1041, 1047, 1057].—From Dárjíling, saddle-cloth, girdle, belts, &c. Made by Tibetans.

3. *Furs, Hairs, &c.*

[1042, 918].—From Dárjíling, a flyflapper. A coat made of sheep-skin.

No. 1042, a horsetail used by Tibetans as a flyflapper. Made by Tibetans.

Div. XIV.—Baskets, Mats, and Straw Work.

The manufacture of baskets, mats, and straw-work is common throughout Bengal. The Monghyr basket ware, the Midnapur matting, and the Farídpur *sital páti* are worth notice. The ivory mat exhibited by Nawab Ahsanulla, of Dacca, is a very fine piece of work.

Baskets, Mats, Matting, &c.

[3807–3809].—From Calcutta, coloured grass mats.

Purchased in the Calcutta bazar. The coloured mats are used by the Hindus during their marriage ceremonies and other holy rites. Plain grass mats are much in demand for covering floors of public offices and dwelling-houses of Europeans and wealthy natives of Calcutta. The stem of the grass (*Papyrus pangorei*, Nees, or *Cyperus tegetum*, Roxb.), called in the Bengali *mádur káti*, is in its green state split into four or five pieces, which are allowed to dry till they contract enough to let their margins overlap each other, and to attain the breadth of a thick needle. They are then ready for weaving.

[21/2, 7/4, 11/5, 13/6, 14/7, & 16/8].—From Champaran, door mats and matting, principally made of fibres.

Nos. 21/2, 11/5, 14/7 and 16/8 are made of *munj* fibres (*Saccharum munja*, Roxb.). The strong and elastic ropes made of this fibre are much valued for their power of resisting moisture. The drab coloured aloe matting is useful for covering floors of houses or saloons of ships and steamers. Its colour never fades.

[1303, 1309, 1310 & 1314–1316]. —From Chittagong, baskets, plates, and fishing traps.

Made of bamboo wickers; 1303 is used for carrying things; 1309 and 1310 are plates used by children; 1314–1316 are traps, locally called *chai*, used for catching fresh-water fishes.

[234, 236].—From Dacca, ivory and *sital páti* mats.

No. 234, an ivory mat with gold embroidery work on the margin, and No. 236, three *sital páti* mats, have been lent by Nawab Ahsanulla, of Dacca. The price of the ivory mat is Rs. 1,500. It is made of narrow and thin ivory strips woven like the ordinary *sital páti* mats No. 236.

[2048, 2049].—From Dinajpur, a grass mat and bamboo fans.

No. 2048, a grass mat made after the copy of celebrated *machhlandi* mat of Midnapur, and No. 2049, a fan, are presented by the Mahárájá of Dinajpur.

[248].—From Farídpur, *sital páti* mats.

Farídpur is the only district in Bengal famous for the manufacture of *sital páti* or "cool mats." Those prepared in Satáir, a fiscal division of Farídpur, are the best of the kind. They are made of a species of cane (*Maranta dichotama*, Wall., *Phrynium dichotomum* Roxb.) known in Eastern Bengal as *Mukta-páti* and *páti-páti*. The canes are split length-wise with a *dáo* (country knife). The surface is well scraped, and the glossy parts remaining under the rind are made into thin and narrow strips, boiled, and finally woven into smooth mats, which, owing to their coolness, are much used in hot seasons for sleeping on. They are chiefly made by women.

[1811, 1813 & 1816].—From Mánbhúm, *dálá* and *khungi* (baskets) and *kulá* (winnower).

No. 1813 is made at Chaki, and Nos. 1811 and 1816 at Gopalpur.

[168, 169, 182, 188, 190, 195–197, 2832 & 2852].—From Muzaffarpur, *siki* grass baskets, betel-pots, plate, and figures of elephant, horse, &c.

[1491, 1492, 4169, 1562/6, **11, 34**, 1554/37, 1551/31, 1563/43]. —From Midnapur, *Machlandi* mats, coir brush mats, &c.

Nos. 1491, 1492, and 4169, the last-named number 4169 has been presented to the Government of Bengal by Rájá Mahendra Lal Khan, of Narajul, are good specimens. *Masland* and *masnad* mats are the other two designations by which they are known in Bengal. The beds on which the rich natives of India sit or recline consist of a richly embroidered cushion and a suite of pillows, and are called *masnads*: hence the name of the *maslandi* mat is supposed to have been derived from the fact of its being so costly and fine that it is only fit for use on beds of rich and wealthy persons. They are prepared by persons of *Byti* caste in Parganás Chetuá and Kásijorá. Men prepare the raw material, and women weave it into mats. Ordinary figured mats are generally made for local use and exportation to other districts, but the best are only made to order, and are woven with silk threads.

The collection of brush door mats made at the Midnapur Jail, by manual labour, from Maldive coir fibre purchased at Calcutta and from country fibres manufactured in the jail, is worthy of notice. They are purchased, in large numbers, both by Europeans and wealthy natives.

[1127–1129, 1131, 1132 & 1134–1138].—From Monghyr, table mats, baskets, bags and fans, made of reed.

Monghyr is celebrated for this industry, and is the only place in India which produces articles of this description. These are made of a kind of grass called in the vernacular *sara* (*Sacchrum sara*).

[3363, 3365, 3370, 3371, 3376, 3380, 3389, 3400, 3402 & 3407–3411].—From Purniah, screen, baskets, boxes made of *siki* grass.

Presented to the Government of Bengal by Babus Achit Chaudhuri and Giridhári Chaudhuri Srilál Jhá, Pánchakri Misra, and Kamal Nath Ghosál, sub-divisional officer of Arrareah.

Parda-nashin ladies of Maithili Brahmins and Chhatri castes make these *siki* grass articles for home use only or for presents to relatives. The grass grows wild in the district. The bark of the straw is stripped off, the stalks are then thoroughly dried and used.

[**98, 3**].—From Sarun.

[1352].—From Tipperah, a *dhuchuni* or bamboo basket.

[1497 & 1505].—From Tipperah Hill Tracts, a basket and a coloured mat.

No. 1505 is a coloured bamboo mat. No. 1497 is a bamboo basket locally called *thurung*. These articles have been presented by the State of Hill Tipperah to the Government of Bengal.

NEPAL.

Div. I.—Fine Arts.

1. *Paintings and Drawings.*

[1-7]. — Native paintings. Paintings or coloured sketch of temples, shrines, gods, goddesses, portraits, &c.

These are done by a class of Newars called Chitrakars, the drawings are neatly finished and the colouring shows some taste, there is, however, little or no idea of perspective.

3. *Photographs.*

[8-43].—Photographs.

Views of Nepal scenery and groups showing types of inhabitants, by Messrs. Johnstone & Hoffmann, Calcutta.

Div. II.—Decorative Art.

1. *Architectural Designs and Models.*

[51-55].—Temple architecture.

These two models are good types of the temple architecture of Nepal.

7. *Decorative Carving as applied to Architecture.*

[56-148].—House-front decoration. Pillars, doorways, arches, balconies, windows, the supports of eaves, beams, friezes, cornices, &c. Figures of divinities, demons, animals, gargoyles, &c., forming part of the decorations of temples. Sometimes a kneeling stone figure of the builder of the temple is seen.

Nos. 56-92 form the front of a Nepalese *pati* or verandah resting-place erected by the pious for the accommodation of travellers and poor persons. It is a copy in *sal* wood of a *pati* in the town of Patan, of some antiquity. Such work is now rarely done in Nepal. Nos. 93-146 forming the screen. Nos. 147 and 148 are copies, the latter on a reduced scale, of windows in the Patan Darbár or Royal residence.

The architectural wood-carving of Nepal is by far the most important decorative art to be found in the country. Unfortunately the industry is fast falling into abeyance from a combination of causes. The carving is artistic in the highest degree. Figures of gods, demons, dragons, snakes, and animals of all sorts, wreaths of flowers and intricate patterns are worked on balconies and windows, the proportions of which are as graceful and true as the details are elaborate. The work is very expensive, and this seems to be the principal reason that so little comparatively is now in demand. This work is done by a class of Newars called Lokarmi, who display a very considerable amount of skill. The figures of demons and gargoyles seen on temples are bold and grotesque.

Div. III.—Musical Instruments.

1. *Wind Instruments.*

[151-159]. — Nepal musical instruments. *Kahal*, a long copper trumpet. *Karnal*, a trumpet made of copper or brass. *Narsingha*, a kind of trumpet. *Hong*, a brass trumpet; *Pong*, a jointed copper trumpet; *Nge-ku*, a buffalo horn.

The instruments enumerated are only those which are believed to be peculiar to the country. In addition, most of the stringed and other instruments in vogue in the plains are used, and some of them manufactured in Nepal.

3. *Instruments of Percussion.*

[160-170]. — *Dhyamaya*, a drum, peculiar to Jaffus. *Koncha khin*, a drum, peculiar to Jaffus. *Naya-knin*, a drum; *Magar-khin*, a tamtam, peculiar to Magars. *Tamra*, a small kettle-drum; *Dango-khin*, a kind of drum; *Bamtal*, a small tambourine; *Dhondhon*, a drum, peculiar to Bhotias. *Panchtal khin*, a large drum; *Khin*, a drum; *Dhak* a drum.

Div. IV.—Jewellery.

1. *Gold and Silversmiths' Work.*

[171-269, 299, also twenty specimens in Mr. Purdon Clarke's collection].

Nepalese gold and silversmiths are not particularly skilful; occasionally some good filigree work is seen on the sheaths of *kookries* and *tulwars*, either in gold or silver. Several of the designs for earrings, head ornaments, &c., are peculiar and not seen elsewhere. *Pandans*, &c., are ornamented with the same grotesque figures, seen in the wood and stone work of the country. The military head-dresses are peculiar to the country, those worn by the highest ranks are of great value and are composed almost entirely of diamonds, pearls, and emeralds set in silver.

Div. V.—Art Manufactures in Metal.

3 *and* 4. *Brass and Copper Wares.*

A hundred and two specimens in Mr. Purdon Clarke's collection. Nepal Pan ware.—*Lotas*, bowls, drinking vessels, bells, lamps of different kinds. Figures of divinities, Puja implements, Censers.

A great deal of brass work is done by Newars at Patan. The designs of some of the lamps are extremely quaint and artistic. The pagoda-like temples are hung with little bells to the clappers of which are attached broad leaf-shaped pieces of brass; these are set in motion by the wind and a continual tinkling is kept up. Besides these, two classes of bells are largely manufactured. One made of brass is in use in Hindu temples; the other of mixed metal is used by Buddhists. The tone of both kinds is generally clear and musical.

5. *Arms and Armour.*

[172-189]. — Nepal Armour. — Bows and arrows, Targets of rhinoceros hide, *Khora. Kookri*, rifles, mountain guns, bayonets, &c.

These may be classed as obsolete arms, although bows and arrows are still in use in some parts of the Terai.

The *Khora* is a curved *tulwar*, the extremity of the blade widening, so as to somewhat resemble the blade of an axe. It was formerly used in warfare, but at present only in beheading buffaloes for sacrifice. The animal's head is taken off at one blow.

The modern national arm of Nepal is the *Kookri*, too well-known to need description. In the Military Arsenal breech-loading rifles, rifled mountain guns, bayonets, &c., are manufactured.

7. *Iron and Steel Wares.*

[190-192].—Locksmith's Ware.

Locks of a peculiar pattern made in the country of Nepalese iron.

Div. VI.—Manufactures in Wood, Ivory, Etc.

2. *Inlaid Work.*

One specimen in Mr. Purdon Clarke's collection.—Inlaid Ware.

But little of this work is done, and it seems to be almost entirely confined to the ornamentation of hookahs, the stems of which are sometimes inlaid with ivory, mother-of-pearl, or brass and ivory.

3. *Ivory Carving.*

[193-197, 202].—Also three specimens in Mr. Purdon Clarke's collection.—Ivory Carvings.

Ivory carving is only carried on to a limited extent. Ivory in the hills is scarce and expensive. Dominoes, almost exactly resembling those in use in Europe, and chopsticks are made for export to Tibet.

5. *Wood Carving.*

[203-205].—Also one specimen in Mr. Purdon Clarke's collection.—Nepal Wood Carving.

Wood carving is little applied except to purposes of architectural decorations.

Small boxes are sometimes carved, and carved black wood *Kookri* handles are now and then seen. The small stands for figures of deities are made to represent thrones.

6. *Miscellaneous.*

(a.) *Horn Carving.*

[198-201].—Also six specimens in Mr. Purdon Clarke's collection.—Horn ware.—Rhinoceros horn cups, *arghas*, and rings.

Drinking cups are made of this material. They are not usually carved. The *argha* is a small shallow cup carved round the edge, it is used in certain religious ceremonies.

Div. VII.—Lapidaries' Work.

1. *Agate, Jasper, and Cornelian Ware.*

[211].—Sri Juntra, or symbol of the Goddess Sursati, in crystal.

Div. IX.—Pottery.

2. *Unglazed Pottery.*

[216-220].—Timmi Pottery.

Good unglazed pottery is made chiefly at Timmi; the patterns resemble those seen in the plains. The lamps are shaped like an *argha.*

Div. XI.—Textiles.

1. *Cotton Fabrics.*

[221-241].—Homespun cloth.

Nos. 238-241 are specimens of Nepalese Homespun Cloth. The other numbers in this section are specimens of clothing. The fabric of which they are composed is not of Nepal manufacture.

2. *Cotton Fabrics.*

[242-253, 297].

The cloth of which (Nos. 246-247 and 297) caps worn by Newars are made is not of Nepal manufacture.

3. *Silk Fabrics.*

[254-262].—The material of which these articles are made is imported.

4. *Other Fabrics.*

[263-267].

No. 263 is a blanket of goat's-hair, manufactured by the hill tribes of Nepal—chiefly by Magars.

Nos. 264-267 are umbrellas of sized cloth of general use in the valley of Nepal.

Div. XIII.—Leathers and Furs.

1. *Shoes.*

[270-277].

No. 270 is intended for the male sentry-box figure.

No. 273 for the opposite female figure.

2. *Poshtins, Belts, Saddlery, &c.*

[298].

No. 298 is a saddle in use in the households of wealthy Nepalese. It is strapped on the backs of male or female servants, whose duty it is to carry their masters and mistresses up and down stairs, or from one part of the house to another. A Nepalese lady of rank will scarcely walk from one room to the next.

3. *Furs.*

[278-284].—Feathers.

Fans manufactured in Khatmandu from Peacock feathers.

Div. XIV.—Baskets, Mats, and Straw Work.

[285-296].

These exhibits are made chiefly by hill tribes inhabiting the mountains round the valley of Nepal, and between it and Tibet.

Nos. 291-292 are baskets called *dhokas*, in which heavy loads are carried on the back, supported by a strap passing across the forehead.

No. 293 is a peculiar arrangement used by the hill tribes of the country as a protection from rain.

THE NORTH-WEST PROVINCES AND OUDH.

Div. I.—Fine Arts.

1. *Paintings and Drawings.*

[401-407].—Paintings on ivory from Benares.

These paintings are done at Benares in gold and colours in the style of manuscript illumination. The subjects usually chosen are scenes from the life of Krishna and illustrations of Hindu festivals. Prices range from Rs.20 to Rs.50 a picture.

3.—*Photographs.*

[419-443.]—Panoramic view of Mussoorie, and views of Bhim Tal; of Naini Tal, before and after the landslip of 1880; of buildings, &c., in Lucknow, La Martiniere, Chattar Mangie, Wingfield Park; of bazars and other noted places in the North-West Provinces and Oudh, Shahjahanpur, Bareilly, Moradabad, Thanstansi, Nagwa, Najibabad, Jaunpur, Lucknow, &c., &c.

Div. II.—Decorative Art.

1. *Architectural Designs and Models.*

[465-471].—Seven examples of stone trellis-work from Agra.

Stone trellis-work in sandstone is a trade largely carried on in Agra. Specimens range from Rs.15 or Rs.18 per slab about 2 ft. 6 in. square. There is some exquisitely fine work in marble and in alabaster in the style of the marble screens of the Taj Mahal. (*Vide* VIII., 1)

4. *Models in Clay, Wax, Terra-cotta, Plaster of Paris.*

[472-526.].—Fifty-five clay figures from Lucknow.

Figures, single and in groups, illustrating trades, castes, and professions, made at Lucknow. These figures are frequently modelled from life, and are very expressive. Colour is sometimes used, and always where fruit is the subject. Prices from 1 rupee a figure to 10 rupees per group, or Rs. 150 to Rs. 250 for any larger work.

No. 522 is a life size figure, and Nos. 524-26 are the figures of three clay modellers of Lucknow, by whom most of the Exhibits in this section have been executed.

[528-529].—About 125 models in clay of fruits and vegetables, from Lucknow.

7. *Decorative Carving.*

[572-573].—(*a*) Carved doorways in wood, from Saharanpur.

[574].—(*b*) Carved façade in wood, from Farrukhabad.

[575-576].—(*c*) Carved façades in wood, from Manipuri.

Wood carving for architectural decoration is carried on in many of the towns of Upper India. The best specimens for the Calcutta Exhibition were obtained from Saharanpur and Aligarh. Prices, according to work and size, up to Rs.600 for such an example as a doorway with doors and framework complete.

[577-579].—(*d*) Wood carvings from Lucknow —façades and doorway.

No. 579 is a carved façade 50 in. × 10 in. with centre doors. The door and the greater part of the carved front were taken from a house lately demolished, and probably not less than 100 years old. The façade truthfully illustrates Bazar architecture.

[580].—(*e*) Carved façade in wood, from Cawnpore.

[581-582].—(*f*) Carved façades in white sandstone, from Muttra.

[583-588].—(*g*) Carved façades in stone, from Agra.

[590].—(*h*) Carved door-frame, from Fatehgarh.

A loan exhibit from J. H. Rivett-Carnac, Esq., B.C.S., C.I.E.

Div. III.—Musical Instruments.

2. *Stringed Instruments.*

[610-612].—*Sitars*, from Lucknow.

A detailed description is scarcely required, and would be too long for insertion here. Considerable art and ingenuity is shown in the adaptation of various material for instruments, such as shells of ostrich eggs, gourds, &c. The chief places of manufacture are Lucknow, Benares, and Rampur.

Div. IV.—Jewellery.

1. *Gold and Silversmith's Work, including Filigrain, Setting of Precious Stones, &c.*

[625-648].—(*a*) Twenty-four anklets, bracelets, necklets, toe-rings, earrings, &c., from Lucknow. (Some of these are in sets of six and twelve).

The best work is obtainable in Lucknow and Rampur, where jewellery set with precious stones can be purchased up to any amount in value. A speciality of Lucknow is that known as diamond-cut silver ornaments. Facets are cut and burnished, which, when in the form of stars, bear at a distance a strong resemblance to the flashing of a diamond. Prices vary from Rs.10 to any amount.

[649].—(*b*) Head ornament, from Rai Bareli.

[650].—(*c*) Silver necklace, from Jhansi.

[651].—(*d*) Purse for personal use, from Faizábád.

[652].—(*e*) Set of bangles, from Gházípur.

These bangles are made of glass, but beautifully ornamented with wires and stars of real gold.

2. *Enamelled Jewellery.*

[666].—Set of enamelled bangles, from Lucknow.

Div. V.—Art Manufactures in Metal.

1. *Gold and Silver Plate.*

[681–723].—(*a*) *Surahis*, jugs, *pandans*, *hukkas*, *atardans*, scent-bottles, plates, saucers, salt-cellars, sugar-basins, milk-pots, tea sets, &c., &c., from Lucknow.

There is a considerable variety in designs and in work, some of which is engraved and some *repoussé*, some in plain silver, others in silver gilt, and others enamelled. Prices from Rs.25 up to Rs.1,000 for such an enamelled *hukkah* as No. 1460 in Section 9.

[751].—Ostrich egg-shell vessel mounted with silver.

[724].—(*b*) Silver fish with gold head, from Fiazábád.

[725–730].—(*c*) Silver fish, from Hamírpur.

[731–750].—(*d*) Silver toys from Gokul, in Muttra, representing animals.

Curious and ingeniously made. Used by the natives as scent-cases.

2. *Koft or Damascened Work.*

[761–788].—*Bidri* ware, from Lucknow.—*Hukkas*, spittoons, *surahis*, plates, saucers, glasses, *pandans*, flower-pots, &c.

Under this head may be classed the *Bidri* ware of Lucknow. On a groundwork of black composite metal silver is worked, both counter-sunk and in relief, in flower and other patterns interspersed with figures of birds and beasts. Gold is also used in the place of silver, and, when not too heavily laid on, with good effect. The metal groundwork is blackened artificially, and a variation lately introduced is that of dull olive green and of blue in the place of black for silver mounted ware.

3. *Brass, Copper, and Mixed Metal Ware.*

[911–1044].—(*a*) Moradabad metal wares.—Vases, flower-pots, *surahis*, jars, *aftabas*, *lotas*, trays, round and oval plates, bowls, saucers, *hukkas*, spittoons, scent-bottles, mugs, tumblers, sugar-basins, and various other articles for ornament and for use, such as shields, photo-frames, wall-brackets, pen-trays, card-trays, cigar-cases, clogs, biscuit boxes, chess-board with pieces, &c., &c.

The effect is produced by chiselling out a pattern on metal and filling in the pattern with lacquer of various colours. This work, commonly known as Moradabad-ware, has advanced in popularity with great strides during the last few years.

[1101–1170].—(*b*) Engraved brass-ware, from Benares.—Vases, salvers, shields, platters, *gharas lotas*, maces, flower-pots, *surahis*, models of temples and mosques, &c., &c.

This is the well-known Benares brasswork.

[1172–1175, 1177, 1181–1183, 1187–1192, 1194–1196].—(*c*) Brass, copper, and mixed metal wares, from Lucknow.—*Lotas*, plain and spouted, plates, mugs, bowls, *hukkas*, *surahis*, *pandans*, banners, single-stick hilts, bells, &c.

Differing from the Benares ware in shapes, suited more for Musulmans than for Hindus.

[1201–1208].—Copper trays, *pandans*, &c., from Lucknow.

Same remarks as above. No. 1206, the large tray, deserves special notice.

[1176, 1179 & 1180].—(*d*) Brass and mixed metal wares, from other places. — Lotas, and cup and saucer, from Sítápur.

[1171].—Sugar-basin, from Bahraich.

[1178, 1184 & 1185].—*Lotas* and cup, from Kheri.

[1186].—*Lota*, from Bara Banki.

[1193].—Brass pen-case, from Gházípur.

[1209–1215].—(*e*) Brass wares, from Jhansi, —*Lotas*, cups, and *Patwaris'* inkstands.

[1216–1224].—(*f*) Metal wares, from Salitpur.—*Lotas*, copper-studded and plain, cups, &c.

Shapes much as elsewhere, the copper-studding in some cases, and the fluted surface in others, constitute the difference. Curious among these, however, are Nos. 1213–14, the inkstands of village accountants.

[1225–1242].—(*g*) Bell metal wares, from Mullipati, Cozamgarh, *Hukkas*, spittoons, *lotas*, plain and fluted, saucers, cups, &c., &c.

This bell-metal, known as *San-Satais*, or "one hundred and twenty-seven," conveys in its name the proportions of the alloy, and can only be obtained in a few places, whereas ordinary bell-metal is common enough.

[1245–1251].—(*h*) Brass images, from Muttra.

Muttra being a place of pilgrimage, a demand for images of Krishna and other deities has fostered skill. Brass and silver toys, in the shape of horses, peacocks, &c., are a speciality of the place.

[1260–1266].—(*i*) Images of mixed metal (Ashtdhat), from Hamírpur.

On a larger scale than those of Muttra and more pretentious in work are the images of mixed metal made in Hamírpur.

5. *Arms and Armour.*

(a.) *Ancient.*

[1301].—Sword and shield with damascened work, from Lucknow.

Specimen of old Lucknow work.

(b.) *Modern.*

[1302–1303 & 1305]. — Sword, shield, and knife, from Agra.

The blades are procured elsewhere, and mounted at Agra.

9. *Enamels other than Jewellery.*

[1451–1464].—Jugs, *surahis*, cups, hukkas, plates, salt-cellars, towel-rings, buckles, &c., from Lucknow.

The best work is that on specimens preserved from the times of the old native Court, of which there are a few in the collection.

DIV. VI.—ART MANUFACTURES IN WOOD, IVORY, ETC.

2. *Inlaid Work.*

[1581-1616].—(*a*) Inlaid works from Manipuri.—Inkstands, pen-trays, plates, watch-cases, boxes, paper-cutters, paper-weights, book-stands, sandals with *lotas*, &c.

Of *shisham* wood, into which patterns are beaten in brass wire and polished. The designs are either of foliage or geometrical. Prices up to Rs. 100. The same work can be introduced with good effect for panelling doors, picture framing, &c.

[1618-1621].—(*b*) Four sandals with *lotas* and bookstands, from Pilibhit.

Work similar to that from Manipuri.

4. *Lacquered Wares.*

[1629-1632 & 1637 & 1640].—(*a*) *Khasdans*, boxes, betel-cases, &c., from Agra.

[1633-1634].—(*b*) Plate and bedstead legs, from Bulandshahr.

[1635-1636].—(*c*) Specimens from Bareilly.

[1638].—(*d*) Set bedstead legs, from Lucknow.

[1641-1648].—(*e*) Painted trays, tea-box, and bracket, from Tilhar, Sháhjahánpur.

[1649-1650].—(*f*) Packs of round playing cards, from Fatehpur.

No particular description called for; each district has a somewhat different style from its neighbour. The lacquering of wood is perhaps more largely applied to the decoration of the legs of *charpais* or native bedsteads than to any other articles.

[1660-1670].—(*g*) *Papier maché* wares,—Trays, cigar-cases, boxes, &c., from Jaunpur.

[1671-1675].—(*h*) *Papier maché* ink-stands, boxes, &c., from Mandawar, Bijnaur.

This work has in both cases been introduced from Cashmere. The Jaunpur work has greatly improved within the last four or five years. That of Mandawar has gradually acquired a distinct character.

5. *Wood Carving.*

[1529-1572]. — Inkstands, envelope-cases, stamp-boxes, clock-cases, book-covers, handkerchief-boxes, glove-boxes, picture-frames, card-trays, tea-caddies, walking-sticks, toilet-boxes, combs, &c., from Nagina, Bijnaur.

This work comes from Nagina, in the Bijnaur district, and has greatly developed of late years. It is now applied to innumerable articles of household and general use. Ebony (*Diospyros melanoxylon*) is especially used. In the more elaborate and expensive work the black is relieved by silver and mother-of-pearl mounts.

[1574].—Specimen of carving, from Sahâranpur.

DIV. VII.—LAPIDARIES' WORK.

1. *Agate, Jasper, and Cornelian Wares.*

[1929-1981].—Paper-weights, knife-handles, knives, paper-cutters, solitaires, brooches, watch-guards, studs, lockets, moss-agates, &c., &c., from Banda. (Most of these are in pairs, and in sets of 6 and 12).

The agates are procured from the bed of the river Ken, in Banda, and are chiefly used for making articles of European design.

DIV. VIII.—MARBLE AND STONE.

1. *Carved objects in Marble.*

[2009-2016].—Carved screens, plate, and boxes, from Agra.

Vide remarks against II., 1.

2. *Inlaid Marble.*

[2029-2044].—Tea-box, plates, boxes, paper-weights inlaid with precious stones and mother-of-pearl.

This industry is peculiar to Agra, and was largely used at the time of building the Taj Mahal. The stones used are procured from all parts of India, and comprise agate, jasper, bloodstone, lapis lazuli, and turquoise.

3. *Carved Stone.*

[2060].—(*a*) Model of a temple, from Mirzapur.

The district of Mirzapur abounds in good stone and good workmen. The model illustrates a Hindu temple, such as is found in various parts of Upper India.

[2061-2067].—(*b*) Carved soapstone wares.—Screens, boxes, plates, &c., from Agra.

This work is executed by the same men who manufacture the inlaid marble wares of Agra.

DIV. IX.—POTTERY.

1. *Glazed Pottery.*

2081-2096].—(*a*) *Surahis*, jars, *lotas*, bowls, basins, cups, and plates, from Khurja, Bulandshahr. (Some of these are in pairs and in sets of 4, 5, and 6).

From Khurja, a town in the Bulandshahr district. There is a greater range of colour and shapes than is found in Rampur work.

[2100 and 2002-2034].—(*b*) *Surahis*, vases, *gubalpashes*, jars, bowls, basins, plates and saucers, &c., from Rampur. (Some are in pairs and in sets of 3, 4, 5, and 9).

The colours are confined to blue and white and claret colour. The style is readily distinguishable.

[2141-2162].—(*c*) *Surahis*, lime jars, ink-bottles, *hukkas*, plates, cups, saucers, teapots, oilcans, &c., from Lucknow. (Some are in pairs and in sets of 4, 5, 6, and 9.)

Have colours and shapes again different to the above.

2. *Unglazed Pottery.*

[2181-2192]. —(*a*) Aligarh black pottery.—Twelve flower vases, jars, *hukkas*, *lotas*, plates &c. (Some are in pairs.)

In plain black or slate colour, carved with raised ornamentation. The colour and appearance is quite special.

[2193-2194].—Aligarh plain red pottery, *surahis* and plates.

[2201-2220].—(*b*) Azamgarh pottery.—*Surahis*, flower-vases, jugs, wine cups, egg cups, butter-dish, soap dish, plates, candlesticks, tea sets, &c. (Most are in pairs.)

A jet black ware covered with floral patterns in silver leaf; a secret process. There are some specimens in which the patterns are worked on a red surface.

[2221-2258].—(*c*) Lucknow painted pottery, *Surahis*, jars, spittoons, glasses, cups, saucers, flower-vases, *abkhoras*, teapots plates, *hukkas*, &c., &c. (Some are in pairs and in sets of 3, 4, 8 and 9.)

[2261-2265]. — (*d*) Gondah painted pottery. —*Surahi*, flower-pots, jars, &c. (All are in pairs with the exception of the *surahi*.)

[2266-2267].—(*e*) Biswan (Sítápur) painted pottery.—Flower-pots and jars. (In pairs.)

Hand-painted in quaint original patterns: a specialty.

[2268-2269].—(*f*) Chunar (Mirzapur) red pottery.—*Surahi* and jar.

Div. XI.—Textiles.

1. *Cotton Fabrics.*

[2721-2727].—(*a*) Sikandarabad (Bulandshahr) muslins.—Turban cloth fringed with gold, handkerchiefs, &c.

Fine, and a distinctive feature is the use of gold thread as a border.

[2728-2735].—(*b*) Masi (Azamgarh) muslins. —Muslins plain and striped.

A large export from this district to Nepal. There is nothing special about the work.

[2736-2745].—(*c*) Lucknow muslins.—Plain and striped, bleached and unbleached.

Muslin is largely manufactured at Lucknow, being preferred for embroidery purposes to English muslin.

[2746-2749].—(*d*) Woven pattern muslins from Jais, Rái Bareli.—Handkerchiefs and check muslins.

[2750-2752].—(*e*) Woven pattern muslin from Benares.—Native caps.

A very delicate loom production, rivalling that of Dacca.

[2756-2762].—(*f*) Rampur *Khes.*

A superior cotton damask, either plain or with borders in coloured thread or interwoven with gold thread. Obtained a Gold Medal at Calcutta.

[2766-2772].—(*g*) Moradabad cloth in dress pieces.

[2774-2785].—(*h*) Coarse cotton fabrics, from Partabgarh in Oudh.—Lehuga cloths, striped and check, &c.

[2791-2792].—Cotton prints, from Partabgarh.

[2786-2788]. — (*i*) Cotton fabrics, from Sítápur.

[2796-2818]. — (*j*) Lucknow chintzes. — Curtains, bed-covers, &c.

[2821-2853].—(*k*) Chintzes from Kanauj and Farrukhabad.—Curtains, bed-covers, &c.

English cloth, hand stamped with patterns of purely native designs, and in fast colours. Farrukhabad and Lucknow command the largest trade, but Kanauj, Bulandshahr, and other towns have a fair amount of trade also, and each place has its own well-recognised styles and patterns.

[2856-2859].—(*l*) Jafarganj (Fatehpur) cotton prints.—Ceiling cloths and curtains.

These are also hand stamped, but are more elaborate in design, and on a larger scale than ordinary chintzes, and are therefore noted separately.

[2862-2904]. — (*m*) Jahangirabad (Bulandshahr) cotton prints.—Chintzes, counterpanes, curtains, table-covers, floor-cloths, &c. (Six of these have each a lining.)

[2920-2925].—(*n*) *Durries* and prayer-rugs, from Agra.

[2926-2933].—(*o*) *Durries* and prayer-rugs, from Aligarh.

[2934-2936].— (*p*) Cotton carpets from Bulandshahr.

These are found of all sizes, but at their best as small prayer carpets for Musalmans. Patterns and work varies with each district.

[3301-3310].—(*q*) Tapestry and fancy *durries*, from Lucknow Jail.

[3311].—(*r*) Fancy *durri*, from Mirzapur Jail.

[3312].—(*s*) Pattern-book of hempen and cotton fabrics, from Lucknow Jail.

2. *Wool Fabrics.*

[3321-3326].—(*a*) Woollen carpets, from the Agra Central Prison.

[3329].—(*b.*) Woollen carpet, from the Lucknow Jail.

[3330-3334]. — (*c*) Woollen carpets and hearthrugs, from the Mirzapur Jail.

These are now a specialty of the Jail Department. The present state of advancement is one far ahead of what was existent in Hindustan immediately previous to the matter being taken up by the jails, and would not, probably if now left to private enterprise, maintain the high standard which the Jail Department, notably at Agra, has attained—witness the productions of Mirzapur and Jhansi. Carpets from the latter city have not been sent, as they are so full of aniline.

[3327-3328].—(*d.*) Woollen pile carpets, from the principal Mirzapur private factory.

Woven from wool on a foundation of cotton, and in the style of Persian carpets.

[3337-3338].—(*e*) Woollen rugs, from Bulandshahr.

[3340].—Felt rug from Bahraich.

Bahraich has a reputation for the excellence of the wool produced in certain parts of the district, and maintains a small trade in felt carpets or rugs of local designs.

3. *Silk Fabrics.*

[3341–3349].—(*a*) Silk fabrics from Benares.—Turban cloths, *chaddars*, dress-pieces, plain and striped, &c.

[3351–3358].—(*b*) Silk fabrics, from Agra.

A large trade maintained, both local and export.

4. *Other Fabrics.*

[3361–3417].—Satinettes in dress-pieces, from Azamgarh.

Of two kinds, (1) silk and cotton; (2) pure silk and *tassar* silk; colours rich, and prices moderate.

DIV. XII.—EMBROIDERY.

1. *Silk, Cotton, and Woollen Thread.*

[3418–3445]. — Native caps, handkerchiefs, jackets, dress-pieces, &c., from Lucknow.

Known as *Chikan* work. Embroidery by hand with silk or cotton thread on muslin of local manufacture. A large trade.

[3347–3348].—Two embroidered alms-bags, from Benares.

2. *Gold and Silver.*

[3453–3459].—(*a*) *Kamdani*, or muslins hand embroidered in gold thread, from Lucknow.—Caps, dress-pieces, *saris*, &c.

[3460–3490].—(*b*) *Zardozi*, velvet and cloth embroidered with gold and silver thread.—Shawls, caps, laces saddle-cloths, mantelpiece fringes, &c., &c., from Lucknow.

[3562–3574].—(*c*) *Kinkhabs*, or cloth of gold from Benares.—Dress-pieces, table-cloths, &c.

Calls for no special remark, but is perhaps the most effective of all fabrics shown.

[3575].—(*d*) Gold and silver embroidered banners from Benares.

The names Lucknow, Agra, and Benares are worked on these. They are intended for the prominent exhibits from those places.

[3576–3580].—(*e*) Embroidered *izarbands* or scarfs from Agra.

[3581–3595].—(*f*) Agra lace, in rolls.

[3598–3600].—(*g*) Ornamental *hukka* pipes, from Agra.

[3601–3605].—(*h*) Whips and walking sticks from Fatehpur.

DIV. XIII.—LEATHERS AND FURS.

1. *Shoes.*

[3491–3492].—Native shoes from Etah. Of horse-hide, and singularly light.

2. *Poshtins, Belts, Saddlery, &c.*

[3501—3508].—Embroidered *sambhar* leather, from Gorakhpur. — Prayer-rugs, cushions, mantelpiece fringes, table-covers, &c.

An art peculiar to the district of Gorakhpur, where the light, buff-coloured leather from the hide of the *sambhar deer* is embroidered with bright-coloured floss silks.

DIV. XIV.—BASKETS, MATS, AND STRAW WORK, ETC.

[3511–3515].—Matting from the Lucknow jail.

[3546–3556]. — Peacock-feather fans from Jhansi.

[3557–3560]. — Peacock-feather fans from Agra.

[3561]. — Peacock-feather trimming, from Jhansi.

THE PUNJAB.

DIV. I.—FINE ARTS.

1. *Paintings and Drawings.*

[2006].—Native figure drawings.

The correctness in matters of detail of these coloured sketches by a self-taught draughtsman of Chiniot (Jhang District) may give them some interest.

[2113.]—Picture of a native woman, exhibited by the Municipal Committee of Amritsar; Artist, Chamlei Kapen Singh.

3. *Photographs.*

[2007].—Photographs from Nature, mounted.

These small pictures by Mr. W. Bull are from both Musalman and Hindu festival scenes, and from the ordinary street life of Lahore.

[2008]. — Photographs from Nature, unmounted.

Dr. Dickson is the author of this series of 19 photographs of street scenes in Lahore, and other subjects.

[2009].—Photographs from Nature, mounted.

The Secretary of the Female Education Committee, Lahore, sends two photographs of the pupils, teachers, &c., of the Central Female School, Lahore.

[2010].—Photographs from Nature, mounted.

Rai Bahadur Kanhya Lal, M.I.C.E., is the photographer of this set of 45 pictures from both the modern and old buildings of Lahore, with some views of Himalayan scenery.

DIV. II.—DECORATIVE ART.

3. *Archæological Drawings and Models.*

[2005].—Copies of inlaid floors from the Hammam, Dehli.

This series of drawings reproduces the most important details of the inlaid marble floors and walls of the Hammam, Dehli, and is by the Mayo School of Art, Lahore.

[2011].—Drawings of old buildings in Lahore. These drawings, sent by the Municipality of Lahore, represent some of the pottery inlay on Lahore brick constructions of the 17th century.

[2012].—Drawings of old Punjab buildings. Drawings by a draughtsman in the Public Works Department of indigenous architecture, sent by the Municipality of Lahore.

[2064]. — 1. Model of Amritsar Golden Temple.

The "Durbar Sahib" of the Sikhs at Amritsar owes its English name, "Golden Temple," to the fact that the upper portion, as shown in this model, is sheathed in embossed copper, gilded. The lower part is covered with marble inlaid in cornelian jasper, and mother o' pearl in Arabesque patterns, similar to those in the Hammam of the Palace at Dehli and in the Taj at Agra. There are, however, notable differences, for the Sikhs not being bound by any Muhammadan canon to exclude representations of living creatures, introduced birds, fishes, and occasionally human figures, into the work. In their treatment of the ordinary forms of Muhammadan architecture they were beginning to make changes, and it is possible that they might have developed an interesting style of their own. This model is the work of Sikh carpenters at Amritsar.

Terra-Cotta and Plaster Busts.

4. *Models in Clay, Terra-cotta, Wax, Plaster of Paris, &c.*

[1986].—Sikh Policeman by G. P. Pinto.

[1987].—*Mehtar* or Sweeper. G. P. Pinto.

[1988].—Hill cultivator, Hindu, from Kangra. G. P. Pinto.

[1989].—Naturalized Pathan, Lahore District. G. P. Pinto.

[1990].—Mussalman Carpenter, Lahore. G. P. Pinto.

[1991]. — Hindu Carpenter, from Nabha. G. P. Pinto.

[1992].—Sikh Carpenter, Lahore. J. L. Kipling.

[1993]. — Lac Turner (Mussalman), from Pakpattan. J. L. Kipling.

These busts are portraits of Punjab working people and others.

Terra-Cotta Statuettes, by G. P. Pinto.

[1994].—Mussalman Fakir.

[1995].—Jatni woman with a child, Sikh.

[1996].—Mussalman Jatni woman with a child.

[1997].—Mussalman Jatni carrying noonday meal to reapers.

[1998].—Punjab Dâk runner.

[1999].—Simla Mail Tonga driver.

[2000].—Hindu Fakir.

[2001].—Soldier, Native Infantry (Pathan).

[2002].—A Sowar, Sikh.

A series of terra-cotta figurines sketched in clay from living models.

5. *Decorative Painting as applied to Architecture.*

[2003].—Sikh wall-paintings—Copies of the work of to-day on the golden temple (Darbar Sahib) of the Sikhs at Amritsar.

These are sent to show the most popular decorative style of wall-painting now in vogue.

[2004].—Copies of fresco wall-paintings from Wazir Khan's Mosque, 17th-century work.

These copies are by the Mayo School of Art, Lahore.

6. *Painting applied to Articles of Domestic Use.*

[97-100]. — Kamágri or Kamángiri work. Painted wood-work. Delhi clothes-chests, cupboard doors, and bed-legs.

[84-85].—Kamágri work. Dera Ghazi Khan bows and arrows.

[86-87].—Kamágri work. Muzaffargarh bows.

[88-92].—Kamágri work. Multan bed-legs, bows, arrows, boxes.

[93].—Kamágri work. Kangra bed-legs.

[94-95].—Kamágri work. Bed-legs and box, Lahore.

[96].—Kamágri work. Jhang. Painted door-panels from Chiniot.

[364-365].—Painted panels, Kashmir.

[362-363]. — Sialkot papier maché work-bowls.

Linseed oil is not used as a vehicle for colour in the Punjab, excepting in the case of the Afridi painted cloths from Peshawar, and in work for Europeans, by whom, as in railway and other workshops, European methods have been introduced. The decoration of the bow-and-arrow, which, till recently, were in ordinary use, and which are still made, has given its name—Kumángiri—vulgarly Kamágri, from Kamán a bow—to the indigenous scheme of painted decoration on wood. It is invariably water-colour, protected by a varnish. Sometimes true gold is used to heighten the effect, and it is occasionally punched and otherwise treated, but more frequently a ground of tin-foil, or of tin levigated, and used like European shell gold or silver, is laid as a preliminary. Over this, transparent and semi-transparent colours acquire a sheen, or, where the foil is left uncoloured, yellow or white varnishes produce the effect of gold or silver. The bows from Multan and other districts show the original and still existent form of the art, and the linen-chest and bed-legs from Delhi, its modern practice. In old houses, doors and chests are sometimes found of a simpler and better type of design, and of a more agreeable colour. Linseed oil is now made in the Punjab, and the European methods of oil-painting are gaining ground everywhere within reach of a railway station. As a curiosity of craftsmanship, it may be mentioned that varnish is invariably applied with the palm of the hand.

7. *Wood Carving applied to Architecture.*

[101-102].—Carved door and window, Bhera (Shahpur District).

[103].—Carved door, Jhelum.

[105].—Bow window, Chiniot (Jhang District).

[106].—Carved window, Rawal Pindi.

[107].—Carved window, Hissar.

[108].—Screen of three arches, Sialkot.

[120].—Carved window, Batala (Gurdaspur District).

[121].—Arcade of three arches, Batala, Gurdaspur.

This group of doors, windows, and arcades represents pretty fairly the architectural woodwork of the Province. As timber is not so plentiful as formerly, house-fronts are not now often built entirely of wood; but in all new houses the doors and windows are carved, and there are no signs of decadence in the wood-carvers' art. Some of the old work is of a finer quality of design and execution, but the difference is mainly one of fashion and style. The present style has succeeded the older manner in a perfectly natural and legitimate way. The cheapness of this work is due to the fact that most Punjab carpenters practice ornamental carving from their infancy. Carving is considered as a part of the carpenters' business, and there are few towns or villages without good examples.

[104].—Carved door, Kamal.

This door-frame, from the southern part of the Punjab, is exceptional, and is copied from an old Hindu stone door. There is scarcely any Hindu sculpture in wood extant, and on the Punjab plains very little Hindu stone carving. The current architectural notions are entirely Mussalman.

[109 to 114].—Six panels in geometrical tracery of joiners' work, *Pinjra*, literally "cage-work." Sialkot, Peshawar, Jhang.

These are specimens of the Arabic geometrical wood work, which is an important feature in Punjab architectural design. The carved panels from Sialkot are intended for use in furniture.

[115 to 119].—Twenty front arches, and four end arcades. Screens forming the frontage of the Punjab Court, made at Lahore, Amritsar, and Udoki.

[2063].—1. Carved door, Amritsar.

8. *Works of Art not specified.*

[2013].—Engraved silver seal. (Indian and Colonial Exhibition.)

This seal is made by Hamam Singh and Partab Singh, of Shahabad, in the Amballa district. The trade of Mohr Kand, or signet cutter, is a common one, but it is almost universally confined to engraving vernacular signatures on blood-stone for the use of those who sign their names by affixing an impression of their seals. The craftsmen mentioned above, however, have carried their practice much further than usual, and can engrave crests, animals, &c., in intaglio, both in stone and metal, with great skill.

DIV. III.—MUSICAL INSTRUMENTS.

1. *Wind Instruments.*

[143-153].—Flageolets, flutes, twin-pipes, snake-charmers, *binjogis*, horns, whistles, &c.

Among these are the twin-pipes, popular in both the hills and plains (148), and the *Binjogi*, a pipe with a gourd air-chamber, best known as the Snake Charmer's instrument.

2. *Stringed Instruments.*

[125-142].—*Madhams, Sitars, Taus, Rasbin, Sarangi, King, Tambura*, &c.

The most characteristic of these instruments are the *Sarangis* (violins) from Bannu and Dera Ghazi Khan (137 to 142). The *Tambura* and *Sitar* are oriental forms of the guitar, used to accompany the voice. The *Taus* (Persian for peacock) is the name given to a stringed instrument terminating in the form of a peacock.

[2117].—A musical instrument, *Taus*, exhibited by the Municipal Committee of Amritsar.

[2065-2066].—Stringed instruments, peacock and understrung guitar, Amritsar.

Madham Sitar, or the understrung guitar, is the commonest and most popular of all instruments now in vogue in the Province.

3. *Instruments of Percussion.*

[155-157].—*Douru, Khanjri*, and *Tapcha*.

Three insignificant instruments, represent inadequately a large class of drums, &c.

DIV. IV.—JEWELLERY.

1. *Gold and Silversmiths' Work, including Filigrain Setting of Precious Stones, &c.*

[1863-1888].—Sialkot jewellery, forehead ornaments, nose ornaments, earrings, gold and silver necklaces, bangles, thumb-rings, anklets, armlets, toe-rings.

[1889-1899, 1936-1938, & 1944].—Lahore jewellery, necklaces, armlets, head ornaments, scent boxes, puzzle rings.

[1900-1906].—Hoshiárpur jewellery, necklaces, head ornaments, bangles, *huka* tube, boxes, walking cane mounts.

[1907-1914].—Gujránwála jewellery, anklets, bracelets, rings, earrings, and nose ring.

[1915-1917]. — Jalandhar jewellery, belt-clasps, ring, silver-wire shoes.

[1918-1921].—Bannu jewellery, silver bird, rings, necklace.

[1922-1923].—Hissar jewellery, earrings.

[1924-1935 & 1939].—Batala (Gurdaspur district) jewellery, anklets, necklaces, bracelets, head and forehead ornaments, earrings, and gold nose ornament.

The selection of gold and silversmiths' work for personal adornment, has been limited by circumstances to purely popular forms. Most of the ornaments in ordinary use in the Punjab will be found, but there are very few of a costly kind.

[1940-1943]. — Hazara jewellery, armlets, bracelets, anklet, forehead ornament.

[1945-1964]. — Rohtak jewellery, belt, *huka* mouth-piece, head and face ornaments, earring, nose-ring, silver necklace, armlet, toe-ring, scent-boxes.

[1862].—Kamal jewellery, a necklace (Pampat beads).

[1984-1985].—Sham jewellery.

2. *Enamelled Jewellery.*

[1966-1974].—Kangra enamel, belt, rings, necklace, forehead ornament, ear and toe-rings.

[1976-1981]. — Multan enamel, necklaces, bracelets, pendants.

[1965].—Hazara enamel, a necklace.

[1975].—Jhang enamel, earrings and rings.

[1982].—Bahawalpur enamel, a scent casket.

Enamelling (Mina Kari) is done in the South Punjab (Multan, Jhang, and Bahawalpur) and also at Kangra. It is also occasionally done by individual workmen elsewhere. The term *Mina* means in Persian a glass vase, or blue glass, also applied to the sky, the azure deep, &c., and hence to the blue vitreous enamel, which is the commonest sort.

Div. V.—Manufactures in Metal.

1. *Gold and Silver Plate.*

[2049 & 2050].—Silver-gilt ewers from the Patiala State.

These are Hindu pattern, and used like the Mussalman *aftàba* as drinking vessels and for ablution.

[2074].—1. A Cashmere ink and pen case (silver).

Wrought by Kashmiris at Amritsar.

2. *Koft or Damascened Work.*

[376-601 & 620-642].—Koft or damascened work from Kotli Loharan (Sialkot) armour, caskets, trays, picture-frames, &c., &c.

[602-619 & 643].—Koft or damascened work from Gujrát.

[644-650].—Koft or damascened work from Lahore.

This art, which takes its European name from Damascus, was formerly extensively practised on the arms and armour made in the chief towns of the Punjab. It is now localized at Kotli (Sialkot) and Gujrat. The articles made are chiefly ornamental small wares for decorative purposes. The art consists in incrusting or inlaying a wire of one metal, usually gold or silver, on another in ornamental patterns: gold and steel are the favourite materials. In the best examples (*tar-i-nishan*) the pattern is first incised, and the wire is laid in. In the ordinary work of the Punjab, the iron or steel is first roughened all over, and the gold or silver wire is laid on in foliated patterns, and burnished into its place. The ground is afterwards blued by heat. The surface of the iron or steel is sometimes chiselled in patterns in relief. Specimens of this variety are shown from Lahore. Two caskets, Nos. 642 & 643, from Sialkot and Gujrat, were made to the order of the Royal Commissioners.

3. *Brass, Copper, and Mixed Metal Wares.*

[1401-1434].—Rewari brass ware; *Hukas*, *pandáns* (betel-nut boxes), water vessels, lamps, pen-cases, cart-bells, cattle-bells, temple-bells, &c., &c.

Rewari, in the Gurgaon district, is the seat of a manufacture of brass ware, the greater part of which, in accordance with modern custom, is tinned. The graven patterns are minute, and comparatively ineffective, and it would seem that Moradabad wares are imitated. The artisans, as in many other trades, are entirely in the hands of Hindu middlemen and dealers, to whom they are always indebted, and their life is practically a long slavery.

[1440].—Bahawalpur brass wares.

Kaul-lotus is the name given to a small brass bowl shaped like a lotus, and hence often to small bowls in general.

[1448-1463].—Sialkot brass ware, cups, *hukas*, drinking vessels, &c.

The brass cups in this series are described as Bahawalpuri Kauls.

[1464-1470].—Dera Ghazi Khan brass wares.

[1471-1474].—Jhang brass wares, locks, shot-mould, and antimony bottle.

The finish of these four articles is seldom met with in wares for native use.

[1476-1478].—Ludhiana brass ware.

A good padlock is an important article in native estimation. Four locks from Ludhiana are in the form of animals with the European lever action. The normal type of native lock is a screw.

[1481-1489 & 1442].—Jhelum brass ware.

These wares are of distinctively Hindu character.

[1490].—Kamal brass ware.

[1491-1494].—Peshawar tinned copper.

Copper engraven and tinned is a favourite material for vessels of Muhammadan use. Persian patterns are in vogue at Peshawar.

[1495].—Dehli brass toys.

This set of forty-nine brass toys includes locomotives, *ekkas*, merry-go-round, toy vessels, &c., as commonly sold.

[2032-2034].—Patiala brass objects.

[1435].—Lahore brass ware.

A paten made for a native Christian church.

[1475].—Gurdaspur brass ware.

[1437].—Amritsar beaten work in copper.

The upper part of the golden Temple at Amritsar (the Darbar Sahib of the Sikhs) is sheathed in beaten work of copper, heavily gilded. This door is in the style of some of the beaten silver doors at this temple.

[1438].—Amritsar beaten work in brass.

The minuteness of this work gives it an unfortunate resemblance to European die-stamped work of Birmingham It is, however, entirely hand-wrought; and like the door mentioned above, is the work of Dooloo, a *chatera* or chaser of Amritsar.

[1436].—An Amritsar Chubb lock in brass. Copy of European original.

[2076–2078 and 2084].—Copper-chased ware, Dehli.

[2079–2083].—Brass-chased ware, Dehli.

4. *Modern Hindu Sacrificial Vessels.*

[1621-1625]. — Gurgaon wares for Hindu worship.

Among these vessels are the *arti*, a sacrificial 5-light lamp, platters for mixing sandal-wood paste, cups, vessels for Ganges water, &c.

[1626–1632]. — Sialkot wares for Hindu worship.

This set comprises the *tashta*, or dish in which idols receive ablutions, the *agha*, a vessel symbolising the feminine principle, the *sangásan*, or stand for idols, the *arti* or sacrificial lamp, the bell, the *chamamti* or spoon, and the *kouli* or vessel for mixing sandal-wood paste.

5. *Arms and Armour.*

1496–1513]. — Peshawar arms — Swords, Afghan knives (*peshkaby* and *chura*), shields, helmet.

Among the arms from Peshawar are some old Persian and Bokhara swords, as well as examples of the heavy Afghan knife.

[1514–1516]. — Kohat arms — Knives and matchlock.

The matchlocks made at Kohat are rather more characteristic than that of any place in the Province.

[1517–1523].—Bannu arms—Waziri matchlock swords, knives, and sword-sticks (*gupti*).

[1524–1529]. — Dera Ghazi Khan arms—Swords, dagger, gun, and shields.

The sword-belt with its numerous appendages (1524) from Dera Ghazi Khan is an exceptionally good example of the taste and skill which on the frontier are often lavished on war trappings.

[1530–1532].—Gujranwala arms.

Gujranwalla has a name for cutlery and arms.

[1533–1542]. — Bhera arms, daggers and knives.

Old files of English manufacture are sometimes forged into daggers and knives of good quality; but country iron is generally used.

[1543–1588].—Sialkot arms—Set of chain armour, swords, daggers, war-quoits, axes, &c.

Chain-mail suits and *char ania*, or four-plate suits of plate armour, are still made for the retinues of some native chiefs and for sale to Europeans.

[2051].—Patiala dagger.

Made in the workshop of the Patiala State.

[2075].—An Akali's headdress, having war quoits, &c.

The Akalis or Nihangs are now a harmless sect of religious devotees, vowed to wear only steel ornaments, such as war quoits, &c., and indigo-dyed clothes. They were formerly a desperate and dangerous band of fanatics. The wearers of this curious headgear protest that they sleep in it.

6. *Cutlery.*

[1589–1595]. — Sialkot Cutlery, tweezers, betel-nut cutters, penknives, &c.

The blacksmiths at this place are greatly dependent upon the Koftgars, to whose order they make their cutlery, such as knives, betel-nut cutter, scissors, &c. They sell very little independently.

[1596–1600].—Gujranwala cutlery.

Nizamabad, in the Gujranwala district, is known for its cutlery. The finish and polish of the articles, though not perfect, is better than the quality of the steel which, although tough, is deficient in hardness, and is often scarcely to be distinguished from good iron.

[1601–1603]. — Gurgaon cutlery, betel-nut cutter, tweezer, and knife.

[1604–1609].—Bhera cutlery, bread and hunting knives, &c.

See Bhera arms.

[1610].—A Jhelum cutlery bit.

A specimen of the cruel bits in ordinary use.

7. *Iron and Steel Wares.*

[1479–1480].—Gurgaon locks.

[2085–2089].—5. Iron bits, Rohtak.

8. *Electro-plated Wares.*

[1611-1619].—Inkstands, trays, goblets, &c., from Sialkot.

These wares from Sialkot are described as electro-plated. Hitherto the chief use of the electro battery in the Punjab has been to renovate the cover dishes of Anglo-Indian dinner services.

[1620].—Ludhiana goblet, with cover electroplated.

9. *Enamels other than Jewellery.*

[1983].—A Bahawalpur enamelled drinking vessel.

This quality of enamel is peculiar to Bahawalpur.

Div. VI.—Art Manufactures in Wood, Etc.

1. *Carved Furniture and Carpentry.*

[367 & 369 & 370].—Lahore carved furniture, cabinet, hanging-shelf, and a chair.

The curious chair, No. 370, is contributed by the Municipality of Lahore, and is a relic of the period of Sikh rule. It belonged to General Ilabi Bakhsh, who commanded the Sikh artillery.

[368].—Dehli carving, *sangásan* or idol-stand.

[371 & 372].—Sialkot carpentry; four walking-sticks.

[373].—Gujranwala cane and horn-sticks.

[374].—A Ludhiana stick.

[375].—Jhelum fancy walking-sticks.

[2028-2031].—Patiala carving box, sticks, sandals and nosegays.

[2090-2092].—Rohtak walking-stick, rosaries of sandalwood, and a wooden figure of a Jat woman.

2. *Inlaid Work.*

[160-189].—Hoshiárpur work, Shisham wood inlaid with ivory, cabinets, chairs, tables, boxes, picture-frames, brackets, rulers, panels, &c.

The ivory inlay of Hoshiárpur is an industry of recent growth, and owes much of its present character to the exertions of Mr. Coldstream, C.S. The panels, 185 to 189, are intended for cabinet-doors or wall-linings.

[190].—A Lahore ivory inlaid box.

Lent by Rai Kanhya Lal Bahadur.

[191 & 192].—Brass inlay, Chiniot (Jhang District).

The five panels and *kajawa* or camel pannier, No. 192, are specimens of brass inlay practised at Chiniot (Jhang District).

[193-195].—Brass inlay Jalandhar boxes.

[196-198].—Wood inlay Lahore and Amritsar tables.

[2027].—A Patiala inlaid box.

Boxwood inlaid in Shisham is the main feature of these three tables and box.

3. *Ivory Carving.*

[1792-1800]. — Dehli ivory carvings, paper-knives, card-cases, combs, animals.

[1801-1816]. — Amritsar ivory carvings, combs, boxes, paper-cutters.

[1780-1785].—Lahore ivory carvings, models, chessmen, earrings, &c.

[1786-1787].—Sialkot ivory carvings, *churis* or bangles.

[1788]. — Multan ivory turnery, *churis* or bangles.

[1789-1791]. — Ludhiana ivory carvings, antimony bottles, &c.

[1777 & 1779].—Dera Ismail Khan ivory carvings, salt-cellars, box.

[1778].—Jalandhar ivory carving, an antimony bottle.

The principal use of ivory in India is for bangle turning. Ivory bangles are worn by some Hindoo castes. Owing to the preponderance of Mussulman ideas there has never been any ivory figure carving in the Punjab. The work of this kind now done at Dehli is copied from Bengal originals. Geometric tracery applied to combs, paper-knives, &c., is the favourite form of ivory treatment. Card-cases and paper-cutters are made at Dehli and Amritsar for sale to Europeans. There are scarcely any uses for ivory in native life.

[2015-2026].—Patiala ivory carvings, figure of a woman, toys, horse, elephant, card cases, paper-cutters, ivory handled sticks.

Among these is an elaborately carved *bartána*, an instrument for adjusting and smoothing the edge folds of the turban of a person of quality.

[2067-2069]. — Ivory carving, Amritsar—comb, stick, handle, and a model of a garden.

At Amritsar great quantities of combs are made, and also paper cutters and card bones ornamented with geometrical open work patterns of some delicacy of execution. No. 2069 is made by one Kadisbaksh, and the comb carvers are generally Sikhs.

4. *Lac Turnery.*

[201-238].—Hoshiárpur lac-turnery. Ninety-one goblets, boxes, *smallies*, flower-pots, candlesticks, &c.

[239-240]. — Jhelum lac-turnery, spinning-wheel and bridal-stool.

[241-245]. — Firozpur lac-turnery, flower-stands, goblets, candlesticks, vases, &c.

[246].—Kasur (Lahore) lac-turnery, a goblet.

[247-249].—Chunian (Lahore) lac-turnery, bridal-stool, spinning-wheel, and bed legs.

[250].—Batala (Gurdaspur) lac-turnery, a bridal-stool.

[251-260].—Dera Ghazi Khan lac-turnery, toys and painted combs.

[261-271]. — Jalandhar lac-turnery, boxes, ornamental ware, &c.

[272-281].— Bannu lac-turnery, boxes, cigar-cases, cups, &c.

[282-283]. — Sialkot lac-turnery, bed-legs, bridal-stool.

[284-305]. — Pakpattan (Montgomery District) lac-turnery, bed-legs, single-stick and buckler, churn, cups, goblets, flower-stands, seed-drill tube, &c.

[306-321].—Sahiwal (Sháhpur District) lac-turnery, tables, toys, &c.

4. *Lacquered Wares.*

[322-323].—Jhelum lac-turnery, cotton spools.

[325-361].—Dera Ismail Khan lac-turnery, caskets, &c.

[324].—Kamal lac-turnery, four bed-legs.

[366].—Gurdaspur lac-turnery, three bed-legs.

Native house furniture is exceedingly simple, being limited usually to a bedstead, one or two low stools, a spinning-wheel, and a few boxes. A part of each marriage outfit in the Punjab is a charpoy, and a quaint, high-backed stool of turned wood, ornamented with lac. Very little painting on wood is now done, and the lac surface, obtained by pressing what is virtually a stick of coloured sealing-wax on an object revolving in the lathe, is a harder and more solid covering than any paint. The heat developed by friction melts the lac; further friction with the dry stem of a palm leaf held endwise, and a final application of an oiled rag of muslin, polish a coat of colour which resists dust, the great heat of the hot weather, and the damp of the rains. But there are many refinements in this most simple art. In Sindh and in the Punjab layer upon layer of coloured lac are laid. Then, with a stylus these coats are scratched through in a manner analogous to Italian *sgraffito* decoration. Supposing red to have been first laid, then green, and, lastly, black, the black is scratched through for green leaves, the green and black for a red flower, and for a white line all are cut through to the wood, and a green pattern with white outlines on a black field is thus produced. The Firozpur pattern scratching is, perhaps, the most skilful, while that of Dera Ismail Khan is the most minute. It is done by women. The wood used is generally shisham (*Dalbergia sissu*), but the tamarind, acacia, and other non-resinous woods are also employed. The workmen have recently discovered that aniline colours can be used, and, in consequence, the Dera Ismail Khan work has lost the sobriety of dark red, black, yellow, and silver, which used to distinguish it.

DIV. VII.—LAPIDARIES WORK.

1. *Agate, Jasper, and Cornelian Wares.*

[1817–1826].—Amritsar lapidaries work in cornelian, agate, jade, &c., knife-handles, sleeve-links, paper-knives, necklaces.

There is some trade in these ornaments, and it is suspected that many are imported and not actually wrought in Amritsar. Possibly the cornelian wares are from Guzerat (Bombay).

[1827–1832].—Bhera (Shahpur), boxes, bracelets, knife-handles, charms.

[2070–2073]. —Jadehead necklaces, sword handles, and paper cutters, Amritsar.

DIV. VIII.—MARBLE AND STONE.

1. *Carved Objects in Marble.*

[2014].—Marble carved book-stand (Rehl).

DIV. IX.—POTTERY—DEHLI POTTERY.

1. *Glazed Pottery.*

[1101–1133].—Dehli pottery.

In its present state is a purely modern product. Though it is clear that it is possible to make a kind of porcelain with the materials to be procured in the neighbourhood, there is no ground for the frequently expressed belief that the manufacture was formerly an important Indian industry. The paste or body is artificial, and is composed for the most part of powdered stone, held together for moulding with a *massala* of gum. It is in consequence deficient in tenacity, and cannot easily be worked on the wheel. The shapes are therefore pressed in moulds. In inferior specimens the glaze frequently separates from the body, but when thoroughly fired the whole substance undergoes an elementary stage of vitrifaction, becomes semi-translucent and approaches porcelain. The prices have steadily risen since it has been brought into notice. The potter is Bhola of Dehli.

[1134–1151].—Gujranwala pottery.

Large jars like these from Gujranwala are occasionally made for storing grain, but it is seldom they are glazed.

[1152–1156].—Peshawar pottery.

At Peshawar and on the frontier glazed pottery is used for eating from. Scarcely anywhere else in the country does this practice obtain. The *tabakh*, a large circular dish, of Persian origin, is the typical piece. Tourists, Anglo-Indians, and the Commissariat Department have asked for wares for use and decoration. The local potters have occasionally attempted to supply the demand, but with no great success.

[1157–1163].—Jalandhar pottery.

This ware is made by Mohamed Sharif. No. 1158 is a large tile copied from a piece of the old pottery mosaic to be found on many mosques and tombs in the Punjab. In the original, however, each leaf and stem is in a separate piece, and is in fact a mosaic of many pieces. Mohamed Sharif does not, apparently, work for any regular market, but now and then produces a few wares to show that he possesses potting secrets.

[1164–1172].—Lahore pottery.

Lahore was once notable for the mosaic of coloured and glazed pottery, with which the mosques and tombs were inlaid, and also for tiles of faience for decorative purposes. There is but little use for glazed pottery in native life, and this series merely shows that the manufacture is possible. But as the brick earth of the neighbourhood is poor in quality, and fuel, with other materials, scarce and dear, it is not likely the trade will grow. This maker is the only potter in Lahore who uses a vitreous glaze, and he complains that, excepting for *huka* bowls, there is no demand for these wares, and his principal trade is in unglazed flower-pots and water vessels.

[1173].—Multan pottery; tomb in blue and white glazed pottery.

[1174–1207].—Multan pottery, vases, *surahis*, &c.

The original and most important use of glazed pottery at Mooltan and in Sind, as elsewhere in the East, was for the decoration of wall surfaces in mosques, tombs, &c. The tomb No. 1173 is by Mohamed Azim, and is copied from an example at Multan. The vases are produced in response to the modern demand for drawing-room ornaments. Except for the *huka* and the *surahi* there is no place in native life for vessels of glazed pottery, and it had never occurred to Oriental potters to make merely decorative vases.

[1208].—Multan pottery.

Pirbaksh, potter of Multan, is the maker of this set of nine pieces of glazed earthenware, which are more like the work of Sind, further south on the Indus, than the typical Multan ware.

[1209–1215].—Sialkot pottery.

2. *Unglazed Pottery.*

[1216].—Bahawalpur pottery.
[1217].—Gurgaon pottery.
[1218].—Jalandhar pottery.
[1219].—Rohtak pottery.

[1220].—Rohtak pottery.

[1221-1223].—Rawal Pindi painted pottery.

Unglazed pottery alone is in really general use. The present series does not include the larger water vessels carried to the well, or the huge cooking vessels used for caste-dinners, &c.

[1224-1247].—Models of snakes, Dehli.

These models are used in district offices for the identification of those poisonous snakes for the destruction of which rewards are offered by the Government.

[1248-1250]. — Sialkot toys and models of fruits sold at festivals.

Div. X.—Glass.

1. *Blown Objects.*

[2052].—Jori Gola. Pair glass globes.

Globes blown and silvered, frequently broken up to furnish the small mirrors sewn into embroidered garments or wrought into the arabesque tracery of plaster wall decoration. Sometimes hung up in houses.

2. *Moulded Articles.*

[2053-2055].—Dehli glass bangles.

[2056-2061].—Dehli lac bangles.

[2062].—A set of Lahore lac bangles.

These are worn by the dozen as bracelets on either arm chiefly by the lower class females, both Hindu and Muhammadan.

[2111].—Set Rohtak lac bangles.

Div. XI.—Textiles (Cotton Prints).

1. *Cotton Fabrics.*

[1-7].—Cotton prints for decorative purposes by Allayár of Kot Kamalia (Montgomery District).

This series was made to order of the Royal Commissioners, and was intended to serve as hangings in one of the vestibules of the Exhibition.

[8-27 & 43-46].—Kot Kamalia cotton prints, floor-clothes, bed-covers, table-cloths, wall-hangings, portières, &c.

[698-700].—Dera Ismail Khan cotton prints, quilts.

[28-32].—Dehli cotton prints.

[33-37].—Multan cotton prints.

[38-39].—Firozpur cotton prints.

[42].—Umballa cotton prints.

[47-55].—Sialkot cotton prints, floor-cloths, and quilt covers.

[56-63].—Lahore cotton prints, curtains, floor-cloths, wall-hanging, &c.

[754].—Gurdaspur cotton prints.

[64-66].—Amritsar cotton prints.

[67-68 & 752-753].—Sultanpur (Kapurthala) cotton prints.

[2101-2109].—9. Rohtak turbans, muslins, and woman's dress, &c.

[2101-2104] Are country-woven fabrics, but the yarn used is English. Their prices vary from 2 anas to Rs. 2 a yard.

Colour printing on cotton cloth is practised in most towns and villages of the Province. The patterns, with one or two insignificant exceptions, are large and coarse, probably because the material usually preferred for a quilt—the decoration of which is the staple of the cotton printers' trade—is the stout and rough hom-spun known as *Khadar*. The dyes used hitherto are simple, being mostly indigo, madder, pomegranate rind, turmeric, safflower, catechu, the sulphates of iron and copper and acacia pods, used with tamarisk galls, alum, and vegetable acids. The blocks are of wood, and are cut by ordinary carpenters as a rule. Some of these prints are suitable for wall hangings, especially because of the boldness of the pattern, which repeat the motives of Muhammadan wall decoration. Those of Kot Kamalia, by Allayar, Nos. 8 to 27 and 43-46, may be noted. Cotton printers form a caste known as *Chhimba* or *Chipi*, distinct from the dyers (*Rangrez*). At the last census 10,199 men and 1,105 women were returned as cotton printers in the Punjab, but probably some of these are only washermen. Aniline colours are liked by natives, and are only kept out of cotton prints by their cost. The average price of cotton print on native cloth in three or four colours is about ten annas per square yard.

Textiles (Tinsel Prints).

1. *Cotton Fabrics.*

[69-71].—Tinsel and gold and silver prints, Dehli.

[72-74].—Tinsel prints, Amritsar.

[76].—Sirsa tinsel print.

[75, 77 & 78].—Hissar tinsel prints.

[684].—Sialkot tinsel print.

Tinsel printing in false gold or silver is extensively practised on cloths worn at weddings. Sometimes colour is used in combination with the foil on white cloths, and occasionally real gold and silver leaf are applied. The method is to stamp the pattern in a glutinous size, on which the foil is afterwards pressed.

[79-83, 651-655 & 761-764].—Rohtak tinsel prints.

The Rohtak foil prints are exceptionally durable; sometimes they are true gold and last for many years.

[765].—Ludhiana tinsel print.

[701-707].—Knot-dyeing, Dehli.

[696-697].—Knot-dyeing, Dera Ismail Khan.

The production of patterns in dyed cloths by means of tying up portions into knots, which are protected from the action of the dye, is probably one of the oldest forms of cloth decoration known. The *Chunnis* of the North-West Provinces are the best known and most largely produced examples, but this mode of colouring is practised in Bombay and elsewhere. The *Chiras* Nos. 701-703 are from Dehli, and are examples of one of the most elaborate forms, stripes in various colours being produced on narrow widths of muslins for turban pieces.

[40–41].—Painted cloths, Firozpur.

The *abras* (quilts Nos. 40–41), are curious examples of a very elementary kind of decoration from Firozpur.

[744–749].—Painted Afridi cloths, Peshawar.

"Afridi lac cloth" is a popular misnomer for cotton cloth decorated with linseed oil painting. This work is not peculiar to the Punjab frontier, but is practised by Hindus at Ahmedabad and Morvi, in the Bombay Presidency. At Nasik a perforated stamp at the end of a tube full of colour produces a pattern on a similar principle to the perforated cylinders used to make patterns in front of thresholds, but in one case the colour is a dry powder, and in the other it is mixed with linseed oil. As the paint dries, powdered mica is sprinkled over it. The Peshawar work is all traced with a stick, no stamps or tubes being used, and the original colours, before the attention of tradespeople was drawn to it, were always good. The work is more durable than might be supposed, and some specimens from Bannu are really fine in colour. Much of the Peshawar work is very poor.

[658–661].—*Khes*, chequered cloth, Muzaffargarh.

[656–657].—Lahore *khes*.

[662].—Sialkot *khes*.

[663–664].—Firozpur *khes*.

[665].—Karnal *khes*.

[666–670].—Jhang *khes*.

[694–695].—Dera Ismail Khan *khes*.

[756].—Gurdaspur *khes*.

[2046].—Patiala *khes*.

Khes is the name by which a stout fabric, woven in coloured chequer patterns is known in the Punjab. The loom for *khes* weaving is wider than usual, and the cloth is prized for winter wraps. It is suitable for some European uses. Dark red, dark blue, and white, are the usual colours. Newer combinations, though often tried, are seldom agreeable in effect. Rs. 19 per hundred yards is an ordinary price, but there are several qualities. These cloths are something like the ginghams and checks of England. They are mostly woven with imported yarn either English or Bombay mill-spun.

[716–731, 750 & 751].—Ludhiana checks.

[713–714].—Jalandhar checks and *gabrúns*.

Susi, Loom-striped Cloths.

[715].—Jalandhar *Susi*.

[755].—Gurdaspur *Susi*.

[672–679].—Sialkot *Susi*.

Susi is the popular name for a peculiar quality of striped cloth (loom coloured), which is in great favour for women's *pyjamas* (drawers) and other articles of dress. Printed imitations of *Susi* are now imported from Europe, but the English cloth, compared with that of native make, is of such poor substance that it does not seriously compete with native cloths. Lines of silk are frequently introduced into the warp,—as in those from Sialkot, Nos. 672, 679.

[711–712].—Rahon *Ghâti*, Jalandhar calico.

Ghâti answers to the best longcloth of England, and was formerly woven of fine quality. The manufacture is naturally declining on account of the competition with European goods, but it is dying hard.

[680–683, & 685–693]. Sialkot *lungis*, *safas* and *lachas*—turban and waist-cloth pieces.

Lungi, *lacha*, *safa*, are names given to pieces woven for turbans, neckcloths (worn flowing loosely) and waist cloths in separate pieces often with coloured or gold thread ends. Many of these are woven with imported mill-spun yarn.

[671].—Sirsa turban.

[708–710].—Jalandhar turbans.

[732–734].—Ludhiana turbans.

[735–742].—Shahpur turbans.

Among the Shahpur turbans, No. 736 is specially devoted to beggars of a particular kind.

[757].—Rohtak turban.

[743].—Gurdaspur bed-cloth *chotahi* (fourfold).

[2044–2045].—Patiala *chotahi* and *khes*, white.

[758].—Rohtak *tanzeb*, muslin.

The Rohtak muslin is nearly the only fine web now woven in the province. Except at Dehli and in the south of the province there never was any considerable production of muslin in the Punjab.

[759–760].—Gurgaon turbans.

Darris.

[1859].—Multan Jail *durree* (floor-cloth).

[1855].—Ludhiana Jail *durree* (floor-cloth).

[1856–1857]. — Rawal Pindi Jail *durrees* (floor-cloth).

[1858].—Kasur (Lahore) *durree*.

[1860–1861].—Umballa *durrees*.

[2047].—Patiala Jail *durree*.

[1853–1854].—Multan cotton-pile carpets.

The cotton *durree* is one of the most popular of Indian floor coverings. It is less liable to the attacks of insects than a woollen carpet, is cooler and can be washed.

2. *Woollen Fabrics.*

[1701–1736]. — Ludhiana shawls, *jamewars* (striped curtains), table-covers (Ahmad Shah and Ahsan Shah).

[1737–1748]. — Amritsar (Daree Sahai and Chamba Mal) shawls, curtains, dressing-gowns, &c.

[1749–1769].—Amritsar (Daree Sahai Prub Dyal) shawls, dressing-gowns, table-cloths, curtains, and dress material.

[1770]. — Peshawar *Jamewar* (striped curtains).

[1771–1773].—Sialkot shawl work.

[1774–1775].—Gurdaspur shawls.

The series of fine woollen goods contributed by three of the most extensive shawl merchants of the province fully display the present state of the manufacture. Many of the shawls sent are of exceptional fineness. The delicate yarn spun by Kashmiri women is supposed to defy imitation by European machinery. Messrs. Daree Sahai Chamba Mal, and Messrs. Daree Sahai Prub Dyal of Amritsar, exhibit specimens of the finest plain shawls now made.

[1776].—Gurgaon wool work with shells.

Cushions or pads on which the water jar is carried.

[1633–1639].—Wool-pile carpets, Dehli Jail.

[1664–1666].—Multan carpets and rugs.

[1640–1643].—Lahore Jail carpets.

[1644].—Multan Jail carpet.

[1645].—Rawal Pindi Jail carpet.

[1646].—Gujrat Jail carpet.

[1647].—Amritsar Jail carpet.

[1648].—Sialkot Jail carpet.

[1653].—Kasur (Lahore).

The carpet weaving of the Punjab jails was first brought into notice at the London Exhibition of 1862. It was virtually a new industry, for with the exception of a few fabrics of inferior quality at Multan, there was then no independent manufacture in the Punjab. There is no caste of carpet weavers, and though there are traditions of carpets having been woven at Lahore during the time of Akbar, but few authentic examples can be found, and the art had entirely died out long before the period of Sikh rule, during which time, of course, there was absolutely no demand for the products of this purely Muhammadan craft. The example set by the jails has occasionally been followed outside, but hitherto no fabrics by independent makers have equalled jail work.

[1649–1652].—Turkistan and Persian carpets imported into Peshawar.

Persian and Turkoman carpets are imported into Peshawar with other products. The warp is frequently of wool and the best examples are remarkable for their velvet-like texture and richness of colour.

[1654 & 1662–1663].—Amritsar carpets (Daree Sahai Chamba Mal).

[1655–1661].—Amritsar carpets (Daree Sahai Prub Dyal).

The Amritsar carpets are woven by Kashmiris, and strongly resemble the ordinary Kashmiri carpet.

[2048].—Patiala Jail carpet.

[1673–1674].—Bannu carpets.

[1675].—Bannu saddle-cloth.

These curious carpets, of a dingy red-ochre colour, are peculiar to the Bannu district.

[1678–1695].—Biluch rugs, saddle-bags, horse and camel gear from Dera Ghazi Khan.

The effect of these trappings can scarcely be appreciated when separated from the animals for which they are devised. The work is wrought by the women of pastoral tribes. Similar articles, also ornamented with shells, are made in some parts of the Balkans. It is unnecessary to point out the peculiarities of the patterns used.

[1676–1677].—Biluch rugs (Dera Ismail Khan).

[1667–1672].—Kohat felts (*Mundas*), floor and saddle cloths.

In Turkistan, felt is extensively used as a protection against the bitter cold of the winter. On the Punjab frontier, although it is not used for tents, it is largely made to serve a floor-cloth. No carpet gives such a sense of warmth. Felts are made also at Shahpur and other places in the North-West Punjab.

[1698].—Country *puttoo* (homespun), Hazara.

[1699].—Country homespun, Rawal Pindi.

[1700].—Country homespun, Bannu.

Loi is the name given to a length of woollen homespun used as a winter wrap or bed-cover. It is made in most parts of the province, while *kambal* stands for a blanket. Rough fabrics of this kind are often woven by the road side on the most elementary form of loom conceivable.

[1696].—Gaddi costume, Kangra, five pieces.

This dress is from Kangra. The flaps of the cap are generally worn turned up against the peak, but are turned down when the weaver is in mourning. The *kalgi* or plume is stuck in the cap.

[2114–2115].—Carpet patterns exhibited by Davee Sahai Chamba Tual.

[2126].—Carpet pattern exhibited by Davee Sahai Rub Dyal.

3. *Silk Fabrics.*

[766–767].—Bridal dress, Batala, nine pieces.

Wedding dress for Hindu bride and bridegroom.

[768–769].—Bridal dress, Batala, eight pieces.

Wedding dress for Muhammadan bride and bridegroom. These, with the above, are from the Gurdaspur district, and are sent to show one of the rustic uses of the local silk manufactured.

[770].—Moollari silks.

Moollari has long had a reputation both for its silks and for a mixture of silk and cotton, which is lawful for Muhammadan wear.

[771 to 775].—Jhelum *lungis* and silks.

The silk fabrics of Jhelum are highly spoken of by native consumers, but there is only a limited production.

[776 to 784].—Lahore silks.

Wider widths and a better quality of silk were formerly produced at Lahore, but there is still a demand for its fabrics. These are specimens of the ordinary *gulbadan* and *daryai*, the former striped and the latter self-coloured. The shot silks are known as *dhúp chhâon*—sun and shade. Lustre is not here considered indispensable in a silk frbric, and many of them are intended to wash. Prices vary from 8 annas to Rs.5 a yard. The ordinary price for a fair Lahore silk is R. 1 8 annas.

[785].—*Khes* silk, Muzaffargarh.

Khes is the generic name for a check pattern. This is from Muzaffargarh, for rustic wear as a quilt.

[786–789].—Bahawalpur silks.

The Bahawalpur silks are generally striped, and frequently interwoven with gold thread, they have good substance, but little lustre; and are not always good in colour. The present samples are exhibited by H. H. the Nawab of Bahawalpur. The prices vary greatly.

[790–795].—Shahpur silks.

The Shahpur silks are mostly *lungis*, intended to be worn as turbans. The production is for rustic use.

[796 & 801–803].—Wazirabad chenille work, cushions, cigar-cases, boxes, balls, &c.

Chenille making (on wire) is said to have been introduced at Wazirabad (Sialkot district) by an English lady many years ago. It still survives, and the results, though unsaleable among either the lower classes of natives or the upper classes of the English, are said to be popular among the educated natives and the Eurasians.

[804–832].—*Patwa* or *Patolis* work.

Under this head is placed a series of the small wares in silk known as patolis work. They are important parts of native dress, including the *Izárband*, a netted silk girdle used by both sexes, the *paranda*, a silk pendant, or queue worked into woman's hair fringes, buttons, and *sezbands*—a tie used to fasten the four corners of bed sheets to the charpoy or bed-frame. They are from Sialkot, Gurdaspur, Lahore, Patiala, and Dehli.

[2043].—Silk bed-ties, Patiala.

[833–838].—Cabul and Bokhara silks.

These are importations, but they form part of the regular trade of Peshawar, and many are used by natives, especially in Sind.

[839–847].—Peshawar *lúngis* and *kullah pech*.

These turban pieces, like those of Kohat, below, are extensively worn on the Punjab frontier, and are often adopted by Southern folk as handsomer than the ordinary white turban. Some of the arrangements of stripes are like the Scottish tartans, distinctive of various khels or clans. The *kullah pech* is a smaller turban, intended to be wound round the conical gold *kullah* or cap. Some native regiments wear the *kullah pech*.

[797–800].—Jalandhar turbans, with gold ends.

[848–862].—Kohat *lúngis*.

The Kohat *lúngis* are more highly prized on the frontier than those of Peshawar. The bulk of these fabrics, it is unnecessary to say, is usually of cotton.

4. *Miscellaneous Fabrics.*

[1838–1852].—*Moonj* matting, Dehli Jail.

[1833].—*Moonj* matting, Ludhiana Jail.

[1834].—*Moonj* matting, Moollari Jail.

[1835].—*Moonj* matting, Umballa Jail.

[1836].—*Monj* matting, Sialkot Jail.

[1837].—*Moonj* matting, Gujrat Jail.

This matting is made from the fibre of *Moonj* grass (*Saccharum Munja*), one of the commonest of road-side and river-bank reeds. The fibre is obtained from the flower stalk. In the Punjab jails attention has been paid to dyeing and weaving the fibre into a useful floor-cloth. If it should find favour for this purpose out of India, a local industry might be developed, since the fibre, though bearing a very definite value, is plentiful.

Div. XII.—Embroidery.

1. *Embroidery in Cotton, Silk, and Wool Thread.*

[863–914].—Amritsar, *phulkari.*

[915–956 & 1028–1043].—Sialkot, *phulkari*

[957–964].—Montgomery, *phulkari.*

[965–966].—Rawal Pindi, *phulkari.*

[967–968 & 1023–1025].—Firozpur, *phulkari.*

[969–971 & 1018–1022]. —Hazara, *phulkari.*

[972–981].—Bannu, *phulkari.*

[982–292].—Hissar, *phulkari.*

[993–1015].—Lahore, *phulkari.*

[1016–1017].—Karnal, *phulkari.*

[1026–1027].—Kohat, *phulkari.*

[1044–1049].—Dera I. Khan, *phulkari.*

[1379–1382].—Rohtak, *phulkari.*

Phulkari, literally flower-work, is the name applied to the embroidery wrought by peasant women on the *ohrni*, or sheet, which forms the most important part of their dress. Originally only three colours of cotton cloth were used—red, from madder; purple, from a combination of madder with indigo and black, and blue-black, which is produced by catechu and indigo. The colours of the silk are—green, two shades of yellow, crimson, white, black, and dark green, and the cloth used for the purpose was almost invariably the homespun *Khadir*, a coarse fabric, the rough texture of which, however, is admirably suited to give depth and solidity of colour when dyed. The *phulkari* stitch is really a darning stitch, and the best patterns were usually those elementary combinations of the square and triangle which seem to come naturally when darning a fabric, the threads of which can be easily counted. In some districts pieces of thin glass, quick-silvered, are inserted, being held in place by a sort of button-hole stich. In others, a variety of the stitch is applied to the ornamentation of woollen fabrics for winter wraps, and in these, human and animal forms are rudely indicated in squares and triangles. Since a demand has arisen for this work on a large scale, the women of the Kashmiri colony at Amritsar have found it a profitable occupation. In the Amritsar work, the stitches of the cloth are not counted, but the pattern is roughly block printed, and the work is therefore much more cheaply done than in the usual domestic way. Mission and other girls' schools also work *phulkari*, and many experiments have been tried with a view to improve on the original type. As a general rule, these are dismal failures. Smooth English Turkey-red calico and other violently coloured grounds are used, and when these are worked over with the most vivid colours procurable, the results are naturally frightful. Besides the *ohrni*, or mantle, the bodice and skirt are often ornamented with embroidery. *Bagh* is the name given to a close all-over or diaper pattern, and *chope* to a deeply bordered fabric with a field of unworked surface, but *phulkari* is the usual and general name. The prices of *phulkaris* have risen slightly with the demand. They were originally a purely domestic product, never intended for sale, and some of the best have occasionally been acquired at prices that can only cover the price of silk and cloth, and leave out of the account the hours of patient toil they have cost. In judging of *phulkari*, native women look at the back and observe the regularity and neatness of the stitch.

[1378].—Kangra embroidery (known as Chamba *Rumáls*).

This embroidery is peculiar to Chamba and the Kangra district. The India Museum already possesses a very large piece of embroidery in this style, wrought in the household of one of the Ranis of Chamba.

[1050–1057].—Bokhara *soznis*.

Quilts of cotton and occasionally of silk, embroidered with brilliantly coloured silks in bold patterns, are imported into Peshawar. The embroidery is imitated at Shikarpur, a town in Sind, which has long had commercial relations with Central Asia.

2. *Embroidery in Gold and Silver Thread.*

[1058].—Dera Ismail Khan gold embroidery.

[1059–1060]. — Peshawar gold-embroidered caps.

The *kullah* is a gold-embroidered cap, round which the Afghan and frontier turban is wound.

[1061–1097].—Dehli gold and silver and silk embroidery.

This well-known Dehli embroidery needs no detailed description. These numbers are exhibited by Messrs. Maniek Chand, and display the most notable varieties of modern work.

[1098].—Dehli gold and silver embroidery.

The dress of a Dehli dancing-girl.

[1099].—Dehli gold and silver embroidery.

A wedding dress (bridegroom's) as worn at Dehli.

[1100].—Dehli gold and silver embroidery.

A *kalgi* or plume, a horse caparisons.

[2035–2042]. — Patiala gold and silver and silk embroidery, horse and saddle-cloths, table covers, and mantle borders.

Div. XIII.—Leather.

1. *Shoes.*

[1251–1268].—Dehli shoes for men, women, and children.

Dehli has long been celebrated for its gold-embroidered shoes. Twenty years ago its annual exports of these wares were valued at four lacs of rupees, and there is every reason to believe that the trade has greatly increased since that time. The present collection shows the principal varieties in shoes for men, women, and children. The prices range from Rs.7 to 7 annas. Jewelled shoes and other costly kinds are only made to order, and none are included in this series.

[1308–1328].—Hoshiarpur shoes.

Hoshiarpur ranks next to Dehli for shoes, and the series shown contains examples in no way inferior to Dehli work.

[1272–1273].—Jhelum shoes.

[1276 & 1278–1280].—Peshawar shoes.

[1281–1283].—Sialkot shoes.

[1284–1289].—Lahore shoes.

[1290–1291].—Rawal Pindi shoes.

[1292–1293].—Jalandhar shoes.

[1298].—Bannu shoes.

[1301–1304].—Dera Ghazi Khan shoes.

[1336–1337].—Gurdaspur shoes.

This series, from nine districts of the Punjab, displays the shoes in general use. Besides these, it may be added that many *mochis* or shoemakers produce boots of European fashion, for which there is a considerable and increasing local demand. None of these have been included.

[1269–1271].—Kohat sandals.

[1274–1275].—Jhelum sandals.

[1277].—Peshawar sandal.

[1299].—Bannu sandal.

[1294–1297].—Bannu gold-embroidered buskins in red leather.

[1300 & 1305–1307].—Dera Ghazi Khan sandals.

The sandal or *chapli* worn in Northern India varies in form, and none of the varieties resemble the classic shape with a separate stall for the big toe, worn in Bombay. In parts of the Himalaya and Kashmir an elaborately laced sandal encloses a sock in soft deer-skin, and forms one of the most comfortable foot-coverings known. The Peshawar sandal is generally embroidered with silk, and specimens of this kind of unusual excellence are shown from Dera Ghazi Khan. From Bannu, another frontier district, pretty gold-embroidered buskins, in soft red leather, are shown. The resemblance of many of these to the sandals on the feet of antique statues need scarcely be pointed out.

2. *Postins, Belts, Saddlery, &c.*

[1338–1343].—Peshawar and frontier belts.

Leathern belts form part of the equipment of every fighting man on the frontier, and they are also worn by those who follow peaceful avocations. Many are embroidered with coloured silk, some with filaments of quills. From Dera Ghazi Khan a very complete specimen is sent, to which are attached embossed leather powder-flasks, cartridge pouches, sword sling, &c., all excellent in design and colour. The other belts are from Peshawar, Bannu, and Kohat.

[1344–1346].—Saddlery.

Three kinds of saddles are shown—1344, the *charjama*, or cloth-covered saddle, chiefly used by Hindus; supposed to prevent contact with leather: 1345, the ordinary saddle of the Punjab: and 1346, a variety peculiar to the frontier.

[1348].—Jhelum whip.

Cutting-whips of English pattern are now used in the Punjab, especially by Potsharis, i.e. residents of the Shahpur, Jhelum, and Rawal Pindi districts.

[2093–2100].—Rohtak leather horse appliances, &c.

[1329–1335].—Hoshiarpur deer-skins.

At Hoshiarpur and Kangra deer-skins are made into a greenish-buff soft leather, used for gloves, coats, breeches, &c. Its local preparation depends on the use of the astringent leaves of the *Conocarpus* and *Rhus cotinus*, which can only be procured in the lower hill ranges. Hawk hoods (*Topi bay*) and gloves are made in this material for the numerous native chiefs and others who keep hawks, and these articles are almost exactly similar to those used in European falconry.

[1350–1356]. — Leather *hukas* metal-bound. Hissar, Kasur, Lahore, and Bannu.

The leather *huka*, bound for its better preservation in metal, is peculiar to the Punjab. It is obviously safer to carry to the field than the earthenware vessel, and the leather being porous, it is supposed to keep the water cooler than the metal *huka*.

[1349].—*Kúpi* ware, Jhang.

Another sort of leather bottle, in the form of large jars, the usual purpose of which is to hold ghee, oil, &c., is made by moulding boiled intestines on clay models. When the bottle is dry the clay is picked out. The six samples here noted are bottles ornamented with various patterns, and are from Maghiana, in the Jhang district.

[1357–1358].—Leather trunks or *yakhdans*, Peshawar.

The *yakhdan* is originally Persian, and leather trunks of this form are only made at Peshawar.

[1347].—Russian leather.

Russia leather skins like this sample find their way to Peshawar overland, and cost about Rs.25 each.

[1359–1377].—Postins and furs.

The Afghan postin, or embroidered sheepskin dolman (jacket?), is the best known item in this group. The rest are the usual furs imported into Peshawar, and include Astrakhan lambskins as well as fox, cat, leopard, and other skins.

Div. XIV.—Baskets.

[2112].—Rohtak palm-leaf hand fans.

Miscellaneous Objects.

[1383–1389].—Lahore sugar-made articles, as plates, penboxes, walnuts, &c.

At fairs, sugar moulded into a variety of fantastic forms is sold.

[1390–1392]. — Native hooka pipes, with Moonj twine.

[1394].—Native hooka pipe, gold embroidered

[1393]. — Native hooka pipe, silver embroidered.

[1395].—Native hooka pipe, plain.

[1396–1397].—Horn-manufacture goblet and powder horns.

[1398–1399].—Peshawar powder horns.

[1400].—Gourd snuff-boxes.

KASHMIR.

Div. II.—Decorative Art.

5. Decorative Painting as applied to Architecture.

[301–310].—1–10. Kashmir painted woodwork, commonly called papier maché.

A set of ten plaques carved and painted, illustrative of the method of decorating ceilings, &c. Price Rs. 4 to 5 per superficial foot.

6. Decorative Painting as applied to Articles of Domestic use.

[311–335].—11–25. Kashmir painted woodwork, commonly called papier maché.

Tables, brackets, writing-cases, vases, &c. This well-known work is a coarse reproduction of the real papier maché work of Persia. Formerly its use seems to have been confined to *kalamdans* (pen cases) and book covers, of which old examples show a close imitation of Persian work. All sorts of articles are now decorated in this way, mainly for sale to European visitors. The bracket 324, and the overmantel 335, represent the latest development of this branch of industry.

7. Decorative Carving as applied to Architecture.

Kashmir carved wood-work (Pinjra work).—Ceilings.

The screen is a complete example of this style of work. The carving is invariably made in deodar wood (*Cedrus deodara*), the *pinjra* or lattice work in *Chil* wood (*Pinus excelsa*), as are the ceilings. It is extremely cheap work; the cost of the last in Kashmir does not exceed one rupee per square yard.

Div. V.—Art Manufactures in Metal.

1. Gold and Silver Plate.

[231–250 & 291–295].—26–45, 46–50. Kashmir silver-gilt plate.—Tea sets, vases, claret-jugs, salt-cellars, muffineers, tray, cruet-stands.

This work is well known, and requires no explanation; 231 is a specimen of the latest style. The price of good work is 6 annas in the rupee, or 37½ per cent. added to the price of the silver.

[251–266].—51–66. Kashmir silver plate.—Claret-jugs, salt-cellars, cups, tea set, sugar basin.

The cost of this work is 4 annas in the rupee, or 25 per cent. added to the price of the silver. An additional anna in the rupee is usually paid for gilding the inside of cups, &c.

3. Brass, Copper, and Mixed Metal.

[402, 412–416].—67, 68–72. Kashmir brass-work—Trays, doors, jar.

This embossed and pierced brass-work is new, and the Kashmiri workman dislikes doing it from the hardness of the brass as compared to copper. The price is Rs. 2-8 a pound.

[404-408, 410, 411, 417, 421, 430 & 431].—73-77, 78-83. Kashmir brass-work.—Lacquered plates, candelabra, ewer and basin, shield vases.

This engraved and lacquered brass-work seems to be indigenous to the valley, the style and coloration being entirely different to Indian work. The price of the best is Rs. 2-12 a pound.

[418-420, 422-426, 428, 429, 432, 439, 440].—83-85, 86-90, 91-95. Kashmir copper-work.—Urn, trays, vases.

An immense quantity of this work is made in Kashmir for sale to visitors. It is not used, untinned, by the people themselves. The price is Rs. 2-3 to Rs. 2-4 a pound.

[401, 403, 409, 433-438].—96-98, 99-104. Kashmir copper-work, tinned.—Bowls, mugs, trays, shield, ewer and basin.

This is the ordinary metal-work for household use in Kashmir as all over Western Asia. It is not equal to the best Persian work, but is better than that of Afghanistan or Turkestan; 403 is a good example. The price of the best work is Rs. 2 to 12 a pound.

9. *Enamels other than Jewellery.*

[201-230].—104-133. Copper, enamelled and gilt.—Vases, jugs, trays, water-bottles.

This is a modern art introduced within the last ten or fifteen years. No. 227 shows the copper enamelled before gilding. Originally dark and light blue only were used, and the designs comparatively simple; but latterly pink, green, yellow, and white have been added, and the patterns elaborated and multiplied on each piece. "The large vase, No. 201 is," writes Sir Oliver St. John, the Resident in Kashmir, "one of the largest and best pieces of work and design that I have seen in Kashmir." The cost of the best copper enamel is 6 annas a tola or rupee weight.

[271-280]. — Silver enamel. — Salt-cellars, tray, coffee-pot, water-bottles, butter-dish, vases.

This work seems to have been borrowed from Persia, where, however, it is not common now, being chiefly used for pipe heads. The cost of the best work is 6 annas a *tola* in addition to the value of the silver.

DIV. VI.—ART MANUFACTURES IN WOOD, IVORY, ETC.

1. *Carved Furniture and Carpentry.*

[351].—Carved furniture.—Chair.

Carved walnut wood chairs are occasionally made to order from European models, to be finished and polished in India or England. The abundance of excellent walnut wood in Kashmir might make this a profitable industry.

DIV. XI.—TEXTILES.

1. *Cotton Fabrics.*

Sambar chintzes.

Although not in the Kashmir Court, the Sambar chintzes, of which one hundred specimens have been sent for decorating the vestibule of the Exhibition, deserve mention here. They are made at Sambar, a small town at the foot of the hills, some thirty miles south of Jummoo. The demand for them has recently been so great that the Kashmir Government has practically made a monopoly of the sale, and now charges Rs. 14 a piece for them, the old price having been from Rs. 9 to 10.

2. *Woollen Fabrics.*

[1-4, 51].—Kashmir shawls.

This manufacture, which formerly brought half a million a year into Kashmir, is now well nigh moribund. Unless means are taken by Government to preserve it, the art of weaving the finest shawl will probably be extinct fifteen or twenty years hence. The warehouses of London and Paris are full of shawls which find no purchasers, and the value in Kashmir has consequently fallen to a third of what it was ten years ago. As an example, see specimen 51, price Rs. 300,—a shawl that would have cost in former days Rs. 800 to Rs. 1,000. The specimens No. 1-4 are from the Maharaja's *toshakhana*, and are of the finest quality, unobtainable nowadays.

[39, 45, 75].—Shawl stuff.

These are specimens of pashmina woven from the unbleached and undyed under-wool. No. 39 is woven of the true *pashm* of the ibex, which is highly valued as making the lightest, warmest, and strongest cloth.

[101-115, 662].—Carpets.

The manufacture of carpets in Kashmir has received a considerable impulse of late years, and numbers of shawl-weavers, unable to find employment in their hereditary craft, are now employed in it. The best are made under the superintendence of M. Bigex, a French merchant. Nos. 1-14 are from his factory, the last nine being of *pashmina*. No. 15 is an ordinary Kashmir rug of purely native manufacture and design, and shows the improvement that has recently taken place.

No. 662 is a portière from the Maharaja's factory at Jummoo, and besides being remarkable for having the pile (of different patterns) on both sides, is a good specimen of local design and colouring. The wholesale price of carpets in Kashmir varies from Rs. 20 (M. Bigex's pashmina carpets) to Rs. 4 a square yard.

[67-73].—Knitted wool work.

Stockings, gloves, and vests of worsted and *pashmina*.

[74-76, 78, 79].—Woollen stuffs.

Specimens of woollen stuffs.

Div. XII.—Embroideries.

1. *Silk, Cotton, or Woollen Thread.*

[5-38, 40-44, 46-66, 80-89].—Shawls, table covers, curtains, floor-cloths, ladies' dresses, strips, &c.

The art of embroidery is nowhere carried to a greater perfection than in Kashmir, taking into consideration execution, colour, design, and price. Specimen 89, an embroidered waistcoat, collar, and cuffs for a lady's dress, is the finest work procurable, and No. 41, a shawl, is also of very good quality. The cheapest style of work is shown in the embroidered strips at 8 annas a yard.

Div. XIII.—Leathers and Furs.

1. *Shoes.*

[91].—Leather sandals and socks.

A specimen of the ordinary foot-gear of the country.

2. *Poshtins, Belts, Saddlery, &c.*

[819].—*Posti* or leather jacket.

3. *Furs.*

[816-818].—Furs.

Three specimens of rugs made in Kashmir. 816 and 881 are skins of the common jackal, *Canis aureus*, and 818 of the Himalayan fox, *Vulpes montanus*.

[801-809].—Heads.

There being no place for these in the catalogue they have been inserted here. The *Ovis Poli* head, 809, is said to be the largest but one known to have been brought from Central Asia. The *Capra Sibirica*, 802, is also a very fine specimen.

CENTRAL PROVINCES.

Div. I.—Fine Arts.

3. *Photographs.*

[2].—Three photographs of Central Provinces buildings and scenery.

An album of views in the Central Provinces prepared by Mr. Blees, photographer, Jabalpur. The views of the Hindu temples on the Narbada at Mandhata and of the Ramtek lake with its fringe of temples and bathing *ghats* are particularly interesting.

Div. II.—Decorative Art.

7. *Decorative carving.*

[3-8].—Carved wooden screens from Nagpur.

Div. IV.—Jewellery.

1. *Gold and Silversmiths' Work.*

[28 & 29].—Gold necklets from Sambalpur.

These are of rough execution, but are interesting as the handiwork of one of the districts in India, most remote from road or railway communication. The Sambalpur district lies on the extreme east of the Provinces, bordering on Orissa, and is 220 miles distant from the nearest railway station. The necklets are, so far as is known, the only jewellery made in these provinces which has any distinctive character. They are largely worn by Brahmin youths, and are considered to possess the virtues of an amulet.

Div. V.—Art Manufactures in Metal.

3. *Brass, Copper, and Mixed Metal.*

[30-33].—Brass work of Bhandara.

Ornamented brass work is made at several places in these Provinces, but nowhere is it of the excellence which distinguishes the manufactures of Benares. Formerly several places bore a local reputation for brass work, amongst which may be mentioned Bhandara, Lodhikhera in the Chhindwára district, Timbunri in the Hoshangábád district, Mandla and Sambalpur. It does not, however, appear that the work turned out at these places ever possessed much artistic merit or was sought after on any other account than its neatness and durability. The manufacture is now greatly depressed by the competition of European goods. The Deputy Commissioner of Bhandara writes that brass working has declined very considerably within the last ten years. Ten years ago there are reported to have been upwards of 200 working firms, whereas now there are only about 50 or 60. The decline in the trade dates from the extension of the railway to Nagpur, since which brass ware has been imported from Bombay. The imported goods are cheaper than those locally made though not perhaps so durable, but they command a ready sale. The importation of rolled brass sheets has also greatly affected the brass-workers of Bhandara, in this way, that formerly many of them were employed in smelting and beating out the metal into sheets; now this occupation is gone, since the sheets are imported ready-made, and all that remains to be done is to convert the brass sheets into vessels by shaping and soldering. There are still however someworkmen in Nagpur and Bhandara who possess some skill in brass graving, and can turn out specimens in the style of those made at Benares, though of vastly inferior merit. The Deputy Commissioner of Chhindwára writes in a similar strain of the brass-workers of Lodhikhera, where "brass-working as a special skilled handicraft has died out since the opening of the railway to Nagpur."

Brass lamps of curious design, but of very rough workmanship, are also made in the Damoh district.

The specimens of Bhandara work now sent illustrate the best work of which the Provinces are now capable.

[34–37].—Brass work of Sambalpur.

The chief characteristic of the brass and bell metal work of Sambalpur is the extreme thinness of the vessels which are made. The *arsis* or small mirrors are used by women and take the place of glass.

Div. VI.—Art Manufactures in Wood, Ivory, Etc.

5. *Wood Carving.*

[38].—Carved bamboo work, Burhanpur.

A fancifully-carved and coloured bamboo walking-stick, made by a carver in Burhanpur.

Div. VIII.—Marble and Stone.

[39–43].—Carved stone ware, Chanda.

Two figures of gods, a model of a temple, and two paper-weights.

Div. IX.—Pottery.

1. *Glazed Pottery.*

[44–56].—Glazed pottery of Burhanpur.

These are samples of the only glazed pottery made in the Provinces, and this industry is, or rather was, an introduction from Ahmadnagar in the Bombay Presidency. It was confined to a single family, and the secret of the glazing process was possessed by one man who has lately died without divulging it. The art, such as it was, is now therefore extinct.

Div. XI.—Textiles.

1. *Cotton Fabrics.*

[57–59 & 169].—Cotton cloth—silk bordered—from the Bhandara district.

[60–62].—Cotton cloth—silk bordered—from the Nagpur district.

[63–69].—Fine cotton cloth from the Chanda district.

The weaving of fine cotton cloth is the most characteristic manufacture of the Nagpur, Bhandara and Chanda districts; the cloths of Umrer (in Nagpur) and Pauni (in Bhandara) being considered especially good. The art of spinning thread of great fineness is one for which these districts have long been well known. In 1867 a piece of Chanda thread was exhibited at a local Exhibition of such fineness that a pound's weight of it would reach a distance of 117 miles. The best compliment to its excellence was paid by some gentlemen in the cotton trade who, notwithstanding that the public were particularly requested not to touch the specimens, succeeded in snipping off pieces of it to carry away as curiosities. The importation of English yarn and the competition of the machine-made yarn of the Nagpur Cotton Mills is reported to have resulted in a great decline in the art of hand-spinning. The weaving industry has not suffered so greatly from this competition, partly because of the intrinsic excellence of the goods manufactured, and partly because of the prejudice in favour of wearing them which exists amongst the better class of Marathas. The greater part of the woven goods turned out consist of turbans and *dhotis*, which are distinguished by bearing a border of (generally) dark red silk, on the breadth of which the value of the fabric in great measure depends. These borders are often woven in intricate patterns of different shades of colour. But the manufacture has fallen off under the competition of English made goods; and it is now not uncommon to attach a locally made silk border to cotton cloths imported from Bombay. The Deputy-Commissioner of Bhandara writes that the cotton weaving industry has declined very considerably during the past ten years. Not only is the number of articles now turned out much less than formerly, but the value of the goods is very much lower. Pauni used to be especially famous for the finely woven broad-bordered and richly ornamented turbans and *dhotis* which it produced. Bhandara, too, used to produce a plentiful supply of turbans and waist cloths of considerable value. Quantity and quality have now fallen off at both places. The opening of railway communication with Bombay has therefore had the same ill effect on local weaving as on brass-working, and has greatly harmed the two principal indigenous handicrafts of the Provinces. It is fair, however, to add that it is only the production of fine cotton cloth which appears to have suffered, and that the weaving of the coarse cotton stuffs worn by the agricultural classes seems to have greatly increased in some places. The Deputy Commissioner of Hoshangábád reports that the number of weavers in that town has increased from 116 to 216, and the officer in charge of the Harda Sub-division of the same district writes that the weaving industry was thought to be dying out, but this is not the case. The coarse fabrics which are made are preferred to imported goods by the labouring class for their greater strength and durability.

The fine cotton cloths made at Pauni and Andhargaon in the Bandhara, and at Umrer in the Nagpur district, bear as a rule a border of silk, which is as a rule of a plain dark red colour, but is occasionally made up in varied colours and patterns. Silk weaving is therefore in these places associated with cotton weaving, and is carried on by the same caste of men (the Koshtas). The dark red colour is obtained by cochineal (*daua kirmani*) and the colour produced at Umrer is considered to be the best, mainly it is said on account of some peculiar property in the water used there which gives a brilliancy of tint unobtainable elsewhere. Under ordinary circumstances then silk weaving in these places is restricted to the weaving of borders, but if plain silk fabrics are required they can be readily made up to order.

[70-74].—Coloured cotton cloths from the Sambalpur district.

These cloths, called *lugas*, are worn by Uria women and are of very curious design. They attracted a good deal of attention at the Calcutta Exhibition.

[75-86].—Cotton prints from Chanda.

[87 & 88].—Cotton prints from Garha in the Jabalpur district.

Cotton printing is only carried on at these two places, and is applied to cloths intended for druggets, curtains, and bed quilts. The patterns are decidedly pretty, though the printing is perhaps not so good as that of Farrukhabad and other places in the North-Western Provinces. With the cloths are shown two specimens of the wooden stamps used by the printers.

3. *Silk Fabrics.*

[89-92].—*Tassar* silk, Bilaspur.

[93-100].—*Tassar* silk, Sambalpur.

This is at the present time the most characteristic of the Provincial manufactures. Its production is largest in the districts of Seoni Bilaspur, Sambalpur and Chanda. The rearing of the worms is entirely in the hands of the Dhimars, men of very low caste; and it is therefore difficult to stimulate production either by the direct encouragement of Government or by increasing the demand for silk. *Tassar* rearing has, however, been specially exempted from duty in Government forests. The worms feed on various kinds of trees, but the one on which they are as a rule reared is the *saj*, *Asan* or *Terminalia tomentosa*. No rearing shed is used. The trees are pollarded and their branches bent down so as to be accessible from the ground. The worms are allowed to wander over the foliage at will, and constant watching is required to protect them from birds and insects. They are also peculiarly liable to disease, and it is no uncommon occurrence for the whole of a crop of worms to die off, leaving the Dhimars without any return for their time and trouble. To prevent this the Dhimars adhere very strictly to certain ceremonial observances while engaged in rearing, and abstain from spirit drinking and from all intercourse with women. Rearing commences on the setting in of the rains, and is started with wild cocoons which have been gathered in the jungles, and never with cocoons saved over from the last year's reared crop. The male and female moths which emerge from these cocoons are allowed to pair, and from the eggs which result a crop of worms is raised during July and August. The cocoons which are thus produced are merely used for rearing a second crop in August and September, the produce of which is the commercial result of the venture. About 80 worms are under favourable circumstances reared from the eggs laid by a single female moth, and about 44 per cent. of the moths are females. Assuming, therefore, that a Dhimar commenced operations in June with 25 female moths, and devoted his first crop entirely to production, his second crop would yield over 70,000 cocoons. It may be noted that on the emerging of the moths which result from the first crop of worms, the males fly off at once, and do not as a rule pair with the females of the same crop. The female moths remain clinging to their empty cocoons and are fertilised by other males from the outside, who are often, it is believed, attracted from very long distances. This peculiarity is shared by several other species of the order (*Bombyces*) to which the *Tassar* moth belongs. The cocoons are sold by the Dhimars to the weavers at from Rs. 3 to 5 Rs. per 1,000. The weavers kill the chrysalides by steaming them, and wind off the silk after soaking the cocoons in an alkaline solution obtained by mixing the ashes of the dried seed pods of the pulse known as *urd* (*Phaseolus radiatus*) in boiling water. This acts as a solvent on the gummy matter which binds the cocoon threads together. The silk is then spun and woven into a fabric, the value of which depends very greatly on its thickness and consistency. As a rule, the cloth is of a plain light buff colour, but it can be made up to order in buff and black lines and checks.

Tassar silk-weaving is carried on at a number of places in Sambalpur district, of which Barpali is the chief. Cloth of good quality is also made in the town of Bilaspur at which a colony of Tassar weavers was settled some years ago by Mr. Chisholm, when Deputy-Commissioner of this district. The material is very largely used in Chhattisgarh for *dhotis* and coats, taking the place which is occupied by Umrer and Pauni fabrics in the Nagpur country. The value of spun *Tassar* silk is from Rs. 6 to Rs. 10 per seer, which is more than the price which it commands in Europe.

4. *Other Fabrics.*

[102-130].—Silk-cotton (mixed)—goods of Burhanpur.

Silk borders for *dhotis*, &c., are as has been already mentioned, woven at several places in the Bhandara and Nagpur districts. But the most important silk weaving of the provinces is that carried on in the town of Burhanpur, situated on the border of the Bombay Presidency to the extreme west of the Provinces, mention of which is also made in connection with the silver-gilt embroidery carried on there. Burhanpur is especially noted for its *saris*, which are commonly woven of silk and cotton mixed, yielding a fabric of great softness of texture. They are made up in a large variety of patterns and colours, the best of which are represented by specimens in the present collection.

[131-146].—Silken goods of Burhanpur.

2. *Gold and Silver.*

[147-160].—Gold and silver embroidery from Burhanpur.

Burhanpur has a name throughout India for its embroidery which is a relic of the days when this town was the headquarters of a Muhammadan Government. The silver and silver-gilt wire used in the manufacture of the *kalabattu* (a silk and wire twist) which is principally used in embroidery work is drawn from bars of silver called *passas* which are made of a uniform size six inches in length and 60 tolas in weight. The *passas* are made up, and the wire partially drawn out under Municipal supervision, and a duty of Rs. 1-8-0 is levied on each *passa*. The purity of the material is ensured by this arrangement, and the Burhanpur wire has maintained a reputation for quality, superior to that of wire made at other places in the Bombay Presidency. On the other hand, it has rendered it impossible to meet competition by lowering the price of the wire, and the sale of the Burhanpur manufacture is said to have been affected by the import of cheap imitations from other places.

Each *passa* receives a gilding, on the thickness of which the price of the wire in great measure depends. The weight of gold used to gild a *passa* varies from 8 to 42 *mashas*. The *passa* is drawn out to a length of 700 yards in the Municipal enclosure, and in this form it is taken home by the wire-drawers. It is subsequently drawn to an astonishing fineness, the degree of which varies with the class of work to which the wire is to be applied. Thus a passa from which "*kalabattu*" (gold and silk twisted thread) is to be manufactured is drawn out to the length of 72,000 yards, while if it is to be used in making flattened wire for braiding (*gota*) it is only drawn out to 48,000 yards.

The process of wire-drawing consists in pulling the wire through a series of holes of decreasing size in an iron plate, the wire being fastened to a wheel which is turned by a winch.

The number of *passas* which have been drawn into wire each year since 1868 has been accurately registered. The results are summarized as follows:—Five years, 1868-1873, 2,879: five years, 1873-1878, 2,987; year 1878-79, 2,527; year 1879-80, 2,865; year 1880-81, 3,114.

The manufacture does not therefore show any signs of declining.

The *choga*, which forms one of the exhibits, is a very fine specimen of cloth of gold and is richly embroidered. The three curtains (*purdahs*) are also excellent specimens of work. The handkerchiefs (*rumals*) made of flattened wire and silk are characteristic of Burhanpur.

Div. XIII.—Leathers and Furs.

[161 and 762].—Embroidered leather shoes, Chanda.

2. *Poshtins, Belts, Saddlery, &c.*

[163].—Embroidered leather saddle cloth, Chanda.

Chanda was once a town of very large size and is surrounded by a massive stone wall seven miles in circumference. It was formerly the capital of a dynasty of rulers representing one of the oldest races in the Provinces—the Gonds. City and race have now alike greatly declined in importance. The greater part of the area within the Chanda wall is now under cultivation, and the town has now only 16,000 inhabitants. The embroidered leather work of Chanda is the only industrial relic of its past magnificence.

Div. XIV.—Baskets, Mats, and Straw Work.

[164-168].—5. Basket work, Chanda.

These are samples of the only fine basket work made in the Provinces, and are of more economic than artistic interest.

ASSAM.

Div. II.—Decorative Art.

8. *Other Works of Decorative Art not specified.*

[765].—Nowgong fan.

[683.]—Cachar plume.

Made of peacocks' feathers.

Div. III. Musical Instruments.

1. *Wind Instruments.*

[668].— Kuki musical instruments.

[686, 687].—Flute, &c.

Used by the Kukis, a tribe inhabiting the North Cachar Hills.

2. *Stringed Instruments.*

[670.]—Cachari musical instruments; harp.

Used by Cacharis.

3. *Instruments of Percussion.*

[506.]—Assamese drum.

Common all over the Assam Valley.

[669 and 688].—Kuki musical instruments.

Used by Kukis, a tribe inhabiting the North Cachar Hills.

Div. IV.—Jewellery.

1. *Gold and Silversmiths' Work, including Filigrain, Setting of Precious Stones, &c.*

[722, 738-741].—Barpeta jewellery, bracelets, earrings, &c.

A peculiarly fine species of gold filigree jewellery is made at Barpeta in the Kámrúp district. The articles are chiefly bracelets and necklaces, the latter being especially beautiful. The gold is sometimes imported direct from Calcutta, but is often obtained from Muhammadan coins brought (to save weight) instead of rupees, by the elephant traders of Rangpur and Purnea.

[554, 555].—Jorhát jewellery, rings, &c.

Made by the enamel workers mentioned below.

[561–567].—Lakhimpur jewellery, gold mohr ring.

Old Assamese coins are constantly used as ornaments for rings.

[401–413.]—Khasia jewellery.

The best known articles of Khasi Hills jewellery are the coral and gold necklaces, so largely worn by the more wealthy of the Khasia women. These necklaces consist of alternate beads (about the size of small marbles) of coral and gold, held together by a thread passing through a hole in the centre of each. The coral is real and comes up from Calcutta. The gold beads are shells of gold filled up with lac. The value of a necklace varies from Rs.50 to 200, and a good specimen would, therefore, have been too expensive to be included amongst the exhibits. A model of one of these necklaces adorns the Khasia figure in the Silk Court. The scallop-shell earring and gold collaret are peculiar to these hills.

[661.]—Cachar earring.

[601.]—Naga Hills Victoria Cross.

The Naga Victoria Cross is worn only by men distinguished for their prowess in fight. It passes over the left shoulder and under the right arm.

[1–21].—Manipur jewellery.

Gold and silver articles are largely made for the native trade at Manipur. The gold used is always pure, but a large number of the articles consist half of gold and half of silver. The ornaments most commonly made are the following: *Kankan.*—A kind of bracelet usually worn in pairs, one on each wrist. The inner surface is usually silver, the outer gold, with elaborate devices of flowers, wreaths, crowns, &c. These are ingeniously worked by hammering the gold on a suitable iron spike. The ends meet in the form of a circle, but are not joined. The bracelet yields to pressure like a ring of steel, so that it can be put on and taken off with facility. A pair of *kankans* generally requires two tolas of gold and an equal quantity of silver. *Kharoo.*—A kind of bracelet very similar to a bangle, made sometimes of gold, and sometimes of silver, and sometimes of both combined. A pair of *kharoos* is generally worn on each arm. *Sunapoki.*—A kind of necklace, formed generally of twenty-one beads. Each bead is a small rounded cone-shaped shell of gold, with a base of silver. The interior is filled with lac. Two small rings of gold at opposite sides of the bead afford the means of uniting the beads to each other with thread and thus of making a necklace; each bead usually contains the one-thirty-second part of a tola of gold. *Bethguta* or *Gulluguta.*—A kind of necklace worn usually by children, the *sunapoki* being generally confined to women. It differs from the *sunapoki* only in the shape of the beads. Each bead resembles a cube with the angles truncated, and is a shell of gold filled with lac. *Bajoo.*—A gold armlet usually worn by women and boys, and always above the elbow. There is no export of the above articles, and the local demand is not very great. The workmen supplement the income derived from their trade by carpentering and horse-dealing. They engage but little in agriculture.

2. *Enamelled Jewellery.*

[742].—Kámrúp enamelled necklace.

[551–553, 556–558].—Jorhat enamelled ware, earrings, &c.

A very fine species of enamelling on gold is done at Jorhat. The colours are blue, green, and white, and the effect is strikingly beautiful. The ornaments produced are lockets, earrings, bracelets, and necklaces. The sale is not extensive, and is only confined to natives. The ornaments are often set with precious stones.

Div. V.—Art Manufactures in Metal.

3. *Brass, Copper, and Mixed Metal.*

[502–505].—Darrang brass ware, plate, &c.

[598–602].—Naga Hills brass bracelets.

[677–681].—Cachar brass ware, chain, &c.

[727 to 737].—Chatibari brass ware, dishes, &c.

These are generally made all over the province. The material used is either brass or bell-metal (a compound of brass and copper). The latter is melted and cast into moulds. *Lotas* and drinking tumblers are the articles usually produced. Brass vessels are made from sheet brass, which is cut and beaten into the required shape. The manufacture of the latter is almost confined to Morios, a Muhammadan caste found all over Assam.

[1–23].—Manipur brass ware.

4. *Brass and Copper Ware for Sacrificial purposes.* (a) *Modern.* (b) *Ancient.*

[636].—Sacrificial knife.

An inlaid knife used in sacrificing goats and buffaloes at religious ceremonies.

5. *Arms and Armour.* (a) *Ancient.* (b) *Modern.*

[725–726].—Bhutia weapons.

A sword and dagger (scabbard of the former, pure silver), used by the bordering tribes of Bhutias. The blades are made from English iron bought in Assam.

[600, 611].—Naga weapons.

[637].—Sylhet inlaid sword.

[665, 699, 701].—Kuki weapons.

Used by Kukis, a race inhabiting the North Cachar Hills.

[571–573].—Lakhimpur *Kukris.*

Made by the Frontier Police of Dibrugarh.

[1–17].—Manipur weapons.

6. *Cutlery.*

[641].—Sylhet cutlery, betel-nut cutter.

The specimen shown is inlaid. The kinds commonly seen are of plain iron, and are in constant use in a country where betel-chewing is universal.

7. *Iron and Steel Wares.*

[667.]—Cachar fish-spear.

Div. VI.—Art Manufactures in Wood, Ivory, Etc.

3. *Ivory Carving.*

[547-550].—Jorhàt ivory work, spoons, combs, &c.

A few carvers in ivory still remain amongst the descendants of those who worked for the Assam kings, but the handicraft appears to be dying out, as there is next to no demand for the articles produced. These are mainly spoons and forks, combs, and sometimes chessmen. The favourite patterns represent a crane in the act of preening, and a crocodile with a fish in its mouth.

[612].—Naga Hills armlet.

4. *Lacquered Wares.*

[631-634, 638-640].—Sylhet lacquer-ware box, toys, &c.

The trade is in the hands of four Mussulmans in the town of Sylhet. The toys are sold in sets of 100 pieces. They are lacquered and quaintly coloured with various patterns. The blow-pipe is a curious article made by one Muhammadan of Sylhet. The pipe is of bamboo, and lacquered with effective colours. The arrows, 100 of which are sold with each pipe for Rs.3-2-0, are made of small strips of bamboo, 8 or 9 inches long, tipped with iron and winged with an inverted cone of paper.

[659].—Cachar beads.

These are worn generally round the neck by women in Cachar.

5. *Wood Carving.*

[766-768, 770].—Nowgong carving, model of tiger-trap, &c.

Parts of Nowgong are infested with tigers, and the model shows the kind of trap generally used. The model of the dug-out boat represents the ordinary vehicle of communication in the province from May to October. The palanquin is rarely used now, but occasionally a member of the priesthood (called a *goshaien*) may be seen carried along by two men. Four men are never required.

[663-664, 666, 676, 682, 684, 689-695, 697-698].—Cachar woodwork, spoon, earrings, &c.

These are all articles of ordinary domestic use in Cachar.

[567-568].—Lakhimpur modelling, model of an Assamese homestead, &c.

The model of the homestead is a very exact representation of the appearance of things on the premises of an ordinary Assamese cultivator. The huts are placed in the relative positions they almost invariably occupy, and show the number which each ryot generally erects. A single family usually occupies one of these homesteads, which is ordinarily separated from the next by a few fields. It is only in very crowded localities that the homesteads are coterminous, and two families never occupy the same premises, unless closely related by blood.

Manipur woodwork.

The Manipuris are the Japanese of this part of India, and possess a marked talent for imitating anything they see. Some of the models shown are very exact representations of the objects copied.

Div. VII.—Lapidaries' Work.

2. *Shells.*

[610].—Naga Hills earrings, with hair.

Naga Hill ornaments and weapons are largely ornamented with dyed goats' hair and shells.

Div. IX.—Pottery.

2. *Unglazed Pottery.*

[662].—Cachari cooking pot.

Div. X.—Glass.

1. *Blown Objects.*

[660].—Cachar white beads.

2. *Moulded Articles.*

[599-603].—Naga bead necklaces.

Div. XI.—Textiles.

1. *Cotton Fabrics.*

[447-453, 455-467, 721].—Goálpára cloths.

Fabrics made of cotton are common all over the province, and their manufacture is as widely distributed as their use. English yarn is said to be rapidly taking the place of homespun thread except when coarse and particularly durable cloths are required; but in the absence of definite statistics it is impossible to be quite certain that this is really the case. The cotton grown in the province is, however, still largely used for domestic purposes, and the spinning-wheel and the loom are to be found in almost every Assamese household.

[586-595].—1-10. Naga cloths.

The articles usually manufactured are noted below: *Dhoties* or waist-cloth.—These are generally unornamented, but occasionally coloured patterns are woven into the end. *Chaddars* or sheets. These are almost invariably quite plain, except when made of the finer kinds of cotton yarn. In this case they are sometimes as fine as muslins, and are only prepared by women of respectability for private use. These carefully woven fabrics are generally decorated with elaborately worked patterns of flowers, fruits and birds in coloured thread, sometimes of silk and sometimes of cotton.

[651-652, 657-658, 671-675].—Cachari and Kuki cloths.

Borkapars.—Large, coarsely woven, heavy, but very durable cloths, generally used by both sexes much in the same way as a shawl is used in Europe. *Khaniva Kapar.*—A highly ornamented shawl, worn double, and generally 21 feet by 4 feet. Usually very finely woven and elaborately adorned along the borders with graceful designs of flowers and creepers. Sometimes the whole of the front sheet of the *Khaniva* is tastefully decorated with flowery spots. The ornamentation is usually made either with silk or coloured thread, or with a mixture of silk and gold or silver. *Chelengs.*—These are similar to the above, but are usually only 3 feet by 10 feet in size. They are finely woven, and ornamented in much the same way as the *Khaniva*, but seldom to the same extent. *Gamocha.*—A species of towel or napkin, usually plain. Riha.—A species of scarf, worn by women only, used as a waist cloth or kamarband. *Mekhla.*—A species of petticoat. The Goálpára (*Babha* and *Mech*) cloths are made by the inhabitants of the eastern Duars at the foot of the Bhutan hills. The Naga cloths shown are worn chiefly by the Angami Nagas. Red, blue, and yellow are the prevailing colours. The Cachar cloths differ but slightly from those worn by Kukis. Both races belong to the district of Cachar.

[1-174]. Manipur cloths.

Almost every description of cotton cloth is made in the little principality, from fine muslins down to coarse *darries* or carpets. All classes of women weave, from the wives and daughters of the maharajah down to the poorest in the country. Little girls begin to learn at a very early age, and soon attain to great skill. Amongst all but the highest classes the women not only supply their families with cloth, but make for sale also. As a rule, coarse cloths are far cheaper than in British territory, but the finer descriptions are much dearer. The latter are generally made from English thread, which for the better fabrics has almost superseded that of native manufacture. Even for the better class of petticoats English thread is now used. This doubles the price. The cheapness of Manipuri cloths is entirely due to the fact that every woman in the valley employs her spare time in making them instead of in idleness. The Naga tribes, who utilise their women for field work, are ceasing to manufacture cloth. They buy it instead from the Manipuris, who are now beginning to imitate the Naga tribal patterns. The Manipuri cloth manufacture is thus artificially kept up by the want of an occupation that pays better.

3. *Silk Fabrics.*

[441-446, 454, 468-481].—Goálpára cloths, turban, &c.

Silk fabrics are exceedingly numerous, and vary greatly in material, workmanship, quality, and colour. There are two species of silk commonly used over the province, and nine species which are also used, but not uncommonly. The two former are known as *Eri* and *Muga*.

[501].—Darrang silk blanket.

[541-544].—Sibsagar cloths.

Eri silk is the produce of a worm believed to be the *Attacus ricini* of scientists. It feeds on the castor-oil plant. No means have yet been discovered of reeling the silk, and thread is therefore always made from it by spinning. As a natural consequence, the thread is uneven and coarse, and the cloth manufactured usually very rough. It is, however, exceedingly durable, and is prized on that account. Women of respectability rarely engage in the manufacture of *Eri* cloths. The following are the principal articles made from this species of silk:—

Borkapar.—The commonest cloth made of this material. It is a large heavy sheet about 21 feet by 5 feet, and universally worn by men of the peasant class during the cold weather. About 1½ *seers* of thread are used generally in the manufacture.

[491].—Garo cloths.

Gamochha.—A species of towel or napkin. *Dukathia.*—A wrapper used by women and children. Takes about ¼ seer of thread.

[653-656].—Kuki cloths.

Mekhla.—Worn as a species of under garment or petticoat by women. It usually takes a little less than ½ a seer of thread. It is generally 7 feet by 4 feet or 6 feet by 3 feet in size.

[414].—Khasi silk jorkin.

[570].—Phakial turban.

Muga silk is the produce of a worm believed to be the *Antheræa Assamæa* of entomologists. The worm feeds on a species of forest tree called the *sum* (*Machilus odoratissima*). The silk is amber in colour, has much more lustre than the *Eri*, and the cocoons can be reeled. *Muga* cloth is largely worn by the upper classes, and is as common amongst them as *Eri* cloth is amongst the peasantry. It is manufactured by women of all ranks. The articles made of *Muga* are usually the following:—

Dhotis.—Waist cloths of various sizes.

Mekhla.—A kind of under garment or petticoat worn by women. It is frequently sewn up like a pillow-case, with one end free and a hole through the other for the head to come through.

Rihas.—Scarfs worn by women. The ends and borders are usually handsomely decorated with ornamental designs worked in bright colours, or in gold or silver thread. Sometimes the whole cloth is elaborately ornamented with designs of flowers.

[1-8].—Manipur cloths.

Gamochhaa.—Used as a handkerchief.

Era Borkapar.—This must not be confounded with *Eri Borkapar*. The latter is made from *Eri* silk, whereas the *Era Borkapar* is woven of a rough thread called *jhutta*, which has been spun from the floss of *Muga* cocoons, and those pierced *Muga* cocoons which do not admit of reeling. This cloth is generally worn folded in two as a warm wrapper by the women of a ryot's household. The processes of ornamentation applied to silk cloths are very much the same as those described above under the head of cotton fabrics, but the materials, especially in the case of *Muga*, are usually much more costly. *Eri* cloths are seldom ornamented except by a coloured design at the two ends. Articles made of *Muga* are generally elaborately decorated, and gold and silver thread are largely used. Besides the two above-named kinds of silk, there are a few more from which textile fabrics are prepared. But these are uncommon, and their manufacture is rapidly dying out. The following is the only kind of any commercial value:—

Pat.—This silk is obtained from two worms, the *Univoltine bombyx textor* and the *Multivoltine bombyx crœsi.* Both kinds are domesticated and are reared on the leaves of a species of mulberry. This silk, which is reeled, not spun, is much rarer and more valuable than either *Eri* or *Muga.* The colour is a pale yellow, like cream. The rearing of the *Univoltine Pat* worm is confined to the Jugi caste and its cultivation is almost unknown outside the district of Sibsagar. The *Multivoltine* variety is also rare. The articles made of the silk are usually the same as those enumerated under the head of *Muga* except that *Pat* silk is never used for a *Borkapar* and rarely as a *Dhoti.* Both *Muga* and *Pat* are used, especially the former, in making the light coats largely worn by Assamese English-speaking clerks.

4. *Other Fabrics.*

[492-493].—Garo bark cloths.
The cloths are made from the bark of the *Artocarpus chaptasa.* A tree two feet in girth is felled and cut into lengths of six feet. Then the pieces are well beaten with heavy sticks, the bark loosened, slit down one side and removed. After washing each piece is placed in the sun, and the material is ready for use. Believed to be peculiar to the Garo Hills.

[596-597].—Naga nettle cloth.
Made at Mazema in the Naga Hills from the fibre of a kind of nettle. It is worn both by men and women.

[769.].—Nowgong tiger net.

Div. XIII.—Leathers and Furs.

2. *Poshtins, Belts, Saddlery, &c.*

[604-609].—Naga skin shields.
Used now mainly for ornament, and only by the Angami Nagas.

[696.]—Kuki square shields.
Made from the skin of the *mithan*, a species of wild cattle found in Assam.

Div. XIV.—Baskets, Mats, and Straw Work.

[723-720, 761-764, 507-508, 545-546].—Assam Valley basket work.
The basket work of the Assam Valley is very varied, and a knowledge of the art is universal. Bamboo is the most commonly used material, but cane is also employed. The *jhapis* of which three are shown, are worn on the head by the Assamese as a protection against sun and rain.

[635].—Sylhet *Sital patti.*
The manufacture of *Sital patti* mats is not peculiar to Sylhet, but the finest specimens are made there. The work is exceedingly tedious and expensive. The material is a kind of reed called in Bengali *Murta.* The manufacture is generally carried on by a caste known as *Das.* The coarser kinds of mats are universally used for sitting and sleeping on, especially during the hot weather. The name *Sital* means "cool."

[685].—Cachar waterproof basket.

BURMA.

Div. I.—Fine Arts.

4. *Sculpture.*

[103-104]. — Models of man and woman, Rangoon.

[1001-1004].—Wood, Rangoon.

See remarks upon wood-carving.

Div. II.—Decorative Art.

8. *Decorative Work in Silk—Decorative Work in Cloth.*

[102].—Silk *kalaga* (hanging), Rangoon.
The best *kalagas* are made in Kemmendine, a suburb of Rangoon, where there are four or five families engaged.

Cloth *kalagas* are red hangings or *purdahs* about 10 or 12 feet long and 4 or 5 feet deep, on which are pourtrayed scenes from one of the mythological plays. The work is technically known as *appliqué* work, and is formed by cutting the figures and foliage of the picture out of vari-coloured cloths and sewing them on to the background. The result in Burma is a gorgeously-colored screen, which is used to decorate the house on festive occasions or to partition off a part of it for a guest. The *kalaga* also forms a gay roof-covering for the bullock-cart when the family travels to one of the large pagoda feasts.

The process of manufacture is as follows: Part of the red cloth ground is stretched by lacing it to the sides of a wooden frame. The leaves and flowers of the border and the strips used to line out the divisions of the picture are marked out on the differently-coloured cloths with chalk and cut out with a pair of scissors. The border running round the edge of the *kalaga*, which is about 15 inches broad, is first lined out with strips of cloth and the leaves and flowers are then added. The detached pieces of the pattern are pasted on with rice paste and afterwards firmly sewn on with thread of the proper colour. When the border is finished the figures are placed in the centre.

As is the case with all Burmese art work, the designs are bold yet graceful, the grotesque element being especially good.

Appliqué Kalagas (Hangings).

[1-6].—118-123.—This *appliqué* work is well adapted for use in dados, *punkah* fringes, screens, and piano-covers.

An ordinary *kalaga* may be bought at the rate of eight annas a square foot and a better quality at 10 annas.

The materials cost about 37.5 per cent. of the ultimate cost, labour costs about the same, leaving 25 per cent. for contingencies and the wages of the master.

Silk *Kalagas.*—In making silk *kalagas* the same designs are used as in the cloth ones; but the details are more carefully worked out, and the colour effect is so improved as to become almost beautiful.

Div. IV.—Jewellery.

1. *Gold and Silversmiths' Work, including Filigrain, Setting of Precious Stones, &c.*

A *Tsal-wee* of twelve chains.

A badge of nobility among the Burmese supposed to be derived from the Brahminical thread. The order consists of six classes; three gold chains of fine open work denote the lowest, three of twisted gold chain the next, then six, nine, and twelve, the latter being the highest grade with the exception of that worn only by the monarch, which consists of twenty-four chains. (Lent by Col. Sladen.)

[58, 59, 60, 61, 63, 64, 65, & 66].—*Dalizans* (necklaces), hair ornaments, earrings, &c., Rangoon.

[62].—*Thongwa, dalizans* (necklaces), hair ornaments, earrings, &c.

[1065].—Rangoon.—*Dalizan* (necklaces).

[2001, 2002, 2005-2007, 2009-2016, 2021, 2024-2030, 2032-2043, 2046-2048, 2053-2060, 2065, 2070, 2071, 2084 & 2085].—Necklaces, chains, bracelets, bangles, &c.—Akyab.

[2003, 2004, 2008, 2022, 2023 & 2086-2388].—Necklaces, chains, bracelets, bangles, &c.—Kyouk-hpyu.

[2004A, 2017-2019, 2031, 2044, 2045, 2061 & 2362].—Necklaces, chains, bracelets, bangles, &c.—Sandoway.

[2020, 2063, 2064 & 2069].—Necklaces, chains, bracelets, bangles, &c.—Arakan Hill Tracts.

The ornaments made by goldsmiths are of filigree, with which are associated small pieces of solid gold either beaten out into the petals of a leaf or cut like a diamond to form the flashing centre of a rosette or a sparkling pendant. In this case the burnished gold retains its proper colour, but in all others it is dyed red with tamarind juice, a barbaric custom to which the Burmese tenaciously cling. The reason given is that no other metal but gold will assume this particular ruddy colour when treated with tamarind juice; it may in fact be regarded as the Hall Mark of Burmese jewellery.

The goldsmiths show great skill and, what is rarer amongst the Burmese, great patience and industry in making their filigree work. For they have first to draw the wire from solid gold, and they then laboriously construct the delicate pieces of which the work is finally formed.

The *dalizan* is perhaps the prettiest of all, and in silver it is sought after by Europeans. It is composed of a collar about half an inch high, from which hang rows of peacocks, rosettes, crescents, &c., linked together and gradually narrowing towards the lower edge.

Ornaments for the hair are of two kinds, those made of sprays of leaves and those made by attaching conventional ornaments to a curved bar by spiral springs. In both kinds a peacock or pheasant is introduced in the centre. Coloured pieces of glass and sometimes precious stones are set in the leaves, and the whole piece vibrates with every movement of the head.

Chains and round necklaces are formed by plaiting flat pieces of gold in various ways and soldering on to the faces small knobs and grains. This kind of work is perhaps the best in design and finish of any made by Burmese goldsmiths.

Most of the gold used is obtained by melting the English sovereign. Chinese gold leaf coming through Upper Burma is usually employed when a purer gold is required. The leaves are about three inches square and are of three qualities, the best being said to be quite pure. A small quantity of pure gold is also obtained from the Shan States and Bangkok; a very soft variety having a slightly green colour. Gold-leaf is sent out from England in some quantity.

Div. V.—Manufactures in Metal.

1. *Gold and Silver Plate.*

[1, 2, 3, 4, 5, 6, 7, 8, 9, 10, 11, 12, 16, 67, 68, 81, 82, 83, 84, and 84A, 114 to 117].—Bowls, boxes, &c., Rangoon.

[1066].—Silver centrepiece.—Rangoon.

[2090].—Bowl.—Prome.

The silver work of Burma is much thought of by connoisseurs all over the world, and under the guidance of Europeans it is being improved, while the national characteristics are zealously preserved. The work is hammered, embossed, chased, and carved, and sometimes cut into open tracery, but it is all made in exactly the same way. It can be applied to any shape, and European patterns are often covered with the Burmese work; but the native demand is entirely for articles of simple shape, such as large round bowls without cover or legs, betel-boxes, small oval lime-boxes, and such like. More intricate shapes are made for use in the palace at Mandalay.

[13, 14, & 15].—Bowls, boxes, &c. Shan States.

The Burmese artist treats silver in the right way, obtaining the greatest effect that the nature of the material allows. The work is either simply embossed and chased, or, in addition, the background may be cut into open tracery and a burnished lining placed within. This will be better understood after reading how an ordinary bowl is made.

The purchaser when giving his order pays for the silver of which the bowl is to be made, and the rupees are melted down in a crucible over a charcoal fire. If, however, the work is to be very good, better silver is bought and is purified over a flaming fire in a flat burnt clay saucer.

When pure the melted metal is allowed to cool in the saucer, which serves as the mould to produce a plate flat on one side and convex on the other about ½ inch or ¾ inch thick. The silver plate is then gradually beaten out on a small iron anvil with an iron hammer until it is of the full diameter of the bowl to be produced.

Throughout this process, and until all hammering is over, it is from time to time heated to red heat and dipped in cold water to preserve its ductility.

The right diameter being attained, the edge or lip is raised by hammering with a straight edged hammer at an angle of 45 deg., and, when the lip has been raised right round, the operator begins beating on the bottom in a narrowing spiral line until the centre is reached, when he steadily works outwards and against inwards, and so on. This process causes the lip or edge to rise, and it is continued until the full height required has been obtained.

The bowl is then beaten with a heavier hammer on a small curved iron anvil until it is of the right shape, when it appears pretty smooth, and covered with innumerable small hammer marks. The old masters laid great stress on the importance of this hammering; and no doubt it is necessary to render the silver ductile enough to withstand the severe handling it afterwards meets with.

A composition of earth-oil, brick-dust, and resin is now prepared and melted into the small bowls, and a short stick is thrust in to serve as a handle. In large bowls an earthenware jar, tapering towards the bottom, is placed about half way down the bowl and the space between the two filled up with the composition.

The lines dividing the surface horizontally are drawn in pencil and then with a graver; in the best shops this is done in the lathe. The surface is divided into the various "houses" or portions for figures, and the borders and the flower-work drawn with a pencil and marked out with a graver. The master generally draws a small portion as pattern, which is repeated by his pupils; he should also draw the figures in pencil, unless he has a skilled pupil. When the entire pattern has been engraved in line, the first embossing takes place, by which all the parts to be lowered are punched in and recede into the plaint composition, which also forces out those portions which are to be in relief.

When this process is over, the composition is melted out, and those parts which are not yet in high or sharp enough relief are punched outwards from inside until the whole is satisfactory.

The bowl is again filled with the wax-like composition and the edges of the embossed portions are defined, and it is handed over to be chased, carved, and cut about until every face has expression, all clothes texture, until the leaves curl over round the gracefully twining tendrils, and the whole composition receives those last touches which show to all the design that has from the beginning been clear in the creative brain of the artist.

When the work is finished it is boiled in a solution of alum for half an hour and then brushed with soap and cold water. The flower-work is burnished with small brass wire brushes and the large smooth portions with steel burnishers, and the whole rubbed with white enamel beads.

There are two kinds of open work; they are both done when the bowl is finished as above. In one kind the intervals between embossed and chased leaves and flowers are cut away, in the other the background around the figures is cut into plate tracery.

In many compositions, such as centrepieces, vases, and candlesticks, figures in the round are introduced. The figure is first shaped and carved in a composition made of beeswax two parts, resin one part.

When correctly modelled, the wax figure is coated over with a thin layer of fine clay well kneaded and mixed with chopped straw and afterwards with a thick layer of ordinary clay. The mould is baked in the fire, the wax melts and runs out through a hole left for the purpose, and the clay becomes as hard as a brick. The melted silver is run in and when cool the mould is broken and the silver figure is patched and corrected as required.

The tools and plant of a worker in silver consist of an open charcoal hearth fanned by English or Burmese bellows. The latter deserve a word or two of description, as they are used in many trades. They are of all sizes, from the tiny model of the goldsmith's, which may be worked with the little finger, to the huge apparatus of the brass-founder, requiring a man to each rod.

The bellows are formed by placing vertically side by side two hollow bamboos plugged at the bottom. From just above the plug two small bamboo pipes converge to the hearth, where they are connected by a fireclay nozzle. The blast is formed by compressing the air in the tubes by an ingenious contrivance which serves at the same time as a piston and as a valve for admitting air. Each tube or cylinder is fitted with a rod, at the end of which is tied a bunch of cock's feathers with the quills upwards; when the rod is forced down the feathers are pressed against the side of the cylinder by the resistance of the air, and an air-tight piston is obtained; when the rod is drawn up again, the feathers trail downwards and the cylinder is filled with air. The rods are worked alternatively and in all, except the largest blowers, are connected at the top by a bar pivoted at a point between them so that a reciprocating movement can be given by pushing up and pulling down one end of the cross-rod by means of a light bamboo. The combined piston and valve closely resembles those feather brushes used for dusting pictures at home.

The other tools used by silversmiths are crucibles, hammers, small anvils, blow-pipe, and a spirit lamp, many sizes of punches and small chisels, a small tapping hammer, and round steel burnishers. Some men are able to use the lathe.

3. *Brass, Copper, and Mixed Metal.*

[80, 111 to 113].—1 to 3. Rangoon.—Images, Gongs.

[1049].—Image.—Mandalay.

The only important manufactures in brass are the castings in that metal of images of Gaudama, bells, and gongs.

A rough solid core of the image to be cast is first made in clay somewhat freely mixed with sand and paddy-husk. A composition made of beeswax 10 parts, resin 7½ parts, to which is added earth-oil, is melted down and in its liquid state thrown into a large shallow basin of water, and on cooling forms a layer of uniform thickness on the surface. The composition is then plastered on the clay core, and with the aid of knives and chisels is carved into the desired shape in all its detail. The composition is now in its turn covered entirely, with the exception of a hole on the crown of the head, with a rather thick layer of clay without any attempt to adhere to the lines of the model. When the outer layer of clay is perfectly dry, the model is heated to allow the composition to melt and run out from a small hole provided for the purpose at the foot of the model. When it has all run out the hole is closed with clay and the molten metal, supplied from furnaces close at hand, poured in at the crown of the clay mould. The casting is then left to cool for a day or so, or longer, according to its size, when the outer and inner mass of clay is removed. The image is next finished off with files and sand-paper, and polished with steel burnishers.

Images are made of a brass consisting of copper in proportion of 60 per cent. and tin 40 per cent., or for a better quality, copper 53·4 per cent., tin 40 per cent., and zinc 6·6.

The flat triangular gongs are made in an open sand mould, which has been formed with a wooden pattern. For round gongs an alloy of one copper and quarter tin.

5. *Arms and Armour* (b, *modern*).

[17, 18, and 19].—Shan States.—Swords, daggers, &c.

[1067].—Swords.—Rangoon.

Foliage and figure work are generally combined in such objects as dagger or sword handles, paper-knives, and table ornaments. Figure work is met with by itself in images of Gaudama.

A curious and intricate effect is obtained by Burmese workmen for *du* handles and table ornaments. The outside of the specimen is carved with foliage and flowers through the interstices of which the inside is hollowed out nearly to the centre, where a figure is carved *in situ*. The figure looks as if it had been carved separately and inserted into a flowery bower, but closer examination shows that this is not the case, and the men may at any time be seen carving the figure through the opening of the tracery.

The elephants' tusks are obtained from Upper Burma and Siam.

9. *Enamels other than Jewellery.*

[20].—Shan States.—*Niello* dagger (silver).

[85].—Rangoon.—*Niello* belt plate (silver).

[87].—Shwegyin.—*Niello* bowl (silver).

[88].—Allanmyo.—*Niello* dagger (silver).

Many of the silversmiths of Burma are proficient in this art, though few are fond of it, because it entails working over a hot furnace and in sulphurous fumes. The design appears as if drawn in silver outline on a black ground. The articles made are cups, lime-boxes, plates, knife-handles, and are all quite smooth, with a good polish.

The black enamel used is made of lead two parts, silver one part, copper one part.

The materials are melted in a fierce fire and sulphur added at discretion.

The object to be treated is made in silver about ⅛ inch thick, and the design is drawn and engraved as before. The lines of the drawing are left alone, but all other parts are punched in and the edges cut sharp with a small chisel. The *niello*, prepared as above, is finely powdered and mixed with borax and placed in all the hollows. The work is then placed under an iron cage in a fierce charcoal fire, where it is fused. It is then filed smooth, polished with sandpaper, then with charcoal-dust, and finally burnished like silver-work.

10. *Block Tin, other Metals, &c.*

[86].—Ramri.—Pipes.

[89].—Shan States.—Pipes.

These pipes are used for purposes of smoking.

[96–101]. — Moulmein. — Block-tin boxes, plates, stands.

This tin is obtained chiefly from the Mergui district.

[2049 - 2052, 2066 - 2068, 2072 - 2083 & 2089].—Bangles (brass), armlets (lead), combs (wooden), belts, earrings, &c. — Arakan Hill Tracts.

Ornaments chiefly worn by the Hill Tribes of Arakan. They are chiefly made of brass and lead.

Div. VI.—Art Manufactures in Wood, Ivory, Etc.

1. *Carved Furniture and Carpentry.*

[31, 32, & 57].—1, 2, and 3. Rangoon.—Cabinet, stand and sideboard back

See remarks upon wood-carving.

[1005].—Steering chair.—Rangoon.

3. *Ivory Carving.*

[1068-1073]. — Images, paper-cutters, &c. Moulmein.

4. *Lacquered Wares.*

[21-30, 69-79, 105-108, & 110]. Prome.—Panels, ducks, boxes, &c.

[1010, 1011, 1050-1064].—Panels, betel-boxes, caskets, and book-case.—Prome.

The lacquer ware used in British Burma is of two kinds—

(i) That in which the article is made of basket work lacquered over;

(ii) That in which the article is made of wood.

With regard to shape alone, a distinction might be drawn between things used in ordinary life and those which are dedicated to the service of the monastery.

All the lacquer ware made on a basket-work form comes from Upper Burma, where it is a very important trade.

In British Burma the trade is confined to the production of wooden articles lacquered over, such as the large, round platter with a raised edge, in which the family dinner is served round, and square boxes and bowls. Another set of artists produce richly gilt boxes used in the monasteries for holding palm-leaf manuscripts, the bowls with a pagoda-shaped cover used for carrying food to monasteries, and pagodas and shrines on which to place images of Gaudama.

The coffers referred to appear as if covered with pictures drawn in black on a gold ground, and the effect is so good that a small demand for tables, panels, and bowls of the same work has sprung up.

The process of manufacture is as follows: A deep red lacquer is made by mixing the sap of the *Melanorrhea usitatissima* with vermilion in the proportion of 12½ parts to 10 parts. The sap or *thitsi* is used alone when a black lacquer is required.

The wooden bowls, platters, &c., are scraped down with fine steel scrapers to make the surface as smooth as possible before laying on the lacquer. All cracks, holes, and chipped edges are filled and built up as it were with a putty made of the lacquer itself mixed with teakwood sawdust. The articles are then put away until the putty is dry and quite hard. The lacquer, the raw *thitsi*, is now rubbed all over the article with the bare hand so that the least particle of sand or stone may be detected, and the article put by in a cool and airy place to dry, not in the sun however, as the lacquer would crack or blister. In about three or four days they are quite dry, and they then receive a thick even coating of *thyo* made up of *thitsi* rice-water, and paddy-husk ashes. Again the article is put away to dry and harden; when the lacquer is quite dry and hard, it is smoothed down with water and paddy-husk ashes and stone polishers of graduated finenes from sandstone to a smooth pebble. This process removes all gloss or polish, and the last coating, or *a yaungtin*, is given to the article, either black or red, as a polish. The grounding is invariably black, and only the last coating red, if red coloured ware is required.

The above process in lacquering bowls, &c., is gone through in preparing boxes and tables. The boxes are generally coated with red lacquer, the tables invariably with black. After the boxes have been well washed and smoothed down, a coating of lacquer, red or black, as the case may be, thick in body, is laid on and the articles put by for a day or two. This coating is to act as a gold size. When the size has sufficiently hardened to permit touching without smearing the fingers, the worker proceeds to paint the design which he wishes to produce on the box or table, the lines standing up above the surface.

The paint used is made from sulphide of arsenic or orpiment, which the worker rubs with a little water on a sandstone palette. To this he adds a small quantity of powdered gum arabic so as to make the paint adhere to the size. The outline must, however, be finished before the *thitsi* groundwork on which he is painting has become too dry to be serviceable as a gold size. The drawings being finished and the paint dry, the process of gilding begins. The gold-leaf is laid on over the whole surface over the size and over the drawings or tracings; the gold adheres to the size but not to the paint. The article is then put away, always in a cool and airy place, until the gold has firmly adhered to the size. The tracings, or rather the paint which rises above the level of the general surface is now washed away with cotton-wool and water, and the design stands out prominently against the gold ground in red or black lines, according as the lacquer beneath the gold is red or black.

Some of the panels are decorated in bas-relief by attaching beadings; figure and foliage work made by mixing *thitsi* and finely powdered bone-ash and taking a cast from a mould cut out in a soapstone slab: a panel so treated looks as if it were made of polished ebony.

The shrines and the priests' begging bowls are first carved or turned in wood and afterwards covered with gold leaf and ornamented with pieces of green and red glass and looking-glass.

Gilt lacquered ware is comparatively cheap, and the artists do not do more than earn enough for a livelihood.

5.—*Wood Carving.*

[50, 90 to 95, and 109].—1 to 7. Rangoon, models of men, women, and carts.

[1006, 1007, 1012-1016]. — Brackets. — Rangoon.

[2091].—Stand.—Prome.

The very best men are masters of all these descriptions of carving, but as a rule the ordinary carver is a proficient at either foliage or figure work.

With work covering such a large range it would be wearisome to describe each variety in even a few of the manifold uses to which it is put. The most characteristic work, both of foliage and figures, is to be found at Buddhist monasteries, where the sacred seven-roofed spire, supported on vermilion and gold-plated pillars, rises above a placed figure of Gaudama; each line of eave and gable is adorned with a many pinnacled piece of carving rising up at the corners over the head of a guardian angel.

It would be difficult, even with the pencil, to represent the beauties of such carving, of which the principal characteristic is the delicacy of the curves which bound the undulating upper edge of the eaves boards where the flame-like pinnacles stand out dark in contrast against the receding roof. The lower edge is generally straight and is marked by a border pattern, while it often drops at the corner into a pendant of open tracery. A good carver will skilfully introduce figures of birds and animals, or the grotesque head of a *belu*, or wild man, into his work. It is easy to imagine how well such carving lends itself to the decoration of furniture.

The designs of the rougher kinds of carving are drawn in chalk or charcoal on the wood itself, and are chiselled out with great rapidity by the workman. The degree of finish depends on the position the work is to occupy and the price the patron can afford to pay. For better kinds of work the design is drawn on paper with a pencil and placed on the wood. The larger holes are gouged or chiselled out, and the rougher work done by the pupil, the master finishing it off. The foliage is conventional, but a good workman is exceedingly particular in obtaining easy-flowing curves and in working out every detail, however roughly, in strict accordance with truth and the propriety of the art. Thus, for example, each tendril should spring from the main branch as it does in nature, and no accidental crossing of another branch can serve as an excuse for introducing a spray which might conveniently fill a space which has hitherto been forgotten.

Div. XI.—Textiles.

1. *Cotton Fabrics.*

[33-52 & 54-56].—1-23. Prome — Clothing, bags, blankets, &c.

Weaving is carried on in almost every house in Burma, though not to such a large extent in the large towns as in the country.

[1008, 1009, 1017-1048 & 1076-1080]. — Clothing (silk).—Prome.

The articles usually made are *putsos*, or waistcloths, worn by men; *tameins*, worn by women. In British Burma, however, most of the silk articles of clothing worn by the people are chiefly of European manufacture; the imported articles being generally cheaper than those locally manufactured, though far less durable.

4. *Other Fabrics.*

[53].—Prome—Clothing.

The cotton-cleaning machine is a very simple and not very effective apparatus. It consists of four posts, a bamboo pedal, a fly-wheel, and two cylinders placed close together. These cylinders work in an opposite and inward direction, the upper one revolving towards and the lower one from the operator. Small quantities of raw cotton are inserted between the cylinders, which catch them up, and whilst passing through between the cylinders the seed which is too large to pass is separated from the wool and left behind. With this apparatus one operator will clean about 12 *viss* (43·80 lbs.) of raw cotton in a day, turning out 4½ viss (16·40 lbs.) of cleaned cotton. The outturn necessarily varies according to the kind and quality of the raw cotton. The wool is then spun into thread with a spool and a wheel in much the same way as used to be done in Europe. The weaving machine is exceedingly simple, and is not unlike the hand-machine formerly in use in Europe. The articles usually made are—

(1) *Putsos*, waistcloths worn by men, about 15 feet long and about 3½ feet broad.
(2) *Tameins*, worn by women, a sheet of two portions sewn together, 4½ feet long by 5½ feet broad.
(3) *Thindaings*, or coverlets, and
(4) *Saungs*, or thick sheets.

The last article is manufactured almost exclusively from the cotton grown in the province. The articles woven are rough but strong, and last longer than the flimsy articles imported, which are, however, more gaudy in their designs and are consequently more sought after by the younger generation and by towns-people who wish to combine effect with economy.

Div. XII.—Embroideries.

2. *Gold and Silver.*

[1074, 1075 & 1081]. — Clothing (embroideries).—Prome.

This kind of work is not carried out in Lower Burma except to supply costumes for the theatre. Gold and silver lace are freely used, as are precious stones, and the result is an exceedingly costly garment. A very ordinary jacket for a "prince" in a marionette company costs Rs. 150.

MADRAS PRESIDENCY.

[Entries in italics refer to *loan* exhibits.]

Div. I., Sect. 1.

Paintings and Drawings.

1. A picture in native oil-painting with scenes from Hindu mythology, &c., and a manuscript description. These pictures are used by itinerant beggars who spread the picture on the ground and explain the scenes to the on-lookers, expecting a few coppers as alms.

2. A native picture in water-colours on crimped paper, representing a different picture when looked at from opposite side.

3 & 4. Six circular paintings on leather.

5. Six circular paintings on leather, Krishna and the Gopis.

6. Six circular paintings on leather.

7. Eight circular paintings on leather.

8. Twelve circular paintings on leather, in paper case.

Large oil-painting of H.H. the Honourable the Maharajah of Vizianagram.

Exhibitor, N. C. Raganatha Naidu, *Pupil of the School of Art.*

9. *An oil-painting representing the "Tree of Life."*

10 to 12. *Water-colour portrait on wood of the former Rajas of Peddapur.*

21. Painting on ivory of H.H. the late Sivaji of Tanjore.

22. Painting on ivory of the Tranquebar Civil Court.

23. Painting on ivory of the Sirangam temple.

24. Painting on ivory of the Trichinopoly rock.

25. Painting on ivory of Trichinopoly.

26. Painting on ivory of the Cape of Good Hope.

27. Painting on ivory of Maharaja Sarfoji.

28. Painting on ivory of a parrot.

29. Painting on ivory of the Trichinopoly rock gate.

30. Painting on ivory of a marriage procession.

31 to 34. Paintings on talc, a book of six.

Div. I.—Sect. 2.

Engravings, Lithographs and Sketches.

Exhibitor, Government Lithographic Department, Madras.

86. Portfolio containing chromo-lithographs, chalk drawings on stone, free-hand drawings on stone, and mapping.

87. Irrigation map of the Madras Presidency.

88. Road map of the Madras Presidency.

89. Design for title-page.

90. Engraving of brass lamp.

Div. I., Sect. 3.

Photographs.

Exhibitor, Colonel H. P. Hawkes, *President, Art Committee.*

91. Book of 50 permanent photographs of Madras and Burmese art ware, prepared by the Madras Government Art Committee.

Exhibitors, Messrs. Nicholas & Co., *Photographers, Madras.*

92. *Book of 60 photographs of architectural subjects in Southern India.*

Exhibitor, F. Dunsterville, Esq.

93. *Permanent photograph carbon process of Hathi Singh's Temple, Ahmedabad.*

94. *Permanent photograph carbon process of Rama Ishwara's Temple, Ahmedabad.*

95. *Permanent photograph carbon process of Chentaraya's Temple, Tadpatri.*

Exhibitor, Madras Irrigation Department.

96 to 100. Five photographs of Kistna Delta Works.

Div. II., Sect. 1.

Architectural Designs and Models.

Exhibitor, Consulting Architect to Government.

102. A model in Carrara marble of the Dharmaraja's Rath at the Seven Pagodas, scale 2 feet to the inch.

103. Model showing a series of wells being sunk on which to found a building. This method of securing a firm foundation in fine sandy mud is peculiar to India.

Div. II., Sect. 2.

Designs for Manufactures.

Exhibitor, E. B. Havell, Esq., *Superintendent Madras School of Arts and Industries.*

170. Twenty blocks for hand-printing the chintz No. 2200.

171. *A collection of six specimens of wood blocks used for hand-printing palampores.*

172. A collection of specimens of wood blocks used for hand-printing palampores.
173. Complete set of specimens of wood blocks for one palampore.
174. Impression of paper of No. 173.
175. Complete set of wood blocks for hand-printing one palampore.
176. Impression on paper of No. 175.
177. Blocks for same as No. 175.
178. Impression same as No. 176.

Exhibitor, C. J. Peters, Esq., *Executive Engineer, Cauvery and Vennar regulators, Grand Anicut, Tanjore.*

179. *A collection of seven wooden blocks used for hand-printing palampores.*
180. A collection of six wooden blocks used for hand-printing palampores.
181. Two blocks for hand-printing the exhibit No. 2396.
182. Two blocks for hand-printing the exhibit No. 2397.
183. Two blocks for hand-printing the exhibit No. 2398.
184. One block for hand-printing the exhibit No. 2399.
185. Two blocks for hand-printing the exhibit No. 2400.
186. Two blocks for hand-printing the exhibit No. 2179.
187. One block for hand-printing the exhibit No. 2180.
188. One block for hand-printing the exhibit No. 2181.
189. One block for hand-printing the exhibit No. 2182.
190. One block for hand-printing the exhibit No. 2183.
191. One block for hand-printing the exhibit No. 2184.
192. One block for hand-printing the exhibit No. 2185.
193. Ten blocks for printing chintzes.
194. Eighteen blocks for printing chintzes.
195. Fourteen blocks for printing chintzes.
196. Ten blocks for printing chintzes.
197. Twelve blocks for printing chintzes.
198. Eight blocks for printing chintzes.
199. Six blocks for printing chintzes.
200. Sixteen blocks for printing chintzes.

Div. II., Sect. 8.

Other works of Decorative Art not specified.

Exhibitor, E. B. Havell, Esq., *Superintendent.*

211. Circular Oriel window in coloured glass, designed, painted, and executed by the pupils of the Madras School of Arts.
212. A stained glass window, designed and executed in the Madras School of Arts for St. Andrew's Kirk.
213. A stained glass window, designed and executed by the pupils of the Madras School of Arts.

Div. III.

Musical Instruments.

221. Drum, ends closed with sheep skin and tightened with rope.
222. Drum, barrel-shaped, ends closed with sheep skin and laced with rope.
223. Tambourine, with cymbals and rattles attached, covered with the skin of a lizard.
224. Brass cymbals.
225. Small cymbals.
226. Flat drum.
227. Conch shell, the mouthpiece mounted in brass, and the other end with an ornamental expansion in the same metal in shape like the tail of a mythical bird often seen in temple carvings.
228. Flute made of bamboo, with nine finger holes.
229. Whistle made of bamboo, with eight finger holes.
230. S-shaped brass trumpet like an ancient Scandinavian horn, used on ceremonial occasions.
231. An oboe-like instrument made of blackwood and brass mounted, the reed being made of the spathe of a palm. It has eight finger holes in front and two in the lower end on one side of the tube.
232. Similar to No. 231, but with seven finger holes.
233. Like No. 232, but covered with cloth, brass mounted, and with the usual palm reed.
234. A small drum chiefly used by beggars.
235. A sort of guitar, the body is semi-globular, made of jackwood, and both it and the neck are inlaid with ivory decorated with floral patterns etched and filled in with red and green pigment. It has four strings and the same number of tuning pegs.
236. Similar to No. 235, but of simpler construction, the body and neck of teakwood, the latter adorned with griffin's head.
237. A guitar. The body is hollowed out of jackwood with belly of the same material, is protracted into a long neck, and has a painted gourd at the upper end fixed below. The strings are of wire and seven in number; four of them run over a bridge, being provided with a number of frets, the remaining three run along the side of the neck, and have an arched bridge of metal, and the scroll is adorned with a painted griffin's head.
238. A guitar, the body a scooped-out gourd, the strings are of wire and five in number, the finger-board has numerous frets made of ligatures of cat-gut and wire passing round the neck.
239. A guitar, with a drum-like body, made out of one piece of wood. The hollow body is traversed by two holes at the base of the neck, and cut so as to form thin wings or scrolls. The bottom of the body is closed with a thin piece of wood, and the belly with parchment. The neck emerges from the body in a deep bracket-like piece and is covered with bright blue cloth

with gilt figures on it, and terminating in the gilded head of a bird. There are nine tuning pegs and cat-gut strings.

240. A violin; the body is hollow and the belly covered with skin. It has cat-gut strings passing over the bridge, and below these are sympathetic wire strings arranged like the string of a harp. It is played on with a bow consisting of hair stretched on a piece of bent cane.

241. Conch shell, same as No. 227.

242. Guitar, same as No. 239.

Div. IV., Sect. 1.

*Special Collection of old Native Jewellery from Madura. Collected for the Committee by M.R.R. Murgesa Pillay.**

271. Gold ear ornament fixed to the upper lobe of the ear, the round part covering the orifice.

272. Gold ear ornament fixed in a hole in the upper lobe of the ear below No. 271.

273. Gold ear ornament fixed in a hole in the side of the ear below No. 272.

274. Gold ear ornament, one of the five jewels worn in a greatly distended hole in the lower lobe of the ear.

275. Gold ear ornament, one of the five jewels worn in a greatly distended hole in the lower lobe of the ear.

276. Gold ear ornament, one of the five jewels worn in a greatly distended hole in the lower lobe of the ear.

277. Gold ear ornament, one of the five jewels worn in a greatly distended hole in the lower lobe of the ear.

278. Gold ear ornament, one of the five jewels worn in a greatly distended hole in the lower lobe of the ear.

279. Gold marriage emblem, a representation of the foot of Krishna.

280. Gold necklet with pendant in the shape of a clove of garlic.

281. Necklet of alternate coral and gold beads, the latter with eight facets each.

282. Silver armlets.

283 & 284. Silver wristlets.

285. Silver finger ring worn on the fourth finger from the thumb.

286. Silver double toe rings connected by chains, worn on the first and last toes, the chain lying between.

287. Silver toe rings, worn on the third from the big toe.

288. Silver toe rings, worn on the fourth from the big toe.

290. Gold ear ornament worn by males.

* The collection of old native jewellery has béen got together by the personal exertions of a member of the Committee, assisted by G. D. Leman, Esq., Collector of Coimbatore, H. G. Turner, Esq., Collector of Vizagapatam, and several other gentlemen of the Madras Civil Service.

The following native gentlemen have also given valuable assistance: M.R.R. P. Murgesa Pillay, Head-quarter Inspector of Police at Madura, M.R R. M. Ramasawmy Naidoo, Comy.-Genl.'s Office, A. Pinto, Esq., Depy. Collector of Chingleput, and Mr. C. Seetharama Iyer, Depy. Collector, Coimbatore.

General Collection of old Native Jewellery from Southern India.

291. Gold ear ornament fixed in the upper lobe of the ear, the round part covering the orifice.

292 to 295. Gold ear ornaments.

296. Gold ear ornament, worn in hole through outer and upper margin of the ear.

297. Gold ear ornament worn as No. 296.

298. Gold ear ornament with pendant, worn as No. 296.

299 & 300. Gold ear ornaments worn as No. 296.

301. Gold ear ornaments (cobra-head), one of the five jewels worn in the distended lobe of the ear.

302 & 303. Gold ear ornaments, same as No. 301.

304. Gold ear ornaments, one of the five jewels.

305. Gold ear ornament.

306. Gold ear studs.

307. Gold ear drops with fringe of false pearls.

308. Gold ear studs and ear drops with fringe of false pearls.

309 & 310. Gold ear drops with fringe of true pearls.

311. Gold nose ornament set with false stones.

312. Gold nose ornament, very finely worked.

313. Gold nose ornament, finely worked.

314. Gold nose ring with one false pearl.

315. Gold nose ring.

316. Gold nose ring worn by Muhammadan women.

317. Gold nose hook worn by Wuddur (tank-digger) women.

318. Gold nose ornament set with coloured stone, worn by Muhammadan women.

319. Gold nose ornament worn by Muhammadan women.

320. Gold nose ornament.

321. Gold ornament for the back of the hair, with imitations of jasmine buds and roses, as worn by Hindus in Malabar.

322. Gold ornament for the back of the hair, with imitation of *chumpaka* flowers, from Malabar.

323. Gold plate for back of the hair.

324 & 325. Gold ornament worn to conceal the parting of the hair, the pendant resting on the forehead.

326. Gold necklet of 25 alternate solid and open work beads.

327. Gold necklet, Vandyke pattern, with drops.

328. Necklet of very thin gold beads threaded on black silk.

329. Silver necklet.

330. Silver necklet from Travancore.

331. Necklet of silver medallions strung on thread, worn by Muhammadan children.

332. Solid silver necklet as worn by Hindus.

333. Solid silver necklet with drops as worn by Muhammadans.

334. Silver pendant.
335. Silver neck-chain of several rows of links.
336. Necklet of glass and gold beads.
337. Necklet of horse hair with two gold studs, worn by Kulla females in Madura.
338 to 340. Two gold beads used as part of necklet from which the *thali* or marriage emblem is suspended.
341. Gold marriage emblem, a representation of the foot of Krishna.
342. Silver necklet of three rows of melon shaped beads.
343. Silver necklet of 31 wheat grain beads.
344. Silver necklet from Travancore—copy in silver of a very old gold necklet.
345. Silver chain of three rows of beads.
346. Silver chain as worn by Parsees.
347. Silver *lingam* case.
348 to 351. Silver armlets.
352. Silver armlets of beads in shape of cloves of garlic with pendant.
353. Silver armlet of double cylinders with pendant.
354. Silver armlet of double cylinders with pointed ends
355. Silver armlet.
356 to 358. Silver wristlets (gauntlet shaped), with filigrain ornamentation.
359. Silver wristlet.
360. Silver wristlet, knob and diamond pattern.
361. Silver wristlet, with filigrain ornament.
362. Silver wristlets, "comb pattern," one pair.
363. Silver wristlet, same as No. 362.
364. Silver wristlets, strung on thread, one pair.
365. Silver wristlets, set with turquoise, &c., one pair.
366. Silver wristlets, strung on thread, one pair.
367. Silver wristlet, "shell pattern."
368. Waist-cord for men of plaited silver.
369. Silver waist-chain with pendants as worn by children.
370 & 371. Silver *pipul* (fig) leaf as worn by girl children.
372 to 384. Silver anklets.
385 to 387. Silver toe rings.
388 to 390. Silver toe ring.
391 to 393. Silver finger ring.
394. Silver filigrain wristlet of Muhammadan pattern.
395. Silver wristlet of Muhammadan pattern.
396 & 397. Silver wristlets.
398. Silver wristlets, "comb pattern."
399. Silver wristlets, plain.
400 & 401. Silver armlet.
402. Silver armlet worn by Vellálas.
403. Child's silver armlet with hook and eye fastening.
404. Adult's silver armlet with hook and eye fastening.
405. Silver *lingam* case.
406. Silver necklet, *swamy* pattern, from Trichinopoly (Modern).
407. Silver wristlet, *swamy* pattern, from Trichinopoly (Modern).
408. Gold ring worn by Muhammadan females on the thumb.
409. Gold ring worn by Muhammadan females on the index finger.
410. Necklet of three rows of gold (wheat ear) and black glass beads.
411. Gold annular studs for the distended lower lobes of ears, worn by females of Reddy caste, one pair.
412. Gold ear ornament worn by females of silk weaver caste.
413. Silver and parcel gilt armlet with filigrain fastening and five round silver bosses as worn by Telugu men in the Vizagapatam district.
414. Silver wristlet composed of two pectinated rings with intermediate cylinder.
415. Gold forehead ornament with drops, worn with the *pimpalum* No. 324.
416 to 421. Silver wristlets, School of Art, Madras.
422 & 423. Silver *shavi-billa* or chatelaines as worn by native women, with 12 keys, charms, &c.
424. Gold marriage necklet of 48 pendants (charms), with 52 rubies and 57 beads.
425. Gold marriage necklet.

Div. IV., Sect. 1.

Special Collection of Jewellery worn by the aboriginal Todas, Badagas, and Kotahs of the Nilgiri Hills.

426 & 427. Gold ear ornament worn by Badaga males.
428. Silver ear ornament worn by Kotah women.
429. Silver necklet (worn by Todas and burned with the body after death).
430. Silver torque or solid necklet of silver and false coral beads, as worn by the aborigines of the Nilgiri Hills.
431. Two necklaces of black glass beads and plaited silver with cowrie shell pendants.
432. Silver armlet worn by Badaga women.
433. Silver wristlet worn by Badaga old females on their left wrist.
434. Silver wristlet worn by Toda women.
435. Silver finger ring worn by Todas and Badagas.
436. Large silver ear-rings worn by Toda women.
437. Brass armlets worn by Toda women and weighing 14 lbs., with cotton guard, ornamented with cowrie shells.
438. Brass wristlet worn by Kotah women on the left wrist.
439. Two copper and two brass wristlets worn by Kotah women.
440. Heavy copper wristlet worn by Kotah women on the right wrist.
441. Seven iron wristlets, of various patterns, worn by Toda women.
442. A brass waist chain worn by Toda women.

General Collection of old Native Jewellery from Southern India.

443. Silver torque or solid necklet with hook and eye fastening.
444. Silver finger ring.
445. Silver pendant worn on the temples attached to the hair.
446. Ear studs of silver gilt, as worn by the Lumbadi women.
447. Four ear-rings with chain and ball pendants, worn in the upper margin of the ear.
448. Breastplate of silver parcel gilt.
449. Wristlet, pectinated pattern.
450. Silver wristlet, old.
451. Waist belt of beaten silver with hook and eye fastening.
452 & 453. Silver wristlets.
454. Hair pendant.
455. Silver finger ring, embossed.
456. Silver finger-ring with oval medallion.
457 & 458. Silver toe rings.
459. Silver necklace, Muhammadan.
460. Silver ornament for top of the head.
461. Silver ornament for top of the head with chignon attached.
462. Silver nose ornament.
463 & 464. Silver armlet.
465. Silver wristlet.
466 to 468. Silver finger ring.
469. Silver waist belt.
470. Silver waist cord made of plaited silver wire, very flexible.
471. Silver coin-case, worn suspended from No. 470.
472 & 473. Silver anklet.
474 & 475. Silver toe rings.
476. Silver *pipul* (fig) leaf as worn by female children.
477. Silver fig leaf.
478. Gold ear-rings.
479 to 481. Ear-rings.
482 to 484. Nose-ring.
485. Silver head ornament with chignon of twisted human hair.
486. Sixteen silver charms to be worn with the chatelaine.

Special Collection of Jewellery from Cochin, exhibited by His Highness the Maharajah.

487. *Gold ornament to cover the queue of plaited hair falling from the back of the head, worn by Brahmins only.*
488. *Gold ornament for the crown of the head, worn immediately above No. 487.*
489. *Gold ornament worn on the top of the head by Brahmin ladies.*
490. *Gold ornament worn below No. 489.*
491 *Gold ornament worn with Nos. 489 and 490.*
492. *Gold ear studs with pendant and fringe of false pearls.*
493. *Gold ear studs worn in the enlarged lobe of the ear by Nair ladies.*
494. *Gold filigrain necklace, comprising three clasps and six rows of chain on each side of the upper portion, and seven in the lower, worn by all castes.*
495. *Gold marriage necklace, consisting of 32 medallions strung on red silk.*
496. *Gold necklace, consisting of 51 medallions of green stone mounted in gold, with 153 rubies, strung on red silk.*
497. *Gold necklace, with 21 medallions, and 22 beads, strung on red silk.*
498. *Gold necklace, with 65 pieces.*
499. *Gold necklace, consisting of 13 medallions representing the avatars of Vishnu, and 14 beads, worn by caste ladies.*
500. *Gold necklace, consisting of three clasps and six rows of chains of faceted beads on each side af the upper and nine on the lower, worn by all castes.*
501. *Gold wristlet representing the story of the bruising of the black serpent.*
502. *Gold wristlet with rattles.*
503. *Gold wristlet with pierced open work ornamentation and rattles.*
504. *Gold waist chain for children, with 28 jingling pendants and 29 beads.*

Silver Jewellery of native make for European wear from Cochin.

505. *Silver hair-pin.*
506. *Silver necklace with 46 filigrain pendants and 44 beads, strung on silver wire.*
507. *Silver necklace with six alternate butterflies and flowers.*
508. *Silver necklace with three rows of imitation coins, 30 in each row, and 30 beads.*
509. *Silver necklace with 10 filigrain flowers and two pendants.*
510. *Silver necklace with 10 filigrain flowers and three pendants.*
511. *Silver rose brooch.*
512. *Silver brooch with four pendants.*
513. *Silver brooch with five pendants.*
514. *Silver brooch vine pattern.*
515. *Silver brooch, Indian lute.*
516. *Silver brooch, Umbrella.*
517. *Silver brooch, Bouquet-holder.*
518. *Silver brooch, Butterfly.*
519. *Silver brooch, flower and leaf.*
520. *Silver brooch, Butterfly.*
521. *Silver brooch, Palanquin.*
522. *Silver locket.*
523. *Silver watch-guard of two rows of imitation coins, 24 in each.*
524. *Silver bracelets, six flowers in each, one pair.*
525. *Silver bracelets, five butterflies in each, one pair.*
526. *Silver bracelets with four rows of frosted beads and two pendants in each, one pair.*
527. *Silver bracelets, double-headed serpents, in filigrain, one pair.*

Special Collection of Jewellery from South Canara.

528. Gold hair-pin, fig-leaf shape.
529. Gold ear studs, fig-leaf shape, worn in the enlarged lobe of the ear by Mapila women.

530. Gold ear studs, clove shape.

531. Gold torque, garlic cloves, faceted beads and flowers, strung on silver wire.

532. Gold wristlets.

533. Silver armlets of silver wire, twisted serpent shape.

534. Silver armlets, bent.

535. Silver armlets, cylinders strung on silver wire.

536. Silver waist belt for little children of plaited silver wire rolled up into seven rows and joined by a silver band.

537. Silver waist belt for little boys, imitation of fruits, &c., strung on red silk.

538. Silver waist belt of little silver balls strung on a chain, worn by little children below No. 536.

539. Silver cylinder worn as a purse round the waist for carrying small coins.

540. Silver fig-leaf as worn by little girls.

541. Silver anklets, Muhammadan pattern.

Special Collection of Native Jewellery from Vizagapatam.

542. Silver ear pendant with stud and fringe of false pearls.

543. Silver necklace.

544. Silver armlet.

545. Silver armlet with large clasp, ornamented in diaper pattern with four bosses on plaited wire.

546. Silver armlet, similar to No. 545, but with gilt front.

547. Silver armlet, Vandyke pattern.

548. Silver armlet, hammer head pattern.

549 to 560. Silver wristlets.

561. Silver waist belt of medallions ornamented with mythological animals and birds, strung between two rows of red cotton thread.

562. Silver waist belt, strung between two rows of black cotton thread.

563. Silver waist belt of plaited wire, with bosses and ornamented buckle.

Div. IV., Sect. 2.

Ornaments in the Baser Metals, &c.

671. Ornament to cover the queue of plaited hair falling from the back of the head.

672. Ornament for the crown of the head.

673. Ornaments for the front of the head, seven pieces, set with false stones and pearls.

674. Ornaments worn from the temple, and fixed to the lower lobe of the ear, set with false stones and pearls.

675. Ear-drops with fringe of false pearls.

676. Nose ornaments worn on the right side of the nose.

677, 688. Necklets with drop of false stones fringed with false pearls, worn tight round the neck.

679. Necklet of false emeralds with drop of the same fringed with false pearls, worn as No. 677.

680. Necklet, string of imitation open-work Rudraksha beads.

681. Necklet, string of eight-faceted brass beads.

682. Necklet, strip of brass with hook and eye attachment, worn tight round the neck.

683. Necklet, string of gilt beads.

684. Necklet to carry the *thali* or marriage token, consisting of two hollow brass tubes (*thaweez*) and brass medallions with floral and mythological ornamentation, strung on black silk with tassel.

685. Head ornament for princes and bridegrooms, worn in the turban above the middle of the forehead, set with false stones.

686. Jewelled breastplate for males, worn suspended from the neck, set with false stones and pearls.

687. Armlet worn on the upper arm, set with false stones.

688. Armlet of brass, with drops of the same, worn on the upper arm.

689. Armlet set with false stones, worn on the upper arm by males.

690, 691. Wristlets.

692. Waist-belt with diaper ornamentation and brass drops.

693. Anklet of chain pattern, in tinned brass wire.

694. Collection of peasant jewellery worn by the poorer classes in the Vizagapatam district.

695. Collection of peasant jewellery from Chingleput.

696. Collection of peasant jewellery from Malabar.

697. Copper anklets.

698. Copper armlet.

699. Collection of peasant jewellery from Tanjore.

700. Head ornament worn at the parting on each side of the forehead.

701. Head ornament worn with No. 700.

702. Seven articles of peasant jewellery from Kistna district.

703. Set of thirteen articles of peasant jewellery from Godavari district.

704. Set of eleven articles of peasant jewellery from Godavari district.

705. Set of peasant jewellery from Trichinopoly.

706. Set of twenty-two articles of peasant jewellery from Cuddapah.

707. Set of twelve articles of peasant jewellery from Cuddapah.

708. Twenty-four articles of peasant jewellery from Ganjam.

Div. V., Sect. 1.

Gold and Silver Plate.

771. Candlestick in solid silver, designed after the manner of a native Hindu lamp, made by Ragavaputtur and Soobroyachary of the Madras School of Art.

772. Water vessel or lotah in solid silver chased and ornamented, made in the Madras School of Art.

773. Spoon of solid silver, bowl supported by parrots and stem ending with five-headed snake overshadowing the *lingam*.

Exhibitor, GATTA SOOBROYADU NAIDU GARU, *Deputy Tahsildar.*

774. *Chased silver muffineer.*
775. *Chased silver muffineer.*

Exhibitor, H.H. THE MAHARAJA OF COCHIN.

776. *Silver scent casket in filigrain.*
777. *Silver bouquet-holder.*
778. *Silver card-case in filigrain.*
779. *Pair of silver crochet needles.*
780. Silver betel-nut box with fluted and embossed ornamentation.
781. Shallow silver bowl with fluted sides and chased centre.

Exhibitor, H.H. THE HONOURABLE THE MAHARAJAH OF VIZIANAGRAM.

Gilt state howdah with canopy used on state and ceremonious occasions.

Silver howdah used for ordinary purposes.

Set of elephant trappings, gilt, used on state and other ceremonious occasions.

Set jewels for elephants, for state and other ceremonious occasions.

Horse saddle cloth, gilt, for state and other ceremonious occasions.

Set of horse jewels.

DIV. V., SECT. 2.

Koft or Damascened Work.

Exhibitor, COL. H. P. HAWKES, *President Exhibition Committee.*

791. *Hookah bottom in old Bidri ware.* This specimen, which appears to be very old, bears curious evidences of the influence of the same Italian art that ornamented the Taj at Agra. The thickness of the silver inlay is noticeable.
792. *Silver snuff-box damascened in gold.*

DIV. V., SECT. 3.

Brass, Copper and Alloys.

LAMPS.

801. Brass lamp of the pattern commonly used in Hindu houses.
802 to 805. Brass lamps surmounted by a figure of the Hansa or sacred goose.
806. Bell-metal lamp with adjustment for raising and lowering.
807. Brass lamp of Muhammadan pattern.
808. Brass lamp of Hindu pattern.
809 to 812. Brass lamps.
813, 814. Brass hanging lamps with chain and hook.
815. Combined oil-pot and hand-lamp, with spoon, used for trimming lamps when in large numbers. The classical shape of this exhibit will be noticed.
816 to 818. Combined oil-pot and lamp.
819. Lamp carried by Muhammadan beggars when asking alms.
820, 821. Brass oil-vessel for feeding torches.

Exhibitor, COL. H. P. HAWKES, *President Exhibition Committee.*

822. *Bronze lamp with 18 branches carrying 98 lights. Height 5 ft. 3 in.* This lamp must be of considerable age, and is interesting from the primitive shape of the reservoirs.

HOUSEHOLD UTENSILS.

Exhibited as specimens of the shapes in general use.

823. Bell-metal *chembu.*
824. Brass *chembu*
825. Brass *chembu*, chased.
826, 827. Brass *chembus.*
828. Brass *chembus*, chased.
829. Brass *chembu.*
830 to 832. Copper *chembus.*
833. *Chembu.*
834. Bell-metal *chembu.*
835. Brass *chembu.*
836. Brass *chembu*, flat bottomed.
837 to 839. Bell-metal *chembus.*
840. Brass *chembu.*
841 to 855. Bell-metal lotahs.
856. Brass *lotah*, with cover, inlaid with copper.

CHEMBUS FOR TRAVELLING, ETC.

857. Bell-metal *chembu* with screw top.
858. Bell-metal *chembu* in two parts.
859. Pewter *lotah* with screw top.
860, 861. Bell-metal water vessel with screw top.
862. Pewter water vessel with screw top.

VESSELS WITH SPOUTS.

863. Copper water vessel with spout.
864 to 867. Bell-metal water vessels with spouts.
868. Bell-metal *aftaba* with *silabchi*, used by Muhammadans for washing the hands before eating.
869. Brass *aftaba.*

Miscellaneous.

870. Large copper vessel, with ring handles, for heating water.
871. Brass water-pot used for bringing water from the well.
872. Copper water-pot used for bringing water from the well.
873 & 874. Brass water-pot used for bringing water from the well.
875. Brass cooking pot.
876. Copper cooking pot.
877, 878. Brass cooking pots.
879, 880. Bell-metal cooking vessels.
881, 882. Brass culinary vessels.
883. Copper cup.
884. Pewter bowl.
885. Brass *chatty.*

Trays, Etc.

886. Circular tray of pierced and engraved brass.

887, 888. Octagonal trays of pierced brass.

889. Oval tray of pierced brass.

890. Brass embossed tray.

891 to 895. Chased brass trays.

896, 897. Chased copper trays.

898. Chased brass tray.

899. Chased copper tray.

900 to 902. Chased brass trays.

903. Chased copper tray.

904. Chased brass tray.

905. Octagonal brass plate inlaid with copper and silver.

906. Circular chased and embossed brass plate.

907. Octagonal pierced brass tray.

908. Bell-metal hookah bottom.

909. Brass hookah bottom.

910. Brass hookah bottom, with silver studs as used by the wandering Lumbadi tribe.

911. Brass spice box.

912. Copper measure.

913. Brass oval box with diagonally fluted ornamentation.

914. Child's toy of brass representing a raja on horseback.

915. Two child's rattles in bell-metal.

916. Betel-nut cutter.

917 to 919. Brass combs.

Exhibitor, Sarabiah, *Brass-smith, Mint Street, Madras.*

920 & 921. *Lotahs in chased brass and copper.*

Div. V., Sect. 3.

921*a*. *Copper tray embossed and chased, from design by E. B. Havell, Esq., School of Art.*

921*b*. *Copper lotah electro-plated, F. B. Havell, Esq., School of Art.*

921*c*. *Two specimens of embossed copper, E. B. Havell, Esq., School of Art.*

922 to 926. Chased brass trays.

927. Old tray in chased brass.

928. Shallow bowl in chased brass.

929. Tray in pierced brass.

930, *a*, *b*. Trays in embossed and pierced brass.

930*c*. Chased *aftaba* with *stlabchi*.

Special Collection of Metal Ware from Malabar.

930*d*, 930*e*. Brass shallow bowls.

930*f*, 930*g*. Bell-metal cups.

930*h*. Bell-metal water vessel for travelling.

930*i*. Bell-metal tobacco-holder.

930*j*. Bell-metal holder for *chunam* (lime to chew with betel-nut).

930*k*. Bell-metal bowl with handle.

930*l*. Brass bowl.

930*m*. & 930*n*. Bell-metal ladles.

930*o*. Bell-metal oil measure.

930*p*. & 930*q*. Brass spittoons.

930*r*. Brass three-armed lamp.

930*s*. Brass lamp.

930*t*. Brass hanging lamp.

930*u*. Brass sacrificial lamp.

930*y*. Drinking vessel in burnished brass.

930*z*. Water-vessel in burnished brass.

930*aa*. Pierced brass plate bearing three candlesticks.

930*ac*. Scent casket in brass, silver gilt.

930*ad*. Betel-nut set of six pieces in pierced brass, silver gilt.

Div. V., Sect. 4.

Brass and Copper Ware for sacrificial purposes.

Sacrificial Utensils.

931. Vishnaivite begging-pot in fluted copper.

932. Original wicker-work type of No. 931.

933. Vishnaivite begging-pot in fluted copper.

934. Copper tray used in Hindu worship.

935. Brass tray used for placing offerings before the idol.

936. Tray in chased copper with lip, for washing the idol.

937. Bell-metal stand for washing the idol.

938. Chased copper sacrificial tray.

Exhibitor, Tanjore Sirkar.

939. *Sacrificial camphor-burner, in the shape of five pagodas, on stand.*

940 to 942. *Sacrificial camphor-burners.*

943. *Sacrificial stand for burning incense tapers.*

944. *Sacrificial camphor-burner.*

945. *Sacrificial stand for burning incense tapers, Goddess on lion.*

946. *Sacrificial stand for burning incense tapers, "Hanuman."*

947. *Sacrificial incense burner, "Garuda."*

948 & 949. *Sacrificial incense burners, Five-headed snakes.*

950. *Sacrificial incense-burner, Goddess on bull.*

951. *Sacrificial incense-burner, the sacred goose.*

952. *A pair of sacrificial incense-burners, bulls.*

953. *A pair of sacrificial incense-burners, goddesses on horses.*

954. *Sacrificial incense-burner, an elephant.*

955. *Sacrificial incense-burner, Krishna.*

956. *Sacrificial incense-burner, a Rishi.*

957. *Sacrificial incense-burner, an idol car.*

958. *Old figure of warrior with winged head-dress.*

959. *A pair of the sandals of Krishna in brass.*

960. *Crown or head-piece surmounted by the sandals of Krishna.*

961. *Miniature crown or head-piece surmounted by sandals of Krishna.*

962. *Brass model of square fan.*

963. *Brass model of round fan.*

964. *Brass comb with handle bearing a tiger and an antelope.*

965. *Crown or head-piece surmounted by sandals of Krishna.*

966. *Small copper model of bull.*
967. *Small brass model of umbrella.*
968. *Two copper models of palmyra leaf fans.*
969. *Two copper models of palmyra leaf fans with handles.*
970. *Two copper models of sacred standards.*
971. *Two copper models of sacrificial standards.*
972. *Copper model of stand for sacred chank shell.*
973. *Copper model of the sacred wheel-standard.*
974. *Two copper models of elephant goad.*
975. *Two copper models of war clubs.*
976. *Copper model of an antelope horn double dagger.*
977. *Copper model of a Kotah dagger.*
978. *Copper model of a bow.*
979. *Copper model of a bichwa dagger.*
980. *Copper model of a curved sword.*
981. *Copper model of straight sword.*
982. *Two copper models of spears.*
983. *Two copper models of tridents.*
984. *Two copper models of battle-axes.*
985. *Two copper models of ploughs.*
986. *Two copper models of swords made in imitation of the snout of the saw-fish.*
987. *Two copper models of Mapila war-knives.*
988. *Copper incense burner.*

Mythological Figures.

989. Brass figure of Kartika-Virasami on elephant.
990. Brass figure of the monkey god carrying Rama and Luchmana.
991. Copper figures of three Hindu gods (Vishnu and wives) on stand.
992. Copper figure of god Venkatapermal under the hood of the seven-headed serpent.
993. Copper figure of Venkatesapermal.
994. Copper figure of Hanuman.
995. Copper figure of Krishna dancing.
996 & 997. Copper figures of Luchmenarayan.
998. Copper figure of Luchmenarayan with *chank* and *chakra.*
999. Copper figure of Krishna dancing.
1000. Copper figure of Kali with drum, trident, sword, and skull.
1001. Copper figure of Luchmenarayan.
1002. Copper figure of Subramanier.
1003, 1004. Copper figures of Krishna.

Sacrificial Utensils.

1005 & 1006. Brass bells used in Hindu temples.
1007. Camphor burner.
1008. Cup for holding sandalwood paste for anointing idols.
1009. Cup or pourer in shape of chank shell.
1010. Cylindrical vessel for sacrificial purposes.
1011. Pigment box.
1012. Incense burner used for sacrificial purposes.
1013. Cylindrical vessel used for sacrificial purposes.
1014 to 1016. Vessels for holding holy water.
1017. Chased sacrificial lotah.
1018. Vessel for holy water.
1019. Chased brass *chembu* used in marking the forehead with the caste symbol.
1020. Vessel for holding holy water, swan on tortoise.
1021. Brass vessel for holy water.
1022. Sacred feet of Krishna, copper plated.
1023 to 1044. House lamps for sacrificial purposes.
1045. Lamp used in Hindu worship.
1046. Flower vase of brass, lightly plated.
1047. House lamp for sacrificial purposes.
1048. Copper figure of the monkey god.
1049. Copper figure of Krishna treading on the serpent.
1050. Copper figure of the kite god.
1051. House lamp for sacrificial purposes.

Marriage Gifts.

1052. Set of 45 "marriage presents" given to a Goomsur Maliah bride.

DIV. V., SECT. 4A.

Articles in Mixed Metals.

1201. Salver in brass and zinc (or type metal), diameter 18 in.
1202. Salver in brass and zinc, diameter 1 ft.
1203. Water vessel or goglet in brass and zinc.
1204. Lotah in brass and zinc.
1205. Round salver of brass with raised figures of Hindu deities in copper, diameter 18 in.
1206. Round salver of brass with raised figures in copper, diameter 12 in.
1207. Octagonal salver of copper with raised figures of Hindu deities in brass, diameter 16 in.
1208. Round salver of copper with raised figures in brass, diameter 12 in.
1209. Round salver of copper with raised figures in silver and brass, diameter 16 in.
1210, 1211. *Lotahs* of brass with raised figures in copper, height 6½ in.
1212. Water vessel of copper with raised silver ornamentation.
1213 & 1214. Water vessels with covers of copper with raised silver ornamentation.
1215. Water vessel of brass ornamented with raised silver and copper flowers. Designed by the Madras School of Art.
1216. Water vessel cover of copper ornament with raised silver figures.
1217. Hexagonal tray, brass inlaid with copper.
1218. Hexagonal tray in copper inlaid with silver.
1219. Oval tray, brass inlaid with silver and copper.
1220. Water vessel of copper inlaid with silver. Designed by the Madras School of Art.
1221. Water vessel of copper, inlaid with silver, designed by the Madras School of Art.

1222 to 1226. Water vessels of brass and copper.

1227, 1228. Water vessels of copper and silver.

1229. Water vessel of brass, inlaid with copper and silver.

1230. Octagonal brass plate of brass and silver.

Div. V., Sect. 5.

Arms and Armour.

1301. Spear in chased steel.
1302. Dagger in chased steel.
1303. Dagger.
1304 to 1306. Spear heads in chased steel.
1307 & 1308. Lance heads.
1309. Bill-hook.

Arms exhibited by H.H. THE MAHARAJAH OF VIZIANAGARAM.

1. Two large spears. Used in warfare.
2. Two medium sized spears. Used in warfare.
3. Two small spears. Used in warfare.
4. Four matchlocks. Used in warfare.
5. Two steel bows and four arrows. Used in warfare.
6. Two double-headed spear-heads. Used in warfare.
7. Two movable spear-heads. Used in warfare.
8. Five battle-axes, of sorts. Used in warfare.
9. Two ivory-handled daggers, wavy blades. Used in warfare.
10. Four straight-bladed, two ivory and silver-topped handles, two plain ivory handles. Used in warfare.
11. Four sacrificial knives. Used in human sacrifice.
12. Two curved-bladed hill swords. Used in warfare.
13. One sickle for cutting corn. Ancients. Used in cutting corn.
14. Two flower bows. At feasts used for throwing flowers.
15. One hill dagger. Used in warfare.
16. Two scimitars (ancient), one less curved than the other. Used in warfare.
17. Two iron hill pikes, bayonet-shaped heads. Used in warfare.
18. Two hill daggers, with side hand-guards. Used in warfare.
19. Two hunting spear heads. Used in warfare.
20. One bamboo bow, six iron-headed arrows, of sorts. Used in warfare.
21. Two circular shields, made of bison hide. Used in warfare.
22. Two circles of iron for throwing in warfare.
23. Two sets of steel armour, consisting of two helmets, two breast-plates, and four arm guards.

Div. VI., Sect. 1.

Carved Furniture and Carpentry.

Exhibitor, MADRAS GOVERNMENT.

1321. Carved wooden screen in two pieces, each 40 ft. long by 12½ ft. high, designed by E. B. Havell, Esq., Superintendent School of Art, and executed under his personal superintendence, Rs. 5000.

1322. Window of carved teak, designed and executed by Minakshi Achary, carver in the Madras School of Art.

1323. Native doorway of carved neem wood.

Exhibitor, Col. H. P. HAWKES, *President Exhibition Committee.*

1324. *Garden seat ornamented with carved wooden figures of Hindu gods, taken from a very old idol car.*

To be presented to the South Kensington Museum at the close of the Exhibition.

Exhibitor, SCHOOL OF ART.

1325. *Carved wooden plaque*, 13 *in. by* 9 *in., by Minakshi Achary.*

1326, 1327. Double comb in sandalwood, roughly carved.

1328, 1329. Carved plaques in sandalwood, mythological subject.

1330. Carving in red-wood (*Pterocarpus santalinus*) representing Krishna with his flute standing alongside a cow.

1331. Carving in red-wood representing Rama, Sita and Lakshmana.

Exhibitors, Messrs. OAKES & Co.

1332. Two carvings in white cedar in frame suitable for door panels.

Div. VI., Sect. 2.

Inlaid Work.

1341. Portfolio in Sandalwood and tortoise-shell ornamented with engraved and perforated ivory.

1342. Portable book-case in sandalwood and engraved and perforated ivory.

1343. Casket in sandalwood and engraved and perforated ivory.

1344. Casket for watch and rings in black buffalo horn and engraved and perforated ivory.

1345. Casket in sandalwood and engraved and perforated ivory, for holding four packets of cards, with two sets of oblong and one set of round markers.

1346. Covered work-basket in sandalwood and engraved ivory.

Div. VI., Sect. 4.

Lacquered Ware.

1361. Circular table top of Kurnul lacquer, diameter 4 ft.

1362. Circular tray on feet, Nossam lacquer, diameter 13 in.

1363. Circular tray on feet, Nossam lacquer, diameter 15 in.

1364, 1365. Circular trays on feet, Nossam lacquer, diameter 13 in.

1366. Octagonal tray on feet, Nossam lacquer, diameter 15 in.

1367. Octagonal oblong tray on feet, Cuddapah lacquer, 15 in. by 11½ in.

1368. Round flat box with cover, Cuddapah lacquer, diameter 9¾ in.

1369. Round flat box with cover, Cuddapah lacquer, diameter 11½ in.

1370, 1371. Boxes of native playing cards in lacquer.

1373 to 1376. Large fans lacquered in four colours.

1377, 1378. Small fans lacquered.

1379 to 1387. Large fans lacquered in colours.

1388. Small fan, lacquered in colours.

1389 and 1390. Palmyra leaf fan painted in diaper pattern.

1391. A set of theatrical ornaments in wood, gilt and lacquered, nine pieces.

1392, 1393. Oblong trays on feet, 1 ft. 6 in. by 1 ft.

1394. Oval tray, 1 ft. 4 in. by 1 ft.

1395. Oval tray on feet, 1 ft. 4 in. by 1 ft.

1396. Glass bangles covered with lacquer and tinsel, 16 pairs.

1397, 1398. Lac bangles covered with tinsel, 56 pairs.

Div. VI., Sect. 6.

Carved Fruit-shells, &c.

1471, 1472. Small caskets of carved cocoanut shell, mounted with silver.

Exhibitor, Sri Rajamani Rajah Deo Garu, C.I.E., *Zemindar of Mandasa.*

1473 to 1475. *Carved cocoanut shells.*

1476 to 1478. *Carved Bael fruit.*

Exhibitor, Raja of Tuni, *Godávari.*

1479. *Miniature cocoanut shell finely carved with the avatars of Vishnu, gold mounted.*

Div. VII., Sect. 1.

Lapidaries' Work.

Exhibitor, J. B. Pennington, Esq., M.C.S.

1481. *Lingam* and *yoni* in rock crystal.

1482. *Brooch of amethystine coloured "Vullum" stone, set in gold.*

1483. *Four cut "Vellum" stones, amethystine colour.*

Div. VIII., Sect. 1.

Carved objects in Marble and Stone.

Exhibitor, Zemindar of Kárvetnagar.

1501. *Small pot in chlorite schist.*

1502 to 1504. Paper-weights in shell marble.

1505. Ruler in shell marble.

1506. Image of Gumata Roya in sienitic granite, being a copy of the colossal monolithic statue at Karkala in South Canara.

1507. Model in soapstone of the *tulsikatta* or altar on which the sacred basil (*Ocymum sanctum*) is grown in the courtyard of Hindu houses.

Div. IX., Sects. 1 & 2.

Glazed and Unglazed Pottery.

Exhibitor, School of Art.

1521. A terra-cotta circular panel, designed and executed in the Madras School of Art.

1522. A pair of terra-cotta panels for a balcony balustrade.

1523. A terra-cotta vase on pedestal, made after the pattern of the sacred silver vessels used in Travancore.

1524 to 1526. Plates in iron-stone china, made at the Madras School of Art, unglazed.

1527. Shallow bowl with cover in iron-stone china, unglazed.

1528. Shallow bowl with cover in iron-stone china, glazed inside.

1529, 1530. Small pots in iron-stone china, glazed inside.

1531, 1532. Spittoon-shaped vases in iron-stone china, glazed inside.

1533. *Lotah*-shaped vase in iron-stone china, glazed inside.

1534, 1535. Small pot, *thamba* shape, in iron-stone china, glazed.

1536. Small pot, spittoon shape, in iron-stone china, glazed.

1537 to 1541. Small pots, *chembu* shape, in iron-stone china, glazed.

1542. *Lotah.*

1543 to 1546. *Chembus.*

1547 to 1550. Water-goglets.

1551, 1552. *Lotahs*, with cover.

1553. Vase.

1554. *Boghna*-shaped pot.

1555. *Boghna*-shaped pot, with cover.

1556, 1557. *Kodum*-shaped pot, &c.

1558. Flower vase-shaped pots, &c.

1559. Flower vase.

1560. Large bowl.

1561. Frame of six encaustic tiles.

1562 & 1563. Goglet-shaped vases in iron-stone china, painted in colour.

1564 to 1566. Goglet-shaped vases with covers in iron-stone china, painted in colour.

1567 & 1568. *Chembu*-shaped pots in iron-stone china, painted in colour.

1569. Vase in iron-stone china, painted in colour.

1570. *Kodum*-shaped pot in iron-stone china, painted in colour.

1571. *Chembu*-shaped pot in iron-stone china, painted in colour.

1572. Plate in iron-stone china, painted in colour.

1573 to 1584. Twelve water goglets with floral ornamentation in mica.

1585 & 1586. Goglets in green glazed earthenware.

1587. Sugar-pot in green glazed earthenware.
1588. Vase in green glazed earthenware.
1589. Flower-pot in green glazed earthenware.
1590. Butter-pot in green glazed earthenware.
1591. Goglet in yellow glazed earthenware.

Div. X., Sect. 1.

Blown objects in Glass.

1651. Glass articles, eleven pieces.

Div. X., Sect. 2.

Moulded articles in Glass.

1671. Glass bangles, green, blue, and black 11 sets of 25 each.

Div. XI., Sect. 1.

Cotton Fabrics.

1691 & 1692. Woman's cloths, red and yellow diaper pattern with red border.
1693. Woman's cloth, green with yellow stripes and maroon border.
1694. Woman's cloth, shot green and red with yellow stripes.
1695 to 1697. Woman's cloths, red and green diaper with yellow and green border.
1698. Woman's cloth, red and green check with maroon border.
1699. Woman's cloth, red and yellow check.
1700 to 1702. Woman's cloths, purple with yellow stripes.
1703. Woman's cloth, shot red and green with crimson border.
1704. Woman's cloth, striped blue and yellow with yellow border.
1705. Woman's cloth, shot green and red with red and yellow border.
1706. Woman's cloth, red and yellow stripes with maroon border.
1707. Woman's cloth, yellow and red check.
1708. Woman's cloth, red and white stripes with yellow border.
1709. Woman's cloth, maroon with yellow border.
1710. Woman's cloth, deep purple blue with white dashes and diapered red border.
1711. Woman's cloth, deep blue with white splashes and red border.
1712. Woman's cloth, plain red with border in several colours.
1713. Woman's cloth, red and blue check with border of various colours.
1714. Woman's cloth, plain white with silk and gold border.
1715. Woman's cloth in graduated tints of pink, gold border.
1716. Woman's cloth, reddish brown with spots, gold and silk border.
1717, 1718. Woman's cloths, black with spots, gold and silk border.
1719. Woman's cloth, plain red with gold border.
1720. Woman's jacket cloth, black with spots.
1721. Man's turban, black with spots.
1722. Man's turban, red with spots.
1723. Men's handkerchiefs, four in one piece.
1724. Petticoat cloth, as worn by Muhammadan women.
1725. Piece of very fine unbleached Arni muslin, 16 yds.
1726. Woman's cloth, red and blue with white splashes.
1727. Woman's cloth, red with yellow check.
1728 to 1730. Woman's cloths, green with yellow stripes.
1731. Woman's cloth, blue with white splashes.
1732. Woman's cloth, blue with yellow border.
1733. Woman's cloth, red with yellow stripes.
1734. Woman's cloth, red with stripes.
1735. Woman's cloth, red with white diaper.
1736, 1737. Woman's cloths, chocolate with yellow stripes.
1738. Man's cloth, white with silk border.
1739, 1740. Woman's jacket cloths.
1741 to 1743. Woman's jacket pieces.
1744. Handkerchiefs, eight in one piece, blue ground with white stripes.
1745. Handkerchiefs, eight in one piece, white ground and blue checks.
1746. Handkerchiefs, eight in one piece, white ground with red stripes.
1747. Handkerchiefs, eight in one piece, yellow ground with red stripes.
1748. Handkerchiefs, eight in one piece, green ground with red and white stripes.
1749. Handkerchiefs, eight in one piece, blue ground with yellow checks and white splashes.
1750 & 1753. Handkerchiefs, eight in one piece, red with red and blue checks.
1751 & 1754. Handkerchiefs, eight in one piece, red ground with blue checks.
1752. Handkerchiefs, eight in one piece, green ground with yellow and red checks.
1755. Handkerchiefs, eight in one piece, red ground with yellow and green checks.
1756. Handkerchiefs, eight in one piece, red ground with blue and white checks.
1757 to 1759. Handkerchiefs, eight in one piece, red ground with white stripes.
1760 to 1764. Handkerchiefs, eight in one piece, tartan pattern.
1765. Waist cloth, tartan pattern, 10½ yds.
1766 to 1769. Waist cloths, tartan pattern, 10½ yds.
1770. Woman's cloth of white Arni muslin with broad silk border, 6 yds. by 3 yds.
1771. Woman's cloth, black and orange check.
1772. Woman's cloth, black ground with yellow checks.
1773. Piece of muslin with red spots.
1774. Piece of muslin with white spots.
1775. Piece of muslin with white stripes.
1776. Piece of muslin, plain.
1777. Woman's cloth with printed border.
1778. Man's cloth with printed border.

1779. Jacket piece, white spots on red ground and lace border.

1780. Similar to No. 1779, but with a black ground.

DIV. XI., SECT. 2.

Wool Fabrics.

CARPETS OR RUGS.

1901. Woollen rug, Kabul pattern, size 4 ft. 10 in. by 2 ft. 9 in.

1902. Woollen carpet or rug of Ramchender-Row-Khanee pattern, size 3 ft. by 2 ft.

1903. Woollen carpet or rug of Bunder-Shah-Nawaz-Khan pattern, size 3 ft. by 3 ft.

1904. Woollen carpet or rug of Hashim-Khanee pattern, size 3 ft. by 3 ft.

1905 to 1919. Small woollen carpets and rugs.

1920, 1921. Woollen carpets, 12 ft. by 9 ft.

DIV. XI., SECT. 3.

Silk Fabrics.

1951. Piece of red and yellow silk for petticoats and *pyjamas*, Muhammadan.

1952 & 1953. Pieces of blue and yellow silk for petticoats and pyjamas, Muhammadan.

1954. Piece of yellow flowered silk for petticoats for Muhammadan females.

1955. Piece of blue flowered silk for petticoats for Muhammadan females.

1956. Piece of red flowered silk for petticoats for Muhammadan females.

1957. Piece of chocolate flowered silk for petticoats for Muhammadan females.

1958. Piece of striped silk for petticoats for Muhammadan females, *kincob* pattern.

1959. Piece of white diapered silk, 12½ yds.

1960. Piece of white silk, 12½ yds.

1961. Woman's jacket, silk.

1962 to 1966. Woman's jacket pieces, silk and cotton.

1967 to 1970. Woman's cloth silks.

1971 to 2001. Silk and cotton checked and striped.

2002 to 2011. Women's jackets, silk and cotton, checked and striped.

2012. Men's handkerchiefs of silk and cotton.

2013. Man's turban, silk and cotton.

2014. Piece of *susi* cloth for *pyjamas* and petticoats for Muhammadans.

2015 & 2016. Pieces of red *susi.*

2017. Piece of check *susi.*

2018. Piece of red *susi.*

2019. Piece of striped *susi.*

2020 to 2022. Pieces of satin for *pyjamas* and petticoats for Muhammadans.

2023. Eighteen pattern lengths of satin.

2024. Woman's jacket cloth, silver and green stripes.

2025. Piece of white Berhampur silk with narrow border, will bear washing.

2026. Piece of red Berhampur silk of fast colour with narrow border, bears washing.

2027. Piece of green Berhampur silk of fast colour with broad border.

2028. Piece of maroon Berhampur silk of fast colour with narrow border.

2029. White silk waist scarf, 9 yds. by 18 in.

2030. Blue silk waist scarf, 6 yds. by 18 in.

2031. Waist scarf of different colours.

2032. Handkerchief of white silk, 1 yd. square.

2033. Handkerchief of orange silk, 1 yd. square.

2034. Handkerchief of purple-brown silk, 1 yd. square.

2035. Handkerchief of red silk, 1 yd. square.

2036. Turban of red silk, 6 yds. by 18 in.

2037. Piece of crimson silk.

2038. A pair of handkerchiefs, silk and cotton, red with gold lace and diaper of birds.

DIV. XI., SECT. 4.

Cotton and Silk Carpets and Hangings, &c.

DHURRIES, CURTAINS AND RUGS.

2101 to 2108. Cotton rugs.

2109. Silk rug measuring 5 ft. 2 in. by 2 ft. 9 in.

2110 to 2147. Cotton purdahs or curtains woven in several colours.

2148 to 2153. Cotton carpets.

2154 to 2157. Cotton tape for cots.

DIV. XI., SECT. 5.

Hand-printed Fabrics.

Exhibitor, H.H. THE RAJA OF PITHAPUR, *Godávari district.*

2161 to 2165. *Hand-printed palampores stamped in gold.*

2166 to 2178. Hand-printed palampores. plain.

2396 to 2185. Hand-printed chintzes.

2179 to 2185. Hand-printed chintzes.

2186 & 2400. Hand-printed handkerchiefs.

2188 & 2189. Hand-printed handkerchiefs, double.

2190. Hand-printed handkerchief.

2191 to 2199. Hand-printed cloths.

2200. Piece of cloth showing various patterns of hand-printing.

PALAMPORES, ETC.

2201, 2202. Hand-printed canopy cloths with scenes from the Ramayanam, measuring 8 ft. by 7½ ft.

2202. Hand-printed canopy cloth, similar to No. 2201.

2203. Hand-printed canopy cloth with scenes from the Ramayanam, measuring 12½ ft. by 11 ft.

2204. Hand-printed canopy cloth with scenes from the Ramayanams, measuring 12 ft. by 11 ft.

2205 to 2208. Hand-printed canopy cloths, Ramayanam series, measuring 7½ ft. by 7½ ft.

2209. Hand-printed canopy cloth, Ramayanan series, 12½ ft. by 11 ft.

2210 to 2212. Hand-printed canopy cloth, Ramayanam series, measuring 13 ft. by 11 ft.

2213. Hand-printed canopy cloth with mythological figures, measuring 9 ft. by 8 ft.

2214, 2215. Hand-printed curtains for doorways in Mussulman houses, 9 ft. by 4 ft.

2216, 2217. Hand-printed palampore, 9 ft. by 4 ft.

2218. Hand-printed canopy cloth, same as No. 2213.

2219. Hand-printed canopy cloth representing scenes from Mahabharata, measuring 6 ft. by 6 ft.

2220. Hand-printed canopy with scenes from Ramayanam, measuring 6 ft. by 6 ft.

2221. Hand-printed canopy cloth with scenes from the Mahabharata, 5½ ft. by 5 ft.

2222.-2246. Hand-printed palampores.

2247. Five so-called palampores from Manchester, imported for sale in Madras and Bengal.

2248 to 2252. Hand-printed palampores.

2253, 2254. Hand-printed muslin.

2255, 2256. Kerchiefs in printed cotton of two colours.

2257, 2258. Kerchiefs in printed cotton of two colours.

2259, 2260. Kerchiefs in two colours.

2261, 2262. Kerchiefs in printed cotton.

2263, 2264. Waist cloths in printed and glazed cotton, blue and red.

2265, 2266. Waist cloths in printed and glazed cotton, blue and red.

2267. Waist cloth in printed and glazed cotton, in three colours, worn by Lubbay Mussulmans.

2268, 2269. Waist cloths in blue with white pattern.

2270 to 2272. Waist cloths in printed cotton of two colours, unglazed.

2273. Pair of handkerchiefs in printed cotton of two shades of brown.

2274 to 2276. Handkerchiefs in two shades of brown.

2277. Pair of handkerchiefs in two shades of brown.

2278. Specimen cloth showing the process of hand-printing on cotton cloth prepared with wax.

2279 to 2284. Turban cloths, hand-printed in ochre, apparently in imitation of the more expensive gold printed fabrics worn by Muhammadans.

2285. Scarf in printed cotton sprinkled with mica, as worn by Muhammadan women.

2286. Cloth in printed cotton as worn by Lubbay women.

2287. Handkerchief in printed cotton.

2288. Woman's cloth in printed cotton.

2289 to 2295. Hand-printed palampores.

2296. Hand-printed woman's cloth.

2297. Stamped cloth piece of eight samples.

2298. Stamped cloth piece of five samples.

2299 to 2302. Hand-printed palampores.

2303 to 2313. Hand-printed woman's cloths.

2314 & 2315. Hand-printed woman's cloths.

2316 to 2327. Hand-printed palampores.

2328 & 2329. Hand-printed woman's cloths.

2330. Hand-printed handkerchief.

Exhibitor, C. J. Peters, Esq., *Executive Engineer Cauvery and Vennar Regulators, Grand Anicut, Tanjore.*

2331 to 2340. *Hand-printed palampores.*

2341 to 2346. *Hand-printed handkerchiefs.*

2347 to 2365. Hand-printed palampores.

2366 to 2391. Hand-printed cloths.

2392 to 2395. Hand-printed palampores.

2396. Mythological palampore from Salem.

Div. XII., Sect. 1.

Embroideries and Laces.

Exhibitor, H.E. Mrs. Grant Duff, *Government House.*

2401. *Imitation of Dutch seventeenth century gauntlets, worked in Madras under Mrs. Firth's superintendence.*

2402. Mantle border in fawn-coloured satin, embroidered in gold and silver.

2403. Embroidery on white silk, 4 yds.

2404. Mantle border in black satin, embroidered with beetle wings.

2405. Tray cover in maroon satin, embroidered in gold and colour.

2406. Ladies' dress in white net, embroidered in gold and beetle wings.

2407. Ladies' dress in black net, embroidered in gold and beetle wings

2408. Small table cover in dark blue cloth, embroidered in gold and silk.

2409. Small table cover in dark blue cloth, embroidered in gold and colours.

2410. Small table cover in black cloth, embroidered in gold and silk.

2411. Small table cover in blue cloth, embroidered in gold and colorus.

2412 & 2413. Small table covers in black cloth, embroidered in gold and colours.

2414. Table cover in black cloth, embroidered in gold and colours.

2415. Mantle border in black cloth, embroidered in gold and colours.

2416 to 2419. Small table covers in blue cotton, embroidered in white chain-stitch.

2420 to 2423. Small table covers in red cotton, embroidered in white chain-stitch.

2424. Head-dress in coloured velvet, profusely embroidered in gold, as worn by native rajas.

2425. Round mat of red cotton, embroidered in gold, &c.

2440. Silk handkerchief, embroidered in red, green, and white silk.

2426 to 2439. Pieces of gold tissue, silver, and silver tape.

2441. Ladies' dress, embroidered in gold and beetle wings.

2442 to 2445. Black silk lace, 4 yds.

2446 to 2452. White lace, 3 yds.

2453. White lace, 1½ yds.

2454 to 2458. White lace, 3 yds.

2459. White lace, 1½ yds.

2460. White lace, 2½ yds.

2461. White lace, 5 yds.

2462. Ladies dress in Arni muslin, embroidered in gold.
2463. Ladies' dress in embroidered China silk.
2464. Piece of muslin, embroidered in Madras.
2465. Piece of tassar silk embroidered like No. 2464.
2466 & 2467. Curtain of blue *dungari* embroidered with yellow silk (*phulkari*).
2468. Canopy, embroidered with mythological figures in cloth of different colours.

Exhibitor, MRS. H. W. BLISS, 32 *Hyde Park Gardens, London, W.*

2469 & 2470. Pair of embroidered curtains, reproduced from an old design by Mrs. Bliss, Madras, mostly worked by Mean Saheb.

Exhibitor, THE HOBART SCHOOL FOR MUHAMMADAN GIRLS.

2471. Embroidered woollen curtain.
2472. Curtain in red *dungari*, embroidered in yellow silk.
2473. Border like No. 2472 adorned with pieces of glass.
2474. Cushion cover in blue satin, embroidered with gold.
2475. Bodice in red muslin, embroidered with gold.
2476. Skull cap in red satin, embroidered with gold.
2477. Set of child's jacket and trousers.
2478. Embroidered child's square.
2479. Pair of embroidered ladies' collarette.
2480. Embroidered handkerchief.
2481. Embroidered antimacassar.
2482. Embroidered muslin dress.

DIV. XIII., SECT. 2.

Saddlery—Leather.

2501. Embroidered saddle in red cloth.

Exhibitors, MESSRS. CROYSDALE & CO., *Madras.*

132. Samples of leather, as prepared by native tanners.

DIV. XIII., SECT. 4.

Articles made of Feathers, Fans, &c.

2511. Fan made of peacocks' feathers.

DIV. XIII., SECT. 5.

Articles in Pith, Mica, &c.

2521. Model in "pith" (*Æschynomene aspera*) of the great Pagoda at Tanjore.
2522 & 2523. Fan of mica with delicate tracery in white pigment.
2524 & 2525. Fan of mica with handle.

DIV. XIV.

Baskets, Mats, &c.

2541. Grass mat made of the split stems of *Cyperus pangorei.*
2542 to 2550. Grass mats.
2551 to 2554. Mats made of the split stems of the *Saccharum* (Sara) black.
2555 to 2558. Mats made of the split stems of the *Saccharum* (?) rose red.

Exhibitor, J. H. GARSTIN, Esq., C.S.I., *Madras Civil Service.*

2559. *Mat made of grass, size 24½ ft. by 4 ft.*
2560. *Mat of similar description, size 27½ ft. by 4 ft.*

Exhibitor, RAMAKRISHNA IYER, *Landholder and Vakil, Tinnevelly.*

2561 & 2562. *Grass mats made of the split stems of Cyperus pangorei.*
2563 to 2568. Grass mats.

Exhibitor, H.H. THE RAJA OF COCHIN.

2569 to 2584. *Grass mats.*

BAMBOOS, CANES, ETC.

Exhibitor, Deputy Surg.-Genl. J. SHORTT, M.D., F.L.S., F.Z.S., *Yercaud, Shevaroys.*

133 & 134. *Bambusa gigantea*, grown from seeds from Burma.
135 to 140. Walking stick of coffee wood.

BUILDING MATERIALS.

Exhibitor, WILLIAM ROSS, *Patentee of "Asphalithos," Bangalore.*

141. "Asphalithos."

TRAVANCORE.

DIV. I., SECT. 1.

Paintings and Drawings.

3001. *Oil-painting, Portrait of a Jew.*

Exhibitor, RAMA VURMA COIL THUMBURAN, TRIVANDRUM, *Travancore.*

3001*a*. Oil-painting, a Hindu devotee.

DIV. I., SECT. 3.

Photographs.

3002. Photograph of fishmongers (Moocava).
3003. Photograph of cocoa-nut tree climber (Thundan).
3004. Photograph of stone-cutter (Chanar).
3005. Photograph of palmyra toddy-drawer (Chanar).

3006. Photograph of sawyer (Thundan).
3007. Photograph of fishmongers (Moocava).
3008. Photograph of hill-tribe (Canicars).
3009. Toddy-drawers (Elavas).
3010. Firewood sellers (Corava).
3011. Photograph of Corava girl with firewood.
3012. Photograph of Poolayars.
3013. Photograph of Poolaya girl.
3014. Photograph of Coshavars (potters) at work.
3015. Photograph of men ploughing a field.
3016. Photograph of State elephant with howdah.
3017. Photograph of Canicars (Hill-tribe).
3018. View of old palace at Neyattinkaray.
3019. View of tank and pagoda, Fort Trivandrum.
3020. View of Pandava idols.
3021. View of public gardens, Trivandrum.
3022. View of pagoda within the Trivandrum Fort.
3023. View of public offices, Trivandrum.
3024. View of road to Chalay from the Eastern Fort Gate, Trivandrum.
3025. View of Poothenaur (Patmanabapuram, South Travancore).
3026. View of interior of marriage pandal of H.H. the late Maharaja's daughters, Trivandrum.
3027. View of H.H. the late Maharaja's palace and gardens.
3028. View of Napier Museum, Trivandrum.
3029. View of Poonalúr Suspension Bridge.
3030. View of interior of Thiruvettar Temple.
3031. View of Poothen Dam (South Travancore).
3032. View of Palace Gate, Trivandrum.
3033. View of the British Presidency at Quilon and Backwater.
3034. View of Temple at Suchindrum.
3035. View of Chalay Bazaar, Trivandrum.
3036. View of Tank and Clock-tower within the fort.
3037. View of Village of Cape Comorin.
3038. View of Wurkullay Cliff.
3039. View of Suchindrum Tank and Mundapum.
3040. View of Ponmanay Dam.
3041. View of Meenmutty River, No. 1, Travancore.
3042. View of Meenmutty River, No. 2, Travancore.
3043. View of Meenmutty River, No. 3, Travancore.
3044. View of Meenmutty River, No. 4, Travancore.
3045. View of Meenmutty River, No. 5.
3046. View of College, Trivandrum, No. 2.
3047. View of Wurkullay Canal cutting.
3048. View of precincts of Pagoda Tank, Trivandrum.
3049. View of Thekkatheravoo Fort, Trivandrum.
3050. View of Jungar and Boat at Fort landing-place, Trivandrum.
3051. View of Car at Suchindrum.
3052. View of Wurkullay Tunnel, No. 2.
3053. View of Pandian Caul (South Travancore).
3054. Portrait of the Installation of H.H. the Maharaja to the Musnud, 19th August 1885.

Div. IV., Sect. 1.

Gold and Silver Jewellery.

3055. *Gold native ear ornament.*
3056. *Necklace set with stones.*
3057. *Necklace set with stones.*
3058. *Gold native necklace, set with stones.*
3059. *Gold native necklace, plain.*
3060. *Gold native necklace, set with stones in front.*
3061 & 3062. *Gold native necklaces, plain.*
3063. *Gold pendant for the neck.*
3064. *Gold necklace.*
3065, 3066. *Gold ear ornaments.*
3067. *Gold anklet.*
3068. *Gold waist ornament.*
3069. *Gold waist ornament of cheetah's teeth, mounted in gold.*
3070. *Gold waist ornament.*
3071. *Gold earrings.*
3072. *Gold tiger-claw earrings, one pair.*
3073. *Gold watch-chain pendant with cocoanut shell inside.*
3074. Gold locket tiger-claw.
3075. Gold brooch (tiger's head).
3076. Gold brooch (heart transfixed by an arrow).
3077. Gold brooch (elephant's head).
3078. Gold earrings (bell), one pair.
3079. Gold earrings (leaf and flower), one pair.
3080. Gold earrings (pigeon), one pair.
3081. Gold earrings (cashew fruit), one pair.
3082. Gold watch-chain pendant with cocoanut shell inside.
3083 & 3084. Silver necklaces (rose and butterfly).
3085 to 3089. Silver necklaces (*chuckrums*).
3090. Silver necklace (butterfly).
3091. Silver necklace of beads (Rudrakshum).
3092. Silver necklace (snake).
3093 & 3094. Silver necklaces (rose).
3095. Silver necklace (jungle almond seeds).
3096. Chuckrum bracelet.
3097, 3098. Rudrakshum bracelets.
3099. Snake bracelets.
3100. Silver bracelets (rose and butterfly).
3101. Silver bracelets (star).
3102. *One bracelet (Kalinji flower).*
3103. *One bracelet (Erukkum flower).*
3104. *One bracelet (Nagathalikai fruit).*
3105. One bracelet (flower and leaves).
3106. One bracelet (buckle).
3107. One bracelet (buckle band).
3108. One silver bracelet (open work).
3109. One silver bracelet (flower).
3110. One silver bracelet (thread band).
3111. Silver bracelets (chain and heart).
3112. Silver bracelets (rose and butterfly).

3113. Silver bracelets (rose).
3114. Silver bracelets (Erukkum flower).
3115. Silver bracelets (butterfly).
3116. Silver bracelets (*chuckyum*).
3117. Silver bracelets (diamond cut).
3118. Silver bracelets (Kalinji flower).
3119. Silver bracelets (Nagathalikai fruit).
3120. *Silver earrings (Nagathalikai).*
3121. Silver earrings (Nagathalikai).
3122. Silver earrings (globe).
3123. Silver earrings (butterfly).
3124. Silver earrings (flower).
3125 to 3127. Silver earrings.
3128. Silver earrings (Munjaadi seeds).
3129 & 3130. Silver earrings (chuckrum).
3131. Silver earrings (jungle almond seeds).
3132. Silver brooch (with three leaves and four pendants).
3133 & 3134. Silver brooches (grapes and vine leaves).
3135. Silver brooch (elephant pattern).
3136. Silver brooch (Veena or lute).
3137. *Silver brooch (with three leaves and five pendants).*
3138. *Silver brooch (Pavakai fruit, Momordica chrantia).*
3139. *Silver brooch (peacock on a bough).*
3140. *Silver brooch (drum).*
3141 & 3142. Silver brooch (little cocoanuts).
3143. Silver brooch (cashew fruit).
3144. Silver brooch (plantain bunch).
3145 to 3147. Silver brooches (butterfly).
3148. Silver brooch (palanquin).
3149. Silver brooch (Pavakai fruit, *Momordica charantia*).
3150. Silver brooch (peacock on a bough).
3151. Silver brooch (tiger's claw).
3152 to 3154. Silver hair-pins.
3155. *Silver hair-pin (Erukkum flower).*
3156 & 3157. Silver hair-pin (Erukkum flower).
3158 & 3159. Silver hair-pins (chuckrum).
3160. *Silver locket (tiger-claw shape).*
3161. Silver locket (tiger-claw shape).
3162. Silver locket (jungle almond seed).
3163 & 3164. Silver bouquet-holder.
3165. Silver card case (vine leaf).
3166. Silver card case (Veena and peacock).
3167. Silver knife-handle.
3168. *Silver bouquet-holder, handle of boar's tusk.*
3169. *Cocoanut-shell scent-bottle with silver filigree work.*

DIV. V., SECT. 1.

Gold and Silver Plate.

3170. Silver casket.

DIV. V., SECT. 2.

Koft or Damascened work.

3171. Iron spear, Koft work.
3172. Ink bottle, Koft work.
3173. *Tumbler, Koft work.*
3174. *Goblet, Koft work.*
3175. *Photo frame.*
3176. *Steel tray (silver Koft work).*
3177. *Steel tray (gilt Koft work), pagoda.*
3178. *Steel tray, musicians.*
3179. Steel tray (10 avatars of Vishnu).
3180. Dagger.
3181. *Weapon with stiletto inside.*
3182. *Knife with copper handle.*
3183. *Dagger in a sheath made of the snout of a sword-fish, ornamented with gold.*
3184. *Knife.*

DIV. V., SECT. 3.

Brass, Copper and Alloys.

3185. Metal mirror.
3186. Copper tumbler.
3187. Copper drinking vessel.

Exhibitor, MR. RUTNASWAMY IYER, *Deputy Peishcar, Salt Department, Trivandrum, Travancore.*

3189. *Copper tumbler.*
3190. *Copper water vessel.*

DIV. V., SECT. 4.

Copper Ware for Sacrificial Purposes.

3491. *Copper vessel used for growing seeds in pagodas during certain ceremonies.*

DIV. V., SECT. 5.

Arms and Armour.

3192. *Sword with iron leaf-shaped handle.*
3193. *Dagger with copper handle, gilt, and inlaid with coloured stones.*
3194. *Ivory-handled knife.*

DIV. V., SECT. 6.

Cutlery.

3195 & 3196. Styles, with knives, &c., for writing on *cadjans.*
3197 & 3198. Sacrificial knives with horn handles.
3199. Ivory-handled table knife.
3200. Pen-knife with four blades and cork-screw.
3201. Ivory-handled pen-knife (double blade).
3202 & 3203. Horn-handled knives.
3204 to 3206. Long knives.
3207 to 3210. Horn-handled table knives.
3211 & 3212. Horn-handled pen-knives (single blade).

Exhibitor, ANANTHA PATMANABHEN KRISHNEN, *Blacksmith, Quilon.*

3213. Small pen-knife, silver handle,
3214. Ivory-handled pen-knife with four blades and a corkscrew.
3215. Ivory-handled pen-knife, double blade.
3216 to 3218. Ivory-handled table knives.
3219. Ivory-handled carver.
3220. Horn-handled table knife.
3221 & 3222. Large *shikar* knives.

Div. VI., Sect. 3.

Ivory Carving.

3223. Picture frame.
3224 to 3229. Glove-stretchers.
3230. Book rack (two sides).
3231 & 3232. Paper-cutters, the handles representing an elk in the coils of a boa.
3233. Paper-cutter (hermit).
3234 & 3235. Paper-cutters (bird's nest).
3236 & 3237. Paper-cutters (areca-nut tree).
3238 & 3239. Paper-cutters (hare and snake).
3240. Paper-cutter (plantain tree).
3241. Paper-cutter (areca bunch).
3242. Paper-cutter (bird and snake).
3243. Paper-cutter (peacock).
3244. Paper-cutter (woman and child).
3245 & 3246. *Paper-cutters.*
3247. Paper-weight (Toucan).
3248. Paper-weight (Tapir).
3249. Paper-weight (Krishna).
3250 Paper-weight (Vishnu).
3251. Paper weight (Elephant carrying Hindu god in procession).

Exhibitor, Mr. J. H. Prince, *Head Government Pleader, Trivandrum, Travancore.*

3252. Paper-weight (Elephant carrying Hindu god in procession.
3253. Paper-weight (calf).
3254. Paper-weight (a cob of cholum).
3255. Paper-weight (sea-shells).
3256. Paper-weight (fruits).
3257. *Paper-weight* (*Sudra woman*).
3258. *Paper-weight* (*State elephant with howdah.*
3259. *Paper-weight* (*ibex*).
3260. *Paper-weight* (*cow*).
3261. *Paper-weight* (*mango with leaves mounted on ebony.*
3262 & 3263. Hand mirrors with carving of "Ganapathi" on the back, mirrors of steel.
3264. Hand mirror (cart and bulls).
3265 & 3266. Hand mirrors (elephant in a bamboo bush).
3267. Hand mirror (elephants drinking water.)
3268. *Brush-back.*
3269. Comb.
3270. Parasol handle.
3271. Handle of walking stick (fish).
3272. Toad (horn).
3273. Elephant (horn).

Div. VI., Sect. 5.

Wood Carving.

3274. *Blackwood flower vase, highly carved.*
3275. *Blackwood mirror frame, highly carved.*
3276. Model of H.H. the Maharaja's State barge.
3277. Model of H.H. the Maharaja's canoe with cabin.
3278. Box containing 20 pairs of models of castes.
3279. Box containing 12 pairs of models of castes.
3280. Wooden tumbler and tray.
3281. *Ebony photo frame.*
3282. *Ebony paper-cutter.*

Div. VI., Sect. 6.

Carved Fruits.

3289. Carved cocoanut shell with lid.
3290 to 3293. Cocoanut shells with lid, carved.
3294 & 3295. Cocoanut shells inlaid with silver.
3296. Cocoanut-shell teapot with tray.
3297. Cocoanut-shell sugar-basin.
3298 & 3299. Cocoanut-shell cups and saucers.
3300. Carved cocoanut-shell cheroot holder.
3301. Cocoanut-shell tea set, inlaid with silver, consisting of 1 teapot, 1 sugar-basin, 1 milk-jug, and 2 cups and 2 saucers.
3302. *Carved cocoanut shell with* 10 *avatars.*
3303. *Carved cocoanut shell mounted on silver stand.*
3304 to 3306. Carved bael shells.
3307. Cocoanut shell, inlaid with silver stars.

Div. XI., Sect. 4.

3308 & 3309. Coir rugs (coloured).

Div. XII., Sect. 1.

Embroidery and Lace.

3310. Infant's robe, embroidered.
3311 to 3313. Strips of embroidery.
3314 & 3315. Embroidered handkerchiefs.
3316 to 3318. Embroidered handkerchiefs with border.
3319. Four yards gold lace.
3320 & 3321. Two yards black and gold lace.
3322. Four yards gold and silver lace.
3323. Gold collar and cuffs.
3324. Gold coiffure.
3325. Gold fichu.
3326. Two yards silver lace.
3327. Two yards silk and silver lace.
3328. Silver fichu and cuffs.
3329. Silver coiffure.
3330 & 3331. Silver fichu.
3332. Three yards black lace.
3333. Fichu and cuffs, white lace.
3334. Fichu, cuffs, and handkerchief-border white lace.
3335–3372. Pieces White Lace.

Div. XIII., Sect. 4.

Articles made of Feathers, Fans, &c.

3373 to 3376. Peacock-feather fans.

Div. XIV.

Baskets, Mats, &c.

3377 to 3382. Specimen of rattaning done in Travancore.

HYDERABAD, DECCAN.

Div. I.—Fine Arts.

2. *Engravings, Lithographs, &c.*

[1-2]—Manuscript inscriptions on grains of rice.

Interesting as showing patience and a steady hand.

3. *Photographs, &c.*

[3-27].—Photographs of Gulbarga and Hyderabad.

Particulars given on photographs.

Div. II.—Decorative Art.

6. *Decorative Painting as applied to Articles of Domestic Use.*

[28-62].—Goblets, drinking vessels, bowls, for *Hukas.*

The earthen vessels are first covered with pipeclay and size; the design is then slightly raised, covered with silver leaf and painted. They are manufactured in Raichor, and are largely used in wedding ceremonies.

[63].—Work in silk thread.

Deserves no special notice.

[64-65].—Blotting pads.

[66-69].—Boxes of playing cards.

These hand-painted articles are much admired, the painting being exceptionally good. The industry is peculiar to India.

[70-72].—Trays.

The painted trays from Kamam are not very good, and are not to be compared to those of Raichor (Baingaupali).

[73-82].—Fans.

The painted Palmyra leaf and *Kas* root fans from India are cheap and handsome.

Div. III.—Musical Instruments.

1-3. *Wind, Stringed, and Percussion Musical Instruments.*

[83-105].—Musical instruments.

No remarks necessary. Nos. 91 and 92, used by professional beggars, are peculiar, the former being simply a dry *calabash* with a wire stretched across. The drums 99 to 104 are constructed from single pieces of wood without a join, and are admirable conductors of sound.

Div. IV.—Jewellery.

1. *Gold and Silversmiths' Work, including Filigrain, Setting of Precious Stones, &c.*

[106-119].—Silver ware.

[120-123].—Silver filigree boxes.

These are all of Aurangabad manufacture. Nos. 106, 114, and 115 are particularly good specimens. These boxes from Zelgandal much resemble the Delhi silver wire work.

Div. V.—Art Manufactures in Metal.

3. *Brass, Copper, and Mixed Metal.*

[124-125].—Drinking vessels.

These vessels, peculiar to Kamam, show alternate layers of brass and copper.

[126-127].—Drinking vessels, lamps, basins, spice boxes, spittoons, travelling companions, *Puja* figures.

From Kamam; not interesting.

[128-136].—From Medduk. The travelling companion is very ingenious.

[137-140].—From Indur. Not interesting. Almost all the brass ware used in Hyderabad is imported from Poona; the local manufactures are not good.

[141-236, 754-756].—*Bidri* ware.

This is an important industry, and commands an extensive demand. No dowry is considered complete, among the better class of Muhammadans, unless a complete set of *Bidri ware,* from bed legs to a spittoon, is included. The high prices often render it necessary for the father of a family to begin his collection years before his daughter is marriageable. The articles are cast in pewter; the designs, often very elaborate, are then chiselled out and silver hammered in; the article is lastly covered with a vegetable acid, mixed with the earth of the place, which is largely impregnated with iron, and the effect is to blacken the pewter and brighten the silver. The insides of all the articles will be found very rough, the manufacturers having no proper implements for smoothing them down. Nos. 754 to 756 are good specimens. An attempt was made to have trays containing illustrations of the Hindu deities. The workmen, however, misunderstood the instructions, and by inserting the silver into the spaces instead of the lines, as shown in the drawings, somewhat marred the effect, and certainly made the work more expensive.

5a. *Arms and Armour.*

[249-280].—Ancient armour.

These arms were purchased in the city of Hyderabad, which is noted for old arms.

5b. *Arms and Armour.*

[281-312].—Modern armour.

The swords and daggers are particularly good. The steel mines in Hyderabad Territory are well known, and the finest Damascus blades are manufactured from Hanam-kunda steel.

Div. VI.—Art Manufactures in Wood, Ivory, Etc.

4. *Lacquered Wares.*

[313-346].—Boxes, fans, sandals, tops, book rests, bed legs, trays, &c.

The beautiful lacquer work of Baingaupali, a

jagir in the Raichor district, is used in ornamenting every article of domestic use. Like the inlaid metal work of Bidar, articles forming part of the wedding dowry are lacquered. The work is of two kinds or classes, one embossed and the other plain, and called respectively *munabathi* and *lajawardi*. The embossing is produced by a tedious process. Shells or slag from the forge are finely ground with some glutinous substance, which is kept a secret, and layer upon layer of this ingredient put on with a brush till the requisite height is attained. The *whole* is then covered with gold-leaf, the designs are picked out in paint, and the article varnished. The prices charged are about Rs. 8 per square foot for *munabathi*, and Rs. 4 for *lajawardi*. The work would be cheaper but for the levying of heavy black mail, a right which few jagirdars fail to exercise. Good specimens of this work will be found in the ornamental screen.

5. *Wood Carving.*

[413-483].—Models of workmen, &c.

The models from Kamam and Zelgandal are fair representations of the different classes, but Zelgandal is decidedly cheaper. Indur sent in a very large collection of models, or more properly toys, but many of them are clearly imitations of European toys, while others are interesting merely because they are grotesque, and bear not the slightest resemblance to the animal intended to be shown. The errors are, however, frequently in the painting. We have yet to see a white pigeon, with tiger-like stripes of ultramarine. Such toys have been eliminated from the collection shown. Nos. 461 and 462 will show the Indur artisan's idea of a lion. The toys are all carved roughly in wood, then shaped with a compound of cow-dung or sawdust, and tamarind pulp or glue.

Div. IX.—Pottery.

2. *Unglazed Pottery.*

[484-494].—Water vessels.

The collection of earthenware is meagre. Nalgonda sent in an immense quantity, from which a small collection was made. These vessels are not sufficiently porous, and do not keep water as cool in the hot season as the rougher manufactures of Hyderabad itself. The vessels are all made on the wheel, as shown in model No. 420 (Class VI. 5).

Div. XI.—Textiles.

1. *Cotton Fabrics.*

[495-505 and 507-508].—Muslins plain and striped.

These kaki-coloured muslins from Raichor are a luxury in the hot weather, and are used by both sexes among the natives, the men using the cloth for their *angrakas* or loose jackets, and the women for wraps. The muslins of Raichor closely resemble those of Nandair, and are about one-fourth the price; but good judges profess to see a great difference.

[509-547].—Muslins.

These are the finest muslins manufactured in the Hyderabad State, and are always salmon coloured; like the Raichor muslins, they are all woven in hand looms.

[548-551].—Quilts.

These quilts, which are hand worked, are much used by the better classes. Need no special remark.

[552-555].—Counterpanes.

The counterpanes from Raichor are very good, and always command a ready sale.

[556-557].—Stamped cloth.

The pieces of stamped cloth from Indur are those commonly used as coverlets and curtains. The stamping is done with a piece of wood on which the pattern has been carved.

[558-560].—Articles of female dress.

Need no special remark.

[561-563].—Towels.

[564-575].—Cloth for suits, &c.

[576].—Model of tent.

Gulbarga jail manufacture. Needs no special remark.

[577-579].—Carpets.

[580-582].—Counterpanes.

[583-585].—Carpets for prayers.

Manufactured in the Gulbarga jail.

As may be expected in a Muhammadan State, a large trade is done in these carpets called "*jai haimaz*," the place of prayer. The Gulbarga jail is the only one which, owing to the energetic Suba of the Western Division, has undertaken and succeeded in turning out fabrics which compare favourably with the work done in the jails in British India.

[586-609].—Cotton carpets.

Kamam, or Warangal, has long been noted for its carpet industry; the texture and make are very good, and the carpets command an extensive sale. Of late years the use of aniline dyes has crept in.

2. *Wool Fabrics.*

[610-617].—Woollen carpets.

3. *Silk Fabrics.*

[620-621].— Silk carpets.

Manufactured in the Gulbarga jail.

[622-626].—*Saris*, Raichor.

[627-631].—*Saris* and bodices, Indur.

[632-633].—Bodices, Zelgandal.

The silk *saris* of Raichor are largely used by the better classes. A mixture of silk and cotton being found cheaper, is often used.

[634-646].—Satin trowsering.

There is a great demand for these satins, which are used solely for trousers by Muhammadan ladies and Parsee gentlemen. They are called *mashru*, and are far more expensive than an inferior kind known as *sangeen*.

[647-648].—Flowered silk.

Aurangabad still maintains its reputation for

embroidery, &c. The silks known as *himru* are still largely used by noblemen for coats, and by females for bodices.

4. *Other Fabrics.*

[649-650].—Gold cloth.

This is another industry for which Aurangabad is justly renowned.

[651-686].—Gold and silver lace.

These laces are always sold by weight, the purest gold and silver being used in their manufacture.

DIV. XII.—EMBROIDERY.

2. *Gold and Silver.*

[687-689].—Embroidered saddle cloth, tray cover, and cushion.

Gulbarga cannot compete with Aurangabad in embroidery. The work in these exhibits is well done, but the metal used is copper-gilt.

[690-703].—Two articles of attire, *saris*, handkerchiefs and turbans.

All these articles of dress are valuable, owing to the handsome embroidered borders worked in gold, for which Aurangabad is famous.

[704-705].—Table cloths.

These exhibits show the gold embroidery of Aurangabad, and the dazzling effect produced by a lavish expenditure of the precious metal is characteristic of Oriental extravagance.

[706-707].—Gold-embroidered caps.

Gold-embroidered caps like the two shown are very commonly used.

[708].—Turban.

[709-710].—2. *Saris.*

[711-717].—Embroidery in gold and beetle wing.

Of these beautiful embroideries Nos. 711-715 are in great demand for ball dresses. The effect by lamplight, especially, is wondrously lovely. The glint of the pieces of the gold-beetles' wings adds considerably to the richness even by day, and forms a relief to the otherwise monotonous effect of the gold.

DIV. XIII.—LEATHER AND FURS.

1. *Shoes.*

[718-725 and 736-737].—Leather slippers and shoes.

Raichor is famous for its leather industry, which, however, does not extend to much more than the manufacture of these indispensable requisites. The leather used is generally dyed red, but is not unfrequently, as in 718 to 720, gilt or silvered.

[726-731].—Slippers.

These slippers are embroidered with gilt copper, and are very commonly used by the middle classes, men and women, especially dancing girls.

[732-735, 738-740].—Country sandals.

No. 732 is an ornamental pair of sandals, seldom seen and never used. 733, also ornamental, may sometimes be met with at village fairs; but Nos. 734, 735, and 738 to 740, are the sandals used by the million throughout the length and breadth of the land.

MYSORE.

DIV. I.—FINE ARTS.

1. *Paintings and Drawings.*

[1-12].—Pictures in oil.

Prices range from Rs. 40 to Rs. 500. Executed by artists taught in English Schools of Art.

DIV. II.—DECORATIVE ART.

3. *Photographs, &c.*

[56-114].—Photographs.

Illustrating scenery and ancient sacred architecture.

[115-120].—Illustrating scenery and ancient sacred architecture, by Mr. C. G Brown, of the "Cubbon" studio.

4. *Archæological Drawings, Models, &c.*

[166-168].—Drawings,

Illustrating temple, fort, and monolith.

[169-178].—Models.

Notable structures and ancient remains.

[174].—9. Model.

A correct representation of Hyder's jail for European prisoners of war, in the Seringapatam fort.

5. *Models in Clay, Wax, Plaster of Paris, &c.*

[176-203]. — Chennapalam ware — fruit, vegetable, and reptiles.

Many of these are not true to nature, but the colouring is in good imitation. A cluster of fruit and leaves costs 5 Rs. Are chiefly made at Chennapalam.

6. *Decorative Painting as applied to Architecture.*

[206-213].—Mysore wall-paintings.

Price per square yard in oils, Rs. 5 to Rs. 10.

7. *Other Works of Decorative Art not Specified.*

[216-221]. — (Melukot) *Kus-kus* hand-punkhas.

Made from roots of *Andropogon muricatus*, ornamented with gilding, peacocks' feathers and coloured silks, and supplied with sandalwood handles. Are usually worked by Brahmins serving in temples. Prices range from 3 Rs. to

15 Rs. for fans, and 10 Rs. to 25 Rs. for handles.

[222].—Bangalore stencil-plates.

To illustrate daily decorations at the entrance to Hindu houses. The plates are filled with finely-powdered quartz and gently tapped on the floor and door-steps, in various combinations, until a square of about 6 feet is obtained. This operation takes the place of pipe-claying English door-steps.

Div. III.—Musical Instruments.

1. *Wind Instruments.*

[224].—Chennapalam Jews-harps.

3. *Instruments of Percussion.*

[225].—Chennapalam bass-drum pot.

Unique as this may appear for a musical instrument, it is in demand both for local use and for export to the Deccan. Value R. 1.

Div. IV.—Jewellery.

1. *Gold and Silversmith's Work.*

[226–295].—Personal ornaments.

These are imitations in base metal and glass, of gold and silver ornaments set with gems, as worn by Hindus. Wages range from ¼ Rupee to 1 Rupee per tola weight for silver jewels; and 1 Rupee to 1¼ Rupees per pagoda weight for gold jewels.

Div. V.—Art Manufactures in Metal.

1. *Gold and Silver Plate.*

[302].—Bangalore ware, cups, *jombus*, and trays.

[303–306].—(*a*) Silver engraved work. (*b*) Silver repoussé work.

French Rocks—French rock ware, trays.

[296].—(*a*) Silver repoussé.

[297–301].—(*b*) Silver engraved.

There is but little variety or originality in form, but great delicacy and ingenuity is displayed in chasing, engraving, and ornamenting the patterns. For superior workmanship in silver, wages equal value of metal paid, and in gold one-half its value.

[307–325, 326–327].—Mysore ware, salvers and *swami* figures.

(*a*) Silver castings. (*b*) Silver chase work.

Manufactured by Venkatrammana, the maker of the Mysore gold trays in his Royal Highness the Prince of Wales's collection.

3. *Brass, Copper, and Mixed Metal.*

[448–451, 478–522].—(*a*) Brass castings.

Nagamangala ware—Lamps, mythological objects, &c.

[445–447].—(*a*) Brass Castings.

Magadi ware.—Lamps.

[331–365, 438–444].—(*a*) Brass castings.

Mysore ware.—*Swami* figures, &c.

[391–437].—(*a*) Brass castings.

[456–477].—(*b*) Engraved and chased.

Shravan-Belgola ware.—Domestic vessels in great variety.

[452–455].—Tumkur locksmiths' work.

The staple work in metals, taking the place of porcelain, glass and silver in a European house. They are mostly rough, without finish or accuracy; circles out, lines never true and marks of the file and burnisher everywhere visible. The best workmen are Jains, and they turn out excellent work for liberal wages. Prices range from ½ Rupee to 1 Rupee per seer of 24 tolas.

4. *Brass and Copper Wares for Sacrificial Purposes.*

[549–571].—(*a*) Brass castings.

Nagamangala ware.—Water vessels, tripods, and mythological animals, &c.

[526–548].—(*a*) Brass castings.

Shravan-Belgola ware.—Cots, stools, cradles, dishes, bells, and lamps, &c.

Specimens are all of ancient patterns, as no innovation is permitted. They are made up to order, as the demand is small. Price 1 Rupee per seer of 24 tolas.

5. *Arms and Armour.*

[576–583].—Mysore make.—Daggers, &c.

There is no demand for these, and the manufacture ceased with the downfall of Muhammadan rule.

7. *Iron and Steel Wares.*

[591].—Chennapalam musical wire.

These wires are in demand all over Southern India for native musical instruments.

[592–597].—Shikarpur ware.—Cutting tools, pans, &c.

Div. VI.—Manufactures in Wood and Ivory.

2. *Inlaid Work.*

[601–615].—Mysore ivory inlaid ebony furniture.

The work consists in introducing pieces of ivory on ebony or on rosewood in conventional Carnatic and Moghal patterns. It has risen in importance since the Calcutta Exhibition of 1883–84, and at present demand is greater than supply. The price of a teapoy is Rs. 50, a chair Rs. 100, and minor articles as low as Rs. 2. A door 6 feet by 12 feet costs Rs. 1,500.

3. *Ivory Carvings.*

[621–622].

This industry has practically died out.

4. *Lacquered Ware.*

[626–630].—Chennapalam toys.

They are made of wood, turned, prettily lacquered in two or three colours, and highly polished. Indian chessmen and chessboards are made of the same ware; and large shields, representing the faces of giants, are supplied to pilgrims to sacred shrines.

5. *Wood Carving.*

[631-663].—Sorab and Sagar sandal-wood ware.—Cabinets, caskets, card, watch, pen and pencil cases, *chowries*, &c.

The carvings, elaborate and minute, represent figures in Hindu mythology, skilfully encircled by intricate foliage, with figures of animals in relief. The details are grouped with quite an Eastern skill, and form an exceedingly rich ornamentation. Prices depend entirely on workmanship. Exhibits Nos. 644 and 646 deserve special mention. The carvings are in illustration of the Puranas.

6. *Horn Inlaid with Metal and Ivory.*

[667]. — Bangalore horn ware. — Buttons, combs, handles, mugs, &c.

Cards containing trade samples by Messrs. Saliah Mahomed Cassim, of Bombay House, Bangalore.

[666, 668, 669].—Mysore horn inlaid ware. —Snuff-boxes, walking-sticks, handles, &c.

The best work is from Mysore town. Prices, Rs. 2 a snuff-box, Rs. 5 a pen-holder, and Rs. 18 a walking-stick.

Div. VIII.—Marble and Stone.

3. *Sculpture.*.

[121-152].—Hindu deities.

Cut in soapstone, in which material sacred sculpture, centuries old, are found in a perfect state of preservation all over the State. Price of an idol 2 feet high is 25 Rs., and in miniature 5 Rs.

4. *Soapstone Vessels.*

[676-681].—Nullur ware.—Cooking vessels.

The exhibits are models on a reduced scale, as full-sized vessels would add greatly to the freight. There was a considerable export trade to other provinces of India at one time, but the demand at present is limited to local requirements. This industry would be capable of indefinite extension by reducing the cost of production and improving the shape of the vessels.

Div. IX.—Pottery.

2. *Unglazed Pottery.*

[686-706]. —Mysore common pottery ware. —Articles of domestic use.

Some of these exhibits are peculiar, in that articles, such as lamps, bells, &c., usually made of metal, are made of pottery ware.

Div. X.—Glass.

2. *Moulded and Drawn Articles.*

[711-718].—Bangles, mugs, phials, &c.

Div. XI.—Textiles.

1. *Cotton Fabrics.*

[721-723].—Ganjam chintz.

These have been specially reproduced from old printing blocks of Hyder's time. They are known as Ganjam chintz, and were originally used for clothing Hyder's and Tippu's Peons.

2. *Wool Fabrics.*

[732].—*Kamblis* for clothing and covering. Davangere goods.

Greatly prized by natives. The best are priced 200 to 300 Rs., and their excellence is proved by a piece measuring 2 yards by 6 yards being rolled up and placed in the hollow of a small bamboo, 1½ ft. by 2½ in.

[726-731].—Kolar goods.

These are partially waterproof, and are principally used for coats and cloaks by natives and by European planters. Price 10 to 12 Rs. a piece, about 15 ft. by 2 ft.

[733-741].—Mandya goods.

These are the cheapest coating *kamblis* Price 1 R. to 3 Rs. a piece.

3. *Carpets.*

[823].—Bangalore woollen carpeting.

Bangalore carpets are a specialty, woven with the same pattern on both sides, and noted for durability. Priced 1 Rs. to 3 Rs. per square yard.

[811-815, 819-822].—Bangalore woollen pile-rugs.

The trade in pile-rugs for export has fallen off since the weavers adopted aniline dyes.

[816-818].—Bangalore cotton carpets.

4. *Silk Fabrics.*

[746].—Bangalore silks—woman's cloth.

Mysore silk is stout and durable. It is sold by weight at 4 and 5 Rs. a tola. The trade has declined owing to disease among the silk-worms.

[747-751].—Tumkur silks—apparel.

5. *Other Fabrics.*

[756-757].—Bangalore woman's cloths.

[758-759].—Tumkur cloths—apparel.

Div. XII.—Embroideries.

1. *Silk, Cotton and Wool.*

[761-763] —Doyleys, &c.

2. *Gold and Silver.*

[765].—Doyleys.

3. *Bead Work.*

[766-768].—Toys.

Div. XIII.—Leather and Furs.

1. *Shoes.*

[769-771].—Shimoga work.
This trade is at its ebb. Most educated Hindus wear European boots and shoes.

Div. XIV.—Basket Work, Floor-mats and Carpets.

1. *Bamboo and Rattan Work.*

[802-810].—Kadur goods—mats and boxes.
[788-801].—Mysore goods—baskets.
[772-780, 781-787]. — Shimoga goods — baskets, boxes, cradles, &c.

Div. XV.—Miscellaneous.

[826].—Mysore moths.
A collection in a box by Mr. W. South, Bangalore.
[831-834].—Models of railway-carriages, tank and channel irrigation.
[835-841].—Mysore perfumes.
[827-830].—Sundries.
[842-843].—Ancient grain seals.
[13-36].—Pictures in water-colours.
The work of a special caste, "*Chitragars*," resident in most chief towns in Mysore. The figures principally represent chiefs, kings, and mythological objects. Prices from Rs. 5 to Rs. 15

2. *Engravings, Lithographs, &c.*

[41-51].—Maps.
District maps of Mysore State, engraved in Mysore.
Topographical map of Mysore.

5. *Educational Appliances.*

[156-162].—Books, &c.
Printed at the Government Press. "The Mysore Gazetteer" and "Inscriptions" are by L. Rice, Esq., C.I.E., Educational Secretary to the Darbar.

COORG.

Div. II.—Decorative Arts.

1. *Architectural Designs and Models.*

[68].—Bethamalé pulp house.
[69].—Coorg dwelling-house.

Div. III.—Musical Instruments.

1. *Wind Instruments.*

[46].—Bell-metal drums.
Small bell-metal drums are made for use as musical instruments by the Coorgs, and cost Rs. 5 each, giving employment to five persons.

Div. IV.—Jewellery.

1. *Gold and Silversmith's Work.*

[7-8, 16-24, & 27.]—Personal ornaments.
These jewels cost from 4 As. to 8 Rs. each.

Div. V.—Art Manufactures in Metal.

3. *Brass, Copper, and Mixed Metal.*

[26].—Pair of flat metal bracelets.
[42].—Spittoon.

5. *Ancient Arms and Armour.*

[9].—Coorg arms.
The Coorg knife (*Piché kathi*) with ornamented handle and sheath, is one foot long, and one and a half inch broad. Worn mostly as an ornament in the cloth (*cummerbund*) tied round the waist. The blade is made of inferior steel. The handle is made usually of silver or ivory; the sheath is made of bamboo or blackwood, and is heavily mounted with silver. The value of silver used in the handle and mounting costs Rs. 10. Occasionally the knives are mounted also with gold, costing Rs. 35 extra. The massive silver chain, with silver tassel and chatelaine and smaller chain, which depend from the sheath, cost Rs. 25.

[10].—Large broad-bladed knife.
The Coorg sword (*Uda katti*), without sheath, but with an ornamental waistbelt and spike behind, into which the sword is fastened, is two feet long and four or five inches broad. It is a powerful weapon, and is used now chiefly for killing pigs. The blade is made of inferior native steel, the handle is generally made of horn. The spike at the back is made generally of brass, occasionally of silver. The belt is made of red cloth mounted with silk and embroidered in gold with silk cords. Ten artisans are employed in making these Coorg weapons. The outturn is estimated at the value of Rs. 1,000 yearly.
[28].—Matchlock.
[29].—Spear.

6. *Cutlery.*

[58].—Axe.
[59].—Billhook.
[60].—Sickle.

Div. VI.—Art Manufactures in Wood and Ivory, Etc.

1. Carved Furniture and Carpentry.

[41].—A wooden plate to hold betel leaf and areca-nut.

5. Wood Carving.

[63].—A wooden bell (*marada thatte*) to fasten round the neck of cattle when out grazing.

Div. IX.—Pottery.

2. Unglazed.

[48].—A double bottomed steam oven for making cakes and puddings.

[50].—A cylindrical earthenware mould with cover for making rice cakes.

[51].—A native earthenware still consisting of boiler, dome, cooler,and wooden receiver to manufacture the strong rice liquor; the paddy (rice in the husk) is soaked in water till it germinates, when the grain is pounded in a mortar and allowed to ferment. It is then boiled in the large vessel, the steam passes through the perforated dome, is precipitated by the super-imposed cooler, which is constantly supplied with cold water, and the liquor falling upon the wooden receptacle is condensed outside.

Div. XIV.—Baskets, Mats, and Straw Work.

[35-38].—Square and round rattan boxes. For keeping clothes, &c.

[39].—Rattan cradle.

A child's cradle made of cane work.

[34].—Rattan shield.

[44].—Square basket.

A square little basket used for carrying rice and milk at marriage ceremonies.

[45].—Open basket.

An open basket for carrying provisions on occasions of journeys made to festivals.

[43].—Coils of coloured straw.

Coils of coloured straw for carrying head loads.

[65].—Basket used for catching fish.

It is placed in front of any channel from which the water of a paddy field runs so as to catch small fish.

[66].—Fish trap made of cane work.

[67].—Conical basket.

CHAPTER VIII.

THE FOREIGN TRADE OF INDIA.

THE foreign trade of India is mostly carried on by the sea, but there is also a smaller trade carried across the land frontiers of the empire into and from the neighbouring countries. The trade carried by sea and that carried by land will be treated separately in this paper.

The foreign trade of India by sea in the last official year, ending on 31st March, 1885, amounted in value to £154,817,192,* of which £69,591,270 represented the value of imports, both merchandise and treasure; while the exports, including re-exports, of merchandise and treasure amounted to £85,225,922. This large excess of exports over imports is an unvarying feature in the trade statistics of India, explained by the fact that India is a debtor to England for capital lent, and has also to remit considerable sums to England yearly for the cost of Military and Civil Administration, for furlough and pension to officers on leave or retired from the service and much of the savings of a great many of the Europeans, official and non-official, living in India. The excess of exports over imports for the last six years has averaged about £18,100,000 annually, while the drawings of the Secretary of State in Council bills for the same period have averaged £19,363,662 annually, which must be taken to be the cost to India of the interest on the debt she has accumulated, and of the other items mentioned above.

The trade has increased more than tenfold during the last fifty years, but the earlier returns were very imperfect, and it will be more accurate to say that the rate of present increase is between four and five per cent. annually, a very fair rate of increase when the generally slow progress of Asiatics is considered. Although the trade has steadily increased to the large sum mentioned above—a sum greatly in excess of the trade value of any other country except England, France, Germany, and the United States—it must be allowed that relatively to the population the trade is very small. It represents a sum of no more than 12*s*. a head of the whole population, a figure which stands in striking contrast to 350*s*. a head in the United Kingdom, 168*s*. a head in France, 145*s*. in Germany, 105*s*. in the United State, and 68*s*. in Italy. These figures point to the extreme poverty of the mass of the Indian people, and it must not be forgotten that the wants and requirements of even well-to-do natives are fewer and simpler than even those of the poorer classes of a backward European country. Comparing Asiatics with Asiatics, which is a truer test, it appears that whereas the foreign trade of India represents a sum of 12*s*. a head of the population, that of China represents no more than 3*s*.

More than half of the whole trade is carried on with the United Kingdom, the proportion last year having been more than fifty-five per cent., while about twenty-five per cent., represents interchange with other Eastern countries, China, the Straits, Ceylon, Mauritius, Arabia, Persia, Egypt, and others. The trade with France represents less than six per cent. of the whole, while the trade with other European countries is even more insignificant. No doubt some of the trade from and to the United Kingdom consists of articles brought from or intended for other European countries or America, but it cannot be traced, and the fact remains that the United Kingdom is India's largest customer, whether as a producer and consumer or as an agent for distribution. Most of the cotton yarn and piece goods, of the woollens and silks, the coal and the salt, the metals, machinery, and railway plant, which form the bulk of the import trade, comes from England.

It has been said above that an important feature in the trade statistics is the large normal excess of exports over imports. Another striking feature is the continued absorption of the precious metals. The flow of gold and silver into India is unintermittent. The total net imports of these metals, that is, deduction made of the quantities again exported, during the last six years amounted to £63½ millions, the proportion of gold to silver being as three to five. The gold is all hoarded, and to a large extent converted into ornaments for the persons of the wives and children of the owner. It is in this form that the suspicious native still prefers to keep his savings secure from the rapacity which traditionary experience of former oppressive Governments taught him to

* In this paper values in rupees are expressed in sterling at the conventional exchange of ten rupees to the pound sterling.

associate with the officials of the State—a conviction which has not even yet departed from him. The silver is mostly all coined into rupees at the Mints, though it does not then all remain in currency, for the silversmith in India works up rupees very largely into ornaments.

Of the whole trade of India about three-fourths is carried on with countries the route to and from which lies through the Suez Canal or round the Cape of Good Hope. The extent to which the Cape route has been abandoned in favour of the Canal since its opening will be apparent from the fact that of a possible trade of 75 per cent. more than 65 per cent. was actually conveyed through the Canal last year; and of this Indian trade through the Canal, amounting to a value of £101½ millions sterling, more than three-fourths was trade to and from the United Kingdom, the value being nearly £77½ millions sterling. These figures attest the high importance of the Canal to the commercial interests of India and England. With the increasing use of the Suez Canal there has been an increasing substitution of steamers for sailing vessels in the Indian carrying trade. The whole number of vessels which entered Indian ports from foreign countries last year was 5,150, aggregating 3,291,000 tons. Of these 1,495 were steamers, aggregating 2,157,000 tons, so that the steam tonnage was two-thirds of the whole. Of the 1,134,000 tons of sailing tonnage a very large proportion consists of small craft trading between India and China, the Eastern Archipelago, Arabia, Persia, and Zanzibar, Mauritius, and other places on the Eastern Coast of Africa. Sailing vessels play but an insignificant part now in the carrying trade between India and the Western World. More than 82 per cent. of the shipping employed in the Indian carrying trade is British and British-Indian.

The bulk of the foreign trade (about 95 per cent. of it) is concentrated in the five principal ports of the country, Bombay, Calcutta, Madras, Rangoon, and Karáchi, more than 80 per cent. flowing in and out of Bombay and Calcutta, the former being now the most important commercial centre in India. Rangoon and Karáchi are rising places, with a fine future in prospect, especially for Rangoon, which may become the main inlet and outlet for the trade of South-Western China.

As already remarked, the wants of the people of India are comparatively few and simple. The bulk of the imports consists of cotton piece goods and yarns, liquors, metals (chiefly copper, iron, and tin), hardware, machinery, railway material, woollen and silk goods, kerosine oil, coal, raw silk, sugar, salt, and spices. The industrial development of India has been slow except in two lines, the manufacture of jute and cotton. The cotton spinning and weaving industry is chiefly concentrated in the Bombay Presidency, though there are a few mills in other provinces also, while the jute manufacturing industry is confined to Calcutta and its neighbourhood. The cotton mills of India now employ 16,496 looms and 2,037,055 spindles, and the jute mills 6,926 looms and 131,740 spindles. The capital invested in cotton mills and jute mills, so far as they are worked on the joint stock principle, is £8,221,725 for the former, and £2,490,000 for the latter.

There can be no doubt that the cotton industry has had an appreciable effect on the import trade in cotton goods and yarns. The revolution which has been effected in this industry is interesting. In the last century India was full of handlooms; cloths produced by cottage industry were worn by the whole population, the better qualities being also exported in considerable quantities to England. The creation of the English cotton industry in Lancashire was followed by a great restriction in the Indian cottage industry, and gradually India not only ceased to export cottons to England, but came to depend herself to a very large extent upon England for the supply of clothing to her own people. This again was followed by the creation of an export trade in raw cotton for the supply of the Lancashire mills—a trade which was enormously stimulated by the interruption in the supplies of American cottons during the War of Secession. Then also was seen the establishment of cotton mills in Western India, the out-turn of which in the coarser yarns and cloths has prevented the increase of the import trade in English cottons, and is likely enough in the not very remote future to reduce that trade to comparative unimportance, and at the same time to quite extinguish the Indian hand-loom industry, which still exists to some small extent in various places. On the other hand, these mills, with the jute mills, and the other few large industries that India possesses, have greatly augmented the imports from England of machinery, metals, and coal.

The re-export trade of India is comparatively very limited. It may be said that of the merchandise received from foreign countries yearly not more than about 5 per cent. is re-shipped abroad. There may be perhaps some 3 per cent. more sent across the land frontiers. And, broadly, quite 90 per cent. of the imports are consumed in India itself. The re-export trade is carried on mainly at Bombay, which is a convenient dépôt between Europe and the coasts of Arabia, Persia, and Africa.

The exports of Indian produce and manufactures were valued last year at £80,313,208. While the largest part of the import trade consists of manufactured goods, about half of them being cotton cloths and yarns; the bulk of the export trade consists of food-stuffs and raw material for manufacture, the principal items being, in addition to opium :—

Food-stuffs: Wheat, rice, tea, sugar, coffee, spices.

Raw material: Cotton, jute, oilseeds (linseed, rape seed, til or sesame, poppy, and others), hides and skins, teakwood, wool.

Goods partly manufactured: Cotton yarn, indigo, vegetable oil (castor and cocoanut), saltpetre, raw silk, tanned hides and skins.

Goods fully manufactured: Cotton piece goods, grey and coloured, bags and sacks of jute, shell lac, silk piece goods.

Drugs and Narcotics: Opium.

The trade in some of these articles has sprung into large dimensions in the course of a few years. Thus the trade in wheat was created not more than twelve years ago, the main factors in its development being the cutting of the Suez Canal and the increase of railways in India, together with the decline in exchange. The export of tea has attained its present dimensions within the last twenty years, the suitability of the waste lands of Assam and Cachar for the cultivation of the tea plant having attracted European capital and suggested an almost unlimited opening for the employment of Europeans. The trade in cotton yarns and cloth is also the creation of the last twelve years, and the extensive manufacture of gunny bags is not older. The export of raw jute on a really large scale only dates from a period subsequent to the Crimean War. The export of oilseeds took large proportions about the same time as the trade in wheat came into existence, its development being favoured by the same causes. The trade in raw cotton was a result of the American War of Secession. On the other hand, while trades like these have risen from nothing and stand forth as the most important components of the Indian export trade, certain other industries which were of the first importance when the East India Company was a great trading corporation a century ago, have either remained without material increase or have fallen away into comparative insignificance, such as for instance, the trade in muslins, in silk goods, in raw silk, in indigo, and in saltpetre.

The figures in the tables appended show at a glance the extent of the import and export trade in the principal articles of merchandise exchanged between India and other countries last year.

TABLE I.—IMPORTS.

Articles.		Quantity.	Value.
			£
Cotton piece-goods, grey	yds.	1,138,343,726	12,276,501
„ white	„	277,875,450	3,698,470
„ coloured	„	315,345,829	4,720,184
Cotton yarn	lbs.	44,799,637	3,360,420
Metals	tons	236,201	4,843,733
Machinery and Millwork		...	1,484,124
Railway material		...	1,592,620
Hardware and Cutlery		...	844,552
Coal and Coke	tons	708,560	1,204,341
Kerosine oil	gallons	26,299,091	1,110,051
Silk piece goods	yds.	12,080,177	1,264,648
„ raw	lbs.	1,831,702	747,563
Woollen piece-goods	yds.	10,700,128	1,002,312
Liquors	gallons	2,310,976	1,217,921
Provisions		...	1,103,321
Apparel		...	942,232
Sugar	cwts.	1,616,874	2,140,838
Salt	tons	412,839	649,233
All other articles		...	8,946,247
Total Value		...	53,149,311

Articles.		Quantity.	Value.
			£
Cotton, raw	cwts.	5,066,057	13,286,367
" yarn	lbs.	65,897,183	2,441,100
" manufactures		...	896,928
Opium	cwts.	118,599	10,882,606
Oilseeds	tons	912,534	10,745,203
Rice	"	1,102,576	7,192,197
Wheat	"	791,537	6,309,140
Jute, raw	cwts.	8,368,686	4,661,368
" bags	No.	82,779,207	1,410,322
Hides and Skins	cwts.	1,010,578	4,934,340
Indigo	"	154,629	4,068,899
Tea	lbs.	64,162,055	4,044,759
Coffee	cwts.	328,317	1,245,506
Wool, raw	lbs.	18,928,173	713,576
All other articles		...	7,480,897
Total Value		...	80,313,208

TABLE III.—VALUE OF TRADE (IN MERCHANDISE) WITH PRINCIPAL COUNTRIES.

Countries.	Imports.	Exports.
	£	£
United Kingdom	42,197,870	32,944,581
China	1,865,759	12,471,893
France	604,246	8,168,508
Italy	418,111	3,485,144
Belgium	247,227	3,120,845
Austria	477,777	2,342,663
United States	1,138,068	3,453,278
Straits Settlements	1,709,596	3,165,666
Mauritius	1,663,627	709,302
Ceylon	410,368	1,783,448
Persia	643,220	318,947
Australia	465,374	773,400
Other Countries	1,308,068	7,575,533
Total	53,149,311	80,313,208

FRONTIER TRADE.

The trade which crosses the land frontiers of India is as yet of no special importance, the whole value of the imports and exports last year amounting to less than £12 millions. This trade has to contend with great difficulties. The routes in many places lead across the highest mountain chain in the world, and are made impracticable by snow for more than half the year. In other places they are caravan tracks across barren deserts or paths cut through primeval forest and malarious jungle, and, whether they pass over desert or jungle, the trader is often subject not only to the risks and difficulties placed in his way by Nature, but to the attacks of freebooters and savages who regard the peaceful trader as lawful prey.

The land frontier stretches over an immense line from Karáchi in the extreme west to the most south-easterly point in British Burma, Mergui. Over this vast line of frontier the current of trade flows, very unequally in its various channels, between India and Baluchistan, Afghanistan, Kashmir, Thibet, Nepal, Sikkim, Bhutan, the Eastern Mountain Country (the home of the savage tribes known as Nagas, Mishmis, Daphlas, Lushais, Abors), Upper Burma, the Karen and Shan Country, and Siam. There are but few points in the line where trade is really safe or is in possession of routes which lend themselves to large future development. These are (1) the railway which is now pushing on towards Quetta, (2) the road through the

Khyber leading into Northern Afghanistan (and here the safety of traders is ensured only by blackmailing the clansmen of the pass), (3) the roads into Kashmir and (4) into Nepal, especially from Bengal, and (5) the great Irrawadi route which leads into Upper Burma and South-Western China. Even on these routes the development of trade is much retarded by the sudden cessation of good roads at the British frontier and by the exactions to which traders are subjected by the States beyond the border. Thus, the trade with Afghanistan would make rapid progress if it were not impeded by Russian fiscal policy which shuts out Indian goods from the Central Asian markets, and by the heavy dues levied by the Amir of Afghanistan. The strict commercial restrictions imposed by the Nepalese durbar and by the Chinese officials in Thibet hamper trade with those countries, and the active intervention of the British Government in Kashmir and Upper Burma has only now succeeded in removing impediments which were paralysing to trade. It is possible that the settlement just concluded with China in regard to commercial intercourse with Thibet may have some effect in increasing trade with that country. Still, considering the natural difficulties of the trade routes, the great distances to be traversed, the cost of transport, and the general poverty of the inhabitants of the regions beyond the Indian frontiers, it would be sanguine to anticipate such a development of trade as would make its value reach real importance.

The bulk of the trade consists of exports from India of cotton goods, metal-ware, tea (to Kabul and Kashmir), rice (to Upper Burma), railway material (for the Sind Peshin line), indigo, and some cattle. The imports are largely food-grains, timber (from Kashmir and Burma), horses, fruits, and drugs. It is impossible to obtain anything like a correct account of the interchange of gold and silver.

The table appended shows the value of the trade in 1884-85 with the principal countries on the other side of the Indian frontiers:—

	Imports into British India.	Exports from British India.
	£	£
Southern Afghanistan and Baluchistan	349,802	1,781,832
Kabul	241,345	469,103
Kashmir	545,913	384,999
Thibet	74,097	30,806
Nepal	1,416,387	986,291
Upper Burma	2,023,933	2,071,424
Karennee	462,825	133,864
N. and S. Shan States	39,738	34,856
Siam	40,864	122,554
Other Countries	319,658	106,620
Total	5,514,562	6,122,349

Part II.

OTHER EXHIBITS.

SILK COURT.

EXHIBITS OF THE GOVERNMENT OF INDIA AND THE ROYAL COMMISSION.

The object of this Imperial and Royal Commission Collection is to illustrate the Silk Industries of India in a two-fold sense.*

First, it is proposed to show the exact state of Sericulture in India at the present moment, the position which it occupies in the output of the raw product, which may be stated to comprise everything that relates to the cocoon and to raw silk, a reeled thread of several cocoons in one.

It is chiefly to the East that Europe has long looked for a supply of this useful material. It is generally conceded that China was the first country to encourage the cultivation of silk, both for domestic purposes and afterwards for exported uses, and through a long expanse of time, slowly travelling westward, this industry has found its way through India, Persia, Arabia, Turkey, and Greece, to Italy and France where, probably in the most perfected state of its development, it still rests unchallenged and triumphant.

Second, its phase in India, as entirely apart from the breeding of the silkworm, in the manufacture of the great variety of fabrics of which silk comprises, if not the whole, the most important part. These may be roughly stated to be the Corah silks of Bengal, rudely produced by looms that would raise the smile and wonder of Europeans, the coarse Tussur fabrics woven in the same district, the magnificent kinkhabs of Benares, Ahmedabad and Surat, in which gold and silver form such important decorative features, the plainer silks of Delhi, the delicate and beautiful silks of Thana (a very ancient Christian Settlement), manufactured by a curious isolated race of weavers, whose story as well as work is so interestingly told and so beautifully illustrated by Mr. Gupte, in his article on the silks of that place, in the Journal of Indian Art, No. 5. (In the sixteenth century there were 4000 weavers at Thana, but now there are, according to Mr. Gupte's paper, only seven families with fourteen looms.) The rich fabrics of Yeola, situated not very far from Thana, the lovely brocades of Surat, incomparable for living beauty and Arabian grace of design, the ruder though not less interesting silks of Peshawar and the surrounding country, the satins of Azimgarh, Ahmedabad, Surat, Dhrangdhra and Kathiawar, the wonderfully constructed patterns of the Patolo weaving with "tie and dye" warp and woof, the silks of Berhampur, Cambay, Cutch, Kathiawar and Bombay, all testify not only to the skill achieved by Indian dyers and weavers during many ages, but also for the fascinations which have held these people spell-bound in the production of their fabrics of mystery and beauty.

The printed silks of India, too, are by a long way not the least of her interesting decorative work. It is a great pity that anything should have superseded the permanent and striking prints of the old-fashioned pocket-handkerchiefs. I have seen them being printed on the squat tables of the Calcutta printers, with indescribable interest, who use their prettily sculptured little blocks with a dexterity and exactness marvellous to see, requiring no pin points to guide them in their repeats of patterns.

The Indians, like the Chinese and Japanese, have never cared so much for what in Europe is termed excellence of quality, which means for the most part mechanical regularity in texture and pattern, and although they have had to weave with threads often much varying in regularity and thickness, yet they have down to to-day managed somehow or other, if they have had a pattern to weave, to put, so to speak, soul into it, and to raise it above the commonplace fabrics so often produced in modern Europe.

For ages, and so long as they continued to use the natural colours which they obtained from their own beautiful dye-stuffs, coupled with an ingenious and traditional taste, they never could go very far wrong in colour. It is now impossible to observe without great regret in passing

* A description of each specimen will be found in the Illustrated Handbook, to be obtained in the Court.

through India how the love of the modern brilliant European dyes has affected, to a serious degree, the products of the native loom of to-day.

This is also to be observed as much in another part of silk decoration in India which is as extensive, if not more so, than weaving—viz., the ornamentation of fabrics of cotton, wool, and silk, by embroidering with a silken floss or thread. Embroidery in India is on a great scale, much of it unknown because unseen. The native ladies of Assam, for example, embroider most beautifully, not for sale, but for domestic uses and for marriage and other presents. It is purely carried on as an art, and not for commerce. It is principally done with a silk that will one day, I feel sure, be in considerable demand in Europe—I mean the silk produced by the worm of the *Antheræa Assama*, or the Muga silkworm. It was not known to the English until recently that any of this silk was exported. It has often been stated by observers in Assam and India, that it was only produced for home consumption, but when I was in Calcutta making inquiries about this silk, which has engaged my attention now for several years, Mr. E. C. Buck, Secretary to the Government of India, Revenue and Agricultural Department, and Mr. H. Z. Darrah, Officiating Director, Department of Agriculture, Assam, discovered, whilst on a tour of inspection and search in the native bazaars of Calcutta, that the embroidered turbans made in Dacca were worked upon a cloth of cotton and Muga silk, wholly embroidered with undyed silk of the same kind. This embroidery, which had been very well known as having been sent down to Calcutta, and largely worn there by the natives, and also exported into Arabia, but kept, and still kept, in the hands of a very few merchants, was previously thought to be worked with Tussur silk, the fawn-like colour of which it closely resembled.

The Special Silk Court of the Government of India, and the Royal Commission for the Colonial and Indian Exhibition, including its adjoining Silk Culture Office, is intended to give ample illustration of all the silk work mentioned in the foregoing lines, and not only that, but to show the recent advances and improvements in the reeling of cocoons, due to the more active enterprise and thought of Western nations, as Italy and France. The application of this thought to the cocoons of India has proved that Bengal silk is capable of a very high degree of refinement, and that it is not inferior in fibre to that of any other country. That it has some points of difference is true, but not such as to make the disparity which has caused Indian silk (I am speaking now of that of the *Bombyx mori* or the silk of Bengal) to take such low rank in comparison with the silks of China, Japan, Italy, Broussa, and France.

That there is a great future in store for Sericulture in India is beyond doubt, and if only the same energy were applied as that brought to bear on the production of Indian wheat and Indian tea, the day would not be far distant when the silk centres of Europe would desire the silks of Bengal more than they now do those of China and Japan.

That India should take a fair position in the supply of the world's demand for silk is not for Englishmen to gainsay. On the contrary, India, with a greatly increasing population, the natural result of a great Continent at peace with itself, and a growing security from depopulation by famine, an improved sanitary administration and more scientific medical enlightenment and instruction, it goes without saying that Englishmen, of all others, should feel the greatest possible interest in the material welfare of India, and especially in everything which tends to the organisation and stimulus of her varied industries, particularly one which is so capable of being more widely spread as Sericulture.

Tussur silk, as adapted for export, has been, during the last ten years, very slow in taking root in India, and large supplies have had to be obtained from China to meet the gradually growing European demand. At the Paris Exhibition of 1878, Sir Philip Cunliffe-Owen determined to give this silk an opportunity of asserting itself, and afterwards in the India Museum he took care that its capabilities and uses should be conspicuously depicted. Not a little of the industrial growth of this useful though wild silk is due to his encouragement, and now in this Exhibition can be seen the fruits of all the care which has been bestowed upon it in various ways.

A number of gentlemen in India are vieing with each other to improve the methods of reeling, and with singular success. In the cases set apart for Tussur silk are shown results which a few years ago would have been thought to be impossible. Already this silk is capable of far more extended uses than ever before, and although it cannot be expected, on account of its structure and properties, to take the place of the more beautiful silk of the *Bombyx mori*, it has its uses and those in a much higher degree than it was ever thought susceptible of.

Besides the silks already mentioned there are others, such as the Eria silk, obtained from the *Attacus ricini* silkworm, which will gradually find extended utility; and great lessons will be learnt by those who care to observe, in these varied exhibits, both in the reeling of the cocoons the spinning of the waste fibres, and the dyeing and weaving of the silks.

One thought is somewhat saddening with regard to silk in India at the present time. I have recently travelled over the greater part of India, and I have everywhere found, in all the silk centres, that for the more ornamental silk fabrics Indian silk is not used, but that the manufacturers procure their supplies from China on the one hand, and Bukhara on the other. This ought not to be. Bengal is capable of producing silk to a vastly extended degree, not only enough for all the requirements of India, which are really very great, both for weaving, embroidery, and minor purposes, but for a greatly increased export trade. Under European careful supervision the native Indian works beautifully. He cares more for patient manual labour and real handicraft traditional work than he does for progressive thought or invention, and it is not to be wondered at that it has been left to the quicker brain and the desire for development that characterises the people of the West, to produce results which find a readier market than his own unaided and unguided efforts can secure.

THOMAS WARDLE.

INDIAN PRIVATE EXHIBITORS' COURT.

Exhibits.	Exhibitors.	London Agents.
Carpets and Fancy Wares	Several Indian Firms	Mawe & Co., Farringdon Road.
Indian Manufactures	Proctor & Co., Bombay	Proctor & Co., 428 Oxford Street.
China Plates painted with miniatures at Delhi	Zoolfekar Khan and Kootboodin Khan, Delhi	Brownfield & Son, Cobridge.
Carved Blackwood Billiard Table	Hemchund Pershotum, Bombay	G. Wright & Co., 162 Westminster Bridge Road.
Silver Bowl	Capt. Colvin, Mondhams Hall, Waltham Abbey	
Jewellery, Silver, &c.	Framjee Pestonjee, Bhumgara	At Exhibition.
Carpets and Mats	Vincent Robinson & Co., Ellore	34 Wigmore Street.
Silk, &c.	T. Wardle & Co., Arrah	T. Wardle & Co., London.
Models of Steamers, &c.	P. & O. S. N. Co.	122 Leadenhall Street.
Arrowroot	Speed & Co., Alipore	Henry S. King & Co., 65 Cornhill.
Teak Wood Articles and Carvings	Bombay and Burmah Trading Co., Rangoon	8 Austin Friars.
Articles dyed with Cutch.		
Condiments	Manockjee Poonjiajee & Sons, Bombay	Phythian & Co., 430 West Strand.
Helmets	C. C. Dass & Co., Calcutta	T. Townend & Co., Lime Street.
Carved Teak Wood Doors, Windows, &c.	Lockwood de Forest, Ahmedabad	Proctor & Co., 428 Oxford Street.
Carved Teak Wood Furniture	Moolchund Bhai, Ahmedabad	Ditto.
Condiments	Framjee Nairojee, Bombay	Aldridge & Co., 4 East India Avenue.
Varnishes	Anglo Indian Copal Varnish Co.	H. S. King & Co.
Surat Ivory and Sandal Wood Carved Work	Moolchund, Cashiram	Liberty & Co., Regent Street.
Bombay Bandhni Silk	Cursetjee S. De Vitre, Bombay.	Ditto.
Indian Medicines	F. H. Bowden, Madras	29 Lansdowne Road, Croydon.
Carpets and Rugs	Lahore Jail	T. Bontor & Co., 35 Old Bond Street, W.
" "	Agra Jail	
2 Carriages	Simpson & Co., Madras	W. C. Wood, 41 Basinghall Street.
Inlaid Carved Boxes and Cast Metal Hieroglyphs	Fisher & Co., Bombay	John R. Fisher, 28 Robert Street, South Kensington, S.W.
Copal Varnish for coachbuilders and best kind of house work	Nobin Chunder Dutt & Co., Calcutta	William Hely, Sevenoaks, Kent.
Foods	Chas. Ady, Moulmein	J. Ernest Ady, c.o. J. F. Aldridge & Co., Billiter Square Buildings.
Moradabad Brass work.	Chiranjee Lal Khanna & Co., Moradabad	Henry S. King & Co.
Arms, &c.	James Buchanan, Hyderabad	J. F. Bremer, 61 Mark Lane.
Weapons, &c.	Manton & Co., Calcutta	Henry S. King & Co.
Oils	Khetter Mohund Bysack & Sons, Calcutta	Ditto.
Condiments	P. Vencatachellum, Madras	A. Monro & Co., 134 Southwark Street.
Leather Shields and Carved Work	Dhalgar Parshotam and Bhagvan Khooshal, Ahmedabad	Henry S. King and Co.

Exhibits.	Exhibitors.	London Agents.
Condiments	C. Stembridge & Co., Calcutta	G. Eyears, 33 Leicester Square.
Boots, Saddlery and Harness	Watts & Co., Calcutta	Ditto.
Carpets and Mats	Vellore Jail	Hampton & Sons, 8 Pall Mall, S.W.
Books printed and published in India	Thacker Spink & Co., Calcutta	W. Thacker & Co., 87 Newgate Street, E.C.
Ale and Porter	Crown Brewery Co., Mussoorie	A. Lawrie & Co., 14 St. Mary Axe.
Condiments	Nujeeb Khan & Co., Calcutta	J. Morison & Co., 4 Fenchurch Street.
Two Carved Wood Sideboards.	East India Art Manufacturing Co., Bombay	Miss Bates, 13 Almorah Road, Islington.
Painted Ivory Figures	Miss Ashcombe	

EXHIBITS OF THE BOMBAY BURMAH TRADING CORPORATION, LIMITED: BURMESE PAVILION, SOUTH PROMENADE.

Rangoon Teak.

Logs in the rough and squared.

Planks.

Examples of application of fine teak scantling in economical construction, viz., bridge, roof truss, girders, shear leg, models of saw mill and church roof, Hatherley patent steps, easels, &c.; also railway keys, railway blocks in the rough and fitted in the wheel.

Flooring, doors, cabinet, &c.

Cutch.

Sections of Cutch trees. Cutch chips and leaves.

Model of Cutch cookery.

Samples of the Corporation's manufactured Cutch.

Velvets, yarns, and hose, showing the colours produced from Cutch; and fishing-net to show its use in tanning.

Elephant skull.

Kalagas, trays, &c., with other articles of domestic use in Burmah.

PRIVATE EXHIBITORS' COURT.

Room wainscoted and parquet-floored in Rangoon Teak, supplied by the Corporation. Executed by Messrs. Gillow & Co.

Fine sideboard of Rangoon carved work.

Various Burmese objects.

INDIAN TEA AND TOBACCO COURT.

TEA EXHIBITS.

Name of Garden.	District.	Proprietor or Managing Agent.
Attah-Barrie	Assam	J. Mackillican & Co.
Bamandanga	Western Dooars	Ditto.
Arcuttipore	Cachar	Ditto.
Amchong	Assam	Ditto.
Kewacherra	Sylhet	Ditto.
Star	Ditto	Ditto.
Lackatoorah	Ditto	Ditto.
East Hopetown	Dehra Doon	Ditto.
Kallacherra	Cachar	Struthers & Co.
Kurseong & Darjeeling Tea Co.	Kurseong	Moran & Co.
Ditto Ditto	Terai	Ditto.
Central Cachar Tea Co.	Cachar	Ditto.
Pathemara	Ditto	Grindlay & Co.
Alyne	Ditto	Ditto.
Aramgurh	Kangra	H. J. Minniken.
Forgri Tea Co.	North Assam	Bird & Co.
Tokai Tea Co.	Assam	Balmer, Lawrie, & Co.
Kousanie Tea Co.	Kumaon	Kousanie Tea Co.
Hathibari Tea Estate	Tezpore, Assam	Finlay, Muir, & Co.
North Sylhet Tea Co.	Jalpaigoori	Ditto.
Bytagool Tea Estate	Ditto	Ditto.
Dooars	Ditto	Ditto.
Balijan	Assam	Planters' Stores and Agency Co., Limited.
Rampore	Cachar	Schoen, Kilburn, & Co.
Darjeeling Tea and Chinchona Association, Limited	Darjeeling	Ditto.
Leesh River Tea Co.	Silligorie	King, Hamilton, & Co.
Phoolbaree Tea Co.	Ditto	Ditto.
Oaklands	Debrooghur	Ditto.
Ramgurh Tea Gardens	Kumaon	W. W. Lee.
Harmutty	Assam	Williamson, Major, & Co.
Mim Tea Co.	Darjeeling	Ditto.
Indian Terai Tea Co.	Ditto	Ditto.
Longview Tea Co.	Ditto	Ditto.
Rambagh Tea Estate	Dehra Doon	Ditto.
Moabund Tea Co.	Assam	Ditto.
Majulighur Tea Estate	Ditto	Ditto.
Ohat Tea Estate	Ditto	Ditto.
Hoolmaree Tea Co.	Ditto	Ditto.
Selim Hill Tea Estate	Darjeeling	Ditto.
Bishnath Tea Co.	Assam	Ditto.
East India Tea Co.	Cachar	Ditto.
Tambulbaree Tea Estate	Assam	Ditto.
Sonapore Tea Concern	Ditto	Ditto.
Borphukhurie Tea Co.	Ditto	Ditto.
Cambrian Tea Association	Darjeeling	Ditto.
Corramore Tea Estate	Assam	Ditto.
Majagram Tea Co.	Cachar	Ditto.
Gillahatin Tea Co.	Assam	Ditto.
Scottish Assam Tea Co.	Ditto	Ditto.
Ghilladharee Tea Concern	Ditto	Ditto.
Borelli Tea Co.	Ditto	Ditto.
Munjha Tea Co.	Darjeeling Terai	Ditto.
Borjoolee Tea Estate	Assam	Ditto.

Name of Garden.	District.	Proprietor or Managing Agent.
dwar Tea Estate	Assam	Williamson, Major, & Co.
o Tea Co.	Ditto	Ditto.
India Tea Co.	Ditto	Ditto.
a Habee Tea Co.	Ditto	Ditto.
1 Tea Co.	Darjeeling	Ditto.
au Tea Co.	Kangra Valley	Nassau Tea Co.
lla Tea Plantation . .	Ditto	T. Barnes Cooke.
m Tea Estate . . .	Ditto	Ditto.
dia	Dehra Doon	J. S. W. Stansfield.
barrie	Tezpur, Assam	Maurice Darker.
h Sylhet Tea Co. . . .	Sylhet	Finlay, Muir, & Co.
ngside Garden, of Springside a Co.	Darjeeling	Jardine, Skinner, & Co.
amookh Garden, of New Mutual a Co.	Cachar	Ditto.
sempore Garden, of New utual Tea Co.	Ditto	Ditto.
loocoorie Garden, of Tezpore d Gogra Tea Co.	Assam	Ditto.
l Hope Garden, of Good Hope a Co.	Western Dooars	Ditto.
orie	Cachar	Ditto.
acherra Garden, of Second utual Tea Co.	Ditto	Ditto.
o Tea Estate	Ditto	Barry & Co.
a Nagpore Tea Co. . . .	Chota, Nagpore	Ditto.
jan Tea Association . .	Assam	Ditto.
t Julinga Tea Estate . .	Cachar	Ditto.
hur Tea Estate	Assam	Ditto.
kote Tea Estate	Ditto	Ditto.
marea Tea Estate	Ditto	Ditto.
in Tea Estate	Cachar	Ditto.
albari Tea Estate	Assam	Ditto.
llajan Tea Estate . .	Ditto	Ditto.
akati Tea Co.	Seebsagur, Assam	Ditto.
roogur Combination Co. .	Assam	Ditto.
oosha Tea Estate	Cachar	Ditto.
ingarh	Ditto	Begg, Dunlop, & Co.
eecherra Tea Co.	Ditto	Ditto.
pacherra	Ditto	Ditto.
mber	Ditto	Ditto.
goorie	Assam	Ditto.
kwah Tea Co.	Ditto	Ditto.
joo Valley	Ditto	Ditto.
gpunnah	Darjeeling	Ditto.
th Sylhet Tea Co.	Sylhet	Finlay, Muir, & Co.
ong Tea Co.	Ditto	Ditto.
nabund	Cachar	Balmer, Lawrie, & Co.
gli Ting	Assam	Harman & Want.
tickcherrie Tea Estate . .	Chittagong	Williamson & Co.
urie	Fiji	Walker, Lambe, & Co.
rmsala	Kangra Valley	Kangra Valley Tea Association.
n Brae	Ditto	Ditto.
ttoo	Ditto	Ditto.
rola	Ditto	Ditto.
chya	Ditto	Ditto.
thiar	Ditto	Ditto.
isdale	Neilgherry Hills	N. G. Benson.
ada	Ditto	E. G. Windle.
asda	Kangra Valley	W. K. Pomeroy.
lanaad	Neilgherry Hills	Thomas G. Hill.
namara	Assam	Jorehaut Tea Co.
maligbur	Ditto	Ditto.
ing	Ditto	Ditto.

Name of Garden.	District.	Proprietor or Managing Agent.
Rungajam	Assam	Jorehaut Tea Co.
Rungagora	Ditto	Ditto.
Hatteechungie	Ditto	Ditto.
Bokahoola	Ditto	Ditto.
Dekhia Tulee	Ditto	Ditto.
Koreekuttea	Ditto	Ditto.
Ambotia	Darjeeling	Darjeeling Co.
Ging	Ditto	Ditto.
Tukdah	Ditto	Ditto.
Phoobsering	Ditto	Ditto.
Turzum	Ditto	Ditto.

TOBACCO EXHIBITS.

Name of Exhibitor.	Address.	Exhibit.
Neelamagum Pillay	Trichinopoly	Cigars.
J. Deb & Co.	Calcutta	Burmese Cigars and Cheroots.
C. W. Eaton & Co.	Coconada	Cigars.
Scott & Co.	Rangoon	Burmese Cheroots.
Assistant Director of Agriculture .	British Burma	Burmese Cigars and Tobacco.
G. Henke & Co.	Calicut	Cigars.
Dewan of Kolhapur	Kolhapur	Samples of Tobacco.
State of Sangli		Ditto.
Beheehardas Veharidas, Desai of Nadiad		Samples of Cigarettes and Tobacco.
Roberts & Co.	Coconada	Cigars and Tobacco.
J. Heimpel	South of India Cigar Factory, Dindigul	Cigars.
Begg, Dunlop, & Co.	Calcutta	Tobacco and Cigarettes.
Maha Lutchmee	Dindigul	Cigars.
Oakes Bros.	Madras	Tobacco and Cigars.
F. W. Cabines	Burma	Cigars and Tobacco.

MADRAS GOVERNMENT.

NARAINSAWMY PILLAY, *Trichinopoly.*

31–37. Cigars.
38. Tobacco.

NEELAMAGA PIDLAY, *Trichinopoly.*

39–48. Cigars.

SAWMINATHA PILLAY & Co., *Worriore, Trichinopoly.*

49–55 Cigars.
56 & 57. Tobacco.

M. SOOBRAMANIA PILLAY & Co., *Worriore, Trichinopoly.*

58. Samples of cigars and tobacco.

T. B. MUTUSAWMY MUDALIAR & Co., *Worriore, Trichinopoly.*

59–72. Cigars and Cigarettes.
73–76. Tobacco.

ETHIRAJULU & BROTHERS, *Poothoor, Trichinopoly.*

77–80. Cigars.

MARIYA PILLAY BROTHERS, *Poothoor, Trichinopoly.*

81–90*a*. Cigars.

CURPUNNAH PILLAY & BROTHERS, *Poothoor, Trichinopoly.*

91–100. Cigars.

Messrs. PARRY & Co., *Madras.*

101–106. Tobacco.

Messrs. G. HENKE & Co., *Calicut.*

107. Box of sample cigars.

M. PARTHASARATHY NAIDU, *Madras.*

107*a*. Havannah cigars.

INDIAN COFFEE EXHIBITORS.

Name of Exhibitor.	Name of Estate.	District.
F. Clifford	Kirkie Coondala	Mysore.
H. W. Raikes	Cheitnully	Ditto.
Gen. G. J. Green, Col. H. Green, & B. Mockett	Ossoor	Ditto.
Col. J. A. Campbell, & D. T. Brett	Hutton Kodigi	Ditto.
Col. J. A. Campbell	Netrokul	Ditto.
Ross Porter, E. Hall & Co.	Umbidy Khan	Ditto.
Syed Ameer Alee Bros.	Goddanbully	Ditto.
O. S. Skirving, K. MacAlpine, G. M. Porter & C. S. Blair	Yellagode	Ditto.
Ross Porter & De Wend	Barekodie	Ditto.
M. V. Charrington	Gootey Khan	Ditto.
Ross Porter & Errington	Bupponji	Ditto.
J. Lee Stewart	Tholulpett	Ditto.
J. & E. Hunt	Cangnoor	Ditto.
Wilson & Co.	Balyarti	Ditto.
J. Hunt	Iggloor	Ditto.
R. Buchanan	Siddra Baunoo	Ditto.
R. C. Sanderson	Engadine	Ditto.
H. Courpalais	Koorken Mutty	Ditto.
A. E. Clifford	Murgaddi Khan	Ditto.
Mysore Estates Co., Limited	Kelagoor	Ditto.
R. C. Sanderson	Canajon	Ditto.
Pearse & Beadon	Gunta Naick	Ditto.
Porter, Hall, & Co.	Santawerry	Ditto.
W. M. Maynard	Hitlow	Ditto.
W. H. Maynard	Gooboor	Ditto.
O. S. Skirving	Coppa	Ditto.
H. Courpalais	H. C.	Ditto.
E. M. Breethampt	Yeurma Gundi	Coorg.
F. G. Arbuthnot	Fischers	Ditto.
Jas. Chisholm	El Dorado	Ditto.
Rev. A. Fennell	Mountain	Ditto.
I. de Vaz	Charlotte	Ditto.
Iver Macpherson	Santi Coopa	Ditto.
Alston, Low & Co.	Coosboor	Ditto.
J. Chisholm	Elkhill	Ditto.
Mathesons	Mattakadu	Ditto.
J. Logan	Pollay Betta	Ditto.
Binney & Co.	Wudderbully	Ditto.
Jas. Chisholm	Fairlands	Ditto.
G. R. Evans	Aalie Topoo	Ditto.
R. J. Rouse & Co.	Guyud	Neilgberry.
Executors of J. Vans Agnew	Glenvans	Ditto.
W. R. Arbuthnot & A. Griffin	Seaforth	Ditto.
G. Arbuthnot & R. F. Phillips	Kotergberry	Ditto.
Ditto ditto	Adderley	Ditto.
E. Walsh	Waverley	Ditto.
Trambacberry Estates Co., Limited	Culloor	Wynaad
G. Romilly	Chulika Mulla	Ditto.
Glenrock Co., Limited	Glenrock	Ditto.
Tambracberry Estates Co., Limited	Eva	Ditto.
Indian Consolidated Gold Mining Co.	Balcarres	Ditto.
Arbuthnot, Latham & Co.	Peermade Placat	Travancore.
Ditto ditto	Glenmore	Ditto.
Travancore Plantation Co., Limited	Hereford	Ditto.
Superintendent, Port Blair & Nicobars	Andaman Coffee Estate	Andamans.

EDUCATIONAL SOCIETIES, ADMINISTRATION COURT.

Exhibitor, School Book Society, *Madras.*

39. English First Book of Lessons.
40. English Second Book of Lessons.
41. Short Account of the Madras Presidency.
42. Naturel History of Animals.
43. The World's History in Tamil.
44. Map of the Madras Presidency, coloured.
45. Tamil reprints from the Janavinodhini, 30 in number.
46. Geikie's Physical Geography in Telugu.
47. Arabian Nights in Hindustani.
48. Persian Lalai-i-Manjuma.

Exhibitor, Christian Vernacular Education Society.

49. English and Tamil Vocabulary of Words and Sentences, in three parts.
50. English First Book.
51. English Second Book.
52. English Fourth Book.
53. Advanced Reader.
54. English New First Book.
55. English New Second Book.
56. English New Third Book.
57. English New Fourth Book.
58. English New Fifth Book.
59. English Primer.
60. English First Reader.
61. English Second Reader.
62. English Third Reader.
63. English Fourth Reader.
64. English Fifth Reader.
65. English Senior Reader.
66. First Book of English Poetry.
67. Grammatical Primer.
68. Manual of Grammar.
69. Translation Exercises.
70. Manual of Geography.
71. Table Book for Madras and Ceylon.
72. The Way to Health.

Exhibitor, Society for Promoting Christian Knowledge, *Madras.*

73. History of India by D. Sinclair.
74. Outlines of Indian History.
75. Outlines of English History.
76. Duncan's Geography of India.
77. Duncan's Geography of Europe.
78. Duncan's Geography of Africa, &c.
79. Duncan's Geography of India.
80. Domestic Economy for Anglo-Indian Schools.
81. Adam's Euclid, Books 1, 2, and 3.
82. English and Tamil First Book.
83. Anglo-Tamil Second Book.
84. Arithmetical Primer.
85. Alphabet, large type, sheet.
86. Tamil Anthology, by Pope.
87. Nanul, by Rev. J. Lazarus.
88. English Tamil Dialogues.
89. Tamil Minor Poets, 1 and 2.
90. Pope's Tamil Grammar, 1 and 2.
91. Persian Munazir-ul-Qavad (Grammar).
92. Persian Zubdut-ul-Qavanin.
93. Persian and English Muhavarat-i-Farsi.
94. Persian Mujmauah-i-Salis.
95. Persian Gulistan.
96. Hindustani Jami-ul-Quavanin (Grammar).
97. Hindustani Kulasat-ul-Quavanin.
98. Hindustani Jami-ul-ashar.
99. Hindustani Chamanistan-i-Ajib.
100. Hindustani Kitab-i-Salis.
101. Hindustani Sinclair's History.
102. Hindustani Catechism of General Geography.

Exhibitor, Religious Tract and Book Society.

103. Progress: a monthly journal for 1884-85.
104. Short Papers for Young Men.
105. Some Elementary Principles of Christianity.
106. "Educate your Children" in Tamil.
107. The Pearl Merchant.
108. Almanac.
109. Bunyan's Pilgrim's Progress.
110. Tamil Hymns and Christian Lyrics.
111. Tamil Life of Christ.
112. Tamil Bible Picture Stories.
113. Telugu History of the True Incarnation.
114. Telugu Story of a Young King.
115. Telugu Line upon Line.
116. Telugu The Peep of Day.
117. Malayalam The Dawn of True Wisdom.

THE NATIONAL INDIAN ASSOCIATION,
Miss E. A. MANNING, Secretary.

Exhibits.	Exhibitor.
Caps embroidered with gold and silver thread, and child's dress in white satin embroidered with silver thread	Lady Jamsetji Jijibhoi, of Bombay.
Caps embroidered with gold and silver threads and pearls, strips of pearl embroidery for trimming dresses, and embroidered pyjamas and jackets	Mrs. C. Jehangir Jessawalla, Bombay.
Jacket embroidered by Mrs. Hassan Ally, a Mohammedan lady, Bombay	Mrs. Hassan Ally.
Bead work and Lace work, by Mrs. Guanapara Kasum, Madras	Mrs. Guanapara Kasum.
A large White Net Veil embroidered in Wool, by Mrs. Gujapathi Rao, Madras	Mrs. Gujapathi Rao.
Silk, used for men's dress	The National Indian Association.
Work done by Students of the Presentation Convent School, Black Town.	Ditto.
Work done by the National Indian Association Home Education Classes	Ditto.
Work done at L. W. N. Girls' School, Kottapettach, Vizagapatam	Ditto.
Work done at Miss Thomas's Girls' School, Tinnevelly .	Ditto.
Work done at the Girls' Boarding School, Battlagunda, Madura	Ditto.
Work done at the Shrinivas Pillars Girls' School, Madras .	Ditto.
Work done at the Government Girls' School, Nellore Town	Ditto.
Work done at the Local Fund Normal School for Masters, Madura	Ditto.
Work done at Six Girls' Schools of H.H. the Maharaja of Vizianagram, Madras	Ditto.

THE TROPHY OF KUCH BEHAR.

Formed by His Highness the Maharajah.

In the Forefront of the Tiger Hunt.—Great Group in the deep grass jungle. A Hunting Elephant, preceding the beaters, has come upon a group of Tigers, one of which is wounded, while another has sprung upon him with deadly grip; others are near, or retreating in the tall grass and bamboo copse.

Among other animals of Kuch Behar are: Leopard, Buffalo, various Deer, Bear, Wild Cat, Boar, Porcupine, Monkeys, &c. Vultures, Pea Fowl, Jungle Fowl, Green Pigeon and other birds.

JUNGLE LIFE.

By the Royal Commission.

Trophies designed to represent generally the Fauna and Flora of India by representative Animals and Birds, picturesquely grouped in illustration of their life habits. Some features of the country, with vegetation, form the foreground, and spaciousness is aimed at by pictorial effect. Among the specimens and groups of Great Game in this Division may be noted: Wounded Boar finding refuge; Cheetahs and Axis; Gaur; Buffalo; Bears and Young; Ovis Ammon; Goral, Nylgai; Markhor; Bara Singha; Hog-Deer; Blackbuck; and Albino Blackbuck; Sambur; Thar; Leopards, &c., &c., and many Birds. Among the Reptiles are Alligators, Pythons and other Snakes, Lizards, &c.

Designed and arranged, and the Specimens Modelled, by

Rowland Ward, F.Z.S

THE INDIAN PALACE.

Previous Exhibitions have served to illustrate some of the multitudinous Arts and products of our Indian Empire, but it has been left for this occasion to bring before us the technical processes of their manufactures, the application and use of objects which otherwise would have remained but beautiful curios, suitable only for the glass cases of a Museum.

For this purpose the Secretary of the Royal Commission made arrangements last year for the utilisation of Indian Art work (as far as possible) in the construction and decoration of the Courts, and submitted for the approval of H.R.H. the President, a plan for the draping of the vestibule with Indian printed cottons, the separation of the Courts by carved wooden and stone screens, the construction of a Palace Durbar Hall in carved wood, and in connection with it the peculiar feature of most oriental Palaces, a "karkhaneh," or workshop, where jewellers, weavers, carvers, and others would carry on their trades, and produce before the visitors the marvellous and beautiful objects of their handiwork.

At the request of H.R.H. the Prince of Wales, the Lords of the Committee of Council on Education gave permission to Mr. C. P. Clarke, C.I.E., the Keeper of the Indian Museum, to visit India, and this gentleman returned in May last, having completed the necessary arrangements, and brought back a party of wood carvers, who immediately commenced the Durbar Hall.

The great stone gateway presented to the South Kensington Museum by His Highness the Maharaja Sindhia having also been lent by the Authorities of the Science and Art Department, a design made by Mr. Purdon Clarke whilst in India was approved, and the gateway incorporated with the Durbar Hall and artisans' shops. The whole now represents a typical Royal Palace and Courtyard with shops overlooked by an Audience Hall, and the public portions of an Indian Palace in the Hindu-Persian style known as Moghal. Protected by two bastion towers and loopholed walls, the courtyard is entered through the Gwalior gateway, a remarkable example of modern Indian Art which would alone merit a visit to the Exhibition from the richness of its decoration, and peculiarity of construction, so completely at variance with our system of masonry. It was designed, and the work of execution superintended, by Major James Keith, the Curator of Antiquities at the Gwalior Fort.

The shops surrounding three sides of the courtyard number thirteen, and seven more line a passage on the right which leads to the Private Exhibitors' Gallery. These are raised about two feet above the level of the pavement, and each front is divided into three openings by columns and foliated arches with lattice panels over. They are occupied by artisans selected by, and under the charge of, Dr. Tyler, C.I.E., of Agra, who ply their several trades, and are desirous not only of inspection of their work, but of the patronage of their visitors.

On the fourth side is a wide porch extending back and on either side; the low ceiling being supported by cross beams, and many columns with bracket capitals. Here are the carpet looms, and office where all arrangements are made and orders received for work to be executed by the artisans in the courtyard.

Passing through the porch, or Hall of Columns, the garden vestibule is reached, a building of somewhat mixed character, partaking more of the form and construction of a large marquee tent than the glimpses of solid masonry showing through the tent-like hangings will admit. The mosaic floor and curious tank fountain again add to this look of solidity, which is confirmed by the red sandstone staircase leading up to the Durbar Hall overlooking the Palace courtyard.

This room is certainly the most remarkable object in the Exhibition, being of foreign origin, yet made in the Exhibition by two natives of Bhera in the Punjab. Entered on the east side through a triple arched opening, the Hall is seen at a *coup-d'œil*, and visitors are bewildered with the mass of intricate ornament which covers the walls and ceiling. The foliated arches of the heads of the thirteen recessed windows are again repeated in the casements, and the peculiar bracketed cornice carries another line of these graceful arches round the room.

LIST OF ARTISANS.

Benares.

Name. — Description.

1. Sha'bán .... Gold brocade weaver (48).*
2. Khádim Hussain .... Ditto (20).
3. Amir 'Ali............ Kinkhab weaver (40).
4. Imámu'ddín .... Kinkhab weaver (45).
5. Ismail .... Kinkhab weaver (40).
6. Asgar Hussain...... Kinkhab weaver (14).

Delhi.

7. Nazir Hasan........ Ivory miniature painter (36).
8. Rahim Baksh........ Gold lace maker.
9. Haji Mi'yak .... Coppersmith (80).
10. Nisar Ahmad .... Seal engraver (24).
11. Mughal Jan .... Silversmith (22).
12. Muhammad Hussain. Coppersmith (24).

Agra.

13. Vilayat Hussain.... Dyer (42).
14. Mukunda .... Calico printer (40).
15. Karan Singh .... Trinket maker (28).
16. Hiralall .... Sweetmeat maker (37).
17. Tulsiràm .... Sweetmeat maker (42).
18. Bákar .... Durri weaver (40).
19. Hemchand .... Goldsmith (42).
20. Bakshiram .... Potter (102).

Cawnpore.

21. Ràmlall .... Carpet weaver (9).
22. Chuta .... Carpet weaver (14).

* The figures between parentheses denote the age.

Mathura.

Name. — Description.

23. Pethàràm .... Carpet reader (22).
24. Ràmphal........... Carpet weaver (9).
25. Bhupla .... Durri weaver (18)
26. Bipat .... Carpet weaver (15).

Bhurtpur.

27. Radha Ballabh...... Builder (36).
28. Nathiràm .... Builder (34).
29. Ghasiràm .... Stone-carver (20).
30. Jogal .... Stone-carver (50).

Bikanir.

31. Kadir Baksh........ Stone-carver (42).

Lucknow.

32. Munnàlàll.......... Clay figure maker (35).
33. Jivanlall .... Decorator (24).

Nagina, Bijnor.

34. Kadir Baksh........ Wood-carver (30).
35. Maullá Baksh....... Wood-carver (20).

Bhavnage.

36. Harji .... Bullock driver (35).
37. Dosa .... Bullock driver (25).

PLATE I.

European Cocoon-reeling machine, diagonal view.
(A Tavelette Consono.)

[*Frontispiece*.

COLONIAL AND INDIAN EXHIBITION.

ROYAL COMMISSION AND GOVERNMENT OF INDIA SILK CULTURE COURT.

DESCRIPTIVE CATALOGUE.

BY

THOMAS WARDLE, F.C.S., F.G.S.

HONORARY SUPERINTENDENT.

LONDON:

WILLIAM CLOWES & SONS, LIMITED,

Printers and Publishers to the Royal Commission,

13 CHARING CROSS, S.W., AND AT THE EXHIBITION.

1886.

INDIAN EMPIRE.

Executive Commissioner,

SIR PHILIP CUNLIFFE-OWEN, K.C.B., K.C.M.G., C.I.E.,

Secretary to the Royal Commission.

Commissioner for the Government of India,

SIR EDWARD C. BUCK, LL.D., B.C.S.

Official Agent for the Government of India,

J. R. ROYLE, ESQ., C.I.E., Assistant Secretary to the Royal Commission.

Special Officer in Charge of the Economic Court,

DR. GEORGE WATT, C.I.E., M.B., C.M.

Honorary Superintendent of the Royal Commission and Government of India Silk Culture Court,

THOMAS WARDLE, ESQ., F.C.S., F.G.S.

(Leek, Staffordshire.)

LIST OF ILLUSTRATIONS.

The larvæ, cocoons, and moths are shown of the actual size.

INTRODUCTION.

Being a Paper on the Silks in the Indian Silk Culture Court at The Colonial and Indian Exhibition, read in the Conference Room on the 24th of June, 1886.

The Chair was taken at 8 o'clock by Mr. (now Sir) Edward C. Buck, LL.D., Secretary to the Government of India Revenue and Agricultural Department, who said: "I consented to preside to-night with the greatest pleasure, because I know, perhaps more than any man, the manner in which Mr. Wardle has devoted his time and labour and his funds towards promoting the cause of the revival of the silk industry in India. I hope the result may be as great as his labours deserve, but whatever improvement may result in the silk trade of India in consequence of his devotion, I am sure he will have the gratitude of both the administrators and the people of India.

We are met here to hear Mr. Wardle's paper, and discuss the influences which may have lead to the decline of the silk industry, and if possible to suggest some means of reviving it. From all I have been able to note, I believe that the silk trade of India has gone down because others have gone up owing to their ability to produce better silk, or as good silk for less money. If this be so, it is not surprising that the trade of India should have decreased, and the question now is whether we can make better silk by improving the silk-worm, or in the processes of reeling and weaving. I will not detain you by attempting to discuss this question, which will be better dealt with by Mr. Wardle and others who may follow him. I will only say that the climate of Bengal is inferior for the *Bombyx mori* worm to that of some other parts of India where experiments are now being made; I hope they will be successful, and in the meantime every effort ought to be made towards improving the existing industry of Bengal. Mr. Wardle's observations may lead us to hope that such may be the case."

Paper.

"The object of this Imperial and Royal Commission Collection is to illustrate the Silk Industries of India in a two-fold sense. First, it proposed to show the exact state of Sericulture in India at the present moment, the position which it occupies in the output of the raw product, which may be stated to comprise everything that relates to the cocoon and to raw silk, which is a reeled thread of several cocoons in one. Second, its phase in India, as entirely apart from the breeding of the silk-worm, in the manufacture of the great variety of fabrics of which silk comprises, if not the whole, the most important part. These may be roughly stated to be the Corah silks of Bengal, rudely produced by looms that would raise the smile and wonder of Europeans, the coarse Tussur fabrics woven in the same and other districts, the magnificent kinkhabs of Benares, Ahmedabad and Surat, in which gold and silver form such important decorative features, the plainer silks of Delhi, the delicate and beautiful silks of Thana (a very ancient Christian Settlement), manufactured by a curious and isolated race of weavers, whose story as well as work is so interestingly told and so beautifully illustrated by Mr. Gupte, in his article on the silks of that place, in the Journal of Indian Art, No. 5. In the sixteenth century there were 4000 weavers at Thana, but now there are only seven families with fourteen looms. The rich fabrics of Yeola, situated not very far from Thana, the lovely brocades of Surat, incomparable for living beauty and Arabian grace of design, the ruder though not less interesting silks of Peshawar and the surrounding country, the satins of Azimgarh, Ahmedabad, Surat, Dhrangdhra and Kathiawar, the wonderfully constructed patterns of the Patolo weaving with 'tie and dye' warp and woof, the silks of Behrampur, Cambay, Cutch, Indore, Kathiawar and Bombay, all testify not only to the skill achieved by Indian dyers and weavers during many ages, but also for the fascinations which have held these people spell-bound in the production of their fabrics of mystery and beauty.

"The printed silks of India, too, are by a long way not the least of her interesting decorative work. It is a great pity that anything should have superseded the permanent and striking prints of the old-fashioned pocket-handkerchiefs. I have seen them being printed on the squat tables of the Calcutta printers, with indescribable interest, who use their prettily sculptured little blocks with a dexterity and exactness marvellous to see, requiring no pin points to guide them in their repeats of patterns.

"The Indians, like the Chinese and Japanese, have never cared so much for what in Europe is termed excellence of quality, which means for the most part mechanical regularity in texture and pattern, and although they have had to weave with threads often much varying in regularity and thickness, yet they have down to to-day managed somehow or other, if they have had a pattern to weave, to put, so to speak, soul into it, and to raise it above the commonplace fabrics so often produced in modern Europe.

"For ages, and so long as they continued to use the natural colours which they obtained from their own beautiful dye-stuffs, coupled with an ingenious and traditional taste, they never could go very far wrong in colour. It is now impossible to observe without great regret in passing through India how the love of the modern brilliant European dyes has affected, to a serious degree, the products of the native loom of to-day.

"This is also to be observed as much in another part of silk decoration in India which is as extensive, if not more so, than weaving—viz., the ornamentation of fabrics of cotton, wool, and silk, by embroidering with a silken floss or thread. Embroidery in India is on a great scale, much of it unknown because unseen. The native ladies of Assam, for example, embroider most beautifully, not for sale, but for domestic uses and for marriage and other presents. It is purely carried on as an art, and not for commerce, and it is principally done with a silk that will one day, I feel sure, be in considerable demand in Europe—I mean the silk produced by the worm of the *Antheræa Assama*, or the Muga silk-worm. It was not known to the English until recently that any of this silk was exported. It has often been stated by observers in Assam and India, that it was only produced for home consumption, but when I was in Calcutta making inquiries about this silk, which has engaged my attention now for several years, Mr. E. C. Buck and Mr. H. Z. Darrah, Officiating Director, Department of Agriculture, Assam, discovered, whilst on a tour of inspection and search in the native bazaars of Calcutta, that the embroidered turbans made in Dacca were worked upon a cloth of cotton and Muga silk, wholly embroidered with undyed silk of the same kind. This embroidery, which had been very well known as having been sent down to Calcutta, and largely worn there by the natives, and also exported into Arabia and other parts of Western Asia, but kept, and still kept, in the hands of a very few merchants, was previously thought to be worked with Tussur silk, the fawn-like colour of which it closely resembled.

"The history of Silk is so well known that it does not require from me more than the most passing notice, merely that which is sufficient to show that whilst we are indebted to the sunny East for this industry, it surely travelled westward, although slowly, until we ourselves have long ceased to be the most westwardly country which has claimed a right to and shown a qualification for the possession of a share of working in this wonderful product of nature; it has followed our kinsmen across the Atlantic, until it almost joins hands with its mother country, which gave it birth in ages so remotely past; for, on first leaving China, it found its way through India, Persia, and Asia Minor to Europe; and in the sixth century it attracted the attention of Justinian, who soon after gave it its first and sure start at Constantinople. We find it afterwards localised in Greece for a long period before the twelfth century, when it was known and practised in Sicily. It reached Italy in the thirteenth century, from whence it spread into France and Spain. We are indebted to the Huguenot persecution for its establishment if not its introduction into England, where it has met with varying fortunes for the past 200 years. On the whole it was never so bad, and, as some think, never so unpromising as now.

"We can claim as much right, although not such an ancient one, to the manufacture of silk in England, as any other European country, but we may not say the same of silk growing or sericulture proper. James I. tried his hand at that, but he made the mistake of thinking more the mulberry tree than of the natural history of the silk-worm, for it certainly was of no use to have silk-worms creeping out of their eggs in a climate where the mulberry leaves were not ready to feed them.

"The silk-worm only thrives where the climate is more congenial than it is here. There is no hope or future for the production of cocoons in England, but there is a good hope of a good future for the retention, development and extension of the making of silk yarns and fabrics. Why not? England possesses a splendid silk manufacturing climate, more humid, or rather less dry, than perhaps any other country, good conditions for winding and weaving silk; brain power not less than other nations, and opportunities of study and technical training gradually although slowly developing. It has examples of ancient and modern art of the best, as well as the worst types; and these should give the best incentives to make beautiful work with either the needle or the loom, by lessons of guidance or avoidance.

"Why should we not resume our fair share in the production of all that silk is capable of in applied use and beauty? I am not one who takes a gloomy view of that which seems to some an impossibility or a hopeless effort. There is much, it cannot be denied, in the revival of this pursuit to attract those who wish to realise happiness of occupation and useful aims, although perhaps not to those who are in search of fortune above other considerations, or of speedy reward.

"My paper thus naturally divides itself into the two aspects of the question with which I started: Silk Manufacturing, which we too, in England, can share with our Indian fellow subjects, and Silk Growing, a field for India, in which we cannot hope to share, but which ought to occupy more of our care and countenance than it does.

"The happiness and prosperity of India is, or ought to be, involved in the happiness and prosperity of England, and contrariwise if Imperial Federation has any meaning, and because of our grave and Christian responsibilities there.

"How Lyons cherishes her Gard, Ardeche, Drome and Vaucluse departments, which send to her dyehouses and looms such carefully reared silk! How these silk-worm rearing districts endeavour, by the most careful attention to all the minutiæ of breeding and feeding, to furnish Lyons with silken fibre of such beautiful quality that the cultured taste gives a ready preference to fabrics produced under such conditions; and so with Italy in both ancient and modern days! I am here to ask, why shall it not be so with us, and the beautiful silk paradise of India committed to our charge and responsibility?

"We are, in our sericultural wealth, through having India, more than equal to France, Italy, or any other country in the world, being in some respects better off than even China; for we are not confined to one species of silk nor to two. India can boast of the greatest silk-producing fauna in the world. She has her varieties of Bombycidæ which feed on the mulberry leaf, both wild and domesticated; she has her jungle broods of worms of many sorts, more or less useful or to become useful by-and-bye; her Tussur silk is now an established and well-rooted industry, a few years ago in exports non-existing; her Assamese women are clad in silks of the Eri and Muga worms, of which as yet we know practically nothing; and silken stuffs are handed down from matron to spinster but little the worse for the wear of a generation. Of all these silks and some others I am here to speak to you; and having been sent out to India to learn of them on the spot, it must not surprise if I return much impressed with the necessity devolving upon us to cherish and develop her industries, so that we may have reason to know that our interests there are not wholly selfish, and that her immense and struggling populations may participate in our comforts and success.

"Too little regard has been paid in recent times to Indian raw silk. Its merits have been overlooked and almost forgotten in the incrustations of defects arising from not keeping pace with the more active thought of the West, and its continually developing appliances for amelioration and improvement of quality, as well as from other but minor causes.

"India sends to Europe but very little raw silk now. It was only 457,600 lbs. in 1885. In 1874 it was 2¼ million lbs., and in 1870 2½ million lbs., against an annual export from China to Europe in 1883 of 7 million lbs., and from Japan of 3 million lbs. Just a hundred years ago, Indian silk was so good in quality as to drive out all competitors from the European market, save China and Italy. In 1884 it was so bad that European manufacturers could not buy it; it had gradually lost its reputation from want of quality. But the silk itself, that is, its fibre as it rested in the cocoon, had not altered in these hundred years; the method of manipulation, I mean the reeling of it from its cocoon, had not kept pace with that of other countries; it had in fact fallen back, gone worse, until Indian silk almost found no place in the world's market; and more, even the manufacturing people of India would not buy it. In a few of the Bengal districts, such as Murshidabad and others, it is used for weaving Corah silks, but generally over India it is not to be found. The manufacturers of Poona told me they bought China silk because Bengal silk was of such defective quality. From the Deccan to Calcutta, and from Calcutta to Benares, and on to Peshawar, I found either China or Bokhara silk; and so down Rajputana to Ahmedabad, Baroda, Surat, Yeola, and Thana, everywhere the native silk avoided, and everywhere the same reason given, its want of thread regularity.

"India only wants the application of progressive observation, and the immediate adoption of whatever method the progress of science and mechanical art bring to produce better results in Europe. That there is ample scope may be inferred from the fact that for the ten years ending 1883 we in England have been purchasing manufactured silks from countries in Europe to the extent of about £11,000,000 annually. I extract the following interesting statement from Mr. J. E. O'Conor's 'Review of the Trade of India in 1884-85':—

"'Silk was imported to a much smaller extent than in the last two previous years, only 1,831,702 lbs., which was 17 per cent. less than in 1883-84, though still a very large quantity for a country which is held to be a great silk-producing country. Whatever may be the capacity of the country for producing silk in large quantities, it is clear that while India imports more silk than it exports (the bulk of the exports being, moreover, only waste or chassam), the country must more properly be called an importer and consumer rather than a present producer of silk. Most of the imported silk comes from China and from Siam, *vid* the Straits for Bombay mainly, and Burma in smaller degree. Even Bengal, however, the great silk-producing province, imported 212,349 lbs. of silk last year.'

"Having convinced myself, by lengthened microscopical study of the structure of Bengal and other cocoons, of the wonderful regularity in which the silk-worm deposits its silken thread, I felt that the fault did not lie with the worm, but in the earliest stage of manufacture, that of reeling or unwinding the silk from the cocoon.

"I have had many opportunities of observing silk-reeling in both France and Italy for many years past, and I felt that if the same care and appliances were used in India as in these countries, silk of proper quality could be obtained.

"In that I perfectly succeeded, and in no case in India was it told me that an improved thread was not the result, in every case it was admitted.

"The use of this little tavelette made the difference. It is simplicity itself, but a simplicity which is the result of prolonged experience and skill. It helps better than any other method I know of to unwind the cocoon regularly and straightly. It is the offspring of the skill of an Italian named Consono, and it is known in Italy as the Tavelette Consono, and is more or less the system of reeling in Italy and France; therefore I am not advocating it as any particular or pet form of instrument; still less must it be considered that I have any but a scientific interest in it; I am not its agent or protector; it passes into my *pot-à-feu* of disinterested work in sericulture for India's good alone.

"I will pause here to consider an objection or two. No effort is ever made at improvement without creating objections and objectors. I anticipated these. I had not had my Tussur experience for nothing. For years at first I heard nothing but objections and prejudices against the utilisation of Tussur silk, some of which ceased only when the objectors found they could object no longer.

"I know I may be told that although this system of reeling yields a better thread of raw silk, the cost of reeling is increased, and that with the present competition it will not pay. I will answer this objection in several ways.

"First, the fault, which I do not admit, lies in the competition and not in the machine.

"Second, I am not disposed to admit that it would be wise to sacrifice any improvement that can be made in quality because the value of the raw silk is enhanced thereby. When I was in Bengal the price of good reeled silk was 11*s.* per lb., now it is 14*s.* 6*d.*,* and this is more than the proportionate increase as compared with the rise of prices of other silks, this excess over others

* During the time that this paper was passing through the press, the price increased to 15*s.* 6*d.*, and, owing to the increased demand, the stocks in London are quite exhausted. The new supply will be from the November bund.

being simply the result of improved reeling, whether with the tavelette or not is of no importance to my argument.

"Third, I am certain that if the Italians ceased to use their tavelette and adopted the one I found in use in India, their silks would at once become of less, probably much less, value in the market. They hold their remarkable values, some 6*s.* per lb. over and above Bengal silks, in a great degree to the beautiful way in which they are reeled. In fact it is possible to buy badly reeled Italian silks at 14*s.* 6*d.* per lb. or only a little more.

"Fourth, I was informed in one large Bengal filature that the cost of reeling by this European method would in all probability be little or nothing in excess of the old method as soon as the reelers had familiarised themselves with its use.

"I have received a letter from Mr. Morey, of the well-known Surdah Filature, in which the following remarks occur:—

"'I have reeled some 10/11 deniers and 25/30 deniers by your European method, and highly approve of it. In fact I am going to reel several bales to test the market. You will be pleased to see the 25/30 deniers, which is a very good silk and unwinds beautifully. You will find no foul places in it, and I sincerely hope that it may prove acceptable to the sewing silk manufacturers. I consider that we have never made such good even size and winding throughout the skein as we get now, and to do this of course there is very little waste.'

"One thing has been proved, and I have been permitted to bring it home to the minds of impartial and unprejudiced manufacturers in England and on the Continent, that the Bengal cocoon has not the inherent imperfections which it was thought pertained to it, and that there is a prospect of a greatly enlarged output of silk from Bengal for several important purposes in the silk trade of Europe and America.

"There may be men in the city who may tell us that Bengal silk, to use a familiar expression, is a thing of the past; but I ask, are they manufacturers? Are they sericulturists? The opinions of practical workers of silk, coupled with my own knowledge of its structure, are of more importance to my argument than what may suit the exigencies of the market to gainsay or to uphold. You have heard what I have got to say about the fibre of Bengal silk—the *practical* opinion which has taken thirty-five years to form, and a *scientific* opinion based upon observed facts. I will now give you the opinions of a few manufacturers who have been recently working better reeled Bengal silks.

"First, Sewing Silk.

"Several of the best manufacturers of silks for sewing purposes in Leek have assured me, after full examination and trial, that this silk is peculiarly applicable to their trade.

"Mr. S. Gibson, a Leek manufacturer, writes:

"'I am very pleased with the five bales of Bengal silk I have just bought; they work very freely, almost running from beginning to end of the skein without breaking down, which means winding without loss. The strand is of nice even size, suitable for the Leek trade, free from rough or slubby places, so much so as to render one important process in the manufacturing unnecessary, viz., cleaning.

"'I am working these new Bengals in both the bright and washed state, and they are coming out at about one-half the cost of original Bengals. If this improved reeling is maintained, it must have a serious influence on the China and Canton raws.'

"Mr. S. Goodwin, another silk manufacturer, and President of the Leek Silk Association, writes:—

"'I have worked the sample skein of Bengal raw silk, and am pleased to say that it is simply perfection. As to reeling, I may say that it wound almost without a break from end to end.'

"This silk was reeled by me in Bengal with the Tavelette Consono.

"The silk of the Bengal worm, by its greater elasticity, is much better adapted for sewing silk than any other. I have estimated, in experiments conducted during the last few days, the tension of the bave, or double fibre deposited by the silk-worm, of the Bengal Madrassee or hot weather cocoons, the Bengal Desi or November bund cocoons, and of Italian cocoons. The results are shown in the following table, each figure being the average of numerous determinations, and representing the number of centimetres, which three decimetres of the bave is capable of extending before it breaks:—

	Tension at the end of the cocoon bave which is at the surface of the cocoon immediately beneath the superficial loose fibres or waste.	Tension at the middle of the cocoon bave.	Tension at the end of the cocoon bave which is nearest the telette or inner envelope.
Madrassee Cocoon . .	4·4	6·3	5·6
Desi Cocoon . . .	3·6	5·7	4·8
Italian Cocoon . . .	2·6	4·9	3·3

"Second, Organzine and Tram for weaving.

"Mr. Nicholson, silk manufacturer, Macclesfield, in a letter to me, writes the following:—

"'In answer to your enquiry, I consider that good Surdah raw, when well reeled with plenty of spin upon it, will work well. It will then be a good substitute for Italian, its cheapness being the reason for its use.'

"In addition to this, I may say that Mr. Nicholson is speaking of a Bengal silk that was not reeled by the Italian method. I contend that there would be no greater evenness of thread in the Italian silk over Bengal if the Italian method of reeling were used.

"Messrs. G. Davenport & Co., of Leek, to whom I sent a portion of the 10 to 12 deniers, which I saw reeled by the Tavelette Consono in Bengal, have thrown it into organzine and tram, and send me the following report:—'The slip winds beautifully. Enclosed are samples of two threads tram and a 500 yards skein of organzine. The silk is very clean. We consider it equal to ordinary Italian. It was running for an hour and only broke down once.'

"Now it is necessary to say that, even with every improvement, Bengal silk may not be expected to rival or supersede the *finest* qualities of silk in the market. An objection or two from me may suffice. It will never be as white as China silk, because one is from a yellow cocoon and the other from a white one. It will not boil-off or condition as well as the silks of Italy, China or Japan, because it contains more gum or grès than these, and this brings me to an entomological point, namely, it is probably not of the same species, but of this further on.

"I must guard myself against being thought slack in acknowledging the claims which at least three well-known Bengal firms have on the consideration of European manufacturers for careful reeling. The excellence of the silk produced at Surdah and its allied factories in the District of Rajshahi and other parts of Bengal, that of the Bengal Silk Company's factories, the chief of which is at Berhampur, and that of the well-known firm of Messrs. Louis Payen & Cie., are too well known to need mention. I acknowledge with much pleasure the kindness I received from them all, and they are well deserving of the confidence of all interested in silk.

"But apart from the efficiency of these well-known firms, there remains the much larger native industry, the reeling that is carried on in the numerous villages under the shade of banyan, palm and mango groves. I visited many of these and found the appliances very rough and rude, the reeling by them varying from 10 to 20 cocoons in almost as many seconds.

"In the Rajshahi District alone, out of 97 filatures, 63 are native and the remaining 34 European, eleven to twelve thousand natives being employed in silk reeling in this district alone, 150 square miles of which exist under mulberry cultivation.

"If these village native filatures can be induced to improve their reeling, a largely extended industry lies waiting for them in their own country; for it goes without saying that the resources of China and Bokhara would not be drawn upon if Bengal silks were of the required quality. Many native manufacturers assured me they would much prefer to buy Indian silk if only the quality were good enough. The consumption of silk for native uses alone is enormous. All Hindoos wear it at meals or worship. The Mahomedans wear Mashru, or cloth of cotton-warp and silk weft, the wearing of pure silk fabrics being forbidden by the Koran.

"Since I was in India another silk-reeling machine has been brought to my notice by the Under Secretary of State for India. Its inventor, Mr. Serrell, of New York, claims for it that unskilled labour can be used with its aid in reeling cocoons. This machine is automatic, and by means of a feeble electric current which controls the feed, takes up another cocoon thread when one breaks, so that a new cocoon is added whenever required to keep up the size of the thread. It is stated to do two and a half times as much work as the present system, at a saving of 2*s.* 9½*d.* per lb. in wages, and one reeler can attend to six bussines. Two of the largest silk-reeling firms in France are in treaty with Mr. Serrell for the examination of this remarkable invention, and are willing to adopt it if its expectations are realized. I am very sorry not to have been permitted to have this machine at work in this Exhibition side by side with the other two. Should it really be able to do what Mr. Serrell claims for it, it will be a valuable addition to the Bengal silk industry, and I commend it to those interested.*

"Indian Sericulture has received a new impetus in a scientific direction. When in Calcutta, I suggested to Mr. Buck the desirability of a scientific investigation of the silk-worm being commenced with a view of enquiry into and amelioration of disease, the breeding of the worms, the growth of the mulberry food, the exorbitant rental of the mulberry lands, and all that relates to the production of good cocoons.

"Mr. Buck acceded, and at once set about organising the means without raising objections. He charged the Indian museum at Calcutta with this enquiry, and Mr. Wood-Mason, the assisting superintendent, immediately began it methodically. The first fruits of it are to be seen, I am delighted to state, in the Indian Silk Culture Court, in a series of cases of moths and cocoons of extreme interest. Hitherto the entomologist has alone occupied this field of research, but now the zoologist takes part with him in the study, and we may confidently anticipate that, when biological and morphological attention has been directed to the subject, we shall be in possession of much valuable information, which in my opinion Bengal sericulture has for a long time greatly needed. Thus the absolutely entomological phase merges into the zoological one, and the morphological study of egg, larva and moth becomes an important adjunct to this industrial pursuit which cannot fail to be greatly strengthened thereby. A sericultural laboratory has been constructed at the Indian Museum, Calcutta, and life studies of various species of silk-worms are being daily conducted.

"Already Mr. Wood-Mason has found a disease in the Bengal worm which proves fatal, to the extent of 60 per cent., and which was not previously suspected. Even its existence was by some observers denied.

"In the published catalogue of the collection he has sent over, he states the Desi or indigenous cold weather moth to be *Bombyx fortunatus*, and the Nistry or Madrassee one *Bombyx crœsi*. The Eria silk-worm he calls *Philosamia ricini* instead of *Attacus ricini* as heretofore, and *Antheræa Assama* is changed into *Antheræopsis Assama.*

"It would be wrong if I did not here mention the great service to the entomology of Indian silk rendered by Mr. F. Moore, to whom is accorded by European consent the highest authority on this subject. For many years Europe has been indebted to him for much patient and laborious investigation, and it is to be hoped that his researches will before long be published.

"In the French report of the Lyons Silk Laboratoire for 1885, of which I shall say more shortly, is the drawing of a new Chinese bivoltine wild silk-moth, feeding on the mulberry tree, which Mr. Moore has named *Rondotia Menciana.* This genus is a new one, and is so named by him as a souvenir of the important works on silk of my old friend and former president, Monsieur Rondot. The specific name is to recall to recollection the old Chinese philosopher Mencius.

"It may turn out that the term "Mori" may have more of a generic significance than specific, indicating simply the mulberry feeders. In fact there is some doubt as to whether we really know what *Bombyx mori* means, or whether it exists at all.

"I feel certain there is a great difference between the mulberry-feeding silk-worms of Bengal and the so-called *Bombyx mori* worm of China and Japan, which is the kind now being acclimatized in North India. The extraordinary difference seen in the respective cocoons shows this plainly enough.

"The Bengal worm I consider to be exactly suited to the Bengal climate.

* I have arranged for a practical trial of it at the Society of Arts in September next, to which gentlemen interested in Sericulture will be invited.

"I do not believe they can be acclimatized in Cashmere, the Panjab, the N.W. Provinces, or in Assam, but without doubt the *Bombyx mori* can, and it is the proper worm to try there. Whether they have structural differences sufficient to be *specific* I must leave to entomology and biology to determine. If they are not *specifically* different, there is sufficient divergence to group them as distinct varieties of the Mori, and I repeat they are exactly suited to those parts of Bengal where they are found, and through which for the most part the Ganges flows. I believe also they are indigenous to this part of India.

"It may be useful here to state that the Bengal silk-worm of the rainy and hot weather bund or season is called locally the Nistry-poloo and Madrassee worm; that of the November or cold weather bund or season is called the Desi or Chota-poloo worm; they are designated by Mr. Wood-Mason respectively *Bombyx cræsi* and *Bombyx fortunatus*, though perhaps only provisionally.*

"Concurrently with this branch of enquiry I most strongly advocate the commencement of a structural one, such as has been started in Lyons, and that the fibres of all kinds of cocoons should undergo systematic examination and be recorded. In this way one enquiry will help and strengthen the other. To be of practical and industrial use, both should be conducted simultaneously; for all manufacturers here will, I am sure, agree with me that it is of the first importance that the strength, elasticity and thickness of fibres should be known, as well as their varying states in health, disease and changing climatic conditions.

"The importance of this would soon be seen in the comparison of Bengal silks with those of Cashmere, the North-West Provinces and the Panjab, and valuable information as to climatic conditions obtained.

"From these comparisons with the better known silks of both East and West would be made, and important data established.

"In England we have done nothing which may be considered to be strictly scientific in silk work. Fortunately we are not long behind France, and I hope Mr. Buck will influence the Government of India in this direction. Besides these points, we do not know much yet about the chemical composition of silk and its gum, or about its properties of combining with other substances, whether as dyes, mordants or adulterants. I am at present at work on spectrum examination of dyed silk and dyes, and on chemical methods for the detection of the amount and nature of the weighting matter too often found in combination with silk.

"The whole subject entails too great a sacrifice on individual enthusiasm. It wants lifting into the sphere of methodical and scientific work, and no one can then doubt of its ultimate usefulness to the silk industry and its entourage.

"The importance of this suggestion, which I desire so much to press at this opportune moment, I may well further emphasize by mentioning that this week I have received from the Lyons Chamber of Commerce the report for the year 1885 of the Administrative Commission of the Laboratory for the study of silk lately founded by this Chamber. I shall be glad to show it to anyone after the lecture.

"It contains three plates of silk-worms, their cocoons and moths, two of them new. Amongst other things I am pleased to observe the prominence given to my examinations for this Chamber of Commerce of the strength, elasticity, and thickness of a large number of silk fibres, which, with the results of their own laboratory, occupy no less than thirty-six pages of the report. I only mention this to show the high importance the Chamber attaches to all that relates to fibre construction. The expenses of this laboratory work have not exceeded £200, which was the estimated sum voted.

"Is it not time we did something in this direction? America, without any real sericulture, but with a rapidly extending silk manufacture, boasts of a splendidly conducted Silk Journal, whilst England remains without one. I feel sure the only way to recover a leading position is to commence original research and collective action and effort.

"We have trusted too much to individual enterprise and effort. This, without collective action, will never get us into the front, or even into a respectable position as compared with France, and both the products of England and India will continue to suffer in comparison with those which are perfectioned by the leaven of applied scientific research.

* It is these worms which produce the Bengal raw silk of commerce.

"That there is a great future in store for Sericulture in India is beyond doubt, and if only the same energy were applied as that brought to bear on the production of Indian wheat and Indian tea, the day would not be far distant when the silk centres of Europe would desire the silks of Bengal as much as they now do those of China and Japan.

"That India should take a fair position in the supply of the world's demand for silk is not for Englishman to gainsay. On the contrary, India, with a greatly increasing population, the natural result of a great Continent at peace with itself, and a growing security from depopulation by famine, an improved sanitary administration and more scientific medical enlightenment and instruction, it goes without saying that Englishmen, of all others, should feel the greatest possible interest in the material welfare of India, and especially in everything which tends to the organisation and stimulus of her varied industries, particularly one which is so capable of being so widely spread as Sericulture.

"Tussur silk, as adapted for export, has been, during the last ten years, very slow in taking root in India, and large supplies have had to be obtained from China to meet the gradually growing European demand. At the Paris Exhibition of 1878, Sir Philip Cunliffe-Owen determined to give this silk an opportunity of asserting itself, and afterwards, in the India Museum, he took care that its capabilities and uses should be conspicuously depicted. Not a little of the industrial growth of this useful though wild silk is due to his encouragement, and now in this Exhibition can be seen the fruits of all the care which has been bestowed upon it in various ways, and I am more than pleased to state that India now has an enormous demand.

"A number of gentlemen in India are vieing with each other to improve the methods of reeling, and with singular success. In the cases set apart for Tussur silk are shown results which a few years ago would have been thought to be impossible. Already this silk is capable of far more extended uses than ever before, and although it cannot be expected, on account of its structure and properties, to take the place of the more beautiful silk of the Bombycidæ, it has its uses, and those in a much higher degree than it was ever thought susceptible of.

"Besides the silks already mentioned, there are others, such as the Eria silk, obtained from the *Attacus ricini* silk-worm, which will gradually find extended utility; and great lessons will be learnt by those who care to observe, in these varied exhibits, both in the reeling of the cocoons, the spinning of the waste fibres, and the dyeing and weaving of the silks.

"On both sides of the Ganges, Bengal is capable of producing silk to a vastly extended degree, not only enough for all the requirements of India, which are really very great, both for weaving, embroidery, and minor purposes, but for a greatly increased export trade. Under European careful supervision, the native Indian works beautifully. He cares more for patient manual labour and real handicraft traditional work than he does for progressive thought or invention, and it is not to be wondered at that it has been left to the quicker brain and the desire for development that characterises the people of the West to produce results which find a readier market than his own unaided and unguided efforts can secure.

"I have spoken before of our responsibilities with regard to India, and I am glad to be one of those who feel more for India in those respects which relate to produce which we can buy from her than in those which we have to sell to her.

"To see the exports from India grow is a duty we owe to this beautiful country, and we should be gainers thereby. Such a practical and unselfish regard for her welfare would constitute the strongest bonds of Empire Federation and enable us to look upon our Indian fellow subjects more in the spirit of the now-a-days too rusty Christian precept of loving our neighbours as ourselves, happily embodied and expressed by Mr. Edwin Arnold in his sonnet preface to his 'India Revisited.'"

"India, farewell! I shall not see again
Thy shining shores, thy peoples of the sun,
Gentle, soft mannered, by a kind word won
To such quick kindness! O'er the Arab main
Our flying flag streams back; and backwards stream
My thoughts to those fair open fields I love,
City and village, maidan, jungle, grove,
The temples and the rivers: must it seem

Too great for one man's heart to say it holds
So many many Indian sisters dear,
So many unknown brothers? that it folds
Lakhs of true friends in parting? Nay! but there
Lingers my heart, leave taking; and it roves
From hut to hut whispering, 'he knows, and loves.'
Good bye! Good night! Sweet may your slumbers be,
Gunga! and Kasi! and Saraswati!"

The paper was illustrated by the aid of a dissolving view apparatus, by examples showing the enlarged microscopic appearance on the screen of the fibres mentioned below.

1. Cotton, showing its flat and twisted fibre of cellulose.

2. Flax. The elementary fibres of flax (*Linium usitatissimum*) are cells of pellucid membranes, joined end to end with cane-like joints, between which form thickened vessels with fibrous matter; along with these are seen the woody fibre or tissue consisting of "elongated cells or tubes, with tapering extremities which overlap each other, and by their union longitudinally form the fibres called hemp or flax."

3. Typical wool fibre, showing the imbrications at its joints.

4. Fibres of Chinese wool.

5. Merino wool, American.

6. Fibres of Mohair. (Mohair is the wool of the Angora goat of Asia Minor).

7. Fibres of Alpaca. (Alpaca wool is from a Llama of Peru).

8. Kempy wool fibres.

9. Diseased wool.

10. Typical mulberry silk.

11. Mulberry silk *baves* of unequal diameter. The *bave* is the double thread as deposited in the cocoon by the silk-worm. The *brin* is either of the single threads or fibres composing the *bave*. The *bave* and consequently the *brins* vary in diameter in the same cocoon, being thinner in the first and last portions reeled and thicker in the middle. The two *brins* are often found to be of unequal diameters, and this occurs mostly in the first and last portions reeled from the cocoon.

12. Silk from cocoon of the *Madrassee* or *Nistri poloo* silk-worm of Bengal (*Bombyx cræsi*). Rainy and hot weather bund.

13. Silk from cocoon of the *Desi* or *Chota poloo* silk-worm of Bengal (*Bombyx fortunatus*). November or cold weather bund.

14. Silk from the cocoon of the mulberry-fed silk-worm of China.

15. Silk from the cocoon of the Tussur silk-worm of India (*Antheræa mylitta*).

16. Silk from the cocoon of the Tussur silk-worm of India (*Antheræa mylitta*), showing the form in which the silk is laid in the cocoon by the silk-worm.

17. Tussur silk, dyed black.

18. Silk from the cocoon of the Muga silk-worm (*Antheræa Assama*).

19. Silk from the cocoon of the Eria silk-worm (*Attacus ricini*).

20. Silk of the spider *Nephilengys malabarensis*, Walck, found at the Lake of Bhím Tál, in Kumáun District, North-Western Provinces, by J. F. Duthie, Esq., of the Botanical Gardens, Saharanpur.

DISCUSSION.

Mr. C. W. Marshall said that Mr. Wardle had compared the silk of a hundred years ago with that of the present time, but it must not be forgotten that whereas the former was produced in the time of the monopoly, and was of equal quality, that produced now was made in great part by the natives only, frequently without supervision, and he did not think there was any falling off in the quality of the silk reeled by European firms; indeed he was quite convinced that there was an improvement. Mr. Wardle had spoken of the market in England at the present time and compared it with that at Calcutta when he was there six months ago, and had suggested that the rise in prices which had taken place in that time was in undue proportion to the rise in the value of the silk generally, and which he attributed to the progress made in the reeling during the time he has been away. It was certain that an improvement had taken place, one of the causes being that the Bengal silk now wound better than formerly; ends had diminished by more than three quarters. He quite agreed that much could be done for Bengal silks, but it must be by the assistance of the Government. For instance, with regard to the diseases of the worm, of which the natives at present knew nothing, something could be done by informing them of the results of European research, pointing out the causes of disease and the methods of preventing them. The natives however would never rear cocoons according to European methods, and anything written on that subject would be so much waste paper. To a great extent the remedy lay with gentlemen in England, because those interested must know that the production of Bengal silk had for some time been almost *nil;* the reason for this state of things was that European firms in India had not been making money, in fact they had great difficulty in existing at all. Of course every man must consider his own interests, and the margin of profit being so small they were compelled to go on in a hand-to-mouth fashion. He thought the buyers would be consulting their own interests in the future if, supposing them to be doing any better in the way of profit, they would make over a little of it to the producers now; unless they did this the reelers could not afford to improve the silk, although it could be done immediately if they met with proper support.

Mr. A. Nicholson, J.P., silk manufacturer of Leek, would not like the meeting to separate without one word from the town of Leek to say how gratified they were to see Mr. Wardle coming to the front to assist India and the silk industry generally. When Mr. Nicholson first went into business, a great part of the silk used was from Bengal, but after a time it became so unworkable that manufacturers were completely at their wits end to get sufficient to meet the demands of the trade, when Canton silk came to their rescue and proved their salvation, for they were enabled to quadruple their output. He was glad to say that they now got silk from Bengal which was nice, level, and clean, and which reeled freely with very little waste. It had come too at an opportune time, for the Canton silk had shown marked deterioration during the last year or two. Here was therefore a good opportunity to take advantage of a silk which would keep up the standard, and perhaps even supplant the Chinese silk. But it was not possible to pay a higher price for Indian than Chinese silk, and the reelers must look to recover their position by improving the quality, and so raising the demand. It was certain that more would be used if the quality were maintained equal to what had been received lately. Some of that sent lacked the "bone" of Chinese silk, and was therefore not suitable for some purposes, but there were many other uses to which it could be put if the quality of 25 or 30 deniers mentioned by Mr. Wardle could be relied upon. Silk of that character was last year about 12*s.*, this season it is 14*s.* 6*d.*, while No. 1 Chinese is only 13*s.* This margin of 1*s.* 6*d.* he did not consider too much because the Indian reeled more freely, but it could not be increased without driving manufacturers back to Chinese; although, other matters being equal, preference would of course be given by English silk manufacturers to the productions of their own Empire.

Mr. S. Gibson stated that he had lately bought a quantity of these better reeled Bengal silks, and had found them most satisfactory. They were amongst the best he had ever had in his machines, and he felt that the Chinese and Japanese silks would find in them a most formidable rival.

Mr. Hewitt (late Commissioner of Chotah Nagpur) testified to the very great assistance Mr. Wardle had given him in suggestions for reeling and developing Tussur silk in his district, which was about the size of Ireland, and contained an abundance of this silk. It would result in spreading the use of the silk, and in re-introducing a most valuable industry to the country. Formerly the natives cultivated a small piece of land in the forests, which were now being cleared, and it was necessary to instruct them that the trees could be as well cultivated near their own homes; no doubt Tussur silk would then reach a position similar to that occupied by other silks. He heartily joined in thanking Mr. Wardle for his disinterested labours.

Mr. T. N. Mukharji, as a native of India, thanked Mr. Wardle for his efforts to revive the Bengal silk trade, and believed his countrymen would join in any organized effort to bring this industry into its proper place. He believed there were three obstacles to this, first the deterioration in the quality of the silk, which could be cured by more careful cultivation; second, the faulty reeling, which could be remedied by the introduction of the process described by Mr.

Wardle; the third obstacle was the price, and he thought the cost of production could be lessened, especially in getting rents reduced from the exorbitant charges now made wherever the mulberry tree was under cultivation. Mr. Mukharji assured Mr. Wardle and the English silk manufacturers present that he would on his return to Bengal do all he could to induce the native reelers to improve their methods, and that he was certain they would be quite determined to take such measures to improve the quality as would bring it up to the desired European standard.

Mr. J. J. J. Keswick, of the firm of Messrs. Jardine, Skinner & Co., Calcutta, thought that the attention Mr. Wardle had attracted to the Indian silks, the hints he had given, and the examples he had shown were likely to be productive of very great good, but he looked to the Government taking up the matter, and being prepared to subject sericulture in India to scientific examination. At the present time England was very much behind France and Italy in this matter, and he was glad to think that the visit to India of Mr. Wardle, and the energy of Mr. Buck had induced the Government to take the matter up, for in the present day scientific research was the guide to everything.

Votes of thanks to Mr. Wardle and to Mr. Buck (proposed by Mr. Vincent Robinson) closed the proceedings.

I have not thought it necessary in the foregoing paper to discuss the obstacles which are purely local, such as the high rentals of mulberry land, which are telling seriously on Bengal sericulture.

These will be found fully treated of, as well as suggestions for overcoming them, in my speech at the Silk Conference in Calcutta on the 8th of January last, and since published by the Government, with illustrations of the improved methods of reeling I suggested.

I am happy in this place to acknowledge the assistance I have received from my esteemed friend Mr. Gupte, of Bombay, whilst writing this catalogue. He has in the kindest manner supplied the explanation and description of those fabrics having local meaning and interest, notably those which contain decorative treatment symbolical of the religious faiths of the peoples of India, such as will be found under Nos. 83–91, 99, 240, which are full of interest, as well as others.

The description of the interesting exhibits of Indo-Persian figure weaving is by Mr. G. Bermingham, Leek.

My thanks are due to my assistants, Mr. Rigby, Mr. Greenwood, and my son Arthur.

All the exhibits will be found under the heads of Provinces, with a few exceptions, which have been unavoidable, owing to the arrangement of the show cases.

I am indebted to Monsieur A. Wailly for several species of living larvæ and cocoons, which, with others I brought from India, have proved of high interest to the public in the Silk Culture Court. Monsieur Wailly, in addition to being an entomological student, is an importer and breeder of and dealer in many species of silkworms, their eggs and larvæ, and it may be useful to the numerous enquirers at the office of the Indian Silk Culture Court and to the public if I give his address. It is Tudor Villa, Tudor Road, Norbiton, Surrey.

I am preparing a report on the Exhibits of Colonial Silk, at the wish of H.R.H. the Executive President, which will be published by the Society of Arts, with other industrial reports.

CATALOGUE.

SINGAPUR AND BURMA.

1. Plaid silk on red ground. Colours, white, yellow, orange and black. From Singapur.

2. Plaid silk on red ground. Colours white, yellow, orange and black. This plaid is arranged very thoughtfully in double white squares, intersected by double squares of black, red, and yellow lines—an excellent disposal of lines intersecting at right angles. This design gives the idea of a cross, in colours, inside white squares, as also in No. 1. From Singapur.

3. Silk piece striped with yellow, white, red, green and black bands in the warp, and red in the weft. Upwards of twenty longitudinal stripes per foot. Each stripe has a neat border on each side. From Singapur.

4. Woven silk with the warp in black, red and yellow stripes, and the weft dyed in bars of yellow and black by steeping it first in the yellow dye, and then tying knots, after the manner of the Gujrati "tie-and-dye" method, to protect that tint in some parts, and finally steeping the yarn in the black dye. This is a curious and very interesting pattern. The appearance of monotony and regularity has been avoided by a shadowy yellow interlacing pattern after the style of the Greek fret having been placed in the longitudinal stripes. From Burma.

5. Striped fabric. The warp in white, yellow, green, orange and maroon bands, and the weft dyed by knot-tying in corresponding tints. From Ava, Burma.

6. Longitudinally striped fabric with green, black, yellow, orange and maroon in the weft (black predominating), and corresponding tints in the weft produced by knot-tying. In all these Burma pieces there is an obvious intention to avoid a distinct line or edge. In this fabric it is done by a slight overlapping of colour at the edges of the stripes, and in No. 12 by shading and unevenness of colour. From Burma.

7. Woman's garment. The warp in white, yellow, blue, purple, and red tints, produced by knot-tying and the weft in bands. The border of this piece is in wavy festoons, perhaps conventional cloud weaving as in China and Japan. From Tennaserim, Burma.

8. Silk shawl from Pegu Burma, with red warp, and yellow, white, green, black, blue, and red weft. The process of weaving this fabric is intricate and interesting; it resembles that followed in weaving some carpets, where one unbroken thread of the weft is not laid from one end of the fabric to the other along the entire breadth of the loom, but is drawn aside and substituted at intervals, and used again when required to produce the figures of fish, birds and animals. This is a splendid specimen of the manipulations of the handlooms of the farther East. The red warp and black weft in certain portions of this fabric produce a very pleasing purple. The conventional appearance of scales of fish, some blue and others green, is remarkably interesting. Fishes, turtles, and lotus flowers, stems, buds and leaves, are also seen in tanks or small lakes, and parrots and peacocks occur in other parts of the design, one part of which consists of the section of a vase filled with deep ruby-coloured silk. On the rim of the vase stand two green parrots facing each other and apparently guarding a chalice which is placed in the centre of the vase on the ruby silk. The pattern work is in white, salmon, green, yellow, blue, ruby and violet on a red silk ground. with here and there Chinese-like embellishments of silver thread lines, sparingly introduced. This is no doubt a Buddhistic cloth, but I am sorry I have not been able to find an explanation of its evident symbolism.

9. Woman's garment from British Burma with designs in conventional figures of elephants, lions and geometrical forms with rosettes resembling some of the sculptures on the English runic crosses. The warp in this example is dyed in white yellow, green, and red, while the weft is used in plain alternate bands of red and white. Economic Museum, Calcutta.

MADRAS PRESIDENCY AND TANJORE.

10. Woman's garment in black and yellow plaid. In this plaid the transverse yellow is predominant and is characteristic of the design. From Tanjore, Madras.

11. Striped silk fabric in red, white, black and green bands. Burma.

12. Striped silk piece in yellow, orange and white bands. Burma.

13. Red *sari*, with an interesting pattern woven in gold. Madras.

14. Green and red silk and cotton *sari*. Madras.

15. Woman's garment from Arni, North Arcot, in red plaids and black lines with yellow borders and ends. This fabric has broad yellow borders with white and black lines, and interesting transverse bands of partial wefting.

16. Silk from Madras with dark blue and yellow stripes, dark blue predominating and interspersed with white streaks.

17. Plain Corah orange handkerchief. From Kistna, Madras.

18. Silk dress piece in very neat plaid, white, green and red. Tanjore, Madras.

19. Red silk jacket piece embroidered with flattened gold and silver wire. From Madras.

20. Black silk embroidered with flattened gold and silver wire. Gold flower sprigs and circular spots. Used for bodices. From Madras.

21. Woman's garment in white, yellow, red, and black, the warp being in yellow, black and white bands, and the weft in corresponding tints. In this example the weft when not yellow (which is the colour of the border) is taken back just as it reaches the inner side of the warp threads of the border on both sides, its place in that part being taken by a new and supplementary yellow weft. The broader bands are made to terminate at the inner border in deep comb-like serrations. From Tanjore.

22. Ruby silk loin cloth with very pretty black and white border. From Berhampur, Madras.

23. Black silk shawl with red, green and white border from Bangalore. From Madras.

24. Red silk shawl with white, green and yellow border. From Bangalore.

25. Figured silk scarf. White figured centre, crimson and white border in cones bounded at the top and bottom with a narrow figured border in black and red. From Bangalore, Mysore State.

26. Woman's garment with forcible black and orange plaid with yellow sides and ends. The transverse black bands terminate in a deep triple serration. From Arni, North Arcot.

27. Silk plaid in white, red and purple. From Tanjore, Madras.

28. Red silk piece with narrow yellow lines intercepted by black cross lines and gold spots. This is an example of the simplest and one of the most primitive types of gold brocade. From Tanjore, Madras.

29. Purple satin mushroo with white zigzag bands and yellow and red-dotted lines. A leasing effect. From Madras.

30. Woman's garment, red with yellow zigzag lines and pretty border. From Bangalore, Mysore State.

31. Woman's yellow and red plaid Sari, with red borders and gold ends. This is a remarkably fine Sari, with very conventional flowering trees in the border. From Tanjore, Madras.

32. Silk plaid in white and sea green. From Tanjore, Madras.

33. Silk piece in green, red, white, and black plaid, green predominating. From Tanjore, Madras.

34. Woman's garment in black, red, and maroon squares, and yellow lines tastefully interspersed with gold thread. From Tanjore.

35. Turban with gold borders. From Salem, Madras.

36. Piece in red and white plaid. From Tanjore, Madras.

37. A plaid in white and black, with red marginal lines. From Tanjore, Madras.

38. Silk piece in white and black stripes woven on a red warp. From Kistna, Madras.

39. Petticoat silk, from Madras. Green and black and yellow, and black shot woven on a black warp with white and purple bands across.

40. Silk *soosee* piece, from Madras, with black and yellow stripes, and also yellow and green lines interspersed with streaks of white.

41. Yellow and red plaid woman's garment. From Cuddalore, Madras.

42. Silk bodice piece. A charming gold and red admixture of colour in repetitions of a narrow pretty border pattern. From Mysore.

43. Purple satin trousering with white bands. This fabric has a purple ground with white wavy transverse bars, intentionally very irregular. From Aurangabad, H.H. the Nizam's territory.

44. White satin *mushroo*. A damask in striped patterning. From Deccan, Hyderabad, H.H. the Nizam's territory.

45. Red satin with stripes of gold thread and pale red silk. From Deccan, Hyderabad.

46. Purple satin brocade, in a pattern of small pretty flower sprigs in frequent repetition. From Deccan, Hyderabad.

47. Blue satin on a red warp, giving a violet effect, striped with gold. From Aurangabad, Nizam's territory.

BOMBAY PRESIDENCY.

48. Silk fabric from Bijapur, Bombay. Gold colour on red ground, used for bodices. The design is called "*ruiphul*," or the flowers of the *Calatropis gigantea*, which (made into a wreath) are required for the marriage ceremony of the high caste Hindus.

All other preparations and ceremonials are but the accessories of the most auspicious and essential one of the bride's putting the sacred wreath of the *rui* round the neck of the bridegroom. Hence this flower is considered very auspicious.

I would call attention to this beautiful fabric, which is a typical specimen of Bijapur designing, colouring, and weaving. There are other examples in the Bombay Court. I am indebted to the Bombay Committee for this very interesting example. A very effective appearance is produced by small spots arranged in diamonds between the flowers. To do full justice to this silk, it should be seen as worn in folds, the most effective disposition of most silks.

49. Child's embroidered shirt or *jhabla*, embroidered with white floss, with yellow spots on black satin ground, from Surat, into which it was introduced in early days by the Parsi settlers; it is hence called the "Parsi *Jhabla*" in India. Surat, Bombay.

50. Silk garment woven by the high caste Gujrati brides during part of their marriage ceremony. It is generally a present from her maternal uncle. The figured designs are produced by a very ingenious and intricate process of weaving, requiring great skill, in which the warp and the weft are separately dyed in bands of colours in the manner of the Gujrati with the help of the *bandana* or knot-tying and dyeing. Surat, Bombay. It is called *patolo*.

51. Silk brocade, white and yellow on red ground. From Surat. The design is called *Khapedi ma phul*, or flowers in zigzag lines. Surat, Bombay.

52. Silk brocade, white and yellow on red ground. From Surat, Bombay.

53. Silk brocade *Himro*, white and red on black and yellow stripes. From Surat, Bombay.

54. Silk brocade *Himro*, yellow and red on black ground. From Surat, Bombay.

55. Silk brocade *Himro*, white and yellow on black ground. From Surat, Bombay.

56. Silk brocade *Himro*, white and yellow on red ground. From Surat, Bombay.

57. Silk brocade *Himro*, yellow and white on black ground. From Surat, Bombay.

58. Silk brocade *Himro*, yellow and white on black ground with red spots. From Surat, Bombay.

51 to 58, with 75 & 77 are a typical series of silk brocades of very thick texture woven in Surat. They are of great beauty and interest, and are much worn by rich Arabs who import them. The colourings are of great delicacy and the designs are very characteristic. In Nos. 51, 52, and 56 is shown great taste in the use of red, gold colour and white, not only in their disposition in the design, but in their respective tones, in which exists thorough harmony. The same may be said of Nos. 54, 55, and 75. No. 52 has a minute green spot for the centre of each flower. They are all studies, and I consider them exquisite stuffs.

With regard to the designs of these brocades, I may describe them as of Arab or Mahomedan forms, chiefly geometrical, for even in those of the more floriated treatment there is more or less of geometrical spacing. Probably the severity of this treatment gave way to an enrichment of foliated forms as in No. 56, in which this idea is worked out in an exceedingly beautiful way. Nearly all of them may be considered to be in or from the diaper manner of design so universal in India.

I selected them very carefully from the small stocks in the hands of the manufacturers in Surat, avoiding those dyed with aniline dyes or kindred derivatives, the colourings of which I found utterly destructive of all beauty and art.

The idea of the central portion of the design of No. 54 is taken from the pine apple.

59. Gold, silver, and red silk Kinkhab. A beautiful treatment of gold and silver in double diaper on crimson silk. The geometric flower is spotted in the centre with blue silk. From Surat, Bombay.

60. Gold, silver, and black silk Kinkhab. This is a most effective treatment of gold and silver weaving on black silk ground. The design is called *Chasam phul*, from a flower of that name. The flower, of eight petals, is in gold, and is in the centre of diamond-shaped lattice work, with silver four-petalled smaller flowers at each intersection. In this as in all the kinkhabs the gold and silver are of the purest description. For the method of the manufacture of gold thread for weaving in India see Nos. 275*a*, *b*, *c*, *d*, *e* and *f*. From Surat, Bombay.

61. Gold, silver, and black silk Kinkhab. From Surat. The design is called *Keri velo*, which means "a creeper with mangoe fruits." Surat, Bombay.

62. Silk and cotton *mashru* (satin) in yellow white, and red lines. From Surat, Bombay. This mixed fabric is specially intended for the use of the Mahomedans who are not allowed by their religion to wear cloth made of pure silk.

63. Silk and cotton *mashru* (satin), in yellow and red lines, the yellow predominating. From Surat, Bombay.

64. Silk and cotton *mashru* (satin), in red, yellow, and white stripes, the red predominating. From Surat, Bombay.

65. Silk and cotton *mashru* (satin), in orange and white stripes, orange predominating. From Surat, Bombay.

66. Silk and cotton *mashru* (satin), in yellow, white, and black stripes. From Surat, Bombay.

67. *Khorji*, or gold and silk kinkhab, from Surat, Bombay. The design is called "*pandadana Kothama ath dani*," that is, an eight petaled flower encircled by leaves. This fabric is specially woven to order for the native princes of Siam alone. The border in which the Buddhist bell ornament is used is in gold on black and red silk, and is most interesting and elaborate.

68. Silk "Sarong," with gold and silver brocades, used by the Siamese princes. In this Sarong fine peacocks are woven in gold on each side of the comb ornament characteristic of Sarongs. Green silk is used in the borders. The fabric is dark crimson silk with gold and silver flower-bosses, the gold ones of two sizes, large and small, and the silver ones all small. They are arranged in diagonal order. From Surat, Bombay.

69. Black silk and gold brocade, with gold border for petticoats. The design is called "*Keri ne Chardani*," which means "mangoes and flowers with four petals. The border of gold is masterly and most effective. Surat, Bombay.

70. Embroidered *sari* borders, from Surat, chiefly used by Parsi women, and sometimes by

the Gujerath women. This variety of embroidery is called "*reshami Bharat Kam*," or work done in hand stitches as opposed to the *Karchobi*, or work done on the frame. From Surat, Bombay.

71. Another embroidered *sári* border. From Surat, Bombay.

72. Silk and cotten *mashru* (satin), for trousering, from Surat, Bombay, in red, yellow, and white stripes.

73. Silk and cotton *mashru* (satin), for trousering, from Surat, Bombay, in red, yellow, and white stripes.

74. Green silk and cotton *mashru* (satin), for trousering. From Surat, Bombay.

75. Silk brocade, yellow, white, and red, on black ground. The design is composed of triangular wedge-shaped characters in white, bordered with yellow, with a small red spot in the centre. The base of the triangles is in an upright position. From Surat, Bombay.

76. Silk brocade, white and yellow, on black ground. The design is called "*Char Khonama chár dáni*," or squares with flowers having four petals. The squares of which this design is composed are set diamond-ways in an exceedingly neat diaper, on violet ground.

77. Silk brocade, white, yellow, and blue. This is the same design as 75, but on a red ground. The spots are green. From Surat, Bombay.

78. Satin with cotton back (*mashru*), in green, white, and yellow stripes. From Surat, Bombay.

79. *Patolo*. This fabric is a duplicate of No. 50, and of the same design. It is a bride's garment, given as a present to a bride, generally by her maternal uncle, during the marriage. It is woven with warp and weft, which have been separately tied and dyed by the bandhana process. The dyer takes a small bundle of warp which has been dyed in the lightest colour found on the warp in the finished piece, and draws in pencil upon it some lines at measured distances according to the design to be produced. His wife then ties the silk, along the spaces marked, tightly round with cotton thread, through which the dye will not penetrate. It is then dyed with the next darker colour found upon the warp, and the process is repeated until the darkest colour is reached. The weft is then treated in the same way, in order that, in the loom, when it crosses the warp, each of its colours may exactly come in contact with the same colour in the warp. The little bundles of warp have next to be arranged in the loom by the weaver, who takes the little bundles of weft one at a time, using each in its own place throughout the design. The *Patolo* is a speciality of a province which includes the territory of H.H. the Gáekwár of Baroda, H.H. the Nabob of Bombay, and the silk weaving districts of Ahmedabad, Surat, and Broach. From Surat, Bombay.

79*a*. Odhani, or silk shawl, beautifully embroidered and ornamented with small circular mirrors. From Cutch. An old piece. Lent by Mr. Wardle.

79*b*. Odhani, or silk shawl, beautifully embroidered with silk on cotton, also old, and with mirrors. Lent by Mr. Wardle.

80. Interesting piece of red satin ornamented with minute white *bandana* spots.

81. *Sári* (woman's garment), red, with plaids in black, worn by Mahomedan women with great precision and neatness. Surat, Bombay.

82. Crimson satin with cotton back (*mashru*). An excellently dyed colour. From Surat, Bombay.

82*a*. Small series of lace borders with gold embroidery. Exhibited by Nam Mian B. Shaikh, Surat, Bombay.

83. Kinkhab. Saddle cloth, from Ahmedabad, Bombay. Gold and silver on dark purple ground. The design is worked in with the emblems of war. The peacock, for instance, is the charger of Kártik Swámi the six headed son of Shiva, and the general of the celestial army. The upright lamp between the peacocks again is emblematic of the eternal monument raised in front of every Shaiva temple to commemorate the victory of *Shiva* over the giant Tripur, which is annually illuminated all round, crowned with a blazing light on the top to remind the devotee how the great enemy was burnt after his fall in the battle. Shiva is the god of destruction, and his name "Har Har Mahádevi" was the war cry of the Marathas. The border of this fabric is elaborate, and is a convolution with seven-petalled flowers, four deep, suggestive of Persian form, interspersed with narrow *motichur*, or herring-bone borders. The whole border is on crimson silk, and is in charming contrast with the purple ground of the centre part or filling of this meaningful kinkhab.

84. Kinkhab table cloth in gold and silver, interspersed with purple, green, and red silk, on black back. It is an adaptation of the saddle cloth, No. 85, to the European drawing-room, and it is the same design. The parrot, which is the chief figure in the design of the border, is a favourite bird in India. The design in the body of the fabric is called "*tara mandal*," or constellation of stars. The border, in five-fold bands, is known in India by the name of *popat-vela*, which means "a creeper," with parrots worked in. In this design the parrots' heads are turned back; but in No. 83 the heads are in their natural position. The Hindoos draw their parrots both ways, the Mahomedans only with the heads turned backwards. From Ahmedabad, Bombay.

85. Kinkhab saddle cloth. This is an older example, of the same pattern as No. 84, and belongs to the South Kensington Museum. From Ahmedabad, Bombay.

86. *Ilaicha*, or satin, with yellow and red dotted lines, and yellow and purple streaks, producing a herring-bone effect. This cloth is used only for the *burkhás* or outer garbs, with which the *Parda* or Zenana women cover themselves from head to foot, having only a couple of small holes, covered with gauze, for the eyes.

This is one of the most curiously woven fabrics in the Court. The lines are in narrow vertical stripes of half-an-inch purple and half-an-inch gold colour, so arranged as to produce diagonal bars of purple and the same of gold alternating across the piece. Each narrow band is bordered with alternating white and red dots. From Surat, Bombay.

87. *Ghagro*, or petticoat, dyed black upon crimson ground, the border part being stopped off by knot tying. Surat, Bombay.

88. Kinkhab, from Ahmedabad, Bombay. Gold or red, superior quality. The design is called *mohor bandi*. from its resemblance to the gold *Mohor* coin of India.

89. Kinkhab, from Ahmedabad, Bombay. Gold, on crimson ground, with green dots.

90. Kinkhab, from Ahmedabad, Bombay. Gold, on crimson ground, with green dots.

91. *Bandhana* silk, from Bombay. White and yellow on red. Bandhana means knot tying, and is derived from the Hindu verb *bandhi*, to tie. The female figures, in the circle at the end, represent *gopis*, or the wives of the cow-herds of Krishna, the eighth incarnation of Vishnu. The elephants and the lotus flowers in the border are sacred to Lakshmi, the goddess of wealth, and the wife of Vishnu. This garment is worn by the Vaishnovite women of Gujrat, who are of the Vaishya or merchant class, the worshippers of the goddess of wealth. The introduction of these symbols into the design can be easily traced to the influence of religion on Indian Art. By this bandhana method the white silk fabric is folded into two, four, eight, or sixteen folds, like folding a letter, corresponding with the number of repetitions of the design required. If two "repeats" are wanted, the fabric is folded once; for four "repeats," twice; for eight "repeats," three times, &c. On the uppermost of these folds the design is printed in lines, with blocks, in red ochre mixed with gum arabic, and then knots are tightly tied at intervals along the lines with cotton thread, in such a way that when the fabric enters the dye beck, the dye will not penetrate to the small portion or spot on the cloth around which the thread is tied. The fabric is then "mordanted" with alum and dyed orange. Then another design is printed upon it in the interspaces of the first which remains tied, knots are tied on the second design, and the fabric dyed red. All the knots are then untied, the fabric spread on a small raised platform, and some of the orange spots touched with indigo to make them green. Bandhani is the name of this process in Gujrat, but in Rajputana and Ulwar, where Hindu is spoken, it is Bandháná.

92. Silk *bandhana*, from Gujrat. Yellow and white, on red. An example of the most rudimentary work done by knot tying, and illustrating the process.

93. Silk handkerchief in *bandhana* work. This is an elaborate design, and is somewhat similar to No. 91 with the addition of green spots, some of the yellow spots having been touched with indigo. Cutch, Bombay.

94. Silk plaid, from Thana, Bombay, in white, red, pink, purple, and black, the red in broad bands across the piece.

95. Figured silk dress piece, in black and white. Chaste geometrical design. From Thana, Bombay.

96. Figured silk dress piece in grey and white. Same design as No. 95. From Thana, Bombay.

97. Silk plaid in white, black and red. Excellent disposition of lines and bands. From Thana, Bombay.

98. Small patterns of Thana silks. Exhibited by Mr. Wardle.

99. Embroidered border from Cutch, Bombay. Hung on the chief entrance of the house of the Indian merchant or Bania, the worshipper of the goddess of wealth, Lakshmi, whose lotus-shaped throne is worked in the design interspersed with bits of silvered glass, producing a pleasing effect. The great *divali* holidays of India, which extend over four to six days, begin with the worship of Lakshmi, when the whole of the town is illuminated, and when the merchants and bankers invite their customers, friends, relations, and acquaintances to their shops, specially decorated with pictures and carpets, and copiously lighted to receive them. After the customary worship of the goddess, and the new account books for the year which commences the next morning, *pan supari*, or betel leaves and nuts, sweet meats, nosegays and perfumes are distributed among the guests, who pour in one after another till midnight, visiting the shops they have been invited to honour with their presence. It is on this day that this specimen is tied to the doorway and its old predecessor removed.

100. Green silk embroidered scarf or shawl from Cutch, Bombay, worn by women. This and No. 99 were lent by Tribhurandas, the son of Sir Mangaldas Nathubhai, of Bombay.

101. Silk bodice piece from Poona, Bombay; white with squares in red, dotted lines, and a gold border.

102. Silk and gold loin cloth from Yeola. This fabric is curiously woven, red on one side and yellow on the other, and its border is of gold and very dignified. Silk loin cloths are worn during the performance of religious ceremonies and during meals, when cotton cloth is considered impure. It is called *pitámbar* in Sanskrit as well as in modern languages. The word *pitmánbar* merely means a yellow cloth, and the probability is that this fabric was always yellow when it was first introduced, and although it is now dyed red, green, purple, orange or black, it still retains its first name, derived in all probability from the natural yellow colour of the *Bombyx mori* silk. Vishnu is called "*Pitambar-dhári*" in mythological books. This name literally means "one who bears a yellow cloth."

103. Green satin with diamond-shaped spots of crimson, with yellow and crimson rings,

white, red and yellow spots produced by bandhana work. The border is red, with white and yellow spots. The larger spots in the centre of the piece are diamond shaped, and composed of concentric crimson and yellow quadrangles. From Porebandar, Bombay.

104. Embroidered *chadar*, with green, purple and orange scrolls, surrounding large red discs representing the full moon. From Shikarpur in Sind, Bombay.

105. Black silk with fine gold border. From Poona, Bombay. Used for bodices.

106. *Shela*, scarf with gold brocade. A very interesting and ornate example of gold weaving The ends bearing very broad gold bands denotes that it is for a woman. From Poona, Bombay.

106*a*. Red silk bodice or pitámbar, a loin piece, gold border. Poona, Bombay.

106*b*. The description of No. 102 applies to this, with the exception that 106*b* is yellow on both sides. Border, gold on red silk ground. The joining of red and yellow weft at the border line is interesting, as the yellow weft does not go further across than the yellow centre. Poona, Bombay.

These two examples 106*a*, and 106*b*, were manufactured in Poona, under the supervision of Mr. E. C. Ozanne, Director of Agriculture, Bombay Presidency, to illustrate native dyes and the types of Poona weaving.

107. Bandhana silk. From Cutch, Bombay. Orange and pink dotted zigzag lines on black ground with red spots.

108. Bodice piece. A very interesting example of decoration. The border has a deep crimson ground, with double rows or bars of white flowers between green and gold coloured lines. The middle part of the cloth is another example of spots arranged in diamond shapes enclosed in yellow squares. Belgaum, Bombay.

109. Embroidered petticoat in yellow, white, and green. Shikarpur, Sind, Bombay.

110. Boy's scarf; purple, with red, green, and yellow border. Shikarpur.

111. Silk scarf (*lungi*), in red, white, and green design, with gold thread, crimson ground. Tatta, Sind, Bombay.

PUNJAB.

112. A dress trimming of English-made net embroidered in Delhi. A fine bold scroll design of flowers and stems worked in undyed but cleaned Bokhara silk floss. A characteristic and good example of the Delhi style of embroidery.

113. Yellow and red shot silk. From Delhi, Punjab.

114. A very large piece of silk embroidery. It is a ceiling cover, and is called Hindi Chandani. From Multan, Punjab.

115. Striped silk, in dull red, gold, and white. From the Punjab.

116. Grey silk. From Lahore, Punjab.

117. Purple piece of silk. From Lahore, Punjab.

118. Green silk piece with white lines. From Lahore, Punjab.

119. Orange and red shot silk piece. From Delhi, Punjab.

120. Crimson silk piece with yellow border. From Lahore, Punjab.

121. Dark grey piece of silk. From Lahore.

122. Light green piece of silk, red border. From Lahore.

123. Red piece of silk, yellow border. From Lahore.

124. Orange piece of silk, red border. From Lahore.

125. Blue and yellow shot silk, yellow border. From Lahore.

126. Purple piece of silk. From Lahore

127. Black and orange shot silk piece. The characteristic of these Lahore silk pieces is their stiff and velvety feel. From Lahore.

128. Man's garment, *lungi*, white with red squares. From Jhelum, Punjab.

129. Salmon-coloured piece of silk. From Lahore.

130. Green and red shot silk piece. From Lahore. A very handsome silk.

131. Red silk piece with white vertical lines. From Amritzur, Punjab.

132. Green silk piece with red lines. From Lahore.

133. Gold coloured and red silk piece worked in serrated bands. From Lahore.

134. A fine Cashmere woollen shawl with embroidered borders of undyed cleaned white silk. Elaborately worked.

135. Blue, yellow, and white printed silk. This has an interesting white scroll pattern on a large scale running over the yellow and black design, which is very peculiar and effective. I bought it in Peshawar, but I think it is probably a Bokhara print.

136. *Sozni* or bed-cover embroidered with silk upon cotton. This remarkably fine piece of embroidery was probably worked away from Peshawar, possibly in Bokhara, although such examples are now made there. The bold treatment of masses of reds, blue, green and yellow are effective, and the design generally denotes a breadth of conception not usual in embroidery. Crimson and scarlet are freely introduced side by side.

137. Black, yellow, and white printed silk, similar to No. 135. Peshawar.

138. Embroidered Sozni or large square silk embroidery, with red and gold coloured silk worked upon a Chinese silk patterned fabric. This is probably the finest sozni exhibited. It is a valuable old piece, with beautifully dyed colours. In possession of Her Majesty the

Queen Empress. It has been well reproduced as an illustration, by chromolithography, by Mr. Griggs in the Journal of Indian Art. It is quite possible this came from Bokhara, although Soznis are now being worked at Peshawar, where I found it.

139. Blue, yellow, and white printed silk, like No. 135. From Peshawar.

140. A very handsome green, yellow, red, and purple plaid. From Peshawar.

141. Silk embroidered *Sozni*. Probably a prayer carpet, as it is embroidered only on the sides, with a plain centre. On a very large scale, like No. 136, the description of which will apply to this. From Peshawar.

142. Embroidered sheepskin overcoat. Lent by Mr. Wardle. The sheepskin is richly embroidered all over in a good design, with gold coloured floss. The wool has not been removed, but forms the interior of the coat. It is worn by military Afghans and others, and is called a postin. It was probably embroidered in Kabul, though I bought it in Peshawar.

143. Printed gauze, in crimson, black, green, and yellow. Bought at Peshawar.

NORTH-WESTERN PROVINCES.

144. A cushion-cover, and a pure example of the Kinkhab weaving of Benares in gold on black silk.

145. A similar Cushion Cover to No. 144, but in gold upon white silk.

146. Gold embroidered black silk cap. From Benares.

147. Gold on coral-coloured silk Kinkhab. Mohor pattern. From Benares.

148. A costly coat of silk cloth richly embroidered with gold. From Benares.

149. Kinkhab, in transverse bands on dark blue silk. An elaborate pattern. From Benares.

150. Kinkhab Turban, most richly woven with gold borders and ends, and very beautiful. From Benares.

BENGAL.

151. *Baluchar Sari.* White brocade on purple ground. Berhampur, Bengal.

152. *Baluchar Sari.* Yellow, white and red silk brocade on green ground. Berhampur, Bengal.

153. *Baluchar Sari.* White and red silk brocade on purple ground. Berhampur, Bengal.

154. *Baluchar Sari.* Orange silk brocade on purple ground, with white and red border, and orange, white and green ends. Berhampur, Bengal.

155. *Baluchar Sari.* Figured brocade in white, red, and yellow on purple ground. Berhampur, Bengal.

156. *Baluchar Sari.* White silk brocade on blue ground, with white and red border. Berhampur, Bengal.

157. *Baluchar Sari.* Orange silk brocade on purple ground, with red, orange, green and white borders and ends.

158. *Baluchar Sari.* Red brocade on red ground, with yellow, green and blue border. Berhampur, Bengal.

159. Man's garment, black, with red, yellow and green bands at the ends. Kagra, Bengal.

151 to 159 are good examples of Berhampur weaving in Saris or women's scarfs; borders most elaborate; with figure weaving of both Hindoo and English subjects. The English subjects are both naval and military. The colouring is very rich, and generally too pronounced for European taste. The borders are all interesting.

160. Purple-shot silk piece. Bankura, Bengal.

161. Black, red, blue and white silk plaid. Murshidabad, Bengal.

162. Purple and buff silk plaid. Murshidabad, Bengal.

163. White and black silk plaid. Bhagalpur, Bengal.

164. White and purple silk plaid. Murshidabad, Bengal.

165. Pink, white and black silk plaid. Murshidabad, Bengal.

166. Purple and white silk plaid. Murshidabad, Bengal.

161 to 166 are an interesting variety of well-thought out forms.

BOKHARA.

166*a*. A curious piece of very narrow silk velvet or plush-like fabric, in conventional carpet design, in green, purple, red, yellow, and cream colour. Bokhara.

Pile-cut fabrics are rare in the East. I have not met with any silk velvets in India of native make.

RAJPUTANA.

166*b*. Old Chenille from Jaipur. Twelve pieces, mats, slippers, boxes and tassels. Well worth examination for bright, effective colouring, design and excellence of dyeing in reds, gold colour, black, green, blue and white.

166*c*. Green velvet bag, embroidered with gold. Jaipur.

166*d*. Purple velvet bag, embroidered with silver. Jaipur.

166*e*. Elaborate specimen of "tie-and-dye" or Bandhana work. Lent by Dewan Sree Ram, Prime Minister of Ulwar.

166*f*. Bi-coloured net. A marriage robe, most curiously dyed red on one side and green on the other. Ornamented with crescents of alternate red and green set off in gold thread embroidered bordering. Ulwar.

166*g*. Gujrati bandhana or "tie-and-dye" work, in spots and borders of four colours. Partly tied. Ulwar.

BENGAL.

167. Tussur silk dress, embroidered with cotton. Hugli, Calcutta.

168. *Charkhona* cloth with white and black squares in the design. (*Chár* means four, and *Khona*, angles.) Bhagalpur, Bengal.

NORTH-WESTERN PROVINCES.

169. *Lungi.* Man's garment with green and yellow zigzag lines and red stripes. Azamgarh, North-Western Provinces.

BENGAL.

170. Tussur silk dress, skirt and bodice, embroidered with Tussur silk. Hugli, Calcutta.

NORTH-WESTERN PROVINCES.

171. Yellow silk and cotton cloth. Azamgarh, North-Western Provinces.

BENGAL.

172. Red silk cloth. Kagra, Bengal.

173. Orange silk cloth, with pretty border. Bought at Calcutta, probably made at Giridi.

174. Satin *mashru*, in white, yellow, black and red bands. Bankura, Bengal.

175. Printed silk handkerchief, black and red on orange ground. Bought at Calcutta.

176. Woman's garment. Bankura, Bengal.

NORTH-WESTERN PROVINCES.

177, 177*a*, 178. Lungis. Men's garments. Azamgarh, North-Western Provinces.

BENGAL.

179. Blue printed silk handkerchief. Calcutta.

180. Printed priest cloth worn by the Vaishnavites, red on orange ground with the footprints of Vishnu, the Protector, and the lotus-shaped symbol of the throne of his wife Lakshmi, the Goddess of Wealth. In the square panels is given the following prayer, which is a repetition of the names of Vishnu in his seventh and eighth incarnations *Ram* and *Krishna.*

"*Hare Rám Hare Rám Ram Ram Hare Hare.*"

"*Hare Krishna Hare Krishna Krishna Krishna Hare Hare.*"

Hare, Krishna and Ram are the names of Vishnu, and they are repeated hundreds of times in the course of the day, the rosary being used for counting the number in hundreds. As a rule 108 beads are strung together to allow a sufficient margin for miscalculation through oversight. It is made of the *rudráksha*, *Elæodendron* seeds or of the wood of *tulsi*, the sacred *Ocymum.*

A priest—Brahman—wears this cloth after bathing during the time he performs his ceremonial worship to his gods and says his *sandhia* or sacred prayer. From Calcutta.

181. Woman's garment, woven in pattern. Bankura, Bengal.

182. Printed silk handkerchief. Calcutta.

183. Printed silk handkerchief. Calcutta.

184. Printed silk handkerchief. Calcutta.

185. Printed silk handkerchief, red on orange ground. Calcutta.

186. Printed silk handkerchief, red and black on orange ground. Calcutta.

187. Printed silk handkerchief, red and black on buff ground. Calcutta.

188. Printed silk handkerchief, red and black on orange ground. Calcutta.

189. Printed silk handkerchief, red and black on yellow ground. Calcutta.

190. Printed silk handkerchief, red and black on orange ground. Calcutta.

191. Printed silk handkerchief, red and black on yellow ground. Calcutta.

192. Printed silk handkerchief, red and blue on yellow ground. Calcutta.

193. Printed silk handkerchief, red on orange ground. Calcutta.

194. Printed silk handkerchief, red and black on orange ground. Calcutta.

195. Printed silk handkerchief, red and black on orange ground. Calcutta.

196. Printed silk handkerchief, red and black on buff ground. Calcutta.

197. Case of exhibits showing the improved reeling of Tussur silk and its appliances. By Mr. T. F. Peppé, Arrah, Bengal. Consisting of Tussur cocoons with pedicles, pierced Tussur cocoons, pedicles of Tussur cocoons softened and prepared for carding, Tussur cocoons prepared for reeling, Tussur raw silk, Tussur silk waste, woven Tussur silk fabrics, Tussur silk lace made at Madras, waist bands, fichus, embroidery, yarns for sewing and stocking-knitting, singlets, socks, &c. London Agents—Tongue & Birkbeck, 34 Southampton Buildings, Chancery Lane, London, W.C.

198. Case containing recent improvements in reeling Tussur silk by various firms in India.

a. By Mr. James Cleghorn, Akra, Calcutta.

b. By C. W. Marshall, Esq., Bengal Silk Company, Berhampur, Bengal.

MADRAS.

c. By the Mylitta Silk Mills Company, Madras, working by a new process invented by Messrs. Ernest Donner and Eugene Corsel.

PUNJAB.

d. By Tubhan Mallik Hashmiri. Exhibited by W. Coldstream, B.C.S. Grown and reeled in the Gurdaspur District.

BENGAL.

e. By Messrs. G. Gauthier & Co., Hazaribagh, Bengal.

f. By Messrs. Louis Payen & Co., Berhampur, Bengal.

199. *Charkana bufta.* Cotton and silk. From Fatwa, Bengal.

200. Tussur marriage *sari*, dyed. Fatwa, Bengal.

201. *Ladhia Charkana bufta.* From Fatwa, Bengal.

202. *Charkana bufta.* From Fatwa, Bengal.
203. *Doaria bufta.* From Fatwa, Bengal.
204. *Istrap bufta.* From Fatwa, Bengal.

NEPAL.

205. Rare piece of undyed silk cloth woven from the silk of the cocoons of the Atlas silk-worm, *Attacus Atlas* in the Nepal Terai by the Mechi people. The warp and weft are spun yarns of long staple. Specially manufactured for this Exhibition and sent by Mr. Phelps.

Owing to the oppression the original manufacturers of this cloth have had to undergo, at the hand of the Nepalese Authority, they have been driven from that part of the country bordering on the Mechi, and are now settling on land across the Teesta.

205*a*. Cloth made from the silk of the Atlas silkworm, like No. 205. Dyed red. Nepal Terai.

205*b*. Cloth of the silk of the Atlas silkworm, like Nos. 205 and 205*a*, woven in pattern in red and yellow. Native weaving and dyes. Nepal Terai.

BENGAL.

206. Cloth woven in squares and embroidered in floral design with the silk of the Muga silk-worm, *Antheræa Assama.* Dacca, Bengal.

207. *Dupata* or turban, embroidered at Dacca, Bengal.

ASSAM.

208. Scarf of Muga silk, with nice border in red, white, gold colour and gold thread. Assam.

BENGAL.

209. Muga silk (*Antheræa Assama*) and cotton fabric. *Bufta.* From Dacca, Bengal.

210. *Dupata* or turban, embroidered at Dacca, Bengal.

211. Muga silk (*Antheræa Assama*) embroidery. Dacca, Bengal.

ASSAM.

212. Muga silk (*Antheræa Assama*) gauze scarf. Assam.

BENGAL.

213. Muga silk (*Antheræa Assama*) embroidery, green, red and gold colour. Dacca, Bengal.

MANIPUR.

214. Silk dress with stripes and interesting border in red, black, gold colour and white. Manipur.

215. Woman's dress, interesting border, principally gold colour. Manipur.

216. Silk and cotton dress, very nicely designed border, principally green. Manipur.

Nos. 214, 215 and 216 are three typical designs of this district. They have been lent by Dr. Watt, C.I.E.

BENGAL.

217. Corah silk for handkerchiefs and *Saris*, cleaned and of excellent quality. Made at Berhampur, Bengal.

218. Gown piece of Corah silk. Berhampur, Bengal.

219. Corah silk, "in gum," or not boiled-off or cleaned.

The word "corah" means "raw," and these silks are all woven in the raw or uncleaned state, as the natural golden colour of this piece shows. The creamy white colour of the cleaned pieces is due to the silk being boiled in water, to which *saji mati* has been added, which dissolves the natural gum from the fibre.

220. Plain Corah silk, ordinary quality.

221. Corah silk of good quality, embroidered in "*chicken*" work at Hugli, Calcutta. From Berhampur, Bengal.

222. White silk *Dhoti*. Murshidabad, Bengal.

223. Piece of Corah cloth. Murshidabad, Bengal.

224. Silk handkerchief. Berhampur, Bengal.

225. Silk handkerchief. Berhampur, Bengal.

226. Thick Tussur silk cloth. Murshidabad, Bengal.

228. Tussur silk *Dhoti*. Giridi.

229 and **230.** Tussur silk fabrics. Bankura, Bengal.

231. Tussur silk fabric. Giridi.

232. Yellow chuddur. Giridi.

233. Dyed Tussur silk fabric. Giridi.

234. Tussur silk dress embroidered with Tussur silk. Hugli, Calcutta.

ASSAM.

235. Silk fabric with deep border woven in stripes, purple centre. Sibgunge, Assam.

236. Silk fabric. Interesting colouring, red and dark blue, with elephant woven in border. Very singular weaving. Sibgunge, Assam.

237. Silk fabric, red centre and gold-coloured border, primitive. Sibgunge, Assam.

MISCELLANEOUS.

238. Leek Tussur embroidery, worked by a young Hindoo widow in the Wesleyan Training Institution, Royapettah, Madras. Lent by J. Wilcox Edge, Esq., Burslem.

239. Handloom, such as has been used for centuries at Benares, in which is woven the sacred ribbon exhibited below it. Lent by Mr. Wardle. This small handloom is used by probably not more than three weavers, who sit in niches in the streets of Benares near the temples weaving the sacred ribbon exhibited below. This ingenious and very curious little loom evidently foreshadowed the application of cards in the Jacquard loom. In this case the cards are little squares of horn, each having four perforations through which four of the warp threads pass and are guided at will to help in forming the intricate pattern. There are in all forty-six horns, indicating 184 warp threads.

Colours of warp green, white and crimson.

Colour of weft crimson, which is knocked up by a small knife-shaped hand-beam.

Length of loom . .	4 ft. 4 in.
Height „ . .	9 in.
Breadth „ .	2½ in.

It is made of wood, and consists only of a base of a carved piece of teak wood, having an upright peg at each end. round which the warp is wound at one end and the woven tape attached at the other.

The only harness is a wooden comb, six inches in length, having 72 teeth, which holds the warp threads sufficiently apart for the horns which are 1¾ in. square to be worked.

240. Sacred Ribbon or Tape woven at Benares in the little loom exhibited above it. It contains, in ornamental borders, twenty-nine names of Vishnu in Sanscrit. They are, when rendered into English characters, as follows:

1. Shri Krishnáyanamha
   Shri Gopijanvallabháyanamha
2. Shri Krishna sharol namaha
   Shri Acháryaji namaha
   Prabhu shri Gosáiji
3. Shri Vithal náthji
   Shri Girdharji
   Shri Govindji
4. Shri Bálkrishnaji
   Shri Gokulnáthji
   Shri Raghunáthji
5. Shri Yadunáthji
   Shri Ghannashyámji
   Shri Dámodarji
6. Shri Govardhananáthji
   Shri Navanita-priyaji
   Shri Madan Mohanji
7. Shri Vithaleshvarayaji
   Shri Dvárkánáthji
   Shri Gokulnáthji
8. Shri Garudhvajaji
   Shri Gokul chandramáji
   Shri Mathuránáthji

   Shri Natavarji
   Shri Bálkrishnaji
   Shri Gokulodhavji

10. Shri Baladevji
    Shri Náthji
    Shri Jamunáji

All these names of Vishnu are written in Sanscrit, some of them having Gujrati terminations. *Shri* means "the beautiful."

Another tape below is intended for Shiva worshippers, and contains only a repetition of *Om Namha Shiváya*, "I bow to Shiva."

These tapes are worn at worship in the Hindoo temples, and at home. Lent by Mr. Wardle.

241. Silk formed by the spider *Nephilengys malabarensis*, Walck., found at the Lake of Bhím Tál, in Kumáun District, North-Western Provinces, by J. F. Duthie, Esq., of the Botanical Gardens, Saharanpur, showing the way in which it was collected on sticks.

242. The same spider-silk as the preceding No., but removed from the sticks. (For information on this silk, see my report of "Researches on Silk Fibre," published by the Government of India, July 9, 1885.)

243. Larvæ, in alcohol, of *Bombyx mori*. *B. fortunatus*, Wood Mason. Government of India. (Pl. III., Fig. 3.)

244. Larvæ of *Bombyx mori* of larger size than No. 243. Government of India.

245. Larvæ of *Antheræa mylitta*, or Tussur silkworms, collected by myself from he *Terminalia tomentosa*, or Saj tree, in the garden of the Rev. A. Campbell, situated in the forest jungles of Manbhum, at Pokhuria, Gobindpur, Bengal. In this jungle district Tussur cocoons are bred and collected by the Santal and Kohl tribes. These caterpillars, when living, were about five inches long, and were of the beautiful pale green colour of the leaves of the Saj tree, and it was consequently very difficult to find them. (Pl. IV.)

246. Larvæ of *Attacus ricini*, which make the Eri silk of Assam. They feed on the leaves of the *Ricinus communis*, or castor-oil plant.

247. Larvæ and Chrysalides of *Cricula trifenestrata*. They feed and make their cocoons in colonies or cluster-bunches, and are found in some parts of Chutia Nagpur in considerable quantity, hanging from the branches of the trees in clusters or bunches like grapes.

248. Silk and cocoons of the mulberry-fed silkworm from Cyprus. These cocoons are remarkably large and the silk good.

249. Sewing silks made from Bengal silk and dyed with Indian dyes. Manufactured from Bengal raw silk by Mr. S. Gibson, Jr., Leek, as is also No. 250.

250. Boiled-off Sewing Silks, showing the excellent quality which the improved reeling of Bengal silk will make.

251. White Silk Handkerchief made entirely with Bengal silk of the improved reeling. This and Nos. 252 to 257 were manufactured by Mr. J. O. Nicholson, Macclesfield.

252. Silk Handkerchief made with well reeled Bengal silk weft, and China silk warp, dyed.

253. Tram made of Bengal silk of the improved reeling. Now in the market.

254. Organzine made of Bengal silk of the improved reeling. Now in the market.

255. Laturi, with boiled Eria cocoons, showing the method of spinning Eria silk in Assam.

256. Takuri, with Eria-spun thread from the Laturi.

257. Laturi, large size, and Takuri, such as are used in spinning Eria silk thread in Assam.

258. Laturi, as used at Ranchi for spinning Tussur silk cord.

259. Bengal Raw Silk reeled with the Tavelette Consono in India. Very fine quality.

260. Tram made of similar raw silk to the preceding No. Thrown by Messrs. George Davenport & Co., Leek.

261. Organzine made of similar raw silk to No. 259.

262. Bara-poloo Silk, 23 deniers. A white univoltine silk, superior either to the Chhotopoloo or the Nistry silks. Unfortunately it is dying out of Bengal.

DECCAN.

263. *Chakmak*, made of bamboo, with caps of portions of Tussur cocoons, used in obtaining a light for smoking. Deccan.

264. Tussur cocoons with pedicles showing

the manner in which the larvæ attach their cocoons to the branches of the trees on which they feed, when they begin to form them.

265. Tussur cocoons softened and prepared for reeling.

266. Tussur cocoons of larvæ which feed on the wild plum tree, *Zizyphus jujuba*. These cocoons are much whiter in colour than those which feed on the Terminalias.

267. Cocoons of the Eria silkworm in masses or attached bunches. Nowgong, Assam.

268. Embroidery floss silk, such as is used in Calcutta, Native dyes.

269. The quantities or lengths of raw silk obtained from various cocoons.

(*a*) Italian White Cocoons, old Italian breed, 725 metres; (*b*) Italian Yellow Cocoons, old Italian breed, 725 metres; (*c*) Bengal Cocoons, Desi worm, 200 metres, very good; (*d*) Bengal Cocoons, Desi worm, 160 metres.

AIDS TO SERICULTURAL STUDY.

270. Aids to sericultural study, consisting of cocoons of thirty-eight varieties of the mulberry-fed silkworm, *Bombyx mori*, other than those of Bengal.

These cocoons are from Mr. Wardle's private collection, and are exhibited here for the purpose of study and comparison with the cocoons of India.

a. Japanese cocoons, Aka-Tiku.
b. " " Ao-Jiku.
c. " " Ko-ischi-Maru.
d. " " Mata-Mukashi.
e. " " Oui-tchi-Zimi.
f. " " Timé San.
g. " " Kin Sei.
h. " " Ki mai san.
i. " " Nikiva San.
j. " " Shi-Kiva-San.
n. Cocoons from Kalamata, Greece.
p. French cocoons, large variety.
q. " " Bione variety.
r. " " Vallerangue.
s. " " des Cevennes.
t. " " Alpes Maritimes.
u. " " de Provence.
v. " " de Sina.
w. Italian cocoons, Sardinia.
x. " " Tuscany.
y. " " Pestellini.
z. Bulgarian cocoons, Roustchouk.
aa. Cocoons from Andros, Greece, Vitaliste.
bb. " " Bagdad, Turkey in Asia.
cc. White cocoons of Corea, raised in France.
ee. " " from Cochin China.
ff. Yellow cocoons, Piedmont.
gg. " " "
hh. White Brianza cocoons, Lombardy.
ii. Green cocoons.
jj. Italian cocoons injured by Camelo beetle.
kk. White Italian cocoons from Japanese eggs.
ll. Yellow cocoons, Milan.
mm. Green Italian cocoons from Japanese eggs.
nn. White cocoons, Milan.
oo. Yellow cocoons, Brianza, Lombardy.

271. Silk; Corah, *i.e.*, cloth woven "in-gum" cloth, made from Madrassee cocoons, Sibgunge.

272. Silk; Corah, *i.e.*, ungummed cloth, made from *Desi* cocoons, Sibgunge.

272 *a*. Raw Silk and Cocoons from the "Lister Grant" Dehra Dun, North-Western Provinces, from French eggs. *See* also Cocoons, 382*a*.

273. Banjetty silk, 16 to 20 deniers, Bengal Silk Company, Berhampur.

Banjetty is the name of one of the factories or filatures of this company.

274. "Pat" silk, *Bombyx textor*, Assam.

275. Stages in the manufacture of Indian gold thread for embroidery and weaving. Sent by E. C. Ozanne, Esq., Director of Agriculture, Bombay Presidency.

a. Silver bar, covered with gold leaf.
b. Thin wire drawn out from the gold leaf covered bar.
c. Finer drawn wire of gold on silver.
d. This is the finer wire flattened by the hammer.
e. China silk thread dyed orange to be covered with the gold and silver wire.
f. Gold thread, consisting of *d* and *e* wound together, for weaving, and embroidery. Its perfected state.

276. Phalki or reel used in India for winding raw silk. (Pl. XLII.)

277. Silk hand reel from Madras, upon which the raw silk is wound from the Phalki. (Pl. XLII.)

278. Tavelette-Consono, as generally used in reeling silk in Italy. (Pl. I.)

This is the tavelette now coming into use in some of the filatures in Bengal, and by which a great improvement in the reeling of Bengal cocoons is effected.

279. Tavelette, showing the method of reeling in the European filatures in Bengal up to the present time.

282. Eleven *kharita* bags, some with seals, obtained from the Foreign Office by Major-General Sir John Watson, V.C., K.C.B.

"*Kharita*" means a letter from a prince, and these bags are used as envelopes by the princes of India. They are beautifully woven in silk, gold and silver.

European Utilizations of Tussur Silk.

283 to 288. Undyed Tussur silk damask, patterned, made from Tussur silk of improved reeling. English and French. Government of India.

289. Undyed Tussur silk damask (with red and blue spots of mulberry silk) made from Tussur silk of improved reeling. Government of India.

290. Tassel and cord made of Tussur silk.

291. Twelve pom-poms of Tussur silk, for millinery purposes. Made by Messrs. Yeomans & Son, London.

292. A facsimile reproduction of a border of very beautiful Italian Florentine embroidery, in Tussur silk floss on Tussur silk cloth, by the

Leek Embroidery Society, from an old piece found in Florence, and lent to this society by Professor Church, of very beautiful design and harmony of colour.

The methods by which the colours of the original were dyed have been re-discovered by Mr. Wardle and applied to the Tussur silk reproduction.

293. Tussur silk fringe in different shades of blue and white.

294. Tussur silk fringe in various colours.

294*a*. Toy chenille dog made of Tussur silk.

294*b*. Toy chenille monkey made of Tussur silk and holding Tussur cocoon.

295. Tussur silk chenille work for upholstery.

295*a*. Tussur patterned cloth, partly dyed.

296. Tussur silk patterned cloth woven in Lyons.

297 to 304. Tussur silk fichus, undyed.

305. Tussur silk fringe, undyed.

306. Tussur silk cloth, partly printed and partly painted by hand.

Leek Embroidery. (Pl. XXXIX.)

307. Case of twenty-two pieces of native woven Tussur silk embroidered upon with Tussur embroidery silk manufactured in England from Indian Tussur cocoons, and dyed by Mr. Wardle with Indian vegetable dyes in permanent colours. Worked and lent by the Leek Embroidery Society, Leek, directed by Mrs. Wardle. 307*a* to 307*t* as follows:—

307*a*. A large design consisting chiefly of birds, pomegranates, lotus flowers and gracefully treated stems, adapted from one of the beautiful fresco borders in the Ajanta caves, Ajanta or Indhyádri hills, Nizam's Dominions, by C. Purdon Clarke, Esq., C.I.E. This pattern is known as the "Ajanta" pattern. It is here worked in reds, greens and greys of lowish tone, with a free use of gold thread. The colouring of this and the whole of these specimens is by Mrs. Wardle.

307*b*. A Damascus design adapted by C. Purdon Clarke, Esq., C.I.E., and coloured by Mrs. Wardle.

307*c*. A Floral border of English design.

307*d*. A Floral border " "

307*e*. A Floral border, Indian design.

307*f*. " " " "

307*g*. A Floral border, with effective herring-bone work, Indian design.

307*h*. A Floral border, Indian design.

307*i*. " " " "

307*j*. " " " "

307*k*. " " " "

307*l*. An Indian design of flowers and interlacing stems in pale shades with gold thread.

307*m*. An old Burgundian design in reds and greens.

307*n*. A Cushion worked in the same design as 307*m* in greens and blues.

307*o*. Satin Bag worked in pale colours.

307*p*. Plush Bag worked in dark colours.

307*q*. Trimmings for a dress worked in pale shades and untarnishable gold thread.

307*r*. Trimmings for a dress worked in deeper shades.

307*s*. Trimmings for a dress worked in gold colour, yellows and gold thread.

307*t*. A Pulpit Hanging in green, blue and gold.

308. "Seal cloth" made in Yorkshire from Tussur silk waste with insertions of white hairs added amongst it. Government of India.

309. Tussur silk cloth, figure woven, undyed. Government of India.

310. "Seal cloth" made in Yorkshire from Tussur silk waste. Government of India.

311. Tussur silk, striped fabric. Government of India.

312. Figured silk fabric, shot with Muga (*Antheræa Assama*) silk of Assam. First Muga silk of English manufacture. Woven in Leek. Lent by Mr. Wardle.

313 and 314. Tussur silk striped fabrics. Government of India.

Sikh Embroideries, etc.

315 to 320. Embroidered petticoats made and worn in Amritsar, Punjab, and the neighbouring villages. Government of India.

321. Embroidered phulcari petticoat made and worn in Amritsar and the neighbouring villages. Government of India.

322 to 325. Embroidered petticoats made and worn in Amritsar and the neighbouring villages. Government of India.

326. Very fine scarlet and yellow phulcari on black ground with very deep border, made and worn in Amritsar and the neighbouring villages. Lent by Sir George Birdwood, C.S.I., LL.D.

327 and 328. Embroidered phulcari petticoat made and worn in Amritsar and the neighbouring villages. Government of India.

329, 329*a* to 329*f*. Very interesting and ancient Indo-Persian figure weaving. 329 Exhibited by South Kensington Museum, Indian section.

These Indo-Persian fabrics are woven in the following manner:—

A main warp forms the black satin ground and rises to allow the weft to come to the face to make the pattern.

A binder warp works simply to fasten the weft figure on the face, and the coloured weft on the back of the cloth. This is almost the oldest method of figure weaving, and not confined to any particular country. It occurs in Japanese and Chinese work, and in many of the Palermitan and Lucca fabrics, particularly the gold brocades, and is also most used at the present day.

These fabrics resemble those which the French call Lampas, and which in England are wrongly termed Brocatelle.

They are not brocades, but are made by the process called lancé, the colours not being put in by independent shuttles, but shot straight from side to side, following each other more or less in bars.

The short and exact repeat of the pattern shows that the fabrics have been made in a modification of the draw loom.

They are all silk, very heavy and expensive to make.

Probably the cloth before being cut was 18 in. to 21 in. wide.

330. Phulcari, embroidered with orange silk on black cotton ground, ornamented with circular pieces of looking-glass, 5 inches apart. Government of India.

331. A good example of a typical phulcari, with most beautiful border in excellent colouring of red and white flowers and gold coloured leaves and stems. The etymology of phulcari is phul, a flower, and cari, embroidery or work. Lent by Mr. Wardle.

332, 332*a* to 350. Embroidered phulcaries made and worn in Amritsar and the neighbouring villages. Government of India.

351. Piece of yellow silk with white spots, effected by the tie and dye or Bandana process.

INDUSTRIAL AND RAW PRODUCTS COLLECTION.
Government of India.

352. Cocoons of the Desi or Chota poloo silkworm of Bengal, *Bombyx fortunatus.* November or cold weather bund. Ovened, i.e., artificially dried. Surdah, Rajshahi, Bengal. Government of India. (See Plate II., Fig. 4.)

353. Cocoons of the Desi or Chota poloo silkworm of Bengal, *Bombyx fortunatus.* November or cold weather bund. Unovened, i.e., sun dried. Surdah, Rajshahi, Bengal. Government of India.

354. Cocoons of the Desi or Chota poloo silkworm of Bengal, *Bombyx fortunatus.* November or cold weather bund. Pierced by the exit of the moth. Surdah, Rajshahi, Bengal. Government of India.

355. Cocoons of the Madrassee or Nistri poloo silkworm of Bengal, *Bombyx cræsi.* Rainy and hot weather bund. Unovened, i.e., sun dried. Surdah, Rajshahi, Bengal. Government of India.

356. Cocoons of the Madrassee or Nistri poloo silkworm of Bengal, *Bombyx cræsi.* Rainy and hot weather bund. Ovened or artificially dried. Surdah, Rajshahi, Bengal. Government of India.

357. Cocoons of the Desi or Chota poloo silkworm of Bengal, *Bombyx fortunatus.* November or cold weather bund. Pierced by the exit of the moth and fly-blown by a dipterous parasite. Surdah, Rajshahi, Bengal. Government of India.

358. Cocoons of the Madrassee or Nistri poloo silkworm of Bengal, *Bombyx cræsi.* Rainy and hot weather bund. Ovened, i.e. artificially dried. Multivoltine, about eight crops a year. Surdah, Rajshahi, Bengal.

359. Hybrid between the cocoons of the Desi or Chota poloo silkworm of Bengal, *Bombyx fortunatus.* November or cold weather bund, and the cocoons of the Madrassee or Mistri poloo silkworm of Bengal, *Bombyx cræsi.* Rainy and hot weather bund. Surdah, Rajshahi, Bengal. Government of India.

360. Cocoons of the mulberry-fed silkworm. Starved or else spun in too cold weather. They contain only a small quantity of silk. Galampore, Bengal. Government of India.

361. "Ordinary" cocoons of the mulberry-fed silkworm. Berhampur, Bengal. Government of India.

362. "Prize" cocoons of the mulberry-fed silkworm. Berhampur, Bengal. Government of India.

363. Cocoons of the mulberry-fed silkworm. Maldah, Bengal. Government of India.

364. Cocoons of the mulberry-fed silkworm. Rangpur, Bengal. Government of India.

365. Cocoons of the mulberry-fed silkworm. Bogra District, Bengal. Government of India.

366. Cocoons of the mulberry-fed silkworm. Pierced by the exit of the moth. Bogra District, Bengal. Government of India.

367. Cocoons of the mulberry-fed silkworm. Pierced by the exit of the moth. Serampur, Bengal. Government of India.

368. Cocoons of the mulberry-fed silkworm, Unovened, i.e. sun-dried. Serampur, Bengal. Government of India.

369. White cocoons of the mulberry-fed silkworm, "Boropolu Morahkoah." Murshidabad, Bengal. Government of India.

370. White cocoons of the mulberry-fed silkworm, "Boropolu kachi koah." Murshidabad, Bengal. Government of India.

371. White cocoons of the mulberry-fed silkworm, "Boropolur lat." Pierced by the exit of the moth. Murshidabad, Bengal. Government of India.

372. Red cocoons of the mulberry-fed silkworm, "Chhotopolur lat." Pierced by the exit of the moth. Murshidabad, Bengal. Government of India.

373. Red cocoons of the mulberry-fed silkworm, "Chhotopolu Morah koah." Murshidabad, Bengal. Government of India.

374. Red cocoons of the mulberry-fed silkworm, "Chhotopolu kachi koah." Murshidabad, Bengal. Government of India.

375. Cocoons of the mulberry-fed silkworm. Pierced by the exit of the moth. Birbhum, Bengal. Government of India.

376. Cocoons of the mulberry-fed silkworm. Birbhum, Bengal. Government of India.

377. Cocoons (*Kóa*) of the mulberry-fed silkworm which obtained a bronze medal at the Doom ran Exhibition 1885. Dinapur, Bengal. Government of India.

378. Cocoons of the mulberry-fed silkworm. Gaya, Bengal. Government of India.

379. Cocoons of the mulberry-fed silkworm, reared in the Sudder subdivision, Howrah, Bengal. Government of India.

380. Cocoons of the mulberry-fed silkworm. Dhantala, Bengal. Government of India.

381. Cocoons of the mulberry-fed silkworm. Prescribed in medicine at Cawnpore as an Aphrodisiac or nervine tonic. Government of India.

381*a*. Cocoons of the mulberry-fed silkworm. Prescribed in medicine at Cawnpore as an Aphrodisiac or nervine tonic, from Bombay, sent by Mr. F C. Ozanne.

382. White and yellow cocoons of the mulberry-fed silkworm. reared from Japanese eggs. Lahore, Punjab. Government of India.

382*a*. Buff Cocoons of the *Bombyx mori*, from French eggs, reared at the "Lister Grant" Dehra Dun. North-Western Provinces.

383. Cocoons of the mulberry-fed silkworm. First crop, raised in February–March, 1884. Eggs received from Dehra Dun. Saharanpur, N.W. Provinces. Government of India.

384. Cocoons of the mulberry-fed silkworm. Second crop. Raised March–April, 1884. Seed raised in Saharanpur, N. W. Provinces, from crop of February–March, 1884. Saharanpur, N. W. Provinces. Government of India.

385. Cocoons of the mulberry-fed silkworm. Third crop. Raised April–May 1884. Seed raised in Saharanpur, N.W. Provinces from crop of March–April 1884. Saharanpur, N. W. Provinces. Government of India.

386. Cocoons of the mulberry-fed silkworm. Dehra Dun, N. W. Provinces. Government of India.

387. Cocoons of the mulberry-fed silkworm, *Bombyx meridionalis*. Coimbatore Jail, Madras. Government of India.

388. Yellow-buff cocoons of the mulberry-fed silkworm, *Bombyx meridionalis*. Cuddapah, Madras. Government of India. I think these Cocoons were wrongly labelled at Madras, and that they are *Bombyx mori*.

389. Cocoons of the mulberry-fed silkworm. Pierced by the exit of the moth. Reared on the Retreat Estate, Yerkad, Madras, from seed received through the Government from Dehra Dun, N. W. Provinces. Exhibited by Deputy Surg.-Genl. J. Shortt, M.D., F.L.S., F.Z.S., Yerkad, Shevaroys.

390. Cocoons of the mulberry-fed silkworm. Pierced by the exit of the moth. Reared on the Retreat Estate, Yerkad, Madras, from Mysore silkworms. Exhibited by Deputy Surg.-Gen. J. Shortt, M.D., F.L.S., F.Z.S., Yerkad, Shevaroys.

391. Cocoons of the mulberry-fed silkworm. Kanara, Madras. Government of India.

392. White and yellow cocoons of the mulberry-fed silkworm. Pierced by the exit of the moth. Burma. Government of India.

392*a*. Green cocoons of *Bombyx mori*. From North Matale, Ceylon. Fifteen hundred feet above the sea level. This part of Ceylon has a rainfall of about 90 inches, and the average temperature is about 75° F. The eggs from which these cocoons are obtained were introduced into Ceylon about two years ago, and come from Japan. Exhibited by the Hon. J. L. Shand, Ceylon Court.

392*b*. White cocoons of *Bombyx mori*. From North Matale, Ceylon. Exhibited by the Hon. J. L. Shand, Ceylon Court.

393. Cocoons of the mulberry-fed silkworm. South Australia. Exhibited by Sir Samuel Davenport.

394. Tussur silk cocoons, "*Muga*." Singbhum, Bengal. Government of India. (Pl. V.)

395. Tussur silk cocoons, "*Daba*." Singbhum, Bengal. Government of India.

396. Tussur silk cocoons, "*Laria*." Singbhum, Bengal. Government of India.

397. Tussur silk cocoons, "*Bogai*." Singbhum, Bengal. Government of India.

398. Pierced Tussur silk cocoons, "*Bugoy*." Singbhum, Bengal. Government of India.

399. Pierced Tussur silk cocoons, "*Daba*." Chaibasa, Singbhum District, Bengal. Government of India.

400. Pierced Tussur silk cocoons, "*Laria*." Chaibasa, Singbhum District, Bengal. Government of India.

401. Tussur silk cocoons. Ranchi, Chutia Nagpur, Bengal. Government of India.

402. Tussur silk cocoons. Santal jungles, Manbhum, Bengal. Government of India.

403. Pierced Tussur silk cocoons. Santal jungles, Manbuhm, Bengal. Government of India.

404. Tussur silk cocoons. Birbhum, Bengal. Government of India.

405. Tussur silk cocoons. Bardwan, Bengal. Government of India.

406. Pierced Tussur silk cocoons. Bardwan, Bengal. Government of India.

407. Tussur silk cocoons. Darjiling, Bengal. Government of India.

408. Tussur silk cocoons. Ganjam District, Madras. Government of India.

409. Tussur silk cocoons. North Arcot, Madras. Government of India.

410. Tussur silk cocoons. Dudhi, Madras. Government of India.

411. Pierced Tussur silk cocoons. Retreat Estate, Yerkad, Madras. Government of India.

412. Tussur silk cocoons. Madras. Government of India.

413. Tussur silk cocoons. Cuddapah, Madras. Government of India.

414. Tussur silk cocoons. Phillaur, Punjab. Government of India.

415. Tussur silk cocoons. Beas, Punjab. Government of India.

416. Tussur silk cocoons. Gaya, Bengal. Government of India.

417. Tussur silk cocoons (very pale in colour). Royal Gardens, Baroda, Bombay. Government of India.

418. Weaver's quills of Tussur silk weft. Murshidabad, Bengal. Government of India. (Pl. XLII.)

419. Pedicles of Tussur silk cocoons, prepared for spinning by boiling. Manbhum, Bengal. Government of India.

420. Pedicles of Tussur silk cocoons, prepared for spinning. Government of India.

421 & 422. Belt and knife-rest used by the wood-cutters of the Kolaba District, Konkan Division, Bombay Presidency, with bells made of Tussur silk cocoons. Lent by J. Griffiths, Esq., Superintendent School of Art, Bombay.

423. Cocoons of the Eria silkworm, *Attacus ricini*. Kamrup, Assam. Government of India.

424. Cocoons of the Eria silkworm, *Attacus ricini*. Assam. Government of India.

425. Cocoons of the Eria silkworm, *Attacus ricini*. Rangpur, Bengal. Government of India.

426. Cocoons of the Eria silkworm, *Attacus*

ricini. Lakhimpur, Assam. Government of India.

427. Red and white cocoons of the Eria silkworm, *Attacus ricini.* Sylhet, Assam. Government of India.

428. Cocoons of the Eria silkworm, *Attacus ricini.* Jalpaiguri, Bengal. Government of India.

429. Red cocoons of the Eria silkworm, *Attacus ricini.* Dinajpur, Bengal. Government of India.

430. Cocoons of the Eria silkworm, *Attacus ricini*, prepared for carding, as sold for manufacturing purposes. Nowgong, Assam. Government of India.

431. Cocoons of the Muga silkworm, *Antheræa Assama*, first quality. Sibsagar, Assam. Government of India. (Pl. VII., Fig. 2.)

432. Cocoons of the Muga silkworm, *Antheræa Assama*, second quality. Sibsagar, Assam. Government of India.

433. Cocoons of the Muga silkworm, *Antheræa Assama*, third quality. Sibsagar, Assam. Government of India.

434. Cocoons of *Cricula trifenestrata.* Exhibited by Deputy Surg.-Genl. J. Shortt, M.D., F.L.S., F.Z.S., Yerkad, Shevaroys. (Pl. XIII.)

435. Cocoons of *Cricula trifenestrata* in cluster-bunches or colonies. Ranchi, Chutia Nagpur. Bengal.

436. Raw silk reeled from the cocoons of the mulberry-fed silkworm by the ordinary method. 12 to 14 cocoons reeled together, size 25/30 deniers. Surdah, Rajshahi, Bengal. Government of India.

437. Raw silk reeled from the cocoons of the mulberry-fed silkworm with Italian appliances. 12 to 14 cocoons reeled together, size 25/30 deniers. Surdah, Rajshahi, Bengal. Government of India.

438. Raw silk reeled from the cocoons of the mulberry-fed silkworm by the ordinary method. Rangpur, Bengal. Government of India.

439. Fine raw silk reeled from the cocoons of the mulberry-fed silkworm, Bogra, Bengal. Government of India.

440. Coarse raw silk reeled from the cocoons of the mulberry-fed silkworm, Bogra, Bengal. Government of India.

441. Raw silk reeled from the cocoons of the mulberry-fed silkworm, lowest quality, Rs. 8 per seer. Maldah, Bengal. Government of India.

442. Raw silk reeled from the cocoons of the mulberry-fed silkworm, middle quality, Rs. 10·8 per seer. Maldah, Bengal. Government of India.

443. Raw silk reeled from the cocoons of the mulberry-fed silkworm, Rs. 11 per seer. Maldah, Bengal. Government of India.

444. Raw silk reeled from the cocoons of the mulberry-fed silkworm, best quality, Rs. 12 per seer. Maldah, Bengal. Government of India.

445. Tram for weaving made from the silk of the mulberry-fed silkworm of Bengal. Jehanabad, Hugli District, Bengal. Government of India.

446. Raw silk reeled from the cocoons of the mulberry-fed silkworm of Bengal. Jangipur, Murshidabad District. Government of India.

447. Raw silk reeled from the cocoons of the mulberry-fed silkworm of Bengal. G. G. McP. Cossimbazaar, 26/30 deniers.

448 & 449. Raw silk reeled from the cocoons of the mulberry-fed silkworm of Bengal. Birbhum, Bengal. Government of India.

450. Tape chassum or waste of the silk of the mulberry-fed silkworm of Bengal. Birbhum, Bengal. Bengal Silk Company.

451. Coarse waste silk of the mulberry-fed silkworm of Bengal. Canpore. Government of India.

452 to 456. Raw silk reeled from the cocoons of the mulberry-fed silkworm. Surdah, Rajshahi, Bengal. Government of India.

457. Coarse raw silk reeled from the cocoons of the mulberry-fed silkworm of Bengal. Radhanagar, Bengal, Government of India.

458. Bharua or Tram thrown from raw silk reeled from the cocoons of the mulberry-fed silkworm of Bengal. Dhantala, Bengal, Government of India.

459. Tana or Warp thrown from raw silk reeled from the cocoons of the mulberry-fed silkworm of Bengal. Dhantala, Bengal, Government of India.

460. Raw silk reeled from the cocoons of the mulberry-fed silkworm of Bengal. Dhantala, Bengal, Government of India.

461. Raw silk reeled from the cocoons of the mulberry-fed silkworm. Dehra Dun, N.W. Provinces. Government of India.

462. White raw silk reeled from the cocoons of the mulberry-fed silkworm of Bengal. Dehra Dun, N. W. Provinces. The seed from which the cocoons were reared was received through the Madras Government. Exhibited by Deputy Surg.-Genl. J. Shortt, M.D., F.L.S., F.Z.S., Yerkad, Shevaroys.

463. Yellow raw silk reeled from the cocoons of the mulberry-fed silkworm of Bengal Dehra Dun, N. W. Provinces. The seed from which the cocoons were reared was received through the Madras Government. Exhibited by Deputy Surg.-Genl. J. Shortt, M.D., F.L.S., F.Z.S., Yerkad, Shevaroys.

464. Straw coloured raw silk reeled from the cocoons of the mulberry-fed silkworm of Bengal. Dehra Dun, N. W. Provinces. The seed from which the cocoons were reared was received through the Madras Government. Exhibited by Deputy Surg.-Genl. J. Shortt, M.D., F.L.S., F.Z.S., Yerkad, Shevaroys.

464*a*. Raw silk reeled from Ceylon green cocoons. See No. 392*a*.

464*b*. Raw silk reeled from Ceylon white cocoons. See No. 392*b*.

465. Native Indian hand-reel for reeling silk cocoons. Government of India.

466. Dyed floss silk (Phalian) in different colours. Rs. 11/12 ann. per seer. Davee Sahai Chumba Mull, Hall Street, Amritsar, Punjab.

467. Floss silk (Katha) imported from

Yerkad, Madras. Rs. 10/4 per seer. Davee Sahai Chumba Mull, Amritsar.

468. Tani silk from Cabul, cleaned. Rs. 16 per seer. Davee Sahai Chumba Mull, Amritsar.

469. Silk (Phalian) imported from Cubul, Rs. 8/4 per seer. Davee Sahai Chumba Mull, Amritsar, Punjab.

470. Silk (Ghatar) imported from Bengal Rs. 8/8 per seer. Davee Sahai Chumba Mull· Amritsar, Punjab.

471. Silk (Vardham) imported from Bukhara. Rs. 12 per seer. Daveo Sahai Chumba Mull, Amritsar, Punjab.

472. Silk (Chappi) imported from Bengal. Rs. 10 per seer. Davee Sahai Chumba Mull, Amritsar, Punjab.

473. Silk (Makhtul) imported from Bengal. Rs. 6 per seer. Daveo Sahai Chumba Mull, Amritsar, Punjab.

474. Silk (Sheesh Mehal) imported from China. Rs. 5/12 per seer. Davee Sahai Chumba Mull, Amritsar, Punjab.

475. Silk (Phul) imported from China. Rs. 11 per seer. Davee Sahai Chumba Mull, Amritsar, Punjab.

476. Silk warp (Tani) imported from Yerkad. Madras, price Rs. 12 per seer. Davee Sahai Chumba Mull, Amritsar, Punjab. Government of India.

477. Silk dyed in different colours with aniline dyes (Vardhan). Rs. 18 per seer. Davee Sahai Chumba Mull, Amritsar, Punjab.

478 & 479. Raw silk of the mulberry-fed silkworm, Kanara, Bombay. Government of India.

480. Coarse raw silk of the mulberry-fed silkworm. Mysore. Government of India.

481. Raw silk of the mulberry-fed silkworm, reeled from cocoons raised from seed obtained locally. Mysore. Exhibited by Deputy-Surg.-Genl. J. Shortt, M.D., F.L.S., F.Z.S., Yerhad, Shevaroys.

482. Rough silk of the mulberry-fed silkworm used for weaving bathing-clothes. Cuddapah, Madras. Government of India.

483. Raw silk reeled from the cocoons of the mulberry-fed silkworm. Cuddapah, Madras, Government of India.

484. Boiled-off silk warp from Koreyal, undyed. Sent by Collector of Coimbatore, Madras. Government of India.

485. Raw mulberry silk from Koreyal. Sent by collector of Coimbatore, Madras. Government of India.

486. Boiled-off silk warp from Koreyal, native-dyed orange.
Sent by collector of Coimbatore, Madras. Government of India.

487. Boiled-off silk warp from Koreyal, native-dyed crimson.
Sent by collector of Coimbatore, Madras. Government of India.

488. Boiled-off silk warp from Koreyal, native-dyed yellow.
Sent by collector of Coimbatore, Madras. Government of India.

489. Boiled-off silk warp from Koreyal, native-dyed orange.
Sent by collector of Coimbatore, Madras. Government of India.

490. Boiled-off silk warp from Koreyal, native-dyed red.
Sent by collector of Coimbatore, Madras, Government of India.

491. Boiled-off silk warp from Koreyal, native-dyed black, with the seeds of *Semecarpus anacardium*.
Sent by collector of Coimbatore, Madras. Government of India.

492. Raw silk of the cocoons of the mulberry-fed silkworm. Tinnevelli, Madras. Government of India.

493. Fine silk of the cocoons of the mulberry-fed silkworm. Cuddapah, Madras. Government of India.

494. Raw silk of the cocoons of the mulberry-fed silkworm. Cuddapah, Madras. Government of India.

495. Raw silk of the cocoons of the mulberry-fed silkworm, after first cleaning. Cuddapah, Madras. Government of India.

496. Raw silk of the cocoons of the mulberry-fed silkworm. Dinapur, Bengal. Government of India.

497. Waste silk of the cocoons of the mulberry-fed silkworm. Stuffing of the bed of the Queen of Burma. Government of India.

498. Tussur silk dyed in Calcutta. Aniline dyes. Government of India.

499. Tussur silk dyed crimson, yellow and violet. Government of India.

500 & 501. Tussur weaving silk, showing the modern improvements in dyeing it. Dyed by Mr. Wardle.

502. Tussar weaving silk, bleached by the most improved process. By Mr. Wardle.

503. Silk cocoons in Colonies, Madagascar. Lent by Mr. Wardle.

505. Tussur silk thread. The Twenty-four Parganas, Bengal. Government of India.

506 & 507. Tussur raw silk, native reeling. Birbhum, Bengal. Government of India.

508. Tussur raw silk, native reeling. Fatwa, Bengal. Government of India.

509. Tussur silk waste. Fatwa, Bengal. Government of India.

510. Tussur silk thread. Bardwan, Bengal. Government of India.

511. Tussur raw silk reeled from "Dhaba" Tussur silk cocoons. Singbhum, Bengal. Government of India.

512. Tussur raw silk reeled from "Bogura" Tussur silk cocoons. Singbhum, Bengal. Government of India.

513. Tussur silk waste. No. 1. Manbhum, Bengal. Sent by T. F. Peppé, Esq.

514. Tussur silk waste. No. 2. Manbhum, Bengal. Sent by T. F. Peppé, Esq.

515. Tussur raw silk, reeled from "Bogoi" Tussur silk cocoons. Singbhum, Bengal. Government of India.

516. Tussur raw silk, reeled from "Laria"

Tussar silk cocoons. Singbhum, Bengal. Government of India.

517. Tussur raw silk. Anandpur, Midnapur Bengal. Government of India.

518. Tussur silk waste. Anandpur, Midnapur, Bengal. Government of India.

519. Tussur raw silk. Baramba State. Orissa. Government of India.

520 & 520a. Tussur raw silk. Rajgram, Bankura. Government of India.

521. Tussur silk waste, (*a*) undyed, (*b*) dyed with magenta. Ranchi, Chutia Nagpur, Bengal. Government of India.

521a. Tussur silk cord, dyed with magenta. Ranchi, Chutia Nagpur, Bengal. Government of India.

522. Tussur raw silk. Midnapur, Bengal. Government of India.

523. Tussur silk of native reeling from Ramdera, near Dehri, Shahabad, Bengal, in the reeling of which castor oil and the alkaline earth, *saji matti*, are used. Sent by T. F. Peppé, Esq.

524. Tussur raw silk. Gaya, Bengal.

525. Dyed Tussur silk warp on hand-reel. Fatwa, Bengal. Government of India.

526. Stiffened Tussur silk warp on hand-reel. Fatwa, Bengal. Government of India.

527. Stiffened and unstiffened Tussur silk warp. Fatwa, Bengal. Government of India.

528. Silk of the Eri silkworm, *Attacus ricini*, spun for weaving into cloth. Not reeled. Lakhimpur, Assam. Government of India.

529. Native made Eria silk cloth. Assam. Government of India.

530. Silk of the Eria silkworm, *Attacus ricini*, spun for weaving into cloth. Not reeled. Lakhimpur, Assam. Government of India.

531. Native made Eria silk cloth. Dinajpur, Bengal. Government of India.

532. Native made Eria silk cloth, embroidered. Lent by Mr. T. F. Peppé, Arrah, Bengal.

533. Warp and weft spun threads of Eria silk, *Attacus ricini*. Nowgong, Assam. Government of India.

534. Native made Eria silk cloth. Nowgong, Assam. Government of India.

535. Native made Eria silk cloth. Nowgong, Assam. Government of India.

536. Waste Eria silk, *Attacus ricini*. Assam. Government of India.

537. Endi cloth, made from the silk of *Attacus ricini*. Assam. Government of India.

538. Balls of waste Eria silk, *Attacus ricini*. Lakhimpur, Assam. Government of India.

539. Silk of the Eria silkworm, *Attacus ricini*, spun for weaving into cloth. Not reeled. Lakhimpur, Assam. Government of India.

540. Ball of raw silk of the Eria silkworm, *Attacas ricini*, spun for weaving into cloth. Not reeled. Lakhimpur, Assam. Government of India.

541 to 543. Silk of the Eria silkworm, *Attacus ricini*, spun for weaving into cloth. Not reeled. Sylhet, Assam. Government of India.

544. Silk of the Eria silkworm, *Attacus ricini*, spun for weaving into cloth. Not reeled. Dinajpur, Assam. Government of India.

545. Silk of the Eria silkworm, *Attacus ricini*, spun for weaving into cloth. Not reeled. Kamrup, Assam. Government of India.

546. Silk of the Eria silkworm, *Attacus ricini*, spun for weaving into cloth. Not reeled. Jalpaiguri, Bengal. Government of India.

547. Silk of the Eria silkworm, *Attacus ricini*, spun for weaving into cloth. Not reeled. (Good quality.) Assam. Government of India.

548. Silk of the Endi or Eria silkworm, *Attacus ricini*, spun for weaving into cloth. Not reeled. Rangpur, Bengal. Government of India.

549. Silk of the Muga silkworm, *Antheræa Assama*. Lakhimpur, Assam. Government of India.

550. Silk of the Muga silkworm, *Antheræa Assama*. Kamrup, Assam. Government of India.

551 & 552. Silk of Muga silkworm (Jutha Muga), *Antheræa Assama*. Lakhimpur, Assam. Government of India.

553. Cloth woven from the silk of the Muga silkworm, *Antheræa Assama*. Government of India.

554. Muga silk turban. Assam. Government of India.

555. Silk of the Muga silkworm, *Antheræa Assama*, spun from pierced cocoons, for weaving into cloth. Not reeled. Assam. Government of India.

556. Silk of the Muga silkworm, *Antheræa Assama*. Sibsagar, Assam. Government of India.

557. Patterned silk damask shot with Muga silk from Assam. Government of India.

558. Tussur moths and cocoons on *Lagerstræmia Indica*. Poona, Bombay. Lent by Lieut.-Col. Counmaker Westwood, Guildford, Surrey, late of Poona.

559. Bengal imperfect Native reeling of raw silk from white and yellow cocoons of the ordinary mulberry-fed silkworm. In the silk, portions of the cocoons will be seen to have been allowed to run up into the reeled hank.

560. Improvement effected in December 1885, in reeling Bengal cocoons with the Tavelette Consono, by Mr. Wardle, showing the high state of refinement of which Bengal silk is susceptible by proper reeling.

561. European yellow raw silk showing the highest standard of reeling attained in Italy. Placed here to show by comparison that the regularity and fineness of thread are quite equalled in Bengal silk when the cocoons are properly reeled.

562. Cocoons of the Desi or Chota poloo silkworm of Bengal, *Bombyx fortunatus*. November or cold weather bund. Used for both the native reeled yellow silk (559), and for that showing the improvement (560).

563. Raw silk reeled at the Surdah Filature of Messrs. R. Watson & Co., Rajshahi, Bengal, with the Tavelette Consono, 25/30 deniers.

Surdah is the name of the head filature of this extensive company, which embraces other filatures in the district. The filatures of

Radnagore, of which the factory at Ghátál is the head, also belong to this company. Ghátál, writes Dr. Hunter, is a municipal town in the Midnapur District, situated on the Silai River near its junction with the Rúpnáráyan, containing a population of about sixteen thousand, nearly all of whom are Hindus. It is an important commercial town, trading in rice, silk, sugar, cotton cloth, &c.

564. Raw silk reeled by the best Indian method at the Surdah Filature of Messrs. R. Watson & Co., Rajshahi, Bengal. 10/11 deniers.

565. Raw silk reeled at the Surdah Filature of Messrs. R. Watson & Co., Rajshahi, Bengal, with the Tavelette Consono, 10/11 deniers.

566. Improved reeling of Tussur silk by Messrs. R. Watson & Co., Surdah Filature, Rajshahi, Bengal.

567. Cocoons from Messrs. R. Watson & Co., Surdah, Rajshahi, Bengal.

a. Cocoons of *Cricula trifenestrata.*

b. Cocoons of the Tussur silkworm.

c. Yellow and white cocoons of the mulberry-fed silkworm. Burma.

d. Desi pierced cocoons of the Mulberry-fed silkworm. November bund.

e. Madrassee or hot weather cocoons of the mulberry-fed silkworm, unovened, i.e. sun dried.

f. Madrassee or hot weather cocoons of the mulberry-fed silkworm, ovened, i.e. artificially dried.

g. Desi or November bund cocoons of the mulberry-fed silkworm, unovened, i.e. sun-dried.

h. Desi or November bund cocoons of the mulberry-fed silkworm, ovened, i.e. artificially dried.

568. Bengal silk waste, from Messrs. R. Watson & Co., Surdah, Rajshahi, Bengal.

569. Tussur silk waste, from Messrs. R. Watson & Co., Surdah, Rajshahi, Bengal.

The Calcutta Agents of this firm are Messrs. Jardine, Skinner & Co. The London Agents, Messrs. Matheson & Co., 3, Lombard Street.

570. Raw silks reeled in the usual Bengal method by the Bengal Silk Company, Behrempore, Bengal.

a. A series of hanks of raw silk, 10 to 13 deniers. Gonatea.

b. A series of hanks of raw silk, 26 to 30 deniers. Cossimbazaar.

c. A series of hanks of raw silk, 11 to 13 deniers. Rangamati.

d. A series of hanks of raw silk, 16 to 20 deniers. Benjeti.

The Manager of this company is Mr. J. W. Stocks of Berhampur, and the Calcutta Agents, Messrs. Lyall, Marshall & Co. The London Agents are Messrs. Anderson Brothers, 16 Philpot Lane, E.C.

571. Gujrati Tie-and-Dye or Bandana work, in various styles of stripes and plaids, effected entirely by tying and dyeing cloth for turbans successively in various ways. These turbans are very beautiful examples of an art for which Ulwar is celebrated, and which is there practised with the greatest ingenuity and patience.

A to C. Turbans produced in Ulwar by the Bandana process. Gold border.

D. Turban produced in Ulwar by the Bandana process, showing the method in which the cloth is tied ready for dyeing. Since the dyeing process it has been untied and partially unrolled.

E. Turban produced in Ulwar by the Bandana process, showing the method in which the cloth is tied ready for dyeing. Since the dyeing process it has been part untied and unrolled.

F. Turban with gold border partially untied.

572. Manchester printed turban sent to India as an imitation of Ulwar Bandana work.

573. Electricity applied to dyeing by Mr. Wardle.

A. shows the application of the galvanic current in printing. The cloth is prepared with a moist precipitate of prussiate of tin and placed on a platinum plate connected with the cathode or negative pole of the battery, and written upon with a platinum pencil connected with the anode or positive pole of the battery. The galvanic current develops the colour.

B is an example of indigo discharged by the galvanic current by the same arrangement as described in A. The cloth is first dyed blue with indigo and then prepared with bichromate of potash.

C is a similar example showing the chemical change which occurs.

D is the same as B, but with saffranine mixed with the solution of bichromate of potash.

E. The cloth is dyed with Munjeet (*Rubia manjista*), and the written part discharged by electrolysis of bichromate of potash with the galvanic pencil.

F is the same kind of indigo discharge as B, but with a pattern cut in platinum plate, connected with the battery, applied to the moist cloth, instead of the galvanic pencil.

G. Green cloth dyed with Indigo and Hursinghar flowers (*Nyctanthes arbortristis*), prepared with bichromate of potash and discharged instantaneously by writing upon it with the galvanic pencil.

H. The same as B, but with the application of a less powerful galvanic current.

I. The same as B, but with the poles reversed. The discharge is therefore at the back of the cloth and penetrates only slightly to the side exhibited.

574. Short-reeled spun native silk for Mutka cloth, boiled off. Jinkra, near Surdah Rajshahi, Bengal. Mutka cloth is woven undyed, and principally at Dacra, six miles from Surdah.

575. Short-reeled spun native silk for Mutka cloth, in gum. Jinkra, near Surdah Rajshahi, Bengal. Mutka cloth is woven undyed, and principally at Dacra, six miles from Surdah, but without the gum having been discharged.

576. Native implement for spinning silk for Mutka cloth. Dacra, near Surdah, Rajshahi Bengal.

578, 578*a* to 578*f*. Seven large Tussur Silk Rugs. Government of India.

579. One small Tussur Silk Rug. Lent by Mr. Wardle.

580. Cocoon reeling machine furnished with the Tavelette Consono, and in daily operation reeling Bengal cocoons worked by a fileuse or cocoon-reeler from the South of France. (Pls. I., XXXVII. to XLI.)

581. Working model of a machine for reeling Indian Tussur silk cocoons, in daily operation, worked by an Indian boy, and furnished with the Tavelette Consono. Suitable for village and cottage reeling in India.

582. THE FIRST INSTALMENT FROM INDIA TOWARDS A COMPLETE ENTOMOLOGICAL COLLECTION ILLUSTRATIVE OF INDIAN SERICULTURE, BY F. WOOD-MASON, ESQ., ASSISTING SUPERINTENDENT OF THE INDIAN MUSEUM, CALCUTTA.

No. of Tray.	No. of Specimen.	Name and Nature of Specimen.	Locality.	REMARKS.
I.	1, *a—j*	*Bombyx mori*, Linn. Cocoons from Indian eggs	Lahore, Panjáb.	
	2, *a—j*	*Bombyx mori*, Linn. Cocoons from Japanese eggs	Ditto.	
	3, *a—e*	*Bombyx* sp. Cocoons .	Kotnaina, Gurdaspur, Panjáb.	Rearer Subhan.
	4, *a—h*	*Bombyx* sp. Cocoons .	Ditto. . .	Ditto.
	5, *a—e*	*Bombyx textor*, Hutton. "Bara Poloo." Cocoons	Gonatea.	
	6, *a—c*	Ditto. Moths 2 ♂, 1 ♀	Ditto . .	Bred in Museum.
	7, *a—f*	Ditto. Cocoons .	Serampore, Hughli District.	
II.	8, *a—h*	*Bombyx meridionalis*. Cocoons	Cuddapah District, Madras.	
	9, *a—h*	Ditto. ditto.	Induradi village, Kollegal Taluk, Koimbatore District.	
	10, *a—j*	*Bombyx* sp. Cocoons .	Serampore, Hughli District.	
	11, *a—c*	*Bombyx fortunatus*. Hutton. "Desi silkworm." Moths 2♂, 1♀	Sadah, Rajshaye .	Bred in Museum. (Pl. II., Figs. 1 and 2.)
	12, *a—h*	Ditto. Cocoons.	Ditto.	
	13, *a—i*	*Bombyx cræsi*, Hutton. "Madrassee silkworm." Cocoons	Sardah, Rajshahye.	
	14, *a—c*	Ditto. Moths 2♂, 1 ♀	Ditto. . .	Bred in Museum.
	15, *a—b*	*Bombyx* sp. Cocoons .	Rungpore.	
III.	16, *a—c*	*Bombyx* sp. "Pat silkworm." Cocoons	Assam . .	? = Bara Poloo.
	17, *a*.	*Theophila Huttoni*, Westw. ♂ ♀ Moths	?	From Hutton's collection.
	18, *a—b*	*Theophila Huttoni*, Westw. Cocoons.	Pokaria, Govindpore.	From wild mulberry.

No. of Tray.	No. of Specimen.	Name and Nature of Specimen.	Locality.	Remarks.
	19, *a*—*e*	*Philosamia ricini*, Jones. Wild Cocoons	Lakhimpore, Assam.	Better known as *Attacus ricini.*
	20, *a.*	Ditto. Moth, ♂ .	Assam . .	Bred in Museum. (Pl. IX.)
	21, *a*—*h*	*Philosamia ricini*, Jones. Cocoons.	Kamrup, Assam.	
	22, *a*—*f*	Ditto. ditto.	Sylhet, Assam.	
IV.	23, *a*—*h*	Ditto. ditto.	Dinagepore.	
	24, *a*—*b*	Ditto. Moths, ♂, ♀ .	Ditto. . .	Bred in Museum. (Pl. IX.)
	25, *a.*	Ditto. Mass of Cocoons	Ditto. . .	Bred in Museum.
	26, *a*—*b*	Ditto. Moths, ♂, ♀ .	Burma . .	Var. *a.*
	27, *a*—*f*	Ditto. Cocoons.	Assam.	
	28, *a*—*b*	Ditto. Moths, 2 ♂ .	Burma . .	Var. *b.*
V.	29, *a*—*f*	*P. cynthia*, Drury. Cocoons.	Near Almora.	(Pl. XIX., Fig. 2.) Better known as *Attacus cynthia.*
	30, *a*—*b*	Ditto. Moths, ♂, ♀ .	Sikkim.	(Pl. XVIII.)
	31, *a*—*b*	*Attacus atlas*, Linn. Moths, ♂, ♀	Burma . .	Var. *a.*
	32, *a*—*b*	*A. atlas*, Linn. Moths, ♂ ♀	Burma . .	Var. *b.* (Pls. X. and XI.)
VI.	33, *a*—*c*	Ditto. Cocoons .	Aligarh.	(Pl. XII., Fig. 2.)
	34, *a*—*b*	Ditto. Moths, ♂, ♀	Sikkim.	
VII.	35, *a*	*A. Edwardsii*, White. Cocoon	Lakhimpur, Assam	"Bun Muga."
	36, *a*—*b*	Ditto. Moths, 2 ♀	Sikkim.	
VIII.	37, *a*	*Actias selene*, Mc'Leay. Cocoon	Sylhet.	(Pl. XIV., Fig. 3.)
	38, *a*—*b*	Ditto. Moths, ♂, ♀	Sikkim.	(Pl. XIV., Fig. 1.; Pl. XV.)
	39, *a*—*b*	*A. leto*, Doubleday, Moths,	Ditto . . .	*A. mænas* is the opposite sex of this species.
IX.	40, *a*—*e*	*Antheræopsis assama*, Helfer. Cocoons	Sibsagar and Kamrup, Assam	3 pale ones = "Mezankoori Muga." Better known as *Antheræa Assama.*
	41, *a*—*d*	Ditto. Cocoons .	Lakhimpur, Assam	On "Hingari" leaves.
	42, *a*—*b*	Ditto. Moths, ♂, ♀ .	Mungaldai, Assam	Bred in Museum. (Pl. VI.)
	43, *a*	*Cricula trifenestrata*, Helfer. Bunch of Cocoons	Ranchi . .	? Winter Cocoons. This silkworm spins its cocoons in cluster bunches or colonies, which are suspended to the small branches of the trees on which the worms feed, by silken cords or shreds.

No. of Tray.	No. of Specimen.	Name and Nature of Specimen.	Locality.	Remarks.
	44, *a—d*	*Cricula trifenestrata*, Helfer. Moths, 1 ♂, 3 ♀	Ranchi . .	Bred in Museum. (Pl. XIII.)
X.	45, *a—e*	*Antheræa mylitta*, Drury. Cocoons.	Singbhoom.	
	46, *a—b*	Ditto. Cocoons	Phillour, Panjáb.	
	47, *a—e*	*A. mylitta*, Drury, Cocoons	Burdwan.	
	48, *a*	*A. mylitta*, Drury, var. Cocoon	Calcutta . .	Showing mode of attachment to shoot of *Terminalia catappa*. At the end of the pedicle of the cocoon is a ring, which, like the pedicle itself, consists of silk, and which firmly clasps the twig, to which the cocoon hangs suspended like a berry. (Pl. V.)
	49, *a*	*Antheræa mylitta*, Drury, var. Cocoon	Calcutta . .	To show mode of attachment to petiole and midrib of leaf of *T. catappa*.
	50, *a*	Ditto. . . .	Ditto. .	Showing 4 successive annular attachments below the pulvinus of as many leaves of a shoot of *Terminalia arjuna*.
	51, *a—b*	Ditto. Moths, ♂, ♀ .	Ditto . .	Bred in Museum from wild cocoons found on *T. catappa* ("Badám"). (Pl. III.)
XI.	52, *a—g*	*Antheræa mylitta*, var. *nebulosa*, Hutton, 1 ♂, 6 ♀ Moths	Maunbhum . .	Differing greatly on the upper surface in the shade of the ground colour, they are all alike below in both sexes. Bred in Museum.
	53, *a—b*	*Antheræa Frithii*, Moore, ♂ Moths	Sikkim . .	Cocoon unknown. (Pl. VIII., Fig. 2.)
XII.	54, *a—b*	*Antheræa Helferi*, Moore, ♂ & ♀ Moths.	Ditto . .	Ditto. (Pl. XVI., Fig. 1.)
	55, *a—b*	*Caligula simla*, Westwood, ♂ & ♀ Moths	N.-W. Himalayas.	♂ from Mussoorie; ♀ from Kumaon from the Hutton collection. (Pl. XVI., Fig. 2.)
	56, *a*	*Neoris Huttoni*, Moore, ♀ Moth	Ditto. . .	From the Hutton collection. (Pl. XIX. Fig. 3.)
	57, *a—b*	*Rinaca zuleika* Hope, ♂ Moth and Cocoon	Sikkim . .	Silk of no practical value.
	58, *a*	*Salassa lola*, Westwood, ♀ Moth	Ditto. . .	Cocoon unknown.

583. Living eggs and cocoons of the Indian Tussur silkworm, *Antheræa mylitta.*

584. Living eggs, larvæ or caterpillars, cocoons and moths of the Chinese Tussur silkworm, *Antheræa pernyi.* The caterpillars are feeding on the leaves of the oak tree. (Pl. XVII.)

585. Living eggs, cocoons and moths of the Eria silkworm, *Attacus ricini.* Assam. (Pl.IX.)

586. Living eggs, cocoons and moths of *Attacus cynthia.* This is the wild form found in the Tarai on the Himalayan slopes. (Pls. XVIII., XIX., Figs. 1 and 2.)

587. Living eggs, caterpillars, cocoons and moths of *Cricula trifenestrata.* Ranchi, Chutiá Nágpur, Bengal. The caterpillars are feeding on the leaves of the plum tree, but their natural food is the leaves of *Oroxylun indicum,* "*Khandan,*" and *Tetranthera monopetala,* "*Pojah.*" (Pl. XIII.)

588. Living eggs, cocoons and moths of *Samia cecropia.*

589. Very rare species of an unnamed *Psychideæ* of Senegal. Living cocoons and moths. The female of this species is wingless and never leaves the cocoon, whilst the male has small transparent wings, and very much resembles the hive bee.

590. Living cocoons and moths of a species of *Psychideæ* from Ranchi, Chutiá Nágpur, Bengal, the caterpillars of which feeds on the tea plant.

591. Living grubs and chrysalides of a parasitic Dipterous fly, which lays its egg in the caterpillar of *Cricula trifenestrata.* If the cocoon of the *Cricula trifenestrata* is to become of commercial importance it will be necessary to protect the worm from the attack of this Dipterous fly. I have found in some of the bunches of cocoons 80 per cent. of the worms killed by it.

592. Living caterpillars and cocoons of *Actias luna,* from North America. The caterpillars are feeding on the walnut tree.

593. Water-colour drawing of the eggs, caterpillars, cocoons and moths of the Indian Tussur silkworm, *Antheræa mylitta,* represented as being attached to a branch of *Lagerstræmia Indica,* upon the leaves of which the caterpillars feed. Lent by Lt.-Col. Coussmaker, Westwood, Guildford, Surrey. Late of Poona, Bombay.

Notes to Plates.

On Pls. XXVIII. and XXIX. will be found drawings of the microscopic appearances of the different fibres of silk, which give a correct idea of their varying structure.

On Pl. XXXVIII. are a few representations of the microscopic appearances of the scales of a few of the silk-producing moths. See also Pl. XXII., Fig. 2.

I have also added, in Pls. XXX. to XXXVII., representations of some of the plants which furnish the food of several species of Indian silkworms.

In the Santal Jungles the leaves of *Terminalia tomentosa* (Pl. XXX.) form the food of those Tussur silkworms whose cocoons are intended to be utilised industrially. The worms whose cocoons are intended for breeding are fed on the leaves of *Shorea robusta* (Pl. XXXI.).

The prices of Tussur cocoons in Fatwa, Manbhum, Gaya, and Chutia Nagpur are shown in the following table (January, 1886):—

Fatwa	120 cocoons per rupee	...	Best cocoons
	160 " "	...	Common cocoons
Manbhum	5 to 7 rupees for 800	...	
Gaya	10 rupees for 1000	...	
Chutia Nagpur ...	320 cocoons per rupee	...	Formerly
	240 " "	...	Recently
	160 to 200 " "	...	Price which the natives are now demanding.

At the beginning of the year the contract price for Indian Tussur waste silk was in France 1*s.* 6*d.* per lb., the highest rate yet obtained, and for Tussur raw silk of the improved reeling 7*s.* 3*d.* per lb., as against 4*s.* 8½*d.* per lb. for Chinese Tussur raw silk.

The Collector of Vizagapatam informed me that immense tracts of country in his district produced Tussur cocoons.

A few particulars of the value of Muga and Eria silks may be useful in this catalogue.

1. Muga. The silk of the Muga cocoon is reeled, not spun. The two principal trees upon which the Muga silkworm feeds are the *Soom* (*Machilus odoratissima*), Pl. XXXIII., and the *Suálu* (*Tetranthera monopetala*). The price for cocoons for reeling is 500 to 800 cocoons for

1. The price for waste cocoons is Rs. 2 per seer containing nearly 3000 cocoons, or 1*s.* 6*d.* per lb. The price of Muga raw silk is from Rs. 8 to Rs. 12 per seer, or 6*s.* to 9*s.* per lb. Muga spun yarn can be bought for Rs. 4 per seer, or 3*s.* per lb. The price of Muga cloth in Assam varies from Rs. 1·8 to Rs. 2 (2*s.* 3*d.* to 3*s.*) per square yard.

2. Eria.—Eria cocoons are sold at Rs. 2·8 to Rs. 3 per seer, containing about 3600 cocoons, or 1s. 10½d. to 2*s.* 3*d.* per lb. Pierced Eria cocoons sell in Calcutta at Rs. 60 to Rs. 70 per maund of 82 lbs., or 1*s.* 1*d.* to 1*s.* 3*d.* per lb. Cocoons containing the dessicated chrysalis sell at the rate of 1200 to 1500 per rupee or at about 9 annas per seer, containing 700 cocoons (5d. per lb). The prices, however, vary much. The value of the thread varies from Rs. 4 to Rs. 7 per seer, or 3*s.* to 5*s.* 3*d.* per lb. Eria thread, I should mention, is made of silk spun from the cocoon and not reeled, as it is not practicable to reel this cocoon. The value of Eria cloth woven with this spun thread varies from Rs. 7 to Rs. 20 for 6 to 7 yards according to quality, or 1*s.* 6*d.* to 5*s.* per yard.

The *Philosamia* or *Attacus cynthia* (Pls. XVIII., XIX. Figs. 1 and 2) is found wild in the Terai.

The *Philosamia* or *Attacus ricini* of Assam (Pl. IX.) is said to owe its difference from *A. cynthia* to domestication.

A few short particulars about Indian Sericulture will not be out of place here, and should be useful hereafter to India.

The *Desi* or *Chota poloo* silkworm of Bengal (*Bombyx fortunatus*), No. 352, &c., is said to have been imported from China, in 1771, by the East India Company, but the pure variety is now only to be found in Bogreo, Midnapur.

The *Madrassee* or *Nistri poloo* silkworm (*Bombyx crœsi*), No. 355, &c., is found throughout the silk districts of Bengal. It is characterised by having round and not crescent marks.

The *Boro poloo* silkworm, the only univoltine variety, No. 369, and others, is found only in parts of Murshidabad, Hugli, Midnapur and Birbhum Dictricts. It is said to have been introduced in 1710, but is gradually being neglected by rearers as precarious and uncertain.

Another variety of the mulberry silkworm, known as *Chini*, is found only in Midnapur, Bengal. This silkworm, as well as the *Boro poloo*, has cresent marks.

Cocoons of Mulberry silkworms for seed, purchased in different districts, are called *Sunchoo*.

The mulberry feeding silkworms of Bengal have four moultings, being in the first stage black, the second blackish-grey, the third grey and the fourth greenish-white or grey. The leaves are given to the worms at first chopped up, after the third moulting detached from the twigs, and after the fourth moulting attached to the twigs. Thirty or forty pounds of cocoons are obtained from an English ounce of eggs. A *bigha** of land gives four crops of leaf in the year, and the produce of cocoons reared per *bigha* in the year is 3 *maunds*.†

In the Punjaub experiments from eggs of French, Italian and Japanese origin yielded 40 lbs. of cocoons per ounce of eggs, and that 16 lbs. of fresh cocoons yielded 1 lb. of raw silk. In Europe 12 lbs. to 14 lbs. of cocoons yield 1 lb. of silk.

In Italy and in France sericulturists obtain 40 to 60 kilogrammes of cocoons per ounce of eggs, but the yields vary with locality and climate. This larger yield is the result of studying the worms, in selection of eggs, in crossing the numerous varieties of the silk-worms.

The mulberry in Bengal (*Morus Indica*), *Tût*, is grown in clayey or sandy soils as a perennial shrub. It is cut down seven to eight times a year. It is planted once and remains in the soil until it wears itself out, or the ryot finds other crops more profitable. New earth is generally put on to renew the soil. The roots belong to the ryot and not to the zamindar.

No. 447. The silks which bear the mark G. G. McP. are from the Bengal Silk Company. This mark is a contraction of G. G. McPherson, who was one of the founders of this industry.

From the 11th to the 16th of January, 1886, an exhibition of silk cocoons was held at Rampore Beauleah, Rajshahi District, Bengal. It was opened and actively supported by Lord H. Ulick Browne, Commissioner of the Rajshahi Division, who believes that it has undoubtedly fostered a spirit of emulation among the cocoon rearers by bringing together the cocoons of various silk producing tracts, and says that there are grounds for hoping that similar Exhibitions held in the different silk producing districts, in different years, may lead to good results.

* There are three *bighas* in an English acre. † A *maund* is about 82 lbs.

A prize of Rs. 50 was awarded to Baboo Roma Nath Sen, the author of the best Bengali essay an the method of rearing silk cocoons. This essay is intended to be printed, and copies distributed among the exhibitors. The money for the prizes was raised by subscriptions in the neighbourhood, to which Government added an equal sum.

The number of exhibits were as under :—

Rajshahi	141
Murshidabad	83
Birbhum	5
Naidya	1
Total	230

The following are the silk districts of Bengal :—

Bardwan.	Jessor.
Bankura.	Murshidabad.
Birbhum.	Rajshahi.
Midnapur.	Rangpur.
Hugli with Howrah and Serampur.	Bogra.
Parganas.	Maldah.
Nadiya.	

Nos. 241 and 242. The spider silk exhibited under these numbers was obtained in 1885, when it was found that in the beginning of October a sufficient number of webs had been spun to make it worth while to commence the collection.

After a certain number of trials it was found best to collect the silk by winding the webs carefully round smooth sticks, from which they may be removed by the application of hot water, but it is impossible to unreel the silk directly from the sticks.

An immense number of webs were collected during the month of October, but so extremely light is the substance that it was impossible to procure anything like the quantity (viz. 200 lbs.) asked for by the Government of India. The amount obtained, including the sticks, was only 28 lbs., the expense of collecting which was Rs. 38 6 0. This silk on sticks was sent to me by the Government of India for experiment. I sent it to Messrs. Brocklehurst & Sons, Macclesfield, who reported that, owing to the small quantity sent and to its being so mixed with refuse matter, they were unable to card and spin it.

I am informed that the French Government has lately sent out forty reeling machines to Madras for reeling Tussur cocoons.

The *Bombyx mori* cocoons, No. 382*a*, have been sent by Mr. S. Cunliffe Lister, of Manningham, Yorkshire, who informs me they are from the "Lister Grant" at Dehra Dun, and reared from French eggs sent out last autumn, and that he has 2000 acres there now under mulberry cultivation, and is planting several hundred acres per annum. It takes five years by his system for the mulberry plants to be of the proper age. These cocoons resemble in size, form and colour the race cultivated in Provence. I have reeled excellent silk from them in the Silk Culture Court here of 10–12 deniers with the Tavelette Consono. *See* Raw Silk, No. 272*a*.

The Exhibits in this Indian Silk Culture Court number upwards of 800.

In addition to the thirty-eight varieties of the cocoons of the mulberry-fed silkworm (*Bombyx mori*), other than those of Bengal, which are described under No. 270, and exhibited as aids to sericultural study, I have received, since the type of this catalogue was set up and too late to be described in their proper place, twenty-three specimens of other varieties, chiefly Italian, and which I am placing in the exhibited collection. They are as follows :—

1. Yellow, from Romagna or Ascoli, reared in Piedmont.
2. Yellow, from Pyrenees, reared in Piedmont.
3. Yellow, from Var, reared in Piedmont.
4. Yellow, from Istria, reared in Friouli.
5. Yellow, from France, reared in Syria.
6. Yellow satinés (oozy), inferior, reared in Piedmont.
7. Yellow muscardinés (chrysalis dried up), reared in Piedmont.

8. Yellow, double, reared in Piedmont.
9. White, from Adrianople, reared in Piedmont.
10. White, from Adrianople, muscardinés, reared in Piedmont.
11. White, from Japan, reared in Piedmont.
12. White, from Japan, seed laid in Italy, reared in Piedmont.
13. Green small cocoons, reared in Piedmont.
14. Green large cocoons, reared in Piedmont.
15. Green inferior satinés, reared in Piedmont.
16. Green inferior rusted (Rouillés), reared in Piedmont.
17. Green, double, reared in Piedmont.
18. Green, white cross, reared in Friouli.
19. Yellow, white cross, reared in Friouli.
20. Yellow, green cross, reared in Friouli.
21. Yellow and white-pierced cocoons, reared in Friouli.
22. Good cocoons, from Romagna.
23. Double cocoons, from Romagna.

ALPHABETICAL LIST OF PLACES IN BRITISH INDIA WHERE SILK IS PRODUCED OR MANUFACTURED.

A.

Adoni (Mad.)
Agra (N. W. P.)
Ahmedabad (Bom.)
Almora (N. W. P.)
Amritsar (Punj.)
Andijon (Punj.)
Arcot (N. W. P.)
Arni (Mad.)
Arrah (Beng.)
Assam
Aurangabad (Nizam.)
Ava (Beng.)
Azamgarh (N. W. P.).

B.

Bagra (Beng.)
Baharapur (Punj.)
Bahawalpur (Punj.)
Balasor (Beng.)
Bamm
Bancoop (Beng.)
Bangalore (Mys.)
Bankura (Beng.)
Baramba (Cuttack, Beng.)
Bardwan, Beng.)
Barhampur (Beng.)
Barhanpur (C. P.)
Baroda (Bom.)
Behar (Beng.)
Bekanir
Belgaum (Bom.)
Bellary (Mad.)
Benares (N. W. P.)
Bengal
Bhandara (C. P.)
Bhagalpur (Beng.)
Bhuj (Bom.)
Bijapur (Bom.)
Birthum (Beng.)
Bishnapur (Beng.)
Bombay
Broach (Bom.)
Bulasor (Beng.)
Bura (C. I.)
Burma.

C.

Calcutta (Beng.)
Cambay (Bom.)
Cashmere
Chamapatna (Mys.)
Champaner (ancient, now in ruins, Bom.)
Chamapatna (Mys.)

C. (*continued.*)

Champawr (Bhogapur, Beng.)
Chanderi (Indore State, Central India).
Chutia Nagpur (Benj.)
Chingleput (Mad.)
Chittagong (Beng.)
Cossimbozor (Beng.)
Cuddelore (Mad.)
Cutch (Bom.)
Cuttach (Beng.)

D.

Dacca (Beng.)
Darjeeling (Beng.)
Darrang (A.)
Dehradun (N. W. P.)
Delhi (Punj.)
Devás (C. I.)
Dhar (C. I.)
Dharwar (Bom.)
Dinapur (Beng.)
Dinajpur (Beng.)

F.

French Rocks (Mys.)
Futwah (Behar, Beng.)

G.

Galampore.
Gaya (Beng.)
Ghátál (Beng.)
Giridi (Beng.)
Goalpara (A.)
Gopinàlhpur (Bankura, Beng.)
Gorakhpore (N. W. P.)
Gujerath (Bom.)
Gurdapore (Punj.)
Gwalior (Scindia).

H.

Hazaribagh
Hill Tipperah
Hugli (Beng.) with Hourah
Hyderabad (Deccan, Nizam).
Hyderabad (Sind, Bom.)

I.

Indore (Holkar)

J.

Jallandar (Punj.)
Jalpaigori (Beng.)
Jamnagar (Bom.)
Jangipur (Beng.)
Jhelam (Punj.)

K.

Kagra (Beng.)
Kalàdgi (Bom.)
Kampli (Mad.)
Kandwa.
Karàchi (Bom.)
Kathiawar (Bom.)
Keonjhar (Cuttach, Beng.)
Kistna (Mad.)
Kohat (Punj.)
Koraad (Mad.)
Kotah State.
Kunegal (Mys.)

L.

Lahore (Punj.)

M.

Madras.
Malda (Beng.)
Manbhum (Beng.)
Manipur (A.)
Mayurbhanj, Cuttach (Beng.)
Maywar (Udepur).
Meerbhung
Midnapur (Beng.)
Mirpur (Beng.)
Moulmein (Bur.)
Multan (Punj.)
Murshidabad (Beng.)
Mysore.

N.

Nadiya.
Naga Hills (A.)
Nagpur (C. P.)
Náráyan Peth (Nizam).
Nasik (Bom.)
Navánagar (Jámnagar (Bom.)
Northern circle (Mad.)

O.

Orrisa (Beng.).
Oudh (N. W. P.)

P.

Paithan (Nizam).
Palampur (Punj.)
Parebanda (Bom.)
Patiala (Punj.)
Patna (Beng.)
Pauni, Bhandara, Nagpur (C. I.)
Pegu (Bur.)
Peome (Beng.)

P. (*continued.*)

Peshawar (Punj.)
Poona (Bom.)
Punjab
Puri (Beng.).

R.

Raichuri (C. P.)
Rajshahi (Beng.)
Rampur Bantia (Beng.)
Ranchi (Beng.)
Rangoon (Bur.)
Rangpur (Beng.)
Rewah (C. I.)
Rewdanda (Bom.)
Royapetta (Beng.).

S.

Salem (Mad.)
Sambalpur (C. P.)
Sángli (Bom.)
Sansmond (Mys.)
Sásvad (Bom.)
Serampur.
Shahapur (Punj.)
Sherpur (Beng.)
Shikarpu (Bom.)
Sholapur (Bom.)
Sial Kot (Punj.)
Sibsagar (A.)
Sibpur (Beng.)
Singapur
Singbhum (Beng.)
Southern circle (Mad.)
Surdah (Beng.)
Surat (Bom.)

T.

Tanjore (Mad.)
Tatta (Bom.)
Tenasserim (Beng.)
Thana (Bom.)
Tigaria, Cuttach (Beng.).

U.

Umrer, near Nagpur (C. P.).

Y.

Yelgundal (Mad.)
Yeola (Bom.)
Yerkah (Mad.)
Yurkund (Punj.).

LIST OF ABBREVIATIONS SHOWING THE NAMES OF THE PROVINCES.

Ben.	=	Bengal.
Punj.	=	Punjab.
Bom.	=	Bombay.
Mad.	=	Madras.
N. W. P.	=	North-Western Provinces.
Nizam.	=	H.H. the Nizam's Territory.
Mys.	=	Mysore.
C. P.	=	Central Provinces.
C. I.	=	Central India.
Scindia.	=	H.H. the Scindia's Territory.
Holkar	=	H.H. the Holkar's Territory.
Jaipur.	=	H.H. the Maharaja of Jaipur's Territory.
Bur.	=	British Burma.

ILLUSTRATIONS.

PLATE II.

Fig. 1.

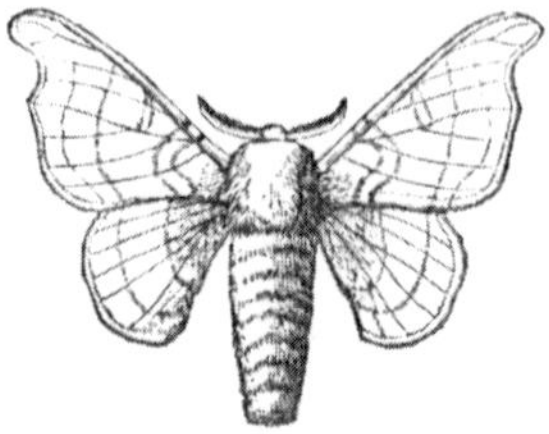

Bombyx mori, or mulberry feeding silkworm (Male).

Fig. 2.

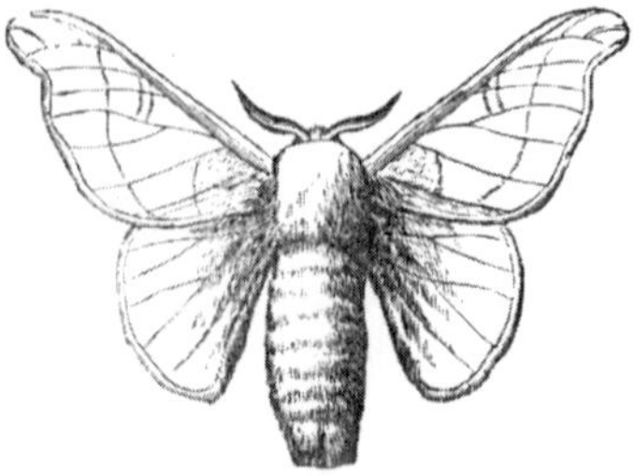

Bombyx mori (Female).

Fig. 3.

Larva of Bombyx mori.
No. in Collection, 243.

Fig. 4.

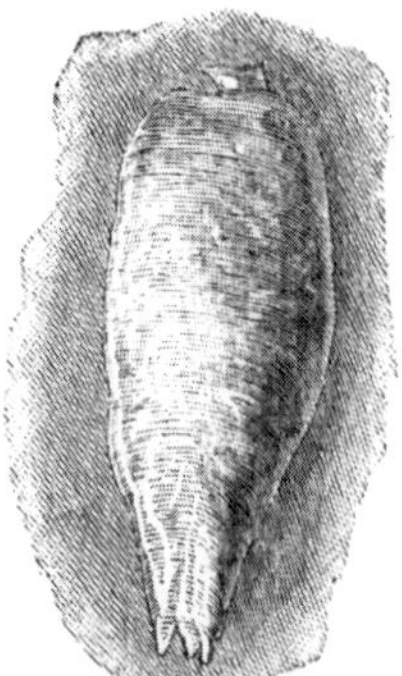

Cocoon of Bombyx fortunatus from Bengal.
No. in Collection, 352.

Fig. 5.

Cocoon of Bombyx mori reared in Italy from Japan seed.
No. in Collection, 270 mm.

PLATE III.

FIG. 1.

Antheræa mylitta or Tussur moth (Male).

No. in Collection, 582. No. in Entomological List, 51a.

FIG. 2.

Antheræa mylitta or Tussur moth (Female).

No. in Collection, 582. No. in Entomological List, 51b.

PLATE IV.

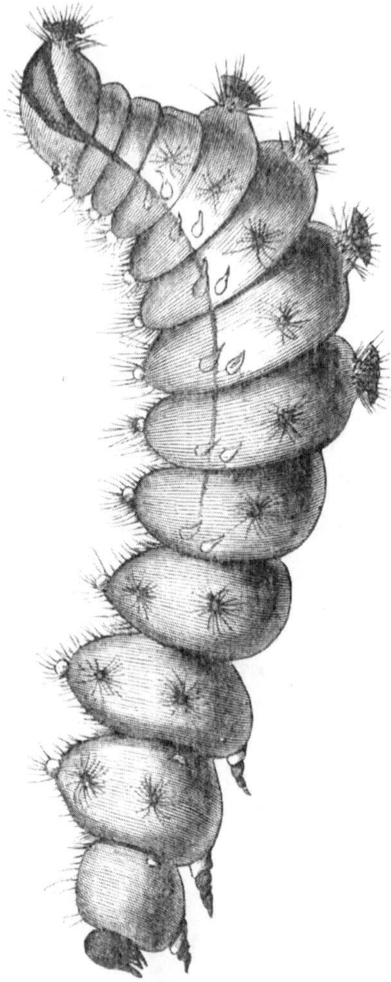

Larva of Antheræa mylitta or Tussur silkworm.

No. in Collection, 245.

PLATE V.

FIG. 1.

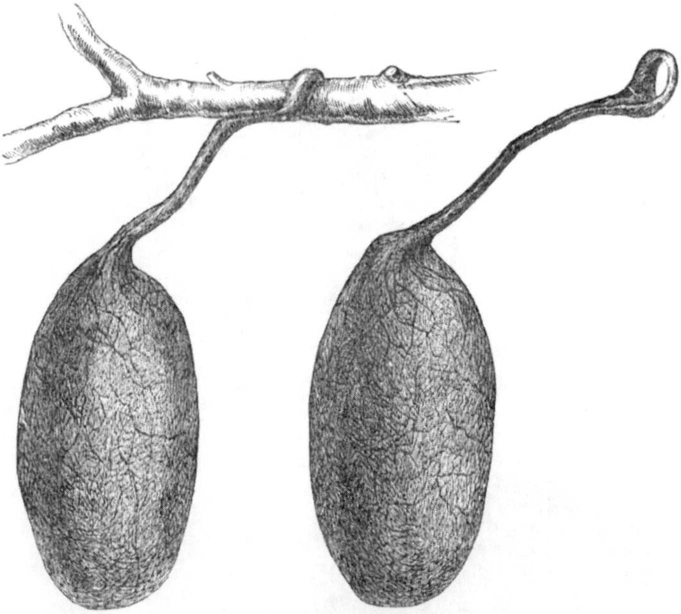

Tussur cocoons.
No. in Collection, 264.

FIG. 2.

Tussur cocoon cut open to show the chrysalis inside.
No. in Collection, 264.

PLATE VI.

FIG. 1.

Antheræopsis or Antheræa Assama or Muga moth (Male).
No. in Collection, 582. No. in Entomological List, 42a.

FIG. 2.

Antheræopsis or Antheræa Assama or Muga moth (Female).
No. in Collection, 582. No. in Entomological List, 42b.

PLATE VII.

FIG. 1.

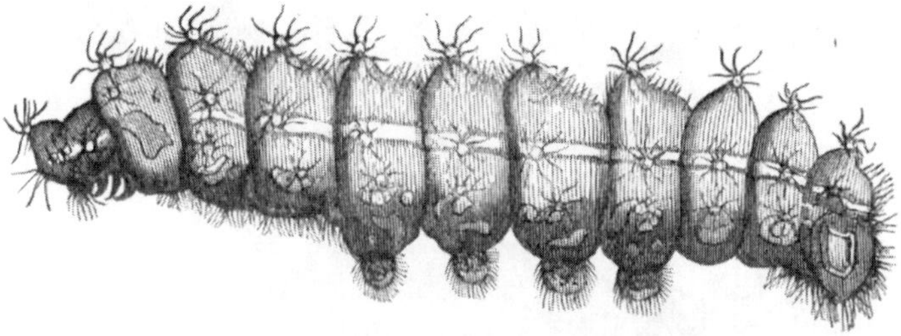

Larva of Antheræopsis or Antheræa Assama or Muga silkworm.

FIG. 2.

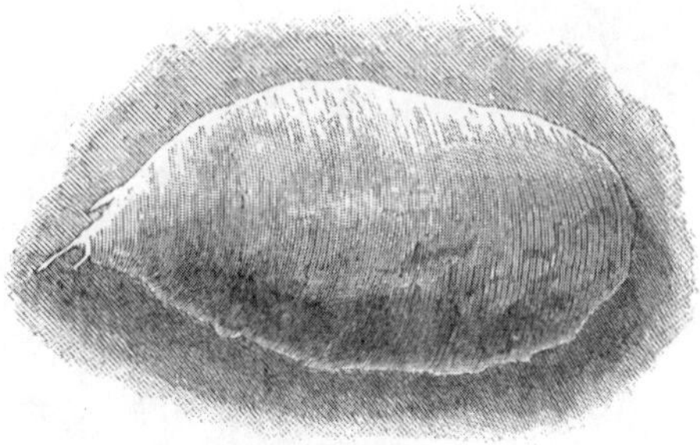

Muga cocoon.

No. in Collection, 431.

PLATE VIII.

FIG. 1.

Antheræa Roylei (Female).

FIG. 2.

Antheræa Frithii (Male).

No. in Collection, 582. No. in Entomological List, 53a.

PLATE IX.

FIG. 1.

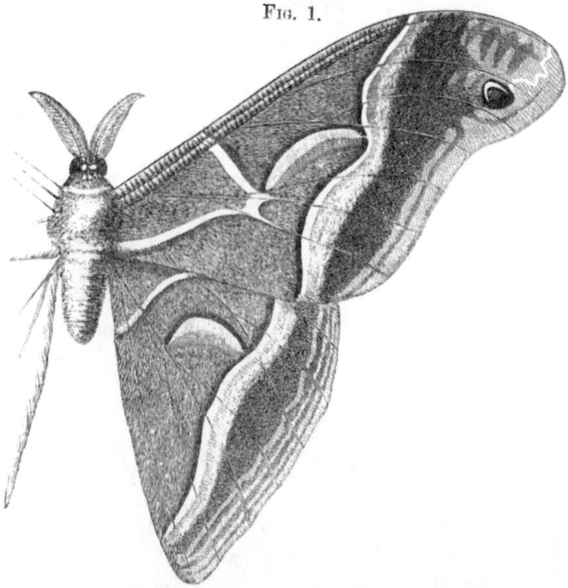

Philosamia or Attacus ricini (Male).

No. in Collection, 582. No. in Entomological List, 24a.

FIG. 2.

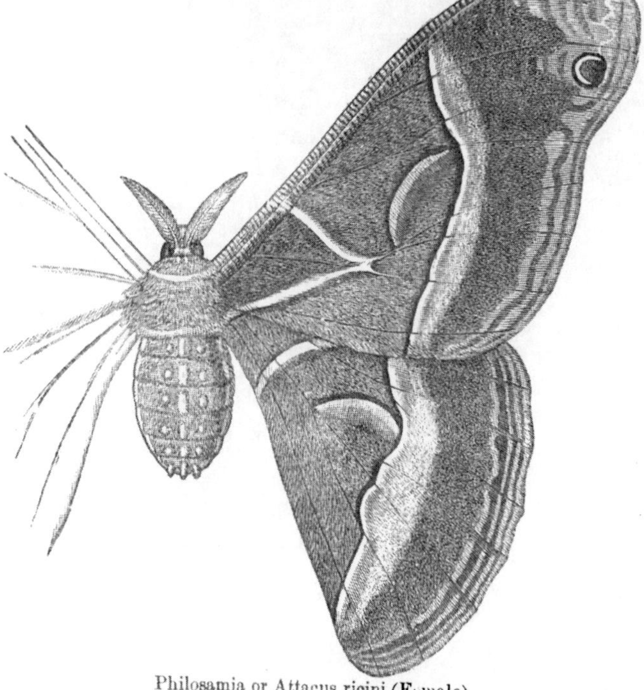

Philosamia or Attacus ricini (Female).

No. in Collection, 582. No. in Entomological List, 24b.

PLATE X

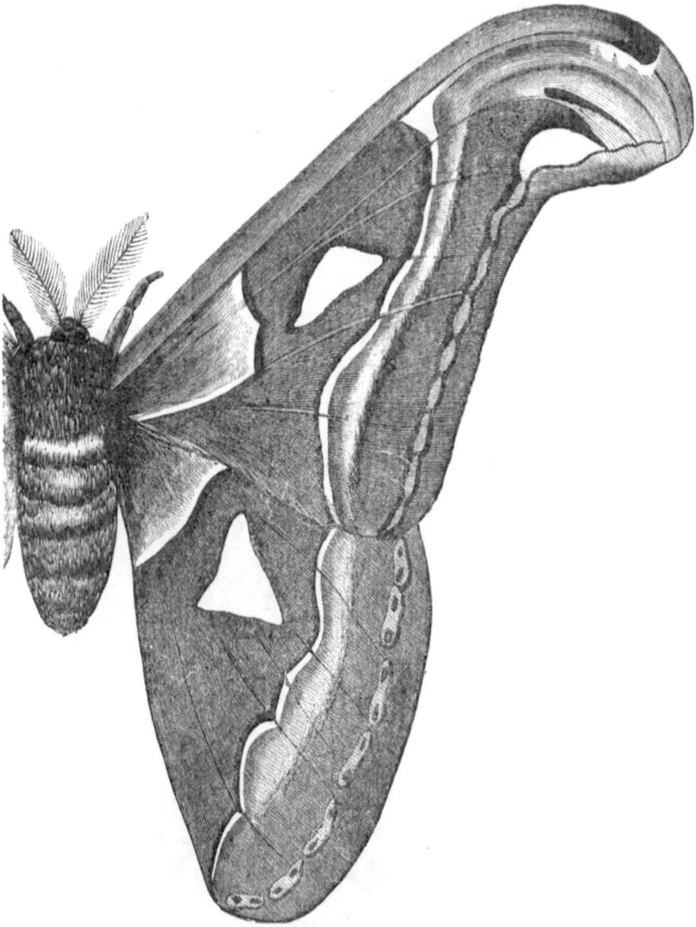

Attacus Atlas (Male).

No. in Collection, 582. No. in Entomological List, 31a.

PLATE XI.

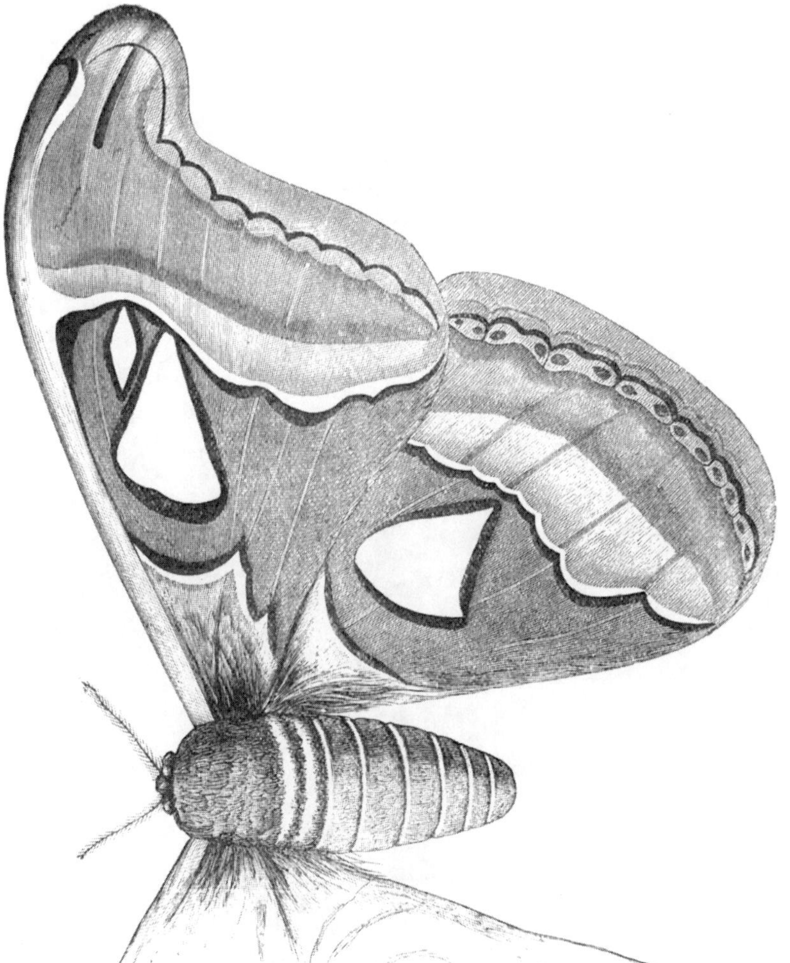

Attacus Atlas (Female).

No. in Collection, 5*2. No. in Entomological List, 31b.

PLATE XII.

FIG. 1.

Larva of Attacus Atlas or Atlas silkworm.

FIG. 2.

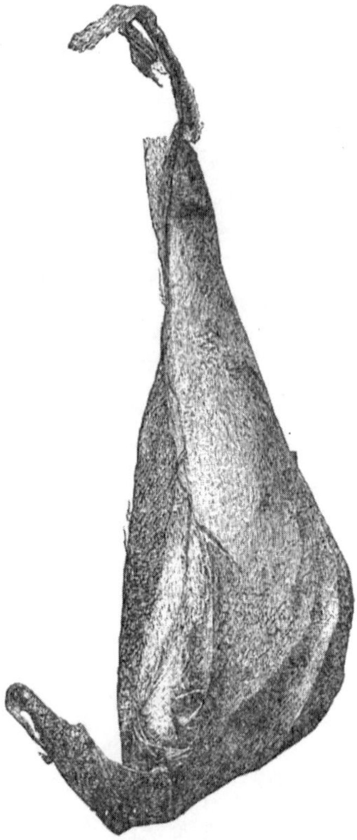

Cocoon of Attacus Atlas.

No. in Collection, 582. No. in Entomological List, 33a.

PLATE XIII.

FIG. 1.

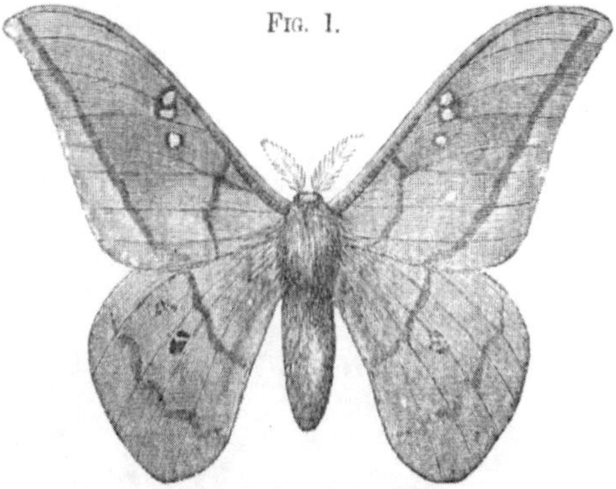

Cricula trifenestrata (Male).

No. in Collection, 582. No. in Entomological List, 44a.

FIG. 2.

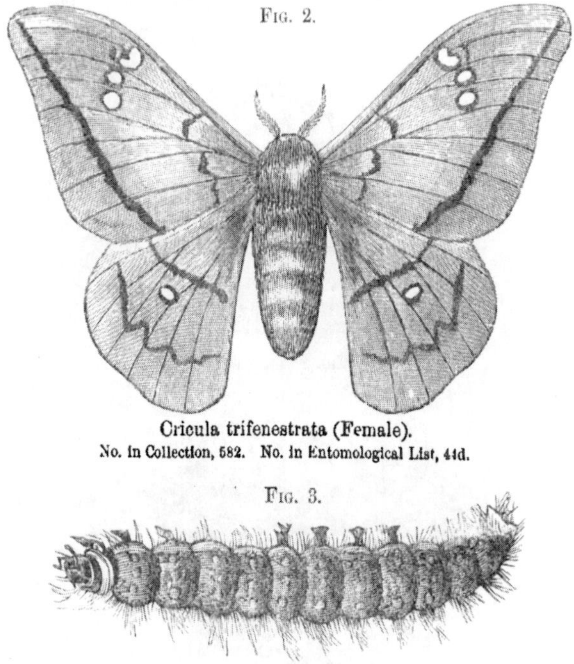

Cricula trifenestrata (Female).

No. in Collection, 582. No. in Entomological List, 44d.

FIG. 3.

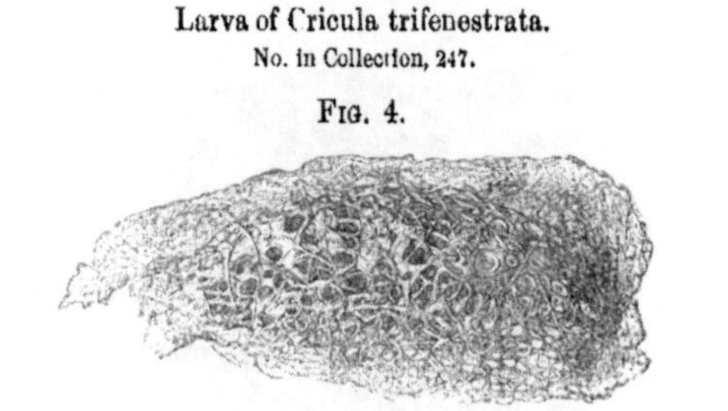

Larva of Cricula trifenestrata.

No. in Collection, 247.

FIG. 4.

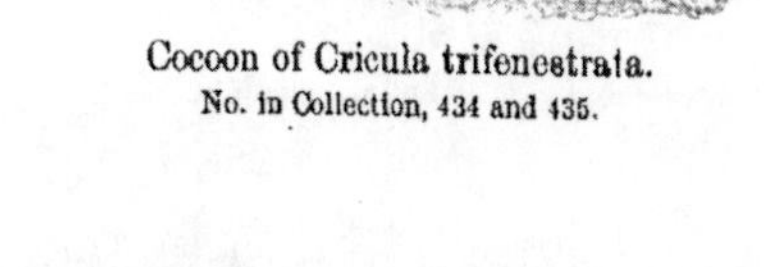

Cocoon of Cricula trifenestrata.

No. in Collection, 434 and 435.

PLATE XIV.

Fig. 1.

Actias selene (Male)

No. in Collection, 582. No. in Entomological List, 37a.

Fig. 2.

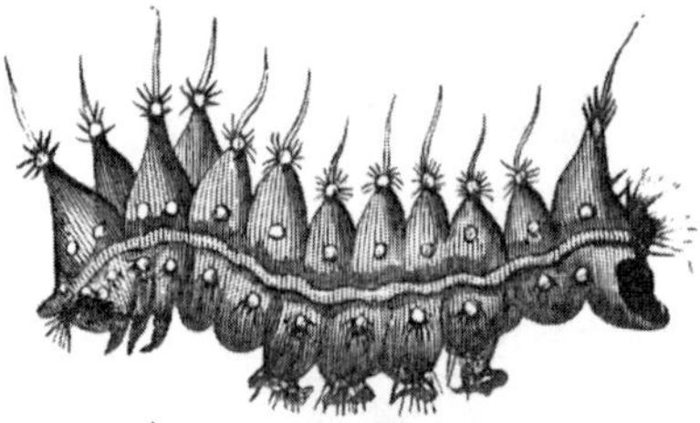

Larva of Actias selene.

Fig. 3.

Cocoon of Selene.

No. in Collection, 582. No. in Entomological List, 37a.

PLATE XV.

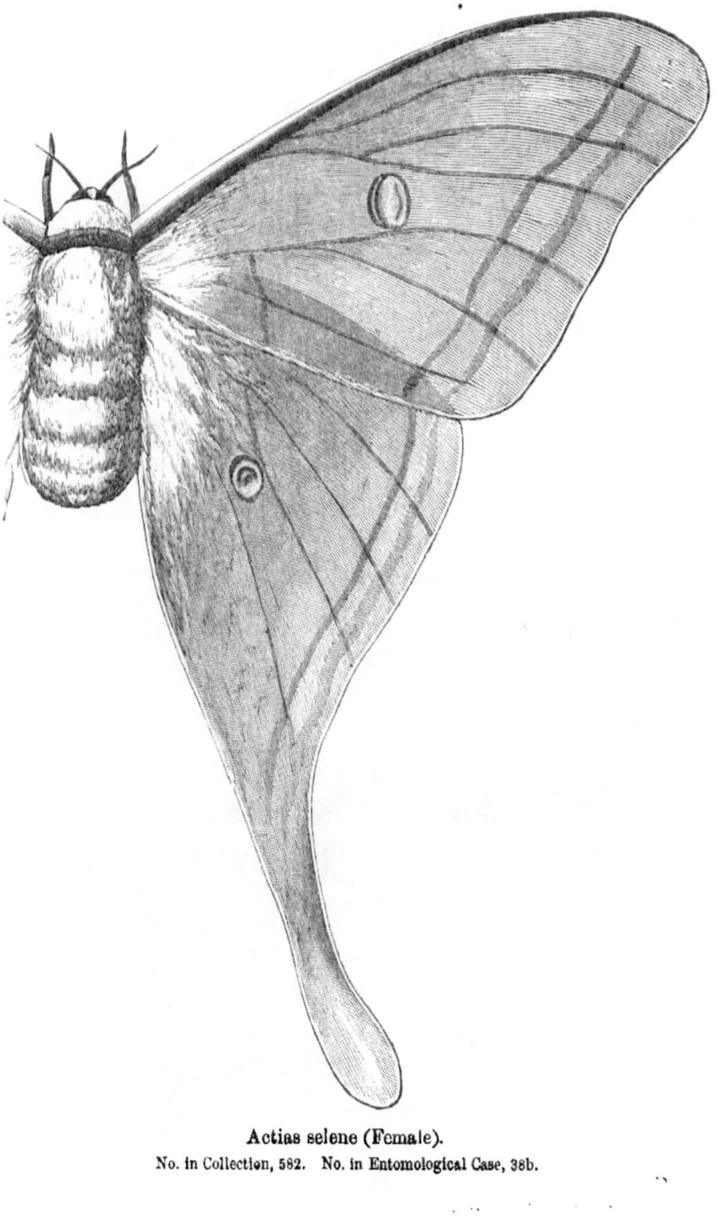

Actias selene (Female).

No. in Collection, 582. No. in Entomological Case, 38b.

PLATE XVI.

FIG. 1.

Antheræa Helferi (Male).

FIG. 2.

Caligula Simla (Female).

PLATE XVII.

Fig. 1.

Antheræa pernyi (Male).

Fig. 2.

Antheræa pernyi (Female).

Fig. 3.

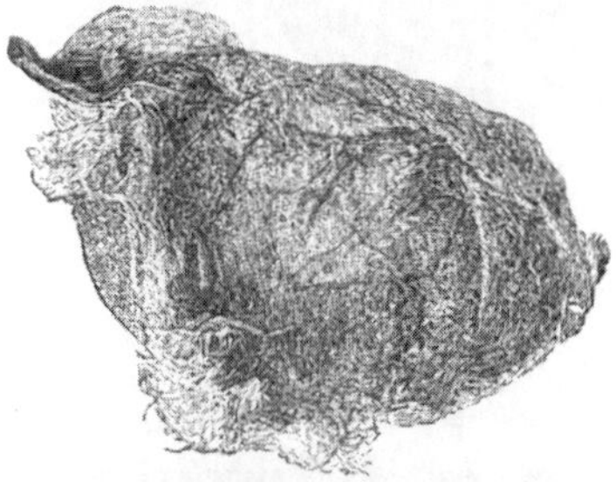

Cocoon of Antheræa pernyi.

PLATE XVIII.

FIG. 1.

Philosamia or Attacus cynthia (Male).

No. in Collection, 582. No. in Entomological List, 30a.

FIG. 2.

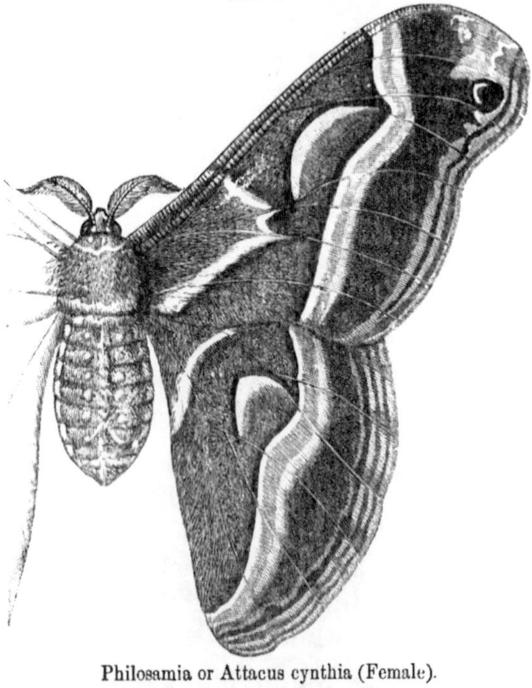

Philosamia or Attacus cynthia (Female).

No. in Collection, 582. No. in Entomological List, 30b.

PLATE XIX.

FIG. 1.

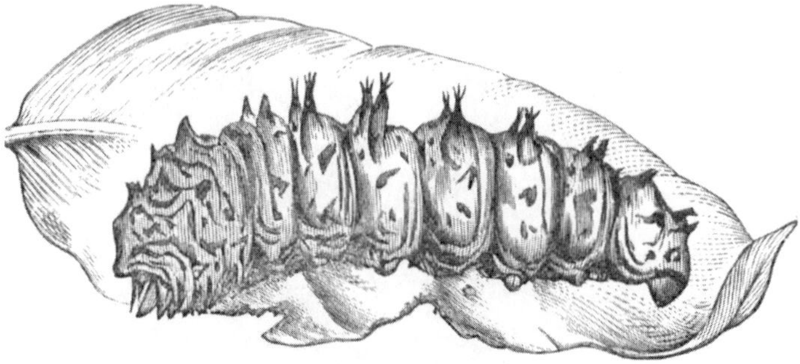

Larva of Philosamia or Attacus cynthia.

FIG. 2.

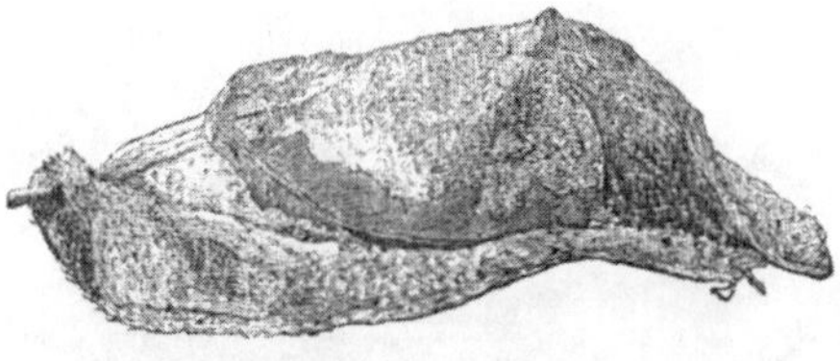

Cocoon of Philosamia or Attacus cynthia.

Fig. 3.

Neoris Huttoni.

No. in Collection, 582. No. in Entomological List, 56a.

PLATE XX.

FIG. 1.

Saturnia carpini (Male).

FIG. 2.

Saturnia carpini (Female).

FIG. 3.

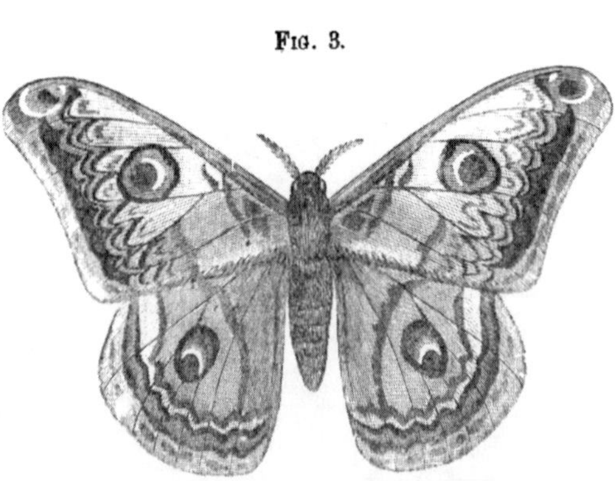

Saturnia Grotei (Female).

PLATE XXXVI

Ailanthus glandulosa, on which the silkworm, Attacus cynthia, feeds.

PLATE XXXV.

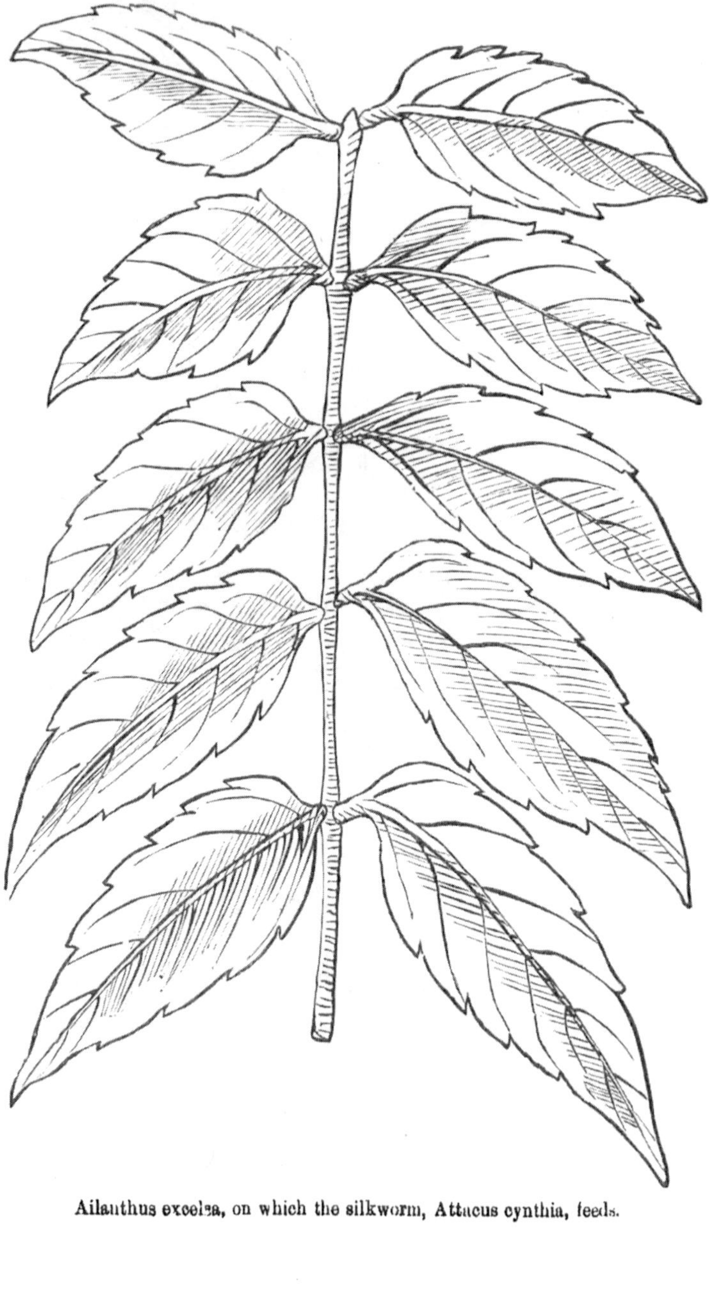

Ailanthus excelsa, on which the silkworm, Attacus cynthia, feeds.

PLATE XXXIV.

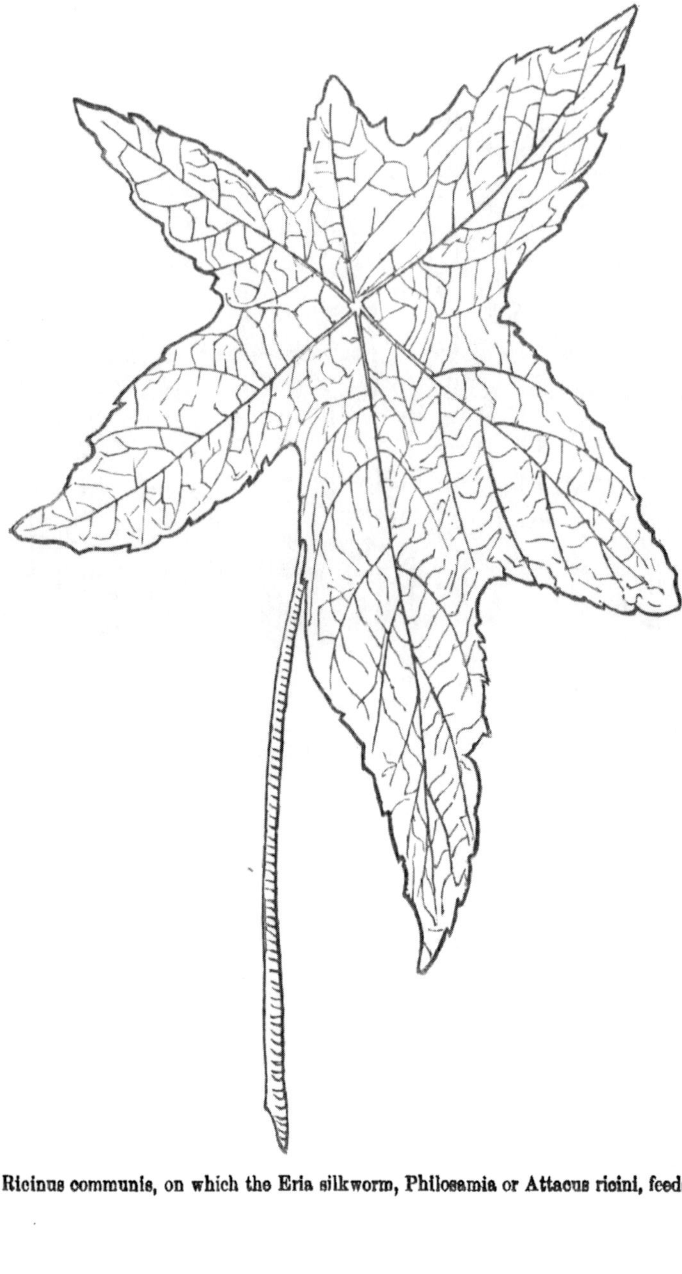

Ricinus communis, on which the Eria silkworm, Philosamia or Attacus ricini, feeds.

PLATE XXXIII.

Machilus odoratissima (*soom* tree), on the leaves of which the Muga silkworm feeds.

PLATE XXXII.

Lagerstræmia Indica, on which the Tussur silkworm feeds.

PLATE XXXI.

Shorea robusta (*sal* tree), on the leaves of which the Tussur silkworm feeds.

PLATE XXX.

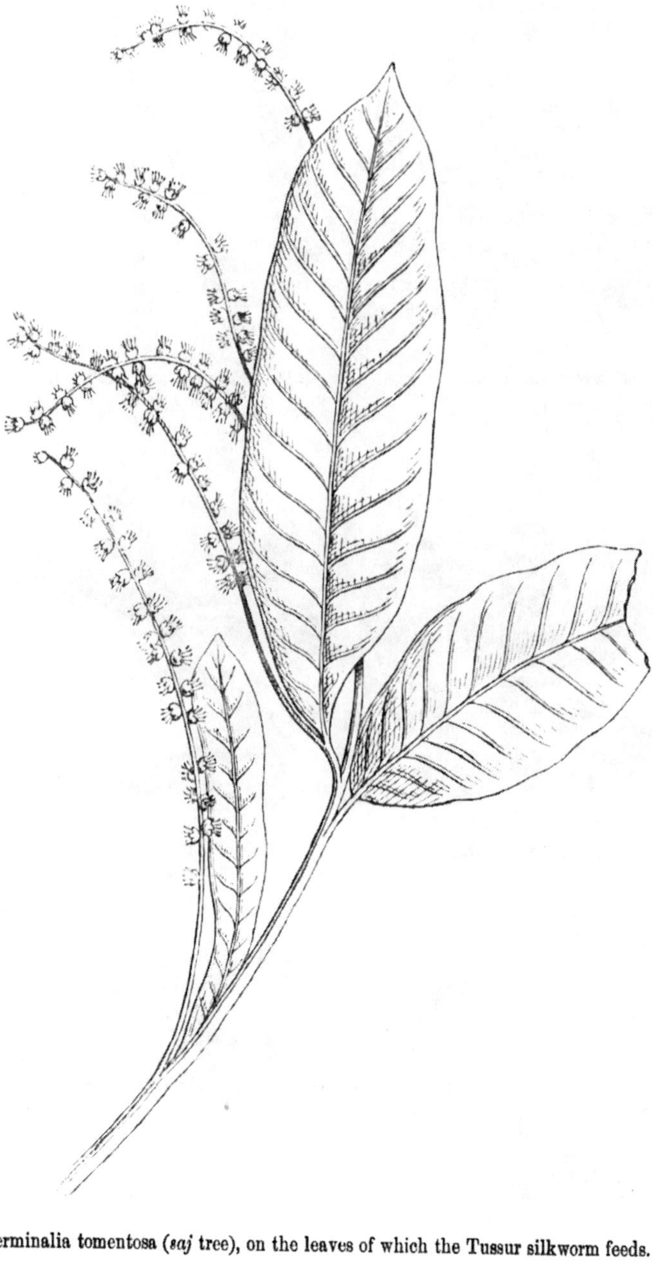

Terminalia tomentosa (*saj* tree), on the leaves of which the Tussur silkworm feeds.

PLATE XXIX.

FIG. 1.

Silk of Actias selene.

FIG. 2.

Silk of Philosamia or Attacus ricini or Eria silk.

FIG. 3.

Silk of Attacus Atlas.

FIG. 4.

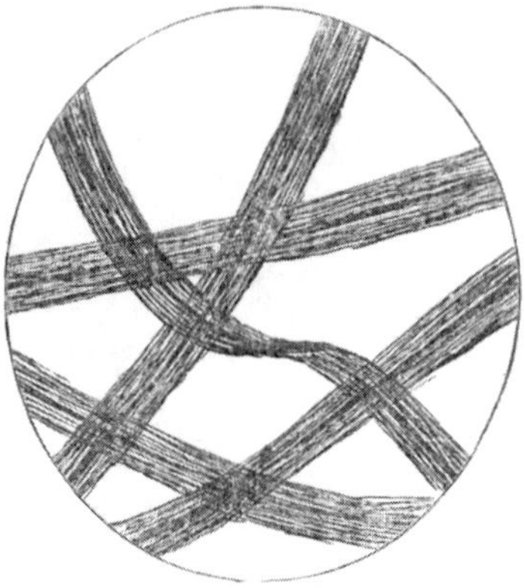

Silk of Cricula trifenestrata.

FIG. 5.

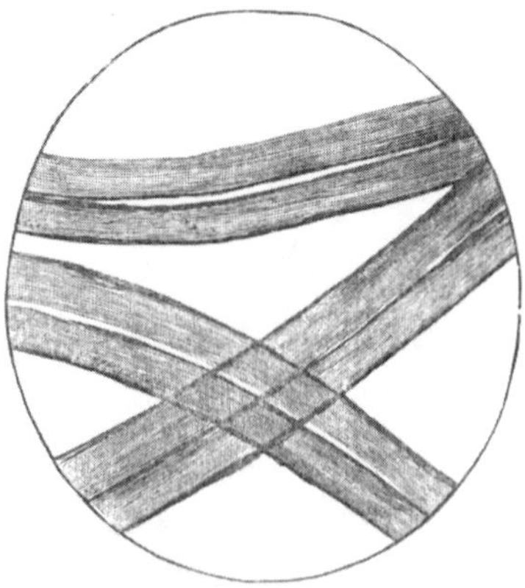

Silk of Antheræa yama-mai.

FIG. 6.

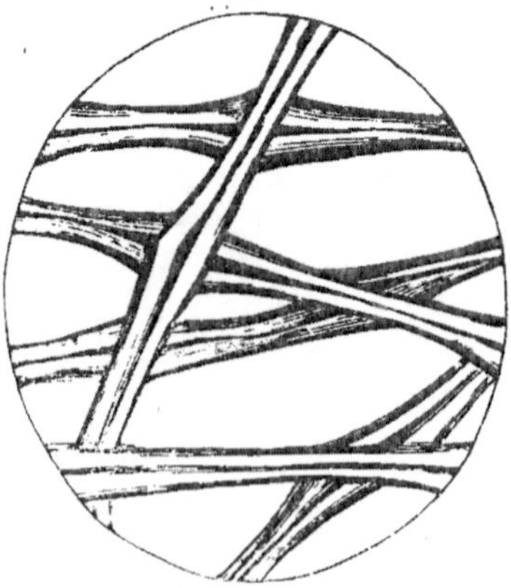

Silk of Saturnia carpini.

PLATE XXVIII.

FIG. 1.

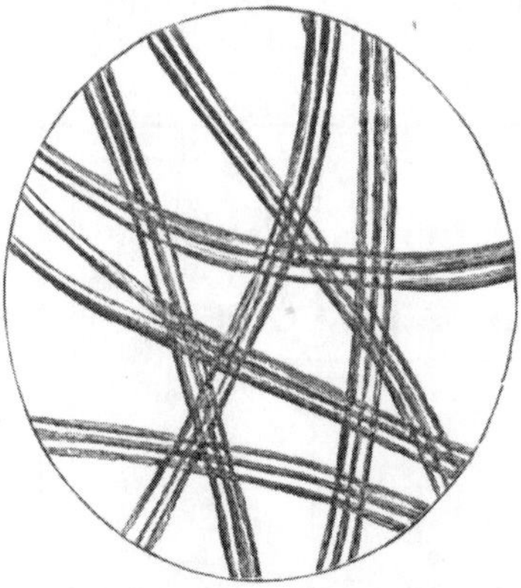

Silk of Bombyx mori, or silk of commerce.

FIG. 2.

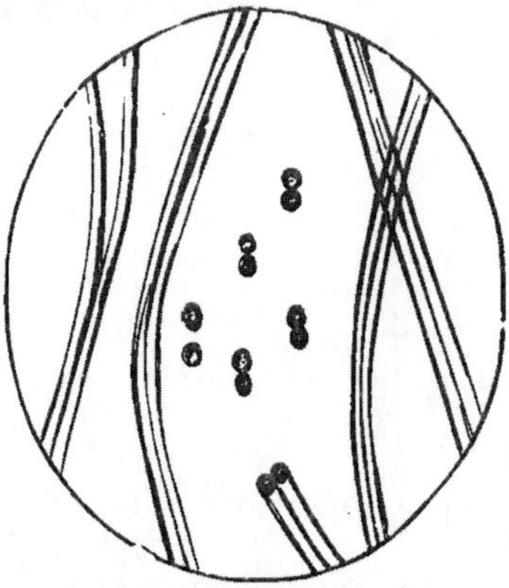

Silk of Bombyx mori, showing transverse sections.

FIG. 3.

Silk of Antheræa mylitta or Tussur silk.

FIG. 4.

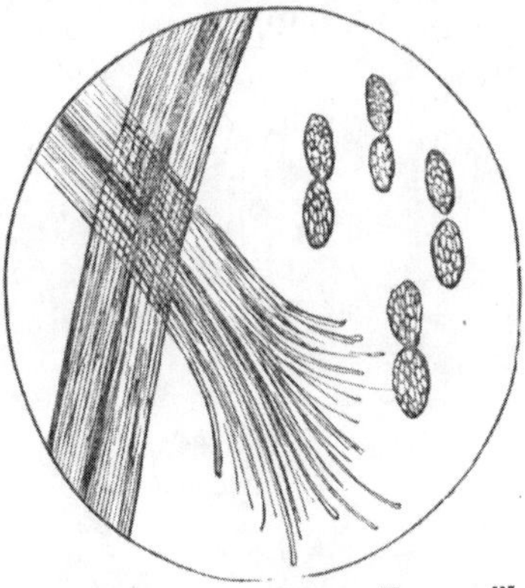

Silk of Antheræa mylitta or Tussur silk, showing fibrets and transverse sections.

FIG. 5.

Silk of Antheræopsis, or Antheræa Assama, or Muga silk.

FIG. 6.

Silk of Antheræopsis or Antheræa pernyi.

PLATE XXVII.

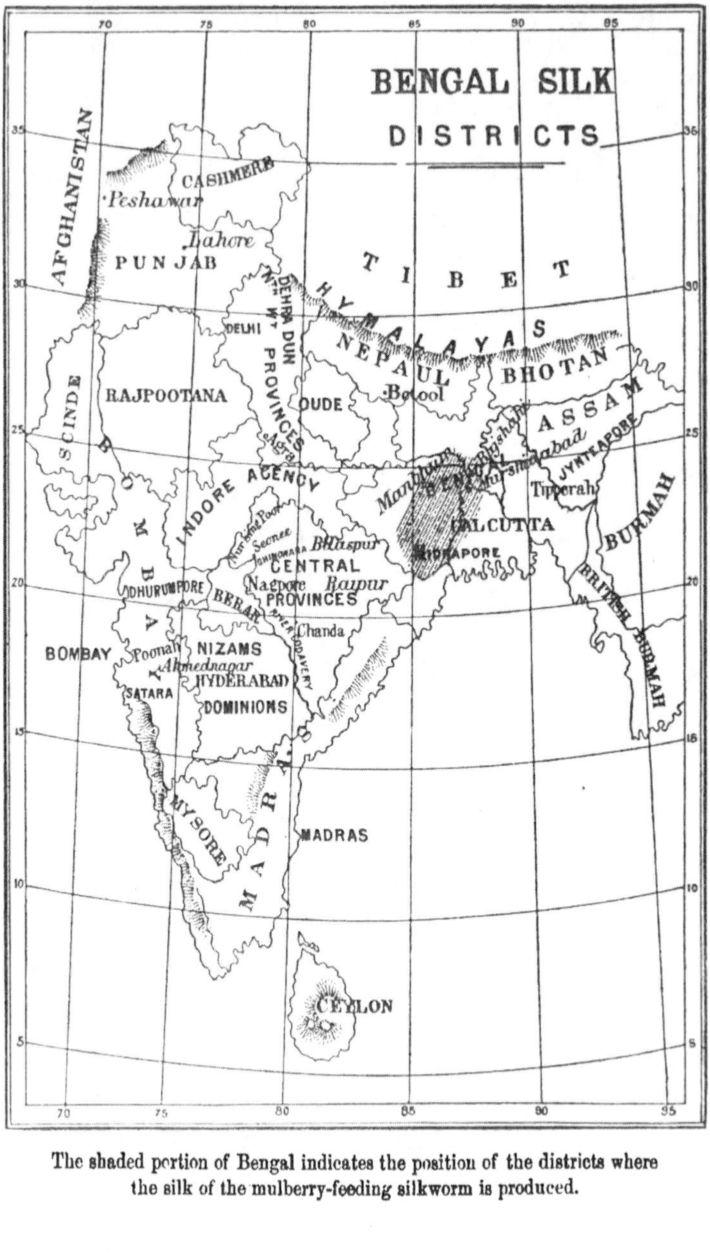

The shaded portion of Bengal indicates the position of the districts where the silk of the mulberry-feeding silkworm is produced.

PLATE XXVI.

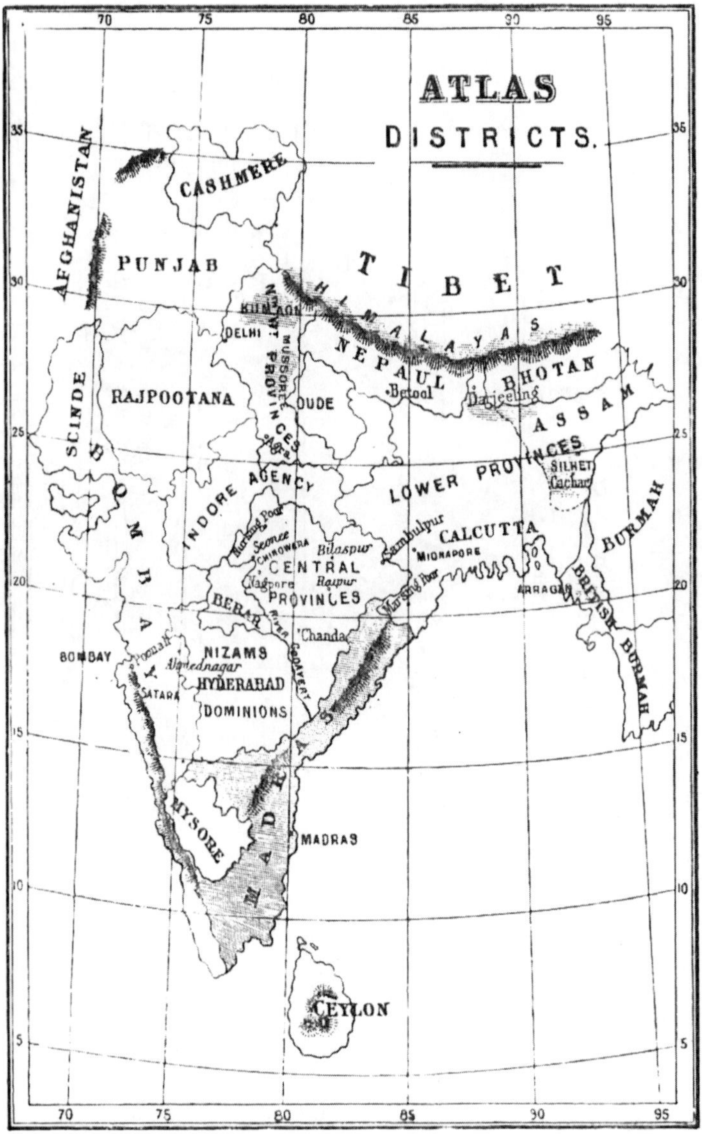

The shaded parts show the districts in which the Atlas moth (*Attacus Atlas*) has been found.

PLATE XXV.

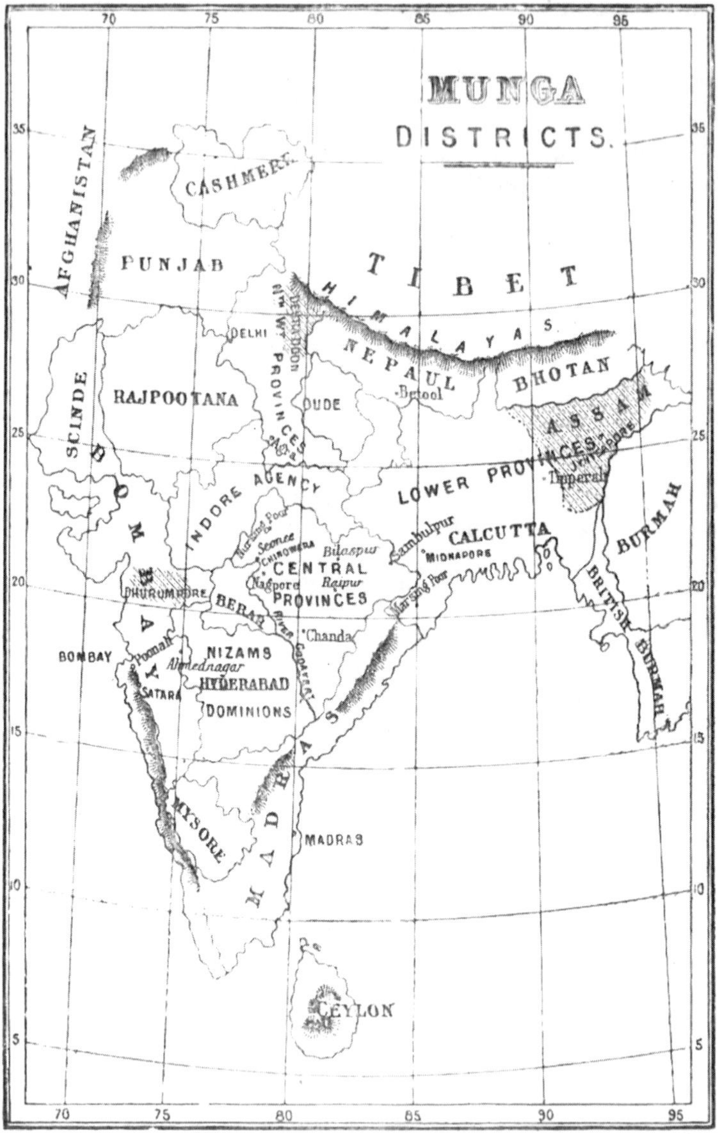

The shaded parts show the districts in which the Munga or Muga moth (*Antheræopsis* or *Antheræa Assama*) has been found.

PLATE XXIV.

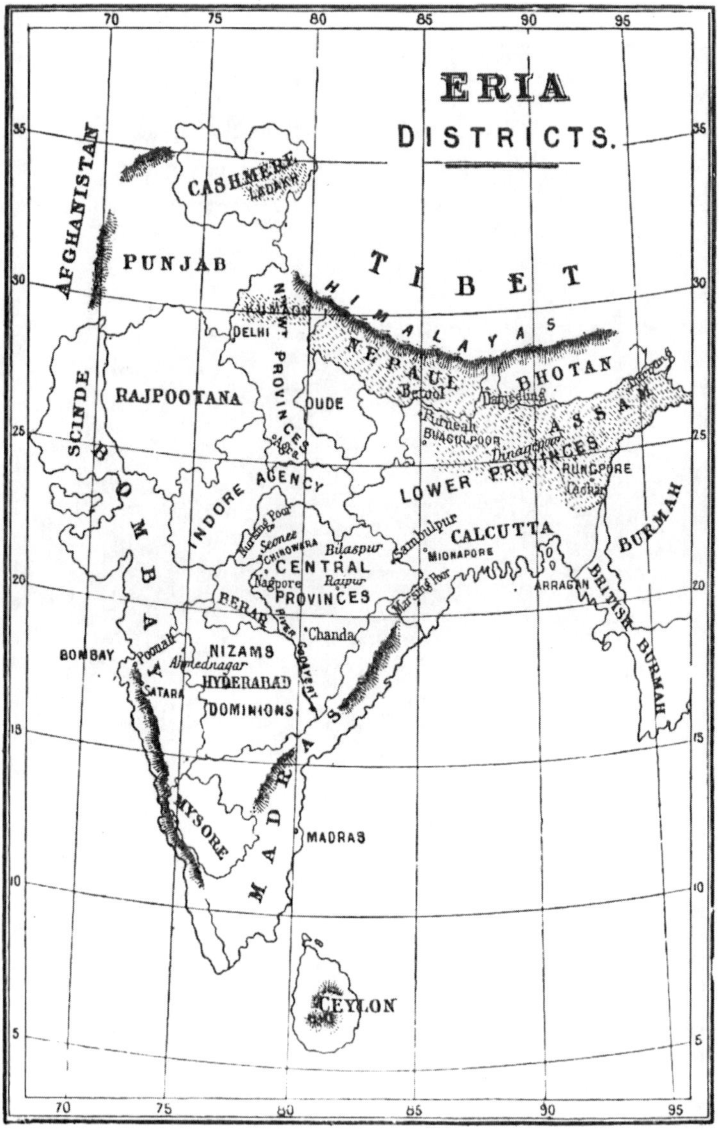

The shaded parts show the districts in which the Eria moth (*Attacus ricini*) has been found.

PLATE XXIII.

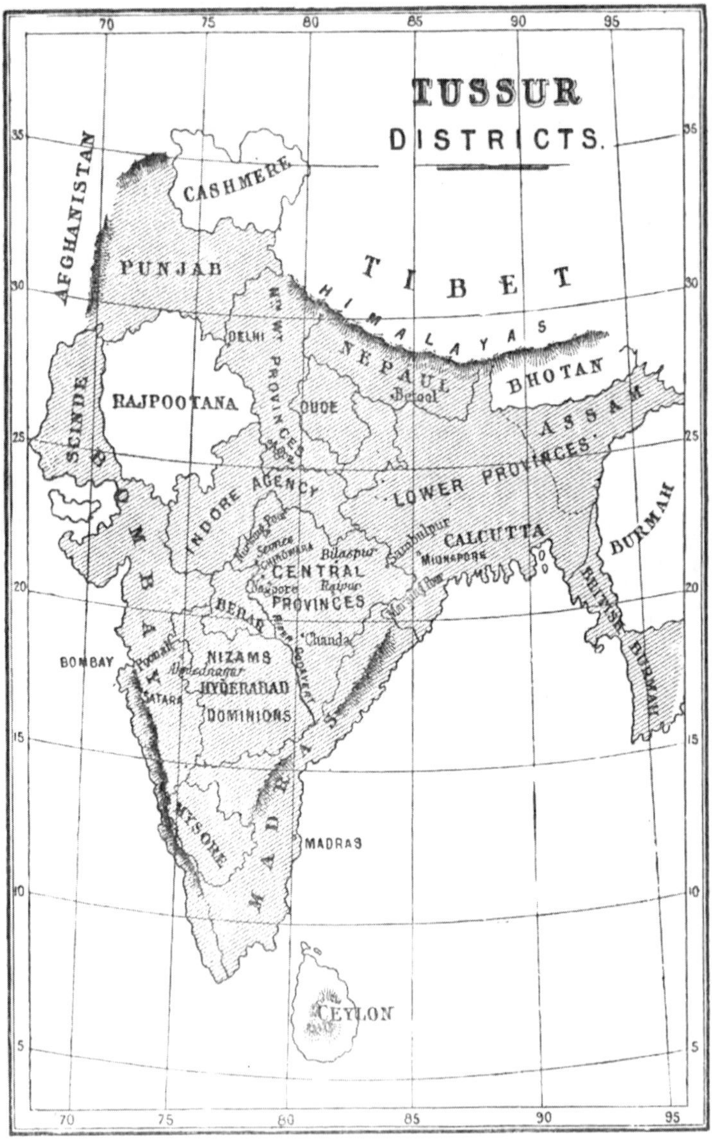

The shaded parts show the districts in which the Tussur moth has been found.

PLATE XXII.

Fig. 1.

Loepa miranda (Male).

Fig. 2.

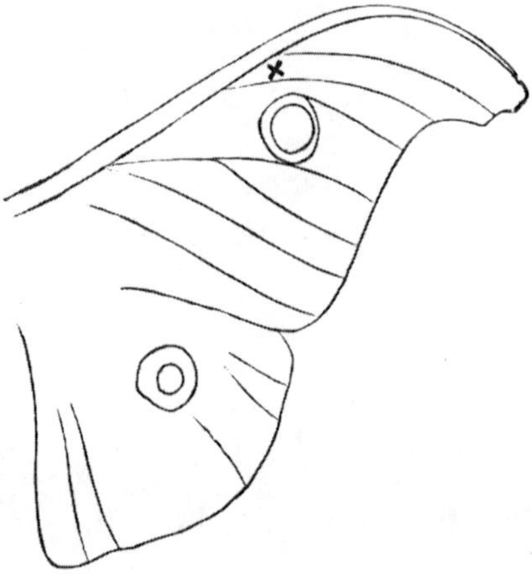

Diagram showing the Point (x) on wing from which the scales have been taken. (*See* Plates XLIX to LIV.)

PLATE XXI.

FIG. 1.

Loepa katinka (Male).

FIG. 2.

Loepa katinka (Female).

FIG. 3.

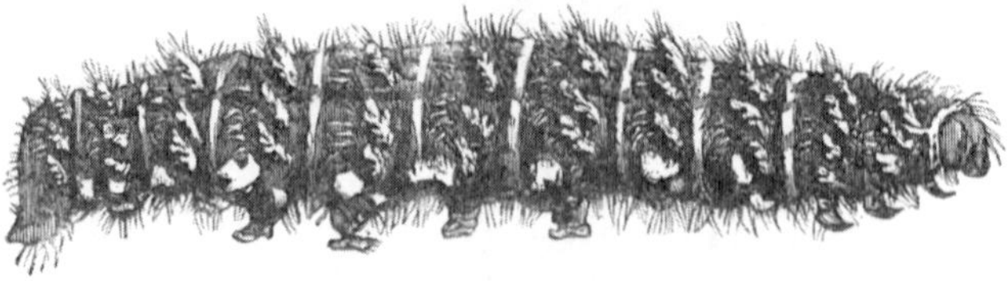

Larva of Loepa katinka.

PLATE XXXVII.

Morus alba (the Mulberry), on which feeds the silkworm which produces the silk of commerce.

PLATE XXXVIII.

FIG. 1.

Bombyx mori (Male).

FIG. 2.

Antheræa mylitta (Male).

FIG. 3.

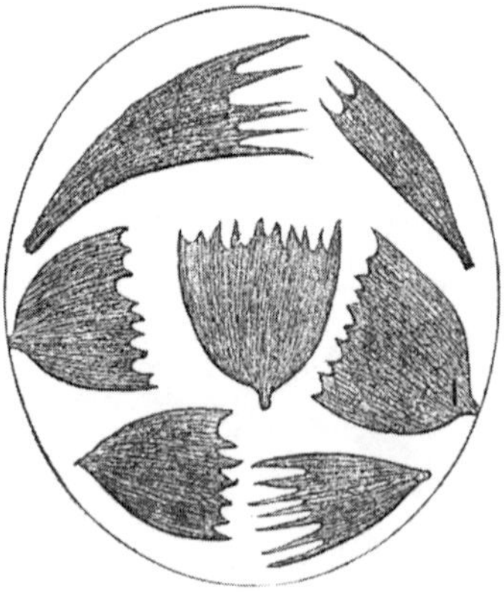

Antheræa mylitta (Female).

FIG. 4.

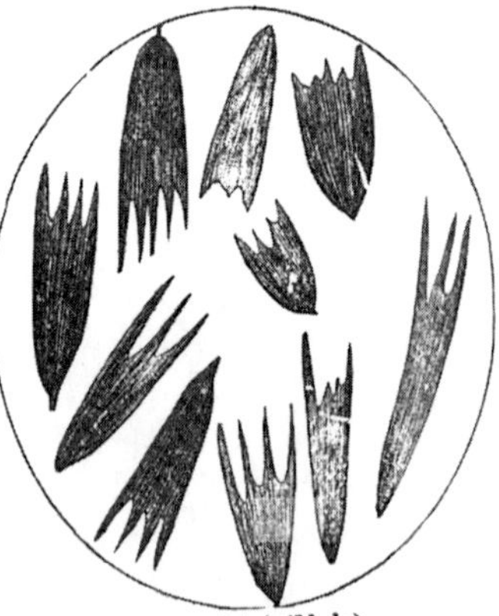

Attacus ricini (Male).

FIG. 5.

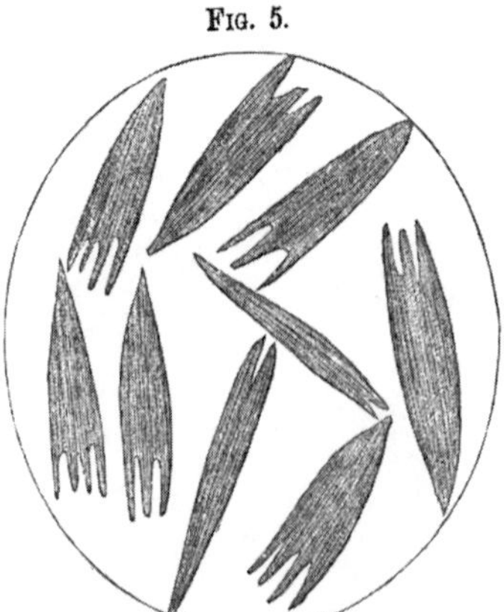

Attacus cynthia (Male).

FIG. 6.

Attacus Atlas (Male).

Scales from Wings magnified 140 diameters.

PLATE XXXIX.

Two examples of "Tussur on Tussur" embroidery by the Leek Embroidery Society, Leek. The designs are Indian, the upper one is a favourite border form of the lotus conventionalised, the lower is an excellent and artistic diaper treatment.

PLATE XI.

European Cocoon-reeling machine, side view. (A. Tavelette Consono.)

PLATE XLI.

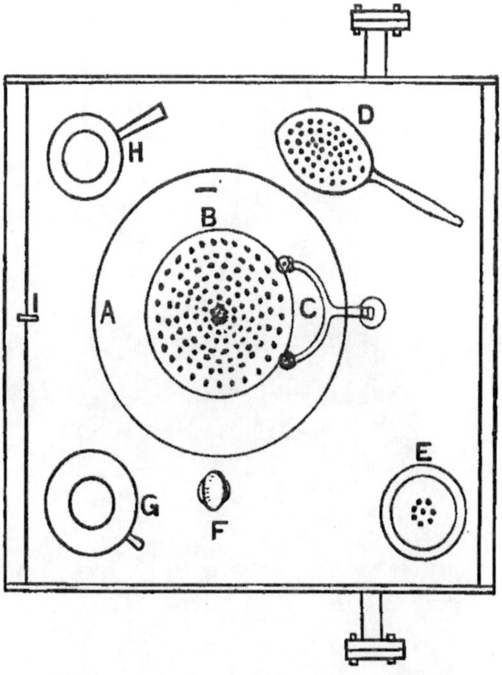

Tray and utensils; mechanical drawing, scale 1 inch to the foot.

PLATE XLII.

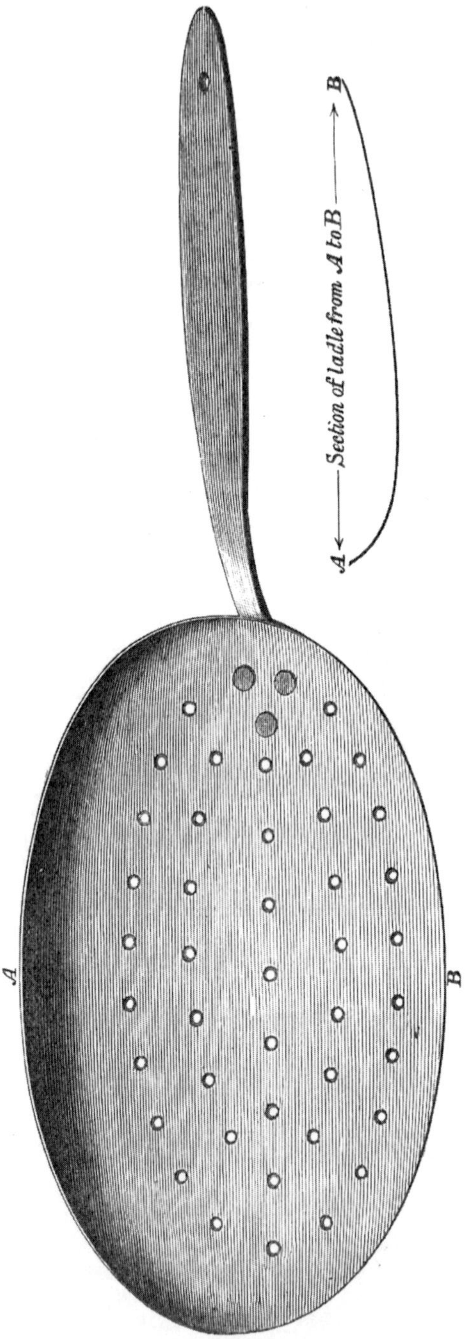

Cocoon ladle for basin; scale ½ of the real size.

PLATE XLIII.

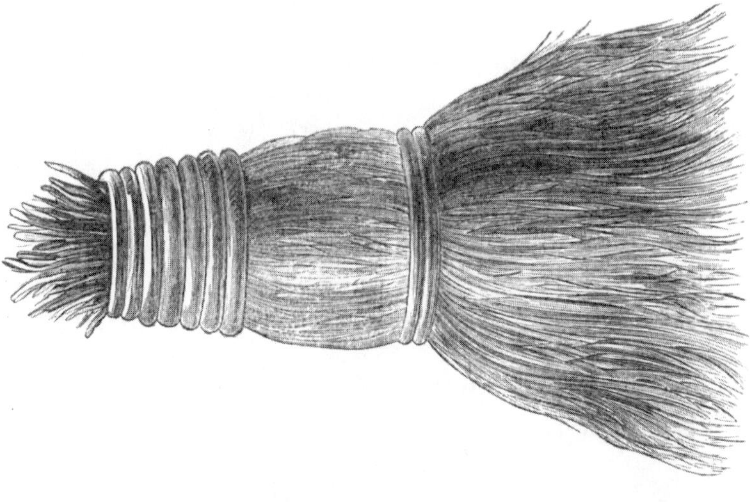

Brushes for the battage; scale ½ of the real size.

Used for collecting the outer and unreelable Cocoon threads, and for finding the reelable ends.

PLATE XLIV.

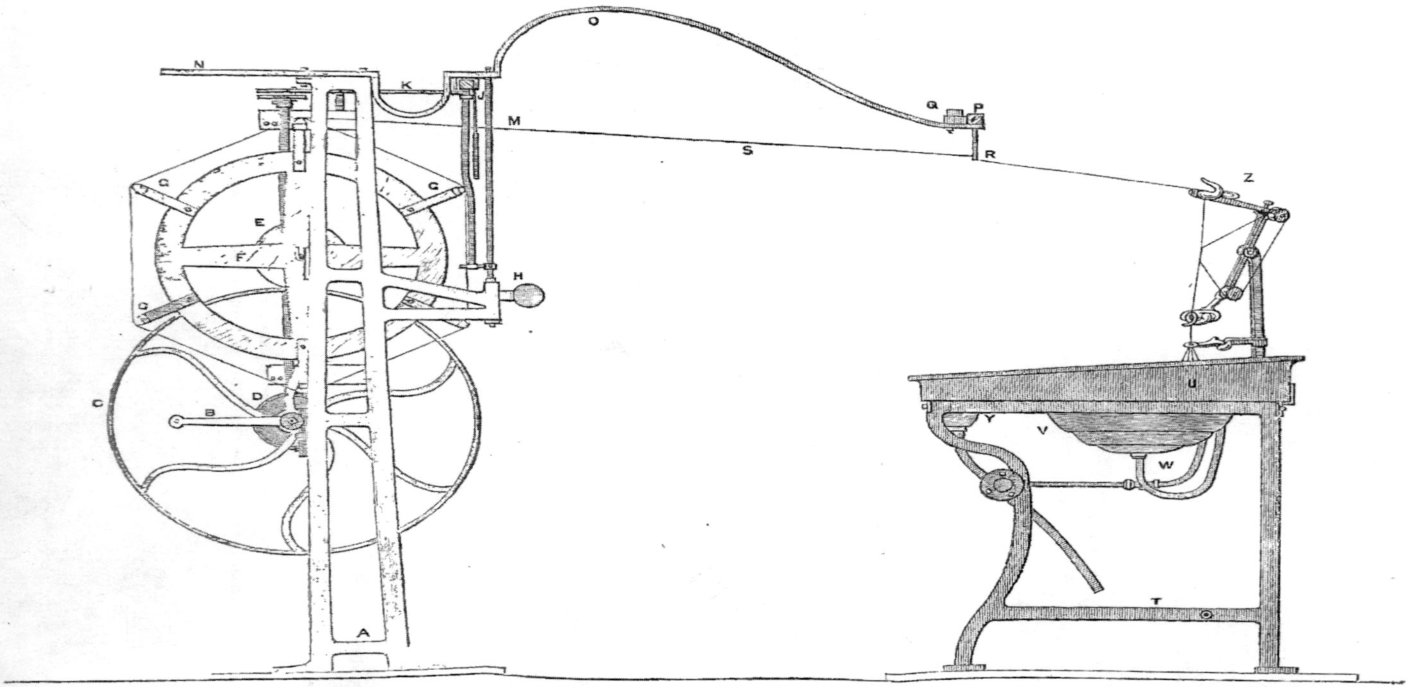

European Cocoon reeling machine, with Tavelette Consono (Z); mechanical drawing, side view, scale 1 inch to the foot.